M000233181

Collins gem

GERMAN
DICTIONARY

Published by Collins
An imprint of HarperCollins Publishers
Westerhill Road
Bishopbriggs
Glasgow G64 2QT

Twelfth Edition 2016

10 9 8 7 6 5 4 3 2 1

© William Collins Sons & Co. Ltd
1978, 1988
© HarperCollins Publishers 1993, 1997,
1999, 2000, 2003, 2006, 2007, 2009,
2012, 2016

ISBN 978-0-00-814186-8

Collins® and Collins Gem®
are registered trademarks of
HarperCollins Publishers Limited

www.collinsdictionary.com

Typeset by RefineCatch Ltd, Bungay,
Suffolk, and Davidson Publishing
Solutions, Glasgow

Printed in Italy by GRAFICA VENETA
S.p.A.

The contents of this publication
are believed correct at the time of
printing. Nevertheless, the Publisher
can accept no responsibility for errors
or omissions, changes in the detail
given or for any expense or loss
thereby caused.

HarperCollins does not warrant that
any website mentioned in this title
will be provided uninterrupted, that
any website will be error free, that
defects will be corrected, or that the
website or the server that makes it
available are free of viruses or bugs.
For full terms and conditions please
refer to the site terms provided on the
website.

A catalogue record for this book is
available from the British Library.

If you would like to comment on any
aspect of this book, please contact us
at the given address or online.
E-mail: dictionaries@harpercollins.co.uk
 facebook.com/harpercollins
 @collinsdict

Acknowledgements

We would like to thank those
authors and publishers who kindly
gave permission for copyright
material to be used in the Collins
Corpus. We would also like to thank
Times Newspapers Ltd for providing
valuable data.

INHALT

CONTENTS

EDITOR/PROJEKTLEITUNG
Susie Beattie

CONTRIBUTORS/MITARBEITER
Christine Bahr
Stuart Fortey
Helen Galloway
Horst Kopleck
Janice McNeillie
Marianne Noble
Britta Nord
Silke Probst
Robin Sawers
Jany Schneider
Veronika Schnorr
Maggie Seaton

FOR THE PUBLISHER/VERLAGSMITARBEITER
Gerry Breslin
Hannah Dove
Kerry Ferguson
Helen Newstead

EINFÜHRUNG

Wir freuen uns sehr, dass Sie sich zum Kauf eines Collins Wörterbuchs Deutsch entschlossen haben. Wir wünschen Ihnen viel Spaß beim Gebrauch in der Schule, zu Hause, im Urlaub und im Beruf.

Diese Einführung wird Ihnen einige nützliche Hinweise dazu geben, wie Sie am besten von Ihrem neuen Wörterbuch profitieren. Schließlich bietet Ihnen das Worterbuch nicht nur Stichwörter und Übersetzungen, sondern auch zahlreiche Zusatzinformationen in jedem einzelnen Eintrag. Mit Hilfe all dieser Informationen können Sie zum einen modernes Deutsch lesen und verstehen, zum anderen auch aktiv auf Deutsch kommunizieren.

Das Collins Wörterbuch Deutsch gibt Ihnen vor dem eigentlichen Wörterbuchtextteil selbst eine Liste aller verwendeten Abkürzungen sowie eine Übersicht zu Aussprache und Gebrauch phonetischer Umschrift. Darüber hinaus finden Sie noch eine Auflistung zu den regelmäßigen deutschen Substantivendungen sowie zu unregelmäßigen englischen und deutschen Verben. Auf den letzten Seiten Ihres Wörterbuchs finden Sie in einem „kleinen Reise-ABC" zahlreiche nützliche Phrasen für verschiedenste Situationen am Urlaubsort.

WIE FINDE ICH WAS?

Die verschiedenen Schriftarten, Schriftgrößen, Symbole, Abkürzungen und Klammern helfen Ihnen dabei, sich innerhalb der Informationen, die das Wörterbuch bietet, zurechtzufinden. Die Konventionen, die diesem Wörterbuch zugrunde liegen, sowie auch der Gebrauch verschiedener Symbole werden im Folgenden näher erläutert.

STICHWÖRTER

Die Wörter, die Sie in Ihrem Wörterbuch nachschlagen, die Stichwörter, sind in alphabetischer Reihenfolge angeordnet. Sie sind fett gedruckt und in blauer Farbe, sodass Sie sie schnell finden. Die Stichwörter, die rechts und links oben auf jeder Seite erscheinen, sind das jeweils erste Stichwort einer Seite, wenn es sich dabei um eine linke Seite handelt, bzw. das letzte Stichwort einer Seite, wenn es sich um eine rechte Seite handelt. Informationen zu Form und Gebrauch des jeweiligen Stichworts werden im Anschluss an die Lautschrift in Klammern angegeben. Normalerweise sind diese

Angaben in abgekürzter Form und *kursiver Schrift* (z.B. (*fam*)) für umgangssprachlich oder (*Comm*) als Sachgebietsangabe für Wirtschaft).

Wo es sich anbietet, werden zusammengehörige Wörter und Wortgruppen in einem Eintrag zusammengefasst (z.B. **gather**, **gathering**; **höflich**, **Höflichkeit**). Hierbei sind die Stichwörter innerhalb des Nests von der Schriftgröße etwas kleiner als das erste Stichwort. Geläufige Ausdrücke, in denen das Stichwort vorkommt, erscheinen ebenfalls **fett**, aber in einer anderen Schriftgröße. Die Tilde (~) steht hierbei für das Hauptstichwort am Anfang eines Eintrags. So steht beispielsweise im Eintrag ‚**Mitte**' der Ausdruck ‚**~ Juni**' für ‚**Mitte Juni**'.

PHONETISCHE UMSCHRIFT

Die Aussprache jedes Stichworts findet sich in phonetischer Umschrift in eckigen Klammern jeweils direkt hinter dem Stichwort selbst (z.B. **mountain** ['maʊntɪn]). Eine Liste der Lautschriftzeichen mit Erklärungen finden Sie auf S. xi.

BEDEUTUNGEN

Die Übersetzung der Stichwörter ist in Normalschrift angegeben. Gibt es mehrere Bedeutungen oder Gebrauchsmöglichkeiten, so sind diese durch einen Strichpunkt voneinander zu unterscheiden. Sie finden oft weitere Angaben in Klammern vor den jeweiligen Übersetzungen. Diese zeigen Ihnen typische Kontexte auf, in denen das Stichwort verwendet werden kann (z.B. **breakup** (*of meeting, organisation*)), oder sie liefern Synonyme (z.B. **fit** (*suitable*)).

GRAMMATISCHE HINWEISE

Die Wortartangabe finden Sie als Abkürzung und in *kursiver Schrift* direkt hinter der Ausspracheinformation zum jeweiligen Stichwort (z.B. *vt, adj, n*).

Die Genusangaben zu deutschen Substantiven werden wie folgt angegeben: *m* für Maskulinum, *f* für Femininum und *nt* für Neutrum. Darüber hinaus finden Sie neben dem Stichwort in Klammern Genitiv- und Pluralform (**Abenteuer** (*-s, -*)).

Die Genusangabe zur deutschen Übersetzung findet sich ebenfalls in *kursiver Schrift* direkt hinter dem Hauptbestandteil der Übersetzung.

INTRODUCTION

We are delighted you have decided to buy the Collins German Dictionary and hope you will enjoy and benefit from using it at school, at home, on holiday or at work.

This introduction gives you a few tips on how to get the most out of your dictionary – not simply from its comprehensive wordlist but also from the information provided in each entry. This will help you to read and understand modern German, as well as to communicate and express yourself in the language.

The Collins German Dictionary begins by listing the abbreviations used in the text and illustrating the sounds shown by the phonetic symbols. Next you will find regular German noun endings and English irregular verbs followed by a section on German irregular verbs. Finally, the new Phrasefinder supplement gives you hundreds of useful phrases which are intended to give you practical help in everyday situations when travelling.

USING YOUR COLLINS DICTIONARY

A wealth of information is presented in the dictionary, using various typefaces, sizes of type, symbols, abbreviations and brackets. The conventions and symbols used are explained in the following sections.

HEADWORDS

The words you look up in the dictionary – 'headwords' – are listed alphabetically. They are printed in **colour** for rapid identification. The headwords appearing at the top of each page indicate the first (if it appears on a left-hand page) and last word (if it appears on a right-hand page) dealt with on the page in question.

Information about the usage or form of certain headwords is given in brackets after the phonetic spelling. This usually appears in abbreviated form and in italics (e.g. (*fam*), (*Comm*)).

Where appropriate, words related to headwords are grouped in the same entry (**gather, gathering; höflich, Höflichkeit**) in a slightly smaller bold type than the headword. Common expressions in which the headword appears are shown in a different size of bold roman type. The swung dash, ~, represents the main headword at the start of each entry. For example, in the entry for '**Mitte**' the phrase '~ **Juni**' should be read '**Mitte Juni**'.

PHONETIC SPELLINGS

The phonetic spelling of each headword (indicating its pronunciation) is given in square brackets immediately after the headword (e.g. **mountain** ['maʊntɪn]). A list of these spellings is given on page xi.

MEANINGS

Headword translations are given in ordinary type and, where more than one meaning or usage exists, they are separated by a semicolon. You will often find other words in italics in brackets before the translations. These offer suggested contexts in which the headword might appear (e.g. **breakup** (*of meeting, organisation*)) or provide synonyms (e.g. **fit** (*suitable*)).

GRAMMATICAL INFORMATION

Parts of speech are given in abbreviated form in italics after the phonetic spellings of headwords (e.g. *vt*, *adj*, *n*).

Genders of German nouns are indicated as follows: *m* for a masculine, *f* for a feminine, and *nt* for a neuter noun. Genitive and plural forms of nouns are also shown next to the headword (**Abenteuer** (-s, -)).

The gender of the German translation appears in *italics* immediately following the key element of the translation.

ABKÜRZUNGEN

ABBREVIATIONS

auch	*a.*	also
Abkürzung	*abk, abbr*	abbreviation
Akronym	*acr*	acronym
Adjektiv	*adj*	adjective
Adverb	*adv*	adverb
Landwirtschaft	*Agr*	agriculture
Akkusativ	*akk*	accusative
Akronym	*akr*	acronym
Anatomie	*Anat*	anatomy
Artikel	*art*	article
Bildende Künste	*Art*	fine arts
Astronomie, Astrologie	*Astr*	astronomy, astrology
Auto, Verkehr	*Auto*	automobiles, traffic
Luftfahrt	*Aviat*	aviation
Biologie	*Bio*	biology
Botanik	*Bot*	botany
britisch	*BRIT*	British
schweizerisch	*CH*	Swiss
Chemie	*Chem*	chemistry
Film	*Cine*	cinema
Wirtschaft	*Comm*	commerce
Konjunktion	*conj*	conjunction
Dativ	*dat*	dative
Eisenbahn	*Eisenb*	railways
Elektrizität	*Elek, Elec*	electricity
besonders	*esp*	especially
und so weiter	*etc*	et cetera
etwas	*etw*	something
Femininum	*f*	feminine
umgangssprachlich	*fam*	familiar, informal
übertragen	*fig*	figurative
Finanzen, Börse	*Fin*	finance
Fotografie	*Foto*	photography
Gastronomie	*Gastr*	cooking, gastronomy
Genitiv	*gen*	genitive
Geographie, Geologie	*Geo*	geography, geology
Geschichte	*Hist*	history
Imperativ	*imper*	imperative
Imperfekt	*imperf*	past tense
Informatik und Computer	*Inform*	computing
Interjektion, Ausruf	*interj*	interjection
unveränderlich	*inv*	invariable
unregelmäßig	*irr*	irregular
jemand, jemandem	*jd, jdm*	someone, somebody
jemanden, jemandes	*jdn, jds*	
Rechtsprechung	*Jur*	law

Konjunktion	konj	conjunction
Bildende Künste	Kunst	fine arts
Sprachwissenschaft, Grammatik	Ling	linguistics, grammar
Maskulinum	m	masculine
Mathematik	Math	mathematics
Medizin	Med	medicine
Meteorologie	Met	meteorology
Maskulinum und Femininum	mf	masculine and feminine
Militär	Mil	military
Musik	Mus	music
Substantiv	n	noun
Seefahrt	Naut	nautical, naval
Neutrum	nt	neuter
Zahlwort	num	numeral
oder	o	or
pejorativ, abwertend	pej	pejorative
Physik	Phys	physics
Plural	pl	plural
Politik	Pol	politics
Partizip Perfekt	pp	past participle
Präfix	pref	prefix
Präposition	prep	preposition
Pronomen	pron	pronoun
1. Vergangenheit	pt	past tense
Eisenbahn	Rail	railways
Religion	Rel	religion
siehe	s.	see
	sb	someone, somebody
schottisch	Scot	Scottish
Singular	sing	singular
Skisport	Ski	skiing
	sth	something
Technik	Tech	technology
Nachrichtentechnik	Tel	telecommunications
Theater	Theat	theatre
Fernsehen	TV	television
Typographie, Buchdruck	Typo	printing
unpersönlich	unpers	impersonal
(nord)amerikanisch	US	(North) American
Verb	vb	verb
Hilfsverb	vb aux	auxiliary verb
intransitives Verb	vi	intransitive verb
reflexives Verb	vr	reflexive verb
transitives Verb	vt	transitive verb
vulgär	vulg	vulgar
Zoologie	Zool	zoology
ungefähre Entsprechung	≈	cultural equivalent
abtrennbares Präfix	|	separable prefix

X

LAUTSCHRIFT

PHONETIC SYMBOLS

[:] Längezeichen, length mark
['] Betonung, stress mark
[*] Bindungs-R, 'r' pronounced before a vowel

alle Vokallaute sind nur ungefähre Entsprechungen
all vowel sounds are approximate only

VOKALE UND DIPHTHONGE

plant, **arm**, **f**ather	[ɑ:]	**Bahn**
fian**cé**	[ɑ̃:]	**En**semble
life	[aɪ]	weit
house	[au]	Haut
man, sad	[æ]	
but, son	[ʌ]	Butler
get, bed	[e]	Metall
name, lame	[eɪ]	
ago, better	[ə]	bitte
bird, her	[ɜ:]	
there, care	[ɛə]	mehr
it, wish	[ɪ]	Bischof
bee, me, beat, belief	[i:]	viel
here	[ɪə]	Bier
no, low	[əu]	
not, long	[ɒ]	Post
law, all	[ɔ:]	Mond
boy, oil	[ɔɪ]	Heu
push, look	[ʊ]	Pult
you, do	[u:]	Hut
poor, sure	[ʊə]	

xi

KONSONANTEN

been, blind	[b]	Ball
do, had	[d]	dann
jam, object	[dʒ]	
father, wolf	[f]	Fass
go, beg	[g]	Gast
house	[h]	Herr
youth, Indian	[j]	ja
keep, milk	[k]	kalt
lamp, oil, ill	[l]	Last
man, am	[m]	Mast
no, manner	[n]	Nuss
long, sing	[ŋ]	lang
El Niño	[ɲ]	El Niño
paper, happy	[p]	Pakt
red, dry	[r]	rot
stand, sand, yes	[s]	Rasse
ship, station	[ʃ]	Schal
tell, fat	[t]	Tal
thank, death	[θ]	
this, father	[ð]	
church, catch	[tʃ]	Rutsch
voice, live	[v]	was
water, we, which	[w]	
loch	[x]	Bach
zeal, these, gaze	[z]	Hase
pleasure	[ʒ]	Genie

xii

REGULAR GERMAN NOUN ENDINGS

nominative		genitive	plural	nominative		genitive	plural
-ade	f	-ade	-aden	-ist	m	-isten	-isten
-ant	m	-anten	-anten	-ium	nt	-iums	-ien
-anz	f	-anz	-anzen	-ius	m	-ius	-iusse
-ar	m	-ars	-are	-ive	f	-ive	-iven
-är	m	-ärs	-äre	-keit	f	-keit	-keiten
-at	nt	-at(e)s	-ate	-lein	nt	-leins	-lein
-atte	f	-atte	-atten	-ling	m	-lings	-linge
-chen	nt	-chens	-chen	-ment	nt	-ments	-mente
-ei	f	-ei	-eien	-mus	m	-mus	-men
-elle	f	-elle	-ellen	-nis	f	-nis	-nisse
-ent	m	-enten	-enten	-nis	nt	-nisses	-nisse
-enz	f	-enz	-enzen	-nom	m	-nomen	-nomen
-ette	f	-ette	-etten	-rich	m	-richs	-riche
-eur	m	-eurs	-eure	-schaft	f	-schaft	-schaften
-euse	f	-euse	-eusen	-sel	nt	-sels	-sel
-heit	f	-heit	-heiten	-tät	f	-tät	-täten
-ie	f	-ie	-ien	-tiv	m, nt	-tivs	-tive
-ik	f	-ik	-iken	-tor	m	-tors	-toren
-in	f	-in	-innen	-tum	m, nt	-tums	-tümer
-ine	f	-ine	-inen	-ung	f	-ung	-ungen
-ion	f	-ion	-ionen	-ur	f	-ur	-uren

Substantive, die mit einem geklammerten 'r' oder 's' enden
(z.B. **Angestellte(r)** mf, **Beamte(r)** m, **Gute(s)** nt) werden wie Adjektive
dekliniert:

Nouns listed with an 'r' or an 's' in brackets (eg **Angestellte(r)** mf,
Beamte(r) m, **Gute(s)** nt) take the same endings as adjectives:

der Angestellte m	**die Angestellte** f	**die Angestellten** pl
ein Angestellter m	**eine Angestellte** f	**Angestellte** pl
der Beamte m		**die Beamten** pl
ein Beamter m		**Beamte** pl
das Gute nt		
ein Gutes nt		

UNREGELMÄSSIGE ENGLISCHE VERBEN

present	past tense	past participle	present	past tense	past participle
arise (arising)	arose	arisen	deal	dealt	dealt
awake (awaking)	awoke	awoken	dig (digging)	dug	dug
be (am, is, are; being)	was, were	been	do (does)	did	done
			draw	drew	drawn
			dream	dreamed (o dreamt)	dreamed (o dreamt)
bear	bore	born(e)			
beat	beat	beaten	drink	drank	drunk
become (becoming)	became	become	drive (driving)	drove	driven
			eat	ate	eaten
begin (beginning)	began	begun	fall	fell	fallen
			feed	fed	fed
bend	bent	bent	feel	felt	felt
bet (betting)	bet	bet	fight	fought	fought
bid (bidding)	bid	bid	find	found	found
bind	bound	bound	flee	fled	fled
bite (biting)	bit	bitten	fling	flung	flung
bleed	bled	bled	fly (flies)	flew	flown
blow	blew	blown	forbid (forbidding)	forbade	forbidden
break	broke	broken	foresee	foresaw	foreseen
breed	bred	bred	forget (forgetting)	forgot	forgotten
bring	brought	brought			
build	built	built	forgive (forgiving)	forgave	forgiven
burn	burnt (o burned)	burnt (o burned)	freeze (freezing)	froze	frozen
burst	burst	burst			
buy	bought	bought	get (getting)	got	got, (US) gotten
can	could	(been able)			
cast	cast	cast	give (giving)	gave	given
catch	caught	caught	go (goes)	went	gone
choose (choosing)	chose	chosen	grind	ground	ground
cling	clung	clung	grow	grew	grown
come (coming)	came	come	hang	hung (o hanged)	hung (o hanged)
cost	cost	cost	have (has; having)	had	had
creep	crept	crept	hear	heard	heard
cut (cutting)	cut	cut			

present	past tense	past participle	present	past tense	past participle
hide (hiding)	hid	hidden	ride (riding)	rode	ridden
hit (hitting)	hit	hit	ring	rang	rung
hold	held	held	rise (rising)	rose	risen
hurt	hurt	hurt	run (running)	ran	run
keep	kept	kept	saw	sawed	sawn
kneel	knelt (o kneeled)	knelt (o kneeled)	say	said	said
know	knew	known	seek	sought	sought
lay	laid	laid	see	saw	seen
lead	led	led	sell	sold	sold
lean	leant (o leaned)	leant (o leaned)	send	sent	sent
leap	leapt (o leaped)	leapt (o leaped)	set (setting)	set	set
learn	learnt (o learned)	learnt (o learned)	shake (shaking)	shook	shaken
leave (leaving)	left	left	shall	should	–
lend	lent	lent	shine (shining)	shone	shone
let (letting)	let	let	shoot	shot	shot
lie (lying)	lay	lain	show	showed	shown
light	lit (o lighted)	lit (o lighted)	shrink	shrank	shrunk
lose (losing)	lost	lost	shut (shutting)	shut	shut
make (making)	made	made	sing	sang	sung
may	might	–	sink	sank	sunk
mean	meant	meant	sit (sitting)	sat	sat
meet	met	met	sleep	slept	slept
mow	mowed	mown (o mowed)	slide (sliding)	slid	slid
must	(had to)	(had to)	sling	slung	slung
pay	paid	paid	slit (slitting)	slit	slit
put (putting)	put	put	smell	smelt (o smelled)	smelt (o smelled)
quit (quitting)	quit (o quitted)	quit (o quitted)	sow	sowed	sown (o sowed)
read	read	read	speak	spoke	spoken
rid (ridding)	rid	rid	speed	sped (o speeded)	sped (o speeded)
			spell	spelt (o spelled)	spelt (o spelled)

present	past tense	past participle	present	past tense	past participle
spend	spent	spent	swell	swelled	swollen (o swelled)
spin (spinning)	spun	spun	swim (swimming)	swam	swum
spit (spitting)	spat	spat	swing	swung	swung
split (splitting)	split	split	take (taking)	took	taken
spoil	spoiled (o spoilt)	spoiled (o spoilt)	teach	taught	taught
			tell	told	told
spread	spread	spread	tear	tore	torn
spring	sprang	sprung	think	thought	thought
stand	stood	stood	throw	threw	thrown
steal	stole	stolen	thrust	thrust	thrust
stick	stuck	stuck	wake (waking)	woke (o waked)	woken (o waked)
sting	stung	stung	wear	wore	worn
stink	stank	stunk	weave (weaving)	wove (o weaved)	woven (o weaved)
strike (striking)	struck	struck	weep	wept	wept
strive (striving)	strove	striven	win (winning)	won	won
swear	swore	sworn	wind	wound	wound
sweep	swept	swept	write (writing)	wrote	written

IRREGULAR GERMAN VERBS

Infinitiv	Präsens 2., 3. Singular	Präteritum	Partizip Perfekt
backen	backst o bäckst, backt o bäckt	backte o buk	gebacken
befehlen	befiehlst, befiehlt	befahl	befohlen
beginnen	beginnst, beginnt	begann	begonnen
beißen	beißt, beißt	biss	gebissen
bergen	birgst, birgt	barg	geborgen
betrügen	betrügst, betrügt	betrog	betrogen
biegen	biegst, biegt	bog	gebogen
bieten	bietest, bietet	bot	geboten
binden	bindest, bindet	band	gebunden
bitten	bittest, bittet	bat	gebeten
blasen	bläst, bläst	blies	geblasen
bleiben	bleibst, bleibt	blieb	geblieben
braten	brätst, brät	briet	gebraten
brechen	brichst, bricht	brach	gebrochen
brennen	brennst, brennt	brannte	gebrannt
bringen	bringst, bringt	brachte	gebracht
denken	denkst, denkt	dachte	gedacht
dringen	dringst, dringt	drang	gedrungen
dürfen	darfst, darf	durfte	gedurft
erschrecken	erschrickst, erschrickt	erschrak	erschrocken
essen	isst, isst	aß	gegessen
fahren	fährst, fährt	fuhr	gefahren
fallen	fällst, fällt	fiel	gefallen
fangen	fängst, fängt	fing	gefangen
finden	findest, findet	fand	gefunden
fliegen	fliegst, fliegt	flog	geflogen
fließen	fließt, fließt	floss	geflossen
fressen	frisst, frisst	fraß	gefressen
frieren	frierst, friert	fror	gefroren
geben	gibst, gibt	gab	gegeben
gehen	gehst, geht	ging	gegangen
gelingen	–, gelingt	gelang	gelungen
gelten	giltst, gilt	galt	gegolten
genießen	genießt, genießt	genoss	genossen
geschehen	–, geschieht	geschah	geschehen
gewinnen	gewinnst, gewinnt	gewann	gewonnen

Infinitiv	Präsens 2., 3. Singular	Präteritum	Partizip Perfekt
gießen	gießt, gießt	goss	gegossen
gleichen	gleichst, gleicht	glich	geglichen
gleiten	gleitest, gleitet	glitt	geglitten
graben	gräbst, gräbt	grub	gegraben
greifen	greifst, greift	griff	gegriffen
haben	hast, hat	hatte	gehabt
halten	hältst, hält	hielt	gehalten
hängen	hängst, hängt	hing	gehangen
heben	hebst, hebt	hob	gehoben
heißen	heißt, heißt	hieß	geheißen
helfen	hilfst, hilft	half	geholfen
kennen	kennst, kennt	kannte	gekannt
klingen	klingst, klingt	klang	geklungen
kommen	kommst, kommt	kam	gekommen
können	kannst, kann	konnte	gekonnt
kriechen	kriechst, kriecht	kroch	gekrochen
laden	lädst, lädt	lud	geladen
lassen	lässt, lässt	ließ	gelassen
laufen	läufst, läuft	lief	gelaufen
leiden	leidest, leidet	litt	gelitten
leihen	leihst, leiht	lieh	geliehen
lesen	liest, liest	las	gelesen
liegen	liegst, liegt	lag	gelegen
lügen	lügst, lügt	log	gelogen
mahlen	mahlst, mahlt	mahlte	gemahlen
meiden	meidest, meidet	mied	gemieden
messen	misst, misst	maß	gemessen
mögen	magst, mag	mochte	gemocht
müssen	musst, muss	musste	gemusst
nehmen	nimmst, nimmt	nahm	genommen
nennen	nennst, nennt	nannte	genannt
pfeifen	pfeifst, pfeift	pfiff	gepfiffen
raten	rätst, rät	riet	geraten
reiben	reibst, reibt	rieb	gerieben
reißen	reißt, reißt	riss	gerissen
reiten	reitest, reitet	ritt	geritten
rennen	rennst, rennt	rannte	gerannt

Infinitiv	Präsens 2., 3. Singular	Präteritum	Partizip Perfekt
riechen	riechst, riecht	roch	gerochen
rufen	rufst, ruft	rief	gerufen
saufen	säufst, säuft	soff	gesoffen
saugen	saugst, saugt	sog o saugte	gesogen o gesaugt
schaffen	schaffst, schafft	schuf	geschaffen
scheiden	scheidest, scheidet	schied	geschieden
scheinen	scheinst, scheint	schien	geschienen
schieben	schiebst, schiebt	schob	geschoben
schießen	schießt, schießt	schoss	geschossen
schlafen	schläfst, schläft	schlief	geschlafen
schlagen	schlägst, schlägt	schlug	geschlagen
schleichen	schleichst, schleicht	schlich	geschlichen
schließen	schließt, schließt	schloss	geschlossen
schmeißen	schmeißt, schmeißt	schmiss	geschmissen
schmelzen	schmilzt, schmilzt	schmolz	geschmolzen
schneiden	schneidest, schneidet	schnitt	geschnitten
schreiben	schreibst, schreibt	schrieb	geschrieben
schreien	schreist, schreit	schrie	geschrien
schweigen	schweigst, schweigt	schwieg	geschwiegen
schwellen	schwillst, schwillt	schwoll	geschwollen
schwimmen	schwimmst, schwimmt	schwamm	geschwommen
schwören	schwörst, schwört	schwor	geschworen
sehen	siehst, sieht	sah	gesehen
sein	bist, ist	war	gewesen
senden	sendest, sendet	sandte	gesandt
singen	singst, singt	sang	gesungen
sinken	sinkst, sinkt	sank	gesunken
sitzen	sitzt, sitzt	saß	gesessen
sollen	sollst, soll	sollte	gesollt
sprechen	sprichst, spricht	sprach	gesprochen
springen	springst, springt	sprang	gesprungen
stechen	stichst, sticht	stach	gestochen
stehen	stehst, steht	stand	gestanden
stehlen	stiehlst, stiehlt	stahl	gestohlen
steigen	steigst, steigt	stieg	gestiegen
sterben	stirbst, stirbt	starb	gestorben

Infinitiv	Präsens 2., 3. Singular	Präteritum	Partizip Perfekt
stinken	stinkst, stinkt	stank	gestunken
stoßen	stößt, stößt	stieß	gestoßen
streichen	streichst, streicht	strich	gestrichen
streiten	streitest, streitet	stritt	gestritten
tragen	trägst, trägt	trug	getragen
treffen	triffst, trifft	traf	getroffen
treiben	treibst, treibt	trieb	getrieben
treten	trittst, tritt	trat	getreten
trinken	trinkst, trinkt	trank	getrunken
tun	tust, tut	tat	getan
verderben	verdirbst, verdirbt	verdarb	verdorben
vergessen	vergisst, vergisst	vergaß	vergessen
verlieren	verlierst, verliert	verlor	verloren
verschwinden	verschwindest, verschwindet	verschwand	verschwunden
verzeihen	verzeihst, verzeiht	verzieh	verziehen
wachsen	wächst, wächst	wuchs	gewachsen
wenden	wendest, wendet	wandte	gewandt
werben	wirbst, wirbt	warb	geworben
werden	wirst, wird	wurde	geworden
werfen	wirfst, wirft	warf	geworfen
wiegen	wiegst, wiegt	wog	gewogen
wissen	weißt, weiß	wusste	gewusst
wollen	willst, will	wollte	gewollt
ziehen	ziehst, zieht	zog	gezogen
zwingen	zwingst, zwingt	zwang	gezwungen

Deutsch – Englisch

German – English

a

à prep +akk at ... each; **4 Tickets ~ 8 Euro** 4 tickets at 8 euros each

A abk = **Autobahn** ~ M (Brit), ~ I (US)

Aal (-(e)s, -e) m eel

○ **SCHLÜSSELWORT**

ab prep +dat from; **Kinder ab 12 Jahren** children from the age of 12; **ab morgen** from tomorrow; **ab sofort** as of now

▷ adv **1** off; **links ab** to the left; **der Knopf ist ab** the button has come off; **ab nach Hause!** off you go home

2 (zeitlich) **von da ab** from then on; **von heute ab** from today, as of today

3 (auf Fahrplänen) **München ab 12.20** leaving Munich 12.20

4 ab und zu o **an** now and then o again

ab|bauen vt (Zelt) to take down; (verringern) to reduce

ab|beißen irr vt to bite off

ab|bestellen vt to cancel

ab|biegen irr vi to turn off; (Straße) to bend; **nach links/rechts ~** to turn left/right

Abbildung f illustration

ab|blasen irr vt (fig) to call off

ab|blenden vt, vi (Auto) (**die Scheinwerfer**) ~ to dip (Brit) (o to dim (US)) one's headlights; **Abblendlicht** nt dipped (Brit) (o dimmed (US)) headlights pl

ab|brechen irr vt to break off; (Gebäude) to pull down; (aufhören) to stop; (Computerprogramm) to abort

ab|bremsen vi to brake, to slow down

ab|bringen irr vt: **jdn von einer Idee ~** to talk sb out of an idea; **jdn vom Thema ~** to get sb away from the subject; **davon lasse ich mich nicht ~** nothing will make me change my mind about it

ab|buchen vt to debit (von to)

ab|danken vi to resign

ab|drehen vt (Gas, Wasser) to turn off; (Licht) to switch off ▷ vi (Schiff, Flugzeug) to change course

Abend (-s, -e) m evening; **am ~** in the evening; **zu ~ essen** to have dinner; **heute/morgen/gestern ~** this/tomorrow/yesterday evening; **guten ~!** good evening; **Abendbrot** nt supper; **Abendessen** nt dinner; **Abendgarderobe** f evening dress (o gown); **Abendkasse** f box office; **Abendkleid** nt evening dress (o gown); **Abendmahl** nt: **das ~** (Holy) Communion; **abends** adv in the evening; **montags ~** on Monday evenings

Abenteuer (-s, -) nt adventure; **Abenteuerurlaub** m adventure holiday

aber conj but; (jedoch) however; **oder ~** alternatively; **~ ja!** (but) of course; **das ist ~ nett von Ihnen** that's really nice of you

abergläubisch adj superstitious

ab|fahren irr vi to leave (o to depart) (nach for); (Ski) to ski down; **Abfahrt** f departure; (von Autobahn) exit; (Ski) descent; (Piste) run; **Abfahrtslauf** m (Ski) downhill; **Abfahrtszeit** f departure time

Abfall m waste; (Müll) rubbish (Brit), garbage (US); **Abfalleimer** m rubbish bin (Brit), garbage can (US)

abfällig adj disparaging; **~ von jdm sprechen** to make disparaging remarks about sb

ab|färben vi (Wäsche) to run; (fig) to rub off

ab|fertigen vt (Pakete) to prepare for dispatch; (an der Grenze) to clear; **Abfertigungsschalter** m (am Flughafen) check-in desk

ab|finden irr vt to pay off ▷ vr: **sich mit etw ~** to come to terms with sth; **Abfindung** f (Entschädigung) compensation; (von Angestellten) redundancy payment

ab|fliegen irr vi (Flugzeug) to take off; (Passagier a.) to fly off; **Abflug** m departure; (Start) takeoff; **Abflughalle** f departure lounge; **Abflugzeit** f departure time

Abfluss m drain; (am Waschbecken) plughole (Brit); **Abflussrohr** nt waste pipe; (außen) drainpipe

ab|fragen vt to test; (Inform) to call up

ab|führen vi (Med) to have a laxative effect ▷ vt (Steuern, Gebühren) to pay; **jdn ~ lassen** to take sb into custody; **Abführmittel** nt laxative

Abgabe f handing in; (von Ball) pass; (Steuer) tax; (einer Erklärung) making; **abgabenfrei** adj tax-free; **abgabenpflichtig** adj liable to tax

Abgase pl (Auto) exhaust fumes pl; **Abgas(sonder)untersuchung** f exhaust emission test

ab|geben vt (Gepäck, Schlüssel) to leave (bei with); (Schularbeit etc) to hand in; (Wärme) to give off; (Erklärung, Urteil) to make ▷ vr: **sich mit jdm ~** to associate with sb; **sich mit etw ~** to bother with sth

abgebildet adj: **wie oben ~** as shown above

ab|gehen irr vi (Post) to go; (Knopf etc) to come off; (abgezogen werden) to be taken off; (Straße) to branch off; **von der Schule ~** to leave school; **sie geht mir ab** I really miss her; **was geht denn hier ab?** (fam) what's going on here?

abgehetzt adj exhausted, shattered

ab|gelaufen adj (Pass) expired; (Zeit, Frist) up; **die Milch ist ~** the milk is past its sell-by date

abgelegen adj remote

abgemacht interj OK, it's a deal, that's settled, then

abgeneigt adj: **einer Sache** (dat) **~ sein** to be averse to sth; **ich wäre nicht ~, das zu tun** I wouldn't mind doing that

Abgeordnete(r) mf Member of Parliament

abgepackt adj prepacked

abgerissen adj: **der Knopf ist ~** the button has come off

abgesehen adj: **es auf jdn/etw ~ haben** to be after sb/sth; **~ von** apart from

abgespannt adj (Person) exhausted, worn out

abgestanden adj stale; (Bier) flat
abgestorben adj (Pflanze) dead; (Finger) numb
abgestumpft adj (Person) insensitive
abgetragen adj (Kleidung) worn
ab|gewöhnen vt: jdm etw ~ to cure sb of sth; **sich etw ~** to give sth up
ab|haken vt to tick off; **das (Thema) ist schon abgehakt** that's been dealt with
ab|halten irr vt (Versammlung) to hold; **jdn von etw ~** (fernhalten) to keep sb away from sth; (hindern) to keep sb from sth
abhanden adj: ~ **kommen** to get lost
Abhang m slope
ab|hängen vt (Bild) to take down; (Anhänger) to uncouple; (Verfolger) to shake off ▷ irr vi: **von jdm/etw ~** to depend on sb/sth; **das hängt davon ab, ob ...** it depends (on) whether ...;
abhängig adj dependent (von on)
ab|hauen irr vt (abschlagen) to cut off ▷ vi (fam: verschwinden) to clear off; **hau ab!** get lost!, beat it!
ab|heben irr vt (Geld) to withdraw; (Telefonhörer, Spielkarte) to pick up ▷ vi (Flugzeug) to take off; (Rakete) to lift off; (Karten) to cut
ab|holen vt to collect; (am Bahnhof etc) to meet; (mit dem Auto) to pick up; **Abholmarkt** m cash and carry
ab|horchen vt (Med) to listen to
ab|hören vt (Vokabeln) to test; (Telefongespräch) to tap; (Tonband etc) to listen to
Abitur (-s, -e) nt German school-leaving examination, ≈ A-levels (Brit), ≈ High School Diploma (US)

ab|kaufen vt: jdm etw ~ to buy sth from sb; **das kauf ich dir nicht ab!** (fam: glauben) I don't believe you
ab|klingen irr vi (Schmerz) to ease; (Wirkung) to wear off
ab|kommen irr vi to get away; **von der Straße ~** to leave the road; **von einem Plan ~** to give up a plan; **vom Thema ~** to stray from the point
Abkommen (-s, -) nt agreement
ab|koppeln vt (Anhänger) to unhitch
ab|kratzen vt to scrape off ▷ vi (fam: sterben) to kick the bucket, to croak
ab|kühlen vi, vt to cool down ▷ vr: **sich ~** to cool down
ab|kürzen vt (Wort) to abbreviate; **den Weg ~** to take a short cut; **Abkürzung** f (Wort) abbreviation; (Weg) short cut
ab|laden irr vt to unload
Ablage f (für Akten) tray; (Aktenordnung) filing system
Ablauf m (Abfluss) drain; (von Ereignissen) course; (einer Frist, Zeit) expiry; **ab|laufen** irr vi (abfließen) to drain away; (Ereignisse) to happen; (Frist, Zeit, Pass) to expire
ab|legen vt to put down; (Kleider) to take off; (Gewohnheit) to get out of; (Prüfung) to take, to sit; (Akten) to file away ▷ vi (Schiff) to cast off
ab|lehnen vt to reject; (Einladung) to decline; (missbilligen)

to disapprove of; (*Bewerber*) to turn down ▷ *vi* to decline

ab|lenken *vt* to distract; **jdn von der Arbeit ~** to distract sb from their work; **vom Thema ~** to change the subject; **Ablenkung** *f* distraction

ab|lesen *vt* (*Text, Rede*) to read; **das Gas/den Strom ~** to read the gas/electricity meter

ab|liefern *vt* to deliver

ab|machen *vt* (*entfernen*) to take off; (*vereinbaren*) to agree; **Abmachung** *f* agreement

ab|melden *vt* (*Zeitung*) to cancel; (*Auto*) to take off the road ▷ *vr*: **sich ~** to give notice of one's departure; (*im Hotel*) to check out; (*vom Verein*) to cancel one's membership

ab|messen *irr vt* to measure

ab|nehmen *irr vt* to take off, to remove; (*Hörer*) to pick up; (*Führerschein*) to take away; (*Geld*) to get (*jdm out of sb*); (*kaufen, umg: glauben*) to buy (*jdm from sb*) ▷ *vi* to decrease; (*schlanker werden*) to lose weight; (*Tel*) to pick up the phone; **fünf Kilo ~** to lose five kilos

Abneigung *f* dislike (*gegen* of); (*stärker*) aversion (*gegen* to)

ab|nutzen *vt* to wear out ▷ *vr*: **sich ~** to wear out

Abonnement (-s, -s) *nt* subscription; **Abonnent(in)** *m(f)* subscriber; **abonnieren** *vt* to subscribe to

ab|raten *irr vi*: **jdm von etw ~** to advise sb against sth

ab|räumen *vt*: **den Tisch ~** to clear the table; **das Geschirr ~** to clear away the dishes; (*Preis etc*) to walk off with

Abrechnung *f* settlement; (*Rechnung*) bill

ab|regen *vr*: **sich ~** (*fam*) to calm

(*o to cool*) down; **reg dich ab!** take it easy

Abreise *f* departure; **ab|reisen** *vi* to leave (*nach* for); **Abreisetag** *m* day of departure

ab|reißen *irr vt* (*Haus*) to pull down; (*Blatt*) to tear off; **den Kontakt nicht ~ lassen** to stay in touch ▷ *vi* (*Knopf etc*) to come off

ab|runden *vt*: **eine Zahl nach oben/unten ~** to round a number up/down

abrupt *adj* abrupt

ABS *nt abk* = **Antiblockiersystem** (*Auto*) ABS

Abs. *abk* = **Absender** from

ab|sagen *vt* to cancel, to call off; (*Einladung*) to turn down ▷ *vi* (*ablehnen*) to decline; **ich muss leider ~** I'm afraid I can't come

Absatz *m* (*Comm*) sales *pl*; (*neuer Abschnitt*) paragraph; (*Schuh*) heel

ab|schaffen *vt* to abolish, to do away with

ab|schalten *vt, vi* (*a. fig*) to switch off

ab|schätzen *vt* to estimate; (*Lage*) to assess

abscheulich *adj* disgusting

ab|schicken *vt* to send off

ab|schieben *irr vt* (*ausweisen*) to deport

Abschied (-(e)s, -e) *m* parting; **~ nehmen** to say good-bye (*von* jdm to sb); **Abschiedsfeier** *f* farewell party

Abschlagszahlung *f* interim payment

Abschleppdienst *m* (*Auto*) breakdown service; **ab|schleppen** *vt* to tow; **Abschleppseil** *nt* towrope; **Abschleppwagen** *m* breakdown truck (*Brit*), tow truck (*US*)

ab|schließen *irr vt* (*Tür*) to lock; (*beenden*) to conclude, to finish; (*Vertrag, Handel*) to conclude;

Abschluss m (Beendigung) close, conclusion; (von Vertrag, Handel) conclusion

ab|schmecken vt (kosten) to taste; (würzen) to season

ab|schminken vr: **sich ~** to take one's make-up off ▷ vt (fam) **sich** (dat) **etw ~** to get sth out of one's mind

ab|schnallen vr: **sich ~** to undo one's seatbelt

ab|schneiden irr vt to cut off ▷ vi: **gut/schlecht ~** to do well/badly

Abschnitt m (von Buch, Text) section; (Kontrollabschnitt) stub

ab|schrauben vt to unscrew

ab|schrecken vt to deter, to put off

ab|schreiben irr vt to copy (bei, von from, off); (verloren geben) to write off; (Comm: absetzen) to deduct

abschüssig adj steep

ab|schwächen vt to lessen; (Behauptung, Kritik) to tone down

ab|schwellen irr vi (Entzündung) to go down; (Lärm) to die down

absehbar adj foreseeable; **in ~er Zeit** in the foreseeable future; **ab|sehen** irr vt (Ende, Folgen) to foresee ▷ vi: **von etw ~** to refrain from sth

abseits adv out of the way; (Sport) offside ▷ prep +gen away from; **Abseits** nt (Sport) offside; **Abseitsfalle** f (Sport) offside trap

ab|senden irr vt to send off; (Post) to post; **Absender(in)** (-s, -) m(f) sender

ab|setzen vt (Glas, Brille etc) to put down; (aussteigen lassen) to drop (off); (Comm) to sell; (Fin) to deduct; (streichen) to drop ▷ vr: **sich ~** (sich entfernen) to clear off; (sich ablagern) to be deposited

Absicht f intention; **mit ~** on

purpose; **absichtlich** adj intentional, deliberate

absolut adj absolute

ab|specken vi (fam) to lose weight

ab|speichern vt (Inform) to save

ab|sperren vt to block (o to close) off; (Tür) to lock; **Absperrung** f (Vorgang) blocking (o closing) off; (Sperre) barricade

ab|spielen vt (CD etc) to play ▷ vr: **sich ~** to happen

ab|springen irr vi to jump down/off; (von einer Geplantem) to drop out (von of)

ab|spülen vt to rinse; (Geschirr) to wash (up)

Abstand m distance; (zeitlich) interval; **~ halten** to keep one's distance

ab|stauben vt, vi to dust; (fam: stehlen) to pinch

Abstecher (-s, -) m detour

ab|steigen irr vi (vom Rad etc) to get off, to dismount; (in Gasthof) to stay (in +dat at)

ab|stellen vt (niederstellen) to put down; (Auto) to park; (ausschalten) to turn (o to switch) off; (Missstand, Unsitte) to stop; **Abstellraum** m store room

Abstieg (-(e)s, -e) m (vom Berg) descent; (Sport) relegation

ab|stimmen vi to vote ▷ vt (Termine, Ziele) to fit in (auf +akk with); **Dinge aufeinander ~** to coordinate things ▷ vr: **sich ~** to come to an agreement (o arrangement)

abstoßend adj repulsive

abstrakt adj abstract

ab|streiten irr vt to deny

Abstrich m (Med) smear; **~e machen** to cut back (an +dat on); (weniger erwarten) to lower one's sights

Absturz m fall; (Aviat, Inform)

crash; **ab**|**stürzen** vi to fall;
(*Aviat, Inform*) to crash

absurd *adj* absurd

Abszess (*-es, -e*) *m* abscess

ab|**tauen** vt, vi to thaw;
(*Kühlschrank*) to defrost

Abtei (*-, -en*) *f* abbey

Abteil (*-(e)s, -e*) *nt* compartment

Abteilung *f* (*in Firma, Kaufhaus*)
department; (*in Krankenhaus*)
section

ab|**treiben** *irr* vt (*Kind*) to abort
▷ vi to be driven off course; (*Med:
Abtreibung vornehmen*) to carry out
an abortion; (*Abtreibung vornehmen
lassen*) to have an abortion;
Abtreibung *f* abortion

ab|**trocknen** vt to dry

ab|**warten** vt to wait for; **das
bleibt abzuwarten** that remains
to be seen ▷ vi to wait

abwärts *adv* down

Abwasch (*-(e)s*) *m* washing-up;
ab|**waschen** *irr* vt (*Schmutz*) to
wash off; (*Geschirr*) to wash (up)

Abwasser (*-s, Abwässer*) *nt*
sewage

ab|**wechseln** vr: **sich ~** to
alternate; **sich mit jdm ~** to take
turns with sb; **abwechselnd** *adv*
alternately; **Abwechslung** *f*
change; **zur ~** for a change

ab|**weisen** vt to turn away;
(*Antrag*) to turn down; **abweisend**
adj unfriendly

abwesend *adj* absent;
Abwesenheit *f* absence

ab|**wiegen** *irr* vt to weigh (out)

ab|**wimmeln** vt (*fam*) **jdn ~** to
get rid of sb, to give sb the elbow

ab|**wischen** vt (*Gesicht, Tisch etc*)
to wipe; (*Schmutz*) to wipe off

ab|**zählen** vt to count; (*Geld*) to
count out

Abzeichen *nt* badge

ab|**zeichnen** vt to draw, to copy;
(*Dokument*) to initial ▷ vr: **sich**

~ to stand out; (*fig: bevorstehen*) to
loom

ab|**ziehen** *irr* vt to take off; (*Bett*)
to strip; (*Schlüssel*) to take out;
(*subtrahieren*) to take away, to
subtract ▷ vi to go away

Abzug *m* (*Foto*) print; (*Öffnung*)
vent; (*Truppen*) withdrawal;
(*Betrag*) deduction; **nach ~ der
Kosten** charges deducted;
abzüglich *prep +gen* minus;
~ 20% Rabatt less 20% discount

ab|**zweigen** vi to branch off ▷ vt
to set aside; **Abzweigung** *f*
junction

Accessoires *pl* accessories *pl*

ach *interj* oh; **~ so!** oh, I see;
~ was! (*Überraschung*) really?;
(*Ärger*) don't talk nonsense

Achse (*-, -n*) *f* axis; (*Auto*) axle

Achsel (*-, -n*) *f* shoulder;
(*Achselhöhle*) armpit

Achsenbruch *m* (*Auto*) broken
axle

acht *num* eight; **heute in ~ Tagen**
in a week('s time), a week from
today

Acht (*-*) *f*: **sich in ~ nehmen** to be
careful (*vor +dat of*), to watch out
(*vor +dat for*); **etw außer ~ lassen**
to disregard sth

achte(r, s) *adj* eighth; *siehe auch*
dritte; **Achtel** (*-s, -*) *nt* (*Bruchteil*)
eighth; (*Wein etc*) eighth of a litre;
(*Glas Wein*) = small glass

achten vt to respect ▷ vi to pay
attention (*auf +akk to*)

Achterbahn *f* big dipper, roller
coaster

acht|**geben** *irr* vi to take care
(*auf +akk of*)

achthundert *num* eight
hundred; **achtmal** *adv* eight
times

Achtung *f* attention; (*Ehrfurcht*)
respect ▷ *interj* look out

achtzehn *num* eighteen;

achtzehnte(r, s) adj
eighteenth; siehe auch **dritte**
achtzig num eighty; **in den ~er Jahren** in the eighties;
achtzigste(r, s) adj eightieth
Acker (-s, Äcker) m field
Action (-, -s) f (fam) action;
Actionfilm m action film
Adapter (-s, -) m adapter
addieren vt to add (up)
Adel (-s) m nobility; **adelig** adj noble
Ader (-, -n) f vein
Adjektiv nt adjective
Adler (-s, -) m eagle
adoptieren vt to adopt;
Adoption f adoption;
Adoptiveltern pl adoptive parents pl; **Adoptivkind** nt adopted child
Adrenalin (-s) nt adrenalin
Adressbuch nt directory;
(persönliches) address book;
Adresse (-, -n) f address;
adressieren vt to address (an +akk to)
ADSL f ADSL
Advent (-s, -) m Advent;
Adventskranz m Advent wreath
Adverb nt adverb
Aerobic nt sg aerobics sing
Affäre (-, -n) f affair
Affe (-n, -n) m monkey
Afghanistan (-s) nt Afghanistan
Afrika (-s) nt Africa;
Afrikaner(in) (-s, -) m(f) African;
afrikanisch adj African
After (-s, -) m anus
Aftershave (-(s), -s) nt aftershave
AG (-, -s) f abk = **Aktiengesellschaft** plc (Brit), corp. (US)
Agent(in) m(f) agent; **Agentur** f agency

aggressiv adj aggressive
Ägypten (-s) nt Egypt
ah interj ah, ooh
aha interj I see, aha
ähneln vi +dat to be like, to resemble ▷ vr: **sich ~** to be alike (o similar)
ahnen vt to suspect; **du ahnst es nicht!** would you believe it?
ähnlich adj similar (dat to); **jdm ~ sehen** to look like sb;
Ähnlichkeit f similarity
Ahnung f idea; (Vermutung) suspicion; **keine ~!** no idea;
ahnungslos adj unsuspecting
Ahorn (-s, -e) m maple
Aids (-) nt Aids; **aidskrank** adj suffering from Aids; **Aidstest** m Aids test
Airbag (-s, -s) m (Auto) airbag;
Airbus m airbus
Akademie (-, -n) f academy;
Akademiker(in) (-s, -) m(f) (university) graduate
akklimatisieren vr: **sich ~** to acclimatize oneself
Akkordeon (-s, -s) nt accordion
Akku (-s, -s) m (storage) battery
Akkusativ m accusative (case)
Akne (-, -) f acne
Akrobat(in) (-s, -en) m(f) acrobat
Akt (-(e)s, -e) m act; (Kunst) nude
Akte (-, -n) f file; **etw zu den ~n legen** (a. fig) to file sth away;
Aktenkoffer m briefcase
Aktie (-, -n) f share;
Aktiengesellschaft f public limited company (Brit), corporation (US)
Aktion f (Kampagne) campaign;
(Einsatz) operation
Aktionär(in) (-s, -e) m(f) shareholder
aktiv adj active; **aktivieren** vt to activate
aktualisieren vt to update;
aktuell adj (Thema) topical;

(*modern*) up-to-date; (*Problem*) current; **nicht mehr ~** no longer relevant

Akupunktur f acupuncture

akustisch adj acoustic; **Akustik** f acoustics sing

akut adj acute

AKW (-s, -s) nt abk = **Atomkraftwerk** nuclear power station

Akzent (-(e)s, -e) m accent; (*Betonung*) stress; **mit starkem schottischen ~** with a strong Scottish accent

akzeptieren vt to accept

Alarm (-(e)s, -e) m alarm; **Alarmanlage** f alarm system; **alarmieren** vt to alarm; **die Polizei ~** to call the police

Albanien (-s) nt Albania

Albatros (-ses, -se) m albatross

albern adj silly

Albtraum m nightmare

Album (-s, Alben) nt album

Algen pl algae pl; (*Meeresalgen*) seaweed sing

Algerien (-s) nt Algeria

Alibi (-s, -s) nt alibi

Alimente pl maintenance sing

Alkohol (-s, -e) m alcohol; **alkoholfrei** adj non-alcoholic; **~es Getränk** soft drink; **Alkoholiker(in)** (-s, -) m(f) alcoholic; **alkoholisch** adj alcoholic; **Alkoholtest** m breathalyser® test (*Brit*), alcohol test

All (-s) nt universe

○ SCHLÜSSELWORT

alle(r, s) adj **1** (*sämtliche*) all; **wir alle** all of us; **alle Kinder waren da** all the children were there; **alle Kinder mögen ...** all children like ...; **alle beide** both of us/them; **sie kamen alle** they all came; **alles Gute** all the best; **alles**

in allem all in all

2 (*mit Zeit- oder Maßangaben*) every; **alle vier Jahre** every four years; **alle fünf Meter** every five metres

▷ pron everything; **alles, was er sagt** everything he says, all that he says

▷ adv (*zu Ende, aufgebraucht*) finished; **die Milch ist alle** the milk's all gone, there's no milk left; **etw alle machen** to finish sth up

Allee (-, -n) f avenue

allein adj, adv alone; (*ohne Hilfe*) on one's own, by oneself; **nicht ~** (*nicht nur*) not only; **allein-erziehend** adj: **~e Mutter** single mother; **Alleinerziehende(r)** mf single mother/father/parent; **alleinstehend** adj single, unmarried

allerbeste(r, s) adj very best

allerdings adv (*zwar*) admittedly; (*gewiss*) certainly, sure (US)

allererste(r, s) adj very first; **zu allererst** first of all

Allergie f allergy; **Allergiker(in)** (-s, -) m(f) allergy sufferer; **allergisch** adj allergic (*gegen* to)

allerhand adj inv (*fam*) all sorts of; **das ist doch ~!** (*Vorwurf*) that's the limit

Allerheiligen (-) nt All Saints' Day

allerhöchste(r, s) adj very highest; **allerhöchstens** adv at the very most; **allerlei** adj inv all sorts of; **allerletzte(r, s)** adj very last; **allerwenigste(r, s)** adj very least

alles pron everything; **~ in allem** all in all; *siehe auch* **alle**

Alleskleber (-s, -) m all-purpose glue

allgemein adj general; **im Allgemeinen** in general;

Allgemeinarzt m,

Allgemeinärztin f GP (Brit), family practitioner (US)

Alligator (-s, -en) m alligator

alljährlich adj annual

allmählich adj gradual ▷ adv gradually

Allradantrieb m all-wheel drive

Alltag m everyday life; **alltäglich** adj everyday; (gewöhnlich) ordinary; (tagtäglich) daily

allzu adv all too

Allzweckreiniger (-s, -) m multi-purpose cleaner

Alpen pl: **die ~** the Alps pl

Alphabet (-(e)s, -e) nt alphabet; **alphabetisch** adj alphabetical

Alptraum m siehe Albtraum

SCHLÜSSELWORT

als konj 1 (zeitlich) when; (gleichzeitig) as; **damals, als ...** (in the days) when ...; **gerade, als ...** just as ...

2 (in der Eigenschaft) than; **als Antwort** as an answer; **als Kind** as a child

3 (bei Vergleichen) than; **ich kam später als er** I came later than he (did) o later than him; **lieber ... als ...** rather ... than ...; **nichts als Ärger** nothing but trouble

4 **als ob/wenn** as if

also conj (folglich) so, therefore ▷ adv, interj so; **~ gut** (o **schön**)! okay then

alt adj old; **wie ~ sind Sie?** how old are you?; **28 Jahre ~** 28 years old; **vier Jahre älter** four years older

Altar (-(e)s, Altäre) m altar

Alter (-s, -) nt age; (hohes) old age; **im ~ von** at the age of; **er ist in meinem ~** he's my age

alternativ adj alternative; (umweltbewusst) ecologically

minded; (Landwirtschaft) organic;
Alternative f alternative

Altersheim nt old people's home

Altglas nt used glass; **Altglascontainer** m bottle bank; **altmodisch** adj old-fashioned; **Altpapier** nt waste paper; **Altstadt** f old town

Alt-Taste f Alt key

Alufolie f (o kitchen) foil

Aluminium (-s) nt aluminium (Brit), aluminum (US)

Alzheimerkrankheit f Alzheimer's (disease)

am kontr von **an dem**; **~ 2. Januar** on January 2(nd); **~ Morgen** in the morning; **~ Strand** on the beach; **~ Bahnhof** at the station; **was gefällt Ihnen ~ besten?** what do you like best?; **~ besten bleiben wir hier** it would be best if we stayed here

Amateur(in) m(f) amateur

ambulant adj outpatient; **kann ich ~ behandelt werden?** can I have it done as an outpatient?; **Ambulanz** f (Krankenwagen) ambulance; (in der Klinik) outpatients' department

Ameise (-, -n) f ant

amen interj amen

Amerika (-s) nt America; **Amerikaner(in)** (-s, -) m(f) American; **amerikanisch** adj American

Ampel (-, -n) f traffic lights pl

Amphitheater nt amphitheatre

Amsel (-, -n) f blackbird

Amt (-(e)s, Ämter) nt (Dienststelle) office, department; (Posten) post; **amtlich** adj official; **Amtszeichen** nt (Tel) dialling tone (Brit), dial tone (US)

amüsant adj amusing; **amüsieren** vt to amuse ▷ vr: **sich ~** to enjoy oneself, to have a good time

○ SCHLÜSSELWORT

an prep +dat **1** (räumlich) (wo?) at;
(auf, bei) on; (nahe bei) near; **an
diesem Ort** at this place; **an der
Wand** on the wall; **zu nahe an
etw** too near to sth; **unten am
Fluss** down by the river; **Köln
liegt am Rhein** Cologne is on the
Rhine
2 (zeitlich: wann?) on; **an diesem
Tag** on this day; **an Ostern** at
Easter
3 arm an Fett low in fat; **an etw
sterben** to die of sth; **an (und für)
sich** actually
▷ prep +akk **1** (räumlich: wohin?) to;
er ging ans Fenster he went
(over) to the window; **etw an die
Wand hängen/schreiben** to
hang/write sth on the wall
2 (woran?) **an etw denken** to think
of sth
3 (gerichtet an) to; **ein Gruß/eine
Frage an dich** greetings/a
question to you
▷ adv **1** (ungefähr) about; **an die
hundert** about a hundred
2 (auf Fahrplänen) Frankfurt an
18.30 arriving Frankfurt 18.30
3 (ab) **von dort/heute an** from
there/today onwards
4 (angeschaltet, angezogen) das
Licht ist an the light is on; **ohne
etwas an** with nothing on; siehe
auch **am**

anal adj anal

analog adj analogous; (Inform)
analog

Analyse (-, -n) f analysis;
analysieren vt to analyse

Ananas (-, - o -se) f pineapple

an|**baggern** vt (fam) to chat up
(Brit), to come on to (US)

Anbau m (Agr) cultivation;

(Gebäude) extension; **an**|**bauen** vt
(Agr) to cultivate; (Gebäudeteil) to
build on

an|**behalten** irr vt to keep on

anbei adv enclosed; **~ sende
ich ...** please find enclosed ...

an|**beten** vt to worship

an|**bieten** irr vt to offer ▷ vr:
sich ~ to volunteer

an|**binden** irr vt to tie up

Anblick m sight

an|**braten** irr vt to brown

an|**brechen** irr vt to start;
(Vorräte, Ersparnisse) to break into;
(Flasche, Packung) to open ▷ vi to
start; (Tag) to break; (Nacht) to fall

an|**brennen** irr vt, vi to burn; **das
Fleisch schmeckt angebrannt**
the meat tastes burnt

an|**bringen** irr vt (herbeibringen)
to bring; (befestigen) to fix, to
attach

Andacht (-, -en) f devotion;
(Gottesdienst) prayers pl

an|**dauern** irr vt to continue, to go
on; **andauernd** adj continual

Andenken (-s, -) nt memory;
(Gegenstand) souvenir

andere(r, s) adj (weitere) other;
(verschieden) different; (folgend)
next; **am ~n Tag** the next day; **von
etw/jmd ~m sprechen** to talk
about sth/sb else; **unter ~m**
among other things; **andererseits**
adv on the other hand

ändern vt to alter, to change
▷ vr: **sich ~** to change

andernfalls adv otherwise

anders adv differently (als from);
jemand/irgendwo ~ someone/
somewhere else; **sie ist ~ als ihre
Schwester** she's not like her
sister; **es geht nicht ~** there's no
other way; **anders(he)rum** adv
the other way round; **anderswo**
adv somewhere else

anderthalb num one and a half

Änderung f change, alteration

an|deuten vt to indicate; (*Wink geben*) to hint at

Andorra (-s) nt Andorra

Andrang m: **es herrschte großer ~** there was a huge crowd

an|drohen vt: **jdm etw ~** to threaten sb with sth

aneinander adv at/on/to one another (*o each other*); **~ denken** think of each other; **sich ~ gewöhnen** to get used to each other; **aneinander|geraten** irr vi to clash; **aneinander|legen** vt to put together

an|erkennen irr vt (*Staat, Zeugnis etc*) to recognize; (*würdigen*) to appreciate; **Anerkennung** f recognition; (*Würdigung*) appreciation

an|fahren irr vt (*fahren gegen*) to run into; (*Ort, Hafen*) to stop (*o call*) at; (*liefern*) to deliver; **jdn ~** (*fig: schimpfen*) to jump on sb ▷ vi to start; (*losfahren*) to drive off

Anfall m (*Med*) attack; **~ für** prone to

Anfang (-(e)s, Anfänge) m beginning, start; **zu/am ~** to start with; **~ Mai** at the beginning of May; **sie ist ~ 20** she's in her early twenties; **an|fangen** irr vt, vi to begin, to start; **damit kann ich nichts ~** that's no use to me; **Anfänger(in)** (-s, -) m(f) beginner; **anfangs** adv at first; **Anfangsbuchstabe** m first (*o initial*) letter

an|fassen vt (*berühren*) to touch ▷ vi: **kannst du mal mit ~?** can you give me a hand?

Anflug m (*Aviat*) approach; (*Hauch*) trace

an|fordern vt to demand; **Anforderung** f request (*von* for); (*Anspruch*) demand

Anfrage f inquiry

an|freunden vr: **sich mit jdm ~** to make (*o* to become) friends with sb

an|fühlen vr: **sich ~** to feel; **es fühlt sich gut an** it feels good

Anführungszeichen pl quotation marks pl

Angabe f (*Tech*) specification; (*fam: Prahlerei*) showing off; (*Tennis*) serve; **~n** pl (*Auskunft*) particulars pl; **die ~n waren falsch** (*Info*) the information was wrong; **an|geben** irr vt (*Name, Grund*) to give; (*zeigen*) to indicate; (*bestimmen*) to set ▷ vi (*fam: prahlen*) to boast; (*Sport*) to serve; **Angeber(in)** (-s, -) m(f) (*fam*) show-off; **angeblich** adj alleged

angeboren adj inborn

Angebot nt offer; (*Comm*) supply (*an +dat of*); **~ und Nachfrage** supply and demand

angebracht adj appropriate

angebunden adj: **kurz ~** curt

angeheitert adj tipsy

an|gehen irr vt to concern; **das geht dich nichts an** that's none of your business; **ein Problem ~** to tackle a problem; **was ihn angeht** as far as he's concerned, for him ▷ vi (*Feuer*) to catch; (*fam: beginnen*) to begin; **angehend** adj prospective

Angehörige(r) mf relative

Angeklagte(r) mf accused, defendant

Angel (-, -n) f fishing rod; (*an der Tür*) hinge

Angelegenheit f affair, matter

Angelhaken m fish hook;

angeln vt to catch ▷ vi to fish; **Angeln** (-s) nt angling, fishing; **Angelrute** (-, -n) f fishing rod

angemessen adj appropriate, suitable

angenehm adj pleasant; **~!** (bei Vorstellung) pleased to meet you

angenommen adj assumed ▷ conj: **~, es regnet, was machen wir dann?** suppose it rains, what do we do then?

angesehen adj respected

angesichts prep +gen in view of, considering

Angestellte(r) mf employee

angetan adj: **von jdm/etw ~ sein** to be impressed by (o taken with) sb/sth

angewiesen adj: **auf jdn/etw ~ sein** to be dependent on sb/sth

an|gewöhnen vt: **sich etw ~** to get used to doing sth; **Angewohnheit** f habit

Angina (-, Anginen) f tonsillitis; **Angina Pectoris** (-) f angina

Angler(in) (-s, -) m(f) angler

Angora (-s) nt angora

an|greifen irr vt to attack; (anfassen) to touch; (beschädigen) to damage; **Angriff** m attack; **etw in ~ nehmen** to get started on sth

Angst (-, Ängste) f fear; **~ haben** to be afraid (o scared) (vor +dat of); **jdm ~ machen** to scare sb; **ängstigen** vt to frighten ▷ vr: **sich ~** to worry (um, wegen +dat about); **ängstlich** adj nervous; (besorgt) worried

an|haben irr vt (Kleidung) to have on, to wear; (Licht) to have on

an|halten irr vi to stop; (andauern) to continue; **anhaltend** adj continuous; **Anhalter(in)** (-s, -) m(f) hitch-hiker; **per ~ fahren** to hitch-hike

anhand prep +gen with; **~ von** by means of

an|hängen vt to hang up; (Eisenb: Wagen) to couple; (Zusatz) to add (on); **jdm etw ~** (fam: unterschieben) to pin sth on sb;

eine Datei an eine E-Mail **~** (Inform) to attach a file to an email; **Anhänger(-s, -)** m (Auto) trailer; (am Koffer) tag; (Schmuck) pendant; **Anhänger(in)** (-s, -) m(f) supporter; **Anhängerkupplung** f towbar; **anhänglich** adj affectionate; (pej) clinging

Anhieb m: **auf ~** straight away; **das kann ich nicht auf ~ sagen** I can't say offhand

an|himmeln vt to idolize

an|hören vt to listen to ▷ vr: **sich ~** to sound; **das hört sich gut an** that sounds good

Animateur(in) m(f) host/hostess

Anis (-es, -e) m aniseed

Anker (-s, -) m anchor; **ankern** vt, vi to anchor; **Ankerplatz** m anchorage

an|klicken vt (Inform) to click on

an|klopfen vi to knock (an +akk on)

an|kommen irr vi to arrive; **bei jdm gut ~** to go down well with sb; **es kommt darauf an** it depends (ob on whether); **darauf kommt es nicht an** that doesn't matter

an|kotzen vt (vulg) **es kotzt mich an** it makes me sick

an|kreuzen vt to mark with a cross

an|kündigen vt to announce

Ankunft (-, Ankünfte) f arrival; **Ankunftszeit** f arrival time

Anlage f (Veranlagung) disposition; (Begabung) talent; (Park) gardens pl; (zu Brief etc) enclosure; (Stereoanlage) stereo; (Tech) plant; (Fin) investment

Anlass (-es, Anlässe) m cause (zu for); (Ereignis) occasion; **aus diesem ~** for this reason; **an|lassen** irr vt (Motor) to start; (Licht, Kleidung) to leave on;

Anlasser (-s, -) m (Auto) starter; **anlässlich** prep +gen on the occasion of

Anlauf m run-up; **anlaufen** irr vi to begin; (Film) to open; (Fenster) to mist up; (Metall) to tarnish

anllegen vt to put (an +akk against/on); (Schmuck) to put on; (Garten) to lay out; (Geld) to invest; (Gewehr) to aim (auf +akk at); **es auf etw** (akk) ~ to be out for sth ▷ vi (Schiff) to berth, to dock ▷ vr: **sich mit jdm** ~ (fam) to pick a quarrel with sb; **Anlegestelle** f moorings pl

anllehnen vt to lean (an +akk against); (Tür) to leave ajar ▷ vr: **sich** ~ to lean (an +akk against)

anlleiern vt: **etw** ~ (fam) to get sth going

Anleitung f instructions pl

Anliegen (-s, -) nt matter; (Wunsch) request

Anlieger(in) (-s, -) m(f) resident; ~ **frei** residents only

anllügen irr vt to lie to

anlmachen vt (befestigen) to attach; (einschalten) to switch on; (Salat) to dress; (den: aufreizen) to turn on; (fam: ansprechen) to chat up (Brit), to come on to (US); (fam: beschimpfen) to have a go at

Anmeldeformular nt application form; (bei Amt) registration form; **anlmelden** vt (Besuch etc) to announce ▷ vr: **sich** ~ (beim Arzt etc) to make an appointment; (bei Amt, für Kurs etc) to register; **Anmeldeschluss** m deadline for applications, registration deadline; **Anmeldung** f registration; (Antrag) application

anlnähen vt: **einen Knopf (an den Mantel)** ~ to sew a button on (one's coat)

annähernd adv roughly; **nicht** ~ nowhere near

Annahme (-, -n) f acceptance; (Vermutung) assumption; **annehmbar** adj acceptable; **anlnehmen** irr vt to accept; (Namen) to take; (Kind) to adopt; (vermuten) to suppose, to assume

Annonce (-, -n) f advertisement

anlöden vt (fam) to bore stiff (o silly)

annullieren vt to cancel

anonym adj anonymous

Anorak (-s, -s) m anorak

anlpacken vt (Problem, Aufgabe) to tackle; **mit** ~ to lend a hand

anlpassen vt (fig) to adapt (dat to) ▷ vr: **sich** ~ to adapt (an +akk to)

anlpfeifen irr vt (Fußballspiel) **das Spiel** ~ to start the game; **Anpfiff** m (Sport) (starting) whistle; (Beginn) kick-off; (fam: Tadel) roasting

anlprobieren vt to try on

Anrede f form of address; **anlreden** vt to address

anlregen vt to stimulate; **Anregung** f stimulation; (Vorschlag) suggestion

Anreise f journey; **anlreisen** vi to arrive; **Anreisetag** m day of arrival

Anreiz m incentive

anlrichten vt (Speisen) to prepare; (Schaden) to cause

Anruf m call; **Anrufbeantworter** (-s, -) m answering machine, answerphone; **anlrufen** irr vt (Tel) to call, to phone, to ring (Brit)

ans kontr von **an das**

Ansage f announcement; (auf Anrufbeantworter) recorded message; **anlsagen** vt to announce; **angesagt sein** to be recommended; (modisch sein) to be the in thing

an|schaffen vt to buy

an|schauen vt to look at

Anschein m appearance; **dem** (o **allem**) ~ **nach** ... it looks as if ...; **den** ~ **erwecken, hart zu arbeiten** to give the impression of working hard; **anscheinend** adj apparent ▷ adv apparently

an|schieben irr vt: **könnten Sie mich mal ~?** (Auto) could you give me a push?

Anschlag m notice; (Attentat) attack; **an|schlagen** irr vt (Plakat) to put up; (beschädigen) to chip ▷ vi (wirken) to take effect; **mit etw an etw** (akk) ~ to bang sth against sth

an|schließen irr vt (Elek, Tech) to connect (an +akk to); (mit Stecker) to plug in ▷ vi, vr (sich) **an etw** (akk) ~ (Gebäude etc) to adjoin sth; (zeitlich) to follow sth ▷ vr: **sich** ~ to join (jdm/einer Gruppe sb/a group); **anschließend** adj adjacent; (zeitlich) subsequent ▷ adv afterwards; ~ **an** (+akk) following; **Anschluss** m (Elek, Eisenb) connection; (von Wasser, Gas etc) supply; **im** ~ **an** (+akk) following; **kein** ~ **unter dieser Nummer** (Tel) the number you have dialled has not been recognized; **Anschlussflug** m connecting flight

an|schnallen vt (Skier) to put on ▷ vr: **sich** ~ to fasten one's seat belt

Anschrift f address

an|schwellen irr vi to swell (up)

an|sehen irr vt to look at; (bei etw ~ zuschauen) to watch; **jdn als etw** ~ to look on sb/sth as sth; **das sieht man ihm an** he looks it

an sein irr vi siehe **an**

an|setzen vt (Termin) to fix; (zubereiten) to prepare ▷ vi (anfangen) to start, to begin; **zu**

etw ~ to prepare to do sth

Ansicht f (Meinung) view, opinion; (Anblick) sight; **meiner** ~ **nach** in my opinion; **zur** ~ on approval; **Ansichtskarte** f postcard

ansonsten adv otherwise

an|spielen vi **auf etw** (akk) ~ to allude to sth; **Anspielung** f allusion (auf +akk to)

an|sprechen irr vt to speak to; (gefallen) to appeal to ▷ vi **auf etw** (akk) ~ (Patient) to respond to sth; **ansprechend** adj attractive; **Ansprechpartner(in)** m(f) contact

an|springen irr vi (Auto) to start

Anspruch m claim; (Recht) right (auf +akk to); **etw in** ~ **nehmen** to take advantage of sth; ~ **auf etw haben** to be entitled to sth; **anspruchslos** adj undemanding; (bescheiden) modest; **anspruchsvoll** adj demanding

Anstalt (-, -en) f institution

Anstand m decency; **anständig** adj decent; (fig, fam) proper; (groß) considerable

an|starren vt to stare at

anstatt prep +gen instead of

an|stecken vt to pin on; (Med) to infect; **jdn mit einer Erkältung** ~ to pass one's cold on to sb ▷ vr: **ich habe mich bei ihm angesteckt** I caught it from him ▷ vi (fig) to be infectious; **ansteckend** adj infectious; **Ansteckungsgefahr** f danger of infection

an|stehen irr vi (in Warteschlange) to queue (Brit), to stand in line (US); (erledigt werden müssen) to be on the agenda

anstelle prep +gen instead of

an|stellen vt (einschalten) to turn on; (Arbeit geben) to employ; (machen) to do; **was hast du**

wieder angestellt? what have you been up to now? ▷ vr: **sich ~** to queue (Brit), to stand in line (US); (fam) **stell dich nicht so an!** stop making such a fuss

Anstoß m impetus; (Sport) kick-off; **an|stoßen** irr vt to push; (mit Fuß) ▷ vi to bump; (mit Gläsern) to drink (a toast) (auf +akk to); **anstößig** adj offensive; (Kleidung etc) indecent

an|strengen vt to strain ▷ vr: **sich ~** to make an effort; **anstrengend** adj tiring

Antarktis f Antarctic

Anteil m share (an +dat in); **~ nehmen an** (+dat) (mitleidig) to sympathize with; (sich interessieren) to take an interest in

Antenne (-, -n) f aerial

Antibabypille f: **die ~** the pill; **Antibiotikum** (-s, Antibiotika) nt (Med) antibiotic

antik adj antique

Antilope (-, -n) f antelope

Antiquariat nt (für Bücher) second-hand bookshop

Antiquitäten pl antiques pl; **Antiquitätenhändler(in)** m(f) antique dealer

Antiviren- adj (Inform) antivirus; **Antivirensoftware** f antivirus software

an|törnen vt (fam) to turn on

Antrag (-(e)s, Anträge) m proposal; (Pol) motion; (Formular) application form; **einen ~ stellen auf** (+akk) to apply for

an|treffen irr vt to find

an|treiben irr vt (Tech) to drive; (anschwemmen) to wash up; **jdn zur Arbeit ~** to make sb work

an|treten irr vt: **eine Reise ~** to set off on a journey

Antrieb m (Tech) drive; (Motivation) impetus

an|tun irr vt: **jdm etwas ~** to do

sth to sb; **sich** (dat) **etwas ~** (Selbstmord begehen) to kill oneself

Antwort (-, -en) f answer, reply; **um ~ wird gebeten** RSVP (répondez s'il vous plaît); **antworten** vi to answer, to reply; **jdm ~** to answer sb; **auf etw** (akk) **~** to answer sth

an|vertrauen vt: **jdm etw ~** to entrust sb with sth

Anwalt (-s, Anwälte) m, **Anwältin** f lawyer

an|weisen irr vt (anleiten) to instruct; (zuteilen) to allocate (jdm etw sth to sb); **Anweisung** f instruction; (von Geld) money order

an|wenden irr vt to use; (Gesetz, Regel) to apply; **Anwender(in)** (-s, -) m(f) user; **Anwendung** f use; (Inform) application

anwesend adj present; **Anwesenheit** f presence

an|widern vt to disgust

Anwohner(in) (-s, -) m(f) resident

Anzahl f number (an +dat of); **an|zahlen** vt to pay a deposit on; **100 Euro ~** to pay 100 euros as a deposit; **Anzahlung** f deposit

Anzeichen nt sign; (Med) symptom

Anzeige (-, -n) f (Werbung) advertisement; (elektronisch) display; (bei Polizei) report; **an|zeigen** vt (Temperatur, Zeit) to indicate, to show; (elektronisch) to display; (bekannt geben) to announce; **einen Autodiebstahl bei der Polizei ~** to report a stolen car to the police

an|ziehen irr vt to attract; (Kleidung) to put on; (Schraube, Seil) to tighten ▷ vr: **sich ~** to get dressed; **anziehend** adj attractive

Anzug m suit

anzüglich adj suggestive

an|zünden vt to light; (Haus etc) to set fire to

an|zweifeln vt to doubt

Aperitif (-s, -s (o -e)) m aperitif

Apfel (-s, Äpfel) m apple;
Apfelbaum m apple tree;
Apfelkuchen m apple cake;
Apfelmus nt apple purée;
Apfelsaft m apple juice; **Apfel-
sine** f orange; **Apfelwein** m cider

Apostroph (-s, -e) m apostrophe

Apotheke (-, -n) f chemist's
(shop) (Brit), pharmacy (US);
apothekenpflichtig adj only
available at the chemist's;
Apotheker(in) (-s, -) m(f)
chemist (Brit), pharmacist (US)

App (-s) f app

Apparat (-(e)s, -e) m (piece of)
apparatus; (Tel) telephone; (Radio,
TV) set; **am ~!** (Tel) speaking; **am
~ bleiben** (Tel) to hold the line

Appartement (-s, -s) nt studio
flat (Brit) (o apartment (US))

Appetit (-(e)s, -e) m appetite;
guten ~! bon appétit; **appetitlich**
adj appetizing

Applaus (-es, -e) m applause

Aprikose (-, -n) f apricot

April (-(s), -e) m April; siehe auch
Juni; ~, ~! April fool!; **Aprilscherz**
(-es, -e) m April fool's joke

apropos adv by the way;
~ Urlaub ... while we're on the
subject of holidays ...

Aquaplaning (-(s)) nt
aquaplaning

Aquarell (-s, -e) nt watercolour

Aquarium (-s, Aquarien) nt
aquarium

Äquator (-s) m equator

Araber(in) (-s, -) m(f) Arab;
arabisch adj Arab; (Ziffer, Sprache)
Arabic; (Meer, Wüste) Arabian

Arbeit (-, -en) f work; (Stelle) job;
(Erzeugnis) piece of work; **arbeiten**
vi to work; **Arbeiter(in)** (-s, -) m(f)
worker; (ungelernt) labourer;
Arbeitgeber(in) (-s, -) m(f)

employer; **Arbeitnehmer(in)**
(-s, -) m(f) employee;
Arbeitsagentur f job agency
(Brit), unemployment agency
(US); **Arbeitsamt** nt job centre
(Brit), employment office (US);
Arbeitserlaubnis f work permit;
arbeitslos adj unemployed;
Arbeitslose(r) mf unemployed
person; **Arbeitslosengeld** nt
(income-related) unemployment
benefit, job-seeker's allowance
(Brit); **Arbeitslosenhilfe** f
(non-income related)
unemployment benefit;
Arbeitslosigkeit f unemploy-
ment; **Arbeitsplatz** m job; (Ort)
workplace; **Arbeitsspeicher** m
(Inform) main memory;
Arbeitszeit f working hours pl;
Arbeitszimmer nt study

Archäologe (-n, -n) m,
Archäologin f archaeologist

Architekt(in) (-en, -en) m(f)
architect; **Architektur** f
architecture

Archiv (-s, -e) nt archives pl

ARD f = **Arbeitsgemeinschaft
der öffentlich-rechtlichen
Rundfunkanstalten der
Bundesrepublik Deutschland**
German broadcasting corporation

arg adj bad; (schrecklich) awful
▷ adv (sehr) terribly

Argentinien (-s) nt Argentina

Ärger (-s) m annoyance;
(stärker) anger; (Unannehmlichkeiten)
trouble; **ärgerlich** adj annoying;
(zornig) angry; **ärgern** vt to annoy
▷ vr: **sich ~** to get annoyed

Argument (-s, -e) nt argument

Arktis (-) f Arctic

arm adj poor

Arm (-(e)s, -e) m arm; (Fluss) branch

Armaturenbrett nt instrument
panel; (Auto) dashboard

Armband nt bracelet;

Armbanduhr f (wrist)watch
Armee (-, -n) f army
Ärmel (-s, -) m sleeve;
Ärmelkanal m (English) Channel
Armut (-) f poverty
Aroma (-s, Aromen) nt aroma
arrogant adj arrogant
Arsch (-es, Ärsche) m (vulg) arse
(Brit), ass (US); **Arschloch** nt
(vulg: Person) asshole (Brit),
asshole (US)
Art (-, -en) f (Weise) way; (Sorte)
kind, sort; (bei Tieren) species;
nach ~ des Hauses à la maison;
auf diese ~ (und Weise) in this
way; **das ist nicht seine ~** that's
not like him
Arterie (-, -n) f artery
artig adj good, well-behaved
Artikel (-s, -) m (Ware) article,
item; (Zeitung) article
Artischocke (-, -n) f artichoke
Artist(in) (-en, -en) m(f) (circus)
performer
Arznei f medicine; **Arzt** (-es,
Ärzte) m doctor; **Arzthelfer(in)**
m(f) doctor's assistant; **Ärztin** f
(female) doctor; **ärztlich** adj
medical; **sich ~ behandeln lassen**
to undergo medical treatment
Asche (-, -n) f ashes pl; (von
Zigarette) ash; **Aschenbecher** m
ashtray; **Aschermittwoch** m
Ash Wednesday
Asiat(in) (-en, -en) m(f) Asian;
asiatisch adj Asian; **Asien** (-s) nt
Asia
Aspekt (-(e)s, -e) m aspect
Asphalt (-(e)s, -e) m asphalt
Aspirin® (-s, -e) nt aspirin
aß imperf von **essen**
Ass (-es, -e) nt (Karten, Tennis) ace
Assistent(in) m(f) assistant
Ast (-(e)s, Äste) m branch
Asthma (-s) nt asthma
Astrologie f astrology;
Astronaut(in) (-en, -en) m(f)

astronaut; **Astronomie** f
astronomy
ASU (-, -s) f abk =
Abgassonderuntersuchung
exhaust emission test
Asyl (-s, -e) nt asylum; (Heim)
home; (für Obdachlose) shelter;
Asylant(in) m(f), **Asylbe-
werber(in)** m(f) asylum seeker
Atelier (-s, -s) nt studio
Atem (-s) m breath; **atembe-
raubend** adj breathtaking;
Atembeschwerden pl breathing
difficulties pl; **atemlos** adj breath-
less; **Atempause** f breather
Athen (-s) nt Athens
Äthiopien (-s) nt Ethiopia
Athlet(in) (-en, -en) m(f) athlete;
Athletik f athletics sing
Atlantik (-s) m Atlantic (Ocean)
Atlas (- o Atlasses, Atlanten) m
atlas
atmen vt, vi to breathe; **Atmung**
f breathing
Atom (-s, -e) nt atom;
Atombombe f atom bomb;
Atomkraftwerk nt nuclear
power station; **Atommüll** m
nuclear waste; **Atomwaffen** pl
nuclear weapons pl
Attentat (-(e)s, -e) nt
assassination (auf +akk of);
(Versuch) assassination attempt
Attest (-(e)s, -e) nt certificate
attraktiv adj attractive
Attrappe (-, -n) f dummy
ätzend adj (fam) revolting;
(schlecht) lousy
au interj ouch; **~ ja!** yeah
Aubergine (-, -n) f aubergine,
eggplant (US)

○ **SCHLÜSSELWORT**

auch adv **1** (ebenfalls) also, too, as
well; **das ist auch schön** that's
nice too o as well; **er kommt — ich**

auch he's coming — so am I, me too; **auch nicht** not ... either; **ich auch nicht** nor I, me neither; **oder auch** or; **auch das noch!** not that as well

2 (*selbst, sogar*) even; **auch wenn das Wetter schlecht ist** even if the weather is bad; **ohne auch nur zu fragen** without even asking

3 (*wirklich*) really; **du siehst müde aus—bin ich auch** you look tired— (so) I am; **so sieht es auch aus** it looks like it too

4 (*auch immer*) **wer auch** whoever; **was auch** whatever; **wie dem auch sei** be that as it may; **wie sehr er sich auch bemühte** however much he tried

audiovisuell *adj* audiovisual

SCHLÜSSELWORT

auf *prep* +*dat* (*wo?*) on; **auf dem Tisch** on the table; **auf der Reise** on the way; **auf der Post/dem Fest** at the post office/party; **auf der Straße** on the road; **auf dem Land/der ganzen Welt** in the country/the whole world
▷ *prep* +*akk* **1** (*wohin?*) on(to); **auf den Tisch** on(to) the table; **auf die Post gehen** to go to the post office; **auf das Land** into the country; **etw auf einen Zettel schreiben** to write sth on a piece of paper

2 auf Deutsch in German; **auf Lebenszeit** for my/his lifetime; **bis auf ihn** except for him; **auf einmal** at once; **auf seinen Vorschlag (hin)** at his suggestion
▷ *adv* **1** (*offen*) open; **auf sein** (*fam*) (*Tür, Geschäft*) to be open; **das Fenster ist auf** the window is open

2 (*hinauf*) up; **auf und ab** up and down; **auf und davon** up and away; **auf!** (*los!*) come on!

3 (*aufgestanden*) up; **auf sein** to be up; **ist er schon auf?** is he up yet?
▷ *konj*: **auf dass** (so) that

auf|atmen *vi* to breathe a sigh of relief

auf|bauen *vt* (*errichten*) to put up; (*schaffen*) to build up; (*gestalten*) to construct; (*gründen*) to found, to base (*auf* +*akk* on); **sich eine Existenz ~** to make a life for oneself

auf|bewahren *vt* to keep, to store

auf|bleiben *irr vi* (*Tür, Laden etc*) to stay open; (*Mensch*) to stay up

auf|blenden *vi, vt*: (**die Scheinwerfer**) **~** to put one's headlights on full beam

auf|brechen *irr vt* to break open
▷ *vi* to burst open; (*gehen*) to leave; (*abreisen*) to set off

auf|drängen *vt*: **jdm etw ~** to force sth on sb ▷ *vr*: **sich ~** to intrude (*jdm* on sb); **aufdringlich** *adj* pushy

aufeinander *adv* (*übereinander*) on top of each other; **~ achten** to look after each other; **~ vertrauen** to trust each other; **aufeinanderfolgen** *vi* to follow one another; **aufeinanderprallen** *vi* to crash into one another

Aufenthalt *m* stay; (*Zug*) stop; **Aufenthaltsgenehmigung** *f* residence permit; **Aufenthaltsraum** *m* lounge

auf|essen *vt* to eat up

auf|fahren *irr vi* (*Auto*) to run (*o* to crash) (*auf* +*akk* into); (*herankommen*) to drive up; **Auffahrt** *f* (*am Haus*) drive; (*Autobahn*) slip road (*Brit*), ramp (*US*); **Auffahrunfall** *m* rear-end

auf|fallen irr vi to stand out; **jdm ~** to strike sb; **das fällt gar nicht auf** nobody will notice; **auffallend** adj striking; **auffällig** adj conspicuous; (Kleidung) striking

auf|fangen irr vt (Ball) to catch; (Stoß) to cushion

auf|fassen vt to understand; **Auffassung** f view; (Meinung) opinion; (Auslegung) concept; (Auffassungsgabe) grasp

auf|fordern vt (befehlen) to call upon; (bitten) to ask

auf|frischen vt to brush up

auf|führen vt (Theat) to perform; (in einem Verzeichnis) to list; (Beispiel) to give ▷ vr: **sich ~** (sich benehmen) to behave; **Aufführung** f (Theat) performance

Aufgabe f job, task; (Schule) exercise; (Hausaufgabe) homework

Aufgang m (Treppe) staircase

auf|geben irr vt (verzichten auf) to give up; (Paket) to post; (Gepäck) to check in; (Bestellung) to place; (Inserat) to insert; (Rätsel, Problem) to set ▷ vi to give up

auf|gehen irr vi (Sonne, Teig) to rise; (sich öffnen) to open; (klar werden) to dawn (jdm on sb)

aufgelegt adj: **gut/schlecht ~** in a good/bad mood

aufgeregt adj excited

aufgeschlossen adj open(minded)

aufgeschmissen adj (fam) in a fix

aufgrund, auf Grund prep +gen on the basis of; (wegen) because of

auf|haben irr vt (Hut etc) to have on; **viel ~** (Schule) to have a lot of homework to do ▷ vi (Geschäft) to be open

auf|halten irr vt (jdn) to detain; (Entwicklung) to stop; (Tür, Hand) to hold open; (Augen) to keep open ▷ vr: **sich ~** (wohnen) to live; (vorübergehend) to stay

auf|hängen irr vt to hang up

auf|heben irr vt (vom Boden etc) to pick up; (aufbewahren) to keep

Aufheiterungen pl (Meteo) bright periods pl

auf|holen vt (Zeit) to make up ▷ vi to catch up

auf|hören vi to stop; **~, etw zu tun** to stop doing sth

auf|klären vt (Geheimnis etc) to clear up; **jdn ~** to enlighten sb; (sexuell) to tell sb the facts of life

Aufkleber (-s, -) m sticker

auf|kommen irr vi (Wind) to come up; (Zweifel, Gefühl) to arise; (Mode etc) to appear on the scene; **für den Schaden ~** to pay for the damage

auf|laden irr vt to load; (Handy etc) to charge; (Handykarte etc) to top up; **Aufladegerät** nt charger

Auflage f edition; (von Zeitung) circulation; (Bedingung) condition

auf|lassen irr vt (Hut, Brille) to keep on; (Tür) to leave open

Auflauf m (Menschen) crowd; (Speise) bake

auf|legen vt (CD, Schminke etc) to put on; (Hörer) to put down ▷ vi (Tel) to hang up

auf|leuchten vi to light up

auf|lösen vt (in Flüssigkeit) to dissolve ▷ vr: **sich ~** (in Flüssigkeit) to dissolve; **der Stau hat sich aufgelöst** traffic is back to normal; **Auflösung** f (von Rätsel) solution; (von Bildschirm) resolution

auf|machen vt to open; (Kleidung) to undo ▷ vr: **sich ~** to set out (nach for)

aufmerksam adj attentive; **jdn auf etw** (akk) **~ machen** to draw sb's attention to sth;

Aufmerksamkeit f attention; (*Konzentration*) attentiveness; (*Geschenk*) small token

auf|muntern vt (*ermutigen*) to encourage; (*aufheitern*) to cheer up

Aufnahme (-, -n) f (*Foto*) photo(graph); (*einzelne*) shot; (*in Verein, Krankenhaus etc*) admission; (*Beginn*) beginning; (*auf Tonband etc*) recording; **Aufnahmeprüfung** f entrance exam; **auf|nehmen** irr vt (*in Krankenhaus, Verein etc*) to admit; (*Musik*) to record; (*beginnen*) to take up; (*in Liste*) to include; (*begreifen*) to take in; **mit jdm Kontakt ~** to get in touch with sb

auf|passen vi (*aufmerksam sein*) to pay attention; (*vorsichtig sein*) to take care; **auf jdn/etw ~** to keep an eye on sb/sth

Aufprall (-s, -e) m impact; **auf|prallen** vi **auf etw** (*akk*) **~** to hit sth, to crash into sth

Aufpreis m extra charge

auf|pumpen vt to pump up

Aufputschmittel nt stimulant

auf|räumen vt, vi (*Dinge*) to clear away; (*Zimmer*) to tidy up

aufrecht adj upright

auf|regen vt to excite; (*ärgern*) to annoy ▷ vr: **sich ~** to get worked up; **aufregend** adj exciting; **Aufregung** f excitement

auf|reißen irr vt (*Tüte*) to tear open; (*Tür*) to fling open; (*fam: Person*) to pick up

Aufruf m (*Aviat, Inform*) call; (*öffentlicher*) appeal; **auf|rufen** irr vt (*auffordern*) to call upon (*zu* for); (*Namen*) to call out; (*Aviat*) to call; (*Inform*) to call up

auf|runden vt (*Summe*) to round up

aufs kontr von **auf das**

Aufsatz m essay

auf|schieben irr vt (*verschieben*)

to postpone; (*verzögern*) to put off; (*Tür*) to slide open

Aufschlag m (*auf Preis*) extra charge; (*Tennis*) service; **auf|schlagen** irr vt (*öffnen*) to open; (*verletzen*) to cut open; (*Zelt*) to pitch, to put up; (*Lager*) to set up ▷ vi (*Tennis*) to serve; **auf etw** (*+akk*) **~** (*aufprallen*) to hit sth

auf|schließen irr vt to unlock, to open up ▷ vi (*aufrücken*) to close up

auf|schneiden irr vt to cut open; (*in Scheiben*) to slice ▷ vi (*angeben*) to boast, to show off

Aufschnitt m (*slices pl of*) cold meat; (*bei Käse*) (assorted) sliced cheeses pl

auf|schreiben irr vt to write down

Aufschrift f inscription; (*Etikett*) label

Aufschub m (*Verzögerung*) delay; (*Vertagung*) postponement

Aufsehen (-s) nt stir; **großes ~ erregen** to cause a sensation; **Aufseher(in)** (-s, -) m(f) guard; (*im Betrieb*) supervisor; (*im Museum*) attendant; (*im Park*) keeper

auf sein irr vi siehe **auf**

auf|setzen vt to put on; (*Dokument*) to draw up ▷ vi (*Flugzeug*) to touch down

Aufsicht f supervision; (*bei Prüfung*) invigilation; **die ~ haben** to be in charge

auf|spannen vt (*Schirm*) to put up

auf|sperren vt (*Mund*) to open wide; (*aufschließen*) to unlock

auf|springen irr vi to jump (*auf +akk* onto); (*hochspringen*) to jump up; (*sich öffnen*) to spring open

auf|stehen irr vi to get up; (*Tür*) to be open

auf|stellen vt (*aufrecht stellen*) to

put up; (aufreihen) to line up; (nominieren) to put up; (Liste, Programm) to draw up; (Rekord) to set up

Aufstieg (-(e)s, -e) m (auf Berg) ascent; (Fortschritt) rise; (beruflich, im Sport) promotion

Aufstrich m spread

auf|tanken vt, vi (Auto) to tank up; (Flugzeug) to refuel

auf|tauchen vi to turn up; (aus Wasser etc) to surface; (Frage, Problem) to come up

auf|tauen vt (Speisen) to defrost ▷ vi to thaw; (fig: Person) to unbend

Auftrag (-(e)s, Aufträge) m (Comm) order; (Arbeit) job; (Anweisung) instructions pl; (Aufgabe) task; **im ~ von** on behalf of; **auf|tragen** irr vt (Salbe etc) to apply; (Essen) to serve

auf|treten irr vi to appear; (Problem) to come up; (sich verhalten) to behave; **Auftritt** m (des Schauspielers) entrance; (fig: Szene) scene

auf|wachen vi to wake up

auf|wachsen irr vi to grow up

Aufwand (-(e)s) m expenditure; (Kosten a.) expense; (Anstrengung) effort; **aufwändig** adj costly; **das ist zu ~** that's too much trouble

auf|wärmen vt to warm up ▷ vr: **sich ~** to warm up

aufwärts adv upwards; **mit etw geht es ~** things are looking up for sth

auf|wecken vt to wake up

aufwendig adj siehe aufwändig

auf|wischen vt to wipe up; (Fußboden) to wipe

auf|zählen vt to list

auf|zeichnen vt to sketch; (schriftlich) to jot down; (auf Band etc) to record; **Aufzeichnung** f

(schriftlich) note; (Tonband etc) recording; (Film) record

auf|ziehen irr vt (öffnen) to pull open; (Uhr) to wind (up); (fam: necken) to tease; (Kinder) to bring up; (Tiere) to rear ▷ vi (Gewitter) to come up

Aufzug m (Fahrstuhl) lift (Brit), elevator (US); (Kleidung) get-up; (Theat) act

Auge (-s, -n) nt eye; **jdm etw aufs ~ drücken** (fam) to force sth on sb; **ins ~ gehen** (fam) to go wrong; **unter vier ~n** in private; **etw im ~ behalten** to keep sth in mind; **Augenarzt** m,

Augenärztin f eye specialist, eye doctor (US); **Augenblick** m moment; **im ~** at the moment; **Augenbraue** (-, -n) f eyebrow; **Augenbrauenstift** m eyebrow pencil; **Augenfarbe** f eye colour; **seine ~** the colour of his eyes; **Augenlid** nt eyelid; **Augenoptiker(in)** (-s, -) m(f) optician; **Augentropfen** pl eyedrops pl; **Augenzeuge** m, **Augenzeugin** f eyewitness

August (-(e)s o -, -e) m August; siehe auch **Juni**

Auktion f auction

 SCHLÜSSELWORT

aus prep +dat 1 (räumlich) out of; (von ... her) from; **er ist aus Berlin** he's from Berlin; **aus dem Fenster** out of the window

2 (gemacht/hergestellt aus) made of; **ein Herz aus Stein** a heart of stone

3 (auf Ursache deutend) out of; **aus Mitleid** out of sympathy; **aus Erfahrung** from experience; **aus Spaß** for fun

4 **aus ihr wird nie etwas** she'll never get anywhere

▷ *adv* **1** (*zu Ende*) finished, over; **aus sein** to be over; **aus und vorbei** over and done with
2 (*ausgeschaltet, ausgezogen*) out; (*Aufschrift an Geräten*) off; **aus sein** (*nicht brennen*) to be out; (*abgeschaltet sein: Radio, Herd*) to be off; **Licht aus!** lights out!
3 (*nicht zu Hause*) **aus sein** to be out
4 (*in Verbindung mit von*) **von Rom aus** from Rome; **vom Fenster aus** out of the window; **von sich aus** (*selbstständig*) of one's own accord; **von ihm aus** as far as he's concerned

Aus (-) *nt* (*Sport*) touch; (*fig*) end
aus|atmen *vi* to breathe out
aus|bauen *vt* (*Haus, Straße*) to extend; (*Motor etc*) to remove
aus|bessern *vt* to repair; (*Kleidung*) to mend
aus|bilden *vt* to educate; (*Lehrling etc*) to train; (*Fähigkeiten*) to develop; **Ausbildung** *f* education; (*von Lehrling etc*) training; (*von Fähigkeiten*) development
Ausblick *m* view; (*fig*) outlook
aus|brechen *irr vi* to break out; **in Tränen ~** to burst into tears; **in Gelächter ~** to burst out laughing
aus|breiten *vt* to spread (out); (*Arme*) to stretch out ▷ *vr*: **sich ~** to spread
Ausbruch *m* (*Krieg, Seuche etc*) outbreak; (*Vulkan*) eruption; (*Gefühle*) outburst; (*von Gefangenen*) escape
aus|buhen *vt* to boo
Ausdauer *f* perseverance; (*Sport*) stamina
aus|dehnen *vt* to stretch; (*fig: Macht*) to extend
aus|denken *irr vt* **sich** (*dat*) **etw ~** to come up with sth

Ausdruck *m* (*Ausdrücke*) expression ▷ *m* (*Ausdrucke, Computerausdruck*) print-out; **aus|drucken** *vt* (*Inform*) to print (out)
aus|drücken *vt* (*formulieren*) to express; (*Zigarette*) to put out; (*Zitrone etc*) to squeeze ▷ *vr*: **sich ~** to express oneself; **ausdrücklich** *adj* express ▷ *adv* expressly
auseinander *adv* (*getrennt*) apart; **~ schreiben** to write as separate words;
auseinander|gehen *irr vi* (*Menschen*) to separate; (*Meinungen*) to differ; (*Gegenstand*) to fall apart;
auseinander|halten *irr vt* to tell apart; **auseinander|setzen** *vt* (*erklären*) to explain;
auseinander|setzen *vr*: **sich ~** (*sich beschäftigen*) to look (mit at); (*sich streiten*) to argue (*mit* with); **Auseinandersetzung** *f* (*Streit*) argument; (*Diskussion*) debate
Ausfahrt *f* (*des Zuges etc*) departure; (*Autobahn, Garage etc*) exit
aus|fallen *irr vi* (*Haare*) to fall out; (*nicht stattfinden*) to be cancelled; (*nicht funktionieren*) to break down; (*Strom*) to be cut off; (*Resultat haben*) to turn out; **groß/klein ~** (*Kleidung, Schuhe*) to be too big/too small
ausfindig machen *vt* to discover
aus|flippen *vi* (*fam*) to freak out
Ausflug *m* excursion, outing; **Ausflugsziel** *nt* destination
Ausfluss *m* (*Med*) discharge
aus|fragen *vt* to question
Ausfuhr (-, -en) *f* export
aus|führen *vt* (*verwirklichen*) to carry out; (*Person*) to take out; (*Comm*) to export; (*darlegen*) to explain

ausführlich adj detailed ▷ adv in detail

ausfüllen vt to fill up; (Fragebogen etc) to fill in (o out)

Ausgabe f (Geld) expenditure; (Inform) output; (Buch) edition; (Nummer) issue

Ausgang m way out, exit; (Flugsteig) gate; (Ende) end; (Ergebnis) result; „**kein ~**" "no exit"

ausgeben irr vt (Geld) to spend; (austeilen) to distribute; **jdm etw ~** (spendieren) to buy sb sth ▷ vr: **sich für etw/jdn ~** to pass oneself off as sth/sb

ausgebucht adj fully booked

ausgefallen adj (ungewöhnlich) unusual

ausgehen irr vi (abends etc) to go out; (Benzin, Kaffee etc) to run out; (Haare) to fall out; (Feuer, Licht etc) to go out; (Resultat haben) to turn out; **davon ~, dass** to assume that; **ihm ging das Geld aus** he ran out of money

ausgelassen adj exuberant

ausgeleiert adj worn out

ausgenommen conj, prep +gen o dat except

ausgerechnet adv: **~ du** you of all people; **~ heute** today of all days

ausgeschildert adj signposted

ausgeschlafen adj: **bist du ~?** have you had enough sleep?

ausgeschlossen adj (unmöglich) impossible, out of the question

ausgesprochen adj (absolut) out-and-out; (unverkennbar) marked ▷ adv extremely; **~ gut** really good

ausgezeichnet adj excellent

ausgiebig adj (Gebrauch) thorough; (Essen) substantial

ausgießen irr vt (Getränk) to pour out; (Gefäß) to empty

ausgleichen irr vt to even out ▷ vi (Sport) to equalize

Ausguss m (Spüle) sink; (Abfluss) outlet

aushalten irr vt to bear, to stand; **nicht auszuhalten sein** to be unbearable ▷ vi to hold out

aushändigen vt: **jdm etw ~** to hand sth over to sb

Aushang m notice

Aushilfe f temporary help; (im Büro) temp

auskennen irr vr: **sich ~** to know a lot (bei, mit about); (an einem Ort) to know one's way around

auskommen irr vi: **gut/schlecht mit jdm ~** to get on well/badly with sb; **mit etw ~** to get by with sth

Auskunft (-, Auskünfte) f information; (nähere) details pl; (Schalter) information desk; (Tel) (directory) enquiries sing (kein Artikel, Brit), information (US)

auslachen vt to laugh at

ausladen irr vt (Gepäck etc) to unload; **jdn ~** (Gast) to tell sb not to come

Auslage f window display; **~n** pl (Kosten) expenses

Ausland nt foreign countries pl; **im/ins ~** abroad; **Ausländer(in)** (-s, -) m(f) foreigner; **ausländerfeindlich** adj hostile to foreigners, xenophobic; **ausländisch** adj foreign; **Auslandsgespräch** nt international call; **Auslandskrankenschein** m health insurance certificate for foreign countries, ≈ E111 (Brit); **Auslandsschutzbrief** m international (motor) insurance cover (documents pl)

auslassen irr vt to leave out; (Wort etc a.) to omit; (überspringen) to skip; (Wut, Ärger) to vent (an +dat on) ▷ vr **sich über etw** (akk) **~** to speak one's mind about sth

aus|laufen irr vi (Flüssigkeit) to run out; (Tank etc) to leak; (Schiff) to leave port; (Vertrag) to expire

aus|legen vt (Waren) to display; (Geld) to lend; (Text etc) to interpret; (technisch ausstatten) to design (für, auf +akk for)

aus|leihen irr vt (verleihen) to lend; **sich** (dat) **etw ~** to borrow sth

aus|loggen vi (Inform) to log out (o off)

aus|lösen vt (Explosion, Alarm) to set off; (hervorrufen) to cause; **Auslöser** (-s, -) m (Foto) shutter release

aus|machen vt (Licht, Radio) to turn off; (vereinbaren) to put out; (Termin, Preis) to fix; (vereinbaren) to agree; (Anteil darstellen, betragen) to represent; (bedeuten) to matter; **macht es Ihnen etwas aus, wenn ...?** would you mind if ...?; **das macht mir nichts aus** I don't mind

Ausmaß nt extent

Ausnahme (-, -n) f exception; **ausnahmsweise** adv as an exception, just this once

aus|nutzen vt (Zeit, Gelegenheit, Einfluss) to use; (jdn, Gutmütigkeit) to take advantage of

aus|packen vt to unpack

aus|probieren vt to try (out)

Auspuff (-(e)s, -e) m (Tech) exhaust; **Auspuffrohr** nt exhaust (pipe); **Auspufftopf** m (Auto) silencer (Brit), muffler (US)

aus|rauben vt to rob

aus|räumen vt (Dinge) to clear away; (Schrank, Zimmer) to empty; (Bedenken) to put aside

aus|rechnen vt to calculate, to work out

Ausrede f excuse

aus|reden vi to finish speaking ▷ vt: **jdm etw ~** to talk sb out of sth

ausreichend adj sufficient, satisfactory; (Schulnote) ≈ D

Ausreise f departure; **bei der ~** on leaving the country; **Ausreiseerlaubnis** f exit visa; **aus|reisen** vi to leave the country

aus|reißen irr vt to tear out ▷ vi to come off; (fam: davonlaufen) to run away

aus|renken vt **sich** (dat) **den Arm ~** to dislocate one's arm

aus|richten vt (Botschaft) to deliver; (Gruß) to pass on; (erreichen) **ich konnte bei ihr nichts ~** I couldn't get anywhere with her; **jdm etw ~** to tell sb sth

aus|rufen irr vt (über Lautsprecher) to announce; **jdn ~ lassen** to page sb; **Ausrufezeichen** nt exclamation mark

aus|ruhen vi to rest ▷ vr: **sich ~** to rest

Ausrüstung f equipment

aus|rutschen vi to slip

aus|schalten vt to switch off; (fig) to eliminate

Ausschau f: **~ halten** to look out (nach for)

aus|scheiden irr vt (Med) to give off, to secrete ▷ vi to leave (aus etw sth); (Sport) to be eliminated

aus|schlafen irr vi to have a lie-in ▷ vr: **sich ~** to have a lie-in ▷ vt to sleep off

Ausschlag m (Med) rash; **den ~ geben** (fig) to tip the balance; **aus|schlagen** irr vt (Zahn) to knock out; (Einladung) to turn down ▷ vi (Pferd) to kick out; **ausschlaggebend** adj decisive

aus|schließen irr vt to lock out; (fig) to exclude; **ausschließlich**

adv exclusively ▷ *prep +gen* excluding

Ausschnitt *m* (*Teil*) section; (*von Kleid*) neckline; (*aus Zeitung*) cutting

Ausschreitungen *pl* riots *pl*

aus|schütten *vt* (*Flüssigkeit*) to pour out; (*Gefäß*) to empty

aus|sehen *irr vi* to look; **krank ~** to look ill; **gut ~** (*Person*) to be good-looking; (*Sache*) to be looking good; **es sieht nach Regen aus** it looks like rain; **es sieht schlecht aus** things look bad

aus sein *irr vi siehe* **aus**

außen *adv* outside; **nach ~** outwards; **von ~** from (the) outside; **Außenbordmotor** *m* outboard motor; **Außenminister(in)** *m(f)* foreign minister, Foreign Secretary (*Brit*); **Außenseite** *f* outside; **Außenseiter(in)** *m(f)* outsider; **Außenspiegel** *m* wing mirror (*Brit*), side mirror (*US*)

außer *prep +dat* (*abgesehen von*) except (for); **nichts ~** nothing but; **~ Betrieb** out of order; **~ sich sein** to be beside oneself (*vor* with); **~ Atem** out of breath ▷ *conj* (*ausgenommen*) except; **~ wenn** unless; **~ dass** except; **außerdem** *conj* besides

äußere(r, s) *adj* outer, external

außergewöhnlich *adj* unusual ▷ *adv* exceptionally; **~ kalt** exceptionally cold; **außerhalb** *prep +gen* outside

äußerlich *adj* external

äußern *vt* to express; (*zeigen*) to show ▷ *vr*: **sich ~** to give one's opinion; (*sich zeigen*) to show itself

außerordentlich *adj* extra-ordinary; **außerplanmäßig** *adj* unscheduled

äußerst *adv* extremely;

äußerste(r, s) *adj* utmost; (*räumlich*) farthest; (*Termin*) last possible

Äußerung *f* remark

aus|setzen *vt* (*Kind, Tier*) to abandon; (*Belohnung*) to offer; **ich habe nichts daran auszusetzen** I have no objection to it ▷ *vi* (*aufhören*) to stop; (*Pause machen*) to drop out; (*beim Spiel*) to miss a turn

Aussicht *f* (*Blick*) view; (*Chance*) prospect; **aussichtslos** *adj* hopeless; **Aussichtsplattform** *f* observation platform; **Aussichtsturm** *m* observation tower

Aussiedler(in) (*-s, -*) *m(f)* émigré (*person of German descent from Eastern Europe*)

aus|spannen *vi* (*erholen*) to relax ▷ *vt*: **er hat ihm die Freundin ausgespannt** (*fam*) he's nicked his girlfriend

aus|sperren *vt* to lock out ▷ *vr*: **sich ~** to lock oneself out

Aussprache *f* (*von Wörtern*) pronunciation; (*Gespräch*) (frank) discussion; **aus|sprechen** *irr vt* to pronounce; (*äußern*) to express ▷ *vr*: **sich ~** to talk (*über +akk* about) ▷ *vi* (*zu Ende sprechen*) to finish speaking

aus|spülen *vt* to rinse (out)

Ausstattung *f* (*Ausrüstung*) equipment; (*Einrichtung*) furnishings *pl*; (*von Auto*) fittings *pl*

aus|stehen *irr vt* to endure; **ich kann ihn nicht ~** I can't stand him ▷ *vi* (*noch nicht da sein*) to be outstanding

aus|steigen *irr vi* to get out (*aus* of); **aus dem Bus/Zug ~** to get off the bus/train; **Aussteiger(in)** *m(f)* dropout

aus|stellen *vt* to display; (*auf Messe, in Museum etc*) to exhibit;

(fam: ausschalten) to switch off; *(Scheck etc)* to make out; *(Pass etc)* to issue; **Ausstellung** *f* exhibition

aus|sterben *irr vi* to die out
aus|strahlen *vt* to radiate; *(Programm)* to broadcast; **Ausstrahlung** *f (Radio, TV)* broadcast; *(fig: von Person)* charisma
aus|strecken *vr:* **sich ~** to stretch out ▷ *vt (Hand)* to reach out *(nach for)*
aus|suchen *vt* to choose
Austausch *m* exchange; **aus|tauschen** *vt* to exchange *(gegen for)*
aus|teilen *vt* to distribute; *(aushändigen)* to hand out
Auster *(-, -n) f* oyster; **Austernpilz** *m* oyster mushroom
aus|tragen *(-s) nt* Australia; **Australier(in)** *(-s, -) m(f)* Australian; **australisch** *adj* Australian
aus|trinken *irr vt (Glas)* to drain; *(Getränk)* to drink up ▷ *vi* to finish one's drink
aus|trocknen *vi* to dry out; *(Fluss)* to dry up
aus|üben *vt (Beruf, Sport)* to practise; *(Einfluss)* to exert
Ausverkauf *m* sale; **ausverkauft** *adj (Karten, Artikel)* sold out
Auswahl *f* selection, choice *(an +dat of)*; **aus|wählen** *vt* to select, to choose
aus|wandern *vi* to emigrate
auswärtig *adj (nicht am/vom Ort)* not local; *(ausländisch)* foreign; **auswärts** *adv (außerhalb der Stadt)* out of town; *(Sport)* **~ spielen** to play away; **Auswärtsspiel** *nt* away match

aus|wechseln *vt* to replace; *(Sport)* to substitute
Ausweg *m* way out
aus|weichen *vi* to get out of the way; **jdm/einer Sache ~** to move aside for sb/sth; *(fig)* to avoid sb/sth
Ausweis *(-es, -e) m (Personalausweis)* identity card, ID; *(für Bibliothek etc)* card; **aus|weisen** *irr vt* to expel ▷ *vr:* **sich ~** to prove one's identity; **Ausweiskontrolle** *f* ID check; **Ausweispapiere** *pl* identification documents pl
auswendig *adv* by heart
aus|wuchten *vt (Auto: Räder)* to balance
aus|zahlen *vt (Summe)* to pay (out); *(Person)* to pay off ▷ *vr:* **sich ~** to be worth it
aus|zeichnen *vt (ehren)* to honour; *(Comm)* to price ▷ *vr:* **sich ~** to distinguish oneself
aus|ziehen *irr vt (Kleidung)* to take off ▷ *vr:* **sich ~** to undress ▷ *vi (aus Wohnung)* to move out
Auszubildende(r) *mf* trainee
authentisch *adj* authentic, genuine
Auto *(-s, -s) nt* car; **~ fahren** to drive; **Autoatlas** *m* road atlas; **Autobahn** *f* motorway *(Brit)*, freeway *(US)*; **Autobahnauffahrt** *f* motorway access road *(Brit)*, on-ramp *(US)*; **Autobahnausfahrt** *f* motorway exit *(Brit)*, off-ramp *(US)*; **Autobahngebühr** *f* toll; **Autobahnkreuz** *nt* motorway interchange; **Autobahnring** *m* motorway ring *(Brit)*, beltway *(US)*; **Autobombe** *f* car bomb; **Autofähre** *f* car ferry; **Autofahrer(in)** *m(f)* driver, motorist; **Autofahrt** *f* drive
Autogramm *(-s, -e) nt* autograph

Automarke f make of car

Automat (-en, -en) m vending machine

Automatik (-, -en) f (Auto) automatic transmission; **Automatikschaltung** f automatic gear change (Brit) (o shift (US)); **Automatikwagen** m automatic

automatisch adj automatic ▷ adv automatically

Automechaniker(in) m(f) car mechanic; **Autonummer** f registration (Brit) (o license (US)) number

Autor (-s, -en) m author

Autoradio nt car radio; **Autoreifen** nt car tyre; **Autoreisezug** m Motorail train® (Brit), auto train (US); **Autorennen** nt motor racing; (einzelnes Rennen) motor race

Autorin f author(ess)

Autoschlüssel m car key; **Autotelefon** nt car phone; **Autounfall** m car accident; **Autoverleih** m, **Autovermietung** f car hire (Brit) (o rental (US)); (Firma) car hire (Brit) (o rental (US)) company; **Autowaschanlage** f car wash; **Autowerkstatt** f car repair shop, garage; **Autozubehör** nt car accessories pl

Avocado (-, -s) f avocado

Axt (-, Äxte) f axe

Azubi (-s, -s) m (-, -s) f akr = **Auszubildende** trainee

B abk = **Bundesstraße**

Baby (-s, -s) nt baby; **Babybett** nt cot (Brit), crib (US); **Babyfläschchen** nt baby's bottle; **Babynahrung** f baby food; **Babysitter(in)** m(f) babysitter; **Babysitz** m child seat; **Babywickelraum** m baby-changing room

Bach (-(e)s, Bäche) m stream

Backblech nt baking tray (Brit), cookie sheet (US)

Backbord nt port (side)

Backe (-, -n) f cheek

backen (backte, gebacken) vt, vi to bake

Backenzahn m molar

Bäcker(in) (-s, -) m(f) baker; **Bäckerei** f bakery; (Laden) baker's (shop)

Backofen m oven; **Backpulver** nt baking powder

Backspace-Taste f (Inform)

backspace key
Backstein m brick
Backwaren pl bread, cakes and pastries pl
Bad (-(e)s, Bäder) nt bath; (Schwimmen) swim; (Ort) spa; **ein ~ nehmen** to have (o take) a bath; **Badeanzug** m swimsuit, swimming costume (Brit); **Badehose** f swimming trunks pl; **Badekappe** f swimming cap; **Bademantel** m bathrobe; **Bademeister(in)** m(f) pool attendant; **Bademütze** f swimming cap
baden vi to have a bath; (schwimmen) to swim; to bathe (Brit) ▷ vt to bath (Brit), to bathe (US)
Baden-Württemberg (-s) nt Baden-Württemberg
Badeort m spa; **Badesachen** pl swimming things pl; **Badeschaum** m bubble bath, bath foam; **Badetuch** nt bath towel; **Badewanne** f bath (tub); **Badezeug** nt swimming gear; **Badezimmer** nt bathroom
Badminton (-s) nt badminton
baff adj: **~ sein** (fam) to be flabbergasted (o gobsmacked)
Bagger (-s, -) m excavator; **Baggersee** m artificial lake in quarry etc, used for bathing
Bahamas pl: **die ~** the Bahamas pl
Bahn (-, -en) f (Eisenbahn) railway (Brit), railroad (US); (Rennbahn) track; (für Läufer) lane; (Astr) orbit; **Deutsche ~** Germany's main railway operator; **bahnbrechend** adj groundbreaking; **BahnCard®** (-, -s) f rail card (allowing 50% or 25% reduction on tickets); **Bahnfahrt** f railway (Brit) (o railroad (US)) journey; **Bahnhof** m station; **am** (o **auf dem**) **~** at the station;

Bahnlinie f railway (Brit) (o railroad (US)) line; **Bahnpolizei** f railway (Brit) (o railroad (US)) police; **Bahnsteig** (-(e)s, -e) m platform; **Bahnstrecke** f railway (Brit) (o railroad (US)) line; **Bahnübergang** m level crossing (Brit), grade crossing (US)
Bakterien pl bacteria pl, germs pl
bald adv (zeitlich) soon; (beinahe) almost; **bis ~!** see you soon (o later); **baldig** adj quick, speedy
Balkan (-s) m: **der ~** the Balkans pl
Balken (-s, -) m beam
Balkon (-s, -s o -e) m balcony
Ball (-(e)s, Bälle) m ball; (Tanz) dance, ball
Ballett (-s) nt ballet
Ballon (-s, -s) m balloon
Ballspiel nt ball game
Ballungsgebiet nt conurbation
Baltikum (-s) nt: **das ~** the Baltic States pl
Bambus (-ses, -se) m bamboo; **Bambussprossen** pl bamboo shoots pl
banal adj banal; (Frage, Bemerkung) trite
Banane (-, -n) f banana
band imperf von **binden**
Band (-(e)s, Bände) m (Buch) volume ▷ (-(e)s, Bänder) nt (aus Stoff) ribbon, tape; (Fließband) production line; (Tonband) tape; (Anat) ligament; **etw auf ~ aufnehmen** to tape sth ▷ (-, -s) f (Musikgruppe) band
Bandage (-, -n) f bandage; **bandagieren** vt to bandage
Bande (-, -n) f (Gruppe) gang
Bänderriss m (Med) torn ligament
Bandscheibe f (Anat) disc; **Bandwurm** m tapeworm
Bank (-, Bänke) f (Sitzbank) bench ▷ (-, -en) f (Fin) bank

Bankautomat m cash dispenser; **Bankkarte** f bank card; **Bankkonto** nt bank account; **Bankleitzahl** f bank sort code; **Banknote** f banknote; **Bankverbindung** f banking (o account) details pl

bar adj: **-es Geld** cash; **etw (in) ~ bezahlen** to pay sth (in) cash

Bar (-, -s) f bar

Bär (-en, -en) m bear

barfuß adj barefoot

barg imperf von **bergen**

Bargeld nt cash; **bargeldlos** adj non-cash

Barkeeper (-s, -) m, **Barmann** m barman, bartender (US)

barock adj baroque

Barometer (-s, -) m barometer

barsch adj brusque

Barsch (-(e)s, -e) m perch

Barscheck m open (o uncrossed) cheque

Bart (-(e)s, Bärte) m beard; **bärtig** adj bearded

Barzahlung f cash payment

Basar (-s, -e) m bazaar

Baseballmütze f baseball cap

Basel (-s) nt Basle

Basilikum (-s) nt basil

Basis (-, Basen) f basis

Baskenland nt Basque region

Basketball m basketball

Bass (-es, Bässe) m bass

basta interj: **und damit ~!** and that's that

basteln vt to make ▷ vi to make things, to do handicrafts; **Bastler** (-s, -) m do-it-yourselfer

bat imperf von **bitten**

Batterie f battery; **batteriebetrieben** adj battery-powered

Bau (-(e)s) m (Bauen) building, construction; (Aufbau) structure; (Baustelle) building site ▷ m (Baue) (Tier) burrow ▷ m (Bauten) (Gebäude) building; **Bauarbeiten** pl construction work sing; (Straßenbau) roadworks pl (Brit), roadwork (US); **Bauarbeiter(in)** m(f) construction worker

Bauch (-(e)s, Bäuche) m stomach; **Bauchnabel** m navel; **Bauchredner(in)** m(f) ventriloquist; **Bauchschmerzen** pl stomach-ache sing; **Bauchspeicheldrüse** f pancreas; **Bauchtanz** m belly dance; (das Tanzen) belly dancing; **Bauchweh** (-s) nt stomach-ache

bauen vt, vi to build; (Tech) to construct

Bauer (-n o -s, -n) m farmer; (Schach) pawn; **Bäuerin** f farmer; (Frau des Bauern) farmer's wife; **Bauernhof** m farm

baufällig adj dilapidated; **Baujahr** adj year of construction; **der Wagen ist ~ 2002** the car is a 2002 model, the car was made in 2002

Baum (-(e)s, Bäume) m tree

Baumarkt m DIY centre

Baumwolle f cotton

Bauplatz m building site; **Baustein** m (für Haus) stone; (Spielzeug) brick; (fig) element; **elektronischer ~** chip; **Baustelle** f building site; (bei Straßenbau) roadworks pl (Brit), roadwork (US); **Bauteil** nt prefabricated part; **Bauunternehmer(in)** m(f) building contractor; **Bauwerk** nt building

Bayern (-s) nt Bavaria

beabsichtigen vt to intend

beachten vt (Aufmerksamkeit schenken) to pay attention to; (Vorschrift etc) to observe; **nicht ~** to ignore; **beachtlich** adj considerable

Beachvolleyball nt beach volleyball

Beamte(r) (-n, -n) m, **Beamtin** f
official; (Staatsbeamter) civil
servant

beanspruchen vt to claim; (Zeit,
Platz) to take up; **jdn ~** to keep sb
busy

beanstanden vt to complain
about; **Beanstandung** f
complaint

beantragen vt to apply for

beantworten vt to answer

bearbeiten vt to work; (Material,
Daten) to process; (Chem) to treat;
(Fall etc) to deal with; (Buch etc) to
revise; (fam: beeinflussen wollen) to
work on; **Bearbeitungsgebühr** f
handling (o service) charge

beatmen vt: **jdn ~** to give sb
artificial respiration

beaufsichtigen vt to supervise;
(bei Prüfung) to invigilate

beauftragen vt to instruct; **jdn
mit etw ~** to give sb the job of
doing sth

Becher (-s, -) m mug; (ohne
Henkel) tumbler; (für Jogurt) pot;
(aus Pappe) tub

Becken (-s, -) nt basin; (Spüle)
sink; (zum Schwimmen) pool; (Mus)
cymbal; (Anat) pelvis

bedanken vr: **sich ~** to say thank
you; **sich bei jdm für etw ~** to
thank sb for sth

Bedarf (-(e)s) m need (an +dat
for); (Comm) demand (an +dat for);
je nach ~ according to demand;
bei ~ if necessary;
Bedarfshaltestelle f request stop

bedauerlich adj regrettable;
bedauern vt to regret;
(bemitleiden) to feel sorry for;
bedauernswert adj (Zustände)
regrettable; (Mensch) unfortunate

bedeckt adj covered; (Himmel)
overcast

bedenken irr vt to consider;
Bedenken (-s, -) nt (Überlegen)

consideration; (Zweifel) doubt;
(Skrupel) scruples pl; **bedenklich**
adj dubious; (Zustand) serious

bedeuten vt to mean; **jdm
nichts/viel ~** to mean nothing/a
lot to sb; **bedeutend** adj
important; (beträchtlich)
considerable; **Bedeutung** f
meaning; (Wichtigkeit) importance

bedienen vt to serve; (Maschine)
to operate ▷ vr: **sich ~** (beim Essen)
to help oneself; **Bedienung** f
service; (Kellner/Kellnerin)
waiter/waitress; (Verkäufer(in))
shop assistant; (Zuschlag) service
(charge); **Bedienungsanleitung**
f operating instructions pl;
Bedienungshandbuch nt
instruction manual

Bedingung f condition; **unter
der ~, dass** on condition that;
unter diesen ~en under these
circumstances

bedrohen vt to threaten

Bedürfnis nt need

Beefsteak (-s, -s) nt steak

beeilen vr: **sich ~** to hurry

beeindrucken vt to impress

beeinflussen vt to influence

beeinträchtigen vt to affect

beenden vt to end; (fertigstellen)
to finish

beerdigen vt to bury; **Beerdigung** f burial; (Feier) funeral

Beere (-, -n) f berry;
(Traubenbeere) grape

Beet (-(e)s, -e) nt bed

befahl imperf von **befehlen**

befahrbar adj passable; (Naut)
navigable; **befahren** irr vt
(Straße) to use; (Pass) to drive over;
(Fluss etc) to navigate ▷ adj:
stark/wenig ~ busy/quiet

Befehl (-(e)s, -e) m order; (Inform)
command; **befehlen** (befahl,
befohlen) vt to order; **jdm ~, etw
zu tun** to order sb to do sth ▷ vi

to give orders
befestigen vt to fix; (mit Schnur, Seil) to attach; (mit Klebestoff) to stick
befeuchten vt to moisten
befinden irr vr: **sich ~** to be
befohlen pp von **befehlen**
befolgen vt (Rat etc) to follow
befördern vt (transportieren) to transport; (beruflich) to promote; **Beförderung** f transport; (beruflich) promotion; **Beförderungsbedingungen** pl conditions pl of carriage
Befragung f questioning; (Umfrage) opinion poll
befreundet adj friendly; **~ sein** to be friends (mit jdm with sb)
befriedigen vt to satisfy; **befriedigend** adj satisfactory; (Schulnote) ≈ C; **Befriedigung** f satisfaction
befristet adj limited (auf +akk to)
befruchten vt to fertilize; (fig) to stimulate
Befund (-(e)s, -e) m findings pl; (Med) diagnosis
befürchten vt to fear
befürworten vt to support
begabt adj gifted, talented; **Begabung** f talent, gift
begann imperf von **beginnen**
begegnen vi to meet (jdm sb), to meet with (einer Sache dat sth)
begehen irr vt (Straftat) to commit; (Jubiläum etc) to celebrate
begehrt adj sought-after; (Junggeselle) eligible
begeistern vt to fill with enthusiasm; (inspirieren) to inspire ▷ vr: **sich für etw ~** to be/get enthusiastic about sth; **begeistert** adj enthusiastic
Beginn (-(e)s) m beginning; **zu ~** at the beginning; **beginnen** (begann, begonnen) vt, vi to start, to begin

beglaubigen vt to certify; **Beglaubigung** f certification
begleiten vt to accompany; **Begleiter(in)** m(f) companion; **Begleitung** f company; (Mus) accompaniment
beglückwünschen vt to congratulate (zu on)
begonnen pp von **beginnen**
begraben irr vt to bury; **Begräbnis** nt burial; (Feier) funeral
begreifen irr vt to understand
Begrenzung f boundary; (fig) restriction
Begriff (-(e)s, -e) m concept; (Vorstellung) idea; **im ~ sein, etw zu tun** to be on the point of doing sth; **schwer von ~ sein** to be slow on the uptake
begründen vt (rechtfertigen) to justify; **Begründung** f explanation; (Rechtfertigung) justification
begrüßen vt to greet; (willkommen heißen) to welcome; **Begrüßung** f greeting; (Empfang) welcome
behaart adj hairy
behalten irr vt to keep; (im Gedächtnis) to remember; **etw für sich ~** to keep sth to oneself
Behälter (-s, -) m container
behandeln vt to treat; **Behandlung** f treatment
behaupten vt to claim, to maintain ▷ vr: **sich ~** to assert oneself; **Behauptung** f claim
beheizen vt to heat
behelfen irr vr: **sich mit/ohne etw ~** to make do with/without sth
beherbergen vt to accommodate
beherrschen vt (Situation, Gefühle) to control; (Instrument) to master ▷ vr: **sich ~** to control

oneself; **Beherrschung** f control (über +akk of); **die ~ verlieren** to lose one's self-control

behilflich adj helpful; **jdm ~ sein** to help sb (bei with)

behindern vt to hinder; (Verkehr, Sicht) to obstruct; **Behinderte(r)** mf person with a disability; **behindertengerecht** adj suitable for disabled people

Behörde (-, -n) f authority; **die ~n** pl the authorities pl

🔵 **SCHLÜSSELWORT**

bei prep +dat (nahe bei) near; (zum Aufenthalt) at, with; (unter, zwischen) among; **bei München** near Munich; **bei uns** at our place; **beim Friseur** at the hairdresser's; **bei seinen Eltern wohnen** to live with one's parents; **bei einer Firma arbeiten** to work for a firm; **etw bei sich haben** to have sth on one; **jdn bei sich haben** to have sb with one; **bei Goethe** in Goethe; **beim Militär** in the army **2** (zeitlich) at, on; (während) during; (Zustand, Umstand) in; **bei Nacht** at night; **bei Nebel** in fog; **bei Regen** if it rains; **bei solcher Hitze** in such heat; **bei meiner Ankunft** on my arrival; **bei der Arbeit** when I'm etc working; **beim Fahren** while driving

bei|behalten irr vt to keep
Beiboot nt dinghy
bei|bringen irr vt: **jdm etw ~** (mitteilen) to break sth to sb; (lehren) to teach sb sth
beide(s) pron both; **meine ~n Brüder** my two brothers, both my brothers; **wir ~** both (o the two) of us; **keiner von ~n** neither of us; **alle ~** both (of them); **~s ist sehr schön** both are very nice; **30**

~ (beim Tennis) 30 all
beieinander adv together
Beifahrer(in) m(f) passenger; **Beifahrerairbag** m passenger airbag; **Beifahrersitz** m passenger seat
Beifall (-(e)s) m applause
beige adj inv beige
Beigeschmack m aftertaste
Beil (-(e)s, -e) nt axe
Beilage f (Gastr) side dish; (Gemüse) vegetables pl; (zu Buch etc) supplement
beiläufig adj casual ▷ adv casually
Beileid nt condolences pl; **(mein) herzliches ~** please accept my sincere condolences
beiliegend adj enclosed
beim kontr von **bei dem**
Bein (-(e)s, -e) nt leg
beinah(e) adv almost, nearly
beinhalten vt to contain
Beipackzettel m instruction leaflet
beisammen adv together; **Beisammensein** (-s) nt get-together
beiseite adv aside; **beiseite|legen** vt: **etw ~** (sparen) to put sth by
Beispiel (-(e)s, -e) nt example; **sich** (dat) **an jdm/etw ein ~ nehmen** to take sb/sth as an example; **zum ~** for example
beißen (biss, gebissen) vt to bite ▷ vi to bite; (stechen: Rauch, Säure) to sting ▷ vr: **sich ~** (Farben) to clash
Beitrag (-(e)s, Beiträge) m contribution; (für Mitgliedschaft) subscription; (Versicherung) premium; **beitragen** irr vt, vi to contribute (zu to)
bekannt adj well-known; (nicht fremd) familiar; **mit jdm ~ sein** to know sb; **~ geben** to announce;

jdn mit jdm ~ machen to introduce sb to sb; **Bekannte(r)** mf friend; (entfernter) acquaintance; **bekanntlich** adv as everyone knows; **Bekanntschaft** f acquaintance
bekiffen vr: **sich ~** (fam) to get stoned
beklagen vr: **sich ~** to complain
Bekleidung f clothing
bekommen irr vt to get; (erhalten) to receive; (Kind) to have; (Zug, Grippe) to catch, to get; **wie viel ~ Sie dafür?** how much is that? ▷ vi: **jdm ~** (Essen) to agree with sb; **wir ~ schon** (bedient werden) we're being served
beladen irr vt to load
Belag (-(e)s, Beläge) m coating; (auf Zähnen) plaque; (auf Zunge) fur
belasten vt to load; (Körper) to strain; (Umwelt) to pollute; (fig: mit Sorgen etc) to burden; (Comm: Konto) to debit; (Jur) to incriminate
belästigen vt to bother; (stärker) to pester; (sexuell) to harass; **Belästigung** f annoyance; **sexuelle ~** sexual harassment
belebt adj (Straße etc) busy
Beleg (-(e)s, -e) m (Comm) receipt; (Beweis) proof; **belegen** vt (Brot) to spread; (Platz) to reserve; (Kurs, Vorlesung) to register for; (beweisen) to prove
belegt adj (Tel) engaged (Brit), busy (US); (Hotel) full; (Zunge) coated; **~es Brötchen** sandwich; **der Platz ist ~** this seat is taken; **Belegzeichen** nt (Tel) engaged tone (Brit), busy tone (US)
beleidigen vt to insult; (kränken) to offend; **Beleidigung** f insult; (Jur) slander; (schriftliche) libel
beleuchten vt to light; (bestrahlen) to illuminate; (fig) to examine; **Beleuchtung** f lighting; (Bestrahlung) illumination

Belgien (-s) nt Belgium; **Belgier(in)** (-s, -) m(f) Belgian; **belgisch** adj Belgian
belichten vt to expose; **Belichtung** f exposure; **Belichtungsmesser** (-s, -) m light meter
Belieben nt: **(ganz) nach ~** (just) as you wish
beliebig adj: **jedes ~e Muster** any pattern; **jeder ~e** anyone ▷ adv: **~ lange** as long as you like; **~ viel** as many (o much) as you like
beliebt adj popular; **sich bei jdm ~ machen** to make oneself popular with sb
beliefern vt to supply
bellen vi to bark
Belohnung f reward
Belüftung f ventilation
belügen irr vt to lie to
bemerkbar adj noticeable; **sich ~ machen** (Mensch) to attract attention; (Zustand) to become noticeable; **bemerken** vt (wahrnehmen) to notice; (sagen) to remark; **bemerkenswert** adj remarkable; **Bemerkung** f remark
bemitleiden vt to pity
bemühen vr: **sich ~** to try (hard), to make an effort; **Bemühung** f effort
bemuttern vt to mother
benachbart adj neighbouring
benachrichtigen vt to inform; **Benachrichtigung** f notification
benachteiligen vt to (put at a) disadvantage; (wegen Rasse etc) to discriminate against
benehmen irr vr: **sich ~** to behave; **Benehmen** (-s) nt behaviour
beneiden vt to envy; **jdn um etw ~** to envy sb sth
Beneluxländer pl Benelux countries pl

benommen adj dazed

benötigen vt to need

benutzen vt to use;
Benutzer(in) (-s, -) m(f) user;
benutzerfreundlich adj user-
friendly; **Benutzerhandbuch** nt
user's guide; **Benutzerkennung** f
user ID; **Benutzerkonto** nt
(Inform) user account;
Benutzername m (Inform) username; **Benutzeroberfläche** f
(Inform) user/system interface;
Benutzung f use;
Benutzungsgebühr f (hire)
charge

Benzin (-s, -e) nt (Auto) petrol
(Brit), gas (US); **Benzinkanister** m
petrol (Brit) (o gas (US)) can;
Benzinpumpe f petrol (Brit) (o
gas (US)) pump; **Benzintank** m
petrol (Brit) (o gas (US)) tank;
Benzinuhr f fuel gauge

beobachten vt to observe;
Beobachtung f observation

bequem adj comfortable;
(Ausrede) convenient; (faul) lazy;
machen Sie es sich ~ make
yourself at home; **Bequemlichkeit**
f comfort; (Faulheit) laziness

beraten irr vt to advise;
(besprechen) to discuss ▷ vr:
sich ~ to consult; **Beratung** f advice;
(bei Arzt etc) consultation

berauben vt to rob

berechnen vt to calculate;
(Comm) to charge

berechtigen vt to entitle (zu to);
(fig) to justify; **berechtigt** adj
justified; **zu etw ~ sein** to be
entitled to sth

bereden vt (besprechen) to discuss

Bereich (-(e)s, -e) m area;
(Ressort, Gebiet) field

bereisen vt to travel through

bereit adj ready; **zu etw ~ sein** to
be ready for sth; **sich ~ erklären,
etw zu tun** to agree to do sth

bereiten vt to prepare; (Kummer)
to cause; (Freude) to give

bereit|legen vt to lay out

bereit|machen vr: **sich ~** to get
ready

bereits adv already

Bereitschaft f readiness;
~ haben (Arzt) to be on call

bereit|stehen vi to be ready

bereuen vt to regret

Berg (-(e)s, -e) m mountain;
(kleiner) hill; **in die ~e fahren** to go
to the mountains; **bergab** adv
downhill; **bergauf** adv uphill;
Bergbahn f mountain railway
(Brit) (o railroad (US))

bergen (barg, geborgen) vt
(retten) to rescue; (enthalten) to
contain

Bergführer(in) m(f) mountain
guide; **Berghütte** f mountain hut;
bergig adj mountainous;
Bergschuh m climbing boot;
Bergsteigen (-s) nt
mountaineering; **Bergsteiger(in)**
(-s, -) m(f) mountaineer;
Bergtour f mountain hike

Bergung f (Rettung) rescue; (von
Toten, Fahrzeugen) recovery

Bergwacht (-, -en) f mountain
rescue service; **Bergwerk** nt
mine

Bericht (-(e)s, -e) m report;
berichten vt, vi to report

berichtigen vt to correct

Bermudadreieck nt Bermuda
triangle; **Bermudainseln** pl
Bermuda sing

Bernstein m amber

berüchtigt adj notorious,
infamous

berücksichtigen vt to take into
account; (Antrag, Bewerber) to
consider

Beruf (-(e)s, -e) m occupation;
(akademischer) profession;
(Gewerbe) trade; **was sind Sie von**

~? what do you do (for a living)?;
beruflich adj professional
Berufsausbildung f vocational training; **Berufsschule** f vocational college; **berufstätig** adj employed; **Berufsverkehr** m commuter traffic
beruhigen vt to calm ▷ vr: **sich ~** (Mensch, Situation) to calm down; **beruhigend** adj reassuring; **Beruhigungsmittel** nt sedative
berühmt adj famous
berühren vt to touch; (gefühlsmäßig bewegen) to move; (betreffen) to affect; (flüchtig erwähnen) to mention, to touch on ▷ vr: **sich ~** to touch
besaufen irr vr: **sich ~** (fam) to get plastered
beschädigen vt to damage
beschäftigen vt to occupy; (beruflich) to employ ▷ vr: **sich mit etw ~** to occupy oneself with sth; (sich befassen) to deal with sth; **beschäftigt** busy, occupied; **Beschäftigung** f (Beruf) employment; (Tätigkeit) occupation; (geistige) preoccupation (mit with)
Bescheid (-(e)s, -e) m information; **~ wissen** to be informed (o know) (über +akk about); **ich weiß ~** I know; **jdm ~ geben** (o sagen) to let sb know
bescheiden adj modest
bescheinigen vt to certify; (bestätigen) to acknowledge; **Bescheinigung** f certificate; (Quittung) receipt
bescheißen irr (vulg) to cheat (um out of)
bescheuert adj (fam, pej) crazy
beschimpfen vt (mit Kraftausdrücken) to swear at
Beschiss (-es) m: **das ist ~** (vulg) that's a rip-off!; **beschissen** adj (vulg) shitty

beschlagnahmen vt to confiscate
Beschleunigung f acceleration; **Beschleunigungsspur** f acceleration lane
beschließen irr vt to decide on; (beenden) to end; **Beschluss** m decision
beschränken vt to limit, to restrict (auf +akk to) ▷ vr: **sich ~** to restrict oneself (auf +akk to); **Beschränkung** f limitation, restriction
beschreiben irr vt to describe; (Papier) to write on; **Beschreibung** f description
beschuldigen vt to accuse (gen of); **Beschuldigung** f accusation
beschummeln vt, vi (fam) to cheat (um out of)
beschützen vt to protect (vor +dat from)
Beschwerde (-, -n) f complaint; **~n** pl (Leiden) trouble sing; **beschweren** vt to weight down; (fig) to burden ▷ vr: **sich ~** to complain
beschwipst adj tipsy
beseitigen vt to remove; (Problem) to get rid of; (Müll) to dispose of; **Beseitigung** f removal; (von Müll) disposal
Besen (-s, -) m broom
besetzen vt (Haus, Land) to occupy; (Platz) to take; (Posten) to fill; (Rolle) to cast; **besetzt** adj full; (Tel) engaged (Brit), busy (US); (Platz) taken; (WC) engaged; **Besetztzeichen** nt engaged tone (Brit), busy tone (US)
besichtigen vt (Museum) to visit; (Sehenswürdigkeit) to have a look at; (Stadt) to tour
besiegen vt to defeat
Besitz (-es) m possession; (Eigentum) property; **besitzen** irr

vt to own; (*Geschäft*) to have;
Besitzer(in) (*-s*, *-*) *m(f)* owner
besoffen *adj* (*fam*) plastered
besondere(r, s) *adj* special;
(*bestimmt*) particular;
(*eigentümlich*) peculiar; **nichts ~s**
nothing special; **Besonderheit** *f*
special feature; (*besondere
Eigenschaft*) peculiarity; **besonders**
adv especially, particularly;
(*getrennt*) separately
besorgen *vt* (*beschaffen*) to get;
(*jdm für sb*); (*kaufen a.*) to purchase;
(*erledigen: Geschäfte*) to deal with
besprechen *irr vt* to discuss;
Besprechung *f* discussion;
(*Konferenz*) meeting; **Besprechungsraum** *m* consultation
room
besser *adj* better; **es geht ihm
~** he feels better; **~ gesagt** or
rather; **~ werden** to improve;
bessern *vt* to improve ▷ *vr:* **sich
~** to improve; (*Mensch*) to mend
one's ways; **Besserung** *f*
improvement; **gute ~!** get well
soon
beständig *adj* constant; (*Wetter*)
settled
Bestandteil *m* component
bestätigen *vt* to confirm;
(*Empfang, Brief*) to acknowledge;
Bestätigung *f* confirmation; (*von
Brief*) acknowledgement
beste(r, s) *adj* best; **das ~ wäre,
wir ...** it would be best if we ...
▷ *adv:* **sie singt am ~n** she sings
best; **so ist es am ~n** it's best that
way; **am ~n gehst du gleich** you'd
better go at once
bestechen *irr vt* to bribe;
Bestechung *f* bribery
Besteck (*-(e)s, -e*) *nt* cutlery
bestehen *irr vi* to be, to exist;
(*andauern*) to last; **~ auf** (*+dat*) to
insist on; **~ aus** to consist of ▷ *vt*
(*Probe, Prüfung*) to pass; (*Kampf*) to

win
bestehlen *irr vt* to rob
bestellen *vt* to order; (*reservieren*)
to book; (*Grüße, Auftrag*) to pass on
(*jdm to sb*); (*kommen lassen*) to send
for; **Bestellnummer** *f* order
number; **Bestellung** *f* (*Comm*)
order; (*das Bestellen*) ordering
bestens *adv* very well
bestimmen *vt* to determine;
(*Regeln*) to lay down; (*Tag, Ort*) to
fix; (*ernennen*) to appoint;
(*vorsehen*) to mean (*für for*);
bestimmt *adj* definite; (*gewiss*)
certain; (*entschlossen*) firm ▷ *adv*
definitely; (*wissen*) for sure;
Bestimmung *f* (*Verordnung*)
regulation; (*Zweck*) purpose
Best.-Nr. *abk* = **Bestellnummer**
order number
bestrafen *vt* to punish
bestrahlen *vt* to illuminate;
(*Med*) to treat with radiotherapy
bestreiten *irr vt* (*leugnen*) to
deny
Bestseller (*-s*, *-*) *m* bestseller
bestürzt *adj* dismayed
Besuch (*-(e)s, -e*) *m* visit; (*Mensch*)
visitor; **~ haben** to have visitors/a
visitor; **besuchen** *vt* to visit;
(*Schule, Kino etc*) to go to;
Besucher(in) (*-s*, *-*) *m(f)* visitor;
Besuchszeit *f* visiting hours *pl*
betäuben *vt* (*Med*) to
anaesthetize; **Betäubung** *f*
anaesthetic; **örtliche ~** local
anaesthetic; **Betäubungsmittel**
nt anaesthetic
Bete (*-, -n*) *f*: **Rote ~** beetroot
beteiligen *vr* **sich an etw** (*dat*)
~ to take part in sth, to participate
in sth ▷ *vt* **jdn an etw** (*dat*) **~** to
involve sb in sth; **Beteiligung** *f*
participation; (*Anteil*) share;
(*Besucherzahl*) attendance
beten *vi* to pray
Beton (*-s, -s*) *m* concrete

betonen vt to stress; (hervorheben) to emphasize; **Betonung** f stress; (fig) emphasis

Betr. abk = **Betreff** re

Betracht m: **in ~ ziehen** to take into consideration; **in ~ kommen** to be a possibility; **nicht in ~ kommen** to be out of the question; **betrachten** vt to look at; **~ als** to regard as; **beträchtlich** adj considerable

Betrag (-(e)s, Beträge) m amount, sum; **betragen** irr vt to amount (o come to) to; vr: **sich ~** to behave

betreffen irr vt to concern; (Regelung etc) to affect; **was mich betrifft** as for me; **betreffend** adj relevant, in question

betreten irr vt to enter; (Bühne etc) to step onto; **„Betreten verboten"** "keep off/out"

betreuen vt to look after; (Reisegruppe, Abteilung) to be in charge of; **Betreuer(in)** (-s, -) m(f) (Pfleger) carer; (von Kind) child minder; (von Reisegruppe) groupleader

Betrieb (-(e)s, -e) m (Firma) firm; (Anlage) plant; (Tätigkeit) operation; (Treiben) bustle; **außer ~ sein** to be out of order; **in ~ sein** to be in operation; **betriebsbereit** adj operational; **Betriebsrat** m (Gremium) works council; **Betriebssystem** nt (Inform) operating system

betrinken irr vr: **sich ~** to get drunk

betroffen adj (bestürzt) shaken; **von etw ~ werden/sein** to be affected by sth

betrog imperf von **betrügen**

betrogen pp von **betrügen**

Betrug (-(e)s, -e) m deception; (Jur) fraud; **betrügen** (betrog, betrogen) vt to deceive; (Jur) to defraud;

(Partner) to cheat on; **Betrüger(in)** (-s, -) m(f) cheat

betrunken adj drunk

Bett (-(e)s, -en) nt bed; **ins** (o zu) **~ gehen** to go to bed; **das ~ machen** to make the bed; **Bettbezug** m duvet cover; **Bettdecke** f blanket

betteln vi to beg

Bettlaken nt sheet

Bettler(in) (-s, -) m(f) beggar

Bettsofa nt sofa bed; **Betttuch** nt sheet; **Bettwäsche** f bed linen; **Bettzeug** nt bedding

beugen vt to bend ▷ vr: **sich ~** to bend; (sich fügen) to submit (dat to)

Beule (-, -n) f (Schwellung) bump; (Delle) dent

beunruhigen vt to worry ▷ vr: **sich ~** to worry

beurteilen vt to judge

Beute (-) f (von Dieb) booty, loot; (von Tier) prey

Beutel (-s, -) m bag

Bevölkerung f population

bevollmächtigt adj authorized (zu etw to do sth)

bevor conj before; **bevor|stehen** irr vi (Schwierigkeiten) to lie ahead; (Gefahr) to be imminent; **jdm ~** (Überraschung etc) to be in store for sb; **bevorstehend** adj forthcoming; **bevorzugen** vt to prefer

bewachen vt to guard; **bewacht** adj: **~er Parkplatz** supervised car park (Brit), guarded parking lot (US)

bewegen vt to move; **jdn dazu ~, etw zu tun** to get sb to do sth ▷ vr: **sich ~** to move; **es bewegt sich etwas** (fig) things are beginning to happen; **Bewegung** f movement; (Phys) motion; (innere) emotion; (körperlich) exercise; **Bewegungsmelder** (-s, -) m sensor (which reacts to *movement)*

Beweis *(-es, -e)* m proof; *(Zeugnis)* evidence; **beweisen** *irr vt* to prove; *(zeigen)* to show

bewerben *irr vr:* **sich ~** to apply *(um* for); **Bewerbung** f application; **Bewerbungsunterlagen** pl application documents pl

bewilligen vt to allow; *(Geld)* to grant

bewirken vt to cause, to bring about

bewohnen vt to live in; **Bewohner(in)** *(-s, -)* m(f) inhabitant; *(von Haus)* resident

bewölkt adj cloudy, overcast; **Bewölkung** f clouds pl

bewundern vt to admire; **bewundernswert** adj admirable

bewusst adj conscious; *(absichtlich)* deliberate; **sich** *(dat)* **einer Sache** *(gen)* ~ **sein** to be aware of sth ▷ adv consciously; *(absichtlich)* deliberately; **bewusstlos** adj unconscious; **Bewusstlosigkeit** f unconsciousness; **Bewusstsein** *(-s)* nt consciousness; **bei** ~ conscious

bezahlen vt to pay; **kann ich bar/mit Kreditkarte ~?** can I pay cash/by credit card?; **sich bezahlt machen** to be worth it; **Bezahlung** f payment

bezeichnen vt *(kennzeichnen)* to mark; *(nennen)* to call; *(beschreiben)* to describe; **Bezeichnung** f *(Name)* name; *(Begriff)* term

beziehen *irr vt (Bett)* to change; *(Haus, Position)* to move into; *(erhalten)* to receive; *(Zeitung)* to take; **einen Standpunkt ~** *(fig)* to take up a position ▷ vr: **sich ~** to refer *(auf +akk* to); **Beziehung** f *(Verbindung)* connection; *(Verhältnis)* relationship; **~en**

haben *(vorteilhaft)* to have connections *(o* contacts); **in dieser** ~ in this respect; **beziehungsweise** adv or; *(genauer gesagt)* or rather

Bezirk *(-(e)s, -e)* m district

Bezug *(-(e)s, Bezüge)* m *(Überzug)* cover; *(von Kopfkissen)* pillowcase; **in ~ auf** *(+akk)* with regard to; **bezüglich** prep *+gen* concerning

bezweifeln vt to doubt

BH *(-s, -s)* m bra

Bhf. abk = **Bahnhof** station

Biathlon *(-s, -s)* m biathlon

Bibel *(-, -n)* f Bible

Biber *(-s, -)* m beaver

Bibliothek *(-, -en)* f library

biegen *(bog, gebogen)* vt to bend ▷ vr: **sich ~** to bend ▷ vi to turn *(in +akk* into); **Biegung** f bend

Biene *(-, -n)* f bee

Bier *(-(e)s, -e)* nt beer; **helles ~** = lager (Brit), beer (US); **dunkles ~** = brown ale (Brit), dark beer (US); **zwei ~, bitte!** two beers, please; **Biergarten** m beer garden; **Bierzelt** nt beer tent

bieten *(bot, geboten)* vt to offer; *(bei Versteigerung)* bid; **sich** *(dat)* **etw ~ lassen** to put up with sth ▷ vr: **sich ~** *(Gelegenheit)* to present itself *(dat* to)

Bikini *(-s, -s)* m bikini

Bild *(-(e)s, -er)* nt picture; *(gedankliches)* image; *(Foto)* photo

bilden vt to form; *(geistig)* to educate; *(ausmachen)* to constitute ▷ vr: **sich ~** *(entstehen)* to form; *(lernen)* to educate oneself

Bilderbuch nt picture book

Bildhauer(in) *(-s, -)* m(f) sculptor

Bildschirm m screen; **Bildschirmschoner** *(-s, -)* m screensaver; **Bildschirmtext** m viewdata, videotext

Bildung f formation; *(Wissen,*

Benehmen) education;
Bildungsurlaub m educational
holiday; (von Firma) study leave
Billard nt billiards sing
billig adj cheap; (gerecht) fair
Billigflieger m budget airline
Billigflug m cheap flight
Binde (-, -n) f bandage;
(Armbinde) band; (Damenbinde)
sanitary towel (Brit), sanitary
napkin (US)
Bindehautentzündung f
conjunctivitis
binden (band, gebunden) vt to tie;
(Buch) to bind; (Soße) to thicken
Bindestrich m hyphen
Bindfaden m string
Bindung f bond, tie
Bio- in zW bio-; **Biokost** f health
food; **Biokraftstoff** m biofuel

○ **BIOLADEN**

- A **Bioladen** is a shop which
- specializes in selling
- environmentally friendly
- products such as
- phosphate-free washing
- powders, recycled paper and
- organically grown vegetables.

Biologie f biology; **biologisch**
adj biological; (Anbau) organic
bipolar adj bipolar
Birke (-, -n) f birch
Birne (-, -n) f (Obst) pear; (Elek)
(light) bulb

○ **SCHLÜSSELWORT**

bis prep +akk, adv **1** (zeitlich) till,
until; (bis spätestens) by; **Sie haben
bis Dienstag Zeit** you have until o
till Tuesday; **bis Dienstag muss es
fertig sein** it must be ready by
Tuesday; **bis auf Weiteres** until
further notice; **bis in die Nacht**

into the night; **bis bald/gleich** see
you later/soon
2 (räumlich) (up) to; **ich fahre bis
Köln** I'm going to o I'm going as far
as Cologne; **bis an unser
Grundstück** (right o up) to our
plot; **bis hierher** this far
3 (bei Zahlen) up to; **bis zu** up to
4 bis auf etw akk (außer) except
sth; (einschließlich) including sth
▷ konj **1** (mit Zahlen) to; **10 bis 20** 10
to 20
2 (zeitlich) till, until; **bis es dunkel
wird** till o until it gets dark; **von ...
bis ...** from ... to ...

Bischof (-s, Bischöfe) m bishop
bisher adv up to now, so far
Biskuit (-(e)s, -s o -e) nt sponge
biss imperf von **beißen**
Biss (-es, -e) m bite
bisschen adj: **ein ~** a bit of; **ein
~ Salz/Liebe** a bit of salt/love; **ich
habe kein ~ Hunger** I'm not a bit
hungry ▷ adv: **ein ~** a bit; **kein
~ not** at all
bissig adj (Hund) vicious;
(Bemerkung) cutting
Bit (-s, -s) nt (Inform) bit
bitte interj please; **(wie) ~?** (I beg
your) pardon?; **~ (schön** o **sehr)!**
(als Antwort auf Dank) you're
welcome; **hier, ~** here you are;
Bitte (-, -n) f request; **bitten**
(bat, gebeten) vt, vi to ask (um for)
bitter adj bitter
Blähungen pl (Med) wind sing
blamieren vr: **sich ~** to make a
fool of oneself ▷ vt: **jdn ~** to make
sb look a fool
Blankoscheck m blank cheque
Blase (-, -n) f bubble; (Med)
blister; (Anat) bladder
blasen (blies, geblasen) vi to blow;
jdm einen ~ (vulg) to give sb a
blow job
Blasenentzündung f cystitis

blass adj pale
Blatt (-(e)s, Blätter) nt leaf; (von Papier) sheet; **blättern** vi (Inform) to scroll; **in etw** (dat) ~ to leaf through sth; **Blätterteig** m puff pastry; **Blattsalat** m green salad; **Blattspinat** m spinach
blau adj blue; (fam: betrunken) plastered; (Gastr) boiled; **~es Auge** black eye; **~er Fleck** bruise; **Blaubeere** f bilberry, blueberry; **Blaulicht** nt flashing blue light; **blau|machen** vi to skip work o school; **Blauschimmelkäse** m blue cheese
Blazer (-s, -) m blazer
Blech (-(e)s, -e) nt sheet metal; (Backblech) baking tray (Brit), cookie sheet (US); **Blechschaden** m (Auto) damage to the bodywork
Blei (-(e)s, -e) nt lead
bleiben (blieb, geblieben) vi to stay; **lass das ~!** stop it; **das bleibt unter uns** that's (just) between ourselves; **mir bleibt keine andere Wahl** I have no other choice
bleich adj pale; **bleichen** vt to bleach
bleifrei adj (Benzin) unleaded; **bleihaltig** adj (Benzin) leaded
Bleistift m pencil
Blende (-, -n) f (Foto) aperture
Blick (-(e)s, -e) m look; (kurz) glance; (Aussicht) view; **auf den ersten ~** at first sight; **einen ~ auf etw** (akk) **werfen** to have a look at sth; **blicken** vi to look; **sich ~ lassen** to show up
blieb imperf von bleiben
blies imperf von blasen
blind adj blind; (Glas etc) dull; **Blinddarm** m appendix; **Blinddarmentzündung** f appendicitis; **Blinde(r)** mf blind person/man/woman; **die ~n** pl the blind pl; **Blindenhund** m guide dog; **Blindenschrift** f

braille
blinken vi (Stern, Lichter) to twinkle; (aufleuchten) to flash; (Auto) to indicate; **Blinker** (-s, -) m (Auto) indicator (Brit), turn signal (US)
blinzeln vi (mit beiden Augen) to blink; (mit einem Auge) to wink
Blitz (-es, -e) m (flash of) lightning; (Foto) flash; **blitzen** vi (Foto) to use a flash; **es blitzte und donnerte** there was thunder and lightning; **Blitzlicht** nt flash
Block (-(e)s, Blöcke) m (a. fig) block; (von Papier) pad; **Blockflöte** f recorder; **Blockhaus** nt log cabin; **blockieren** vt to block ▷ vi to jam; (Räder) to lock
blöd adj stupid; **blödeln** vi (fam) to fool around
Blog (-s, -s) nt (Inform) blog; **bloggen** vi to blog
Blogosphäre (-, -n) f blogosphere
blond adj blond; (Frau) blonde

⊙ SCHLÜSSELWORT

bloß adj **1** (unbedeckt) bare; (nackt) naked; **mit der bloßen Hand** with one's bare hand; **mit bloßem Auge** with the naked eye **2** (alleinig, nur) mere; **der bloße Gedanke** the very thought; **bloßer Neid** sheer envy ▷ adv only, merely; **lass das bloß!** just don't do that!; **wie ist das bloß passiert?** how on earth did that happen?

blühen vi to bloom; (fig) to flourish
Blume (-, -n) f flower; (von Wein) bouquet; **Blumenbeet** nt flower bed; **Blumengeschäft** nt florist's (shop); **Blumenkohl** m cauliflower; **Blumenladen** m flower shop; **Blumenstrauß** m

bunch of flowers; **Blumentopf** m
flowerpot; **Blumenvase** f vase
Bluse (-, -n) f blouse
Blut (-(e)s) nt blood; **Blutbild** nt
blood count; **Blutdruck** m blood
pressure; **Blutorange** f blood
orange
Blüte (-, -n) f (Pflanzenteil) flower,
bloom; (Baumblüte) blossom; (fig)
prime
bluten vi to bleed
Blütenstaub m pollen
Bluter (-s, -) m (Med)
haemophiliac; **Blutguss** m
haematoma; (blauer Fleck) bruise;
Blutgruppe f blood group; **blutig**
adj bloody; **Blutkonserve** f unit
of stored blood; **Blutprobe** f
blood sample; **Blutspende** f
blood donation; **Bluttransfusion**
f blood transfusion; **Blutung** f
bleeding; **Blutvergiftung** f
blood poisoning; **Blutwurst** f
black pudding (Brit), blood
sausage (US)
BLZ abk = **Bankleitzahl**
Bob (-s, -s) m bob(sleigh)
Bock (-(e)s, Böcke) m (Reh) buck;
(Schaf) ram; (Gestell) trestle; (Sport)
vaulting horse; **ich hab keinen
~ (drauf)** (fam) I don't feel like it
Boden (-s, Böden) m ground;
(Fußboden) floor; (von Meer, Fass)
bottom; (Speicher) attic;
Bodennebel m ground mist;
Bodenpersonal nt ground staff;
Bodenschätze pl mineral
resources pl
Bodensee m: **der ~** Lake
Constance
Body (-s, -s) m body;
Bodybuilding (-s) nt
bodybuilding
bog imperf von **biegen**
Bogen (-s, -) m (Biegung) curve;
(in der Architektur) arch; (Waffe,
Instrument) bow; (Papier) sheet

Bohne (-, -n) f bean; **grüne ~n** pl
green (o French (Brit)) beans pl;
weiße ~n pl haricot beans pl;
Bohnenkaffee m real coffee;
Bohnensprosse f bean sprout
bohren vt to drill; **Bohrer** (-s, -)
m drill
Boiler (-s, -) m water heater
Boje (-, -n) f buoy
Bolivien (-s) nt Bolivia
Bombe (-, -n) f bomb
Bon (-s, -s) m (Kassenzettel)
receipt; (Gutschein) voucher,
coupon
Bonbon (-s, -s) nt sweet (Brit),
candy (US)
Bonus (- o -ses, -se o Boni) m
bonus; (Punktvorteil) bonus points
pl; (Schadenfreiheitsrabatt)
no-claims bonus
Boot (-(e)s, -e) nt boat;
Bootsverleih m boat hire (Brit) (o
rental (US))
Bord (-(e)s, -e) m: **an ~** (eines
Schiffes) on board (a ship); **an
~ gehen** (Schiff) to go on board;
(Flugzeug) to board; **von ~ gehen**
to disembark; **Bordcomputer** m
dashboard computer
Bordell (-s, -e) nt brothel
Bordkarte f boarding card
Bordstein m kerb (Brit), curb (US)
borgen vt to borrow; **jdm etw
~** to lend sb sth; **sich** (dat) **etw ~** to
borrow sth
Börse (-, -n) f stock exchange;
(Geldbörse) purse
bös adj siehe **böse**; **bösartig** adj
malicious; (Med) malignant
Böschung f slope; (Uferböschung)
embankment
böse adj bad; (stärker) evil;
(Wunde) nasty; (zornig) angry; **bist
du mir ~?** are you angry with me?
boshaft adj malicious
Bosnien (-s) nt Bosnia;
Bosnien-Herzegowina (-s) nt

Bosnia-Herzegovina

böswillig adj malicious

bot imperf von **bieten**

botanisch adj: **~er Garten** botanical gardens pl

Botschaft f message; (Pol) embassy; **Botschafter(in)** m(f) ambassador

Botsuana (-s) nt Botswana

Bouillon (-, -s) f stock

Boutique (-, -n) f boutique

Bowle (-, -n) f punch

Box (-, -en) f (Behälter, Pferdebox) box; (Lautsprecher) speaker; (bei Autorennen) pit

boxen vi to box; **Boxer** (-s, -) m (Hund, Sportler) boxer; **Boxershorts** pl boxer shorts pl; **Boxkampf** m boxing match

Boykott (-s, -e) m boycott

brach imperf von **brechen**

brachte imperf von **bringen**

Brainstorming (-s) nt brainstorming

Branchenverzeichnis nt yellow pages® pl

Brand (-(e)s, Brände) m fire; **einen ~ haben** (fam) to be parched

Brandenburg (-s) nt Brandenburg

Brandsalbe f ointment for burns

Brandung f surf

Brandwunde f burn

brannte imperf von **brennen**

Brasilien (-s) nt Brazil

braten (briet, gebraten) vt to roast; (auf dem Rost) to grill; (in der Pfanne) to fry; **Braten** (-s, -) m roast; (roher) joint; **Bratensoße** f gravy; **Brathähnchen** nt roast chicken; **Bratkartoffeln** pl fried potatoes pl; **Bratpfanne** f frying pan; **Bratspieß** m spit; **Bratwurst** f fried sausage; (gegrillte) grilled sausage

Brauch (-s, Bräuche) m custom

brauchen vt (nötig haben) to need

(für, zu for); (erfordern) to require; (Zeit) to take; (gebrauchen) to use; **wie lange wird er ~?** how long will it take him?; **du brauchst es nur zu sagen** you only need to say; **das braucht (seine) Zeit** it takes time; **ihr braucht es nicht zu tun** you don't have (o need) to do it; **sie hätte nicht zu kommen ~** she needn't have come

brauen vt to brew; **Brauerei** f brewery

braun adj brown; (von Sonne) tanned; **Bräune** (-, -n) f brownness; (von Sonne) tan; **Bräunungsstudio** nt tanning studio

Brause (-, -n) f (Dusche) shower; (Getränk) fizzy drink (Brit), soda (US)

Braut (-, Bräute) f bride; **Bräutigam** (-s, -e) m bridegroom

brav adj (artig) good, well-behaved

bravo interj well done

BRD (-) f abk = **Bundesrepublik Deutschland** FRG

○ **BRD**
○
○ The **BRD** is the official name for
○ the Federal Republic of
○ Germany. It comprises 16
○ **Länder** (see **Land**). It was the
○ name given to the former West
○ Germany as opposed to East
○ Germany (the **DDR**). The two
○ Germanies were reunited on 3rd
○ October 1990.

brechen (brach, gebrochen) vt to break; (erbrechen) to bring up; **sich** (dat) **den Arm ~** to break one's arm ▷ vi to break; (erbrechen) to vomit, to be sick; **Brechreiz** m nausea

Brei (-(e)s, -e) m (Breimasse) mush, pulp; (Haferbrei) porridge; (für

Kinder) pap

breit *adj* wide; *(Schultern)* broad; **zwei Meter ~** two metres wide; **Breite** (-, -n) *f* breadth; *(bei Maßangaben)* width; *(Geo)* latitude; **der ~ nach** widthways; **Breitengrad** *m* (degree of) latitude

Bremen (-s) *nt* Bremen

Bremsbelag *m* brake lining; **Bremse** (-, -n) *f* brake; *(Zool)* horsefly; **bremsen** *vi* to brake ▷ *vt (Auto)* to brake; *(fig)* to slow down; **Bremsflüssigkeit** *f* brake fluid; **Bremslicht** *nt* brake light; **Bremspedal** *nt* brake pedal; **Bremsspur** *f* tyre marks *pl*; **Bremsweg** *m* braking distance

brennen (brannte, gebrannt) *vi* to burn; *(in Flammen stehen)* to be on fire; **es brennt!** fire!; **mir ~ die Augen** my eyes are smarting; **das Licht ~ lassen** to leave the light on; **Brennholz** *nt* firewood; **Brennnessel** *f* stinging nettle; **Brennspiritus** *m* methylated spirits *pl*; **Brennstab** *m* fuel rod; **Brennstoff** *m* fuel

Brett (-(e)s, -er) *nt (länger)* plank; *(Regal)* shelf; *(Spielbrett)* board; **Schwarzes ~** notice board, bulletin board (US); **~er** *pl (ski)* skis *pl*; **Brettspiel** *nt* board game

Brezel (-, -n) *f* pretzel

Brief (-(e)s, -e) *m* letter; **Briefbombe** *f* letter bomb; **Brieffreund(in)** *m(f)* penfriend, pen pal; **Briefkasten** *m* letterbox (Brit), mailbox (US); **elektronischer ~** electronic mailbox; **Briefmarke** *f* stamp; **Briefpapier** *nt* writing paper; **Brieftasche** *f* wallet; **Briefträger(in)** *m(f)* postman/-woman; **Briefumschlag** *m* envelope; **Briefwaage** *f* letter scales *pl*

briet *imperf von* **braten**

Brille (-, -n) *f* glasses *pl*; *(Schutzbrille)* goggles *pl*; **Brillenetui** *nt* glasses case

bringen (brachte, gebracht) *vt (herbringen)* to bring; *(mitnehmen, vom Sprecher aus)* to take; *(holen, herbringen)* to get, to fetch; *(Theat, Cine)* to show; *(Radio, TV)* to broadcast; **~ Sie mir bitte noch ein Bier** could you bring me another beer, please?; **jdn nach Hause ~** to take sb home; **jdn dazu ~, etw zu tun** to make sb do sth; **jdn auf eine Idee ~** to give sb an idea

Brise (-, -n) *f* breeze

Brite (-n, -n) *m*, **Britin** *f* British person, Briton; **er ist ~** he is British; **die ~n** the British; **britisch** *adj* British

Brocken (-s, -) *m* bit; *(größer)* lump, chunk

Brokkoli *m* broccoli

Brombeere *f* blackberry

Bronchitis (-) *f* bronchitis

Bronze (-, -n) *f* bronze

Brosche (-, -n) *f* brooch

Brot (-(e)s, -e) *nt* bread; *(Laib)* loaf; **Brotaufstrich** *m* spread; **Brötchen** *nt* roll; **Brotzeit** *f* *(Pause)* break; *(Essen)* snack; **~ machen** to have a snack

Browser (-s, -) *m (Inform)* browser

Bruch (-(e)s, Brüche) *m (Brechen)* breaking; *(Bruchstelle; mit Partei, Tradition etc)* break; *(Med: Eingeweidebruch)* rupture, hernia; *(Knochenbruch)* fracture; *(Math)* fraction; **brüchig** *adj* brittle

Brücke (-, -n) *f* bridge

Bruder (-s, Brüder) *m* brother

Brühe (-, -n) *f (Suppe)* (clear) soup; *(Grundlage)* muck; *(pej: Getränk)* muck; **Brühwürfel** *m* stock cube

brüllen vi to roar; (Stier) to bellow; (vor Schmerzen) to scream (with pain)

brummen vi (Bär, Mensch) to growl; (brummeln) to mutter; (Insekt) to buzz; (Motor, Radio) to drone ▷ vt to growl

brünett adj brunette

Brunnen (-s, -) m fountain; (tief) well; (natürlich) spring

Brust (-, Brüste) f breast; (beim Mann) chest; **Brustschwimmen** (-s) nt breaststroke; **Brustwarze** f nipple

brutal adj brutal

brutto adv gross

BSE (-) nt abk = **bovine spongiforme Enzephalopathie** BSE

Bube (-n, -n) m boy, lad; (Karten) jack

Buch (-(e)s, Bücher) nt book

Buche (-, -n) f beech (tree)

buchen vt to book; (Betrag) to enter

Bücherei f library

Buchfink m chaffinch

Buchhalter(in) m(f) accountant

Buchhandlung f bookshop

Büchse (-, -n) f tin (Brit), can

Buchstabe (-ns, -n) m letter; **buchstabieren** vt to spell

Bucht (-, -en) f bay

Buchung f booking; (Comm) entry

Buckel (-s, -) m hump

bücken vr: **sich ~** to bend down

Buddhismus (-) m Buddhism

Bude (-, -en) f (auf Markt) stall; (fam: Wohnung) pad, place

Büfett (-s, -s) nt sideboard; **kaltes ~** cold buffet

Büffel (-s, -) m buffalo

Bügel (-s, -) m (Kleidung) hanger; (Steigbügel) stirrup; (Brille) sidepiece; (von Skilift) T-bar; **Bügelbrett** nt ironing board;

Bügeleisen nt iron; **Bügelfalte** f crease; **bügelfrei** adj non-iron; **bügeln** vt, vi to iron

buh interj boo

Bühne (-, -n) f stage; **Bühnenbild** nt set

Bulgare (-n, -n) m, **Bulgarin** f Bulgarian; **Bulgarien** (-s) nt Bulgaria; **bulgarisch** adj Bulgarian; **Bulgarisch** nt Bulgarian

Bulimie f bulimia

Bulle (-n, -n) m bull; (fam: Polizist) cop

Bummel (-s, -) m stroll; **bummeln** vi (trödeln) to dawdle; (faulenzen) to loaf around; **Bummelzug** m slow train

bums interj bang

bumsen vi (vulg) to screw

Bund[1] (-(e)s, Bünde) m (von Hose, Rock) waistband; (Freundschaftsbund) bond; (Organisation) association; (Pol) confederation; **der ~** (fam: Bundeswehr) the army ▷ (-(e)s, -e) nt bunch; (von Stroh etc) bundle

Bundes- in zW Federal; (auf Deutschland bezogen a.) German; **Bundeskanzler(in)** m(f) Chancellor; **Bundesland** nt state, Land; **Bundesliga** f **erste/zweite ~** First/Second Division; **Bundespräsident(in)** m(f) President; **Bundesrat** m (in Deutschland) Upper House of the German Parliament); (in der Schweiz) Council of Ministers; **Bundesregierung** f Federal Government; **Bundesrepublik** f Federal Republic; **~ Deutschland** Federal Republic of Germany; **Bundesstraße** f ≈ A road (Brit), ≈ state highway (US); **Bundestag** m Lower House (of the German Parliament); **Bundeswehr** f (German) armed forces pl

● **BUNDESWEHR**
●
● The **Bundeswehr** is the name
● for the German armed forces. It
● was established in 1955, first of
● all for volunteers, but from 1956
● until 2011, there was compulsory
● military service for all
● able-bodied young men of 18. In
● peacetime the Defence Minister
● is the head of the 'Bundeswehr',
● but in wartime the
● **Bundeskanzler** takes over. The
● 'Bundeswehr' comes under the
● jurisdiction of NATO.

Bündnis nt alliance
Bungalow (-s, -s) m bungalow
Bungeejumping (-s) nt bungee
jumping
bunt adj colourful; (von Programm
etc) varied; **~e Farben** bright
colours ▷ adv (anstreichen) in
bright colours; **Buntstift** m
crayon, coloured pencil
Burg (-, -en) f castle
Bürger(in) (-s, -) m(f) citizen;
bürgerlich adj (Rechte, Ehe etc)
civil; (vom Mittelstand)
middle-class; (pej) bourgeois;
Bürgermeister(in) m(f) mayor;
Bürgersteig (-(e)s, -e) m
pavement (Brit), sidewalk (US)
Büro (-s, -s) nt office;
Büroklammer f paper clip
Bürokratie f bureaucracy
Bursche (-n, -n) m lad; (Typ) guy
Bürste (-, -n) f brush; **bürsten**
vt to brush
Bus (-ses, -se) m bus; (Reisebus)
coach (Brit), bus; **Busbahnhof** m
bus station
Busch (-(e)s, Büsche) m bush;
(Strauch) shrub
Busen (-s, -) m breasts pl, bosom
Busfahrer(in) m(f) bus driver;
Bushaltestelle f bus stop

Businessclass (-) f business
class
Buslinie f bus route; **Busreise** f
coach tour (Brit), bus tour
Bußgeld nt fine
Büstenhalter (-s, -) m bra
Busverbindung f bus
connection
Butter (-) f butter; **Butterbrot**
nt slice of bread and butter;
Butterkäse m type of mild, full-fat
cheese; **Buttermilch** f
buttermilk; **Butterschmalz** nt
clarified butter
Button (-s, -s) m badge (Brit),
button (US)
b. w. abk = **bitte wenden** pto
Byte (-s, -s) nt byte
bzw. adv abk = **beziehungsweise**

C

ca. adv abk = **circa** approx
Cabrio (-s, -s) nt convertible
Café (-s, -s) nt café
Cafeteria (-, -s) f cafeteria
Call-Center (-s, -) nt call centre
campen vi to camp; **Camping**
(-s) nt camping; **Campingbus** m
camper; **Campingplatz** m
campsite, camping ground (US)
Cappuccino (-s, -) m
cappuccino
Carving (-s) nt (Ski) carving;
Carvingski m carving ski
CD (-, -s) f abk = **Compact Disc**
CD; **CD-Brenner** (-s, -) m CD
burner; **CD-Player**
(-s, -) m CD player; **CD-ROM**
(-, -s) f abk = **Compact Disc Read
Only Memory** CD-ROM;
CD-ROM-Laufwerk nt CD-ROM
drive; **CD-Spieler** m CD player
Cello (-s, -s o Celli) nt cello
Celsius nt celsius; **20 Grad ~** 20

degrees Celsius, 68 degrees
Fahrenheit
Cent (-, -s) m (von Dollar und Euro)
cent
Chamäleon (-s, -s) nt
chameleon
Champagner (-s, -) m
champagne
Champignon (-s, -s) m
mushroom
Champions League (-, -s) f
Champions League
Chance (-, -n) f chance; **die ~n
stehen gut** the prospects are good
Chaos (-) nt chaos; **Chaot(in)**
(-en, -en) m(f) (fam) disorganized
person, scatterbrain; **chaotisch**
adj chaotic
Charakter (-s, -e) m character;
charakteristisch adj character-
istic (für of)
Charisma (-s, Charismen o
Charismata) nt charisma
charmant adj charming
Charterflug m charter flight;
chartern vt to charter
Chat (-s, -s) m (Inform) chat;
chatten vi (Inform) to chat
checken vt (überprüfen) to check;
(fam: verstehen) to get
Check-in (-s, -s) m check-in;
Check-in-Schalter m check-in
desk
Chef(in) (-s, -s) m(f) boss;
Chefarzt m, **Chefärztin** f senior
consultant (Brit), medical director
(US)
Chemie (-) f chemistry;
chemisch adj chemical; **~e
Reinigung** f dry cleaning
Chemotherapie f
chemotherapy
Chicorée (-s) m chicory
Chiffre (-, -n) f (Geheimzeichen)
cipher; (in Zeitung) box number
Chile (-s) nt Chile
Chili (-s, -s) m chilli

China (-s) nt China; **Chinakohl** m Chinese leaves pl (Brit), bok choy (US); **Chinarestaurant** nt Chinese restaurant; **Chinese** (-n, -n) m Chinese; **Chinesin** (-, -nen) f Chinese (woman); **sie ist ~** she's Chinese; **chinesisch** adj Chinese; **Chinesisch** nt Chinese

Chip (-s, -s) m (Inform) chip; **Chipkarte** f smart card

Chips pl (Kartoffelchips) crisps pl (Brit), chips pl (US)

Chirurg(in) (-en, -en) m(f) surgeon

Chlor (-s) nt chlorine

Choke (-s, -s) m choke

Cholera (-) f cholera

Cholesterin (-s) nt cholesterol

Chor (-(e)s, Chöre) m choir; (Theat) chorus

Choreografie f choreography

Christ(in) (-en, -ep) m(f) Christian; **Christbaum** m Christmas tree; **Christi Himmelfahrt** f the Ascension (of Christ); **Christkind** nt baby Jesus; (das Geschenke bringt) ≈ Father Christmas, Santa Claus; **christlich** adj Christian

Chrom (-s) nt chrome; (Chem) chromium

chronisch adj chronic

chronologisch adj chronological ▷ adv in chronological order

Chrysantheme (-, -n) f chrysanthemum

circa adv about, approximately

City (-) f city centre, downtown (US)

Clementine (-, -n) f clementine

clever adj clever, smart

Clique (-, -n) f group; (pej) clique; **David und seine ~** David and his lot or crowd

Clown (-s, -s) m clown

Club (-s, -s) m club; **Cluburlaub** m club holiday (Brit), club vacation (US)

Cocktail (-s, -s) m cocktail; **Cocktailtomate** f cherry tomato

Cognac (-s) m cognac

Cola (-, -s) f Coke®, cola

Comic (-s, -s) m comic strip; (Heft) comic

Compact Disc (-, -s) f compact disc

Computer (-s, -) m computer; **Computerfreak** m computer nerd; **computergesteuert** adj computer-controlled; **Computergrafik** f computer graphics pl; **computerlesbar** adj machine-readable; **Computerspiel** nt computer game; **Computertomografie** f computer tomography, scan; **Computervirus** m computer virus

Container (-s, -) m (zum Transport) container; (für Bauschutt etc) skip

Control-Taste f control key

Cookie (-s, -s) nt (Inform) cookie

cool adj (fam) cool

Cornflakes pl cornflakes pl

Couch (-, -en) f couch; **Couchtisch** m coffee table

Coupé (-s, -s) nt coupé

Coupon (-s, -s) m coupon

Cousin (-s, -s) m cousin; **Cousine** f cousin

Crack (-s) nt (Droge) crack

Creme (-, -s) f cream; (Gastr) mousse

Creutzfeld-Jakob-Krankheit f Creutzfeld-Jakob disease, CJD

Croissant (-s, -s) nt croissant

Curry (-s) m curry powder ▷ (-s) nt (indisches Gericht) curry; **Currywurst** f fried sausage with ketchup and curry powder

Cursor (-s, -s) m (Inform) cursor

Cybercafé nt cybercafé; **Cyberspace** (-) m cyberspace

d

da adv 1 (örtlich) there; (hier) here; **da draußen** out there; **da sein** to be there; **da bin ich** here I am; **da, wo** where; **ist noch Milch da?** is there any milk left?
2 (zeitlich) then; (folglich) so
3 **da haben wir Glück gehabt** we were lucky there; **da kann man nichts machen** nothing can be done about it
▷ konj (weil) as, since

dabei adv (räumlich) close to it; (zeitlich) while (obwohl, doch) though; **sie hörte Radio und rauchte ~** she was listening to the radio and smoking (at the same time); **~ fällt mir ein ...** that reminds me ...; **~ kam es zu einem Unfall** this led to an accident; **... und ~ hat er gar keine Ahnung ...**

even though he has no idea; **ich finde nichts ~** I don't see anything wrong with it; **es bleibt ~** that's settled; **~ sein** (anwesend) to be present; (beteiligt) to be involved; **ich bin ~!** count me in; **er war gerade ~ zu gehen** he was just (o on the point of) leaving

dabei|bleiben irr vi to stick with it; **ich bleibe dabei** I'm not changing my mind

dabei|haben irr vt: **er hat seine Schwester dabei** he's brought his sister; **ich habe kein Geld dabei** I haven't got any money on me

Dach (-(e)s, Dächer) nt roof; **Dachboden** m attic, loft; **Dachgepäckträger** m roofrack; **Dachrinne** f gutter

Dachs (-es, -e) m badger

dachte imperf von **denken**

Dackel (-s, -) m dachshund

dadurch adv (räumlich) through it; (durch diesen Umstand) in that way; (deshalb) because of that, for that reason ▷ conj: **~, dass** because; **~, dass er hart arbeitete** (indem) by working hard

dafür adv for it; (anstatt) instead; **~ habe ich 50 Euro bezahlt** I paid 50 euros for it; **ich bin ~ zu bleiben** I'm for (o in favour of) staying; **~ ist er ja da** that's what he's there for; **er kann nichts ~** he can't help it

dagegen adv against it; (im Vergleich damit) in comparison; (bei Tausch) for it; **ich habe nichts ~** I don't mind

daheim adv at home

daher adv (räumlich) from there; (Ursache) that's why ▷ conj (deshalb) that's why

dahin adv (räumlich) there; (zeitlich) then; (vergangen) gone; **bis ~** (zeitlich) till then; (örtlich) up to there; **bis ~ muss die Arbeit fertig**

sein the work must be finished by then

dahinter adv behind it; **~ kommen** to find out

Dahlie f dahlia

Dalmatiner (-s, -) m dalmatian

damals adv at that time, then

Dame (-, -n) f lady; (Karten) queen; (Spiel) draughts sing (Brit), checkers sing (US); **Damenbinde** f sanitary towel (Brit), sanitary napkin (US); **Damenkleidung** f ladies' wear; **Damentoilette** f ladies' toilet (o restroom (US))

damit adv with it; (begründend) by that; **was meint er ~?** what does he mean by that?; **genug ~!** that's enough ▷ conj so that

Damm (-(e)s, Dämme) m dyke; (Staudamm) dam; (am Hafen) mole; (Bahn-, Straßendamm) embankment

Dämmerung f twilight; (am Morgen) dawn; (am Abend) dusk

Dampf (-(e)s, Dämpfe) m steam; (Dunst) vapour; **Dampfbad** nt Turkish bath; **Dampfbügeleisen** nt steam iron; **dampfen** vi to steam

dämpfen vt (Gastr) to steam; (Geräusch) to deaden; (Begeisterung) to dampen

Dampfer (-s, -) m steamer

Dampfkochtopf m pressure cooker

danach adv after that; (zeitlich a.) afterwards; (demgemäß) accordingly; **mir ist nicht ~** I don't feel like it; **~ sieht es aus** that's what it looks like

Däne (-n, -n) m Dane

daneben adv beside it; (im Vergleich) in comparison

Dänemark (-s) nt Denmark; **Dänin** f Dane, Danish woman/girl; **dänisch** adj Danish; **Dänisch** nt Danish

dank prep +dat o gen thanks to; **Dank** (-(e)s) m thanks pl; **vielen ~!** thank you very much; **jdm ~ sagen** to thank sb; **dankbar** adj grateful; (Aufgabe) rewarding; **danke** interj thank you, thanks; **~ schön** (o sehr) thank you very much; **nein ~!** no, thank you; **~, gerne!** yes, please; **~, gleichfalls!** thanks, and the same to you; **danken** vi: **jdm für etw ~** to thank sb for sth; **nichts zu ~!** you're welcome

dann adv then; **bis ~!** see you (later); **~ eben nicht** okay, forget it, suit yourself

daran adv (räumlich) on it; (befestigen) to it; (stoßen) against it; **es liegt ~, dass ...** it's because ...

darauf adv (räumlich) on it; (zielgerichtet) towards it; (danach) afterwards; **es kommt ganz ~ an, ob ...** it all depends whether ...; **ich freue mich ~** I'm looking forward to it; **am Tag ~** the next day; **~ folgend** (Tag, Jahr) next, following

darauffolgend adj (Tag, Jahr) next, following

daraus adv from it; **was ist ~ geworden?** what became of it?

darin adv in it; **das Problem liegt ~, dass ...** the basic problem is that ...

Darlehen (-s, -) nt loan

Darm (-(e)s, Därme) m intestine; (Wurstdarm) skin; **Darmgrippe** f gastroenteritis

dar|stellen vt to represent; (Theat) to play; (beschreiben) to describe; **Darsteller(in)** m(f) actor/actress; **Darstellung** f representation; (Beschreibung) description

darüber adv (räumlich) above it, over it; (fahren) over it; (mehr) more; (*währenddessen*) meanwhile; (*sprechen, streiten, sich freuen*) about it

darum *adv* (*deshalb*) that's why; **es geht ~, dass ...** the point (*o thing*) is that ...

darunter *adv* (*räumlich*) under it; (*dazwischen*) among them; (*weniger*) less; **was verstehen Sie ~?** what do you understand by that?; **~ fallen** to be included

darunterfallen *vi* to be included

das *art* the; **~ Auto da** that car; **er hat sich ~ Bein gebrochen** he's broken his leg; **vier Euro ~ Kilo** four euros a kilo ▷ *pron* that (*one*), this (*one*); (*relativ, Sache*) that, which; (*relativ, Person*) who, that; (*demonstrativ*) this/that one; **~ Auto da** that car; **ich nehme ~ da** I'll take that one; **~ Auto, ~ er kaufte** the car (that *o which*) he bought; **~ Mädchen, ~ nebenan wohnt** the girl who (*o that*) lives next door; **~ heißt** that is; **~ sind Amerikaner** they're American

da sein *vi* siehe **da**

dass *conj* that; **so ~** so that; **es sei denn, ~** unless; **ohne ~ er grüßte** without saying hello

dasselbe *pron* the same

Datei *f* (*Inform*) file; **Dateimanager** *m* file manager

Daten *pl* data *pl*; **Datenbank** *f* database; **Datenmissbrauch** *m* misuse of data; **Datenschutz** *m* data protection; **Datenträger** *m* data carrier; **Datenverarbeitung** *f* data processing

datieren *vt* to date

Dativ *m* dative (case)

Dattel (-, -*n*) *f* date

Datum (-*s, Daten*) *nt* date

Dauer (-, -*n*) *f* duration; (*Länge*) length; **auf die ~** in the long run; **für die ~ von zwei Jahren** for (a

period of) two years; **Dauerauftrag** *m* (*Fin*) standing order; **dauerhaft** *adj* lasting; (*Material*) durable; **Dauerkarte** *f* season ticket; **dauern** *vi* to last; (*Zeit benötigen*) to take; **es hat sehr lange gedauert, bis er ...** it took him a long time to ...; **wie lange dauert es denn noch?** how much longer will it be?; **das dauert mir zu lange** I can't wait that long; **dauernd** *adj* lasting; (*ständig*) constant ▷ *adv* always, constantly; **er lachte ~** he kept laughing; **unterbrich mich nicht ~** stop interrupting me; **Dauerwelle** *f* perm (*Brit*), permanent (*US*)

Daumen (-*s*, -) *m* thumb

Daunendecke *f* eiderdown

davon *adv* of it; (*räumlich*) away; (*weg von*) from it; (*Grund*) because of it; **ich hätte gerne ein Kilo ~** I'd like one kilo of that; **~ habe ich gehört** I've heard of it; (*Geschehen*) I've heard about it; **das kommt ~, wenn ...** that's what happens when ...; **was habe ich ~?** what's the point?; **auf und ~** up and away; **davonlaufen** *irr vi* to run away

davor *adv* (*räumlich*) in front of it; (*zeitlich*) before; **ich habe Angst ~** I'm afraid of it

dazu *adv* (*zusätzlich*) on top of that, as well; (*zu diesem Zweck*) for it, for that purpose; **ich möchte Reis ~** I'd like rice with it; **und ~ noch** in addition; **~ fähig sein, etw zu tun** to be capable of doing sth; **wie kam es ~?** how did it happen?; **dazugehören** *vi* to belong to it; **dazukommen** *irr vi* (*zu jdm ~*) to join sb; **kommt noch etwas dazu?** anything else?

dazwischen *adv* in between; (*Unterschied etc*) between them; (*in einer Gruppe*) among them

dazwischen|kommen irr vi:
wenn nichts dazwischenkommt
if all goes well; **mir ist etwas
dazwischengekommen**
something has cropped up

DDR (-) f abk = **Deutsche
Demokratische Republik** (Hist)
GDR

dealen vi (fam: mit Drogen) to deal
in drugs; **Dealer(in)** (-s, -) m(f)
(fam) dealer, pusher

Deck (-(e)s, -s o -e) nt deck

Decke (-, -n) f cover; (für Bett)
blanket; (für Tisch) tablecloth; (von
Zimmer) ceiling

Deckel (-s, -) m lid

decken vt to cover; (Tisch) to lay,
to set ▷ vr: **sich ~** (Interessen) to
coincide; (Aussagen) to correspond
▷ vi (den Tisch decken) to lay (o set)
the table

Decoder (-s, -) m decoder

defekt adj faulty; **Defekt** (-(e)s,
-e) m fault, defect

definieren vt to define;
Definition (-, -en) f definition

deftig adj (Preise) steep; **ein ~es
Essen** a good solid meal

dehnbar adj flexible, elastic;
dehnen vt to stretch ▷ vr: **sich
~** to stretch

Deich (-(e)s, -e) m dyke

dein pron (adjektivisch) your;
deine(r, s) pron (substantivisch)
yours; (of you); **deiner** pron gen
von **du**; of you; **deinetwegen** adv
(wegen dir) because of you; (dir
zuliebe) for your sake; (um dich)
about you

deinstallieren vt (Programm) to
uninstall

Dekolleté (-s, -s) nt low neckline

Dekoration f decoration; (in
Laden) window dressing;
dekorativ adj decorative;
dekorieren vt to decorate;
(Schaufenster) to dress

Delfin (-s, -e) m dolphin

delikat adj (lecker) delicious;
(heikel) delicate

Delikatesse (-, -n) f delicacy

Delle (-, -en) f (fam) dent

Delphin (-s, -e) m dolphin

dem dat sing von **der/das**; **wie
~ auch sein mag** be that as it may

demnächst adv shortly, soon

Demo (-, -s) f (fam) demo

Demokratie (-, -n) f democracy;
demokratisch adj democratic

demolieren vt to demolish

Demonstration f demonstration; **demonstrieren** vt, vi to
demonstrate

den art akk sing acc, dat pl von **der**; **sie
hat sich ~ Arm gebrochen** she's
broken her arm ▷ pron him;
(Sache) that one; (relativ: Person)
who, that, whom; (relativ: Sache)
which, that; **~ hab ich schon ewig
nicht mehr gesehen** I haven't
seen him in ages ▷ pron (Person)
who, that, whom; (Sache) which,
that; **der Typ, auf ~ sie steht** the
guy (who) she fancies; **der Berg,
auf ~ wir geklettert sind** the
mountain (that) we climbed

denkbar adj: **das ist ~** that's
possible ▷ adv: **~ einfach**
extremely simple; **denken** (dachte,
gedacht) vt, vi to think (über +akk
about); **an jdn/etw ~** to think of
sb/sth; (sich erinnern,
berücksichtigen) to remember
sb/sth; **woran denkst Du?** what
are you thinking about?; **denk an
den Kaffee** don't forget the coffee
▷ vr: **sich ~** (sich vorstellen) to
imagine; **das kann ich mir ~** I can
(well) imagine

Denkmal (-s, Denkmäler) nt
monument; **Denkmalschutz** m
monument preservation; **unter
~ stehen** to be listed

denn conj for, because ▷ adv

then; (*nach Komparativ*) than; **was ist ~?** what's wrong?; **ist das ~ so schwierig?** is it really that difficult?
dennoch *conj* still, nevertheless
Deo (-s, -s) *nt*, **Deodorant** (-s, -s) *nt* deodorant; **Deoroller** *m* roll-on deodorant; **Deospray** *m o nt* deodorant spray
Deponie (-, -*n*) *f* waste disposal site, tip
Depressionen *pl:* **an ~ leiden** to suffer from depression *sing;* **deprimieren** *vt* to depress

SCHLÜSSELWORT

der (*f* **die**, *nt* **das**, *gen* **des, der, des,** *dat* **dem, der, dem,** *akk* **den, die, das**, *pl* **die**) *def art* the; **der Rhein** the Rhine; **der Klaus** (*fam*) Klaus; **die Frau** (*im Allgemeinen*) women; **der Tod/das Leben** death/life; **der Fuß des Berges** the foot of the hill; **gib es der Frau** give it to the woman; **er hat sich die Hand verletzt** he has hurt his hand
▷ *relativ pron* (*bei Menschen*) who, that; (*bei Tieren, Sachen*) which, that; **der Mann, den ich gesehen habe** the man who *o* whom *o* that I saw
▷ *demonstrativ pron* he/she/it (*jener, dieser*) that; (*pl*) those; **der/die war es** it was him/her; **der mit der Brille** the one with glasses; **ich will den (da)** I want that one

derart *adv* so; (*solcher Art*) such; **derartig** *adj:* **ein ~er Fehler** such a mistake, a mistake like that
derart *adv* so; (*solcher Art*) such; **derartig** *adj:* **ein ~er Fehler** such a mistake, a mistake like that
deren *gen von* **die** ▷ *pron* (*Person*) her; (*Sache*) its; (*Plural*) *pron* ▷ *pron* (*Person*) whose; (*Sache*) of which; **meine Freundin und ~ Mutter** my friend and her mother; **das sind**

~ Sachen that's their stuff; **die Frau, ~ Tochter ...** the woman whose daughter ...; **ich bin mir ~ bewusst** I'm aware of that
dergleichen *pron:* **und ~ mehr** and the like, and so on; **nichts ~** no such thing
derjenige *pron* the one; **~, der** (*relativ*) the one who *o* that
dermaßen *adv* so much; (*mit Adj*) so
derselbe *pron* the same (person/thing)
deshalb *adv* therefore; **~ frage ich ja** that's why I'm asking
Design (-s, -s) *nt* design; **Designer(in)** (-s, -s) *m(f)* designer
Desinfektionsmittel *nt* disinfectant; **desinfizieren** *vt* to disinfect
Desktop (-, -(s)) *m* (*Inform*) desktop
dessen *gen von* **der, das** ▷ *pron* (*Person*) his; (*Sache*) its; **ich bin mir ~ bewusst** I'm aware of that ▷ *pron* (*Person*) whose; (*Sache*) of which; **mein Freund und ~ Mutter** my friend and his mother; **der Mann, ~ Tochter ...** the man whose daughter ...; **ich bin mir ~ bewusst** I'm aware of that
Dessert (-s, -s) *nt* dessert; **zum** (*o* **als**) **~** for dessert
destilliert *adj* distilled
desto *adv:* **je eher, ~ besser** the sooner, the better
deswegen *conj* therefore
Detail (-s, -s) *nt* detail; **ins ~ gehen** to go into detail
Detektiv(in) (-s, -*e*) *m(f)* detective
deutlich *adj* clear; (*Unterschied*) distinct
deutsch *adj* German; **Deutsch** *nt* German; **auf ~** in German; **ins ~e übersetzen** to translate into German; **Deutsche(r)** *mf*

German; **Deutschland** nt
Germany
Devise (-, -n) f motto; **~n** pl (Fin)
foreign currency sing;
Devisenkurs m exchange rate
Dezember (-(s), -) m December;
siehe auch **Juni**
dezent adj discreet
d.h. abk von **das heißt** i.e.
(gesprochen: i.e. oder that is)
Dia (-s, -s) nt slide
Diabetes (-, -) m (Med) diabetes;
Diabetiker(in) (-s, -) m(f)
diabetic
Diagnose (-, -n) f diagnosis
diagonal adj diagonal
Dialekt (-(e)s, -e) m dialect
Dialog (-(e)s, -e) m dialogue;
(Inform) dialog
Dialyse (-, -n) f (Med) dialysis
Diamant m diamond
Diaprojektor m slide projector
Diät (-, -en) f diet; **eine ~ machen**
to be on a diet; (anfangen) to go on
a diet
dich pron akk von **du** you;
~ (selbst) (reflexiv) yourself; **pass
auf ~ auf** look after yourself; **reg
~ nicht auf** don't get upset
dicht adj dense; (Nebel) thick;
(Gewebe) close; (wasserdicht)
watertight; (Verkehr) heavy ▷ adv:
~ an/bei close to; **~ bevölkert**
densely populated
Dichter(in) (-s, -) m(f) poet;
(Autor) writer
Dichtung f (Auto) gasket;
(Dichtungsring) washer; (Gedichte)
poetry
Dichtungsring m (Tech) washer
dick adj thick; (Person) fat; **jdn
~ haben** to be sick of sb;
Dickdarm m colon; **Dickkopf** m
stubborn (o pig-headed) person;
Dickmilch f sour milk
die art the; **~ arme Sarah** poor
Sarah ▷ pron (sing, Person, als

Subjekt) she; (Person, als Subjekt,
Plural) they; (Person, als Objekt) her;
(Person, als Objekt, Plural) them;
(Sache) that (one), this (one);
(Plural) those (ones); (Sache, Plural)
those (ones); (relativ, auf Person)
who, that; (relativ, auf Sachen)
which, that; **~ mit den langen
Haaren** the one (o her) with the
long hair; **sie war ~ erste, ~ es
erfuhr** she was the first to know;
ich nehme ~ da I'll take that
one/those ▷ pl von **der, die, das**
Dieb(in) (-(e)s, -e) m(f) thief;
Diebstahl (-(e)s, Diebstähle) m
theft; **Diebstahlsicherung** f
burglar alarm
diejenige pron the one; **~, die**
(relativ) the one who (o that); **~n** pl
those pl, the ones
Diele (-, -n) f hall
Dienst (-(e)s, -e) m service; **außer
~** retired; **~ haben** to be on duty
Dienstag m Tuesday; siehe auch
Mittwoch; **dienstags** adv on
Tuesdays; siehe auch **mittwochs**
Dienstbereitschaft f: **~ haben**
(Arzt) to be on call; **diensthabend**
adj: **der ~e Arzt** the doctor on
duty; **Dienstleistung** f service;
dienstlich adj official; **er ist
~ unterwegs** he's away on
business; **Dienstreise** f business
trip; **Dienststelle** f department;
Dienstwagen m company car;
Dienstzeit f office hours pl; (Mil)
period of service
diesbezüglich adj (formell) on
this matter
diese(r, s) pron this (one); pl
these; **~ Frau** this woman; **~r
Mann** this man; **~s Mädchen** this
girl; **~ Leute** these people; **ich
nehme ~/-n/-s (hier)** I'll take this
one; (dort) I'll take that one; **ich
nehme ~ pl (hier)** I'll take these
(ones); (dort) I'll take those (ones)

Diesel (-s, -) m (Auto) diesel

dieselbe pron the same; **es sind immer ~** it's always the same people

Dieselmotor m diesel engine; **Dieselöl** nt diesel (oil)

diesig adj hazy, misty

diesmal adv this time

Dietrich (-s, -e) m skeleton key

Differenz (-, -en) f difference

digital adj digital; **Digital-** in zW (Anzeige etc) digital;
Digitalfernsehen nt digital television, digital TV;
Digitalkamera f digital camera

Diktat (-(e)s, -e) nt dictation

Diktatur f dictatorship

Dill (-s) m dill

DIN abk = **Deutsche Industrienorm** DIN; **~ A4** A4

Ding (-(e)s, -e) nt thing; **vor allen ~en** above all; **der Stand der ~e** the state of affairs; **das ist nicht mein ~** (fam) it's not my sort of thing (o cup of tea); **Dingsbums** (-) nt (fam) thingy, thingummybob

Dinkel (-s, -) m (Bot) spelt

Dinosaurier (-s, -) m dinosaur

Diphtherie (-, -n) f diphtheria

Diplom (-(e)s, -e) nt diploma

Diplomat(in) (-en, -en) m(f) diplomat

dir pron dat von **du** (to) you; **hat er ~ geholfen?** did he help you?; **ich werde es ~ erklären** I'll explain it to you; (reflexiv) **wasch ~ die Hände** go and wash your hands; **ein Freund von ~** a friend of yours

direkt adj direct; (Frage) straight; **~e Verbindung** through service ▷ adv directly; (sofort) immediately; **~ am Bahnhof** right next to the station; **Direktflug** m direct flight

Direktor(in) m(f) director; (Schule) headmaster/-mistress

(Brit), principal (US)

Direktübertragung f live broadcast

Dirigent(in) m(f) conductor; **dirigieren** vt to direct; (Mus) to conduct

Discman® (-s, -s) m Discman®

Diskette f disk, diskette; **Diskettenlaufwerk** nt disk drive

Diskjockey (-s, -s) m disc jockey; **Disko** (-, -s) f (fam) disco, club; **Diskothek** (-, -en) f discotheque, club

diskret adj discreet

diskriminieren vt to discriminate against

Diskussion f discussion; **diskutieren** vt, vi to discuss

Display (-s, -s) nt display

disqualifizieren vt to disqualify

Distanz f distance

Distel (-, -n) f thistle

Disziplin (-, -en) f discipline

divers adj various

dividieren vt to divide (durch by); **8 dividiert durch 2 ist 4** 8 divided by 2 is 4

DJ (-s, -s) m abk = **Diskjockey** DJ

○ SCHLÜSSELWORT

doch adv **1** (dennoch) after all; (sowieso) anyway; **er kam doch noch** he came after all; **du weißt es ja doch besser** you know better than I do anyway; **und doch ...** and yet ...
2 (als bejahende Antwort) yes I do/it does etc; **das ist nicht wahr — doch!** that's not true — yes it is!
3 (auffordernd) **komm doch** do come; **lass ihn doch** just leave him; **nicht doch!** oh no!
4 sie ist doch noch so jung but she's still so young; **Sie wissen doch, wie das ist** you know how

it is(, don't you?); **wenn doch** if only
▷ *konj* (*aber*) but; (*trotzdem*) all the same; **und doch hat er es getan** but still he did it

Doktor(in) *m(f)* doctor
Dokument *nt* document;
Dokumentarfilm *m* documentary (film); **dokumentieren** *vt* to document;
Dokumentvorlage *f* (*Inform*) document template
Dollar (-(s), -s) *m* dollar
dolmetschen *vt, vi* to interpret;
Dolmetscher(in) (-s, -) *m(f)* interpreter
Dolomiten *pl* Dolomites *pl*
Dom (-(e)s, -e) *m* cathedral
Domäne (-, -n) *f* domain, province; (*Inform: Domain*) domain
Dominikanische Republik *f* Dominican Republic
Domino (-s, -s) *nt* dominoes *sing*
Donau (-) *f* Danube
Döner (-s, -) *m*, **Döner Kebab** (-(s), -s) *m* doner kebab
Dongle *m* (*Inform*) dongle
Donner (-s, -) *m* thunder;
donnern *vi*: **es donnert** it's thundering
Donnerstag *m* Thursday; *siehe auch* **Mittwoch**; **donnerstags** *adv* on Thursdays; *siehe auch* **mittwochs**
doof *adj* (*fam*) stupid
dopen *vt* to dope; **Doping** (-s) *nt* doping; **Dopingkontrolle** *f* drugs test
Doppel (-s, -) *nt* duplicate; (*Sport*) doubles *sing*; **Doppelbett** *nt* double bed; **Doppeldecker** *m* double-decker; **Doppelhaushälfte** *f* semi-detached house (*Brit*), duplex (*US*); **doppelklicken** *vi* to double-click; **Doppelname** *m* double-barrelled name;

Doppelpunkt *m* colon;
Doppelstecker *m* two-way adaptor; **doppelt** *adj* double; **in ~er Ausführung** in duplicate;
Doppelzimmer *nt* double room
Dorf (-(e)s, Dörfer) *nt* village
Dorn (-(e)s, -en) *m* (*Bot*) thorn
Dörrobst *nt* dried fruit
Dorsch (-(e)s, -e) *m* cod
dort *adv* there; **~ drüben** over there; **dorther** *adv* from there
Dose (-, -n) *f* box; (*Blechdose*) tin (*Brit*), can; (*Bierdose*) can
dösen *vi* to doze
Dosenbier *nt* canned beer;
Dosenöffner *m* tin opener (*Brit*), can opener
Dotter (-s, -) *m* (egg) yolk
downloaden *vt* to download
Downsyndrom (-(e)s, -e) *nt* (*Med*) Down's syndrome
Dozent(in) *m(f)* lecturer
Dr. *abk* = **Doktor**
Drache (-n, -n) *m* dragon;
Drachen (-s, -) *m* (*Spielzeug*) kite; (*Sport*) hang-glider;
Drachenfliegen (-s) *nt* hang-gliding; **Drachenflieger(in)** (-s, -) *m(f)* hang-glider
Draht (-(e)s, Drähte) *m* wire;
drahtlos *adj* wireless;
Drahtseilbahn *f* cable railway
Drama (-s, Dramen) *nt* drama;
dramatisch *adj* dramatic
dran *adv* (*fam*) *kontr von* **daran**;
gut ~ sein (*reich*) to be well-off; (*glücklich*) to be fortunate; (*gesundheitlich*) to be well;
schlecht ~ sein to be in a bad way; **wer ist ~?** whose turn is it?; **ich bin ~** it's my turn; **bleib ~!** (*Tel*) hang on
drang *imperf von* **dringen**
Drang (-(e)s, Dränge) *m* (*Trieb*) urge (*nach* for); (*Druck*) pressure
drängeln *vt, vi* to push
drängen *vt* (*schieben*) to push;

(antreiben) to urge ▷ *vi (eilig sein)* to be urgent; *(Zeit)* to press; **auf etw** *(akk)* **~** to press for sth

dran|kommen *irr vi:* **wer kommt dran?** who's turn is it?, who's next?

drauf *(fam)* kontr von **darauf**; **gut/schlecht ~ sein** to be in a good/bad mood

Draufgänger(in) *(-s, -)* m(f) daredevil

drauf|kommen *irr vi* to remember; **ich komme nicht drauf** I can't think of it

drauf|machen *vi (fam)* **einen ~** to go on a binge

draußen *adv* outside

Dreck *(-(e)s)* m dirt, filth; **dreckig** *adj* dirty, filthy

drehen *vt, vi* to turn; *(Zigaretten)* to roll; *(Film)* to shoot ▷ *vr:* **sich ~** to turn; *(um Achse)* to rotate; **sich ~ um** *(handeln von)* to be about

Drehstrom m three-phase current; **Drehtür** f revolving door; **Drehzahlmesser** m rev counter

drei *num* three; **~ viertel voll** three-quarters full; **es ist ~ viertel neun** it's a quarter to nine; **Drei** *(-, -en)* f three; *(Schulnote)* = C; **Dreieck** nt triangle; **dreieckig** *adj* triangular; **dreifach** *adj* triple ▷ *adv* three times; **dreihundert** *num* three hundred; **Dreikönigstag** m Epiphany; **dreimal** *adv* three times; **Dreirad** nt tricycle; **dreispurig** *adj* three-lane

dreißig *num* thirty; **dreißigste(r, s)** *adj* thirtieth; *siehe auch* **dritte**

Dreiviertelstunde f: **eine ~** three quarters of an hour

dreizehn *num* thirteen; **dreizehnte(r, s)** *adj* thirteenth; *siehe auch* **dritte**

dressieren *vt* to train

Dressing *(-s, -s)* nt *(salad)* dressing

Dressman *(-s, Dressmen)* m *(male)* model

Dressur *(-, -en)* f training

drin *(fam)* kontr von **darin** in it; **mehr war nicht ~** that was the best I could do

dringen *(drang, gedrungen)* vi *(Wasser, Licht, Kälte)* to penetrate *(durch* through, *in* +*akk* into); **auf etw** *(akk)* **~** to insist on sth; **dringend, dringlich** *adj* urgent

drinnen *adv* inside

dritt *adv:* **wir sind zu ~** there are three of us; **dritte(r, s)** *adj* third; **die Dritte Welt** the Third World; **3. Juni** 3(rd) June *(gesprochen: on the third of June)*; **am 3. Juni** on 3(rd) June, on June 3(rd) *(gesprochen: on the third of June)*; **München, den 3. Juni** Munich, June 3(rd); **Drittel** *(-s, -)* nt *(Bruchteil)* third; **drittens** *adv* thirdly

Droge *(-, -n)* f drug; **drogenabhängig, drogensüchtig** *adj* addicted to drugs

Drogerie f chemist's *(Brit)*, drugstore *(US)*; **Drogeriemarkt** m discount chemist's *(Brit)* (o drugstore *(US)*)

● **DROGERIE**
●
● The **Drogerie** as opposed to the
● **Apotheke** sells medicines not
● requiring a prescription. It
● tends to be cheaper and also
● sells cosmetics, perfume and
● toiletries.

drohen *vi* to threaten *(jdm* sb); **mit etw ~** to threaten to do sth

dröhnen *vi (Motor)* to roar; *(Stimme, Musik)* to boom; *(Raum)* to resound

Drohung f threat

Drossel (-, -n) f thrush
drüben adv over there; *(auf der anderen Seite)* on the other side
drüber *(fam)* kontr von **darüber**
Druck (-(e)s, Drücke) m *(Phys)* pressure; *(fig: Belastung)* stress; **jdn unter ~ setzen** to put sb under pressure ▸ (-(e)s, -e) m *(Typo: Vorgang)* printing; *(Produkt, Schriftart)* print; **Druckbuchstabe** m block letter; **in ~n schreiben** to print; **drucken** vt, vi to print
drücken vt, vi *(Knopf, Hand)* to press; *(zu eng sein)* to pinch; *(fig: Preise)* to keep down; **jdm etw in die Hand ~** to press sth into sb's hand ▸ vr **sich ~** to get out of sth; **drückend** adj oppressive
Drucker (-s, -) m *(Inform)* printer; **Druckertreiber** m printer driver
Druckknopf m press stud *(Brit)*, snap fastener *(US)*; **Drucksache** f printed matter; **Druckschrift** f block letters pl
drunten adv down there
drunter *(fam)* kontr von **darunter**
Drüse (-, -n) f gland
Dschungel (-s, -) m jungle
du pron you; **bist ~ es?** is it you?; **wir sind per ~** we're on first-name terms
Dübel (-s, -) m Rawlplug®
ducken vt to duck ▸ vr: **sich ~** to duck
Dudelsack m bagpipes pl
Duett (-(e)s, -e) m duet
Duft (-(e)s, Düfte) m scent; **duften** vi to smell nice; **es duftet nach ...** it smells of ...
dulden vt to tolerate
dumm adj stupid; **Dummheit** f stupidity; *(Tat)* stupid thing; **Dummkopf** m idiot
dumpf adj *(Ton)* muffled; *(Erinnerung)* vague; *(Schmerz)* dull
Düne (-, -n) f dune

Dünger (-s, -) m fertilizer
dunkel adj dark; *(Stimme)* deep; *(Ahnung)* vague; *(rätselhaft)* obscure; *(verdächtig)* dubious; **im Dunkeln tappen** *(fig)* to be in the dark; **dunkelblau** adj dark blue; **dunkelblond** adj light brown; **dunkelhaarig** adj dark-haired; **Dunkelheit** f darkness
dünn adj thin; *(Kaffee)* weak
Dunst (-es, Dünste) m haze; *(leichter Nebel)* mist; *(Chem)* vapour
dünsten vt *(Gastr)* to steam
Duo (-s, -s) nt duo
Dur (-) nt *(Mus)* major (key); **in G-~** in G major

○ SCHLÜSSELWORT

durch prep +akk **1** *(hindurch)* through; **durch den Urwald** through the jungle; **durch die ganze Welt reisen** to travel all over the world
2 *(mittels)* through, by (means of); *(aufgrund)* due to, owing to; **Tod durch Herzschlag/den Strang** death from a heart attack/by hanging; **durch die Post** by post; **durch seine Bemühungen** through his efforts
▸ adv **1** *(hindurch)* through; **die ganze Nacht durch** all through the night; **den Sommer durch** during the summer; **8 Uhr durch** past 8 o'clock; **durch und durch** completely
2 *(durchgebraten etc)* **(gut) durch** well-done

durchaus adv absolutely; **~ nicht** not at all
Durchblick m view; **den ~ haben** *(fig)* to know what's going on; **durch|blicken** vi to look through; *(fam: verstehen)* to understand *(bei etw sth)*; **etw**

~ lassen (fig) to hint at sth
Durchblutung f circulation
durch|brennen irr vi (Sicherung) to blow; (Draht) to burn through; (fam: davonlaufen) to run away
durchdacht adv: **gut ~** well thought-out
durch|drehen vt (Fleisch) to mince ▷ vi (Räder) to spin; (fam: nervlich) to crack up
durcheinander adv in a mess; (fam: verwirrt) confused; **Durcheinander** (-s) nt (Verwirrung) confusion; (Unordnung) mess; **durcheinander|bringen** irr vt to mess up; (verwirren) to confuse; **durcheinander|reden** vi to talk all at the same time; **durcheinander|trinken** irr vi to mix one's drinks
Durchfahrt f way through; **„~ verboten!"** "no thoroughfare"
Durchfall m (Med) diarrhoea
durch|fallen irr vi to fall through; (in Prüfung) to fail
durch|fragen vr: **sich ~** to ask one's way
durch|führen vt to carry out
Durchgang m passage; (Sport) round; (bei Wahl) ballot; **Durchgangsverkehr** m through traffic
durchgebraten adj well done
durchgefroren adj frozen to the bone
durch|gehen irr vi to go through (durch etw sth); (ausreißen: Pferd) to break loose; (Mensch) to run away; **durchgehend** adj (Zug) through; **~ geöffnet** open all day
durch|halten irr vi to hold out ▷ vt (Tempo) to keep up; **etw ~** (bis zum Schluss) to see sth through
durch|kommen irr vi to get through; (Patient) to pull through

durch|lassen irr vt (jdn) to let through; (Wasser) to let in
durch|lesen irr vt to read through
durchleuchten vt to X-ray
durch|machen vt to go through; (Entwicklung) to undergo; **die Nacht ~** to make a night of it, to have an all-nighter
Durchmesser (-s, -) m diameter
Durchreise f journey through; **auf der ~** passing through; (Güter) in transit; **Durchreisevisum** nt transit visa
durch|reißen irr vt, vi to tear (in two)
durchs kontr von **durch das**
Durchsage (-, -n) f announcement
durchschauen vt (jdn, Lüge) to see through
durch|schlagen irr vr: **sich ~** to struggle through
durch|schneiden irr vt to cut (in two)
Durchschnitt m (Mittelwert) average; **im ~** on average; **durchschnittlich** adj average ▷ adv (im Durchschnitt) on average; **Durchschnittsgeschwindigkeit** f average speed
durch|setzen vt to get through ▷ vr: **sich ~** (Erfolg haben) to succeed; (sich behaupten) to get one's way
durchsichtig adj transparent, see-through
durch|stellen vt (Tel) to put through
durch|streichen irr vt to cross out
durchsuchen vt to search (nach for); **Durchsuchung** f search
durchwachsen adj (Speck) streaky; (fig: mittelmäßig) so-so
Durchwahl f direct dialling; (Nummer) extension

durch|ziehen *irr vt* (*Plan*) to carry through
Durchzug *m* draught

○ **SCHLÜSSELWORT**

dürfen *unreg vi* **1** (*Erlaubnis haben*) to be allowed to; **ich darf das** I'm allowed to (do that); **darf ich?** may I?; **darf ich ins Kino?** can o may I go to the cinema?; **es darf geraucht werden** you may smoke **2** (*in Verneinungen*) **er darf das nicht** he's not allowed to (do that); **das darf nicht geschehen** that must not happen; **da darf sie sich nicht wundern** that shouldn't surprise her
3 (*in Höflichkeitsformeln*) **darf ich Sie bitten, das zu tun?** may o could I ask you to do that?; **was darf es sein?** what can I do for you?
4 (*können*) **das dürfen Sie mir glauben** you can believe me **5** (*Möglichkeit*) **das dürfte genug sein** that should be enough; **es dürfte Ihnen bekannt sein, dass ...** as you will probably know ...

dürftig *adj* (*ärmlich*) poor; (*unzulänglich*) inadequate
dürr *adj* dried-up; (*Land*) arid; (*mager*) skinny
Durst (*-(e)s*) *m* thirst; **~ haben** to be thirsty; **durstig** *adj* thirsty
Dusche (*-, -n*) *f* shower; **duschen** *vi* to have a shower ▷ *vr*: **sich ~** to have a shower; **Duschgel** *nt* shower gel; **Duschvorhang** *m* shower curtain
Düse (*-, -n*) *f* nozzle; (*Tech*) jet; **Düsenflugzeug** *nt* jet (aircraft)
Dussel (*-s, -*) *m* (*fam*) dope; **duss(e)lig** *adj* (*fam*) stupid

düster *adj* dark; (*Gedanken, Zukunft*) gloomy
Dutyfreeshop (*-s, -s*) *m* duty-free shop
Dutzend (*-s, -e*) *nt* dozen
duzen *vt* to address as "du" ▷ *vr*: **sich ~** (*mit jdm*) to address each other as "du", to be on first-name terms
DVD (*-, -s*) *f abk* = **Digital Versatile Disk** DVD; **DVD-Player** (*-s, -*) *m* DVD player; **DVD-Rekorder** (*-s, -*) *m* DVD recorder
dynamisch *adj* dynamic
Dynamo (*-s, -s*) *m* dynamo
D-Zug *m* fast train

e

Ebbe (-, -n) f low tide
eben adj level; (glatt) smooth ▷ adv just; (bestätigend) exactly
Ebene (-, -n) f plain; (fig) level
ebenfalls adv also, as well; (Antwort: gleichfalls!) you too; **ebenso** adv just as; ~ **gut** just as well; ~ **viel** just as much
Eber (-s, -) m boar
E-Book (-s, -s) nt e-book
E-Book-Reader m e-reader
EC (-, -s) m abk = **Eurocityzug**
Echo (-s, -s) nt echo
echt adj (Leder, Gold) real, genuine; **ein ~er Verlust** a real loss
EC-Karte f ≈ debit card
Ecke (-, -n) f corner; (Math) angle; **an der ~** at the corner; **gleich um die ~** just round the corner; **eckig** adj rectangular; **Eckzahn** m canine
Economyclass (-) f coach (class), economy class

Ecstasy (-) f (Droge) ecstasy
edel adj noble; **Edelstein** m precious stone
EDV (-) f abk = **elektronische Datenverarbeitung** EDP
Efeu (-s) m ivy
Effekt (-s, -e) m effect
egal adj: **das ist ~** it doesn't matter; **das ist mir ~** I don't care, it's all the same to me; ~ **wie teuer** no matter how expensive
egoistisch adj selfish
ehe conj before
Ehe (-, -n) f marriage; **Ehefrau** f wife; (verheiratete Frau) married woman; **Eheleute** pl married couple sing
ehemalig adj former; **ehemals** adv formerly
Ehemann m husband; (verheirateter Mann) married man; **Ehepaar** nt married couple
eher adv (früher) sooner; (lieber) rather, sooner; (mehr) more; **je ~, desto besser** the sooner the better
Ehering m wedding ring
eheste(r, s) adj (früheste) first ▷ adv: **am ~n** (am wahrscheinlichsten) most likely
Ehre (-, -n) f honour; **ehren** vt to honour; **ehrenamtlich** adj voluntary; **Ehrengast** m guest of honour; **Ehrenwort** nt word of honour; ~**!** I promise
ehrgeizig adj ambitious
ehrlich adj honest
Ei (-(e)s, -er) nt egg; **hart gekochtes/weiches** ~ hard-boiled/soft-boiled egg
Eiche (-, -n) f oak (tree); **Eichel** (-, -n) f acorn
Eichhörnchen nt squirrel
Eid (-(e)s, -e) m oath
Eidechse (-, -n) f lizard
Eierbecher m eggcup; **Eierstock** m ovary; **Eieruhr** f egg timer
Eifersucht f jealousy;

eifersüchtig adj jealous (auf +akk of)

Eigelb (-(e)s, -) nt egg yolk

eigen adj own; (typisch) characteristic (jdm of sb); (eigenartig) peculiar; **eigenartig** adj peculiar; **Eigenschaft** f quality; (Chem, Phys) property; (Merkmal) characteristic

eigentlich adj actual, real ▷ adv actually, really; **was denken Sie sich ~ dabei?** what on earth do you think you're doing?

Eigentum nt property; **Eigentümer(in)** m(f) owner; **Eigentumswohnung** f owner-occupied flat (Brit), condominium (US)

eignen vr: **sich ~ für** to be suited for; **er würde sich als Lehrer ~** he'd make a good teacher

Eilbrief m express letter, special-delivery letter; **Eile** (-) f hurry; **eilen** vi (dringend sein) to be urgent; **es eilt nicht** there's no hurry; **eilig** adj hurried; (dringlich) urgent; **es ~ haben** to be in a hurry

Eimer (-s, -) m bucket

ein adv: **nicht ~ noch aus wissen** not to know what to do; **~ aus** (Schalter) on - off

ein(e) art a; (vor gesprochenem Vokal) an; **~ Mann** a man; **~ Apfel** an apple; **~e Stunde** an hour; **~ Haus** a house; **~ (gewisser) Herr Miller** a (certain) Mr Miller; **~es Tages** one day

einander pron one another, each other

ein|arbeiten vt to train ▷ vr: **sich ~** to get used to the work

ein|atmen vt, vi to breathe in

Einbahnstraße f one-way street

ein|bauen vt to build in; (Motor etc) to install, to fit; **Einbauküche**

f fitted kitchen

ein|biegen irr vi to turn (in +akk into)

ein|bilden vt: **sich** (dat) **etw ~** to imagine sth

ein|brechen irr vi (in Haus) to break in; (Dach etc) to fall in; to collapse; **Einbrecher(in)** (-s, -) m(f) burglar

ein|bringen irr vt (Ernte) to bring in; (Gewinn) to yield; **jdm etw ~** to bring o earn) sb sth ▷ vr **sich in** (akk) **etw ~** to make a contribution to sth

Einbruch m (Haus) break-in, burglary; **bei ~ der Nacht** at nightfall

Einbürgerung f naturalization

ein|checken vt to check in

ein|cremen vt to put some cream on ▷ vr: **sich ~** to put some cream on

eindeutig adj clear, obvious ▷ adv clearly; **~ falsch** clearly wrong

ein|dringen irr vi (gewaltsam) to force one's way in (in +akk -to); (in Haus) to break in (in +akk -to); (Gas, Wasser) to get in (in +akk -to)

Eindruck m impression; **großen ~ auf jdn machen** to make a big impression on sb

eine(r, s) pron one; (jemand) someone; **~r meiner Freunde** one of my friends; **~ nach dem andern** one after the other

einig adj (Zwillinge) identical

eineinhalb one and a half

einerseits adv on the one hand

einfach adj (nicht kompliziert) simple; (Mensch) ordinary; (Essen) plain; (nicht mehrfach) single; **~e Fahrkarte** single ticket (Brit), one-way ticket (US) ▷ adv simply; (nicht mehrfach) once

Einfahrt f (Vorgang) driving in; (eines Zuges) arrival; (Ort) entrance

Einfall m (Idee) idea; **ein|fallen** irr vi (Licht etc) to fall in; (einstürzen) to collapse; **ihm fiel ein, dass ...** it occurred to him that ...; **ich werde mir etwas ~ lassen** I'll think of something; **was fällt Ihnen ein!** what do you think you're doing?

Einfamilienhaus nt detached house

einfarbig adj all one colour; (Stoff etc) self-coloured

Einfluss m influence

ein|frieren irr vt, vi to freeze

ein|fügen vt to fit in; (zusätzlich) to add; (Inform) to insert; **Einfügetaste** f (Inform) insert key

Einfuhr (-, -en) f import; **Einfuhrbestimmungen** pl import regulations pl

ein|führen vt to introduce; (Ware) to import; **Einführung** f introduction

Eingabe f (Dateneingabe) input; **Eingabetaste** f (Inform) return (o enter) key

Eingang m entrance; **Eingangshalle** f entrance hall, lobby (US)

ein|geben irr vt (Daten etc) to enter, to key in

eingebildet adj imaginary; (eitel) arrogant

Eingeborene(r) mf native

ein|gehen irr vi (Sendung, Geld) to come in, to arrive; (Tier, Pflanze) to die; (Stoff) to shrink; **auf etw** (akk) **~ to** agree to sth; **auf jdn ~** to respond to sb ▷ vt (Vertrag) to enter into; (Wette) to make; (Risiko) to take

eingelegt adj (in Essig) pickled

eingeschaltet adj (switched) on

eingeschlossen adj locked in; (inklusive) included

ein|gewöhnen vr: **sich ~ to** settle in

ein|gießen irr vt to pour

ein|greifen irr vi to intervene; **Eingriff** m intervention; (Operation) operation

ein|halten irr vt (Versprechen etc) to keep

einheimisch adj (Produkt, Mannschaft) local; **Einheimische(r)** mf local

Einheit f (Geschlossenheit) unity; (Maß) unit; **einheitlich** adj uniform

ein|holen vt (Vorsprung aufholen) to catch up with; (Verspätung) to make up for; (Rat, Erlaubnis) to ask for

Einhorn nt unicorn

einhundert num one (o a) hundred

einig adj (vereint) united; **sich** (dat) **~ sein** to agree

einige pron pl some; (mehrere) several ▷ adj some; **nach ~er Zeit** after some time; **~e hundert Euro** some hundred euros

einigen vr: **sich ~** to agree (auf +akk on)

einigermaßen adv fairly, quite; (leidlich) reasonably

einiges pron something; (ziemlich viel) quite a bit; (mehreres) a few things; **es gibt noch ~ zu tun** there's still a fair bit to do

Einkauf m purchase; **Einkäufe** (machen) to do one's shopping; **ein|kaufen** vt to buy ▷ vi to go shopping; **Einkaufsbummel** m shopping trip; **Einkaufstasche** f, **Einkaufstüte** f shopping bag; **Einkaufswagen** m shopping trolley (Brit) (o cart (US)); **Einkaufszentrum** nt shopping centre (Brit) (o mall (US))

ein|klemmen vt to jam; **er hat sich** (dat) **den Finger eingeklemmt** he got his finger caught

Einkommen (-s, -) nt income

ein|laden irr vt (jdn) to invite; (Gegenstände) to load; **jdn zum Essen ~** to take sb out for a meal; **ich lade dich ein** (bezahle) it's my treat; **Einladung** f invitation

Einlass (-es, Einlässe) m admittance; **~ ab 18 Uhr** doors open at 6 pm; **ein|lassen** irr vr **sich ~ mit jdm/auf etw** (akk) **~** to get involved with sb/sth

ein|leben vr: **sich ~** to settle down

ein|legen vt (Film etc) to put in; (marinieren) to marinate; **eine Pause ~** to take a break

ein|leiten vt to start; (Maßnahmen) to introduce; (Geburt) to induce; **Einleitung** f introduction; (von Geburt) induction

ein|leuchten vi: **jdm ~** to be (o become) clear to sb; **einleuchtend** adj clear

ein|loggen vi (Inform) to log on (o in)

ein|lösen vt (Scheck) to cash; (Gutschein) to redeem; (Versprechen) to keep

einmal adv once; (früher) before; (in Zukunft) some day; (erstens) first; **~ im Jahr** once a year; **noch ~** once more, again; **ich war schon ~ hier** I've been here before; **warst du schon ~ in London?** have you ever been to London?; **nicht ~** not even; **auf ~** suddenly; (gleichzeitig) at once; **einmalig** adj unique; (einmal geschehend) single; (prima) fantastic

ein|mischen vr: **sich ~** to interfere (in +akk with)

Einnahme (-, -n) f (Geld) takings pl; (von Medizin) taking; **ein|nehmen** vt irr (Medizin) to take; (Geld) to take in; (Standpunkt, Raum) to take up; **jdn für sich ~** to win sb over

ein|ordnen vt to put in order; (klassifizieren) to classify; (Akten) to file ⊳ vr: **sich ~** (Auto) to get into lane; **sich rechts/links ~** to get into the right/left lane

ein|packen vt to pack (up)

ein|parken vt, vi to park

ein|planen vt to allow for

ein|prägen vt **sich** (dat) **etw ~** to remember (o memorize) sth

ein|räumen vt (Bücher, Geschirr) to put away; (Schrank) to put things in

ein|reden vt: **jdm/sich etw ~** to talk sb/oneself into (believing) sth

ein|reiben irr vt: **sich mit etw ~** to rub sth into one's skin

ein|reichen vt to hand in; (Antrag) to submit

Einreise f entry; **Einreisebestimmungen** pl entry regulations pl; **Einreiseerlaubnis** f, **Einreisegenehmigung** f entry permit; **ein|reisen** vi to enter (in ein Land a country); **Einreisevisum** nt entry visa

ein|renken vt (Arm, Bein) to set

ein|richten vt (Wohnung) to furnish; (gründen) to establish, to set up; (arrangieren) to arrange ⊳ vr: **sich ~** (im Haus) to furnish one's home; (sich vorbereiten) to prepare oneself (auf +akk for); (sich anpassen) to adapt (auf +akk to); **Einrichtung** f (Wohnung) furnishings pl; (öffentliche Anstalt) institution; (Schwimmbad etc) facility

eins num one; **Eins** (-, -en) f one; (Schulnote) ≈ A

einsam adj lonely

ein|sammeln vt to collect

Einsatz m (Teil) insert; (Verwendung) use; (Spieleinsatz) stake; (Risiko) risk; (Mus) entry

ein|schalten vt (Elek) to switch on

ein|schätzen vt to estimate, to assess

ein|schenken vt to pour

ein|schiffen vr: **sich ~** to embark (nach für)

ein|schlafen irr vi to fall asleep, to drop off; **mir ist der Arm eingeschlafen** my arm's gone to sleep

ein|schlagen irr vt (Fenster) to smash; (Zähne, Schädel) to smash in; (Weg, Richtung) to take ▷ vi to hit (in etw akk sth, auf jdn sb); (Blitz) to strike; (Anklang finden) to be a success

ein|schließen irr vt (jdn) to lock in; (Gegenstand) to lock away; (umgeben) to surround; (fig: beinhalten) to include; **einschließlich** adj inclusive ▷ prep +gen including; **von Montag bis ~ Freitag** from Monday up to and including Friday, Monday through Friday (US)

ein|schränken vt to limit, to restrict; (verringern) to cut down on ▷ vr: **sich ~** to cut down (on expenditure)

ein|schreiben irr vr: **sich ~** to register; (Schule) to enrol; **Einschreiben** (-s, -) nt registered letter; **etw per ~ schicken** to send sth by special delivery

ein|schüchtern vt to intimidate

ein|sehen irr vt (verstehen) to see; (Fehler) to recognize; (Akten) to have a look at

einseitig adj one-sided

ein|senden irr vt to send in

ein|setzen vt to put in; (in Amt) to appoint; (Geld) to stake; (verwenden) to use ▷ vi (beginnen) to set in; (Mus) to enter, to come in ▷ vr: **sich ~** to work hard; **sich für jdn/etw ~** to support sb/sth

Einsicht f insight; **zu der**

~ kommen, dass ... to come to realize that ...

ein|sperren vt to lock up

ein|spielen vt (Geld) to bring in

ein|springen irr vi (aushelfen) to step in (für for)

Einspruch m objection (gegen to)

einspurig adj single-lane

Einstand m (Tennis) deuce

ein|stecken vt (Elek: Stecker) to plug in; (Brief) to post, to mail (US); (mitnehmen) to take; (hinnehmen) to swallow

ein|steigen irr vi (in Auto) to get in; (in Bus, Flugzeug) to get on; (sich beteiligen) to get involved

ein|stellen vt (beenden) to stop; (Geräte) to adjust; (Kamera) to focus; (Sender, Radio) to tune in; (unterstellen) to put; (in Firma) to employ, to take on ▷ vr: **sich auf jdn/etw ~** to adapt to sb/prepare oneself for sth; **Einstellung** f (von Gerät) adjustment; (von Kamera) focusing; (von Arbeiter) taking on; (Meinung) attitude

ein|stürzen vi to collapse

eintägig adj one-day

ein|tauschen vt to exchange (gegen for)

eintausend num one (o a) thousand

ein|teilen vt (in Teile) to divide (up) (in +akk into); (Zeit) to organize

eintönig adj monotonous

Eintopf m stew

ein|tragen irr vt (in eine Liste) to put down, to enter ▷ vr: **sich ~** to put one's name down, to register

ein|treffen irr vi to happen; (ankommen) to arrive

ein|treten irr vi (hineingehen) to enter (in etw akk sth); (in Klub, Partei) to join (in etw akk sth); (sich ereignen) to occur; **~ für** to support; **Eintritt** m admission; **„~ frei"**

"admission free"; **Eintrittskarte** f (entrance) ticket; **Eintrittspreis** m admission charge

einverstanden interj okay, all right ▷ adj: **mit etwas ~ sein** to agree to sth, **to accept sth**

Einwanderer m, **Einwanderin** f immigrant; **ein|wandern** vi to immigrate

einwandfrei adj perfect, flawless

Einwegflasche f non-returnable bottle

ein|weichen vt to soak

ein|weihen vt (Gebäude) to inaugurate, to open; **jdn in etw** (akk) **~ lassen** to let sb in on sth; **Einweihungsparty** f house-warming party

ein|werfen irr vt (Ball, Bemerkung etc) to throw in; (Brief) to post, to mail (US); (Geld) to put in, to insert; (Fenster) to smash

ein|wickeln vt to wrap up; (fig) **jdn ~** to take sb in

Einwohner(in) (-s, -) m(f) inhabitant; **Einwohnermeldeamt** nt registration office for residents

Einwurf m (Öffnung) slot; (Sport) throw-in

Einzahl f singular

ein|zahlen vt to pay in (auf ein Konto -to an account)

Einzel (-s, -) nt (Tennis) singles sing; **Einzelbett** nt single bed; **Einzelfahrschein** m single ticket (Brit), one-way ticket (US); **Einzelgänger(in)** m(f) loner; **Einzelhandel** m retail trade; **Einzelkind** nt only child

einzeln adj individual; (getrennt) separate; (einzig) single; **~e ...** several ..., some ...; **der/die Einzelne** the individual; **im Einzelnen** in detail ▷ adv separately; (verpacken, aufführen) individually; **~ angeben** to specify; **~ eintreten** to enter one by one

Einzelzimmer nt single room; **Einzelzimmerzuschlag** m single-room supplement

ein|ziehen irr vt: **den Kopf ~** to duck ▷ vi (in ein Haus) to move in

einzig adj only; (einzeln) single; (einzigartig) unique; **kein -er Fehler** not a single mistake; **das Einzige** the only thing; **der/die Einzige** the only person ▷ adv only; **die ~ richtige Lösung** the only correct solution; **einzigartig** adj unique

Eis (-es, -) nt ice; (Speiseeis) ice-cream; **Eisbahn** f ice(skating) rink; **Eisbär** m polar bear; **Eisbecher** m (ice-cream) sundae; **Eisberg** m iceberg; **Eisbergsalat** m iceberg lettuce; **Eiscafé** nt, **Eisdiele** f ice-cream parlour

Eisen (-s, -) nt iron; **Eisenbahn** f railway (Brit), railroad (US); **eisern** adj iron

eisgekühlt adj chilled; **Eishockey** nt ice hockey; **Eiskaffee** m iced coffee; **eiskalt** adj ice-cold; (Temperatur) freezing; **Eiskunstlauf** m figure skating; **eis|laufen** vi to skate; **Eisschokolade** f iced chocolate; **Eisschrank** m fridge, ice-box (US); **Eistee** m iced tea; **Eiswürfel** m ice cube; **Eiszapfen** m icicle

eitel adj vain

Eiter (-s) m pus

Eiweiß (-es, -e) nt egg white; (Chem, Bio) protein

ekelhaft, **ek(e)lig** adj disgusting, revolting; **ekeln** vr: **sich ~** to be disgusted (vor +dat at)

EKG (-s, -s) nt abk = **Elektrokardiogramm** ECG

Ekzem (-s, -e) nt (Med) eczema

elastisch adj elastic

Elch (-(e)s, -e) m elk; (nordamerikanischer) moose

Elefant m elephant

elegant adj elegant

Elektriker(in) (-s, -) m(f) electrician; **elektrisch** adj electric; **Elektrizität** f electricity; **Elektroauto** nt electric car; **Elektrogerät** nt electrical appliance; **Elektrogeschäft** nt electrical shop; **Elektroherd** m electric cooker; **Elektromotor** m electric motor; **Elektronik** f electronics sing; **elektronisch** adj electronic; **Elektrorasierer** (-s, -) m electric razor

Element (-s, -e) nt element

elend adj miserable; **Elend** (-(e)s) nt misery

elf num eleven; **Elf** (-, -en) f (Sport) eleven

Elfenbein nt ivory

Elfmeter m (Sport) penalty (kick)

elfte(r, s) adj eleventh; siehe auch **dritte**

Ell(en)bogen m elbow

Elster (-, -n) f magpie

Eltern pl parents pl; **Elternteil** m parent

EM f abk = **Europameisterschaft** European Championship(s)

E-Mail (-, -s) f (Inform) e-mail; **jdm eine ~ schicken** to e-mail sb, to send sb an e-mail; **jdm etwas per ~ schicken** to e-mail sth to sb; **E-Mail-Adresse** f e-mail address; **e-mailen** vt to e-mail

Emoticon (-s, -s) nt emoticon

emotional adj emotional

empfahl imperf von **empfehlen**

empfand imperf von **empfinden**

Empfang (-(e)s, Empfänge) m reception; (Erhalten) receipt; **in ~ nehmen** to receive; **empfangen** (empfing, empfangen) vt to receive; **Empfänger(in)** (-s, -) m(f) recipient; (Adressat) addressee ▷ m

(Tech) receiver; **Empfängnisverhütung** f contraception; **Empfangshalle** f reception area

empfehlen (empfahl, empfohlen) vt to recommend; **Empfehlung** f recommendation

empfinden (empfand, empfunden) vt to feel; **empfindlich** adj (Mensch) sensitive; (Stelle) sore; (reizbar) touchy; (Material) delicate

empfing imperf von **empfangen**

empfohlen pp von **empfehlen**

empfunden pp von **empfinden**

empört adj indignant (über +akk at)

Ende (-s, -n) nt end; (Film, Roman) ending; **am ~** at the (end); (schließlich) in the end; **~ Mai** at the end of May; **~ der Achtzigerjahre** in the late eighties; **sie ist ~ zwanzig** she's in her late twenties; **zu ~** over, finished; **enden** vi to end; **der Zug endet hier** this service (o train) terminates here; **endgültig** adj final; (Beweis) conclusive

Endivie f endive

endlich adv at last, finally; (am Ende) eventually; **Endspiel** nt final; (Endrunde) finals pl; **Endstation** f terminus; **Endung** f ending

Energie f energy; **~sparend** energy-saving; **Energiebedarf** m energy requirement; **Energieverbrauch** m energy consumption

energisch adj (entschlossen) forceful

eng adj narrow; (Kleidung) tight; (fig: Freundschaft, Verhältnis) close; **das wird ~** (fam: zeitlich) we're running out of time, it's getting tight ▷ adv: **~ befreundet sein** to be close friends

engagieren vt to engage ▷ vr: **sich ~** to commit oneself, to be

committed (*für* to)
Engel (-s, -) *m* angel
England *nt* England;
Engländer(in) (-s, -) *m(f)*
Englishman/ -woman; **die ~** *pl* the
English *pl*; **englisch** *adj* English;
(*Gastr*) rare; **Englisch** *nt* English;
ins ~e übersetzen to translate
into English
Enkel (-s, -) *m* grandson; **Enkelin**
f granddaughter
enorm *adj* enormous; (*fig*)
tremendous
Entbindung *f* (*Med*) delivery
entdecken *vt* to discover;
Entdeckung *f* discovery
Ente (-, -n) *f* duck
Enter-Taste *f* (*Inform*) enter (*or*
return) key
entfernen *vt* to remove; (*Inform*)
to delete ▷ *vr*: **sich ~** to go away;
entfernt *adj* distant; **15 km von X
~** 15 km away from X; **20 km
voneinander ~** 20 km apart;
Entfernung *f* distance; **aus der
~** from a distance
entführen *vt* to kidnap;
Entführer(in) *m(f)* kidnapper;
Entführung *f* kidnapping
entgegen *prep* +*dat* contrary to
▷ *adv* towards; **dem Wind
~** against the wind;
entgegengesetzt *adj* (*Richtung*)
opposite; (*Meinung*) opposing;
entgegenkommen *irr vi*: **jdm
~** to come to meet sb; (*fig*) to
accommodate sb;
entgegenkommend *adj* (*Verkehr*)
oncoming; (*fig*) obliging
entgegnen *vt* to reply (*auf* +*akk*
to)
entgehen *irr vi*: **jdm ~** to escape
sb's notice; **sich** (*dat*) **etw ~ lassen**
to miss sth
entgleisen *vi* (*Eisenb*) to be
derailed; (*fig*: *Mensch*) to
misbehave

Enthaarungscreme *f* hair
remover
enthalten *irr vt* (*Behälter*) to
contain; (*Preis*) to include ▷ *vr*:
sich ~ to abstain (*gen* from)
entkoffeiniert *adj*
decaffeinated
entkommen *irr vi* to escape
entkorken *vt* to uncork
entlang *prep* +*akk o dat* **~ dem
Fluss, den Fluss ~** along the river;
entlang|gehen *irr vi* to walk
along
entlassen *irr vt* (*Patient*) to
discharge; (*Arbeiter*) to dismiss
entlasten *vt*: **jdn ~** (*Arbeit
abnehmen*) to relieve sb of some of
his/her work
entmutigen *vt* to discourage
entnehmen *irr vt* to take (*dat* from)
entrahmt *adj* (*Milch*) skimmed
entschädigen *vt* to
compensate; **Entschädigung** *f*
compensation
entscheiden *irr vt, vi* to decide
▷ *vr*: **sich ~** to decide; **sich
für/gegen etw ~** to decide
on/against sth; **wir haben uns
entschieden, nicht zu gehen** we
decided not to go; **das
entscheidet sich morgen** that'll
be decided tomorrow;
entscheidend *adj* decisive;
(*Stimme*) casting; (*Frage, Problem*)
crucial; **Entscheidung** *f*
decision
entschließen *irr vr*: **sich ~** to
decide (*zu, für* on), to make up
one's mind; **Entschluss** *m*
decision
entschuldigen *vt* to excuse
▷ *vr*: **sich ~** to apologize; **sich bei
jdm für etw ~** to apologize to sb
for sth ▷ *vi*: **entschuldige!, ~ Sie!**
(*vor einer Frage*) excuse me;
(*Verzeihung*) (I'm) sorry, excuse me
(*US*); **Entschuldigung** *f* apology;

entsetzlich | 68

(Grund) excuse; **jdn um ~ bitten** to apologize to sb; **~!** (bei Zusammenstoß) (I'm) sorry, excuse me (US); (vor einer Frage) excuse me; (wenn man etw nicht verstanden hat) (I beg your) pardon?

entsetzlich adj dreadful, appalling
entsorgen vt to dispose of
entspannen vt (Körper) to relax; (Pol: Lage) to ease ▷ vr: **sich ~** to relax; (fam) to chill out; **Entspannung** f relaxation
entsprechen irr vi +dat to correspond to; (Anforderungen, Wünschen etc) to comply with; **entsprechend** adj appropriate ▷ adv accordingly ▷ prep +dat according to, in accordance with
entstehen irr vi (Schwierigkeiten) to arise; (gebaut werden) to be built; (hergestellt werden) to be created
enttäuschen vt to disappoint; **Enttäuschung** f disappointment
entweder conj: **~ ... oder ...** either ... or ...; **~ oder!** take it or leave it
entwerfen irr vt (Möbel, Kleider) to design; (Plan, Vertrag) to draft
entwerten vt to devalue; (Fahrschein) to cancel; **Entwerter** (-s, -) m ticket-cancelling machine
entwickeln vt (a. Foto) to develop; (Mut, Energie) to show, to display ▷ vr: **sich ~** to develop; **Entwicklung** f development; (Foto) developing; **Entwicklungshelfer(in)** (-s, -) m(f) development worker; **Entwicklungsland** nt developing country
Entwurf m outline; (Design) design; (Vertragsentwurf) draft
entzückend adj delightful, charming
Entzug m withdrawal; (Behandlung) detox;

Entzugserscheinung f withdrawal symptom
entzünden vr: **sich ~** to catch fire; (Med) to become inflamed; **Entzündung** f (Med) inflammation
Epidemie (-, -n) f epidemic
Epilepsie (-, -n) f epilepsy
epilieren vt to remove body hair, to depilate
er pron (Person) he; (Sache) it; **er ist's** it's him; **wo ist mein Mantel? — ~ ist ...** where's my coat? — it's ...
Erbe (-n, -n) m heir ▷ (-s) nt inheritance; (fig) heritage; **erben** vt to inherit; **Erbin** f heiress; **erblich** adj hereditary
erblicken vt to catch sight of
erbrechen irr vt to vomit ▷ vr: **sich ~** to vomit; **Erbrechen** nt vomiting
Erbschaft f inheritance
Erbse (-, -n) f pea
Erdapfel m potato; **Erdbeben** nt earthquake; **Erdbeere** f strawberry; **Erde** (-, -n) f (Planet) earth; (Boden) ground; **Erdgas** nt natural gas; **Erdgeschoss** nt ground floor (Brit), first floor (US); **Erdkunde** f geography; **Erdnuss** f peanut; **Erdöl** nt (mineral) oil; **Erdrutsch** m landslide; **Erdteil** m continent
E-Reader m e-reader
ereignen vr: **sich ~** to happen, to take place; **Ereignis** nt event
erfahren irr vt to learn, to find out; (erleben) to experience ▷ adj experienced; **Erfahrung** f experience
erfinden irr vt to invent; **erfinderisch** adj inventive, creative; **Erfindung** f invention
Erfolg m (-(e)s, -(e)) m success; (Folge) result; **~ versprechend** promising; **viel ~!** good luck;

erfolglos adj unsuccessful;
erfolgreich adj successful
erforderlich adj necessary
erforschen vt to explore;
(untersuchen) investigate
erfreulich adj pleasing, pleasant;
(Nachricht) good;
erfreulicherweise adv
fortunately
erfrieren irr vi to freeze to death;
(Pflanzen) to be killed by frost
Erfrischung f refreshment
erfüllen vt (Raum) to fill; (Bitte,
Wunsch etc) to fulfil ▷ vr: **sich ~** to
come true
ergänzen vt (hinzufügen) to add;
(vervollständigen) to complete ▷ vr:
sich ~ to complement one
another; **Ergänzung** f
completion; (Zusatz) supplement
ergeben irr vt (Betrag) to come
to; (zum Ergebnis haben) to result in
▷ irr vr: **sich ~** to surrender;
(folgen) to result (aus from) ▷ adj
devoted; (demütig) humble
Ergebnis nt result
ergreifen irr vt to seize; (Beruf) to
take up; (Maßnahme, Gelegenheit) to
take; (rühren) to move
erhalten irr vt (bekommen) to
receive; (bewahren) to preserve;
gut ~ sein to be in good
condition; **erhältlich** adj
available
erheblich adj considerable
erhitzen vt to heat (up)
erhöhen vt to raise; (verstärken)
to increase ▷ vr: **sich ~** to
increase
erholen vr: **sich ~** to recover; (sich
ausruhen) to have a rest; **erholsam**
adj restful; **Erholung** f recovery;
(Entspannung) relaxation, rest
erinnern vt to remind (an +akk
of) ▷ vr: **sich ~** to remember (an
etw akk sth); **Erinnerung** f
memory; (Andenken) souvenir;

(Mahnung) reminder
erkälten vr: **sich ~** to catch a
cold; **erkältet** adj: **(stark) ~ sein**
to have a (bad) cold; **Erkältung** f
cold
erkennen irr vt to recognize;
(sehen, verstehen) to see; **~, dass ...**
to realize that ...; **erkenntlich**
adj: **sich ~ zeigen** to show one's
appreciation
Erker (-s, -) m bay
erklären vt to explain; (kundtun)
to declare; **Erklärung** f
explanation; (Aussage) declaration
erkundigen vr: **sich ~** to enquire
(nach about)
erlauben vt to allow, to permit;
jdm ~, etw zu tun to allow (o
permit) sb to do sth; **sich** (dat) **etw
~** to permit oneself sth; **~ Sie(,
dass ich rauche)?** do you mind (if I
smoke)?; **was ~ Sie sich?** what do
you think you're doing?; **Erlaubnis**
f permission
Erläuterung f explanation; (zu
Text) comment
erleben vt to experience; (schöne
Tage etc) to have; (Schlimmes) to go
through; (miterleben) to witness;
(noch miterleben) to live to see;
Erlebnis nt experience
erledigen vt (Angelegenheit,
Aufgabe) to deal with; (fam:
ruinieren) to finish; **erledigt** adj
(beendet) finished; (gelöst) dealt
with; (fam: erschöpft) whacked,
knackered (Brit)
erleichtert adj relieved
Erlös (-es, -e) m proceeds pl
ermahnen vt (warnend) to warn
ermäßigt adj reduced;
Ermäßigung f reduction
ermitteln vt to find out; (Täter)
to trace ▷ vi (Jur) to investigate
ermöglichen vt to make
possible (dat for)
ermorden vt to murder

ermüdend adj tiring
ermutigen vt to encourage
ernähren vt to feed; (Familie) to support ▷ vr: **sich ~** to support oneself; **sich ~ von** to live on; **Ernährung** f (Essen) food; **Ernährungsberater(in)** m(f) nutritional (o dietary) adviser
erneuern vt to renew; (restaurieren) to restore; (renovieren) to renovate; (auswechseln) to replace
ernst adj serious ▷ adv: **jdn/etw ~ nehmen** take sb/sth seriously; **Ernst** (-es) m seriousness; **das ist mein ~** I'm quite serious; **im ~?** seriously?; **ernsthaft** adj serious ▷ adv seriously
Ernte (-, -n) f harvest; **Erntedankfest** nt harvest festival (Brit), Thanksgiving (Day) (US: 4. Donnerstag im November); **ernten** vt to harvest; (Lob etc) to earn
erobern vt to conquer
eröffnen vt to open; **Eröffnung** f opening
erogen adj erogenous
erotisch adj erotic
erpressen vt (jdn) to blackmail; (Geld etc) to extort; **Erpressung** f blackmail; (von Geld) extortion
erraten irr vt to guess
erregen vt to excite; (sexuell) to arouse; (ärgern) to annoy; (hervorrufen) to arouse ▷ vr: **sich ~** to get worked up; **Erreger** (-s, -) m (Med) germ; (Virus) virus
erreichbar adj: **~ sein** to be within reach; (Person) to be available; **das Stadtzentrum ist zu Fuß/mit dem Wagen leicht ~** the city centre is within easy walking/driving distance; **erreichen** vt to reach; (Zug etc) to catch
Ersatz (-es) m replacement; (auf

Zeit) substitute; (Ausgleich) compensation; **Ersatzreifen** m (Auto) spare tyre; **Ersatzteil** nt spare (part)
erscheinen irr vi to appear; (wirken) to seem
erschöpft adj exhausted; **Erschöpfung** f exhaustion
erschrecken vt to frighten ▷ (erschrak, erschrocken) vi to get a fright; **erschreckend** adj alarming; **erschrocken** adj frightened
erschwinglich adj affordable
ersetzen vt to replace; (Auslagen) to reimburse

SCHLÜSSELWORT

erst adv **1** first; **mach erst mal die Arbeit fertig** finish your work first; **wenn du das erst mal hinter dir hast** once you've got that behind you
2 (nicht früher als, nur) only; (nicht bis) not till; **erst gestern** only yesterday; **erst morgen** not until tomorrow; **erst als** only when, not until; **wir fahren erst später** we're not going until later; **er ist (gerade) erst angekommen** he's only just arrived
3 **wäre er doch erst zurück!** if only he were back!

erstatten vt (Kosten) to refund; **Bericht ~** to report (über +akk on); **Anzeige gegen jdn ~** to report sb to the police
erstaunlich adj astonishing; **erstaunt** adj surprised
erstbeste(r, s) adj: **das ~ Hotel** any old hotel; **der Erstbeste** just anyone
erste(r, s) adj first; siehe auch **dritte; zum ~n Mal** for the first time; **er wurde Erster** he came

first; **auf den ~n Blick** at first sight

erstens adv first(ly), in the first place

ersticken vi (Mensch) to suffocate; **in Arbeit ~** to be snowed under with work

erstklassig adj first-class; **erstmals** adv for the first time

erstrecken vr: **sich ~** to extend, to stretch (auf +akk over; über +akk over)

ertappen vt to catch

erteilen vt (Rat, Erlaubnis) to give

Ertrag (-(e)s, Erträge) m yield; (Gewinn) proceeds pl; **ertragen** irr vt (Schmerzen) to bear, to stand; (dulden) to put up with; **erträglich** adj bearable; (nicht zu schlecht) tolerable

ertrinken irr vi to drown

erwachsen adj grown-up; **~ werden** to grow up; **Erwachsene(r)** mf adult, grown-up

erwähnen vt to mention

erwarten vt to expect; (warten auf) to wait for; **ich kann den Sommer kaum ~** I can hardly wait for the summer

erwerbstätig adj employed

erwidern vt to reply; (Gruß, Besuch) to return

erwischen vt (fam) to catch (bei etw doing sth)

erwünscht adj desired; (willkommen) welcome

Erz (-es, -e) nt ore

erzählen vt to tell (jdm etw sb sth); **Erzählung** f story, tale

erzeugen vt to produce; (Strom) to generate; **Erzeugnis** nt product

erziehen irr vt to bring up; (geistig) to educate; (Tier) to train; **Erzieher(in)** (-s, -) m(f) educator; (Kindergarten) (nursery school)

teacher; **Erziehung** f upbringing; (Bildung) education

es pron (Sache, im Nom und Akk) it; (Baby, Tier) he/she; **ich bin ~** it's me; **~ ist kalt** it's cold; **~ gibt ...** there is .../there are ...; **ich hoffe ~** I hope so; **ich kann ~** I can do it

Escape-Taste f (Inform) escape key

Esel (-s, -) m donkey

Espresso (-s, -) m espresso

essbar adj edible; **essen** (aß, gegessen) vt, vi to eat; **zu Mittag/Abend ~** to have lunch/dinner; **was gibt's zu ~?** what's for lunch/dinner?; **~ gehen** to eat out; **gegessen sein** (fig, fam) to be history; **Essen** (-s, -) nt (Mahlzeit) meal; (Nahrung) food

Essig (-s, -e) m vinegar

Esslöffel m dessert spoon; **Esszimmer** nt dining room

Estland nt Estonia

Etage (-, -n) f floor, storey; **in** (o **auf**) **der ersten ~** on the first (Brit) (o second (US)) floor; **Etagenbett** nt bunk bed

Etappe (-, -n) f stage

ethnisch adj ethnic

Etikett (-(e)s, -e) nt label

etliche pron pl several, quite a few; **etliches** pron quite a lot

etwa adv (ungefähr) about; (vielleicht) perhaps; (beispielsweise) for instance

etwas pron something; (verneinend, fragend) anything; (ein wenig) a little; **~ Neues** something/anything new; **~ zu essen** something to eat; **~ Salz** some salt; **wenn ich noch ~ tun kann ...** if I can do anything else ... ▷ adv a bit, a little; **~ mehr** a little more

EU (-) f abk = **Europäische Union** EU

euch pron sich, dat von **ihr**; you, (to)

you; ~ **(selbst)** *(reflexiv)* yourselves;
wo kann ich ~ treffen? where can
I meet you?; **sie schickt es ~** she'll
send it to you; **ein Freund von ~** a
friend of yours; **setzt ~ bitte**
please sit down; **habt ihr
~ amüsiert?** did you enjoy
yourselves?

euer *pron (adjektivisch)* your;
~ David *(am Briefende)* Yours, David
▷ *pron gen von* **ihr**; of you; **euere(r,
s)** *pron siehe* **eure**

Eule *(-, -n)* f owl

eure(r, s) *pron (substantivisch)*
yours; **das ist ~** that's yours;
euretwegen *adv (wegen euch)*
because of you; *(euch zuliebe)* for
your sake; *(um euch)* about you

Euro *(-, -)* m *(Währung)* euro;
Eurocent *m* eurocent; **Eurocity**
(-(s), -s) m, **Eurocityzug** *m*
European Intercity train; **Europa**
(-s) *nt* Europe; **Europäer(in)** *(-s, -)*
m(f) European; **europäisch** *adj*
European; **Europäische Union**
European Union;
Europameister(in) *m(f)* Euro-
pean champion; *(Mannschaft)*
European champions pl;
Europaparlament *nt* European
Parliament

Euter *(-s, -)* *nt* udder

evangelisch *adj* Protestant

eventuell *adj* possible ▷ *adv*
possibly, perhaps

ewig *adj* eternal; **er hat
~ gebraucht** it took him ages;
Ewigkeit f eternity

Ex *mf* ex

Ex- *in zW* ex-, former; **~frau**
ex-wife; **~freund** m ex-boyfriend;
~minister former minister

exakt *adj* precise

Examen *(-s, -)* *nt* exam

Exemplar *(-s, -e)* *nt* specimen;
(Buch) copy

Exil *(-s, -e)* *nt* exile

Existenz f existence; *(Unterhalt)*
livelihood, living; **existieren** *vi*
to exist

exklusiv *adj* exclusive; **exklusive**
adv, prep +gen excluding

exotisch *adj* exotic

Experte *(-n, -n)* m, **Expertin** f
expert

explodieren *vi* to explode;
Explosion f explosion

Export *(-(e)s, -e)* m export;
exportieren *vt* to export

Express *(-es)* m, **Expresszug** m
express (train)

extra *adj inv (fam: gesondert)*
separate; *(zusätzlich)* extra ▷ *adv*
(gesondert) separately; *(speziell)*
specially; *(absichtlich)* on purpose;
Extra *(-s, -s)* *nt* extra

extrem *adj* extreme ▷ *adv*
extremely; **~ kalt** extremely cold

exzellent *adj* excellent

Eyeliner *(-s, -)* m eyeliner

E-Zigarette f e-cigarette

f

fabelhaft adj fabulous, marvellous

Fabrik f factory

Fach (-(e)s, Fächer) nt compartment; (Schulfach, Sachgebiet) subject; **Facharzt** m, **Fachärztin** f specialist; **Fachausdruck** (-s, Fachausdrücke) m technical term

Fächer (-s, -) m fan

Fachfrau f specialist, expert; **Fachmann** (-leute) m specialist, expert; **Fachwerkhaus** nt half-timbered house

Fackel (-, -n) f torch

fad(e) adj (Essen) bland; (langweilig) dull

Faden (-s, Fäden) m thread

fähig adj capable (zu, gen of); **Fähigkeit** f ability

Fahndung f search

Fahne (-, -n) f flag

Fahrausweis m ticket

Fahrbahn f road; (Spur) lane

Fähre (-, -n) f ferry

fahren (fuhr, gefahren) vt to drive; (Rad) to ride; (befördern) to drive, to take; **50 km/h ~** to drive at (o do) 50 kph ▷ vi (sich bewegen) to go; (Autofahrer) to drive; (Schiff) to sail; (abfahren) to leave; **mit dem Auto/Zug ~** to go by car/train; **rechts ~!** keep to the right; **Fahrer(in)** (-s, -) m(f) driver; **Fahrerairbag** m driver airbag; **Fahrerflucht** f: **~ begehen** to fail to stop after an accident; **Fahrersitz** m driver's seat

Fahrgast m passenger; **Fahrgeld** nt fare; **Fahrgemeinschaft** f car pool; **Fahrkarte** f ticket; **Fahrkartenautomat** m ticket machine; **Fahrkartenschalter** m ticket office

fahrlässig adj negligent

Fahrlehrer(in) m(f) driving instructor; **Fahrplan** m timetable; **Fahrplanauszug** m individual timetable; **fahrplanmäßig** adj (Eisenb) scheduled; **Fahrpreis** m fare; **Fahrpreisermäßigung** f fare reduction; **Fahrrad** nt bicycle; **Fahrradschlauch** m bicycle tube; **Fahrradschloss** nt bicycle lock; **Fahrradverleih** m cycle hire (Brit) (o rental (US)); **Fahrradweg** m cycle path; **Fahrschein** m ticket; **Fahrscheinautomat** m ticket machine; **Fahrscheinentwerter** m ticket-cancelling machine; **Fahrschule** f driving school; **Fahrschüler(in)** m(f) learner (driver) (Brit), student driver (US); **Fahrspur** f lane; **Fahrstreifen** m lane; **Fahrstuhl** m lift (Brit), elevator (US)

Fahrt (-, -en) f journey; (kurz) trip; (Auto) drive; **auf der ~ nach London** on the way to London; **nach drei Stunden ~** after travelling for three hours; **gute ~!** have a good trip; **Fahrtkosten** pl travelling expenses pl; **Fahrtrichtung** f direction of travel

fahrtüchtig f (*Person*) fit to drive; (*Fahrzeug*) roadworthy

Fahrtunterbrechung f break in the journey, stop

Fahrverbot nt: **~ erhalten/ haben** to be banned from driving; **Fahrzeug** nt vehicle; **Fahrzeugbrief** m (vehicle) registration document; **Fahrzeughalter(in)** m(f) registered owner; **Fahrzeugpapiere** pl vehicle documents pl

fair adj fair

Fakultät f faculty

Falke (-n, -n) m falcon

Fall (-(e)s, Fälle) m (*Sturz*) fall; (*Sachverhalt, juristisch*) case; **auf jeden ~, auf alle Fälle** in any case; (*bestimmt*) definitely; **auf keinen ~** on no account; **für den ~, dass ...** in case ...

Falle (-, -n) f trap

fallen (fiel, gefallen) vi to fall; **etw ~ lassen** to drop sth

fällig adj due

falls adv if; (*für den Fall, dass*) in case

Fallschirm m parachute; **Fallschirmspringen** nt parachuting, parachute jumping; **Fallschirmspringer(in)** m(f) parachutist

falsch adj (*unrichtig*) wrong; (*unehrlich, unecht*) false; (*Schmuck*) fake; **~ verbinden** sorry, wrong number; **fälschen** vt to forge; **Falschfahrer(in)** m(f) person driving the wrong way on the motorway; **Falschgeld** nt counterfeit money; **Fälschung** f forgery, fake

Faltblatt nt leaflet

Falte (-, -n) f (*Knick*) fold; (*Haut*) wrinkle; (*Rock*) pleat; (*Bügel*) crease; **falten** vt to fold; **faltig** adj (*zerknittert*) creased; (*Haut, Gesicht*) wrinkled

Familie f family; **Familienangehörige(r)** mf family member; **Familienname** m surname; **Familienstand** m marital status

Fan (-s, -s) m fan

fand imperf von **finden**

fangen (fing, gefangen) vt to catch ▷ vr: **sich ~** (*nicht fallen*) to steady oneself; (*fig*) to compose oneself

Fantasie f imagination

fantastisch adj fantastic

Farbdrucker m colour printer; **Farbe** (-, -n) f colour; (*zum Malen etc*) paint; (*für Stoff*) dye; **färben** vt to colour; (*Stoff, Haar*) to dye; **Farbfernsehen** nt colour television; **Farbfilm** m colour film; **farbig** adj coloured; **Farbkopierer** m colour copier; **farblos** adj colourless; **Farbstoff** m dye; (*für Lebensmittel*) colouring

Farn (-(e)s, -e) m fern

Fasan (-(e)s, -e(n)) m pheasant

Fasching (-s, -e) m carnival, Mardi Gras (US); **Faschingsdienstag** (-s, -e) m Shrove Tuesday, Mardi Gras (US)

Faschismus m fascism

Faser (-, -n) f fibre

Fass (-es, Fässer) nt barrel; (*Öl*) drum

fassen vt (*ergreifen*) to grasp; (*enthalten*) to hold; (*Entschluss*) to take; (*verstehen*) to understand; **nicht zu ~** unbelievable ▷ vr: **sich ~** to compose oneself; **Fassung** f (*Umrahmung*) mount; (*Brille*) frame; (*Lampe*) socket; (*Wortlaut*) version; (*Beherrschung*) composure; **jdn aus der ~ bringen**

to throw sb; **die ~ verlieren** to lose one's cool

fast adv almost, nearly

fasten vi to fast; **Fastenzeit** f: **die ~** (christlich) Lent; (muslimisch) Ramadan

Fast Food (-s) nt fast food

Fastnacht f (Fasching) carnival

fatal adj (verhängnisvoll) disastrous; (peinlich) embarrassing

faul adj (Obst, Gemüse) rotten; (Mensch) lazy; (Ausrede) lame; **faulen** vi to rot

faulenzen vi to do nothing, to hang around; **Faulheit** f laziness

faulig adj rotten; (Geruch, Geschmack) foul

Faust (-, Fäuste) f fist; **Fausthandschuh** m mitten

Fax (-, -(e)) nt fax; **faxen** vi, vt to fax; **Faxgerät** nt fax machine; **Faxnummer** f fax number

FCKW (-, -s) nt abk = **Fluorchlorkohlenwasserstoff** CFC

Februar (-(s), -e) m February; siehe auch **Juni**

Fechten f fencing

Feder (-, -n) f feather; (Schreibfeder) (pen-)nib; (Tech) spring; **Federball** m (Ball) shuttlecock; (Spiel) badminton; **Federung** f suspension

Fee (-, -n) f fairy

fegen vi, vt to sweep

fehl adj: **~ am Platz** (o Ort) out of place

fehlen vi (abwesend sein) to be absent; **etw fehlt jdm** sb lacks sth; **was fehlt ihm?** what's wrong with him?; **du fehlst mir** I miss you; **es fehlt an ...** there's no...

Fehler (-s, -) m mistake, error; (Mangel, Schwäche) fault; **Fehlerbeseitigung** f (Inform) debugging; **Fehlermeldung** f (Inform) error message

Fehlzündung f (Auto) misfire

Feier (-, -n) f celebration; (Party) party; **Feierabend** m end of the working day; **~ haben** to finish work; **nach ~** after work; **feierlich** adj solemn; **feiern** vt, vi to celebrate, to have a party; **Feiertag** m holiday; **gesetzlicher ~** public holiday

feig(e) adj cowardly

Feige (-, -n) f fig

Feigling m coward

Feile (-, -n) f file

fein adj fine; (vornehm) refined; **~!** great!; **das schmeckt ~** that tastes delicious

Feind(in) (-(e)s, -e) m(f) enemy; **feindlich** adj hostile

Feinkost (-) f delicacies pl; **Feinkostladen** m delicatessen; **Feinschmecker(in)** (-s, -) m(f) gourmet; **Feinstaub** m particulate matter; **Feinwaschmittel** nt washing powder for delicate fabrics

Feld (-(e)s, -er) nt field; (Schach) square; (Sport) pitch; **Feldsalat** m lamb's lettuce; **Feldweg** m path across the fields

Felge (-, -n) f (wheel) rim

Fell (-(e)s, -e) nt fur; (von Schaf) fleece

Fels (-en, -en) m, **Felsen** (-s, -) m rock; (Klippe) cliff; **felsig** adj rocky

feminin adj feminine; **Femininum** (-s, Feminina) nt (Ling) feminine noun

feministisch adj feminist

Fenchel (-s, -) m fennel

Fenster (-s, -) nt window; **Fensterbrett** nt windowsill; **Fensterladen** m shutter; **Fensterplatz** m windowseat; **Fensterscheibe** f windowpane

Ferien pl holidays pl (Brit), vacation sing (US); **~ haben/ machen** to be/go on holiday (Brit)

(o vacation (US)); **Ferienhaus** nt
holiday (Brit) (o vacation (US))
home; **Ferienkurs** m holiday
(Brit) (o vacation (US)) course;
Ferienlager nt holiday camp
(Brit), vacation camp (US); (für
Kinder im Sommer) summer camp;
Ferienort m holiday (Brit) (o
vacation (US)) resort;
Ferienwohnung f holiday flat
(Brit), vacation apartment (US)

Ferkel (-s, -) nt piglet

fern adj distant, far-off; **von**
~ from a distance; **Fernabfrage** f
remote-control access;
Fernbedienung f remote control;
Ferne f distance; **aus der** ~ from
a distance

ferner adj, adv further; (außerdem)
besides

Fernflug m long-distance flight;
Ferngespräch nt long-distance
call; **ferngesteuert** adj
remote-controlled; **Fernglas** nt
binoculars pl; **Fernlicht** nt full
beam (Brit), high beam (US)

Fernsehapparat m TV (set);
fern|sehen irr vi to watch
television; **Fernsehen** nt
television; **im** ~ on television;
Fernseher m TV (set);
Fernsehkanal m TV channel;
Fernsehprogramm nt (Sendung)
TV programme; (Zeitschrift) TV
guide; **Fernsehserie** f TV series
sing; **Fernsehturm** m TV tower;
Fernsehzeitschrift f TV guide

Fernstraße f major road;
Ferntourismus m long-haul
tourism; **Fernverkehr** m
long-distance traffic

Ferse (-, -n) f heel

fertig adj (bereit) ready; (beendet)
finished; (gebrauchsfertig)
ready-made; ~ **machen** (beenden)
to finish; **sich** ~ **machen** to get
ready; **mit etw** ~ **werden** to be

able to cope with sth; **auf die
Plätze, ~, los!** on your marks, get
set, go!; **Fertiggericht** nt ready
meal; **fertig|machen** vt (jdn
kritisieren) to give sb hell; (jdn zur
Verzweiflung bringen) to drive sb
mad; (jdn deprimieren) to get sb
down

fest adj firm; (Nahrung) solid;
(Gehalt) regular; (Schuhe) sturdy;
(Schlaf) sound

Fest (-(e)s, -e) nt party; (Rel)
festival

Festbetrag m fixed amount
fest|binden irr vt to tie (an +dat
to); **fest|halten** irr vt to hold
onto ▷ vr: **sich** ~ to hold on (an
+dat to)

Festiger (-s, -) m setting lotion

Festival (-s, -s) nt festival

Festland nt mainland; **das
europäische** ~ the (European)
continent

fest|legen vt to fix ▷ vr: **sich**
~ to commit oneself

festlich adj festive

fest|machen vt to fasten;
(Termin etc) to fix; **fest|nehmen** irr
vt to arrest; **Festnetz** nt (Tel)
landline; **Festplatte** f (Inform)
hard disk

fest|setzen vt to fix

Festspiele pl festival sing

fest|stehen irr vi to be fixed

fest|stellen vt to establish;
(sagen) to remark

Feststelltaste f shift lock

Festung f fortress

Festzelt nt marquee

Fete (-, -n) f party

fett adj (dick) fat; (Essen etc)
greasy; (Schrift) bold; **Fett** (-(e)s,
-e) nt fat; (Tech) grease; **fettarm**
adj low-fat; **fettig** adj fatty;
(schmierig) greasy

feucht adj damp; (Luft) humid;
Feuchtigkeit f dampness;

(*Luftfeuchtigkeit*) humidity; **Feuchtigkeitscreme** f moisturizing cream

Feuer (-s, -) nt fire; **haben Sie ~?** have you got a light?; **Feueralarm** m fire alarm; **feuerfest** adj fireproof; **Feuerlöscher** (-s, -) m fire extinguisher; **Feuermelder** (-s, -) m fire alarm; **Feuertreppe** f fire escape; **Feuerwehr** (-, -en) f fire brigade; **Feuerwehrfrau** f firewoman, fire fighter; **Feuerwehrmann** m fireman, fire fighter; **Feuerwerk** nt fireworks pl; **Feuerzeug** nt (cigarette) lighter

Fichte (-, -n) f spruce

ficken vt, vi (vulg) to fuck

Fieber (-s, -) nt temperature, fever; **~ haben** to have a high temperature; **Fieberthermometer** nt thermometer

fiel imperf von **fallen**

fies adj (fam) nasty

Figur (-, -en) f figure; (im Schach) piece

Filet (-s, -s) nt fillet; **filetieren** vt to fillet; **Filetsteak** nt fillet steak

Filiale (-, -n) f (Comm) branch

Film (-(e)s, -e) m film, movie; **filmen** vt, vi to film

Filter (-s, -) m filter; **Filterkaffee** m filter coffee; **filtern** vt to filter; **Filterpapier** nt filter paper

Filz (-es, -e) m felt; **Filzschreiber** m, **Filzstift** m felt(-tip) pen, felt-tip

Finale (-s, -) nt (Sport) final

Finanzamt nt tax office; **finanziell** adj financial; **finanzieren** vt to finance

finden (fand, gefunden) vt to find; (meinen) to think; **ich finde nichts dabei, wenn ...** I don't see what's

wrong if ...; **ich finde es gut/schlecht** I like/don't like it ▷ vr: **es fanden sich nur wenige Helfer** there were only a few helpers

fing imperf von **fangen**

Finger (-s, -) m finger; **Fingerabdruck** m fingerprint; **Fingerhandschuh** m glove; **Fingernagel** m fingernail

Fink (-en, -en) m finch

Finne (-n, -n) m, **Finnin** f Finn, Finnish man/woman; **finnisch** adj Finnish; **Finnisch** nt Finnish; **Finnland** nt Finland

finster adj dark; (verdächtig) dubious; (verdrossen) grim; (Gedanke) dark; **Finsternis** f darkness

Firewall (-, -s) f (Inform) firewall

Firma (-, Firmen) f firm

Fisch (-(e)s, -e) m fish; **~e** pl (Astr) Pisces sing; **fischen** vt, vi to fish; **Fischer(in)** (-s, -) m(f) fisherman/ -woman; **Fischerboot** nt fishing boat; **Fischgericht** nt fish dish; **Fischhändler(in)** m(f) fishmonger; **Fischstäbchen** nt fish finger (Brit) (o stick US)

Fisole (-, -n) f French bean

fit adj fit; **Fitness** (-) f fitness; **Fitnesscenter** (-s, -) nt fitness centre; **Fitnesstrainer(in)** m(f) fitness trainer, personal trainer

fix adj (schnell) quick; **~ und fertig** exhausted

fixen vi (fam) to shoot up; **Fixer(in)** (-s, -) m(f) (fam) junkie

FKK f abk = **Freikörperkultur** nudism; **FKK-Strand** m nudist beach

flach adj flat; (Gewässer, Teller) shallow; **~er Absatz** low heel; **Flachbildschirm** m flat screen

Fläche (-, -n) f area; (Oberfläche) surface

Flagge (-, -n) f flag

flambiert adj flambé(ed)

Flamme (-, -n) f flame

Flanell (-s) m flannel

Flasche (-, -n) f bottle; **eine ~ sein** (fam) to be useless; **Flaschenbier** nt bottled beer; **Flaschenöffner** m bottle opener; **Flaschenpfand** nt deposit; **Flaschentomate** f plum tomato

flatterhaft adj fickle; **flattern** vi to flutter

flauschig adj fluffy

Flausen pl (fam) daft ideas pl

Flaute (-, -n) f calm; (Comm) recession

Flechte (-, -n) f plait; (Med) scab; (Bot) lichen; **flechten** (flocht, geflochten) vt to plait; (Kranz) to bind

Fleck (-(e)s, -e) m, **Flecken** (-s, -) m spot; (Schmutz) stain; (Stoff~) patch; (Makel) blemish; **Fleckentferner** (-s, -) m stain remover; **fleckig** adj spotted; (mit Schmutzflecken) stained

Fledermaus f bat

Fleisch (-(e)s) nt flesh; (Essen) meat; **Fleischbrühe** f meat stock; **Fleischer(in)** (-s, -) m(f) butcher; **Fleischerei** f butcher's (shop); **Fleischtomate** f beef tomato

fleißig adj diligent, hard-working

flennen vi (fam) to cry, to howl

flexibel adj flexible

flicken vt to mend; **Flickzeug** nt repair kit

Flieder (-s, -) m lilac

Fliege (-, -n) f fly; (Krawatte) bow tie

fliegen (flog, geflogen) vt, vi to fly

Fliese (-, -n) f tile

Fließband nt conveyor belt; (als Einrichtung) production (or assembly) line; **fließen** (floss, geflossen) vi to flow; **fließend** adj fluent; (Übergänge) smooth; **~(es) Wasser** running water

Flipper (-s, -) m pinball machine; **flippern** vi to play pinball

flippig adj (fam) eccentric

flirten vi to flirt

Flitterwochen pl honeymoon sing

flocht imperf von **flechten**

Flocke (-, -n) f flake

flog imperf von **fliegen**

Floh (-(e)s, Flöhe) m flea; **Flohmarkt** m flea market

Flop (-s, -s) m flop

Floskel (-, -n) f empty phrase

floss imperf von **fließen**

Floß (-es, Flöße) nt raft

Flosse (-, -n) f fin; (Schwimmflosse) flipper

Flöte (-, -n) f flute; (Blockflöte) recorder

flott adj lively; (elegant) smart; (Naut) afloat

Fluch (-(e)s, Flüche) m curse; **fluchen** vi to swear, to curse

Flucht (-, -en) f flight; **flüchten** vi to flee (vor +dat from); **flüchtig** adj: **ich kenne ihn nur ~** I don't know him very well at all; **Flüchtling** m refugee

Flug (-(e)s, Flüge) m flight; **Flugbegleiter(in)** (-s, -) m(f) flight attendant; **Flugblatt** nt leaflet

Flügel (-s, -) m wing; (Mus) grand piano

Fluggast m passenger (on a plane); **Fluggesellschaft** f airline; **Flughafen** m airport; **Flugkarte** f airline ticket; **Fluglotse** m air-traffic controller; **Flugnummer** f flight number; **Flugplan** m flight schedule; **Flugplatz** m airport; (klein) airfield; **Flugschein** m plane ticket; **Flugschreiber** m flight recorder, black box; **Flugsteig** (-s, -e) m gate; **Flugstrecke** f air route; **Flugticket** nt plane ticket; **Flugverbindung** f flight connection; **Flugverkehr** m air traffic; **Flugzeit** f flying time; **Flugzeug** nt plane; **Flugzeugentführung** f hijacking

Flunder (-, -n) f flounder

Fluor (-s) nt fluorine

Flur (-(e)s, -e) m hall

Fluss (-es, Flüsse) m river; (*Fließen*) flow

flüssig adj liquid; **Flüssigkeit** (-, -en) f liquid; **Flüssigseife** f liquid soap

flüstern vt, vi to whisper

Flut (-, -en) f (a. fig) flood; (*Gezeiten*) high tide; **Flutlicht** nt floodlight

Fohlen (-s, -) nt foal

Föhn (-(e)s, -e) m hairdryer; (*Wind*) foehn; **föhnen** vt to dry; (*beim Friseur*) to blow-dry

Folge (-, -n) f (*Reihe, Serie*) series sing; (*Aufeinanderfolge*) sequence; (*Fortsetzung eines Romans*) instalment; (*Fortsetzung einer Fernsehserie*) episode; (*Auswirkung*) result; **etw zur ~ haben** to result in sth; **~n haben** to have consequences; **folgen** vi to follow (*jdm sb*); (*gehorchen*) to obey (*jdm sb*); **jdm ~ können** (fig) to be able to follow sb; **folgend** adj following; **folgendermaßen** adv as follows; **folglich** adv consequently

Folie f foil; (*für Projektor*) transparency

Fön® m siehe **Föhn**

Fondue (-s, -s) nt fondue

fönen vt siehe **föhnen**

fordern vt to demand

fördern vt to promote; (*unterstützen*) to help

Forderung f demand

Forelle f trout

Form (-, -en) f form; (*Gestalt*) shape; (*Gussform*) mould; (*Backform*) baking tin (Brit) (o pan

(US)); **in ~ sein** to be in good form; **Formalität** f formality; **Format** nt format; **von internationalem ~** of international standing; **formatieren** vt (*Diskette*) to format; (*Text*) to edit

Formblatt nt form; **formen** vt to form, to shape; **förmlich** adj formal; (*buchstäblich*) real; **formlos** adj informal; **Formular** (-s, -e) nt form; **formulieren** vt to formulate

forschen vi to search (*nach* for); (*wissenschaftlich*) to (do) research; **Forscher(in)** m(f) researcher; **Forschung** f research

Förster(in) (-s, -) m(f) forester; (*für Wild*) gamekeeper

fort adv away; (*verschwunden*) gone; **fort|bewegen** vt to move away ▷ vr: **sich ~** to move; **Fortbildung** f further education; (*im Beruf*) further training; **fort|fahren** irr vi to go away; (*weitermachen*) to continue; **fort|gehen** irr vi to go away; **fortgeschritten** adj advanced; **Fortpflanzung** f reproduction

Fortschritt m progress; **~e machen** to make progress; **fortschrittlich** adj progressive

fort|setzen vt to continue; **Fortsetzung** f continuation; (*folgender Teil*) instalment; **~ folgt** to be continued

Foto (-s, -s) nt photo ▷ (-s, -s) m (*Fotoapparat*) camera; **Fotograf(in)** (-en, -en) m(f) photographer; **Fotografie** f photography; (*Bild*) photograph; **fotografieren** vt to photograph ▷ vi to take photographs; **Fotohandy** nt camera phone; **Fotokopie** f photocopy; **fotokopieren** vt to photocopy

Foul (-s, -s) nt foul

Foyer (-s, -s) nt foyer

Fr. f abk = **Frau** Mrs; (unverheiratet, neutral) Ms

Fracht (-, -en) f freight; (Naut) cargo; (Preis) carriage; **Frachter** (-s, -) m freighter

Frack (-(e)s, Fräcke) m tails pl

Fracking nt fracking

Frage (-, -n) f question; **das ist eine ~ der Zeit** that's a matter (o question) of time; **das kommt nicht in ~** that's out of the question; **Fragebogen** m questionnaire; **fragen** vt, vi to ask; **Fragezeichen** nt question mark; **fragwürdig** adj dubious

Franken (-s, -) m (Schweizer Währung) Swiss franc ▷ (-s) nt (Land) Franconia

frankieren vt to stamp; (maschinell) to frank

Frankreich (-s) nt France; **Franzose** (-n, -n) m, **Französin** f Frenchman/-woman; **die ~n** pl the French pl; **französisch** adj French; **Französisch** nt French

fraß imperf von **fressen**

Frau (-, -en) f woman; (Ehefrau) wife; (Anrede) Mrs; (unverheiratet, neutral) Ms; **Frauenarzt** m, **Frauenärztin** f gynaecologist; **Frauenbewegung** f women's movement; **frauenfeindlich** adj misogynous; **Frauenhaus** nt refuge (for battered women)

Fräulein nt (junge Dame) young lady; (veraltet als Anrede) Miss

Freak (-s, -s) m (fam) freak

frech adj cheeky; **Frechheit** f cheek; **so eine ~!** what a cheek

Freeclimbing (-s) nt free climbing

frei adj free; (Straße) clear; (Mitarbeiter) freelance; **ein ~er Tag** a day off; **~e Arbeitsstelle** vacancy; **Zimmer ~** room(s) to let (Brit), room(s) for rent (US); **im Freien** in the open air; **Freibad** nt open-air (swimming) pool; **freiberuflich** adj freelance; **freig(i)ebig** adj generous; **Freiheit** f freedom; **Freikarte** f free ticket; **freilassen** irr vt to (set) free

freilich adv of course

Freilichtbühne f open-air theatre; **freimachen** vr: **sich ~** to undress; **freinehmen** irr vt: **sich** (dat) **einen Tag ~** to take a day off; **Freisprechanlage** f hands-free phone; **Freistoß** m free kick

Freitag m Friday; siehe auch **Mittwoch**; **freitags** adv on Fridays; siehe auch **mittwochs**

freiwillig adj voluntary

Freizeichen nt (Tel) ringing tone

Freizeit f spare (o free) time; **Freizeithemd** nt sports shirt; **Freizeitkleidung** f leisure wear; **Freizeitpark** m leisure park

fremd adj (nicht vertraut) strange; (ausländisch) foreign; (nicht eigen) someone else's; **Fremde(r)** mf (Unbekannter) stranger; (Ausländer) foreigner; **fremdenfeindlich** adj anti-foreigner, xenophobic; **Fremdenführer(in)** m(f) (tourist) guide; **Fremdenverkehr** m tourism; **Fremdenverkehrsamt** nt tourist information office; **Fremdenzimmer** nt (guest) room; **Fremdsprache** f foreign language; **Fremdsprachenkenntnisse** pl knowledge sing of foreign languages; **Fremdwort** nt foreign word

fressen (fraß, gefressen) vt, vi (Tier) to eat; (Mensch) to guzzle

Freude (-, -n) f joy, delight; **freuen** vt to please; **es freut mich, dass ...** I'm pleased that ... ▷ vr: **sich ~** to be pleased (über +akk about); **sich auf etw** (akk) **~** to look forward to sth

Freund (-(e)s, -e) m friend; (in Beziehung) boyfriend; **Freundin** f friend; (in Beziehung) girlfriend; **freundlich** adj friendly; (liebenswürdig) kind; **freundlicherweise** adv kindly; **Freundlichkeit** f friendliness; (Liebenswürdigkeit) kindness; **Freundschaft** f friendship

Frieden (-s, -) m peace; **Friedhof** m cemetery; **friedlich** adj peaceful

frieren (fror, gefroren) vt, vi to freeze; **ich friere, es friert mich** I'm freezing

Frikadelle f rissole

Frisbee® nt, **Frisbeescheibe®** f frisbee®

frisch adj fresh; (lebhaft) lively; **„~ gestrichen" "wet paint"; sich ~ machen** to freshen up; **Frischhaltefolie** f clingfilm® (Brit), plastic wrap (US); **Frischkäse** m cream cheese

Friseur(in) (-s, -e) m(f) hairdresser; **frisieren** vt: **jdn ~** to do sb's hair ▷ vr: **sich ~** to do one's hair

Frist (-, -en) f period; (Zeitpunkt) deadline; **innerhalb einer ~ von zehn Tagen** in a ten-day period; **eine ~ einhalten** to meet a deadline; **die ~ ist abgelaufen** the deadline has expired; **fristgerecht** adj, adv within the specified time; **fristlos** adj: **~e Entlassung** dismissal without notice

Frisur f hairdo, hairstyle

frittieren vt to deep-fry

Frl. f abk = **Fräulein** Miss

froh adj happy; **~e Weihnachten!** Merry Christmas

fröhlich adj happy, cheerful

Fronleichnam (-(e)s) m Corpus Christi

frontal adj frontal

fror imperf von **frieren**

Frosch (-(e)s, Frösche) m frog

Frost (-(e)s, Fröste) m frost; **bei ~** in frosty weather; **Frostschutzmittel** nt anti-freeze

Frottee nt terry(cloth); **Frottier(hand)tuch** nt towel

Frucht (-, Früchte) f (a. fig) fruit; (Getreide) corn; **Fruchteis** nt fruit-flavoured ice-cream; **Früchtetee** m fruit tea; **fruchtig** adj fruity; **Fruchtpresse** f juicer; **Fruchtsaft** m fruit juice; **Fruchtsalat** m fruit salad

früh adj, adv early; **heute ~** this morning; **um fünf Uhr ~** at five (o'clock) in the morning; **~ genug** soon enough; **früher** adj earlier; (ehemalig) former ▷ adv formerly, in the past; **frühestens** adv at the earliest

Frühjahr nt, **Frühling** m spring; **Frühlingsrolle** f spring roll; **Frühlingszwiebel** f spring onion (Brit), scallion (US)

frühmorgens adv early in the morning

Frühstück nt breakfast; **frühstücken** vi to have breakfast; **Frühstücksbüfett** nt breakfast buffet; **Frühstücksfernsehen** nt breakfast television; **Frühstücksspeck** m bacon

frühzeitig adj early

Frust (-s) m (fam) frustration; **frustrieren** vt to frustrate

Fuchs (-es, Füchse) m fox

fühlen vt, vi to feel ▷ vr: **sich ~** to feel

fuhr imperf von **fahren**

führen vt to lead; (Geschäft) to run; (Name) to bear; (Buch) to keep ▷ vi to lead, to be in the lead ▷ vr: **sich ~** to behave; **Führerschein** m driving licence (Brit), driver's license (US); **Führung** f leadership; (eines Unternehmens) management; (Mil) command; (in Museum, Stadt) guided tour; **in ~ liegen** to be in the lead

füllen vt to fill; (Gastr) to stuff ▷ vr: **sich ~** to fill

Füller (-s, -) m, **Füllfederhalter** (-s, -) m fountain pen

Füllung f filling

Fund (-(e)s, -e) m find; **Fundbüro** nt lost property office (Brit), lost and found (US); **Fundsachen** pl lost property sing

fünf num five; **Fünf** (-, -en) f five; (Schulnote) ≈ E; **fünfhundert** num five hundred; **fünfmal** adv five times; **fünfte(r, s)** adj fifth; siehe auch **dritte; Fünftel** (-s, -) nt (Bruchteil) fifth; **fünfzehn** num fifteen; **fünfzehnte(r, s)** adj fifteenth; siehe auch **dritte; fünfzig** num fifty; **fünfzigste(r, s)** adj fiftieth

Funk (-s) m radio; **über ~** by radio

Funke (-ns, -n) m spark; **funkeln** vi to sparkle

Funkgerät nt radio set; **Funktaxi** nt radio taxi, radio cab

Funktion f function; **funktionieren** vi to work, to function; **Funktionstaste** f (Inform) function key

für prep +akk for; **was ~ (ein) ...?** what kind (o sort) of ...?; **Tag ~ Tag** day after day

Furcht (-) f fear; **furchtbar** adj terrible; **fürchten** vt to be afraid of, to fear ▷ vr: **sich ~** to be afraid (vor +dat of); **fürchterlich** adj awful

füreinander adv for each other

fürs kontr von **für das**

Fürst(in) (-en, -en) m(f) prince/princess; **Fürstentum** nt principality; **fürstlich** adj (fig) splendid

Furunkel (-s, -) nt boil

Furz (-es, -e) m (vulg) fart; **furzen** vi (vulg) to fart

Fuß (-es, Füße) m foot; (von Glas, Säule etc) base; (von Möbel) leg; **zu ~** on foot; **zu ~ gehen** to walk; **Fußball** m football (Brit), soccer; **Fußballmannschaft** f football (Brit) (o soccer) team; **Fußballplatz** m football pitch (Brit), soccer field (US); **Fußballspiel** nt football (Brit) (o soccer) match; **Fußballspieler(in)** m(f) footballer (Brit), soccer player; **Fußboden** m floor; **Fußgänger(in)** (-s, -) m(f) pedestrian; **Fußgängerüberweg** m pedestrian crossing (Brit), crosswalk (US); **Fußgängerzone** f pedestrian precinct (Brit) (o zone (US)); **Fußgelenk** nt ankle; **Fußpilz** m athlete's foot; **Fußtritt** m kick; **jdm einen ~ geben** to give sb a kick, to kick sb; **Fußweg** m footpath

Futon (-s, -s) m futon

Futter (-s, -) nt feed; (Heu etc) fodder; (Stoff) lining; **füttern** vt to feed; (Kleidung) to line

Futur (-s, -e) nt (Ling) future (tense)

Fuzzi (-s, -s) m (fam) guy

g

gab imperf von **geben**

Gabe (-, -n) f gift

Gabel (-, -n) f fork; **Gabelung** f fork

Gage (-, -n) f fee

gähnen vi to yawn

Galerie f gallery

Galle (-, -n) f gall; (Organ) gall bladder; **Gallenstein** m gallstone

Galopp (-s) m gallop; **galoppieren** vi to gallop

galt imperf von **gelten**

Gameboy® (-s, -s) m Gameboy®

Gamer(in) (-s, -) m(f) (Inform) gamer

Gameshow f game show

gammeln vi to loaf around; **Gammler(in)** (-s, -) m(f) layabout

gang adj: **~ und gäbe sein** to be quite normal

Gang (-(e)s, Gänge) m walk; (im Flugzeug) aisle; (Essen, Ablauf) course; (Flur etc) corridor;

(Durchgang) passage; (Auto) gear; **den zweiten ~ einlegen** to change into second (gear); **etw in ~ bringen** to get sth going; **Gangschaltung** f gears pl; **Gangway** (-, -s) f (Aviat) steps pl; (Naut) gangway

Gans (-, Gänse) f goose; **Gänseblümchen** nt daisy; **Gänsehaut** f goose pimples pl (Brit), goose bumps pl (US)

ganz adj whole; (vollständig) complete; **~ Europa** all of Europe; **sein ~es Geld** all his money; **den ~en Tag** all day; ▷ adv quite; (völlig) completely; **es hat mir ~ gut gefallen** I quite liked it; **~ schön viel** quite a lot; **~ und gar nicht** not at all; **das ist etwas ~ anderes** that's a completely different matter; **ganztägig** adj all-day; (Arbeit, Stelle) full-time; **ganztags** adv (arbeiten) full-time; **Ganztagsschule** f all-day school; **Ganztagsstelle** f full-time job

gar adj done, cooked ▷ adv at all; **~ nicht/nichts** not/nothing at all; **~ nicht schlecht** not bad at all

Garage (-, -n) f garage

Garantie f guarantee; **garantieren** vt to guarantee

Garderobe (-, -n) f (Kleidung) wardrobe; (Abgabe) cloakroom

Gardine f curtain

Garn (-(e)s, -e) nt thread

Garnele (-, -n) f shrimp

garnieren vt to decorate; (Speisen) to garnish

Garten (-s, Gärten) m garden; **Gärtner(in)** (-s, -) m(f) gardener; **Gärtnerei** f nursery; (Gemüsegärtnerei) market garden (Brit), truck farm (US)

Gas (-es, -e) nt gas; **~ geben** (Auto) to accelerate; (fig) to get a move on; **Gasanzünder** m gas lighter; **Gasbrenner** m gas burner;

Gasflasche f gas bottle;
Gasheizung f gas heating;
Gasherd m gas stove, gas cooker
(Brit); **Gaskocher** (-s, -) m
camping stove; **Gaspedal** nt
accelerator, gas pedal (US)
Gasse (-, -n) f alley
Gast (-es, Gäste) m guest; **Gäste
haben** to have guests;
Gastarbeiter(in) m(f) foreign
worker; **Gästebett** nt spare bed;
Gästebuch nt visitors' book;
Gästehaus nt guest house;
Gästezimmer nt guest room;
gastfreundlich adj hospitable;
Gastfreundschaft f hospitality;
Gastgeber(in) (-s, -) m(f) host/
hostess; **Gasthaus** nt, **Gasthof** m
inn; **Gastland** nt host country
Gastritis (-) f gastritis
Gastronomie f catering trade
Gastspiel nt (Sport) away game;
Gaststätte f restaurant;
(Trinklokal) pub (Brit), bar;
Gastwirt(in) m(f) landlord/-lady
GAU (-s, -s) m akr = **größter
anzunehmender Unfall** MCA
Gaumen (-s, -) m palate
Gaze (-, -n) f gauze
geb. adj abk = **geboren** b. ▷ adj
abk = **geborene** née; siehe **geboren**
Gebäck (-(e)s, -e) nt pastries pl;
(Kekse) biscuits pl (Brit), cookies pl
(US)
gebacken pp von **backen**
Gebärdensprache f sign
language
Gebärmutter f womb
Gebäude (-s, -) nt building
geben (gab, gegeben) vt, vi to give
(jdm etw sb sth, sth to sb); (Karten)
to deal; **lass dir eine Quittung
~** ask for a receipt ▷ vt impers: **es
gibt** there is/are; (in Zukunft) there
will be; **das gibt's nicht** I don't
believe it ▷ vr: **sich ~** (sich
verhalten) to behave, to act; **das

gibt sich wieder it'll sort itself out
Gebet (-(e)s, -e) nt prayer
gebeten pp von **bitten**
Gebiet (-(e)s, -e) nt area;
(Hoheitsgebiet) territory; (fig) field
gebildet adj educated; (belesen)
well-read
Gebirge (-s, -) nt mountains pl;
gebirgig adj mountainous
Gebiss (-es, -e) nt teeth pl;
(künstlich) dentures pl; **gebissen**
pp von **beißen**; **Gebissreiniger** m
denture tablets pl
Gebläse (-s, -) nt fan, blower
geblasen pp von **blasen**
geblieben pp von **bleiben**
gebogen pp von **biegen**
geboren pp von **gebären** ▷ adj
born; **Andrea Jordan, geborene
Christian** Andrea Jordan, née
Christian
geborgen pp von **bergen** ▷ adj
secure, safe
geboten pp von **bieten**
gebracht pp von **bringen**
gebrannt pp von **brennen**
gebraten pp von **braten**
gebrauchen vt to use;
Gebrauchsanweisung f direc-
tions pl for use; **gebrauchsfertig**
adj ready to use; **gebraucht** adj
used; **etw ~ kaufen** to buy sth
secondhand; **Gebrauchtwagen**
m secondhand (o used) car
gebräunt adj tanned
gebrochen pp von **brechen**
Gebühr (-, -en) f charge; (Maut)
toll; (Honorar) fee; **Gebühren-
einheit** f (Tel) unit;
gebührenfrei adj free of charge;
(Telefonnummer) freefone® (Brit),
toll-free (US); **gebührenpflichtig**
adj subject to charges; **~e Straße**
toll road
gebunden pp von **binden**
Geburt (-, -en) f birth; **gebürtig**
adj: **er ist ~er Schweizer** he is

Swiss by birth; **Geburtsdatum**
nt date of birth; **Geburtsjahr** nt
year of birth; **Geburtsname** m
birth name; (einer Frau) maiden
name; **Geburtsort** m birthplace;
Geburtstag m birthday;
herzlichen Glückwunsch zum ~!
Happy Birthday; **Geburtsurkunde**
f birth certificate
Gebüsch (-(e)s, -e) nt bushes pl
gedacht pp von **denken**
Gedächtnis (-ses, -se) nt memory; **im
~ behalten** to remember
Gedanke (-ns, -n) m thought;
sich (dat) **über etw** (akk) **~n
machen** to think about sth;
(besorgt) to be worried about sth;
Gedankenstrich m dash
Gedeck (-(e)s, -e) nt place
setting; (Speisenfolge) set meal
Gedenkstätte f memorial;
Gedenktafel f commemorative
plaque
Gedicht (-(e)s, -e) nt poem
Gedränge (-s) nt crush, crowd
gedrungen pp von **dringen**
Geduld (-) f patience; **geduldig**
adj patient
gedurft pp von **dürfen**
geehrt adj: **Sehr ~er Herr Young**
Dear Mr Young
geeignet adj suitable
Gefahr (-, -en) f danger; **auf
eigene ~** at one's own risk; **außer
~** out of danger; **gefährden** vt to
endanger
gefahren pp von **fahren**
gefährlich adj dangerous
Gefälle (-s, -) nt gradient, slope
gefallen pp von **fallen** ▷ irr vi:
jdm ~ to please sb; **er/es gefällt
mir** I like him/it; **sich** (dat) **etw
~ lassen** to put up with sth
Gefallen (-s, -) m: **jdm
einen ~ tun** to do sb a favour
gefälligst adv ..., will you!
~ still! be quiet, will you!

gefangen pp von **fangen**
Gefängnis (-ses, -se) nt prison
Gefäß (-es, -e) nt (Behälter)
container, receptacle; (Anat, Bot)
vessel
gefasst adj composed, calm; **auf
etw** (akk) **~ sein** to be prepared (o
ready) for sth
geflochten pp von **flechten**
geflogen pp von **fliegen**
geflossen pp von **fließen**
Geflügel (-s) nt poultry
gefragt adj in demand
gefressen pp von **fressen**
Gefrierbeutel m freezer bag;
gefrieren irr vi to freeze;
Gefrierfach nt freezer
compartment; **Gefrierschrank**
m (upright) freezer; **Gefriertruhe**
f (chest) freezer
gefroren pp von **frieren**
Gefühl (-(e)s, -e) nt feeling
gefunden pp von **finden**
gegangen pp von **gehen**
gegeben pp von **geben**
gegebenenfalls adv if need
be

O   SCHLÜSSELWORT

gegen prep +akk 1 against; **nichts
gegen jdn haben** to have nothing
against sb; **X gegen Y** (Sport, Jur) X
versus Y; **ein Mittel gegen
Schnupfen** something for colds
2 (in Richtung auf) towards; **gegen
Osten** to(wards) the east; **gegen
Abend** towards evening; **gegen
einen Baum fahren** to drive into a
tree
3 (ungefähr) round about; **gegen 3
Uhr** around 3 o'clock
4 (gegenüber) around; (ungefähr)
around; **gerecht gegen alle** fair to
all
5 (im Austausch für) for; **gegen bar**
for cash; **gegen Quittung** against

a receipt
6 (verglichen mit) compared with

Gegend (-, -en) f area; **hier in der ~** around here

gegeneinander adv against one another

Gegenfahrbahn f opposite lane; **Gegenmittel** nt remedy (gegen for); **Gegenrichtung** f opposite direction; **Gegensatz** m contrast; **im ~ zu** in contrast to; **gegensätzlich** adj conflicting; **gegenseitig** adj mutual; **sich ~ helfen** to help each other

Gegenstand m object; (Thema) subject

Gegenteil nt opposite; **im ~ on** the contrary; **gegenteilig** adj opposite, contrary

gegenüber prep +dat opposite; (zu jdm) to(wards); (angesichts) in the face of ▷ adv opposite; **gegenüber|stehen** vt to face; (Problemen) to be faced with; **gegenüber|stellen** vt to confront (dat with); (fig) compare (dat with)

Gegenverkehr m oncoming traffic; **Gegenwart** (-) f present (tense)

Gegenwind m headwind

gegessen pp von **essen**
geglichen pp von **gleichen**
geglitten pp von **gleiten**
Gegner(in) (-s, -) m(f) opponent
gegolten pp von **gelten**
gegossen pp von **gießen**
gegraben pp von **graben**
gegriffen pp von **greifen**
gehabt pp von **haben**
Gehackte(s) nt mince(d meat) (Brit), ground meat (US)
Gehalt ▷ (-(e)s, Gehälter) nt salary
gehalten pp von **halten**
gehangen pp von **hängen**

gehässig adj spiteful, nasty
gehauen pp von **hauen**
gehbehindert adj: **sie ist ~** she can't walk properly

geheim adj secret; **etw ~ halten** to keep sth secret; **Geheimnis** nt secret; (rätselhaft) mystery; **geheimnisvoll** adj mysterious; **Geheimnummer** f, **Geheimzahl** f (von Kreditkarte) PIN number

geheißen pp von **heißen**

gehen (ging, gegangen) vt, vi to go; (zu Fuß) to walk; (funktionieren) to work; **über die Straße ~** to cross the street; **~ nach** (Fenster) to face ▷ vi impers: **wie geht es (dir)?** how are you (o things)?; **mir/ihm geht es gut** I'm/he's (doing) fine; **geht das?** is that possible?; **geht's noch?** can you still manage?; **es geht** not too bad, OK; **das geht nicht** that's not on; **es geht um ...** it's about ...

Gehirn (-(e)s, -e) nt brain; **Gehirnerschütterung** f concussion

gehoben pp von **heben**
geholfen pp von **helfen**
Gehör (-(e)s) nt hearing
gehorchen vi to obey (jdm sb)
gehören vi to belong (jdm to sb); **wem gehört das Buch?** whose book is this?; **gehört es dir?** is it yours? ▷ vr impers: **das gehört sich nicht** it's not done
gehörlos adj deaf
gehorsam adj obedient
Gehsteig, Gehweg (-s, -e) m pavement (Brit), sidewalk (US)
Geier (-s, -) m vulture
Geige (-, -n) f violin
geil adj randy (Brit), horny (US); (fam: toll) fantastic
Geisel (-, -n) f hostage
Geist (-(e)s, -er) m spirit; (Gespenst) ghost; (Verstand) mind; **Geisterbahn** f ghost train, tunnel

of horror (US); **Geisterfahrer(in)** m(f) person driving the wrong way on the motorway

geizig adj stingy

gekannt pp von **kennen**

geklungen pp von **klingen**

geknickt adj (fig) dejected

gekniffen pp von **kneifen**

gekommen pp von **kommen**

gekonnt pp von **können** ▷ adj skilful

gekrochen pp von **kriechen**

Gel (-s, -s) nt gel

Gelächter (-s, -) nt laughter

geladen pp von **laden** ▷ adj loaded; (Elek) live; (fig) furious

gelähmt adj paralysed

Gelände (-s, -) nt land, terrain; (Fabrik, Sportgelände) grounds pl; (Baugelände) site

Geländer (-s, -) nt railing; (Treppengeländer) banister

Geländewagen m off-road vehicle

gelang imperf von **gelingen**

gelassen pp von **lassen** ▷ adj calm, composed

Gelatine f gelatine

gelaufen pp von **laufen**

gelaunt adj: **gut/schlecht ~** in a good/bad mood

gelb adj yellow; (Ampel) amber, yellow (US); **gelblich** adj yellowish; **Gelbsucht** f jaundice

Geld (-(e)s, -er) nt money; **Geldautomat** m cash machine (o dispenser (Brit)), ATM (US); **Geldbeutel** m, **Geldbörse** f purse; **Geldbuße** f fine; **Geldschein** m (bank)note (Brit), bill (US); **Geldstrafe** f fine; **Geldstück** nt coin; **Geldwechsel** m exchange of money; (Ort) bureau de change; **Geldwechselautomat** m, **Geldwechsler** (-s, -) m change machine

Gelee (-s, -s) nt jelly

gelegen pp von **liegen** ▷ adj situated; (passend) convenient; **etw kommt jdm ~** sth is convenient for sb

Gelegenheit f opportunity; (Anlass) occasion

gelegentlich adj occasional ▷ adv occasionally; (bei Gelegenheit) some time (or other)

Gelenk (-(e)s, -e) nt joint

gelernt adj skilled

gelesen pp von **lesen**

geliehen pp von **leihen**

gelingen (gelang, gelungen) vi to succeed; **es ist mir gelungen, ihn zu erreichen** I managed to get hold of him

gelitten pp von **leiden**

gelockt adj curly

gelogen pp von **lügen**

gelten (galt, gegolten) vt (wert sein) to be worth; **jdm viel/wenig ~** to mean a lot/not to mean much to sb ▷ vi (gültig sein) to be valid; (erlaubt sein) to be allowed; **jdm ~** (gemünzt sein auf) to be meant for (o aimed at) sb); **etw ~ lassen** to accept sth; **als etw ~** to be considered to be sth; **Geltungsdauer f: eine ~ von fünf Tagen haben** to be valid for five days

gelungen pp von **gelingen**

gemahlen pp von **mahlen**

Gemälde (-s, -) nt painting, picture

gemäß prep +dat in accordance with ▷ adj appropriate (dat to)

gemein adj (niederträchtig) mean, nasty; (gewöhnlich) common

Gemeinde (-, -n) f district, community; (Pfarrgemeinde) parish; (Kirchengemeinde) congregation

gemeinsam adj joint, common ▷ adv together, jointly; **das Haus**

gehört uns beiden ~ the house belongs to both of us
Gemeinschaft f community; **~ Unabhängiger Staaten** Commonwealth of Independent States
gemeint pp von **meinen**; **das war nicht so ~** I didn't mean it like that
gemessen pp von **messen**
gemieden pp von **meiden**
gemischt adj mixed
gemocht pp von **mögen**
Gemüse (-s, -) nt vegetables pl; **Gemüsehändler(in)** m(f) greengrocer
gemusst pp von **müssen**
gemustert adj patterned
gemütlich adj comfortable, cosy; (Mensch) good-natured, easy-going; **mach es dir ~** make yourself at home
genannt pp von **nennen**
genau adj exact, precise ▷ adv exactly, precisely; **~ in der Mitte** right in the middle; **es mit etw ~ nehmen** to be particular about sth; **~ genommen** strictly speaking; **ich weiß es ~** I know for certain (o for sure); **genauso** adv exactly the same (way); **~ gut/viel/viele Leute** just as well/much/many people (wie as)
genehmigen vt to approve; **sich** (dat) **etw ~** to indulge in sth; **Genehmigung** f approval
Generalkonsulat nt consulate general
Generation f generation
Genf (-s) nt Geneva; **~er See** Lake Geneva
Genforschung f genetic research
genial adj brilliant
Genick (-(e)s, -e) nt (back of the) neck
Genie (-s, -s) nt genius
genieren vr: **sich ~** to feel

awkward; **ich geniere mich vor ihm** he makes me feel embarrassed
genießen (genoss, genossen) vt to enjoy
Genitiv m genitive (case)
genmanipuliert adj genetically modified, GM
Genom (-s, -e) nt genome
genommen pp von **nehmen**
genoss imperf von **genießen**
genossen pp von **genießen**
Gentechnik f genetic technology; **gentechnisch** adv; **~ verändert** genetically modified, GM
genug adv enough
genügen vi to be enough (jdm for sb); **danke, das genügt** thanks, that's enough (o that will do)
Genuss (-es, Genüsse) m pleasure; (Zusichnehmen) consumption
geöffnet adj (Geschäft etc) open
Geografie f geography
Geologie f geology
Georgien (-s) nt Georgia
Gepäck (-(e)s) nt luggage (Brit), baggage; **Gepäckabfertigung** f luggage (Brit) (o baggage) check-in; **Gepäckablage** f luggage (o baggage) rack; **Gepäckannahme** f (zur Beförderung) luggage (Brit) (o baggage) office; (zur Aufbewahrung) left-luggage office (Brit), baggage checkroom (US); **Gepäckaufbewahrung** f left-luggage office (Brit), baggage checkroom (US); **Gepäckausgabe** f luggage (Brit) (o baggage) office; (am Flughafen) baggage reclaim; **Gepäckband** nt luggage (Brit) (o baggage) conveyor; **Gepäckkontrolle** f luggage (Brit) (o baggage) check; **Gepäckstück** nt item of luggage (Brit) (o baggage (US)); **Gepäckträger** m porter; (an Fahrrad) carrier;

Gepäckversicherung f luggage (Brit) (o baggage) insurance;
Gepäckwagen m luggage van (Brit), baggage car (US)
gepfiffen pp von **pfeifen**
gepflegt adj well-groomed; (Park) well looked after
gequollen pp von **quellen**

⭕ SCHLÜSSELWORT

gerade adj straight; (aufrecht)
upright; **eine gerade Zahl** an even number
▷ adv 1 (genau) just, exactly;
(speziell) especially; **gerade deshalb** that's just o exactly why;
das ist es ja gerade! that's just it!;
gerade du you especially; **warum gerade ich?** why me (of all people)?; **jetzt gerade nicht!** not now!; **gerade neben** right next to
2 (eben, soeben) just; **er wollte gerade aufstehen** he was just about to get up; **gerade erst** only just; **gerade noch** (only) just

geradeaus adv straight ahead
gerannt pp von **rennen**
geraspelt adj grated
Gerät (-(e)s, -e) nt device, gadget; (Werkzeug) tool; (Radio, Fernseher) set; (Zubehör) equipment
geraten pp von **raten** ▷ irr vi to turn out; **gut/schlecht ~** to turn out well/badly; **an jdn ~** to come across sb; **in etw** (akk) ~ to get into sth
geräuchert adj smoked
geräumig adj roomy
Geräusch (-(e)s, -e) nt sound; (unangenehm) noise
gerecht adj fair; (Strafe, Belohnung) just; **jdm/einer Sache ~ werden** to do justice to sb/sth
gereizt adj irritable

Gericht (-(e)s, -e) nt (Jur) court; (Essen) dish
gerieben pp von **reiben**
gering adj small; (unbedeutend) slight; (niedrig) low; (Zeit) short;
geringfügig adj slight, minor
▷ adv slightly
gerissen pp von **reißen**
geritten pp von **reiten**
gern(e) adv willingly, gladly; **etw ~ tun** to like doing sth;
~ geschehen you're welcome;
gern haben, gern mögen irr vt to like
gerochen pp von **riechen**
Gerste (-, -n) f barley;
Gerstenkorn nt (im Auge) stye
Geruch (-(e)s, Gerüche) m smell
Gerücht (-(e)s, -e) nt rumour
gerufen pp von **rufen**
Gerümpel (-s) nt junk
gerungen pp von **ringen**
Gerüst (-(e)s, -e) nt (auf Bau) scaffolding; (Gestell) trestle; (fig) framework (zu of)
gesalzen pp von **salzen**
gesamt adj whole, entire; (Kosten) total; (Werke) complete;
Gesamtschule f = comprehensive school
gesandt pp von **senden**
Gesäß (-es, -e) nt bottom
geschaffen pp von **schaffen**
Geschäft (-(e)s, -e) nt business; (Laden) shop; (Geschäftsabschluss) deal; **geschäftlich** adj commercial
▷ adv on business; **Geschäftsfrau** f businesswoman; **Geschäftsführer(in)** m(f) managing director; (von Laden) manager;
Geschäftsleitung f executive board; **Geschäftsmann** m businessman; **Geschäftsreise** f business trip; **Geschäftsstraße** f shopping street; **Geschäftszeiten** pl business (o opening) hours pl

geschehen *(geschah, geschehen)* vi to happen

Geschenk *(-(e)s, -e)* nt present, gift; **Geschenkgutschein** m gift voucher; **Geschenkpapier** nt gift-wrapping paper, giftwrap

Geschichte *(-, -n)* f story; *(Sache)* affair; *(Hist)* history

geschickt *adj* skilful

geschieden *pp von* **scheiden**
▷ *adj* divorced

geschienen *pp von* **scheinen**

Geschirr *(-(e)s, -e)* nt crockery; *(zum Kochen)* pots and pans *pl*; *(von Pferd)* harness; **~ spülen** to do (o wash) the dishes, to do the washing-up *(Brit)*; **Geschirrspülmaschine** f dishwasher; **Geschirrspülmittel** nt washing-up liquid *(Brit)*, dishwashing liquid *(US)*; **Geschirrtuch** nt tea towel *(Brit)*, dish towel *(US)*

geschissen *pp von* **scheißen**

geschlafen *pp von* **schlafen**

geschlagen *pp von* **schlagen**

Geschlecht *(-(e)s, -er)* nt sex; *(Ling)* gender; **Geschlechtskrankheit** f sexually transmitted disease, STD; **Geschlechtsorgan** nt sexual organ; **Geschlechtsverkehr** m sexual intercourse

geschlichen *pp von* **schleichen**

geschliffen *pp von* **schleifen**

geschlossen *adj* closed

Geschmack *(-(e)s, Geschmäcke)* m taste; **geschmacklos** *adj* tasteless; **Geschmack(s)sache** f: **das ist ~** that's a matter of taste; **geschmackvoll** *adj* tasteful

geschmissen *pp von* **schmeißen**

geschmolzen *pp von* **schmelzen**

geschnitten *pp von* **schneiden**

geschoben *pp von* **schieben**

Geschoss *(-es, -e)* nt *(Stockwerk)* floor

geschossen *pp von* **schießen**

Geschrei *(-s)* nt cries *pl*; *(fig)* fuss

geschrieben *pp von* **schreiben**

geschrie(e)n *pp von* **schreien**

geschützt *adj* protected

Geschwätz *(-es)* nt chatter; *(Klatsch)* gossip; **geschwätzig** *adj* talkative, gossipy

geschweige *adv:* **~ (denn)** let alone

geschwiegen *pp von* **schweigen**

Geschwindigkeit f speed; *(Phys)* velocity; **Geschwindigkeitsbegrenzung** f speed limit

Geschwister *pl* brothers and sisters *pl*

geschwollen *adj (angeschwollen)* swollen; *(Rede)* pompous

geschwommen *pp von* **schwimmen**

geschworen *pp von* **schwören**

Geschwulst *(-, Geschwülste)* f growth

Geschwür *(-(e)s, -e)* nt ulcer

gesehen *pp von* **sehen**

gesellig *adj* sociable; **Gesellschaft** f society; *(Begleitung)* company; *(Abend~)* party; **~ mit beschränkter Haftung** limited company *(Brit)*, limited corporation *(US)*

gesessen *pp von* **sitzen**

Gesetz *(-es, -e)* nt law; **gesetzlich** *adj* legal; **~er Feiertag** public (o bank *(Brit)* o legal *(US)*) holiday; **gesetzwidrig** *adj* illegal

Gesicht *(-(e)s, -er)* nt face; *(Miene)* expression; **mach doch nicht so ein ~!** stop pulling such a face; **Gesichtscreme** f face cream; **Gesichtswasser** nt toner

gesoffen *pp von* **saufen**

gesogen *pp von* **saugen**

gespannt *adj* tense; *(begierig)* eager; **ich bin ~, ob ...** I wonder if ...; **auf etw/jdn ~ sein** to look

forward to sth/to seeing sb
Gespenst (-(e)s, -er) nt ghost
gesperrt adj closed
gesponnen pp von **spinnen**
Gespräch (-(e)s, -e) nt talk,
conversation; (Diskussion)
discussion; (Anruf) call
gesprochen pp von **sprechen**
gesprungen pp von **springen**
Gestalt (-, -en) f form, shape;
(Mensch) figure
gestanden pp von **stehen**,
gestehen
Gestank (-(e)s) m stench
gestatten vt to permit, to allow;
~ **Sie?** may I?
Geste (-, -n) f gesture
gestehen irr vt to confess
gestern adv yesterday;
~ **Abend/Morgen** yesterday
evening/morning
gestiegen pp von **steigen**
gestochen pp von **stechen**
gestohlen pp von **stehlen**
gestorben pp von **sterben**
gestört adj disturbed; (Empfang)
poor
gestoßen pp von **stoßen**
gestreift adj striped
gestrichen pp von **streichen**
gestritten pp von **streiten**
gestunken pp von **stinken**
gesund adj healthy; **wieder**
~ **werden** to get better;
Gesundheit f health; ~! bless
you!; **gesundheitsschädlich** adj
unhealthy
gesungen pp von **singen**
gesunken pp von **sinken**
getan pp von **tun**
getragen pp von **tragen**
Getränk (-(e)s, -e) nt drink;
Getränkeautomat m drinks
machine; **Getränkekarte** f list
of drinks
Getreide (-s, -) nt cereals pl,
grain

getrennt adj separate; ~ **leben**
to live apart; ~ **zahlen** to pay
separately
getreten pp von **treten**
Getriebe (-s, -) nt (Auto) gearbox
getrieben pp von **treiben**
Getriebeschaden m gearbox
damage
getroffen pp von **treffen**
getrunken pp von **trinken**
Getue nt fuss
geübt adj experienced
gewachsen pp von **wachsen**
▷ adj: **jdm/einer Sache** ~ **sein** to
be a match for sb/up to sth
Gewähr (-) f guarantee; **keine**
~ **übernehmen für** to accept no
responsibility for
Gewalt (-, -en) f (Macht) power;
(Kontrolle) control; (große Kraft)
force; (~taten) violence; **mit aller**
~ with all one's might; **gewaltig**
adj tremendous; (Irrtum) huge
gewandt pp von **wenden** ▷ adj
(flink) nimble; (geschickt) skilful
gewann imperf von **gewinnen**
gewaschen pp von **waschen**
Gewebe (-s, -) nt (Stoff) fabric;
(Bio) tissue
Gewehr (-(e)s, -e) nt rifle, gun
Geweih (-(e)s, -e) nt antlers pl
gewellt adj (Haare) wavy
gewendet pp von **wenden**
Gewerbe (-s, -) nt trade;
Gewerbegebiet nt industrial
estate (Brit) (o park (US));
gewerblich adj commercial
Gewerkschaft f trade union
gewesen pp von **sein**
Gewicht (-(e)s, -e) nt weight;
(fig) importance
gewiesen pp von **weisen**
Gewinn (-(e)s, -e) m profit; (bei
Spiel) winnings pl; **gewinnen**
(gewann, gewonnen) vt to win;
(erwerben) to gain; (Kohle, Öl) to
extract ▷ vi to win; (profitieren) to

gain; **Gewinner(in)** (-s, -) m(f) winner

gewiss adj certain ▷ adv certainly

Gewissen (-s, -) nt conscience; **ein gutes/schlechtes ~ haben** to have a clear/bad conscience

Gewitter (-s, -) nt thunderstorm; **gewittern** vi impers: **es gewittert** it's thundering

gewogen pp von **wiegen**

gewöhnen vt jdn an etw (akk) ~ to accustom sb to sth ▷ vr: **sich an jdn/etw ~** to get used (o accustomed) to sb/sth; **Gewohnheit** f habit; (Brauch) custom; **gewöhnlich** adj usual; (durchschnittlich) ordinary; (pej) common; **wie ~** as usual; **gewohnt** adj usual; **etw ~ sein** to be used to sth

gewonnen pp von **gewinnen**

geworben pp von **werben**

geworden pp von **werden**

geworfen pp von **werfen**

Gewürz (-es, -e) nt spice; **Gewürznelke** f clove; **gewürzt** adj seasoned

gewusst pp von **wissen**

Gezeiten pl tides pl

gezogen pp von **ziehen**

gezwungen pp von **zwingen**

Gibraltar (-s) nt Gibraltar

Gicht (-) f gout

Giebel (-s, -) m gable

gierig adj greedy

gießen (goss, gegossen) vt to pour; (Blumen) to water; (Metall) to cast; **Gießkanne** f watering can

Gift (-(e)s, -e) nt poison; **giftig** adj poisonous

Gigabyte nt gigabyte

Gin (-s, -s) m gin

ging imperf von **gehen**

Gin Tonic (-(s), -s) m gin and tonic

Gipfel (-s, -) m summit, peak; (Pol) summit; (fig: Höhepunkt)

height

Gips (-es, -e) m (a. Med) plaster; **Gipsbein** nt: **sie hat ein ~** she's got her leg in plaster; **Gipsverband** m plaster cast

Giraffe (-, -n) f giraffe

Girokonto nt current account (Brit), checking account (US)

Gitarre (-, -n) f guitar

Gitter (-s, -) nt bars pl

glänzen vi (a. fig) to shine; **glänzend** adj shining; (fig) brilliant

Glas (-es, Gläser) nt glass; (Marmelade) jar; **zwei ~ Wein** two glasses of wine; **Glascontainer** m bottle bank; **Glaser(in)** m(f) glazier; **Glasscheibe** f pane (of glass); **Glassplitter** m splinter of glass

Glasur f glaze; (Gastr) icing

glatt adj smooth; (rutschig) slippery; (Lüge) downright; **Glatteis** nt (black) ice; **Glätteisen** nt hair straighteners pl

Glatze (-, -n) f bald head; (fam: Skinhead) skinhead

glauben vt, vi to believe (an +akk in); (meinen) to think; **jdm ~** to believe sb

gleich adj equal; (identisch) same, identical; **alle Menschen sind ~** all people are the same; **es ist mir ~** it's all the same to me ▷ adv equally; (sofort) straight away; (bald) in a minute; **~ groß/alt** the same size/age; **~ nach/an** after/at; **Gleichberechtigung** f equal rights pl; **gleichen** (glich, geglichen) vi: **jdm/einer Sache ~** to be like sb/sth ▷ vr: **sich ~** to be alike; **gleichfalls** adv likewise; **danke ~!** thanks, and the same to you; **gleichgültig** adj indifferent; **gleichmäßig** adj regular; (Verteilung) even, equal;

gleichzeitig adj simultaneous ▷ adv at the same time
Gleis (-es, -e) nt track, rails pl; (Bahnsteig) platform
gleiten (glitt, geglitten) vi to glide; (rutschen) to slide; **Gleitschirmfliegen** (-s) nt paragliding
Gletscher (-s, -) m glacier; **Gletscherskifahren** nt glacier skiing; **Gletscherspalte** f crevasse
glich imperf von **gleichen**
Glied (-(e)s, -er) nt (Arm, Bein) limb; (von Kette) link; (Penis) penis; **Gliedmaßen** pl limbs pl
glitschig adj slippery
glitt imperf von **gleiten**
glitzern vi to glitter; (Sterne) to twinkle
Glocke (-, -n) f bell; **Glockenspiel** nt chimes pl
Glotze (-, -n) f (fam: TV) box; **glotzen** vi (fam) to stare
Glück (-(e)s) nt luck; (Freude) happiness; ~ **haben** to be lucky; **viel** ~! good luck; **zum** ~ fortunately; **glücklich** adj lucky; (froh) happy; **glücklicherweise** adj fortunately; **Glückwunsch** m congratulations pl; **herzlichen** ~ **zur bestandenen Prüfung** congratulations on passing your exam; **herzlichen** ~ **zum Geburtstag!** Happy Birthday
Glühbirne f light bulb; **glühen** vi to glow; **Glühwein** m mulled wine
GmbH (-, -s) f abk = **Gesellschaft mit beschränkter Haftung** ≈ Ltd (Brit), ≈ Inc (US)
Gokart (-(s), -s) m go-kart
Gold (-(e)s) nt gold; **golden** adj gold; (fig) golden; **Goldfisch** m goldfish; **Goldmedaille** f gold medal

Golf (-(e)s, -e) m gulf; **der** ~ **von Biskaya** the Bay of Biscay ▷ (-s) nt golf; **Golfplatz** m golf course; **Golfschläger** m golf club
Gondel (-, -n) f gondola; (Seilbahn) cable-car
gönnen vt: **ich gönne es ihm** I'm really pleased for him; **sich** (dat) **etw** ~ to allow oneself sth
googeln vt to google
goss imperf von **gießen**
gotisch adj Gothic
Gott (-es, Götter) m God; (Gottheit) god; **Gottesdienst** m service; **Göttin** f goddess
Grab (-(e)s, Gräber) nt grave
graben (grub, gegraben) vt to dig; **Graben** (-s, Gräben) m ditch
Grabstein m gravestone
Grad (-(e)s, -e) m degree; **wir haben 30** ~ **Celsius** it's 30 degrees Celsius, it's 86 degrees Fahrenheit; **bis zu einem gewissen** ~ up to a certain extent
Graf (-en, -en) m count; (in Großbritannien) earl
Graffiti pl graffiti sing
Grafik (-, -en) f graph; (Kunstwerk) graphic; (Illustration) diagram; **Grafikkarte** f (Inform) graphics card; **Grafikprogramm** nt (Inform) graphics software
Gräfin (-, -nen) f countess
Gramm (-s) nt gram(me)
Grammatik f grammar
Grapefruit (-, -s) f grapefruit
Graphik f siehe **Grafik**
Gras (-es, Gräser) nt grass
grässlich adj horrible
Gräte (-, -n) f (fish)bone
gratis adj, adv free (of charge)
gratulieren vi: **jdm** (zu etw) ~ to congratulate sb (on sth); (ich) **gratuliere!** congratulations!
grau adj grey, gray (US); **grauhaarig** adj grey-haired
grausam adj cruel

gravierend adj (Fehler) serious

greifen (griff, gegriffen) vt to
seize; **zu etw ~** (fig) to resort to
sth ▷ vi (Regel etc) to have an
effect (bei on)

grell adj harsh

Grenze (-, -n) f boundary; (Staat)
border; (Schranke) limit; **grenzen**
vi to border (an +akk on);
Grenzkontrolle f border control;
Grenzübergang m border
crossing point; **Grenzverkehr** m
border traffic

Grieche (-n, -n) m Greek;
Griechenland nt Greece;
Griechin f Greek; **griechisch** adj
Greek; **Griechisch** nt Greek

griesgrämig adj grumpy

Grieß (-es, -e) m (Gastr) semolina

griff imperf von **greifen**

Griff (-(e)s, -e) m grip; (Tür etc)
handle; **griffbereit** adj handy

Grill (-s, -s) m grill; (im Freien)
barbecue

Grille (-, -n) f cricket

grillen vt to grill ▷ vi to have a
barbecue; **Grillfest** nt, **Grillfete** f
barbecue; **Grillkohle** f charcoal

grinsen vi to grin; (höhnisch) to
sneer

Grippe (-, -n) f flu;
Grippeschutzimpfung f flu
vaccination

grob adj coarse; (Fehler, Verstoß)
gross; (Einschätzung) rough

Grönland (-s) nt Greenland

groß adj big, large; (hoch) tall;
(fig) great; (Buchstabe) capital;
(erwachsen) grown-up; **im Großen
und Ganzen** on the whole ▷ adv
greatly; **großartig** adj
wonderful

Großbritannien (-s) nt (Great)
Britain

Großbuchstabe m capital letter

Größe (-, -n) f size; (Länge)
height; (fig) greatness; **welche**

~ haben Sie? what size do you
take?

Großeltern pl grandparents pl;
Großhandel m wholesale trade;
Großmarkt m hypermarket;
Großmutter f grandmother;
Großraum m: **der ~ Manchester**
Greater Manchester;
groß|schreiben irr vt to write
with a capital letter; **Großstadt** f
city; **Großvater** m grandfather;
großzügig adj generous;
(Planung) on a large scale

Grotte (-, -n) f grotto

grub imperf von **graben**

Grübchen nt dimple

Grube (-, -n) f pit

grüezi interj (schweizerisch) hello

Gruft (-, -¨e) f vault

grün adj green; **~er Salat** lettuce;
~e Bohnen French beans; **der ~e
Punkt** symbol for recyclable
packaging; **im ~en Bereich**
hunky-dory

● **GRÜNER PUNKT**
●
● The **grüner Punkt** is the green
● spot symbol which appears on
● packaging, indicating that the
● packaging should not be
● thrown into the normal
● household refuse but kept
● separate to be recycled through
● the **DSD** (Duales System
● Deutschland) system. The
● recycling is financed by licences
● bought by the manufacturer
● from the 'DSD' and the cost of
● this is often passed on to the
● consumer.

Grünanlage f park

Grund (-(e)s, Gründe) m (Ursache)
reason; (Erdboden) ground; (See,
Gefäß) bottom; (Grundbesitz) land,
property; **aus gesundheitlichen**

Gründen for health reasons; **im ~e basically**; **aus diesem ~** for this reason

gründen vt to found; **Gründer(in)** m(f) founder

Grundgebühr f basic charge; **Grundgesetz** nt (German) Constitution

gründlich adj thorough

Gründonnerstag m Maundy Thursday

grundsätzlich adj fundamental, basic; **sie kommt ~ zu spät** she's always late; **Grundschule** f primary school; **Grundstück** nt plot; (Anwesen) estate; (Baugrundstück) site; **Grundwasser** nt ground water

Grüne(n) mf (Pol) Green; **die ~n** the Green Party

Gruppe (-, -n) f group; **Gruppenermäßigung** f group discount; **Gruppenreise** f group tour

Gruselfilm m horror film

Gruß (-es, Grüße) m greeting; **viele Grüße** best wishes; **Grüße an** (+akk) regards to; **mit freundlichen Grüßen** Yours sincerely (Brit), Sincerely yours (US); **sag ihm einen schönen ~ von mir** give him my regards; **grüßen** vt to greet; **grüß deine Mutter von mir** give your mother my regards; **Julia lässt (euch) ~** Julia sends (you) her regards

gucken vi to look

Gulasch (-(e)s, -e) nt goulash

gültig adj valid

Gummi (-s, -s) m or nt rubber; **Gummiband** nt rubber (o elastic (Brit)) band; **Gummibärchen** pl gums (in the shape of a bear) (Brit), gumdrops pl (in the shape of a bear) (US); **Gummihandschuhe** pl rubber gloves pl; **Gummistiefel** m wellington (boot) (Brit), rubber

boot (US)

günstig adj favourable; (Preis) good

gurgeln vi to gurgle; (im Mund) to gargle

Gurke (-, -n) f cucumber; **saure ~** gherkin

Gurt (-(e)s, -e) m belt

Gürtel (-s, -) m belt; (Geo) zone; **Gürtelrose** f shingles sing

GUS (-) f akr = **Gemeinschaft Unabhängiger Staaten** CIS

 SCHLÜSSELWORT

gut adj good; **alles Gute** all the best; **also gut** all right then
▷ adv well; **gut gehen** to work, to come off; **es geht jdm gut** sb's doing fine; **gut gemeint** well meant; **gut schmecken** to taste good; **jdm guttun** to do sb good; **gut, aber ...** OK, but ...; **(na) gut, ich komme** all right, I'll come; **gut drei Stunden** a good three hours; **das kann gut sein** that may well be; **lass es gut sein** that'll do

Gutachten (-s, -) nt report; **Gutachter(in)** (-s, -) m(f) expert

gutartig adj (Med) benign

Güter pl goods pl; **Güterbahnhof** m goods station; **Güterzug** m goods train

gutgläubig adj trusting; **Guthaben** (-s) nt (credit) balance

gutmütig adj good-natured

Gutschein m voucher; **Gutschrift** f credit

GV-Pflanzen pl GM crops

Gymnasium nt = grammar school (Brit), ≈ high school (US)

Gymnastik f exercises pl, keep-fit

Gynäkologe m, **Gynäkologin** f gynaecologist

Gyros (-, -) nt doner kebab

h

Haar (-(e)s, -e) nt hair; **um ein ~ nearly**; **sich** (dat) **die ~e schneiden lassen** to have one's hair cut; **Haarbürste** f hairbrush; **Haarfestiger** m setting lotion; **Haargel** nt hair gel; **Haarglätter** m hair straighteners pl; **haarig** adj hairy; (fig) nasty; **Haarschnitt** m haircut; **Haarspange** f hair slide (Brit), barrette (US); **Haarspliss** m split ends pl; **Haarspray** nt hair spray; **Haartrockner** (-s, -) m hairdryer; **Haarwaschmittel** nt shampoo

haben (hatte, gehabt) vt, vaux to have; **Hunger/Angst ~** to be hungry/afraid; **Ferien ~** to be on holiday (Brit) (o vacation (US)); **welches Datum ~ wir heute?** what's the date today?; **ich hätte gerne ...** I'd like ...; **hätten Sie etwas dagegen, wenn ...?** would

you mind if ...?; **was hast du denn?** what's the matter (with you)?

Haben nt (Comm) credit

Habicht (-(e)s, -e) m hawk

Hacke (-, -n) f (im Garten) hoe; (Ferse) heel; **hacken** vt to chop; (Loch) to hack; (Erde) to hoe; **Hacker(in)** (-s, -) m(f) (Inform) hacker; **Hackfleisch** nt mince(d meat) (Brit), ground meat (US)

Hafen (-s, Häfen) m harbour; (großer) port; **Hafenstadt** f port

Hafer (-s, -) m oats pl; **Haferflocken** pl rolled oats pl

Haft (-) f custody; **haftbar** adj liable, responsible; **haften** vi to stick; **~ für** to be liable (o responsible) for; **Haftnotiz** f Post-it®; **Haftpflichtversicherung** f third party insurance; **Haftung** f liability

Hagebutte (-, -n) f rose hip

Hagel (-s) m hail; **hageln** vi impers to hail

Hahn (-(e)s, Hähne) m cock; (Wasserhahn) tap (Brit), faucet (US); **Hähnchen** nt cockerel; (Gastr) chicken

Hai(fisch) (-(e)s, -e) m shark

häkeln vi, vt to crochet; **Häkelnadel** f crochet hook

Haken (-s, -) m hook; (Zeichen) tick

halb adj half; **~ eins** half past twelve; (fam) half twelve; **eine ~e Stunde** half an hour; **~ offen** half-open; **Halbfinale** nt semifinal; **halbieren** vt to halve; **Halbinsel** f peninsula; **Halbjahr** nt half-year; **halbjährlich** adj half-yearly; **Halbmond** m (Astr) half-moon; (Symbol) crescent; **Halbpension** f half board; **halbseitig** adj: **~ gelähmt** paralyzed on one side; **halbtags**

adv (arbeiten) part-time; **halbwegs** *adv* (leidlich) reasonably; **Halbzeit** f half; (Pause) half-time

half *imperf von* **helfen**; **Hälfte** (-, -n) f half

Halle (-, -n) f hall; **Hallenbad** *nt* indoor (swimming) pool

hallo *interj* hello, hi

Halogenlampe f halogen lamp; **Halogenscheinwerfer** *m* halogen headlight

Hals (-es, Hälse) *m* neck; (Kehle) throat; **Halsband** *nt* (für Tiere) collar; **Halsentzündung** f sore throat; **Halskette** f necklace; **Hals-Nasen-Ohren-Arzt** *m*, **Hals-Nasen-Ohren-Ärztin** f ear, nose and throat specialist; **Halsschmerzen** *pl* sore throat sing; **Halstuch** *nt* scarf

halt *interj* stop ▷ *adv*: **das ist ~ so** that's just the way it is; **Halt** (-(e)s, -e) *m* stop; (fester) hold; (innerer) stability

haltbar *adj* durable; (Lebensmittel) non-perishable; **Haltbarkeitsdatum** *nt* best-before date

halten (hielt, gehalten) *vt* to keep; (festhalten) to hold; **~ für** to regard as; **~ von** to think of; **den Elfmeter ~** to save the penalty; **eine Rede ~** to give (o make) a speech ▷ *vi* to hold; (frisch bleiben) to keep; (stoppen) to stop; **zu jdm ~** to stand by sb ▷ *vr*: **sich ~** (frisch bleiben) to keep; (sich behaupten) to hold out

Haltestelle f stop; **Halteverbot** *nt*: **hier ist ~** you can't stop here

Haltung f (Körper) posture; (fig) attitude; (Selbstbeherrschung) composure; **~ bewahren** to keep one's composure

Hamburg (-s) *nt* Hamburg; **Hamburger** (-s, -) *m* (Gastr) hamburger

Hammelfleisch *nt* mutton

Hammer (-s, Hämmer) *m* hammer; (fig, fam: Fehler) howler; **das ist der ~** (unerhört) that's a bit much

Hämorr(ho)iden *pl* haemorrhoids *pl*, piles *pl*

Hamster (-s, -) *m* hamster

Hand (-, Hände) f hand; **jdm die ~ geben** to shake hands with sb; **jdn bei der ~ nehmen** to take sb by the hand; **eine ~ voll Reis/Leute** a handful of rice/people; **zu Händen von** attention; **Handarbeit** f (Schulfach) handicraft; **~ sein** to be handmade; **Handball** *m* handball; **Handbremse** f handbrake; **Handbuch** *nt* handbook, manual; **Handcreme** f hand cream; **Händedruck** *m* handshake

Handel (-s) *m* trade; (Geschäft) transaction; **handeln** *vi* to act; (Comm) to trade; **~ von** to be about ▷ *vr impers*: **sich ~ um** to be about; **es handelt sich um ...** it's about ...; **Handelskammer** f chamber of commerce; **Handelsschule** f business school

Handfeger (-s, -) *m* brush; **Handfläche** f palm; **Handgelenk** *nt* wrist; **handgemacht** *adj* handmade; **Handgepäck** *nt* hand luggage (Brit) (o baggage)

Händler(in) (-s, -) *m(f)* dealer

handlich *adj* handy

Handlung f act, action; (von Roman, Film) plot

Handschellen *pl* handcuffs *pl*; **Handschrift** f handwriting; **Handschuh** *m* glove; **Handschuhfach** *nt* glove compartment; **Handtasche** f handbag, purse (US); **Handtuch** *nt* towel; **Handwerk** *nt* trade; (Kunst~) craft; **Handwerker** (-s, -)

m workman

Handy (-s, -s) *nt* mobile (phone) (Brit), cell phone (US); **Handynummer** *f* mobile number (Brit), cell phone number (US)

Hanf (-(e)s) *m* hemp

Hang (-(e)s, Hänge) *m* (Abhang) slope; (fig) tendency

Hängebrücke *f* suspension bridge; **Hängematte** *f* hammock

hängen (hing, gehangen) *vi* to hang; **an der Wand/an der Decke ~** to hang on the wall/from the ceiling; **an jdm ~** (fig) to be attached to sb; **~ bleiben** to get caught (an +dat on); (fig) to get stuck ▷ *vt* to hang (an +akk on)

Hantel (-, -n) *f* dumbbell

Hardware (-, -s) *f* (Inform) hardware

Harfe (-, -n) *f* harp

harmlos *adj* harmless

harmonisch *adj* harmonious

Harn (-(e)s, -e) *m* urine; **Harnblase** *f* bladder

Harpune (-, -n) *f* harpoon

hart *adj* hard; (fig) harsh; **zu jdm ~ sein** to be hard on sb; **~ gekocht** (Ei) hard-boiled; **hartnäckig** *adj* stubborn

Haschee (-s, -s) *nt* hash

Haschisch (-) *nt* hashish

Hase (-n, -n) *m* hare

Haselnuss *f* hazelnut

Hasenscharte *f* (Med) harelip

Hashtag (-s, -s) *m* (auf Twitter) hashtag

Hass (-es) *m* hatred (auf, gegen +akk of), hate; **einen ~ kriegen** (fam) to see red; **hassen** *vt* to hate

hässlich *adj* ugly; (gemein) nasty

Hast (-) *f* haste, hurry; **hastig** *adj* hasty

hatte *imperf von* **haben**

Haube (-, -n) *f* hood; (Mütze) cap; (Auto) bonnet (Brit), hood (US)

Hauch (-(e)s, -e) *m* breath; (Luft~)

breeze; (fig) trace; **hauchdünn** *adj* (Schicht, Scheibe) wafer-thin

hauen (haute, gehauen) *vt* to hit

Haufen (-s, -) *m* pile; **ein ~ Geld** (viel Geld) a lot of money

häufig *adj* frequent ▷ *adv* frequently, often

Haupt- *in zW* main; **Hauptbahnhof** *m* central (o main) station; **Hauptdarsteller(in)** *m(f)* leading actor/lady; **Haupteingang** *m* main entrance; **Hauptgericht** *nt* main course; **Hauptgeschäftszeiten** *pl* peak shopping hours *pl*; **Hauptgewinn** *m* first prize

Häuptling *m* chief

Hauptquartier *nt* headquarters *pl*; **Hauptreisezeit** *f* peak tourist season; **Hauptrolle** *f* leading role; **Hauptsache** *f* main thing; **hauptsächlich** *adv* mainly, chiefly; **Hauptsaison** *f* high (o peak) season; **Hauptsatz** *m* main clause; **Hauptschule** *f* ≈ secondary school (Brit), ≈ junior high school (US); **Hauptspeicher** *m* (Inform) main storage (o memory); **Hauptstadt** *f* capital; **Hauptstraße** *f* main road; (im Stadtzentrum) main street; **Hauptverkehrszeit** *f* rush hour

Haus (-es, Häuser) *nt* house; **nach ~e** home; **zu ~e** at home; **jdn nach ~e bringen** to take sb home; **bei uns zu ~e** (Heimat) where we come from; (Familie) in my family; (Haus) at our place; **Hausarbeit** *f* housework; **Hausaufgabe** *f* (Schule) homework; **~n** *pl* homework *sing*; **Hausbesitzer(in)** (-s, -) *m(f)* house owner; (Vermieter) landlord/-lady; **Hausbesuch** *m* home visit; **Hausbewohner(in)** (-s, -) *m(f)* occupant; **Hausflur** *m* hall; **Hausfrau** *f* housewife;

hausgemacht adj homemade;
Haushalt m household; (Pol)
budget; **Herr(in)** m(f)
host/hostess; (Vermieter)
landlord/-lady

häuslich adj domestic

Hausmann m house-husband;
Hausmannskost f good plain
cooking; **Hausmeister(in)** m(f)
caretaker (Brit), janitor (US);
Hausnummer f house number;
Hausordnung f (house) rules pl;
Hausschlüssel m front-door key;
Hausschuh m slipper; **Haustier**
nt pet; **Haustür** f front door

Haut (-, Häute) f skin; (Tier) hide;
Hautarzt m, **Hautärztin** f
dermatologist; **Hautausschlag**
m skin rash; **Hautcreme** f skin
cream; **Hautfarbe** f skin colour;
Hautkrankheit f skin disease

Hawaii (-s) nt Hawaii

Hbf. abk = **Hauptbahnhof** central
station

Hebamme (-, -n) f midwife

Hebel (-s, -) m lever

heben (hob, gehoben) vt to raise,
to lift

Hebräisch (-) nt Hebrew

Hecht (-(e)s, -e) m pike

Heck (-(e)s, -e) nt (von Boot) stern;
(von Auto) rear; **Heckantrieb** m
rear-wheel drive

Hecke (-, -n) f hedge

Heckklappe f tailgate;
Hecklicht nt tail-light;
Heckscheibe f rear window

Hefe (-, -n) f yeast

Heft (-(e)s, -e) nt notebook,
exercise book; (Ausgabe) issue

heftig adj violent; (Kritik, Streit)
fierce

Heftklammer f paper clip;
Heftpflaster nt plaster (Brit),
Band-Aid® (US)

Heide (-, -n) f heath, moor;
Heidekraut nt heather

Heidelbeere f bilberry, blueberry

heidnisch adj (Brauch) pagan

heikel adj (Angelegenheit)
awkward; (wählerisch) fussy

heil adj (Sache) in one piece,
intact; (Person) unhurt; **heilbar**
adj curable

Heilbutt (-(e)s, -e) m halibut

heilen vt to cure ▷ vi to heal

heilig adj holy; **Heiligabend** m
Christmas Eve; **Heilige(r)** mf
saint

Heilmittel nt remedy, cure (gegen
for); **Heilpraktiker(in)** (-s, -) m(f)
non-medical practitioner

heim adv home; **Heim** (-(e), -e) nt
home

Heimat f home
(town/country); **Heimatland** nt
home country

heim|fahren irr vi to drive
home; **Heimfahrt** f journey
home; **heimisch** adj
(Bevölkerung, Brauchtum) local;
(Tiere, Pflanzen) native;
heim|kommen irr vi to come (o
return) home

heimlich adj secret

Heimreise f journey home;
Heimspiel nt (Sport) home game;
Heimvorteil m (Sport) home
advantage; **Heimweg** m way
home; **Heimweh** (-s) nt
homesickness; **~ haben** to be
homesick; **Heimwerker(in)** m(f)
DIY enthusiast

Heirat (-, -en) f marriage;
heiraten vi to get married ▷ vt
to marry; **Heiratsantrag** m
proposal; **er hat ihr einen
~ gemacht** he proposed to her

heiser adj hoarse

heiß adj hot; (Diskussion) heated;
mir ist ~ I'm hot

heißen (hieß, geheißen) vi to be
called; (bedeuten) to mean; **ich
heiße Tom** my name is Tom; **wie**

~ Sie? what's your name?; **wie heißt sie mit Nachnamen?** what's her surname?; **wie heißt das auf Englisch?** what's that in English? ▷ vi impers: **es heißt** (man sagt) it is said; **es heißt in dem Brief ...** it says in the letter ...; **das heißt** that is

Heißluftherd m fan-assisted oven

heiter adj cheerful; (Wetter) bright

heizen vt to heat; **Heizkissen** m (Med) heated pad; **Heizkörper** m radiator; **Heizöl** nt fuel oil; **Heizung** f heating

Hektar (-s, -) nt hectare

Hektik (-, -en) f: **nur keine ~!** take it easy; **hektisch** adj hectic

Held (-en, -en) m hero; **Heldin** f heroine

helfen (half, geholfen) vi to help (jdm bei etw sb with sth); (nützen) to be of use; **sie weiß sich** (dat) **zu ~** she can manage ▷ vi impers: **es hilft nichts, du musst ...** it's no use, you have to ...; **Helfer(in)** m(f) helper; (Mitarbeiter) assistant

Helikopter-Skiing (-s) nt heliskiing, helicopter skiing

hell adj bright; (Farbe) light; (Hautfarbe) fair; **hellblau** adj light blue; **hellblond** adj ash-blond; **hellgelb** adj pale yellow; **hellgrün** adj light green; **Hellseher(in)** m(f) clairvoyant

Helm (-(e)s, -e) m helmet; **Helmpflicht** f compulsory wearing of helmets

Hemd (-(e)s, -en) nt shirt; (Unter~) vest

hemmen vt to check; (behindern) to hamper; **gehemmt sein** to be inhibited; **Hemmung** f (psychisch) inhibition; **sie hatte keine ~, ihn zu betrügen** she had no scruples about deceiving him; (moralisch) scruple

Henkel (-s, -) m handle

Henna (-s) nt henna

Henne (-, -n) f hen

Hepatitis (-, Hepatitiden) f hepatitis

her adv **1** (Richtung) **komm her zu mir** come here (to me); **von England her** from England; **von weit her** from a long way away; **her damit!** hand it over!; **wo hat er das her?** where did he get that from?; **wo bist du her?** where do you come from?

2 (Blickpunkt) **von der Form her** as far as the form is concerned

3 (zeitlich) **das ist 5 Jahre her** that was 5 years ago; **ich kenne ihn von früher her** I know him from before

herab adv down; **herablassend** adj (Bemerkung) condescending; **herab|sehen** irr vt: **auf jdn ~** to look down on sb; **herab|setzen** vt to reduce; (fig) to disparage

heran adv: **näher ~** to come closer; **heran|kommen** irr vi to approach; **~ an** (+akk) to be able to get at; (fig) to be able to get hold of; **heran|wachsen** irr vi to grow up

herauf adv up; **herauf|beschwören** irr vt to evoke; (verursachen) to cause; **herauf|ziehen** irr vt to pull up ▷ vi to approach; (Sturm) to gather

heraus adv out; **heraus|bekommen** irr vt (Geheimnis) to find out; (Rätsel) to solve; **ich bekomme noch zwei Euro heraus** I've got two euros change to come; **heraus|bringen** irr vt to bring out; **heraus|finden** irr vt to find out

irr vt to find out; **heraus|fordern**
vt to challenge; **Herausforderung**
f challenge; **heraus|geben** *irr vt*
(*Buch*) to edit; (*veröffentlichen*) to
publish; **jdm zwei Euro ~** to give
sb two euros change; **geben Sie**
mir bitte auf 20 Euro heraus
could you give me change for 20
euros, please?; **heraus|holen** *vt*
to get out (*aus* of); **heraus|-**
kommen *irr vi* to come
out; **dabei kommt nichts heraus**
nothing will come of it;
heraus|stellen *vr*: **sich ~** to turn
out (*als* to be); **heraus|ziehen** *irr*
vt to pull out
Herbergseltern *pl* (youth hostel)
wardens *pl*
Herbst (*-(e)s, -e*) *m* autumn, fall
(*US*)
Herd (*-(e)s, -e*) *m* cooker, stove
Herde (*-, -n*) *f* herd; (*Schafe*) flock
herein *adv in*; **~!** come in;
herein|fallen *irr vi*: **wir sind auf**
einen Betrüger hereingefallen
we were taken in by a swindler;
herein|legen *vt*: **jdn ~** (*fig*) to
take sb for a ride
Herfahrt *f* journey here; **auf der**
~ on the way here
Hergang *m* course (of events);
schildern Sie mir den ~ tell me
what happened
Hering (*-s, -e*) *m* herring
her|kommen *irr vi* to come; **wo**
kommt sie her? where does she
come from?
Heroin (*-s*) *nt* heroin
Herpes (*-*) *m* (*Med*) herpes
Herr (*-(e)n, -en*) *m* (*vor Namen*) Mr;
(*Mann*) gentleman; (*Adliger, Gott*)
Lord; **mein ~!** sir; **meine ~en!**
gentlemen; **Sehr geehrte Damen**
und ~en Dear Sir or Madam;
herrenlos *adj* (*Gepäck*) abandoned;
(*Tier*) stray; **Herrentoilette** *f*
men's toilet, gents

her|richten *vt* to prepare
herrlich *adj* marvellous, splendid
Herrschaft *f* rule; (*Macht*) power;
meine ~en! ladies and gentlemen!
herrschen *vi* to rule; (*bestehen*) to
be
her|stellen *vt* to make;
(*industriell*) to manufacture; **Her-**
steller(in) *m(f)* manufacturer;
Herstellung *f* production
herüber *adv* over
herum *adv* around; (*im Kreis*)
round; **um etw ~** around sth; **du**
hast den Pulli falsch ~ an your
sweater's inside out; **anders ~** the
other way round; **herum|fahren**
irr vi to drive around; **herum|**
führen *vt*: **jdn in der Stadt ~** to
show sb around the town ▷ *vi*:
die Straße führt ums das Zentrum
herum the road goes around the
city centre; **herum|kommen** *irr*
vi: **sie ist viel in der Welt**
herumgekommen she's been
around the world; **um etw**
~ (*vermeiden*) to get out of sth;
herum|kriegen *vt* to talk round;
herum|treiben *irr vr*: **sich ~** to
hang around
herunter *adv* down;
heruntergekommen *adj* (*Gebäude*,
Gegend) run-down; (*Person*)
down-at-heel; **herunter|handeln**
vt to get down; **herunter|holen**
vt to bring down;
herunter|kommen *irr vi* to come
down; **herunterladbar** *adj*
(*Inform*) downloadable;
herunter|laden *irr vt* (*Inform*) to
download
hervor *adv* out; **hervor|bringen**
irr vt to produce; (*Wort*) to utter;
hervor|heben *irr vt* to
emphasize; **hervorragend** *adj*
excellent; **hervor|rufen** *irr vt* to
cause, to give rise to
Herz (*-ens, -en*) *nt* heart; (*Karten*)

hearts pl; **von ganzem ~en**
wholeheartedly; **sich** (dat) **etw zu
~en nehmen** to take sth to heart;
Herzanfall m heart attack;
Herzbeschwerden pl heart
trouble sing; **Herzfehler** m heart
defect; **herzhaft** adj (Essen)
substantial; **~ lachen** to have a
good laugh; **Herzinfarkt** m
heart attack; **Herzklopfen** (-s) nt
(Med) palpitations pl; **ich hatte
~ (vor Aufregung)** my heart was
pounding (with excitement);
herzkrank adj: **sie ist ~** she's got
a heart condition; **herzlich** adj
(Empfang, Mensch) warm; **~en
Glückwunsch** congratulations

Herzog(in) (-s, Herzöge) m(f)
duke/duchess

Herzschlag m heartbeat;
(Herzversagen) heart failure;
Herzschrittmacher m pacemaker; **Herzstillstand** m
cardiac arrest

Hessen (-s) nt Hessen

heterosexuell adj heterosexual;
Heterosexuelle(r) mf
heterosexual

Hetze (-, -n) f (Eile) rush; **hetzen**
vt to rush ▷ vr: **sich ~** to rush

Heu (-(e)s) nt hay

heuer adv this year

heulen vi to howl; (weinen) to cry

Heuschnupfen m hay fever;
Heuschrecke (-, -n) f grasshopper; (größer) locust

heute adv today; **~ Abend/früh**
this evening/morning; **~ Morgen**
this morning; **~ Nacht** tonight;
(letzte Nacht) last night; **~ in acht
Tagen** a week (from) today; **sie
hat bis ~ nicht bezahlt** she hasn't
paid to this day; **heutig** adj: **die
~e Zeitung/Generation** today's
paper/generation; **heutzutage**
adv nowadays

Hexe (-, -n) f witch;

Hexenschuss m lumbago

hielt imperf von **halten**

hier adv here; **~ entlang** this way;
ich bin auch nicht von ~ I'm a
stranger here myself; **hier|bleiben**
irr vi to stay here; **hier|lassen** irr
vt to leave here; **hierher** adv
here; **das gehört nicht ~** that
doesn't belong here; **hiermit** adv
with this; **hierzulande** adv in
this country

hiesig adj local

hieß imperf von **heißen**

Hi-Fi-Anlage f hi-fi (system)

high adj (fam) high; **Highlife** (-s)
nt high life; **~ machen** to live it
up; **Hightech** (-s) nt high tech

Hilfe (-, -n) f help; (für Notleidende,
finanziell) aid; **~! I** help!; **Erste
~ leisten** to give first aid; **um
~ bitten** to ask for help; **hilflos**
adj helpless; **hilfsbereit** adj
helpful; **Hilfsmittel** nt aid

Himbeere f raspberry

Himmel (-s, -) m sky; (Rel)
heaven; **Himmelfahrt** f
Ascension; **Himmelsrichtung** f
direction; **himmlisch** adj
heavenly

SCHLÜSSELWORT

hin adv **1** (Richtung) **hin und zurück**
there and back; **hin und her** to
and fro; **bis zur Mauer hin** up to
the wall; **wo ist er hin?** where has
he gone? **Geld hin, Geld her**
money or no money
2 (auf … hin) **auf meine Bitte hin**
at my request; **auf seinen Rat hin**
on the basis of his advice
3 **mein Glück ist hin** my happiness
has gone

hinab adv down; **hinab|gehen** irr
vi to go down

hinauf adv up; **hinauf|gehen** irr

vi, vt to go up; **hinauf|steigen** *irr vi* to climb (up)

hinaus *adv* out; **hinaus|gehen** *irr vi* to go out; **das Zimmer geht auf den See hinaus** the room looks out onto the lake; **~ über** (+*akk*) to exceed; **hinaus|laufen** *irr vi* to run out; **~ auf** (+*akk*) to come to, to amount to; **hinaus|schieben** *irr vt* to put off, postpone; **hinaus|werfen** *irr vt* to throw out; (*aus Firma*) to fire, to sack (*Brit*); **hinaus|zögern** *vr*: **sich ~** to take longer than expected

Hinblick *m* in (*o im*) **~ auf** (+*akk*) with regard to; (*wegen*) in view of

hin|bringen *irr vt*: **ich bringe Sie hin** I'll take you there

hindern *vt* to prevent; **jdn daran ~, etw zu tun** to stop (*o prevent*) sb from doing sth; **Hindernis** *nt* obstacle

Hinduismus *m* Hinduism

hindurch *adv* through; **das ganze Jahr ~** throughout the year, all year round; **die ganze Nacht ~** all night (long)

hinein *adv* in; **hinein|gehen** *irr vi* to go in; **~ in** (+*akk*) to go into, to enter; **hinein|passen** *vi* to fit in; **~ in** (+*akk*) to fit into

hin|fahren *irr vi* to go there ▷ *vt* to take there; **Hinfahrt** *f* outward journey

hin|fallen *irr vi* to fall (down)

Hinflug *m* outward flight

hing *imperf von* **hängen**

hin|gehen *irr vi* to go there; (*Zeit*) to pass; **hin|halten** *irr vt* to hold out; (*warten lassen*) to put off

hinken *vi* to limp; **der Vergleich hinkt** the comparison doesn't work

hin|knien *vr*: **sich ~** to kneel down; **hin|legen** *vt* to put down ▷ *vr*: **sich ~** to lie down; **hin|nehmen** *irr vt* (*fig*) to put up

with, to take; **Hinreise** *f* outward journey; **hin|setzen** *vr*: **sich ~** to sit down; **hinsichtlich** *prep* +*gen* with regard to; **hin|stellen** *vt* to put (down) ▷ *vr*: **sich ~** to stand

hinten *adv* at the back; (*im Auto*) in the back; (*dahinter*) behind

hinter *prep* +*dat o akk* behind; (*nach*) after; **~ jdm her sein** to be after sb; **etw ~ sich** (*akk*) **bringen** to get sth over (and done) with; **Hinterachse** *f* rear axle; **Hinterausgang** *m* rear exit; **Hinterbein** *nt* hind leg; **Hinterbliebene(r)** *mf* dependant; **hintere(r, s)** *adj* rear, back; **hintereinander** *adv* (*in einer Reihe*) one behind the other; (*hintereinander her*) one after the other; **drei Tage ~** three days running (*o* in a row); **Hintereingang** *m* rear entrance; **Hintergedanke** *m* ulterior motive; **hintergehen** *irr vt* to deceive; **Hintergrund** *m* background; **hinterher** *adv* (*zeitlich*) afterwards; **~ los, ~I** come on, after him/her/them; **Hinterkopf** *m* back of the head; **hinterlassen** *irr vt* to leave; **jdm eine Nachricht ~** to leave a message for sb; **hinterlegen** *vt* to leave (*bei* with)

Hintern (-, -) *m* (*fam*) backside, bum

Hinterradantrieb *m* (*Auto*) rear-wheel drive; **Hinterteil** *nt* back (*part*); (*Hintern*) behind; **Hintertür** *f* back door

hinüber *adv* over; **~ sein** (*fam: kaputt*) to be ruined; (*verdorben*) to have gone bad; **hinüber|gehen** *irr vi* to go over

hinunter *adv* down; **hinunter|gehen** *irr vi, vt* to go down; **hinunter|schlucken** *vt*

(a. fig) to swallow
Hinweg m outward journey
hinweg|setzen vr **sich über etw** (akk) **~** to ignore sth
Hinweis (-es, -e) m (Andeutung) hint; (Anweisung) instruction; (Verweis) reference; **hin|weisen** irr vi **jdn auf etw** (acc) **~** to point sth out to sb; **jdn nochmal auf etw ~** to remind sb of sth
hinzu adv in addition; **hinzu|fügen** vt to add; **hinzu|kommen** irr vi: **zu jdm ~** to join sb; **es war kalt, hinzu kam, dass es auch noch regnete** it was cold, and on top of that it was raining
Hirn (-(e)s, -e) nt brain; (Verstand) brains pl; **Hirnhautentzündung** f meningitis
Hirsch (-(e)s, -e) m deer; (als Speise) venison
Hirte (-n, -n) m shepherd
historisch adj historical
Hit (-s, -s) m (fig, Mus, Inform) hit; **Hitliste** f, **Hitparade** f charts pl
Hitze (-) f heat; **hitzebeständig** adj heat-resistant; **Hitzewelle** f heatwave; **hitzig** adj hot-tempered; (Debatte) heated; **Hitzschlag** m heatstroke
HIV (-(s), -(s)) nt abk = **Human Immunodeficiency Virus** HIV; **HIV-negativ** adj HIV-negative; **HIV-positiv** adj HIV-positive
H-Milch f long-life milk
hob imperf von **heben**
Hobby (-s, -s) nt hobby
Hobel (-s, -) m plane
hoch adj high; (Baum) tall; (Schnee) deep; **der Zaun ist drei Meter ~** the fence is three metres high; **~auflösend** high-resolution; **~ begabt** extremely gifted; **das ist mir zu ~** that's above my head; **~ soll sie leben!, sie lebe ~!** three cheers for her; **4 ~ 2 ist 16** 4 squared

is 16; **4 ~ 5** 4 to the power of 5
Hoch (-s, -s) nt (Ruf) cheer; (Meteo) high; **hochachtungsvoll** adv (in Briefen) yours faithfully; **Hochbetrieb** m: **es herrscht ~** they/we are extremely busy; **Hochdeutsch** nt High German; **Hochgebirge** nt high mountains pl; **Hochgeschwindigkeitszug** m high-speed train; **Hochhaus** nt high rise; **hoch|heben** irr vt to lift (up); **hoch|laden** irr vt (Inform) to upload; **Hochsaison** f high season; **Hochschule** f college; (Universität) university; **Hochschulreife** f **er hat (die) ~** he's got his A-levels (Brit), he's graduated from high school (US); **Hochsommer** m midsummer; **Hochspannung** f great tension; (Elek) high voltage; **Hochsprung** m high jump
höchst adv highly, extremely; **höchste(r, s)** adj highest; (äußerste) extreme; **höchstens** adv at the most; **Höchstform** f (Sport) top form; **Höchstgeschwindigkeit** f maximum speed; **Höchstparkdauer** f maximum stay
Hochstuhl m high chair
höchstwahrscheinlich adv very probably
Hochwasser nt high water; (Überschwemmung) floods pl; **hochwertig** adj high-quality
Hochzeit (-, -en) f wedding; **Hochzeitsnacht** f wedding night; **Hochzeitsreise** f honeymoon; **Hochzeitstag** m wedding day; (Jahrestag) wedding anniversary
hocken vi to squat, to crouch
Hocker (-s, -) m stool
Hockey (-s) nt hockey
Hoden (-s, -) m testicle
Hof (-(e)s, Höfe) m (Hinterhof) yard;

(*Innenhof*) courtyard; (*Bauernhof*) farm; (*Königshof*) court

hoffen vi to hope (*auf +akk* for); **ich hoffe es** I hope so; **hoffentlich** adv hopefully; **~ nicht** I hope not; **Hoffnung** f hope; **hoffnungslos** adj hopeless

höflich adj polite; **Höflichkeit** f politeness

hohe(r, s) adj siehe **hoch**

Höhe (-, -n) f height; (*Anhöhe*) hill; (*einer Summe*) amount; **in einer ~ von 5000 Metern** at an altitude of 5,000 metres; (*Flughöhe*) altitude; **Höhenangst** f vertigo

Höhepunkt m (*einer Reise*) high point; (*einer Veranstaltung*) highlight; (*eines Films; sexuell*) climax

höher adj, adv higher

hohl adj hollow

Höhle (-, -n) f cave

holen vt to get, to fetch; (*abholen*) to pick up; (*Atem*) to catch; **die Polizei ~** to call the police; **jdn/etw ~ lassen** to send for sb/sth

Holland nt Holland; **Holländer(in)** (-s, -) m(f) Dutchman/-woman; **holländisch** adj Dutch

Hölle (-, -n) f hell

Hologramm nt hologram

holperig adj bumpy

Holunder (-s, -) m elder

Holz (-es, Hölzer) nt wood; **Holzboden** m wooden floor; **hölzern** adj wooden; **holzig** adj (*Stängel*) woody; **Holzkohle** f charcoal

Homebanking (-s) nt home banking, online banking; **Homepage** (-, -s) f home page; **Hometrainer** m exercise machine

Homoehe f (*fam*) gay marriage

homöopathisch adj homeopathic

homosexuell adj homosexual; **Homosexuelle(r)** mf homosexual

Honig (-s, -e) m honey; **Honigmelone** f honeydew melon

Honorar (-s, -e) nt fee

Hopfen (-s, -) m (*Bot*) hop; (*beim Brauen*) hops pl

hoppla interj whoops, oops

horchen vi to listen (*auf +akk* to); (*an der Tür*) to eavesdrop

hören vt, vi (*passiv, mitbekommen*) to hear; (*zufällig*) to overhear; (*aufmerksam zuhören; Radio, Musik*) to listen to; **ich habe schon viel von Ihnen gehört** I've heard a lot about you; **Hörer** m (*Tel*) receiver; **Hörer(in)** m(f) listener; **Hörgerät** nt hearing aid

Horizont (-(e)s, -e) m horizon; **das geht über meinen ~** that's beyond me

Hormon (-s, -e) nt hormone

Hornhaut f hard skin; (*des Auges*) cornea

Hornisse (-, -n) f hornet

Horoskop (-s, -e) nt horoscope

Hörsaal m lecture hall; **Hörsturz** m acute hearing loss; **Hörweite** f: **in/außer ~** within/out of earshot

Höschenwindel (-, -n) f nappy (*Brit*), diaper (*US*)

Hose (-, -n) f trousers pl (*Brit*), pants pl (*US*); (*Unterhose*) (under)pants pl; **eine ~** a pair of trousers/pants; **kurze ~** (pair of) shorts pl; **Hosenanzug** m trouser suit (*Brit*), pantsuit (*US*); **Hosenschlitz** m fly, flies (*Brit*); **Hosentasche** f trouser pocket (*Brit*), pant pocket (*US*); **Hosenträger** m braces pl (*Brit*), suspenders pl (*US*)

Hospital (-s, Hospitäler) nt hospital

Hotdog (-s, -s) nt o m hot dog

Hotel (-s, -s) nt hotel; **in welchem ~ seid ihr?** which hotel are you staying at?; **Hoteldirektor(in)** m(f) hotel manager; **Hotelkette** f hotel chain; **Hotelzimmer** nt hotel room

Hotline (-, -s) f hot line; **Hotspot** m (wireless) hotspot

Hubraum m cubic capacity

hübsch adj (Mädchen, Kind, Kleid) pretty; (gutaussehend: Mann, Frau) good-looking, cute

Hubschrauber (-s, -) m helicopter

Huf (-(e)s, -e) m hoof; **Hufeisen** nt horseshoe

Hüfte (-, -n) f hip

Hügel (-s, -) m hill; **hügelig** adj hilly

Huhn (-(e)s, Hühner) nt hen; (Gastr) chicken; **Hühnchen** nt chicken; **Hühnerauge** nt corn; **Hühnerbrühe** f chicken broth

Hülle (-, -n) f cover; (für Ausweis) case; (Zellophan) wrapping

Hummel (-, -n) f bumblebee

Hummer (-s, -) m lobster; **Hummerkrabbe** f king prawn

Humor (-s) m humour; **~ haben** to have a sense of humour; **humorlos** adj humourless; **humorvoll** adj humorous

humpeln vi hobble

Hund (-(e)s, -e) m dog; **Hundeleine** f dog lead (Brit), dog leash (US)

hundert num hundred; **Hundertjahrfeier** f centenary; **hundertprozentig** adj, adv one hundred per cent; **hundertste(r, s)** adj hundredth

Hündin f bitch

Hunger (-s) m hunger; **~ haben/bekommen** to be/get hungry; **hungern** vi to go

hungry; (ernsthaft, dauernd) to starve

Hupe (-, -n) f horn; **hupen** vi to sound one's horn

Hüpfburg f bouncy castle®; **hüpfen** vi to hop; (springen) to jump

Hürde (-, -n) f hurdle

Hure (-, -n) f whore (pej)

hurra interj hooray

husten vi to cough; **Husten** (-s) m cough; **Hustenbonbon** nt cough sweet; **Hustensaft** m cough mixture

Hut (-(e)s, Hüte) m hat

hüten vt to look after ▷ vr: **sich ~** to watch out; **sich ~, etw zu tun** to take care not to do sth; **sich ~ vor** (+dat) to beware of

Hütte (-, -n) f hut, cottage; **Hüttenkäse** m cottage cheese

Hyäne (-, -n) f hyena

Hydrant m hydrant

hygienisch adj hygienic

Hyperlink (-s, -s) m hyperlink

Hypnose (-, -n) f hypnosis; **Hypnotiseur(in)** m(f) hypnotist; **hypnotisieren** vt to hypnotize

Hypothek (-, -en) f mortgage

hysterisch adj hysterical

I

Igel (-s, -) m hedgehog
ignorieren vt to ignore
ihm pron dat sing von **er/es**; (to) him, (to) it; **wie geht es ~?** how is he?; **ein Freund von ~** a friend of his ▷ pron dat von **es**; (to) it
ihn pron akk sing von **er**; (Person) him; (Sache) it
ihnen pron dat pl von **sie**; (to) them; **wie geht es ~?** how are they?; **ein Freund von ~** a friend of theirs
Ihnen pron dat sing u pl von **Sie**; (to) you; **wie geht es ~?** how are you?; **ein Freund von ~** a friend of yours

○ SCHLÜSSELWORT

ihr pron **1** (nom pl) you; **ihr seid es** it's you
2 (dat von sie) to her; **gib es ihr** give it to her; **er steht neben ihr** he is standing beside her
▷ possessiv pron **1** (sg) her; (bei Tieren, Dingen) its; **ihr Mann** her husband
2 (pl); **die Bäume und ihre Blätter** the trees and their leaves

Ihr pron von **Sie**; (adjektivisch) your; **~(e) XY** (am Briefende) Yours, XY
ihre(r, s) pron (substantivisch, sing) hers; (pl) theirs; **das ist ~/~r/ihr(e)s** that's hers; (pl) that's theirs
Ihre(r, s) pron (substantivisch) yours; **das ist ~/~r/Ihr(e)s** that's yours
ihretwegen adv (wegen ihr) because of her; (ihr zuliebe) for her sake; (um sie) about her; (von ihr aus) as far as she is concerned ▷ adv (wegen ihnen) because of them; (ihnen zuliebe) for their sake; (um sie) about them; (von ihnen aus)

i. A. abk = **im Auftrag** pp
IC (-, -s) m abk = **Intercityzug** Intercity (train)
ICE (-, -s) m abk = **Intercityexpresszug** German high-speed train
ich pron I; **~ bin's** it's me; **~ nicht** not me; **du und ~** you and me; **hier bin ~!** here I am; **~ Idiot!** stupid me
Icon (-s, -s) nt (Inform) icon
IC-Zuschlag m Intercity supplement
ideal adj ideal
Idee (-, -n) f idea
identifizieren vt to identify ▷ vr: **sich mit jdm/etw ~** to identify with sb/sth
identisch adj identical
Identität f identity
Idiot(in) (-en, -en) m(f) idiot; **idiotisch** adj idiotic
Idol (-s, -e) nt idol
Idylle f idyll; **idyllisch** adj idyllic

as far as they are concerned;
Ihretwegen adv (wegen Ihnen)
because of you; (Ihnen zuliebe) for
your sake; (um Sie) about you; (von
Ihnen aus) as far as you are
concerned

Ikone (-, -n) f icon
illegal adj illegal
Illusion f illusion; **sich** (dat) **~en
machen** to delude oneself;
illusorisch adj illusory
Illustration f illustration
Illustrierte (-n, -n) f (glossy)
magazine
im kontr von **in dem**; **~ Bett** in bed;
~ Fernsehen on TV; **~ Radio** on
the radio; **~ Bus/Zug** on the
bus/train; **~ Januar** in January;
~ Stehen (while) standing up
Imam (-s, -e) m imam
Imbiss (-es, -e) m snack;
Imbissbude f, **Imbissstube** f
snack bar
Imbussschlüssel m hex key
immer adv always; **~ mehr** more
and more; **~ wieder** again and
again; **~ noch** still; **~ noch nicht**
still not; **für ~** forever; **~ wenn
ich ...** every time I ...; **~ schöner/
trauriger** more and more
beautiful/sadder and sadder;
**was/wer/wo/wann (auch)
~** whatever/whoever/wherever/
whenever; **immerhin** adv after
all; **immerzu** adv all the time
Immigrant(in) m(f) immigrant
Immobilien pl property sing, real
estate sing; **Immobilien-
makler(in)** m(f) estate
agent (Brit), realtor (US)
immun adj immune (gegen to);
Immunschwäche f immunodeficiency; **Immun-
schwächekrankheit** f immune
deficiency syndrome;
Immunsystem nt immune
system

impfen vt to vaccinate; **ich muss
mich gegen Pocken ~ lassen** I've
got to get myself vaccinated
against smallpox; **Impfpass** m
vaccination card; **Impfstoff** m
vaccine; **Impfung** f vaccination
imponieren vi to impress (jdm
sb)
Import (-(e)s, -e) m import;
importieren vt to import
impotent adj impotent
imstande adj: **~ sein** to be
in a position; (fähig) to be
able

⭕ **SCHLÜSSELWORT**

in prep +akk **1** (räumlich: wohin?) in,
into; **in die Stadt** into town; **in die
Schule gehen** to go to school
2 (zeitlich) **bis ins 20. Jahrhundert**
into o up to the 20th century
▷ prep +dat **1** (räumlich: wo?) in; **in
der Stadt** in town; **in der Schule
sein** to be at school
2 (zeitlich: wann?) **in diesem Jahr**
this year; (in jenem Jahr) in that
year; **heute in zwei Wochen** two
weeks today

inbegriffen adj included
indem conj: **sie gewann, ~ sie
mogelte** she won by cheating
Inder(in) (-s, -) m(f) Indian
Indianer(in) (-s, -) m(f)
American Indian, Native
American; **indianisch** adj
American Indian, Native American
Indien (-s) nt India
indirekt adj indirect
indisch adj Indian
indiskret adj indiscreet
individuell adj individual
Indonesien (-s) nt Indonesia
Industrie f industry; **Industrie-
in** zW industrial; **Industriegebiet**
nt industrial area; **industriell** adj

industrial
ineinander adv in(to) one another (o each other)
Infarkt (-(e)s, -e) m (Herzinfarkt) heart attack
Infektion f infection;
Infektionskrankheit f infectious disease; **infizieren** vt to infect
▷ vr: **sich ~** to be infected
Info (-, -s) f (fam) info
infolge prep as a result of, owing to; **infolgedessen** adv consequently
Infomaterial nt (fam) bumf, info
Informatik f computer science;
Informatiker(in) (-s, -) m(f) computer scientist
Information f information;
Informationsschalter m information desk; **informieren** vt to inform; **falsch ~** to misinform
▷ vr: **sich ~** to find out (über +akk about)
infrage adv: **das kommt nicht ~** that's out of the question; **etw ~ stellen** to question sth
Infrastruktur f infrastructure
Infusion f infusion
Ingenieur(in) m(f) engineer
Ingwer (-s) m ginger
Inhaber(in) (-s, -) m(f) owner; (Haus~) occupier; (von Lizenz) holder; (Fin) bearer
Inhalt (-(e)s, -e) m contents pl; (eines Buchs etc) content; (Math) volume; (Flächeninhalt) area;
Inhaltsangabe f summary;
Inhaltsverzeichnis nt table of contents
Initiative f initiative; **die ~ ergreifen** to take the initiative
Injektion f injection
inklusive adv, prep inclusive (gen of)
inkonsequent adj inconsistent
Inland nt (Pol, Comm) home; **im ~** at home; (Geo) inland;

inländisch adj domestic;
Inlandsflug m domestic flight;
Inlandsgespräch nt national call
Inliner pl, **Inlineskates** pl (Sport) Rollerblades® pl, in-line skates pl
innen adv inside;
Innenarchitekt(in) m(f) interior designer; **Innenhof** m (inner) courtyard; **Innenminister(in)** m(f) minister of the interior, Home Secretary (Brit); **Innenseite** f inside; **Innenspiegel** m rearview mirror; **Innenstadt** f town centre; (von Großstadt) city centre
innere(r, s) adj inner; (im Körper, inländisch) internal; **Innere(s)** nt inside; (Mitte) centre; (fig) heart
Innereien pl innards pl
innerhalb adv, prep +gen within; (räumlich) inside
innerlich adj internal; (geistig) inner
innerste(r, s) adj innermost
Innovation f innovation;
innovativ adj innovative
inoffiziell adj unofficial; (zwanglos) informal
ins kontr von **in das**
Insasse (-n, -n) m, **Insassin** f (Auto) passenger; (Anstalt) inmate
insbesondere adv particularly, in particular
Inschrift f inscription
Insekt (-(e)s, -en) nt insect, bug (US); **Insektenschutzmittel** nt insect repellent; **Insektenstich** m insect bite
Insel (-, -n) f island
Inserat nt advertisement
insgesamt adv altogether, all in all
Insider(in) (-s, -) m(f) insider
insofern adv in that respect; (deshalb) (and) so ▷ conj if; **~ als** in so far as

Installateur(in) m(f) (Klempner) plumber; (Elektroinstallateur) electrician; **installieren** vt (Inform) to install

Instinkt (-(e)s, -e) m instinct

Institut (-(e)s, -e) nt institute

Institution f institution

Instrument nt instrument

Insulin (-s) nt insulin

Inszenierung f production

intakt adj intact

intellektuell adj intellectual

intelligent adj intelligent; **Intelligenz** f intelligence

intensiv adj (gründlich) intensive; (Gefühl, Schmerz) intense; **Intensivkurs** m crash course; **Intensivstation** f intensive care unit

interaktiv adj interactive

Intercityexpress(zug) m German high-speed train; **Intercityzug** m Intercity (train); **Intercityzuschlag** m Intercity supplement

interessant adj interesting; **Interesse** (-s, -n) nt interest; ~ **haben an** (+dat) to be interested in; **interessieren** vt to interest ▷ vr: **sich** ~ to be interested (für in)

Interface (-, -s) nt (Inform) interface

Internat nt boarding school

international adj international

Internet (-s) nt internet, net; **im** ~ **on the internet**; **im** ~ **surfen** to surf the net; **Internetanschluss** m internet connection; **Internetauktion** f internet auction; **Internetcafé** nt internet café, cybercafé; **Internetfirma** f dotcom company; **Internethandel** m e-commerce; **Internetseite** f web page; **Internetzugang** m internet access

interpretieren vt to interpret (als as)

Interpunktion f punctuation

Interview (-s, -s) nt interview; **interviewen** vt to interview

intim adj intimate

intolerant adj intolerant

investieren vt to invest

inwiefern adv in what way; (in welchem Ausmaß) to what extent; **inwieweit** adv to what extent

inzwischen adv meanwhile

iPod® m iPod®

Irak (-(s)) m: (**der**) ~ Iraq

Iran (-(s)) m: (**der**) ~ Iran

Ire (-n, -n) m Irishman

irgend adv: ~ **so ein Idiot** some idiot; **wenn** ~ **möglich** if at all possible; **irgendein** pron, **irgendeine(r, s)** adj some; (fragend, im Bedingungssatz; beliebig) any; **irgendetwas** pron something; (fragend, im Bedingungssatz) anything; **irgendjemand** pron somebody; (fragend, im Bedingungssatz) anybody; **irgendwann** adv sometime; (zu beliebiger Zeit) any time; **irgendwie** adv somehow; **irgendwo** adv somewhere; (fragend, im Bedingungssatz) anywhere

Irin f Irishwoman; **irisch** adj Irish; **Irland** nt Ireland

ironisch adj ironic

irre adj crazy, mad; (toll) terrific; **Irre(r)** mf lunatic; **irreführen** irr vt to mislead; **irremachen** vt to confuse; **irren** vi to be mistaken; (umherirren) to wander ▷ vr: **sich** ~ to be mistaken; **wenn ich mich nicht irre** if I'm not mistaken; **sich in der Nummer** ~ (Telefon) to get the wrong number; **irrsinnig** adj mad, crazy; **Irrtum** (-s, -tümer) m mistake, error; **irrtümlich** adj mistaken ▷ adv by mistake

ISBN (-) nt abk = **industrial standard business network** ISBN

▷ (-) f abk = **Internationale Standard Buchnummer** ISBN

Ischias (-) m sciatica

ISDN (-) nt abk = **integrated services digital network** ISDN

Islam (-s) m Islam; **islamisch** adj Islamic

Island nt Iceland; **Isländer(in)** (-s, -) m(f) Icelander; **isländisch** adj Icelandic; **Isländisch** nt Icelandic

Isolierband nt insulating tape; **isolieren** vt to isolate; (Elek) to insulate

Isomatte f thermomat, karrymat®

Israel (-s) nt Israel; **Israeli** (-(s), -(s)) m (-, -(s)) f Israeli; **israelisch** adj Israeli

IT (-) f abk = **Informationstechnologie** IT

Italien (-s) nt Italy; **Italiener(in)** (-s, -) m(f) Italian; **italienisch** adj Italian; **Italienisch** nt Italian

○ SCHLÜSSELWORT

ja adv 1 yes; **haben Sie das gesehen? — ja** did you see it? — yes(, I did); **ich glaube ja** (yes,) I think so

2 (fragend) really?; **ich habe gekündigt — ja?** I've quit — have you?; **du kommst, ja?** you're coming, aren't you?

3 **sei ja vorsichtig** do be careful; **Sie wissen ja, dass ...** as you know, ...; **tu das ja nicht!** don't do that!; **ich habe es ja gewusst** I just knew it; **ja, also ...** well you see ...

Jacht (-, -en) f yacht; **Jachthafen** m marina

Jacke (-, -n) f jacket; (Wolljacke) cardigan

Jackett (-s, -s o -e) nt jacket

Jagd (-, -en) f hunt; (Jagen) hunting; **jagen** vi to hunt ▷ vt to hunt; (*verfolgen*) to chase; **Jäger(in)** *m(f)* hunter

Jaguar (-s, -e) *m* jaguar

Jahr (-(e)s, -e) *nt* year; **ein halbes ~** six months *pl*; **Anfang der neunziger ~e** in the early nineties; **mit sechzehn ~en** (at the age of) sixteen; **Jahrestag** *m* anniversary; **Jahreszahl** *f* date, year; **Jahreszeit** *f* season; **Jahrgang** *m* (*Wein*) year, vintage; **der ~ 1989** (*Personen*) those born in 1989; **Jahrhundert** (-s, -e) *nt* century; **jährlich** *adj* yearly, annual; **Jahrmarkt** *m* fair; **Jahrtausend** *nt* millennium; **Jahrzehnt** *nt* decade

jähzornig *adj* hot-tempered

Jakobsmuschel *f* scallop

Jalousie *f* (venetian) blind

Jamaika (-s) *nt* Jamaica

jämmerlich *adj* pathetic

jammern *vi* to moan

Januar (-(s), -e) *m* January; *siehe auch* **Juni**

Japan (-s) *nt* Japan; **Japaner(in)** (-s, -) *m(f)* Japanese; **japanisch** *adj* Japanese; **Japanisch** *nt* Japanese

jaulen *vi* to howl

jawohl *adv* yes (of course)

Jazz (-) *m* jazz

 SCHLÜSSELWORT

je *adv* **1** (*jemals*) ever; **hast du so was je gesehen?** did you ever see anything like it?
2 (*jeweils*) every, each; **sie zahlten je 3 Euro** they paid 3 euros each
▷ *konj* **1 je nach** depending on; **je nachdem** it depends; **je nachdem, ob ...** depending on whether ...
2 je eher, desto o **umso besser** the sooner the better

Jeans (-, -) *f* jeans *pl*

jede(r, s) *unbest Zahlwort* (*insgesamt gesehen*) every; (*einzeln gesehen*) each; (*jede(r, s) beliebige*) any; **~s Mal** every time, each time; **~n zweiten Tag** every other day; **sie hat an ~m Finger einen Ring** she's got a ring on each finger; **~r Computer reicht aus** any computer will do; **bei ~m Wetter** in any weather ▷ *pron* everybody; (*jeder Einzelne*) each; **~r von euch/uns** each of you/us; **jedenfalls** *adv* in any case; **jederzeit** *adv* at any time; **jedesmal** *adv* every time

jedoch *adv* however

jemals *adv* ever

jemand *pron* somebody; (*in Frage und Verneinung*) anybody

Jemen (-(s)) *m* Yemen

jene(r, s) *adj* that, those *pl* ▷ *pron* that (one), those *pl*

jenseits *adv* on the other side ▷ *prep* +*gen* on the other side of; (*fig*) beyond

Jetlag (-s) *m* jet lag

jetzig *adj* present

jetzt *adv* now; **erst ~** only now; **~ gleich** right now; **bis ~** so far, up to now; **von ~ an** from now on

jeweils *adv* **~ zwei zusammen** two at a time; **zu ~ 5 Euro** at 5 euros each

Job (-s, -s) *m* job; **jobben** *vi* (*fam*) to work, to have a job

Jod (-(e)s) *nt* iodine

joggen *vi* to jog; **Jogging** (-s) *nt* jogging; **Jogginganzug** *m* jogging suit, tracksuit; **Jogginghose** *f* jogging pants *pl*

Jog(h)urt (-s, -s) *m* o *nt* yoghurt

Johannisbeere *f*: **Schwarze ~** blackcurrant; **Rote ~** redcurrant

Joint (-s, -s) *m* (*fam*) joint

jonglieren *vi* to juggle

Jordanien (-s) *nt* Jordan

Journalist(in) *m(f)* journalist

Joystick (-s, -s) m (Inform) joystick

jubeln vi to cheer

Jubiläum (-s, Jubiläen) nt jubilee; (Jahrestag) anniversary

jucken vi to itch ▷ vt: **es juckt mich am Arm** my arm is itching; **das juckt mich nicht** (fam) I couldn't care less; **Juckreiz** m itch

Jude (-n, -n) m, **jüdin** f Jew; **sie ist Jüdin** she's Jewish; **jüdisch** adj Jewish

Judo (-(s)) nt judo

Jugend (-) f youth; **jugendfrei** adj: **ein ~er Film** a U-rated film (Brit), a G-rated film (US); **ein nicht ~er Film** an X-rated film; **Jugendgruppe** f youth group; **Jugendherberge** (-, -n) f youth hostel; **Jugendherbergsausweis** m youth hostel card; **jugendlich** adj youthful; **Jugendliche(r)** mf young person; **Jugendstil** m art nouveau; **Jugendzentrum** nt youth centre

Jugoslawien (-s) nt (Hist) Yugoslavia; **das ehemalige ~** the former Yugoslavia

Juli (-(s), -s) m July; siehe auch **Juni**

jung adj young

Junge (-n, -n) m boy

Junge(s) (-n, -n) nt young animal; **die ~n** pl the young pl

Jungfrau f virgin; (Astr) Virgo

Junggeselle (-n, -n) m bachelor; **Junggesellin** f single woman

Juni (-(s), -s) m June; **im ~** in June; **am 4. ~** on 4(th) June, on June 4(th) (gesprochen: on the fourth of June); **Anfang/Mitte/Ende ~** at the beginning/in the middle/at the end of June; **letzten/nächsten ~** last/next June

Jupiter (-s) m Jupiter

Jura ohne Artikel (Studienfach) law;

~ studieren to study law; **Jurist(in)** m(f) lawyer; **juristisch** adj legal

Justiz (-) f justice; **Justizminister(in)** m(f) minister of justice

Juwel (-s, -en) nt jewel; **Juwelier(in)** (-s, -e) m(f) jeweller

k

Kabel (-s, -) nt (Elek) wire; (stark) cable; **Kabelfernsehen** nt cable television

Kabeljau (-s, -e o -s) m cod

kabellos adj wireless

Kabine f cabin; (im Schwimmbad) cubicle

Kabrio (-s, -s) nt convertible

Kachel (-, -n) f tile; **Kachelofen** m tiled stove

Käfer (-s, -) m beetle, bug (US)

Kaff (-s, -s) nt dump, hole

Kaffee (-s, -s) m coffee; ~ **kochen** to make some coffee; **Kaffeefilter** m coffee filter; **Kaffeekanne** f coffeepot; **Kaffeeklatsch** (-(e)s, -e) m chat over coffee and cakes, coffee klatch (US); **Kaffeelöffel** m coffee spoon; **Kaffeemaschine** f coffee maker (o machine); **Kaffeetasse** f coffee cup

Käfig (-s, -e) m cage

kahl adj bald; (Baum, Wand) bare

Kahn (-(e)s, Kähne) m boat; (Lastkahn) barge

Kai (-s, -e o -s) m quay

Kaiser (-s, -) m emperor; **Kaiserin** f empress; **Kaiserschnitt** m (Med) caesarean (section)

Kajak (-s, -s) m kayak; **Kajakfahren** nt kayaking

Kajüte (-, -n) f cabin

Kakao (-s, -s) m cocoa; (Getränk) (hot) chocolate

Kakerlake (-, -n) f cockroach

Kaki (-, -s) f kaki

Kaktee (-, -n) f, **Kaktus** (-, -se) m cactus

Kalb (-(e)s, Kälber) nt calf; **Kalbfleisch** nt veal; **Kalbsbraten** m roast veal; **Kalbsschnitzel** nt veal cutlet; (paniert) escalope of veal

Kalender (-s, -) m calendar; (Taschenkalender) diary

Kalk (-(e)s, -e) m lime; (in Knochen) calcium

Kalorie f calorie; **kalorienarm** adj low-calorie

kalt adj cold; **mir ist (es)** ~ I'm cold; **kaltblütig** adj cold-blooded; **Kälte** (-) f cold; (fig) coldness

kam imperf von **kommen**

Kambodscha (-s) nt Cambodia

Kamel (-(e)s, -e) nt camel

Kamera (-, -s) f camera

Kamerad(in) (-en, -en) m(f) friend; (als Begleiter) companion

Kamerafrau f camerawoman; **Kamerahandy** nt cameraphone; **Kameramann** m cameraman

Kamille f camomile; **Kamillentee** m camomile tea

Kamin (-s, -e) m (außen) chimney; (innen) fireplace

Kamm (-(e)s, Kämme) m comb; (Berg) ridge; (Hahn) crest; **kämmen** vr **sich** ~, **sich** (dat) **die Haare** ~ to comb one's hair; **Kammermusik** f chamber music

Kampf (-(e)s, Kämpfe) m fight; (Schlacht) battle; (Wettbewerb) contest; (fig: Anstrengung) struggle; **kämpfen** vi to fight (für, um for); **Kampfsport** m martial art

Kanada (-s) nt Canada; **Kanadier(in)** (-s, -) m(f) Canadian; **kanadisch** adj Canadian

Kanal (-s, Kanäle) m (Fluss) canal; (Rinne, TV) channel; (für Abfluss) drain; **der ~** (Ärmelkanal) the (English) Channel; **Kanalinseln** pl Channel Islands pl; **Kanalisation** f sewerage system; **Kanaltunnel** m Channel Tunnel

Kanarienvogel m canary

Kandidat(in) (-en, -en) m(f) candidate

Kandis(zucker) (-) m rock candy

Känguru (-s, -s) nt kangaroo

Kaninchen (-s, -) nt rabbit

Kanister (-s, -) m can

Kännchen nt pot; **ein ~ Kaffee/Tee** a pot of coffee/tea; **Kanne** (-, -n) f (Krug) jug; (Kaffeekanne) pot; (Milchkanne) churn; (Gießkanne) can

kannte imperf von **kennen**

Kante (-, -n) f edge

Kantine f canteen

Kanton (-s, -e) m canton

Kanu (-s, -s) nt canoe

Kanzler(in) (-s, -) m(f) chancellor

Kap (-s, -s) nt cape

Kapazität f capacity; (Fachmann) authority

Kapelle f (Gebäude) chapel; (Mus) band

Kaper (-, -n) f caper

kapieren vt, vi (fam) to understand; **kapiert?** got it?

Kapital (-s, -e o -ien) nt capital

Kapitän (-s, -e) m captain

Kapitel (-s, -) nt chapter

Kappe (-, -n) f cap

Kapsel (-, -n) f capsule

kaputt adj (fam) broken; (Mensch) exhausted; **kaputt|gehen** irr vi to break; (Schuhe) to fall apart; (Firma) to go bust; (Stoff) to wear out; **kaputt|machen** vt to break; (jdn) to wear out

Kapuze (-, -n) f hood

Kap Verde (-s) nt Cape Verde

Karaffe (-, -n) f carafe; (mit Stöpsel) decanter

Karamell (-s) m caramel, toffee

Karaoke (-(s)) nt karaoke

Karat (-s, -e) nt carat

Karate (-s) nt karate

Kardinal (-s, Kardinäle) m cardinal

Karfreitag m Good Friday

kariert adj checked; (Papier) squared

Karies (-) f (tooth) decay

Karikatur f caricature

Karneval (-s, -e o -s) m carnival

Kärnten (-s) nt Carinthia

Karo (-s, -s) nt square; (Karten) diamonds pl

Karosserie f (Auto) body(work)

Karotte (-, -n) f carrot
Karpfen (-s, -) m carp
Karriere (-, -n) f career
Karte (-, -n) f card; (Landkarte) map; (Speisekarte) menu; (Eintrittskarte, Fahrkarte) ticket; **mit ~ bezahlen** to pay by credit card; **~n spielen** to play cards; **die ~n mischen/geben** to shuffle/deal the cards
Kartei f card index; **Karteikarte** f index card
Kartenspiel nt card game; **Kartentelefon** nt cardphone; **Kartenvorverkauf** m advance booking
Kartoffel (-, -n) f potato; **Kartoffelbrei** m mashed potatoes pl; **Kartoffelchips** pl crisps pl (Brit), chips pl (US); **Kartoffelpuffer** m potato cake (made from grated potatoes); **Kartoffelpüree** nt mashed potatoes pl; **Kartoffelsalat** m potato salad
Karton (-s, -s) m cardboard; (Schachtel) (cardboard) box
Kartusche (-, -n) f cartridge
Karussell (-s, -s) nt roundabout (Brit), merry-go-round
Kaschmir (-s, e) m (Stoff) cashmere
Käse (-s, -) m cheese; **Käsekuchen** m cheesecake; **Käseplatte** f cheeseboard
Kasino (-s, -s) nt (Spielkasino) casino
Kaskoversicherung f comprehensive insurance
Kasper(l) (-s, -) m Punch; (fig) clown; **Kasper(l)etheater** nt (Vorstellung) Punch and Judy show; (Gebäude) Punch and Judy theatre
Kasse (-, -n) f (in Geschäft) till, cash register; (im Supermarkt) checkout; (Geldkasten) cashbox;

(Theater) box office; (Kino) ticket office; (Krankenkasse) health insurance; (Spar~) savings bank; **Kassenbon** (-s, -s) m, **Kassenzettel** m receipt
Kassette f (small) box; (Tonband) cassette; **Kassettenrekorder** m cassette recorder
kassieren vt to take ▷ vi: **darf ich ~?** would you like to pay now?; **Kassierer(in)** m(f) cashier
Kastanie f chestnut
Kasten (-s, Kästen) m (Behälter) box; (Getränkekasten) crate
Kat m abk = **Katalysator**
Katalog (-(e)s, -e) m catalogue
Katalysator m (Auto) catalytic converter; (Phys) catalyst
Katar (-s) nt Qatar
Katarr(h) (-s, -e) m catarrh
Katastrophe (-, -n) f catastrophe, disaster
Kategorie (-, -n) f category
Kater (-s, -) m tomcat; (fam: nach zu viel Alkohol) hangover
Kathedrale (-, -n) f cathedral
Katholik(in) m(f) Catholic; **katholisch** adj Catholic
Katze (-, -n) f cat
Kauderwelsch (-(s)) nt (unverständlich) gibberish; (Fachjargon) jargon
kauen vt, vi to chew
Kauf (-(e)s, Käufe) m purchase; (Kaufen) buying; **ein guter ~** a bargain; **etw in ~ nehmen** to put up with sth; **kaufen** vt to buy; **Käufer(in)** m(f) buyer; **Kauffrau** f businesswoman; **Kaufhaus** nt department store; **Kaufmann** m businessman; (im Einzelhandel) shopkeeper (Brit), storekeeper (US); **Kaufpreis** m purchase price; **Kaufvertrag** m purchase agreement
Kaugummi m chewing gum
Kaulquappe (-, -n) f tadpole

kaum *adv* hardly, scarcely
Kaution *f* deposit; (*Jur*) bail
Kaviar *m* caviar
KB (-, -) *nt*, **Kbyte** (-, -) *nt abk* = **Kilobyte** KB
Kebab (-(s), -s) *m* kebab
Kegel (-s, -) *m* skittle; (*beim Bowling*) pin; (*Math*) cone;
Kegelbahn *f* bowling alley;
kegeln *vi* to play skittles; (*bowlen*) to bowl
Kehle (-, -n) *f* throat; **Kehlkopf** *m* larynx
Kehre (-, -n) *f* sharp bend
kehren *vt* (*fegen*) to sweep
Keilriemen *m* (*Auto*) fan belt
kein *pron* no, not ... any; **ich habe ~ Geld** I have no money, I don't have any money; **~ Mensch** no one; **du bist ~ Kind mehr** you're not a child any more; **keine(r, s)** *pron* (*Person*) no one, nobody; (*Sache*) not ... any, none; **~r von ihnen** none of them; (*bei zwei Personen/Sachen*) neither of them; **ich will keins von beiden** I don't want either of them; **keinesfalls** *adv* on no account, under no circumstances
Keks (-es, -e) *m* biscuit (*Brit*), cookie (*US*); **jdm auf den ~ gehen** (*fam*) to get on sb's nerves
Keller (-s, -) *m* cellar; (*Geschoss*) basement
Kellner (-s, -) *m* waiter;
Kellnerin *f* waitress
Kenia (-s) *nt* Kenya
kennen (*kannte, gekannt*) *vt* to know; **wir ~ uns seit 1990** we've known each other since 1990; **wir ~ uns schon** we've already met; **kennst du mich noch?** do you remember me?; **kennenlernen** *vt* to get to know; **sich ~** to get to know each other; (*zum ersten Mal*) to meet
Kenntnis *f* knowledge; **seine ~se** his knowledge

Kennwort *nt* (*a. Inform*) password; **Kennzeichen** *nt* mark, sign; (*Auto*) number plate (*Brit*), license plate (*US*); **besondere ~** distinguishing marks
Kerl (-s, -e) *m* guy, bloke (*Brit*)
Kern (-(e)s, -e) *m* (*Pfirsich, Kirsche etc*) stone; (*Nuss*) kernel; (*Atomkern*) nucleus; (*fig*) heart, core
Kernenergie *f* nuclear energy;
Kernkraft *f* nuclear power;
Kernkraftwerk *nt* nuclear power station
Kerze (-, -n) *f* candle; (*Zündkerze*) plug
Ket(s)chup (-(s), -s) *m o nt* ketchup
Kette (-, -n) *f* chain; (*Halskette*) necklace
keuchen *vi* to pant;
Keuchhusten *m* whooping cough
Keule (-, -n) *f* club; (*Gastr*) leg; (*von Hähnchen a.*) drumstick
Keyboard (-s, -s) *nt* (*Mus*) keyboard
Kfz *nt abk* = **Kraftfahrzeug**
Kfz-Brief *m* = logbook
Kfz-Steuer *f* = road tax (*Brit*), vehicle tax (*US*)
KG (-, -s) *f abk* = **Kommanditgesellschaft** limited partnership
Kichererbse *f* chick pea
kichern *vi* to giggle
Kickboard® (-s, -s) *nt* micro scooter
Kicker (-s, -) *m* (*Spiel*) table football (*Brit*), foosball (*US*)
kidnappen *vt* to kidnap
Kidney-Bohne *f* kidney bean
Kiefer (-s, -) *m* jaw ▶ (-, -n) *f* pine; **Kieferchirurg(in)** *m(f)* oral surgeon

Kieme (-, -n) f gill

Kies (-es, -e) m gravel; **Kiesel** (-s, -) m, **Kieselstein** m pebble

Kilo (-s, -(s)) nt kilo; **Kilobyte** nt kilobyte; **Kilogramm** nt kilogram; **Kilometer** m kilometre; **Kilometerstand** m ≈ mileage; **Kilometerzähler** m ≈ mileometer; **Kilowatt** nt kilowatt

Kind (-(e)s, -er) nt child; **sie bekommt ein ~** she's having a baby; **Kinderarzt** m, **Kinderärztin** f paediatrician; **Kinderbetreuung** f childcare; **Kinderbett** nt cot (Brit), crib (US); **Kinderfahrkarte** f child's ticket; **Kindergarten** m nursery school, kindergarten; **Kindergärtner(in)** m(f) nursery-school teacher; **Kindergeld** nt child benefit; **Kinderkrippe** f crèche (Brit), daycare center (US); **Kinderlähmung** f polio; **Kindermädchen** nt nanny (Brit), nurse(maid); **kindersicher** adj childproof; **Kindersicherung** f childproof safety catch; (an Flasche) childproof cap; **Kindersitz** m child seat; **Kindertagesstätte** f day nursery; **Kinderteller** m (im Restaurant) children's portion; **Kinderwagen** m pram (Brit), baby carriage (US); **Kinderzimmer** nt children's (bed)room; **Kindheit** f childhood; **kindisch** adj childish; **kindlich** adj childlike

Kinn (-(e)s, -e) nt chin

Kino (-s, -s) nt cinema (Brit), movie theater (US); **ins ~ gehen** to go to the cinema (Brit) (o to the movies (US))

Kiosk (-(e)s, -e) m kiosk

Kippe f (fam: Zigarettenstummel) cigarette end, fag end (Brit)

kippen vi to tip over ▷ vt to tilt; (Regierung, Minister) to topple

Kirche (-, -n) f church; **Kirchturm** m church tower; (mit Spitze) steeple; **Kirchweih** f fair

Kirmes (-, -sen) f fair

Kirsche (-, -n) f cherry; **Kirschtomate** f cherry tomato

Kissen (-s, -) nt cushion; (Kopfkissen) pillow; **Kissenbezug** m cushion cover; (für Kopfkissen) pillowcase

Kiste (-, -n) f box; (Truhe) chest

KITA (-, -s) f abk = **Kindertagesstätte** day-care centre (Brit), day-care center (US)

kitschig adj kitschy, cheesy

kitzelig adj (a. fig) ticklish; **kitzeln** vt, vi to tickle

Kiwi (-, -s) f (Frucht) kiwi (fruit)

Klage (-, -n) f complaint; (Jur) lawsuit; **klagen** vi to complain (über +akk about, bei to); **kläglich** adj wretched

Klammer (-, -n) f (in Text) bracket; (Büroklammer) clip; (Wäscheklammer) peg (Brit), clothespin (US); (Zahnklammer) brace; **Klammeraffe** m (fam) at-sign, @; **klammern** vr: **sich ~** to cling (an +akk to)

Klamotten pl (fam: Kleider) clothes pl

klang imperf von **klingen**

Klang (-(e)s, Klänge) m sound

Klappbett nt folding bed

klappen vi impers (gelingen) to work; **es hat gut geklappt** it went well

klappern vi to rattle; (Geschirr) to clatter; **Klapperschlange** f rattlesnake

Klapprad nt folding bicycle; **Klappstuhl** m folding chair

klar adj clear; **sich (dat) im Klaren sein** to be clear (über +akk about); **alles ~?** everything okay?

klären vt (Flüssigkeit) to purify; (Probleme, Frage) to clarify ▷ vr:

sich ~ to clear itself up
Klarinette (-, -n) f clarinet
klar|kommen irr vi: **mit etw ~** to cope with something; **kommst du klar?** are you managing all right?; **mit jdm ~** to get along with sb; **klar|machen** vt: **jdm etw ~** to make sth clear to sb; **klar|stellen** vt to clarify
Klärung f (von Frage, Problem) clarification
klasse adj inv (fam) great, brilliant
Klasse (-, -n) f class; (Schuljahr) form (Brit), grade (US); **erster ~ reisen** to travel first class; **in welche ~ gehst du?** which form (Brit) (o grade (US)) are you in?; **Klassenarbeit** f test; **Klassenlehrer(in)** m(f) class teacher; **Klassenzimmer** nt classroom
Klassik f (Zeit) classical period; (Musik) classical music
Klatsch (-(e)s, -e) m (Gerede) gossip; **klatschen** vi (schlagen) to smack; (Beifall) to applaud, to clap; (reden) to gossip; **klatschnass** adj soaking (wet)
Klaue (-, -n) f claw; (fam: Schrift) scrawl; **klauen** vt (fam) to pinch
Klavier (-s, -e) nt piano
Klebeband nt adhesive tape; **kleben** vt to stick (an +akk to) ▷ vi (klebrig sein) to be sticky; **klebrig** adj sticky; **Klebstoff** m glue; **Klebstreifen** m adhesive tape
Klecks (-es, -e) m blob; (Tinte) blot
Klee (-s) m clover
Kleid (-(e)s, -er) nt (Frauen-) dress; **~er** pl (Kleidung) clothes pl; **Kleiderbügel** m coat hanger; **Kleiderschrank** m wardrobe (Brit), closet (US); **Kleidung** f clothing
klein adj small, little; (Finger) little; **mein ~er Bruder** my little (o younger) brother; **als ich noch**

~ war when I was a little boy/girl; **etw ~ schneiden** to chop sth up; **Kleinanzeige** f classified ad; **Kleinbuchstabe** m small letter; **Kleinbus** m minibus; **Kleingeld** nt change; **Kleinigkeit** f trifle; (Zwischenmahlzeit) snack; **Kleinkind** nt toddler; **klein|schreiben** vt (mit kleinem Anfangsbuchstaben) to write with a small letter; **Kleinstadt** f small town
Kleister (-s, -) m paste
Klempner(in) m(f) plumber
klettern vi to climb
Klettverschluss m Velcro® fastening
klicken vi (a. Inform) to click
Klient(in) (-en, -en) m(f) client
Klima (-s, -s) nt climate; **Klimaanlage** f air conditioning; **klimatisiert** adj air-conditioned; **Klimawandel** m climate change
Klinge (-, -n) f blade
Klingel (-, -n) f bell; **klingeln** vi to ring
klingen (klang, geklungen) vi to sound
Klinik f clinic; (Krankenhaus) hospital
Klinke (-, -n) f handle
Klippe (-, -n) f cliff; (im Meer) reef; (fig) hurdle
Klischee (-s, -s) nt (fig) cliché
Klo (-s, -s) nt (fam) loo (Brit), john (US); **Klobrille** f toilet seat; **Klopapier** nt toilet paper
klopfen vt, vi to knock; (Herz) to thump
Kloß (-es, Klöße) m (im Hals) lump; (Gastr) dumpling
Kloster (-s, Klöster) nt (für Männer) monastery; (für Frauen) convent
Klub (-s, -s) m club
klug adj clever
knabbern vt, vi to nibble

Knäckebrot nt crispbread
knacken vt, vi to crack
Knall (-(e)s, -e) m bang; **knallen** vi to bang
knapp adj (kaum ausreichend) scarce; (Sieg) narrow; ~ **bei Kasse sein** to be short of money; ~ **zwei Stunden** just under two hours
Knauf (-s, Knäufe) m knob
kneifen (kniff, gekniffen) vt, vi to pinch; (sich drücken) to back out (vor +dat of); **Kneifzange** f pincers pl
Kneipe (-, -n) f (fam) pub (Brit), bar
Knete (-) f (fam: Geld) dough; **kneten** vt to knead; (formen) to mould
knicken vt, vi (brechen) to break; (Papier) to fold; **geknickt sein** (fig) to be downcast
Knie (-s, -) nt knee; **in die ~ gehen** to bend one's knees; **Kniebeuge** f knee bend; **Kniegelenk** nt knee joint; **Kniekehle** f back of the knee; **knien** vi to kneel; **Kniescheibe** f kneecap; **Knieschoner** (-s, -) m, **Knieschützer** (-s, -) m knee pad; **Kniestrumpf** m knee-length sock
kniff imperf von **kneifen**
knipsen vt to punch; (Foto) to snap ▷ vi (Foto) to take snaps
knirschen vi to crunch; **mit den Zähnen ~** to grind one's teeth
knitterfrei adj non-crease; **knittern** vi to crease
Knoblauch m garlic; **Knoblauchbrot** nt garlic bread; **Knoblauchzehe** f clove of garlic
Knöchel (-s, -) m (Finger) knuckle; (Fuß) ankle
Knochen (-s, -) m bone; **Knochenbruch** m fracture; **Knochenmark** nt marrow
Knödel (-s, -) m dumpling
Knollensellerie m celeriac

Knopf (-(e)s, Knöpfe) m button; **Knopfdruck** m: **auf ~** at the touch of a button; **Knopfloch** nt buttonhole
Knospe (-, -n) f bud
knoten vt to knot; **Knoten** (-s, -) m knot; (Med) lump
Know-how (-(s)) nt know-how, expertise
knurren vi (Hund) to growl; (Magen) to rumble; (Mensch) to grumble
knusprig adj crisp; (Keks) crunchy
knutschen vi (fam) to smooch
k. o. adj inv (Sport) knocked out; (fig) knackered
Koalition f coalition
Koch (-(e)s, Köche) m cook; **Kochbuch** nt cookery book, cookbook; **kochen** vt, vi to cook; (Wasser) to boil; (Kaffee, Tee) to make; **Köchin** f cook; **Kochlöffel** m wooden spoon; **Kochnische** f kitchenette; **Kochplatte** f hotplate; **Kochrezept** nt recipe; **Kochtopf** m saucepan
Kode (-s, -s) m code
Köder (-s, -) m bait
Koffein nt caffeine; **koffeinfrei** adj decaffeinated
Koffer (-s, -) m (suit)case; **Kofferraum** m (Auto) boot (Brit), trunk (US)
Kognak (-s, -s) m brandy
Kohl (-(e)s, -e) m cabbage
Kohle (-, -n) f coal; (Holzkohle) charcoal; (Chem) carbon; (fam: Geld) cash, dough; **Kohlehydrat** nt carbohydrate; **Kohlendioxid** nt carbon dioxide; **Kohlensäure** f (in Getränken) fizz; **ohne ~** still, non-carbonated (US); **mit ~** sparkling, carbonated (US); **Kohletablette** f charcoal tablet
Kohlrabi (-(s), -(s)) m kohlrabi
Koje (-, -n) f cabin; (Bett) bunk

Kokain (-s) nt cocaine
Kokosnuss f coconut
Kolben (-s, -) m (Tech) piston; (Mais~) cob
Kolik (-, -en) f colic
Kollaps (-es, -e) m collapse
Kollege (-n, -n) m, **Kollegin** f colleague
Köln (-s) nt Cologne; **Kölnischwasser** nt eau du cologne
Kolonne (-, -n) f convoy
Kölsch (-, -) nt (Bier) (strong) lager (from the Cologne region)
Kolumbien (-s) nt Columbia
Koma (-s, -s) nt coma
Kombi (-(s)s, -s) m estate (car) (Brit), station wagon (US)
Kombination f combination; (Folgerung) deduction; (Hemdhose) combinations pl; (Aviat) flying suit; **kombinieren** vt to combine ▷ vi to reason; (vermuten) to guess; **Kombizange** f (pair of) pliers pl
Komfort (-s) m conveniences pl; (Bequemlichkeit) comfort
Komiker(in) m(f) comedian, comic; **komisch** adj funny
Komma (-s, -s) nt comma
Kommanditgesellschaft f limited partnership
kommen (kam, gekommen) vi to come; (näher kommen) to approach; (passieren) to happen; (gelangen, geraten) to get; (erscheinen) to appear; (in die Schule, das Gefängnis etc) to go; ~ **lassen** to send for; **zu sich** ~ to come round (o to); **zu etw** ~ (bekommen) to acquire sth; (Zeit dazu finden) to get round to sth; **wer kommt zuerst?** who's first?; **kommend** adj coming; ~e **Woche** next week; **in den** ~en **Jahren** in the years to come
Kommentar m commentary; **kein** ~ no comment
Kommilitone (-n, -n) m,

Kommilitonin f fellow student
Kommissar(in) m(f) inspector
Kommode (-, -n) f chest of drawers
Kommunikation f communication
Kommunion f (Rel) communion
Kommunismus m communism
Komödie f comedy
kompakt adj compact
Kompass (-es, -e) m compass
kompatibel adj compatible
kompetent adj competent
komplett adj complete
Kompliment nt compliment; **jdm ein** ~ **machen** to pay sb a compliment; ~! congratulations
Komplize (-n, -n) m accomplice
kompliziert adj complicated
Komponist(in) m(f) composer
Kompost (-(e)s, -e) m compost; **Komposthaufen** m compost heap; **kompostierbar** adj biodegradable
Kompott (-(e)s, -e) nt stewed fruit
Kompresse (-, -n) f compress
Kompromiss (-es, -e) m compromise
Kondensmilch f condensed milk, evaporated milk
Kondition f (Leistungsfähigkeit) condition; **sie hat eine gute** ~ she's in good shape
Konditorei f cake shop; (mit Café) café
Kondom (-s, -e) nt condom
Konfektionsgröße f size
Konferenz f conference
Konfession f religion; (christlich) denomination
Konfetti (-(s)) nt confetti
Konfirmation f (Rel) confirmation
Konfitüre (-, -n) f jam
Konflikt (-(e)s, -e) m conflict
konfrontieren vt to confront

k

Kongress (-es, -e) m conference;
der ~ (Parlament der USA)
Congress
König (-(e)s, -e) m king; **Königin**
f queen; **königlich** adj royal;
Königreich nt kingdom
Konkurrenz f competition

🔵 SCHLÜSSELWORT

können (pt **konnte**, pp **gekonnt** o
(als Hilfsverb) **können**) vt, vi 1 to be
able to; **ich kann es machen** I can
do it, I am able to do it; **ich kann
es nicht machen** I can't do it, I'm
not able to do it; **ich kann nicht ...**
I can't ..., I cannot ...; **ich kann
nicht mehr** I can't go on
2 (wissen, beherrschen) to know;
können Sie Deutsch? can you
speak German?; **er kann gut
Englisch** he speaks English well;
sie kann keine Mathematik she
can't do mathematics
3 (dürfen) to be allowed to; **kann
ich gehen?** can I go?; **könnte ich
...?** could I ...?; **kann ich mit?** (fam)
can I come with you?
4 (möglich sein) **Sie könnten recht
haben** you may be right; **das kann
sein** that's possible; **kann sein**
maybe

konsequent adj consistent;
Konsequenz f consequence
konservativ adj conservative
Konserven pl tinned food sing
(Brit), canned food sing;
Konservendose f tin (Brit), can
konservieren vt to preserve;
Konservierungsmittel nt
preservative
Konsonant m consonant
Konsul(in) (-s, -n) m(f) consul;
Konsulat nt consulate
Kontakt (-(e)s, -e) m contact;
kontaktarm adj: **er ist ~** he lacks

contact with other people;
kontaktfreudig adj sociable;
Kontaktlinsen pl contact lenses
pl
Kontinent m continent
Konto (-s, **Konten**) nt account;
Kontoauszug m (bank)
statement;
Kontoauszugsdrucker m
bank-statement machine;
Kontoinhaber(in) m(f) account
holder; **Kontonummer** f
account number; **Kontostand** m
balance
Kontrabass m double bass
Kontrast (-(e)s, -e) m contrast
Kontrolle (-, -n) f control;
(Aufsicht) supervision;
(Passkontrolle) passport control;
kontrollieren vt to control;
(nachprüfen) to check
Konzentration f concentra-
tion; **Konzentrationslager** nt
(Hist) concentration camp;
konzentrieren vt to concentrate
▷ vr: **sich ~** to concentrate
Konzept (-(e)s, -e) nt rough draft;
jdn aus dem ~ bringen to put sb
off
Konzern (-(e)s, -e) m firm
Konzert (-(e)s, -e) nt concert;
(Stück) concerto; **Konzertsaal** m
concert hall
koordinieren vt to coordinate
Kopf (-(e)s, **Köpfe**) m head; **pro
~** per person; **sich den
~ zerbrechen** to rack one's brains;
Kopfhörer m headphones pl;
Kopfkissen nt pillow; **Kopfsalat**
m lettuce; **Kopfschmerzen** pl
headache sing; **Kopfstütze** f
headrest; **Kopftuch** nt
headscarf; **kopfüber** adv
headfirst
Kopie f copy; **kopieren** vt (a.
Inform) to copy; **Kopierer** (-s, -) m,
Kopiergerät nt copier

Kopilot(in) m(f) co-pilot

Koralle (-, -n) f coral

Koran (-s) m (Rel) Koran

Korb (-(e)s, Körbe) m basket; **jdm einen ~ geben** (fig) to turn sb down

Kord (-(e)s, -e) m corduroy

Kordel (-, -n) f cord

Kork (-(e)s, -e) m cork; **Korken** (-s, -) m cork; **Korkenzieher** (-s, -) m corkscrew

Korn (-(e)s, Körner) nt grain; **Kornblume** f cornflower

Körper (-s, -) m body; **Körperbau** m build; **Körpergeruch** m body odour; **Körpergröße** f height; **körperlich** adj physical; **Körperteil** m part of the body; **Körperverletzung** f physical injury

korrekt adj correct

Korrespondent(in) m(f) correspondent; **Korrespondenz** f correspondence

korrigieren vt to correct

Kosmetik f cosmetics pl; **Kosmetikkoffer** m vanity case; **Kosmetiksalon** m beauty parlour; **Kosmetiktuch** nt paper tissue

Kost (-) f (Nahrung) food; (Verpflegung) board

kostbar adj precious; (teuer) costly, expensive

kosten vt to cost ▷ vt, vi (versuchen) to taste; **Kosten** pl costs pl, cost; (Ausgaben) expenses pl; **auf ~ von** at the expense of; **kostenlos** adj free (of charge); **Kostenvoranschlag** m estimate

köstlich adj (Essen) delicious; (Einfall) delightful; **sich ~ amüsieren** to have a marvellous time

Kostprobe f taster; (fig) sample; **kostspielig** adj expensive

Kostüm (-s, -e) nt costume;

(Damenkostüm) suit

Kot (-(e)s) m excrement

Kotelett (-(e)s, -e o -s) nt chop, cutlet

Koteletten pl sideboards pl (Brit), sideburns pl (US)

Kotflügel m (Auto) wing

kotzen vi (vulg) to puke, to throw up

Krabbe (-, -n) f shrimp; (größer) prawn; (Krebs) crab

krabbeln vi to crawl

Krach (-(e)s, -s o -e) m crash; (andauernd) noise; (fam: Streit) row

Kraft (-, Kräfte) f strength; (Pol, Phys) force; (Fähigkeit) power; (Arbeits~) worker; **in ~ treten** to come into effect; **Kraftausdruck** m swearword; **Kraftfahrzeug** nt motor vehicle; **Kraftfahrzeugbrief** m ≈ logbook; **Kraftfahrzeugschein** m vehicle registration document; **Kraftfahrzeugsteuer** f ≈ road tax (Brit), vehicle tax (US); **Kraftfahrzeugversicherung** f car insurance; **kräftig** adj strong; (gesund) healthy; (Farben) intense, strong; **Kraftstoff** m fuel; **Kraftwerk** nt power station

Kragen (-s, -) m collar

Krähe (-, -n) f crow

Kralle (-, -n) f claw; (Parkkralle) wheel clamp

Kram (-(e)s) m stuff

Krampf (-(e)s, Krämpfe) m cramp; (zuckend) spasm; **Krampfader** f varicose vein

Kran (-(e)s, Kräne) m crane

Kranich (-s, -e) m (Zool) crane

krank adj ill, sick

kränken vt to hurt

Krankengymnastik f physiotherapy; **Krankenhaus** nt hospital; **Krankenkasse** f health insurance; **Krankenpfleger** (-s, -) m (male) nurse;

Krankenschein m health insurance certificate; **Krankenschwester** f nurse; **Krankenversicherung** f health insurance; **Krankenwagen** m ambulance; **Krankheit** f illness; (durch Infektion hervorgerufen) disease

Kränkung f insult

Kranz (-es, Kränze) m wreath

krass adj crass; (fam: toll) wicked

kratzen vt, vi to scratch; **Kratzer** (-s, -) m scratch

kraulen vi (schwimmen) to do the crawl ▷ vt (streicheln) to pet

Kraut (-(e)s, Kräuter) nt plant; (Gewürz) herb; (Gemüse) cabbage; **Kräuter** pl herbs pl; **Kräuterbutter** f herb butter; **Kräutertee** m herbal tea; **Krautsalat** m coleslaw

Krawatte f tie

kreativ adj creative

Krebs (-es, -e) m (Zool) crab; (Med) cancer; (Astr) Cancer

Kredit (-(e)s, -e) m credit; **auf ~** on credit; **einen ~ aufnehmen** to take out a loan; **Kreditkarte** f credit card

Kreide (-, -n) f chalk

Kreis (-es, -e) m circle; (Bezirk) district

kreischen vi to shriek; (Bremsen, Säge) to screech

Kreisel (-s, -) m (Spielzeug) top; (Verkehrskreisel) roundabout (Brit), traffic circle (US)

Kreislauf m (Med) circulation; (fig: der Natur etc) cycle; **Kreislaufstörungen** pl (Med) **ich habe ~** I've got problems with my circulation; **Kreisverkehr** m roundabout (Brit), traffic circle (US)

Kren (-s) m horseradish

Kresse (-, -n) f cress

Kreuz (-es, -e) nt cross; (Anat) small of the back; (Karten) clubs pl;

mir tut das ~ weh I've got backache; **Kreuzband** m cruciate ligament; **kreuzen** vt to cross ▷ vr: **sich ~** to cross ▷ vi (Naut) to cruise; **Kreuzfahrt** f cruise; **Kreuzgang** m cloisters pl; **Kreuzotter** (-, -n) f adder; **Kreuzschlitzschraubenzieher** m Phillips® screwdriver; **Kreuzschlüssel** m (Auto) wheel brace; **Kreuzschmerzen** pl backache sing; **Kreuzung** f (Verkehrskreuzung) crossroads sing, intersection; (Züchtung) cross; **Kreuzworträtsel** nt crossword (puzzle)

kriechen (kroch, gekrochen) vi to crawl; (unauffällig) to creep; (fig, pej) (vor jdm) **~** to crawl (to sb); **Kriechspur** f crawler lane

Krieg (-(e)s, -e) m war

kriegen vt (fam) to get; (erwischen) to catch; **sie kriegt ein Kind** she's having a baby; **ich kriege noch Geld von dir** you still owe me some money

Krimi (-s, -s) m (fam) thriller; **Kriminalität** f criminality; **Kriminalpolizei** f detective force, **~ CID** (Brit), **~ FBI** (US); **Kriminalroman** m detective novel; **kriminell** adj criminal

Krippe (-, -n) f (Futterkrippe) manger; (Weihnachtskrippe) crib (Brit), crèche (US); (Kinderkrippe) crèche (Brit), daycare center (US)

Krise (-, -n) f crisis

Kristall (-s, -e) m crystal ▷ (-s) nt (Glas) crystal

Kritik f criticism; (Rezension) review; **Kritiker(in)** m(f) critic; **kritisch** adj critical

kritzeln vt, vi to scribble, to scrawl

Kroate (-n, -n) m Croat; **Kroatien** (-s) nt Croatia; **Kroatin** f Croat; **kroatisch** adj Croatian;

Kroatisch nt Croatian

kroch imperf von **kriechen**

Krokodil (-s, -e) nt crocodile

Krokus (-, - o -se) m crocus

Krone (-, -n) f crown;
Kronleuchter m chandelier

Kropf (-(e)s, Kröpfe) m (Med)
goitre; (von Vogel) crop

Kröte (-, -n) f toad

Krücke (-, -n) f crutch

Krug (-(e)s, Krüge) m jug;
(Bierkrug) mug

Krümel (-s, -) m crumb

krumm adj crooked

Krüppel (-s, -) m cripple (pej)

Kruste (-, -n) f crust

Kruzifix (-es, -e) nt crucifix

Kuba (-s) nt Cuba

Kübel (-s, -) m tub; (Eimer) bucket

Kubikmeter m cubic metre

Küche (-, -n) f kitchen; (Kochen)
cooking

Kuchen (-s, -) m cake; (mit
Teigdeckel) pie; **Kuchengabel** f
cake fork

Küchenmaschine f food
processor; **Küchenpapier** nt
kitchen roll; **Küchenschrank** m
(kitchen) cupboard

Kuckuck (-s, -e) m cuckoo

Kugel (-, -n) f ball; (Math) sphere;
(Mil) bullet; (Weihnachtskugel)
bauble; **Kugellager** nt ball
bearing; **Kugelschreiber** m
(ball-point) pen, biro® (Brit);
Kugelstoßen (-s) nt shot put

Kuh (-, Kühe) f cow

kühl adj cool; **Kühlakku** (-s, -s) m
ice pack; **Kühlbox** f cool box;
kühlen vt to cool; **Kühler** (-s, -)
m (Auto) radiator; **Kühlerhaube**
f (Auto) bonnet (Brit), hood (US);
Kühlschrank m fridge,
refrigerator; **Kühltasche** f cool
bag; **Kühltruhe** f freezer;
Kühlwasser nt (Auto) radiator
water

Kuhstall m cowshed

Küken (-s, -) nt chick

Kuli (-s, -s) m (fam: Kugelschreiber)
pen, biro® (Brit)

Kulisse (-, -n) f scenery

Kult (-s, -e) m cult; **Kultfigur** f
cult figure

Kultur f culture; (Lebensform)
civilization; **Kulturbeutel** m
toilet bag (Brit), washbag;
kulturell adj cultural

Kümmel (-s, -) m caraway
seeds pl

Kummer (-s) m grief, sorrow

kümmern vr: **sich um jdn ~** to
look after sb; **sich um etw ~** to see
to sth ▷ vt to concern; **das
kümmert mich nicht** that doesn't
worry me

Kumpel (-s, -) m (fam) mate, pal

Kunde (-n, -n) m customer;
Kundendienst m after-sales (o
customer) service;
Kunden(kredit)karte f storecard, chargecard; **Kunden-
nummer** f customer number

kündigen vi to hand in one's
notice; (Mieter) to give notice that
one is moving out; **jdm ~** to give
sb his/her notice; (Vermieter) to
give sb notice to quit ▷ vt to
cancel; (Vertrag) to terminate; **jdm
die Stellung ~** to give sb his/her
notice; **jdm die Wohnung ~** to
give sb notice to quit; **Kündigung**
f (Arbeitsverhältnis) dismissal;
(Vertrag) termination;
(Abonnement) cancellation; (Frist)
notice; **Kündigungsfrist** f
period of notice

Kundin f customer; **Kundschaft**
f customers pl

künftig adj future

Kunst (-, Künste) f art; (Können)
skill; **Kunstausstellung** f art
exhibition; **Kunstgewerbe** nt arts
and crafts pl; **Künstler(in)** (-s, -)

m(f) artist; **künstlerisch** *adj* artistic

künstlich *adj* artificial

Kunststoff *m* synthetic material; **Kunststück** *nt* trick; **Kunstwerk** *nt* work of art

Kupfer (-s, -) *nt* copper

Kuppel (-, -n) *f* dome

kuppeln *vi* (*Auto*) to operate the clutch; **Kupplung** *f* coupling; (*Auto*) clutch

Kur (-, -en) *f* course of treatment; (*am Kurort*) cure

Kür (-, -en) *f* (*Sport*) free programme

Kurbel (-, -n) *f* crank; (*von Rollo, Fenster*) winder

Kürbis (-ses, -se) *m* pumpkin

Kurierdienst *m* courier service

kurieren *vt* to cure

Kurort *m* health resort

Kurs (-es, -e) *m* course; (*Fin*) rate; (*Wechselkurs*) exchange rate

kursiv *adj* italic ▷ *adv* in italics

Kursleiter(in) *m(f)* course tutor; **Kursteilnehmer(in)** *m(f)* (*course*) participant; **Kurswagen** *m* (*Eisenb*) through carriage

Kurve (-, -n) *f* curve; (*Straßenkurve*) bend; **kurvenreich** *adj* (*Straße*) winding

kurz *adj* short; (*zeitlich a.*) brief; **~ vorher/darauf** shortly before/after; **kannst du ~ kommen?** could you come here for a minute?; **~ gesagt** in short; **kurzärmelig** *adj* short-sleeved; **kürzen** *vt* to cut short; (*in der Länge*) to shorten; (*Gehalt*) to reduce; **kurzerhand** *adv* on the spot; **kurzfristig** *adj* short-term; **das Konzert wurde ~ abgesagt** the concert was called off at short notice; **Kurzgeschichte** *f* short story; **kurzhaarig** *adj* short-haired; **kürzlich** *adv* recently; **Kurzparkzone** *f*

short-stay (*Brit*) (*o* short-term (*US*)) parking zone; **Kurzschluss** *m* (*Elek*) short circuit; **kurzsichtig** *adj* short-sighted; **Kurztrip** *m* trip, break; **Kurzurlaub** *m* short holiday (*Brit*), short vacation (*US*); **Kurzwelle** *f* short wave

Kusine *f* cousin

Kuss (-es, Küsse) *m* kiss; **küssen** *vt* to kiss ▷ *vr*: **sich ~** to kiss

Küste (-, -n) *f* coast; (*Ufer*) shore; **Küstenwache** *f* coastguard

Kutsche (-, -n) *f* carriage; (*geschlossene*) coach

Kuvert (-s, -s) *nt* envelope

Kuvertüre (-, -n) *f* coating

Kuwait (-s) *nt* Kuwait

KZ (-s, -s) *nt abk* = **Konzentrationslager** (*Hist*) concentration camp

L

Labor (-s, -e o -s) nt lab

Labyrinth (-s, -e) nt maze

Lache (-, -n) f (Pfütze) puddle; (Blut~, Öl~) pool

lächeln vi to smile; **Lächeln** (-s) nt smile; **lachen** vi to laugh; **lächerlich** adj ridiculous

Lachs (-es, -e) m salmon

Lack (-(e)s, -e) m varnish; (Farblack) lacquer; (an Auto) paint; **lackieren** vt to varnish; (Auto) to spray; **Lackschaden** m scratch (on the paintwork)

Ladegerät nt (battery) charger; **laden** (lud, geladen) vt (a. Inform) to load; (einladen) to invite; (Handy etc) to charge

Laden (-s, Läden) m shop; (Fensterladen) shutter; **Ladendieb(in)** m(f) shoplifter; **Ladendiebstahl** m shoplifting; **Ladenschluss** m closing time

Ladung f load; (Naut, Aviat)

cargo; (Jur) summons sing

lag imperf von **liegen**

Lage (-, -n) f position, situation; (Schicht) layer; **in der ~ sein zu** to be in a position to

Lager (-s, -) nt camp; (Comm) warehouse; (Tech) bearing; **Lagerfeuer** nt campfire; **lagern** vi (Dinge) to be stored; (Menschen) to camp ▷ vt to store

Lagune f lagoon

lahm adj lame; (langweilig) dull; **lähmen** vt to paralyse; **Lähmung** f paralysis

Laib (-s, -e) m loaf

Laie (-n, -n) m layman

Laken (-s, -) nt sheet

Lakritze (-, -n) f liquorice

Lamm (-(e)s, Lämmer) nt lamb

Lampe (-, -n) f lamp; (Glühbirne) bulb; **Lampenfieber** nt stage fright; **Lampenschirm** m lampshade

Lampion (-s, -s) m Chinese lantern

Land (-(e)s, Länder) nt (Gelände) land; (Nation) country; (Bundesland) state, Land; **auf dem ~(e)** in the country

○ **LAND**
○
○ A **Land** (plural **Länder**) is a
○ member state of the **BRD**. There
○ are 16 **Länder**, namely
○ Baden-Württemberg, Bayern,
○ Berlin, Brandenburg, Bremen,
○ Hamburg, Hessen,
○ Mecklenburg-Vorpommern,
○ Niedersachsen,
○ Nordrhein-Westfalen,
○ Rheinland-Pfalz, Saarland,
○ Sachsen, Sachsen-Anhalt,
○ Schleswig-Holstein and
○ Thüringen. Each "Land" has its
○ own parliament and
○ constitution.

Landebahn f runway; **landen** vt, vi to land; (Schiff) to dock

Länderspiel nt international (match)

Landesgrenze f national border, frontier; **Landesinnere** nt interior; **landesüblich** adj customary; **Landeswährung** f national currency; **landesweit** adj nationwide

Landhaus nt country house; **Landkarte** f map; **Landkreis** m administrative region, ≈ district

ländlich adj rural

Landschaft f countryside; (schöne) scenery; (Kunst) landscape; **Landstraße** f country road, B road (Brit)

Landung f landing; **Landungsbrücke** f, **Landungssteg** m gangway

Landwirt(in) m(f) farmer; **Landwirtschaft** f agriculture, farming; **landwirtschaftlich** adj agricultural

lang adj long; (Mensch) tall; **ein zwei Meter ~er Tisch** a table two metres long; **den ganzen Tag ~** all day long; **die Straße ~** along the street; **langärmelig** adj long-sleeved; **lange** adv (for) a long time; **ich musste ~ warten** I had to wait (for) a long time; **ich bleibe nicht ~** I won't stay long; **es ist ~ her, dass wir uns gesehen haben** it's a long time since we saw each other; **Länge** (-, -n) f length; (Geo) longitude

langen vi (fam: ausreichen) to be enough; (fam: fassen) to reach (nach for); **mir langt's** I've had enough

Langeweile f boredom

langfristig adj long-term ▷ adv in the long term

Langlauf m cross-country skiing

längs prep +gen **die Bäume ~ der Straße** the trees along(side) the road ▷ adv: **die Streifen laufen ~ über das Hemd** the stripes run lengthways down the shirt

langsam adj slow ▷ adv slowly

Langschläfer(in) (-s, -) m(f) late riser

längst adv: **das ist ~ fertig** that was finished a long time ago; **sie sollte ~ da sein** she should have been here long ago; **als sie kam, waren wir ~ weg** when she arrived we had long since left

Langstreckenflug m long-haul flight

Languste (-, -n) f crayfish, crawfish (US)

langweilen vt to bore; **ich langweile mich** I'm bored; **langweilig** adj boring; **Langwelle** f long wave

Laos (-) nt Laos

Lappen (-s, -) m cloth, rag; (Staublappen) duster

läppisch (Summe) ridiculous

Laptop (-s, -s) m laptop

Lärche (-, -n) f larch

Lärm (-(e)s) m noise

las imperf von lesen

Lasche (-, -n) f flap

Laser (-s, -) m laser; **Laserdrucker** m laser printer

🔵 SCHLÜSSELWORT

lassen (pt **ließ**, pp **gelassen** o (als Hilfsverb) **lassen**) vt **1** (unterlassen) to stop; (momentan) to leave; **lass das (sein)!** don't (do it)!; (hör auf!) stop it!; **lass mich!** leave me alone; **lassen wir das!** let's leave it; **er kann das Trinken nicht lassen** he can't stop drinking **2** (zurücklassen) to leave; **etw lassen, wie es ist** to leave sth (just) as it is

3 (*überlassen*) **jdn ins Haus lassen** to let sb into the house
▷ *vi* ; **lass mal**, ich mache das schon leave it, I'll do it
▷ *Hilfsverb* 1 (*veranlassen*) **etw machen lassen** to have o get sth done; **sich *dat* etw schicken lassen** to have sth sent (to one)
2 (*zulassen*) **jdn etw wissen lassen** to let sb know sth; **das Licht brennen lassen** to leave the light on; **jdn warten lassen** to keep sb waiting; **das lässt sich machen** that can be done
3 **lass uns gehen** let's go

lässig *adj* casual
Last (-, -en) *f* load; (*Bürde*) burden; (*Naut, Aviat*) cargo
Laster (-s, -) *nt* vice; (*fam*) truck, lorry (Brit)
lästern *vi*: **über jdn/etw ~** to make nasty remarks about sb/sth
lästig *adj* annoying; (*Person*) tiresome
Last-Minute-Angebot *nt* last-minute offer; **Last-Minute-Flug** *m* last-minute flight; **Last-Minute-Ticket** *nt* last-minute ticket
Lastwagen *m* truck, lorry (Brit)
Latein (-s) *nt* Latin
Laterne (-, -n) *f* lantern; (*Straßenlaterne*) streetlight
Latte (-, -n) *f* slat; (*Sport*) bar
Latz (-es, Lätze) *m* bib; **Lätzchen** *nt* bib; **Latzhose** *f* dungarees pl
lau *adj* (*Wind, Luft*) mild
Laub (-(e)s) *nt* foliage; **Laubfrosch** *m* tree frog; **Laubsäge** *f* fretsaw
Lauch (-(e)s) *m* leek; **eine Stange ~** a leek; **Lauchzwiebel** *f* spring onions pl (Brit), scallions pl (US)
Lauf (-(e)s, Läufe) *m* run; (*Wettlauf*) race; (*Entwicklung*) course; (*von*

Gewehr) barrel; **Laufbahn** *f* career; **laufen** (*lief, gelaufen*) *vi, vt* to run; (*gehen*) to walk; (*funktionieren*) to work; **mir läuft die Nase** my nose is running; **was läuft im Kino?** what's on at the cinema?; **wie läuft's so?** how are things?; **laufend** *adj* running; (*Monat, Ausgaben*) current; **auf dem Laufenden sein/halten** to be/to keep up-to-date; **Läufer** (-s, -) *m* (*Teppich*) rug; (*Schach*) bishop; **Läufer/in** *m(f)* (*Sport*) runner; **Laufmasche** *f* ladder (Brit), run (US); **Laufwerk** *nt* (*Inform*) drive
Laune (-, -n) *f* mood; **gute/schlechte ~ haben** to be in a good/bad mood; **launisch** *adj* moody
Laus (-, Läuse) *f* louse
lauschen *vi* to listen; (*heimlich*) to eavesdrop
laut *adj* loud ▷ *adv* loudly; (*lesen*) aloud ▷ *prep* +*gen o dat* according to
läuten *vt, vi* to ring
lauter *adv* (*fam: nichts als*) nothing but
Lautsprecher *m* loudspeaker; **Lautstärke** *f* loudness; (*Radio, TV*) volume
lauwarm *adj* lukewarm
Lava (-, *Laven*) *f* lava
Lavendel (-s, -) *m* lavender
Lawine *f* avalanche
LCD-Anzeige *f* LCD-display
leasen *vt* to lease; **Leasing** (-s) *nt* leasing
leben *vt, vi* to live; (*am Leben sein*) to be alive; **wie lange ~ Sie schon hier?** how long have you been living here?; **von ... ~** (*Nahrungsmittel etc*) to live on ...; (*Beruf, Beschäftigung*) to make one's living from ...; **Leben** (-s, -) *nt* life; **lebend** *adj* living; **lebendig** *adj* alive; (*lebhaft*) lively;

lebensgefährlich adj very dangerous; (Verletzung) critical;
Lebensgefährte m, **Lebensgefährtin** f partner;
Lebenshaltungskosten pl cost sing of living; **lebenslänglich** adj for life; **~ bekommen** to get life;
Lebenslauf m curriculum vitae (Brit), CV (Brit), resumé (US);
Lebensmittel pl food sing;
Lebensmittelgeschäft nt grocer's (shop); **Lebensmittelvergiftung** f food poisoning;
lebensnotwendig adj vital;
Lebensretter(in) m(f) rescuer;
Lebensstandard m standard of living; **Lebensunterhalt** m livelihood; **Lebensversicherung** f life insurance (o assurance (Brit));
Lebenszeichen nt sign of life
Leber (-, -n) f liver; **Leberfleck** m mole; **Leberpastete** f liver pâté

Lebewesen nt living being
lebhaft adj lively; (Erinnerung, Eindruck) vivid; **Lebkuchen** m gingerbread; **ein ~** a piece of gingerbread; **leblos** adj lifeless
Leck nt leak
lecken vi (Loch haben) to leak ▷ vt, vi (schlecken) to lick
lecker adj delicious, tasty
Leder (-s, -) nt leather
ledig adj single
leer adj empty; (Seite) blank; (Batterie) dead; **leeren** vt to empty ▷ vr: **sich ~** to empty;
Leerlauf m (Gang) neutral;
Leertaste f space bar; **Leerung** f emptying; (Briefkasten) collection; **Leerzeichen** nt blank, space
legal adj legal, lawful
legen vt to put, to place; (Eier) to lay ▷ vr: **sich ~** to lie down; (Sturm, Begeisterung) to die down; (Schmerz, Gefühl) to wear off

Legende (-, -n) f legend
leger adj casual
Lehm (-(e)s, -e) m loam; (Ton) clay
Lehne (-, -n) f arm(rest); (Rückenlehne) back(rest); **lehnen** vt to lean ▷ vr: **sich ~** to lean (an/gegen +akk against); **Lehnstuhl** m armchair

Lehrbuch nt textbook; **Lehre** (-, -n) f teaching; (beruflich) apprenticeship; (moralisch) lesson;
lehren vt to teach; **Lehrer(in)** (-s, -) m(f) teacher; **Lehrgang** m course; **Lehrling** m apprentice;
lehrreich adj instructive
Leib (-(e)s, -er) m body;
Leibgericht nt, **Leibspeise** f favourite dish; **Leibwächter(in)** m(f) bodyguard
Leiche (-, -n) f corpse;
Leichenhalle f mortuary;
Leichenwagen m hearse
leicht adj light; (einfach) easy, simple; (Erkrankung) slight; **es sich** (dat) **~ machen** to take the easy way out ▷ adv (mühelos, schnell) easily; (geringfügig) slightly;
Leichtathletik f athletics sing;
leicht|fallen irr vi: **jdm ~** to be easy for sb; **leichtsinnig** adj careless; (stärker) reckless
leid adj: **jdn/etw ~ sein** to be tired of sb/sth; **Leid** (-(e)s) nt grief, sorrow; **leiden** (litt, gelitten) vi, vt to suffer (an, unter +dat from);
ich kann ihn/es nicht ~ I can't stand him/it; **Leiden** (-s, -) nt suffering; (Krankheit) illness
Leidenschaft f passion;
leidenschaftlich adj passionate
leider adv unfortunately; **wir müssen jetzt ~ gehen** I'm afraid we have to go now; **~ ja/nein** I'm afraid so/not
leid|tun vi: **es tut mir/ihm leid** I'm/he's sorry; **er tut mir leid** I'm sorry for him

Leihbücherei f lending library
leihen (lieh, geliehen) vt: **jdm etw ~** to lend sb sth; **sich** (dat) **etw von jdm ~** to borrow sth from sb;
Leihfrist f lending period;
Leihgebühr f hire charge; (für Buch) lending charge; **Leihwagen** m hire car (Brit), rental car (US)
Leim (-(e)s, -e) m glue
Leine (-, -n) f cord; (für Wäsche) line; (Hundeleine) lead (Brit), leash (US)
Leinen (-s, -) nt linen; **Leintuch** nt (für Bett) sheet; **Leinwand** f (Kunst) canvas; (Cine) screen
leise adj quiet; (sanft) soft ▷ adv quietly
Leiste (-, -n) f ledge; (Zierleiste) strip; (Anat) groin
leisten vt (Arbeit) to do; (vollbringen) to achieve; **jdm Gesellschaft ~** to keep sb company; **sich** (dat) **etw ~** (gönnen) to treat oneself to sth; **ich kann es mir nicht ~** I can't afford it
Leistenbruch m hernia
Leistung f performance; (gute) achievement
Leitartikel m leading article (Brit), editorial (US)
leiten vt to lead; (Firma) to run; (in eine Richtung) to direct; (Elek) to conduct
Leiter (-, -n) f ladder
Leiter(in) (-s, -) m(f) (von Geschäft) manager
Leitplanke (-, -n) f crash barrier
Leitung f (Führung) direction; (Tel) line; (von Firma) management; (Wasserleitung) pipe; (Kabel) cable; **eine lange ~ haben** to be slow on the uptake; **Leitungswasser** nt tap water
Lektion (-, -en) f lesson
Lektüre (-, -n) f (Lesen) reading; (Lesestoff) reading matter

Lende (-, -n) f (Speise) loin; (vom Rind) sirloin; **die ~n pl** (Med) the lumbar region sing
lenken vt to steer; (Blick) to direct (auf +akk towards); **jds Aufmerksamkeit auf etw** (akk) **~** to draw sb's attention to sth; **Lenker** m (von Fahrrad, Motorrad) handlebars pl; **Lenkrad** nt steering wheel; **Lenkradschloss** nt steering lock; **Lenkstange** f handlebars pl
Leopard (-en, -en) m leopard
Lepra (-) f leprosy
Lerche (-, -n) f lark
lernen vt, vi to learn; (für eine Prüfung) to study, to revise
lesbisch adj lesbian
Lesebuch nt reader; **lesen** (las, gelesen) vi, vt to read; (ernten) to pick; **Leser(in)** m(f) reader; **Leserbrief** m letter to the editor; **leserlich** adj legible; **Lesezeichen** nt bookmark
Lettland nt Latvia
letzte(r, s) adj last; (neueste) latest; (endgültig) final; **zum ~n Mal** for the last time; **am ~n Montag** last Monday; **in ~r Zeit** lately, recently; **letztens** adv (vor kurzem) recently; **letztere(r, s)** adj the latter
Leuchtanzeige f illuminated display; **Leuchte** (-, -n) f lamp, light; **leuchten** vi to shine; (Feuer, Zifferblatt) to glow; **Leuchter** (-s, -) m candlestick; **Leuchtfarbe** f fluorescent colour; (Anstrichfarbe) luminous paint; **Leuchtreklame** f neon sign; **Leuchtstoffröhre** f strip light; **Leuchtturm** m lighthouse
leugnen vt to deny ▷ vi to deny everything
Leukämie f leukaemia (Brit), leukemia (US)

Leukoplast® (-(e)s, -e) nt
Elastoplast® (Brit), Band-Aid®
(US)

Leute pl people pl

Lexikon (-s, Lexika) nt encyclopaedia (Brit), encyclopedia (US);
(Wörterbuch) dictionary

Libanon (-s) m: **der ~** Lebanon

Libelle f dragonfly

liberal adj liberal

Libyen (-s) nt Libya

Licht (-(e)s, -er) nt light;
Lichtblick m ray of hope;
lichtempfindlich adj sensitive to
light; **Lichtempfindlichkeit** f
(Foto) speed; **Lichthupe** f: **die
~ betätigen** to flash one's lights;
Lichtjahr nt light year;
Lichtmaschine f dynamo;
Lichtschalter m light switch;
Lichtschranke f light barrier;
Lichtschutzfaktor m sun
protection factor, SPF

Lichtung f clearing

Lid (-(e)s, -er) nt eyelid;
Lidschatten m eyeshadow

lieb adj (nett) nice; (teuer, geliebt)
dear; (liebenswert) sweet; **das ist
~ von dir** that's nice of you; **Lieber
Herr X** Dear Mr X; **Liebe** (-, -n) f
love; **lieben** vt to love; (sexuell) to
make love to; **liebenswürdig** adj
kind; **lieber** adv rather; **ich
möchte ~ nicht** I'd rather not;
welches ist dir ~? which one do
you prefer?; siehe auch **gern, lieb**;
Liebesbrief m love letter;
Liebeskummer m: **~ haben** to be
lovesick; **Liebespaar** nt lovers pl;
liebevoll adj loving;
Liebhaber(in) (-s, -) m(f) lover;
lieblich adj lovely; (Wein) sweet;
Liebling m darling; (Günstling)
favourite; **Lieblings-** in zW
favourite; **liebste(r, s)** adj
favourite; **liebsten** adv: **am
~ esse ich ...** my favourite food

is ...; **am ~ würde ich bleiben** I'd
really like to stay

Liechtenstein (-s) nt
Liechtenstein

Lied (-(e)s, -er) nt song; (Rel) hymn

lief imperf von **laufen**

Lieferant(in) m(f) supplier

lieferbar adj available

liefern vt to deliver; (beschaffen)
to supply

Lieferschein m delivery note;
Lieferung f delivery;
Lieferwagen m delivery van

Liege (-, -n) f (beim Arzt) couch;
(Notbett) campbed; (Gartenliege)
lounger; **liegen** (lag, gelegen) vi to
lie; (sich befinden) to be; **mir liegt
nichts/viel daran** it doesn't
matter to me/it matters a lot to
me; **woran liegt es nur, dass ...?**
why is it that ...?; **~ bleiben**
(Mensch) to stay lying down; (im
Bett) to stay in bed; (Ding) to be left
(behind); **~ lassen** (vergessen) to
leave behind; **Liegestuhl** m deck
chair; **Liegestütz** m press-up
(Brit), push-up (US); **Liegewagen**
m (Eisenb) couchette car

lieh imperf von **leihen**

ließ imperf von **lassen**

Lift (-(e)s, -e o -s) m lift, elevator
(US)

Liga (-, Ligen) f league, division

light adj (Cola) diet; (fettarm)
low-fat; (kalorienarm) low-calorie;
(Zigaretten) mild

Likör (-s, -e) m liqueur

lila adj inv purple

Lilie f lily

Limette (-, -n) f lime

Limo (-, -s) f (fam) fizzy drink
(Brit), soda (US); **Limonade** f
fizzy drink (Brit), soda (US); (mit
Zitronengeschmack) lemonade

Limone (-, -n) f lime

Limousine (-, -n) f saloon (car)
(Brit), sedan (US); (fam) limo

Linde (-, -n) f lime tree
lindern vt to relieve, to soothe
Lineal (-s, -e) nt ruler
Linie f line; **Linienflug** m scheduled flight; **liniert** adj ruled, lined
Link (-s, -s) m (Inform) link
Linke (-n, -n) f left-hand side; (Hand) left hand; (Pol) left (wing); **linke(r, s)** adj left; **auf der -n Seite** on the left, on the left-hand side; **links** adv on the left; **~ abbiegen** to turn left; **~ von** to the left of; **~ oben** at the top left; **Linkshänder(in)** (-s, -) m(f) left-hander; **linksherum** adv to the left, anticlockwise; **Linksverkehr** m driving on the left
Linse (-, -n) f lentil; (optisch) lens
Lippe (-, -n) f lip; **Lipgloss** nt lip gloss; **Lippenstift** m lipstick
lispeln vi to lisp
List (-, -en) f cunning; (Trick) trick
Liste (-, -n) f list
Litauen (-s) nt Lithuania
Liter (-s, -) m on t litre
literarisch adj literary; **Literatur** f literature
Litschi (-, -s) f lychee, litchi
litt imperf von **leiden**
live adv (Radio, TV) live
Lizenz f licence
Lkw (-(s), (-s)) m abk = **Lastkraftwagen** truck, lorry (Brit); **Lkw-Maut** f heavy goods vehicle toll
Lob (-(e)s) nt praise; **loben** vt to praise
Loch (-(e)s, Löcher) nt hole; **lochen** vt to punch; **Locher** (-s, -) m (hole) punch
Locke (-, -n) f curl; **locken** vt (anlocken) to lure; (Haare) to curl; **Lockenstab** m curling tongs pl (Brit), curling irons pl (US); **Lockenwickler** (-s, -) m curler

locker adj (Schraube, Zahn) loose; (Haltung) relaxed; (Person) easy-going; **das schaffe ich ~** (fam) I'll manage it, no problem; **lockern** vt to loosen ▷ vr: **sich ~** to loosen
lockig adj curly
Löffel (-s, -) m spoon; **einen ~ Mehl zugeben** add a spoonful of flour; **Löffelbiskuit** (-s, -s) m sponge finger
log imperf von **lügen**
Loge (-, -n) f (Theat) box
logisch adj logical
Logo (-s, -s) nt logo
Lohn (-(e)s, Löhne) m reward; (Arbeitslohn) pay, wages pl
lohnen vr: **sich ~** to be worth it; **es lohnt sich nicht zu warten** it's no use waiting
Lohnerhöhung f pay rise (Brit), pay raise (US); **Lohnsteuer** f income tax
Lokal (-(e)s, -e) nt (Gaststätte) restaurant; (Kneipe) pub (Brit), bar
Lokomotive f locomotive
London (-s) nt London
Lorbeer (-s, -en) m laurel; **Lorbeerblatt** nt (Gastr) bay leaf
los adj loose; **~! go on!; jdn/etw ~ sein** to be rid of sb/sth; **was ist ~?** what's the matter?, what's up?; **dort ist nichts/viel ~** there's nothing/a lot going on there
Los (-es, -e) nt (Schicksal) lot, fate; (Lotterie etc) ticket
losbinden irr vt to untie
löschen vt (Feuer, Licht) to put out, to extinguish; (Durst) to quench; (Tonband) to erase; (Daten, Zeile) to delete; **Löschtaste** f delete key
lose adj loose
Lösegeld nt ransom
losen vi to draw lots
lösen vt (lockern) to loosen; (Rätsel) to solve; (Chem) to

dissolve; (Fahrkarte) to buy ▷ vr: **sich ~** (abgehen) to come off; (Zucker etc) to dissolve; (Problem, Schwierigkeit) to (re)solve itself

los|fahren irr vi to leave; **los|gehen** irr vi to set out; (anfangen) to start; **los|lassen** irr vt to let go

löslich adj soluble

Lösung f (eines Rätsels, Problems, Flüssigkeit) solution

los|werden irr vt to get rid of

Lotterie f lottery; **Lotto** (-s) nt National Lottery; **~ spielen** to play the lottery

Löwe (-n, -n) m (Zool) lion; (Astr) Leo; **Löwenzahn** m dandelion

Luchs (-es, -e) m lynx

Lücke (-, -n) f gap; **Lückenbüßer(in)** (-s, -) m(f) stopgap

lud imperf von **laden**

Luft (-, Lüfte) f air; (Atem) breath; **Luftballon** m balloon; **Luftblase** f (air) bubble; **luftdicht** adj airtight; **Luftdruck** m (Meteo) atmospheric pressure; (in Reifen) air pressure

lüften vt to air; (Geheimnis) to reveal

Luftfahrt f aviation; **Luftfeuchtigkeit** f humidity; **Luftfilter** m air filter; **Luftfracht** f air freight; **Luftkissenboot** nt, **Luftkissenfahrzeug** nt hovercraft; **Luftlinie** f: **10 km ~** 10 km as the crow flies; **Luftmatratze** f airbed; **Luftpirat(in)** m(f) hijacker; **Luftpost** f airmail; **Luftpumpe** f (bicycle) pump; **Luftröhre** f windpipe

Lüftung f ventilation

Luftveränderung f change of air; **Luftverschmutzung** f air pollution; **Luftwaffe** f air force; **Luftzug** m draught (Brit), draft (US)

Lüge (-, -n) f lie; **lügen** (log, gelogen) vi to lie; **Lügner(in)** (-s, -) m(f) liar

Luke (-, -n) f hatch

Lumpen (-s, -) m rag

Lunchpaket nt packed lunch

Lunge (-, -n) f lungs pl; **Lungenentzündung** f pneumonia

Lupe (-, -n) f magnifying glass; **etw unter die ~ nehmen** (fig) to have a close look at sth

Lust (-, Lüste) f joy, delight; (Neigung) desire; **~ auf etw** (akk) **haben** to feel like sth; **~ haben, etw zu tun** to feel like doing sth

lustig adj (komisch) amusing, funny; (fröhlich) cheerful

lutschen vt to suck ▷ vi **~ an** (+dat) to suck; **Lutscher** (-s, -) m lollipop

Luxemburg (-s) nt Luxembourg

luxuriös adj luxurious

Luxus (-) m luxury

Lymphdrüse f lymph gland; **Lymphknoten** m lymph node

Lyrik (-) f poetry

m

machbar adj feasible

🔵 **SCHLÜSSELWORT**

machen vt 1 to do; (herstellen, zubereiten) to make; **was machst du da?** what are you doing (there)?; **das ist nicht zu machen** that can't be done; **das Radio leiser machen** to turn the radio down; **aus Holz gemacht** made of wood

2 (verursachen, bewirken) to make; **jdm Angst machen** to make sb afraid; **das macht die Kälte** it's the cold that does that

3 (ausmachen) to matter; **das macht nichts** that doesn't matter; **die Kälte macht mir nichts** I don't mind the cold

4 (kosten, ergeben) to be; **3 und 5 macht 8** 3 and 5 are 8; **was o wie viel macht das?** how much

does that make?

5 was macht die Arbeit? how's the work going?; **was macht dein Bruder?** how is your brother doing?; **das Auto machen lassen** to have the car done; **mach's gut!** take care!; (viel Glück) good luck! ▷ vi: **mach schnell!** hurry up!; **Schluss machen** to finish (off); **mach schon!** come on!; **das macht müde** it makes you tired; **in etw** dat **machen** to be o deal in sth ▷ vr to come along (nicely) **sich an etw** akk **machen** to set about sth; **sich verständlich machen** to make o.s. understood; **sich dat viel aus jdm/etw machen** to like sb/sth

Macho (-s, -s) m (fam) macho (type)

Macht (-s, Mächte) f power; **mächtig** adj powerful; (fam: ungeheuer) enormous; **machtlos** adj powerless; **da ist man ~** there's nothing you can do (about it)

Mädchen nt girl; **Mädchenname** m maiden name

Made (-, -n) f maggot

Magazin (-s, -e) nt magazine

Magen (-s, - o Mägen) m stomach; **Magenbeschwerden** pl stomach trouble sing; **Magen-Darm-Infektion** f gastroenteritis; **Magengeschwür** nt stomach ulcer; **Magenschmerzen** pl stomachache sing

mager adj (Fleisch, Wurst) lean; (Person) thin; (Käse, Joghurt) low-fat; **Magermilch** f skimmed milk; **Magersucht** f anorexia; **magersüchtig** adj anorexic

magisch adj magical

Magnet (-s o -en, -en) m magnet

mähen vt, vi to mow

mahlen *(mahlte, gemahlen)* vt to grind

Mahlzeit f meal; *(für Baby)* feed ▷ *interj (guten Appetit)* enjoy your meal

Mähne *(-, -n)* f mane

mahnen vt to urge; **jdn schriftlich ~** to send sb a reminder; **Mahngebühr** f fine; **Mahnung** f warning; *(schriftlich)* reminder

Mai *(-(s), -e)* m May; *siehe auch* **Juni**; **Maifeiertag** m May Day; **Maiglöckchen** nt lily of the valley; **Maikäfer** m cockchafer

Mail *(-, -s)* f e-mail; **jdm eine~ schicken** to mail sb, to e-mail sb; **Mailbox** f *(Inform)* mailbox; **mailen** vi, vt to e-mail

Mais *(-es, -e)* m maize, corn (US); **Maiskolben** m corn cob; *(Gastr)* corn on the cob

Majestät *(-, -en)* f Majesty

Majonäse *(-, -n)* f mayonnaise

Majoran *(-s, -e)* m marjoram

makaber *(-, -n)* adj macabre

Make-up *(-s, -s)* nt make-up

Makler(in) *(-s, -)* m(f) broker; *(Immobilienmakler)* estate agent (Brit), Realtor® (US)

Makrele *(-, -n)* f mackerel

Makro *(-s, -s)* nt *(Inform)* macro

Makrone *(-, -n)* f macaroon

mal adv *(beim Rechnen)* times, multiplied by; *(beim Messen)* by; *(fam: einmal = früher)* once; *(einmal = zukünftig)* some day; **4 ~ 3 ist 12** 4 times 3 is (o equals) twelve; **da habe ich ~ gewohnt** I used to live there; **irgendwann ~ werde ich dort hinfahren** I'll go there one day; **das ist nun ~ so** that's just the way it is (o goes); **Mal** *(-(e)s, -e)* nt *(Zeitpunkt)* time; *(Markierung)* mark; **jedes ~** every time; **ein paar ~** a few times; **ein einziges ~** just once

Malaria *(-)* f malaria

Malaysia *(-s)* nt Malaysia

Malbuch nt colouring book

Malediven pl Maldives pl

malen vt, vi to paint; **Maler(in)** *(-s, -)* m(f) painter; **Malerei** f painting; **malerisch** adj picturesque

Mallorca *(-s)* nt Majorca, Mallorca

mal\|nehmen irr vt to multiply *(mit by)*

Malta *(-s)* nt Malta

Malventee m mallow tea

Malz *(-es)* nt malt; **Malzbier** nt malt beer

Mama *(-, -s)* f mum(my) (Brit), mom(my) (US)

man pron you; *(förmlich)* one; *(jemand)* someone, somebody; *(die Leute)* they, people pl; **wie schreibt ~ das?** how do you spell that?; **~ hat ihr das Fahrrad gestohlen** someone stole her bike; **~ sagt, dass ...** they (o people) say that ...

managen vt *(fam)* to manage; **Manager(in)** *(-s, -)* m(f) manager

manche(r, s) adj many a; *(mit pl)* a number of, some ▷ pron *(einige)* some; *(viele)* many; **~ Politiker** many politicians pl, many a politician; **manchmal** adv sometimes

Mandant(in) m(f) client

Mandarine f mandarin, tangerine

Mandel *(-, -n)* f almond; **~n** *(Anat)* tonsils pl; **Mandelentzündung** f tonsillitis

Manege *(-, -n)* f ring

Mangel *(-s, Mängel)* m *(Fehlen)* lack; *(Knappheit)* shortage *(an +dat of)*; *(Fehler)* defect, fault; **mangelhaft** adj *(Ware)* faulty; *(Schulnote)* ≈ E

Mango *(-, -s)* f mango

Mangold *(-s)* m mangel(wurzel)

Manieren pl manners pl

Maniküre (-, -n) f manicure

manipulieren vt to manipulate

Manko (-s, -s) nt deficiency

Mann (-(e)s, Männer) m man; (Ehemann) husband; **Männchen** nt: **es ist ein ~** (Tier) it's a he; **männlich** adj masculine; (Bio) male

Mannschaft f (Sport, fig) team; (Naut, Aviat) crew

Mansarde (-, -n) f attic

Manschettenknopf m cufflink

Mantel (-s, Mäntel) m coat; (Tech) casing, jacket

Mappe (-, -n) f briefcase; (Aktenmappe) folder

Maracuja (-, -s) f passion fruit

Marathon (-s, -s) m marathon

Märchen (-) nt fairy tale

Marder (-s, -) m marten

Margarine f margarine

Marienkäfer m ladybird (Brit), ladybug (US)

Marihuana (-s) nt marijuana

Marille (-, -n) f apricot

Marinade (-, -n) f marinade

Marine f navy

marinieren vt to marinate

Marionette f puppet

Mark (-(e)s) nt (Knochenmark) marrow; (Fruchtmark) pulp

Marke (-, -n) f (Warensorte) brand; (Fabrikat) make; (Briefmarke) stamp; (Essenmarke) voucher, ticket; (aus Metall etc) disc; (Messpunkt) mark; **Markenartikel** m branded item, brand name product; **Markenzeichen** nt trademark

markieren vt to mark; **Markierung** f marking; (Zeichen) mark

Markise (-, -n) f awning

Markt (-(e)s, Märkte) m market; **auf den ~ bringen** to launch; **Markthalle** f covered market;

Marktlücke f gap in the market; **Marktplatz** m market place; **Marktwirtschaft** f market economy

Marmelade f jam; (Orangenmarmelade) marmalade

Marmor (-s, -e) m marble; **Marmorkuchen** m marble cake

Marokko (-s) nt Morocco

Marone (-, -n) f chestnut

Mars (-) m Mars

Marsch (-(e)s, Märsche) m march; **Märtyrer(in)** (-s, -) m(f) martyr

März (-(es), -e) m March; siehe auch **Juni**

Marzipan (-s, -e) nt marzipan

Maschine f machine; (Motor) engine; **maschinell** adj mechanical, machine-; **Maschinenbau** m mechanical engineering

Masern pl (Med) measles sing

Maske f mask; **Maskenball** m fancy-dress ball; **maskieren** vr: **sich ~** (Maske aufsetzen) to put on a mask; (verkleiden) to dress up

Maskottchen nt mascot

maß imperf von **messen**

Maß (-es, -e) nt measure; (Mäßigung) moderation; (Grad) degree, extent; **~e** (Person) measurements; (Raum) dimensions; **in gewissem/hohem ~e** to a certain/high degree; **in zunehmendem ~e** increasingly

Mass (-, -(en)) f (Bier) litre of beer

Massage (-, -n) f massage

Masse (-, -n) f mass; (von Menschen) crowd; (Großteil) majority; **massenhaft** adv masses (o loads) of; **am See sind ~ Mücken** there are masses of mosquitoes at the lake; **Massenkarambolage** f pile-up; **Massenmedien** pl mass media pl; **Massenproduktion** f mass

production; **Massentourismus**
m mass tourism

Masseur(in) m(f)
masseur/masseuse

maßgeschneidert adj (Kleidung) made-to-measure

massieren vt to massage

mäßig adj moderate

massiv adj solid; (fig) massive

maßlos adj extreme

Maßnahme (-, -n) f measure,
step

Maßstab m rule, measure; (fig)
standard; **im ~ von 1:5** on a scale
of 1:5

Mast (-(e)s, -e(n)) m mast; (Elek)
pylon

Material (-s, -ien) nt material;
(Arbeitsmaterial) materials pl;
materialistisch adj materialistic

Materie (-, -n) f matter; **materiell** adj
material

Mathe (-) f (fam) maths (Brit),
math (US); **Mathematik** f
mathematics sing; **Mathe-
matiker(in)** m(f) mathematician

Matinee (-, -n) f = matinee

Matratze (-, -n) f mattress

Matrose (-n, -n) m sailor

Matsch (-(e)s) m mud; (Schnee)
slush; **matschig** adj muddy;
(Schnee) slushy; (Obst) mushy

matt adj weak; (glanzlos) dull;
(Foto) matt; (Schach) mate

Matte (-, -n) f mat

Matura (-) f Austrian
school-leaving examination; ≈
A-levels (Brit), ≈ High School
Diploma (US)

Mauer (-, -n) f wall

Maul (-(e)s, Mäuler) nt mouth;
(fam) gob; **halt's ~!** shut your face
(o gob); **Maulbeere** f mulberry;
Maulesel m mule; **Maulkorb** m
muzzle; **Maul- und Klauenseuche**
f foot-and-mouth disease;
Maulwurf m mole

Maurer(in) (-s, -) m(f) bricklayer

Mauritius (-) nt Mauritius

Maus (-, Mäuse) f mouse;
Mausefalle f mousetrap;
Mausklick (-s, -s) m mouse click;
Mauspad (-s, -s) nt mouse mat (o
pad); **Maustaste** f mouse key (o
button)

Maut (-, -en) f toll; **Mautgebühr**
f toll; **mautpflichtig** adj: **~e
Straße** toll road, turnpike (US);
Mautstelle f tollbooth, tollgate;
Mautstraße f toll road, turnpike
(US)

maximal adv: **ihr habt ~ zwei
Stunden Zeit** you've got two
hours at (the) most; **~ vier Leute** a
maximum of four people

Mayonnaise f siehe **Majonäse**

Mazedonien (-s) nt Macedonia

MB (-, -) nt, **Mbyte** (-, -) nt abk =
Megabyte MB

Mechanik f mechanics sing;
(Getriebe) mechanics pl;
Mechaniker(in) (-s, -) m(f) mechanic;
mechanisch adj mechanical;
Mechanismus m mechanism

meckern vi (Ziege) to bleat; (fam:
schimpfen) to moan

Mecklenburg-Vorpommern
(-s) nt Mecklenburg-Western
Pomerania

Medaille (-, -n) f medal

Medien pl media pl

Medikament nt medicine

Meditation f meditation;
meditieren vi to meditate

medium adj (Steak) medium

Medizin (-, -en) f medicine (gegen
for); **medizinisch** adj medical

Meer (-(e)s, -e) nt sea; **am ~** by
the sea; **Meerenge** f straits pl;
Meeresfrüchte pl seafood sing;
Meeresspiegel m sea level;
Meerrettich m horseradish;
Meerschweinchen nt guinea
pig; **Meerwasser** nt seawater

Megabyte nt megabyte;
Megahertz nt megahertz

Mehl (-(e)s, -e) nt flour;
Mehlspeise f sweet dish made from
flour, eggs and milk

mehr pron, adv more; **~ will ich
nicht ausgeben** I don't want to
spend any more, that's as much as I
want to spend; **was willst du ~?**
what more do you want? ▷ adv:
immer ~ (Leute) more and more
(people); **~ als fünf Minuten** more
than five minutes; **je ~ ..., desto
besser** the more, the better; **ich
kann nicht ~ stehen** I can't stand
any more (o longer); **es ist kein
Brot ~ da** there's no bread left; **nie
~** never again; **mehrdeutig** adj
ambiguous; **mehrere** pron
several; **mehreres** pron several
things; **mehrfach** adj multiple;
(wiederholt) repeated;
Mehrfachstecker m multiple
plug; **Mehrheit** f majority;
mehrmals adv repeatedly;
mehrsprachig adj multilingual;
Mehrwegflasche f returnable
bottle, deposit bottle;
Mehrwertsteuer f value added
tax, VAT; **Mehrzahl** f majority;
(Plural) plural

meiden (mied, gemieden) vt to
avoid

Meile (-, -n) f mile

mein pron (adjektivisch) my;
meine(r, s) pron (substantivisch)
mine

meinen vt, vi (glauben, der Ansicht
sein) to think; (sagen) to say; (sagen
wollen, beabsichtigen) to mean; **das
war nicht so gemeint** I didn't
mean it like that

meinetwegen adv (wegen mir)
because of me; (mir zuliebe) for my
sake; (von mir aus) as far as I'm
concerned

Meinung f opinion; **meiner**

~ nach in my opinion;
Meinungsumfrage f opinion
poll; **Meinungsverschiedenheit**
f disagreement (über +akk about)

Meise (-, -n) f tit; **eine ~ haben**
(fam) to be crazy

Meißel (-s, -) m chisel

meist adv mostly; **meiste(r, s)**
pron (adjektivisch) most; **die ~n**
(Leute) most people; **die ~ Zeit**
most of the time; **das ~ (davon)**
most of it; **die ~n von ihnen** most
of them; (substantivisch) most of
them; **am ~n** (the) most;
meistens adv mostly; (zum
größten Teil) for the most part

Meister(in) (-s, -) m(f) master;
(Sport) champion; **Meisterschaft**
f championship; **Meisterwerk**
nt masterpiece

melden vt to report ▷ vr: **sich
~** to report (bei to); (Schule) to put
one's hand up; (freiwillig) to
volunteer; (auf etw, am Telefon) to
answer; **Meldung** f
announcement; (Bericht) report;
(Inform) message

Melodie f tune, melody

Melone (-, -n) f melon

Memoiren pl memoirs pl

Menge (-, -n) f quantity;
(Menschen) crowd; **eine ~** (große
Anzahl) a lot (gen of);
Mengenrabatt m bulk discount

Meniskus (-, Menisken) m
meniscus

Mensa (-, Mensen) f canteen,
cafeteria (US)

Mensch (-en, -en) m human
being, man; (Person) person; **kein
~** nobody; **~!** (bewundernd) wow!;
(verärgert) bloody hell!;
Menschenmenge f crowd;
Menschenrechte pl human
rights pl; **Menschenverstand** m:
gesunder ~ common sense;
Menschheit f humanity,

mankind; **menschlich** adj
human; (human) humane

Menstruation f menstruation

Mentalität f mentality, mindset

Menthol (-s) nt menthol

Menü (-s, -s) nt set meal; (Inform)
menu; **Menüleiste** f (Inform)
menu bar

Merkblatt nt leaflet; **merken** vt
(bemerken) to notice; **sich** (dat) etw
~ to remember sth; **Merkmal** nt
feature

Merkur (-s) m Mercury

merkwürdig adj odd

Messbecher m measuring jug

Messe (-, -n) f fair; (Rel) mass;
Messebesucher(in) m(f) visitor
to a/the fair; **Messegelände** nt
exhibition site

messen (maß, gemessen) vt to
measure; (Temperatur, Puls) to take
▷ vr: **sich ~** to compete; **sie kann
sich mit ihm nicht ~** she's no
match for him

Messer (-s, -) nt knife

Messgerät nt measuring device,
gauge

Messing (-s) nt brass

Metall (-s, -e) nt metal

Meteorologe m, **Meteorologin**
f meteorologist

Meter (-s, -) m o nt metre;
Metermaß nt tape measure

Methode (-, -n) f method

Metzger(in) (-s, -) m(f) butcher;
Metzgerei f butcher's (shop)

Mexiko (-s) nt Mexico

MEZ f abk = **mitteleuropäische
Zeit** CET

miau interj miaow

mich pron akk von **ich** me;
~ **(selbst)** (reflexiv) myself; **stell
dich hinter ~** stand behind me;
ich fühle ~ wohl I feel fine

mied imperf von **meiden**

Miene (-, -n) f look, expression

mies adj (fam) lousy

Miesmuschel f mussel

Mietauto nt siehe **Mietwagen**;
Miete (-, -n) f rent; **mieten** vt to
rent; (Auto) to hire (Brit), to rent
(US); **Mieter(in)** (-s, -) m(f)
tenant; **Mietshaus** nt block of
flats (Brit), apartment house (US);
Mietvertrag m rental
agreement; **Mietwagen** m hire
car (Brit), rental car (US); **sich** (dat)
einen ~ nehmen to hire (Brit) (o
rent (US)) a car

Migräne (-, -n) f migraine

Migrant(in) (-en, -en) m(f)
migrant (worker)

Mikrofon (-s, -e) nt microphone

Mikrowelle (-, -n) f,
Mikrowellenherd m microwave
(oven)

Milch (-) f milk; **Milcheis** nt
ice-cream (made with milk);
Milchglas nt (dickes, trübes Glas)
frosted glass; **Milchkaffee** m
milky coffee; **Milchprodukte** pl
dairy products pl; **Milchpulver** nt
powdered milk; **Milchreis** m rice
pudding; **Milchshake** m milk
shake; **Milchstraße** f Milky Way

mild adj mild; (Richter) lenient;
(freundlich) kind

Militär (-s) nt military, army

Milliarde (-, -n) f billion;
Milligramm nt milligram;
Milliliter m millilitre; **Millimeter**
m millimetre; **Million** f million;
Millionär(in) m(f) millionaire

Milz (-, -en) f spleen

Mimik f facial expression(s)

Minderheit f minority

minderjährig adj underage

minderwertig adj inferior;
Minderwertigkeitskomplex m
inferiority complex

Mindest- in zW minimum;
mindeste(r, s) adj least;
mindestens adv at least;
Mindesthaltbarkeitsdatum nt

best-before date, sell-by date (Brit)

Mine (-, -n) f mine; (Bleistift) lead; (Kugelschreiber) refill

Mineralwasser nt mineral water

Minibar f minibar; **Minigolf** nt miniature golf, crazy golf (Brit)

minimal adj minimal

Minimum (-s, Minima) nt minimum

Minirock m miniskirt

Minister(in) (-s, -) m(f) minister; **Ministerium** (-s, Ministerien) nt ministry; **Ministerpräsident(in)** m(f) (von Bundesland) Minister President (Prime Minister of a Bundesland)

minus adv minus; **Minus** (-, -) nt deficit; **im ~ sein** to be in the red; (Konto) to be overdrawn

Minute (-, -n) f minute

Minze (-, -n) f mint

Mio. nt abk von **Million(en)** m

mir pron dat von **ich** (to) me; **kannst du ~ helfen?** can you help me?; **kannst du es ~ erklären?** can you explain it to me?; **ich habe ~ einen neuen Rechner gekauft** I bought (myself) a new computer; **ein Freund von ~** a friend of mine

Mirabelle (-, -n) f mirabelle (small yellow plum)

mischen vt to mix; (Karten) to shuffle; **Mischmasch** m (fam) hotchpotch; **Mischung** f mixture (aus of)

missachten vt to ignore; **Missbrauch** m abuse; (falscher Gebrauch) misuse; **missbrauchen** vt to misuse (zu for); (sexuell) to abuse; **Misserfolg** m failure; **Missgeschick** nt (Panne) mishap; **misshandeln** vt to ill-treat

Mission f mission

misslingen (misslang, misslungen) vi to fail; **der Versuch ist mir misslungen** my attempt failed;

misstrauen vt +dat to distrust; **Misstrauen** (-s) nt mistrust, suspicion (gegenüber of); **misstrauisch** adj distrustful; (argwöhnisch) suspicious; **Missverständnis** nt misunderstanding; **missverstehen** irr vt to misunderstand

Mist (-(e)s) m (fam) rubbish; (von Kühen) dung; (als Dünger) manure

Mistel (-, -n) f mistletoe

mit prep +dat with; (mittels) by; **~ der Bahn** by train; **~ der Kreditkarte bezahlen** to pay by credit card; **~ 10 Jahren** at the age of 10; **wie wärs ~ ...?** how about ...? ▷ adv along, too; **wollen Sie ~?** do you want to come along?

Mitarbeiter(in) m(f) (Angestellter) employee; (an Projekt) collaborator; (freier) freelancer

mit|bekommen irr vt (fam: aufschnappen) to catch; (hören) to hear; (verstehen) to get

mit|benutzen vt to share

Mitbewohner(in) m(f) (in Wohnung) flatmate (Brit), roommate (US)

mit|bringen irr vt to bring along; **Mitbringsel** (-s, -) nt small present

miteinander adv with one another; (gemeinsam) together

mit|erleben vt to see (with one's own eyes)

Mitesser (-s, -) m blackhead

Mitfahrgelegenheit f = lift, ride (US); **Mitfahrzentrale** f agency for arranging lifts

mit|geben irr vt: **jdm etw ~** to give sb sth (to take along)

Mitgefühl nt sympathy

mit|gehen irr vi to go/come along

mitgenommen adj worn out, exhausted

Mitglied nt member

mithilfe prep +gen ~ **von** with the help of

mit|kommen irr vi to come along; (verstehen) to follow

Mitleid nt pity; ~ **haben mit** to feel sorry for

mit|machen vt to take part in ▷ vi to take part

mit|nehmen irr vt to take along; (anstrengen) to wear out, to exhaust

mit|schreiben irr vi to take notes ▷ vt to take down

Mitschüler(in) m(f) schoolmate

mit|spielen vi (in Mannschaft) to play; (bei Spiel) to join in; **in einem Film/Stück ~** to act in a film/play

Mittag m midday; **gestern ~ at** midday yesterday, yesterday lunchtime; **über ~ geschlossen** closed at lunchtime; **zu ~ essen** to have lunch; **Mittagessen** nt lunch; **mittags** adv at lunchtime, at midday; **Mittagspause** f lunch break

Mitte (-, -n) f middle; ~ **Juni** in the middle of June; **sie ist ~ zwanzig** she's in her mid-twenties

mit|teilen vt: **jdm etw ~** to inform sb of sth; **Mitteilung** f notification

Mittel (-s -) nt means sing; (Maßnahme, Methode) method; (Med) remedy (gegen for); **das ist ein gutes ~,** (um) **junge Leute zu erreichen** that's a good way of engaging with young people

Mittelalter nt Middle Ages pl; **mittelalterlich** adj medieval; **Mittelamerika** nt Central America; **Mitteleuropa** nt Central Europe; **Mittelfeld** nt midfield; **Mittelfinger** m middle finger; **mittelmäßig** adj mediocre; **Mittelmeer** nt Mediterranean (Sea);

Mittelohrentzündung f inflammation of the middle ear; **Mittelpunkt** m centre; **im ~ stehen** to be the centre of attention

mittels prep +gen by means of

Mittelstreifen m central reservation (Brit), median (US); **Mittelstürmer(in)** m(f) striker, centre-forward; **Mittelwelle** f medium wave

mitten adv in the middle; ~ **auf der Straße/in der Nacht** in the middle of the street/night

Mitternacht f midnight

mittlere(r, s) adj middle; (durchschnittlich) average

mittlerweile adv meanwhile

Mittwoch (-s, -e) m Wednesday; (**am**) ~ on Wednesday; (**am**) ~ **Morgen/Nachmittag/Abend** (on) Wednesday morning/afternoon/evening; **diesen/letzten/nächsten** ~ this/last/next Wednesday; **jeden** ~ every Wednesday; ~ **in einer Woche** a week on Wednesday, Wednesday week; **mittwochs** adv on Wednesdays; ~ **abends** (jeden Mittwochabend) on Wednesday evenings

mixen vt to mix; **Mixer** (-s, -) m (Küchengerät) blender

MKS f abk = **Maul- und Klauenseuche** FMD

mobben vt to harass (to bully) (at work)

Mobbing (-s) nt workplace bullying (o harassment)

Möbel (-s, -) nt piece of furniture; **die ~** pl the furniture sing; **Möbelwagen** m removal van

mobil adj mobile

Mobilfunknetz nt cellular network; **Mobiltelefon** nt mobile phone

möblieren vt to furnish

mochte *imperf von* **mögen**
Mode (-, -n) f fashion
Model (-s, -s) nt model
Modell (-s, -e) nt model
Modem (-s, -s) nt (Inform) modem
Mode(n)schau f fashion show
Moderator(in) m(f) presenter
modern adj modern; (modisch) fashionable
Modeschmuck m costume jewellery; **modisch** adj fashionable
Modus (-, Modi) m (Inform) mode; (fig) way
Mofa (-s, -s) nt moped
mogeln vi to cheat

○ SCHLÜSSELWORT

mögen (pt **mochte**, pp **gemocht** o (als Hilfsverb) **mögen**) vt, vi to like; **magst du/mögen Sie ihn?** do you like him?; **ich möchte ...** I would like ..., I'd like ...; **er möchte in die Stadt** he'd like to go into town; **ich möchte nicht, dass du ...** I wouldn't like you to ...; **ich mag nicht mehr** I've had enough ▷ Hilfsverb to like to; (wollen) to want; **möchtest du etwas essen?** would you like something to eat?; **sie mag nicht bleiben** she doesn't want to stay; **das mag wohl sein** that may well be; **was mag das heißen?** what might that mean?; **Sie möchten zu Hause anrufen** could you please call home?

möglich adj possible; **so bald wie ~** as soon as possible; **möglicherweise** adv possibly; **Möglichkeit** f possibility; **möglichst** adv as ... as possible
Mohn (-(e)s, -e) m (Blume) poppy; (Samen) poppy seed

Möhre (-, -n) f, **Mohrrübe** f carrot
Mokka (-s, -s) m mocha
Moldawien (-s) nt Moldova
Molkerei (-, -en) f dairy
Moll (-) nt minor (key); **a-~** A minor
mollig adj cosy; (dicklich) plump
Moment (-(e)s, -e) m moment; **im ~** at the moment; **einen ~ bitte!** just a minute; **momentan** adj momentary ▷ adv at the moment
Monaco (-s) nt Monaco
Monarchie f monarchy
Monat (-(e)s, -e) m month; **sie ist im dritten ~** (schwanger) she's three months pregnant; **monatlich** adj, adv monthly; **~ 100 Euro zahlen** to pay 100 euros a month (o every month); **Monatskarte** f monthly season ticket
Mönch (-s, -e) m monk
Mond (-(e)s, -e) m moon; **Mondfinsternis** f lunar eclipse
Mongolei (-) f: **die ~** Mongolia
Monitor m (Inform) monitor
monoton adj monotonous
Monsun (-s, -e) m monsoon
Montag m Monday; siehe auch **Mittwoch**; **montags** adv on Mondays; siehe auch **mittwochs**
Montenegro (-s) nt Montenegro
Monteur(in) (-s, -e) m(f) fitter; **montieren** vt to assemble, to set up
Monument nt monument
Moor (-(e)s, -e) nt moor
Moos (-es, -e) nt moss
Moped (-s, -s) nt moped
Moral (-) f (Werte) morals pl; (einer Geschichte) moral; **moralisch** adj moral
Mord (-(e)s, -e) m murder;

Mörder(in) (-s, -) m(f) murderer/murderess

morgen adv tomorrow; **~ früh** tomorrow morning

Morgen (-s, -) m morning; **am ~** in the morning; **Morgenmantel** m, **Morgenrock** m dressing gown; **Morgenmuffel** m: **er ist ein ~** he's not a morning person; **morgens** adv in the morning; **um 3 Uhr ~** at 3 (o'clock) in the morning, at 3 am

Morphium (-s) nt morphine

morsch adj rotten

Mosaik (-s, -e(n)) nt mosaic

Mosambik (-s) nt Mozambique

Moschee (-, -n) f mosque

Moskau (-s) nt Moscow

Moskito (-s, -s) m mosquito; **Moskitonetz** nt mosquito net

Moslem (-s, -s) m, **Moslime** (-, -n) f Muslim

Most (-(e)s, -e) m (unfermented) fruit juice; (Apfelwein) cider

Motel (-s, -s) nt motel

motivieren vt to motivate

Motor m engine; (Elek) motor; **Motorboot** nt motorboat; **Motoröl** nt engine oil; **Motorhaube** f bonnet (Brit), hood (US); **Motorrad** nt motorbike, motorcycle; **Motorradfahrer(in)** m(f) motorcyclist; **Motorroller** m (motor) scooter; **Motorschaden** m engine trouble

Motte (-, -n) f moth

Motto (-s, -s) nt motto

Mountainbike (-s, -s) nt mountain bike

Möwe (-, -n) f (sea)gull

MP3-Player (-s, -) m MP3 player

Mrd. f abk = **Milliarde(n)**

MS (-) f abk = **multiple Sklerose** MS

Mücke (-, -n) f midge; (tropische) mosquito; **Mückenstich** m mosquito bite

müde adj tired

muffig adj (Geruch) musty; (Gesicht, Mensch) grumpy

Mühe (-, -n) f trouble, pains pl; **sich** (dat) **große ~ geben** to go to a lot of trouble

muhen vi to moo

Mühle (-, -n) f mill; (Kaffeemühle) grinder

Müll (-(e)s) m rubbish (Brit), garbage (US); **Müllabfuhr** f rubbish (Brit) (o garbage (US)) disposal

Mullbinde f gauze bandage

Müllcontainer m waste container; **Mülldeponie** f rubbish (Brit) (o garbage (US)) dump; **Mülleimer** m rubbish bin (Brit), garbage can (US); **Mülltonne** f dustbin (Brit), garbage can (US); **Mülltrennung** f sorting and collecting household waste according to type of material; **Müllverbrennungsanlage** f incineration plant; **Müllwagen** m dustcart (Brit), garbage truck (US)

multikulturell adj multicultural

Multimedia- in zW multimedia

Multiple-Choice-Verfahren nt multiple choice

multiple Sklerose (-n, -n) f multiple sclerosis

Multiplexkino nt multiplex (cinema)

multiplizieren vt to multiply (mit by)

Mumie f mummy

Mumps (-) m mumps sing

München (-s) nt Munich

Mund (-(e)s, Münder) m mouth; **halt den ~!** shut up; **Mundart** f dialect; **Munddusche** f dental water jet

münden vi to flow (in +akk into)

Mundgeruch m bad breath; **Mundharmonika** (-, -s) f mouth organ

mündlich adj oral
Mundschutz m mask;
Mundwasser nt mouthwash
Munition f ammunition
Münster (-s, -) nt minster,
cathedral
munter adj lively
Münzautomat m vending
machine; **Münze** (-, -n) f coin;
Münzeinwurf m slot;
Münzrückgabe f coin return;
Münztelefon nt pay phone;
Münzwechsler m change
machine
murmeln vt, vi to murmur, to
mutter
Murmeltier nt marmot
mürrisch adj sullen, grumpy
Mus (-es, -e) nt puree
Muschel (-, -n) f mussel; (~schale)
shell
Museum (-s, Museen) nt
museum
Musical (-s, -s) nt musical
Musik f music; **musikalisch** adj
musical; **Musiker(in)** (-s, -) m(f)
musician; **Musikinstrument** nt
musical instrument; **musizieren**
vi to play music
Muskat (-(e)s) m nutmeg
Muskel (-s, -n) m muscle;
Muskelkater m: ~ **haben** to be
stiff; **Muskelriss** m torn muscle;
Muskelzerrung f pulled muscle;
muskulös adj muscular
Müsli (-s, -) nt muesli
Muslim(in) (-s, -) m(f) Muslim
Muss nt [?] must

○ **SCHLÜSSELWORT**

müssen (pt **musste**, pp **gemusst**
o (als Hilfsverb) **müssen**) vi
1 (Zwang) must; (nur im Präsens) to
have to; **ich muss es tun** I must do
it, I have to do it; **ich musste es
tun** I had to do it; **er muss es**

nicht tun he doesn't have to do it;
muss ich? must I?, do I have to?;
wann müsst ihr zur Schule?
when do you have to go to
school?; **er hat gehen müssen** he
(has) had to go; **muss das sein?** is
that really necessary?; **ich muss
mal** (fam) I need the toilet
2 (sollen) **das musst du nicht tun!**
you oughtn't to o shouldn't do
that; **Sie hätten ihn fragen
müssen** you should have asked
him
3 es muss geregnet haben it
must have rained; **es muss nicht
wahr sein** it needn't be true

Muster (-s, -) nt (Dessin) pattern,
design; (Probe) sample; (Vorbild)
model; **mustern** vt to have a
close look at; **jdn ~** to look sb up
and down
Mut (-(e)s) m courage; **jdm
~ machen** to encourage sb; **mutig**
adj brave, courageous
Mutter (-, Mütter) f mother
▷ (-, -n) f (Schraubenmutter) nut;
Muttersprache f mother
tongue; **Muttertag** m Mother's
Day; **Mutti** f mum(my) (Brit),
mom(my) (US)
mutwillig adj deliberate
Mütze (-, -n) f cap
MwSt. abk = **Mehrwertsteuer**
VAT
Myanmar (-s) nt Myanmar

m

und nach gradually, little by little; **nach wie vor** still

nach|ahmen vt to imitate

Nachbar(in) (-n, -n) m(f) neighbour; **Nachbarschaft** f neighbourhood

nach|bestellen vt to order some more

nachdem conj after; (weil) since; **je ~ (ob/wie)** depending on (whether/how)

nach|denken irr vi to think (über +akk about); **nachdenklich** adj thoughtful

nacheinander adv one after another (o the other)

Nachfolger(in) (-s, -) m(f) successor

nach|forschen vt to investigate

Nachfrage f inquiry; (Comm) demand; **nach|fragen** vi to inquire

nach|geben irr vi to give in (jdm to sb)

Nachgebühr f surcharge; (für Briefe etc) excess postage

nach|gehen irr vi to follow (jdm sb); (erforschen) to inquire (einer Sache dat into sth); **die Uhr geht (zehn Minuten) nach** this watch is (ten minutes) slow

nachher adv afterwards; **bis ~!** see you later

Nachhilfe f extra tuition

nach|holen vt to catch up with; (Versäumtes) to make up for

nach|kommen irr vi to follow; **einer Verpflichtung** (dat) **~ to** fulfil an obligation

nach|lassen irr vt (Summe) to take off ▷ vi to decrease, to ease off; (schlechter werden) to deteriorate; **nachlässig** adj negligent, careless

nach|laufen irr vi to run after, to chase (jdm sb)

N abk = **Nord** N

na interj: ~ **also!**, ~ **bitte!** see?, what did I tell you?; ~ **ja** well; ~ **und?** so what?

Nabel (-s, -) m navel

 SCHLÜSSELWORT

nach prep +dat **1** (örtlich) to; **nach Berlin** to Berlin; **nach links/rechts** (to the) left/right; **nach oben/hinten** up/back **2** (zeitlich) after; **einer nach dem anderen** one after the other; **nach Ihnen!** after you!; **zehn (Minuten) nach drei** ten (minutes) past three **3** (gemäß) according to; **nach dem Gesetz** according to the law; **dem Namen nach** judging by his/her name; **nach allem, was ich weiß** as far as I know

▷ adv: **ihm nach!** after him!; **nach**

nach|lösen vt: **eine Fahrkarte ~** to buy a ticket on the bus/train

nach|machen vt to imitate, to copy (jdm etw sth from sb); (fälschen) to counterfeit

Nachmittag m afternoon; **heute ~** this afternoon; **am ~** in the afternoon; **nachmittags** adv in the afternoon; **um 3 Uhr ~** at 3 (o'clock) in the afternoon, at 3 pm

Nachnahme (-, -n) f cash on delivery; **per ~** COD

Nachname m surname

nach|prüfen vt to check

nach|rechnen vt to check

Nachricht (-, -en) f (piece of) news sing; (Mitteilung) message; **Nachrichten** pl news sing

Nachsaison f off-season

nach|schauen vi: **jdm ~** to gaze after sb ▷ vt (prüfen) to check

nach|schicken vt to forward

nach|schlagen irr vt to look up

nach|sehen irr vt (prüfen) to check

Nachspeise f dessert

nächstbeste(r, s) adj: **der ~ Zug/Job** the first train/job that comes along; **nächste(r, s)** adj next; (nächstgelegen) nearest

Nacht (-, Nächte) f night; **in der ~** during the night; (bei Nacht) at night; **Nachtclub** m nightclub; **Nachtdienst** m night duty; **~ haben** (Apotheke) to be open all night

Nachteil m disadvantage

Nachtflug m night flight; **Nachtfrost** m overnight frost; **Nachthemd** nt (für Damen) nightdress; (für Herren) nightshirt

Nachtigall (-, -en) f nightingale

Nachtisch m dessert, sweet (Brit), pudding (Brit); **Nachtleben** nt nightlife

nach|tragen irr vt: **jdm etw ~** (übel nehmen) to hold sth against sb

nachträglich adv: **~ alles Gute zum Geburtstag!** Happy belated birthday

nachts at night; **um 11 Uhr ~** at 11 (o'clock) at night, at 11 pm; **um 2 Uhr ~** at 2 (o'clock) in the morning, at 2 am; **Nachtschicht** f night shift; **Nachttarif** m off-peak rate; **Nachttisch** m bedside table; **Nachtzug** m night train

Nachweis (-es, -e) m proof

Nachwirkung f after-effect

nach|zahlen vi to pay extra ▷ vt: **20 Euro ~** to pay 20 euros extra

nach|zählen vt to check

Nacken (-s, -) m (nape of the) neck

nackt adj naked; (Tatsachen) plain, bare; **Nacktbadestrand** m nudist beach

Nadel (-, -n) f needle; (Stecknadel) pin; **Nadelstreifen** pl pinstripes pl

Nagel (-s, Nägel) m nail; **Nagelbürste** f nail brush; **Nagelfeile** f nail-file; **Nagellack** m nail varnish (o polish); **Nagellackentferner** (-s, -) m nail-varnish (o nail-polish) remover; **Nagelschere** f nail scissors pl

nah(e) adj, adv (räumlich) near(by); (zeitlich) near; (Verwandte, Freunde) close; **Nähe** (-) f (Umgebung) vicinity; **in der ~** nearby; **in der ~ von** near to; **nahe|gehen** irr vi: **jdm ~** to upset sb; **nahe|legen** vt: **jdm etw ~** to suggest sth to sb; **nahe|liegen** irr vi to be obvious ▷ prep +dat near (to), close to

nähen vt, vi to sew

nähere(r, s) adj (Erklärung, Erkundung) more detailed; **die ~ Umgebung** the immediate area;

Nähere(s) nt details pl; **nähern**
vr: **sich ~** to approach

nahezu adv virtually, almost

nahm imperf von **nehmen**

Nähmaschine f sewing
machine

nahrhaft adj nourishing,
nutritious; **Nahrung** f food;
Nahrungsmittel nt food

Naht (-, **Nähte**) f seam; (Med)
stitches pl, suture; (Tech) join

Nahverkehr m local traffic;
Nahverkehrszug m local train

Nähzeug nt sewing kit

naiv adj naive

Name (-ns, -n) m name

nämlich adv that is to say,
namely; (denn) since

nannte imperf von **nennen**

Napf (-(e)s, **Näpfe**) m bowl, dish

Narbe (-, -n) f scar

Narkose (-, -n) f anaesthetic

Narzisse (-, -n) f narcissus

naschen vt, vi to nibble;
Naschkatze f (fam) nibbler; **eine
~ sein** to have a sweet tooth

Nase (-, -n) f nose; **Nasenbluten**
(-s) nt nosebleed; **~ haben** to
have a nosebleed; **Nasenloch** nt
nostril; **Nasentropfen** pl nose
drops pl

Nashorn nt rhinoceros

nass adj wet; **Nässe** (-) f
wetness; **nässen** vi (Wunde) to
weep

Nation (-, -en) f nation; **national**
adj national; **Nationalfeiertag** m
national holiday; **Nationalhymne**
(-, -n) f national anthem;
Nationalität f nationality;
Nationalmannschaft f national
team; **Nationalpark** m National
Park; **Nationalspieler(in)** m(f)
international (player)

NATO f abk = **North Atlantic
Treaty Organization** NATO, Nato

Natur f nature; **Naturkost** f
health food; **natürlich** adj natural
▷ adv naturally; (selbstverständlich)
of course; **Naturpark** m nature
reserve; **naturrein** adj natural,
pure; **Naturschutz** m
conservation; **Naturschutzgebiet**
nt nature reserve; **Naturwissenschaft** f (natural) science;
Naturwissenschaftler(in) m(f)
scientist

Navigationssystem nt (Auto)
navigation system

n. Chr. abk = **nach Christus** AD

Nebel (-s, -) m fog, mist; **neblig**
adj foggy, misty; **Nebelschein-
werfer** m foglamp; **Nebelschlussleuchte** f (Auto) rear foglight

neben prep +akk o dat next to;
(außer) apart from, besides;
nebenan adv next door;
Nebenausgang m side exit;
nebenbei adv at the same time;
(außerdem) additionally; (beiläufig)
incidentally; **nebeneinander** adv
side by side; **Nebeneingang** m
side entrance; **Nebenfach** nt
subsidiary subject

nebenher adv (zusätzlich)
besides; (gleichzeitig) at the same
time; (daneben) alongside

Nebenkosten pl extra charges
pl, extras pl; **Nebensache** f
minor matter; **nebensächlich**
adj minor; **Nebensaison** f low
season; **Nebenstraße** f side
street; **Nebenwirkung** f side
effect

neblig adj foggy, misty

necken vt to tease

Neffe (-n, -n) m nephew

negativ adj negative; **Negativ**
nt (Foto) negative

nehmen (nahm, genommen) vt to
take; **wie man's nimmt** it
depends on how you look at it;
den Bus/Zug ~ to take the
bus/train; **jdn/etw ernst ~** to

take sb/sth seriously; **etw zu sich ~ to eat sth; jdn zu sich ~** to have sb come and live with one; **jdn an die Hand ~** to take sb by the hand

neidisch adj envious

neigen vi: **zu etw ~** to tend towards sth; **Neigung** f (des Geländes) slope; (Tendenz) inclination; (Vorliebe) liking

nein adv no

Nektarine f nectarine

Nelke (-, -n) f carnation; (Gewürz) clove

nennen (nannte, genannt) vt to name; (Namen) to call

Neonazi (-s, -s) m neo-Nazi

Nepal (-s) nt Nepal

Neptun (-s) m Neptune

Nerv (-s, -en) m nerve; **jdm auf die ~en gehen** to get on sb's nerves; **nerven** vt: **jdn ~** (fam) to get on sb's nerves; **Nervenzusammenbruch** m nervous breakdown; **nervös** adj nervous

Nest (-(e)s, -er) nt nest; (pej: Ort) dump

nett adj nice; (freundlich) kind; **sei so ~ und ...** do me a favour and ...

netto adv net

Netz (-es, -e) nt net; (für Einkauf) string bag; (System) network; (Stromnetz) mains, power (US); **Netzanschluss** m mains connection; **Netzbetreiber(in)** m(f) network operator; (Inform) Internet operator; **Netzgerät** nt power pack; **Netzkarte** f season ticket; **Netzwerk** nt (Inform) network; **Netzwerken** nt (social) networking; **Netzwerkkarte** f network card

neu adj new; (Sprache, Geschichte) modern; **die ~esten Nachrichten** the latest news; **Neubau** m new building; **neuerdings** adv recently; **Neueröffnung** f

new business; **Neuerung** f innovation; (Reform) reform

Neugier f curiosity; **neugierig** adj curious (auf +akk about); **ich bin ~, ob ...** I wonder whether (o if) ...; **ich bin ~, was du dazu sagst** I'll be interested to hear what you have to say about it

Neuheit f novelty; **Neuigkeit** f news sing; **eine ~** a piece of news; **Neujahr** nt New Year; **prosit ~!** Happy New Year; **neulich** adv recently, the other day; **Neumond** m new moon

neun num nine; **neunhundert** num nine hundred; **neunmal** adv nine times; **neunte(r, s)** adj ninth; siehe auch **dritte; Neuntel** (-s, -) nt ninth; **neunzehn** num nineteen; **neunzehnte(r, s)** adj nineteenth; siehe auch **dritte; neunzig** num ninety; **in den ~er Jahren** in the nineties; **Neunzigerjahre** pl nineties pl; **neunzigste(r, s)** adj ninetieth

neureich adj nouveau riche

Neurologe m, **Neurologin** f neurologist; **Neurose** (-, -n) f neurosis; **neurotisch** adj neurotic

Neuseeland nt New Zealand

Neustart m (Inform) restart, reboot

neutral adj neutral

neuwertig adj nearly new

Nicaragua (-s) nt Nicaragua

○ SCHLÜSSELWORT

nicht adv 1 (Verneinung) not; **er ist es nicht** it's not him, it isn't him; **er raucht nicht** (gerade) he isn't smoking; (gewöhnlich) he doesn't smoke; **ich kann das nicht — ich auch nicht** I can't do it — neither o nor can I; **es regnet nicht mehr** it's not raining any more; **nicht rostend** stainless

n

2 (Bitte, Verbot) **nicht!** don't!, no!;
nicht berühren! do not touch!;
nicht doch! don't!
3 (rhetorisch) **du bist müde, nicht
(wahr)?** you're tired, aren't you?;
das ist schön, nicht (wahr)? it's
nice, isn't it?
4 was du nicht sagst! the things
you say!

Nichte (-, -n) f niece
Nichtraucher(in) m(f) non-
smoker; **Nichtraucherzone** f
non-smoking area
nichts pron nothing; **für ~ und
wieder ~** for nothing at all; **ich
habe ~ gesagt** I didn't say
anything; **macht ~** never mind
Nichtschwimmer(in) m(f)
non-swimmer
nichtssagend adj meaningless
Nick (-s) username
nicken vi to nod
Nickerchen nt nap
Nickname (-ns, -n) m username
nie adv never; **~ wieder** (o mehr)
never again; **fast ~** hardly ever
nieder adj (niedrig) low; (gering)
inferior ▷ adv down;
niedergeschlagen adj depressed;
Niederlage f defeat
Niederlande pl Netherlands pl;
Niederländer(in) m(f) Dutch-
man/Dutchwoman;
niederländisch adj Dutch;
Niederländisch nt Dutch
Niederlassung f branch
Niederösterreich nt Lower
Austria; **Niedersachsen** nt
Lower Saxony
Niederschlag m (Meteo)
precipitation; (Regen) rainfall
niedlich adj sweet, cute
niedrig adj low; (Qualität)
inferior
niemals adv never
niemand pron nobody, no one;

ich habe ~en gesehen I haven't
seen anyone; **~ von ihnen** none of
them
Niere (-, -n) f kidney;
Nierenentzündung f kidney
infection; **Nierensteine** pl
kidney stones pl
nieseln vi impers to drizzle;
Nieselregen m drizzle
niesen vi to sneeze
Niete (-, -n) f (Los) blank; (Reinfall)
flop; (pej:Mensch) failure; (Tech) rivet
Nigeria (-s) nt Nigeria
Nikotin (-s) nt nicotine
Nilpferd nt hippopotamus
nippen vi to sip; **an etw** (dat) **~** to
sip sth
nirgends adv nowhere
Nische (-, -n) f niche
Niveau (-s, -s) nt level; **sie hat
~** she's got class
nobel adj (großzügig) generous;
(fam: luxuriös) classy, posh;
Nobelpreis m Nobel Prize

○ **SCHLÜSSELWORT**

noch adv **1** (weiterhin) still; **noch
nicht** not yet; **noch nie** never
(yet); **noch immer** o **immer noch**
still; **bleiben Sie doch noch** stay a
bit longer
2 (in Zukunft) still, yet; **das kann
noch passieren** that might still
happen; **er wird noch kommen**
he'll come (yet)
3 (nicht später als) **noch vor einer
Woche** a week ago; **noch am
selben Tag** the very same day;
noch im 19. Jahrhundert as late
as the 19th century; **noch heute**
today
4 (zusätzlich) **wer war noch da?**
who else was there?; **noch einmal**
once more, again; **noch dreimal**
three more times; **noch einer**
another one

5 (bei Vergleichen) **noch größer** even bigger; **das ist noch besser** that's better still; **und wenn es noch so schwer ist** however hard it is

6 Geld noch und noch heaps (and heaps) of money; **sie hat noch und noch versucht, ...** she tried again and again to ...

▷ konj: **weder A noch B** neither A nor B

nochmal(s) adv again, once more

Nominativ m nominative (case)

Nonne (-, -n) f nun

Nonstop-Flug m nonstop flight

Nord north; **Nordamerika** nt North America; **Norddeutschland** nt Northern Germany; **Norden** (-s) m north; **im ~ Deutschlands** in the north of Germany; **Nordeuropa** nt Northern Europe

Nordic Walking nt (Sport) Nordic Walking

Nordirland nt Northern Ireland; **nordisch** adj (Völker, Sprache) Nordic; **Nordkorea** (-s) nt North Korea; **nördlich** adj northern; (Kurs, Richtung) northerly; **Nordost(en)** m northeast; **Nordpol** m North Pole; **Nordrhein-Westfalen** (-s) nt North Rhine-Westphalia; **Nordsee** f North Sea; **nordwärts** adv north, northwards; **Nordwest(en)** m northwest; **Nordwind** m north wind

nörgeln vi to grumble

Norm (-, -en) f norm; (Größenvorschrift) standard

normal adj normal; **Normalbenzin** nt regular (petrol (Brit) o gas (US)); **normalerweise** adv normally

normen vt to standardize

Norwegen (-s) nt Norway;

Norweger(in) m(f) Norwegian; **norwegisch** adj Norwegian; **Norwegisch** nt Norwegian

Not (-, Nöte) f need; (Armut) poverty; (Elend) hardship; (Bedrängnis) trouble; (Mangel) want; (Mühe) trouble; (Zwang) necessity; **zur ~** if necessary; (gerade noch) just about

Notar(in) m(f) public notary; **notariell** adj: **~ beglaubigt** attested by a notary

Notarzt m, **Notärztin** f emergency doctor;

Notarztwagen m emergency ambulance; **Notaufnahme** f A&E, casualty (Brit), emergency room (US); **Notausgang** m emergency exit; **Notbremse** f emergency brake; **Notdienst** m emergency service, after-hours service; **notdürftig** adj scanty; (behelfsmäßig) makeshift

Note (-, -n) f note; (in Schule) mark, grade (US); (Mus) note

Notebook (-(s), -s) nt (Inform) notebook

Notfall m emergency; **notfalls** adv if necessary

notieren vt to note down

nötig adj necessary; **etw ~ haben** to need sth

Notiz (-, -en) f note; (Zeitungs~) item; **Notizblock** m notepad; **Notizbuch** nt notebook

Notlage f crisis; (Elend) plight; **notlanden** vi to make a forced (o emergency) landing; **Notlandung** f emergency landing; **Notruf** m emergency call; **Notrufnummer** f emergency number; **Notrufsäule** f emergency telephone

notwendig adj necessary

Nougat (-s, -s) m od nt nougat

November (-(s), -) m November; siehe auch **Juni**

Nr. abk = **Nummer** No., no.

Nu m: **im ~** in no time

nüchtern adj sober; (Magen) empty

Nudel (-, -n) f noodle; **~n** pl (italienische) pasta sing

null num zero; (Tel) O (Brit), zero (US); **~ Fehler** no mistakes; **~ Uhr** midnight; **Null** (-, -en) f nought, zero; (pej: Mensch) dead loss; **Nulltarif** m: **zum ~** free of charge

Numerus clausus (-) m restriction on the number of students allowed to study a particular subject

Nummer (-, -n) f number; **nummerieren** vt to number; **Nummernschild** nt (Auto) number plate (Brit), license plate (US)

nun adv now; **von ~ an** from now on ▷ interj well; **~ gut!** all right, then; **es ist ~ mal so** that's the way it is

nur adv only; **nicht ~ ..., sondern auch ...** not only ..., but also ...; **~ Anna nicht** except Anna

Nürnberg (-s) nt Nuremberg

Nuss (-, Nüsse) f nut; **Nussknacker** (-s, -) m nutcracker; **Nuss-Nougat-Creme** f chocolate nut cream

Nutte (-, -n) f (fam) tart

nutz, nütze adj: **zu nichts ~ sein** to be useless; **nutzen, nützen** vt to use (zu etw for sth); **was nützt es?** what use is it? ▷ vi to be of use; **das nützt nicht viel** that doesn't help much; **es nützt nichts(, es zu tun)** it's no use (doing it); **Nutzen** (-s, -) m usefulness; (Gewinn) profit; **nützlich** adj useful

Nylon (-s) nt nylon

O

o interj oh

O abk = **Ost** E

Oase (-, -n) f oasis

ob conj if, whether; **so als ~** as if; **er tut so, als ~ er krank wäre** he's pretending to be sick; **und ~!** you bet

obdachlos adj homeless

oben adv (am oberen Ende) at the top; (obenauf) on (the) top; (im Haus) upstairs; (in einem Text) above; **~ erwähnt** (o **genannt**) above-mentioned; **mit dem Gesicht nach ~** face up; **da ~** up there; **von ~ bis unten** from top to bottom; **siehe ~** see above

Ober (-s, -) m waiter

obere(r, s) adj upper, top

Oberfläche f surface; **oberflächlich** adj superficial; **Obergeschoss** nt upper floor

oberhalb adv, prep +gen above

Oberhemd nt shirt; **Oberkörper**

m upper body; **Oberlippe** f upper lip; **Oberösterreich** nt Upper Austria; **Oberschenkel** m thigh

oberste(r, s) adj very top, topmost

Oberteil nt top

obig adj above(-mentioned)

Objekt (-(e)s, -e) nt object

objektiv adj objective; **Objektiv** nt lens

obligatorisch adj compulsory, obligatory

Oboe (-, -n) f oboe

Observatorium nt observatory

Obst (-(e)s) nt fruit; **Obstkuchen** m fruit tart; **Obstsalat** m fruit salad

obszön adj obscene

obwohl conj although

Ochse (-n, -n) m ox; **Ochsenschwanzsuppe** f oxtail soup

ocker adj ochre

öd(e) adj waste; (unbebaut) barren; (fig) dull

oder conj or; **~ aber** or else; **er kommt doch, ~?** he's coming, isn't he?

Ofen (-s, Öfen) m oven; (Heizofen) heater; (Kohleofen) stove; (Herd) cooker, stove; **Ofenkartoffel** f baked (o jacket) potato

offen adj open; (aufrichtig) frank; (Stelle) vacant ▷ adv frankly; **~ gesagt** to be honest

offenbar adj obvious; **offensichtlich** adj evident, obvious

öffentlich adj public; **Öffentlichkeit** f (Leute) public; (einer Versammlung etc) public nature

offiziell adj official

offline adv (Inform) offline

öffnen vt to open ▷ vr: **sich ~** to open; **Öffner** (-s, -) m opener; **Öffnung** f opening;

Öffnungszeiten pl opening times pl

oft adv often; **schon ~** many times; **öfter** adv more often (o frequently); **öfters** adv often, frequently

ohne conj, prep +akk without; **~ weiteres** without a second thought; (sofort) immediately; **~ ein Wort zu sagen** without saying a word; **~ mich** count me out

Ohnmacht (-machten) f unconsciousness; (Hilflosigkeit) helplessness; **in ~ fallen** to faint; **ohnmächtig** adj unconscious; **sie ist ~** she has fainted

Ohr (-(e)s, -en) nt ear; (Gehör) hearing

Öhr (-(e)s, -e) nt eye

Ohrenarzt m, **Ohrenärztin** f ear specialist; **Ohrenschmerzen** pl earache; **Ohrentropfen** pl ear drops pl; **Ohrfeige** f slap (in the face); **Ohrläppchen** nt earlobe; **Ohrringe** pl earrings pl

oje interj oh dear

okay interj OK, okay

Ökoladen m health food store; **ökologisch** adj ecological; **~e Landwirtschaft** organic farming

ökonomisch adj economic; (sparsam) economical

Ökosteuer f green tax

Ökostrom m green electricity; **Ökosystem** nt ecosystem

Oktanzahl f (bei Benzin) octane rating

Oktober (-(s), -) m October; siehe auch **Juni**

- **OKTOBERFEST**

- The annual October beer
- festival, the **Oktoberfest**,
- takes place in Munich on a
- huge field where beer tents,

- roller coasters and many other
- amusements are set up. People
- sit at long wooden tables, drink
- beer from enormous litre beer
- mugs, eat pretzels and listen
- to brass bands. It is a great
- attraction for tourists and locals
- alike.

Öl (-(e)s, -e) nt oil; **Ölbaum** m
olive tree; **ölen** vt to oil; (Tech) to
lubricate; **Ölfarbe** f oil paint;
Ölfilter m oil filter; **Ölgemälde**
nt oil painting; **Ölheizung** f
oil-fired central heating; **ölig** adj
oily

oliv adj inv olive-green; **Olive**
(-, -n) f olive; **Olivenöl** nt olive oil

Ölmessstab m dipstick; **Ölofen**
m oil stove; **Ölpest** f oil
pollution; **Ölsardine** f sardine in
oil; **Ölstandanzeiger** m (Auto)
oil gauge; **Ölteppich** m oil slick;
Ölwechsel m oil change

Olympiade f Olympic Games pl;
olympisch adj Olympic

Oma f, **Omi** (-s, -s) f grandma,
gran(ny)

Omelett (-(e)s, -s) nt, **Omelette**
f omelette

Omnibus m bus

onanieren vi to masturbate

Onkel (-s, -) m uncle

online adv (Inform) online;
Onlinedienst m (Inform) online
service

OP (-s, -s) m abk =
Operationssaal operating
theatre (Brit) (o room US))

Opa m, **Opi** (-s, -s) m grandpa,
grandad

Open-Air-Konzert nt open-air
concert

Oper (-, -n) f opera; (Gebäude)
opera house

Operation f operation

Operette f operetta

operieren vi to operate ▷ vt to
operate on

Opernhaus nt opera house,
opera; **Opernsänger(in)** m(f)
opera singer

Opfer (-s, -) nt sacrifice; (Mensch)
victim; **ein ~ bringen** to make a
sacrifice

Opium (-s) nt opium

Opposition f opposition

Optiker(in) (-s, -) m(f) optician

optimal adj optimal, optimum

optimistisch adj optimistic

oral adj oral; **Oralverkehr** m
oral sex

orange adj inv orange; **Orange**
(-, -n) f orange; **Orangenmarmelade** f marmalade;
Orangensaft m orange juice

Orchester (-s, -) nt orchestra

Orchidee (-, -n) f orchid

Orden (-s, -) m (Rel) order; (Mil)
decoration

ordentlich adj (anständig)
respectable; (geordnet) tidy, neat;
(fam: annehmbar) not bad; (fam:
tüchtig) proper ▷ adv properly

ordinär adj common, vulgar;
(Witz) dirty

ordnen vt to sort out; **Ordner**
(-s, -) m (bei Veranstaltung)
steward; (Aktenordner) file;
Ordnung f order; (Geordnetsein)
tidiness; **(geht) in ~!** (that's) all
right; **mit dem Drucker ist etwas
nicht in ~** there's something
wrong with the printer

Oregano (-s) m oregano

Organ (-s, -e) nt organ; (Stimme)
voice

Organisation f organization;
organisieren vt to organize;
(fam: beschaffen) to get hold of
▷ vr: **sich ~** to organize

Organismus m organism

Orgasmus m orgasm

Orgel (-, -n) f organ

Orgie f orgy
orientalisch adj oriental
orientieren vr: **sich ~** to get one's bearings; **Orientierung** f orientation; **Orientierungssinn** m sense of direction
original adj original; (echt) genuine; **Original** (-s, -e) nt original
originell adj original; (komisch) witty
Orkan (-(e)s, -e) m hurricane
Ort (-(e)s, -e) m place; (Dorf) village; **an ~ und Stelle, vor ~** on the spot
Orthopäde (-n, -n) m, **Orthopädin** f orthopaedist
örtlich adj local; **Ortschaft** f village, small town; **Ortsgespräch** nt local call; **Ortstarif** m local rate; **Ortszeit** f local time

OSSI

Ossi is a colloquial and rather derogatory word used to describe a German from the former **DDR**.

Ost east; **Ostdeutschland** nt (als Landesteil) Eastern Germany; (Hist) East Germany; **Osten** (-s) m east
Osterei nt Easter egg; **Osterglocke** f daffodil; **Osterhase** m Easter bunny; **Ostermontag** m Easter Monday; **Ostern** (-, -) nt Easter; **an** (o **zu**) **~** at Easter; **frohe ~** Happy Easter
Österreich (-s) nt Austria; **Österreicher(in)** (-s, -) m(f) Austrian; **österreichisch** adj Austrian
Ostersonntag m Easter Sunday
Osteuropa nt Eastern Europe; **Ostküste** f east coast; **östlich** adj eastern; (Kurs, Richtung) easterly; **Ostsee** f: **die ~** the Baltic (Sea); **Ostwind** m east(erly) wind
OSZE (-) f abk = **Organisation für Sicherheit und Zusammenarbeit in Europa** OSCE
Otter (-s, -) m otter
out adj (fam) out; **outen** vt to out
oval adj oval
Overheadprojektor m overhead projector
Ozean (-s, -e) m ocean; **der Stille ~** the Pacific (Ocean)
Ozon (-s) nt ozone; **Ozonbelastung** f ozone level; **Ozonloch** nt hole in the ozone layer; **Ozonschicht** f ozone layer; **Ozonwerte** pl ozone levels pl

p

paar adj inv **ein ~** a few; **ein ~ Mal** a few times; **ein ~ Äpfel** some apples

Paar (-(e)s, -e) nt pair; (Ehepaar) couple; **ein ~ Socken** a pair of socks

pachten vt to lease

Päckchen nt package; (Zigaretten) packet; (zum Verschicken) small parcel; **packen** vt to pack; (fassen) to grasp, to seize; (fam: schaffen) to manage; (fig: fesseln) to grip; **Packpapier** nt brown paper; **Packung** f packet, pack (US); **Packungsbeilage** f package insert, patient information leaflet

Pädagoge (-n, -n) m, **Pädagogin** f teacher; **pädagogisch** adj educational; **~e Hochschule** college of education

Paddel (-s, -) nt paddle; **Paddelboot** nt canoe; **paddeln**

vi to paddle

Paket (-(e)s, -e) nt packet; (Postpaket) parcel; (Inform) package; **Paketbombe** f parcel bomb; **Paketkarte** f dispatch form (to be filled in with details of the sender and the addressee when handing in a parcel at the post office)

Pakistan (-s) nt Pakistan

Palast (-es, Paläste) m palace

Palästina (-s) nt Palestine; **Palästinenser(in)** (-s, -) m(f) Palestinian

Palatschinken pl filled pancakes pl

Palette f (von Maler) palette; (Ladepalette) pallet; (Vielfalt) range

Palme (-, -n) f palm (tree); **Palmsonntag** m Palm Sunday

Pampelmuse (-, -n) f grapefruit

pampig adj (fam: frech) cheeky; (breiig) gooey

Panda(bär) (-s, -s) m panda

Pandemie (-, -n) f pandemic

panieren vt (Gastr) to coat with breadcrumbs; **paniert** adj breaded

Panik f panic

Panne (-, -n) f (Auto) breakdown; (Missgeschick) slip; **Pannendienst** m, **Pannenhilfe** f breakdown (o rescue) service

Pant(h)er (-s, -) m panther

Pantomime (-, -n) f mime

Panzer (-s, -) m (Panzerung) armour (plating); (Mil) tank

Papa (-s, -s) m dad(dy), pa (US)

Papagei (-s, -en) m parrot

Papaya (-, -s) f papaya

Papier (-s, -e) nt paper; **~e** pl (Ausweispapiere) papers pl; (Dokumente, Urkunden) papers pl, documents pl; **Papiercontainer** m paper bank; **Papierformat** nt paper size; **Papiergeld** nt paper money; **Papierkorb** m wastepaper basket; (Inform)

recycle bin; **Papiertaschentuch**
nt (paper) tissue; **Papiertonne** f
paper bank
Pappbecher m paper cup;
Pappe (-, -n) f cardboard;
Pappkarton m cardboard box;
Pappteller m paper plate
Paprika (-s, -s) m (Gewürz)
paprika; (Schote) pepper
Papst (-(e)s, Päpste) m pope
Paradeiser (-s, -) m tomato
Paradies (-es, -e) nt paradise
Paragliding (-s) nt paragliding
Paragraph (-en, -en) m
paragraph; (Jur) section
parallel adj parallel
Paranuss f Brazil nut
Parasit (-en, -en) m parasite
parat adj ready; **etw ~ haben** to
have sth ready
Pärchen nt couple
Parfüm (-s, -s o -e) nt perfume;
Parfümerie f perfumery;
parfümieren vt to scent, to
perfume
Pariser (-s, -) m (fam: Kondom)
rubber
Park (-s, -s) m park
Park-and-ride-System nt
park-and-ride system; **Parkbank** f
park bench; **Parkdeck** nt parking
level; **parken** vt, vi to park
Parkett (-s, -e) nt parquet
flooring; (Theat) stalls pl (Brit),
parquet (US)
Parkhaus nt multi-storey car
park (Brit), parking garage (US)
parkinsonsche Krankheit f
Parkinson's disease
Parkkralle f (Auto) wheel clamp;
Parklicht nt parking light;
Parklücke f parking space;
Parkplatz m (für ein Auto) parking
space; (für mehrere Autos) car park
(Brit), parking lot (US);
Parkscheibe f parking disc;
Parkscheinautomat m pay

point; (Parkscheinausgabegerät)
ticket machine; **Parkuhr** f
parking meter; **Parkverbot** nt
(Stelle) no-parking zone; **hier ist
~** you can't park here
Parlament nt parliament
Parmesan (-s) m Parmesan
(cheese)
Partei f party
Parterre (-s, -s) nt ground floor
(Brit), first floor (US)
Partie f part; (Spiel) game; (Mann,
Frau) catch; **mit von der ~ sein** to
be in on it
Partitur f (Mus) score
Partizip (-s, -ien) nt participle
Partner(in) (-s, -) m(f) partner;
Partnerschaft f partnership;
eingetragene ~ civil partnership;
Partnerstadt f twin town
Party (-, -s) f party; **Partymuffel**
(-s, -) m party pooper;
Partyservice m catering service
Pass (-es, Pässe) m pass; (Ausweis)
passport
passabel adj reasonable
Passagier (-s, -e) m passenger
Passamt nt passport office
Passant(in) m(f) passer-by;
Passbild nt passport photo
passen vi (Größe) to fit; (Farbe,
Stil) to go (zu with); (auf Frage) to
pass; **passt (es) dir morgen?** does
tomorrow suit you?; **das passt
mir gut** that suits me fine;
passend adj suitable;
(zusammenpassend) matching;
(angebracht) fitting; (Zeit)
convenient; **haben Sie es nicht ~?**
(Kleingeld) have you got the right
change?
passieren vi to happen
passiv adj passive
Passkontrolle f passport
control
Passwort nt password
Paste (-, -n) f paste

Pastellfarbe f pastel colour

Pastete (-, -n) f (warmes Gericht) pie; (Pastetchen) vol-au-vent; (ohne Teig) pâté

Pastor, in (-s, -en) m(f) minister, vicar

Pate (-n, -n) m godfather; **Patenkind** nt godchild

Patient(in) m(f) patient

Patin f godmother

Patrone (-, -n) f cartridge

patsch interj splat; **patschnass** adj soaking wet

pauschal adj (Kosten) inclusive; (Urteil) sweeping; **Pauschale** (-, -n) f flat rate; **Pauschalgebühr** f flat rate (charge); **Pauschalpreis** m flat rate; (für Hotel, Reise) all-inclusive price; **Pauschalreise** f package tour

Pause (-, -n) f break; (Theat) interval; (Kino etc) intermission; (Innehalten) pause

Pavian (-s, -e) m baboon

Pavillon (-s, -s) m pavilion

Pay-TV (-s) nt pay-per-view television, pay TV

Pazifik (-s) m Pacific (Ocean)

PC (-s, -s) m abk = **Personal Computer** PC

Pech (-s, -e) nt (fig) bad luck; **~ haben** to be unlucky; **~ gehabt!** tough (luck)

Pedal (-s, -e) nt pedal

Pediküre (-, -n) f pedicure

Peeling (-s, -s) nt (facial/body) scrub

peinlich adj (unangenehm) embarrassing, awkward; (genau) painstaking; **es war mir sehr ~** I was totally embarrassed

Peitsche (-, -n) f whip

Pelikan (-s, -e) m pelican

Pellkartoffeln pl potatoes pl boiled in their skins

Pelz (-es, -e) m fur; **pelzig** adj (Zunge) furred

pendeln vi (Zug, Bus) to shuttle; (Mensch) to commute; **Pendelverkehr** m shuttle traffic; (für Pendler) commuter traffic; **Pendler(in)** (-s, -) m(f) commuter

penetrant adj sharp; (Mensch) pushy

Penis (-, -se) m penis

Pension f (Geld) pension; (Ruhestand) retirement; (für Gäste) guesthouse, B&B; **pensioniert** adj retired; **Pensionsgast** m guest (in a guesthouse)

Peperoni (-, -) f chilli

per prep +akk by, per; (pro) per; (bis) by

perfekt adj perfect

Pergamentpapier nt grease-proof paper

Periode (-, -n) f period

Perle (-, -n) f (a. fig) pearl

perplex adj dumbfounded

Person (-, -en) f person; **ein Tisch für drei -en** a table for three; **Personal** (-s) nt staff, personnel; (Bedienung) servants pl; **Personalausweis** m identity card; **Personalien** pl particulars pl; **Personenschaden** m injury to persons; **Personenwaage** f (bathroom) scales pl; **Personenzug** m passenger train; **persönlich** adj personal; (auf Briefen) private ▷ adv personally; (selbst) in person; **Persönlichkeit** f personality

Peru (-s) nt Peru

Perücke (-, -n) f wig

pervers adj perverted

pessimistisch adj pessimistic

Pest (-) f plague

Petersilie f parsley

Petroleum (-s) nt paraffin (Brit), kerosene (US)

Pfad (-(e)s, -e) m path; **Pfadfinder** (-s, -) m boy scout;

Pfadfinderin f girl guide
Pfahl (-(e)s, Pfähle) m post, stake
Pfand (-(e)s, Pfänder) nt security; (Flaschenpfand) deposit; (im Spiel) forfeit; **Pfandflasche** f returnable bottle
Pfanne (-, -n) f (frying) pan
Pfannkuchen m pancake
Pfarrei f parish; **Pfarrer(in)** (-s, -) m(f) priest
Pfau (-(e)s, -en) m peacock
Pfeffer (-s, -) m pepper; **Pfefferkuchen** m gingerbread; **Pfefferminze** (-e) f peppermint; **Pfefferminztee** m peppermint tea; **Pfeffermühle** f pepper mill; **pfeffern** vt to put pepper on/in; **Pfefferstreuer** (-s, -) m pepper pot
Pfeife (-, -n) f whistle; (für Tabak, von Orgel) pipe; **pfeifen** (pfiff, gepfiffen) vt, vi to whistle
Pfeil (-(e)s, -e) m arrow
Pfeiltaste f (Inform) arrow key
Pferd (-(e)s, -e) nt horse; **Pferdeschwanz** m (Frisur) ponytail; **Pferdestall** m stable; **Pferdestärke** f horsepower
pfiff imperf von **pfeifen**
Pfifferling m chanterelle
Pfingsten (-, -) nt Whitsun, Pentecost (US); **Pfingstmontag** m Whit Monday; **Pfingstsonntag** m Whit Sunday, Pentecost (US)
Pfirsich (-s, -e) m peach
Pflanze (-, -n) f plant; **pflanzen** vt to plant; **Pflanzenfett** nt vegetable fat
Pflaster (-s, -) nt (für Wunde) plaster, Band Aid® (US); (Straßenpflaster) road surface, pavement (US)
Pflaume (-, -n) f plum
Pflege (-, -n) f care; (Krankenpflege) nursing; (von Autos, Maschinen) maintenance; **pflegebedürftig** adj in need of

care; **pflegeleicht** adj easy-care; (fig) easy to handle; **pflegen** vt to look after; (Kranke) to nurse; (Beziehungen) to take care of; (Daten) to maintain; **Pflegepersonal** nt nursing staff; **Pflegeversicherung** f long-term care insurance
Pflicht (-, -en) f duty; (Sport) compulsory section; **pflicht-bewusst** adj conscientious; **Pflichtfach** nt (Schule) compulsory subject; **Pflicht-versicherung** f compulsory insurance
pflücken vt to pick
Pforte (-, -n) f gate; **Pförtner(in)** (-s, -) m(f) porter
Pfosten (-s, -) m post
Pfote (-, -n) f paw
pfui interj ugh
Pfund (-(e)s, -e) nt pound
pfuschen vi (fam) to be sloppy
Pfütze (-, -n) f puddle
Phantasie f siehe **Fantasie**; **phantastisch** adj siehe **fantastisch**
Phase (-, -n) f phase
Philippinen pl Philippines pl
Philosophie f philosophy
Photo nt siehe **Foto**
pH-neutral adj pH-balanced; **pH-Wert** m pH-value
Physalis (-, Physalen) f physalis
Physik f physics sing
physisch adj physical
Pianist(in) (-en, -en) m(f) pianist
Pickel (-s, -) m pimple; (Werkzeug) pickaxe; (Berg~) ice-axe
Picknick (-s, -e o -s) nt picnic; **ein ~ machen** to have a picnic
piepsen vi to chirp
piercen vt: **sich die Nase ~ lassen** to have one's nose pierced; **Piercing** (-s) nt (body) piercing
pieseln vi (fam) to pee

Pik (-, -) nt (Karten) spades pl

pikant adj spicy

Pilates nt (Sport) Pilates

Pilger(in) m(f) pilgrim;
Pilgerfahrt f pilgrimage

Pille (-, -n) f pill; **sie nimmt die
~** she's on the pill

Pilot(in) (-en, -en) m(f) pilot

Pils (-, -) nt (Pilsner) lager

Pilz (-es, -e) m (essbar) mushroom;
(giftig) toadstool; (Med) fungus

PIN (-, -s) f PIN (number)

pingelig adj (fam) fussy

Pinguin (-s, -e) m penguin

Pinie f pine; **Pinienkern** m pine
nut

pink adj shocking pink

pinkeln vi (fam) to pee

Pinsel (-s, -) m (paint)brush

Pinzette f tweezers pl

Pistazie (-, -n) f pistachio

Piste (-, -n) f (Ski) piste; (Aviat)
runway

Pistole (-, -n) f pistol

Pixel (-s) nt (Inform) pixel

Pizza (-, -s) f pizza; **Pizzaservice**
m pizza delivery service; **Pizzeria**
(-, Pizzerien) f pizzeria

Pkw (-(s), -(s)) m abk =
Personenkraftwagen car

Plakat nt poster

Plakette f (Schildchen) badge;
(Aufkleber) sticker

Plan (-(e)s, Pläne) m plan; (Karte)
map; **planen** vt to plan

Planet (-en, -en) m planet;
Planetarium nt planetarium

planmäßig adj scheduled

Plan(t)schbecken nt paddling
pool; **plan(t)schen** vi to splash
around

Planung f planning

Plastik f sculpture ▷ (-s) nt
plastic; **Plastikfolie** f plastic film;
Plastiktüte f plastic bag

Platin (-s) nt platinum

platsch interj splash

platt adj flat; (fam: überrascht)
flabbergasted; (fig: geistlos) flat,
boring

Platte (-, -n) f (Foto, Tech, Gastr)
plate; (Steinplatte) flag;
(Schallplatte) record;
Plattenspieler m record player

Plattform f platform; **Plattfuß**
m flat foot; (Reifen) flat (tyre)

Platz (-es, Plätze) m place;
(Sitzplatz) seat; (freier Raum) space,
room; (in Stadt) square; (Sportplatz)
playing field; **nehmen Sie ~** please
sit down, take a seat; **ist dieser
~ frei?** is this seat taken?;
Platzanweiser(in) m(f)
usher/usherette

Plätzchen nt spot; (Gebäck)
biscuit

platzen vi to burst; (Bombe) to
explode

Platzkarte f seat reservation;
Platzreservierung f seat
reservation; **Platzverweis** m: **er
erhielt einen ~** he was sent off;
Platzwunde f laceration, cut

plaudern vi to chat, to talk

pleite adj (fam) broke; **Pleite**
(-, -n) f (Bankrott) bankruptcy;
(fam: Reinfall) flop

Plombe (-, -n) f lead seal;
(Zahnplombe) filling; **plombieren**
vt (Zahn) to fill

plötzlich adj sudden ▷ adv suddenly,
all at once

plump adj clumsy; (Hände)
ungainly; (Körper) shapeless

plumps interj thud; (in Flüssigkeit)
plop

Plural (-s, -e) m plural

plus adv plus; **fünf ~ sieben ist
zwölf** five plus seven is (o are)
twelve; **zehn Grad ~** ten degrees
above zero; **Plus** (-, -) nt plus;
(Fin) profit; (Vorteil) advantage

Plüsch (-(e)s, -e) m plush

Pluto (-) m Pluto

PLZ *abk* = **Postleitzahl** postcode (Brit), zip code (US)

Po (-s, -s) *m* (fam) bottom, bum

Pocken *pl* smallpox *sing*

Podcast (-s, -n) *f* podcast

poetisch *adj* poetic

Pointe (-, -n) *f* punch line

Pokal (-s, -e) *m* goblet; (Sport) cup

pökeln *vt* to pickle

Pol (-s, -e) *m* pole

Pole (-n, -n) *m* Pole; **Polen** (-s) *nt* Poland

Police (-, -n) *f* (insurance) policy

polieren *vt* to polish

Polin *f* Pole, Polish woman

Politik *f* politics *sing*; (eine bestimmte) policy; **Politiker(in)** *m(f)* politician; **politisch** *adj* political

Politur *f* polish

Polizei *f* police *pl*; **Polizeibeamte(r)** *m*, **Polizeibeamtin** *f* police officer; **polizeilich** *adj* police; **sie wird ~ gesucht** the police are looking for her; **Polizeirevier** *nt*, **Polizeiwache** *f* police station; **Polizeistunde** *f* closing time; **Polizeiwache** *f* police station; **Polizist(in)** *m(f)* policeman/ -woman

Pollen (-s, -) *m* pollen; **Pollenflug** (-s) *m* pollen count

polnisch *adj* Polish; **Polnisch** *nt* Polish

Polo (-s) *nt* polo; **Polohemd** *nt* polo shirt

Polster (-s, -) *nt* cushion; (Polsterung) upholstery; (in Kleidung) padding; (fig: Geld) reserves *pl*; **polstern** *vt* to upholster; (Kleidung) to pad

Polterabend *m* party prior to a wedding, at which old crockery is smashed to bring good luck

poltern *vi* (Krach machen) to crash; (schimpfen) to rant

Polyester (-s, -) *m* polyester

Polypen *pl* (Med) adenoids *pl*

Pommes frites *pl* chips (Brit), French fries (US)

Pony (-s, -s) *m* (Frisur) fringe (Brit), bangs *pl* (US) ▷ (-s, -s) *nt* (Pferd) pony

Popcorn (-s) *nt* popcorn

Popmusik *f* pop (music)

populär *adj* popular

Pore (-, -n) *f* pore

Pornografie *f* pornography

Porree (-s, -s) *m* leeks *pl*; **eine Stange ~** leeks

Portemonnaie, Portmonee (-s, -s) *nt* purse

Portier (-s, -s) *m* porter

Portion *f* portion, helping

Porto (-s, -s) *nt* postage

Portrait, Porträt (-s, -s) *nt* portrait

Portugal (-s) *nt* Portugal; **Portugiese** (-n, -n) *m* Portuguese; **Portugiesin** (-, -nen) *f* Portuguese; **portugiesisch** *adj* Portuguese; **Portugiesisch** *nt* Portuguese

Portwein (-s, -e) *m* port

Porzellan (-s, -e) *nt* china

Posaune (-, -n) *f* trombone

Position *f* position

positiv *adj* positive

Post® (-, -en) *f* post office; (Briefe) post (Brit), mail (US); **Postamt** *nt* post office; **Postanweisung** *f* postal order (Brit), money order (US); **Postbank** *f* German post office bank; **Postbote** *m*, **-botin** *f* postman/-woman

posten *vt* (auf Forum, Blog) to post

Posten (-s, -) *m* post, position; (Comm) item; (auf Liste) entry

Poster (-s, -s) *m* poster

Postfach *nt* post-office box, PO box; **Postkarte** *f* postcard;

postlagernd adv poste restante; **Postleitzahl** f postcode (Brit), zip code (US)

postmodern adj postmodern

Postsparkasse f post office savings bank; **Poststempel** m postmark; **Postweg** m: **auf dem ~ by** mail

Potenz f (Math) power; (eines Mannes) potency

PR (-, -s) f abk = **Public Relations** PR

prächtig adj splendid

prahlen vi to boast, to brag

Praktikant(in) m(f) trainee; **Praktikum** (-s, Praktika) nt practical training; **praktisch** adj practical; **~er Arzt** general practitioner

Praline f chocolate

Prämie f (bei Versicherung) premium; (Belohnung) reward; (von Arbeitgeber) bonus

Präparat nt (Med) medicine; (Bio) preparation

Präservativ nt condom

Präsident(in) m(f) president

Praxis (-, Praxen) f practice; (Behandlungsraum) surgery; (von Anwalt) office; **Praxisgebühr** f surgery surcharge

präzise adj precise, exact

predigen vt, vi to preach; **Predigt** (-, -en) f sermon

Preis (-es, -e) m (zu zahlen) price; (bei Sieg) prize; **den ersten ~ gewinnen** to win first prize; **Preisausschreiben** nt competition

Preiselbeere f cranberry

preisgünstig adj inexpensive; **Preislage** f price range; **Preisliste** f price list; **Preisschild** nt price tag; **Preisträger(in)** m(f) prizewinner; **preiswert** adj inexpensive

Prellung f bruise

Premiere (-, -n) f premiere, first night

Premierminister(in) m(f) prime minister, premier

Prepaidhandy nt prepaid mobile (Brit), prepaid cell phone (US); **Prepaidkarte** f prepaid card

Presse (-, -n) f press

pressen vt to press

prickeln vi to tingle

Priester(in) (-s, -) m(f) priest/(woman) priest

Primel (-, -n) f primrose

primitiv adj primitive

Prinz (-en, -en) m prince; **Prinzessin** f princess

Prinzip (-s, -ien) nt principle; **im ~** basically; **aus ~** on principle

Priorität f priority

privat adj private; **Privatfernsehen** nt commercial television; **Privatgrundstück** nt private property; **privatisieren** vt to privatize

pro prep +akk per; **5 Euro ~ Stück/Person** 5 euros each/per person; **Pro** (-s) nt pro

Probe (-, -n) f test; (Teststück) sample; (Theat) rehearsal; **Probefahrt** f test drive; **eine ~ machen** to go for a test drive; **Probezeit** f trial period; **probieren** vt, vi to try; (Wein, Speise) to taste, to sample

Problem (-s, -e) nt problem

Produkt (-(e)s, -e) nt product; **Produktion** f production; (produzierte Menge) output; **produzieren** vt to produce

Professor(in) (-s, -en) m(f) professor

Profi (-s, -s) m pro

Profil (-s, -e) nt profile; (von Reifen, Schuhsohle) tread

Profit (-(e)s, -e) m profit; **profitieren** vi to profit (von from)

Prognose (-, -n) f prediction; (Wetter) forecast
Programm (-s, -e) nt programme; (Inform) program; (TV) channel; **Programmheft** nt programme; **programmieren** vt to program; **Programmierer(in)** (-s, -) m(f) programmer; **Programmkino** nt arts (o repertory US) cinema
Projekt (-(e)s, -e) nt project
Projektor m projector
Promenade (-, -n) f promenade
Promille (-(s), -) nt (blood) alcohol level; **0,8 ~** 0,08 per cent; **Promillegrenze** f legal alcohol limit
prominent adj prominent; **Prominenz** f VIPs pl, (famous figures pl; (fam: Stars) the glitterati pl
Propeller (-s, -) m propeller
prosit interj cheers
Prospekt (-(e)s, -e) m leaflet, brochure
prost interj cheers
Prostituierte(r) mf prostitute
Protest (-(e)s, -e) m protest
Protestant(in) m(f) Protestant; **protestantisch** adj Protestant
protestieren vi to protest (gegen against)
Prothese (-, -n) f artificial arm/leg; (Gebiss) dentures pl
Protokoll (-s, -e) nt (bei Sitzung) minutes pl; (diplomatisch, Inform) protocol; (bei Polizei) statement
protzen vi to show off; **protzig** adj flashy
Proviant (-s, -e) m provisions pl
Provider (-s, -) m (Inform) (service) provider
Provinz (-, -en) f province
Provision f (Comm) commission
provisorisch adj provisional; **Provisorium** (-s, Provisorien) nt stopgap; (Zahn) temporary filling

provozieren vt to provoke
Prozent (-(e)s, -e) nt per cent
Prozess (-es, -e) m (Vorgang) process; (Jur) trial; (Rechtsfall) (court) case; **prozessieren** vi to go to law (mit against)
Prozession f procession
Prozessor (-s, -en) m (Inform) processor
prüde adj prudish
prüfen vt to test; (nachprüfen) to check; **Prüfung** f (Schul) exam; (Überprüfung) check; **eine ~ machen** (Schule) to take an exam
Prügelei f fight; **prügeln** vt to beat ▷ vr: **sich ~** to fight
PS abk = **Pferdestärke** hp; = **Postskript(um)** PS
pseudo- präf pseudo-; **Pseudokrupp** (-s) m (Med) pseudocroup; **Pseudonym** (-s, -e) nt pseudonym
pst interj ssh
Psychiater(in) (-s, -) m(f) psychiatrist; **psychisch** adj psychological; (Krankheit) mental;
Psychoanalyse f psychoanalysis; **Psychologe** (-n, -n) m, **Psychologin** f psychologist; **Psychologie** f psychology
Psychopharmaka pl mind-affecting drugs pl, psychotropic drugs pl; **psychosomatisch** adj psychosomatic; **Psychoterror** m psychological intimidation; **Psychotherapie** f psychotherapy
Pubertät f puberty
Publikum (-s) nt audience; (Sport) crowd
Pudding (-s, -e o -s) m blancmange
Pudel (-s, -) m poodle
Puder (-s, -) m powder; **Puderzucker** m icing sugar
Puerto Rico (-s) nt Puerto Rico
Pulli (-s, -s) m, **Pullover** (-s, -) m sweater, pullover, jumper (Brit)

Puls (-es, -e) m pulse

Pulver (-s, -) nt powder;
Pulverkaffee m instant coffee;
Pulverschnee m powder snow

pummelig adj chubby

Pumpe (-, -n) f pump; **pumpen**
vt to pump; (fam: verleihen) to lend;
(fam: sich ausleihen) to borrow

Pumps pl court shoes pl (Brit),
pumps pl (US)

Punk (-s, -s) m (Musik, Mensch)
punk

Punkt (-(e)s, -e) m point; (bei
Muster) dot; (Satzzeichen) full stop
(Brit), period (US); **~ zwei Uhr** at
two o'clock sharp

pünktlich adj punctual, on time;
Pünktlichkeit f punctuality

Punsch (-(e)s, -e) m punch

Pupille (-, -n) f pupil

Puppe (-, -n) f doll

pur adj pure; (völlig) sheer;
(Whisky) neat

Püree (-s, -s) nt puree;
(Kartoffelpüree) mashed potatoes pl

Puste (-) f (fam) puff; **außer
~ sein** to be puffed

Pustel (-, -n) f pustule; (Pickel)
pimple; **pusten** vi to blow;
(keuchen) to puff

Pute (-, -n) f turkey;
Putenschnitzel nt turkey
escalope

Putsch (-es, -e) m putsch

Putz (-es) m (Mörtel) plaster

putzen vt to clean; **sich** (dat) **die
Nase ~** to blow one's nose; **sich**
(dat) **die Zähne ~** to brush one's
teeth; **Putzfrau** f cleaner;
Putzlappen m cloth, **Putzmann**
m cleaner; **Putzmittel** nt
cleaning agent, cleaner

Puzzle (-s, -s) nt jigsaw (puzzle)

Pyjama (-s, -s) m pyjamas pl

Pyramide (-, -n) f pyramid

Python (-s, -s) m python

q

Quadrat nt square; **quadratisch**
adj square; **Quadratmeter** m
square metre

quaken vi (Frosch) to croak; (Ente)
to quack

Qual (-, -en) f pain, agony;
(seelisch) anguish; **quälen** vt to
torment ▷ vr: **sich ~** to struggle;
(geistig) to torment oneself;
Quälerei f torture, torment

qualifizieren vt to qualify;
(einstufen) to label ▷ vr: **sich ~** to
qualify

Qualität f quality

Qualle (-, -n) f jellyfish

Qualm (-(e)s) m thick smoke;
qualmen vt, vi to smoke

Quantität f quantity

Quarantäne (-, -n) f quarantine

Quark (-s) m quark; (fam: Unsinn)
rubbish

Quartett (-s, -e) nt quartet;
(Kartenspiel) happy families sing

Quartier (-s, -e) nt accommodation

quasi adv more or less

Quatsch (-es) m (fam) rubbish; **quatschen** vi (fam) to chat

Quecksilber nt mercury

Quelle (-, -n) f spring; (eines Flusses) source

quellen vi to pour

quer adv crossways, diagonally; (rechtwinklig) at right angles; **~ über die Straße** straight across the street; **querfeldein** adv across country; **Querflöte** f flute; **Querschnitt** m cross section; **querschnittsgelähmt** adj paraplegic; **Querstraße** f side street

quetschen vt to squash, to crush; (Med) to bruise; **Quetschung** f bruise

Queue (-s, -s) m (billiard) cue

quietschen vi to squeal; (Tür, Bett) to squeak; (Bremsen) to screech

quitt adj quits, even

Quitte (-, -n) f quince

Quittung f receipt

Quiz (-, -) nt quiz

Quote (-, -n) f rate; (Comm) quota

r

Rabatt (-(e)s, -e) m discount

Rabbi (-(s), -s) m rabbi; **Rabbiner** (-s, -) m rabbi

Rabe (-n, -n) m raven

Rache (-) f revenge, vengeance

Rachen (-s, -) m throat

rächen vt to avenge ▷ vr: **sich ~** to take (one's) revenge (an +dat on)

Rad (-(e)s, Räder) nt wheel; (Fahrrad) bike; **~ fahren** to cycle; **mit dem ~ fahren** to go by bike

Radar (-s) m o nt radar; **Radarfalle** f speed trap; **Radarkontrolle** f radar speed check

radeln vi (fam) to cycle; **Radfahrer(in)** m(f) cyclist; **Radfahrweg** m cycle track (o path)

Radicchio (-s) m (Salatsorte) radicchio

radieren vt to rub out, to erase;
Radiergummi m rubber (Brit),
eraser; **Radierung** f (Kunst)
etching
Radieschen nt radish
radikal adj radical
Radio (-s, -s) nt radio; **im ~ on**
the radio
radioaktiv adj radioactive
Radiologe (-n, -n) m, **Radiologin**
f radiologist
Radiorekorder m radio cassette
recorder; **Radiosender** m radio
station; **Radiowecker** m radio
alarm (clock)
Radkappe f (Auto) hub cap
Radler(in) (-s, -) m(f) cyclist
Radler (-s, -) nt ≈ shandy
Radlerhose f cycling shorts pl;
Radrennen nt cycle racing;
(einzelnes Rennen) cycle race;
Radtour f cycling tour; **Radweg**
m cycle track (o path)
raffiniert adj crafty, cunning;
(Zucker) refined
Rafting (-s) nt white water
rafting
Ragout (-s, -s) nt ragout
Rahm (-s) m cream
rahmen vt to frame; **Rahmen**
(-s, -) m frame
Rakete (-, -n) f rocket
rammen vt to ram
Rampe (-, -n) f ramp
ramponieren vt (fam) to
damage, to batter
Ramsch (-(e)s, -e) m junk
ran (fam) kontr von **heran**
Rand (-(e)s, Ränder) m edge; (von
Brille, Tasse etc) rim; (auf Papier)
margin; (Schmutzrand, unter Augen)
ring; (fig) verge, brink
randalieren vi to (go on the)
rampage; **Randalierer(in)** (-s, -)
m(f) hooligan
Randstein m kerb (Brit), curb
(US); **Randstreifen** m shoulder

rang imperf von **ringen**
Rang (-(e)s, Ränge) m rank; (in
Wettbewerb) place; (Theat) circle
rannte imperf von **rennen**
ranzig adj rancid
Rap (-s, -s) m (Mus) rap; **rappen**
vi (Mus) to rap; **Rapper(in)** (-s, -)
m(f) (Mus) rapper
rar adj rare, scarce
rasant adj quick, rapid
rasch adj quick
rascheln vi to rustle
rasen vi (sich schnell bewegen)
to race; (toben) to rave; **gegen
einen Baum ~** to crash into a
tree
Rasen (-s, -) m lawn
rasend adj (vor Wut) furious
Rasenmäher (-s, -) m
lawnmower
Rasierapparat m razor;
(elektrischer) shaver; **Rasiercreme**
f shaving cream; **rasieren** vt to
shave ▸ vr: **sich ~** to shave;
Rasierer m shaver; **Rasiergel** nt
shaving gel; **Rasierklinge** f
razor blade; **Rasiermesser** nt
(cutthroat) razor; **Rasierpinsel**
m shaving brush; **Rasierschaum**
m shaving foam; **Rasierzeug** nt
shaving tackle, shaving
equipment
Rasse (-, -n) f race; (Tiere) breed
Rassismus m racism;
Rassist(in) m(f) racist;
rassistisch adj racist
Rast (-, -en) f rest, break;
~ machen to have a rest (o break);
rasten vi to rest; **Rastplatz** m
(Auto) rest area; **Raststätte** f
(Auto) service area; (Gaststätte)
motorway (Brit) (o highway (US))
restaurant
Rasur f shave
Rat (-(e)s, Ratschläge) m (piece of)
advice; **sie hat mir einen
~ gegeben** she gave me some

advice; **um ~ fragen** to ask for advice

Rate (-, -n) f instalment; **etw auf ~n kaufen** to buy sth in instalments (Brit), to buy sth on the instalment plan (US)

raten (riet, geraten) vt, vi to guess; (empfehlen) to advise (jdm sb)

Rathaus nt town hall

Ration f ration

ratlos adj at a loss, helpless; **ratsam** adj advisable

Rätsel (-s, -) nt puzzle; (Worträtsel) riddle; **das ist mir ein ~** it's a mystery to me; **rätselhaft** adj mysterious

Ratte (-, -n) f rat

rau adj rough, coarse; (Wetter) harsh

Raub (-(e)s) m robbery; (Beute) loot, booty; **rauben** vt to steal; **jdm etw ~** to rob sb of sth; **Räuber(in)** (-s, -) m(f) robber; **Raubfisch** m predatory fish; **Raubkopie** f pirate copy; **Raubmord** m robbery with murder; **Raubtier** nt predator; **Raubüberfall** m mugging; **Raubvogel** m bird of prey

Rauch (-(e)s) m smoke; (Abgase) fumes pl; **rauchen** vt, vi to smoke; **Raucher(in)** (-s, -) m(f) smoker; **Raucherabteil** nt smoking compartment

Räucherlachs m smoked salmon; **räuchern** vt to smoke

rauchig adj smoky; **Rauchmelder** m smoke detector; **Rauchverbot** nt smoking ban; **hier ist ~** there's no smoking here

rauf (fam) kontr von **herauf**

rauh adj siehe **rau**; **Rauhreif** m siehe **Raureif**

Raum (-(e)s, Räume) m space; (Zimmer, Platz) room; (Gebiet) area

räumen vt to clear; (Wohnung, Platz) to vacate; (wegbringen) to shift, to move; (in Schrank etc) to put away

Raumfähre f space shuttle; **Raumfahrt** f space travel; **Raumschiff** nt spacecraft, spaceship; **Raumsonde** f space probe; **Raumstation** f space station

Raumtemperatur f room temperature

Räumungsverkauf m clearance sale, closing-down sale

Raupe (-, -n) f caterpillar

Raureif m hoarfrost

raus (fam) kontr von **heraus**, **hinaus**; **~!** (get) out!

Rausch (-(e)s, Räusche) m intoxication; **einen ~ haben/kriegen** to be/get drunk

rauschen vi (Wasser) to rush; (Baum) to rustle; (Radio etc) to hiss; **Rauschgift** nt drug; **Rauschgiftsüchtige(r)** mf drug addict

rausfliegen irr vi (fam) to be kicked out

raushalten irr vr (fam) **halt du dich da raus!** you (just) keep out of it

räuspern vr: **sich ~** to clear one's throat

rausschmeißen irr vt (fam) to throw out

Razzia (-, Razzien) f raid

reagieren vi to react (auf +akk to); **Reaktion** f reaction

real adj real; **realisieren** vt (merken) to realize; (verwirklichen) to implement; **realistisch** adj realistic; **Realität** (-, -en) f reality; **Reality-TV** (-s) nt reality TV

Realschule f ≈ secondary school, junior high (school) (US)

Rebe (-, -n) f vine

rebellieren vi to rebel

Rebhuhn nt partridge

rechnen vt, vi to calculate; **~ mit** to expect; (bauen auf) to count on ▷ vr: **sich ~** to pay off, to turn out to be profitable; **Rechner** (-s, -) m calculator; (Computer) computer; **Rechnung** f calculation(s); (Comm) bill (Brit), check (US); **die ~, bitte!** can I have the bill, please?; **das geht auf meine ~** this is on me

recht adj (richtig, passend) right; **~ haben** to be right; **jdm ~ geben** to agree with sb; **mir soll's ~ sein** it's alright by me; **mir ist es ~** I don't mind ▷ adv really, quite; (richtig) rightly; **ich weiß nicht ~** I don't really know; **es geschieht ihm ~** it serves him right

Recht (-(e)s, -e) nt right; (Jur) law

Rechte (-n, -n) f right-hand side; (Hand) right hand; (Pol) right (wing); **rechte(r, s)** adj right; **auf der ~n Seite** on the right, on the right-hand side; **Rechte(s)** nt right thing; **etwas/nichts ~s** something/nothing proper

Rechteck (-s, -e) nt rectangle; **rechteckig** adj rectangular

rechtfertigen vt to justify ▷ vr: **sich ~** to justify oneself

rechtlich adj legal; **rechtmäßig** adj legal, lawful

rechts adv on the right; **~ abbiegen** to turn right; **~ von** to the right of; **~ oben** at the top right

Rechtsanwalt m, **-anwältin** f lawyer

Rechtschreibung f spelling

Rechtshänder(in) (-s, -) m(f) right-hander; **rechtsherum** adv to the right, clockwise; **rechtsradikal** adj (Pol) extreme right-wing

Rechtsschutzversicherung f legal costs insurance

Rechtsverkehr m driving on the right

rechtswidrig adj illegal

rechtwinklig adj right-angled; **rechtzeitig** adj timely ▷ adv in time

recyclebar adj recyclable; **recyceln** vt to recycle; **Recycling** (-s) nt recycling; **Recyclingpapier** nt recycled paper

Redakteur(in) m(f) editor; **Redaktion** f editing; (Leute) editorial staff; (Büro) editorial office(s)

Rede (-, -n) f speech; (Gespräch) talk; **eine ~ halten** to make a speech; **reden** vi to talk, to speak ▷ vt to say; (Unsinn etc) to talk; **Redewendung** f idiom; **Redner(in)** m(f) speaker

reduzieren vt to reduce

Referat (-s, -e) nt paper; **ein ~ halten** to give a paper (über +akk on)

reflektieren vt to reflect

Reform (-, -en) f reform; **Reformhaus** nt health food shop; **reformieren** vt to reform

Regal (-s, -e) nt shelf; (Möbelstück) shelves pl

Regel (-, -n) f rule; (Med) period; **regelmäßig** adj regular; **regeln** vt to regulate, to control; (Angelegenheit) to settle ▷ vr: **sich von selbst ~** to sort itself out; **Regelung** f regulation

Regen (-s, -) m rain; **Regenbogen** m rainbow; **Regenmantel** m raincoat; **Regenrinne** f gutter; **Regenschauer** m shower; **Regenschirm** m umbrella; **Regenwald** m rainforest; **Regenwurm** m earthworm

Regie f direction

regieren vt, vi to govern, to rule;

Regierung f government; (von Monarch) reign

Region f region; **regional** adj regional

Regisseur(in) m(f) director

registrieren vt to register; (bemerken) to notice

regnen vi impers to rain; **regnerisch** adj rainy

regulär adj regular; **regulieren** vt to regulate, to adjust

Reh (-(e)s, -e) nt deer; (Fleisch) venison

Rehabilitationszentrum nt (Med) rehabilitation centre

Reibe (-, -n) f, **Reibeisen** nt grater; **reiben** (rieb, gerieben) vt to rub; (Gastr) to grate; **reibungslos** adj smooth

reich adj rich

Reich (-(e)s, -e) nt empire; (eines Königs) kingdom

reichen vi to reach; (genügen) to be enough, to be sufficient (jdm for sb) ▷ vt to hold out; (geben) to pass, to hand; (anbieten) to offer

reichhaltig adj ample, rich; **reichlich** adj (Trinkgeld) generous; (Essen) ample; **~ Zeit** plenty of time; **Reichtum** (-s, -tümer) m wealth

reif adj ripe; (Mensch, Urteil) mature

Reif (-(e)s, -e) m (Raureif) hoarfrost ▷ (-(e)s, -e) m (Ring) ring, hoop

reifen vi to mature; (Obst) to ripen

Reifen (-s, -) m ring, hoop; (von Auto) tyre; **Reifendruck** m tyre pressure; **Reifenpanne** m puncture; **Reifenwechsel** m tyre change

Reihe (-, -n) f row; (von Tagen etc, fam: Anzahl) series sing; **der ~ nach** one after the other; **er ist an der ~** it's his turn; **Reihenfolge** f

order, sequence; **Reihenhaus** nt terraced house (Brit), row house (US)

Reiher (-s, -) m heron

rein (fam) kontr von **herein, hinein** ▷ adj pure; (sauber) clean

Reinfall m (fam) letdown; **rein|fallen** irr vi (fam) **auf etw** (akk) **~** to fall for sth

reinigen vt to clean; **Reinigung** f cleaning; (Geschäft) (dry) cleaner's; **Reinigungsmittel** nt cleaning agent, cleaner

rein|legen vt: **jdn ~** to take sb for a ride

Reis (-es, -e) m rice

Reise (-, -n) f journey; (auf Schiff) voyage; **Reiseapotheke** f first-aid kit; **Reisebüro** nt travel agent's; **Reisebus** m coach; **Reiseführer(in)** m(f) (Mensch) courier; (Buch) guide(book); **Reisegepäck** nt luggage (Brit), baggage; **Reisegesellschaft** f (Veranstalter) tour operator; **Reisegruppe** f tourist party; (mit Reisebus) coach party; **Reiseleiter(in)** m(f) courier; **reisen** vi to travel; **~ nach** to go to; **Reisende(r)** m traveller; **Reisepass** m passport; **Reiseroute** f route, itinerary; **Reiserücktrittversicherung** f holiday cancellation insurance; **Reisescheck** m traveller's cheque; **Reisetasche** f holdall (Brit), carryall (US); **Reiseveranstalter** m tour operator; **Reiseverkehr** m holiday traffic; **Reiseversicherung** f travel insurance; **Reiseziel** nt destination

Reiskocher (-s, -) m rice steamer

reißen (riss, gerissen) vt, vi to tear; (ziehen) to pull, to drag; (Witz) to crack

Reißnagel m drawing pin (Brit), thumbtack (US); **Reißverschluss** m zip (Brit), zipper (US); **Reißzwecke** f drawing pin (Brit), thumbtack (US)

reiten (ritt, geritten) vt, vi to ride; **Reiter(in)** m(f) rider; **Reithose** f riding breeches pl; **Reitsport** m riding; **Reitstiefel** m riding boot

Reiz (-es, -e) m stimulus; (angenehm) charm; (Verlockung) attraction; **reizen** vt to stimulate; (unangenehm) to annoy; (verlocken) to appeal to, to attract; **reizend** adj charming; **Reizgas** nt irritant gas; **Reizung** f irritation

Reklamation f complaint

Reklame (-, -n) f advertising; (Einzelwerbung) advertisement; (im Fernsehen) commercial

reklamieren vi to complain (wegen about)

Rekord (-(e)s, -e) m record

relativ adj relative ▷ adv relatively

relaxen vi to relax, to chill out

Religion f religion; **religiös** adj religious

Remoulade (-, -n) f tartar sauce

Renaissance f renaissance, revival; (Hist) Renaissance

Rennbahn f racecourse; (Auto) racetrack; **rennen** (rannte, gerannt) vt, vi to run; **Rennen** (-s, -) nt running; (Wettbewerb) race; **Rennfahrer(in)** m(f) racing driver; **Rennrad** nt racing bike; **Rennwagen** m racing car

renommiert adj famous, noted (wegen, für for)

renovieren vt to renovate; **Renovierung** f renovation

rentabel adj profitable

Rente (-, -n) f pension; **Rentenversicherung** f pension scheme

Rentier nt reindeer

rentieren vr: **sich ~** to pay, to be profitable

Rentner(in) (-s, -) m(f) pensioner, senior citizen

Reparatur f repair; **Reparaturwerkstatt** f repair shop; (Auto) garage; **reparieren** vt to repair

Reportage f report; **Reporter(in)** (-s, -) m(f) reporter

Reptil (-s, -ien) nt reptile

Republik f republic

Reservat (-s, -e) nt nature reserve; (für Ureinwohner) reservation; **Reserve** (-, -n) f reserve; **Reservekanister** m spare can; **Reserverad** nt (Auto) spare wheel; **reservieren** vt to reserve; **Reservierung** f reservation

resignieren vi to give up; **resigniert** adj resigned

Respekt (-(e)s, no pl) m respect; **respektieren** vt to respect

Rest (-(e)s, -e) m rest, remainder; (Überreste) remains pl; **der ~ ist für Sie** keep the change

Restaurant (-s, -s) nt restaurant

restaurieren vt to restore

Restbetrag m balance; **restlich** adj remaining; **restlos** adj complete; **Restmüll** m non-recyclable waste

Resultat nt result

retten vt to save, to rescue

Rettich (-s, -e) m radish

Rettung f rescue; (Hilfe) help; (Rettungsdienst) ambulance service; **Rettungsboot** nt lifeboat; **Rettungshubschrauber** m rescue helicopter; **Rettungsring** m lifebelt, life preserver (US); **Rettungswagen** m ambulance

retweeten vt (auf Twitter) to retweet

Reue (-) f remorse; (Bedauern)

regret; **reuen** vt: **es reut ihn** he regrets it

revanchieren vr: **sich ~** (*sich rächen*) to get one's own back, to get one's revenge; (*für Hilfe etc*) to return the favour

Revolution f revolution

Rezept (-(e)s, -e) nt (*Gastr*) recipe; (*Med*) prescription; **rezeptfrei** adj over-the-counter, non-prescription

Rezeption f (*im Hotel*) reception

rezeptpflichtig adj available only on prescription

R-Gespräch (-(e)s, -e) nt reverse-charge (*Brit*) (o collect (*US*)) call

Rhabarber (-s) m rhubarb

Rhein (-s) m Rhine; **Rheinland-Pfalz** (-) nt Rhineland-Palatinate

Rheuma (-s) nt rheumatism

Rhythmus m rhythm

richten vt (*lenken*) to direct (*auf +akk to*); (*Waffe, Kamera*) to point (*auf +akk at*); (*Brief, Anfrage*) to address (*an +akk to*); (*einstellen*) to adjust; (*instand setzen*) to repair; (*zurechtmachen*) to prepare ▷ vr: **sich ~ nach** (*Regel etc*) to keep to; (*Mode, Beispiel*) to follow; (*abhängen von*) to depend on

Richter(in) (-s, -) m(f) judge

Richtgeschwindigkeit f recommended speed

richtig adj right, correct; (*echt*) proper ▷ adv (*fam: sehr*) really; **richtig stellen** vt: **etw ~** (*berichtigen*) to correct sth

Richtlinie f guideline

Richtung f direction; (*Tendenz*) tendency; **Richtungstaste** f arrow key

rieb imperf von **reiben**

riechen (*roch, gerochen*) vt, vi to smell; **nach etw ~** to smell of sth; **an etw** (*dat*) **~** to smell sth

rief imperf von **rufen**

Riegel (-s, -) m bolt; (*Gastr*) bar

Riemen (-s, -) m strap; (*Gürtel*) belt

Riese (-n, -n) m giant; **Riesengarnele** f king prawn; **riesengroß** adj gigantic, huge; **Riesenrad** nt big wheel; **riesig** adj enormous, huge

riet imperf von **raten**

Riff (-(e)s, -e) nt reef

Rind (-(e)s, -er) nt cow; (*Bulle*) bull; (*Gastr*) beef; **~er** pl cattle pl

Rinde (-, -n) f (*Baum*) bark; (*Käse*) rind; (*Brot*) crust

Rinderbraten m roast beef; **Rinderwahn(sinn)** m mad cow disease; **Rindfleisch** nt beef

Ring (-(e)s, -e) m ring; (*Straße*) ring road; **Ringbuch** nt ring binder

ringen (*rang, gerungen*) vi to wrestle; **Ringer(in)** m(f) wrestler; **Ringfinger** m ring finger; **Ringkampf** m wrestling match; **ringsherum** adv round about

Rippe (-, -n) f rib; **Rippenfellentzündung** f pleurisy

Risiko (-s, -s o Risiken) nt risk; **auf eigenes ~** at one's own risk; **riskant** adj risky; **riskieren** vt to risk

riss imperf von **reißen**

Riss (-es, -e) m tear; (*in Mauer, Tasse etc*) crack; **rissig** adj cracked; (*Haut*) chapped

ritt imperf von **reiten**

Ritter (-s, -) m knight

Rivale (-n, -n) m, **Rivalin** f rival

Rizinusöl nt castor oil

Robbe (-, -n) f seal

Roboter (-s, -) m robot

robust adj robust

roch imperf von **riechen**

Rock (-(e)s, Röcke) m skirt

Rockband f (*Musikgruppe*) rock band; **Rockmusik** f rock (music)

Rodelbahn f toboggan run; **rodeln** vi to toboggan

Roggen (-s, -) m rye; **Roggenbrot** nt rye bread

roh adj raw; (Mensch) coarse, crude; **Rohkost** f raw vegetables and fruit pl

Rohr (-(e)s, -e) nt pipe; (Bot) cane; (Schilf) reed; **Röhre** (-, -n) f tube; (Leitung) pipe; (Elek) valve; (Backröhre) oven; **Rohrzucker** m cane sugar

Rohstoff m raw material

Rokoko (-s) nt rococo

Rollbrett nt skateboard

Rolle (-, -n) f (etw Zusammengerolltes) roll; (Theat) role

rollen vt, vi to roll

Roller (-s, -) m scooter

Rollerblades® pl Rollerblades® pl; **Rollerskates** pl roller skates pl

Rollkragenpullover m polo-neck (Brit) or turtleneck (US)) sweater; **Rollladen** m, **Rollo** (-s, -s) m (roller) shutters pl; **Rollschuh** m roller skate; **Rollstuhl** m wheelchair; **rollstuhlgerecht** adj suitable for wheelchairs; **Rolltreppe** f escalator

Roman (-s, -e) m novel

Romantik f romance; **romantisch** adj romantic

römisch-katholisch adj Roman Catholic

röntgen vt to X-ray; **Röntgenaufnahme** f, **Röntgenbild** nt X-ray; **Röntgenstrahlen** pl X-rays pl

rosa adj inv pink

Rose (-, -n) f rose

Rosenkohl m (Brussels) sprouts pl

Rosé(wein) m rosé (wine)

rosig adj rosy

Rosine (-, -n) f raisin

Rosmarin (-s) m rosemary

Rosskastanie f horse chestnut

Rost (-(e)s, -e) m rust; (zum Braten) grill, gridiron; **Rostbratwurst** f grilled sausage; **rosten** vi to rust; **rösten** vt to roast, to grill; (Brot) to toast; **rostfrei** adj rustproof; (Stahl) stainless; **rostig** adj rusty; **Rostschutz** m rustproofing

rot adj red; ~ **werden** to blush; **Rote Karte** red card; **Rote Bete** beetroot; **bei Rot über die Ampel fahren** to jump the lights; **das Rote Kreuz** the Red Cross

Röteln pl German measles sing

röten vt to redden ▷ vr: **sich** ~ to redden

rothaarig adj red-haired

rotieren vi to rotate; **am Rotieren sein** (fam) to be rushing around like a mad thing

Rotkehlchen nt robin; **Rotkohl** m, **Rotkraut** nt red cabbage; **Rotlichtviertel** nt red-light district; **Rotwein** m red wine

Rouge (-s, -s) nt rouge

Route (-, -n) f route

Routine f experience; (Trott) routine

Rubbellos nt scratchcard; **rubbeln** vt to rub

Rübe (-, -n) f turnip; **Gelbe** ~ carrot; **Rote** ~ beetroot

rüber (fam) kontr von **herüber, hinüber**

rückbestätigen vt (Flug etc) to reconfirm

rücken vt, vi to move; **könntest du ein bisschen ~?** could you move over a bit?

Rücken (-s, -) m back; **Rückenlehne** f back(rest); **Rückenmark** nt spinal cord; **Rückenschmerzen** pl backache sing; **Rückenschwimmen** (-s) nt backstroke; **Rückenwind** m tailwind

Rückerstattung f refund; **Rückfahrkarte** f return ticket (Brit), round-trip ticket (US); **Rückfahrt** f return journey; **Rückfall** m relapse; **Rückflug** m return flight; **Rückgabe** f return; **rückgängig** adj: **etw ~ machen** to cancel sth; **Rückgrat** (-(e)s, -e) nt spine, backbone; **Rückkehr** (-, -en) f return; **Rücklicht** nt rear light; **Rückreise** f return journey; **auf der ~** on the way back

Rucksack m rucksack, backpack; **Rucksacktourist(in)** m(f) backpacker

Rückschritt m step back; **Rückseite** f back; (hinterer Teil) rear; **siehe ~** see overleaf; **Rücksicht** f consideration; **~ nehmen auf** (+akk) to show consideration for; **rücksichtslos** adj inconsiderate; (Fahren) reckless; (unbarmherzig) ruthless; **rücksichtsvoll** adj considerate; **Rücksitz** m back seat; **Rückspiegel** m (Auto) rear-view mirror; **Rückstand** m: **sie sind zwei Tore im ~** they're two goals down; **im ~ sein mit** (Arbeit, Miete) to be behind with; **Rücktaste** f backspace key; **Rückvergütung** f refund; **rückwärts** adv backwards, back; **Rückwärtsgang** m (Auto) reverse (gear); **Rückweg** m return journey, way back; **Rückzahlung** f repayment

Ruder (-s, -) nt oar; (Steuer) rudder; **Ruderboot** nt rowing boat (Brit), rowboat (US); **rudern** vt, vi to row

Ruf (-(e)s, -e) m call, cry; (Ansehen) reputation; **rufen** (rief, gerufen) vt, vi to call; (schreien) to cry; **Rufnummer** f telephone number

Ruhe (-) f rest; (Ungestörtheit) peace, quiet; (Gelassenheit, Stille) calm; (Schweigen) silence; **lass mich in ~!** leave me alone; **ruhen** vi to rest; **Ruhestand** m retirement; **im ~ sein** to be retired; **Ruhestörung** f disturbance of the peace; **Ruhetag** m closing day; **montags ~ haben** to be closed on Mondays

ruhig adj quiet; (bewegungslos) still; (Hand) steady; (gelassen) calm

Ruhm (-(e)s) m fame, glory

Rührei nt scrambled egg(s); **rühren** vt to move; (umrühren) to stir ▸ vr: **sich ~** to move; (sich bemerkbar machen) to say something; **rührend** adj touching, moving; **Rührung** f emotion

Ruine (-, -n) f ruin; **ruinieren** vt to ruin

rülpsen vi to burp, to belch

rum (fam) kontr von **herum**

Rum (-s, -s) m rum

Rumänien (-s) nt Romania

Rummel (-s) m (Trubel) hustle and bustle; (Jahrmarkt) fair; (Medienrummel) hype; **Rummelplatz** m fairground

rumoren vi: **es rumort in meinem Bauch/Kopf** my stomach is rumbling/my head is spinning

Rumpf (-(e)s, Rümpfe) m (Anat) trunk; (Aviat) fuselage; (Naut) hull

rümpfen vt: **die Nase ~** to turn one's nose up (über at)

Rumpsteak nt rump steak

rund adj round ▸ adv (etwa) around; **~ um etw** (a)round sth; **Runde** (-, -n) f round; (in Rennen) lap; **Rundfahrt** f tour (durch of); **Rundfunk** m broadcasting; (Rundfunkanstalt) broadcasting service; **im ~** on the radio; **Rundgang** m tour (durch of); (von Wächter) round

rundlich *adj* plump; **Rundreise**
f tour (durch of)
runter (*fam*) *kontr von* **herunter,**
hinunter; **runterscrollen** *vt*
(*Inform*) to scroll down
runzeln *vt*: **die Stirn ~** to frown;
runzelig *adj* wrinkled
ruppig *adj* gruff
Rüsche (-, -*n*) f frill
Ruß (-*es*) *m* soot
Russe (-*n*, -*n*) *m* Russian
Rüssel (-*s*, -) *m* (*Elefant*) trunk;
(*Schwein*) snout
Russin f Russian; **russisch** *adj*
Russian; **Russisch** *nt* Russian;
Russland *nt* Russia
Rüstung f (*mit Waffen*) arming;
(*Ritterrüstung*) armour; (*Waffen*)
armaments *pl*
Rutsch (-(*e*)*s*, -*e*) *m*: **guten ~** (**ins**
neue Jahr)**!** Happy New Year;
Rutschbahn f, **Rutsche** f slide;
rutschen *vi* to slide; (*ausrutschen*)
to slip; **rutschig** *adj* slippery
rütteln *vt, vi* to shake

S

S *abk* = **Süd** S
s. *abk* = **siehe** see; = **Seite** p.
Saal (-(*e*)*s*, *Säle*) *m* hall; (*für*
Sitzungen) room
Saarland *nt* Saarland
sabotieren *vt* to sabotage
Sache (-, -*n*) f thing;
(*Angelegenheit*) affair, business;
(*Frage*) matter; **bei der ~ bleiben**
to keep to the point; **sachkundig**
adj competent; **Sachlage** f
situation; **sachlich** *adj* (*objektiv*)
objective; (*nüchtern*)
matter-of-fact; (*inhaltlich*) factual;
sächlich *adj* (*Ling*) neuter;
Sachschaden *m* material
damage
Sachsen (-*s*) *nt* Saxony;
Sachsen-Anhalt (-*s*) *nt*
Saxony-Anhalt
sacht(e) *adv* softly, gently
Sachverständige(r) *mf* expert
Sack (-(*e*)*s*, *Säcke*) *m* sack; (*pej*:

Mensch) bastard, bugger;
Sackgasse f dead end, cul-de-sac
Safe ⟨-s, -s⟩ m safe
Safer Sex m safe sex
Safran ⟨-s, -e⟩ m saffron
Saft ⟨-(e)s, Säfte⟩ m juice; **saftig**
adj juicy
Sage ⟨-, -n⟩ f legend
Säge ⟨-, -n⟩ f saw; **Sägemehl** nt
sawdust
sagen vt, vi to say (jdm to sb),
to tell (jdm sb); **wie sagt man ...
auf Englisch?** what's ... in
English?
sägen vt, vi to saw
sagenhaft adj legendary; (fam:
großartig) fantastic
sah imperf von **sehen**
Sahne ⟨-⟩ f cream
Saison ⟨-, -s⟩ f season;
außerhalb der ~ out of season
Saite ⟨-, -n⟩ f string
Sakko ⟨-s, -s⟩ nt jacket
Salami ⟨-, -s⟩ f salami
Salat ⟨-(e)s, -e⟩ m salad;
(Kopfsalat) lettuce; **Salatbar** f
salad bar; **Salatschüssel** f salad
bowl; **Salatsoße** f salad
dressing
Salbe ⟨-, -n⟩ f ointment
Salbei ⟨-s⟩ m sage
Salmonellenvergiftung f
salmonella (poisoning)
salopp adj (Kleidung) casual;
(Sprache) slangy
Salsamusik f salsa (music)
Salto ⟨-s, -s⟩ m somersault
Salz ⟨-es, -e⟩ nt salt; **salzarm** adj
low-salt; **salzen** (salzte, gesalzen)
vt to salt; **Salzgurke** f pickled
gherkin; **Salzhering** m pickled
herring; **salzig** adj salty;
Salzkartoffeln pl boiled potatoes
pl; **Salzstange** f pretzel stick;
Salzstreuer m salt cellar (Brit) (o
shaker (US)); **Salzwasser** nt salt
water

Samba ⟨-, -s⟩ f samba
Samen ⟨-s, -⟩ m seed; (Sperma)
sperm
sammeln vt to collect;
Sammler(in) m(f) collector;
Sammlung f collection;
(Ansammlung, Konzentration)
concentration
Samstag m Saturday; siehe auch
Mittwoch; samstags adv on
Saturdays; siehe auch **mittwochs**
samt prep +dat (along) with,
together with
Samt ⟨-(e)s, -e⟩ m velvet
sämtliche(r, s) adj all (the)
Sanatorium ⟨-s, Sanatorien⟩ nt
sanatorium (Brit), sanitarium (US)
Sand ⟨-(e)s, -e⟩ m sand
Sandale ⟨-, -n⟩ f sandal
sandig adj sandy; **Sandkasten**
m sandpit (Brit), sandbox (US);
Sandpapier nt sandpaper;
Sandstrand m sandy beach
sandte imperf von **senden**
sanft adj soft, gentle
sang imperf von **singen**
Sänger(in) ⟨-s, -⟩ m(f) singer
Sangria ⟨-, -s⟩ f sangria
sanieren vt to redevelop;
(Gebäude) to renovate; (Betrieb) to
restore to profitability
sanitär adj sanitary; **~e Anlagen**
pl sanitation
Sanitäter(in) ⟨-s, -⟩ m(f) ambu-
lance man/woman, paramedic
sank imperf von **sinken**
Sankt Gallen ⟨-s⟩ nt St Gallen
Saphir ⟨-s, -e⟩ m sapphire
Sardelle f anchovy
Sardine f sardine
Sarg ⟨-(e)s, Särge⟩ m coffin
saß imperf von **sitzen**
Satellit ⟨-en, -en⟩ m satellite;
Satellitenfernsehen nt satellite
TV; **Satellitenschüssel** f (fam)
satellite dish
Satire ⟨-, -n⟩ f satire (auf +akk on)

s

satt adj full; (Farbe) rich, deep;
~ **sein** (gesättigt) to be full;
~ **machen** to be filling; **jdn/etw**
~ **sein** to be fed up with sb/sth

Sattel (-s, Sättel) m saddle

satt|haben irr vt: **jdn/etw**
~ (nicht mehr mögen) to be fed up
with sb/sth

Saturn (-s) m Saturn

Satz (-es, Sätze) m (Ling) sentence;
(Mus) movement; (Tennis) set;
(Kaffee) grounds pl; (Comm) rate;
(Sprung) jump; (Comm) rate

Satzzeichen nt punctuation
mark

Sau (-, Säue) f sow; (pej: Mensch)
dirty bugger

sauber adj clean; (ironisch) fine;
~ **machen** to clean; **Sauberkeit** f
cleanness; (von Person) cleanliness;
säubern vt to clean

saublöd adj (fam) really stupid,
dumb

Sauce (-, -n) f sauce; (zu Braten)
gravy

Saudi-Arabien (-s) nt Saudi
Arabia

sauer adj sour; (Chem) acid; (fam:
verärgert) cross; **saurer Regen** acid
rain; **Sauerkirsche** f sour
cherry; **Sauerkraut** nt
sauerkraut; **säuerlich** adj
slightly sour; **Sauermilch** f
sour milk; **Sauerrahm** m sour
cream; **Sauerstoff** m oxygen

saufen (soff, gesoffen) vt to drink;
(fam: Mensch) to knock back ▷ vi
to drink; (fam: Mensch) to booze

saugen (sog o saugte, gesogen o
gesaugt) vt, vi to suck; (mit
Staubsauger) to vacuum, to hoover
(Brit); **Sauger** (-s, -) m (auf Flasche)
teat; **Säugetier** nt mammal;
Säugling m infant, baby

Säule (-, -n) f column, pillar

Saum (-s, Säume) m hem; (Naht)
seam

Sauna (-, -s) f sauna

Säure (-, -n) f acid

sausen vi (Ohren) to buzz; (Wind)
to howl; (Mensch) to rush

Saustall m pigsty; **Sauwetter**
nt: **was für ein** ~ (fam) what lousy
weather

Saxophon (-s, -e) nt saxophone

S-Bahn f suburban railway;
S-Bahn-Haltestelle f, **S-Bahnhof**
m suburban (train) station

scannen vt to scan; **Scanner**
(-s, -) m scanner

schäbig adj shabby

Schach (-s, -s) nt chess; (Stellung)
check; **Schachbrett** nt
chessboard; **Schachfigur** f
chess piece; **schachmatt** adj
checkmate

Schacht (-(e)s, Schächte) m shaft

Schachtel (-, -n) f box

schade interj what a pity

Schädel (-s, -) m skull;
Schädelbruch m fractured skull

schaden vi to damage, to harm
(jdm sb); **das schadet nichts** it
won't do any harm; **Schaden**
(-s, Schäden) m damage;
(Verletzung) injury; (Nachteil)
disadvantage; **einen**
~ **verursachen** to cause damage;
Schadenersatz m compensation, damages pl; **schadhaft** adj
faulty; (beschädigt) damaged;
schädigen vt to damage; (jdn) to
do harm to, to harm; **schädlich**
adj harmful (für to); **Schadstoff**
m harmful substance;
schadstoffarm adj low-emission

Schaf (-(e)s, -e) nt sheep;
Schafbock m ram; **Schäfer** (-s, -)
m shepherd; **Schäferhund** m
Alsatian (Brit), German shepherd;
Schäferin f shepherdess

schaffen (schuf, geschaffen) vt to
create; (Platz) to make ▷ vt
(erreichen) to manage, to do;

(erledigen) to finish; (Prüfung) to pass; (transportieren) to take; **jdm zu ~ machen** to cause sb trouble

Schaffner(in) (-s, -) m(f) (in Bus) conductor/conductress; (Eisenb) guard

Schafskäse m sheep's (milk) cheese

schal adj (Getränk) flat

Schal (-s, -e o -s) m scarf

Schälchen nt (small) bowl

Schale (-, -n) f skin; (abgeschält) peel; (Nuss, Muschel, Ei) shell; (Geschirr) bowl, dish

schälen vt to peel; (Tomate, Mandel) to skin; (Erbsen, Eier, Nüsse) to shell; (Getreide) to husk ▷ vr: **sich ~** to peel

Schall (-(e)s, -e) m sound; **Schalldämpfer** (-s, -) m (Auto) silencer (Brit), muffler (US); **Schallplatte** (-, -n) f record

Schalotte (-, -n) f shallot

schalten vt to switch ▷ vi (Auto) to change gear; (fam: begreifen) to catch on; **Schalter** (-s, -) m (auf Post, Bank) counter; (an Gerät) switch; **Schalterhalle** f main hall; **Schalteröffnungszeiten** pl business hours pl

Schaltfläche f (Inform) button; **Schalthebel** m gear lever (Brit) o shift (US); **Schaltjahr** nt leap year; **Schaltknüppel** m gear lever (Brit) o shift (US); **Schaltung** f gear change (Brit), gearshift (US)

Scham (-) f shame; (Schamgefühl) modesty; **schämen** vr: **sich ~** to be ashamed

Schande (-) f disgrace

Schanze (-, -n) f ski jump

Schar (-, -en) f (von Vögeln) flock; (Menge) crowd; **in ~en** in droves

scharf adj (Messer, Kritik) sharp; (Essen) hot; **auf etw** (akk) **~ sein** (fam) to be keen on sth

Schärfe (-, -n) f sharpness; (Strenge) rigour; (Foto) focus

Scharlach (-s) m (Med) scarlet fever

Scharnier (-s, -e) nt hinge

Schaschlik (-s, -s) m o nt (shish) kebab

Schatten (-s, -) m shadow; **30 Grad im ~** 30 degrees in the shade; **schattig** adj shady

Schatz (-es, Schätze) m treasure; (Mensch) love

schätzen vt (abschätzen) to estimate; (Gegenstand) to value; (würdigen) to value, to esteem; (vermuten) to reckon; **Schätzung** f estimate; (das Schätzen) estimation; (von Wertgegenstand) valuation; **schätzungsweise** adv roughly, approximately

Schau (-, -en) f show; (Ausstellung) exhibition

schauen vi to look; **ich schau mal, ob ...** I'll go and have a look whether ...; **schau, dass ...** see (to it) that ...

Schauer (-s, -) m (Regen) shower; (Schreck) shudder

Schaufel (-, -n) f shovel; **~ und Besen** dustpan and brush; **schaufeln** vt to shovel; **Schnee ~** to clear the snow away

Schaufenster nt shop window; **Schaufensterbummel** m window-shopping expedition

Schaukel (-, -n) f swing; **schaukeln** vi to rock; (mit Schaukel) to swing

Schaulustige(r) mf gawper (Brit), rubbernecker (US)

Schaum (-(e)s, Schäume) m foam; (Seifenschaum) lather; (Bierschaum) froth; **Schaumbad** nt bubble bath; **schäumen** vi to foam; **Schaumfestiger** (-s, -) m styling mousse; **Schaumgummi** m foam (rubber); **Schaumwein** m sparkling wine

Schauplatz m scene; **Schauspiel** nt spectacle; (Theat) play; **Schauspieler(in)** m(f) actor/actress

Scheck (-s, -s) m cheque; **Scheckheft** nt chequebook; **Scheckkarte** f cheque card

Scheibe (-, -n) f disc; (von Brot, Käse etc) slice; (Glasscheibe) pane; **Scheibenbremse** f (Auto) disc brake; **Scheibenwaschanlage** f (Auto) windscreen (Brit) (o windshield (US)) washer unit; **Scheibenwischer** (-s, -) m (Auto) windscreen (Brit) (o windshield (US)) wiper

Scheich (-s, -s) m sheik(h)

Scheide (-, -n) f (Anat) vagina

scheiden (schied, geschieden) vt (trennen) to separate; (Ehe) to dissolve; **sich ~ lassen** to get a divorce; **sie hat sich von ihm ~ lassen** she divorced him; **Scheidung** f divorce

Schein (-(e)s, -e) m light; (Anschein) appearance; (Geld) (bank)note; **scheinbar** adj apparent; **scheinen** (schien, geschienen) vi (Sonne) to shine; (den Anschein haben) to seem; **Scheinwerfer** (-s, -) m floodlight; (Theat) spotlight; (Auto) headlight

Scheiß- in zW (vulg) damned, bloody (Brit); **Scheiße** (-) f (vulg) shit, crap; **Scheißegal** adj (vulg) **das ist mir ~** I don't give a damn (o toss); **scheißen** (schiss, geschissen) vi (vulg) to shit

Scheitel (-s, -) m parting (Brit), part (US)

scheitern vi to fail (an +dat because of)

Schellfisch m haddock

Schema (-s, -s o Schemata) nt

scheme, plan; (Darstellung) diagram

Schenkel (-s, -) m thigh

schenken vt to give; **er hat es mir geschenkt** he gave it to me (as a present); **sich** (dat) **etw ~** (fam: weglassen) to skip sth

Scherbe (-, -n) f broken piece, fragment

Schere (-, -n) f scissors pl; (groß) shears pl; **eine ~** a pair of scissors/shears

Scherz (-es, -e) m joke

scheu adj shy

scheuen vr **sich ~ vor** (+dat) to be afraid of, to shrink from ▷ vt to shun ▷ vi (Pferd) to shy

scheuern vt to scrub; **jdm eine ~** (fam) to slap sb in the face

Scheune (-, -n) f barn

scheußlich adj dreadful

Schi (-s, -er) m siehe **Ski**

Schicht (-, -en) f layer; (in Gesellschaft) class; (in Fabrik etc) shift

schick adj stylish, chic

schicken vt to send ▷ vr: **sich ~** (sich beeilen) to hurry up

Schickimicki (-(s), -s) m (fam) trendy

Schicksal (-s, -e) nt fate

Schiebedach nt (Auto) sunroof; **schieben** (schob, geschoben) vt, vi to push; **die Schuld auf jdn ~** to put the blame on sb; **Schiebetür** f sliding door

schied imperf von **scheiden**

Schiedsrichter(in) m(f) referee; (Tennis) umpire; (Schlichter) arbitrator

schief adj crooked; (Blick) funny ▷ adv crooked(ly); **schiefgehen** irr vi (fam: misslingen) to go wrong

schielen vi to squint

schien imperf von **scheinen**

Schienbein nt shin

Schiene (-, -n) f rail; (Med) splint

schier adj pure; (fig) sheer ▷ adv nearly, almost

schießen (schoss, geschossen) vt to shoot; (Ball) to kick; (Tor) to score; (Foto) to take ▷ vi to shoot (auf +akk at)

Schiff (-(e)s, -e) nt ship; (in Kirche) nave; **Schifffahrt** f shipping; **Schiffsreise** f voyage

schikanieren vt to harass; (Schule) to bully

Schild (-(e)s, -e) m (Schutz) shield ▷ (-(e)s, -er) nt sign; **was steht auf dem ~?** what does the sign say?

Schilddrüse f thyroid gland

schildern vt to describe

Schildkröte f tortoise; (Wasserschildkröte) turtle

Schimmel (-s, -) m mould; (Pferd) white horse; **schimmeln** vi to go mouldy

schimpfen vt to tell off ▷ vi (sich beklagen) to complain; **mit jdm ~** to tell sb off; **Schimpfwort** nt swearword

Schinken (-s, -) m ham

Schirm (-(e)s, -e) m (Regenschirm) umbrella; (Sonnenschirm) parasol, sunshade

schiss imperf von **scheißen**

Schlacht (-, -en) f battle; **schlachten** vt to slaughter; **Schlachter(in)** (-s, -) m(f) butcher

Schlaf (-(e)s) m sleep; **Schlafanzug** m pyjamas pl; **Schlafcouch** f bed settee

Schläfe (-, -n) f temple

schlafen (schlief, geschlafen) vi to sleep; **schlaf gut!** sleep well; **hast du gut geschlafen?** did you sleep all right?; **er schläft noch** he's still asleep; **~ gehen** to go to bed

schlaff adj slack; (kraftlos) limp; (erschöpft) exhausted

Schlafgelegenheit f place to sleep; **Schlaflosigkeit** f

sleeplessness; **Schlafmittel** nt sleeping pill; **schläfrig** adj sleepy

Schlafsaal m dormitory; **Schlafsack** m sleeping bag; **Schlaftablette** f sleeping pill; **er ist eine richtige ~** (fam: langweilig) he's such a bore; **Schlafwagen** m sleeping car, sleeper; **Schlafzimmer** nt bedroom

Schlag (-(e)s, Schläge) m blow; (Puls) beat; (Elek) shock; (fam: Portion) helping; (Art) kind, type; **Schlagader** f artery; **Schlaganfall** m (Med) stroke; **schlagartig** adj sudden

schlagen (schlug, geschlagen) vt to hit; (besiegen) to beat; (Sahne) to whip; **jdn zu Boden ~** to knock sb down ▷ vi (Herz) to beat; (Uhr) to strike; **mit dem Kopf gegen etw ~** to bang one's head against sth ▷ vr: **sich ~** to fight

Schläger (-s, -) m (Sport) bat; (Tennis) racket; (Golf) (golf) club; (Hockey) hockey stick; (Mensch) brawler; **Schlägerei** f fight, brawl

schlagfertig adj quick-witted; **Schlagloch** nt pothole; **Schlagsahne** f whipping cream; (geschlagen) whipped cream; **Schlagzeile** f headline; **Schlagzeug** nt drums pl; (in Orchester) percussion

Schlamm (-(e)s, -e) m mud

schlampig adj (fam) sloppy

schlang imperf von **schlingen**

Schlange (-, -n) f snake; (von Menschen) queue (Brit), line (US); **~ stehen** to queue (Brit), to stand in line (US); **Schlangenlinie** f wavy line; **in ~n fahren** to swerve about

schlank adj slim

schlapp adj limp; (locker) slack

Schlappe (-, -n) f (fam) setback

schlau adj clever, smart; (raffiniert) crafty, cunning

Schlauch (-(e)s, Schläuche) m hose; (in Reifen) inner tube; **Schlauchboot** nt rubber dinghy

schlecht adj bad; **mir ist ~** I feel sick; **die Milch ist ~** the milk has gone off ▷ adv badly; **es geht ihm ~** he's having a hard time; (gesundheitlich) he's not feeling well; (finanziell) he's pretty hard up; **schlecht|machen** vt: **jdn ~** (herabsetzen) to run sb down

schleichen (schlich, geschlichen) vi to creep

Schleier (-s, -) m veil

Schleife (-, -n) f (Inform, Aviat, Elek) loop; (Band) bow

schleifen vt (ziehen, schleppen) to drag ▷ (schliff, geschliffen) vt (schärfen) to grind; (Edelstein) to cut

Schleim (-(e)s, -e) m slime; (Med) mucus; **Schleimer** (-s, -) m (fam) creep; **Schleimhaut** f mucous membrane

schlendern vi to stroll

schleppen vt to drag; (Auto, Schiff) to tow; (tragen) to lug; **Schlepplift** m ski tow

Schleswig-Holstein (-s) nt Schleswig-Holstein

Schleuder (-, -n) f catapult; (für Wäsche) spin-dryer; **schleudern** vt to hurl; (Wäsche) to spin-dry ▷ vi (Auto) to skid; **Schleudersitz** m ejector seat

schlich imperf von **schleichen**

schlicht adj simple, plain

schlichten vt (Streit) to settle

schlief imperf von **schlafen**

schließen (schloss, geschlossen) vt, vi to close, to shut; (beenden) to close; (Freundschaft, Ehe) to enter into; (folgern) to infer (aus from) ▷ vr: **sich ~** to close, to shut; **Schließfach** nt locker

schließlich adv finally; (schließlich doch) after all

schliff imperf von **schleifen**

schlimm adj bad; **schlimmer** adj worse; **schlimmste(r, s)** adj worst; **schlimmstenfalls** adv at (the) worst

Schlinge (-, -n) f loop; (Med) sling

Schlips (-es, -e) m tie

Schlitten (-s, -) m sledge, toboggan; (mit Pferden) sleigh; **Schlittenfahren** (-s) nt tobogganing

Schlittschuh m ice skate; **~ laufen** to ice-skate

Schlitz (-es, -e) m slit; (für Münze) slot; (an Hose) flies pl

schloss imperf von **schließen**

Schloss (-es, Schlösser) nt lock; (Burg) castle

Schlosser(in) m(f) mechanic

Schlucht (-, -en) f gorge, ravine

schluchzen vi to sob

Schluck (-(e)s, -e) m swallow; **Schluckauf** (-s) m hiccups pl; **schlucken** vt, vi to swallow

schludern vi (fam) to do sloppy work

schlug imperf von **schlagen**

Schlüpfer (-s, -) m panties pl

schlüpfen vi, vt to slip

Schluss (-es, Schlüsse) m end; (Schlussfolgerung) conclusion; **am ~** at the end; **mit jdm ~ machen** to finish (o split up) with sb

Schlüssel (-s, -) m (a. fig) key; **Schlüsselbein** nt collarbone; **Schlüsselbund** m bunch of keys; **Schlüsseldienst** m key-cutting service; **Schlüsselloch** nt keyhole

Schlussfolgerung f conclusion; **Schlusslicht** nt tail-light; (fig) tail-ender; **Schlussverkauf** m clearance sale

schmächtig adj frail

schmal adj narrow; (Mensch, Buch etc) slim; (karg) meagre

Schmalz (-es, -e) nt dripping, lard; (fig: Sentimentalitäten) schmaltz

schmatzen vi to eat noisily

schmecken vt, vi to taste (nach of); **es schmeckt ihm** he likes it; **lass es dir ~!** bon appétit

Schmeichelei f flattery; **schmeichelhaft** adj flattering; **schmeicheln** vi: **jdm ~** to flatter sb

schmeißen (schmiss, geschmissen) vt (fam) to chuck, to throw

schmelzen (schmolz, geschmolzen) vt, vi to melt; (Metall, Erz) to smelt; **Schmelzkäse** m cheese spread

Schmerz (-es, -en) m pain; (Trauer) grief; **~en haben** to be in pain; **~en im Rücken haben** to have a pain in one's back; **schmerzen** vt, vi to hurt; **Schmerzensgeld** nt compensation; **schmerzhaft, schmerzlich** adj painful; **schmerzlos** adj painless; **Schmerzmittel** nt painkiller; **schmerzstillend** adj painkilling; **Schmerztablette** f painkiller

Schmetterling m butterfly

Schmied(in) m(-(e)s, -e) m(f) blacksmith; **schmieden** vt to forge; (Pläne) to make

schmieren vt to smear; (ölen) to lubricate, to grease; (bestechen) to bribe ▷ vt, vi (unsauber schreiben) to scrawl; **Schmiergeld** nt (fam) bribe; **schmierig** adj greasy; **Schmierseife** f soft soap

Schminke (-, -n) f make-up; **schminken** vr: **sich ~** to put one's make-up on

schmiss imperf von **schmeißen**

schmollen vi to sulk; **schmollend** adj sulky

schmolz imperf von **schmelzen**

Schmuck (-(e)s, -e) m jewellery (Brit), jewelry (US); (Verzierung)

decoration; **schmücken** vt to decorate

schmuggeln vt, vi to smuggle

schmunzeln vi to smile

schmusen vi to (kiss and) cuddle

Schmutz (-es) m dirt, filth; **schmutzig** adj dirty

Schnabel (-s, Schnäbel) m beak, bill; (Ausguss) spout

Schnake (-, -n) f mosquito

Schnalle (-, -n) f buckle

Schnäppchen nt (fam) bargain; **schnappen** vt (fangen) to catch ▷ vi: **nach Luft ~** to gasp for breath; **Schnappschuss** m (Foto) snap(shot)

Schnaps (-es, Schnäpse) m schnapps

schnarchen vi to snore

schnaufen vi to puff, to pant

Schnauzbart m moustache; **Schnauze** (-, -n) f snout, muzzle; (Ausguss) spout; (fam: Mund) trap; **die ~ voll haben** to have had enough

schnäuzen vr: **sich ~** to blow one's nose

Schnecke (-, -n) f snail; **Schneckenhaus** nt snail's shell

Schnee (-s) m snow; **Schneeball** m snowball; **Schneebob** m snowmobile; **Schneebrille** f snow goggles pl; **Schneeflocke** f snowflake; **Schneegestöber** (-s, -) nt snow flurry; **Schneeglöckchen** nt snowdrop; **Schneegrenze** f snowline; **Schneekanone** f snow thrower; **Schneekette** f (Auto) snow chain; **Schneemann** m snowman; **Schneepflug** m snowplough; **Schneeregen** m sleet; **Schneeschmelze** f thaw; **Schneesturm** m snowstorm, blizzard; **Schneetreiben** nt light blizzards pl; **Schneewehe** f snowdrift

Schneide (-, -n) f edge; (Klinge) blade; **schneiden** (schnitt, geschnitten) vt to cut; **sich** (dat) **die Haare ~ lassen** to have one's hair cut ▷ vr: **sich ~** to cut oneself; **Schneider(in)** (-s, -) m(f) tailor; (für Damenmode) dressmaker; **Schneiderin** f dressmaker; **Schneidezahn** m incisor

schneien vi impers to snow

schnell adj quick, fast ▷ adv quickly, fast; **mach ~!** hurry up; **Schnelldienst** m express service; **Schnellhefter** m loose-leaf binder; **Schnellimbiss** m snack bar; **Schnellkochtopf** m pressure cooker; **Schnellreinigung** f express dry cleaning; (Geschäft) express (dry) cleaner's; **Schnellstraße** f expressway; **Schnellzug** m fast train

schneuzen vr siehe **schnäuzen**

schnitt imperf von **schneiden**

Schnitt (-(e)s, -e) m cut; (Schnittpunkt) intersection; (Querschnitt) (cross) section; (Durchschnitt) average; (eines Kleides) style; **Schnitte** (-, -n) f slice; (belegt) sandwich; **Schnittkäse** m cheese slices pl; **Schnittlauch** m chives pl; **Schnittmuster** nt pattern; **Schnittstelle** f (Inform, fig) interface; **Schnittwunde** f cut, gash

Schnitzel (-s, -) nt (Papier) scrap; (Gastr) escalope

schnitzen vt to carve

Schnorchel (-s, -) m snorkel; **schnorcheln** vi to go snorkelling, to snorkel

schnüffeln vi to sniff

Schnuller (-s, -) m dummy (Brit), pacifier (US)

Schnulze (-, -n) f (Film, Roman) weepie

Schnupfen (-s, -) m cold

schnuppern vi to sniff

Schnur (-, Schnüre) f string, cord; (Elek) lead; **schnurlos** adj (Telefon) cordless

Schnurrbart m moustache

schnurren vi to purr

Schnürsenkel (-s, -) m shoelace

schob imperf von **schieben**

Schock (-(e)s, -e) m shock; **unter ~ stehen** to be in a state of shock; **schockieren** vt to shock

Schokolade f chocolate; **Schokoriegel** m chocolate bar

Scholle (-, -n) f (Fisch) plaice; (Eis) ice floe

SCHLÜSSELWORT

schon adv 1 (bereits) already; **er ist schon da** he's there already, he's already there; **ist er schon da?** is he there yet?; **warst du schon einmal da?** have you ever been there?; **ich war schon einmal da** I've been there before; **das war schon immer so** that has always been the case; **schon oft** often; **hast du schon gehört?** have you heard?

2 (bestimmt) all right; **du wirst schon sehen** you'll see (all right); **das wird schon noch gut** that'll be OK

3 (bloß) just; **allein schon das Gefühl** ... just the very feeling ...; **schon der Gedanke** the very thought; **wenn ich das schon höre** I've been to hear that

4 (einschränkend) **ja schon, aber ...** yes (well), but ...

5 **schon möglich** possible; **schon gut!** OK!; **du weißt schon** you know; **komm schon!** come on!

schön adj beautiful; (nett) nice; (Frau) beautiful, pretty; (Mann)

beautiful, handsome; (Wetter) fine;
~e Grüße best wishes; **~es
Wochenende** have a nice
weekend

schonen vt (pfleglich behandeln) to
look after ▷ vr: **sich ~** to take it
easy

Schönheit f beauty

Schonkost f light diet

schöpfen vt to scoop; (mit Kelle)
to ladle; **Schöpfkelle** f,
Schöpflöffel m ladle

Schöpfung f creation

Schoppen (-s, -) m glass (of
wine)

Schorf (-(e)s, -e) m scab

Schorle (-, -n) f spritzer

Schornstein m chimney;
Schornsteinfeger(in) (-s, -) m(f)
chimney sweep

schoss imperf von **schießen**

Schoß (-es, Schöße) m lap

Schotte (-n, -n) m Scot,
Scotsman; **Schottin** f Scot,
Scotswoman; **schottisch** adj
Scottish, Scots; **Schottland** nt
Scotland

schräg adj slanting; (Dach)
sloping; (Linie) diagonal; (fam:
unkonventionell) wacky

Schrank (-(e)s, Schränke) m
cupboard; (Kleiderschrank)
wardrobe (Brit), closet (US)

Schranke (-, -n) f barrier

Schrankwand f wall unit

Schraube (-, -n) f screw;
schrauben vt to screw; **Schrau-
bendreher** (-s, -) m screwdriver;
Schraubenschlüssel m spanner;
Schraubenzieher (-s, -) m screwdriver; **Schraubverschluss** m
screw top, screw cap

Schreck (-(e)s, -e) m, **Schrecken**
(-s, -) m terror; (Angst) fright; **jdm
einen ~ einjagen** to give sb a
fright; **schreckhaft** adj jumpy;
schrecklich adj terrible, dreadful

Schrei (-(e)s, -e) m scream; (Ruf)
shout

Schreibblock m writing pad;
schreiben (schrieb, geschrieben) vt,
vi to write; (buchstabieren) to spell;
wie schreibt man ...? how do you
spell ...?; **Schreiben** (-s, -) nt
writing; (Brief) letter;
Schreibfehler m spelling
mistake; **schreibgeschützt** adj
(Diskette) write-protected;
Schreibtisch m desk;
Schreibwaren pl stationery sing;
Schreibwarenladen m
stationer's

schreien (schrie, geschrie(e)n) vt, vi
to scream; (rufen) to shout

Schreiner(in) m(f) joiner;
Schreinerei f joiner's workshop

schrie imperf von **schreien**

schrieb imperf von **schreiben**

Schrift (-, -en) f writing;
(Handschrift) handwriting;
(Schriftart) typeface; (Schrifttyp)
font; **schriftlich** adj written ▷ adv
in writing; **würden Sie uns das
bitte ~ geben?** could we have
that in writing, please?; **Schrift-
steller(in)** (-s, -) m(f) writer

Schritt (-(e)s, -e) m step; **~ für
~** step by step; **~e gegen etw
unternehmen** to take steps
against sth; **Schrittgeschwind-
igkeit** f walking speed;
Schrittmacher m (Med)
pacemaker

Schrott (-(e)s, -e) m scrap metal;
(fig) rubbish

schrubben vi, vt to scrub;
Schrubber (-s, -) m scrubbing
brush

schrumpfen vi to shrink

Schubkarren (-s, -) m wheelbarrow; **Schublade** f drawer

schubsen vt to shove, to push

schüchtern adj shy

schuf imperf von **schaffen**

Schuh (-(e)s, -e) m shoe;
Schuhcreme f shoe polish;
Schuhgeschäft nt shoe shop;
Schuhgröße f shoe size;
Schuhlöffel m shoehorn
Schulabschluss m school-
leaving qualification
schuld adj: **wer ist ~ daran?**
whose fault is it?; **er ist ~** it's his
fault, he's to blame; **Schuld** (-) f
guilt; (Verschulden) fault; **~ haben**
to be to blame (an +dat for); **er hat
~** it's his fault; **sie gibt mir die
~ an dem Unfall** she blames me
for the accident; **schulden** vt to
owe (jdm etw sb sth); **Schulden**
debts pl; **~ haben** to be in debt;
~ machen to run up debts; **seine
~ bezahlen** to pay off one's debts;
schuldig adj guilty (an +dat of);
(gebührend) due; **jdm etw ~ sein** to
owe sb sth
Schule (-, -n) f school; **in der ~** at
school; **in die ~ gehen** to go to
school; **Schüler(in)** (-s, -) m(f)
(jüngerer) pupil; (älterer) student;
Schüleraustausch m school
exchange; **Schulfach** nt subject;
Schulferien pl school holidays pl
(Brit) (o vacation (US)); **schulfrei**
adj: **morgen ist ~** there's no school
tomorrow; **Schulfreund(in)** m(f)
schoolmate; **Schuljahr** nt school
year; **Schulkenntnisse** pl: **~ in
Französisch** school-(level) French;
Schulklasse f class; **Schul-
leiter(in)** m(f) headmaster/
headmistress (Brit), principal (US)
Schulter (-, -n) f shoulder;
Schulterblatt nt shoulder blade
Schulung f training;
(Veranstaltung) training course
schummeln vi (fam) to cheat
Schuppe (-, -n) f (von Fisch) scale;
schuppen vt to scale ▷ vr: **sich
~** to peel; **Schuppen** pl (im Haar)
dandruff sing

Schürfwunde f graze
Schürze (-, -n) f apron
Schuss (-es, Schüsse) m shot; **mit
einem ~ Wodka** with a dash of
vodka
Schüssel (-, -n) f bowl
Schuster(in) (-s, -) m(f)
shoemaker
Schutt (-(e)s) m rubble
Schüttelfrost m shivering fit;
schütteln vt to shake ▷ vr: **sich
~** to shake
schütten vt to pour; (Zucker, Kies
etc) to tip ▷ vi impers to pour
(down)
Schutz (-es) m protection (gegen,
vor against, from); (Unterschlupf)
shelter; **jdn in ~ nehmen** to stand
up for sb; **Schutzblech** nt
mudguard; **Schutzbrief** m travel
insurance document for drivers;
Schutzbrille f (safety) goggles pl
Schütze (-n, -n) m (beim Fußball)
scorer; (Astr) Sagittarius
schützen vt: **jdn gegen/vor etw
~** to protect sb against/from sth;
Schutzimpfung f inoculation,
vaccination
schwach adj weak; **~e Augen**
poor eyesight sing; **Schwäche**
(-, -n) f weakness; **Schwachstelle**
f weak point; **Schwachstrom** m
low-voltage current
Schwager (-s, Schwäger) m
brother-in-law; **Schwägerin** f
sister-in-law
Schwalbe (-, -n) f swallow; (beim
Fußball) dive
schwamm imperf von
schwimmen
Schwamm (-(e)s, Schwämme) m
sponge; **~ drüber!** (fam) let's forget
it!
Schwan (-(e)s,
Schwäne) m swan
schwanger adj pregnant; **im
vierten Monat ~ sein** to be four

months pregnant; **Schwanger-schaft** f pregnancy; **Schwanger-schaftsabbruch** m abortion; **Schwangerschaftstest** m pregnancy test

schwanken vi to sway; (Preise, Zahlen) to fluctuate; (zögern) to hesitate; (taumeln) to stagger; **ich schwanke zwischen A und B** I can't decide between A and B

Schwanz (-es, Schwänze) m tail; (vulg: Penis) cock

Schwarm (-(e)s, Schwärme) m swarm; (fam: angehimmelte Person) heartthrob; **schwärmen** vi to swarm; **~ für** to be mad about

schwarz adj black; **mir wurde ~ vor Augen** everything went black; **Schwarzarbeit** f illicit work; **Schwarzbrot** nt black bread; **schwarz|fahren** irr vi to travel without a ticket; (ohne Führerschein) to drive without a licence; **Schwarzfahrer(in)** m(f) fare-dodger; **Schwarzmarkt** m black market; **schwarz|sehen** irr vi (fam: pessimistisch sein) to be pessimistic (für about); **Schwarzwald** m Black Forest; **schwarzweiß** adj black and white

schwatzen vi to chatter; **Schwätzer(in)** (-s, -) m(f) chatterbox; (Schwafler) gasbag; (Klatschmaul) gossip

Schwebebahn f suspension railway; **schweben** vi to float; (hoch) to soar

Schwede (-n, -n) m Swede; **Schweden** (-s) nt Sweden; **Schwedin** f Swede; **schwedisch** adj Swedish; **Schwedisch** nt Swedish

Schwefel (-s) m sulphur

schweigen (schwieg, geschwiegen) vi to be silent; (nicht mehr reden) to stop talking; **Schweigen** (-s) nt

silence; **Schweigepflicht** f duty of confidentiality; **die ärztliche ~** medical confidentiality

Schwein (-(e)s, -e) nt pig; (fam: Glück) luck; (fam: gemeiner Mensch) swine; **Schweinebraten** m roast pork; **Schweinefleisch** nt pork; **Schweinegrippe** f swine flu; **Schweinerei** f mess; (Gemeinheit) dirty trick

Schweiß (-es) m sweat

schweißen vt, vi to weld

Schweiz (-) f: **die ~** Switzerland; **Schweizer(in)** (-s, -) m(f) Swiss; **Schweizerdeutsch** nt Swiss German; **schweizerisch** adj Swiss

Schwelle (-, -n) f doorstep; (a. fig) threshold

schwellen vi to swell (up); **Schwellung** f swelling

schwer adj heavy; (schwierig) difficult, hard; (schlimm) serious, bad; **er ist ~ zu verstehen** it's difficult to understand what he's saying ▷ adv (sehr) really; (verletzt etc) seriously, badly; **etw ~ nehmen** to take sth hard; **Schwerbehinderte(r)** mf person with a severe disability; **schwer|fallen** irr vi (Schwierigkeiten bereiten bereiten) **jdm ~** to be difficult for sb; **schwerhörig** adj hard of hearing

Schwert (-(e)s, -er) nt sword; **Schwertlilie** f iris

Schwester (-, -n) f sister; (Med) nurse

schwieg imperf von **schweigen**

Schwiegereltern pl parents-in-law pl; **Schwiegermutter** f mother-in-law; **Schwiegersohn** m son-in-law; **Schwiegertochter** f daughter-in-law; **Schwiegervater** m father-in-law

schwierig adj difficult, hard; **Schwierigkeit** f difficulty; **in ~en kommen** to get into trouble; **jdm**

~en machen to make things difficult for sb

Schwimmbad nt swimming pool; **Schwimmbecken** nt swimming pool; **schwimmen** (schwamm, geschwommen) vi to swim; (treiben) to float; (fig: unsicher sein) to be all at sea; **Schwimmer(in)** m(f) swimmer; **Schwimmflosse** f flipper; **Schwimmflügel** m water wing; **Schwimmreifen** m rubber ring; **Schwimmweste** f life jacket

Schwindel (-s) m dizziness; (Anfall) dizzy spell; (Betrug) swindle; **schwindelfrei** adj: **nicht ~ sein** to suffer from vertigo; **~ sein** to have a head for heights; **schwindlig** adj dizzy; **mir ist ~** I feel dizzy

Schwips m: **einen ~ haben** to be tipsy

schwitzen vi to sweat

schwoll imperf von **schwellen**

schwor imperf von **schwören**

schwören (schwor, geschworen) vt, vi to swear; **einen Eid ~** to take an oath

schwul adj gay

schwül adj close

Schwung (-(e)s, Schwünge) m swing; (Triebkraft) momentum; (fig: Energie) energy; (fam: Menge) batch; **in ~ kommen** to get going

Schwur (-s, Schwüre) m oath

Screenshot m (Inform) screenshot

scrollen vi (Inform) to scroll

sechs num six; **Sechs** (-, -en) f six; (Schulnote) ≈ F; **Sechserpack** m sixpack; **sechshundert** num six hundred; **sechsmal** adv six times; **sechste(r, s)** adj sixth; siehe auch **dritte**; **Sechstel** (-s, -) nt sixth; **sechzehn** num sixteen; **sechzehnte(r, s)** adj sixteenth; siehe auch **dritte**; **sechzig** num

sixty; **in den ~er Jahren** in the sixties; **sechzigste(r, s)** adj sixtieth

Secondhandladen m second-hand shop

See (-, -n) f sea; **an der ~** by the sea ▷ (-s, -n) m lake; **am ~** by the lake; **Seegang** m waves; **hoher/schwerer/leichter ~** rough/heavy/calm seas pl; **Seehund** m seal; **Seeigel** m sea urchin; **seekrank** adj seasick

Seele (-, -n) f soul

Seeleute pl seamen pl, sailors pl

seelisch adj mental, psychological

Seelöwe m sea lion; **Seemann** m sailor, seaman; **Seemeile** f nautical mile; **Seemöwe** f seagull; **Seenot** f distress (at sea); **Seepferdchen** nt sea horse; **Seerose** f water lily; **Seestern** m starfish; **Seezunge** f sole

Segel (-s, -) nt sail; **Segelboot** nt yacht; **Segelfliegen** (-s) nt gliding; **Segelflugzeug** nt glider; **segeln** vt, vi to sail; **Segelschiff** nt sailing ship

sehbehindert adj partially sighted

sehen (sah, gesehen) vt, vi to see; (in bestimmte Richtung) to look; **gut/schlecht ~** to have good/bad eyesight; **auf die Uhr ~** to look at one's watch; **kann ich das mal ~?** can I have a look at it?; **wir ~ uns morgen!** see you tomorrow!; **ich kenne sie nur vom Sehen** I only know her by sight; **Sehenswürdigkeiten** pl sights pl

Sehne (-, -n) f tendon; (an Bogen) string

sehnen vr: **sich ~** to long (nach for)

Sehnenscheidenentzündung f (Med) tendovaginitis;

Sehnenzerrung f (Med) pulled tendon

Sehnsucht f longing; **sehnsüchtig** adj longing

sehr adv (vor Adjektiv, Adverb) very; (mit Verben) a lot, very much; **zu ~** too much

seicht adj shallow

Seide (-, -n) f silk

Seife (-, -n) f soap; **Seifenoper** f soap (opera); **Seifenschale** f soap dish

Seil (-(e)s, -e) nt rope; (Kabel) cable; **Seilbahn** f cable railway

⊙ SCHLÜSSELWORT

sein¹ (pt **war**, pp **gewesen**) vi **1** to be; **ich bin** I am; **du bist** you are; **er/sie/es ist** he/she/it is; **wir sind/ihr seid/sie sind** we/you/they are; **wir waren** we were; **wir sind gewesen** we have been

2 seien Sie nicht böse don't be angry; **sei so gut und ...** be so kind as to ...; **das wäre gut** that would be a good thing; **wenn ich Sie wäre** if I were o was you; **das wär's** that's all, that's it; **morgen bin ich in Rom** tomorrow I'll o I will o I shall be in Rome; **waren Sie mal in Rom?** have you ever been to Rome?

3 wie ist das zu verstehen? how is that to be understood?; **er ist nicht zu ersetzen** he cannot be replaced; **mit ihr ist nicht zu reden** you can't talk to her

4 mir ist kalt I'm cold; **was ist?** what's the matter?, what is it?; **ist was?** is something the matter?; **es sei denn, dass ...** unless ...; **wie dem auch sei** be that as it may; **wie wäre es mit ...?** how o what about ...?; **lass das sein!** stop that!

sein² pron possessiv von **er**; (adjektivisch) his ▷ pron possessiv von **es**; (adjektivisch) its; (adjektivisch, männlich) her; (weiblich) her; (sächlich) its; **das ist ~e Tasche** that's his bag; **jeder hat ~e Sorgen** everyone has their problems; **seine(r, s)** pron possessiv von **er**; (substantivisch) his ▷ pron possessiv von **es**; (substantivisch) its; (substantivisch, männlich) his; (weiblich) hers; **das ist ~r/~/~s** that's his/hers; **seiner** pron gen von **er**; of him ▷ pron gen von **es**; of it; **seinetwegen** adv (wegen ihm) because of him; (ihm zuliebe) for his sake; (um ihn) about him; (von ihm aus) as far as he is concerned

seit conj (bei Zeitpunkt) since; (bei Zeitraum) for; **er ist ~ Montag hier** he's been here since Monday; **er ist ~ einer Woche hier** he's been here for a week; **~ langem** for a long time; **seitdem** adv, conj since

Seite (-, -n) f side; (in Buch) page; **zur ~ gehen** to step aside; **Seitenairbag** m side-impact airbag; **Seitenaufprallschutz** m (Auto) side-impact protection; **Seitensprung** m affair; **Seitenstechen** (-s) nt: **~ haben/ bekommen** to have/get a stitch; **Seitenstraße** f side street; **Seitenstreifen** m hard shoulder (Brit), shoulder (US); **Seitenwind** m crosswind

seither adv since (then)

seitlich adj side

Sekretär(in) m(f) secretary; **Sekretariat** (-s, -e) nt secretary's office

Sekt (-(e)s, -e) m sparkling wine (similar to champagne)

Sekte (-, -n) f sect

Sekunde (-, -n) f second;
Sekundenkleber (-s, -) m superglue; **Sekundenschnelle** f: **es
geschah alles in ~** it was all over
in a matter of seconds

O SCHLÜSSELWORT

selbst pron **1 ich/er/wir selbst** I
myself/he himself/we ourselves;
sie ist die Tugend selbst she's
virtue itself; **er braut sein Bier
selbst** he brews his own beer; **wie
geht's? — gut, und selbst?** how
are things? — fine, and yourself?
2 (ohne Hilfe) alone, on
my/his/one's etc own; **von selbst**
by itself; **er kam von selbst** he
came of his own accord; **selbst
gemacht** home-made
▷ adv even; **selbst wenn** even if;
selbst Gott even God (himself)

selbständig adj siehe
selbstständig
Selbstauslöser (-s, -) m (Foto)
self-timer; **Selbstbedienung** f
self-service; **Selbstbefriedigung** f
masturbation;
Selbstbeherrschung f
self-control; **Selbstbeteiligung** f
(einer Versicherung) excess;
selbstbewusst adj
(self-)confident; **Selbstbräuner**
(-s, -) m self-tanning lotion;
selbstgemacht adj self-made;
selbstklebend adj self-adhesive;
Selbstlaut m vowel; **Selbstmord**
m suicide; **Selbstmordattentat**
nt suicide bombing; **Selbstmord-
attentäter(in)** m(f) suicide
bomber; **selbstsicher** adj
self-assured; **selbstständig** adj
independent; (arbeitend)
self-employed; **Selbstverpflegung**
f self-catering;
selbstverständlich adj obvious;

ich halte das für ~ I take that for
granted ▷ adv naturally;
Selbstvertrauen nt
self-confidence
Selfie nt selfie
Sellerie (-s, -(s)) m (-, -n) f (Knollensellerie) celeriac; (Stangensellerie)
celery
selten adj rare ▷ adv rarely
seltsam adj strange;
~ schmecken/riechen to
taste/smell strange
Semester (-s, -) nt semester;
Semesterferien pl vacation sing
Semikolon (-s, Semikola) nt
semicolon
Seminar (-s, -e) nt seminar
Semmel (-, -n) f roll;
Semmelbrösel pl breadcrumbs
Senat (-(e)s, -e) m senate
senden (sandte, gesandt) vt to
send ▷ vt, vi (Radio, TV) to
broadcast; **Sender** (-s, -) m (TV)
channel; (Radio) station; (Anlage)
transmitter; **Sendung** f (Radio,
TV) broadcasting; (Programm)
programme
Senf (-(e)s, -e) m mustard
Senior(in) m(f) senior citizen;
Seniorenpass m senior citizen's
travel pass
senken vt to lower ▷ vr: **sich
~ to** sink
senkrecht adj vertical
Sensation (-, -en) f sensation
sensibel adj sensitive
sentimental adj sentimental
separat adj separate
September (-(s), -) m
September; siehe auch **Juni**
Serbien (-s) nt Serbia
Serie f series sing
seriös adj (ernsthaft) serious;
(anständig) respectable
Serpentine f hairpin (bend)
Serum (-s, Seren) nt serum
Server (-s, -) m (Inform) server

Service (-(s), -) nt (Geschirr)
service ▷ (-, -s) m service
servieren vt, vi to serve
Serviette f napkin, serviette
Servolenkung f (Auto) power
steering
Sesam (-s, -s) m sesame seeds pl
Sessel (-s, -) m armchair;
Sessellift m chairlift
Set (-s, -s) m o nt set; (Tischset)
tablemat
setzen vt to put; (Baum etc) to
plant; (Segel) to set ▷ vr: **sich ~** to
settle; (hinsetzen) to sit down; **~ Sie
sich doch** please sit down
Seuche (-, -n) f epidemic
seufzen vt, vi to sigh
Sex (-(es)) m sex; **Sexismus** m
sexism; **sexistisch** adj sexist;
Sextourismus m sex tourism;
Sexualität f sexuality; **sexuell**
adj sexual
Seychellen pl Seychelles pl
sfr abk = **Schweizer Franken** Swiss
franc(s)
Shampoo (-s, -s) nt shampoo
Shareware (-, -s) f (Inform)
shareware
Shorts f shorts pl
Shuttlebus m shuttle bus

🔵 SCHLÜSSELWORT

sich pron 1 (akk) **er/sie/es ... sich**
he/she/it ... himself/herself/itself;
sie pl/man ... sich they/one ...
themselves/oneself; **Sie ... sich**
you ... yourself/yourselves pl; **sich
wiederholen** to repeat
oneself/itself
2 (dat) **er/sie/es ... sich** he/she/it
... to himself/herself/itself; **sie**
pl/man ... sich they/one ... to
themselves/oneself; **Sie ... sich**
you ... to yourself/yourselves pl;
**sie hat sich einen Pullover
gekauft** she bought herself a

jumper; **sich die Haare waschen**
to wash one's hair
3 (mit Präposition) **haben Sie Ihren
Ausweis bei sich?** do you have
your pass on you?; **er hat nichts
bei sich** he's got nothing on him;
sie bleiben gern unter sich they
keep themselves to themselves
4 (einander) each other, one
another; **sie bekämpfen sich** they
fight each other o one another
5 **dieses Auto fährt sich gut** this
car drives well; **hier sitzt es sich
gut** it's good to sit here

sicher adj safe (vor +dat from);
(gewiss) certain (gen of);
(zuverlässig) reliable; (selbstsicher)
confident; **aber ~!** of course, sure;
Sicherheit f safety; (Aufgabe von
Sicherheitsbeamten) (Fin) security;
(Gewissheit) certainty;
(Selbstsicherheit) confidence; **mit
~** definitely; **Sicherheitsabstand**
m safe distance; **Sicherheitsgurt**
m seat belt; **sicherheitshalber**
adv just to be on the safe side;
Sicherheitsnadel f safety pin;
Sicherheitsvorkehrung f safety
precaution; **sicherlich** adv
certainly; (wahrscheinlich) probably
sichern vt to secure (gegen
against); (schützen) to protect;
(Daten) to back up; **Sicherung** f
(Sichern) securing; (Vorrichtung)
safety device; (an Waffen) safety
catch; (Elek) fuse; (Inform) backup;
die ~ ist durchgebrannt the fuse
has blown
Sicht (-) f sight; (Aussicht) view;
sichtbar adj visible; **sichtlich**
adj evident, obvious;
Sichtverhältnisse pl visibility
sing; **Sichtweite** f: **in/außer
~** within/out of sight
sie pron (3. Person sing) she; (3.
Person pl) they; (akk von sing) her;

(akk von pl) them; *(für eine Sache)* it;
da ist ~ ja there she is; **da sind ~ ja**
there they are; **ich kenne ~** *(Frau)* I
know her; *(mehrere Personen)* I
know them; **~ lag gerade noch
hier** *(meine Jacke, Uhr)* it was here
just a minute ago; **ich hab
~ gefunden** *(meine Jacke, Uhr)* I've
found it; **hast du meine
Brille/Hose gesehen? — ich kann
~ nirgends finden** have you seen
my glasses/trousers? — I can't
find them anywhere

Sie *pron (Höflichkeitsform, Nom und
Akk)* you

Sieb *(-(e)s, -e)* nt sieve; *(Teesieb)*
strainer

sieben num seven;
siebenhundert num seven
hundred; **siebenmal** adv seven
times; **siebte(r, s)** adj seventh;
siehe auch **dritte**; **Siebtel** *(-s, -)* nt
seventh; **siebzehn** num
seventeen; **siebzehnte(r, s)** adj
seventeenth; siehe auch **dritte**;
siebzig num seventy; **in den ~er
Jahren** in the seventies;
siebzigste(r, s) adj
seventieth

Siedlung *(-, -en)* f *(Wohngebiet)*
housing estate (Brit) *(o
development (US))*

Sieg *(-(e)s, -e)* m victory; **siegen**
vi to win; **Sieger(in)** *(-s, -)* m(f)
winner; **Siegerehrung** f
presentation ceremony

siehe imper see

siezen vt to address as "Sie"

Signal *(-s, -e)* nt signal

Silbe *(-, -n)* f syllable

Silber *(-s)* nt silver;
Silberhochzeit f silver wedding;
Silbermedaille f silver medal

Silikon *(-s, -e)* nt silicone

Silvester *(-s, -)* nt,
Silvesterabend m New Year's
Eve, Hogmanay *(Scot)*

○ **SILVESTER**
○
○ **Silvester** is the German name
○ for New Year's Eve. Although
○ not an official holiday, most
○ businesses close early and
○ shops shut at midday. Most
○ Germans celebrate in the
○ evening and at midnight they
○ let off fireworks and rockets;
○ the revelry usually lasts until the
○ early hours of the morning.

Simbabwe *(-s)* nt Zimbabwe
SIM-Karte f SIM card
simpel adj simple
simultan adj simultaneous
simsen vi, vt *(fam)* to text
Sinfonie *(-, -n)* f symphony;
Sinfonieorchester nt symphony
orchestra
Singapur *(-s)* nt Singapore
singen *(sang, gesungen)* vt, vi to
sing; **richtig/falsch ~** to sing in
tune/out of tune
Single *(-, -s)* f *(CD)* single ▷ *(-s, -s)*
m *(Mensch)* single
Singular m singular
sinken *(sank, gesunken)* vi to sink;
(Preise etc) to fall, to go down
Sinn *(-(e)s, -e)* m *(Denken)* mind;
(Wahrnehmung) sense; *(Bedeutung)*
sense, meaning; **~ machen** to
make sense; **das hat keinen ~** it's
no use; **sinnlich** adj sensuous;
(erotisch) sensual; *(Wahrnehmung)*
sensory; **sinnlos** adj *(unsinnig)*
stupid; *(Verhalten)* senseless;
(zwecklos) pointless; *(bedeutungslos)*
meaningless; **sinnvoll** adj
meaningful; *(vernünftig)* sensible
Sirup *(-s, -e)* m syrup
Sitte *(-, -n)* f custom
Situation f situation
Sitz *(-es, -e)* m seat; **sitzen** *(saß,
gesessen)* vi to sit; *(Bemerkung,
Schlag)* to strike home; *(Gelerntes)*
to have sunk in; **der Rock sitzt**

gut the skirt is a good fit;
~ bleiben (Schule) to have to repeat
a year; **Sitzgelegenheit** f place to
sit down; **Sitzplatz** m seat;
Sitzung f meeting

Sizilien (-s) nt Sicily

Skandal (-s, -e) m scandal

Skandinavien (-s) nt
Scandinavia

Skateboard (-s, -s) nt
skateboard: **skateboarden** vi to
skateboard

Skelett (-s, -e) nt skeleton

skeptisch adj sceptical

Ski (-s, -er) m ski; **~ laufen** (o
fahren) to ski; **Skianzug** m ski
suit; **Skibrille** f ski goggles pl;
Skifahren (-s) nt skiing; **Skigebiet**
(-s, -e) nt skiing area; **Skihose** f
skiing trousers pl; **Skikurs** m
skiing course; **Skilanglauf** m
cross-country skiing; **Skiläufer(in)**
m(f) skier; **Skilehrer(in)** m(f) ski
instructor; **Skilift** m ski-lift

Skinhead (-s, -s) m skinhead

Skipiste f ski run; **Skischanze**
(-, -n) f ski jump; **Skischuh** m
ski boot; **Skischule** f ski school;
Skispringen (-s, -n) nt ski jumping;
Skistiefel (-s, -) m ski boot;
Skistock m ski pole; **Skiträger** m
ski rack; **Skiurlaub** m skiing
holiday (Brit) (o vacation (US))

Skizze (-, -n) f sketch

Skonto (-, -s) m o nt discount

Skorpion (-s, -e) m (Zool)
scorpion; (Astr) Scorpio

Skulptur (-, -en) f sculpture

S-Kurve f double bend

Slalom (-s, -s) m slalom

Slip (-s, -s) m (pair of) briefs pl;
Slipeinlage f panty liner

Slowakei (-) f Slovakia;
slowakisch adj Slovakian;
S~ Republik Slovak Republic;
Slowakisch nt Slovakian

Slowenien (-s) nt Slovenia;

slowenisch adj Slovenian;
Slowenisch nt Slovenian

Smartphone nt smartphone

Smog (-s) m smog; **Smogalarm**
m smog alert

Smoking (-s, -s) m dinner jacket
(Brit), tuxedo (US)

SMS nt abk = **Short Message
Service** ▷ f (Nachricht) text
message; **ich schicke dir eine ~** I'll
text you, I'll send you a text

Snowboard (-s, -s) nt snowboard; **snowboarden** vi to
snowboard; **Snowboardfahren**
(-s) nt snowboarding;
Snowboardfahrer(in) m(f)
snowboarder

○ SCHLÜSSELWORT

so adv 1 (so sehr) so; **so groß/schön**
etc so big/nice etc; **so groß/schön
wie ...** as big/nice as ...; **so viel
(wie)** as much as; **rede nicht so
viel** don't talk so much; **so weit
sein** to be ready; **so weit wie** o **als
möglich** as far as possible; **ich bin
so weit zufrieden** by and large I'm
quite satisfied; **so wenig (wie)** as
little (as); **das hat ihn so
geärgert, dass ...** that annoyed
him so much that ...; **so einer wie
ich** somebody like me; **na so was!**
well, well!

2 (auf diese Weise) like this; **mach
es nicht so** don't do it like that; **so
oder so** in one way or the other;
und so weiter and so on; **... oder
so was** ... or something like that;
das ist gut so that's fine

3 (fam) (umsonst) **ich habe es so
bekommen** I got it for nothing

▷ konj: **sodass** so that; **so wie es
jetzt ist** as things are at the
moment

▷ excl: **so?** really?; **so, das wär's**
so, that's it then

s. o. *abk* = **siehe oben** see above

sobald *conj* as soon as

Social Media *pl* social media

Socke (-, -n) *f* sock

Sodbrennen (-s) *nt* heartburn

Sofa (-s, -s) *nt* sofa

sofern *conj* if, provided (that)

soff *imperf von* **saufen**

sofort *adv* immediately, at once; **Sofortbildkamera** *f* instant camera

Softeis *nt* soft ice-cream

Software (-, -s) *f* software

sog *imperf von* **saugen**

sogar *adv* even; **kalt, ~ sehr kalt** cold, in fact very cold

sogenannt *adj* so-called

Sohle (-, -n) *f* sole

Sohn (-(e)s, Söhne) *m* son

Soja (-, Sojen) *f* soya; **Sojasprossen** *pl* bean sprouts *pl*

solang(e) *conj* as long as

Solarium *nt* solarium

Solarzelle *f* solar cell

solche(r, s) *pron* such; **eine ~ Frau, solch eine Frau** such a woman, a woman like that; **~ Sachen** things like that, such things; **ich habe ~ Kopfschmerzen** I've got such a headache; **ich habe ~n Hunger** I'm so hungry

Soldat(in) (-en, -en) *m(f)* soldier

solidarisch *adj* showing solidarity; **sich ~ erklären mit** to declare one's solidarity with

solid(e) *adj* solid; (*Leben, Mensch*) respectable

Soll (-(s), -(s)) *nt* (*Fin*) debit; (*Arbeitsmenge*) quota, target

SCHLÜSSELWORT

sollen (*pt* **sollte**, *pp* **gesollt** *o* (*als Hilfsverb*) **sollen**) *Hilfsverb* **1** (*Pflicht, Befehl*) to be supposed to; **du hättest nicht gehen sollen** you shouldn't have gone, you oughtn't

to have gone; **soll ich?** shall I?; **soll ich dir helfen?** shall I help you?; **sag ihm, er soll warten** tell him he's to wait; **was soll ich machen?** what should I do?

2 (*Vermutung*) **sie soll verheiratet sein** she's said to be married; **was soll das heißen?** what's that supposed to mean?; **man sollte glauben, dass ...** you would think that ...; **sollte das passieren, ...** if that should happen ...

▷ *vt, vi*: **was soll das?** what's all this?; **das sollst du nicht** you shouldn't do that; **was soll's?** what the hell

Solo (-s, -s) *nt* solo

Sommer (-s, -) *m* summer; **Sommerfahrplan** *m* summer timetable; **Sommerferien** *pl* summer holidays *pl* (*Brit*) (*o* vacation *sing* (*US*)); **sommerlich** *adj* summery; (*Sommer-*) summer; **Sommerreifen** *m* normal tyre; **Sommersprossen** *pl* freckles *pl*; **Sommerzeit** *f* summertime; (*Uhrzeit*) daylight saving time

Sonderangebot *nt* special offer; **sonderbar** *adj* strange, odd; **Sondermarke** *f* special stamp; **Sondermaschine** *f* special plane; **Sondermüll** *m* hazardous waste

sondern *conj* but; **nicht nur ..., ~ auch** not only ..., but also

Sonderpreis *m* special price; **Sonderschule** *f* special school; **Sonderzeichen** *nt* (*Inform*) special character; **Sonderzug** *m* special train

Song (-s, -s) *m* song

Sonnabend *m* Saturday; *siehe auch* **Mittwoch**; **sonnabends** *adv* on Saturdays; **~ morgens** on Saturday mornings; *siehe auch* **mittwochs**

Sonne (-, -n) f sun; **sonnen** vr:
sich ~ to sunbathe;
Sonnenaufgang m sunrise;
Sonnenblume f sunflower;
Sonnenblumenkern m sunflower seed; **Sonnenbrand** m
sunburn; **Sonnenbrille** f
sunglasses pl, shades pl;
Sonnencreme f sun cream;
Sonnendach nt (an Haus)
awning; (Auto) sunroof; **Sonnendeck** nt sun deck; **Sonnenmilch** f
suntan lotion; **Sonnenöl** nt
suntan oil; **Sonnenschein** m
sunshine; **Sonnenschirm** m
parasol, sunshade; **Sonnenschutzcreme** f sunscreen; **Sonnenstich**
m sunstroke; **Sonnenstudio** nt
solarium; **Sonnenuhr** f sundial;
Sonnenuntergang m sunset;
sonnig adj sunny
Sonntag m Sunday; siehe auch
Mittwoch; **sonntags** adv on
Sundays; siehe auch **mittwochs**
sonst adv, conj (außerdem) else;
(andernfalls) otherwise; (or) else;
(mit Pron, in Fragen) else;
(normalerweise) normally, usually;
~ noch etwas? anything else?;
~ nichts nothing else
sooft conj whenever
Sopran (-s, -e) m soprano
Sorge (-, -n) f worry; (Fürsorge)
care; **sich** (dat) **um jdn ~n machen**
to be worried about sb; **sorgen**
vi: **für jdn ~** to look after sb; **für**
etw ~ to take care of sth, to see to
sth ▷ vr: **sich ~** to worry (um
about); **sorgfältig** adj careful
sortieren vt to sort (out)
Sortiment nt assortment
sosehr conj however much
Soße (-, -n) f sauce; (zu Braten)
gravy
Soundkarte f (Inform) sound card
Souvenir (-s, -s) nt souvenir
soviel conj as far as

soweit conj as far as
sowie conj (wie auch) as well as;
(sobald) as soon as
sowohl conj: **~ ... als** (o wie) **auch**
both ... and
sozial adj social; **~er**
Wohnungsbau public-sector
housing (programme); **~es**
Netzwerk social networking site;
Sozialhilfe f income support
(Brit), welfare (aid) (US);
Sozialismus m socialism;
Sozialkunde f social studies pl;
Sozialversicherung f social
security; **Sozialwohnung** f
council flat (Brit), state-subsidized
apartment (US)
Soziologie f sociology
sozusagen adv so to speak
Spachtel (-s, -) m spatula
Spag(h)etti pl spaghetti sing
Spalte (-, -n) f crack; (Gletscher)
crevasse; (in Text) column
spalten vt to split
Spam (-s, -s) nt (Inform) spam
Spange (-, -n) f clasp; (Haar-
spange) slide (Brit), barrette (US)
Spanien (-s) nt Spain;
Spanier(in) (-s, -) m(f) Spaniard;
spanisch adj Spanish; **Spanisch**
nt Spanish
spann imperf von **spinnen**
spannen vt (straffen) to tighten;
(befestigen) to brace ▷ vi to be tight
spannend adj exciting, gripping;
Spannung f tension; (Elek)
voltage; (fig) suspense
Sparbuch nt savings book;
(Konto) savings account; **sparen**
vt, vi to save
Spargel (-s, -) m asparagus
Sparkasse f savings bank;
Sparkonto f savings account
spärlich adj meagre; (Bekleidung)
scanty
sparsam adj economical;
Sparschwein nt piggy bank

Spaß (-es, Späße) m joke; (Freude)
fun; **es macht mir ~** I enjoy it, it's
(great) fun; **viel ~!** I have fun

spät adj, adv late; **zu ~ kommen**
to be late

Spaten (-s, -) m spade

später adj, adv later; **spätestens**
adv at the latest; **Spätvorstellung**
f late-night performance

Spatz (-en, -en) m sparrow

spazieren vi to stroll, to walk;
~ gehen to go for a walk;
Spaziergang m walk

Specht (-(e)s, -e) m woodpecker

Speck (-(e)s, -e) m bacon fat;
(durchwachsen) bacon

Spedition f (für Umzug) removal
firm

Speiche (-, -n) f spoke

Speichel (-s) m saliva

Speicher (-s, -) m storehouse;
(Dachboden) attic; (Inform)
memory; **Speicherkarte** f
memory card; **speichern** vt
(Inform) to store; (sichern) to save

Speise (-, -n) f food; (Gericht)
dish; **Speisekarte** f menu;
Speiseröhre f gullet,
oesophagus; **Speisesaal** m
dining hall; **Speisewagen** m
dining car

Spende (-, -n) f donation;
spenden vt to donate, to give

spendieren vt: **jdm etw ~** to
treat sb to sth

Sperre (-, -n) f barrier; (Verbot)
ban; **sperren** vt to block; (Sport)
to suspend; (verbieten) to ban

Sperrgepäck nt bulky luggage;
Sperrstunde f closing time;
Sperrung f closing

Spesen pl expenses pl

spezialisieren vr: **sich ~** to
specialize (auf +akk in);
Spezialist(in) m(f) specialist;
Spezialität f speciality (Brit),
specialty (US); **speziell** adj

special ▷ adv especially

Spiegel (-s, -) m mirror;
Spiegelei nt fried egg (sunny-side
up (US)); **spiegelglatt** adj very
slippery; **Spiegelreflexkamera** f
reflex camera

Spiel (-(e)s, -e) nt game; (Tätigkeit)
play(ing); (Karten) pack, deck;
(Tech) (free) play; **Spielautomat** m
(ohne Geldgewinn) gaming
machine; (mit Geldgewinn) slot
machine; **spielen** vt, vi to play;
(um Geld) to gamble; (Theat) to
perform, to act; **Klavier ~** to play
the piano; **spielend** adv easily;
Spieler(in) (-s, -) m(f) player; (um
Geld) gambler; **Spielfeld** nt (für
Fußball, Hockey) field; (für
Basketball) court; **Spielfilm** m
feature film; **Spielkasino** nt
casino; **Spielkonsole** f games
console; **Spielplatz** m
playground; **Spielraum** m room to
manoeuvre; **Spielregel** f rule;
sich an die ~n halten to stick to
the rules; **Spielsachen** pl toys pl;
Spielzeug nt toys pl; (einzelnes)
toy

Spieß (-es, -e) m spear; (Bratspieß)
spit; **Spießer(in)** (-s, -) m(f)
square, stuffy type; **spießig** adj
square, uncool

Spikes pl (Sport) spikes pl; (Auto)
studs pl

Spinat (-(e)s, -e) m spinach

Spinne (-, -n) f spider; **spinnen**
(spann, gesponnen) vt, vi to spin;
(fam: Unsinn reden) to talk rubbish;
(verrückt sein) to be crazy; **du
spinnst!** you must be mad;
Spinnwebe (-, -n) f cobweb

Spion(in) (-s, -e) m(f) spy;
spionieren vi to spy; (fig) to
snoop around

Spirale (-, -n) f spiral; (Med) coil

Spirituosen pl spirits pl, liquor
sing (US)

Spiritus (-, -se) *m* spirit
spitz *adj* (Nase, Kinn) pointed; (Bleistift, Messer) sharp; (Winkel) acute; **Spitze** (-, -n) *f* point; (von Finger, Nase) tip; (Bemerkung) taunt, dig; (erster Platz) lead; (Gewebe) lace; **Spitzer** (-s, -) *m* pencil sharpener; **Spitzname** *m* nickname
Spliss (-) *m* split ends *pl*
sponsern *vt* to sponsor; **Sponsor(in)** (-s, -en) *m(f)* sponsor
spontan *adj* spontaneous
Sport (-(e)s, -e) *m* sport; **~ treiben** to do sport; **Sportanlage** *f* sports grounds *pl*; **Sportart** *f* sport; **Sportbekleidung** *f* sportswear; **Sportgeschäft** *nt* sports shop; **Sporthalle** *f* gymnasium, gym; **Sportlehrer(in)** (-s, -) *m(f)* sports instructor; (Schule) PE teacher; **Sportler(in)** (-s, -) *m(f)* sportsman/-woman; **sportlich** *adj* sporting; (Mensch) sporty; **Sportplatz** *m* playing field; **Sporttauchen** *nt* (skin-)diving; (mit Gerät) scuba-diving; **Sportverein** *m* sports club; **Sportwagen** *m* sports car
sprach *imperf von* **sprechen**
Sprache (-, -n) *f* language; (Sprechen) speech; **Sprachenschule** *f* language school; **Sprachführer** *m* phrasebook; **Sprachkenntnisse** *pl* knowledge *sing* of languages; **gute englische ~ haben** to have a good knowledge of English; **Sprachkurs** *m* language course; **Sprachunterricht** *m* language teaching
sprang *imperf von* **springen**
Spray (-s, -s) *m* ont spray
Sprechanlage *f* intercom; **sprechen** (sprach, gesprochen) *vt, vi*

to speak (jdn, mit jdm to sb); (sich unterhalten) to talk (mit to, über, von about); **~ Sie Deutsch?** do you speak German?; **kann ich bitte mit David ~?** (am Telefon) can I speak to David, please?; **Sprecher(in)** *m(f)* speaker; (Ansager) announcer; **Sprechstunde** *f* consultation; (Arzt) surgery hours *pl*; (Anwalt etc) office hours *pl*; **Sprechzimmer** *nt* consulting room
Sprengstoff *m* explosive
Sprichwort *nt* proverb
Springbrunnen *m* fountain
springen (sprang, gesprungen) *vi* to jump; (Glas) to crack; (mit Kopfsprung) to dart
Sprit (-(e)s, -e) *m* (fam: Benzin) petrol (Brit), gas (US)
Spritze (-, -n) *f* (Gegenstand) syringe; (Injektion) injection; (an Schlauch) nozzle; **spritzen** *vt* to spray; (Med) to inject ▷ *vi* to splash; (Med) to give injections
Spruch (-(e)s, Sprüche) *m* saying
Sprudel (-s, -) *m* sparkling mineral water; (süßer) fizzy drink (Brit), soda (US); **sprudeln** *vi* to bubble
Sprühdose *f* aerosol (can); **sprühen** *vt, vi* to spray; (fig) to sparkle; **Sprühregen** *m* drizzle
Sprung (-(e)s, Sprünge) *m* jump; (Riss) crack; **Sprungbrett** *nt* springboard; **Sprungschanze** *f* ski jump; **Sprungturm** *m* diving platforms *pl*
Spucke (-) *f* spit; **spucken** *vt, vi* to spit; (fam: sich erbrechen) to vomit; **Spucktüte** *f* sick bag
spuken *vi* (Geist) to walk; **hier spukt es** this place is haunted
Spülbecken *nt* sink
Spule (-, -n) *f* spool; (Elek) coil
Spüle (-, -n) *f* sink; **spülen** *vt, vi* to rinse; (Geschirr) to wash up;

(*Toilette*) to flush; **Spülmaschine** f dishwasher; **Spülmittel** nt washing-up liquid (Brit), dishwashing liquid (US); **Spültuch** nt dishcloth; **Spülung** f (von WC) flush

Spur (-, -en) f trace; (Fußspur, Radspur) track; (Fährte) trail; (Fahrspur) lane; **die ~ wechseln** to change lanes pl

spüren vt to feel; (merken) to notice; **Spürhund** m sniffer dog

Squash (-) nt squash; **Squashschläger** m squash racket

Sri Lanka (-s) nt Sri Lanka

Staat (-(e)s, -en) m state; **staatlich** adj state(-); (vom Staat betrieben) state-run; **Staatsangehörigkeit** f nationality; **Staatsanwalt** m, **-anwältin** f prosecuting counsel (Brit), district attorney (US); **Staatsbürger(in)** m(f) citizen; **Staatsbürgerschaft** f nationality; **doppelte ~** dual nationality; **Staatsexamen** nt final exam taken by trainee teachers, medical and law students

Stab (-(e)s, Stäbe) m rod; (Gitter) bar; **Stäbchen** nt (Essstäbchen) chopstick; **Stabhochsprung** m pole vault

stabil adj stable; (Möbel) sturdy

stach imperf von **stechen**

Stachel (-s, -n) m spike; (von Tier) spine; (von Insekten) sting; **Stachelbeere** f gooseberry; **Stacheldraht** m barbed wire; **stachelig** adj prickly

Stadion (-s, Stadien) nt stadium

Stadt (-, Städte) f town; (groß) city; **in der ~** in town; **Stadtautobahn** f urban motorway (Brit) (o expressway (US)); **Stadtbummel** (-s, -) m: **einen ~ machen** to go round town; **Stadtführer** m (Heft) city

guide; **Stadtführung** f city sightseeing tour; **Stadthalle** f municipal hall; **städtisch** adj municipal; **Stadtmauer** f city wall(s); **Stadtmitte** f town/city centre, downtown (US); **Stadtplan** m (street) map; **Stadtrand** m outskirts pl; **Stadtrundfahrt** f city tour; **Stadtteil** m, **Stadtviertel** nt district, part of town; **Stadtzentrum** nt town/city centre, downtown (US)

stahl imperf von **stehlen**

Stahl (-(e)s, Stähle) m steel

Stall (-(e)s, Ställe) m stable; (Kaninchen) hutch; (Schweine) pigsty; (Hühner) henhouse

Stamm (-(e)s, Stämme) m (Baum) trunk; (von Menschen) tribe; **stammen** vi: **~ aus** to come from; **Stammgast** m regular (guest); **Stammkunde** m, **Stammkundin** f regular (customer); **Stammtisch** m table reserved for regulars

stampfen vt, vi to stamp; (mit Werkzeug) to pound; (stapfen) to tramp

stand imperf von **stehen**

Stand (-(e)s, Stände) m (Wasser, Benzin) level; (Stehen) standing position; (Zustand) state; (Spielstand) score; (auf Messe etc) stand; (Klasse) class; **im ~e sein** to be in a position; (fähig) to be able

Stand-by-Betrieb m stand-by; **Stand-by-Ticket** nt stand-by ticket

Ständer (-s, -) m (Gestell) stand; (fam: Erektion) hard-on

Standesamt nt registry office

ständig adj permanent; (ununterbrochen) constant, continual

Standlicht nt sidelights pl (Brit), parking lights pl (US); **Standort** m position; **Standpunkt** m standpoint; **Standspur** f (Auto) hard shoulder (Brit), shoulder (US)

Stange (-, -n) f stick; (Stab) pole; (Metall) bar; (Zigaretten) carton; **Stangenbohne** f runner (Brit) (o string (US)) bean; **Stangenbrot** nt French stick; **Stangensellerie** m celery

stank imperf von **stinken**

Stapel (-s, -) m pile

Star (-(e)s, -e) m (Vogel) starling; (Med) cataract ▷ (-s, -s) m (in Film etc) star

starb imperf von **sterben**

stark adj strong; (heftig, groß) heavy; (Maßangabe) thick; **Stärke** (-, -n) f strength; (Dicke) thickness; (Wäschestärke, Speisestärke) starch; **stärken** vt to strengthen; (Wäsche) to starch; **Starkstrom** m high-voltage current; **Stärkung** f strengthening; (Essen) refreshment

starr adj stiff; (unnachgiebig) rigid; (Blick) staring

starren vi to stare

Start (-(e)s, -e) m start; (Aviat) takeoff; **Startautomatik** f automatic choke; **Startbahn** f runway; **starten** vt, vi to start; (Aviat) to take off; **Starthilfekabel** nt jump leads pl (Brit), jumper cables pl (US); **Startmenü** nt (Inform) start menu

Station f (Haltestelle) stop; (Bahnhof) station; (im Krankenhaus) ward; **stationär** adj stationary; **~e Behandlung** in-patient treatment; **jdn ~ behandeln** to treat sb as an in-patient

Statistik f statistics pl

Stativ nt tripod

statt conj, prep +gen o dat instead of; **~ zu arbeiten** instead of working

statt|finden irr vi to take place

Statue (-, -n) f statue

Statusleiste f. **Statuszeile** f (Inform) status bar

Stau (-(e)s, -e) m (im Verkehr) (traffic) jam; **im ~ stehen** to be stuck in a traffic jam

Staub (-(e)s) m dust; **~ wischen** to dust; **staubig** adj dusty; **staubsaugen** vt, vi to vacuum, to hoover (Brit); **Staubsauger** m vacuum cleaner, Hoover® (Brit); **Staubtuch** nt duster

Staudamm m dam

staunen vi to be astonished (über +akk at)

Stausee m reservoir; **Stauung** f (von Wasser) damming-up; (von Blut, Verkehr) congestion; **Stauwarnung** f traffic report

Std. abk = **Stunde** h

Steak (-s, -s) nt steak

stechen (stach, gestochen) vt, vi (mit Nadel etc) to prick; (mit Messer) to stab; (mit Finger) to poke; (Biene) to sting; (Mücke) to bite; (Sonne) to burn; (Kartenspiel) to trump; **Stechen** (-s, -) nt sharp pain, stabbing pain; **Stechmücke** f mosquito

Steckdose f socket; **stecken** vt to put; (Nadel) to stick; (beim Nähen) to pin ▷ vi (festsitzen) to be stuck; (Nadeln) to be (sticking); **der Schlüssel steckt** the key is in the door; **Stecker** (-s, -) m plug; **Steckrübe** f swede (Brit), rutabaga (US)

Steg (-s, -e) m bridge

stehen (stand, gestanden) vi to stand (zu by); (sich befinden) to be; (stillstehen) to have stopped; **was steht im Brief?** what does it say in the letter?; **jdm (gut) ~** to suit sb; **~ bleiben** (Uhr) to stop; **~ lassen** to leave ▷ vi impers: **wie steht's?** (Sport) what's the score?

stehlen (stahl, gestohlen) vt to steal

Stehplatz m (im Konzert etc) standing ticket

Steiermark (-) f Styria

steif adj stiff

steigen (stieg, gestiegen) vi (Preise, Temperatur) to rise; (klettern) to climb; **~ in/auf** (+akk) to get in/on

steigern vt to increase ▷ vr: **sich ~** to increase

Steigung f incline, gradient

steil adj steep; **Steilhang** m steep slope; **Steilküste** f steep coast

Stein (-(e)s, -e) m stone; **Steinbock** m (Zool) ibex; (Astr) Capricorn; **steinig** adj stony; **Steinschlag** m falling rocks pl

Stelle (-, -n) f place, spot; (Arbeit) post, job; (Amt) office; **ich an deiner ~** if I were you; **auf der ~** straightaway; **stellen** vt to put; (Uhr etc) to set (auf +akk to); (zur Verfügung stellen) to provide ▷ vr: **sich ~** (bei Polizei) to give oneself up; **sich schlafend ~** to pretend to be asleep; **Stellenangebot** nt job offer, vacancy; **stellenweise** adv in places; **Stellenwert** m (fig) status; **einen hohen ~ haben** to play an important role; **Stellplatz** m parking space; **Stellung** f position; **zu etw ~ nehmen** to comment on sth; **Stellvertreter(in)** m(f) representative; (amtlich) deputy; (von Arzt) locum (Brit), locum tenens (US)

Stempel (-s, -) m stamp; **stempeln** vt to stamp; (Briefmarke) to cancel

sterben (starb, gestorben) vi to die

Stereoanlage f stereo (system)

steril adj sterile; **sterilisieren** vt to sterilize

Stern (-(e)s, -e) m star; **ein Hotel mit vier ~en** a four-star hotel; **Sternbild** nt constellation; (Sternzeichen) star sign, sign of the zodiac; **Sternfrucht** f star fruit; **Sternschnuppe** (-, -n) f shooting star; **Sternwarte** (-e, -n) f observatory; **Sternzeichen** nt star sign, sign of the zodiac; **welches ~ bist du?** what's your star sign?

stets adv always

Steuer (-s, -) nt (Auto) steering wheel ▷ (-, -n) f tax; **Steuerberater(in)** m(f) tax adviser; **Steuerbord** nt starboard; **Steuererklärung** f tax declaration; **steuerfrei** adj tax-free; (Waren) duty-free; **Steuerknüppel** m control column; (Aviat, Inform) joystick; **steuern** vt, vi to steer; (Flugzeug) to pilot; (Entwicklung, Tonstärke) (Inform) to control; **steuerpflichtig** adj taxable; **Steuerung** f (Auto) steering; (Vorrichtung) controls pl; (Aviat) piloting; (fig) control; **Steuerungstaste** f (Inform) control key

Stich (-(e)s, -e) m (von Insekt) sting; (von Mücke) bite; (durch Messer) stab; (beim Nähen) stitch; (Färbung) tinge; (Kartenspiel) trick; (Kunst) engraving

sticken vt, vi to embroider

Sticker (-s, -) m sticker

Stickerei f embroidery

stickig adj stuffy, close

Stiefbruder m stepbrother

Stiefel (-s, -) m boot

Stiefmutter f stepmother

Stiefmütterchen nt pansy

Stiefschwester f stepsister; **Stiefsohn** m stepson; **Stieftochter** f stepdaughter; **Stiefvater** m stepfather

stieg imperf von **steigen**

Stiege (-, -n) f steps pl
Stiel (-(e)s, -e) m handle; (Bot) stalk; **ein Eis am ~** an ice lolly (Brit), a Popsicle® (US)
Stier (-(e)s, -e) m (Zool) bull; (Astr) Taurus; **Stierkampf** m bullfight
stieß imperf von **stoßen**
Stift (-(e)s, -e) m (aus Holz) peg; (Nagel) tack; (zum Schreiben) pen; (Farbstift) crayon; (Bleistift) pencil
Stil (-s, -e) m style
still adj quiet; (unbewegt) still
stillen vt (Säugling) to breast-feed
still|halten irr vi to keep still; **still|stehen** irr vi to stand still
Stimme (-, -n) f voice; (bei Wahl) vote
stimmen vi to be right; **stimmt!** that's right; **hier stimmt was nicht** there's something wrong here; **stimmt so!** keep the change
Stimmung f mood; (Atmosphäre) atmosphere
Stinkefinger m (fam) **jdm den ~ zeigen** to give sb the finger (o bird (US))
stinken (stank, gestunken) vi to stink (nach of)
Stipendium nt scholarship; (als Unterstützung) grant
Stirn (-, -en) f forehead; **Stirnhöhle** f sinus
Stock (-(e)s, Stöcke) m stick; (Bot) stock ▷ m (Stockwerke) floor, storey; **Stockbett** nt bunk bed; **Stöckelschuhe** pl high-heels; **Stockwerk** nt floor; **im ersten ~** on the first floor (Brit), on the second floor (US)
Stoff (-(e)s, -e) m (Gewebe) material; (Materie) matter; (von Buch etc) subject (matter); (fam: Rauschgift) stuff
stöhnen vi to groan (vor with)
stolpern vi to stumble, to trip
stolz adj proud

stopp interj hold it; (Moment mal!) hang on a minute; **stoppen** vt, vi to stop; (mit Uhr) to time; **Stoppschild** nt stop sign; **Stoppuhr** f stopwatch
Stöpsel (-s, -) m plug; (für Flaschen) stopper
Storch (-(e)s, Störche) m stork
stören vt to disturb; (behindern) to interfere with; **darf ich dich kurz ~?** can I trouble you for a minute?; **stört es dich, wenn ...?** do you mind if ...?
stornieren vt to cancel; **Stornogebühr** f cancellation fee
Störung f disturbance; (in der Leitung) fault
Stoß (-es, Stöße) m (Schub) push; (Schlag) blow; (mit Fuß) kick; (Haufen) pile; (zerkleinern) to pulverize ▷ vr: **sich ~** to bang oneself; **sich ~ an** (+dat) (fig) to take exception to
stoßen (stieß, gestoßen) vt (mit Druck) to shove, to push; (mit Schlag) to knock; (mit Fuß) to kick; (anstoßen) to bump; (zerkleinern) to pulverize ▷ vr: **sich ~** to bang oneself; **sich ~ an** (+dat) (fig) to take exception to
Stoßstange f (Auto) bumper
stottern vt, vi to stutter
Str. abk von **Straße** St, Rd
Strafe (-, -n) f punishment; (Sport) penalty; (Gefängnisstrafe) sentence; (Geldstrafe) fine; **strafen** vt to punish; **Straftat** f (criminal) offence; **Strafzettel** m ticket
Strahl (-s, -en) m ray, beam; (Wasser) jet; **strahlen** vi to radiate; (fig) to beam
Strähne (-, -n) f strand; (weiß, gefärbt) streak
Strand (-(e)s, Strände) m beach; **am ~** on the beach; **Strandcafé** nt beach café; **Strandkorb** m wicker beach chair with a hood; **Strandpromenade** f promenade

strapazieren vt (Material) to be hard on; (Mensch, Kräfte) to be a strain on

Straße (-, -n) f road; (in der Stadt) street; **Straßenarbeiten** pl roadworks pl (Brit), road repairs pl (US); **Straßenbahn** f tram (Brit), streetcar (US); **Straßencafé** nt pavement café (Brit), sidewalk café (US); **Straßenfest** nt street party; **Straßenglätte** f slippery roads pl; **Straßenkarte** f road map; **Straßenrand** m: **am ~** at the roadside; **Straßenschild** nt street sign; **Straßensperre** f roadblock; **Straßenverhältnisse** pl road conditions pl

Strategie (-, -n) f strategy

Strauch (-(e)s, Sträucher) m bush, shrub; **Strauchtomate** f vine-ripened tomato

Strauß (-es, Sträuße) m bunch; (als Geschenk) bouquet ▷ m (Strauße) (Vogel) ostrich

Strecke (-, -n) f route; (Entfernung) distance; (Eisenb) line

strecken vt to stretch ▷ vr: **sich ~** to stretch

streckenweise adv (teilweise) in parts; (zeitweise) at times

Streich (-(e)s, -e) m trick, prank

streicheln vt to stroke

streichen (strich, gestrichen) vt (anmalen) to paint; (berühren) to stroke; (auftragen) to spread; (durchstreichen) to delete; (nicht genehmigen) to cancel

Streichholz nt match; **Streichholzschachtel** f matchbox; **Streichkäse** m cheese spread

Streifen (-s, -) m (Linie) stripe; (Stück) strip; (Film) film

Streifenwagen m patrol car

Streik (-(e)s, -s) m strike; **streiken** vi to be on strike

Streit (-(e)s, -e) m argument (um, wegen about, over); **streiten** (stritt, gestritten) vi to argue (um, wegen about, over) ▷ vr: **sich ~** to argue (um, wegen about, over)

streng adj (Blick) severe; (Lehrer) strict; (Geruch) sharp

Stress (-es) m stress; **stressen** vt to stress (out); **stressig** adj (fam) stressful

Stretching (-s) nt (Sport) stretching exercises pl

streuen vt to scatter; **die Straßen ~** to grit the roads; (mit Salz) to put salt down on the roads; **Streufahrzeug** nt gritter lorry (Brit), salt truck (US)

strich imperf von **streichen**

Strich (-(e)s, -e) m (Linie) line; **Stricher** m (fam: Strichjunge) rent boy (Brit), boy prostitute; **Strichkode** (-s, -s) m bar code; **Stricherin** f (fam: Strichmädchen) hooker; **Strichpunkt** m semicolon

Strick (-(e)s, -e) m rope

stricken vt, vi to knit; **Strickjacke** f cardigan; **Stricknadel** f knitting needle

String (-s, -s) m, **Stringtanga** m G-string

Stripper(in) m(f) stripper; **Striptease** (-) m striptease

stritt imperf von **streiten**

Stroh (-(e)s) nt straw; **Strohdach** nt thatched roof; **Strohhalm** m (drinking) straw

Strom (-(e)s, Ströme) m river; (fig) stream; (Elek) current; **Stromanschluss** m connection; **Stromausfall** m power failure

strömen vi to stream, to pour; **Strömung** f current

Stromverbrauch m power consumption; **Stromzähler** m electricity meter

Strophe (-, -n) f verse

Strudel (-s, -) m (in Fluss) whirlpool; (Gebäck) strudel

Struktur f structure; (von Material) texture

Strumpf (-(e)s, Strümpfe) m (Damenstrumpf) stocking; (Socke) sock; **Strumpfhose** f (pair of) tights pl (Brit), pantyhose (US)

Stück (-(e)s, -e) nt piece; (von Zucker) lump; (etwas) bit; (Zucker) lump; (Theat) play; **ein ~ Käse** a piece of cheese

Student(in) m(f) student; **Studentenausweis** m student card; **Studentenwohnheim** nt hall of residence (Brit), dormitory (US); **Studienabschluss** m qualification (at the end of a course of higher education); **Studienfahrt** f study trip; **Studienplatz** m university/college place; **studieren** vt, vi to study; **Studium** nt studies pl; **während seines ~s** while he is/was studying

Stufe (-, -n) f step; (Entwicklungsstufe) stage

Stuhl (-(e)s, Stühle) m chair

stumm adj silent

stumpf adj blunt; (teilnahmslos, glanzlos) dull; **stumpfsinnig** adj dull

Stunde (-, -n) f hour; (Unterricht) lesson; **eine halbe ~** half an hour; **Stundenkilometer** m: **80 ~** 80 kilometres an hour; **stundenlang** adv for hours; **Stundenlohn** m hourly wage; **Stundenplan** m timetable; **stündlich** adj hourly

Stuntman (-s, Stuntmen) m stuntman; **Stuntwoman** (-, Stuntwomen) f stuntwoman

stur adj stubborn; (stärker) pigheaded

Sturm (-(e)s, Stürme) m storm; **stürmen** vi (Wind) to blow hard; (rennen) to storm; **Stürmer(in)** m(f) striker, forward; **Sturmflut** f storm tide; **stürmisch** adj stormy; (fig) tempestuous; (Zeit) turbulent; (Liebhaber) passionate; (Beifall, Begrüßung) tumultuous; **Sturmwarnung** f gale warning

Sturz (-es, Stürze) m fall; (Pol) overthrow; **stürzen** vt (werfen) to hurl; (Pol) to overthrow; (umkehren) to overturn ▷ vi to fall; (rennen) to dash; **Sturzhelm** m crash helmet

Stute (-, -n) f mare

Stütze (-, -n) f support; (Hilfe) help; (fam: Arbeitslosenunterstützung) dole (Brit), welfare (US)

stützen vt to support; (Ellbogen) to prop

stutzig adj perplexed, puzzled; (misstrauisch) suspicious

Styropor® (-s) nt polystyrene (Brit), styrofoam (US)

subjektiv adj subjective

Substanz (-, -en) f substance

subtrahieren vt to subtract

Subvention f subsidy; **subventionieren** vt to subsidize

Suche f search (nach for); **auf der ~ nach etw sein** to be looking for sth; **suchen** vt to look for; (Inform) to search ▷ vi to look, to search (nach for); **Suchmaschine** f (Inform) search engine

Sucht (-, Süchte) f mania; (Med) addiction; **süchtig** adj addicted; **Süchtige(r)** mf addict

Süd south; **Südafrika** nt South Africa; **Südamerika** nt South America; **Süddeutschland** nt Southern Germany; **Süden** (-s) m south; **im ~ Deutschlands** in the south of Germany; **Südeuropa** nt Southern Europe; **Südkorea** (-s) nt South Korea; **südlich** adj southern; (Kurs, Richtung) southerly; **Verkehr in ~er**

Richtung southbound traffic; **Südost(en)** m southeast; **Südpol** m South Pole; **Südstaaten** pl (der USA) the Southern States pl, the South sing; **südwärts** adv south, southwards; **Südwest(en)** m southwest; **Südwind** m south wind

Sülze (-, -n) f jellied meat

Summe (-, -n) f sum; (Gesamtsumme) total

summen v (-e)s, Sümpfe) m hum; (Insekt) to buzz

Sumpf (-(e)s, Sümpfe) m marsh; (subtropischer) swamp; **sumpfig** adj marshy

Sünde (-, -n) f sin

super adj (fam) super, great; **Super** (-s) nt (Benzin) four star (petrol) (Brit), premium (US); **Supermarkt** m supermarket

Suppe (-, -n) f soup; **Suppengrün** nt bunch of herbs and vegetables for flavouring soup; **Suppenlöffel** m soup spoon; **Suppenschüssel** f soup tureen; **Suppentasse** f soup cup; **Suppenteller** m soup plate; **Suppenwürfel** m stock cube

Surfbrett nt surfboard; **surfen** vi to surf; **im Internet ~** to surf the Internet; **Surfer(in)** (-s, -) m(f) surfer

Surrealismus m surrealism

Sushi (-s, -s) nt sushi

süß adj sweet; **süßen** vt to sweeten; **Süßigkeit** f (Bonbon etc) sweet (Brit), candy (US); **Süßkartoffel** f sweet potato (Brit), yam (US); **süßsauer** adj sweet-and-sour; **Süßspeise** f dessert; **Süßstoff** m sweetener; **Süßwasser** nt fresh water

Sweatshirt (-s, -s) nt sweatshirt

Swimmingpool (-s, -s) m (swimming) pool

Sylvester nt siehe **Silvester**

Symbol (-s, -e) nt symbol; **Symbolleiste** f (Inform) toolbar

Symmetrie (-, -n) f symmetry; **symmetrisch** adj symmetrical

sympathisch adj nice; **jdn ~ finden** to like sb

Symphonie (-, -n) f symphony

Symptom (-s, -e) nt symptom (für of)

Synagoge (-, -n) f synagogue

synchronisiert adj (Film) dubbed; **Synchronstimme** f dubbing voice

Synthetik (-, -en) f synthetic (fibre); **synthetisch** adj synthetic

Syrien (-s) nt Syria

System (-s, -e) nt system; **systematisch** adj systematic; **Systemsteuerung** f (Inform) control panel

Szene (-, -n) f scene

t

Tabak (-s, -e) *m* tobacco;
Tabakladen *m* tobacconist's
Tabelle *f* table
Tablet (-s, -s) *nt* (Inform) tablet
Tablett (-(e)s, -s) *nt* tray
Tablette *f* tablet, pill
Tabulator *m* tabulator, tab
Tacho(meter) (-s, -) *m* (Auto) speedometer
Tafel (-, -n) *f* (a. Math) table; (Anschlagtafel) board; (Wandtafel) blackboard; (Schiefer~) slate; (Gedenktafel) plaque; **eine ~ Schokolade** a bar of chocolate; **Tafelwasser** *nt* table water
Tag (-(e)s, -e) *m* day; (Tageslicht) daylight; **guten ~!** good morning/afternoon; **am ~** during the day; **sie hat ihre ~e** she's got her period; **eines ~es** one day; **~ der Arbeit** Labour Day; **Tagebuch** *nt* diary; **tagelang** *adj* for days (on end);

Tagesanbruch *m* daybreak;
Tagesausflug *m* day trip;
Tagescreme *f* day cream;
Tagesdecke *f* bedspread;
Tagesgericht *nt* dish of the day;
Tageskarte *f* (Fahrkarte) day ticket; **die ~** (Speisekarte) today's menu; **Tageslicht** *nt* daylight;
Tagesmutter *f* child minder;
Tagesordnung *f* agenda;
Tagestour *f* day trip;
Tageszeitung *f* daily newspaper;
täglich *adj*, *adv* daily; **tags(über)** *adv* during the day; **Tagung** *f* conference
Tai Chi (-) *nt* tai chi
Taille (-, -n) *f* waist
Taiwan (-s) *nt* Taiwan
Takt (-(e)s, -e) *m* (Taktgefühl) tact; (Mus) time
Taktik (-, -en) *f* tactics *pl*
taktlos *adj* tactless; **taktvoll** *adj* tactful
Tal (-(e)s, Täler) *nt* valley
Talent (-(e)s, -e) *nt* talent; **talentiert** *adj* talented
Talkmaster(in) (-s, -) *m(f)* talk-show host; **Talkshow** (-, -s) *f* talkshow
Tampon (-s, -s) *m* tampon
Tandem (-s, -s) *nt* tandem
Tang (-s, -e) *m* seaweed
Tanga (-s, -s) *m* thong
Tank (-s, -s) *m* tank;
Tankanzeige *f* fuel gauge;
Tankdeckel *m* fuel cap; **tanken** *vi* to get some petrol (Brit) (o gas (US)); (Aviat) to refuel; **Tanker** (-s, -) *m* (oil) tanker; **Tankstelle** *f* petrol station (Brit), gas station (US); **Tankwart(in)** (-s, -e) *m(f)* petrol pump attendant (Brit), gas station attendant (US)
Tanne (-, -n) *f* fir; **Tannenzapfen** *m* fir cone
Tansania (-s) *nt* Tanzania
Tante (-, -n) *f* aunt;
Tante-Emma-Laden *m* corner

shop (Brit), grocery store (US)

Tanz (-es, *Tänze*) m dance; **tanzen**
vt, vi to dance; **Tänzer(in)** m(f)
dancer; **Tanzfläche** f dance floor;
Tanzkurs m dancing course;
Tanzlehrer(in) m(f) dancing
instructor; **Tanzstunde** f
dancing lesson

Tapete (-, -n) f wallpaper;
tapezieren vt, vi to wallpaper

Tarantel (-, -n) f tarantula

Tarif (-s, -e) m tariff, (scale of)
fares/charges pl

Tasche (-, -n) f bag; (*Hosentasche*)
pocket; (*Handtasche*) bag (Brit),
purse (US)

Taschen- in zW pocket;
Taschenbuch nt paperback;
Taschendieb(in) m(f) pick-
pocket; **Taschengeld** nt pocket
money; **Taschenlampe** f torch
(Brit), flashlight (US);
Taschenmesser nt penknife;
Taschenrechner m pocket
calculator; **Taschentuch** nt
handkerchief

Tasse (-, -n) f cup; **eine ~ Kaffee**
a cup of coffee

Tastatur f keyboard; **Taste**
(-, -n) f button; (*von Klavier,
Computer*) key; **Tastenfeld** nt
keypad; **Tastenkombination** f
(*Inform*) shortcut

tat imperf von **tun**

Tat (-, -en) f action

Tatar (-s, -s) m raw minced beef

Täter(in) (-s, -) m(f) culprit

tätig adj active; **in einer Firma
~ sein** to work for a firm;
Tätigkeit f activity; (*Beruf*)
occupation

tätowieren vt to tattoo;
Tätowierung f tattoo (*an +dat* on)

Tatsache f fact; **tatsächlich** adj
actual ▷ adv really

Tau (-(e)s, -e) nt (*Seil*) rope ▷ (-(e)s)
m dew

taub adj deaf; (*Füße etc*) numb (vor
Kälte with cold)

Taube (-, -n) f pigeon; (*Turtel~,*
fig: *Friedenssymbol*) dove

taubstumm adj with a hearing
and speech impairment

tauchen vt to dip ▷ vi to dive;
(*Naut*) to submerge; **Tauchen** (-s)
nt diving; **Taucher(in)** (-s, -) m(f)
diver; **Taucheranzug** m diving
(o wet) suit; **Taucherbrille** f
diving goggles pl; **Tauchermaske**
f diving mask; **Tauchkurs** m
diving course; **Tauchsieder** (-s, -)
m portable immersion coil for heating
water

tauen vi impers to thaw

Taufe (-, -n) f baptism; **taufen**
vt to baptize; (*nennen*) to christen

taugen vi to be suitable (*für* for);
nichts ~ to be no good

Tausch (-(e)s, -e) m exchange;
tauschen vt to exchange, to
swap

täuschen vt to deceive ▷ vi to
be deceptive ▷ vr: **sich ~** to be
wrong; **täuschend** adj
deceptive; **Täuschung** f
deception; (*optisch*) illusion

tausend num a thousand;
vier~ four thousand; **~ Dank!**
thanks a lot; **tausendmal** adv a
thousand times; **tausendste(r, s)**
adj thousandth; **Tausendstel**
(-s, -) nt (*Bruchteil*) thousandth

Taxi nt taxi; **Taxifahrer(in)** m(f)
taxi driver; **Taxistand** m taxi
rank (Brit), taxi stand (US)

Team (-s, -s) nt team;
Teamarbeit f team work;
teamfähig adj able to work in a
team

Technik f technology;
(*angewandte*) engineering;
(*Methode*) technique;
Techniker(in) (-s, -) m(f) engineer; (*Sport, Mus*) technician;

technisch adj technical

Techno (-s) m (Mus) techno

Teddybär m teddy bear

TEE abk = **Trans-Europ-Express** Trans-Europe-Express

Tee (-s, -s) m tea; **Teebeutel** m teabag; **Teekanne** f teapot; **Teelöffel** m teaspoon

Teer (-(e)s, -e) m tar

Teesieb nt tea strainer; **Teetasse** f teacup

Teich (-(e)s, -e) m pond

Teig (-(e)s, -e) m dough; **Teigwaren** pl pasta sing

Teil (-(e)s, -e) m part; (Anteil) share; **zum ~** partly ▷ (-(e)s, -e) part; (Bestandteil) component; **teilen** vt to divide; **teil|nehmen** irr vi to take part (an +dat in); **Teilnehmer(in)** (-s, -) m(f) participant

Teilkaskoversicherung f third party, fire and theft insurance

teilmöbliert adj partly furnished

Teilnahme (-, -n) f participation (an +dat in); **teil|nehmen** irr vi to take part (an +dat in); **Teilnehmer(in)** (-s, -) m(f) participant

teils adv partly; **teilweise** adv partially, in part; **Teilzeit** f: **~ arbeiten** to work part-time

Teint (-s, -s) m complexion

Tel. abk von **Telefon** tel.

Telefon (-s, -e) nt telephone; **Telefonanruf** m, **Telefonat** nt (tele)phone call; **Telefonanschluss** m telephone connection; **Telefonauskunft** f directory enquiries pl (Brit), directory assistance (US); **Telefonbuch** nt telephone directory; **Telefongebühren** pl telephone charges pl; **Telefongespräch** nt telephone conversation; **telefonieren** vi: **ich telefoniere gerade (mit ...)** I'm on the phone (to ...);

telefonisch adj telephone; (Benachrichtigung) by telephone; **Telefonkarte** f phonecard; **Telefonnummer** f (tele)phone number; **Telefonrechnung** f phone bill; **Telefonverbindung** f telephone connection; **Telefonzelle** f phone box (Brit), phone booth; **Telefonzentrale** f switchboard; **über die ~** through the switchboard

Telegramm nt telegram; **Teleobjektiv** nt telephoto lens; **Teleshopping** (-s) nt teleshopping; **Teleskop** (-s, -e) nt telescope

Teller (-s, -) m plate

Tempel (-s, -) m temple

Temperament nt temperament; (Schwung) liveliness; **temperamentvoll** adj lively

Temperatur f temperature; **bei ~en von 30 Grad** at temperatures of 30 degrees; **~ haben** to have a temperature; **~ bei jdm messen** to take sb's temperature

Tempo (-s, -s) nt (Geschwindigkeit) speed; **Tempolimit** (-s, -s) nt speed limit

Tempotaschentuch® nt (Papiertaschentuch) (paper) tissue

Tendenz f tendency; (Absicht) intention

Tennis nt tennis; **Tennisball** m tennis ball; **Tennisplatz** m tennis court; **Tennisschläger** m tennis racket; **Tennisspieler(in)** m(f) tennis player

Tenor (-s, Tenöre) m tenor

Teppich (-s, -e) m carpet; **Teppichboden** m (fitted) carpet

Termin (-s, -e) m (Zeitpunkt) date; (Frist) deadline; (Arzttermin etc) appointment

Terminal (-s, -s) nt (Inform, Aviat) terminal

Terminkalender m diary;

Terminplaner m (in Buchform) personal organizer, Filofax®; (Taschencomputer) personal digital assistant, PDA

Terpentin (-s, -e) nt turpentine, turps sing

Terrasse (-, -n) f terrace; (hinter einem Haus) patio

Terror (-s) m terror; **Terroranschlag** m terrorist attack; **terrorisieren** vt to terrorize; **Terrorismus** m terrorism; **Terrorist(in)** m(f) terrorist

Tesafilm® m ≈ sellotape® (Brit), ≈ Scotch tape® (US)

Test (-s, -e) m test

Testament nt will; **das Alte/Neue ~** the Old/New Testament

testen vt to test; **Testergebnis** nt test results pl

Tetanus (-) m tetanus; **Tetanusimpfung** f (anti-)tetanus injection

teuer adj expensive, dear (Brit)

Teufel (-s, -) m devil; **was/wo zum ~** what/where the devil; **Teufelskreis** m vicious circle

Text (-(e)s, -e) m text; (Liedertext) words pl, lyrics pl; **Textmarker** (-s, -) m highlighter; **Textverarbeitung** f word processing; **Textverarbeitungsprogramm** nt word processing program

Thailand nt Thailand

Theater (-s, -) nt theatre; (fam) fuss; **ins ~ gehen** to go to the theatre; **Theaterkasse** f box office; **Theaterstück** nt (stage) play; **Theatervorstellung** f (stage) performance

Theke (-, -n) f (Schanktisch) bar; (Ladentisch) counter

Thema (-s, Themen) nt subject, topic; **kein ~!** no problem

Themse (-) f Thames

Theologie f theology

theoretisch adj theoretical; **~ stimmt das** that's right in theory; **Theorie** f theory

Therapeut(in) m(f) therapist; **Therapie** f therapy; **eine ~ machen** to undergo therapy

Thermalbad nt thermal bath; (Ort) thermal spa; **Thermometer** (-s, -) nt thermometer

Thermosflasche® f. **Thermoskanne®** f Thermos® (flask); **Thermostat** (-(e)s, -e) m thermostat

These (-, -n) f theory

Thron (-(e)s, -e) m throne

Thunfisch m tuna

Thüringen (-s) nt Thuringia

Thymian (-s, -e) m thyme

Tick (-(e)s, -e) m tic; (Eigenart) quirk; (Fimmel) craze; **ticken** vi to tick; **er tickt nicht ganz richtig** he's off his rocker

Ticket (-s, -s) nt (plane) ticket

tief adj deep; (Ausschnitt, Ton, Sonne) low; **2 Meter ~** 2 metres deep; **Tief** (-s, -s) nt (Meteo) low; (seelisch) depression; **Tiefdruck** m (Meteo) low pressure; **Tiefe** (-, -n) f depth; **Tiefgarage** f underground car park (Brit) (o garage (US)); **tiefgekühlt** adj frozen; **Tiefkühlfach** nt freezer compartment; **Tiefkühlkost** f frozen food; **Tiefkühltruhe** f freezer; **Tiefpunkt** m low

Tier (-(e)s, -e) nt animal; **Tierarzt** m, **Tierärztin** f vet; **Tiergarten** m zoo; **Tierhandlung** f pet shop; **Tierheim** nt animal shelter; **tierisch** adj animal ▷ adv (fam) really; **~ ernst** deadly serious; **ich hatte ~ Angst** I was dead scared; **Tierkreiszeichen** nt sign of the zodiac; **Tierpark** m zoo; **Tierquälerei** f cruelty to animals;

Tierschützer(in) (-s, -) m(f) animal rights campaigner; **Tierversuch** m animal experiment

Tiger (-s, -) m tiger

timen vt to time; **Timing** (-s) nt timing

Tinte (-, -n) f ink; **Tintenfisch** m cuttlefish; (klein) squid; (achtarmig) octopus; **Tintenfischringe** pl calamari pl; **Tintenstrahldrucker** m ink-jet printer

Tipp (-s, -s) m tip; **tippen** vt, vi to tap; (fam: schreiben) to type; (fam: raten) to guess

Tirol (-s) nt Tyrol

Tisch (-(e)s, -e) m table; **Tischdecke** f tablecloth; (Arbeit) joinery; **Tischtennis** nt table tennis; **Tischtennisschläger** m table-tennis bat

Titel (-s, -) m title; **Titelbild** nt cover picture

Toast (-(e)s, -s) m toast; **toasten** vt to toast; **Toaster** (-s, -) m toaster

Tochter (-, Töchter) f daughter

Tod (-(e)s, -e) m death; **Todesopfer** nt casualty; **Todesstrafe** f death penalty; **todkrank** adj terminally ill; (sehr krank) seriously ill; **tödlich** adj deadly, fatal; **er ist ~ verunglückt** he was killed in an accident; **todmüde** adj (fam) dead tired; **todsicher** adj (fam) dead certain

Tofu (-(s)) m tofu, bean curd

Toilette (-, -n) f toilet, restroom (US); **Toilettenpapier** nt toilet paper

toi, toi, toi interj good luck

tolerant adj tolerant (gegen of)

toll adj mad; (Treiben) wild; (fam: großartig) great; **Tollkirsche** f deadly nightshade; **Tollwut** f rabies sing

Tomate (-, -n) f tomato; **Tomatenmark** nt tomato purée (Brit) (o paste (US)); **Tomatensaft** m tomato juice

Tombola (-, -s) f raffle, tombola (Brit)

Ton (-(e)s, -e) m (Erde) clay ▷ m (Töne; Laut) sound; (Mus) note; (Redeweise) tone; (Farbton, Nuance) shade; **Tonband** nt tape; **Tonbandgerät** nt tape recorder

tönen vi to sound ▷ vt to shade; (Haare) to tint

Toner (-s, -) m toner; **Tonerkassette** f toner cartridge

Tonne (-, -n) f (Fass) barrel; (Gewicht) tonne, metric ton

Tontechniker(in) m(f) sound engineer

Tönung f hue; (für Haar) rinse

Top (-s, -s) nt top

Topf (-(e)s, Töpfe) m pot

Töpfer(in) (-s, -) m(f) potter; **Töpferei** f pottery; (Gegenstand) piece of pottery

Tor (-(e)s, -e) nt gate; (Sport) goal; **ein ~ schießen** to score a goal; **Torhüter(in)** m(f) goalkeeper

torkeln vi to stagger

Tornado (-s, -s) m tornado

Torschütze m, **Torschützin** f (goal)scorer

Torte (-, -n) f cake; (Obsttorte) flan; (Sahnetorte) gateau

Torwart(in) (-s, -e) m(f) goalkeeper

tot adj dead; **~er Winkel** blind spot

total adj total, complete; **Totalschaden** m complete write-off

Tote(r) mf dead man/woman; (Leiche) corpse; **töten** vt, vi to kill; **Totenkopf** m skull

tot|lachen vr: **sich ~** to kill oneself laughing

Toto (-s, -s) m o nt pools pl

tot|schlagen irr vt to beat to death; **die Zeit ~** to kill time

Touchscreen (-s, -s) m touch screen

Tour (-, -en) f trip; (Rundfahrt) tour; **eine ~ nach York machen** to go on a trip to York; **Tourenski** m touring ski

Tourismus m tourism; **Tourist(in)** m(f) tourist; **Touristenklasse** f tourist class; **touristisch** adj tourist; (pej) touristy

traben vi to trot

Tournee (-, -n) f tour

Tracht (-, -en) f (Kleidung) traditional costume

Trackball (-s, -s) m (Inform) trackball

Tradition f tradition; **traditionell** adj traditional

traf imperf von **treffen**

Trafik (-, -en) f tobacconist's

Tragbahre (-, -n) f stretcher

tragbar adj portable

träge adj sluggish, slow

tragen (trug, getragen) vt to carry; (Kleidung, Brille, Haare) to wear; (Namen, Früchte) to bear; **Träger** (-s, -) m (an Kleidung) strap; (Hosen~) braces pl (Brit), suspenders pl (US); (in der Architektur) beam; (Stahl~, Eisen~) girder

Tragfläche f wing; **Tragflügelboot** nt hydrofoil

tragisch adj tragic; **Tragödie** f tragedy

Trainer(in) (-s, -) m(f) trainer, coach; **trainieren** vt, vi to train; (jdn a.) to coach; (Übung) to practise; **Training** (-s, -s) nt training; **Trainingsanzug** m tracksuit

Traktor m tractor

Trambahn f tram (Brit), streetcar (US)

trampen vi to hitchhike; **Tramper(in)** m(f) hitchhiker

Träne (-, -n) f tear; **tränen** vi to water; **Tränengas** nt teargas

trank imperf von **trinken**

Transfusion f transfusion

Transitverkehr m transit traffic; **Transitvisum** nt transit visa

Transplantation f transplant; (Hauttransplantation) graft

Transport (-(e)s, -e) m transport; **transportieren** vt to transport; **Transportmittel** nt means sing of transport; **Transportunternehmen** nt haulage firm

Transvestit (-en, -en) m transvestite

trat imperf von **treten**

Traube (-, -n) f (einzelne Beere) grape; (ganze Frucht) bunch of grapes; **Traubensaft** m grape juice; **Traubenzucker** m glucose

trauen vi: **jdm/einer Sache ~** to trust sb/sth; **ich traute meinen Ohren nicht** I couldn't believe my ears ▷ vr: **sich ~** to dare ▷ vt to marry; **sich ~ lassen** to get married

Trauer (-) f sorrow; (für Verstorbenen) mourning

Traum (-(e)s, Träume) m dream; **träumen** vt, vi to dream (von of, about); **traumhaft** adj dreamlike; (fig) wonderful

traurig adj sad (über +akk about)

Trauschein m marriage certificate; **Trauung** f wedding ceremony; **Trauzeuge** m, **Trauzeugin** f witness (at wedding ceremony); **~** best man/maid of honour

Travellerscheck m traveller's cheque

treffen (traf, getroffen) vr: **sich ~** to meet ▷ vt, vi to hit; (Bemerkung) to hurt; (begegnen) to meet; (Entscheidung) to make; (Maßnahmen) to take; **Treffen** (-s, -) nt meeting; **Treffer** (-s, -) m (Tor) goal; **Treffpunkt** m meeting place

treiben (trieb, getrieben) vt to drive; (Sport) to do ▷ vi (im Wasser) to drift; (Pflanzen) to sprout; (Tee, Kaffee) to be diuretic; **Treiber** (-s, -) m (Inform) driver

Treibgas nt propellant; **Treibhaus** nt greenhouse; **Treibstoff** m fuel

trennen vt to separate; (teilen) to divide ▷ vr: **sich ~** to separate; **sich von jdm ~** to leave sb; **sich von etw ~** to part with sth; **Trennung** f separation

Treppe (-, -n) f stairs pl; (im Freien) steps pl; **Treppengeländer** nt banister; **Treppenhaus** nt staircase

Tresen (-s, -) m (in Kneipe) bar; (in Laden) counter

Tresor (-s, -e) m safe

Tretboot nt pedal boat; **treten** (trat, getreten) vi to step; **mit jdm in Verbindung ~** to get in contact with sb ▷ vt to kick; (nieder-) to tread

treu adj (gegenüber Partner) faithful; (Kunde, Fan) loyal; **Treue** (-) f (eheliche) faithfulness; (von Kunde, Fan) loyalty

Triathlon (-s, -s) m triathlon

Tribüne (-, -n) f stand; (Rednertribüne) platform

Trick (-s, -e o -s) m trick; **Trickfilm** m cartoon

trieb imperf von **treiben**

Trieb (-(e)s, -e) m urge; (Instinkt) drive; (Neigung) inclination; (an Baum etc) shoot; **Triebwerk** nt engine

Trikot (-s, -s) nt shirt, jersey

Trimm-Dich-Pfad m fitness trail

trinkbar adj drinkable; **trinken** (trank, getrunken) vt, vi to drink; **einen ~ gehen** to go out for a drink; **Trinkgeld** nt tip; **Trinkhalm** m (drinking) straw; **Trinkwasser** nt drinking water

Trio (-s, -s) nt trio

Tripper (-s, -) m gonorrhoea

Tritt (-(e)s, -e) m (Schritt) step; (Fußtritt) kick; **Trittbrett** nt running board

Triumph (-(e)s, -e) m triumph; **triumphieren** vi to triumph (über +akk over)

trivial adj trivial

trocken adj dry; **Trockenhaube** f hair-dryer; **Trockenheit** f dryness; **trocken|legen** vt (Baby) to change; **trocknen** vt, vi to dry; **Trockner** (-s, -) m dryer

Trödel (-s) m (fam) junk; **Trödelmarkt** m flea market

trödeln vi (fam) to dawdle

Trommel (-, -n) f drum; **Trommelfell** nt eardrum; **trommeln** vt, vi to drum

Trompete (-, -n) f trumpet

Tropen pl tropics pl

Tropf (-(e)s, -e) m (Med) drip; **am ~ hängen** to be on a drip; **tröpfeln** vi to drip; **es tröpfelt** it's drizzling; **tropfen** vt, vi to drip; **Tropfen** (-s, -) m drop; **tropfenweise** adv drop by drop; **tropfnass** adj dripping wet; **Tropfsteinhöhle** f stalactite cave

tropisch adj tropical

Trost (-es) m consolation, comfort; **trösten** vt to console, to comfort; **trostlos** adj bleak; (Verhältnisse) wretched; **Trostpreis** m consolation prize

Trottoir (-s, -s) nt pavement (Brit), sidewalk (US)

trotz prep +gen o dat in spite of; **Trotz** (-es) m defiance; **trotzdem** adv nevertheless ▷ conj although;

trotzig adj defiant

trüb adj dull; (Flüssigkeit, Glas) cloudy; (fig) gloomy

Trüffel (-, -n) f truffle

trug imperf von **tragen**

trügerisch adj deceptive

Truhe (-, -n) f chest

Trümmer pl wreckage sing; (Bau~) ruins pl

Trumpf (-(e)s, Trümpfe) m trump

Trunkenheit f intoxication; ~ **am Steuer** drink driving (Brit), drunk driving (US)

Truthahn m turkey

Tscheche (-n, -n) m, **Tschechin** f Czech; **Tschechien** (-s) nt Czech Republic; **tschechisch** adj Czech; **Tschechische Republik** Czech Republic; **Tschechisch** nt Czech

Tschetschenien (-s) nt Chechnya

tschüs(s) interj bye

T-Shirt (-s, -s) nt T-shirt

Tube (-, -n) f tube

Tuberkulose (-, -n) f tuberculosis, TB

Tuch (-(e)s, Tücher) nt cloth; (Halstuch) scarf; (Kopftuch) headscarf

tüchtig adj competent; (fleißig) efficient; (fam: kräftig) good

Tugend (-, -en) f virtue; **tugendhaft** adj virtuous

Tulpe (-, -n) f tulip

Tumor (-s, -en) m tumour

tun (tat, getan) vt (machen) to do; (legen) to put; **was tust du da?** what are you doing?; **das tut man nicht** you shouldn't do that; **jdm etw ~** (antun) to do sth to sb; **das tut es auch** that'll do ▷ vi to act; **so ~, als ob** to act as if ▷ vr impers: **es tut sich etwas/viel** something/a lot is happening

Tuner (-s, -) m tuner

Tunesien (-s) nt Tunisia

Tunfisch m siehe **Thunfisch** tuna

Tunnel (-s, -s o -) m tunnel

Tunte (-, -n) f (pej, fam) fairy

tupfen vt, vi to dab; (mit Farbe) to dot; **Tupfen** (-s, -) m dot

Tür (-, -en) f door; **vor/an der ~** at the door; **an die ~ gehen** to answer the door

Türke (-n, -n) m Turk; **Türkei** (-) f: **die ~** Turkey; **Türkin** f Turk

Türkis (-es, -e) m turquoise

türkisch adj Turkish; **Türkisch** nt Turkish

Turm (-(e)s, Türme) m tower; (spitzer Kirchturm) steeple; (Sprung~) diving platform; (Schach) rook, castle

turnen vi to do gymnastics; **Turnen** (-s) nt gymnastics sing; (Schule) physical education, PE; **Turner(in)** m(f) gymnast; **Turnhalle** f gym(nasium); **Turnhose** f gym shorts pl

Turnier (-s, -e) nt tournament

Turnschuh m gym shoe, sneaker (US)

Türschild nt doorplate; **Türschloss** nt lock

tuscheln vt, vi to whisper

Tussi (-, -s) f (pej, fam) chick

Tüte (-, -n) f bag

TÜV (-s, -s) m akr **Technischer Überwachungsverein** ≈ MOT (Brit), vehicle inspection (US)

○ **TÜV**
○
○ The **TÜV** is the organization
○ responsible for checking the
○ safety of machinery, particularly
○ vehicles. Cars over three years
○ old have to be examined every
○ two years for their safety and
○ for their exhaust emissions.
○ **TÜV** is also the name given to
○ the test itself.

TÜV-Plakette f badge attached to a vehicle's numberplate, indicating that it has passed the "TÜV"

Tweed (-s, -s) m tweed

twittern vi (auf Twitter) to tweet

Typ (-s, -en) m type; (Auto) model; (Mann) guy, bloke

Typhus (-) m typhoid

typisch adj typical (für of); **ein ~er Fehler** a common mistake; **~ Marcus!** that's just like Marcus; **~ amerikanisch!** that's so American

u. abk = **und**

u. a. abk = **und andere(s)** and others; = **unter anderem, unter anderen** among other things

u. A. w. g. abk = **um Antwort wird gebeten** RSVP

U-Bahn f underground (Brit), subway (US)

übel adj bad; (moralisch) wicked; **mir ist ~** I feel sick; **diese Bemerkung hat er mir ~ genommen** he took offence at my remark; **Übelkeit** f nausea

üben vt, vi to practise

○ SCHLÜSSELWORT

über prep +dat **1** (räumlich) over, above; **zwei Grad über null** two degrees above zero **2** (zeitlich) over; **über der Arbeit einschlafen** to fall asleep over one's work

▷ prep +akk **1** (räumlich) over; (hoch über auch) above; (quer über auch) across

2 (zeitlich) over; **über Weihnachten** over Christmas; **über kurz oder lang** sooner or later

3 (mit Zahlen) **Kinder über 12 Jahren** children over o above 12 years of age; **ein Scheck über 200 Euro** a cheque for 200 euros

4 (auf dem Wege) via; **nach Köln über Aachen** to Cologne via Aachen; **ich habe es über die Auskunft erfahren** I found out from information

5 (betreffend) about; **ein Buch über ...** a book about o on ...; **über jdn/etw lachen** to laugh about o at sb/sth

6 Macht über jdn haben to have power over sb; **sie liebt ihn über alles** she loves him more than everything

▷ adv over; **über und über** over and over; **den ganzen Tag über** all day long; **jdm in etw** dat **über sein** to be superior to sb in sth

überall adv everywhere
überanstrengen vr: **sich ~** to overexert oneself
überbacken adj: **(mit Käse) ~** au gratin; **überbelichten** vt (Foto) to overexpose; **überbieten** irr vt to outbid; (übertreffen) to surpass; (Rekord) to break
Überbleibsel (-s, -) nt remnant
Überblick m overview; (fig: in Darstellung) survey; (Fähigkeit zu verstehen) grasp (über +akk of)
überbuchen vt to overbook; **Überbuchung** f overbooking
überdurchschnittlich adj above average
übereinander adv on top of each other; (sprechen etc) about each other

überein|stimmen vi to agree (mit with)
überempfindlich adj hypersensitive
überfahren irr vt (Auto) to run over; **Überfahrt** f crossing
Überfall m (Banküberfall) robbery; (Mil) raid; (auf jdn) assault; **überfallen** irr vt to attack; (Bank) to raid
überfällig adj overdue
überfliegen irr vt to fly over; (Buch) to skim through
Überfluss m overabundance, excess (an +dat of); **überflüssig** adj superfluous
überfordern vt to demand too much of; (Kräfte) to overtax; **da bin ich überfordert** (bei Antwort) you've got me there
Überführung f (Brücke) flyover (Brit), overpass (US)
überfüllt adj overcrowded
Übergabe f handover
Übergang m crossing; (Wandel, Überleitung) transition; **Übergangslösung** f temporary solution, stopgap
übergeben irr vt to hand over
▷ vr: **sich ~** to be sick, to vomit
Übergepäck nt excess baggage
Übergewicht nt excess weight; **(10 Kilo) ~ haben** to be (10 kilos) overweight
überglücklich adj overjoyed; (fam) over the moon
Übergröße f outsize
überhaupt adv at all; (im Allgemeinen) in general; (besonders) especially; **was willst du ~?** what is it you want?
überheblich adj arrogant
überholen vt to overtake; (Tech) to overhaul; **Überholspur** f overtaking (Brit) o passing (US) lane; **überholt** adj outdated

Überholverbot nt: **hier herrscht ~** you can't overtake here
überhören vt to miss, not to catch; (absichtlich) to ignore;
überladen irr vt to overload ▷ adj (fig) cluttered; **überlassen** irr vt: **jdm etw ~** to leave sth to sb; **über|laufen** irr vi (Flüssigkeit) to overflow
überleben vt, vi to survive; **Überlebende(r)** mf survivor
überlegen vt to consider; **sich** (dat) **etw ~** to think about sth; **er hat es sich** (dat) **anders überlegt** he's changed his mind ▷ adj superior (dat to); **Überlegung** f consideration
überm kontr von **über dem**
übermäßig adj excessive
übermorgen adv the day after tomorrow
übernächste(r, s) adj: **~ Woche** the week after next
übernachten vi to spend the night (bei jdm at sb's place); **übernächtigt** adj bleary-eyed, very tired; **Übernachtung** f overnight stay; **~ mit Frühstück** bed and breakfast
übernehmen irr vt to take on; (Amt, Geschäft) to take over ▷ vr: **sich ~** to take on too much
überprüfen vt to check; **Überprüfung** f check; (Überprüfen) checking
überqueren vt to cross
überraschen vt to surprise; **Überraschung** f surprise
überreden vt to persuade; **er hat mich überredet** he talked me into it
überreichen vt to hand over
übers kontr von **über das**
überschätzen vt to overestimate; **überschlagen** irr vt (berechnen) to estimate; (auslassen: Seite) to skip ▷ vr: **sich**

~ to somersault; (Auto) to overturn; (Stimme) to crack; **überschneiden** irr vr: **sich ~** (Linien etc) to intersect; (Termine) to clash
Überschrift f heading
Überschwemmung f flood
Übersee f: **nach/in ~** overseas
übersehen irr vt (Gelände) to look (out) over; (nicht beachten) to overlook
übersetzen vt to translate (aus from, in +akk into); **Übersetzer(in)** (-s, -) m(f) translator; **Übersetzung** f translation
Übersicht f overall view; (Darstellung) survey; **übersichtlich** adj clear
überstehen irr vt (durchstehen) to get over; (Winter etc) to get through
Überstunden pl overtime sing
überstürzt adj hasty
überteuert adj overpriced
übertragbar adj transferable; (Med) infectious; **übertragen** irr vt to transfer (auf +akk to); (Radio) to broadcast; (Krankheit) to transmit ▷ vr to spread (auf +akk to) ▷ adj figurative; **Übertragung** f (Radio) broadcast; (von Daten) transmission
übertreffen irr vt to surpass
übertreiben irr vt, vi to exaggerate; to overdo; **Übertreibung** f exaggeration; **übertrieben** adj exaggerated, overdone
überwachen vt to supervise; (Verdächtigen) to keep under surveillance
überwand imperf von **überwinden**
überweisen irr vt to transfer; (Patienten) to refer (an +akk to); **Überweisung** f transfer; (von Patienten) referral

u

überwiegend adv mainly

überwinden (überwand, überwunden) vt to overcome ▷ vr: **sich ~** to make an effort, to force oneself; **überwunden** pp von **überwinden**

Überzelt nt flysheet

überzeugen vt to convince; **Überzeugung** f conviction

überziehen irr vt (bedecken) to cover; (Jacke etc) to put on; (Konto) to overdraw; **die Betten frisch ~** to change the sheets

üblich adj usual

übrig adj remaining; **ist noch Saft ~?** is there any juice left?; **die Übrigen** pl the rest pl; **im Übrigen** besides; **~ bleiben** to be left (over); **mir blieb nichts anderes ~, als zu gehen)** I had no other choice (but to go); **übrigens** adv besides; (nebenbei bemerkt) by the way; **übrig haben** irr vt: **für jdn etwas ~** (fam: jdn mögen) to have a soft spot for sb

Übung f practice; (im Sport, Aufgabe etc) exercise

Ufer (-s, -) nt (Fluss) bank; (Meer, See) shore; **am ~** on the bank/shore

Ufo (-(s), -s) nt akr = **unbekanntes Flugobjekt** UFO

Uhr (-, -en) f clock; (am Arm) watch; **wie viel ~ ist es?** what time is it?; **1 ~** 1 o'clock; **20 ~** 8 o'clock, 8 pm; **Uhrzeigersinn** m: **im ~** clockwise; **gegen den ~** anticlockwise (Brit), counterclockwise (US); **Uhrzeit** f time (of day)

Ukraine (-) f: **die ~** the Ukraine

UKW abk = **Ultrakurzwelle** VHF

Ulme (-, -n) f elm

Ultrakurzwelle f very high frequency; **Ultraschallaufnahme** f (Med) scan

○ SCHLÜSSELWORT

um prep +akk **1** (um herum) (a)round; **um Weihnachten** around Christmas; **er schlug um sich** he hit about him

2 (mit Zeitangabe) at; **um acht (Uhr)** at eight (o'clock)

3 (mit Größenangabe) by; **etw um 4 cm kürzen** to shorten sth by 4 cm; **um 10% teurer** 10% more expensive; **um vieles besser** better by far; **um so besser** so much the better

4 der Kampf um den Titel the battle for the title; **um Geld spielen** to play for money; **Stunde um Stunde** hour after hour; **Auge um Auge** an eye for an eye

▷ prep +gen: **um ... willen** for the sake of ...; **um Gottes willen** for goodness' o (stärker) God's sake

▷ konj: **um ... zu** (in order) to ...; **zu klug, um zu ...** too clever to ...; siehe **umso**

▷ adv **1** (ungefähr) about; **um (die) 30 Leute** about o around 30 people

2 (vorbei) **die 2 Stunden sind um** the two hours are up

umarmen vt to embrace

Umbau m rebuilding; (zu etwas) conversion (zu into); **umbauen** vt to rebuild; (zu etwas) to convert (zu into)

um|blättern vt, vi to turn over

um|bringen irr vt to kill

um|buchen vi to change one's reservation/flight

um|drehen vt to turn (round); (obere Seite nach unten) to turn over ▷ vr: **sich ~** to turn (round); **Umdrehung** f turn; (Phys, Auto) revolution

um|fahren irr vt to knock down

um|fallen irr vi to fall over

Umfang m (Ausmaß) extent; (von Buch) size; (Reichweite) range; (Math) circumference; **umfangreich** adj extensive

Umfeld nt environment

Umfrage f survey

Umgang m company; (mit jdm) dealings pl; **umgänglich** adj sociable; **Umgangssprache** f colloquial language, slang

Umgebung f surroundings pl; (Milieu) environment; (Personen) people around one

umgehen irr vi (Gerücht) to go round; ~ (**können**) **mit** (know how to) handle ▷ vt to avoid; (Schwierigkeit, Verbot) to get round

um|gehen irr vi: **mit etw** ~ to handle sth; **Umgehungsstraße** f bypass

umgekehrt adj reverse; (gegenteilig) opposite ▷ adv the other way round; **und** ~ and vice versa

um|hören vr: **sich** ~ to ask around; **um|kehren** vi to turn back ▷ vt to reverse; (Kleidungsstück) to turn inside out; **um|kippen** vt to tip over ▷ vi to overturn; (fig) to change one's mind; (fam: ohnmächtig werden) to pass out

Umkleidekabine f changing cubicle (Brit), dressing room (US); **Umkleideraum** m changing room

Umkreis m neighbourhood; **im** ~ **von** within a radius of

um|leiten vt to divert; **Umleitung** f diversion

um|rechnen vt to convert (in +akk into); **Umrechnung** f conversion; **Umrechnungskurs** m rate of exchange

Umriss m outline

um|rühren vi, vt to stir

ums kontr von **um das**

Umsatz m turnover

um|schalten vi to turn over

Umschlag m cover; (Buch) jacket; (Med) compress; (Brief) envelope

Umschulung f retraining

um|sehen irr vr: **sich** ~ to look around; (suchen) to look out (nach for)

umso adv all the; ~ **mehr** all the more; ~ **besser** so much the better

umsonst adv (vergeblich) in vain; (gratis) for nothing

Umstand m circumstance; **Umstände** (pl) (fig) fuss; **in anderen Umständen sein** to be pregnant; **jdm Umstände machen** to cause sb a lot of trouble; **machen Sie bitte keine Umstände** please, don't put yourself out; **unter diesen/ keinen Umständen** under these/no circumstances; **unter Umständen** possibly; **umständlich** adj (Methode) complicated; (Ausdrucksweise) long-winded; (Mensch) ponderous; **Umstandsmode** f maternity wear

um|steigen irr vi to change (trains/buses)

um|stellen vt (an anderen Ort) to change round; (Tech) to convert ▷ vr: **sich** ~ to adapt (auf +akk to); **Umstellung** f change; (Umgewöhnung) adjustment; (Tech) conversion

Umtausch m exchange; **um|tauschen** vt to exchange; (Währung) to change

Umweg m detour

Umwelt f environment; **Umweltbelastung** f ecological damage; **umweltbewusst** adj environmentally aware;

u

umweltfreundlich adj environment-friendly;
Umweltpapier nt recycled paper;
umweltschädlich adj harmful to the environment; **Umweltschutz** m environmental protection;
Umweltschützer(in) (-s, -) m(f) environmentalist;
Umweltsteuer f green tax;
Umweltverschmutzung f pollution; **umweltverträglich** adj environment-friendly

um|werfen irr vt to knock over; (fig: ändern) to upset; (fig, fam: jdn) to flabbergast

um|ziehen irr vt to change ▷ vr: **sich ~** to change ▷ vi to move (house); **Umzug** m (Straßenumzug) procession; (Wohnungsumzug) move

unabhängig adj independent; **Unabhängigkeitstag** m Independence Day, Fourth of July (US)

unabsichtlich adv unintentionally

unangenehm adj unpleasant; **Unannehmlichkeit** f inconvenience; **~en** pl trouble sing

unanständig adj indecent; **unappetitlich** adj (Essen) unappetizing; (abstoßend) off-putting; **unbeabsichtigt** adj unintentional; **unbedeutend** adj insignificant, unimportant; (Fehler) slight

unbedingt adj unconditional ▷ adv absolutely

unbefriedigend adj unsatisfactory; **unbegrenzt** adj unlimited; **unbekannt** adj unknown; **unbeliebt** adj unpopular; **unbemerkt** adj unnoticed; **unbequem** adj (Stuhl, Mensch) uncomfortable; (Regelung) inconvenient; **unbeständig** adj (Wetter)

unsettled; (Lage) unstable; (Mensch) unreliable; **unbestimmt** adj indefinite; **unbeteiligt** adj (nicht dazugehörig) uninvolved; (innerlich nicht berührt) indifferent, unconcerned; **unbewacht** adj unguarded; **unbewusst** adj unconscious; **unbezahlt** adj unpaid; **unbrauchbar** adj useless

und conj and; **~ so weiter** and so on; **na ~?** so what?

undankbar adj (Person) ungrateful; (Aufgabe) thankless; **undenkbar** adj inconceivable; **undeutlich** adj indistinct; **undicht** adj leaky; **uneben** adj uneven; (Schmuck etc) fake; **unehelich** adj (Kind) illegitimate; **unendlich** adj endless; (Math) infinite; **unentbehrlich** adj indispensable; **unentgeltlich** adj free (of charge); **unentschieden** adj undecided; **~ enden** (Sport) to end in a draw **unerfreulich** adj unpleasant; **unerhört** adj unheard-of; (Bitte) outrageous; **unerlässlich** adj indispensable; **unerträglich** adj unbearable; **unerwartet** adj unexpected **unerwünscht** adj unwelcome; (Eigenschaften) undesirable; **unfähig** adj incompetent; **~ sein, etw zu tun** to be incapable of doing sth; **unfair** adj unfair **Unfall** m accident; **Unfallflucht** f failure to stop after an accident; **Unfallhergang** m: **den ~ schildern** to give details of the accident; **Unfallstation** f casualty ward; **Unfallstelle** f scene of the accident; **Unfallversicherung** f accident insurance

unfreundlich adj unfriendly

Ungarn (-s) nt Hungary

Ungeduld f impatience;
ungeduldig adj impatient
ungeeignet adj unsuitable
ungefähr adj approximate ▷ adv
approximately; **~ 10 Kilometer**
about 10 kilometres; **wann ~?**
about what time?; **wo ~?**
whereabouts?
ungefährlich adj harmless;
(sicher) safe
ungeheuer adj huge ▷ adv (fam)
enormously; **Ungeheuer** (-s, -) nt
monster
ungehorsam adj disobedient
(gegenüber to)
ungelegen adj inconvenient;
ungemütlich adj unpleasant;
(Mensch) disagreeable;
ungenießbar adj inedible;
(Getränk) undrinkable;
ungenügend adj unsatisfactory;
(Schulnote) ≈ F; **ungepflegt** adj
(Garten) untended; (Aussehen)
unkempt; (Hände) neglected;
ungerade adj odd
ungerecht adj unjust;
ungerechtfertigt adj unjusti-
fied; **Ungerechtigkeit** f
injustice, unfairness
ungern adv reluctantly;
ungeschickt adj clumsy;
ungeschminkt adj without
make-up; **ungesund** adj
unhealthy; **ungewiss** adj
uncertain; **ungewöhnlich** adj
unusual
Ungeziefer (-s) nt vermin pl
ungezogen adj ill-mannered
ungezwungen adj relaxed
ungiftig adj non-toxic
unglaublich adj incredible
Unglück (-(e)s, -e) nt (Unheil)
misfortune; (Pech) bad luck;
(Unglücksfall) disaster; (Verkehrs~)
accident; **das bringt ~** that's
unlucky; **unglücklich** adj
unhappy; (erfolglos) unlucky;

(unerfreulich) unfortunate;
unglücklicherweise adv
unfortunately
ungültig adj invalid
ungünstig adj inconvenient
unheilbar adj incurable; **~ krank
sein** to be terminally ill
unheimlich adj eerie ▷ adv (fam)
incredibly
unhöflich adj impolite
uni adj plain
Uni (-, -s) f uni
Uniform (-, -en) f uniform
Universität f university
Unkenntnis f ignorance
unklar adj unclear
Unkosten pl expenses pl;
Unkostenbeitrag m contribution (towards expenses)
Unkraut nt weeds pl, ~art, weed
unlogisch adj illogical
unmissverständlich adj
unambiguous
unmittelbar adj immediate;
~ darauf immediately afterwards
unmöbliert adj unfurnished
unmöglich adj impossible
unnahbar adj unapproachable
unnötig adj unnecessary
UNO (-) f abkr = **United Nations
Organization** UN
unordentlich adj untidy;
Unordnung f disorder
unpassend adj inappropriate;
(Zeit) inconvenient; **unpersönlich**
adj impersonal; **unpraktisch** adj
impractical
Unrecht nt wrong; **zu ~** wrongly;
im ~ sein to be wrong; **unrecht**
adj wrong; **~ haben** to be
wrong
unregelmäßig adj irregular;
unreif adj unripe; **unruhig** adj
restless; **~ schlafen** to have a bad
night
uns pron akk, dat von **wir**; us; (to)
us; **~ (selbst)** (reflexiv) ourselves;

sehen Sie ~? can you see us?; **er schickte es ~** he sent it to us; **lasst ~ in Ruhe** leave us alone; **ein Freund von ~** a friend of ours; **wir haben ~ hingesetzt** we sat down; **wir haben ~ amüsiert** we enjoyed ourselves; **wir mögen ~** we like each other

unscharf adj (Foto) blurred, out of focus

unscheinbar adj insignificant; (Aussehen) unprepossessing

unschlüssig adj undecided

unschuldig adj innocent

unser pron (adjektivisch) our
▷ pron gen von **wir**; of us; **unsere(r, s)** pron (substantivisch) ours; **unseretwegen** adv (wegen uns) because of us; (uns zuliebe) for our sake; (um uns) about us; (von uns aus) as far as we are concerned

unseriös adj dubious; **unsicher** adj (ungewiss) uncertain; (Person, Job) insecure

Unsinn m nonsense

unsterblich adj immortal; **~ verliebt** madly in love

unsympathisch adj unpleasant; **er ist mir ~** I don't like him

unten adv below; (im Haus) downstairs; (an der Treppe etc) at the bottom; **nach ~** down

SCHLÜSSELWORT

unter prep +dat 1 (räumlich, mit Zahlen) under; (drunter) underneath, below; **unter 18 Jahren** under 18 years
2 (zwischen) among(st); **sie waren unter sich** they were by themselves; **einer unter ihnen** one of them; **unter anderem** among other things
▷ prep +akk under, below

Unterarm m forearm

unterbelichtet adj (Foto) underexposed

Unterbewusstsein nt subconscious

unterbrechen irr vt to interrupt; **Unterbrechung** f interruption; **ohne ~** nonstop

unterdrücken vt to suppress; (Leute) to oppress

unterdurchschnittlich adj below average

untere(r, s) adj lower

untereinander adv (räumlich) one below the other; (gegenseitig) each other; (miteinander) among themselves/yourselves/ourselves

Unterführung f underpass

untergehen irr vi to go down; (Sonne) to set; (Volk) to perish; (Welt) to come to an end; (im Lärm) to be drowned out

Untergeschoss nt basement; **Untergewicht** nt: (**3 Kilo**) **~ haben** to be (3 kilos) underweight; **Untergrund** m foundation; (Pol) underground; **Untergrundbahn** f underground (Brit), subway (US)

unterhalb adv, prep +gen below; **~ von** below

Unterhalt m maintenance; **unterhalten** irr vt to maintain; (belustigen) to entertain ▷ vr: **sich ~ to talk**; (sich belustigen) to enjoy oneself; **Unterhaltung** f (Belustigung) entertainment; (Gespräch) talk, conversation

Unterhemd nt vest (Brit), undershirt (US); **Unterhose** f underpants pl; (für Damen) briefs pl

unterirdisch adj underground

Unterkiefer m lower jaw

Unterkunft (-, -künfte) f accommodation

Unterlage f (Beleg) document; (Schreibunterlage) pad

unterlassen irr vt: **es ~, etw zu tun** (versäumen) to fail to do sth; (bleiben lassen) to refrain from doing sth

unterlegen adj inferior (dat to); (besiegt) defeated

Unterleib m abdomen

Unterlippe f lower lip

Untermiete f: **zur ~ wohnen** to be a subtenant; **Untermieter(in)** m(f) subtenant

unternehmen irr vt (Reise) to go on; (Versuch) to make; **etwas ~** to do something (gegen about); **Unternehmen** (-s, -) nt undertaking; (Comm) company; **Unternehmensberater(in)** (-s, -) m(f) management consultant; **Unternehmer(in)** (-s, -) m(f) entrepreneur

Unterricht (-(e)s, -e) m lessons pl; **unterrichten** vt to teach

unterschätzen vt to underestimate

unterscheiden irr vt to distinguish (von from, zwischen +dat between) ▷ vr: **sich ~** to differ (von from)

Unterschenkel m lower leg

Unterschied (-(e)s, -e) m difference; **im ~ zu dir** unlike you; **unterschiedlich** adj different

unterschreiben irr vt to sign; **Unterschrift** f signature

Untersetzer (-s, -) m tablemat; (für Gläser) coaster

unterste(r, s) adj lowest, bottom

unter|stellen vr: **sich ~** to take shelter

unterstellen vt (rangmäßig) to subordinate (dat to); (fig) to impute (jdm etw sth to sb)

unterstreichen irr vt (a. fig) to underline

Unterstrich m (Inform) underscore

unterstützen vt to support; **Unterstützung** f support

untersuchen vt (Med) to examine; (Polizei) to investigate; **Untersuchung** f examination; (polizeiliche) investigation

untertags adv during the day

Untertasse f saucer

Unterteil nt lower part, bottom

Untertitel m subtitle

untervermieten vt to sublet

Unterwäsche f underwear

unterwegs adv on the way

unterzeichnen vt to sign

untreu adj unfaithful

untröstlich adj inconsolable; **unüberlegt** adj ill-considered ▷ adv without thinking; **unüblich** adj unusual; **unverantwortlich** adj irresponsible; (unentschuldbar) inexcusable

unverbindlich adj not binding; (Antwort) noncommittal ▷ adv (Comm) without obligation

unverbleit adj unleaded; **unverheiratet** adj unmarried, single; **unvermeidlich** adj unavoidable; **unvernünftig** adj silly; **unverschämt** adj impudent; **unverständlich** adj incomprehensible; **unverträglich** adj (Person) quarrelsome; (Essen) indigestible

unverwüstlich adj indestructible; (Mensch) irrepressible

unverzeihlich adj unpardonable; **unverzüglich** adj immediate; **unvollständig** adj incomplete; **unvorsichtig** adj careless

unwahrscheinlich adj improbable, unlikely ▷ adv (fam) incredibly

Unwetter nt thunderstorm

unwichtig adj unimportant

unwiderstehlich adj irresistible

unwillkürlich adj involuntary
▷ adv instinctively; **ich musste
~ lachen** I couldn't help laughing
unwohl adj unwell, ill
unzählig adj innumerable,
countless
unzerbrechlich adj unbreak-
able; **unzertrennlich** adj
inseparable; **unzufrieden** adj
dissatisfied; **unzugänglich** adj
inaccessible; **unzumutbar** adj
unacceptable
unzusammenhängend adj
disconnected; (Äußerung)
incoherent; **unzutreffend** adj
inapplicable; (unwahr) incorrect;
unzuverlässig adj unreliable
Update (-s, -s) nt (Inform) update
üppig adj (Essen) lavish;
(Vegetation) lush
uralt adj ancient, very old
Uran (-s) nt uranium
Uranus (-) m Uranus
Uraufführung f premiere
Urenkel m great-grandson;
Urenkelin f great-grand-
daughter; **Urgroßeltern** pl
great-grandparents pl;
Urgroßmutter f great-grandmother; **Urgroßvater** m
great-grandfather
Urheber(in) (-s, -) m(f) origin-
ator; (Autor) author
Urin (-s, -e) m urine; **Urinprobe**
f urine specimen
Urkunde (-, -n) f document
Urlaub (-(e)s, -e) m holiday (Brit),
vacation (US); **im ~** on holiday
(Brit), on vacation (US); **in ~ fahren**
to go on holiday (Brit) (o vacation
(US)); **Urlauber(in)** (-s, -) m(f)
holiday-maker (Brit), vacationer
(US); **Urlaubsort** m holiday
resort; **urlaubsreif** adj ready for
a holiday (Brit) (o vacation (US));
Urlaubszeit f holiday season
(Brit), vacation period (US)

Urne (-, -n) f urn
Urologe m, **Urologin** f
urologist
Ursache f cause (für of); **keine ~!**
not at all; (bei Entschuldigung) that's
all right
Ursprung m origin; (von Fluss)
source; **ursprünglich** adj
original ▷ adv originally;
Ursprungsland adj country of
origin
Urteil (-s, -e) nt (Meinung)
opinion; (Jur) verdict; (Strafmaß)
sentence; **urteilen** vi to judge
Uruguay (-s) nt Uruguay
Urwald m jungle
USA pl USA sing
User(in) (-s, -) m(f) (Inform) user
usw. abk = **und so weiter** etc
Utensilien pl utensils pl

V

vage adj vague

Vagina (-, Vaginen) f vagina

Valentinstag m St Valentine's Day

Vandalismus m vandalism

Vanille (-) f vanilla

variieren vt, vi to vary

Vase (-, -n) f vase

Vaseline (-) f Vaseline®

Vater (-s, Väter) m father; **väterlich** adj paternal; **Vaterschaft** f fatherhood; (Jur) paternity; **Vatertag** m Father's Day; **Vaterunser** nt: **das ~ (beten)** (to say) the Lord's Prayer

V-Ausschnitt m V-neck

v. Chr. abk = **vor Christus** BC

Veganer(in) (-s, -) m(f) vegan; **Vegetarier(in)** (-s, -) m(f) vegetarian; **vegetarisch** adj vegetarian

Veilchen nt violet

Velo (-s, -s) nt (schweizerisch) bicycle

Vene (-, -n) f vein

Venedig (-s) nt Venice

Venezuela (-s) nt Venezuela

Ventil (-s, -e) nt valve

Ventilator m ventilator

Venus (-) f Venus

Venusmuschel f clam

verabreden vt to arrange ▷ vr: **sich ~** to arrange to meet (mit jdm sb); **ich bin schon verabredet** I'm already meeting someone; **Verabredung** f arrangement; (Termin) appointment; (zum Ausgehen) date

verabschieden vt (Gäste) to say goodbye to; (Gesetz) to pass ▷ vr: **sich ~** to say goodbye

verachten vt to despise; **verächtlich** adj contemptuous; (verachtenswert) contemptible; **Verachtung** f contempt

verallgemeinern vt to generalize

Veranda (-, Veranden) f veranda, porch (US)

veränderlich adj changeable; **verändern** vt to change ▷ vr: **sich ~** to change; **Veränderung** f change

veranlassen vt to cause

veranstalten vt to organize; **Veranstalter(in)** (-s, -) m(f) organizer; **Veranstaltung** f event; **Veranstaltungsort** m venue

verantworten vt to take responsibility for ▷ vr: **sich für etw ~** to answer for sth; **verantwortlich** adj responsible (für for); **Verantwortung** f responsibility (für for)

verärgern vt to annoy

verarschen vt (fam) to take the piss out of (Brit), to make a sucker out of (US)

Verb (-s, -en) nt verb

Verband m (Med) bandage; (Bund) association; **Verband(s)kasten** m first-aid box; **Verband(s)zeug** nt dressing material

verbessern vt to improve; (berichtigen) to correct ▷ vr: **sich ~** to improve; (berichtigen) to correct oneself; **Verbesserung** f improvement; (Berichtigung) correction

verbiegen irr vi to bend ▷ vr: **sich ~** to bend

verbieten irr vt to forbid; **jdm ~, etw zu tun** to forbid sb to do sth

verbinden irr vt to connect; (kombinieren) to combine; (Med) to bandage; **können Sie mich mit ... ~?** (Tel) can you put me through to ...?; **ich verbinde** (Tel) I'm putting you through ▷ vr (Chem) **sich ~** to combine

verbindlich adj binding; (freundlich) friendly; **Verbindung** f connection

verbleit adj leaded

verblüffen vt to amaze

verblühen vi to fade

verborgen adj hidden

Verbot (-(e)s, -e) nt ban (für, von on); **verboten** adj forbidden; **es ist ~** it's not allowed; **es ist ~, hier zu parken** you're not allowed to park here; **Rauchen ~** no smoking

verbrannt adj burnt

Verbrauch (-(e)s) m consumption; **verbrauchen** vt to use up; **Verbraucher(in)** (-s, -) m(f) consumer

Verbrechen (-s, -) nt crime; **Verbrecher(in)** (-s, -) m(f) criminal

verbreiten vt to spread ▷ vr: **sich ~** to spread

verbrennen irr vt to burn; **Verbrennung** f burning; (in Motor) combustion

verbringen irr vt to spend

verbunden adj: **falsch ~** sorry, wrong number

Verdacht (-(e)s) m suspicion; **verdächtig** adj suspicious; **verdächtigen** vt to suspect

verdammt interj (fam) damn

verdanken vt: **jdm etw ~** to owe sth to sb

verdarb imperf von **verderben**

verdauen vt (a. fig) to digest; **verdaulich** adj digestible; **das ist schwer ~** that is hard to digest; **Verdauung** f digestion

Verdeck (-(e)s, -e) nt top

verderben (verdarb, verdorben) vt to spoil; (schädigen) to ruin; (moralisch) to corrupt; **es sich** (dat) **mit jdm ~** to get into sb's bad books; **ich habe mir den Magen verdorben** I've got an upset stomach ▷ vi (Lebensmittel) to go off

verdienen vt to earn; (moralisch) to deserve; **Verdienst** (-(e)s, -e) m earnings pl ▷ (-(e)s, -e) nt merit; (Leistung) service (um to)

verdoppeln vt to double

verdorben pp von **verderben** ▷ adj spoilt; (geschädigt) ruined; (moralisch) corrupt

verdrehen vt to twist; (Augen) to roll; **jdm den Kopf ~** (fig) to turn sb's head

verdünnen vt to dilute

verdunsten vi to evaporate

verdursten vi to die of thirst

verehren vt to admire; (Rel) to worship; **Verehrer(in)** (-s, -) m(f) admirer

Verein (-(e)s, -e) m association; (Klub) club

vereinbar adj compatible

vereinbaren vt to arrange; **Vereinbarung** f agreement, arrangement

vereinigen vt to unite ▷ vr: **sich ~** to unite; **Vereinigtes Königreich** nt United Kingdom; **Vereinigte Staaten (von Amerika)** pl United States sing (of America); **Vereinigung** f union; (Verein) association; **Vereinte Nationen** pl United Nations pl

vereisen vi (Straße) to freeze over; (Fenster) to ice up ▷ vt (Med) to freeze

vererben irr vt: **jdm etw ~** to leave sth to sb; (Bio) to pass sth on to sb ▷ vr: **sich ~** to be hereditary; **vererblich** adj hereditary

verfahren irr vi to proceed ▷ vr: **sich ~** to get lost; **Verfahren** (-s, -) nt procedure; (Tech) method; (Jur) proceedings pl

verfallen irr vi to decline; (Haus) to be falling apart; (Fin) to lapse; (Fahrkarte etc) to expire; **~ in** (+akk) to lapse into; **Verfallsdatum** nt expiry (Brit) (o expiration (US)) date; (von Lebensmitteln) best-before date

verfärben vr: **sich ~** to change colour; (Wäsche) to discolour

Verfasser(in) (-s, -) m(f) author, writer; **Verfassung** f (gesundheitlich) condition; (Pol) constitution

verfaulen vi to rot

verfehlen vt to miss

verfeinern vt to refine

Verfilmung f film (o screen) version

verfluchen vt to curse

verfolgen vt to pursue; (Pol) to persecute

verfügbar adj available; **verfügen** vi **über etw** (akk) **~** to have sth at one's disposal; **Verfügung** f order; **jdm zur ~ stehen** to be at sb's disposal; **jdm etw zur ~ stellen** to put sth at sb's disposal

verführen vt to tempt; (sexuell) to seduce; **verführerisch** adj seductive

vergangen adj past; **~e Woche** last week; **Vergangenheit** f past

Vergaser (-s, -) m (Auto) carburettor

vergaß imperf von **vergessen**

vergeben irr vt to forgive (jdm etw sb for sth); (weggeben) to award, to allocate; **vergebens** adv in vain; **vergeblich** adv in vain ▷ adj vain, futile

vergehen irr vi to pass ▷ vr: **sich an jdm ~** to indecently assault sb; **Vergehen** (-s, -) nt offence

Vergeltung f retaliation

vergessen (vergaß, vergessen) vt to forget; **vergesslich** adj forgetful

vergeuden vt to squander, to waste

vergewaltigen vt to rape; **Vergewaltigung** f rape

vergewissern vr: **sich ~** to make sure

vergiften vt to poison; **Vergiftung** f poisoning

Vergissmeinnicht (-(e)s, -e) nt forget-me-not

Vergleich (-(e)s, -e) m comparison; (Jur) settlement; **im ~ zu** compared to (o with); **vergleichen** irr vt to compare (mit to, with)

Vergnügen (-s, -) nt pleasure; **viel ~!** enjoy yourself; **vergnügt** adj cheerful; **Vergnügungspark** m amusement park

vergoldet adj gold-plated

vergriffen adj (Buch) out of print; (Ware) out of stock

vergrößern vt to enlarge; (*Menge*) to increase; (*mit Lupe*) to magnify; **Vergrößerung** f enlargement; (*Menge*) increase; (*mit Lupe*) magnification; **Vergrößerungsglas** nt magnifying glass

verh. adj abk = **verheiratet** married

verhaften vt to arrest

verhalten irr vr: **sich ~** (*sich benehmen*) to behave; (*Sache*) to be; **Verhalten** (-s) nt behaviour

Verhältnis nt relationship (*zu* with); (*Math*) ratio; **-se** pl circumstances pl, conditions pl; **im ~ von 1 zu 2** in a ratio of 1 to 2; **verhältnismäßig** adj relative ▷ adv relatively

verhandeln vi to negotiate (*über etw akk* sth); **Verhandlung** f negotiation

verheimlichen vt to keep secret (*jdm* from sb)

verheiratet adj married

verhindern vt to prevent; **sie ist verhindert** she can't make it

Verhör (-(e)s, -e) nt interrogation; (*gerichtlich*) examination; **verhören** vt to interrogate; (*bei Gericht*) to examine ▷ vr: **sich ~** to mishear

verhungern vi to starve to death

verhüten vt to prevent; **Verhütung** f prevention; (*mit Pille, Kondom etc*) contraception; **Verhütungsmittel** nt contraceptive

verirren vr: **sich ~** to get lost

Verkauf m sale; **verkaufen** vt to sell; **zu ~** for sale; **Verkäufer(in)** m(f) seller; (*beruflich*) salesperson; (*in Laden*) shop assistant (Brit), salesperson (US); **verkäuflich** adj for sale

Verkehr (-s, -e) m traffic; (*Sex*) intercourse; (*Umlauf*) circulation; **verkehren** vi (*Bus etc*) to run; **~ in** to frequent; **~ mit** to associate (o mix) with; **Verkehrsampel** f traffic lights pl; **Verkehrsamt** nt tourist information office; **verkehrsfrei** adj traffic-free; **Verkehrsfunk** m travel news sing; **Verkehrsinsel** f traffic island; **Verkehrsmeldung** f traffic report; **Verkehrsmittel** nt means sing of transport; **öffentliche ~** pl public transport sing; **Verkehrsschild** nt traffic sign; **Verkehrstote(r)** mf road casualty; **die Zahl der ~n** the number of deaths on the road; **Verkehrsunfall** m road accident; **Verkehrszeichen** nt traffic sign

verkehrt adj wrong; (*verkehrt herum*) the wrong way round; (*Pullover etc*) inside out; **du machst es ~** you're doing it wrong

verklagen vt to take to court

verkleiden vt to dress up (*als* as) ▷ vr: **sich ~** to dress up (*als* as); (*um unerkannt zu bleiben*) to disguise oneself; **Verkleidung** f (*Karneval*) fancy dress; (*um nicht erkannt zu werden*) disguise

verkleinern vt to reduce; (*Zimmer, Gebiet etc*) to make smaller

verkneifen vr: **sich** (dat) **etw ~** (*Lachen*) to stifle sth; (*Schmerz*) to hide sth; (*sich versagen*) to do without sth; **verkommen** irr vi to deteriorate; (*Mensch*) to go downhill ▷ adj (*Haus*) dilapidated; (*moralisch*) depraved; **verkraften** vt to cope with

verkratzt adj scratched

verkühlen vr: **sich ~** to get a chill

verkürzen vt to shorten

Verlag (-(e)s, -e) m publishing company

verlangen vt (*fordern*) to

demand; (wollen) to want; (Preis) to ask; (Qualifikation) to require; (erwarten) to ask (von of); (fragen nach) to ask for; (Pass etc) to ask to see; **~ Sie Herrn X** ask for Mr X ▷ vi: **~ nach** to ask for

verlängern vt to extend; (Pass, Erlaubnis) renew; **Verlängerung** f extension; (Sport) extra time; (von Pass, Erlaubnis) renewal; **Verlängerungsschnur** f extension cable; **Verlängerungswoche** f extra week

verlassen irr vt to leave ▷ irr vr: **sich ~** to rely (auf +akk on) ▷ adj desolate; (Mensch) abandoned; **verlässlich** adj reliable

Verlauf m course; **verlaufen** irr vi (Weg, Grenze) to run (entlang along); (zeitlich) to pass; (Farben) to run ▷ vr: **sich ~** to get lost; (Menschenmenge) to disperse

verlegen vt to move; (verlieren) to mislay; (Buch) to publish ▷ adj embarrassed; **Verlegenheit** f embarrassment; (Situation) difficulty

Verleih (-(e)s, -e) m (Firma) hire company (Brit), rental company (US); **verleihen** irr vt to lend; (vermieten) to hire out (Brit), to rent (out) (US); (Preis, Medaille) to award

verleiten vt: **jdn dazu ~, etw zu tun** to induce sb to do sth

verlernen vt to forget

verletzen vt to injure; (fig) to hurt; **Verletzte(r)** mf injured person; **Verletzung** f injury; (Verstoß) violation

verlieben vr: **sich ~** to fall in love (in jdn with sb); **verliebt** adj in love

verlieren (verlor, verloren) vt, vi to lose

verloben vr: **sich ~** to get engaged (mit to); **Verlobte(r)** mf

fiancé/fiancée; **Verlobung** f engagement

verlor imperf von **verlieren** ▷ adj **verloren** pp von **verlieren** ▷ adj lost; (Eier) poached; **~ gehen** to go missing

verlosen vt to raffle; **Verlosung** f raffle

Verlust (-(e)s, -e) m loss

vermehren vt to multiply; (Menge) to increase ▷ vr: **sich ~** to multiply; (Menge) to increase

vermeiden irr vt to avoid

vermeintlich adj supposed

vermieten vt to rent (out), to let (out) (Brit); (Auto) to hire (out) (Brit), to rent (out) (US); **Vermieter(in)** m(f) landlord/-lady

vermischen vt to mix ▷ vr: **sich ~** to mix

vermissen vt to miss; **vermisst** adj missing; **jdn als ~ melden** to report sb missing

Vermittlung f (bei Streit) mediation; (Herbeiführung) arranging; (Stelle) agency

Vermögen (-s, -) nt fortune

vermuten vt to suppose; (argwöhnen) to suspect; **vermutlich** adj probable ▷ adv probably; **Vermutung** f supposition; (Verdacht) suspicion

vernachlässigen vt to neglect

vernichten vt to destroy; **vernichtend** adj (fig) crushing; (Blick) withering; (Kritik) scathing

Vernunft (-) f reason; **ich kann ihn nicht zur ~ bringen** I can't make him see reason; **vernünftig** adj sensible; (Preis) reasonable

veröffentlichen vt to publish

verordnen vt (Med) to prescribe; **Verordnung** f order; (Med) prescription

verpachten vt to lease (out) (an +akk to)

verpacken vt to pack;
(*einwickeln*) to wrap up

Verpackung f packaging;
Verpackungskosten pl packing
charges pl

verpassen vt to miss

verpflegen vt to feed;
Verpflegung f feeding; (*Kost*)
food; (*in Hotel*) board

verpflichten vt to oblige;
(*anstellen*) to engage ▷ vr: **sich
~** to commit oneself (*etw zu tun*
to doing sth)

verprügeln vt to beat up

verraten irr vt to betray;
(*Geheimnis*) to divulge; **aber nicht
~!** but don't tell anyone ▷ vr: **sich
~** to give oneself away

verrechnen vt: **~ mit** to set off
against ▷ vr: **sich ~** to
miscalculate; **Verrechnungs-
scheck** m crossed cheque (*Brit*),
check for deposit only (*US*)

verregnet adj rainy

verreisen vi to go away (*nach* to);
sie ist (geschäftlich) verreist
she's away (on business);

verrenken vt to contort; (*Med*) to
dislocate; **sich** (*dat*) **den Knöchel
~** to sprain (o twist) one's ankle;
verringern vt to reduce

verrostet adj rusty

verrückt adj mad, crazy; **es
macht mich ~** it's driving me mad

versagen vt to fail; **Versagen** (-s)
nt failure; **Versager(in)** (-s, -) m(f)
failure

versalzen irr vt to put too much
salt in/on

versammeln vt to assemble, to
gather ▷ vr: **sich ~** to assemble,
to gather; **Versammlung** f
meeting

Versand (-(e)s) m dispatch;
(*Abteilung*) dispatch department;
Versandhaus nt mail-order
company

versäumen vt to miss;
(*unterlassen*) to neglect; **~, etw zu
tun** to fail to do sth

verschätzen vr: **sich ~** to
miscalculate

verschenken vt to give away;
(*Chance*) to waste

verschicken vt to send off

verschieben vt irr (*auf später*) to
postpone, to put off; (*an anderen
Ort*) to move

verschieden adj (*unterschiedlich*)
different; (*mehrere*) various; **sie
sind ~ groß** they are of different
sizes; **Verschiedene** pl various
people/things pl; **Verschiedenes**
various things pl

verschimmelt adj mouldy

verschlafen irr vt to sleep
through; (*fig*) to miss ▷ vi to
oversleep

verschlechtern vr: **sich ~** to
deteriorate, to get worse;
Verschlechterung f
deterioration

Verschleiß (-es) m wear and tear

verschließbar adj lockable;
verschließen irr vt to close; (*mit
Schlüssel*) to lock

verschlimmern vt to make
worse ▷ vr: **sich ~** to get worse

verschlossen adj locked; (*fig*)
reserved

verschlucken vt to swallow
▷ vr: **sich ~** to choke (*an +dat* on)

Verschluss m lock; (*von Kleid*)
fastener; (*Foto*) shutter; (*Stöpsel*)
stopper

verschmutzen vt to get dirty;
(*Umwelt*) to pollute

verschnaufen vi: **ich muss mal
~** I need to get my breath back

verschneit adj snow-covered

verschnupft adj: **~ sein** to have
a cold; (*fam: beleidigt*) to be peeved

verschonen vt to spare (*jdn mit
etw sb sth*)

verschreiben irr vt (Med) to prescribe;
verschreibungspflichtig adj available only on prescription
verschwand imperf von **verschwinden**
verschweigen irr vt to keep secret; **jdm etw ~** to keep sth from sb
verschwenden vt to waste; **Verschwendung** f waste
verschwiegen adj discreet; (Ort) secluded
verschwinden (verschwand, verschwunden) vi to disappear, to vanish; **verschwinde!** get lost!; **verschwunden** pp von **verschwinden**
Versehen (-s, -) nt: **aus ~** by mistake; **versehentlich** adv by mistake
versenden irr vt to send off
versessen adj: **~ auf** (+akk) mad about
versetzen vt to transfer; (verpfänden) to pawn; (fam: bei Verabredung) to stand up ▷ vr: **sich in jdn** (o jds Lage) **~** to put oneself in sb's place
verseuchen vt to contaminate
versichern vt to insure; (bestätigen) to assure; **versichert sein** to be insured; **Versichertenkarte** f health-insurance card; **Versicherung** f insurance; **Versicherungskarte** f: **grüne ~** green card (Brit), insurance document for driving abroad; **Versicherungspolice** f insurance policy
versilbert adj silver-plated
versinken irr vi to sink
Version f version
versöhnen vt to reconcile ▷ vr: **sich ~** to become reconciled
versorgen vt to provide, to supply (mit with); (Familie) to look

after ▷ vr: **sich ~** to look after oneself; **Versorgung** f provision; (Unterhalt) maintenance; (für Alter etc) benefit
verspäten vr: **sich ~** to be late; **verspätet** adj late; **Verspätung** f delay; **(eine Stunde) ~ haben** to be (an hour) late
versprechen irr vt to promise ▷ vr: **ich habe mich versprochen** I didn't mean to say that
Verstand m mind; (Vernunft) (common) sense; **den ~ verlieren** to lose one's mind; **verständigen** vt to inform ▷ vr: **sich ~** to communicate; (sich einigen) to come to an understanding; **Verständigung** f communication; **verständlich** adj understandable; **Verständnis** nt understanding (für of); (Mitgefühl) sympathy; **verständnisvoll** adj understanding
verstauchen vt to sprain; **verstaucht** pp von **verstauchen** sprained
Versteck (-(e)s, -e) nt hiding place; **~ spielen** to play hide-and-seek; **verstecken** vt to hide (vor +dat from) ▷ vr: **sich ~** to hide (vor +dat from)
verstehen irr vt to understand; **falsch ~** to misunderstand ▷ vr: **sich ~** to get on (mit with)
Versteigerung f auction
verstellbar adj adjustable; **verstellen** vt to move; (Uhr) to adjust; (versperren) to block; (Stimme, Handschrift) to disguise ▷ vr: **sich ~** to pretend, to put on an act
verstopfen vt to block up; (Med) to constipate; **Verstopfung** f obstruction; (Med) constipation
Verstoß m infringement, violation (gegen of)

Versuch (-(e)s, -e) m attempt; (*wissenschaftlich*) experiment; **versuchen** vt to try

vertauschen vt to exchange; (*versehentlich*) to mix up

verteidigen vt to defend; **Verteidiger(in)** (-s, -) m(f) (*Sport*) defender; (*Jur*) defence counsel; **Verteidigung** f defence

verteilen vt to distribute

Vertrag (-(e)s, Verträge) m contract; (*Pol*) treaty

vertragen irr vt to stand, to bear ▷ vr: **sich ~** to get along (with each other); (*sich aussöhnen*) to make it up

verträglich adj (*Mensch*) good-natured; (*Speisen*) digestible

vertrauen vi: **jdm/einer Sache ~** to trust sb/sth; **Vertrauen** (-s) nt trust (*in +akk*, in zu in); **ich habe kein ~ zu ihm** I don't trust him; **ich hab's ihm im ~ gesagt** I told him in confidence; **vertraulich** adj (*geheim*) confidential; **vertraut** adj: **sich mit etw ~ machen** to familiarize oneself with sth

vertreten irr vt to represent; (*Ansicht*) to hold; **Vertreter(in)** (-s, -) m(f) representative

Vertrieb (-(e)s, -e) m (*Abteilung*) sales department

vertrocknen vi to dry up

vertun irr vr: **sich ~** to make a mistake

vertuschen vt to cover up

verunglücken vi to have an accident; **tödlich ~** to be killed in an accident

verunsichern vt to make uneasy

verursachen vt to cause

verurteilen vt to condemn

vervielfältigen vt to make copies of

verwählen vr: **sich ~** to dial the wrong number

verwalten vt to manage; (*behördlich*) to administer; **Verwalter(in)** (-s, -) m(f) manager; (*Vermögens~*) trustee; **Verwaltung** f management; (*amtlich*) administration

verwandt adj related (mit to); **Verwandte(r)** mf relative, relation; **Verwandtschaft** f relationship; (*Menschen*) relations pl

verwarnen vt to warn; (*Sport*) to caution

verwechseln vt to confuse (mit with); (*halten für*) to mistake (mit for)

verweigern vt to refuse

verwenden vt to use; (*Zeit*) to spend; **Mühe auf etw** (akk) **~** to take trouble over sth; **Verwendung** f use

verwirklichen vt to realize; **sich selbst ~** to fulfil oneself

verwirren vt to confuse; **Verwirrung** f confusion

verwitwet adj widowed

verwöhnen vt to spoil

verwunderlich adj surprising; **Verwunderung** f astonishment

verwüsten vt to devastate

verzählen vr: **sich ~** to miscount

verzehren vt to consume

Verzeichnis nt (*Liste*) list; (*Katalog*) catalogue; (*in Buch*) index; (*Inform*) directory

verzeihen (verzieh, verziehen) vt, vi to forgive (jdm etw sb for sth); **~ Sie bitte, ...** (*vor Frage etc*) excuse me, ...; **~ Sie die Störung** sorry to disturb you; **Verzeihung** f: **~!** sorry; **~, ...** (*vor Frage etc*) excuse me, ...; (*jdn*) **um ~ bitten** to apologize (to sb)

verzichten vi: **auf etw** (akk) **~** to do without sth; (*aufgeben*) to give sth up

verzieh imperf von **verzeihen**
verziehen pp von **verzeihen**
verziehen irr vt (Kind) to spoil; **das Gesicht ~** to pull a face ▷ vr: **sich ~** to go out of shape; (Gesicht) to contort; (verschwinden) to disappear
verzieren vt to decorate
verzögern vt to delay ▷ vr: **sich ~** to be delayed; **Verzögerung** f delay
verzweifeln vi to despair (an +dat of); **verzweifelt** adj desperate; **Verzweiflung** f despair
Veterinär(in) (-s, -e) m(f) veterinary surgeon (Brit), veterinarian (US)
Vetter (-s, -n) m cousin
vgl. abk = **vergleiche**
Viagra® (-s) nt Viagra®
Vibrator (-s, -en) m vibrator; **vibrieren** vi to vibrate
Video (-s, -s) nt video; **auf ~ aufnehmen** to video; **Videoclip** (-s, -s) m video clip; **Videofilm** m video; **Videogerät** nt video (recorder); **Videokamera** f video camera; **Videokassette** f video (cassette); **Videorekorder** m video recorder; **Videospiel** nt video game; **Videothek** f (-, -en) f video library
Vieh (-(e)s) nt cattle
viel pron a lot (of), lots of; **~ Arbeit** a lot of work, lots of work; **~e Leute** a lot of people, lots of people, many people; **zu ~** too much; **zu ~e** too many; **sehr ~** a great deal of; **sehr ~e** a great many; **ziemlich ~/-e** quite a lot of; **nicht ~** not much, not a lot of; **nicht ~e** not many, not a lot of ▷ pron a lot; **sie sagt nicht ~** she doesn't say a lot; **nicht ~** not much, not a lot of; **nicht ~e** not many, not a lot of; **gibt es ~?** is

there much?, is there a lot?; **gibt es ~e?** are there many?, are there a lot? ▷ adv a lot; **er geht ~ ins Kino** he goes a lot to the cinema; **sehr ~** a great deal; **ziemlich ~** quite a lot; **~ besser** much better; **~ teurer** much more expensive; **~ zu ~** far too much
vielleicht adv perhaps; **~ ist sie krank** perhaps she's ill, she might be ill; **weißt du ~, wo er ist?** do you know where he is (by any chance)?
vielmal(s) adv many times; **danke ~s** many thanks; **vielmehr** adv rather; **vielseitig** adj very varied; (Mensch, Gerät) versatile
vier num four; **auf allen ~en** on all fours; **unter ~ Augen** in private, privately; **Vier** (-, -en) f four; (Schulnote) = D; **Vierbettzimmer** nt four-bed room; **Viereck** (-(e)s, -e) nt four-sided figure; (Quadrat) square; **viereckig** adj four-sided; (quadratisch) square; **vierfach** adj: **die ~e Menge** four times the amount; **vierhundert** num four hundred; **viermal** adv four times; **vierspurig** adj four-lane
viert adv: **wir sind zu ~** there are four of us; **vierte(r, s)** adj fourth; siehe auch **dritte**
Viertel (-s, -) nt (Stadtviertel) quarter, district; (Bruchteil) quarter; (Viertelliter) quarter-litre; (Uhrzeit) quarter; **~ vor/nach drei** a quarter to/past three; **viertel drei** a quarter past two; **drei ~ drei** a quarter to three; **Viertelfinale** nt quarter-final; **vierteljährlich** adj quarterly; **Viertelstunde** f quarter of an hour
vierzehn num fourteen; **in ~ Tagen** in two weeks, in a fortnight (Brit); **vierzehntägig** adj two-week, fortnightly (Brit);

vierzehnte(r, s) *adj* fourteenth;
siehe auch **dritte**; **vierzig** *num*
forty; **vierzigste(r, s)** *adj*
fortieth

Vietnam (-s) *nt* Vietnam

Vignette *f* (Autobahn~)
motorway (Brit) (o freeway (US))
permit

Villa (-, Villen) *f* villa

violett *adj* purple

Violine *f* violin

viral *adj* (Inform) viral

Virus (-, Viren) *m* o *nt* virus

Visitenkarte *f* card

Visum (-s, Visa o Visen) *nt* visa

Vitamin (-s, -e) *nt* vitamin

Vitrine (-, -n) *f* (glass) cabinet;
(Schaukasten) display case

Vogel (-s, Vögel) *m* bird;
Vogelgrippe *f* bird flu, avian flu;
vögeln *vi, vt* (vulg) to screw

Voicemail (-, -s) *f* voice mail

Vokal (-s, -e) *m* vowel

Volk (-(e)s, Völker) *nt* people *pl*;
(Nation) nation; **Volksfest** *nt*
festival; (Jahrmarkt) funfair;
Volkshochschule *f* adult
education centre; **Volkslied** *nt*
folksong; **Volksmusik** *f* folk
music; **volkstümlich** *adj* (einfach
und beliebt) popular; (herkömmlich)
traditional; (Kunst) folk

voll *adj* full (von of); **voll|machen**
vt to fill (up); **voll|tanken** *vi* to
fill up

Vollbart *m* beard; **Vollbremsung**
f: **eine ~ machen** to slam on the
brakes; **vollends** *adv* completely

Volleyball *m* volleyball

Vollgas *nt*: **mit ~** at full throttle;
~ geben to step on it

völlig *adj* complete ▷ *adv*
completely

volljährig *adj* of age;
Vollkaskoversicherung *f* fully
comprehensive insurance;
vollklimatisiert *adj* fully

air-conditioned; **vollkommen**
adj perfect; **~er Unsinn** complete
rubbish ▷ *adv* completely

Vollkornbrot *nt* wholemeal
(Brit) (o whole wheat (US)) bread

Vollmacht (-, -en) *f* authority;
(Urkunde) power of attorney

Vollmilch *f* full-fat milk (Brit),
whole milk (US);
Vollmilchschokolade *f* milk
chocolate; **Vollmond** *m* full
moon; **Vollnarkose** *f* general
anaesthetic; **Vollpension** *f* full
board

vollständig *adj* complete

Volltreffer *m* direct hit;
Vollwertkost *f* wholefood;
vollzählig *adj* complete

Volt (-, -) *nt* volt

Volumen (-s, -) *nt* volume

vom *kontr von* **von dem** (räumlich,
zeitlich, Ursache) from; **ich kenne
sie nur ~ Sehen** I only know her by
sight

⭕ SCHLÜSSELWORT

von *prep* +dat 1 (Ausgangspunkt)
from; **von ... bis** from ... to; **von
morgens bis abends** from
morning till night; **von ... nach ...**
from ... to ...; **von ... an** from ...;
von ... aus from ...; **von dort aus**
from there; **etw von sich aus tun**
to do sth of one's own accord; **von
mir aus** (fam) if you like, I don't
mind; **von wo/wann ...?**
where/when ... from?

2 (Ursache, im Passiv) by; **ein
Gedicht von Schiller** a poem by
Schiller; **von etw müde** tired from
sth

3 (als Genitiv) of; **ein Freund von
mir** a friend of mine; **nett von dir**
nice of you; **jeweils zwei von zehn**
two out of every ten

4 (über) about; **er erzählte vom**

Urlaub he talked about his holiday
5 **von wegen!** (fam) no way!

voneinander adv from each
other

🅞 SCHLÜSSELWORT

vor prep +dat 1 (räumlich) in front
of; **vor der Kirche links abbiegen**
turn left before the church
2 (zeitlich) before; **ich war vor ihm
da** I was there before him; **vor 2
Tagen** 2 days ago; **5 (Minuten) vor
4** 5 (minutes) to 4; **vor Kurzem** a
little while ago
3 (Ursache) with; **vor Wut/Liebe**
with rage/love; **vor Hunger
sterben** to die of hunger; **vor
lauter Arbeit** because of work
4 **vor allem, vor allen Dingen**
most of all
▷ prep +akk (räumlich) in front of
▷ adv: **vor und zurück** backwards
and forwards

voran|gehen irr vi to go ahead;
einer Sache (dat) **~** to precede sth;
voran|kommen irr vi to make
progress
Vorarlberg (-s) nt Vorarlberg
voraus adv ahead ; **im Voraus** in
advance; **voraus|fahren** irr vi to
drive on ahead; **vorausgesetzt**
conj provided (that); **Voraussage**
f prediction; (Wetter) forecast;
voraus|sagen vt to predict;
voraus|sehen irr vt to foresee;
voraus|sein irr vi: **jdm ~** to be
ahead of sb; **voraus|setzen** vt to
assume; **Voraussetzung** f
requirement, prerequisite;
voraussichtlich adj expected
▷ adv probably; **voraus|zahlen**
vt to pay in advance
Vorbehalt (-(e)s, -e) m
reservation; **vor|behalten** irr vt:

sich/jdm etw ~ to reserve sth (for
oneself)/for sb
vorbei adv past, over, finished;
vorbei|bringen irr vt to drop by
(o in); **vorbei|fahren** irr vi to
drive past; **vorbei|gehen** irr vi to
pass by, to go past; (verstreichen,
aufhören) to pass; **vorbei|kommen**
irr vi to drop by; **vorbei|lassen** irr
vt: **kannst du die Leute ~?** would
you let these people pass?; **lässt
du mich bitte mal vorbei?** can I
get past, please?; **vorbei|reden**
vi: **aneinander ~** to talk at
cross-purposes
vor|bereiten vt to prepare ▷ vr:
sich ~ to get ready (auf +akk, für
for); **Vorbereitung** f preparation
vor|bestellen vt to book in
advance; (Essen) to order in
advance; **Vorbestellung** f
booking, reservation
vor|beugen vt to prevent (dat
sth); **vorbeugend** adj preven-
tive; **Vorbeugung** f prevention
Vorbild nt (role) model;
vorbildlich adj model, ideal
Vorderachse f front axle;
vordere(r, s) adj front;
Vordergrund m foreground;
Vorderradantrieb m (Auto)
front-wheel drive; **Vorderseite** f
front; **Vordersitz** m front seat;
Vorderteil m o nt front (part)
Vordruck m form
voreilig adj hasty, rash; **~e
Schlüsse ziehen** to jump to
conclusions; **voreingenommen**
adj biased
vor|enthalten irr vt: **jdm etw
~** to withhold sth from sb
vorerst adv for the moment
vor|fahren irr vi (vorausfahren) to
drive on ahead; **vor das Haus ~** to
drive up to the house; **fahren Sie
bis zur Ampel vor** drive as far as
the traffic lights

Vorfahrt f (Auto) right of way;
~ achten give way (Brit), yield
(US); **Vorfahrtsschild** nt give
way (Brit) o yield (US) sign;
Vorfahrtsstraße f major road

Vorfall m incident

vor|führen vt to demonstrate;
(Film) to show; (Theaterstück, Trick)
to perform

Vorgänger(in) m(f) predecessor

vor|gehen irr vi (vorausgehen) to
go on ahead; (nach vorn) to go
forward; (handeln) to act, to
proceed; (Uhr) to be fast; (Vorrang
haben) to take precedence;
(passieren) to go on; **Vorgehen** (-s)
nt procedure

Vorgesetzte(r) mf superior

vorgestern adv the day before
yesterday

vor|haben irr vt to plan; **hast du
schon was vor?** have you got
anything on?; **ich habe vor, nach
Rom zu fahren** I'm planning to go
to Rome

vor|halten irr vt: **jdm etw ~** to
accuse sb of sth

Vorhand f forehand

vorhanden adj existing;
(erhältlich) available

Vorhang m curtain

Vorhaut f foreskin

vorher adv before; **zwei Tage
~** two days before; **~ essen wir**
we'll eat first; **Vorhersage** f
forecast; **vorher|sehen** irr vt to
foresee

vorhin adv just now, a moment
ago

Vorkenntnisse pl previous
knowledge sing

vor|kommen irr vi (nach vorne
kommen) to come forward;
(geschehen) to happen; (sich finden)
to occur; (scheinen) to seem (to
be); **sich** (dat) **dumm ~** to feel
stupid

Vorlage f model

vor|lassen irr vt: **jdn ~** to let sb
go first

vorläufig adj temporary

vor|lesen irr vt to read out

Vorlesung f lecture

vorletzte(r, s) adj last but one;
am ~n Samstag (on) the Saturday
before last

Vorliebe f preference

vor|machen vt: **kannst du es
mir ~?** can you show me how to do
it?; **jdm etwas ~** (fig: täuschen) to
fool sb

vor|merken vt to note down;
(Plätze) to book

Vormittag m morning; **am ~ in
the morning; heute ~** this
morning; **vormittags** adv in the
morning; **um 9 Uhr ~** at 9 (o'clock)
in the morning, at 9 am

vorn(e) adv in front; **von
~ anfangen** to start at the
beginning; **nach ~** to the front;
weiter ~ further up; **von ~ bis
hinten** from beginning to end

Vorname m first name; **wie
heißt du mit ~** what's your first
name?

vornehm adj (von Rang)
distinguished; (Benehmen) refined;
(fein, elegant) elegant

vor|nehmen irr vt **sich** (dat) **etw
~** to start on sth; **sich** (dat) ~, **etw
zu tun** (beschließen) to decide to do
sth

vornherein adv: **von ~** from the
start

Vorort m suburb

vorrangig adj priority

Vorrat m stock, supply; **vorrätig**
adj in stock

Vorrecht nt privilege

Vorruhestand m early
retirement

Vorsaison f early season

Vorsatz m intention; (Jur) intent;

vorsätzlich *adj* intentional; *(Jur)* premeditated

Vorschau *f* preview; *(Film)* trailer

Vorschlag *m* suggestion, proposal; **vorschlagen** *irr vt* to suggest, to propose; **ich schlage vor, dass wir gehen** I suggest we go

vor|schreiben *irr vt (befehlen)* to stipulate; **jdm etw ~** to dictate sth to sb

Vorschrift *f* regulation, rule; *(Anweisung)* instruction; **vorschriftsmäßig** *adj* correct

Vorschule *f* nursery school, pre-school *(US)*

Vorsicht *f* care; **~!** look out; *(Schild)* caution; **~ Stufe!** mind the step; **vorsichtig** *adj* careful; **vorsichtshalber** *adv* just in case

Vorsorge *f* precaution; *(Vorbeugung)* prevention; **Vorsorgeuntersuchung** *f* checkup; **vorsorglich** *adv* as a precaution

Vorspann *(-(e)s, -e)* *m* credits *pl*

Vorspeise *f* starter

Vorsprung *m* projection; *(Abstand)* lead

vor|stellen *vt (bekannt machen)* to introduce; *(Uhr)* to put forward; *(vor etw)* to put in front; **sich** *(dat)* **etw ~** to imagine sth; **Vorstellung** *f (Bekanntmachung)* introduction; *(Theat)* performance; *(Gedanke)* idea; **Vorstellungsgespräch** *nt* interview

vor|täuschen *vt* to feign

Vorteil *m* advantage *(gegenüber* over); **die Vor- und Nachteile** the pros and cons; **vorteilhaft** *adj* advantageous

Vortrag *(-(e)s, Vorträge)* *m* talk *(über +akk* on); *(akademisch)* lecture; **einen ~ halten** to give a talk

vorüber *adv* over; **vorüber|gehen** *irr vi* to pass; **vorübergehend** *adj* temporary

▷ *adv* temporarily, for the time being

Vorurteil *nt* prejudice

Vorverkauf *m* advance booking

vor|verlegen *vt* to bring forward

Vorwahl *f (Tel)* dialling code *(Brit)*, area code *(US)*

Vorwand *(-(e)s, Vorwände)* *m* pretext, excuse; **unter dem ~, dass** with the excuse that

vorwärts *adv* forward; **vorwärts|gehen** *irr vi (fig)* to progress

vorweg *adv* in advance; **vorweg|nehmen** *irr vt* to anticipate

Vorweihnachtszeit *f* pre-Christmas period, run-up to Christmas *(Brit)*

vor|werfen *irr vt:* **jdm etw ~** to accuse sb of sth

vorwiegend *adv* mainly

Vorwort *nt* preface

Vorwurf *m* reproach; **sich** *(dat)* **Vorwürfe machen** to reproach oneself; **jdm Vorwürfe machen** to accuse sb; **vorwurfsvoll** *adj* reproachful

vor|zeigen *vt* to show

vorzeitig *adj* premature, early

vor|ziehen *irr vt (lieber haben)* to prefer

Vorzug *m* preference; *(gute Eigenschaft)* merit; *(Vorteil)* advantage

vorzüglich *adj* excellent

vulgär *adj* vulgar

Vulkan *(-s, -e)* *m* volcano; **Vulkanausbruch** *m* volcanic eruption

V

W _abk_ = **West** W

Waage (-, -n) _f_ scales _pl_; (_Astr_) Libra; **waagerecht** _adj_ horizontal

wach _adj_ awake; **~ werden** to wake up; **Wache** (-, -n) _f_ guard

Wachs (-es, -e) _nt_ wax

wachsen (wuchs, gewachsen) _vi_ to grow

wachsen _vt_ (_Skier_) to wax

Wachstum _nt_ growth

Wachtel (-, -n) _f_ quail

Wächter(in) (-s, -) _m(f)_ guard; (_auf Parkplatz_) attendant

wackelig _adj_ wobbly; (_fig_) shaky; **Wackelkontakt** _m_ loose connection; **wackeln** _vi_ to be wobbly; (_Zahn, Schraube_) to be loose; **mit dem Kopf ~** to waggle one's head

Wade (-, -n) _f_ (_Anat_) calf

Waffe (-, -n) _f_ weapon

Waffel (-, -n) _f_ waffle; (_Keks, Eiswaffel_) wafer

wagen _vt_ to risk; **es ~, etw zu tun** to dare to do sth

Wagen (-s, -) _m_ (_Auto_) car; (_Eisenb_) carriage; **Wagenheber** (-s, -) _m_ jack; **Wagentyp** _m_ model, make

Wahl (-, -en) _f_ choice; (_Pol_) election

wählen _vt_ to choose; (_Tel_) to dial; (_Pol_) to vote for; (_durch Wahl ermitteln_) to elect ▷ _vi_ to choose; (_Tel_) to dial; (_Pol_) to vote; **Wähler(in)** (-s, -) _m(f)_ voter; **wählerisch** _adj_ choosy

Wahlkampf _m_ election campaign; **wahllos** _adv_ at random; **Wahlwiederholung** _f_ redial

Wahnsinn _m_ madness; **~!** amazing!; **wahnsinnig** _adj_ insane, mad ▷ _adv_ (_fam_) incredibly

wahr _adj_ true; **das darf doch nicht ~ sein!** I don't believe it!; **nicht ~?** that's right, isn't it?

während _prep_ +_gen_ during ▷ _conj_ while; **währenddessen** _adv_ meanwhile, in the meantime

Wahrheit _f_ truth

wahrnehmbar _adj_ noticeable, perceptible; **wahr|nehmen** _irr vt_ to perceive

Wahrsager(in) (-s, -) _m(f)_ fortune-teller

wahrscheinlich _adj_ probable, likely ▷ _adv_ probably; **ich komme ~ zu spät** I'll probably be late; **Wahrscheinlichkeit** _f_ probability

Währung _f_ currency

Wahrzeichen _nt_ symbol

Waise (-, -n) _f_ orphan

Wal (-(e)s, -e) _m_ whale

Wald (-(e)s, Wälder) _m_ wood; (_groß_) forest; **Waldbrand** _m_ forest fire; **Waldsterben** (-s) _nt_ forest dieback

Wales (-) nt Wales; **Waliser(in)** m(f) Welshman/Welshwoman; **walisisch** adj Welsh; **Walisisch** nt Welsh

Walkie-Talkie (-(s), -s) nt walkie-talkie

Walkman® (-s, -s) m walkman®, personal stereo

Wall (-(e)s, Wälle) m embankment

Wallfahrt f pilgrimage; **Wallfahrtsort** m place of pilgrimage

Walnuss f walnut

Walross (-es, -e) nt walrus

wälzen vt to roll; (Bücher) to pore over; (Probleme) to deliberate on ▷ vr: **sich ~** to wallow; (vor Schmerzen) to roll about; (im Bett) to toss and turn

Walzer (-s, -) m waltz

Wand (-, Wände) f wall; (Trenn~) partition; (Berg~) (rock) face

Wandel (-s) m change; **wandeln** vt to change ▷ vr: **sich ~** to change

Wanderer (-s, -) m, **Wanderin** f hiker; **Wanderkarte** f hiking map; **wandern** vi to hike; (Blick) to wander; (Gedanken) to stray; **Wanderschuh** m walking shoe; **Wanderstiefel** m hiking boot; **Wanderung** f hike; **eine ~ machen** to go on a hike; **Wanderweg** m walking (o hiking) trail

Wandleuchte f wall lamp; **Wandmalerei** f mural; **Wandschrank** m built-in cupboard (Brit), closet (US)

wandte imperf von **wenden**

Wange (-, -n) f cheek

wann adv when; **seit ~ ist sie da?** how long has she been here?; **bis ~ bleibt ihr?** how long are you staying?

Wanne (-, -n) f (bath) tub

Wappen (-s, -) nt coat of arms

war imperf von **sein**

warb imperf von **werben**

Ware (-, -n) f product; **~n** goods pl; **Warenhaus** nt department store; **Warenprobe** f sample; **Warenzeichen** nt trademark

warf imperf von **werfen**

warm adj warm; (Essen) hot; **~ laufen** to warm up; **mir ist es zu ~** I'm too warm; **Wärme** (-, -n) f warmth; **wärmen** vt to warm; (Essen) to warm (o to heat) up ▷ vi (Kleidung, Sonne) to be warm ▷ vr: **sich ~** to warm up; (gegenseitig) to keep each other warm; **Wärmflasche** f hot-water bottle; **Warmstart** m (Inform) warm start

Warnblinkanlage f (Auto) warning flasher; **Warndreieck** nt (Auto) warning triangle; **warnen** vt to warn (vor +dat about, of); **Warnung** f warning

Warteliste f waiting list; **warten** vi to wait (auf +akk for); **warte mal!** wait (o hang on) a minute ▷ vt (Tech) to service

Wärter(in) m(f) attendant

Wartesaal m, **Wartezimmer** nt waiting room

Wartung f service; (das Warten) servicing

warum adv why

Warze (-, -n) f wart

was pron what; (fam: etwas) something; **~ kostet das?** what does it cost? how much is it?; **~ für ein Auto ist das?** what kind of car is that?; **~ für eine Farbe/Größe?** what colour/size?; **~?** (fam: wie bitte?) what?; **~ ist/gibt's?** what is it? what's up? **du weißt, ~ ich meine** you know what I mean; **~ (auch) immer** whatever; **soll ich dir ~ mitbringen?** do you want me to bring you anything?; **alles, ~ er hat** everything he's got

w

Waschanlage f (Auto) car wash;
waschbar adj washable;
Waschbär m raccoon;
Waschbecken nt washbasin

Wäsche (-, -n) f washing;
(schmutzig) laundry; (Bettwäsche)
linen; (Unterwäsche) underwear; **in
der ~** in the wash;
Wäscheklammer f clothes peg
(Brit) (o pin (US)); **Wäscheleine** f
clothesline

waschen (wusch, gewaschen) vt, vi
to wash ▷ vr: **sich ~** to (have a)
wash; **sich** (dat) **die Haare ~** to
wash one's hair

Wäscherei f laundry;
Wäscheständer m clothes horse;
Wäschetrockner m tumble-drier

Waschgelegenheit f washing
facilities pl; **Waschlappen** m
flannel (Brit), washcloth (US); (fam:
Mensch) wet blanket;
Waschmaschine f washing
machine; **Waschmittel** nt,
Waschpulver nt washing
powder; **Waschraum** m
washroom; **Waschsalon** (-s, -s) m
launderette (Brit), laundromat
(US); **Waschstraße** f car wash

Wasser (-s, -) nt water;
fließendes ~ running water;
Wasserball m (Sport) water polo;
Wasserbob m jet ski;
wasserdicht adj watertight; (Uhr
etc) waterproof; **Wasserfall** m
waterfall; **Wasserfarbe** f
watercolour; **wasserfest** adj
watertight, waterproof;
Wasserhahn m tap (Brit), faucet
(US); **wässerig** adj watery;
Wasserkessel (-s, -) m kettle;
Wasserkocher (-s, -) m electric
kettle; **Wasserleitung** f water
pipe; **wasserlöslich** adj
water-soluble; **Wassermann** m
(Astr) Aquarius; **Wassermelone** f
water melon; **Wasserrutschbahn** f

f water chute; **Wasserschaden**
m water damage; **wasserscheu**
adj scared of water; **Wasserski**
nt water-skiing; **Wasserspiegel**
m surface of the water;
(Wasserstand) water level;
Wassersport m water sports pl;
wasserundurchlässig adj
watertight, waterproof;
Wasserverbrauch m water
consumption;
Wasserversorgung f water
supply; **Wasserwaage** f spirit
level; **Wasserwerk** nt
waterworks pl

waten vi to wade

Watt (-(e)s, -en) nt (Geo) mud flats
pl ▷ (-s, -) nt (Elek) watt

Watte (-, -n) f cotton wool;
Wattepad (-s, -s) m cotton pad;
Wattestäbchen nt cotton bud,
Q-tip® (US)

WC (-s, -s) nt toilet, restroom
(US); **WC-Reiniger** m toilet
cleaner

Web (-s) nt (Inform) Web;
Webadresse f (Inform) web
address; **Webseite** f (Inform) web
page

Wechsel (-s, -) m change;
(Spieler~: Sport) substitution;
Wechselgeld nt change;
wechselhaft adj (Wetter)
changeable; **Wechseljahre** pl
menopause sing; **Wechselkurs** m
exchange rate; **wechseln** vt to
change; (Blicke) to exchange; **Geld
~** to change some money; (in
Kleingeld) to get some change;
Euro in Pfund ~ to change euros
into pounds ▷ vi to change;
kannst du ~? can you change this?;
Wechselstrom m alternating
current, AC; **Wechselstube** f
bureau de change

Weckdienst m wake-up call
service; **wecken** vt to wake (up);

Wecker (-s, -) m alarm clock; Weckruf m wake-up call

wedeln vi (Ski) to wedel; **mit etw ~** to wave sth; **mit dem Schwanz ~** to wag its tail; **der Hund wedelte mit dem Schwanz** the dog wagged its tail

weder conj: **~ ... noch ...** neither ... nor ...

weg adv (entfernt, verreist) away; (los, ab) off; **er war schon ~** he had already left (o gone); **Hände ~!** hands off!; **weit ~** a long way away (o off)

Weg (-(e)s, -e) m way; (Pfad) path; (Route) route; **jdn nach dem ~ fragen** to ask sb the way; **auf dem ~ sein** to be on the way

weg|bleiben irr vi to stay away; weg|bringen irr vt to take away

wegen prep +gen o dat because of

weg|fahren irr vi to drive away; (abfahren) to leave; (in Urlaub) to go away; Wegfahrsperre f (Auto) (engine) immobilizer; weg|gehen irr vi to go away; weg|kommen irr vi to get away; (fig) **gut/schlecht ~** to come off well/badly; weg|lassen irr vt to leave out; weg|laufen irr vi to run away; weg|legen vt to put aside; weg|machen vt (fam) to get rid of; weg|müssen irr vi: **ich muss weg** I've got to go; weg|nehmen irr vt to take away; weg|räumen vt to clear away; weg|rennen irr vi to run away; weg|schicken vt to send away; weg|schmeißen irr vt to throw away; weg|sehen irr vi to look away; weg|tun irr vt to put away

Wegweiser (-s, -) m signpost

weg|werfen irr vt to throw away; weg|wischen vt to wipe off; weg|ziehen irr vi to move (away)

weh adj sore; siehe auch wehtun

wehen vt, vi to blow; (Fahne) to flutter

Wehen pl labour pains pl

Wehrdienst m military service

wehren vr: **sich ~** to defend oneself

weh|tun irr vi to hurt; **jdm/sich ~** to hurt sb/oneself

Weibchen nt: **es ist ein ~** (Tier) it's a she; **weiblich** adj feminine; (Bio) female

weich adj soft; **~ gekocht** (Ei) soft-boiled

Weichkäse m soft cheese; (Streichkäse) cheese spread; weichlich adj soft; (körperlich) weak; Weichspüler (-s, -) m (für Wäsche) (fabric) softener

Weide (-, -n) f (Baum) willow; (Grasfläche) meadow

weigern vr: **sich ~** to refuse; Weigerung f refusal

Weiher (-s, -) m pond

Weihnachten (-, -) nt Christmas; Weihnachtsabend m Christmas Eve; Weihnachtsbaum m Christmas tree;

Weihnachtsfeier f Christmas party; Weihnachtsferien pl Christmas holidays pl (Brit), Christmas vacation sing (US); Weihnachtsgeld nt Christmas bonus; Weihnachtsgeschenk nt Christmas present; Weihnachtskarte f Christmas card; Weihnachtslied nt Christmas carol; Weihnachtsmann m Father Christmas, Santa (Claus)

● **WEIHNACHTSMARKT**

● The **Weihnachtsmarkt** is a
● market held in most large
● towns in Germany in the weeks
● prior to Christmas. People visit
● it to buy presents, toys and

w

- Christmas decorations, and to
- enjoy the festive atmosphere.
- Food and drink associated with
- the Christmas festivities can
- also be eaten and drunk then,
- for example, gingerbread and
- mulled wine.

Weihnachtsstern m (Bot)
poinsettia; **Weihnachtstag** m:
erster ~ Christmas Day; **zweiter
~** Boxing Day; **Weihnachtszeit** f
Christmas season
weil conj because
Weile (-) f while, short time; **es
kann noch eine ~ dauern** it could
take some time
Wein (-(e)s, -e) m wine; (Pflanze)
vine; **Weinbeere** f grape;
Weinberg m vineyard;
Weinbergschnecke f snail;
Weinbrand m brandy
weinen vt, vi to cry
Weinglas nt wine glass;
Weinkarte f wine list;
Weinkeller m wine cellar;
Weinlese (-, -n) f vintage;
Weinprobe f wine tasting;
Weintraube f grape
weise adj wise
Weise (-, -n) f manner, way; **auf
diese (Art und) ~** this way
weisen (wies, gewiesen) vt to
show
Weisheit f wisdom;
Weisheitszahn m wisdom
tooth
weiß adj white; **Weißbier** nt ≈
wheat beer; **Weißbrot** nt white
bread; **weißhaarig** adj
white-haired; **Weißkohl** m,
Weißkraut nt (white) cabbage;
Weißwein m white wine
weit adj wide; (Begriff) broad;
(Reise, Wurf) long; (Kleid) loose; **wie
~ ist es ...?** how far is it ...?; **so
~ sein** to be ready ▷ adv far;

~ verbreitet widespread;
~ gereist widely travelled; **~ offen**
wide open; **das geht zu ~** that's
going too far, that's pushing it
weiter adj wider; (~ weg) farther
(away); (zusätzlich) further; **~e
Informationen** further
information sing ▷ adv further; **~!**
go on; (weitergehen) keep moving;
~ nichts/niemand
nothing/nobody else; **und so
~** and so on; **weiter|arbeiten** vi
to carry on working;
Weiterbildung f further training
(o education); **weiter|empfehlen**
irr vt to recommend;
weiter|erzählen vt: **nicht ~!**
don't tell anyone; **weiter|fahren**
irr vi to go on (nach to, bis as far
as); **weiter|geben** irr vt to pass
on; **weiter|gehen** irr vi to go on;
weiter|helfen irr vi: **jdm ~** to
help sb; **weiterhin** adv: **etw
~ tun** to go on doing sth;
weiter|machen vt, vi to
continue; **weiter|reisen** vi to
continue one's journey
weitgehend adj considerable
▷ adv largely; **weitsichtig** adj
long-sighted; (fig) far-sighted;
Weitsprung m long jump;
Weitwinkelobjektiv nt (Foto)
wide-angle lens
Weizen (-s, -) m wheat;
Weizenbier nt ≈ wheat beer

SCHLÜSSELWORT

welche(r, s) interrogativ pron
which; **welcher von beiden?**
which (one) of the two?; **welchen
hast du genommen?** which (one)
did you take?; **welche eine ...!**
what a ...!; **welche Freude!** what
joy! ▷ indef pron some; (in Fragen)
any; **ich habe welche** I have some;
haben Sie welche? do you have

any? ▷ *relativ pron (bei Menschen)* who; *(bei Sachen)* which, that; **welche(r, s) auch** immer whoever/whichever/whatever

welk *adj* withered; **welken** *vi* to wither

Welle (-, -n) *f* wave; **Wellengang** *m* waves *pl*; **starker ~** heavy seas *pl*; **Wellenlänge** *f* (*a. fig*) wavelength; **Wellenreiten** *nt* surfing; **Wellensittich** (-s, -e) *m* budgerigar, budgie; **wellig** *adj* wavy

Wellness *f* health and beauty (Brit), wellness (US)

Welpe (-n, -n) *m* puppy

Welt (-, -en) *f* world; **auf der ~** in the world; **auf die ~ kommen** to be born; **Weltall** *nt* universe; **weltbekannt**, **weltberühmt** *adj* world-famous; **Weltkrieg** *m* world war; **Weltmacht** *f* world power; **Weltmeister(in)** *m(f)* world champion; **Weltmeisterschaft** *f* world championship; *(im Fußball)* World Cup; **Weltraum** *m* space; **Weltreise** *f* trip round the world; **Weltrekord** *m* world record; **Weltstadt** *f* metropolis; **weltweit** *adj* worldwide, global

wem *pron dat von* **wer** who ..., (to) whom; **~ hast du's gegeben?** who did you give it to?; **~ gehört es?** who does it belong to?, whose is it?; **~ auch immer es gehört** whoever it belongs to

wen *pron akk von* **wer** who, whom; **~ hast du besucht?** who did you visit?; **~ möchten Sie sprechen?** who would you like to speak to?

Wende (-, -n) *f* turning point; *(Veränderung)* change; **die ~** *(Hist)* the fall of the Berlin Wall; **Wendekreis** *m (Auto)* turning circle

Wendeltreppe *f* spiral staircase

wenden (wendete o wandte, gewendet o gewandt) *vt, vi* to turn (round); *(um 180°)* to make a U-turn; **sich an jdn ~** to turn to sb; **bitte ~!** please turn over, PTO ▷ *vr*: **sich ~** to turn; **sich an jdn ~** to turn to sb

wenig *pron, adv* little; **~(e)** *pl* few; **(nur) ein (klein) ~** (just) a little (bit); **ein ~ Zucker** a little bit of sugar, a little sugar; **wir haben ~ Zeit** we haven't got much time; **zu ~** too little; *pl* too few; **nur ~ wissen** only a few know ▷ *adv*: **er spricht ~** he doesn't talk much; **~ bekannt** little known; **wenige** *pron pl* few *pl*; **wenigste(r, s)** *adj* least; **wenigstens** *adv* at least

⬤ **SCHLÜSSELWORT**

wenn *konj* 1 *(falls, bei Wünschen)* if; **wenn auch ...**, **selbst wenn ...** even if ...; **wenn ich doch ...** if only I ...

2 *(zeitlich)* when; **immer wenn** whenever

wennschon *adv*: **na ~** so what?

wer *pron* who; **~ war das?** who was that?; **~ von euch?** which (one) of you? ▷ *pron* anybody who, anyone who; **~ das glaubt, ist dumm** anyone who believes that is stupid; **~ auch immer** whoever ▷ *pron* somebody, someone; *(in Fragen)* anybody, anyone; **ist da ~?** is (there) anybody there?

Werbefernsehen *nt* TV commercials *pl*; **Werbegeschenk** *nt* promotional gift; **werben** (warb, geworben) *vt* to win; *(Mitglied)* to recruit ▷ *vi* to advertise; **Werbespot** (-s, -s) *m* commercial; **Werbung** *f* advertising

W

○ SCHLÜSSELWORT

werden (pt **wurde**, pp **geworden** o (bei Passiv) **worden**) vi to become; **was ist aus ihm/aus der Sache geworden?** what became of him/it?; **es ist nichts/gut geworden** it came to nothing/turned out well; **es wird Nacht/Tag** it's getting dark/light; **mir wird kalt** I'm getting cold; **mir wird schlecht** I feel ill; **Erster werden** to come o be first; **das muss anders werden** that'll have to change; **rot/zu Eis werden** to turn red/to ice; **was willst du (mal) werden?** what do you want to be?; **die Fotos sind gut geworden** the photos have come out nicely

▷ als Hilfsverb **1** (bei Futur) **er wird es tun** he will o he'll do it; **er wird das nicht tun** he will not o he won't do it; **es wird gleich regnen** it's going to rain

2 (bei Konjunktiv) **ich würde ...** I would ...; **er würde gern ...** he would o he'd like to ...; **ich würde lieber ...** I would o I'd rather ...

3 (bei Vermutung) **sie wird in der Küche sein** she will be in the kitchen

4 (bei Passiv) **gebraucht werden** to be used; **er ist erschossen worden** he has o he's been shot; **mir wurde gesagt, dass ...** I was told that ...

werfen (warf, geworfen) vt to throw

Werft (-, -en) f shipyard; dockyard

Werk (-(e)s, -e) nt (Kunstwerk, Buch etc) work; (Fabrik) factory; (Mechanismus) works pl; **Werkstatt** (-, -stätten) f workshop; (Auto)

garage; **Werktag** m working day; **werktags** adv on weekdays, during the week; **Werkzeug** nt tool; **Werkzeugkasten** m toolbox

wert adj worth; **es ist etwa 50 Euro ~** it's worth about 50 euros; **das ist nichts ~** it's worthless; **Wert** (-(e)s, -e) m worth; (Zahlen~) (Fin) value; **~ legen auf** (+akk) to attach importance to; **es hat doch keinen ~** (Sinn) it's pointless; **Wertangabe** f declaration of value; **Wertbrief** m insured letter; **Wertgegenstand** m valuable object; **wertlos** adj worthless; **Wertmarke** f token; **Wertpapiere** pl securities pl; **Wertsachen** pl valuables pl; **Wertstoff** m recyclable waste; **wertvoll** adj valuable

Wesen (-s, -) nt being; (Natur, Charakter) nature

wesentlich adj significant; (beträchtlich) considerable ▷ adv considerably

weshalb adv why

Wespe (-, -n) f wasp; **Wespenstich** m wasp sting

wessen pron gen von **wer**; whose

● WESSI

● A **Wessi** is a colloquial and often
● derogatory word used to
● describe a German from the
● former West Germany. The
● expression 'Besserwessi' is used
● by East Germans to describe a
● West German who is considered
● to be a know-all.

West west; **Westdeutschland** nt (als Landesteil) Western Germany; (Hist) West Germany **Weste** (-, -n) f waistcoat (Brit), vest (US); (Wollweste) cardigan

Westen (-s) *m* west; **im ~ Englands** in the west of England; **der Wilde ~** the Wild West; **Westeuropa** *nt* Western Europe; **Westküste** *f* west coast; **westlich** *adj* western; (*Kurs, Richtung*) westerly; **Westwind** *m* west(erly) wind

weswegen *adv* why

Wettbewerb *m* competition; **Wettbüro** *nt* betting office; **Wette** (-, -n) *f* bet; **eine ~ abschließen** to make a bet; **die ~ gilt!** you're on; **wetten** *vt, vi* to bet (*auf +akk* on); **ich habe mit ihm gewettet, dass ...** I bet him that ...; **ich wette mit dir um 50 Euro** I'll bet you 50 euros; **~, dass?** wanna bet?

Wetter (-s, -) *nt* weather; **Wetterbericht** *m*, **Wettervorhersage** *f* weather forecast; **Wetterkarte** *f* weather map; **Wetterlage** *f* weather situation; **Wettervorhersage** *f* weather forecast

Wettkampf *m* contest; **Wettlauf** *m* race; **Wettrennen** *nt* race

WG (-, -s) *f abk* = **Wohngemeinschaft**

Whirlpool® (-s, -s) *m* Jacuzzi®

Whisky (-s, -s) *m* (*schottisch*) whisky; (*irisch, amerikanisch*) whiskey

wichtig *adj* important

wickeln *vt* (*Schnur*) to wind (*um* round); (*Schal, Decke*) to wrap (*um* round); **ein Baby ~** to change a baby's nappy (*Brit*) (o diaper (US)); **Wickelraum** *m* baby-changing room; **Wickeltisch** *m* baby-changing table

Widder (-s, -) *m* (*Zool*) ram; (*Astr*) Aries *sing*

wider *prep +akk* against

widerlich *adj* disgusting

widerrufen *irr vt* to withdraw; (*Auftrag, Befehl etc*) to cancel

widersprechen *irr vi* to contradict (*jdm* sb); **Widerspruch** *m* contradiction

Widerstand *m* resistance; **widerstandsfähig** *adj* resistant (*gegen* to)

widerwärtig *adj* disgusting

widerwillig *adj* unwilling

widmen *vt* to dedicate ▷ *vr*: **sich jdm/etw ~** to devote oneself to sb/sth; **Widmung** *f* dedication

○ SCHLÜSSELWORT

wie *adv* how; **wie groß/schnell?** how big/fast?; **wie wär's?** how about it?; **wie ist er?** what's he like?; **wie gut du das kannst!** you're very good at it; **wie bitte?** pardon?; (*entrüstet*) I beg your pardon!; **und wie!** and how!; **wie viel** how much; **wie viele Menschen** how many people; **wie weit** to what extent

▷ *konj* 1 (*bei Vergleichen*) **so schön wie ...** as beautiful as ...; **wie ich schon sagte** as I said; **wie du wie** you; **singen wie ein ...** to sing like a ...; **wie (zum Beispiel)** such as (for example)

2 (*zeitlich*) **wie er das hörte, ging er** when he heard that he left; **er hörte, wie der Regen fiel** he heard the rain falling

wieder *adv* again; **~ ein(e) ...** another ...; **~ erkennen** to recognize; **etw ~ gutmachen** to make up for sth; **~ verwerten** to recycle

wieder|bekommen *irr vt* to get back

wiederbeschreibbar *adj* (*CD, DVD*) rewritable

W

wiederholen vt to repeat;
Wiederholung f repetition
Wiederhören nt (Tel) **auf
~ goodbye**
wieder|kommen irr vi to come
back
wieder|sehen irr vt to see
again; (wieder treffen) to meet
again; **Wiedersehen** (-s) nt
reunion; **auf ~!** goodbye
Wiedervereinigung f
reunification
Wiege (-, -n) f cradle; **wiegen**
(wog, gewogen) vt, vi to weigh
Wien (-s) nt Vienna
wies imperf von **weisen**
Wiese (-, -n) f meadow
Wiesel (-s, -) nt weasel
wieso adv why
wievielmal adv how often;
wievielte(r, s) adj: **zum ~n Mal?**
how many times?; **den
Wievielten haben wir heute?**
what's the date today?; **am
Wievielten hast du Geburtstag?**
which day is your birthday?
wieweit conj to what extent
Wi-Fi nt Wi-Fi
wild adj wild
Wild (-(e)s) nt game
wildfremd adj (fam) **ein ~er
Mensch** a complete (o total)
stranger; **Wildleder** nt suede;
Wildpark m game park;
Wildschwein nt (wild) boar;
Wildwasserfahren (-s) nt
whitewater rafting
Wille (-ns, -n) m will
willen prep +gen **um ... ~** for the
sake of ...; **um Himmels ~!**
(vorwurfsvoll) for heaven's sake!;
(betroffen) goodness me
willkommen adj welcome; **jdn
~ heißen** to welcome sb
Wimper (-, -n) f eyelash;
Wimperntusche f mascara
Wind (-(e)s, -e) m wind

Windel (-, -n) f nappy (Brit),
diaper (US)
windgeschützt adj sheltered
from the wind; **windig** adj windy;
(fig) dubious; **Windjacke** f
windcheater; **Windmühle** f
windmill; **Windpark** m wind
farm; **Windpocken** pl chickenpox
sing; **Windschutzscheibe** f (Auto)
windscreen (Brit), windshield (US);
Windstärke f wind force;
Windsurfen (-s) nt windsurfing;
Windsurfer(in) m(f) windsurfer
Winkel (-s, -) m (Math) angle;
(Gerät) set square; (in Raum)
corner; **im rechten ~ zu** at right
angles to
winken vt, vi to wave
Winter (-s, -) m winter;
Winterausrüstung f (Auto)
winter equipment;
Winterfahrplan m winter
timetable; **winterlich** adj
wintry; **Wintermantel** m winter
coat; **Winterreifen** m winter
tyre; **Winterschlussverkauf** m
winter sales pl; **Wintersport** m
winter sports pl
Winterzeit f (Uhrzeit) winter
time (Brit), standard time (US)
winzig adj tiny
wir pron we; **~ selbst** we
ourselves; **~ alle** all of us; **~ drei**
the three of us; **~ sind's** it's us;
~ nicht not us
Wirbel (-s, -) m whirl; (Trubel)
hurly-burly; (Aufsehen) fuss; (Anat)
vertebra; **Wirbelsäule** f spine
wirken vi to be effective;
(erfolgreich sein) to work; (scheinen)
to seem
wirklich adj real; **Wirklichkeit** f
reality
wirksam adj effective; **Wirkung**
f effect
wirr adj confused; **Wirrwarr** (-s)
m confusion

Wirsing (-s) m savoy cabbage
Wirt (-(e)s, -e) m landlord; **Wirtin**
f landlady
Wirtschaft f (Comm) economy;
(Gaststätte) pub; **wirtschaftlich**
adj (Pol, Comm) economic;
(sparsam) economical
Wirtshaus nt pub
wischen vt, vi to wipe; **Wischer**
(-s, -) m wiper
wissen (wusste, gewusst) vt to
know; **weißt du schon, ...?** did
you know ...?; **woher weißt du
das?** how do you know?; **das
musst du selbst ~** that's up to
you; **Wissen** (-s) nt knowledge
Wissenschaft f science;
Wissenschaftler(in) (-s, -) m(f)
scientist; (Geisteswissenschaftler)
academic; **wissenschaftlich** adj
scientific; (geisteswissenschaftlich)
academic
Witwe (-, -n) f widow; **Witwer**
(-s, -) m widower
Witz (-(e)s, -e) m joke; **mach
keine ~e!** you're kidding!; **das soll
wohl ein ~ sein** you've got to be
joking; **witzig** adj funny
wo adv where; **zu einer Zeit, ~ ...**
at a time when ...; **überall, ~ ich
hingehe** wherever I go ▷ conj:
jetzt, ~ du da bist now that you're
here; **~ ich gerade spreche**
while I'm talking to you;
woanders adv somewhere else
wobei adv: **~ mir einfällt ...**
which reminds me ...
Woche (-, -n) f week; **während** (o
unter) **der ~** during the week;
einmal die ~ once a week;
Wochenende nt weekend; **am
~** at (Brit) (o on (US)) the weekend;
wir fahren übers ~ weg we're
going away for the weekend;
Wochenendhaus nt weekend
cottage; **Wochenendtrip** m
weekend trip; **Wochenendurlaub**

m weekend break; **Wochenkarte**
f weekly (season) ticket;
wochenlang adv for weeks (on
end); **Wochenmarkt** m weekly
market; **Wochentag** m weekday;
wöchentlich adj, adv
weekly
Wodka (-s, -s) m vodka
wodurch adv: **~ unterscheiden
sie sich?** what's the difference
between them?; **~ hast du es
gemerkt?** how did you notice?;
wofür adv (relativ) for which;
(Frage) what ... for; **~ brauchst du
das?** what do you need that for?
wog imperf von **wiegen**
woher adv where ... from; **wohin**
adv where ... to

⊙ SCHLÜSSELWORT

wohl adv 1 wohl oder übel
whether one likes it or not
2 (wahrscheinlich) probably; (gewiss)
certainly; (vielleicht) perhaps; **sie
ist wohl zu Hause** she's probably
at home; **das ist doch wohl nicht
dein Ernst!** surely you're not
serious; **das mag wohl sein** that
may well be; **ob das wohl stimmt?**
I wonder if that's true; **er weiß das
sehr wohl** he knows that perfectly
well

Wohl (-(e)s) nt: **zum ~!** cheers;
wohlbehalten adv safe and
sound; **wohl|fühlen** vr: **sich
~ (zufrieden)** to feel happy;
(gesundheitlich) to feel well;
Wohlstand m prosperity,
affluence; **wohl|tun** irr vi: **jdm
~** to do sb good; **Wohlwollen** nt
goodwill
Wohnblock m block of flats
(Brit), apartment house (US);
wohnen vi to live;
Wohngemeinschaft f shared flat

(Brit) (o apartment (US)); **ich wohne in einer ~** I share a flat (o apartment); **wohnhaft** adj resident; **Wohnküche** f kitchen-cum-living-room; **Wohnmobil** (-s, -e) nt camper, RV (US); **Wohnort** m place of residence; **Wohnsitz** m place of residence; **Wohnung** f flat (Brit), apartment (US); **Wohnungstür** f front door; **Wohnwagen** m caravan; **Wohnzimmer** nt living room

Wolf (-(e)s, Wölfe) m wolf
Wolke (-, -n) f cloud; **Wolkenkratzer** m skyscraper; **wolkenlos** adj cloudless; **wolkig** adj cloudy
Wolldecke f (woollen) blanket; **Wolle** (-, -n) f wool

○ SCHLÜSSELWORT

wollen (pt **wollte**, pp **gewollt** o (als Hilfsverb) **wollen**) vt, vi to want; **ich will nach Hause** I want to go home; **er will nicht** he doesn't want to; **er wollte das nicht** he didn't want it; **wenn du willst** if you like; **ich will, dass du mir zuhörst** I want you to listen to me ▷ Hilfsverb: **er will ein Haus kaufen** he wants to buy a house; **ich wollte, ich wäre ...** I wish I were ...; **etw gerade tun wollen** to be going to do sth

Wolljacke f cardigan
womit adv what ... with; **~ habe ich das verdient?** what have I done to deserve that?
womöglich adv possibly
woran adv: **~ denkst du?** what are you thinking of?; **~ ist er gestorben?** what did he die of?; **~ sieht man das?** how can you tell?

worauf adv: **~ wartest du?** what are you waiting for?
woraus adv: **~ ist das gemacht?** what is it made of?
Workshop (-s, -s) m workshop
World Wide Web nt World Wide Web
Wort (-(e)s, Wörter) nt (Vokabel) word ▷ (-(e)s, -e) nt (Äußerung) word; **mit anderen ~en** in other words; **jdn beim ~ nehmen** to take sb at his/her word; **Wörterbuch** nt dictionary; **wörtlich** adj literal
worüber adv: **~ redet sie?** what is she talking about?
worum adv: **~ gehts?** what is it about?
worunter adv: **~ leidet er?** what is he suffering from?
wovon adv (relativ) from which; **~ redest du?** what are you talking about?; **wozu** adv (relativ) to/for which; (interrogativ) what ... for/to; (warum) why; **~?** what for?; **~ brauchst du das?** what do you need it for?; **~ soll das gut sein?** what's it for?; **~ hast du Lust?** what do you feel like doing?
Wrack (-(e)s, -s) nt wreck
Wucher (-s) m profiteering; **das ist ~!** that's daylight robbery!
wuchs imperf von **wachsen**
wühlen vi to rummage; (Tier) to root; (Maulwurf) to burrow
Wühltisch m bargain counter
wund adj sore; **Wunde** (-, -n) f wound
Wunder (-s, -) nt miracle; **es ist kein ~** it's no wonder; **wunderbar** adj wonderful, marvellous; **Wunderkerze** f sparkler; **Wundermittel** nt wonder cure; **wundern** vr: **sich ~** to be surprised (über +akk at) ▷ vt to surprise; **wunderschön** adj

beautiful; **wundervoll** *adj* wonderful

Wundsalbe *f* antiseptic ointment; **Wundstarrkrampf** *m* tetanus

Wunsch (-(e)s, Wünsche) *m* wish (*nach* for); **wünschen** *vt* to wish; **sich** (*dat*) **etw ~** to want sth; **ich wünsche dir alles Gute** I wish you all the best; **wünschenswert** *adj* desirable

wurde *imperf von* **werden**

Wurf (-s, Würfe) *m* throw; (*Zool*) litter

Würfel (-s, -) *m* dice; (*Math*) cube; **würfeln** *vi* to throw (the dice); (*Würfel spielen*) to play dice ▷ *vt* (*Zahl*) to throw; (*Gastr*) to dice; **Würfelzucker** *m* lump sugar

Wurm (-(e)s, Würmer) *m* worm

Wurst (-, Würste) *f* sausage; **das ist mir ~** (*fam*) I couldn't care less

Würstchen *nt* frankfurter

Würze (-, -n) *f* seasoning, spice

Wurzel (-, -n) *f* root; **Wurzelbehandlung** *f* root canal treatment

würzen *vt* to season, to spice; **würzig** *adj* spicy

wusch *imperf von* **waschen**

wusste *imperf von* **wissen**

wüst *adj* (*unordentlich*) chaotic; (*ausschweifend*) wild; (*öde*) desolate; (*fam: heftig*) terrible

Wüste (-, -n) *f* desert

Wut (-) *f* rage, fury; **ich habe eine ~ auf ihn** I'm really mad at him; **wütend** *adj* furious

WWW (-) *nt abk* = **World Wide Web** WWW

X-Beine *pl* knock-knees *pl*; **x-beinig** *adj* knock-kneed

x-beliebig *adj*: **ein ~es Buch** any book (you like)

x-mal *adv* umpteen times

Xylophon (-s, -e) *nt* xylophone

y z

Yoga (-(s)) *m o nt* yoga
Yuppie (-s, -s) *m* (-, -s) *f* yuppie

zackig *adj* (*Linie etc*) jagged; (*fam:
Tempo*) brisk
zaghaft *adj* timid
zäh *adj* tough; (*Flüssigkeit*) thick
Zahl (-, -en) *f* number; **zahlbar**
adj payable; **zahlen** *vt, vi* to pay;
~ bitte! could I have the bill (*Brit*)
(o check (*US*)) please?; **bar ~** to pay
cash; **zählen** *vt, vi* to count (*auf
+akk* on); **~ zu** to be one of;
Zahlenschloss *nt* combination
lock; **Zähler** (-s, -) *m* (*Gerät*)
counter; (*für Strom, Wasser*) meter;
zahlreich *adj* numerous;
Zahlung *f* payment;
Zahlungsanweisung *f* money
order; **Zahlungsbedingungen** *pl*
terms *pl* of payment
zahm *adj* tame; **zähmen** *vt* to
tame
Zahn (-(e)s, *Zähne*) *m* tooth;
Zahnarzt *m*, **Zahnärztin** *f*
dentist; **Zahnbürste** *f*

toothbrush; **Zahncreme** f
toothpaste; **Zahnersatz** m
dentures pl; **Zahnfleisch** nt gums
pl; **Zahnfleischbluten** nt bleeding
gums pl; **Zahnfüllung** f filling;
Zahnklammer f brace;
Zahnpasta f, **Zahnpaste** f
toothpaste; **Zahnradbahn** f rack
railway (Brit) o railroad (US);
Zahnschmerzen pl toothache
sing; **Zahnseide** f dental floss;
Zahnspange f brace;
Zahnstocher (-s, -) m toothpick
Zange (-, -n) f pliers pl;
(Zuckerzange) tongs pl; (Beißzange,
Zool) pincers pl; (Med) forceps pl
zanken vi to quarrel
Zäpfchen nt (Anat) uvula; (Med)
suppository
zapfen vt (Bier) to pull; **Zapfsäule**
f petrol (Brit) o gas (US) pump
zappeln vi to wriggle; (unruhig
sein) to fidget
zappen vi to zap, to channel-hop
zart adj (weich, leise) soft; (Braten
etc) tender; (fein, schwächlich)
delicate; **zartbitter** adj
(Schokolade) plain, dark
zärtlich adj tender, affectionate;
Zärtlichkeit f tenderness; **~en** pl
hugs and kisses pl
Zauber (-s, -) m magic; (Bann)
spell; **Zauberei** f magic; **Zauberer**
(-s, -) m magician; (Künstler)
conjuror; **Zauberformel** f (magic)
spell; **zauberhaft** adj enchanting;
Zauberin f sorceress;
Zauberkünstler(in) m(f) magician,
conjuror; **Zaubermittel** nt magic
cure; **zaubern** vi to do magic; (als
Künstler) to do conjuring tricks;
Zauberspruch m (magic) spell
Zaun (-(e)s, Zäune) m fence
z. B. abk = **zum Beispiel** e.g., eg
ZDF nt = **Zweites Deutsches
Fernsehen** second German television
channel

Zebra (-s, -s) nt zebra;
Zebrastreifen m zebra crossing
(Brit), crosswalk (US)
Zecke (-, -n) f tick
Zehe (-, -n) f toe; (Knoblauch)
clove; **Zehennagel** m toenail;
Zehenspitze f tip of the toes
zehn num ten; **Zehnerkarte** f
ticket valid for ten trips; **Zehnkampf**
m decathlon; **Zehnkämpfer(in)**
m(f) decathlete; **zehnmal** adv ten
times; **zehntausend** num ten
thousand; **zehnte(r, s)** adj
tenth; siehe auch **dritte**; **Zehntel**
(-s, -) nt tenth; **Zehntelsekunde** f
tenth of a second
Zeichen (-s, -) nt sign;
(Schriftzeichen) character;
Zeichenblock m sketch pad;
Zeichenerklärung f key;
Zeichensetzung f punctuation;
Zeichensprache f sign language;
Zeichentrickfilm m cartoon
zeichnen vt, vi to draw;
Zeichnung f drawing
Zeigefinger m index finger;
zeigen vt to show; **sie zeigte uns
die Stadt** she showed us around
the town; **zeig mal!** let me see
▷ vi to point (auf +akk to, at) ▷ vr:
sich ~ to show oneself; **es wird
sich ~** time will tell; **Zeiger** (-s, -)
m pointer; (Uhr) hand
Zeile (-, -n) f line
Zeit (-, -en) f time; **ich habe keine
~** I haven't got time; **lass dir ~** take
your time; **das hat ~** there's no
rush; **von ~ zu ~** from time to
time; **Zeitansage** f (Tel)
speaking clock (Brit), correct time
(US); **Zeitarbeit** f temporary
work; **zeitgenössisch** adj
contemporary, modern; **zeitgleich**
adj simultaneous ▷ adv at exactly
the same time; **zeitig** adj early;
Zeitkarte f season ticket;
zeitlich adj (Reihenfolge)

chronological; **es passt ~ nicht** it isn't a convenient time; **ich schaff es ~ nicht** I'm not going to make it; **Zeitlupe** f slow motion; **Zeitplan** m schedule; **Zeitpunkt** m point in time; **Zeitraum** m period (of time); **Zeitschrift** f magazine; (wissenschaftliche) periodical

Zeitung f newspaper; **es steht in der ~** it's in the paper(s); **Zeitungsanzeige** f newspaper advertisement; **Zeitungsartikel** m newspaper article; **Zeitungskiosk** m, **Zeitungsstand** m newsstand

Zeitunterschied m time difference; **Zeitverschiebung** f time lag; **Zeitvertreib** (-(e)s, -e) m: **zum ~** to pass the time; **zeitweise** adv occasionally; **Zeitzone** f time zone

Zelle (-, -n) f cell

Zellophan® (-s) nt cellophane®

Zelt (-(e)s, -e) nt tent; **zelten** vi to camp, to go camping; **Zeltplatz** m campsite, camping site

Zement (-(e)s, -e) m cement

Zentimeter m or nt centimetre

Zentner (-s, -) m (metric) hundredweight; (in Deutschland) fifty kilos; (in Österreich und der Schweiz) one hundred kilos

zentral adj central; **Zentrale** (-, -n) f central office; (Tel) exchange; **Zentralheizung** f central heating; **Zentralverriegelung** f (Auto) central locking; **Zentrum** (-s, Zentren) nt centre

zerbrechen irr vt, vi to break; **zerbrechlich** adj fragile

Zeremonie (-, -n) f ceremony

zergehen irr vi to dissolve; (schmelzen) to melt

zerkleinern vt to cut up; (zerhacken) to chop (up);

chronological; **es passt ~ nicht** it isn't a convenient time; **ich schaff es ~ nicht**

zerkratzen vt to scratch; **zerlegen** vt to take to pieces; (Fleisch) to carve; (Gerät, Maschine) to dismantle; **zerquetschen** vt to squash; **zerreißen** irr vt to tear to pieces ▷ vi to tear

zerren vt to drag; **sich** (dat) **einen Muskel ~** to pull a muscle ▷ vi to tug (an +dat at); **Zerrung** f (Med) pulled muscle

zerschlagen irr vt to smash ▷ vr: **sich ~** to come to nothing

zerschneiden irr vt to cut up

zerstören vt to destroy; **Zerstörung** f destruction

zerstreuen vt to scatter; (Menge) to disperse; (Zweifel etc) to dispel ▷ vr: **sich ~** (Menge) to disperse; **zerstreut** adj scattered; (Mensch) absent-minded; (kurzfristig) distracted

zerteilen vt to split up

Zertifikat (-(e)s, -e) nt certificate

Zettel (-s, -) m piece of paper; (Notizzettel) note

Zeug (-(e)s, -e) nt (fam) stuff; (Ausrüstung) gear; **dummes ~** nonsense

Zeuge (-n, -n) m, **Zeugin** f witness

Zeugnis nt certificate; (Schule) report; (Referenz) reference

z. H(d). abk = **zu Händen von** attn

zickig adj (fam) touchy, bitchy

Zickzack (-(e)s, -e) m: **im ~ fahren** to zigzag (across the road)

Ziege (-, -n) f goat

Ziegel (-s, -) m brick; (Dach) tile

Ziegenkäse m goat's cheese; **Ziegenpeter** m mumps

ziehen (zog, gezogen) vt to draw; (zerren) to pull; (Spielfigur) to move; (züchten) to rear ▷ vi (zerren) to pull; (sich bewegen) to move; (Rauch, Wolke etc) to drift; **den Tee**

~ lassen to let the tea stand ▷ vi impers: **es zieht** there's a draught ▷ vr: **sich** ~ (Treffen, Rede) to drag on

Ziel (-(e)s, -e) nt (Reise) destination; (Sport) finish; (Absicht) goal, aim; **zielen** vi to aim (auf +akk at); **Zielgruppe** f target group; **ziellos** adj aimless; **Zielscheibe** f target

ziemlich adj considerable; **ein ~es Durcheinander** quite a mess; **mit ~er Sicherheit** with some certainty ▷ adv rather, quite; **~ viel** quite a lot

zierlich adj dainty; (Frau) petite

Ziffer (-, -n) f figure; **arabische/römische ~n** pl Arabic/Roman numerals pl; **Zifferblatt** nt dial, face

zig adj (fam) umpteen

Zigarette f cigarette; **Zigarettenautomat** m cigarette machine; **Zigarettenpapier** nt cigarette paper; **Zigarettenschachtel** f cigarette packet; **Zigarettenstummel** m cigarette end; **Zigarillo** (-s, -s) m cigarillo; **Zigarre** (-, -n) f cigar

Zigeuner(in) (-s, -) m(f) gipsy

Zimmer (-s, -) nt room; **haben Sie ein ~ für zwei Personen?** do you have a room for two?; **Zimmerlautstärke** f reasonable volume; **Zimmermädchen** nt chambermaid; **Zimmermann** m carpenter; **Zimmerpflanze** f house plant; **Zimmerschlüssel** m room key; **Zimmerservice** m room service; **Zimmervermittlung** f accommodation agency

Zimt (-(e)s, -e) m cinnamon; **Zimtstange** f cinnamon stick

Zink (-(e)s) nt zinc

Zinn (-(e)s) nt (Element) tin; (legiertes) pewter

Zinsen pl interest sing

Zipfel (-s, -) m corner; (spitz) tip; (Hemd) tail; (Wurst) end; **Zipfelmütze** f pointed hat

zirka adv about, approximately

Zirkel (-s, -) m (Math) (pair of) compasses pl

Zirkus (-, -se) m circus

zischen vi to hiss

Zitat (-(e)s, -e) nt quotation (aus from); **zitieren** vt to quote

Zitronat nt candied lemon peel; **Zitrone** (-, -n) f lemon; **Zitronenlimonade** f lemonade; **Zitronensaft** m lemon juice

zittern vi to tremble (vor +dat with)

zivil adj civilian; (Preis) reasonable; **Zivil** (-s) nt plain clothes pl; (Mil) civilian clothes pl; **Zivildienst** m community service (for conscientious objectors)

zocken vi (fam) to gamble

Zoff (-s) m (fam) trouble

zog imperf von **ziehen**

zögerlich adj hesitant; **zögern** vi to hesitate

Zoll (-(e)s, Zölle) m customs pl; (Abgabe) duty; **Zollabfertigung** f customs clearance; **Zollamt** nt customs office; **Zollbeamte(r)** m, **-beamtin** f customs official; **Zollerklärung** f customs declaration; **zollfrei** adj duty-free; **Zollgebühren** pl customs duties pl; **Zollkontrolle** f customs check; **Zöllner(in)** m(f) customs officer; **zollpflichtig** adj liable to duty

Zone (-, -n) f zone

Zoo (-s, -s) m zoo

Zoom (-s, -s) nt zoom (shot); (Objektiv) zoom (lens)

Zopf (-(e)s, Zöpfe) m plait (Brit), braid (US)

Zorn (-(e)s) m anger; **zornig** adj angry (über etw akk about sth, auf jdn with sb)

○ SCHLÜSSELWORT

zu prep +dat **1** (örtlich) to; **zum Bahnhof/Arzt gehen** to go to the station/doctor; **zur Schule/Kirche gehen** to go to school/church; **sollen wir zu euch gehen?** shall we go to your place?; **sie sah zu ihm hin** she looked towards him; **zum Fenster herein** through the window; **zu meiner Linken** to o on my left

2 (zeitlich) at; **zu Ostern** at Easter; **bis zum 1. Mai** until May 1st; (nicht später als) by May 1st; **zu meiner Zeit** in my time

3 (Zusatz) with; **Wein zum Essen trinken** to drink wine with one's meal; **sich zu jdm setzen** to sit down beside sb; **setz dich doch zu uns** (come and) sit with us; **Anmerkungen zu etw** notes on sth

4 (Zweck) for; **Wasser zum Waschen** water for washing; **Papier zum Schreiben** paper to write on; **etw zum Geburtstag bekommen** to get sth for one's birthday

5 (Veränderung) into; **zu etw werden** to turn into sth; **jdn zu etw machen** to make sb (into) sth; **zu Asche verbrennen** to burn to ashes

6 (mit Zahlen) **3 zu 2** (Sport) 3-2; **das Stück zu 5 Euro** at 5 euros each; **zum ersten Mal** for the first time

7 **zu meiner Freude** etc to my joy etc; **zum Glück** luckily; **zu Fuß** on foot; **es ist zum Weinen** it's enough to make you cry

▷ konj to; **etw zu essen** sth to eat; **um besser sehen zu können** in order to see better; **ohne es zu wissen** without knowing it; **noch zu bezahlende Rechnungen** bills

that are still to be paid

▷ adv **1** (allzu) too; **zu sehr** too much; **zu viel** too much; **zu wenig** too little

2 (örtlich) toward(s); **er kam auf mich zu** he came up to me

3 (geschlossen) shut, closed; **die Geschäfte haben zu** the shops are closed; **"auf/zu"** (Wasserhahn etc) "on/off"

4 (fam) (los) **nur zu!** just keep on!; **mach zu!** hurry up!

zuallererst adv first of all; **zuallerletzt** adv last of all

Zubehör (-(e)s, -e) nt accessories pl

zu|bereiten vt to prepare; **Zubereitung** f preparation

zu|binden irr vt to do (o tie) up

Zucchini pl courgettes pl (Brit), zucchini pl (US)

züchten vt (Tiere) to breed; (Pflanzen) to grow

zucken vi to jerk; (krampfhaft) to twitch; (Strahl etc) to flicker; **mit den Schultern ~** to shrug (one's shoulders)

Zucker (-s, -) m sugar; (Med) diabetes sing; **Zuckerdose** f sugar bowl; **zuckerkrank** adj diabetic; **Zuckerrohr** nt sugar cane; **Zuckerrübe** f sugar beet; **Zuckerwatte** f candy-floss (Brit), cotton candy (US)

zu|decken vt to cover up

zu|drehen vt to turn off

zueinander adv to one another; (mit Verb) together; **zueinander|halten** irr vi to stick together

zuerst adv first; (zu Anfang) at first; **~ einmal** first of all

Zufahrt f access; (Einfahrt) drive(way); **Zufahrtsstraße** f access road; (Autobahn) slip road (Brit), ramp (US)

Zufall m chance; (Ereignis) coincidence; **durch ~** by accident; **so ein ~!** what a coincidence; **zufällig** adj chance ▷ adv by chance; **weißt du ~, ob ...?** do you happen to know whether ...?

zufrieden adj content(ed); (befriedigt) satisfied; **lass sie ~** leave her alone; **zufrieden|geben** irr vr: **sich mit etw ~** to settle for sth; **Zufriedenheit** f contentment; (Befriedigtsein) satisfaction; **zufrieden|stellen** vt: **sie ist schwer zufriedenzustellen** she is hard to please

zu|fügen vt to add (dat to); **jdm Schaden/Schmerzen ~** to cause sb harm/pain

Zug (-(e)s, Züge) m (Eisenb) train; (Luft) draught; (Ziehen) pull; (Gesichtszug) feature; (Schach) move; (Charakterzug) trait; (an Zigarette) puff, drag; (Schluck) gulp

Zugabe f extra; (in Konzert etc) encore

Zugabteil nt train compartment

Zugang m access; **„kein ~!"** "no entry!"

Zugauskunft f (Stelle) train information office/desk; **Zugbegleiter(in)** m(f) guard (Brit), conductor (US)

zu|geben irr vt to admit; **zugegeben** adv admittedly

zu|gehen irr vi (schließen) to shut; **auf jdn/etw ~** to walk towards sb/sth; **dem Ende ~** to be coming to a close ▷ vi impers (sich ereignen) to happen; **es ging lustig zu** we/they had a lot of fun; **dort geht es streng zu** it's strict there

Zügel (-s, -) m rein

Zugführer(in) m(f) guard (Brit), conductor (US)

zugig adj draughty

zügig adj speedy

zugleich adv (zur gleichen Zeit) at the same time; (ebenso) both

Zugluft f draught

Zugpersonal nt train staff

zu|greifen irr vi (fig) to seize the opportunity; (beim Essen) to help oneself; **~ auf** (+akk) (Inform) to access

Zugrestaurant nt dining car, diner (US)

Zugriffsberechtigung f (Inform) access right

zugrunde adv: **~ gehen** to perish; **~ gehen an** (+dat) (sterben) to die of

Zugschaffner(in) m(f) ticket inspector; **Zugunglück** nt train crash

zugunsten prep +gen o dat in favour of

Zugverbindung f train connection

zu|haben irr vi to be closed

zu|halten irr vt: **sich (dat) die Nase ~** to hold one's nose; **sich (dat) die Ohren ~** to hold one's hands over one's ears; **die Tür ~** to hold the door shut

Zuhause (-s) nt home

zu|hören vi to listen (dat to); **Zuhörer(in)** m(f) listener

zu|kleben vt to seal

zu|kommen irr vi to come up (auf +akk to); **jdm etw ~ lassen** to give/send sb sth; **etw auf sich** (akk) **~ lassen** to take sth as it comes

zu|kriegen vt: **ich krieg den Koffer nicht zu** I can't shut the case

Zukunft (-, Zukünfte) f future; **zukünftig** adj future ▷ adv in future

zu|lassen irr vt (hereinlassen) to admit; (erlauben) to permit; (Auto) to license; (fam: nicht öffnen) to keep shut; **zulässig** adj permissible, permitted

zuletzt adv finally, at last
zuliebe adv: **jdm ~** for sb's sake
zum kontr von **zu dem**; **~ dritten Mal** for the third time; **~ Scherz** as a joke; **~ Trinken** for drinking
zu|machen vt to shut; (Kleidung) to do up ▷ vi to shut
zumindest adv at least
zu|muten vt: **jdm etw ~** to expect sth of sb ▷ vr **sich** (dat) **zu viel ~** to overdo things
zunächst adv first of all; **~ einmal** to start with
Zunahme (-, -n) f increase
Zuname m surname, last name
zünden vt, vi (Auto) to ignite, to fire; **Zündkabel** f (Auto) ignition cable; **Zündkerze** f (Auto) spark plug; **Zündschloss** nt ignition lock; **Zündschlüssel** m ignition key; **Zündung** f ignition
zu|nehmen irr vi to increase; (Mensch) to put on weight ▷ vt: **5 Kilo ~** to put on 5 kilos
Zunge (-, -n) f tongue
Zungenkuss m French kiss
zunichte|machen vt (zerstören) to ruin
zunutze adv **sich** (dat) **etw ~ machen** to make use of sth
zu|parken vt to block
zur kontr von **zu der**
zurecht|finden irr vr: **sich ~** to find one's way around;
zurecht|kommen irr vi to cope (mit etw with sth);
zurecht|machen vt to prepare ▷ vr: **sich ~** to get ready
Zürich (-s) nt Zurich
zurück adv back
zurück|bekommen irr vt to get back; **zurück|blicken** vi to look back (auf +akk at); **zurück|bringen** irr vt (hierhin) to bring back; (woandershin) to take back; **zurück|erstatten** vt to refund; **zurück|fahren** irr vi to go back;

zurück|geben irr vt to give back; (antworten) to answer; **zurück|gehen** irr vi to go back; (zeitlich) to date back (auf +akk to); **zurück|halten** irr vt to hold back; (hindern) to prevent ▷ vr: **sich ~** to hold back; **zurückhaltend** adj reserved
zurück|holen vt to fetch back; **zurück|kommen** irr vi to come back; **auf etw** (akk) **~** to return (o get back) to sth; **zurück|lassen** irr vt to leave behind; **zurück|legen** vt to put back; (Geld) to put by; (reservieren) to keep back; (Strecke) to cover; **zurück|nehmen** irr vt to take back; **zurück|rufen** irr vt to call back; **zurück|schicken** vt to send back; **zurück|stellen** vt to put back; **zurück|treten** irr vi to step back; (von Amt) to retire; **zurück|verlangen** vt: **etw ~** to ask for sth back; **zurück|zahlen** vt to pay back
zurzeit adv at present
Zusage f promise; (Annahme) acceptance; **zu|sagen** vt to promise ▷ vi to accept; **jdm ~** (gefallen) to appeal to sb
zusammen adv together
Zusammenarbeit f collaboration; **zusammen|arbeiten** vi to work together
zusammen|brechen irr vi to collapse; (psychisch) to break down; **Zusammenbruch** m collapse; (psychischer) breakdown
zusammen|fassen vt to summarize; (vereinigen) to unite; **zusammenfassend** adj summarizing ▷ adv to summarize; **Zusammenfassung** f summary
zusammen|gehören vi to belong together; **zusammen|halten** irr vi to stick together

Zusammenhang m connection; **im/aus dem ~** in/out of context; **zusammen|hängen** irr vi to be connected; **zusammenhängend** adj coherent; **zusammenhang(s)los** adj incoherent

zusammen|klappen vi, vt to fold up

zusammen|knüllen vt to screw up

zusammen|kommen irr vi to meet; (sich ereignen) to happen together; **zusammen|legen** vt to fold up ▷ vi (Geld sammeln) to club together; **zusammen|nehmen** irr vt to summon up; **alles zusammengenommen** all in all ▷ vr: **sich ~** to pull oneself together; (fam) to get a grip, to get one's act together; **zusammen|passen** vi to go together; (Personen) to be suited; **zusammen|rechnen** vt to add up

Zusammensein (-s) nt get-together

zusammen|setzen vt to put together ▷ vr: **sich ~ aus** to be composed of; **Zusammensetzung** f composition

Zusammenstoß m crash, collision; **zusammen|stoßen** irr vi to crash (mit into)

zusammen|zählen vt to add up

zusammen|ziehen irr vi (in Wohnung etc) to move in together

Zusatz m addition; **zusätzlich** adj additional ▷ adv in addition

zu|schauen vi to watch; **Zuschauer(in)** (-s, -) m(f) spectator; **die ~** (pl) (Theat) the audience sing; **Zuschauertribüne** f stand

zu|schicken vt to send

Zuschlag m extra charge; (Fahrkarte) supplement

zuschlagpflichtig adj subject to an extra charge; (Eisenb) subject to a supplement

zu|schließen irr vt to lock up

zu|sehen irr vi to watch (jdm sb); **~, dass** (dafür sorgen) to make sure that

zu|sichern vt: **jdm etw ~** to assure sb of sth

Zustand m state, condition; **sie bekommt Zustände, wenn sie das sieht** (fam) she'll have a fit if she sees that

zustande adv: **~ bringen** to bring about; **~ kommen** to come about

zuständig adj (Behörde) relevant; **~ für** responsible for

Zustellung f delivery

zu|stimmen vi to agree (einer Sache dat to sth, jdm with sb); **Zustimmung** f approval

zu|stoßen irr vi (fig) to happen (jdm to sb)

Zutaten pl ingredients pl

zu|trauen vt: **jdm etw ~** to think sb is capable of sth; **das hätte ich ihm nie zugetraut** I'd never have thought he was capable of it; **ich würde es ihr ~** (etw Negatives) I wouldn't put it past her; **Zutrauen** (-s) nt confidence (zu in); **zutraulich** adj trusting; (Tier) friendly

zu|treffen irr vi to be correct; **~ auf** (+akk) to apply to; **Zutreffendes bitte streichen** please delete as applicable

Zutritt m entry; (Zugang) access; **~ verboten!** no entry

zuverlässig adj reliable; **Zuverlässigkeit** f reliability

Zuversicht f confidence; **zuversichtlich** adj confident

zuvor adv before; (zunächst) first; **zuvor|kommen** irr vi: **jdm ~** to

beat sb to it; **zuvorkommend**
adj obliging

Zuwachs (-es, Zuwächse) *m*
increase, growth; (*fam: Baby*)
addition to the family

zuwider *adv:* **es ist mir ~** I hate (*o*
detest) it

zu|winken *vi:* **jdm ~** to wave to
sb

zuzüglich *prep +gen* plus

zwang *imperf von* **zwingen**

Zwang (-(e)s, Zwänge) *m* (*innerer*)
compulsion; (*Gewalt*) force

zwängen *vt* to squeeze (*in +akk*
into) ▷ *vr:* **sich ~** to squeeze (*in*
+*akk* into)

zwanglos *adj* informal

zwanzig *num* twenty;
zwanzigste(r, s) *adj* twentieth;
siehe auch **dritte**

zwar *adv:* **und ~ ...** (*genauer*) ...,
to be precise; **das ist ~ schön,
aber ...** it is nice, but ...; **ich kenne
ihn ~, aber ...** I know him all right,
but ...

Zweck (-(e)s, -e) *m* purpose;
zwecklos *adj* pointless

zwei *num* two; **Zwei** (-, -en) *f*
two; (*Schulnote*) ≈ B;
Zweibettzimmer *nt* twin room;
zweideutig *adj* ambiguous;
(*unanständig*) suggestive;
zweifach *adj, adv* double

Zweifel (-s, -) *m* doubt;
zweifellos *adv* undoubtedly;
zweifeln *vi* to doubt (*an etw dat*
sth); **Zweifelsfall** *m:* **im ~** in case
of doubt

Zweig (-(e)s, -e) *m* branch

Zweigstelle *f* branch

zweihundert *num* two hundred;
zweimal *adv* twice; **zweisprachig**
adj bilingual; **zweispurig** *adj*
(*Auto*) two-lane; **zweit** *adv:* **wir
sind zu ~** there are two of us;
zweite(r, s) *adj* second; *siehe
auch* **dritte eine ~ Portion** a

second helping; **zweitens** *adv*
secondly; (*bei Aufzählungen*)
second; **zweitgrößte(r, s)** *adj*
second largest; **Zweitschlüssel**
m spare key

Zwerchfell *nt* diaphragm

Zwerg(in) (-(e)s, -e) *m(f)* dwarf
(*pej*)

Zwetschge (-, -n) *f* plum

zwicken *vt* to pinch

Zwieback (-(e)s, -e) *m* rusk

Zwiebel (-, -n) *f* onion; (*von
Blume*) bulb; **Zwiebelsuppe** *f*
onion soup

Zwilling (-s, -e) *m* twin; **~e** (*pl*)
(*Astr*) Gemini *sing*

zwingen (zwang, gezwungen) *vt*
to force

zwinkern *vi* to blink; (*absichtlich*)
to wink

zwischen *prep* +*akk o dat*
between

Zwischenablage *f* (*Inform*)
clipboard

zwischendurch *adv* in between

Zwischenfall *m* incident

Zwischenlandung *f* stopover

zwischenmenschlich *adj*
interpersonal

Zwischenraum *m* space

Zwischenstopp (-s, -s) *m*
stopover

Zwischensumme *f* subtotal

Zwischenzeit *f:* **in der ~** in the
meantime

zwitschern *vt, vi* to twitter, to
chirp

zwölf *num* twelve; **zwölfte(r, s)**
adj twelfth; *siehe auch* **dritte**

Zylinder (-s, -) *m* cylinder; (*Hut*)
top hat

zynisch *adj* cynical

Zypern (-s) *nt* Cyprus

Zyste (-, -n) *f* cyst

Phrasefinder

Sprachführer

TOPICS | THEMEN

TOPICS | THEMEN

Hello!	Guten Tag!
Good evening!	Guten Abend!
Good night!	Gute Nacht!
Goodbye!	Auf Wiedersehen!
What's your name?	Wie heißen Sie?
My name is ...	Mein Name ist ...
This is ...	Das ist ...
my wife.	*meine Frau.*
my husband.	*mein Mann.*
my partner.	*mein Partner/ meine Partnerin.*
Where are you from?	Wo kommen Sie her?
I come from ...	Ich komme aus ...
How are you?	Wie geht es Ihnen?
Fine, thanks.	Danke, gut.
And you?	Und Ihnen?
Do you speak English?	Sprechen Sie Englisch?
I don't understand German.	Ich verstehe kein Deutsch.
Thanks very much!	Vielen Dank!
Pleasure to meet you.	Ich freue mich, Sie kennenzulernen.
I'm British.	Ich bin Brite/Britin.
What do you do for a living?	Was machen Sie beruflich?

Asking the Way — Erkundigungen

Where is the nearest ...?	Wo ist der/die/das nächste ...?
How do I get to ...?	Wie komme ich zum/zur/ nach ...?
Is it far?	Ist es weit?
How far is it?	Wie weit ist es?
Is this the right way to ...?	Bin ich hier richtig zum/zur/ nach ...?
I'm lost.	Ich habe mich verlaufen/ verfahren.
Can you show me on the map?	Können Sie mir das auf der Karte zeigen?
You have to turn round.	Kehren Sie um.
Go straight on.	Fahren Sie geradeaus.
Turn left/right.	Biegen Sie nach links/rechts ab.
Take the second street on the left/right.	Nehmen Sie die zweite Straße links/rechts.

Car Hire — Autovermietung

I want to hire ...	Ich möchte ... mieten.
a car.	*ein Auto.*
a moped.	*ein Moped*
How much is it for ...?	Was kostet das für ...?
one day	*einen Tag*
a week	*eine Woche*
Is there a kilometre charge?	Verlangen Sie eine Kilometer- gebühr?
What is included in the price?	Was ist alles im Preis inbegriffen?
I'd like a child seat for a ... -year-old child.	Ich hätte gerne einen Kindersitz für ein ... Jahre altes Kind.
What do I do if I have an accident/if I break down?	Was tue ich bei einem Unfall/ einer Panne?

Breakdowns — Pannen

My car has broken down.	Ich habe eine Panne.
Where is the next garage?	Wo ist die nächste Werkstatt?
The exhaust	*Der Auspuff*
The gearbox	*Das Getriebe*
The windscreen	*Die Windschutzscheibe*
... is broken.	*... ist kaputt.*
The brakes	*Die Bremsen*
The headlights	*Die Scheinwerfer*
The windscreen wipers	*Die Scheibenwischer*
... are not working.	*... funktionieren nicht.*
The battery is flat.	Die Batterie ist leer.
The car won't start.	Der Motor springt nicht an.
The engine is overheating.	Der Motor wird zu heiß.
I have a flat tyre.	Ich habe einen Platten.
Can you repair it?	Können Sie das reparieren?
When will the car be ready?	Wann ist das Auto fertig?

Parking — Parken

Can I park here?	Kann ich hier parken?
Do I need to buy a (parking) ticket?	Muss ich einen Parkschein lösen?
Where is the ticket machine?	Wo ist der Parkscheinautomat?
The ticket machine isn't working.	Der Parkscheinautomat funktioniert nicht.

Petrol Station — Tankstelle

Where is the nearest petrol station?	Wo ist die nächste Tankstelle?
Fill it up, please.	Volltanken bitte.

40 euros' worth of ..., please.	Für 40 Euro ... bitte.
diesel	*Diesel*
unleaded (economy) petrol	*Normalbenzin*
premium unleaded	*Super*
Pump number ... please.	Säule Nummer ... bitte.
Please check ...	Bitte überprüfen Sie ...
the tyre pressure.	*den Reifendruck.*
the oil.	*das Öl.*
the water.	*das Wasser.*

Accidents — Unfälle

Please call ...	Bitte rufen Sie ...
the police.	*die Polizei.*
an ambulance.	*einen Krankenwagen.*
Here are my insurance details.	Hier sind meine Versicherungsangaben.
Give me your insurance details, please.	Bitte geben Sie mir Ihre Versicherungsangaben.
Can you be a witness for me?	Würden Sie das bezeugen?
You were driving too fast.	Sie sind zu schnell gefahren.
It wasn't your right of way.	Sie haben die Vorfahrt nicht beachtet.

Car Travel — Unterwegs mit dem Auto

What's the best route to ...?	Wie kommt man am besten nach/zu ...?
I'd like a motorway tax sticker ...	Ich hätte gerne einen Aufkleber für die Autobahngebühr/ eine Vignette ...
for a week.	*für eine Woche.*
for a month.	*für einen Monat.*
Do you have a road map of this area?	Haben Sie eine Straßenkarte von dieser Gegend?

Cycling	Fahrrad
Where is the cycle path to ...?	Wo ist der Radwanderweg nach ...?
Can I keep my bike here?	Kann ich hier mein Fahrrad unterstellen?
My bike has been stolen.	Mein Fahrrad ist gestohlen worden.
Where is the nearest bike repair shop?	Wo gibt es hier eine Fahrradwerkstatt?
The brakes aren't working.	Die Bremse funktioniert nicht.
The gears aren't working.	Die Gangschaltung funktioniert nicht.
The chain is broken.	Die Kette ist gerissen.
I've got a flat tyre.	Ich habe einen Platten.
I need a puncture repair kit.	Ich brauche Reifenflickzeug.

Train	Eisenbahn
How much is ...?	Wie viel kostet ...?
a single	*eine einfache Fahrt*
a return	*eine Rückfahrkarte*
A single to ..., please.	Eine einfache Fahrt nach ... bitte.
Two returns to ..., please.	Zwei Rückfahrkarten nach ... bitte.
Is there a reduction ...?	Gibt es eine Ermäßigung ...?
for students	*für Studenten*
for pensioners	*für Rentner*
for children	*für Kinder*
with this pass	*mit diesem Pass*
I'd like to reserve a seat on the train to ..., please.	Ich würde gerne einen Platz für den Zug nach ... reservieren bitte.
I want to book a sleeper to ...	Ich möchte einen Schlafwagenplatz nach ... buchen.

When is the next train to ...?	Wann geht der nächste Zug nach ...?
Is there a supplement to pay?	Muss ich einen Zuschlag zahlen?
Do I need to change?	Muss ich umsteigen?
Where do I change?	Wo muss ich umsteigen?
Which platform does the train for ... leave from?	Von welchem Gleis fährt der Zug nach ... ab?
Is this the train for ...?	Ist das der Zug nach ...?
Excuse me, that's my seat.	Entschuldigen Sie, das ist mein Platz.
I have a reservation.	Ich habe eine Reservierung.
Is this seat taken/free?	Ist dieser Platz besetzt/noch frei?
Where is the buffet car?	Wo ist der Speisewagen?
Where is coach number ...?	Wo ist Wagen Nummer ...?

Ferry / Fähre

Is there a ferry to ...?	Gibt es eine Fähre nach ...?
When is the next ferry to ...?	Wann geht die nächste Fähre nach ...?
When is the first/last ferry to ...?	Wann geht die erste/letzte Fähre nach ...?
How much is ...?	Was kostet ...?
a single	*die einfache Fahrt*
a return	*die Hin- und Rückfahrt*
How much is it for a car/ camper with ... people?	Was kostet es für ein Auto/ Wohnmobil mit ... Personen?
How long does the crossing take?	Wie lange dauert die Überfahrt?
Where is ...?	Wo ist ...?
the restaurant	*das Restaurant*
the duty-free shop	*der Duty-free-Shop*
Where is cabin number ...?	Wo ist Kabine Nummer ...?

Plane | Flugzeug

Where is ...?	*Wo ist ...?*
the taxi rank	*der Taxistand*
the bus stop	*die Bushaltestelle*
the information office	*die Information*
Where do I check in for the flight to ...?	Wo ist das Check-in für den Flug nach ...?
Which gate for the flight to ...?	Von welchem Gate geht der Flug nach ...?
When does boarding begin?	Wann beginnt das Boarding?
Window/aisle, please.	Fenster/Gang bitte.
I've lost my boarding pass/ my ticket.	Ich habe meine Bordkarte/ mein Flugticket verloren.
Where is the baggage carousel?	Wo ist die Gepäckausgabe?
My luggage hasn't arrived.	Mein Gepäck ist nicht angekommen.

Local Public Transport | Öffentlicher Nahverkehr

How do I get to ...?	Wie komme ich zum/zur/ nach ...?
Where is the nearest ...?	*Wo ist die nächste ...?*
bus stop	*Bushaltestelle*
tram stop	*Straßenbahnhaltestelle*
underground station	*U-Bahn-Station*
Which line goes to ...?	Welche Linie fährt nach ...?
Where is the bus station?	Wo ist der Busbahnhof?
A ticket to ..., please.	Eine Fahrkarte nach ... bitte.
Is there a reduction ...?	*Gibt es eine Ermäßigung ...?*
for students	*für Studenten*
for pensioners	*für Rentner*
for children	*für Kinder*
with this card	*mit diesem Ausweis*

How does the ticket machine work?	Wie funktioniert der Fahrkartenautomat?
Do you have a map of the rail network?	Haben Sie eine Karte mit dem Streckennetz?
Please tell me when to get off.	Bitte sagen Sie mir, wann ich aussteigen muss.
What is the next stop?	Was ist die nächste Haltestelle?

Taxi | Taxi

Where can I get a taxi?	Wo bekomme ich hier ein Taxi?
Call me a taxi, please.	Bitte rufen Sie mir ein Taxi.
Please order me a taxi for ... o'clock.	Bitte bestellen Sie mir ein Taxi für ... Uhr.
To the airport/station, please.	Zum Flughafen/Bahnhof, bitte.
I'm in a hurry.	Ich habe es sehr eilig.
Straight ahead/to the left/ to the right.	Geradeaus/links/rechts.
Stop here, please.	Bitte halten Sie hier.
Please could you wait for me?	Könnten Sie bitte auf mich warten?
How much is it?	Was kostet die Fahrt?
I need a receipt.	Ich brauche eine Quittung.
Keep the change.	Stimmt so.

Camping	Camping
Is there a campsite here?	Gibt es hier einen Campingplatz?
We'd like a site for ...	Wir hätten gerne einen Platz für ...
a tent.	*ein Zelt.*
a camper van.	*ein Wohnmobil.*
a caravan.	*einen Wohnwagen.*
We'd like to stay one night/ ... nights.	Wir möchten eine Nacht/ ... Nächte bleiben.
How much is it per night?	Was kostet die Nacht?
Where are ...?	Wo sind ...?
the toilets	*die Toiletten*
the showers	*die Duschen*
Where is ...?	Wo ist ...?
the shop	*der Laden*
the site office	*die Verwaltung*
Can we camp here overnight?	Können wir über Nacht hier zelten?

Self-Catering	Ferienwohnung/-haus
Where do we get the key for the house?	Wo bekommen wir den Schlüssel für das Haus?
Do we have to pay extra for electricity/gas?	Müssen wir Strom/Gas extra bezahlen?
How does ... work?	Wie funktioniert ...?
the washing machine	*die Waschmaschine*
the heating	*die Heizung*
Who do I contact if there are any problems?	An wen kann ich mich bei Problemen wenden?
We need ...	Wir brauchen ...
a second key.	*einen zweiten Schlüssel.*
more sheets.	*mehr Bettwäsche.*

The gas has run out.	Das Gas ist alle.
There is no electricity.	Es gibt keinen Strom.
Where do we hand in the keys when we're leaving?	Wo geben wir die Schlüssel bei der Abreise ab?
Do we have to clean the apartment/the house before we leave?	Müssen wir die Wohnung/ das Haus vor der Abreise sauber machen?

Hotel | Hotel

Do you have a ... for tonight?	Haben Sie ein ... für heute Nacht?
single room	*Einzelzimmer*
double room	*Doppelzimmer*
Do you have a room ...?	Haben Sie ein Zimmer ...?
with a bath	*mit Bad*
with a shower	*mit Dusche*
I want to stay for one night/ ... nights.	Ich möchte eine Nacht/ ... Nächte bleiben.
I booked a room in the name of ...	Ich habe ein Zimmer auf den Namen ... reserviert.
I'd like another room.	Ich möchte ein anderes Zimmer.
What time is breakfast?	Wann gibt es Frühstück?
Where is breakfast served?	Wo gibt es Frühstück?
Can I have breakfast in my room?	Können Sie mir das Frühstück aufs Zimmer bringen?
Where is ...?	Wo ist ...?
the restaurant	*das Restaurant*
the bar	*die Bar*
the gym	*der Fitnessraum*
the swimming pool	*der Swimmingpool*
I'd like an alarm call tomorrow morning at ...	Bitte wecken Sie mich morgen früh um ...
Room number ...	Zimmer Nummer ...

SHOPPING | EINKAUFEN

I'm looking for ...	Ich suche ...
I'd like ...	Ich hätte gerne ...
Do you have ...?	Haben Sie ...?
Do you have this ...?	Haben Sie das ...?
in another size	*in einer anderen Größe*
in another colour	*in einer anderen Farbe*
in another design	*mit einem anderen Muster*
I take size ...	Ich trage Größe ...
My feet are size ...	Meine Schuhgröße ist ...
I'll take it.	Ich nehme das.
Do you have anything else?	Haben Sie noch etwas anderes?
That's too expensive.	Das ist zu teuer.
I'm just looking.	Ich sehe mich nur um.
Do you take credit cards?	Nehmen Sie Kreditkarten?

Food Shopping	Lebensmittel
Where is the nearest ...?	Wo ist hier ...?
supermarket	*ein Supermarkt*
baker's	*eine Bäckerei*
butcher's	*eine Metzgerei*
greengrocer's	*ein Obst- und Gemüseladen*
Where is the market?	Wo ist der Markt?
When is the market on?	Wann ist Markt?
a kilo of ...	ein Kilo ...
a pound of ...	ein Pfund ...
200 grams of ...	200 Gramm ...
... slices ...	... Scheiben ...
a litre of ...	ein Liter ...
a bottle of ...	eine Flasche ...
a packet of ...	ein Päckchen ...

Photography | Fotografie

I need passport-sized photos.	Ich brauche Passfotos.
I'm looking for a cable for a digital camera.	Ich suche ein Kabel für eine Digitalkamera.
Do you sell brand-name chargers?	Verkaufen Sie Marken-Ladekabel?
I'd like to buy a memory card.	Ich würde gerne eine Speicherkarte kaufen.
Can I print my digital photos here?	Kann ich meine Digitalfotos hier drucken lassen?
I'd like the photos ...	Ich hätte die Bilder gern ...
matt.	matt.
glossy.	Hochglanz.
ten by fifteen centimetres.	im Format zehn mal fünfzehn.
How much do the photos cost?	Wie viel kosten die Bilder?
Are you allowed to take photos here?	Darf man hier fotografieren?
Could you take a photo of us, please?	Könnten Sie bitte ein Foto von uns machen?

Post Office | Post

Where is the nearest post office?	Wo ist die nächste Post?
When does the post office open?	Wann hat die Post geöffnet?
I'd like ... stamps for postcards/letters to the UK/the US.	Ich hätte gerne ... Briefmarken für Postkarten/Briefe nach Großbritannien/in die USA.
Where is the nearest postbox?	Wo ist hier ein Briefkasten?

Sightseeing	Besichtigungen
Where is the tourist office?	Wo ist die Touristen-information?
Do you have any leaflets about ...?	Haben Sie Broschüren über ...?
What sights can you visit here?	Welche Sehenswürdigkeiten gibt es hier?
Is there a guided tour in English?	Gibt es eine Stadtrundfahrt/ einen Stadtrundgang auf Englisch?
When is ... open?	Wann ist ... geöffnet?
the museum	*das Museum*
the church	*die Kirche*
the castle	*das Schloss*
How much does it cost to get in?	Was kostet der Eintritt?
Are there any reductions ...?	Gibt es eine Ermäßigung ...?
for students	*für Studenten*
for children	*für Kinder*
for pensioners	*für Rentner*
for the unemployed	*für Arbeitslose*
I'd like a catalogue.	Ich hätte gerne einen Katalog.
Can I take photos here?	Kann ich hier fotografieren?
Can I film here?	Kann ich hier filmen?

Entertainment	Unterhaltung
What is there to do here?	Was kann man hier unter-nehmen?
Do you have a list of events?	Haben Sie einen Veranstal-tungskalender?
Where can we ...?	Wo kann man hier ...?
go dancing	*tanzen gehen*
hear live music	*Livemusik hören*

Where is there ...?	*Wo gibt es hier ... ?*
a nice pub	*eine nette Kneipe*
a good disco	*eine gute Disko*
What's on tonight ...?	*Was gibt es heute Abend ...?*
at the cinema	*im Kino*
at the theatre	*im Theater*
at the opera	*in der Oper*
at the concert hall	*in der Konzerthalle*
Where can I buy tickets	*Wo kann ich Karten für ...*
for ...?	*kaufen?*
the theatre	*das Theater*
the concert	*das Konzert*
the opera	*die Oper*
the ballet	*das Ballett*
How much is it to get in?	*Was kostet der Eintritt?*
I'd like a ticket/... tickets	*Ich hätte gerne eine Karte/*
for ...	*... Karten für ...*
Are there any reductions	*Gibt es eine Ermäßigung*
for ...?	*für ...?*
children	*Kinder*
pensioners	*Rentner*
students	*Studenten*
the unemployed	*Arbeitslose*

At the Beach | Am Strand

Can you swim here/	*Kann man hier/in diesem*
in this lake?	*See baden?*
Where is the nearest quiet	*Wo gibt es hier einen*
beach?	*ruhigen Strand?*
How deep is the water?	*Wie tief ist das Wasser?*
What is the water	*Wie viel Grad hat das Wasser?*
temperature?	

LEISURE	FREIZEIT
Are there currents?	Gibt es hier Strömungen?
Is there a lifeguard?	Gibt es hier einen Rettungs-schwimmer?
Where can you ...?	Wo kann man hier ...?
go surfing	*surfen*
go waterskiing	*Wasserski fahren*
go diving	*tauchen*
go paragliding	*Gleitschirm fliegen*
I'd like to hire ...	Ich möchte ... mieten.
a beach chair.	*einen Strandkorb*
a deckchair.	*einen Liegestuhl*
a sunshade.	*einen Sonnenschirm*
I'd like to hire ...	Ich möchte ... ausleihen.
a surfboard.	*ein Surfbrett*
a jet-ski.	*einen Jetski*
a rowing boat.	*ein Ruderboot*
a pedal boat.	*ein Tretboot*

Skiing	Ski
Where can I hire skiing equipment?	Wo kann ich eine Skiaus-rüstung ausleihen?
I'd like to hire ...	Ich möchte ... ausleihen.
downhill skis.	*Abfahrtski*
cross-country skis.	*Langlaufski*
ski boots.	*Skischuhe*
Please can you tighten my bindings?	Könnten Sie bitte meine Bindung enger stellen?
Where can I buy a ski pass?	Wo kann ich einen Skipass kaufen?
I'd like a ski pass ...	Ich hätte gerne einen Skipass ...
for a day.	*für einen Tag.*
for five days.	*für fünf Tage.*
for a week.	*für sieben Tage.*

How much is a ski pass?	Wie viel kostet der Skipass?
Do you have a map of the ski runs?	Haben Sie eine Pistenkarte?
What time is the first/last lift?	Wann fährt der erste/letzte Lift?
Where are the beginners' slopes?	Wo sind die Abfahrten für Anfänger?
How difficult is this slope?	Welchen Schwierigkeitsgrad hat diese Abfahrt?
Is there a ski school?	Gibt es eine Skischule?
What's the weather forecast?	Wie ist der Wetterbericht?
What is the snow like?	Wie ist der Schnee?
Is there a danger of avalanches?	Besteht Lawinengefahr?

Sport | Sport

Where can we ...?	Wo kann man hier ...?
play tennis/golf	*Tennis/Golf spielen*
go swimming	*schwimmen*
go riding	*reiten*
How much is it per hour?	Wie viel kostet es pro Stunde?
Where can I book a court?	Wo kann ich einen Platz buchen?
Where can I hire rackets?	Wo kann ich Schläger ausleihen?
Where can I hire a rowing boat/a pedal boat?	Wo kann ich ein Ruderboot/ ein Tretboot mieten?
Do you need a fishing permit?	Braucht man einen Angelschein?
I'd like to see ...	Ich möchte ... ansehen.
a football match.	*ein Fußballspiel*
a horse race.	*ein Pferderennen*

A table for ... people, please.	Einen Tisch für ... Personen bitte.
The menu, please.	Die Speisekarte bitte.
The wine list, please.	Die Weinkarte bitte.
What do you recommend?	Was empfehlen Sie?
Do you have ...?	Haben Sie ...?
any vegetarian dishes	*vegetarische Gerichte*
children's portions	*Kinderportionen*
Does that contain ...?	Enthält das ...?
peanuts	*Erdnüsse*
alcohol	*Alkohol*
Can you bring (more) ..., please?	Bitte bringen Sie (noch) ...
I'll have ...	Ich nehme ...
The bill, please.	Zahlen bitte.
All together, please.	Bitte alles zusammen.
Separate bills, please.	Getrennte Rechnungen bitte.
Keep the change.	Stimmt so.
I didn't order this.	Das habe ich nicht bestellt.
The bill is wrong.	Die Rechnung stimmt nicht.
The food is cold/too salty.	Das Essen ist kalt/versalzen.
I'd like the steak rare/medium/well-done, please.	Ich hätte das Steak gern blutig/halbdurch/durchgebraten bitte.
A bottle of sparkling/still water, please.	Eine Flasche Wasser mit/ohne Kohlensäure bitte.

see also MENU READER   *siehe auch* SPEISEKARTE

Telephone · Telefon

Where can I make a phone call?	Wo kann ich hier telefonieren?
Hello.	Hallo.
This is ...	Hier ist ...
Who's speaking, please?	Wer spricht dort bitte?
Can I speak to Mr/Ms ..., please?	Kann ich bitte mit Herrn/Frau ... sprechen?
Extension ..., please.	Apparat ... bitte.
I'll phone back later.	Ich rufe später wieder an.
Where can I charge my mobile (phone)?	Wo kann ich mein Handy aufladen?
I need a new battery.	Ich brauche einen neuen Akku.
I can't get a network.	Hier ist kein Netz.
You're breaking up.	Die Verbindung ist sehr schlecht.
I'd like to buy a SIM card with/without subscription.	Ich möchte eine SIM-Karte mit/ohne Vertragsbindung kaufen.

Internet · Internet

I'd like to send an email.	Ich würde gern eine E-Mail verschicken.
I'd like to print out a document.	Ich würde gern ein Dokument ausdrucken.
How do you change the language of the keyboard?	Wie ändert man die Sprache der Tastatur?
What's the Wi-Fi password?	Was ist das WLAN-Passwort?

Passport/Customs | Pass/Zoll

Here is ...	Hier ist ...
my passport.	*mein Pass.*
my identity card.	*mein Personalausweis.*
my driving licence.	*mein Führerschein.*
Here are my vehicle documents.	Hier sind meine Fahrzeugpapiere.
This is a present.	Das ist ein Geschenk.
It's for my own personal use.	Das ist für meinen persönlichen Gebrauch.

At the Bank | Bank

Where can I change money?	Wo kann ich hier Geld wechseln?
Is there a bank/bureau de change here?	Gibt es hier eine Bank/eine Wechselstube?
When is the bank/bureau de change open?	Wann ist die Bank/Wechselstube geöffnet?
I'd like ... euros.	Ich hätte gerne ... Euro.
What's the commission?	Wie hoch ist die Gebühr?
Can I use my credit card to get cash?	Kann ich hier mit meiner Kreditkarte Bargeld bekommen?
Where is the nearest cash machine?	Wo gibt es hier einen Geldautomaten?
The cash machine swallowed my card.	Der Geldautomat hat meine Karte geschluckt.
Can you give me some change, please.	Bitte geben Sie mir etwas Kleingeld.

Emergency Services	Notfalldienste
Help!	Hilfe!
Fire!	Feuer!
Please call ...	Bitte rufen Sie ...
an ambulance.	*einen Krankenwagen.*
the fire brigade.	*die Feuerwehr.*
the police.	*die Polizei.*
I need to make an urgent phone call.	Ich muss dringend telefonieren.
I need an interpreter.	Ich brauche einen Dolmetscher.
Where is the police station?	Wo ist die Polizeiwache?
Where is the nearest hospital?	Wo ist das nächste Krankenhaus?
Where is the A&E department?	Wo ist die Notaufnahme?
I want to report a theft.	Ich möchte einen Diebstahl melden.
... has been stolen.	... ist gestohlen worden.
There's been an accident.	Es ist ein Unfall passiert.
There are ... people injured.	Es gibt ... Verletzte.
My location is ...	Mein Standort ist ...
I've been ...	Ich bin ... worden.
robbed	*beraubt*
attacked	*überfallen*
raped	*vergewaltigt*
I'd like to phone my embassy.	Ich möchte mit meiner Botschaft sprechen.

Pharmacy	Apotheke
Where is the nearest pharmacy?	Wo gibt es hier eine Apotheke?
Which pharmacy provides emergency service?	Welche Apotheke hat Bereitschaft?
I'd like something for ...	Ich hätte gerne etwas gegen ...
diarrhoea.	*Durchfall.*
a temperature.	*Fieber.*
travel sickness.	*Reisekrankheit.*
a headache.	*Kopfschmerzen.*
a cold.	*Erkältung.*
I'd like ...	Ich hätte gerne ...
plasters.	*Pflaster.*
a bandage.	*einen Verband.*
I can't take ...	Ich vertrage kein ...
aspirin.	*Aspirin.*
penicillin.	*Penizillin.*
Is it safe to give to children?	Kann man das Kindern geben?
How should I take it?	Wie soll ich das einnehmen?

At the Doctor's	Beim Arzt
I need a doctor.	Ich brauche einen Arzt.
I have a pain here.	Ich habe hier Schmerzen.
I feel ...	Mir ist ...
hot.	*heiß.*
cold.	*kalt.*
sick.	*übel.*
dizzy.	*schwindlig.*

I'm allergic to ...	Ich bin allergisch gegen ...
I am ...	Ich bin ...
pregnant.	*schwanger.*
diabetic.	*Diabetiker.*
HIV-positive.	*HIV-positiv.*
I'm on this medication.	Ich nehme dieses Medikament.
My blood group is ...	Meine Blutgruppe ist ...

At the Hospital | Krankenhaus

Which ward is ... in?	Auf welcher Station liegt ...?
When are visiting hours?	Wann ist die Besuchszeit?
I'd like to speak to ...	Ich möchte mit ... sprechen.
a doctor.	*einem Arzt*
a nurse.	*einer Krankenschwester*
I'd like headphones for the TV, please.	Ich hätte gerne Kopfhörer für den Fernseher, bitte.
When will I be discharged?	Wann werde ich entlassen?

At the Dentist's | Beim Zahnarzt

I need a dentist.	Ich brauche einen Zahnarzt.
This tooth hurts.	Dieser Zahn tut weh.
One of my fillings has fallen out.	Mir ist eine Füllung herausgefallen.
I have an abscess.	Ich habe einen Abszess.
I want/don't want an injection for the pain.	Ich möchte eine/keine Spritze gegen die Schmerzen.
Can you repair my dentures?	Können Sie mein Gebiss reparieren?
I need a receipt for the insurance.	Ich brauche eine Quittung für die Versicherung.

Business Travel | Dienstreisen

I'd like to arrange a meeting with ...	Ich möchte eine Besprechung mit ... ausmachen.
I have an appointment with Mr/Ms ...	Ich haben einen Termin mit Herrn/Frau ...
Here is my card.	Hier ist meine Karte.
I work for ...	Ich arbeite für ...
How do I get to ...?	Wie komme ich ...?
your office	*zu Ihrem Büro*
Mr/Ms ...'s office	*zum Büro von Herrn/Frau ...*
the canteen	*zur Kantine*
I need an interpreter.	Ich brauche einen Dolmetscher.
Can you copy that for me, please?	Bitte kopieren Sie das für mich.
May I use ...?	Darf ich ... benutzen?
your phone	*Ihr Telefon*
your computer	*Ihren Computer*
your desk	*Ihren Schreibtisch*
Do you have an Internet connection/Wi-Fi?	Haben Sie eine Internetverbindung/WLAN?

Disabled Travellers | Behinderte

Where is the wheelchair-accessible entrance?	Wo ist der Eingang für Rollstuhlfahrer?
Is your hotel accessible to wheelchairs?	Ist Ihr Hotel rollstuhlgerecht?
I need a room ...	Ich brauche ein Zimmer ...
on the ground floor.	*im Erdgeschoss.*
with wheelchair access.	*für Rollstuhlfahrer.*
Do you have a lift for wheelchairs?	Haben Sie einen Aufzug für Rollstühle?
Where is the disabled toilet?	Wo ist die Behindertentoilette?

Is the train wheelchair accessible?	Kann ich als Rollstuhlfahrer in diesem Zug mitfahren?
Can you help me get on/ off please?	Bitte helfen Sie mir beim Einsteigen/Aussteigen.

Travelling with Children — Reisen mit Kindern

Is it OK to bring children here?	Können wir die Kinder mitbringen?
Are children allowed in too?	Ist der Eintritt auch Kindern gestattet?
Is there a reduction for children?	Gibt es eine Ermäßigung für Kinder?
Do you have children's portions?	Haben Sie Kinderportionen?
Do you have ...?	Haben Sie ...?
a high chair	*einen Kinderstuhl*
a cot	*ein Kinderbett*
a child's seat	*einen Kindersitz*
a baby's changing table	*einen Wickeltisch*
Where can I change the baby?	Wo kann ich das Baby wickeln?
Where can I breast-feed the baby?	Wo kann ich das Baby stillen?
Can you warm this up, please?	Können Sie das bitte aufwärmen?
What is there for children to do?	Was können Kinder hier unternehmen?
Where is the nearest playground?	Wo gibt es hier einen Spielplatz?
Is there a child-minding service?	Gibt es hier eine Kinderbetreuung?
My son/daughter is ill.	Mein Sohn/meine Tochter ist krank.

I'd like to make a complaint.	Ich möchte mich beschweren.
To whom should I speak in order to make a complaint?	An wen kann ich mich mit einer Beschwerde wenden?
I'd like to speak to the manager, please.	Ich möchte mit dem Geschäftsführer sprechen.
The light	*Das Licht*
The heating	*Die Heizung*
The shower	*Die Dusche*
... doesn't work.	... funktioniert nicht.
The room is ...	Das Zimmer ist ...
dirty.	*schmutzig.*
too small.	*zu klein.*
too cold.	*zu kalt.*
Can you clean the room, please?	Bitte machen Sie das Zimmer sauber.
Can you turn down the TV/the radio, please?	Bitte stellen Sie den Fernseher/ das Radio leiser.
The food is ...	Das Essen ist ...
cold.	*kalt.*
too salty.	*versalzen.*
This isn't what I ordered.	Das habe ich nicht bestellt.
We've been waiting for a very long time.	Wir warten schon sehr lange.
The bill is wrong.	Die Rechnung stimmt nicht.
I want my money back.	Ich möchte mein Geld zurück.
I'd like to exchange this.	Ich möchte das umtauschen.
I'm not satisfied with this.	Ich bin damit nicht zufrieden.

Alsterwasser lager shandy

Apfelkorn apple brandy

arme Ritter French toast

Auflauf baked dish, which can be sweet or savoury

Backpflaumen prunes

Bauernfrühstück cooked breakfast of scrambled eggs, bacon, diced potatoes, onions, tomatoes

Berliner doughnut filled with jam

Bierwurst Bavarian boiled sausage

Birchermüsli muesli with yoghurt (Switzerland)

Blätterteig puff pastry

Bockwurst boiled sausage; a popular snack served with a bread roll

Brathähnchen roast chicken

Bratkartoffeln fried potatoes

Dunkles dark beer

Eierkuchen pancakes

Eintopf stew

Eisbein boiled pork knuckle, often served with sauerkraut

Eiswein a rich, naturally sweet white wine made from grapes harvested after a period of frost

Fünfkornbrot wholemeal bread made with five different cereals

geschmort braised

Gewürzgurken gherkins

Hackbraten meatloaf

Hefeweizen wheat beer

Helles light beer

Heuriger new wine

Jägerschnitzel escalope served with mushrooms and a wine sauce

Kaiserschmarren strips of pancake served with raisins, sugar and cinnamon

Kartoffelpuffer potato pancakes

Knackwurst hot spicy sausage; a popular snack served with bread

Knödel dumpling

Kroketten croquettes

Leberkäse pork liver meatloaf

Leinsamenbrot wholemeal bread with linseed

Linzer Torte latticed tart with jam topping

Malzbier dark malt beer

Maß a litre of beer

Melange milky coffee (Austria)

Mischbrot grey bread made with rye and wheat flour

Nockerln small dumplings

Pils, Pilsner a strong, slightly bitter lager

Pumpernickel very dark bread made with coarse wholemeal rye flour

Raclette melted cheese and potatoes

Radler beer with lemonade, shandy

Räucherkäse smoked cheese

Reibekuchen potato cakes

Rösti fried grated potatoes

Roulade beef olive

Rührei scrambled eggs

Sachertorte rich chocolate gâteau

Sauerbraten braised pickled beef served with dumplings and vegetables

Schwertfisch swordfish

Spanferkel suckling pig

Spiegelei fried egg

Steinbutt turbot

Steinpilze porcini mushrooms

Stollen spiced loaf with candied peel traditionally eaten at Christmas

Vollkorn wholemeal

Wiener Schnitzel escalope fried in breadcrumbs

Wildbraten roast venison

Zervelatwurst fine beef and pork salami

bangers and mash Kartoffelpüree mit Bratwurst, Zwiebeln und Soße

banoffee pie Törtchen mit einer Füllung aus Bananen, Toffee und Sahne

BLT (sandwich) Sandwich mit Schinkenspeck, Salat und Tomaten

bubble and squeak gebratene Fleischreste und Gemüse

butternut squash Butternusskürbis

Caesar salad Salatgericht aus Römersalat, Eiern, Parmesankäse und Vinaigrette

chocolate brownie kleiner Schokoladenkuchen

chicken nuggets Hähnchen-Nuggets

chowder dicke Suppe aus Meeresfrüchten oder Gemüse, oft mit Milch oder Sahne verfeinert

club sandwich dreilagiges, mit Toastbrot zubereitetes Sandwich

Cornish pasty Gebäckstück aus Blätterteig mit Fleischfüllung

cottage pie zweilagiger Auflauf aus Rinderhack und Kartoffelbrei

cream tea kleine Mahlzeit bestehend aus Tee, Hefegebäck, Streichrahm und Marmelade

English breakfast warmes Frühstück aus Bohnen in Tomatensoße, Speck, Eiern und Würstchen

filo pastry Blätterteig

haggis mit gehackten Schafsinnereien und Haferschrot gefüllter Schafsmagen

hash browns Rösti-Ecken

hotpot Fleischeintopf mit Kartoffeln

Irish stew Eintopf mit Hammelfleisch, Kartoffeln und Zwiebeln

monkfish Seeteufel

oatcake Haferkeks

pavlova Baisertorte, mit Sahne und Früchten gefüllt

purée Püree

Quorn® proteinreicher Fleischersatz aus Gemüsesubstanz

savoy cabbage Wirsing

Scotch egg hart gekochtes Ei in Wurstbrät, paniert und ausgebacken

scrumpy starker Cider aus Südwestengland

sea bass Wolfsbarsch

shortcrust pastry Mürbeteig

spare ribs Schälrippchen

Stilton englischer Blauschimmelkäse

sundae Eisbecher mit Nüssen und Sirup

toad in the hole in Teig gebackene Bratwürste

turbot Steinbutt

Welsh rarebit überbackene Käseschnitte

Yorkshire pudding im Backofen ausgebackener Teig als Beilage zu Fleischgerichten

English – German

Englisch – Deutsch

a

abandon [əˈbændən] vt
(desert) verlassen; (give up)
aufgeben
abbey [ˈæbɪ] n Abtei f
abbreviate [əbriːˈvɪeɪt] vt
abkürzen; **abbreviation**
[əbriːvɪˈeɪʃən] n Abkürzung f
ABC [ˈeɪbiːˈsiː] n (a. fig) Abc nt
abdicate [ˈæbdɪkeɪt] vi (king)
abdanken; **abdication**
[æbdɪˈkeɪʃən] n Abdankung f
abdomen [ˈæbdəmən] n Unterleib m
ability [əˈbɪlɪtɪ] n Fähigkeit f;
able [ˈeɪbl] adj fähig; **to be ~ to
do sth** etw tun können
abnormal [æbˈnɔːml] adj
anormal
aboard [əˈbɔːd] adv, prep an Bord
+gen
abolish [əˈbɒlɪʃ] vt abschaffen
aborigine [æbəˈrɪdʒɪniː] n Ur-
einwohner(in) m(f) (Australiens)
abort [əˈbɔːt] vt (Med: foetus)
abtreiben; (Space: mission)
abbrechen; **abortion** [əˈbɔːʃən] n
Abtreibung f

a [eɪ, ə; æn, ən] (before vowel or
silent h: **an**) indef art **1** ein,
eine; **a woman** eine Frau; **a
book** ein Buch; **an eagle** ein
Adler; **she's a doctor** sie ist
Ärztin
2 (instead of the number "one") ein,
eine; **a year ago** vor einem Jahr; **a
hundred/thousand** etc pounds
(ein) hundert/(ein) tausend etc
Pfund
3 (in expressing ratios, prices etc) pro;
3 a day/week 3 pro Tag/Woche, 3
am Tag/in der Woche; **10 km an
hour** 10 km pro Stunde/in der
Stunde

AA abbr = **Automobile
Association** britischer
Automobilklub, ≈ ADAC m
aback adv: **taken ~** erstaunt

about [əˈbaʊt] adv **1**
(approximately) etwa, ungefähr;
about a hundred/thousand etc
etwa hundert/tausend etc; **at
about 2 o'clock** etwa um 2 Uhr;
I've just about finished ich bin
gerade fertig
2 (referring to place) herum, umher;
to leave things lying about
Sachen herumliegen lassen; **to
run/walk** etc **about**
herumrennen/gehen etc
3 (to be about to do sth** im Begriff
sein, etw zu tun; **he was about to
go to bed** er wollte gerade ins Bett
gehen

▷ prep **1** (relating to) über +akk; **a book about London** ein Buch über London; **what is it about?** worum geht es?; (book etc) wovon handelt es?; **we talked about it** wir haben darüber geredet; **what o how about doing this?** wollen wir das machen?
2 (referring to place) um (... herum); **to walk about the town** in der Stadt herumgehen; **her clothes were scattered about the room** ihre Kleider waren über das ganze Zimmer verstraut

above [ə'bʌv] adv oben; **children aged 8 and ~** Kinder ab 8 Jahren; **on the floor ~** ein Stockwerk höher ▷ prep über; **~ 40 degrees** über 40 Grad; **~ all** vor allem ▷ adj obig

abroad [ə'brɔːd] adv im Ausland; **to go ~** ins Ausland gehen

abrupt [ə'brʌpt] adj (sudden) plötzlich, abrupt

abscess ['æbsɪs] n Geschwür nt

absence ['æbsəns] n Abwesenheit f; **absent** ['æbsənt] adj abwesend; **to be ~** fehlen; **absent-minded** adj zerstreut

absolute ['æbsəluːt] adj absolut; (power) unumschränkt; (rubbish) vollkommen, total; **absolutely** adv absolut; (true, stupid) vollkommen, **~! genau!; you're ~ right** du hast/Sie haben völlig recht

absorb [əb'zɔːb] vt absorbieren; (fig: information) in sich aufnehmen; **absorbed** adj: **~ in sth** in etw vertieft; **absorbent** adj absorbierend; **~ cotton** (US) Watte f; **absorbing** adj (fig) faszinierend, fesselnd

abstain [əb'steɪn] vi: **to ~ (from voting)** sich (der Stimme) enthalten

abstract ['æbstrækt] adj abstrakt

absurd [əb'sɜːd] adj absurd

abundance [ə'bʌndəns] n Reichtum m (of +dat)

abuse [ə'bjuːs] n (rude language) Beschimpfungen pl; (mistreatment) Missbrauch m ▷ [ə'bjuːz] vt (misuse) missbrauchen; **abusive** [ə'bjuːsɪv] adj beleidigend

AC abbr = **alternating current** Wechselstrom m ▷ abbr = **air conditioning** Klimaanlage

a/c abbr = **account** Kto.

academic [ækə'demɪk] n Wissenschaftler(in) m(f) ▷ adj akademisch, wissenschaftlich

accelerate [æk'seləreɪt] vi (car etc) beschleunigen; (driver) Gas geben; **acceleration** [ækselə'reɪʃən] n Beschleunigung f; **accelerator** [æk'seləreɪtə°] n Gas(pedal) nt

accent ['æksent] n Akzent m

accept [ək'sept] vt annehmen; (agree to) akzeptieren; (responsibility) übernehmen; **acceptable** [ək'septəbl] adj annehmbar

access ['ækses] n Zugang m; (Inform) Zugriff m; **accessible** [æk'sesəbl] adj (leicht) zugänglich/erreichbar; (place) (leicht) erreichbar

accessory [æk'sesərɪ] n Zubehörteil nt

access road n Zufahrtsstraße f

accident ['æksɪdənt] n Unfall m; **by ~** zufällig; **accidental** [æksɪ'dentl] adj unbeabsichtigt; (meeting) zufällig; (death) durch Unfall; **~ damage** Unfallschaden m; **accident-prone** adj vom Pech verfolgt

acclimatize [ə'klaɪmətaɪz] vt: **to ~ oneself** sich gewöhnen (to an +akk)

accommodate [əˈkɒmədeɪt] vt unterbringen;
accommodation(s) [əkɒməˈdeɪʃən(z)] n Unterkunft f

accompany [əˈkʌmpənɪ] vt begleiten

accomplish [əˈkʌmplɪʃ] vt erreichen

accord [əˈkɔːd] n: **of one's own ~** freiwillig; **accordance** [əˈkɔːdəns] prep nach, laut +dat

account [əˈkaʊnt] n (in bank etc) Konto nt; (narrative) Bericht m; **on ~** wegen; **no no ~** auf keinen Fall; **to take into ~** berücksichtigen, in Betracht ziehen; **accountant** [əˈkaʊntənt] n Buchhalter(in m(f)); **account for** vt (explain) erklären; (expenditure) Rechenschaft ablegen für; **account number** n Kontonummer f

accumulate [əˈkjuːmjʊleɪt] vt ansammeln ▷ vi sich ansammeln

accuracy [ˈækjʊrəsɪ] n Genauigkeit f; **accurate** [ˈækjʊrɪt] adj genau

accusation [ækjʊˈzeɪʃən] n Anklage f, Beschuldigung f

accusative [əˈkjuːzətɪv] n Akkusativ m

accuse [əˈkjuːz] vt beschuldigen; (Jur) anklagen (of wegen +gen); **~ sb of doing sth** jdn beschuldigen, etw getan zu haben; **accused** n (Jur) Angeklagte(r) m(f)

accustom [əˈkʌstəm] vt gewöhnen (to an +akk); **accustomed** adj gewohnt; **to get ~ to sth** sich an etw akk gewöhnen

ace [eɪs] n Ass nt ▷ adj Star-

ache [eɪk] n Schmerz m ▷ vi wehtun

achieve [əˈtʃiːv] vt erreichen; **achievement** n Leistung f

acid [ˈæsɪd] n Säure f ▷ adj sauer; **~ rain** saurer Regen

acknowledge [əkˈnɒlɪdʒ] vt (recognize) anerkennen; (admit) zugeben; (receipt of letter etc) bestätigen; **acknowledgement** n Anerkennung f; (of letter) Empfangsbestätigung f

acne [ˈæknɪ] n Akne f

acorn [ˈeɪkɔːn] n Eichel f

acoustic [əˈkuːstɪk] adj akustisch; **acoustics** [əˈkuːstɪks] npl Akustik f

acquaintance [əˈkweɪntəns] n (person) Bekannte(r) m f

acquire [əˈkwaɪə*] vt erwerben, sich aneignen; **acquisition** [ækwɪˈzɪʃn] n (of skills etc) Erwerb m; (object) Anschaffung f

acrobat [ˈækrəbæt] n Akrobat(in) m(f)

across [əˈkrɒs] prep über +akk; **he lives ~ the street** er wohnt auf der anderen Seite der Straße ▷ adv hinüber, herüber; **~** 100m = 100m breit

act [ækt] n (deed) Tat f; (Jur: law) Gesetz nt; (Theat) Akt m; (fig: pretence) Schau f; **it's all an ~** es ist alles nur Theater; **to be in the ~ of doing sth** gerade dabei sein, etw zu tun ▷ vi (take action) handeln; (behave) sich verhalten; (Theat) spielen; **~ to ~ as** (person) fungieren als; (thing) dienen als ▷ vt (a part) spielen

action [ˈækʃən] n (of play, novel etc) Handlung f; (in film etc) Action f; (Mil) Kampf m; **to take ~** etwas unternehmen; **out of ~** (machine) außer Betrieb; **to put a plan into ~** einen Plan in die Tat umsetzen; **action replay** n (Sport, TV) Wiederholung f

activate [ˈæktɪveɪt] vt aktivieren; **active** [ˈæktɪv] adj aktiv; (child) lebhaft; **activity** [ækˈtɪvɪtɪ] n Aktivität f; (occupation) Beschäftigung f; (organized event) Veranstaltung f

actor ['æktə⁹] n Schauspieler(in) m(f); **actress** ['æktrɪs] n Schauspielerin f

actual ['æktjʊəl] adj wirklich; **actually** adv eigentlich; (said in surprise) tatsächlich

acupuncture [ˌækjʊpʌŋktʃə⁹] n Akupunktur f

acute [ə'kjuːt] adj (pain) akut; (sense of smell) fein; (Math: angle) spitz

ad [æd] abbr = **advertisement**
AD abbr = **Anno Domini** nach Christi, n. Chr.

adapt [ə'dæpt] vi sich anpassen (to +akk) ▷ vt anpassen (to +dat); (rewrite) bearbeiten (for für); **adaptable** adj anpassungsfähig; **adaptation** n (of book etc) Bearbeitung f; **adapter** n (Elec) Zwischenstecker m, Adapter m

add [æd] vt (ingredient) hinzufügen; (numbers) addieren; **add up** vi (make sense) stimmen ▷ vt (numbers) addieren

addict ['ædɪkt] n Süchtige(r) mf; **addicted** [ə'dɪktɪd] adj: ~ **to alcohol/drugs** alkohol-/ drogensüchtig

addition [ə'dɪʃən] n Zusatz m; (to bill) Aufschlag m; (Math) Addition f; **in ~** außerdem, zusätzlich (to zu); **additional** adj zusätzlich, weiter; **additive** ['ædɪtɪv] n Zusatz m; **add-on** ['ædɒn] n Zusatzgerät nt

address [ə'dres] n Adresse f ▷ vt (letter) adressieren; (person) anreden

adequate ['ædɪkwɪt] adj (appropriate) angemessen; (sufficient) ausreichend; (time) genügend

adhesive [əd'hiːsɪv] n Klebstoff m; **adhesive tape** n Klebstreifen m

adjacent [ə'dʒeɪsənt] adj benachbart

adjective ['ædʒəktɪv] n Adjektiv nt

adjoining [ə'dʒɔɪnɪŋ] adj benachbart, Neben-

adjust [ə'dʒʌst] vt einstellen; (put right also) richtig stellen; (speed, flow) regulieren; (in position) verstellen ▷ vi sich anpassen (to +dat); **adjustable** adj verstellbar

admin ['ædmɪn] n (fam) Verwaltung f; **administration** [ədmɪnɪs'treɪʃən] n Verwaltung f; (Pol) Regierung f

admirable ['ædmərəbl] adj bewundernswert; **admiration** [ædmɪ'reɪʃən] n Bewunderung f; **admire** [əd'maɪə⁹] vt bewundern

admission [əd'mɪʃən] n (entrance) Zutritt m; (to university etc) Zulassung f; (fee) Eintritt m; (confession) Eingeständnis nt; **admission charge**, **admission fee** n Eintrittspreis m; **admit** [əd'mɪt] vt (let in) hereinlassen (to in +akk); (to university etc) zulassen; (confess) zugeben, gestehen; **to be ~ted to hospital** ins Krankenhaus eingeliefert werden

adolescent [ædə'lesnt] n Jugendliche(r) mf

adopt [ə'dɒpt] vt (child) adoptieren; (idea) übernehmen; **adoption** [ə'dɒpʃn] n (of child) Adoption f; (of idea) Übernahme f

adorable [ə'dɔːrəbl] adj entzückend; **adore** [ə'dɔː⁹] vt anbeten; (person) über alles lieben, vergöttern

ADSL abbr = **asymmetric digital subscriber line** ADSL f

adult ['ædʌlt] adj erwachsen; (film etc) für Erwachsene ▷ n Erwachsene(r) mf

adultery [ə'dʌltərɪ] n Ehebruch m

advance [əd'vɑːns] n (money) Vorschuss m; (progress) Fortschritt

_m_; **in ~** im Voraus; **to book in ~**
vorbestellen ▷ _vi_ (_move forward_)
vorrücken ▷ _vt_ (_money_)
vorschießen; **advance booking** _n_
Reservierung _f_; (_Theat_) Vorverkauf
_m_; **advanced** [əd'vɑːnst] _adj_ (_modern_)
fortschrittlich; (_course, study_) für
Fortgeschrittene; **advance**
payment _n_ Vorauszahlung _f_
advantage [əd'vɑːntɪdʒ] _n_
Vorteil _m_; **to take ~ of** (_exploit_)
ausnutzen; (_profit from_) Nutzen
ziehen aus; **it's to your ~** es ist in
deinem/Ihrem Interesse
adventure [əd'ventʃə*] _n_
Abenteuer _nt_; **adventure holiday**
_n_ Abenteuerurlaub _m_; **adventure**
playground _n_ Abenteuerspiel-
platz _m_; **adventurous**
[əd'ventʃərəs] _adj_ (_person_)
abenteuerlustig
adverb ['ædvɜːb] _n_ Adverb _nt_
adverse ['ædvɜːs] _adj_ (_conditions
etc_) ungünstig; (_effect, comment etc_)
negativ
advert ['ædvɜːt] _n_ Anzeige _f_;
advertise ['ædvətaɪz] _vt_ werben
für; (_in newspaper_) inserieren; (_job_)
ausschreiben ▷ _vi_ Reklame
machen; (_in newspaper_)
annoncieren (_for_ für);
advertisement [əd'vɜːtɪsmənt]
_n_ Werbung _f_; (_announcement_)
Anzeige _f_; **advertising** _n_
Werbung _f_
advice [əd'vaɪs] _n_ Rat(schlag) _m_;
word o **piece of ~** Ratschlag _m_;
take my ~ hör auf mich;
advisable [əd'vaɪzəbl] _adj_ ratsam; **advise** [əd'vaɪz] _vt_ raten
(_sb_ jdm); **to ~ sb to do sth/not to**
do sth jdm zuraten/abraten, etw
zu tun
Aegean [iː'dʒiːən] _n_: **the ~ (Sea)**
die Ägäis
aerial ['eərɪəl] _n_ Antenne _f_ ▷ _adj_
Luft-

aerobatics [eərəʊ'bætɪks] _npl_
Kunstfliegen _nt_
aerobics [eə'rəʊbɪks] _nsing_
Aerobic _nt_
aeroplane ['eərəpleɪn] _n_
Flugzeug _nt_
afaik _abbr_ = **as far as I know**;
(_SMS_) = soweit ich weiß
affair [ə'feə*] _n_ (_matter, business_)
Sache _f_, Angelegenheit _f_; (_scandal_)
Affäre _f_; (_love affair_) Verhältnis _nt_
affect [ə'fekt] _vt_ (_influence_)
(ein)wirken auf +_akk_; (_health,
organ_) angreifen; (_move deeply_)
berühren; (_concern_) betreffen;
affection [ə'fekʃən] _n_ Zuneigung
_f_; **affectionate** [ə'fekʃənɪt] _adj_
liebevoll
affluent ['æfluənt] _adj_
wohlhabend
afford [ə'fɔːd] _vt_ sich leisten; **I**
can't ~ it ich kann es mir nicht
leisten; **affordable** [ə'fɔːdəbl]
adj erschwinglich
Afghanistan [æf'gænɪstæn] _n_
Afghanistan _nt_
aforementioned
[əfɔː'menʃənd] _adj_ oben genannt
afraid [ə'freɪd] _adj_: **to be ~** Angst
haben (_of_ vor +_dat_); **to be ~ that ...**
fürchten, dass ...; **I'm ~ I don't**
know das weiß ich leider nicht
Africa ['æfrɪkə] _n_ Afrika _nt_;
African _adj_ afrikanisch ▷ _n_
Afrikaner(in) _m(f)_; **African**
American, **Afro-American** ▷ _n_
Afroamerikaner(in) _m(f)_
after ['ɑːftə*] _prep_ nach; **ten**
~ five (_US_) zehn nach fünf; **to be**
~ sb/sth (_following, seeking_) hinter
jdm/etw her sein; **~ all**
schließlich; (_in spite of everything_)
(schließlich) doch ▷ _conj_
nachdem ▷ _adv_: **soon ~** bald
danach; **aftercare** _n_
Nachbehandlung _f_; **after-effect** _n_
Nachwirkung _f_

afternoon n Nachmittag m; ~,
good ~ guten Tag!; **in the**
~ nachmittags

afters npl Nachtisch m;
after-sales service n
Kundendienst m; **after-shave
(lotion)** n Rasierwasser nt;
aftersun n After-Sun-Lotion f;
afterwards adv nachher; (after
that) danach

again [əˈgen] adv wieder; (one
more time) noch einmal; **not ~!**
(nicht) schon wieder; **~ and**
~ immer wieder; **the same**
~ **please** das Gleiche noch mal
bitte

against [əˈgenst] prep gegen;
~ **my will** wider Willen; **~ the law**
unrechtmäßig, illegal

age [eɪdʒ] n Alter nt; (period of
history) Zeitalter nt; **at the ~ of
four** im Alter von vier (Jahren);
what ~ is she?, what is her ~? wie
alt ist sie?; **to come of ~** volljährig
werden; **under ~** minderjährig
▷ vi altern, alt werden; **aged** adj;
~ **thirty** dreißig Jahre alt; **a son
~ twenty** ein zwanzigjähriger
Sohn ▷ adj [ˈeɪdʒɪd] (elderly)
betagt; **age group** n
Altersgruppe f; **ageism** n
Diskriminierung f aufgrund des
Alters; **age limit** n Altersgrenze f

agency [ˈeɪdʒənsɪ] n Agentur f

agenda [əˈdʒendə] n Tagesordnung f

agent [ˈeɪdʒənt] n (Comm)
Vertreter(in) m(f); (for writer, actor
etc) Agent(in) m(f)

aggression [əˈgreʃn] n Aggression f; **aggressive** [əˈgresɪv] adj
aggressiv

agitated adj aufgeregt; **to get
~** sich aufregen

AGM abbr = **Annual General
Meeting** JHV f

ago [əˈgəʊ] adv: **two days ~**

heute vor zwei Tagen; **not long
~** (erst) vor Kurzem

agonize [ˈægənaɪz] vi sich den
Kopf zerbrechen (over über dat);
agonizing adj qualvoll; **agony**
[ˈægənɪ] n Qual f

agree [əˈgriː] vt (date, price etc)
vereinbaren; **to ~ to do sth** sich
bereit erklären, etw zu tun; **to
~ that ...** sich dat einig sein,
dass ...; (decide) beschließen,
dass ...; (admit) zugeben, dass ...
▷ vi (have same opinion, correspond)
übereinstimmen (with mit);
(consent) zustimmen; (come to an
agreement) sich einigen (about, on
auf +akk); (food) **not to ~ with sb**
jdm nicht bekommen; **agreement**
n (agreeing) Übereinstimmung f;
(contract) Abkommen nt,
Vereinbarung f

agricultural [ægrɪˈkʌltʃərəl] adj
landwirtschaftlich,
Landwirtschafts-; **agriculture**
[ˈægrɪkʌltʃə°] n Landwirtschaft f

ahead [əˈhed] adv: **to be ~**
führen, vorne liegen; **~ of** vor
+dat; **to be ~ of sb** (person) jdm
voraus sein; (thing) vor jdm liegen;
to be 3 metres ~ 3 Meter
Vorsprung haben

aid [eɪd] n Hilfe f; **in ~ of**
zugunsten +gen; **with the ~ of**
mithilfe +gen ▷ vt helfen +dat;
(support) unterstützen

Aids [eɪdz] n acr = **acquired
immune deficiency syndrome**
Aids nt

aim [eɪm] vt (gun, camera) richten
(at auf +akk) ▷ vi: **to ~ at** (with gun
etc) zielen auf +akk; (fig) abzielen
auf +akk; **to ~ to do sth**
beabsichtigen, etw zu tun ▷ n
Ziel nt

air [eə°] n Luft f; **in the open ~** im
Freien; (Radio, TV) **to be on the
~** (programme) auf Sendung sein;

(station) senden ▷ vt lüften;
airbag n (Auto) Airbag m;
air-conditioned adj mit
Klimaanlage; **air-conditioning** n
Klimaanlage f; **aircraft** n
Flugzeug nt; **airfield** n Flugplatz
m; **air force** n Luftwaffe f;
airgun n Luftgewehr nt;
airline n Fluggesellschaft f;
airmail n Luftpost f; **by ~** mit
Luftpost; **airplane** n (US)
Flugzeug nt; **air pollution** n
Luftverschmutzung f; **airport** n
Flughafen m; **airsick** adj
luftkrank; **airtight** adj luftdicht;
air-traffic controller n Fluglotse
m, Fluglotsin f; **airy** adj luftig;
(manner) lässig

aisle [aıl] n Gang m; (in church)
Seitenschiff nt; **~ seat** Sitz m am
Gang

ajar [ə'dʒɑː°] adj (door) angelehnt

alarm [ə'lɑːm] n (warning) Alarm
m; (bell etc) Alarmanlage f ▷ vt
beunruhigen; **alarm clock** n
Wecker m; **alarmed** adj (protected)
alarmgesichert; **alarming** adj
beunruhigend

Albania [æl'beɪnɪə] n Albanien
nt; **Albanian** adj albanisch ▷ n
(person) Albaner(in) m(f); (language)
Albanisch nt

album ['ælbəm] n Album nt

alcohol ['ælkəhɒl] n Alkohol m;
alcohol-free adj alkoholfrei;
alcoholic [ælkə'hɒlık] adj (drink)
alkoholisch ▷ n Alkoholiker(in)
m(f); **alcoholism** n Alkoholismus
m

ale [eɪl] n Ale nt (helles englisches
Bier)

alert [ə'lɜːt] adj wachsam ▷ n
Alarm m ▷ vt warnen (to vor +dat)

algebra ['ældʒıbrə] n Algebra f

Algeria [æl'dʒıərɪə] n Algerien nt

alibi ['ælıbaı] n Alibi nt

alien ['eɪlɪən] n (foreigner)

Ausländer(in) m(f); (from space)
Außerirdische(r) mf

align [ə'laın] vt ausrichten (with
auf +akk)

alike [ə'laık] adj, adv gleich;
(similar) ähnlich

alive [ə'laıv] adj lebendig; **to
keep sth** ~ etw am Leben
erhalten; **he's still** ~ er lebt noch

○ **KEYWORD**

all [ɔːl] adj alle(r, s); **all day/night**
den ganzen Tag/die ganze Nacht;
all men are equal alle Menschen
sind gleich; **all five came** alle fünf
kamen; **all the books/food** die
ganzen Bücher/das ganze Essen;
all the time die ganze Zeit (über);
all his life sein ganzes Leben
(lang)

▷ pron 1 alles; **I ate it all, I ate all of
it** ich habe alles gegessen; **all of
us/the boys went** wir gingen
alle/alle Jungen gingen; **we all sat
down** wir setzten uns alle

2 (in phrases) **above all** vor allem;
after all schließlich; **at all:** not at
all (in answer to question)
überhaupt nicht; (in answer to
thanks) gern geschehen; **I'm not at
all tired** ich bin überhaupt nicht
müde; **anything at all will do** es
ist egal, welche(r, s); **all in all** alles
in allem

▷ adv ganz; **all alone** ganz allein;
it's not as hard as all that so
schwer ist es nun auch wieder
nicht; **all the more/the better**
umso mehr/besser; **all but** fast;
the score is 2 all es steht 2 zu 2

allegation [ælı'geɪʃən] n
Behauptung f; **alleged** adj
angeblich

allergic [ə'lɜːdʒık] adj allergisch

(to gegen); **allergy** ['ælədʒɪ] n
Allergie f

alleviate [ə'liːvɪeɪt] vt (pain)
lindern

alley ['ælɪ] n (enge) Gasse;
(passage) Durchgang m; (bowling)
Bahn f

alliance [ə'laɪəns] n Bündnis nt

alligator ['ælɪɡeɪtə°] n Alligator
m

all-night adj (café, cinema) die
ganze Nacht geöffnet

allocate ['æləkeɪt] vt zuweisen,
zuteilen (to dat)

allotment n (plot)
Schrebergarten m

allow [ə'laʊ] vt (permit) erlauben
(sb jdm); (grant) bewilligen; (time)
einplanen; **allow for** vt
berücksichtigen; (cost etc)
einkalkulieren; **allowance** n (from
state) Beihilfe f; (from parent)
Unterhaltsgeld nt

all right [ɔːl'raɪt] adj okay, in
Ordnung; **I'm ~** mir geht's gut
▷ adv (satisfactorily) ganz gut
▷ interj okay

all-time adj (record, high) aller
Zeiten

allusion [ə'luːʒn] n Anspielung f
(to auf +akk)

ally ['ælaɪ] n Verbündete(r) mf;
(Hist) Alliierte(r) mf

almond ['ɑːmənd] n Mandel f

almost ['ɔːlməʊst] adv fast

alone [ə'ləʊn] adj, adv allein

along [ə'lɒŋ] prep entlang
+akk; **~ the river** den Fluss
entlang; (position) am Fluss
entlang ▷ adv (onward) weiter;
~ with zusammen mit; **all ~** die
ganze Zeit, von Anfang an;
alongside prep neben +dat ▷ adv
(walk) nebenher

aloud [ə'laʊd] adv laut

alphabet ['ælfəbet] n Alphabet
nt

alpine ['ælpaɪn] adj alpin; **Alps**
[ælps] npl: **the ~** die Alpen

already [ɔːl'redɪ] adv schon,
bereits

Alsace ['ælsæs] n Elsass nt;
Alsatian [æl'seɪʃən] adj
elsässisch ▷ n Elsässer(in) m(f);
(Brit: dog) Schäferhund m

also ['ɔːlsəʊ] adv auch

altar ['ɔːltə°] n Altar m

alter ['ɔːltə°] vt ändern;
alteration [ɔːltə'reɪʃən] n
Änderung f; **~s (to building)** Umbau
m

alternate [ɔːl'tɜːnət] adj
abwechselnd ▷ ['ɔːltəneɪt] vi
abwechseln (with mit);
alternating current n
Wechselstrom m

alternative [ɔːl'tɜːnətɪv] adj
Alternativ- ▷ n Alternative f

although [ɔːl'ðəʊ] conj obwohl

altitude ['æltɪtjuːd] n Höhe f

altogether [ɔːltə'ɡeðə°] adv (in
total) insgesamt; (entirely) ganz
und gar

aluminium [æljʊ'mɪnɪəm], **aluminum** (US)
[ə'luːmɪnəm] n
Aluminium nt

always ['ɔːlweɪz] adv immer

am [æm] present of **be**; bin

am, a.m. abbr = **ante meridiem**
vormittags, vorm.

amateur ['æmətə°] n Amateur(in) m(f) ▷ adj Amateur-;
(theatre, choir) Laien-

amaze [ə'meɪz] vt erstaunen;
amazed adj erstaunt (at über
+akk); **amazing** adj erstaunlich

Amazon ['æməzən] n: **~ (river)**
Amazonas m

ambassador [æm'bæsədə°] n
Botschafter m

amber ['æmbə°] n Bernstein m

ambiguity [æmbɪ'ɡjuːɪtɪ] n
Zweideutigkeit f; **ambiguous**
[æm'bɪɡjʊəs] adj zweideutig

ambition [æm'bɪʃən] n Ambition f; (ambitious nature) Ehrgeiz m; **ambitious** [æm'bɪʃəs] adj ehrgeizig

ambulance [ˈæmbjʊləns] n Krankenwagen m

amend [əˈmend] vt (law etc) ändern

America [əˈmerɪkə] n Amerika nt; **American** adj amerikanisch ⊳ n Amerikaner(in) m(f); **native ~** Indianer(in) m(f)

amiable [ˈeɪmɪəbl] adj liebenswürdig

amicable [ˈæmɪkəbl] adj freundlich; (relations) freundschaftlich; (Jur: settlement) gütlich

amnesia [æmˈniːzɪə] n Gedächtnisverlust m

among(st) [əˈmʌŋ(st)] prep unter +dat

amount [əˈmaʊnt] n (quantity) Menge f; (of money) Betrag m; **a large/small ~ of ...** ziemlich viel/wenig ... ⊳ vi: **to ~ to** (total) sich belaufen auf +akk

amp, ampere [æmp, ˈæmpeə⁹] n Ampere nt

amplifier [ˈæmplɪfaɪə⁹] n Verstärker m

amputate [ˈæmpjʊteɪt] vt amputieren

Amtrak® [ˈæmtræk] n amerikanische Eisenbahngesellschaft

amuse [əˈmjuːz] vt amüsieren; (entertain) unterhalten; **amused** adj: **I'm not ~** das finde ich gar nicht lustig; **amusement** n (enjoyment) Vergnügen nt; (recreation) Unterhaltung f; **amusement arcade** n Spielhalle f; **amusement park** n Vergnügungspark m; **amusing** adj amüsant

an [æn, ən] art ein(e)

anaemic [əˈniːmɪk] adj blutarm

anaesthetic [ænɪsˈθetɪk] n

Narkose f; (substance) Narkosemittel nt

analyse, analyze [ˈænəlaɪz] vt analysieren; **analysis** [əˈnælɪsɪs] n Analyse f

anatomy [əˈnætəmɪ] n Anatomie f; (structure) Körperbau m

ancestor [ˈænsestə⁹] n Vorfahr m

anchor [ˈæŋkə⁹] n Anker m ⊳ vt verankern; **anchorage** n Ankerplatz m

anchovy [ˈæntʃəvɪ] n Sardelle f

ancient [ˈeɪnʃənt] adj alt; (fam: person, clothes etc) uralt

and [ænd, ənd] conj und

Andorra [ænˈdɔːrə] n Andorra nt

anemic adj (US) see **anaemic**

anesthetic n (US) see **anaesthetic**

angel [ˈeɪndʒəl] n Engel m

anger [ˈæŋgə⁹] n Zorn m ⊳ vt ärgern

angina, angina pectoris [ænˈdʒaɪnə(ˈpektərɪs)] n Angina Pectoris f

angle [ˈæŋgl] n Winkel m; (fig) Standpunkt m

angler [ˈæŋglə⁹] n Angler(in) m(f); **angling** [ˈæŋglɪŋ] n Angeln nt

angry [ˈæŋgrɪ] adj verärgert; (stronger) zornig; **to be ~ with sb** auf jdn böse sein

angular [ˈæŋgjʊlə⁹] adj eckig; (face) kantig

animal [ˈænɪməl] n Tier nt; **animal rights** npl Tierrechte pl

animated [ˈænɪmeɪtɪd] adj lebhaft; **~ film** Zeichentrickfilm m

aniseed [ˈænɪsiːd] n Anis m

ankle [ˈæŋkl] n (Fuß)knöchel m

annex [ˈæneks] n Anbau m

anniversary [ænɪˈvɜːsərɪ] n Jahrestag m

announce [əˈnaʊns] vt bekannt geben; (officially) bekannt machen; (on radio, TV etc) (Radio,

TV) ansagen; **announcement** n
Bekanntgabe f; (official)
Bekanntmachung f; (Radio, TV)
Ansage f; **announcer** n (Radio, TV)
Ansager(in) m(f)

annoy [əˈnɔɪ] vt ärgern;
annoyance n Ärger m; **annoyed**
adj ärgerlich; **to be ~ with sb**
(about sth) sich über jdn (über
etw) ärgern; **annoying** adj
ärgerlich; (person) lästig, nervig

annual [ˈænjʊəl] adj jährlich
▷ n Jahrbuch n

anonymous [əˈnɒnɪməs] adj
anonym

anorak [ˈænəræk] n Anorak m

anorexia [ænəˈreksɪə] n Magersucht f; **anorexic** adj
magersüchtig

another [əˈnʌðə*] adj, pron
(different) ein(e) andere(r, s);
(additional) noch eine(r, s); **let me**
put it ~ way lass es mich anders
sagen

answer [ˈɑːnsə*] n Antwort f (to
auf +akk); (solution) Lösung f +gen
▷ vi antworten; (on phone) sich
melden ▷ vt (person) antworten
+dat; (letter, question) beantworten;
(telephone) gehen an +akk,
abnehmen; (door) öffnen; **answer**
back vi widersprechen;
answering machine,
answerphone n Anrufbeantworter m

ant [ænt] n Ameise f

Antarctic [ænˈtɑːktɪk] n
Antarktis f; **Antarctic Circle** n
südlicher Polarkreis

antelope [ˈæntɪləʊp] n Antilope f

antenna [ænˈtenə] (pl **antennae**)
n (Zool) Fühler m; (Radio) Antenne f

anti- [ˈæntɪ] pref Anti-, anti-;
antibiotic [ˈæntɪbaɪˈɒtɪk] n
Antibiotikum n

anticipate [ænˈtɪsɪpeɪt] vt (expect:
trouble, question) erwarten,

rechnen mit; **anticipation**
[æntɪsɪˈpeɪʃən] n Erwartung f

anticlimax [æntɪˈklaɪmæks] n
Enttäuschung f; **anticlockwise**
[æntɪˈklɒkwaɪz] adv entgegen
dem Uhrzeigersinn

antidote [ˈæntɪdəʊt] n Gegenmittel nt; **antifreeze** n
Frostschutzmittel nt

Antipodes [ænˈtɪpədiːz] npl
Australien und Neuseeland

antiquarian [æntɪˈkwɛərɪən]
adj: **~ bookshop** Antiquariat nt

antique [ænˈtiːk] n Antiquität f
▷ adj antik; **antique shop** n
Antiquitätengeschäft nt

anti-Semitism [æntɪˈsemɪtɪzm]
n Antisemitismus m; **antiseptic**
[æntɪˈseptɪk] n Antiseptikum nt
▷ adj antiseptisch; **antisocial** adj
(person) ungesellig; (behaviour)
unsozial, asozial; **antivirus** adj
(Inform) Antiviren-; **antivirus**
software n Antivirensoftware f

antlers [ˈæntləz] npl Geweih nt

anxiety [æŋˈzaɪətɪ] n Sorge f
(about um); **anxious** [ˈæŋkʃəs] adj
besorgt (about um); (apprehensive)
ängstlich

⭕ **KEYWORD**

any [ˈenɪ] adj **1** (in questions etc)
have you any butter? haben Sie
(etwas) Butter?; **have you any**
children? haben Sie Kinder?; **if**
there are any tickets left falls
noch Karten da sind
2 (with negative) **I haven't any**
money ich habe kein Geld
3 (no matter which) jede(r, s)
(beliebige); **any colour (at all)**
jede beliebige Farbe; **choose any**
book you like nehmen Sie ein
beliebiges Buch
4 (in phrases) **in any case** in jedem

Fall; **any day now** jeden Tag; **at any moment** jeden Moment; **at any rate** auf jeden Fall ▷ *pron* **1** (*in questions etc*) **have you got any?** haben Sie welche?; **can any of you sing?** kann (irgend)einer von euch singen? **2** (*with negative*) **I haven't any (of them)** ich habe keinen/keines (davon) **3** (*no matter which one(s)*): **take any of those books (you like)** nehmen Sie irgendeines dieser Bücher ▷ *adv* **1** (*in questions etc*) **do you want any more soup/ sandwiches?** möchten Sie noch Suppe/Brote?; **are you feeling any better?** fühlen Sie sich etwas besser? **2** (*with negative*) **I can't hear him any more** ich kann ihn nicht mehr hören

anybody *pron* (*whoever one likes*) irgendjemand; (*everyone*) jeder; (*in question*) jemand;

anyhow *adv* **I don't want to talk about it, not now ~** ich möchte nicht darüber sprechen, jedenfalls nicht jetzt; **they asked me not to go, but I went ~** sie baten mich, nicht hinzugehen, aber ich bin trotzdem hingegangen; **anyone** *pron* (*whoever one likes*) irgendjemand; (*everyone*) jeder; (*in question*) jemand; **isn't there ~ you can ask?** gibt es denn niemanden, den du fragen kannst/den Sie fragen können?; **anyplace** *adv* (*US*) irgendwo; (*direction*) irgendwohin; (*everywhere*) überall

○ **KEYWORD**

anything ['enιθιη] *pron* **1** (*in questions etc*) (irgend)etwas; **can**

you see anything? können Sie etwas sehen? **2** (*with negative*) **I can't see anything** ich kann nichts sehen **3** (*no matter what*) **you can say anything you like** Sie können sagen, was Sie wollen; **anything will do** irgendetwas (wird genügen); irgendeine(r, s) (wird genügen); **he'll eat anything** er isst alles

anytime *adv* jederzeit; **anyway** *adv*: **I didn't want to go there ~** ich wollte da sowieso nicht hingehen; **thanks ~** trotzdem danke; **~, as I was saying, ...** jedenfalls, wie ich schon sagte, ...; **anywhere** *adv* irgendwo; (*direction*) irgendwohin; (*everywhere*) überall **apart** [ə'pɑːt] *adv* auseinander; **~ from** außer; **live ~** getrennt leben **apartment** [ə'pɑːtmənt] *n* (*esp US*) Wohnung *f*; **apartment block** *n* (*esp US*) Wohnblock *m* **ape** [eɪp] *n* (Menschen)affe *m* **aperitif** [ə'perɪtɪf] *n* Aperitif *m* **apologize** [ə'pɒlədʒaɪz] *vi* sich entschuldigen; **apology** *n* Entschuldigung *f* **apostrophe** [ə'pɒstrəfɪ] *n* Apostroph *m* **app** [æp] (*for mobile phone*) App *f* **appalled** [ə'pɔːld] *adj* entsetzt (*at über* +*akk*); **appalling** *adj* entsetzlich **apparatus** [æpə'reɪtəs] *n* Apparat *m*; (*piece of apparatus*) Gerät *nt* **apparent** [ə'pærənt] *adj* (*obvious*) offensichtlich (*to* für); (*seeming*) scheinbar; **apparently** *adv* anscheinend **appeal** [ə'piːl] *vi* (dringend)

bitten (for um, to +akk); (Jur)
Berufung einlegen; **to ~ sb** (be
attractive) jdm zusagen ▷ n Aufruf
m (to an +akk); (Jur) Berufung f;
(attraction) Reiz m; **appealing** adj
ansprechend, attraktiv

appear [əˈpɪə*] vi erscheinen;
(Theat) auftreten; (seem) scheinen;
appearance n Erscheinen nt;
(Theat) Auftritt m; (look) Aussehen
nt

appendicitis [əpendɪˈsaɪtɪs] n
Blinddarmentzündung f;
appendix [əˈpendɪks] n Blinddarm m; (to book) Anhang m

appetite [ˈæpɪtaɪt] n Appetit m;
(fig: desire) Verlangen nt; (sexual)
Lust f; **appetizing** [ˈæpɪtaɪzɪŋ]
adj appetitlich, appetitanregend

applause [əˈplɔːz] n Beifall m,
Applaus m

apple [ˈæpl] n Apfel m; **apple
crumble** n mit Streuseln bestreutes
Apfeldessert; **apple juice** n
Apfelsaft m; **apple pie** n
gedeckter Apfelkuchen m; **apple
puree, apple sauce** n Apfelmus
nt; **apple tart** n Apfelkuchen m;
apple tree n Apfelbaum m

appliance [əˈplaɪəns] n Gerät nt;
applicable [əˈplɪkəbl] adj
anwendbar; (on forms) zutreffend;
applicant [ˈæplɪkənt] n Bewer-
ber(in) m(f); **application**
[æplɪˈkeɪʃən] n (request) Antrag m
(for auf +akk); (for job) Bewerbung f
(for um); **application form** n
Anmeldeformular nt; **apply**
[əˈplaɪ] vi (be relevant) zutreffen (to
auf +akk); (for job etc) sich
bewerben (for um) ▷ vt (cream,
paint etc) auftragen; (put into
practice) anwenden; (brakes)
betätigen

appoint [əˈpɔɪnt] vt (to post)
ernennen; **appointment** n
Verabredung f; (at doctor, hairdresser

etc, in business) Termin m; **by
~** nach Vereinbarung

appreciate [əˈpriːʃɪeɪt] vt (value)
zu schätzen wissen; (understand)
einsehen; **to be much ~d** richtig
gewürdigt werden ▷ vi (increase in
value) im Wert steigen;
appreciation [əpriːʃɪˈeɪʃən] n
(esteem) Anerkennung f,
Würdigung f; (of person also)
Wertschätzung f

apprehensive [æprɪˈhensɪv] adj
ängstlich

apprentice [əˈprentɪs] n Lehrling m

approach [əˈprəʊtʃ] vi sich
nähern ▷ vt (place) sich nähern
+dat; (person) herantreten an +akk;
(problem) angehen

appropriate [əˈprəʊprɪət] adj
passend; (to occasion) angemessen;
(remark) treffend; **appropriately**
adv passend; (expressed) treffend

approval [əˈpruːvəl] n (show of
satisfaction) Anerkennung f;
(permission) Zustimmung f (of zu);
approve [əˈpruːv] vt billigen
▷ vi: **to ~ of sth/sb** etw
billigen/von jdm etwas halten; **I
don't ~** ich missbillige das

approx [əˈprɒks] abbr =
approximately ca.; **approximate**
[əˈprɒksɪmɪt] adj ungefähr;
approximately adv ungefähr,
circa

apricot [ˈeɪprɪkɒt] n Aprikose f

April [ˈeɪprəl] n April m; see also
September

apron [ˈeɪprən] n Schürze f

aptitude [ˈæptɪtjuːd] n Begabung
f

aquaplaning [ˈækwəpleɪnɪŋ] n
(Auto) Aquaplaning nt

aquarium [əˈkweərɪəm] n
Aquarium nt

Aquarius [əˈkweərɪəs] n (Astr)
Wassermann m

Arab ['ærəb] n Araber(in) m(f); (horse) Araber m; **Arabian** [ə'reɪbɪən] adj arabisch; **Arabic** ['ærəbɪk] n (language) Arabisch nt ▷ adj arabisch

arbitrary ['ɑːbɪtrərɪ] adj willkürlich

arcade [ɑː'keɪd] n Arkade f; (shopping arcade) Einkaufspassage f

arch [ɑːtʃ] n Bogen m

archaeologist, **archeologist** (US) [ɑːkɪ'ɒlədʒɪst] n Archäologe m, Archäologin f; **archaeology**, **archeology** (US) [ɑːkɪ'ɒlədʒɪ] n Archäologie f

archaic [ɑː'keɪɪk] adj veraltet

archbishop [ɑːtʃ'bɪʃəp] n Erzbischof m

archery ['ɑːtʃərɪ] n Bogenschießen nt

architect ['ɑːkɪtekt] n Architekt(in) m(f); **architecture** [ɑːkɪ'tektʃə] n Architektur f

archive(s) ['ɑːkaɪv(z)] n(pl) Archiv nt

archway ['ɑːtʃweɪ] n Torbogen m

Arctic ['ɑːktɪk] n Arktis f; **Arctic Circle** n nördlicher Polarkreis

are [ə, unstressed ɑː'] present of **be**

area ['ɛərɪə] n (region, district) Gebiet nt, Gegend f; (amount of space) Fläche f; (part of building etc) Bereich m, Zone f; (fig: field) Bereich m; **the London ~** der Londoner Raum; **area code** n (US) Vorwahl f

aren't [ɑːnt] contr of **are not**

Argentina [ɑːdʒən'tiːnə] n Argentinien nt

argue ['ɑːgjuː] vi streiten (about, over über +akk); **to ~ that ...** behaupten, dass ...; **to ~ for/against ...** sprechen für/gegen ...; **argument** n (reasons) Argument nt; (quarrel) Streit m; **to have an ~** sich streiten

Aries ['ɛəriːz] nsing (Astr) Widder m

arise [ə'raɪz] (**arose, arisen**) vi sich ergeben, entstehen; (problem, question, wind) aufkommen

aristocracy [ærɪs'tɒkrəsɪ] n (class) Adel m; **aristocrat** ['ærɪstəkræt] n Adlige(r) mf; **aristocratic** [ærɪstə'krætɪk] adj aristokratisch, adlig

arm [ɑːm] n Arm m; (sleeve) Ärmel m; (of armchair) Armlehne f ▷ vt bewaffnen; **armchair** [ɑːmtʃɛə°] n Lehnstuhl m

armed [ɑːmd] adj bewaffnet

armpit ['ɑːmpɪt] n Achselhöhle f

arms [ɑːmz] npl Waffen pl

army ['ɑːmɪ] n Armee f, Heer nt

A road ['eɪrəʊd] n (Brit) ≈ Bundesstraße f

aroma [ə'rəʊmə] n Duft m, Aroma nt; **aromatherapy** [ərəʊmə'θerəpɪ] n Aromatherapie f

arose [ə'rəʊz] pt of **arise**

around [ə'raʊnd] adv herum, umher; (present) hier (irgendwo); (approximately) ungefähr; (with time) gegen; **he's ~ somewhere** er ist hier irgendwo in der Nähe ▷ prep (surrounding) um ... (herum); (about in) in ... herum

arr. abbr = **arrival**, **arrives** Ank.

arrange [ə'reɪndʒ] vt (put in order) (an)ordnen; (alphabetically) ordnen; (artistically) arrangieren; (agree to: meeting etc) vereinbaren, festsetzen; (holidays) festlegen; (organize) planen; **to ~ that ...** es so einrichten, dass ...; **we ~d to meet at eight o'clock** wir haben uns für acht Uhr verabredet; **it's all ~d** es ist alles arrangiert; **arrangement** n (layout) Anordnung f; (agreement)

Vereinbarung f, Plan m; **make ~s** Vorbereitungen treffen

arrest [əˈrest] vt (person) verhaften ▷ n Verhaftung f; **under ~** verhaftet

arrival [əˈraɪvəl] n Ankunft f; **new ~** (person) Neuankömmling m; **arrivals** n (airport) Ankunftshalle f; **arrive** [əˈraɪv] vi ankommen (at bei, in +dat); **to ~ at a solution** eine Lösung finden

arrogant [ˈærəgənt] adj arrogant

arrow [ˈærəʊ] n Pfeil m

arse [ɑːs] n (vulg) Arsch m

art [ɑːt] n Kunst f, **the ~s** (pl) Geisteswissenschaften pl

artery [ˈɑːtəri] n Schlagader f, Arterie f

art gallery n Kunstgalerie f, Kunstmuseum nt

arthritis [ɑːˈθraɪtɪs] n Arthritis f

artichoke [ˈɑːtɪtʃəʊk] n Artischocke f

article [ˈɑːtɪkl] n Artikel m; (object) Gegenstand m

artificial [ɑːtɪˈfɪʃəl] adj künstlich, Kunst-; (smile etc) gekünstelt

artist [ˈɑːtɪst] n Künstler(in) m(f); **artistic** [ɑːˈtɪstɪk] adj künstlerisch

○ **KEYWORD**

as [æz, əz] conj 1 (referring to time) als; **as the years went by** mit den Jahren; **he came in as I was leaving** als er hereinkam, ging ich gerade; **as from tomorrow** ab morgen

2 (in comparisons) **as big as** so groß wie; **twice as big as** zweimal so groß wie; **as much/many as** so viel/so viele wie; **as soon as** sobald

3 (since, because) da; **he left early as he had to be home by 10** er

ging früher, da er um 10 zu Hause sein musste

4 (referring to manner, way) wie; **do as you wish** mach was du willst; **as she said** wie sie sagte

5 (concerning) **as for o to that** was das betrifft o angeht

6 **as if o though** als ob

▷ prep als; see also **long**; **he works as a driver** er arbeitet als Fahrer; see also **such**; **he gave it to me as a present** er hat es mir als Geschenk gegeben; see also **well**

asap [eɪeseɪˈpiː, ˈeɪsæp] acr = **as soon as possible** möglichst bald

ascertain [æsəˈteɪn] vt feststellen

ash [æʃ] n (dust) Asche f; (tree) Esche f

ashamed [əˈʃeɪmd] adj beschämt; **to be ~ (of sb/sth)** sich (für jdn/etw) schämen

ashore [əˈʃɔː] adv an Land

ashtray [ˈæʃtreɪ] n Aschenbecher m

Asia [ˈeɪʃə] n Asien nt; **Asian** adj asiatisch ▷ n Asiat(in) m(f)

aside [əˈsaɪd] adv beiseite, zur Seite; **~ from** (esp US) außer

ask [ɑːsk] vt, vi fragen; (question) stellen; (request) bitten um; (invite) einladen; **to ~ sb the way** jdn nach dem Weg fragen; **to ~ sb to do sth** jdn darum bitten, etw zu tun; **ask for** vt bitten um

asleep [əˈsliːp] adj, adv: **to be ~** schlafen; **to fall ~** einschlafen

asparagus [əsˈpærəgəs] n Spargel m

aspect [ˈæspekt] n Aspekt m

aspirin [ˈæsprɪn] n Aspirin® f

ass [æs] n (a. fig) Esel m; (US vulg) Arsch m

assassinate [əˈsæsɪneɪt] vt ermorden; **assassination**

[əˈsæsɪneɪʃn] n Ermordung f; ~ **attempt** Attentat nt

assault [əˈsɔːlt] n Angriff m; (Jur) Körperverletzung f ▷ vt überfallen, herfallen über +akk

assemble [əˈsembl] vt (parts) zusammensetzen; (people) zusammenrufen ▷ vi sich versammeln; **assembly** [əˈsemblɪ] n (of people) Versammlung f; (of parts) Zusammensetzen nt; **assembly hall** n Aula f

assert [əˈsɜːt] vt behaupten; **assertion** [əˈsɜːʃən] n Behauptung f

assess [əˈses] vt einschätzen; **assessment** n Einschätzung f

asset [ˈæset] n Vermögenswert m; (fig) Vorteil m; ~s pl Vermögen nt

assign [əˈsaɪn] vt zuweisen; **assignment** n Aufgabe f; (mission) Auftrag m

assist [əˈsɪst] vt helfen +dat; **assistance** n Hilfe f; **assistant** n Assistent(in) m(f), Mitarbeiter(in) m(f); (in shop) Verkäufer(in) m(f); **assistant referee** n (Sport) Schiedsrichterassistent(in) m(f)

associate [əˈsəʊʃɪeɪt] vt verbinden (with mit); **association** [əsəʊsɪˈeɪʃən] n (organization) Verband m, Vereinigung f; **in ~ with ...** in Zusammenarbeit mit ...

assorted [əˈsɔːtɪd] adj gemischt; **assortment** n Auswahl f (of an +dat); (of sweets) Mischung f

assume [əˈsjuːm] vt annehmen (that ... dass ...); (role, responsibility) übernehmen; **assumption** [əˈsʌmpʃən] n Annahme f

assurance [əˈʃʊərəns] n Versicherung f; (confidence) Zuversicht f; **assure** [əˈʃʊə] vt (say confidently) versichern +dat; **to**

~ **sb of sth** jdm etw zusichern; **to be ~d of sth** einer Sache sicher sein

asterisk [ˈæstərɪsk] n Sternchen nt

asthma [ˈæsmə] n Asthma nt

astonish [əˈstɒnɪʃ] vt erstaunen; **astonished** adj erstaunt (at über); **astonishing** adj erstaunlich; **astonishment** n Erstaunen nt

astound [əˈstaʊnd] vt sehr erstaunen; **astounding** adj erstaunlich

astray [əˈstreɪ] adv: **to go ~** (letter etc) verloren gehen; (person) vom Weg abkommen; **to lead ~** irreführen, verführen

astrology [əˈstrɒlədʒɪ] n Astrologie f

astronaut [ˈæstrənɔːt] n Astronaut(in) m(f)

astronomy [əˈstrɒnəmɪ] n Astronomie f

asylum [əˈsaɪləm] n (home) Anstalt f; (political asylum) Asyl nt; **asylum seeker** n Asylbewerber(in) m(f)

○ **KEYWORD**

at [æt] prep 1 (referring to position, direction) an +dat; bei +dat; (with place) in +dat; **at the top** an der Spitze; **at home/school** zu Hause, zuhause (österreichisch, schweizerisch)/in der Schule; **at the baker's** beim Bäcker; **to look at sth** auf etw akk blicken; **to throw sth at sb** etw nach jdm werfen

2 (referring to time) **at 4 o'clock** um 4 Uhr; **at night** bei Nacht; **at Christmas** zu Weihnachten; **at times** manchmal

3 (referring to rates, speed etc) **at £1 a kilo** zu £1 pro Kilo; **two at a time**

zwei auf einmal; **at 50 km/h** mit 50 km/h

4 (referring to manner) **at a stroke** mit einem Schlag; **at peace** in Frieden

5 (referring to activity) **to be at work** bei der Arbeit sein; **to play at cowboys** Cowboy spielen; **to be good at sth** gut in etw dat sein

6 (referring to cause) **surprised/ annoyed at sth** überrascht/ verärgert über etw akk; **I went at his suggestion** ich ging auf seinen Vorschlag hin

7 (@ symbol) At-Zeichen nt

ate [et, eɪt] pt of **eat**

athlete ['æθliːt] n Athlet(in) m(f); (track and field) Leichtathlet(in) m(f); (sportsman) Sportler(in) m(f); **~'s foot** Fußpilz m; **athletic** [æθ'letɪk] adj sportlich; (build) athletisch; **athletics** npl Leichtathletik f

Atlantic [ət'læntɪk] n: **the ~ (Ocean)** der Atlantik

atlas ['ætləs] n Atlas m

ATM abbr = **automated teller machine** Geldautomat m

atmosphere ['ætməsfɪə] n Atmosphäre f; (fig) Stimmung f

atom ['ætəm] n Atom nt; **atomic** [ə'tɒmɪk] adj Atom-; **~ energy** Atomenergie f; **~ power** Atomkraft f

A to Z® [eɪ tə 'zed] n Stadtplan m (in Buchform)

atrocious [ə'trəʊʃəs] adj grauenhaft; **atrocity** [ə'trɒsɪtɪ] n Grausamkeit f; (deed) Gräueltat f

attach [ə'tætʃ] vt befestigen, anheften (to an +dat); **to ~ importance to sth** Wert auf etw akk legen; **to be ~ed to sb** sich zu jdm/etw hingezogen fühlen; **attachment** [ə'trækʃən] n Anziehungskraft f; (thing) Attraktion f; **attractive** adj attraktiv; (thing, idea) reizvoll

(affection) Zuneigung f; (Inform) Attachment m, Anhang m, Anlage f

attack [ə'tæk] vt, vi angreifen ▷ n Angriff m (on auf +akk); (Med) Anfall m

attempt [ə'tempt] n Versuch m; **to make an ~ to do sth** versuchen, etw zu tun ▷ vt versuchen

attend [ə'tend] vt (go to) teilnehmen an +dat; (lectures, school) besuchen ▷ vi (be present) anwesend sein; **attend to** vt sich kümmern um; (customer) bedienen; **attendance** n (presence) Anwesenheit f; (people present) Teilnehmerzahl f; **attendant** n (in car park etc) Wächter(in) m(f); (in museum) Aufseher(in) m(f)

attention [ə'tenʃən] n Aufmerksamkeit f; **(your) ~ please** Achtung!; **to pay ~ to sth** etw beachten; **to pay ~ to sb** jdm aufmerksam zuhören; (listen) jdm/etw aufmerksam zuhören; **for the ~ of ...** zu Händen von ...; **attentive** [ə'tentɪv] adj aufmerksam

attic ['ætɪk] n Dachboden m; (lived in) Mansarde f

attitude ['ætɪtjuːd] n (mental) Einstellung f (to, towards zu); (more general, physical) Haltung f

attorney [ə'tɜːnɪ] n (US: lawyer) Rechtsanwalt m, Rechtsanwältin f

attract [ə'trækt] vt anziehen; (attention) erregen; **to be ~ed to by sb** sich zu jdm hingezogen fühlen; **attraction** [ə'trækʃən] n Anziehungskraft f; (thing) Attraktion f; **attractive** adj attraktiv; (thing, idea) reizvoll

aubergine ['əʊbəʒiːn] n Aubergine f

auction ['ɔːkʃən] n Versteigerung f, Auktion f ▷ vt versteigern

audible ['ɔːdɪbl] adj hörbar
audience ['ɔːdɪəns] n Publikum nt; (Radio) Zuhörer pl; (TV) Zuschauer pl
audio ['ɔːdɪəʊ] adj Ton-
audition [ɔːˈdɪʃən] n Probe f ▷ vi (Theat) vorspielen, vorsingen
auditorium [ɔːdɪˈtɔːrɪəm] n Zuschauerraum m
Aug abbr = **August**
August ['ɔːgəst] n August m; see also **September**
aunt [ɑːnt] n Tante f
au pair [əʊˈpeə*] n Aupairmädchen nt, Aupairjunge m
Australia [ɒsˈtreɪlɪə] n Australien nt; **Australian** adj australisch ▷ n Australier(in) m(f)
Austria ['ɒstrɪə] n Österreich nt; **Austrian** adj österreichisch ▷ n Österreicher(in) m(f)
authentic [ɔːˈθentɪk] adj echt; (signature) authentisch; **authenticity** [ɔːθenˈtɪsɪtɪ] n Echtheit f
author ['ɔːθə*] n Autor(in) m(f); (of report etc) Verfasser(in) m(f)
authority [ɔːˈθɒrɪtɪ] n (power, expert) Autorität f; **an ~ on sth** eine Autorität auf dem Gebiet einer Sache; **the authorities** (pl) die Behörden pl; **authorize** ['ɔːθəraɪz] vt (permit) genehmigen; **be ~d to do sth** offiziell berechtigt sein, etw zu tun
auto ['ɔːtəʊ] (pl **-s**) n (US) Auto nt
autobiography [ɔːtəʊbaɪˈɒɡrəfɪ] n Autobiographie f; **autograph** ['ɔːtəɡrɑːf] n Autogramm nt
automatic [ɔːtəˈmætɪk] adj automatisch; **~ gear change** (Brit), **~ gear shift** (US) Automatikschaltung f ▷ n (car) Automatikwagen m
automobile ['ɔːtəməbiːl] n (US) Auto(mobil) nt; **autotrain**

['ɔːtəʊtreɪn] n (US) Autoreisezug m
autumn ['ɔːtəm] n (Brit) Herbst m
auxiliary [ɔːɡˈzɪlɪərɪ] adj Hilfs-; **~ verb** Hilfsverb nt ▷ n Hilfskraft f
availability [əveɪləˈbɪlɪtɪ] n (of product) Lieferbarkeit f; (of resources) Verfügbarkeit f; **available** [əˈveɪləbl] adj erhältlich; (existing) vorhanden; (product) lieferbar; (person) erreichbar; **to be/make ~ to sb** jdm zur Verfügung stehen/stellen; **they're only ~ in black** es gibt sie nur in Schwarz, sie sind nur in Schwarz erhältlich
avalanche ['ævəlɑːnʃ] n Lawine f
Ave abbr = **avenue**
avenue ['ævənjuː] n Allee f
average ['ævərɪdʒ] n Durchschnitt m; **on ~** im Durchschnitt ▷ adj durchschnittlich; **~ speed** Durchschnittsgeschwindigkeit f; **of ~ height** von mittlerer Größe
avian flu ['eɪvɪənˈfluː] n Vogelgrippe f
aviation [eɪvɪˈeɪʃən] n Luftfahrt f
avocado [ævəˈkɑːdəʊ] (pl **-s**) n Avocado f
avoid [əˈvɔɪd] vt vermeiden; **to ~ sb** jdm aus dem Weg gehen; **avoidable** adj vermeidbar
awake [əˈweɪk] (awoke, awoken) vi aufwachen ▷ adj wach
award [əˈwɔːd] n (prize) Preis m; (for bravery etc) Auszeichnung f ▷ vt zuerkennen (to sb jdm); (present) verleihen (to sb jdm)
aware [əˈweə*] adj bewusst; **to be ~ of sth** sich dat einer Sache gen bewusst sein; **I was not ~ that ...** es war mir nicht klar, dass ...
away [əˈweɪ] adv weg; **to look ~** wegsehen; **he's ~** er ist nicht da; (on a trip) er ist verreist; (from school, work) er fehlt; (Sport) **they**

are (**playing**) ~ sie spielen auswärts; (*with distance*) **three miles** ~ drei Meilen (von hier) entfernt; **to work** ~ drauflos arbeiten

awful [ˈɔːfʊl] *adj* schrecklich, furchtbar; **awfully** *adv* furchtbar

awkward [ˈɔːkwəd] *adj* (*clumsy*) ungeschickt; (*embarrassing*) peinlich; (*difficult*) schwierig

awning [ˈɔːnɪŋ] *n* Markise *f*

awoke [əˈwəʊk] *pt of* **awake**; **awoken** [əˈwəʊkən] *pp of* **awake**

ax (*US*), **axe** [æks] *n* Axt *f*

axle [ˈæksl] *n* (*Tech*) Achse *f*

BA *abbr* = **Bachelor of Arts**
BSc *abbr* = **Bachelor of Science**

babe [beɪb] *n* (*fam*) Baby *nt*; (*fam: affectionate*) Schatz *m*, Kleine(r) *mf*

baby [ˈbeɪbɪ] *n* Baby *nt*; (*of animal*) Junge(s) *nt*; (*fam: affectionate*) Schatz *m*, Kleine(r) *mf*; **to have a** ~ ein Kind bekommen; **it's your** ~ (*fam: responsibility*) das ist dein Bier; **baby carriage** *n* (*US*) Kinderwagen *m*; **baby food** *n* Babynahrung *f*; **babyish** *adj* kindisch; **baby shower** *n* (*US*) Party für die werdende Mutter; **baby-sit** *irr vi* babysitten; **baby-sitter** *n* Babysitter(in) *m(f)*

bachelor [ˈbætʃələ°] *n* Junggeselle *m*; **Bachelor of Arts/Science** erster akademischer Grad, ≈ Magister/Diplom; **bachelorette** *n* Junggesellin *f*; **bachelorette party** *n* (*US*)

Junggesellinnenabschied; **bachelor party** n (US) Junggesellenabschied
back [bæk] n (of person, animal) Rücken m; (of house, coin etc) Rückseite f; (of chair) Rückenlehne f; (of car) Rücksitz m; (of train) Ende nt; (Sport: defender) Verteidiger(in) m(f); **at the ~ of ...**, (US) **in ~ of** (inside) hinten in ...; (outside) hinter ...; **~ to front** verkehrt herum ▷ vt (support) unterstützen; (car) rückwärtsfahren ▷ vi (go backwards) rückwärtsgehen o rückwärtsfahren ▷ adj Hinter-; **~ wheel** Hinterrad nt ▷ adv zurück; **they're ~** sie sind wieder da; **back away** vi sich zurückziehen; **back down** vi nachgeben; **back up** vi (car etc) zurücksetzen ▷ vt (support) unterstützen; (Inform) sichern; (car) zurückfahren
backache n Rückenschmerzen pl; **backbone** n Rückgrat nt; **backdate** vt zurückdatieren; **backdoor** n Hintertür f; **backfire** vi (plan) fehlschlagen; (Auto) fehlzünden; **background** n Hintergrund m; **backhand** n (Sport) Rückhand f; **backlog** n (of work) Rückstand m; **backpack** n (US) Rucksack m; **backpacker** n Rucksacktourist(in) m(f);
backpacking n Rucksacktourismus m; **back seat** n Rücksitz m; **backside** n (fam) Po m; **back street** n Seitenstraße nt; **backstroke** n Rückenschwimmen nt; **back-up** n (support) Unterstützung f; **~ (copy)** (Inform) Sicherungskopie f; **backward** adj (child) zurückgeblieben; (region) rückständig; **~ movement** Rückwärtsbewegung f;
backwards adv rückwärts; **backyard** n Hinterhof m

bacon ['beɪkən] n Frühstücksspeck m
bacteria [bæk'tɪərɪə] npl Bakterien pl
bad [bæd] (**worse, worst**) adj schlecht, schlimm; (smell) übel; **I have a ~ back** mir tut der Rücken weh; **I'm ~ at maths/sport** ich bin schlecht in Mathe/Sport; **to go ~** schlecht werden, verderben
badge [bædʒ] n Abzeichen nt
badger ['bædʒə'] n Dachs m
badly ['bædlɪ] adv schlecht; **~ wounded** schwer verwundet; **to need sth ~** etw dringend brauchen; **bad-tempered** ['bæd'tempəd] adj schlecht gelaunt
bag [bæg] n (small) Tüte f; (larger) Beutel m; (handbag) Tasche f; **my ~s** (luggage) mein Gepäck
baggage ['bægɪdʒ] n Gepäck nt; **baggage allowance** n Freigepäck nt; **baggage (re)claim** n Gepäckrückgabe f
baggy ['bægɪ] adj (zu) weit; (trousers, suit) ausgebeult
bag lady ['bæɡleɪdɪ] n Stadtstreicherin f
bagpipes ['bægpaɪps] npl Dudelsack m
Bahamas [bə'hɑ:məz] npl: **the ~** die Bahamas pl
bail [beɪl] n (money) Kaution f
bait [beɪt] n Köder m
bake [beɪk] vt, vi backen; **baked beans** npl weiße Bohnen in Tomatensoße; **baked potato** (pl **-es**) n in der Schale gebackene Kartoffel, Ofenkartoffel f; **baker** ['beɪkə'] n Bäcker(in) m(f); **bakery** ['beɪkərɪ] n Bäckerei f; **baking powder** n Backpulver nt
balance ['bæləns] n (equilibrium) Gleichgewicht nt ▷ vt (make up for) ausgleichen; **balanced** adj

ausgeglichen; **balance sheet** n
Bilanz f

balcony ['bælkənɪ] n Balkon m

bald [bɔːld] adj kahl; **to be** ~ eine
Glatze haben

Balkans ['bɔːlkənz] npl: **the** ~
der Balkan, die Balkanländer pl

ball [bɔːl] n Ball m; **to have a** ~
(fam) sich prima amüsieren

ballet ['bæleɪ] n Ballett nt; **ballet
dancer** n Balletttänzer(in) m(f)

balloon [bə'luːn] n (Luft)ballon
m

ballot ['bælət] n (geheime)
Abstimmung; **ballot box** n
Wahlurne f; **ballot paper** n
Stimmzettel m

ballpoint (pen) ['bɔːlpɔɪnt] n
Kugelschreiber m

ballroom ['bɔːlruːm] n Tanzsaal
m

Baltic ['bɔːltɪk] adj: ~ **Sea** Ostsee
f; **the** ~ **States** die baltischen
Staaten

Baltics ['bɔːltɪks] n: **the** ~ das
Baltikum nt

bamboo [bæm'buː] n Bambus m;
bamboo shoots npl
Bambussprossen pl

ban [bæn] n Verbot nt ⊳ vt
verbieten

banana [bə'nɑːnə] n Banane f;
he's ~**s** er ist völlig durchgeknallt;
banana split n Bananensplit nt

band [bænd] n (group) Gruppe f;
(of criminals) Bande f; (Mus) Kapelle
f; (pop, rock etc) Band f; (strip) Band
nt

bandage ['bændɪdʒ] n Verband
m; (elastic) Bandage f ⊳ vt
verbinden

B & B abbr = **bed and breakfast**

bang [bæŋ] n (noise) Knall m;
(blow) Schlag m ⊳ vt, vi knallen;
(door) zuschlagen, zuknallen;
banger [bæŋə°] n (Brit fam:
firework) Knallkörper m; (sausage)

Würstchen nt; (fam: old car)
Klapperkiste f

bangs [bæŋz] npl (US: of hair)
Pony m

banish ['bænɪʃ] vt verbannen

banister(s) ['bænɪstə°] n (Treppen)geländer nt

bank [bæŋk] n (Fin) Bank f; (of
river etc) Ufer nt; **bank account** n
Bankkonto nt; **bank balance** n
Kontostand m; **bank card** n
Bankkarte f; **bank code** n
Bankleitzahl f; **bank holiday** n
gesetzlicher Feiertag

> **BANK HOLIDAY**
>
> • Als **bank holiday** wird in
> • Großbritannien ein gesetzlicher
> • Feiertag bezeichnet, an dem die
> • Banken geschlossen sind. Die
> • meisten dieser Feiertage,
> • abgesehen von Weihnachten
> • und Ostern, fallen auf Montage
> • im Mai und August. An diesen
> • langen Wochenenden (bank
> • holiday weekends) fahren viele
> • Briten in Urlaub, sodass dann
> • auf den Straßen, Flughäfen und
> • bei der Bahn sehr viel Betrieb
> • ist.

bank manager n Filialleiter(in)
m(f); **banknote** n Banknote f

bankrupt vt ruinieren; **to go**
~ Pleite gehen

bank statement n
Kontoauszug m

baptism ['bæptɪzəm] n Taufe f;
baptize ['bæptaɪz] vt taufen

bar [bɑː°] n (for drinks) Bar f; (less
smart) Lokal nt; (rod) Stange f; (of
chocolate etc) Riegel m, Tafel f; (of
soap) Stück nt; (counter) Theke f
⊳ prep außer; ~ **none** ohne
Ausnahme

barbecue ['bɑːbɪkjuː] n (device)

Grill m; (party) Barbecue nt,
Grillfete f; **to have a ~** grillen

barbed wire ['bɑːbd'waɪə°] n
Stacheldraht m

barber ['bɑːbə°] n (Herren)friseur m

bar code ['bɑːkəʊd] n
Strichkode m

bare [beə°] adj nackt; **~ patch**
kahle Stelle; **barefoot** adj, adv
barfuß; **bareheaded** adj, adv
ohne Kopfbedeckung; **barely** adv
kaum; (with age) knapp

bargain ['bɑːgɪn] n (cheap offer)
günstiges Angebot, Schnäppchen
nt; (transaction) Geschäft nt; **what
a ~** das ist aber günstig! ▷ vi
(ver)handeln

barge [bɑːdʒ] n (for freight)
Lastkahn m; (unpowered)
Schleppkahn m

bark [bɑːk] n (of tree) Rinde f;
(of dog) Bellen nt ▷ vi (dog)
bellen

barley ['bɑːlɪ] n Gerste f

barmaid ['bɑːmeɪd] n Bar-
keeperin f; **barman** ['bɑːmən] (pl
-men) n Barkeeper m

barn [bɑːn] n Scheune f

barometer [bə'rɒmɪtə°] n Barometer nt

baroque [bə'rɒk] adj barock,
Barock-

barracks ['bærəks] npl Kaserne f

barrel ['bærəl] n Fass nt; **barrel
organ** n Drehorgel f

barricade [bærɪ'keɪd] n Bar-
rikade f

barrier ['bærɪə°] n (obstruction)
Absperrung f, Barriere f; (across
road etc) Schranke f

barrow ['bærəʊ] n (cart)
Schubkarren m

bartender [bɑː'tendə°] n (US)
Barkeeper(in) m(f)

base [beɪs] n Basis f; (of lamp,
pillar etc) Fuß m; (Mil) Stützpunkt m

▷ vt gründen (on auf +akk); **to be
~d on sth** auf etw dat basieren;
baseball n Baseball m; **baseball
cap** n Baseballmütze f;
basement n Kellergeschoss nt

bash [bæʃ] (fam) n Schlag m; (fam)
Party f ▷ vt hauen

basic ['beɪsɪk] adj einfach;
(fundamental) Grund-; (importance,
difference) grundlegend; (in
principle) grundsätzlich; **the
accomodation is very ~** die
Unterkunft ist sehr bescheiden;
basically adv im Grunde; **basics**
npl: **the ~** das Wesentliche

basil ['bæzl] n Basilikum nt

basin ['beɪsn] n (for washing,
valley) (Wasch)becken nt

basis ['beɪsɪs] n Basis f; **on the
~ of** aufgrund +gen; **on a monthly
~** monatlich

basket ['bɑːskɪt] n Korb m;
basketball n Basketball m

Basque [bæsk] n (person) Baske
m, Baskin f; (language) Baskisch nt
▷ adj baskisch

bass [beɪs] n (Mus) Bass m; (Zool)
Barsch m ▷ adj (Mus) Bass-

bastard ['bɑːstəd] n (vulg: awful
person) Arschloch nt

bat [bæt] n (Zool) Fledermaus f;
(Sport: cricket, baseball) Schlagholz
nt; (table tennis) Schläger m

batch [bætʃ] n Schwung m; (fam:
of letters, books etc) Stoß m

bath [bɑːθ] n Bad nt; (tub)
Badewanne f; **to have a ~** baden
▷ vt (child etc) baden

bathe [beɪð] vt, vi (wound etc)
baden; **bath foam** ['bɑːθfəʊm] n
Badeschaum m; **bathing cap** n
Badekappe f; **bathing costume,
bathing suit** (US) n Badeanzug m

bathmat ['bɑːθmæt] n Badevor-
leger m; **bathrobe** n Bademantel
m; **bathroom** n Bad(ezimmer) nt;
baths [bɑːðz] npl (Schwimm)bad

nt; **bath towel** n Badetuch nt;
bathtub n Badewanne f

baton ['bætən] n (Mus) Taktstock
m; (police) Schlagstock m

batter ['bætə°] n Teig m ▷ vt
heftig schlagen; **battered** adj
übel zugerichtet; (hat, car)
verbeult; (wife, baby) misshandelt

battery ['bætərɪ] n (Elec) Batterie
f; **battery charger** n Ladegerät nt

battle ['bætl] n Schlacht f; (fig)
Kampf m (for um +akk); **battlefield**
n Schlachtfeld m; **battlements**
npl Zinnen pl

Bavaria [bə'veərɪə] n Bayern nt;
Bavarian adj bay(e)risch ▷ n
Bayer(in) m(f)

bay [beɪ] n (of sea) Bucht f; (on
house) Erker m; (tree) Lorbeerbaum
m; **bay leaf** n Lorbeerblatt nt; **bay
window** n Erkerfenster nt

BBC abbr = **British Broadcasting
Corporation** BBC f

BC abbr = **before Christ** vor Christi
Geburt, v. Chr.

○ **KEYWORD**

be [biː] (pt **was, were,** pp **been**) vb
aux 1 (with present participle: forming
continuous tenses): **what are you
doing?** was machst du (gerade)?;
it is raining es regnet; **I've been
waiting for you for hours** ich
warte schon seit Stunden auf dich
2 (with pp: forming passives): **to be
killed** getötet werden; **the thief
was nowhere to be seen** der Dieb
war nirgendwo zu sehen
3 (in tag questions): **it was fun,
wasn't it?** es hat Spaß gemacht,
nicht wahr?
4 (+to +infin) **the house is to be
sold** das Haus soll verkauft
werden; **he's not to open it** er darf
es nicht öffnen

▷ vb +complement 1 (usu) sein; **I'm
tired** ich bin müde; **I'm hot/cold**
mir ist heiß/kalt; **he's a doctor** er
ist Arzt; **2 and 2 are 4** 2 und 2 ist o
sind 4; **she's tall/pretty** sie ist
groß/hübsch; **be careful/quiet**
sei vorsichtig/ruhig
2 (of health) **how are you?** wie geht
es dir?; **he's very ill** er ist sehr
krank; **I'm fine now** jetzt geht es
mir gut
3 (of age) **how old are you?** wie alt
bist du?; **I'm sixteen (years old)**
ich bin sechzehn (Jahre alt)
4 (cost) **how much was the meal?**
was o wie viel hat das Essen
gekostet?; **that'll be £5.75, please**
das macht £5.75, bitte

▷ vi 1 (exist, occur etc) sein; **is there
a God?** gibt es einen Gott?; **be
that as it may** wie dem auch sei;
so be it also gut
2 (referring to place) sein; **I won't be
here tomorrow** ich werde morgen
nicht hier sein
3 (referring to movement) **where
have you been?** wo bist du
gewesen?; **I've been in the
garden** ich war im Garten
▷ impers vb 1 (referring to time,
distance, weather) sein; **it's 5
o'clock** es ist 5 Uhr; **it's 10 km to
the village** es sind 10 km bis zum
Dorf; **it's too hot/cold** es ist zu
heiß/kalt
2 (emphatic) **it's me** ich bin's; **it's
the postman** es ist der Briefträger

beach [biːtʃ] n Strand m;
beachwear n Strandkleidung f

bead [biːd] n (of glass, wood etc)
Perle f; (drop) Tropfen m

beak [biːk] n Schnabel m

beam [biːm] n (of wood etc) Balken
m; (of light) Strahl m ▷ vi (smile etc)
strahlen

bean [biːn] n Bohne f; **bean curd**
n Tofu m

bear [beə^r] *vt* (*carry*) tragen; (*tolerate*) ertragen ▷ *n* Bär *m*; **bearable** *adj* erträglich

beard [bɪəd] *n* Bart *m*

beast [biːst] *n* Tier *nt*; (*brutal person*) Bestie *f*; (*disliked person*) Biest *nt*

beat [biːt] (**beat, beaten**) *vt* schlagen; (*as punishment*) prügeln; **to ~ sb at tennis** jdn im Tennis schlagen ▷ *n* (*of heart, drum etc*) Schlag *m*; (*Mus*) Takt *m*; (*type of music*) Beat *m*; **beat up** *vt* zusammenschlagen

beaten ['biːtn] *pp of* **beat**; **off the ~ track** abgelegen

beautiful ['bjuːtɪful] *adj* schön; (*splendid*) herrlich; **beauty** ['bjuːtɪ] *n* Schönheit *f*; **beauty spot** *n* (*place*) lohnendes Ausflugsziel

beaver ['biːvə^r] *n* Biber *m*

became [bɪ'keɪm] *pt of* **become**

because [bɪ'kɒz] *adv, conj* weil ▷ *prep*: **~ of** wegen +*gen o dat*

become [bɪ'kʌm] (**became, become**) *vt* werden; **what's ~ of him?** was ist aus ihm geworden?

bed [bed] *n* Bett *nt*; (*in garden*) Beet *nt*; **bed and breakfast** *n* Übernachtung *f* mit Frühstück; **bedclothes** *npl* Bettwäsche *f*; **bedding** *n* Bettzeug *nt*; **bed linen** *n* Bettwäsche *f*; **bedroom** *n* Schlafzimmer *nt*; **bed-sit(ter)** *n* (*fam*) möblierte Einzimmerwohnung *f*; **bedspread** *n* Tagesdecke *f*; **bedtime** *n* Schlafenszeit *f*

bee [biː] *n* Biene *f*

beech [biːtʃ] *n* Buche *f*

beef [biːf] *n* Rindfleisch *nt*; **beefburger** *n* Hamburger *m*; **beef tomato** *n* (*pl* **-es**) *n* Fleischtomate *f*

beehive ['biːhaɪv] *n* Bienenstock *m*

been [biːn] *pp of* **be**

beer [bɪə^r] *n* Bier *nt*; **beer garden** *n* Biergarten *m*

beetle ['biːtl] *n* Käfer *m*

beetroot ['biːtruːt] *n* Rote Bete *f*

before [bɪ'fɔː^r] *prep*; **the year ~ last** vorletztes Jahr; **the day ~ yesterday** vorgestern ▷ *conj* bevor ▷ *adv* (*of time*) vorher; **have you been there ~?** waren Sie/warst du schon einmal dort?; **beforehand** *adv* vorher

beg [beg] *vt*: **to ~ sb to do sth** jdn inständig bitten, etw zu tun ▷ *vi* (*beggar*) betteln (*for* um +*akk*)

began [bɪ'gæn] *pt of* **begin**

beggar ['begə^r] *n* Bettler(in) *m(f)*

begin [bɪ'gɪn] (**began, begun**) *vt, vi* anfangen, beginnen; **to ~ to do sth** anfangen, etw zu tun; **beginner** *n* Anfänger(in) *m(f)*; **beginning** *n* Anfang *m*

begun [bɪ'gʌn] *pp of* **begin**

behalf [bɪ'hɑːf] *n*: **on ~ of, in ~ of** (*US*) im Namen/Auftrag von; **on my ~** für mich

behave [bɪ'heɪv] *vi* sich benehmen; **~ yourself!** benimm dich!; **behavior** (*US*), **behaviour** [bɪ'heɪvjə^r] *n* Benehmen *nt*

behind [bɪ'haɪnd] *prep* hinter; **to be ~ time** Verspätung haben ▷ *adv* hinten; **to be ~ with one's work** mit seiner Arbeit im Rückstand sein ▷ *n* (*fam*) Hinterteil *nt*

beige [beɪʒ] *adj* beige

being ['biːɪŋ] *n* (*existence*) Dasein *nt*; (*person*) Wesen *nt*

Belarus [belə'rʊs] *n* Weißrussland *nt*

belch [beltʃ] *n* Rülpser *m* ▷ *vi* rülpsen

belfry ['belfrɪ] *n* Glockenturm *m*

Belgian ['beldʒən] *adj* belgisch ▷ *n* Belgier(in) *m(f)*; **Belgium** ['beldʒəm] *n* Belgien *nt*

belief [brˈliːf] n Glaube m (in an +akk); (conviction) Überzeugung f; **it's my ~ that ...** ich bin der Überzeugung, dass ...; **believe** [brˈliːv] vt glauben; **believe in** vi glauben an +akk; **believer** n (Rel) Gläubige(r) mf

bell [bel] n (church) Glocke f; (bicycle, door) Klingel f; **bellboy** ['belbɔɪ] n (esp US) Page m

bellows ['belauz] npl (for fire) Blasebalg m

belly ['belɪ] n Bauch m; **bellyache** n Bauchweh nt ▷ vi (fam) meckern; **belly button** n (fam) Bauchnabel m; **bellyflop** n (fam) Bauchklatscher m

belong [brˈlɒŋ] vi gehören (to sb jdm); (to club) angehören +dat; **belongings** npl Habe f

below [brˈləʊ] prep unter ▷ adv unten

belt [belt] n (round waist) Gürtel m; (safety belt) Gurt m; **below the ~** unter der Gürtellinie ▷ vi (fam: go fast) rasen, düsen; **beltway** n (US) Umgehungsstraße f

bench [bentʃ] n Bank f

bend [bend] n Biegung f; (in road) Kurve f ▷ vt (bent, bent) (curve) biegen; (head, arm) beugen ▷ vi sich biegen; (person) sich beugen; **bend down** vi sich bücken

beneath [brˈniːθ] prep unter ▷ adv darunter

beneficial [benrˈfɪʃl] adj gut, nützlich (to für); **benefit** ['benɪfɪt] n (advantage) Vorteil m; (profit) Nutzen m; **for your/his ~** deinetwegen/seinetwegen; **unemployment ~** Arbeitslosengeld nt ▷ vt guttun +dat ▷ vi Nutzen ziehen (from aus)

benign [brˈnaɪn] adj (person) gütig; (climate) mild; (Med) gutartig

bent [bent] pt, pp of **bend** ▷ adj krumm; (fam) korrupt

beret ['bereɪ] n Baskenmütze f

Bermuda [bəˈmjuːdə] n the **~s** pl die Bermudas pl ▷ adj **~ shorts** pl Bermudashorts pl; **the ~ triangle** das Bermudadreieck

berry ['berɪ] n Beere f

berth [bɜːθ] n (for ship) Ankerplatz m; (in ship) Koje f; (in train) Bett nt ▷ vt an Kai festmachen ▷ vi anlegen

beside [brˈsaɪd] prep neben; **~ the sea/lake** am Meer/See; **besides** [brˈsaɪdz] prep außer ▷ adv außerdem

besiege [brˈsiːdʒ] vt belagern

best [best] adj beste(r, s); **my ~ friend** mein bester o engster Freund; **the ~ thing to do would be to ...** das Beste wäre zu ...; (on food packaging) **~ before ...** mindestens haltbar bis ... ▷ n der/die/das Beste; **all the ~** alles Gute; **to make the ~ of it** das Beste daraus machen ▷ adv am besten; **I like this ~** das mag ich am liebsten; **best-before date** n Mindesthaltbarkeitsdatum nt; **best man** n ['best'mæn] (pl **men**) n Trauzeuge m; **bestseller** ['bestselə°] n Bestseller m

bet [bet] (bet, bet) vt, vi wetten (on auf +akk); **I ~ him £5 that ...** ich habe mit ihm um 5 Pfund gewettet, dass ...; **you ~** (fam) und ob!; **I ~ he'll be late** er kommt mit Sicherheit zu spät ▷ n Wette f

betray [brˈtreɪ] vt verraten; **betrayal** [brˈtreɪəl] n Verrat m

better ['betə°] adj, adv besser; **to get ~** (healthwise) sich erholen, wieder gesund werden; (improve) sich verbessern; **I'm much ~ today** es geht mir heute viel besser; **you'd ~ go** du solltest/Sie sollten lieber gehen; **a change for the ~** eine Wendung zum Guten

betting ['bɛtɪŋ] n Wetten pl

between [bɪ'twiːn] prep zwischen; (among) unter; **~ you and me, ...** unter uns gesagt, ...
▷ adv: **(in) ~** dazwischen

beverage ['bɛvərɪdʒ] n (formal) Getränk nt

beware [bɪ'wɛəʳ] vt: **to ~ of sth** sich vor etw +dat hüten; **"~ of the dog"** Vorsicht, bissiger Hund!"

bewildered [bɪ'wɪldəd] adj verwirrt

beyond [bɪ'jɒnd] prep (place) jenseits +gen; (time) über ...
hinaus; (out of reach) außerhalb +gen; **it's ~ me** da habe ich keine Ahnung, da bin ich überfragt
▷ adv darüber hinaus

bias ['baɪəs] n (prejudice) Vorurteil nt, Voreingenommenheit f

bias(s)ed ['baɪəst] adj voreingenommen

bib [bɪb] n Latz m

Bible ['baɪbl] n Bibel f

bicycle ['baɪsɪkl] n Fahrrad nt

bid [bɪd] (bid, bid) vt (offer) bieten
▷ n (attempt) Versuch m; (offer) Gebot nt

big [bɪg] adj groß; **it's no ~ deal** (fam) es ist nichts Besonderes;
big-headed [bɪg'hɛdɪd] adj eingebildet

bike [baɪk] n (fam) Rad nt

bikini [bɪ'kiːnɪ] n Bikini m

bilingual [baɪ'lɪŋgwəl] adj zweisprachig

bill [bɪl] n (account) Rechnung f;
(US: banknote) Banknote f; (Pol) Gesetzentwurf m; (Zool) Schnabel m; **billfold** ['bɪlfəʊld] n (US) Brieftasche f

billiards ['bɪljədz] nsing Billard nt; **billiard table** Billardtisch m

billion ['bɪljən] n Milliarde f

bin [bɪn] n Behälter m; (rubbish bin) (Müll)eimer m; (for paper)

Papierkorb m

bind [baɪnd] (**bound, bound**) vt binden; (bind together) zusammenbinden; (wound) verbinden; **binding** n (ski) Bindung f; (book) Einband m

binge [bɪndʒ] n (fam: drinking) Sauferei f; **to go on a ~** auf Sauftour gehen

bingo ['bɪngəʊ] n Bingo nt

binoculars [bɪ'nɒkjʊləz] npl Fernglas nt

biodegradable ['baɪəʊdɪ'greɪdəbl] adj biologisch abbaubar

biofuel ['baɪəʊ'fjuəl] n Bio-kraftstoff m

biography [baɪ'ɒgrəfɪ] n Bio-grafie f

biological [baɪə'lɒdʒɪkəl] adj biologisch; **biology** [baɪ'ɒlədʒɪ] n Biologie f

bipolar [baɪ'pəʊlə] adj bipolar

birch [bɜːtʃ] n Birke f

bird [bɜːd] n Vogel m; (Brit fam: girl, girlfriend) Tussi f; **bird flu** n Vogelgrippe f; **bird watcher** n Vogelbeobachter(in) m(f)

birth [bɜːθ] n Geburt f; **birth certificate** n Geburtsurkunde f;
birth control n Geburtenkontrolle f; **birthday** n Geburtstag m; **happy ~** herzlichen Glückwunsch zum Geburtstag;
birthday card n Geburtstagskarte f; **birthday party** n Geburtstagsfeier f;
birthplace n Geburtsort m

biscuit ['bɪskɪt] n (Brit) Keks m

bisexual [baɪ'sɛksjʊəl] adj bisexuell

bishop ['bɪʃəp] n Bischof m; (in chess) Läufer m

bit [bɪt] pt of **bite** n (piece) Stück(chen) nt; (Inform) Bit nt; **a ~ (of ...)** (small amount) ein bisschen ...; **a ~ tired** etwas müde;

~ by = allmählich; (*time*) **for a ~** ein Weilchen; **quite a ~** (*a lot*) ganz schön viel

bitch [bɪtʃ] n (*dog*) Hündin f; (*pej: woman*) Miststück nt, Schlampe f; **son of a ~** (*US: vulg*) Hurensohn m, Scheißkerl m; **bitchy** adj gemein, zickig

bite [baɪt] (**bit, bitten**) vt, vi beißen ▷ n Biss m; (*mouthful*) Bissen m; (*insect*) Stich m; **to have a ~** eine Kleinigkeit essen; **bitten** pp of **bite**

bitter [ˈbɪtə°] adj bitter; (*memory etc*) schmerzlich ▷ n (*Brit: beer*) halbdunkles Bier; **bitter lemon** n Bitter Lemon nt

bizarre [bɪˈzɑː°] adj bizarr

black [blæk] adj schwarz; **blackberry** n Brombeere f; **blackbird** n Amsel f; **blackboard** n (*Wand*)tafel f; **black box** n (*Aviat*) Flugschreiber m; **blackcurrant** n Schwarze Johannisbeere; **black eye** n blaues Auge; **Black Forest** n Schwarzwald m; **Black Forest gateau** n Schwarzwälder Kirschtorte f; **blackmail** n Erpressung f ▷ vt erpressen; **black market** n Schwarzmarkt m; **blackout** n (*Med*) Ohnmacht f; **to have a ~** ohnmächtig werden; **black pudding** n = Blutwurst f; **Black Sea** n: **the ~** das Schwarze Meer; **blacksmith** n Schmied(in) m(f); **black tie** n Abendanzug m, Smoking m; **is it ~?** ist/besteht da Smokingzwang?

bladder [ˈblædə°] n Blase f

blade [bleɪd] n (*of knife*) Klinge f; (*of propeller*) Blatt nt; (*of grass*) Halm m

blame [bleɪm] n Schuld f ▷ vt: **to ~ sb on sb** jdm die Schuld an etw dat geben; **he is to ~** er ist daran schuld

~ by = allmählich; (*time*) **for a ~** ein Weilchen; **quite a ~** (*a lot*) ganz schön viel

bland [blænd] adj (*taste*) fade; (*comment*) nichtssagend

blank [blæŋk] adj (*page, space*) leer, unbeschrieben; (*look*) ausdruckslos; **~ cheque** n Blankoscheck m

blanket [ˈblæŋkɪt] n (*Woll*)decke f

blast [blɑːst] n (*of wind*) Windstoß m; (*of explosion*) Druckwelle f ▷ vt (*blow up*) sprengen; **~!** (*fam*) Mist!, verdammt!

blatant [ˈbleɪtənt] adj (*undisguised*) offen; (*obvious*) offensichtlich

blaze [bleɪz] vi lodern; (*sun*) brennen ▷ n (*building*) Brand m; (*other fire*) Feuer nt; **a ~ of colour** eine Farbenpracht

blazer [ˈbleɪzə°] n Blazer m

bleach [bliːtʃ] n Bleichmittel nt ▷ vt bleichen

bleak [bliːk] adj öde, düster; (*future*) trostlos

bleary [ˈblɪərɪ] adj (*eyes*) trübe, verschlafen

bleed [bliːd] (**bled, bled**) vi bluten

blend [blend] n Mischung f ▷ vt mischen ▷ vi sich mischen; **blender** n Mixer m

bless [bles] vt segnen; **~ you!** Gesundheit!; **blessing** n Segen m

blew [bluː] pt of **blow**

blind [blaɪnd] adj blind; (*corner*) unübersichtlich; **to turn a ~ eye to sth** bei etw ein Auge zudrücken ▷ n (*for window*) Rollo nt ▷ vt blenden; **blind alley** n Sackgasse f; **blind spot** n (*Auto*) toter Winkel; (*fig*) schwacher Punkt

blink [blɪŋk] vi blinzeln; (*light*) blinken

bliss [blɪs] n (*Glück*)seligkeit f

blister [ˈblɪstə°] n Blase f

blizzard ['blɪzəd] n Schneesturm m
bloated ['bləʊtɪd] adj aufgedunsen
block [blɒk] n (of wood, stone, ice)
Block m, Klotz m; (of buildings)
Häuserblock m; ~ **of flats** (Brit)
Wohnblock m ▷ vt (road etc)
blockieren; (pipe, nose) verstopfen;
blockage ['blɒkɪdʒ] n Verstopfung f; **blockbuster** ['blɒkbʌstə⁰]
n Knüller m; **block letters** npl
Blockschrift f

blog [blɒg] n (Inform) Blog m,
Weblog m ▷ vi bloggen; **blogger**
n Blogger(in) m(f)
blogosphere ['blɒgəsfɪə⁰] n
Blogosphäre f
bloke [bləʊk] n (Brit fam) Kerl m,
Typ m
blond(e) [blɒnd] adj blond ▷ n
(person) Blondine f, blonder Typ
blood [blʌd] n Blut nt; **blood
count** n Blutbild nt; **blood donor**
n Blutspender(in) m(f); **blood
group** n Blutgruppe f; **blood
orange** n Blutorange f; **blood
poisoning** n Blutvergiftung f;
blood pressure n Blutdruck m;
blood sample n Blutprobe f;
bloodsports npl Sportarten, bei
denen Tiere getötet werden;
bloodthirsty adj blutrünstig;
bloody adj (Brit fam) verdammt,
Scheiß-; (literal sense) blutig
bloom [bluːm] n Blüte f ▷ vi
blühen
blossom ['blɒsəm] n Blüte f ▷ vi
blühen
blot [blɒt] n (of ink) Klecks m;
(fig) Fleck m
blouse [blaʊz] n Bluse f; **big
girl's ~** (fam) Schwächling m
blow [bləʊ] n Schlag m ▷ vi, vt
(**blew, blown**) (wind) wehen,
blasen; (person: trumpet etc) blasen;
to ~ one's nose sich dat die Nase
putzen; **blow out** vt (candle etc)
ausblasen; **blow up** vi

explodieren ▷ vt sprengen;
(balloon, tyre) aufblasen; (Foto:
enlarge) vergrößern; **blow-dry** vt
föhnen; **blowjob** n (fam) **to give
sb a ~** jdm einen blasen; **blown**
[bləʊn] pp of **blow**; **blow-out** n
(Auto) geplatzter Reifen
BLT n abbr = **bacon, lettuce and
tomato sandwich** mit
Frühstücksspeck, Kopfsalat und
Tomaten belegtes Sandwich
blue [bluː] adj blau; (fam:
unhappy) trübsinnig,
niedergeschlagen; (film)
pornografisch; (joke) anzüglich;
(language) derb; **bluebell** n
Glockenblume f; **blueberry** n
Blaubeere f; **blue cheese** n
Blauschimmelkäse m; **blues** npl:
the ~ (Mus) der Blues; **to have the
~** (fam) niedergeschlagen sein
blunder ['blʌndə⁰] n Schnitzer m
blunt [blʌnt] adj (knife) stumpf;
(fig) unverblümt; **bluntly** adv
geradeheraus
blurred [blɜːd] adj verschwommen, unklar
blush [blʌʃ] vi erröten
board [bɔːd] n (of wood) Brett nt;
(committee) Ausschuss m; (of firm)
Vorstand m; **~ and lodging**
Unterkunft und Verpflegung f; **on
~** - an Bord ▷ vt (train, bus)
einsteigen in +akk; (ship) an Bord
+gen gehen; **boarder** n (school)
Internatsschüler(in) m(f); **board
game** n Brettspiel nt; **boarding
card, boarding pass** n Bordkarte
f, Einsteigekarte f; **boarding
school** n Internat nt; **board
meeting** n Vorstandssitzung f;
boardroom n Sitzungssaal m
(des Vorstands)
boast [bəʊst] vi prahlen (about
mit) ▷ n Prahlerei f
boat [bəʊt] n Boot nt; (ship) Schiff
nt; **boatman** n (hirer)

Bootsverleiher m; **boat race** n Regatta f; **boat train** n Zug m mit Schiffsanschluss

bob(sleigh) ['bɒbsleɪ] n Bob m

bodily ['bɒdɪlɪ] adj körperlich ▷ adv (forcibly) gewaltsam; **body** ['bɒdɪ] n Körper m; (dead) Leiche f; (of car) Karosserie f; **bodybuilding** n Bodybuilding n; **bodyguard** n Leibwächter m; (group) Leibwache f; **body jewellery** n Intimschmuck m; **body odour** n Körpergeruch m; **body piercing** n Piercing nt; **bodywork** n Karosserie f

boil [bɔɪl] vt, vi kochen ▷ n (Med) Geschwür nt; **boiler** n Boiler m; **boiling** adj (water etc) kochend (heiß); **I was ~** (hot) mir war fürchterlich heiß; (with rage) ich kochte vor Wut; **boiling point** n Siedepunkt m

bold [bəʊld] adj kühn, mutig; (colours) kräftig; (type) fett

Bolivia [bə'lɪvɪə] n Bolivien nt

bolt [bəʊlt] n (lock) Riegel m; (screw) Bolzen m ▷ vt verriegeln

bomb [bɒm] n Bombe f ▷ vt bombardieren

bond [bɒnd] n (link) Bindung f; (Fin) Obligation f

bone [bəʊn] n Knochen m; (of fish) Gräte f; **boner** n (US fam) Schnitzer m; (vulg: erection) Ständer m

bonfire ['bɒnfaɪə°] n Feuer nt (im Freien)

bonnet ['bɒnɪt] n (Brit Auto) Haube f; (for baby) Häubchen nt

bonny ['bɒnɪ] adj (esp Scottish) hübsch

bonus ['bəʊnəs] n Bonus m, Prämie f

boo [buː] vt auspfeifen, ausbuhen ▷ vi buhen ▷ n Buhruf m

book [bʊk] n Buch nt; (of tickets, stamps) Heft n ▷ vt (ticket etc) bestellen; (hotel, flight etc) buchen; (Sport) verwarnen; **fully ~ed (up)** ausgebucht; (performance) ausverkauft; **book in** vi eintragen; **to be ~ed in at a hotel** ein Zimmer in einem Hotel bestellt haben; **bookcase** n Bücherregal nt; **booking** n Buchung f; **booking office** n (Rail) Fahrkartenschalter m; (Theat) Vorverkaufsstelle f; **book-keeping** n Buchhaltung f; **booklet** n Broschüre f; **bookmark** n (a. Inform) Lesezeichen nt; **bookshelf** n Bücherbord nt; **bookshelves** Bücherregal nt; **bookshop**, **bookstore** n (esp US) Buchhandlung f

boom [buːm] n (of business) Boom m; (noise) Dröhnen nt ▷ vi (business) boomen; (fam) florieren; (voice etc) dröhnen

boomerang ['buːməræŋ] n Bumerang m

boost [buːst] n Auftrieb m ▷ vt (production, sales) ankurbeln; (power, profits etc) steigern; **booster (injection)** n Wiederholungsimpfung f

boot [buːt] n Stiefel m; (Brit Auto) Kofferraum m ▷ vt (Inform) laden, booten

booth [buːð] n (at fair etc) Bude f; (at trade fair etc) Stand m

booze [buːz] n (fam) Alkohol m ▷ vi (fam) saufen

border ['bɔːdə°] n Grenze f; (edge) Rand m; **north/south of the Border** in Schottland/England; **borderline** n Grenze f

bore [bɔː°] pt of **bear** ▷ vt (hole etc) bohren; (person) langweilen ▷ n (person) Langweiler(in) m(f). langweiliger Mensch; (thing) langweilige Sache; **bored** adj: **to be ~** sich langweilen; **boredom** n

Langeweile f; **boring** adj
langweilig

born [bɔːn] adj: **he was ~ in London** er ist in London geboren

borne [bɔːn] pp of **bear**

borough ['bʌrə] n Stadtbezirk m

borrow ['bɒrəʊ] vt borgen

Bosnia-Herzegovina ['bɒznɪəhɜːtsəɡəʊ'viːnə] n Bosnien-Herzegowina nt; **Bosnian** ['bɒznɪən] adj bosnisch ▷ n Bosnier(in) m(f)

boss [bɒs] n Chef(in) m(f), Boss m; **boss around** vt herumkommandieren; **bossy** adj herrisch

botanical [bə'tænɪkəl] adj botanisch; **~ garden(s)** botanischer Garten

both [bəʊθ] adj beide; **the books** beide Bücher ▷ pron (people) beide; (things) beides; **~ (of) the boys** die beiden Jungs; **I like ~ of them** ich mag sie (alle) beide ▷ adv: **~ X and Y** sowohl X als auch Y

bother ['bɒðə*] vt ärgern, belästigen; **it doesn't ~ me** das stört mich nicht; **he can't be ~ed with details** mit Details gibt er sich nicht ab; **I'm not ~ed** das ist mir egal ▷ vi sich kümmern (about um); **don't ~** (das ist) nicht nötig, lass es! ▷ n (trouble) Mühe f; (annoyance) Ärger m

bottle ['bɒtl] n Flasche f ▷ vt (in Flaschen) abfüllen; **bottle out** vi (fam) den Mut verlieren, aufgeben; **bottle bank** n Altglascontainer m; **bottled** adj in Flaschen; **~ beer** Flaschenbier nt; **bottleneck** n (fig) Engpass m; **bottle opener** n Flaschenöffner m

bottom ['bɒtəm] n (of container) Boden m; (underside) Unterseite f; (fam: of person) Po m; **at the ~ of the sea/table/page** auf dem

Meeresgrund/am Tabellenende/unten auf der Seite ▷ adj unterste(r, s); **to be ~ of the class/league** Klassenletzte(r)/Tabellenletzte(r) sein; **~ gear** (Auto) erster Gang

bought [bɔːt] pt, pp of **buy**

bounce [baʊns] vi (ball) springen, aufprallen; (cheque) platzen; **~ up and down** (person) herumhüpfen; **bouncy** adj (ball) gut springend; (person) munter; **bouncy castle®** nt Hüpfburg f

bound [baʊnd] pt, pp of **bind** ▷ adj (tied up) gebunden; (obliged) verpflichtet; **to be ~ to do sth** (sure to) etw bestimmt tun (werden); (have to) etw tun müssen; **it's ~ to happen** es muss so kommen; **to be ~ for** auf dem Weg nach ... sein; **boundary** ['baʊndərɪ] n Grenze f

bouquet [bʊ'keɪ] n (flowers) Strauß m; (of wine) Blume f

boutique [buːˈtiːk] n Boutique f

bow [bəʊ] n (ribbon) Schleife f; (instrument, weapon) Bogen m ▷ [baʊ] vi sich verbeugen ▷ [baʊ] n (with head) Verbeugung f; (of ship) Bug m

bowels ['baʊəlz] npl Darm m

bowl [bəʊl] n (basin) Schüssel f; (shallow) Schale f; (for animal) Napf m ▷ vt, vi (in cricket) werfen

bowler ['bəʊlə*] n (in cricket) Werfer(in) m(f); (hat) Melone f

bowling ['bəʊlɪŋ] n Kegeln nt; **bowling alley** n Kegelbahn f; **bowling green** n Rasen m zum Bowling-Spiel; **bowls** ['bəʊlz] nsing (game) Bowling-Spiel nt

bow tie [bəʊ'taɪ] n Fliege f

box [bɒks] n Schachtel f; (cardboard) Karton m; (bigger) Kasten m; (space on form) Kästchen nt; (Theat) Loge f; **boxer** n Boxer(in) m(f); **boxers, boxer**

shorts npl Boxershorts pl; **boxing** n (Sport) Boxen nt; **Boxing Day** n zweiter Weihnachtsfeiertag

○ **BOXING DAY**
○
○ **Boxing Day** ist ein Feiertag in
○ Großbritannien. Fällt
○ Weihnachten auf ein
○ Wochenende, wird der Feiertag
○ am nächsten Wochentag
○ nachgeholt. Der Name geht auf
○ einen alten Brauch zurück:
○ früher erhielten Händler und
○ Lieferanten an diesem Tag ein
○ Geschenk, die sogenannte
○ Christmas Box.

boxing gloves npl
Boxhandschuhe pl; **boxing ring** n
Boxring m
box number n Chiffre f
box office n (cinema, theatre)
Kasse f
boy [bɔɪ] n Junge m
boycott ['bɔɪkɒt] n Boykott m
▷ vt boykottieren
boyfriend ['bɔɪfrɛnd] n (fester)
Freund m; **boy scout** n
Pfadfinder m
bra [brɑː] n BH m
brace [breɪs] n (on teeth) Spange f
bracelet ['breɪslɪt] n Armband nt
braces ['breɪsɪz] npl (Brit)
Hosenträger pl
bracket ['brækɪt] n (in text)
Klammer f; (Tech) Träger m ▷ vt
einklammern
brag [bræg] vi angeben
Braille [breɪl] n Blindenschrift f
brain [breɪn] n (Anat) Gehirn nt;
(mind) Verstand m, **-s** (pl)
(intelligence) Grips m; **brainwave**
n Geistesblitz m; **brainy** adj schlau,
clever
braise [breɪz] vt schmoren
brake [breɪk] n Bremse f ▷ vi

bremsen; **brake fluid** n
Bremsflüssigkeit f; **brake light** n
Bremslicht nt; **brake pedal** n
Bremspedal nt
branch [brɑːntʃ] n (of tree) Ast m;
(of family, subject) Zweig m; (of firm)
Filiale f, Zweigstelle f; **branch off**
vi (road) abzweigen
brand [brænd] n (Comm) Marke f
brand-new ['brænd'njuː] adj
(funkel)nagelneu
brandy ['brændɪ] n Weinbrand m
brass [brɑːs] n Messing nt; (Brit
fam: money) Knete f; **brass band** n
Blaskapelle f
brat [bræt] n (pej, fam) Gör nt
brave [breɪv] adj tapfer, mutig;
bravery ['breɪvərɪ] n Mut m
brawl [brɔːl] n Schlägerei f
brawn [brɔːn] n (strength)
Muskelkraft f; (Gastr) Sülze f;
brawny adj muskulös
Brazil [brə'zɪl] n Brasilien nt;
Brazilian adj brasilianisch ▷ n
Brasilianer(in) m(f); **brazil nut** n
Paranuss f
bread [brɛd] n Brot nt; **breadbin**
(Brit), **breadbox** (US) n
Brotkasten m; **breadcrumbs** pl
Brotkrumen pl; (Gastr) Paniermehl
nt; **breaded** adj paniert;
breadknife n Brotmesser nt
breadth [brɛdθ] n Breite f
break [breɪk] n (fracture) Bruch
m; (rest) Pause f; (short holiday)
Kurzurlaub m; **give me a ~** gib mir
eine Chance, hör auf damit! ▷ vt
(**broke, broken**) (fracture) brechen;
(in pieces) zerbrechen; (toy, device)
kaputt machen; (promise) nicht
halten; (silence) brechen; (law)
verletzen; (journey) unterbrechen;
(news) mitteilen (to sb jdm); **I
broke my leg** ich habe mir das
Bein gebrochen; **he broke it to
her gently** er hat es ihr schonend
beigebracht ▷ vi (come apart)

(auseinander)brechen; (in pieces) zerbrechen; (toy, device) kaputtgehen; (day, dawn) anbrechen; (news) bekannt werden; **break down** vi (car) eine Panne haben; (machine) versagen; (person) zusammenbrechen; **break in** vi (burglar) einbrechen; **break into** vt einbrechen in +akk; **break off** vi, vt abbrechen; **break out** vi ausbrechen; **to ~ in a rash** einen Ausschlag bekommen; **break up** vi aufbrechen; (meeting, organisation) sich auflösen; (marriage) in die Brüche gehen; (couple) sich trennen; **school breaks up on Friday** am Freitag beginnen die Ferien ▷ vt aufbrechen; (marriage) zerstören; (meeting) auflösen; **breakable** adj zerbrechlich; **breakage** n Bruch m; **breakdown** n (of car) Panne f; (of machine) Störung f; (of person, relations, system) Zusammenbruch m; **breakdown service** n Pannendienst m; **breakdown truck** n Abschleppwagen m

breakfast ['brekfəst] n Frühstück nt; **to have ~** frühstücken; **breakfast cereal** n Cornflakes, Muesli etc; **breakfast television** n Frühstücksfernsehen nt

break-in ['breɪkɪn] n Einbruch m; **breakup** ['breɪkʌp] n (of meeting, organization) Auflösung f; (of marriage) Zerrüttung f

breast [brest] n Brust f; **breastfeed** vt stillen; **breaststroke** n Brustschwimmen nt

breath [breθ] n Atem m; **out of ~** außer Atem; **breathalyse, breathalyze** ['breθəlaɪz] vt (ins Röhrchen) blasen lassen; **breathalyser, breathalyzer** n

vt, vi atmen; **breathe in** vt, vi einatmen; **breathe out** vt, vi ausatmen; **breathless** ['breθlɪs] adj atemlos; **breathtaking** ['breθteɪkɪŋ] adj atemberaubend

bred [bred] pt, pp of **breed**

breed [briːd] n (race) Rasse f ▷ vi (**bred, bred**) sich vermehren ▷ vt züchten; **breeder** n Züchter(in) m(f); (fam) Hetero m; **breeding** n (of animals) Züchtung f; (of person) (gute) Erziehung f

breeze [briːz] n Brise f

brevity ['brevɪtɪ] n Kürze f

brew [bruː] vt (beer) brauen; (tea) kochen; **brewery** n Brauerei f

bribe [braɪb] n Bestechungsgeld nt ▷ vt bestechen; **bribery** ['braɪbərɪ] n Bestechung f

brick [brɪk] n Backstein m; **bricklayer** n Maurer(in) m(f)

bride [braɪd] n Braut f; **bridegroom** n Bräutigam m; **bridesmaid** n Brautjungfer f

bridge [brɪdʒ] n Brücke f; (cards) Bridge nt

brief [briːf] adj kurz ▷ vt instruieren (on über +akk); **briefcase** n Aktentasche f; **briefs** npl Slip m

bright [braɪt] adj hell; (colour) leuchtend; (cheerful) heiter; (intelligent) intelligent; (idea) glänzend; **brighten up** vt aufhellen; (person) aufheitern ▷ vi sich aufheitern; (person) fröhlicher werden

brilliant ['brɪljənt] adj (sunshine, colour) strahlend; (person) brillant; (idea) glänzend; (Brit fam) **it was ~** es war fantastisch

brim [brɪm] n Rand m

bring [brɪŋ] (**brought, brought**) vt bringen; (with one) mitbringen; **bring about** vt herbeiführen, bewirken; **bring back** vt zurückbringen; (memories) wecken; **bring down** vt (reduce) senken; (*government etc*) zu Fall bringen; **bring in** vt hereinbringen; (*introduce*) einführen; **bring out** vt herausbringen; **bring round, bring to** vt wieder zu sich bringen; **bring up** vt (*child*) aufziehen; (*question*) zur Sprache bringen

brisk [brɪsk] *adj* (*trade*) lebhaft; (*wind*) frisch

bristle ['brɪsl] *n* Borste *f*

Brit [brɪt] *n* (*fam*) Brite *m*, Britin *f*; **Britain** ['brɪtn] *n* Großbritannien *nt*; **British** ['brɪtɪʃ] *adj* britisch; **the ~ Isles** (*pl*) die Britischen Inseln *pl* ▷ *n* **the ~** (*pl*) die Briten *pl*

brittle ['brɪtl] *adj* spröde

broad [brɔːd] *adj* breit; (*accent*) stark; **in ~ daylight** am helllichten Tag ▷ (*US fam*) Frau *f*

B road [biːrəʊd] *n* (*Brit*) ≈ Landstraße *f*

broadcast ['brɔːdkɑːst] *n* Sendung *f* ▷ *irr* vt, vi senden; (*event*) übertragen

broaden ['brɔːdn] vt: **to ~ the mind** den Horizont erweitern; **broad-minded** *adj* tolerant

broccoli ['brɒkəlɪ] *n* Brokkoli *pl*

brochure ['brəʊʃjʊə°] *n* Prospekt *m*, Broschüre *f*

broke [brəʊk] *pt of* **break** ▷ *adj* (*Brit fam*) pleite; **broken** ['brəʊkən] *pp of* **break**; **broken-hearted** *adj* untröstlich

broker ['brəʊkə°] *n* Makler(in) *m(f)*

brolly ['brɒlɪ] *n* (*Brit*) Schirm *m*

bronchitis [brɒŋ'kaɪtɪs] *n* Bronchitis *f*

bronze [brɒnz] *n* Bronze *f*

brooch [brəʊtʃ] *n* Brosche *f*

broom [bruːm] *n* Besen *m*

Bros [brɒs] *abbr* = **brothers** Gebr.

broth [brɒθ] *n* Fleischbrühe *f*

brothel ['brɒθl] *n* Bordell *nt*

brother ['brʌðə°] *n* Bruder *m*; **~s** (*pl*) (*Comm*) Gebrüder *pl*; **brother-**

in-law (*pl* **brothers-in-law**) *n* Schwager *m*

brought [brɔːt] *pt, pp of* **bring**

brow [braʊ] *n* (*eyebrow*) (Augen)braue *f*; (*forehead*) Stirn *f*

brown [braʊn] *adj* braun; **brown bread** *n* Mischbrot *nt*; (*wholemeal*) Vollkornbrot *nt*; **brownie** ['braʊnɪ] *n* (*Gastr*) Brownie *m*; (*Brit*) junge Pfadfinderin; **brown paper** *n* Packpapier *nt*; **brown rice** *n* Naturreis *m*; **brown sugar** *n* brauner Zucker

browse [braʊz] vi (*in book*) blättern; (*in shop*) schmökern, herumschauen; **browser** *n* (*Inform*) Browser *m*

bruise [bruːz] *n* blauer Fleck ▷ vt: **to ~ one's arm** sich *dat* einen blauen Fleck (am Arm) holen

brunette [bruː'net] *n* Brünette *f*

brush [brʌʃ] *n* Bürste *f*; (*for sweeping*) Handbesen *m*; (*for painting*) Pinsel *m* ▷ vt bürsten; (*sweep*) fegen; **to ~ one's teeth** sich *dat* die Zähne putzen; **brush up** vt (*French etc*) auffrischen

Brussels sprouts [brʌsl'spraʊts] *npl* Rosenkohl *m*, Kohlsprossen *pl*

brutal ['bruːtl] *adj* brutal; **brutality** [bruː'tælɪti] *n* Brutalität *f*

BSE *abbr* = **bovine spongiform encephalopathy** BSE *f*

bubble ['bʌbl] *n* Blase *f*; **bubble bath** *n* Schaumbad *nt*, Badeschaum *m*; **bubbly** ['bʌblɪ] *adj* sprudelnd; (*person*) temperamentvoll ▷ *n* (*fam*) Schampus *m*

buck [bʌk] *n* (*animal*) Bock *m*; (*US fam*) Dollar *m*

bucket ['bʌkɪt] *n* Eimer *m*; **bucket list** *n* Liste von Dingen, die man vor seinem Tod gerne gemacht haben würde

BUCKINGHAM PALACE

Der **Buckingham Palace** ist die offizielle Londoner Residenz der britischen Monarchen und liegt am St James's Park. Der Palast wurde 1703 für den Herzog von Buckingham erbaut, 1762 von George III gekauft, zwischen 1821 und 1836 und Anfang des 20. Jahrhunderts teilweise neu gestaltet. Teile des Buckingham Palace sind heute der Öffentlichkeit zugänglich.

buckle ['bʌkl] n Schnalle f ⊳ vi (Tech) sich verbiegen ⊳ vt zuschnallen
bud [bʌd] n Knospe f
Buddhism ['budɪzəm] n Buddhismus m; **Buddhist** adj buddhistisch ⊳ n Buddhist(in) m(f)
buddy ['bʌdɪ] n (fam) Kumpel m
budget ['bʌdʒɪt] n Budget nt ⊳ adj preisgünstig; **budget airline** n Billigflieger m
budgie ['bʌdʒɪ] n Wellensittich m
buff [bʌf] adj (US) muskulös; **in the ~** nackt ⊳ n (enthusiast) Fan m
buffalo ['bʌfələʊ] (pl **-es**) n Büffel m
buffer ['bʌfə*] n (a. Inform) Puffer m
buffet ['bʊfeɪ] n (food) (kaltes) Büfett nt
bug [bʌg] n (Inform) Bug m, Programmfehler m; (listening device) Wanze f; (US: insect) Insekt nt; (fam: illness) Infektion f ⊳ vt (fam) nerven
bugger ['bʌgə*] n (vulg) Scheißkerl m ⊳ interj (vulg) Scheiße f; **bugger off** vi (vulg) abhauen, Leine ziehen
buggy® ['bʌgɪ] n (for baby) Buggy® m

build [bɪld] n (**built, built**) vt bauen; **build up** vt aufbauen; **builder** n Bauunternehmer(in) m(f); **building** n Gebäude nt; **building site** n Baustelle f; **building society** n Bausparkasse f
built pt, pp of **build**; **built-in** adj (cupboard) Einbau-, eingebaut
bulb [bʌlb] n (Bot) (Blumen)zwiebel f; (Elec) Glühbirne f
Bulgaria [bʌl'gɛərɪə] n Bulgarien nt; **Bulgarian** adj bulgarisch ⊳ n (person) Bulgare m, Bulgarin f; (language) Bulgarisch nt
bulimia [bə'lɪmɪə] n Bulimie f
bulk [bʌlk] n (size) Größe f; (greater part) Großteil m (of +gen); **in ~** en gros; **bulky** adj (goods) sperrig; (person) stämmig
bull [bʊl] n Stier m; **bulldog** n Bulldogge f; **bulldoze** ['bʊldəʊz] vt planieren; **bulldozer** n Planierraupe f
bullet ['bʊlɪt] n Kugel f
bulletin ['bʊlɪtɪn] n Bulletin nt; (announcement) Bekanntmachung f; (Med) Krankenbericht m; **bulletin board** n (US: Inform) schwarzes Brett
bullfight ['bʊlfaɪt] n Stierkampf m; **bullshit** (fam) Scheiß m; **bully** ['bʊlɪ] n Tyrann m
bum [bʌm] n (Brit fam: backside) Po m; (US: vagrant) Penner m; (worthless person) Rumtreiber m; **bum around** vi herumgammeln
bumblebee ['bʌmblbi:] n Hummel f
bumf [bʌmf] (fam) n Infomaterial nt, Papierkram m
bump [bʌmp] n (swelling) Beule f; (road) Unebenheit f; (blow) Stoß m ⊳ vt stoßen; **to ~ one's head** sich dat den Kopf anschlagen (on an +dat); **bump into** vt stoßen gegen; (fam: meet)

(zufällig) begegnen +dat; **bumper**
n (Auto) Stoßstange f ▷ adj
(edition etc) Riesen-; (crop etc)
Rekord-; **bumpy** ['bʌmpɪ] adj
holp(e)rig

bun [bʌn] n süßes Brötchen

bunch [bʌntʃ] n (of flowers)
Strauß m; (fam: of people) Haufen m;
~ of keys Schlüsselbund m; **~ of
grapes** Weintraube f

bundle ['bʌndl] n Bündel nt

bungalow ['bʌŋɡələu] n Bungalow m

bungee jumping ['bʌndʒɪ-
dʒʌmpɪŋ] n Bungeejumping nt

bunk [bʌŋk] n Koje f; **bunk
bed(s)** n(pl) Etagenbett nt

bunker ['bʌŋkə°] n (Mil) Bunker
m

bunny ['bʌnɪ] n Häschen nt

buoy [bɔɪ] n Boje f; **buoyant**
['bɔɪənt] adj (floating)
schwimmend

BUPA ['buːpə] abbr (Brit) private
Krankenkasse

burden ['bɜːdn] n Last f

bureau ['bjuːrəu] n Büro nt;
(government department) Amt nt;
bureaucracy [bjuːˈrɔkrəsɪ] n
Bürokratie f; **bureaucratic**
[bjuːrəˈkrætɪk] adj bürokratisch;
bureau de change ['bjuːrəu də
ʃɑ̃ʒ] n Wechselstube f

burger ['bɜːɡə°] n Hamburger m

burglar ['bɜːɡlə°] n Einbre-
cher(in) m(f); **burglar alarm** n
Alarmanlage f; **burglarize** vt (US)
einbrechen in +akk; **burglary** n
Einbruch m; **burgle** ['bɜːɡl] vt
einbrechen in +akk

burial ['berɪəl] n Beerdigung f

burn [bɜːn] (burnt o burned,
burnt o burned) vt verbrennen;
(food, slightly) anbrennen; **to
~ one's hand** sich dat die Hand
verbrennen ▷ vi brennen ▷ n
(injury) Brandwunde f; (on material)

verbrannte Stelle; **burn down** vt,
vi abbrennen

burp [bɜːp] vi rülpsen ▷ vt (baby)
aufstoßen lassen

bursary ['bɜːsərɪ] n Stipendium nt

burst [bɜːst] (burst, burst) vt
platzen lassen ▷ vi platzen;
to ~ into tears in Tränen
ausbrechen

bury ['berɪ] vt begraben; (in grave)
beerdigen; (hide) vergraben

bus [bʌs] n Bus m; **bus driver** n
Busfahrer(in) m(f)

bush [buʃ] n Busch m

business ['bɪznɪs] n Geschäft nt;
(enterprise) Unternehmen nt;
(concern, affair) Sache f; **I'm here on
~** ich bin geschäftlich hier; **it's
none of your ~** das geht dich
nichts an; **business card** n
Visitenkarte f; **business class** n
(Aviat) Businessclass f;
businessman (pl **-men**) n
Geschäftsmann m; **business
studies** npl Betriebswirtschaft-
slehre f; **businesswoman** (pl
-women) n Geschäftsfrau f

bus service n Busverbindung f;
bus shelter n Wartehäuschen nt;
bus station n Busbahnhof m; **bus
stop** n Bushaltestelle f

bust [bʌst] n Büste f ▷ adj
(broken) kaputt; **to go ~** (fam)
gehen; **bust-up** n (fam) Krach m

busy ['bɪzɪ] adj beschäftigt;
(street, place) belebt; (esp US:
telephone) besetzt; **~ signal** (US)
Besetztzeichen nt

KEYWORD

but [bʌt, bət] conj 1 (yet) aber; **not
X but Y** nicht X sondern Y
2 (however) I'd love to come, but
I'm busy ich würde gern kommen,
bin aber beschäftigt
3 (showing disagreement, surprise etc)

but that's fantastic! (aber) das ist ja fantastisch!
▷ prep (apart from, except): **nothing but trouble** nichts als Ärger; **no-one but him can do it** niemand außer ihm kann es machen; **but for you/your help** ohne dich/deine Hilfe; **anything but that** alles, nur das nicht
▷ adv (just, only) **she's but a child** sie ist noch ein Kind; **had I but known** wenn ich es nur gewusst hätte; **I can but try** ich kann es immerhin versuchen; **all but finished** so gut wie fertig

butcher ['butʃə°] n Fleischer(in) m(f), Metzger(in) m(f)
butler ['bʌtlə°] n Butler m
butt [bʌt] (US fam) n Hintern m
butter ['bʌtə°] n Butter f ▷ vt buttern; **buttercup** n Butterblume f; **butterfly** n Schmetterling m
buttocks ['bʌtəks] npl Gesäß nt
button ['bʌtn] n Knopf m; (badge) Button m ▷ vt zuknöpfen; **buttonhole** n Knopfloch nt
buy [baɪ] n Kauf m ▷ vt (bought, bought) kaufen (from von); **he bought me a ring** er hat mir einen Ring gekauft; **buyer** n Käufer(in) m(f)
buzz [bʌz] n Summen nt; **to give sb a ~** (fam) jdn anrufen ▷ vi summen; **buzzer** ['bʌzə°] n Summer m; **buzz word** n (fam) Modewort nt

🔵 **KEYWORD**

by [baɪ] prep **1** (referring to cause, agent) von, durch; **killed by lightning** vom Blitz getötet; **a painting by Picasso** ein Gemälde von Picasso
2 (referring to method, manner) **by bus/car/train** mit dem Bus/Auto/Zug; **to pay by cheque** per Scheck bezahlen; **by moonlight** bei Mondschein; **by saving hard, he ...** indem er eisern sparte, ... er ...
3 (via, through) über +akk; **he came in by the back door** er kam durch die Hintertür herein
4 (close to, past) bei, an +dat; **a holiday by the sea** ein Urlaub am Meer; **she rushed by me** sie eilte an mir vorbei
5 (not later than) **by 4 o'clock** bis 4 Uhr; **by this time tomorrow** morgen um diese Zeit; **by the time I got here it was too late** als ich hier ankam, war es zu spät
6 (during) **by day** bei Tag
7 (amount) **by the kilo/metre** kiloweise/meterweise; **paid by the hour** stundenweise bezahlt
8 (math, measure) **to divide by 3** durch 3 teilen; **to multiply by 3** mit 3 malnehmen; **a room 3 metres by 4** ein Zimmer 3 mal 4 Meter; **it's broader by a metre** es ist (um) einen Meter breiter
9 (according to) nach; **it's all right by me** von mir aus gern
10 (all) **by oneself** etc ganz allein
11 **by the way** übrigens
▷ adv **1** see **go**; **pass** etc
2 **by and by** irgendwann; (with past tenses) nach einiger Zeit; **by and large** (on the whole) im Großen und Ganzen

bye-bye ['baɪ'baɪ] interj (fam) Wiedersehen, tschüss
by-election n Nachwahl f; **bypass** n Umgehungsstraße f; (Med) Bypass m; **byproduct** n Nebenprodukt nt; **byroad** n Nebenstraße f; **bystander** n Zuschauer(in) m(f)
byte [baɪt] n Byte nt

C

C [si:] *abbr* = **Celsius** C

c *abbr* = **circa** ca

cab [kæb] *n* Taxi *nt*

cabbage ['kæbɪdʒ] *n* Kohl *m*

cabin ['kæbɪn] *n* (*Naut*) Kajüte *f*; (*Aviat*) Passagierraum *m*; (*wooden house*) Hütte *f*; **cabin crew** *n* Flugbegleitpersonal *nt*; **cabin cruiser** *n* Kajütboot *nt*

cabinet ['kæbɪnɪt] *n* Schrank *m*; (*for display*) Vitrine *f*; (*Pol*) Kabinett *nt*

cable ['keɪbl] *n* (*Elec*) Kabel *nt*; **cable-car** *n* Seilbahn *f*; **cable railway** *n* Drahtseilbahn *f*; **cable television, cablevision** (*US*) *n* Kabelfernsehen *nt*

cactus ['kæktəs] *n* Kaktus *m*

CAD *abbr* = **computer-aided design** CAD *nt*

Caesarean [si:'zɛərɪən] *adj*: **~ (section)** Kaiserschnitt *m*

café ['kæfeɪ] *n* Café *nt*; **cafeteria** [kæfɪ'tɪərɪə] *n* Cafeteria *f*; **cafetiere** [kæfə'tjɛə°] *n* Kaffeebereiter *m*

cage [keɪdʒ] *n* Käfig *m*

Cairo ['kaɪərəʊ] *n* Kairo *nt*

cake [keɪk] *n* Kuchen *m*; **cake shop** *n* Konditorei *f*

calamity [kə'læmɪtɪ] *n* Katastrophe *f*

calculate ['kælkjʊleɪt] *vt* berechnen; (*estimate*) kalkulieren; **calculating** *adj* berechnend; **calculation** [kælkjʊ'leɪʃən] *n* Berechnung *f*; (*estimate*) Kalkulation *f*; **calculator** ['kælkjʊleɪtə°] *n* Taschenrechner *m*

calendar ['kælɪndə°] *n* Kalender *m*

calf [kɑːf] (*pl* **calves**) *n* Kalb *nt*; (*Anat*) Wade *f*

California [kælɪ'fɔːnɪə] *n* Kalifornien *nt*

call [kɔːl] *vt* rufen; (*name, describe as*) nennen; (*Tel*) anrufen; (*Inform, Aviat*) aufrufen; **what's this ~ed?** wie heißt das?; **that's what I ~ service** das nenne ich guten Service ▷ *vi* (*shout*) rufen (*for help* um Hilfe); (*visit*) vorbeikommen; **to ~ at the doctor's** beim Arzt vorbeigehen; (*of train*) **to ~ at ...** in ... halten ▷ *n* (*shout*) Ruf *m*; (*Tel*) Anruf *m*; (*Inform, Aviat*) Aufruf *m*; **to make a ~** telefonieren; **to give sb a ~** jdn anrufen; **to be on ~** Bereitschaftsdienst haben; **call back** *vt, vi* zurückrufen; **call for** *vt* (*come to pick up*) abholen; (*demand, require*) verlangen; **call off** *vt* absagen

call centre *n* Callcenter *nt*; **caller** *n* Besucher(in) *m(f)*; (*Tel*) Anrufer(in) *m(f)*

calm [kɑːm] *n* Stille *f*; (*also of person*) Ruhe *f*; (*of sea*) Flaute *f* ▷ *vt* beruhigen ▷ *adj* ruhig; **calm down** *vi* sich beruhigen

calorie ['kælərɪ] *n* Kalorie *f*

calves [kɑːvz] *pl of* **calf**

Cambodia [kæm'bəʊdɪə] *n* Kambodscha *f*

camcorder ['kæmkɔːdə°] *n* Camcorder *m*

came [keɪm] *pt of* **come**

camel ['kæməl] *n* Kamel *nt*

camera ['kæmərə] *n* Fotoapparat *m*, Kamera *f*; **camera phone** ['kæmərəfəʊn] *n* Fotohandy *nt*

camomile ['kæməmaɪl] *n* Kamille *f*

camouflage ['kæməflɑːʒ] *n* Tarnung *f*

camp [kæmp] *n* Lager *nt*; (camping place) Zeltplatz *m* ▷ *vi* zelten, campen ▷ *adj* (fam) theatralisch, tuntig

campaign [kæm'peɪn] *n* Kampagne *f*; (Pol) Wahlkampf *m* ▷ *vi* sich einsetzen (for/against für/gegen)

campbed ['kæmpbed] *n* Campingliege *f*; **camper** ['kæmpə°] *n* (person) Camper(in) *m(f)*; (van) Wohnmobil *nt*; **camping** ['kæmpɪŋ] *n* Zelten *nt*, Camping *nt*; **campsite** ['kæmpsaɪt] *n* Zeltplatz *m*, Campingplatz *m*

campus ['kæmpəs] *n* (of university) Universitätsgelände *nt*, Campus *m*

⟳ KEYWORD

can [kæn] (negative **cannot**, **can't**, conditional **could**) *vb aux* **1** (be able to, know how to) können; **I can see you tomorrow, if you like** ich könnte Sie morgen sehen, wenn Sie wollen; **I can swim** ich kann schwimmen; **can you speak German?** sprechen Sie Deutsch?

2 (may) können, dürfen; **could I have a word with you?** könnte ich Sie kurz sprechen?

Canada ['kænədə] *n* Kanada *nt*; **Canadian** [kə'neɪdjən] *adj* kanadisch ▷ *n* Kanadier(in) *m(f)*

canal [kə'næl] *n* Kanal *m*

canary [kə'nɛərɪ] *n* Kanarienvogel *m*

cancel ['kænsəl] *vt* (plans) aufgeben; (meeting, event) absagen; (Comm: order etc) stornieren; (contract) kündigen; (Inform) löschen; (Aviat: flight) streichen; **to be ~led** (event, train, bus) ausfallen; **cancellation** [kænsə'leɪʃən] *n* Absage *f*; (Comm) Stornierung *f*; (Aviat) gestrichener Flug

cancer ['kænsə°] *n* (Med) Krebs *m*; **Cancer** *n* (Astr) Krebs *m*

candid ['kændɪd] *adj* (person, conversation) offen

candidate ['kændɪdət] *n* (for post) Bewerber(in) *m(f)*; (Pol) Kandidat(in) *m(f)*

candle ['kændl] *n* Kerze *f*; **candlelight** *n* Kerzenlicht *nt*; **candlestick** *n* Kerzenhalter *m*

candy ['kændɪ] *n* (US) Bonbon *nt*; (quantity) Süßigkeiten *pl*; **candy-floss** *n* (Brit) Zuckerwatte *f*

cane [keɪn] *n* Rohr *nt*; (stick) Stock *m*

cannabis ['kænəbɪs] *n* Cannabis *m*

canned [kænd] *adj* Dosen-

cannot ['kænɒt] *contr of* **can not**

canny ['kænɪ] *adj* (shrewd) schlau

canoe [kə'nuː] *n* Kanu *nt*; **canoeing** *n* Kanufahren *nt*

can opener ['kænəʊpnə°] *n* Dosenöffner *m*

canopy ['kænəpɪ] *n* Baldachin *m*; (awning) Markise *f*; (over entrance) Vordach *nt*

can't | 292

can't [kɑːnt] *contr of* **can not**

canteen [kænˈtiːn] *n (in factory)* Kantine *f*; *(in university)* Mensa *f*

canvas ['kænvəs] *n (for sails, shoes)* Segeltuch *nt*; *(for tent)* Zeltstoff *m*; *(for painting)* Leinwand *f*

canvass ['kænvəs] *vi um* Stimmen werben *(for für)*

canyon ['kænjən] *n* Felsenschlucht *f*; **canyoning** ['kænjənɪŋ] *n* Canyoning *nt*

cap [kæp] *n* Mütze *f*; *(lid)* Verschluss *m*, Deckel *m*

capability [keɪpəˈbɪlɪtɪ] *n* Fähigkeit *f*; **capable** ['keɪpəbl] *adj* fähig; **to be ~ of sth** zu etw fähig *(o imstande)* sein; **to be ~ of doing sth** etw tun können

capacity [kəˈpæsɪtɪ] *n (of building, container)* Fassungsvermögen *nt*; *(ability)* Fähigkeit *f*

cape [keɪp] *n (garment)* Cape *nt*, Umhang *m*; *(Geo)* Kap *nt*

caper ['keɪpə°] *n (for cooking)* Kaper *f*

capital ['kæpɪtl] *n (Fin)* Kapital *nt*; *(letter)* Großbuchstabe *m*; **~ (city)** Hauptstadt *f*; **capitalism** *n* Kapitalismus *m*; **capital punishment** *n* die Todesstrafe

Capricorn ['kæprɪkɔːn] *n (Astr)* Steinbock *m*

capsize [kæpˈsaɪz] *vi* kentern

capsule ['kæpsjuːl] *n* Kapsel *f*

captain ['kæptɪn] *n* Kapitän *m*; *(army)* Hauptmann *m*

caption ['kæpʃən] *n* Bildunterschrift *f*

captive ['kæptɪv] *n* Gefangene(r) *mf*; **capture** ['kæptʃə°] *vt (person)* fassen, gefangen nehmen; *(town etc)* einnehmen; *(Inform: data)* erfassen ▷ *n* Gefangennahme *f*; *(Inform)* Erfassung *f*

car [kɑː°] *n* Auto *nt*; *(US Rail)* Wagen *m*

carafe [kəˈræf] *n* Karaffe *f*

caramel ['kærəmel] *n* Karamelle *f*

caravan ['kærəvæn] *n* Wohnwagen *m*; **caravan site** *n* Campingplatz *m* für Wohnwagen

caraway (seed) ['kærəweɪ] *n* Kümmel *m*

carbohydrate [kɑːbəʊˈhaɪdreɪt] *n* Kohle(n)hydrat *nt*

car bomb *n* Autobombe *f*

carbon ['kɑːbən] *n* Kohlenstoff *m*; **carbon footprint** *n* ökologischer Fußabdruck; **carbon-neutral** *adj* CO2-neutral

car boot sale *n* auf einem Parkplatz stattfindender Flohmarkt

carburettor, carburetor (US) ['kɑːbjʊretə°] *n* Vergaser *m*

card [kɑːd] *n* Karte *f*; *(material)* Pappe *f*; **cardboard** *n* Pappe *f*; **~ (box)** Karton *m*; *(smaller)* Pappschachtel *f*; **card game** *n* Kartenspiel *nt*

cardigan ['kɑːdɪgən] *n* Strickjacke *f*

card index *n* Kartei *f*; **cardphone** ['kɑːdfəʊn] *n* Kartentelefon *nt*

care [keə°] *n (worry)* Sorge *f*; *(carefulness)* Sorgfalt *f*; *(looking after things, people)* Pflege *f*; **with ~** sorgfältig; *(cautiously)* vorsichtig; **to take ~** *(watch out)* vorsichtig sein; *(in address)* **~ of** bei; **to take ~ of** sorgen für, sich kümmern um ▷ *vi*: **I don't ~** es ist mir egal; **to ~ about sth** Wert auf etw *akk* legen; **he ~s about her** sie liegt ihm am Herzen; *give about* sorgen für, sich kümmern um; *(like)* mögen

career [kəˈrɪə°] *n* Karriere *f*, Laufbahn *f*; **career woman** *(pl* **women***)* *n* Karrierefrau *f*; **careers adviser** *n* Berufsberater(in) *m(f)*

carefree ['keəfriː] *adj* sorgenfrei; **careful, carefully** *adj, adv* sorgfältig; *(cautious, cautiously)*

vorsichtig; **careless, carelessly**
adj, adv nachlässig; (driving etc)
leichtsinnig; (remark)
unvorsichtig; **carer** ['kɛərə°] n
Betreuer(in) m(f), Pfleger(in) m(f);
caretaker ['kɛəteɪkə°] n Hausmeister(in) m(f); **careworker** n
Pfleger(in) m(f)

car-ferry ['kɑːfɛrɪ] n Autofähre f

cargo ['kɑːgəʊ] pl **-(e)s** n
Ladung f

car hire, car hire company n
Autovermietung f

Caribbean [kærɪˈbiːən] n Karibik
f ▷ adj karibisch

caring ['kɛərɪŋ] adj mitfühlend;
(parent, partner) liebevoll; (looking
after sb) fürsorglich

car insurance n
Kraftfahrzeugversicherung f

carnation [kɑːˈneɪʃən] n Nelke f

carnival ['kɑːnɪvəl] n Volksfest
nt; (before Lent) Karneval m

carol ['kærəl] n Weihnachtslied nt

carp [kɑːp] n (fish) Karpfen m

car park n (Brit) Parkplatz m;
(multi-storey car park) Parkhaus nt

carpenter ['kɑːpəntə°] n Zimmermann m

carpet ['kɑːpɪt] n Teppich m

car phone n Autotelefon nt

carpool n Fahrgemeinschaft f;
(vehicles) Fuhrpark m ▷ vi eine
Fahrgemeinschaft bilden; **car
rental** n Autovermietung f

carriage ['kærɪdʒ] n (Brit Rail:
coach) Wagen m; (compartment)
Abteil nt; (horse-drawn) Kutsche f;
(transport) Beförderung f;
carriageway n (Brit: on road)
Fahrbahn f

carrier ['kærɪə°] n (Comm)
Spediteur(in) m(f); **carrier bag** n
Tragetasche f

carrot ['kærət] n Karotte f

carry ['kærɪ] vt tragen; (in vehicle)
befördern; (have on one) bei sich

haben; **carry on** vi (continue)
weitermachen; (fam: make a scene)
ein Theater machen ▷ vt
(continue) fortführen; **to ~ on
working** weiter arbeiten; **carry
out** vt (orders, plan) ausführen,
durchführen

carrycot n Babytragetasche f

carsick ['kɑːsɪk] adj: **he gets
~** ihm wird beim Autofahren übel

cart [kɑːt] n Wagen m, Karren m;
(US: shopping trolley)
Einkaufswagen m

carton ['kɑːtən] n (Papp)karton
m; (of cigarettes) Stange f

cartoon [kɑːˈtuːn] n Cartoon m
nt; (one drawing) Karikatur f; (film)
(Zeichen)trickfilm m

cartridge ['kɑːtrɪdʒ] n (for film)
Kassette f; (for gun, pen, printer)
Patrone f; (for copier) Kartusche f

carve [kɑːv] vt, vi (wood)
schnitzen; (stone) meißeln; (meat)
schneiden, tranchieren; **carving**
n (in wood) Schnitzerei f; (in stone)
Skulptur f; (Ski) Carving nt

car wash n Autowaschanlage f

case [keɪs] n (crate) Kiste f; (box)
Schachtel f; (for jewels) Schatulle f;
(for spectacles) Etui nt; (Jur: matter)
Fall m; **in ~** falls; **in that ~** in dem
Fall; **in ~ of fire** bei Brand; **it's a
~ of ...** es handelt sich hier um ...

cash [kæʃ] n Bargeld nt; **in ~** bar;
~ on delivery per Nachnahme
▷ vt (cheque) einlösen; **cash desk**
n Kasse f; **cash dispenser** n
Geldautomat m; **cashier** [kæˈʃɪə°]
n Kassierer(in) m(f); **cash
machine** n (Brit) Geldautomat m

cashmere ['kæʃmɪə°] n Kaschmirwolle f

cash payment n Barzahlung f;
cashpoint n (Brit) Geldautomat m

casing ['keɪsɪŋ] n Gehäuse nt

casino [kəˈsiːnəʊ] (pl **-s**) n
Kasino nt

cask [kɑːsk] n Fass nt
casserole [ˈkæsərəʊl] n Kasserole f; (food) Schmortopf m
cassette [kæˈset] n Kassette f; **cassette recorder** n Kassettenrekorder m
cast [kɑːst] (vb: **cast, cast**) vt (throw) werfen; (Theat, Cine) besetzen; (roles) verteilen ▷ n (Theat, Cine) Besetzung f; (Med) Gipsverband m; **cast off** vi (Naut) losmachen
caster [ˈkɑːstəˈ] n: ~ **sugar** Streuzucker m
castle [ˈkɑːsl] n Burg f
castrate [kæsˈtreɪt] vt kastrieren
casual [ˈkæʒjʊəl] adj (arrangement, remark) beiläufig; (attitude, manner) (nach)lässig, zwanglos; (dress) leger; (work, earnings) Gelegenheits-; (look, glance) flüchtig; ~ **wear** Freizeitkleidung f; ~ **sex** Gelegenheitssex m; **casually** adv (remark, say) beiläufig; (meet) zwanglos; (dressed) leger
casualty [ˈkæʒjʊəltɪ] n Verletzte(r) m(f); (dead) Tote(r) m(f); (department in hospital) Notaufnahme f
cat [kæt] n Katze f; (male) Kater m
catalog (US), **catalogue** [ˈkætəlɒg] n Katalog m ▷ vt katalogisieren
cataract [ˈkætərækt] n Wasserfall m; (Med) grauer Star
catarrh [kəˈtɑːˈ] n Katarr(h) m
catastrophe [kəˈtæstrəfɪ] n Katastrophe f
catch [kætʃ] n (fish etc) Fang m ▷ vt (caught, caught) fangen; (thief) fassen; (train, bus etc) nehmen; (not miss) erreichen; (hear, understand) mitbekommen, verstehen; ~ **a cold** sich erkälten; to ~ **fire** Feuer fangen; **I didn't ~ that** das habe ich nicht verstanden; **catch on** vi (become popular) Anklang finden; **catch up** vt, vi: to ~ **with**

sb jdn einholen; **to ~ on sth** etw nachholen; **catching** adj ansteckend
category [ˈkætɪgərɪ] n Kategorie f
cater [ˈkeɪtəˈ] vi die Speisen und Getränke liefern (for für); **cater for** vt (have facilities for) eingestellt sein auf +akk; **catering** n Versorgung f mit Speisen und Getränken, Gastronomie f; **catering service** n Partyservice m
caterpillar [ˈkætəpɪləˈ] n Raupe f
cathedral [kəˈθiːdrəl] n Kathedrale f, Dom m
Catholic [ˈkæθəlɪk] adj katholisch ▷ Katholik(in) m(f)
cat nap n (Brit) kurzer Schlaf; **cat's eyes** [ˈkætsaɪz] npl (in road) Katzenaugen pl, Reflektoren pl
catsup [ˈkætsʌp] n (US) Ketchup nt o m
cattle [ˈkætl] npl Vieh nt
caught [kɔːt] pt, pp of **catch**
cauliflower [ˈkɒlɪflaʊəˈ] n Blumenkohl m; **cauliflower cheese** n Blumenkohl m in Käsesoße
cause [kɔːz] n (origin) Ursache f (of für); (reason) Grund m (for zu); (purpose) Sache f; **for a good** ~ für wohltätige Zwecke; **no ~ for alarm/complaint** kein Grund zur Aufregung/Klage ▷ vt verursachen
causeway [ˈkɔːzweɪ] n Damm m
caution [ˈkɔːʃən] n Vorsicht f; (Jur, Sport) Verwarnung f ▷ vt (ver)warnen; **cautious** [ˈkɔːʃəs] adj vorsichtig
cave [keɪv] n Höhle f; **cave in** vi einstürzen
cavity [ˈkævɪtɪ] n Hohlraum m; (in tooth) Loch nt
cayenne (pepper) [keɪˈen] n Cayennepfeffer m

CCTV abbr = **closed circuit television** Video-überwachungsanlage f

CD abbr = **Compact Disc** CD f; **CD player** n CD-Spieler m; **CD-ROM** abbr = **Compact Disc Read Only Memory** CD-ROM f; **CD-RW** abbr = **Compact Disc Rewritable** CD-RW f

cease [siːs] vi aufhören ▷ vt beenden; **to ~ doing sth** aufhören, etw zu tun; **cease fire** n Waffenstillstand m

ceiling ['siːlɪŋ] n Decke f

celebrate ['sɛlɪbreɪt] vt, vi feiern; **celebrated** adj gefeiert; **celebration** [sɛlɪ'breɪʃən] n Feier f; **celebrity** [sɪ'lɛbrɪtɪ] n Berühmtheit f, Star m

celeriac [sə'lɛrɪæk] n (Knollen)sellerie m o f; **celery** ['sɛlərɪ] n (Stangen)sellerie m o f

cell [sɛl] n Zelle f; (US) see **cellphone**

cellar ['sɛlə°] n Keller m

cello ['tʃɛləʊ] (pl -s) n Cello nt

cellphone ['sɛlfəʊn], **cellular phone** ['sɛljʊlə'fəʊn] n Mobiltelefon nt, Handy nt

Celt [kɛlt] n Kelte m, Keltin f; **Celtic** ['kɛltɪk] adj keltisch ▷ n (language) Keltisch nt

cement [sɪ'mɛnt] n Zement m

cemetery ['sɛmɪtrɪ] n Friedhof m

censorship ['sɛnsəʃɪp] n Zensur f

cent [sɛnt] n (of dollar, euro etc) Cent m

center n (US) see **centre**

centiliter (US), **centilitre** ['sɛntiːliːtə°] n Zentiliter m; **centimeter** (US), **centimetre** ['sɛntiːmiːtə°] n Zentimeter m

central ['sɛntrəl] adj zentral; **Central America** n Mittelamerika nt; **Central Europe** n

Mitteleuropa nt; **central heating** n Zentralheizung f; **centralize** vt zentralisieren; **central locking** n (Auto) Zentralverriegelung f; **central reservation** n (Brit) Mittelstreifen m; **central station** n Hauptbahnhof m

centre ['sɛntə°] n Mitte f; (building, of city) Zentrum nt ▷ vt zentrieren; **centre forward** n (Sport) Mittelstürmer m

century ['sɛntjʊrɪ] n Jahrhundert nt

ceramic [sɪ'ræmɪk] adj keramisch

cereal ['sɪərɪəl] n (any grain) Getreide nt; (breakfast cereal) Frühstücksflocken pl

ceremony ['sɛrɪmənɪ] n Feier f, Zeremonie f

certain ['sɜːtən] adj sicher (of +gen); (particular) bestimmt; **for ~** mit Sicherheit; **certainly** adv sicher; (without doubt) bestimmt; **~l** aber sicher!; **~ not** ganz bestimmt nicht!

certificate [sə'tɪfɪkɪt] n Bescheinigung f; (in school, of qualification) Zeugnis nt; **certify** ['sɜːtɪfaɪ] vt, vi bescheinigen

cervical smear ['sɜːvɪkəl smɪə°] n Abstrich m

CFC abbr = **chlorofluorocarbon** FCKW nt

chain [tʃeɪn] n Kette f ▷ vt: **to ~ (up)** anketten; **chain reaction** n Kettenreaktion f; **chain store** n Kettenladen m

chair [tʃeə°] n Stuhl m; (university) Lehrstuhl m; (armchair) Sessel m; (chairperson) Vorsitzende(r) mf; **chairlift** n Sessellift m; **chairman** (pl -men) n Vorsitzende(r) m; (of firm) Präsident m; **chairperson** n Vorsitzende(r) mf; (of firm) Präsident(in) m(f); **chairwoman**

(*pl* **-women**) *n* Vorsitzende *f*; (*of firm*) Präsidentin *f*

chalet ['ʃæleɪ] *n* (*in mountains*) Berghütte *f*; (*holiday dwelling*) Ferienhäuschen *nt*

chalk ['tʃɔːk] *n* Kreide *f*

challenge ['tʃælɪndʒ] *n* Herausforderung *f* ▷ *vt* (*person*) herausfordern; (*statement*) bestreiten

chambermaid ['tʃeɪmbə'meɪd] *n* Zimmermädchen *nt*

chamois leather ['ʃæmwɑː'leðə'] *n* (*for windows*) Fensterleder *nt*

champagne [ʃæm'peɪn] *n* Champagner *m*

champion ['tʃæmpɪən] *n* (*Sport*) Meister(in) *m(f)*; **championship** *n* Meisterschaft *f*

chance [tʃɑːns] *n* (*fate*) Zufall *m*; (*possibility*) Möglichkeit *f*; (*opportunity*) Gelegenheit *f*; (*risk*) Risiko *nt*; **by ~** zufällig; **he doesn't stand a ~ (of winning)** er hat keinerlei Chance(, zu gewinnen)

chancellor ['tʃɑːnsələ'] *n* Kanzler(in) *m(f)*

chandelier [ʃændɪ'lɪə'] *n* Kronleuchter *m*

change [tʃeɪndʒ] *vt* verändern; (*alter*) ändern; (*money, wheel, nappy*) wechseln; (*exchange*) (um)tauschen; **to ~ one's clothes** sich umziehen; **to ~ trains** umsteigen; **to ~ gear** (*Auto*) schalten ▷ *vi* sich ändern; (*esp outwardly*) sich verändern; (*get changed*) sich umziehen ▷ *n* Veränderung *f*; (*alteration*) Änderung *f*; (*money*) Wechselgeld *nt*; (*coins*) Kleingeld *nt*; **for a ~** zur Abwechslung; **can you give me ~ for £10?** können Sie mir auf 10 Pfund herausgeben?; **change down** *vi* (*Brit Auto*) herunterschalten; **change over** *vi*

sich umstellen (**to** auf +*akk*); **change up** *vi* (*Brit Auto*) hochschalten

changeable *adj* (*weather*) veränderlich, wechselhaft; **change machine** *n* Geldwechsler *m*; **changing room** *n* Umkleideraum *m*

channel ['tʃænl] *n* Kanal *m*; (*Radio, TV*) Kanal *m*, Sender *m*; **the (English) Channel** der Ärmelkanal; **the Channel Islands** die Kanalinseln; **the Channel Tunnel** der Kanaltunnel; **channel-hopping** *n* Zappen *nt*

chaos ['keɪɒs] *n* Chaos *nt*; **chaotic** [keɪ'ɒtɪk] *adj* chaotisch

chap [tʃæp] *n* (*Brit fam*) Bursche *m*, Kerl *m*

chapel ['tʃæpl] *n* Kapelle *f*

chapped ['tʃæpt] *adj* (*lips*) aufgesprungen

chapter ['tʃæptə'] *n* Kapitel *nt*

character ['kærəktə'] *n* Charakter *m*, Wesen *nt*; (*in a play, novel etc*) Figur *f*; (*Typo*) Zeichen *nt*; **he's a real ~** er ist ein echtes Original; **characteristic** [kærəktə'rɪstɪk] *n* typisches Merkmal

charcoal ['tʃɑːkəʊl] *n* Holzkohle *f*

charge [tʃɑːdʒ] *n* (*cost*) Gebühr *f*; (*Jur*) Anklage *f*; **free of ~** gratis, kostenlos; **to be in ~ of** verantwortlich sein für ▷ *vt* (*money*) verlangen; (*Jur*) anklagen; (*battery*) laden; **charge card** *n* Kundenkreditkarte *f*

charity ['tʃærɪtɪ] *n* (*institution*) wohltätige Organisation *f*; **a collection for ~** eine Sammlung für wohltätige Zwecke; **charity shop** *n* Geschäft einer 'charity', in dem freiwillige Helfer gebrauchte Kleidung, Bücher etc verkaufen

charm [tʃɑːm] *n* Charme *m* ▷ *vt* bezaubern; **charming** *adj* reizend, charmant

chart [tʃɑːt] n Diagramm nt; (map) Karte f; **the ~s** pl die Charts, die Hitliste

charter [ˈtʃɑːtə°] n Urkunde f ⊳ vt (Naut, Aviat) chartern; **charter flight** n Charterflug m

chase [tʃeɪs] vt jagen, verfolgen ⊳ n Verfolgungsjagd f; (hunt) Jagd f

chassis [ˈʃæsɪ] n (Auto) Fahrgestell nt

chat [tʃæt] vi plaudern; (Inform) chatten ⊳ n Plauderei f; (Inform) Chat m; **chat up** vt anmachen, anbaggern; **chatroom** n (Inform) Chatroom m; **chat show** n Talkshow f; **chatty** adj geschwätzig

chauffeur [ˈʃəʊfə°] n Chauffeur(in) m(f), Fahrer(in) m(f)

cheap [tʃiːp] adj billig; (of poor quality) minderwertig

cheat [tʃiːt] vt, vi betrügen; (in school, game) mogeln

Chechen [ˈtʃetʃen] adj tschetschenisch ⊳ n Tschetschene m, Tschetschenin f

Chechnya [ˈtʃetʃnɪə] n Tschetschenien nt

check [tʃek] vt (examine) überprüfen (for auf +akk); (Tech: adjustment etc) kontrollieren; (US: tick) abhaken; (Aviat: luggage) einchecken; (US: coat) abgeben ⊳ n (examination, restraint) Kontrolle f; (US: restaurant bill) Rechnung f; (pattern) Karo(muster) nt; (US) see **cheque**; **check in** vi, vt (Aviat) einchecken; (into hotel) sich anmelden; **check out** vi sich abmelden, auschecken; **check up** vi nachprüfen; **to ~ on sb** Nachforschungen über jdn anstellen

checkers [ˈtʃekəz] nsing (US) Damespiel nt

check-in [ˈtʃekɪn] n (airport) Check-in m; (hotel) Anmeldung f; **check-in desk** n

Abfertigungsschalter m; **checking account** n (US) Scheckkonto nt; **check list** n Kontrollliste f; **checkout** n (supermarket) Kasse f; **checkout time** n (hotel) Abreise(zeit) f; **checkpoint** n Kontrollpunkt m; **checkroom** n (US) Gepäckaufbewahrung f; **checkup** n (Med) (ärztliche) Untersuchung

cheddar [ˈtʃedə°] n Cheddarkäse m

cheek [tʃiːk] n Backe f, Wange f; (insolence) Frechheit f; **what a ~** so eine Frechheit!; **cheekbone** n Backenknochen m; **cheeky** adj frech

cheer [tʃɪə°] n Beifallsruf m; **~s** (when drinking) prost!; (Brit fam: thanks) danke; (Brit: goodbye) tschüs ⊳ vt zujubeln +dat ⊳ vi jubeln; **cheer up** vt aufmuntern ⊳ vi fröhlicher werden; **~! Kopf** hoch!; **cheerful** [ˈtʃɪəfʊl] adj fröhlich

cheese [tʃiːz] n Käse m; **cheeseboard** n Käsebrett nt; (as course) (gemischte) Käseplatte; **cheesecake** n Käsekuchen m

chef [ʃef] n Koch m; (in charge of kitchen) Küchenchef(in) m(f)

chemical [ˈkemɪkl] adj chemisch ⊳ Chemikalie f; **chemist** [ˈkemɪst] n (pharmacist) Apotheker(in) m(f); (industrial chemist) Chemiker(in) m(f); **~'s (shop)** Apotheke f; **chemistry** n Chemie f

cheque [tʃek] n (Brit) Scheck m; **cheque account** n (Brit) Girokonto nt; **cheque book** n (Brit) Scheckheft nt; **cheque card** n (Brit) Scheckkarte f

chequered [ˈtʃekəd] adj kariert

cherish [ˈtʃerɪʃ] vt (look after) liebevoll sorgen für; (hope) hegen; (memory) bewahren

cherry ['tʃerɪ] n Kirsche f; **cherry tomato** (pl **-es**) n Kirschtomate f

chess [tʃes] n Schach nt; **chessboard** n Schachbrett nt

chest [tʃest] n Brust f; (box) Kiste f; **~ of drawers** Kommode f

chestnut ['tʃesnʌt] n Kastanie f

chew [tʃuː] vt, vi kauen; **chewing gum** n Kaugummi m

chick [tʃɪk] n Küken nt; **chicken** n Huhn nt; (food: roast) Hähnchen nt; (coward) Feigling m; **chicken breast** n Hühnerbrust f; **chicken Kiev** n paniertes Hähnchen, mit Knoblauchbutter gefüllt; **chickenpox** n Windpocken pl; **chickpea** n Kichererbse f

chicory ['tʃɪkərɪ] n Chicorée f

chief [tʃiːf] n (of department etc) Leiter(in) m(f); (boss) Chef(in) m(f); (of tribe) Häuptling m ⊳ adj Haupt-; **chiefly** adv hauptsächlich

child [tʃaɪld] (pl **children**) n Kind nt; **child abuse** n Kindesmisshandlung f; **child allowance**, **child benefit** (Brit) n Kindergeld nt; **childbirth** n Geburt f, Entbindung f; **childhood** n Kindheit f; **childish** adj kindisch; **child lock** n Kindersicherung f; **childproof** adj kindersicher; **children** ['tʃɪldrən] pl of **child**; **child seat** n Kindersitz m

Chile ['tʃɪlɪ] n Chile nt

chill [tʃɪl] n Kühle f; (Med) Erkältung f ⊳ vt (wine) kühlen; **chill out** vi (fam) chillen, relaxen; **chilled** adj gekühlt

chilli ['tʃɪlɪ] n Pepperoni pl; (spice) Chili m; **chilli con carne** ['tʃɪlɪkɒn'kɑːnɪ] n Chili con carne nt

chilly ['tʃɪlɪ] adj kühl, frostig

chimney ['tʃɪmnɪ] n Schornstein m; **chimneysweep** n Schornsteinfeger(in) m(f)

chimpanzee [tʃɪmpæn'ziː] n Schimpanse m

chin [tʃɪn] n Kinn nt

china ['tʃaɪnə] n Porzellan nt

China ['tʃaɪnə] n China nt; **Chinese** [tʃaɪ'niːz] adj chinesisch ⊳ n (person) Chinese m, Chinesin f; (language) Chinesisch nt; **Chinese leaves** npl Chinakohl m

chip [tʃɪp] n (of wood etc) Splitter m; (damage) angeschlagene Stelle; (Inform) Chip m; **~s** (Brit: potatoes) Pommes (frites) pl; (US: crisps) Kartoffelchips pl ⊳ vt anschlagen, beschädigen; **chippie** (fam), **chip shop** n Frittenbude f

chiropodist [kɪ'rɒpədɪst] n Fußpfleger(in) m(f)

chirp [tʃɜːp] vi zwitschern

chisel ['tʃɪzl] n Meißel m

chitchat ['tʃɪtʃæt] n Gerede nt

chives ['tʃaɪvz] npl Schnittlauch m

chlorine ['klɔːriːn] n Chlor nt

chocaholic, **chocoholic** ['tʃɒkə'hɒlɪk] n Schokoladenfreak m; **choc-ice** ['tʃɒkaɪs] n Eis nt mit Schokoladenüberzug; **chocolate** ['tʃɒklɪt] n Schoko-lade f; (chocolate-coated sweet) Praline f; **a bar of ~** eine Tafel Schokolade; **a box of ~s** eine Schachtel Pralinen; **chocolate cake** n Schokoladenkuchen m; **chocolate sauce** n Schokoladensoße f

choice [tʃɔɪs] n Wahl f; (selection) Auswahl f ⊳ adj auserlesen; (product) Qualitäts-

choir ['kwaɪə] n Chor m

choke [tʃəʊk] vi sich verschlucken; (Sport) die Nerven verlieren ⊳ vt erdrosseln ⊳ n (Auto) Choke m

cholera ['kɒlərə] n Cholera f

cholesterol [kə'lestərəl] n Cholesterin nt

chook [tʃʊk] n (Aust, NZ fam) Huhn nt

choose [tʃuːz] (**chose, chosen**) vt wählen; (pick out) sich aussuchen; **there are three to ~ from** es stehen drei zur Auswahl

chop [tʃɒp] vt (zer)hacken; (meat etc) klein schneiden ▷ n (meat) Kotelett nt; **to get the ~** gefeuert werden; **chopper** n Hackbeil nt; (fam: helicopter) Hubschrauber m; **chopsticks** npl Essstäbchen pl

chorus ['kɔːrəs] n Chor m; (in song) Refrain m

chose, chosen [tʃəʊz, 'tʃəʊzn] pt, pp of **choose**

chowder ['tʃaʊdə*] n (US) dicke Suppe mit Meeresfrüchten

christen ['krɪsn] vt taufen; **christening** n Taufe f; **Christian** ['krɪstɪən] adj christlich ▷ n Christ(in) m(f); **Christian name** n (Brit) Vorname m

Christmas ['krɪsməs] n Weihnachten pl; **Christmas card** n Weihnachtskarte f; **Christmas carol** n Weihnachtslied nt; **Christmas Day** n der erste Weihnachtstag; **Christmas Eve** n Heiligabend m; **Christmas pudding** n Plumpudding m; **Christmas tree** n Weihnachtsbaum m

chronic ['krɒnɪk] adj (Med, fig) chronisch; (fam: very bad) miserabel

chrysanthemum [krɪ'sænθɪməm] n Chrysantheme f

chubby ['tʃʌbɪ] adj (child) pummelig; (adult) rundlich

chuck [tʃʌk] vt (fam) schmeißen; **chuck in** vt (fam: job) hinschmeißen; **chuck out** vt

(fam) rausschmeißen; **chuck up** vi (fam) kotzen

chunk [tʃʌŋk] n Klumpen m; (of bread) Brocken m; (of meat) Batzen m; **chunky** adj (person) stämmig

church [tʃɜːtʃ] n Kirche f; **churchyard** n Kirchhof m

chute [ʃuːt] n Rutsche f

chutney ['tʃʌtnɪ] n Chutney m

CIA abbr = **Central Intelligence Agency** (US) CIA f

CID abbr = **Criminal Investigation Department** (Brit) ≈ Kripo f

cider ['saɪdə*] n ≈ Apfelmost m

cigar [sɪ'gɑː*] n Zigarre f; **cigarette** [sɪgə'ret] n Zigarette f

cinema ['sɪnəmə] n Kino nt

cinnamon ['sɪnəmən] n Zimt m

circle ['sɜːkl] n Kreis m ▷ vi kreisen; **circuit** ['sɜːkɪt] n Rundfahrt f; (on foot) Rundgang m; (for racing) Rennstrecke f; (Elec) Stromkreis m; **circular** ['sɜːkjʊlə*] adj (kreis)rund, kreisförmig ▷ n Rundschreiben nt; **circulation** [sɜːkjʊ'leɪʃən] n (of blood) Kreislauf m; (of newspaper) Auflage f

circumstances ['sɜːkəmstənsəz] npl (facts) Umstände pl; (financial condition) Verhältnisse pl; **in/under the ~** unter den Umständen; **under no ~** auf keinen Fall

circus ['sɜːkəs] n Zirkus m

cissy ['sɪsɪ] n (fam) Weichling m

cistern ['sɪstən] n Zisterne f; (of WC) Spülkasten m

citizen ['sɪtɪzn] n Bürger(in) m(f); (of nation) Staatsangehörige(r) mf; **citizenship** n Staatsangehörigkeit f

city ['sɪtɪ] n Stadt f; (large) Großstadt f; **the ~** (London's financial centre) die (Londoner)

City; **city centre** n Innenstadt f,
Zentrum nt

civil ['sɪvl] adj (of town) Bürger-;
(of state) staatsbürgerlich; (not
military) zivil; **civil ceremony** n
standesamtliche Hochzeit; **civil
engineering** n Hoch- und Tiefbau
m, Bauingenieurwesen nt; **civilian**
[sɪ'vɪljən] n Zivilist(in) m(f);
civilization [sɪvɪlaɪˈzeɪʃən] n
Zivilisation f, Kultur f; **civilized**
['sɪvɪlaɪzd] adj zivilisiert,
kultiviert; **civil partnership** n
eingetragene Partnerschaft; **civil
rights** npl Bürgerrechte pl; **civil
servant** n (Staats)beamte(r) m,
(Staats)beamtin f; **civil service** n
Staatsdienst m; **civil war** n
Bürgerkrieg m

CJD abbr = **Creutzfeld-Jakob
disease** = Creutzfeld-
Jakob-Krankheit f

cl abbr = **centilitre(s)** cl

claim [kleɪm] vt beanspruchen;
(apply for) beantragen; (demand)
fordern; (assert) behaupten (that
dass) ▷ n (demand) Forderung f
(for für); (right) Anspruch m (to auf
+akk); ~ **for damages**
Schadenersatzforderung f; **to
make** o **put in a ~** (insurance)
Ansprüche geltend machen;
claimant n Antragsteller(in) m(f)

clam [klæm] n Venusmuschel f;
clam chowder n (US) dicke
Muschelsuppe (mit Sellerie, Zwiebeln
etc)

clap [klæp] vi (Beifall) klatschen

claret ['klærɪt] n roter
Bordeaux(wein)

clarify ['klærɪfaɪ] vt klären

clarinet [klærɪ'net] n Klarinette f

clarity ['klærɪtɪ] n Klarheit f

clash [klæʃ] vi (physically)
zusammenstoßen (with mit);
(argue) sich auseinandersetzen
(with mit); (fig: colours) sich beißen

▷ n Zusammenstoß m; (argument)
Auseinandersetzung f

clasp [klɑːsp] n (on belt) Schnalle f

class [klɑːs] n Klasse f ▷ vt
einordnen, einstufen

classic ['klæsɪk] adj (mistake,
example etc) klassisch ▷ n
Klassiker m; **classical** ['klæsɪkəl]
adj (music, ballet etc) klassisch

classification [klæsɪfɪ'keɪʃn] n
Klassifizierung f; **classify**
['klæsɪfaɪ] vt klassifizieren;
classified advertisement n
Kleinanzeige f

classroom ['klɑːsrʊm] n Klassenzimmer nt

classy ['klɑːsɪ] adj (fam) nobel,
exklusiv

clatter ['klætə°] vi klappern

clause [klɔːz] n (Ling) Satz m; (Jur)
Klausel f

claw [klɔː] n Kralle f

clay [kleɪ] n Lehm m; (for pottery)
Ton m

clean [kliːn] adj sauber;
~ **driving licence** Führerschein
ohne Strafpunkte ▷ vt sauber
machen; (carpet etc) reinigen;
(window, shoes, vegetables) putzen;
(wound) säubern; **clean up** vt
sauber machen ▷ vi aufräumen;
cleaner n (person) Putzmann m,
Putzfrau f; (substance) Putzmittel
nt; ~**'s** (firm) Reinigung f

cleanse [klɛnz] vt reinigen;
(wound) säubern; **cleanser** n
Reinigungsmittel nt

clear [klɪə°] adj klar; (distinct)
deutlich; (conscience) rein; (free,
road etc) frei; **to be ~ about sth**
sich über etw im Klaren sein
▷ adv: **to stand ~** zurücktreten
▷ vt (road, room etc) räumen; (table)
abräumen; (Jur: find innocent)
freisprechen (of von) ▷ vi (fog,
mist) sich verziehen; (weather)
aufklaren; **clear away** vt

wegräumen; (dishes) abräumen; **clear off** vi (fam) abhauen; **clear up** vi (tidy up) aufräumen; (weather) sich aufklären ▷ vt (room) aufräumen; (litter) wegräumen; (matter) klären

clearing n Lichtung f; **clearly** adv klar; (speak, remember) deutlich; (obviously) eindeutig; **clearout** n Entrümpelungsaktion f; **clearway** n (Brit) Straße f mit Halteverbot nt

clench [klɛntʃ] vt (fist) ballen; (teeth) zusammenbeißen

clergyman ['klɜːdʒɪmæn] (pl **-men**) n Geistliche(r) m; **clergywoman** ['klɜːdʒɪwʊmən] (pl **-women**) n Geistliche f

clerk [klɑːk], (US) [klɜːk] n (in office) Büroangestellte(r) m/f; (US: salesperson) Verkäufer(in) m(f)

clever ['klevə°] adj schlau, klug; (idea) clever

cliché ['kliːʃeɪ] n Klischee nt

click [klɪk] n Klicken nt; (Inform) Mausklick m ▷ vi klicken; **to ~ on sth** (Inform) etw anklicken; **it ~ed** (fam) ich hab's/er hat's etc geschnallt, es hat gefunkt, es hat Klick gemacht; **they ~ed** sie haben sich gleich verstanden; **click on** vt (Inform) anklicken

client ['klaɪənt] n Kunde m, Kundin f; (Jur) Mandant(in) m(f)

cliff [klɪf] n Klippe f

climate ['klaɪmɪt] n Klima nt; **climate change** n Klimawandel m

climax ['klaɪmæks] n Höhepunkt m

climb [klaɪm] vi (person) klettern; (aircraft, sun) steigen; (road) ansteigen ▷ vt (mountain) besteigen; (tree etc) klettern auf +akk ▷ n Aufstieg m; **climber** n (mountaineer) Bergsteiger(in) m(f); **climbing** n Klettern nt,

Bergsteigen nt; **climbing frame** n Klettergerüst nt

cling [klɪŋ] (**clung, clung**) vi sich klammern (to an +akk); **cling film®** n Frischhaltefolie f

clinic ['klɪnɪk] n Klinik f; **clinical** adj klinisch

clip [klɪp] n Klammer f ▷ vt (fix) anklemmen (to an +akk); (fingernails) schneiden; **clipboard** n Klemmbrett nt; **clippers** npl Schere f; (for nails) Zwicker m

cloak [kləʊk] n Umhang m; **cloakroom** n (for coats) Garderobe f

clock [klɒk] n Uhr f; (Auto: fam) Tacho m; **round the ~** rund um die Uhr; **clockwise** adv im Uhrzeigersinn

clog [klɒg] n Holzschuh m ▷ vt verstopfen

cloister ['klɔɪstə°] n Kreuzgang m

clone [kləʊn] n Klon m ▷ vt klonen

close [kləʊs] adj nahe (to +dat); (friend, contact) eng; (resemblance) groß; **~ to the beach** in der Nähe des Strandes; **~ win** knapper Sieg; **on ~r examination** bei näherer o genauerer Untersuchung ▷ adv [kləʊs] dicht; **he lives ~ by** er wohnt ganz in der Nähe ▷ vt [kləʊz] schließen; (road) sperren; (discussion, matter) abschließen ▷ vi [kləʊz] schließen ▷ n [kləʊz] Ende nt; **close down** vi schließen; (factory) stillgelegt werden ▷ vt (shop) schließen; (factory) stilllegen; **closed** adj (road) gesperrt; (shop etc) geschlossen; **circuit television** n Videoüberwachungsanlage f; **closely** adv (related) eng, nah; (packed, follow) dicht; (attentively) genau

closet ['klɒzɪt] n (esp US) Schrank m

close-up ['kləʊsʌp] n Nahaufnahme f

closing ['kləʊzɪŋ] adj: ~ **date** letzter Termin; (for competition) Einsendeschluss m; ~ **time** (of shop) Ladenschluss m; (Brit: of pub) Polizeistunde f

closure ['kləʊʒə°] n Schließung f; Abschluss m; **to look for** ~ mit etw abschließen wollen

clot [klɒt] n (blood) ~ Blutgerinnsel nt; (fam: idiot) Trottel m ▷ vi (blood) gerinnen

cloth [klɒθ] n (material) ▷ Tuch nt; (for cleaning) Lappen m

clothe [kləʊð] vt kleiden; **clothes** [kləʊðz] npl Kleider pl, Kleidung f; **clothes line** n Wäscheleine f; **clothes peg, clothespin** (US) n Wäscheklammer f; **clothing** ['kləʊðɪŋ] n Kleidung f

clotted ['klɒtɪd] adj: ~ **cream** dicke Sahne (aus erhitzter Milch)

cloud [klaʊd] n Wolke f; **cloudy** adj (sky) bewölkt; (liquid) trüb

clove [kləʊv] n Gewürznelke f; ~ **of garlic** Knoblauchzehe f

clover ['kləʊvə°] n Klee m; **cloverleaf** (pl -**leaves**) n Kleeblatt nt

clown [klaʊn] n Clown m

club [klʌb] n (weapon) Knüppel m; (society) Klub m, Verein m; (nightclub) Disko f; (golf club) Golfschläger m; ~**s** (Cards) Kreuz nt; **clubbing**: **to go** ~ in die Disko gehen; **club class** n (Aviat) Businessclass f

clue [kluː] n Anhaltspunkt m, Hinweis m; **he hasn't a** ~ er hat keine Ahnung

clumsy ['klʌmzɪ] adj unbeholfen, ungeschickt

clung [klʌŋ] pt, pp of **cling**

clutch [klʌtʃ] n (Auto) Kupplung f ▷ vt umklammern; (book etc) an sich akk klammern

cm abbr = **centimetre(s)** cm

c/o abbr = **care of** bei

Co abbr = **company** Co

coach [kəʊtʃ] n (Brit: bus) Reisebus m; (Rail) (Personen)wagen m; (Sport: trainer) Trainer(in) m(f) ▷ vt Nachhilfeunterricht geben +dat; (Sport) trainieren; **coach (class)** n (Aviat) Economyclass f; **coach driver** n Busfahrer(in) m(f); **coach party** n Reisegruppe f (Bus); **coach station** n Busbahnhof m; **coach trip** n Busfahrt f; (tour) Busreise f

coal [kəʊl] n Kohle f

coalition [kəʊə'lɪʃən] n (Pol) Koalition f

coalmine ['kəʊlmaɪn] n Kohlenbergwerk nt; **coalminer** n Bergarbeiter m

coast [kəʊst] n Küste f; **coastguard** n Küstenwache f; **coastline** n Küste f

coat [kəʊt] n Mantel m; (jacket) Jacke f; (on animals) Fell nt, Pelz m; (of paint) Schicht f; ~ **of arms** Wappen nt; **coathanger** n Kleiderbügel m; **coating** n Überzug m; (layer) Schicht f

cobble(stone)s ['kɒbl(stəʊn)z] npl Kopfsteine pl; (surface) Kopfsteinpflaster nt

cobweb ['kɒbweb] n Spinnennetz nt

cocaine [kə'keɪn] n Kokain nt

cock [kɒk] n Hahn m; (vulg: penis) Schwanz m; **cock up** vt (Brit fam) vermasseln, versauen; **cockerel** ['kɒkərəl] n junger Hahn

cockle ['kɒkl] n Herzmuschel f

cockpit ['kɒkpɪt] n (in plane, racing car) Cockpit m; **cockroach** ['kɒkrəʊtʃ] n Kakerlake f; **cocktail**

['kɒkteɪl] n Cocktail m; **cock-up** n (Brit fam) **to make a ~ of sth** bei etw Mist bauen; **cocky** ['kɒkɪ] adj großspurig, von sich selbst überzeugt

cocoa ['kəʊkəʊ] n Kakao m

coconut ['kəʊkənʌt] n Kokosnuss f

cod [kɒd] n Kabeljau m

COD abbr = **cash on delivery** per Nachnahme

code [kəʊd] n Kode m

coeducational [kəʊedjʊ'keɪʃənl] adj (school) gemischt

coffee ['kɒfɪ] n Kaffee m; **coffee bar** n Café nt; **coffee break** n Kaffeepause f; **coffee maker** n Kaffeemaschine f; **coffee pot** n Kaffeekanne f; **coffee shop** n Café nt; **coffee table** n Couchtisch m

coffin ['kɒfɪn] n Sarg m

coil [kɔɪl] n Rolle f; (Elec) Spule f; (Med) Spirale f

coin [kɔɪn] n Münze f

coincide [kəʊɪn'saɪd] vi (happen together) zusammenfallen (with mit); **coincidence** [kəʊ'ɪnsɪdəns] n Zufall m

coke [kəʊk] n Koks m; **Coke®** Cola f

cola ['kəʊlə] n Cola f

cold [kəʊld] adj kalt; **I'm ~** mir ist kalt, ich friere ▷ n Kälte f; (illness) Erkältung f, Schnupfen m; **to catch a ~** sich erkälten; **cold box** n Kühlbox f; **cold sore** n Herpes m; **cold turkey** n (fam) Totalentzug m; (symptoms) Entzugserscheinungen pl

coleslaw ['kəʊlslɔ:] n Krautsalat m

collaborate [kə'læbəreɪt] vi zusammenarbeiten (with mit); **collaboration** [kəlæbə'reɪʃən] n Zusammenarbeit f; (of one party) Mitarbeit f

collapse [kə'læps] vi zusammenbrechen; (building etc) einstürzen ▷ n Zusammenbruch m; (of building) Einsturz m; **collapsible** [kə'læpsəbl] adj zusammenklappbar, Klapp-

collar ['kɒlə'] n Kragen m; (for dog, cat) Halsband nt; **collarbone** n Schlüsselbein nt

colleague ['kɒli:g] n Kollege m, Kollegin f

collect [kə'lekt] vt sammeln; (fetch) abholen ▷ vi sich sammeln; **collect call** n (US) R-Gespräch nt; **collected** adj (works) gesammelt; (person) gefasst; **collector** n Sammler(in) m(f); **collection** [kə'lekʃən] n Sammlung f; (Rel) Kollekte f; (from postbox) Leerung f

college ['kɒlɪdʒ] n (residential) College nt; (specialist) Fachhochschule f; (vocational) Berufsschule f; (US: university) Universität f; **to go to ~** (US) studieren

collide [kə'laɪd] vi zusammenstoßen; **collision** [kə'lɪʒən] n Zusammenstoß m

colloquial [kə'ləʊkwɪəl] adj umgangssprachlich

Cologne [kə'ləʊn] n Köln nt

colon ['kəʊlən] n (punctuation mark) Doppelpunkt m

colonial [kə'ləʊnɪəl] adj Kolonial-; **colonize** ['kɒlənaɪz] vt kolonisieren; **colony** ['kɒlənɪ] n Kolonie f

color n (US), **colour** ['kʌlə'] n Farbe f; (of skin) Hautfarbe f ▷ vt anmalen; (bias) färben; **colour-blind** adj farbenblind; **coloured** adj farbig; (biased) gefärbt; **colour film** n Farbfilm m; **colourful** adj (lit, fig) bunt; (life, past) bewegt; **colouring** n (in food etc) Farbstoff m; (complexion) Gesichtsfarbe f; **colourless** adj (*lit, fig*) farblos; **colour photo(graph)** *n* Farbfoto *nt*; **colour television** *n* Farbfernsehen *nt*

column ['kɒləm] *n* Säule *f*; (*of print*) Spalte *f*

comb [kəum] *n* Kamm *m* ▷ *vt* kämmen; **to ~ one's hair** sich kämmen

combination [kɒmbɪ'neɪʃən] *n* Kombination *f*; (*mixture*) Mischung *f* (*of aus*); **combine** [kəm'baɪn] *vt* verbinden (*with* mit); (*two things*) kombinieren

come [kʌm] (**came**, **come**) *vi* kommen; (*arrive*) ankommen; (*on list, in order*) stehen; (*with adjective: become*) werden; **~ and see us** besuchen Sie uns mal; **coming** in komm ja schon!; **to ~ first/second** erster/zweiter werden; **to ~ true** wahr werden; **to ~ loose** sich lockern; **the years to ~** die kommenden Jahre; **there's one more to ~** es kommt noch eins/noch einer; **how ~ ...?** (*fam*) wie kommt es, dass ...?; **~ to think of it** (*fam*) wo es mir gerade einfällt; **come across** *vt* (*find*) stoßen auf +*akk*; **come back** *vi* zurückkommen; **I'll ~ to that** ich komme darauf zurück; **come down** *vi* herunterkommen; (*rain, snow, price*) fallen; **come from** *vt* (*result*) kommen von; **where do you ~?** wo kommen Sie her?; **I ~ London** ich komme aus London; **come in** *vi* hereinkommen; (*arrive*) ankommen; (*in race*) **to ~ fourth** Vierter werden; **come off** *vi* (*button, handle etc*) abgehen; (*succeed*) gelingen; **to ~ well/badly** gut/schlecht wegkommen; **come on** *vi* (*progress*) vorankommen; **~!** komm!; (*hurry*) beeil dich!; (*encouraging*) los!; **come out** *vi*

herauskommen; (*photo*) was werden; (*homosexual*) sich outen; **come round** *vi* (*visit*) vorbeikommen; (*regain consciousness*) wieder zu sich kommen; **come to** *vi* (*regain consciousness*) wieder zu sich kommen ▷ *vt* (*sum*) sich belaufen auf +*akk*; **when it comes to ...** wenn es um ... geht; **come up** *vi* hochkommen; (*sun, moon*) aufgehen; **to ~ (for discussion)** zur Sprache kommen; **come up to** *vt* (*approach*) zukommen auf +*akk*; (*water*) reichen bis zu; (*expectations*) entsprechen +*dat*; **come up with** *vt* (*idea*) haben; (*solution, answer*) kommen auf +*akk*; **to ~ a suggestion** einen Vorschlag machen

comedian [kə'miːdɪən] *n* Komiker(in) *m(f)*

comedown ['kʌmdaun] *n* Abstieg *m*

comedy ['kɒmədɪ] *n* Komödie *f*, Comedy *f*

comfort ['kʌmfət] *n* Komfort *m*; (*consolation*) Trost *m* ▷ *vt* trösten; **comfortable** *adj* bequem; (*income*) ausreichend; (*temperature, life*) angenehm; **comforting** *adj* tröstlich

comic ['kɒmɪk] *n* (*magazine*) Comic(heft) *nt*; (*comedian*) Komiker(in) *m(f)* ▷ *adj* komisch

coming ['kʌmɪŋ] *adj* kommend; (*event*) bevorstehend

comma ['kɒmə] *n* Komma *nt*

command [kə'mɑːnd] *n* Befehl *m*; (*control*) Führung *f*; (*Mil*) Kommando *nt* ▷ *vt* befehlen +*dat*

commemorate [kə'meməreɪt] *vt* gedenken +*gen*; **commemoration** [kəmemə'reɪʃən] *n*: **in ~ of** in Gedenken an +*akk*

comment ['kɒment] *n* (*remark*)

Bemerkung f; (note) Anmerkung f; (official) Kommentar m (on zu); **no ~** kein Kommentar ▷ vi sich äußern (on zu); **commentary** ['kɒməntrɪ] n Kommentar m (on zu); (TV, Sport) Livereportage f; **commentator** ['kɒmənteɪtə°] n Kommentator(in) m(f); (TV, Sport) Reporter(in) m(f)

commerce ['kɒmɜːs] n Handel m; **commercial** [kə'mɜːʃəl] adj kommerziell; (training) kaufmännisch; **~ break** Werbepause f; **~ vehicle** Lieferwagen m ▷ n (TV) Werbespot m

commission [kə'mɪʃən] n Auftrag m; (fee) Provision f; (reporting body) Kommission f ▷ vt beauftragen

commit [kə'mɪt] vt (crime) begehen ▷ vr: (undertake) sich verpflichten (to zu); **commitment** n Verpflichtung f; (Pol) Engagement nt

committee [kə'mɪtɪ] n Ausschuss m, Komitee nt

commodity [kə'mɒdɪtɪ] n Ware f

common ['kɒmən] adj (experience) allgemein, alltäglich; (shared) gemeinsam; (widespread, frequent) häufig; (pej) gewöhnlich, ordinär; **to have sth in ~** etw gemein haben ▷ n (Brit: land) Gemeindewiese f; **commonly** adv häufig, allgemein; **commonplace** adj alltäglich; (pej) banal; **commonroom** n Gemeinschaftsraum m; (Brit Pol) **the (House of) ~** das Unterhaus; **common sense** n gesunder Menschenverstand; **Commonwealth** n Commonwealth nt; **~ of Independent**

States Gemeinschaft f Unabhängiger Staaten

communal ['kɒmjunl] adj gemeinsam; (of a community) Gemeinschafts-, Gemeinde-

communicate [kə'mjuːnɪkeɪt] vi kommunizieren (with mit); **communication** [kəmjuːnɪ'keɪʃən] n Kommunikation f, Verständigung f; **communications satellite** n Nachrichtensatellit m; **communications technology** n Nachrichtentechnik f; **communicative** adj gesprächig

communion [kə'mjuːnɪən] n: **(Holy) Communion** Heiliges Abendmahl; (Catholic) Kommunion f

communism ['kɒmjunɪzəm] n Kommunismus m; **communist** ['kɒmjunɪst] adj kommunistisch ▷ n Kommunist(in) m(f)

community [kə'mjuːnɪtɪ] n Gemeinschaft f; **community centre** n Gemeindezentrum nt; **community service** n (Jur) Sozialdienst m

commutation ticket [kɒmjuˈteɪʃəntɪkɪt] n (US) Zeitkarte f; **commute** [kə'mjuːt] vi pendeln; **commuter** n Pendler(in) m(f)

compact [kəm'pækt] adj kompakt ▷ ['kɒmpækt] n (for make-up) Puderdose f; (US: car) ~ Mittelklassewagen m; **compact camera** n Kompaktkamera f; **compact disc** n Compact Disc f, CD f

companion [kəm'pænɪən] n Begleiter(in) m(f)

company ['kʌmpənɪ] n Gesellschaft f; (Comm) Firma f; **to keep sb ~** jdm Gesellschaft leisten; **company car** n Firmenauto nt

comparable ['kɒmpərəbl] adj
vergleichbar (*with*, to mit)

comparative [kəm'pærətɪv] adj
relativ ▷ n (*Ling*) Komparativ m;
comparatively adv
verhältnismäßig

compare [kəm'peə°] vt vergleichen (*with*, to mit); **~d with** o
to im Vergleich zu; **beyond**
~ unvergleichlich; **comparison**
[kəm'pærɪsn] n Vergleich m; **in**
~ with im Vergleich mit (o zu)

compartment [kəm'pɑːtmənt]
n (*Rail*) Abteil nt; (*in desk etc*) Fach
nt

compass ['kʌmpəs] n Kompass
m; **~es** pl Zirkel m

compassion [kəm'pæʃən] n
Mitgefühl nt

compatible [kəm'pætɪbl] adj
vereinbar (*with* mit); (*Inform*)
kompatibel; **we're not ~** wir
passen nicht zueinander

compensate ['kɒmpenseɪt] vt
(*person*) entschädigen (*for* für) ▷ vi:
to ~ for sth Ersatz für etw leisten;
(*make up for*) etw ausgleichen;
compensation [kɒmpenˈseɪʃən]
n Entschädigung f; (*money*)
Schadenersatz m; (*Jur*) Abfindung f

compete [kəm'piːt] vi konkur-
rieren (*for* um); (*Sport*) kämpfen (*for*
um); (*take part*) teilnehmen (*in* an
+*dat*)

competence ['kɒmpɪtəns] n
Fähigkeit f; (*Jur*) Zuständigkeit f;
competent adj fähig; (*Jur*)
zuständig

competition [kɒmpɪ'tɪʃən] n
(*contest*) Wettbewerb m; (*Comm*)
Konkurrenz f (*for* um);
competitive [kəm'petɪtɪv] adj
(*firm*, *price*, *product*)
konkurrenzfähig; **competitor**
[kəm'petɪtə°] n (*Comm*)
Konkurrent(in) m(f); (*Sport*)
Teilnehmer(in) m(f)

complain [kəm'pleɪn] vi klagen;
(*formally*) sich beschweren (*about*
über +*akk*); **complaint** n Klage f;
Beanstandung f; (*formal*)
Beschwerde f; (*Med*) Leiden nt

complement vt ergänzen

complete [kəm'pliːt] adj vollständig; (*finished*) fertig; (*failure*,
disaster) total; (*happiness*)
vollkommen; **are we ~?** sind wir
vollzählig? ▷ vt vervollständigen;
(*finish*) beenden; (*form*) ausfüllen;
completely adv völlig; **not ~ ...**
nicht ganz ...

complex ['kɒmpleks] adj komplex; (*task*, *theory etc*) kompliziert
▷ n Komplex m

complexion [kəm'plekʃən] n
Gesichtsfarbe f, Teint m

complicated ['kɒmplɪkeɪtɪd] adj
kompliziert; **complication**
['kɒmplɪkeɪʃən] n Komplikation
f

compliment ['kɒmplɪmənt] n
Kompliment nt; **complimentary**
[kɒmplɪ'mentərɪ] adj lobend;
(*free of charge*) Gratis-; **~ ticket**
Freikarte f

comply [kəm'plaɪ] vi: **to ~ with**
the regulations den Vorschriften
entsprechen

component [kəm'pəʊnənt] n
Bestandteil m

compose [kəm'pəʊz] vt (*music*)
komponieren; **to ~ oneself** sich
zusammennehmen; **composed**
adj gefasst; **to be ~ of** bestehen
aus; **composer** n Komponist(in)
m(f); **composition** [kɒmpə'zɪʃən]
n (*of a group*) Zusammensetzung f;
(*Mus*) Komposition f

comprehend [kɒmprɪ'hend] vt
verstehen; **comprehension**
[kɒmprɪ'henʃən] n Verständnis nt

comprehensive
[kɒmprɪ'hensɪv] adj umfassend;
~ school Gesamtschule f

compress [kəm'pres] vt komprimieren

comprise [kəm'praɪz] vt umfassen, bestehen aus

compromise ['kɒmprəmaɪz] n Kompromiss m ▷ vi einen Kompromiss schließen

compulsory [kəm'pʌlsərɪ] adj obligatorisch; **~ subject** Pflichtfach nt

computer [kəm'pju:tə°] n Computer m; **computer-aided** adj computergestützt; **computer-controlled** adj rechnergesteuert; **computer game** n Computerspiel nt; **computer-literate** adj: **to be ~** mit dem Computer umgehen können; **computer scientist** n Informatiker(in) m(f); **computing** n (subject) Informatik f

con [kɒn] (fam) n Schwindel m ▷ vt betrügen (out of um)

conceal [kən'si:l] vt verbergen (from vor +dat)

conceivable [kən'si:vəbl] adj denkbar, vorstellbar; **conceive** [kən'si:v] vt (imagine) sich vorstellen; (child) empfangen

concentrate ['kɒnsəntreɪt] vi sich konzentrieren (on auf +akk); **concentration** [kɒnsən'treɪʃən] n Konzentration f

concept ['kɒnsept] n Begriff m

concern [kən'sɜ:n] n (affair) Angelegenheit f, (worry) Sorge f; (Comm: firm) Unternehmen nt; **it's not my ~** das geht mich nichts an; **there's no cause for ~** kein Grund zur Beunruhigung ▷ vt (affect) angehen; (have connection with) betreffen; (be about) handeln von; **those ~ed** die Betroffenen; **as far as I'm ~ed** was mich betrifft; **concerned** adj (anxious) besorgt; **concerning** prep bezüglich, hinsichtlich +gen

concert ['kɒnsət] n Konzert nt; **~ hall** Konzertsaal m

concession [kən'seʃən] n Zugeständnis nt; (reduction) Ermäßigung f

concise [kən'saɪs] adj knapp gefasst, prägnant

conclude [kən'klu:d] vt (end) beenden, (ab)schließen; (infer) folgern (from aus); **to ~ that ...** zu dem Schluss kommen, dass ...; **conclusion** [kən'klu:ʒən] n Schluss m, Schlussfolgerung f

concrete ['kɒnkri:t] n Beton m ▷ adj konkret

concussion [kən'kʌʃən] n Gehirnerschütterung f

condemn [kən'dem] vt verdammen, (esp Jur) verurteilen

condensed milk n Kondensmilch f, Dosenmilch f

condition [kən'dɪʃən] n (state) Zustand m; (requirement) Bedingung f; **on ~ that ...** unter der Bedingung, dass ...; **~s** pl (circumstances, weather) Verhältnisse pl; **conditional** adj bedingt; (Ling) Konditional-; **conditioner** n Weichspüler m; (for hair) Pflegespülung f

condo ['kɒndəʊ] (pl **-s**) n see **condominium**

condolences [kən'dəʊlənsɪz] npl Beileid nt

condom ['kɒndəm] n Kondom nt

condominium [kɒndə'mɪnɪəm] n (US: apartment) Eigentumswohnung f

conduct ['kɒndʌkt] n (behaviour) Verhalten nt ▷ [kən'dʌkt] vt führen, leiten; (orchestra) dirigieren; **conductor** [kən'dʌktə°] n (of orchestra) Dirigent(in) m(f); (Brit: in bus) Schaffner(in) m(f); (US: on train) Zugführer(in) m(f)

cone [kəʊn] n Kegel m; *(for ice cream)* Waffeltüte f; *(fir cone)* (Tannen)zapfen m

conference ['kɒnfərəns] n Konferenz f

confess [kən'fes] vt, vi: **to ~ that ...** gestehen, dass ...; **confession** [kən'feʃən] n Geständnis nt; *(Rel)* Beichte f

confetti [kən'feti] n Konfetti nt

confidence ['kɒnfɪdəns] n Vertrauen nt *(in zu)*; *(assurance)* Selbstvertrauen nt; **confident** adj *(sure)* zuversichtlich *(that ... dass ...)*, überzeugt *(of von)*; *(self-assured)* selbstsicher; **confidential** [kɒnfɪ'denʃəl] adj vertraulich

confine [kən'faɪn] vt beschränken *(to auf +akk)*

confirm [kən'fɜːm] vt bestätigen; **confirmation** [kɒnfə'meɪʃən] n Bestätigung f; *(Rel)* Konfirmation f; **confirmed** adj überzeugt; *(bachelor)* eingefleischt

confiscate ['kɒnfɪskeɪt] vt beschlagnahmen, konfiszieren

conflict ['kɒnflɪkt] n Konflikt m

confuse [kən'fjuːz] vt verwirren; *(sth with sth)* verwechseln *(with mit)*; *(several things)* durcheinanderbringen; **confused** adj *(person)* konfus, verwirrt; *(account)* verworren; **confusing** adj verwirrend; **confusion** [kən'fjuːʒən] n Verwirrung f; *(of two things)* Verwechslung f; *(muddle)* Chaos nt

congested [kən'dʒestɪd] adj verstopft; *(overcrowded)* überfüllt; **congestion** [kən'dʒestʃən] n Stau m

congratulate [kən'grætjʊleɪt] vt gratulieren *(on zu)*; **congratulations** [kəngrætjʊ'leɪʃənz] npl Glück-

wünsche pl; **~!** gratuliere!, herzlichen Glückwunsch!

congregation [kɒngrɪ'geɪʃən] n *(Rel)* Gemeinde f

congress ['kɒngres] n Kongress m; *(US)* **Congress** der Kongress; **congressman** (pl **-men**), **congresswoman** (pl **-women**) n *(US)* Mitglied nt des Repräsentantenhauses

conifer ['kɒnɪfə°] n Nadelbaum m

conjunction [kən'dʒʌŋkʃən] n *(Ling)* Konjunktion f; **in ~ with** in Verbindung mit

conk out [kɒŋk 'aʊt] vi *(fam: appliance, car)* den Geist aufgeben, streiken; *(person: die)* ins Gras beißen

connect [kə'nekt] vt verbinden *(with, to mit)*; *(Elec, Tech: appliance etc)* anschließen *(to an +akk)* ▷ vi *(train, plane)* Anschluss haben *(with an +akk)*; **~ing flight** Anschlussflug m; **~ing train** Anschlusszug m; **connection** [kə'nekʃən] n Verbindung f; *(link)* Zusammenhang m; *(for train, plane, electrical appliance)* Anschluss m *(with, to an +akk)*; *(business etc)* Beziehung f; **in ~ with** in Zusammenhang mit; **bad ~** *(Tel)* schlechte Verbindung; *(Elec)* Wackelkontakt m; **connector** n *(Inform: computer)* Stecker m

conscience ['kɒnʃəns] n Gewissen nt; **conscientious** [kɒnʃɪ'enʃəs] adj gewissenhaft

conscious ['kɒnʃəs] adj *(act)* bewusst; *(Med)* bei Bewusstsein; **to be ~** bei Bewusstsein sein; **consciousness** n Bewusstsein nt

consecutive [kən'sekjʊtɪv] adj aufeinanderfolgend

consent [kən'sent] n Zustimmung f ▷ vi zustimmen *(to dat)*

consequence ['kɒnsɪkwəns] *n*
Folge *f*, Konsequenz *f*;
consequently ['kɒnsɪkwəntli]
adv folglich, deshalb

conservation [kɒnsə'veɪʃən] *n*
Erhaltung *f*; (*nature conservation*)
Naturschutz *m*; **conservation
area** *n* Naturschutzgebiet *nt*

conservative [kən'sɜːvətɪv] *adj* konservativ

Conservative [kən'sɜːvətɪv]
(*Pol*) **Conservative** *adj* konservativ

conservatory [kən'sɜːvətrɪ] *n*
(*greenhouse*) Gewächshaus *nt*;
(*room*) Wintergarten *m*

consider [kən'sɪdə*] *vt* (*reflect
on*) nachdenken über, sich
überlegen; (*take into account*) in
Betracht ziehen; (*regard*) halten
für; **he is ~ed (to be) ...** er gilt als
...; **considerable** [kən'sɪdərəbl]
adj beträchtlich; **considerate**
[kən'sɪdərɪt] *adj* aufmerksam,
rücksichtsvoll; **consideration**
[kənsɪdə'reɪʃən] *n* (*thoughtfulness*)
Rücksicht *f*; (*thought*) Überlegung
f; **to take sth into ~** etw in
Betracht ziehen; **considering**
[kən'sɪdərɪŋ] *prep* in Anbetracht
+*gen* ▷ *conj* da

consist [kən'sɪst] *vi*: **to ~ of ...**
bestehen aus ...

consistent [kən'sɪstənt] *adj*
(*behaviour, process etc*)
konsequent; (*statements*)
übereinstimmend; (*argument*)
folgerichtig; (*performance, results*)
beständig

consolation [kɒnsə'leɪʃən] *n*
Trost *m*; **console** [kən'səʊl] *vt*
trösten

consolidate [kən'sɒlɪdeɪt] *vt*
festigen

consonant ['kɒnsənənt] *n*
Konsonant *m*

conspicuous [kən'spɪkjʊəs] *adj*
auffällig, auffallend

conspiracy [kən'spɪrəsɪ] *n*
Komplott *nt*; **conspire**

[kən'spaɪə*] *vi* sich verschwören
(*against gegen*)

constable ['kʌnstəbl] *n* (*Brit*)
Polizist(in) *m(f)*

Constance ['kɒnstəns] *n* Konstanz *nt*; **Lake ~** der Bodensee

constant ['kɒnstənt] *adj* (*continual*) ständig, dauernd;
(*unchanging: temperature etc*)
gleichbleibend; **constantly** *adv*
dauernd

consternation [kɒnstə'neɪʃən]
n (*dismay*) Bestürzung *f*

constituency [kən'stɪtjʊənsɪ]
n Wahlkreis *m*

constitution [kɒnstɪ'tjuːʃən] *n*
Verfassung *f*; (*of person*)
Konstitution *f*

construct [kən'strʌkt] *vt* bauen;
construction [kən'strʌkʃən] *n*
(*process, result*) Bau *m*; (*method*)
Bauweise *f*; **under ~** im Bau
befindlich; **construction site**
n Baustelle *f*; **construction worker**
n Bauarbeiter(in) *m(f)*

consulate ['kɒnsjʊlət] *n* Konsulat *nt*

consult [kən'sʌlt] *vt* um Rat
fragen; (*doctor*) konsultieren;
(*book*) nachschlagen in +*dat*;
consultant [kən'sʌltənt] *n* (*Med*) Facharzt *m*,
Fachärztin *f*; **consultation**
[kɒnsəl'teɪʃən] *n* Beratung *f*;
(*Med*) Konsultation *f*; **~ room**
Besprechungsraum,
Sprechzimmer

consume [kən'sjuːm] *vt* verbrauchen; (*food*) konsumieren;
consumer *n* Verbraucher(in)
m(f); **consumer-friendly** *adj*
verbraucherfreundlich

contact ['kɒntækt] *n* (*touch*)
Berührung *f*; (*communication*)
Kontakt *m*; (*person*) Kontaktperson
f; **to be/keep in ~ (with sb)** (mit
jdm) in Kontakt sein/bleiben ▷ *vt*
sich in Verbindung setzen mit;

contact lenses npl Kontaktlinsen pl

contagious [kən'teɪdʒəs] adj ansteckend

contain [kən'teɪn] vt enthalten; container n Behälter m; (for transport) Container m

contaminate [kən'tæmɪneɪt] vt verunreinigen; (chemically) verseuchen; ~d by radiation strahlenverseucht, verstrahlt; contamination [kəntæmɪ'neɪʃən] n Verunreinigung f; (by radiation) Verseuchung f

contemporary [kən'tempərərɪ] adj zeitgenössisch

contempt [kən'tempt] n Verachtung f; contemptuous adj verächtlich; to be ~ voller Verachtung sein (of für)

content [kən'tent] adj zufrieden

content(s) ['kɒntent(s)] n pl Inhalt m

contest ['kɒntest] n (Wett)kampf m (for um); (competition) Wettbewerb m ▷ [kən'test] vt kämpfen um +akk; (dispute) bestreiten; contestant [kən'testənt] n Teilnehmer(in) m(f)

context ['kɒntekst] n Zusammenhang m; out of ~ aus dem Zusammenhang gerissen

continent ['kɒntɪnənt] n Kontinent m, Festland nt; the Continent (Brit) das europäische Festland, der Kontinent; continental [kɒntɪ'nentl] adj kontinental; ~ breakfast kleines Frühstück mit Brötchen und Marmelade, Kaffee oder Tee

continual [kən'tɪnjʊəl] adj (endless) ununterbrochen; (constant) dauernd, ständig; continually adv dauernd; (again and again) immer wieder; continuation [kəntɪnjʊ'eɪʃən] n

Fortsetzung f; continue [kən'tɪnjuː] vi weitermachen (with mit); (esp talking) fortfahren (with mit); (travelling) weiterfahren; (state, conditions) fortdauern, anhalten ▷ vt fortsetzen; to be ~d Fortsetzung folgt; continuous [kən'tɪnjʊəs] adj (endless) ununterbrochen; (constant) ständig

contraceptive [kɒntrə'septɪv] n Verhütungsmittel nt

contract ['kɒntrækt] n Vertrag m

contradict [kɒntrə'dɪkt] vt widersprechen +dat; contradiction [kɒntrə'dɪkʃən] n Widerspruch m

contrary ['kɒntrərɪ] n Gegenteil nt; on the ~ im Gegenteil ▷ adj: ~ to entgegen +dat

contrast ['kɒntrɑːst] n Kontrast m, Gegensatz m; in ~ to im Gegensatz zu ▷ [kən'trɑːst] vt entgegensetzen

contribute [kən'trɪbjuːt] vt, vi beitragen (to zu); (money) spenden (to für); contribution [kɒntrɪ'bjuːʃən] n Beitrag m

control [kən'trəʊl] vt (master) beherrschen; (temper etc) im Griff haben; (esp Tech) steuern; to ~ oneself sich beherrschen ▷ n Kontrolle f; (mastery) Beherrschung f; (esp Tech) Steuerung f; ~s pl (knobs, switches etc) Bedienungselemente pl; (collectively) Steuerung f; to be out of ~ außer Kontrolle sein; control knob n Bedienungsknopf m; control panel n Schalttafel f

controversial [kɒntrə'vɜːʃəl] adj umstritten

convalesce [kɒnvə'les] vi gesund werden; convalescence n Genesung f

convenience [kən'viːnɪəns] n (quality, thing) Annehmlichkeit f; at

your ~ wann es Ihnen passt; **with all modern ~s** mit allem Komfort; **convenience food** n Fertiggericht nt; **convenient** adj günstig, passend

convent ['kɒnvənt] n Kloster nt

convention [kənˈvenʃən] n (custom) Konvention f; (meeting) Konferenz f; **the Geneva Convention** die Genfer Konvention; **conventional** adj herkömmlich, konventionell

conversation [kɒnvəˈseɪʃən] n Gespräch nt, Unterhaltung f

conversion [kənˈvɜːʃən] n Umwandlung f (into in +akk); (of building) Umbau m (into zu); (calculation) Umrechnung f; **conversion table** f; **convert** [kənˈvɜːt] vt umwandeln; (person) bekehren; (Inform) konvertieren; **to ~ into euros** in Euro umrechnen; **convertible** n (Auto) Kabrio nt ▷ adj umwandelbar

convey [kənˈveɪ] vt (carry) befördern; (feelings) vermitteln; **conveyor belt** n Förderband nt, Fließband nt

convict [kənˈvɪkt] vt verurteilen (of wegen) ▷ ['kɒnvɪkt] n Strafgefangene(r) mf; **conviction** n (Jur) Verurteilung f; (strong belief) Überzeugung f

convince [kənˈvɪns] vt überzeugen (of von); **convincing** adj überzeugend

cook [kʊk] vt, vi kochen ▷ n Koch m, Köchin f; **cookbook** n Kochbuch nt; **cooker** n Herd m; **cookery** n Kochkunst f; **~ book** Kochbuch nt; **cookie** n (US) Keks m; **cooking** n Kochen nt; (style of cooking) Küche f

cool [kuːl] adj kühl, gelassen; (fam: brilliant) cool, stark ▷ vt, vi (ab)kühlen; **~ it** reg dich ab! ▷ n:

to keep/lose one's ~ (fam) ruhig bleiben/durchdrehen; **cool down** vi abkühlen; (calm down) sich beruhigen

cooperate [kəʊˈɒpəreɪt] vi zusammenarbeiten, kooperieren; **cooperation** [kəʊˈpəˈreɪʃən] n Zusammenarbeit f, Kooperation f; **cooperative** [kəʊˈɒpərətɪv] adj hilfsbereit ▷ n Genossenschaft f

coordinate [kəʊˈɔːdɪneɪt] vt koordinieren

cop [kɒp] n (fam: policeman) Bulle m

cope [kəʊp] vi zurechtkommen, fertig werden (with mit)

Copenhagen [kəʊpənˈheɪgən] n Kopenhagen nt

copier ['kɒpɪə] n Kopierer m

copper ['kɒpə] n Kupfer nt; (Brit fam: policeman) Bulle m; (fam: coin) Kupfermünze f; **~s** Kleingeld nt

copy ['kɒpɪ] n Kopie f; (of book) Exemplar nt ▷ vt kopieren; (imitate) nachahmen; **copyright** n Urheberrecht nt

coral ['kɒrəl] n Koralle f

cord [kɔːd] n Schnur f; (material) Kordsamt m; **cordless** ['kɔːdlɪs] adj (phone) schnurlos

core [kɔː] n (a. fig) Kern m; (of apple, pear) Kerngehäuse nt; **core business** n Kerngeschäft nt

cork [kɔːk] n (material) Kork m; (stopper) Korken m; **corkscrew** ['kɔːkskruː] n Korkenzieher m

corn [kɔːn] n Getreide nt, Korn nt; (US: maize) Mais m; (on foot) Hühnerauge nt; **~ on the cob** (gekochter) Maiskolben; **corned beef** n Cornedbeef nt

corner ['kɔːnə] n Ecke f; (on road) Kurve f; (Sport) Eckstoß m ▷ vt in die Enge treiben; **corner shop** n Laden m an der Ecke

cornflakes ['kɔːfleɪks] npl Cornflakes pl

Cornish ['kɔ:nɪʃ] *adj* kornisch; **~ pasty** mit Fleisch und Kartoffeln gefüllte Pastete; **Cornwall** ['kɔ:nwəl] *n* Cornwall *nt*

coronation [kɔrə'neɪʃən] *n* Krönung *f*

corporation [kɔ:pə'reɪʃən] *n* (US Comm) Aktiengesellschaft *f*

corpse [kɔ:ps] *n* Leiche *f*

correct [kə'rekt] *adj* (accurate) richtig; (proper) korrekt ▷ *vt* korrigieren, verbessern; **correction** *n* (esp written) Korrektur *f*

correspond [kɔrɪ'spɒnd] *vi* entsprechen (to dat); (two things) übereinstimmen; (exchange letters) korrespondieren; **corresponding** *adj* entsprechend

corridor ['kɔrɪdɔ:°] *n* (in building) Flur *m*; (in train) Gang *m*

corrupt [kə'rʌpt] *adj* korrupt

cosmetic [kɒz'metɪk] *adj* kosmetisch; **cosmetics** *npl* Kosmetika *pl*; **cosmetic surgeon** *n* Schönheitschirurg(in) *m(f)*; **cosmetic surgery** *n* Schönheitschirurgie *f*

cosmopolitan [kɒzmə'pɒlɪtən] *adj* international; (attitude) weltoffen

cost [kɒst] (**cost, cost**) *vt* kosten ▷ *n* Kosten *pl*; **at all ~s, at any ~** um jeden Preis; **~ of living** Lebenshaltungskosten *pl*; **costly** *adj* kostspielig

costume ['kɒstju:m] *n* (Theat) Kostüm *nt*

cosy ['kəʊzɪ] *adj* gemütlich

cot [kɒt] *n* (Brit) Kinderbett *nt*; (US) Campingliege *f*

cottage ['kɒtɪdʒ] *n* kleines Haus; (country cottage) Landhäuschen *nt*; **cottage cheese** *n* Hüttenkäse *m*; **cottage pie** *n* Hackfleisch mit Kartoffelbrei überbacken

cotton ['kɒtn] *n* Baumwolle *f*;

cotton candy *n* (US) Zuckerwatte *f*; **cotton wool** *n* (Brit) Watte *f*

couch [kaʊtʃ] *n* Couch *f*; (sofa) Sofa *nt*; **couchette** [ku:'ʃet] *n* Liegewagen(platz) *m*

cough [kɒf] *vi* husten ▷ *n* Husten *m*; **cough mixture** *n* Hustensaft *m*; **cough sweet** *n* Hustenbonbon *nt*

could [kʊd] *pt of* **can** konnte; conditional könnte; **~ you come earlier?** könntest du/könnten Sie früher kommen?

couldn't *contr of* **could not**

council ['kaʊnsl] *n* (Pol) Rat *m*; (local ~) Gemeinderat *m*; (town ~) Stadtrat *m*; **council estate** *n* Siedlung *f* des sozialen Wohnungsbaus; **council house** *n* Sozialwohnung *f*; **councillor** ['kaʊnsɪlə°] *n* Gemeinderat *m*, Gemeinderätin *f*; **council tax** *n* Gemeindesteuer *f*

count [kaʊnt] *vt, vi* zählen; (include) mitrechnen ▷ *n* Zählung *f*; (noble) Graf *m*; **count on** *vt* (rely on) sich verlassen auf +akk; (expect) rechnen mit

counter ['kaʊntə°] *n* (in shop) Ladentisch *m*; (in café) Theke *f*; (in bank, post office) Schalter *m*; **counter attack** *n* Gegenangriff *m* ▷ *vi* zurückschlagen; **counter-clockwise** *adv* (US) entgegen dem Uhrzeigersinn

counterpart ['kaʊntəpɑ:t] *n* Gegenstück *nt* (of zu)

countess *n* Gräfin *f*

countless ['kaʊntlɪs] *adj* zahllos, unzählig

country ['kʌntrɪ] *n* Land *nt*; **in the ~** auf dem Land(e); **in this ~** hierzulande; **country cousin** *n* (fam) Landei *nt*; **country dancing** *n* Volkstanz *m*; **country house** *n* Landhaus *nt*; **countryman** *n* (compatriot) Landsmann *m*;

country music n Countrymusic f;
country road n Landstraße f;
countryside n Landschaft f; (rural area) Land nt
county ['kaʊntɪ] n (Brit) Grafschaft f; (US) Verwaltungsbezirk m; **county town** n (Brit) = Kreisstadt f
couple ['kʌpl] n Paar nt; **a ~ of** ein paar
coupon ['kuːpɒn] n (voucher) Gutschein m
courage ['kʌrɪdʒ] n Mut m; **courageous** [kə'reɪdʒəs] adj mutig
courgette [kʊə'ʒet] n (Brit) Zucchini f
courier ['kʊrɪə'] n (for tourists) Reiseleiter(in) m(f); (messenger) Kurier m
course [kɔːs] n (of study) Kurs m; (for race) Strecke f; (Naut, Aviat) Kurs m; (at university) Studiengang m; (in meal) Gang m; **of ~** natürlich; **in the ~ of** während
court [kɔːt] n (Sport) Platz m; (Jur) Gericht nt
courteous ['kɜːtɪəs] adj höflich; **courtesy** ['kɜːtəsɪ] n Höflichkeit f; **~ bus/coach** (gebührenfreier) Zubringerbus
courthouse ['kɔːthaʊs] n (US) Gerichtsgebäude nt; **court order** n Gerichtsbeschluss m; **courtroom** n Gerichtssaal m
courtyard ['kɔːtjɑːd] n Hof m
cousin ['kʌzn] n (male) Cousin m; (female) Cousine f
cover ['kʌvə'] n (to bedecken (in, with mit); (distance) zurücklegen; (loan, costs) decken ▷ n (for bed etc) Decke f; (of cushion) Bezug m; (lid) Deckel m; (of book) Umschlag m; (insurance) ~ Versicherungsschutz m; **cover up** vt zudecken; (error etc) vertuschen; **coverage** n Berichterstattung f (of über +akk);

cover charge n Kosten pl für ein Gedeck; **covering** n Decke f; **covering letter** n Begleitbrief m; **cover story** n (newspaper) Titelgeschichte f
cow [kaʊ] n Kuh f
coward ['kaʊəd] n Feigling m; **cowardly** adj feig(e)
cowboy ['kaʊbɔɪ] n Cowboy m
coy [kɔɪ] adj gespielt schüchtern, kokett
cozy ['kəʊzɪ] adj (US) gemütlich
CPU abbr = **central processing unit** Zentraleinheit f
crab [kræb] n Krabbe f
crabby ['kræbɪ] adj mürrisch, reizbar
crack [kræk] n Riss m; (in pottery, glass) Sprung m; (drug) Crack nt; **to have a ~ at sth** etw ausprobieren ▷ vi (pottery, glass) einen Sprung bekommen; (wood, ice etc) einen Riss bekommen; **to get ~ing** (fam) loslegen ▷ vt (bone) anbrechen; (nut, code) knacken
cracker ['krækə'] n (biscuit) Kräcker m; (Christmas ~) Knallbonbon nt; **crackers** adj (fam) verrückt, bekloppt; **he's ~** er hat nicht alle Tassen im Schrank
crackle ['krækl] vi knistern; (telephone, radio) knacken; **crackling** n (Gastr) Kruste f (des Schweinebratens)
cradle ['kreɪdl] n Wiege f
craft [krɑːft] n Handwerk nt; (art) Kunsthandwerk nt; (Naut) Boot nt; **craftsman** (pl **-men**) n Handwerker m; **craftsmanship** n Handwerkskunst f; (ability) handwerkliches Können
crafty ['krɑːftɪ] adj schlau
cram [kræm] vt stopfen (into in +akk); **to be ~med with ...** mit ... vollgestopft sein ▷ vi (revise for exam) pauken (for für)
cramp [kræmp] n Krampf m

cranberry ['krænbərɪ] n Preiselbeere f
crane [kreɪn] n (machine) Kran m; (bird) Kranich m
crap [kræp] n (vulg) Scheiße f; (rubbish) Mist m ▷ adj beschissen, Scheiß-
crash [kræʃ] vi einen Unfall haben; (two vehicles) zusammenstoßen; (plane, computer) abstürzen; (economy) zusammenbrechen; **to ~ into sth** gegen etw knallen ▷ vt einen Unfall haben mit ▷ n (car) Unfall m; (train) Unglück nt; (collision) Zusammenstoß m; (Aviat, Inform) Absturz m; (noise) Krachen nt; **crash barrier** n Leitplanke f; **crash course** n Intensivkurs m; **crash helmet** n Sturzhelm m; **crash landing** n Bruchlandung f
crate [kreɪt] n Kiste f; (of beer) Kasten m
crater ['kreɪtə°] n Krater m
craving ['kreɪvɪŋ] n starkes Verlangen, Bedürfnis nt
crawl [krɔːl] vi kriechen; (baby) krabbeln ▷ n (swimming) Kraul nt; **crawler lane** n Kriechspur f
crayfish ['kreɪfɪʃ] n Languste f
crayon ['kreɪən] n Buntstift m
crazy ['kreɪzɪ] adj verrückt (about nach)
cream [kriːm] n (from milk) Sahne f, Rahm m; (polish, cosmetic) Creme f ▷ adj cremefarben; **cream cake** n (small) Sahnetörtchen nt; (big) Sahnetorte f; **cream cheese** n Frischkäse m; **creamer** n Kaffeeweißer m; **cream tea** n (Brit) Nachmittagstee mit Törtchen, Marmelade und Schlagsahne; **creamy** adj sahnig
crease [kriːs] n Falte f ▷ vt falten; (untidy) zerknittern
create [kriːˈeɪt] vt schaffen; (cause) verursachen; **creative**

[kriːˈeɪtɪv] adj schöpferisch; (person) kreativ; **creature** ['kriːtʃə°] n Geschöpf nt
crèche [kreʃ] n Kinderkrippe f
credible ['kredɪbl] adj (person) glaubwürdig; **credibility** n Glaubwürdigkeit f
credit ['kredɪt] n (Fin: amount allowed) Kredit m; (amount possessed) Guthaben nt; (recognition) Anerkennung f; **~s** (of film) Abspann m; **credit card** n Kreditkarte f; **credit crunch** n Kreditklemme f
creep [kriːp] (**crept, crept**) vi kriechen; **creeps** n: **he gives me the ~** er ist mir nicht ganz geheuer; **creepy** ['kriːpɪ] adj (frightening) gruselig, unheimlich
crept [krept] pt, pp of **creep**
cress [kres] n Kresse f
crest [krest] n Kamm m; (of coat of arms) Wappen nt
crew [kruː] n Besatzung f, Mannschaft f
crib [krɪb] n (US) Kinderbett nt
cricket ['krɪkɪt] n (insect) Grille f; (game) Cricket m
crime [kraɪm] n Verbrechen nt; **criminal** ['krɪmɪnl] n Verbrecher(in) m(f) ▷ adj kriminell, strafbar
cripple ['krɪpl] n (pej) Krüppel m ▷ vt verkrüppeln, lähmen
crisis ['kraɪsɪs] (pl **crises**) n Krise f
crisp [krɪsp] adj knusprig; **crisps** npl (Brit) Chips pl; **crispbread** n Knäckebrot nt
criterion [kraɪˈtɪərɪən] n Kriterium nt
critic ['krɪtɪk] n Kritiker(in) m(f); **critical** adj kritisch; **critically** adv kritisch; **~ ill/injured** schwer krank/verletzt; **criticism** ['krɪtɪsɪzəm] n Kritik f; **criticize** ['krɪtɪsaɪz] vt kritisieren
Croat [ˈkrəʊæt] n Kroate m,

Kroatin f; **Croatia** [krəʊˈeɪʃə] n Kroatien nt; **Croatian** [krəʊˈeɪʃən] adj kroatisch

crockery [ˈkrɒkərɪ] n Geschirr nt

crocodile [ˈkrɒkədaɪl] n Krokodil nt

crocus [ˈkrəʊkəs] n Krokus m

crop [krɒp] n (harvest) Ernte f; **crops** npl Getreide nt; **crop up** vi auftauchen

croquette [krəˈket] n Krokette f

cross [krɒs] n Kreuz nt; **to mark sth with a ~** etw ankreuzen (to zu, gegen); (road, river etc) überqueren; (legs) übereinanderschlagen; **it ~ed my mind** es fiel mir ein; **to ~ one's fingers** die Daumen drücken ▷ adj ärgerlich, böse; **cross out** vt durchstreichen

crossbar n (of bicycle) Stange f; (Sport) Querlatte f; **cross-country** adj: **~ running** Geländelauf m; **~ skiing** Langlauf m; **cross-examination** n Kreuzverhör nt; **cross-eyed** adj: **to be ~** schielen; **crossing** n (crossroads) (Straßen)kreuzung f; (for pedestrians) Fußgängerüberweg m; (on ship) Überfahrt f; **crossroads** nsing o pl Straßenkreuzung f; **cross section** n Querschnitt m; **crosswalk** n (US) Fußgängerüberweg m; **crossword (puzzle)** n Kreuzworträtsel nt

crouch [kraʊtʃ] vi hocken

crouton [ˈkruːtɒn] n Croûton m

crow [krəʊ] n Krähe f

crowbar [ˈkrəʊbɑː°] n Brecheisen nt

crowd [kraʊd] n Menge f ▷ vi sich drängen (into in +akk; round um); **crowded** adj überfüllt

crown [kraʊn] n Krone f ▷ vt krönen; (fam) **and to ~ it all ...** und als Krönung ...

crucial [ˈkruːʃəl] adj entscheidend

crude [kruːd] adj primitiv; (humour, behaviour) derb, ordinär ▷ n: **~ (oil)** Rohöl nt

cruel [ˈkrʊəl] adj grausam (to zu, gegen); (unfeeling) gefühllos; **cruelty** n Grausamkeit f; **~ to animals** Tierquälerei f

cruise [kruːz] n Kreuzfahrt f ▷ vi (ship) kreuzen; (car) mit Reisegeschwindigkeit fahren; **cruise liner** n Kreuzfahrtschiff nt; **cruise missile** n Marschflugkörper m; **cruising speed** n Reisegeschwindigkeit f

crumb [krʌm] n Krume f

crumble [ˈkrʌmbl] vt, vi zerbröckeln ▷ n mit Streuseln überbackenes Kompott

crumpet [ˈkrʌmpɪt] n weiches Hefegebäck zum Toasten; (fam: attractive woman) Schnecke f

crumple [ˈkrʌmpl] vt zerknittern

crunchy [ˈkrʌntʃɪ] adj (Brit) knusprig

crusade [kruːˈseɪd] n Kreuzzug m

crush [krʌʃ] vt zerdrücken; (finger etc) quetschen; (spices, stone) zerstoßen ▷ n: **to have a ~ on sb** in jdn verknallt sein; **crushing** adj (defeat, remark) vernichtend

crust [krʌst] n Kruste f; **crusty** adj knusprig

crutch [krʌtʃ] n Krücke f

cry [kraɪ] vi (call) rufen; (scream) schreien; (weep) weinen ▷ n (call) Ruf m; (louder) Schrei m

crypt [krɪpt] n Krypta f

crystal [ˈkrɪstl] n Kristall m

cu abbr = **see you** (SMS, e-mail) bis bald

Cuba [ˈkjuːbə] n Kuba nt

cube [kjuːb] n Würfel m

cubic [ˈkjuːbɪk] adj Kubik-

cubicle [ˈkjuːbɪkl] n Kabine f

cuckoo ['kuku:] n Kuckuck m

cucumber ['kju:kʌmbə*] n Salatgurke f

cuddle ['kʌdl] vt in den Arm nehmen; (amorously) schmusen mit ▷ n Liebkosung f, Umarmung f; **to have a ~** schmusen; **cuddly** adj verschmust; **cuddly toy** n Plüschtier nt

cuff [kʌf] n Manschette f; (US: trouser ~) Aufschlag m; **off the ~** aus dem Stegreif; **cufflink** n Manschettenknopf m

cuisine [kwɪ'zi:n] n Kochkunst f, Küche f

cul-de-sac ['kʌldəsæk] n (Brit) Sackgasse f

culprit ['kʌlprɪt] n Schuldige(r) mf; (fig) Übeltäter(in) m(f)

cult [kʌlt] n Kult m

cultivate ['kʌltɪveɪt] vt (Agr: land) bebauen; (crop) anbauen; **cultivated** adj (person) kultiviert, gebildet

cultural ['kʌltʃərəl] adj kulturell, Kultur-; **culture** ['kʌltʃə*] n Kultur f; **cultured** adj gebildet, kultiviert; **culture vulture** (Brit fam) n Kulturfanatiker(in) m(f)

cumbersome ['kʌmbəsəm] adj (object) unhandlich

cumin ['kʌmɪn] n Kreuzkümmel m

cunning ['kʌnɪŋ] adj schlau; (person a.) gerissen

cup [kʌp] n Tasse f; (prize) Pokal m; **it's not his ~ of tea** das ist nicht sein Fall; **cupboard** ['kʌbəd] n Schrank m; **cup final** n Pokalendspiel nt; **cup tie** n Pokalspiel nt

cupola ['kju:pələ] n Kuppel f

curable ['kjʊərəbl] adj heilbar

curb [kɜ:b] n (US) see **kerb**

curd [kɜ:d] n: ~ **cheese**, **~s =** Quark m

cure [kjʊə*] n Heilmittel nt (for

gegen); (process) Heilung f ▷ vt heilen; (Gastr) pökeln; (smoke) räuchern

curious ['kjʊərɪəs] adj neugierig; (strange) seltsam

curl [kɜ:l] n Locke f ▷ vi sich kräuseln; **curly** adj lockig

currant ['kʌrənt] n (dried) Korinthe f; (red, black) Johannisbeere f

currency ['kʌrənsɪ] n Währung f; **foreign ~** Devisen pl

current ['kʌrənt] n (in water) Strömung f; (electric ~) Strom m ▷ adj (issue, affairs) aktuell, gegenwärtig; (expression) gängig; **current account** n Girokonto nt; **currently** adv zur Zeit

curriculum [kə'rɪkjʊləm] n Lehrplan m; **curriculum vitae** [kə'rɪkjʊləm'vi:taɪ] n (Brit) Lebenslauf m

curry ['kʌrɪ] n Currygericht nt; **curry powder** n Curry(pulver) nt

curse [kɜ:s] vi (swear) fluchen (at auf +akk) ▷ n Fluch m

cursor ['kɜ:sə*] n (Inform) Cursor m

curt [kɜ:t] adj schroff, kurz angebunden

curtain ['kɜ:tn] n Vorhang m; **it was ~s for Benny** für Benny war alles vorbei

curve [kɜ:v] n Kurve f ▷ vi einen Bogen machen; **curved** adj gebogen

cushion ['kʊʃən] n Kissen nt

custard ['kʌstəd] n dicke Vanillesoße, die warm oder kalt zu vielen englischen Nachspeisen gegessen wird

custom ['kʌstəm] n Brauch m; (habit) Gewohnheit f; **customary** ['kʌstəmərɪ] adj üblich; **custom-built** adj nach Kundenangaben gefertigt; **customer** ['kʌstəmə*] n Kunde m, Kundin f; **customer loyalty card** n Kundenkarte f; **customer service** n Kundendienst m

customs ['kʌstəmz] npl (*organization, location*) Zoll m; **to pass through ~** durch den Zoll gehen; **customs officer** n Zollbeamte(r) m, Zollbeamtin f

cut [kʌt] (**cut**, **cut**) vt schneiden; (*cake*) anschneiden; (*wages, benefits*) kürzen; (*prices*) heruntersetzen ▷ n **~ my finger** ich habe mir in den Finger geschnitten ▷ n Schnitt m; (*wound*) Schnittwunde f; (*reduction*) Kürzung f (*in gen*); **price/tax ~** Preissenkung/Steuersenkung f; **to be a ~ above the rest** eine Klasse besser als die anderen sein; **cut back** vt (*workforce etc*) reduzieren; **cut down** vt (*tree*) fällen; **to ~ on sth** etwas einschränken; **cut in** vi (*Auto*) scharf einscheren; **to ~ on sb** jdn schneiden; **cut off** vt abschneiden; (*gas, electricity*) abdrehen, abstellen; (*Tel*) **I was ~** ich wurde unterbrochen

cutback n Kürzung f

cute [kjuːt] adj putzig, niedlich; (*US: shrewd*) clever

cutlery ['kʌtləri] n Besteck nt

cutlet ['kʌtlɪt] n (*pork*) Kotelett nt; (*veal*) Schnitzel nt

cut-price adj verbilligt

cutting ['kʌtɪŋ] n (*from paper*) Ausschnitt m; (*of plant*) Ableger m ▷ adj (*comment*) verletzend

CV abbr = **curriculum vitae**

cwt abbr = **hundredweight** = Zentner, Ztr.

cybercafé [saɪbə'kæfeɪ] n Internetcafé nt; **cyberspace** n Cyberspace m

cycle ['saɪkl] n Fahrrad nt ▷ vi Rad fahren; **cycle lane, cycle path** n Radweg m; **cycling** n

Radfahren nt; **cyclist** ['saɪklɪst] n Radfahrer(in) m(f)

cylinder ['sɪlɪndə] n Zylinder m

cynical ['sɪnɪkəl] adj zynisch

cypress ['saɪprɪs] n Zypresse f

Cypriot ['sɪprɪət] adj zypriotisch ▷ n Zypriote m, Zypriotin f; **Cyprus** ['saɪprəs] n Zypern nt

czar [zɑː°] n Zar m; **czarina** [zɑː'riːnə] n Zarin f

Czech [tʃek] adj tschechisch ▷ n (*person*) Tscheche m, Tschechin f; (*language*) Tschechisch nt; **Czech Republic** n Tschechische Republik, Tschechien nt

d

dab [dæb] vt (wound, nose etc) betupfen (with mit)

dachshund ['dækshʊnd] n Dackel m

dad(dy) ['dæd(ɪ)] n Papa m, Vati m; **daddy-longlegs** nsing (Brit) Schnake; (US) Weberknecht m

daffodil ['dæfədɪl] n Osterglocke f

daft [dɑːft] adj (fam) blöd, doof

dahlia ['deɪlɪə] n Dahlie f

daily ['deɪlɪ] adj, adv täglich ▷ n (paper) Tageszeitung f

dairy ['dɛərɪ] n (on farm) Molkerei f; **dairy products** npl Milchprodukte pl

daisy ['deɪzɪ] n Gänseblümchen nt

dam [dæm] n Staudamm m ▷ vt stauen

damage ['dæmɪdʒ] n Schaden m; **~s** pl (Jur) Schadenersatz m ▷ vt beschädigen; (reputation, health) schädigen, schaden +dat

damn [dæm] adj (fam) verdammt ▷ vt (condemn) verurteilen; **~ (it)!** verflucht! ▷ n: **he doesn't give a ~** es ist ihm völlig egal

damp [dæmp] adj feucht ▷ n Feuchtigkeit f; **dampen** ['dæmpən] vt befeuchten

dance [dɑːns] n Tanz m; (event) Tanzveranstaltung f ▷ vi tanzen; **dance floor** n Tanzfläche f; **dancer** n Tänzer(in) m(f); **dancing** n Tanzen nt

dandelion ['dændɪlaɪən] n Löwenzahn m

dandruff ['dændrəf] n Schuppen pl

Dane [deɪn] n Däne m, Dänin f

danger ['deɪndʒəʳ] n Gefahr f; **~ (sign)** Achtung!; **to be in ~** in Gefahr sein; **dangerous** adj gefährlich

Danish ['deɪnɪʃ] adj dänisch ▷ n (language) Dänisch nt; **the ~** pl die Dänen; **Danish pastry** n Plundergebäck nt

Danube ['dænjuːb] n Donau f

dare [dɛəʳ] vi: **to ~ (to) do sth** es wagen, etw zu tun; **I didn't ~ ask** ich traute mich nicht, zu fragen; **how ~ you** was fällt dir ein!; **daring** adj (person) mutig; (film, clothes etc) gewagt

dark [dɑːk] adj dunkel; (gloomy) düster, trübe; (sinister) finster; **~ chocolate** Bitterschokolade f; **~ green/blue** dunkelgrün/dunkelblau ▷ n Dunkelheit f; **in the ~** im Dunkeln; **dark glasses** npl Sonnenbrille f; **darkness** n Dunkelheit nt

darling ['dɑːlɪŋ] n Schatz m; (also favourite) Liebling m

darts [dɑːts] nsing (game) Darts nt

dash [dæʃ] vi stürzen, rennen

▷ vt: **to ~ hopes** Hoffnungen zerstören ▷ n (in text) Gedankenstrich m; (of liquid) Schuss m; **dashboard** n Armaturenbrett nt

data ['deɪtə] npl Daten pl; **data bank**, **data base** n Datenbank f; **data capture** n Datenerfassung f; **data processing** n Datenverarbeitung f; **data protection** n Datenschutz m

date [deɪt] n Datum nt; (for meeting, delivery etc) Termin m; (with person) Verabredung f; (with girlfriend/boyfriend etc) Date nt; (fruit) Dattel f; **what's the ~ (today)?** der Wievielte ist heute?; **out of ~** adj (news) aktuell; (fashion) zeitgemäß ▷ vt (letter etc) datieren; (person) gehen mit; **dated** adj altmodisch; **date of birth** n Geburtsdatum nt; **dating agency** n Partnervermittlung f

dative ['deɪtɪv] n Dativ m

daughter ['dɔːtə*] n Tochter f; **daughter-in-law** (pl **daughters-in-law**) n Schwiegertochter f

dawn [dɔːn] n Morgendämmerung f ▷ vi dämmern; **it ~ed on me** mir ging ein Licht auf

day [deɪ] n Tag m; **one ~** eines Tages; **by ~** bei Tage; **~ after ~**, **~ by ~** Tag für Tag; **the ~ after/before** am Tag danach/zuvor; **the ~ before yesterday** vorgestern; **the ~ after tomorrow** übermorgen; **these ~s** heutzutage; **in those ~s** damals; **let's call it a ~** Schluss für heute!; **daybreak** n Tagesanbruch m; **day-care center** (US), **day-care centre** n (Brit) Kita f (Kindertagesstätte); **daydream** n Tagtraum m ▷ vi (mit offenen Augen) träumen; **daylight** n

Tageslicht nt; **in ~** bei Tage; **day nursery** n Kita f (Kindertagesstätte); **day return** n (Brit Rail) Tagesrückfahrkarte f; **daytime** n: **in the ~** bei Tage, tagsüber; **daytrip** n Tagesausflug m

dazed [deɪzd] adj benommen

dazzle ['dæzl] vt blenden; **dazzling** adj blendend, glänzend

dead [ded] adj tot; (limb) abgestorben ▷ adv genau; (fam) total, völlig; **~ tired** todmüde; **~ slow** (sign) Schritt fahren; **dead end** n Sackgasse f; **deadline** n Termin m; (period) Frist f; **~ for applications** Anmeldeschluss m; **deadly** adj tödlich ▷ adv: **~ dull** todlangweilig

deaf [def] adj taub; **deafen** vt taub machen; **deafening** adj ohrenbetäubend

deal [diːl] (**dealt**, **dealt**) vt, vi (cards) geben, austeilen ▷ n (business ~) Geschäft nt; (agreement) Abmachung f; **it's a ~** abgemacht!; **a good/great ~ of** ziemlich/sehr viel; **deal in** vt handeln mit; **deal with** vt (matter) sich beschäftigen mit; (book, film) behandeln; (successfully: person, problem) fertig werden mit; (matter) erledigen; **dealer** n (Comm) Händler(in) m(f); (drugs) Dealer(in) m(f); **dealings** npl (Comm) Geschäfte pl

dealt [delt] pt, pp of **deal**

dear [dɪə*] adj lieb, teuer; **Dear Sir or Madam** Sehr geehrte Damen und Herren; **Dear David** Lieber David ▷ n Schatz m; (as address) mein Schatz, Liebling; **dearly** adv (love) (heiß und) innig; (pay) teuer

death [deθ] n Tod m; (of project, hopes) Ende nt; (in accident) Todesfall m, Todesopfer nt; **death certificate** n Totenschein m;

death penalty n Todesstrafe f;
death toll n Zahl f der Todesopfer; **death trap** n Todesfalle f
debatable [dɪˈbeɪtəbl] adj
fraglich; (question) strittig; **debate**
[dɪˈbeɪt] n Debatte f ▷ vt
debattieren
debauched [dɪˈbɔːtʃt] adj
ausschweifend
debit [ˈdebɪt] n Soll nt ▷ vt
(account) belasten; **debit card** n
Geldkarte f
debris [ˈdebriː] n Trümmer pl
debt [det] n Schuld f; **to be in
~** verschuldet sein
debug [diːˈbʌg] vt (Inform) Fehler
beseitigen in +dat
decade [ˈdekeɪd] n Jahrzehnt nt
decadent [ˈdekədənt] adj
dekadent
decaff [ˈdiːkæf] n (fam) koffein-
freier Kaffee; **decaffeinated**
[diːˈkæfɪneɪtɪd] adj koffeinfrei
decanter [dɪˈkæntə°] n Dekanter
m, Karaffe f
decay [dɪˈkeɪ] n Verfall m;
(rotting) Verwesung f; (of tooth)
Karies f ▷ vi verfallen; (rot)
verwesen; (wood) vermodern;
(teeth) faulen; (leaves) verrotten
deceased [dɪˈsiːst] n: **the ~**
der/die Verstorbene
deceit [dɪˈsiːt] n Betrug m;
deceive [dɪˈsiːv] vt täuschen
December [dɪˈsembə°] n
Dezember m; see also **September**
decent [ˈdiːsənt] adj anständig
deception [dɪˈsepʃən] n Betrug
m; **deceptive** [dɪˈseptɪv] adj
täuschend, irreführend
decide [dɪˈsaɪd] vt (question)
entscheiden; (body of people)
beschließen; **I can't ~ what to do**
ich kann mich nicht entscheiden,
was ich tun soll ▷ vi sich
entscheiden; **to ~ on sth** (in favour
of sth) sich für etw entscheiden,

sich zu etw entschließen; **decided**
adj entschieden; (clear) deutlich;
decidedly adv entschieden
decimal [ˈdesɪml] adj Dezimal-;
decimal system n
Dezimalsystem nt
decipher [dɪˈsaɪfə°] vt entziffern
decision [dɪˈsɪʒn] n Entscheidung f (on über +akk); (of committee,
jury etc) Beschluss m; **to make a
~** eine Entscheidung treffen;
decisive [dɪˈsaɪsɪv] adj entscheidend; (person)
entscheidungsfreudig
deck [dek] n (Naut) Deck nt; (of
cards) Blatt nt; **deckchair** n
Liegestuhl m
declaration [deklɑˈreɪʃən] n
Erklärung f; **declare** [dɪˈkleə°] vt
erklären; (state) behaupten (that
dass); (at customs) **have you
anything to ~?** haben Sie etwas
zu verzollen?
decline [dɪˈklaɪn] n Rückgang m
▷ vt (invitation, order) ablehnen ▷ vi
(become less) sinken, abnehmen;
(health) sich verschlechtern
decode [diːˈkəʊd] vt
entschlüsseln
decompose [diːkəmˈpəʊz] vi sich
zersetzen
decontaminate
[diːkənˈtæmɪneɪt] vt entgiften;
(from radioactivity) entseuchen
decorate [ˈdekəreɪt] vt
(aus)schmücken; (wallpaper)
tapezieren; (paint) anstreichen;
decoration [dekəˈreɪʃən] n
Schmuck m; (process) Schmücken
nt; (wallpapering) Tapezieren nt;
(painting) Anstreichen nt;
Christmas ~s Weihnachts-
schmuck m; **decorator** n
Maler(in) m(f)
decrease [ˈdiːkriːs] n Abnahme f
▷ [diːˈkriːs] vi abnehmen
dedicate [ˈdedɪkeɪt] vt widmen

(to sb jdm); **dedicated** adj (person) engagiert; **dedication** [dedɪˈkeɪʃən] n Widmung f; (commitment) Hingabe f, Engagement nt

deduce [dɪˈdjuːs] vt folgern, schließen (from aus, that dass)

deduct [dɪˈdʌkt] vt abziehen (from von); **deduction** [dɪˈdʌkʃən] n (of money) Abzug m; (conclusion) (Schluss)folgerung f

deed [diːd] n Tat f

deep [diːp] adj tief; **deepen** vt vertiefen; **deep-freeze** n Tiefkühltruhe f; (upright) Gefrierschrank m; **deep-fry** vi frittieren

deer [dɪəᵊ] n Reh nt; (with stag) Hirsch m

defeat [dɪˈfiːt] n Niederlage f; **to admit ~** sich geschlagen geben ▷ vt besiegen

defect [ˈdiːfekt] n Defekt m, Fehler m; **defective** [dɪˈfektɪv] adj fehlerhaft

defence [dɪˈfens] n Verteidigung f; **defend** [dɪˈfend] vt verteidigen; **defendant** [dɪˈfendənt] n (Jur) Angeklagte(r) mf; **defender** n (Sport) Verteidiger(in) m(f); **defensive** [dɪˈfensɪv] adj defensiv

deficiency [dɪˈfɪʃənsɪ] n Mangel m; **deficient** adj mangelhaft; **deficit** [ˈdefɪsɪt] n Defizit nt

define [dɪˈfaɪn] vt (word) definieren; (duties, powers) bestimmen; **definite** [ˈdefɪnɪt] adj (clear) klar, eindeutig; (certain) sicher; **it's ~** es steht fest; **definitely** adv bestimmt; **definition** [defɪˈnɪʃən] n Definition f; (Foto) Schärfe f

defrost [diːˈfrɒst] vt (fridge) abtauen; (food) auftauen

degrading [dɪˈgreɪdɪŋ] adj erniedrigend

degree [dɪˈgriː] n Grad m; (at university) akademischer Grad; **a certain/high ~ of** ein gewisses/hohes Maß an +dat; **to a certain ~** einigermaßen; **I have a ~ in chemistry** = ich habe einen Abschluss in Chemie

dehydrated [diːhaɪˈdreɪtɪd] adj (food) getrocknet, Trocken-; (person) ausgetrocknet

de-ice [diːˈaɪs] vt enteisen

delay [dɪˈleɪ] vt (postpone) verschieben, aufschieben; **to be ~ed** (event) sich verzögern; **the train/flight was ~ed** der Zug/die Maschine hatte Verspätung ▷ vi warten; (hesitate) zögern ▷ n Verzögerung f; (of train etc) Verspätung f; **without ~** unverzüglich; **delayed** adj (train etc) verspätet

delegate [ˈdelɪgət] n Delegierte(r) mf ▷ [ˈdelɪgeɪt] vt delegieren; **delegation** [delɪˈgeɪʃən] n Abordnung f, (foreign) Delegation f

delete [dɪˈliːt] vt (aus)streichen; (Inform) löschen; **deletion** n Streichung f; (Inform) Löschung f

deli [ˈdelɪ] n (fam) Feinkostgeschäft nt

deliberate [dɪˈlɪbərət] adj (intentional) absichtlich; **deliberately** adv mit Absicht, extra

delicate [ˈdelɪkɪt] adj (fine) fein; (fragile) zart; (a. Med) empfindlich; (situation) heikel

delicatessen [delɪkəˈtesn] nsing Feinkostgeschäft nt

delicious [dɪˈlɪʃəs] adj köstlich, lecker

delight [dɪˈlaɪt] n Freude f ▷ vt entzücken; **delighted** adj sehr erfreut (with über +akk); **delightful** adj entzückend; (weather, meal etc) herrlich

deliver [dɪ'lɪvə*] vt (goods) liefern
(to sb jdm); (letter, parcel) zustellen;
(speech) halten; (baby) entbinden;
delivery n Lieferung f; (of letter,
parcel) Zustellung f; (of baby)
Entbindung f; **delivery van** n
Lieferwagen m

delude [dɪ'luːd] vt täuschen;
don't ~ yourself mach dir nichts
vor; **delusion** n Irrglaube m

de luxe [dɪ'lʌks] adj Luxus-

demand [dɪ'maːnd] vt verlangen
(from von); (time, patience etc)
erfordern ▷ n (request) Forderung
f, Verlangen nt (for nach); (Comm:
for goods) Nachfrage f; **on ~** auf
Wunsch; **very much in ~** sehr
gefragt; **demanding** adj
anspruchsvoll

demented [dɪ'mentɪd] adj
wahnsinnig

demerara [demə'reərə] n:
~ (sugar) brauner Zucker

demister n Defroster m

demo [deməʊ] (pl **-s**) n (fam)
Demo f

democracy [dɪ'mɒkrəsɪ] n
Demokratie f; **democrat**,
Democrat (US Pol) ['deməkræt]
Demokrat(in) m(f); **democratic**
adj demokratisch; **the
Democratic Party** (US Pol) die
Demokratische Partei

demolish [dɪ'mɒlɪʃ] vt abreißen;
(fig) zerstören; **demolition**
[demə'lɪʃən] n Abbruch m

demonstrate ['demənstreɪt] vt,
vi demonstrieren, beweisen;
demonstration n Demonstration f

demoralize [dɪ'mɒrəlaɪz] vt
demoralisieren

denial [dɪ'naɪəl] n Leugnung f;
(official ~) Dementi nt

denim ['denɪm] n Jeansstoff m;
denim jacket n Jeansjacke f;
denims npl Bluejeans pl

Denmark ['denmaːk] n Dänemark nt

denomination [dɪnɒmɪ'neɪʃən]
n (Rel) Konfession f; (Comm)
Nennwert m

dense [dens] adj dicht; (fam:
stupid) schwer von Begriff; **density**
['densɪtɪ] n Dichte f

dent [dent] n Beule f, Delle f ▷ vt
einbeulen

dental ['dentl] adj Zahn-; **~ care**
Zahnpflege f; **~ floss** Zahnseide f;
dentist ['dentɪst] n Zahnarzt m,
Zahnärztin; **dentures** ['dentʃəz]
npl Zahnprothese f; (full) Gebiss nt

deny [dɪ'naɪ] vt leugnen,
bestreiten; (refuse) ablehnen

deodorant [diː'əʊdərənt] n
Deo(dorant) nt

depart [dɪ'paːt] vi abreisen; (bus,
train) abfahren (for nach, from von);
(plane) abfliegen (for nach, from
von)

department [dɪ'paːtmənt] n
Abteilung f; (at university) Institut
nt; (Pol: ministry) Ministerium nt;
department store n Kaufhaus nt

departure [dɪ'paːtʃə*] n (of
person) Weggang m; (on journey)
Abreise f (for nach); (of train etc)
Abfahrt f (for nach); (of plane)
Abflug m (for nach); **departure
lounge** n (Aviat) Abflughalle f;
departure time n Abfahrtzeit f;
(Aviat) Abflugzeit f

depend [dɪ'pend] vi: **it ~s** es
kommt darauf an (whether, if ob);
depend on vt (thing) abhängen
von; (person: rely on) sich verlassen
auf +akk; (person, area etc)
angewiesen sein auf +akk; **it ~s on
the weather** es kommt auf das
Wetter an; **dependable** adj
zuverlässig; **dependence** n
Abhängigkeit f (on von);
dependent adj abhängig (on von)

deport [dɪ'pɔːt] vt ausweisen,

abschieben; **deportation**
[di:po:'teɪʃən] n Abschiebung f
deposit [dɪ'pɔzɪt] n (down
payment) Anzahlung f; (security)
Kaution f; (for bottle) Pfand nt; (to
bank account) Einzahlung f; (in river
etc) Ablagerung f ▷ vt (put down)
abstellen, absetzen; (to bank
account) einzahlen; (sth valuable)
deponieren; **deposit account** n
Sparkonto nt
depot ['depəʊ] n Depot nt
depreciate [dɪ'pri:ʃɪeɪt] vi an
Wert verlieren
depress [dɪ'pres] vt (in mood)
deprimieren; **depressed** adj
(person) niedergeschlagen,
deprimiert; **~ area**
Notstandsgebiet nt; **depressing**
adj deprimierend; **depression**
[dɪ'preʃən] n (mood) Depression f;
(Meteo) Tief nt
deprive [dɪ'praɪv] vt: **to ~ sb of
sth** jdn einer Sache berauben;
deprived adj (child) (sozial)
benachteiligt
dept abbr = **department** Abt.
depth [depθ] n Tiefe f
deputy ['depjʊtɪ] adj stell-
vertretend, Vize- ▷ n
Stellvertreter(in) m(f); (US Pol)
Abgeordnete(r) mf
derail [dɪ'reɪl] vt entgleisen
lassen; **to be ~ed** entgleisen
deranged [dɪ'reɪndʒd] adj
geistesgestört
derivation [derɪ'veɪʃən] n
Ableitung f; **derive** [dɪ'raɪv] vt
ableiten (from von) ▷ abstammen
(from von)
dermatitis [dɜ:mə'taɪtɪs] n
Hautentzündung f
derogatory [dɪ'rɒgətərɪ] adj
abfällig
descend [dɪ'send] vt, vi
hinabsteigen, hinuntergehen;
(person) **to ~ o** be **~ed from**

abstammen von; **descendant** n
Nachkomme m; **descent** [dɪ'sent]
n (coming down) Abstieg m; (origin)
Abstammung f
describe [dɪs'kraɪb] vt beschreiben; **description**
[dɪ'skrɪpʃən] n Beschreibung f
desert ['dezət] n Wüste f
▷ [dɪ'zɜ:t] vt verlassen; (abandon)
im Stich lassen; **deserted** adj
verlassen; (empty) menschenleer
deserve [dɪ'zɜ:v] vt verdienen
design [dɪ'zaɪn] n (plan) Entwurf
m; (of vehicle, machine)
Konstruktion f; (of object) Design
nt; (planning) Gestaltung f ▷ vt
entwerfen; (machine etc)
konstruieren; **~ed for sb/sth**
(intended) für jdn/etw konzipiert
designate ['dezɪgneɪt] vt
bestimmen
designer [dɪ'zaɪnə°] n
Designer(in) m(f); (Tech)
Konstrukteur(in) m(f); **designer
drug** n Designerdroge f
desirable [dɪ'zaɪərəbl] n
wünschenswert; (person)
begehrenswert; **desire** [dɪ'zaɪə°]
n Wunsch m (for nach); (esp sexual)
Begierde f (for nach) ▷ vt
wünschen; (ask for) verlangen; **if
~d** auf Wunsch
desk [desk] n Schreibtisch m;
(reception ~) Empfang m; (at airport
etc) Schalter m; **desktop** n
Desktop m; (Inform) Desktop m;
desktop publishing n
Desktoppublishing nt
desolate ['desəlɪt] adj trostlos
despair [dɪs'peə°] n Verzweiflung f (at über +akk) ▷ vi
verzweifeln (of an +dat)
despatch [dɪ'spætʃ] see **dispatch**
desperate ['despərɪt] adj
verzweifelt; (situation)
hoffnungslos; **to be ~ for sth** etw
dringend brauchen, unbedingt
wollen; **desperation**

[dɪspə'reɪʃən] n Verzweiflung f

despicable [dɪ'spɪkəbl] adj verachtenswert; **despise** [dɪ'spaɪz] vt verachten

despite [dɪ'spaɪt] prep trotz +gen

dessert [dɪ'zɜːt] n Nachtisch m; **dessert spoon** n Dessertlöffel m

destination [destɪ'neɪʃən] n (of person) (Reise)ziel nt; (of goods) Bestimmungsort m

destiny ['destɪnɪ] n Schicksal nt

destroy [dɪ'strɔɪ] vt zerstören; (completely) vernichten; **destruction** [dɪ'strʌkʃən] n Zerstörung f; (complete) Vernichtung f; **destructive** [dɪ'strʌktɪv] adj zerstörerisch; (esp fig) destruktiv

detach [dɪ'tætʃ] vt abnehmen; (from form etc) abtrennen; (free) lösen (from von); **detachable** adj abnehmbar; (from form etc) abtrennbar; **detached** adj (attitude) distanziert, objektiv; ~ **house** Einzelhaus nt

detail ['diːteɪl, (US) dɪ'teɪl] n Einzelheit f, Detail nt; (further) ~**s from ...** Näheres erfahren Sie bei ...; **to go into ~** ins Detail gehen; **in ~** ausführlich; **detailed** adj detailliert, ausführlich

detain [dɪ'teɪn] vt aufhalten; (police) in Haft nehmen

detect [dɪ'tekt] vt entdecken; (notice) wahrnehmen; **detective** [dɪ'tektɪv] n Detektiv(in) m(f); **detective story** n Krimi m

detention [dɪ'tenʃən] n Haft f; (Sch) Nachsitzen nt

deter [dɪ'tɜː] vt abschrecken (from von)

detergent [dɪ'tɜːdʒənt] n Reinigungsmittel nt; (soap powder) Waschmittel nt

deteriorate [dɪ'tɪərɪəreɪt] vi sich verschlechtern

determination [dɪtɜːmɪ'neɪʃən] n Entschlossenheit f; **determine** [dɪ'tɜːmɪn] vt bestimmen; **determined** adj (fest) entschlossen

deterrent [dɪ'terənt] n Abschreckungsmittel nt

detest [dɪ'test] vt verabscheuen; **detestable** adj abscheulich

detour ['diːtʊə] n Umweg m; (of traffic) Umleitung f

detox ['diːtɒks] n Entzug m

deuce [djuːs] n (Tennis) Einstand m

devalue [diː'væljuː] vt abwerten

devastate ['devəsteɪt] vt verwüsten; **devastating** ['devəsteɪtɪŋ] adj verheerend

develop [dɪ'veləp] vt entwickeln; (illness) bekommen ▷ vi sich entwickeln; **developing country** n Entwicklungsland nt; **development** n Entwicklung f; (of land) Erschließung f

device [dɪ'vaɪs] n Vorrichtung f, Gerät nt

devil ['devl] n Teufel m; **devilish** adj teuflisch

devote [dɪ'vəʊt] vt widmen (to dat); **devoted** adj liebend; (servant etc) treu ergeben; **devotion** n Hingabe f

devour [dɪ'vaʊə] vt verschlingen

dew [djuː] n Tau m

diabetes [daɪə'biːtiːz] n Diabetes m, Zuckerkrankheit f; **diabetic** [daɪə'betɪk] adj zuckerkrank, für Diabetiker ▷ n Diabetiker(in) m(f)

diagnosis (diagnoses) [daɪəg'nəʊsɪs] (pl **diagnoses**) n Diagnose f

diagonal [daɪ'æɡənl] adj diagonal

diagram ['daɪəɡræm] n Diagramm nt

dial ['daɪəl] n Skala f; (of clock)

Zifferblatt nt ▷ vt (Tel) wählen;
dial code n (US) Vorwahl f
dialect ['daɪəlekt] n Dialekt m
dialling code n (Brit) Vorwahl f;
dialling tone n (Brit) Amtszeichen nt
dialogue, dialog (US) ['daɪəlɒg]
n Dialog m
dial tone n (US) Amtszeichen nt
dialysis [daɪ'æləsɪs] n (Med)
Dialyse f
diameter [daɪ'æmɪtə°] n
Durchmesser m
diamond ['daɪəmənd] n Diamant m; (Cards) Karo nt
diaper ['daɪpə°] n (US) Windel f
diarrhoea [daɪə'riːə] n Durchfall
m
diary ['daɪərɪ] n (Taschen)ka-
lender m; (account) Tagebuch nt
dice [daɪs] npl Würfel pl; **diced**
adj in Würfel geschnitten
dictate [dɪk'teɪt] vt diktieren;
dictation [dɪk'teɪʃən] n Diktat nt
dictator [dɪk'teɪtə°] n Dikta-
tor(in) m(f); **dictatorship**
[dɪk'teɪtəʃɪp] n Diktatur f
dictionary ['dɪkʃənrɪ] n
Wörterbuch nt
did [dɪd] pt of **do**
didn't ['dɪdnt] contr of **did not**
die [daɪ] vi sterben (of an +dat);
(plant, animal) eingehen; (engine)
absterben; **to be dying to do sth**
darauf brennen, etw zu tun; **I'm
dying for a drink** ich brauche
unbedingt was zu trinken; **die
away** vi schwächer werden;
(wind) sich legen; **die down** vi
nachlassen; **die out** vi aussterben
diesel ['diːzəl] n (fuel, car) Diesel
m; **~ engine** n Dieselmotor m
diet ['daɪət] n Kost f; (special food)
Diät f ▷ vi eine Diät machen
differ ['dɪfə°] vi (be different) sich
unterscheiden; (disagree) anderer
Meinung sein; **difference**

['dɪfrəns] n Unterschied m; **it
makes no ~ (to me)** es ist (mir)
egal; **it makes a big ~** es macht
viel aus; **different** adj andere(r, s);
(with pl) verschieden; **to be quite
~** ganz anders sein (from als); (two
people, things) völlig verschieden
sein; **a ~ person** ein anderer
Mensch; **differentiate**
[dɪfə'renʃɪeɪt] vt, vi
unterscheiden; **differently**
['dɪfrəntlɪ] adv anders (from als);
(from one another) unterschiedlich
difficult ['dɪfɪkəlt] adj schwierig; **I find it ~** es fällt mir schwer;
difficulty n Schwierigkeit f; **with
~** nur schwer; **to have ~ in doing
sth** etw nur mit Mühe machen
können
dig [dɪg] (dug, dug) vt, vi (hole)
graben; **dig in** vi (fam: to food)
reinhauen; **~I** greif(t) zu!; **dig up** vt
ausgraben
digest [daɪ'dʒest] vt (a. fig)
verdauen; **digestible** [dɪ'dʒestəbl]
adj verdaulich; **digestion**
[dɪ'dʒestʃən] n Verdauung f;
digestive [dɪ'dʒestɪv] adj: **~ biscuit** (Brit) Vollkornkeks m
digit ['dɪdʒɪt] n Ziffer f; **digital**
['dɪdʒɪtəl] adj digital; **~ computer**
n Digitalrechner m; **~ watch/clock**
n Digitaluhr f; **digital camera** n
Digitalkamera f; **digital
television, digital TV** n
Digitalfernsehen nt
dignified ['dɪgnɪfaɪd] adj
würdevoll; **dignity** ['dɪgnɪtɪ] n
Würde f
dilapidated [dɪ'læpɪdeɪtɪd] adj
baufällig
dilemma [daɪ'lemə] n Dilemma
nt
dill [dɪl] n Dill m
dilute [daɪ'luːt] vt verdünnen
dim [dɪm] adj (light) schwach;
(outline) undeutlich; (stupid)

schwer von Begriff ▷ vt
verdunkeln; (US Auto) abblenden;
~med headlights (US)
Abblendlicht nt

dime [daɪm] n (US)
Zehncentstück nt

dimension [daɪˈmenʃən] n
Dimension f; **~s** pl Maße pl

diminish [dɪˈmɪnɪʃ] vt
verringern ▷ vi sich verringern

dimple [ˈdɪmpl] n Grübchen nt

dine [daɪn] vi speisen; **dine out**
vi außer Haus essen; **diner** n Gast
m; (Rail) Speisewagen m; (US)
Speiselokal nt

dinghy [ˈdɪŋgɪ] n Ding(h)i nt;
(inflatable) Schlauchboot nt

dingy [ˈdɪndʒɪ] adj düster; (dirty)
schmuddelig

dining car [ˈdaɪnɪŋka:°] n
Speisewagen m; **dining room** n
Esszimmer nt; (in hotel)
Speiseraum m; **dining table** n
Esstisch m

dinkum [ˈdɪŋkəm] adj (Aust, NZ
fam): **(fair) ~** echt, wirklich;
he's a ~ Aussie er ist ein
waschechter Australier (fam)

dinner [ˈdɪnə°] n Abendessen nt;
(lunch) Mittagessen nt; (public)
Diner nt; **to be at ~** beim Essen
sein; **to have ~** zu Abend/Mittag
essen; **dinner jacket** n Smoking
m; **dinner party** n
Abendgesellschaft f (mit Essen);
dinnertime n Essenszeit f

dinosaur [ˈdaɪnəsɔ:°] n Dinosaurier m

dip [dɪp] vt tauchen (in in +akk);
to ~ (one's headlights (Brit Auto)
abblenden; **~ped headlights**
Abblendlicht nt ▷ n (in ground)
Bodensenke f; (sauce) Dip m

diploma [dɪˈpləʊmə] n Diplom nt

diplomat [ˈdɪpləmæt] n Diplo-
mat(in) m(f); **diplomatic**
[dɪpləˈmætɪk] adj diplomatisch

dipstick [ˈdɪpstɪk] n Ölmessstab
m

direct [daɪˈrekt] adj direkt;
(cause, consequence) unmittelbar;
~ debit (mandate)
Einzugsermächtigung f;
(transaction) Abbuchung f im
Lastschriftverfahren; **~ train**
durchgehender Zug ▷ vt (aim,
send) richten (at, to an +akk); (film)
die Regie führen bei; (traffic)
regeln; **direct current** n (Elec)
Gleichstrom m

direction [dɪˈrekʃən] n (course)
Richtung f; (Cine) Regie f; **in
the ~ of ...** in Richtung ...; **~s**
pl (to a place) Wegbeschreibung f

directly [dɪˈrektlɪ] adv direkt; (at
once) sofort

director [dɪˈrektə°] n Direk-
tor(in) m(f), Leiter(in) m(f); (of film)
Regisseur(in) m(f)

directory [dɪˈrektərɪ] n Adressbuch nt; (Tel) Telefonbuch nt;
~ enquiries o (US) **assistance** (Tel)
Auskunft f

dirt [dɜ:t] n Schmutz m, Dreck m;
dirt cheap adj spottbillig; **dirt
road** n unbefestigte Straße; **dirty**
adj schmutzig

disability [dɪsəˈbɪlɪtɪ] n
Behinderung f; **disabled**
[dɪsˈeɪbld] adj behindert,
Behinderten-; **~ people**
Behinderte

disadvantage [dɪsədˈvɑ:ntɪdʒ]
n Nachteil m; **at a ~** benachteiligt

disagree [dɪsəˈgri:] vi anderer
Meinung sein; (two people) sich
nicht einig sein; (two reports etc)
nicht übereinstimmen; **to ~ with
sb** mit jdm nicht übereinstimmen;
(food) jdm nicht bekommen;
disagreeable adj unangenehm;
(person) unsympathisch;
disagreement n Meinungsverschiedenheit f

disappear [dɪsə'pɪə°] vi verschwinden; **disappearance** n Verschwinden nt

disappoint [dɪsə'pɔɪnt] vt enttäuschen; **disappointing** adj enttäuschend; **disappointment** n Enttäuschung f

disapproval [dɪsə'pruːvl] n Missbilligung f; **disapprove** [dɪsə'pruːv] vi missbilligen (of akk)

disarm [dɪs'ɑːm] vt entwaffnen ▷ vi (Pol) abrüsten; **disarmament** n Abrüstung f; **disarming** adj (smile, look) gewinnend

disaster [dɪ'zɑːstə°] n Katastrophe f; **disastrous** [dɪ'zɑːstrəs] adj katastrophal

disbelief [dɪsbə'liːf] n Unglaübigkeit f

disc [dɪsk] n Scheibe f, CD f; see also **disk**; (Anat) Bandscheibe f; **disc brake** n Scheibenbremse f

discharge ['dɪstʃɑːdʒ] n (Med) Ausfluss m ▷ [dɪs'tʃɑːdʒ] vt (person) entlassen; (emit) ausstoßen; (Med) ausscheiden

discipline ['dɪsɪplɪn] n Disziplin f

disc jockey n ['dɪskdʒɒkɪ] n Diskjockey m

disclose [dɪs'kləʊz] vt bekannt geben; (secret) enthüllen

disco ['dɪskəʊ] (pl -s) n Disko f, Diskomusik f

discomfort [dɪs'kʌmfət] n (slight pain) leichte Schmerzen pl; (unease) Unbehagen nt

disconnect [dɪskə'nekt] vt (electricity, gas, phone) abstellen; (unplug) **to ~ the TV (from the mains)** den Stecker des Fernsehers herausziehen; (Tel) **I've been ~ed** das Gespräch ist unterbrochen worden

discontent [dɪskən'tent] n Unzufriedenheit f; **discontented** adj unzufrieden

discontinue [dɪskən'tɪnjuː] vt einstellen; (product) auslaufen lassen

discount ['dɪskaʊnt] n Rabatt m

discover [dɪs'kʌvə°] vt entdecken; **discovery** n Entdeckung f

discredit [dɪs'kredɪt] vt in Verruf bringen ▷ n Misskredit m

discreet [dɪs'kriːt] adj diskret

discrepancy [dɪs'krepənsɪ] n Unstimmigkeit f, Diskrepanz f

discriminate [dɪs'krɪmɪneɪt] vi unterscheiden; **to ~ against sb** jdn diskriminieren; **discrimination** [dɪskrɪmɪ'neɪʃən] n (different treatment) Diskriminierung f

discus ['dɪskəs] n Diskus m

discuss [dɪs'kʌs] vt diskutieren, besprechen; **discussion** [dɪs'kʌʃən] n Diskussion f

disease [dɪ'ziːz] n Krankheit f

disembark [dɪsɪm'bɑːk] vi von Bord gehen

disentangle [dɪsɪn'tæŋgl] vt entwirren

disgrace [dɪs'greɪs] n Schande f ▷ vt Schande machen +dat; (family etc) Schande bringen über +akk; (less strong) blamieren; **disgraceful** adj skandalös

disguise [dɪs'gaɪz] vt verkleiden; (voice) verstellen ▷ n Verkleidung f; **in ~** verkleidet

disgust [dɪs'gʌst] n Abscheu m; (physical) Ekel m ▷ vt anekeln, anwidern; **disgusting** adj widerlich; (physically) ekelhaft

dish [dɪʃ] n Schüssel f; (food) Gericht nt; **~es** pl (crockery) Geschirr nt; **to do/wash the ~es** abwaschen; **dishcloth** n (for washing) Spültuch nt; (for drying) Geschirrtuch nt

dishearten [dɪs'hɑːtən] vt entmutigen; **don't be ~ed** lass den Kopf nicht hängen!

dishonest [dɪs'ɒnɪst] adj unehrlich

dishonour [dɪs'ɒnə°] n Schande f

dish towel n (US) Geschirrtuch nt; **dish washer** n Geschirrspülmaschine f

dishy ['dɪʃɪ] adj (Brit fam) gut aussehen

disillusioned [dɪsɪ'luːʒənd] adj desillusioniert

disinfect [dɪsɪn'fekt] vt desinfizieren; **disinfectant** n Desinfektionsmittel nt

disintegrate [dɪs'ɪntɪgreɪt] vi zerfallen; (group) sich auflösen

disjointed [dɪs'dʒɔɪntɪd] adj unzusammenhängend

disk [dɪsk] n (Inform: floppy) Diskette f; **disk drive** n Diskettenlaufwerk nt; **diskette** [dɪ'sket] n Diskette f

dislike [dɪs'laɪk] n Abneigung f ▷ vt nicht mögen; **to ~ doing sth** etw ungern tun

dislocate ['dɪsləʊkeɪt] vt (Med) verrenken, ausrenken

dismal ['dɪzməl] adj trostlos

dismantle [dɪs'mæntl] vt auseinandernehmen; (machine) demontieren

dismay [dɪs'meɪ] n Bestürzung f; **dismayed** adj bestürzt

dismiss [dɪs'mɪs] vt (employee) entlassen; **dismissal** n Entlassung f

disobedience [dɪsə'biːdɪəns] n Ungehorsam m; **disobedient** adj ungehorsam; **disobey** [dɪsə'beɪ] vt nicht gehorchen +dat

disorder [dɪs'ɔːdə°] n (mess) Unordnung f, (riot) Aufruhr m; (Med) Störung f, Leiden nt

disorganized [dɪs'ɔːgənaɪzd] adj chaotisch

disparaging adj geringschätzig

dispatch [dɪ'spætʃ] vt abschicken, abfertigen

dispensable [dɪ'spensəbl] adj entbehrlich; **dispense** vt verteilen; **dispense with** vt verzichten auf +akk; **dispenser** n Automat m

disperse [dɪ'spɜːs] vi sich zerstreuen

display [dɪ'spleɪ] n (exhibition) Ausstellung f, Show f; (of goods) Auslage f; (Tech) Anzeige f, Display nt ▷ vt zeigen; (goods) ausstellen

disposable [dɪ'spəʊzəbl] adj (container, razor etc) Wegwerf-; **~ nappy** Wegwerfwindel f; **disposal** [dɪ'spəʊzəl] n Loswerden nt; (of waste) Beseitigung f; **to be at sb's ~** jdm zur Verfügung stehen; **to have at one's ~** verfügen über; **dispose of** vt loswerden; (goods etc) beseitigen

dispute [dɪ'spjuːt] n Streit m; (industrial) Auseinandersetzung f ▷ vt bestreiten

disqualification [dɪskwɒlɪfɪ'keɪʃən] n Disqualifikation f; **disqualify** [dɪs'kwɒlɪfaɪ] vt disqualifizieren

disregard [dɪsrɪ'gɑːd] vt nicht beachten

disreputable [dɪs'repjʊtəbl] adj verrufen

disrespect [dɪsrɪ'spekt] n Respektlosigkeit f

disrupt [dɪs'rʌpt] vt stören; (interrupt) unterbrechen; **disruption** [dɪs'rʌpʃən] n Störung f, (interruption) Unterbrechung f

dissatisfied [dɪs'sætɪsfaɪd] adj unzufrieden

dissent [dɪ'sent] n Widerspruch m

dissolve [dɪˈzɒlv] vt auflösen
▷ vi sich auflösen

dissuade [dɪˈsweɪd] vt (davon abbringen) **to ~ sb from doing sth** jdn davon abbringen, etw zu tun

distance [ˈdɪstəns] n Entfernung f; **in the/from a ~** in/aus der Ferne; **distant** adj (a. in time) fern; (relative etc) entfernt; (person) distanziert

distaste [dɪsˈteɪst] n Abneigung f (for gegen)

distil [dɪsˈtɪl] vt destillieren; **distillery** n Brennerei f

distinct [dɪsˈtɪŋkt] adj verschieden; (clear) klar, deutlich; **distinction** [dɪsˈtɪŋkʃən] n (difference) Unterschied m; (in exam etc) Auszeichnung f; **distinctive** adj unverkennbar; **distinctly** adv deutlich

distinguish [dɪsˈtɪŋgwɪʃ] vt unterscheiden (sth from sth etw von etw)

distort [dɪsˈtɔːt] vt verzerren; (truth) verdrehen

distract [dɪsˈtrækt] vt ablenken; **distraction** [dɪsˈtrækʃən] n Ablenkung f; (diversion) Zerstreuung f

distress [dɪsˈtrɛs] n (need, danger) Not f; (suffering) Leiden nt; (mental) Qual f; (worry) Kummer m ▷ vt mitnehmen, erschüttern; **distressed area** n Notstandsgebiet nt; **distress signal** n Notsignal nt

distribute [dɪsˈtrɪbjuːt] vt verteilen; (Comm: goods) vertreiben; **distribution** [dɪstrɪˈbjuːʃən] n Verteilung f; (Comm: of goods) Vertrieb m; **distributor** n (Auto) Verteiler m; (Comm) Händler(in) m(f)

district [ˈdɪstrɪkt] n Gegend f; (administrative) Bezirk m; **district attorney** n (US) Staatsanwalt m, Staatsanwältin f

distrust [dɪsˈtrʌst] vt misstrauen +dat ▷ n Misstrauen nt

disturb [dɪsˈtɜːb] vt stören; (worry) beunruhigen; **disturbance** n Störung f; **disturbing** adj beunruhigend

ditch [dɪtʃ] n Graben m ▷ vt (fam: person) den Laufpass geben +dat; (plan etc) verwerfen

ditto [ˈdɪtəʊ] n dito, ebenfalls

dive [daɪv] n (into water) Kopfsprung m; (Aviat) Sturzflug m; (fam) zwielichtiges Lokal n ▷ vi (under water) tauchen; **diver** n Taucher(in) m(f)

diverse [daɪˈvɜːs] adj verschieden; **diversion** [daɪˈvɜːʃən] n (of traffic) Umleitung f; (distraction) Ablenkung f; **divert** [daɪˈvɜːt] vt ablenken; (traffic) umleiten

divide [dɪˈvaɪd] vt teilen; (in several parts, between people) aufteilen ▷ vi sich teilen; **dividend** [ˈdɪvɪdend] n Dividende f

divine [dɪˈvaɪn] adj göttlich

diving [ˈdaɪvɪŋ] n (Sport-) tauchen nt; (jumping in) Springen nt; (Sport: from board) Kunstspringen nt; **diving board** n Sprungbrett nt; **diving goggles** npl Taucherbrille f; **diving mask** n Tauchmaske f

division [dɪˈvɪʒən] n Teilung f; (Math) Division f; (department) Abteilung f; (Sport) Liga f

divorce [dɪˈvɔːs] n Scheidung f ▷ vt sich scheiden lassen von; **divorced** adj geschieden; **to get ~** sich scheiden lassen; **divorcee** [dɪvɔːˈsiː] n Geschiedene(r) mf

DIY [diːaɪˈwaɪ] abbr =

do-it-yourself; DIY centre n
Baumarkt m

dizzy ['dɪzɪ] adj schwindlig

DJ [di:'dʒeɪ] abbr = **dinner jacket**
Smoking m ▷ abbr = **disc jockey**
Diskjockey m, DJ m

DNA abbr = **desoxyribonucleic
acid** DNS f

🔵 **KEYWORD**

do [du:] (pt **did**, pp **done**) n (inf)
(party etc) Fete f
▷ vb aux **1** (in negative constructions
and questions) **I don't understand**
ich verstehe nicht; **didn't you
know?** wusstest du das nicht?;
what do you think? was meinen
Sie?
2 (for emphasis, in polite phrases) **she
does seem rather tired** sie
scheint wirklich sehr müde zu
sein; **do sit down/help yourself**
setzen Sie sich doch hin/greifen
Sie doch zu
3 (used to avoid repeating vb) **she
swims better than I do** sie
schwimmt besser als ich; **she
lives in Glasgow — so do I** sie
wohnt in Glasgow — ich auch
4 (in tag questions) **you like him,
don't you?** du magst/Sie mögen
ihn doch, oder?
▷ vt **1** (carry out, perform etc) tun,
machen; **what are you doing
tonight?** was machst du/machen
Sie heute Abend?; **I've got
nothing to do** ich habe nichts zu
tun; **to do one's hair/nails** sich
die Haare/Nägel machen
2 (car etc) fahren
▷ vi **1** (act, behave) **do as I do** mach
es wie ich
2 (get on, fare) **he's doing
well/badly at school** er ist
gut/schlecht in der Schule; **how
do you do?** guten Tag

3 (be suitable) gehen; (be sufficient)
reichen; **to make do (with)**
auskommen mit

do away with vt (kill)
umbringen; (abolish: law etc)
abschaffen

do up vt (laces, dress, buttons)
zumachen; (renovate: room, house)
renovieren

do with vt (need) brauchen; (be
connected) zu tun haben mit

do without vt, vi auskommen
ohne

do up vt (fasten) zumachen;
(parcel) verschnüren; (renovate)
wiederherstellen

do with vt (need) brauchen; **I
could ~ a drink** ich könnte einen
Drink gebrauchen

do without vt auskommen
ohne; **I can ~ your comments**
auf deine Kommentare kann ich
verzichten

dock [dɒk] n Dock nt; (Jur)
Anklagebank f; **docker** n
Hafenarbeiter m; **dockyard** n
Werft f

doctor ['dɒktə°] n Arzt m, Ärztin f;
(in title, also academic) Doktor m

document ['dɒkjʊmənt] n
Dokument nt; **documentary**
[dɒkjʊ'mentərɪ] n Dokumentarfilm m; **documentation**
[dɒkjʊmen'teɪʃən] n Dokumen-
tation f

docusoap ['dɒkjʊsəʊp] n
Reality-Serie f, Dokusoap f

doddery ['dɒdərɪ] adj tatterig

dodgem ['dɒdʒəm] n Auto-
skooter m

dodgy ['dɒdʒɪ] adj nicht ganz in
Ordnung; (dishonest, unreliable)
zwielichtig; **he has a ~ stomach**
er hat sich den Magen verdorben

dog [dɒg] n Hund m; **dog food** n
Hundefutter nt; **doggie bum**

['dɒgɪ'bæg] n Tüte oder Box, in der Essensreste aus dem Restaurant mit nach Hause genommen werden können

do-it-yourself ['du:ɪtjə'self] n Heimwerken nt, Do-it-yourself nt ▷ adj Heimwerker-; **do-it-yourselfer** n Bastler(in) m(f), Heimwerker(in) m(f)

doll [dɒl] n Puppe f

dollar ['dɒlə*] n Dollar m

dolphin ['dɒlfɪn] n Delphin m

domain [də'meɪn] n Domäne f; (Inform) Domain f

dome [dəʊm] n Kuppel f

domestic [də'mestɪk] adj häuslich; (within country) Innen-, Binnen-; **domestic animal** n Haustier nt; **domesticated** [də'mestɪkeɪtɪd] adj (person) häuslich; (animal) zahm; **domestic flight** n Inlandsflug m

domicile ['dɒmɪsaɪl] n (ständiger) Wohnsitz

dominant ['dɒmɪnənt] adj dominierend, vorherrschend; **dominate** ['dɒmɪneɪt] vt beherrschen

dominoes ['dɒmɪnəʊz] npl Domino(spiel) nt

donate [dəʊ'neɪt] vt spenden; **donation** n Spende f

done [dʌn] pp of **do** ▷ adj (cooked) gar; **well ~** durchgebraten

doner (kebab) ['dɒnəkə'bæb] n Döner (Kebab) m

dongle ['dɒŋgəl] n (Inform) Dongle m

donkey ['dɒŋkɪ] n Esel m

donor ['dəʊnə] n Spender(in) m(f)

don't [dəʊnt] contr of **do not**

doom [du:m] n Schicksal nt; (downfall) Verderben nt

door [dɔ:*] n Tür f; **doorbell** n Türklingel f; **door handle** n Türklinke f; **doorknob** n Türknauf m; **doormat** n Fußabtreter m;

doorstep n Türstufe f; **right on our ~** direkt vor unserer Haustür

dope [dəʊp] (Sport) n (for athlete) Aufputschmittel nt ▷ vt dopen

dormitory ['dɔ:mɪtrɪ] n Schlafsaal m; (US) Studentenwohnheim nt

dosage ['dəʊsɪdʒ] n Dosierung f; **dose** [dəʊs] n Dosis f

dot [dɒt] n Punkt m; **on the ~** auf die Minute genau, pünktlich

dotcom ['dɒtkɒm] n: **~ (company)** Internetfirma f, Dotcom-Unternehmen nt

dote on [dəʊt ɒn] vt abgöttisch lieben

dotted line n punktierte Linie

double ['dʌbl] adj, adv doppelt; **~ the quantity** die zweifache Menge, doppelt so viel ▷ vt verdoppeln ▷ vi (person) Doppelgänger(in) m(f); (Cine) Double nt; **double bass** n Kontrabass m; **double bed** n Doppelbett nt; **double-click** n (Inform) doppelklicken; **double cream** n Sahne mit hohem Fettgehalt; **doubledecker** n Doppeldecker m; **double glazing** n Doppelverglasung f; **double-park** vi in zweiter Reihe parken; **double room** n Doppelzimmer nt; **doubles** npl (Sport: also match) Doppel nt

doubt [daʊt] n Zweifel m; **no ~** ohne Zweifel, zweifellos, wahrscheinlich; **to have one's ~s** Bedenken haben ▷ vt bezweifeln; (statement, word) anzweifeln; **I ~ it** das bezweifle ich; **doubtful** adj zweifelhaft, zweifelnd; **it is ~ whether ...** es ist fraglich, ob ...; **doubtless** adv ohne Zweifel, sicherlich

dough [dəʊ] n Teig m; **doughnut** n Donut m (rundes Hefegebäck)

dove [dʌv] n Taube f

down [daʊn] n Daunen pl; (fluff)
Flaum m ▷ adv unten; (motion)
nach unten; (towards speaker)
herunter; (away from speaker)
hinunter; **~ here/there** hier/dort
unten; (downstairs) **they came
~ for breakfast** sie kamen zum
Frühstück herunter; (southwards)
he came ~ from Scotland er kam
von Schottland herunter ▷ prep
(towards speaker) herunter; (away
from speaker) hinunter; **to drive
~ the hill/road** den Berg/die
Straße hinunter fahren; (along) **to
walk ~ the street** die Straße
entlang gehen; **he's ~ the pub**
(fam) er ist in der Kneipe ▷ vt
(fam: drink) runterkippen ▷ adj
niedergeschlagen, deprimiert

down-and-out adj
heruntergekommen ▷ n
Obdachlose(r) mf, Penner(in) m(f);
downcast adj niedergeschlagen;
downfall n Sturz m;
down-hearted adj entmutigt;
downhill adv bergab; **he's going
~** (fig) mit ihm geht es bergab

download [daʊnˈləʊd] vt
herunterladen; **downloadable** adj
(Inform) herunterladbar;
downmarket adj für den
Massenmarkt; **down payment** n

Anzahlung f; **downpour** n
Platzregen m; **downs** npl Hügel-
land nt; **downsize** vt verkleinern
▷ vi sich verkleinern

Down's syndrome
[ˈdaʊnzˈsɪndrəʊm] n (Med)
Downsyndrom nt

downstairs [daʊnˈsteəz] adv
unten; (motion) nach unten;
downstream adv flussabwärts;
downtime n Ausfallzeit f;
downtown adv (be, work etc) in
der Innenstadt; (go) in die
Innenstadt ▷ adj (US) in der
Innenstadt; **~ Chicago** die
Innenstadt von Chicago; **down
under** adv (fam: in/to Australia)
in/nach Australien; (in/to New
Zealand) in/nach Neuseeland;
downwards adv nach unten;
(movement, trend) Abwärts-

doze [dəʊz] vi dösen ▷ n
Nickerchen nt

dozen [ˈdʌzn] n Dutzend nt; **two
~ eggs** zwei Dutzend Eier; **~s of
times** x-mal

DP abbr = **data processing** DV f

drab [dræb] adj trist; (colour)
düster

draft [drɑːft] n (outline) Entwurf
m; (US Mil) Einberufung f

drag [dræg] vt schleppen ▷ n (fam)
to be a ~ (boring) stinklangweilig
sein; (laborious) ein ziemlicher
Schlauch sein; **drag on** vi sich in
die Länge ziehen

dragon [ˈdrægən] n Drache m;
dragonfly n Libelle f

drain [dreɪn] n Abfluss m ▷ vt
(water, oil) ablassen; (vegetables etc)
abgießen; (land) entwässern,
trockenlegen ▷ vi (of water)
abfließen; **drainpipe** n
Abflussrohr nt

drama [ˈdrɑːmə] n (a. fig) Drama
nt; **dramatic** [drəˈmætɪk] adj
dramatisch

drank [dræŋk] pt of **drink**

drapes [dreɪps] npl (US) Vorhänge pl

drastic ['dræstɪk] adj drastisch

draught [drɑːft] n (Luftzug m; **there's a ~** es zieht; **on ~** (beer) vom Fass; **draughts** nsing Damespiel nt; **draughty** adj zugig

draw [drɔː] (**drew, drawn**) vt (pull) ziehen; (crowd) anlocken, anziehen; (picture) zeichnen ▷ vi (Sport) unentschieden spielen ▷ vi (Sport) Unentschieden nt; (attraction) Attraktion f; (for lottery) Ziehung f; **draw out** vt herausziehen; (money) abheben; **draw up** vt (formulate) entwerfen; (list) erstellen ▷ vi (car) anhalten; **drawback** n Nachteil m; **drawbridge** n Zugbrücke f

drawer ['drɔː] n Schublade f

drawing ['drɔːɪŋ] n Zeichnung f; **drawing pin** n Reißzwecke f

drawn [drɔːn] pp of **draw**

dread [dred] n Furcht f (of vor +dat) ▷ vt sich fürchten vor +dat; **dreadful** adj furchtbar; **dreadlocks** npl Rastalocken pl

dream [driːm] (**dreamed** o **dreamt, dreamed** o **dreamt**) vt, vi träumen (about von) ▷ n Traum m; **dreamt** [dremt] pt, pp of **dream**

dreary ['drɪərɪ] adj (weather, place) trostlos; (book etc) langweilig

drench [drentʃ] vt durchnässen

dress [dres] n Kleidung f; (garment) Kleid nt ▷ vt anziehen; (Med: wound) verbinden; **to get ~ed** sich anziehen; **dress up** vi sich fein machen; (in costume) sich verkleiden (as als); **dress circle** n (Theat) erster Rang; **dresser** n Anrichte f; (US: dressing table) (Frisier)kommode f; **dressing** n (Gastr) Dressing nt, Soße f; (Med) Verband m; **dressing gown** n

Bademantel m; **dressing room** n (Theat) Künstlergarderobe f; **dressing table** n Frisierkommode f; **dress rehearsal** n (Theat) Generalprobe f

drew [druː] pt of **draw**

dried [draɪd] adj getrocknet; (milk, flowers) Trocken-; **~ fruit** Dörrobst nt; **drier** ['draɪə] n see **dryer**

drift [drɪft] vi treiben ▷ n (of snow) Verwehung f; (fig) Tendenz f; **if you get my ~** wenn du mich richtig verstehst/wenn Sie mich richtig verstehen

drill [drɪl] n Bohrer m ▷ vt, vi bohren

drink [drɪŋk] (**drank, drunk**) vt, vi trinken ▷ n Getränk nt; (alcoholic) Drink m; **drink-driving** n (Brit) Trunkenheit f am Steuer; **drinking water** n Trinkwasser nt

drip [drɪp] n Tropfen m ▷ vi tropfen; **drip-dry** adj bügelfrei; **dripping** n Bratenfett nt ▷ adj: **~ (wet)** tropfnass

drive [draɪv] (**drove, driven**) vt (car, person in car) fahren; (force: person, animal) treiben; (Tech) antreiben; **to ~ sb mad** jdn verrückt machen ▷ vi fahren ▷ n Fahrt f; (entrance) Einfahrt f, Auffahrt f; (Inform) Laufwerk nt; **to go for a ~** spazieren fahren; **drive away** vi, **drive off** vi wegfahren ▷ vt vertreiben

drive-in adj Drive-in-; **~ cinema** (US) Autokino nt

driven ['drɪvn] pp of **drive**

driver ['draɪvə] n Fahrer(in) m(f); (Inform) Treiber m; **~'s license** (US) Führerschein m; **~'s seat** Fahrersitz m; **driving** ['draɪvɪŋ] n (Auto)fahren nt; **he likes ~** er fährt gern Auto; **driving lesson** n

Fahrstunde f; **driving licence** n (Brit) Führerschein m; **driving school** n Fahrschule f; **driving seat** n (Brit) Fahrersitz m; **to be in the ~** alles im Griff haben; **driving test** n Fahrprüfung f

drizzle ['drɪzl] n Nieselregen m ▷ vi nieseln

drop [drɔp] n (of liquid) Tropfen m; (fall in price etc) Rückgang m ▷ vt (a. fig: give up) fallen lassen ▷ vi (fall) herunterfallen; (figures, temperature) sinken, zurückgehen; **drop by, drop in** vi vorbeikommen; **drop off** vi (to sleep) einnicken; **drop out** vi (withdraw) aussteigen; (university) das Studium abbrechen; **dropout** n Aussteiger(in) m(f)

drought [draut] n Dürre f

drove [drəuv] pt of **drive**

drown [draun] vi ertrinken ▷ vt ertränken

drowsy ['drauzɪ] adj schläfrig

drug [drʌg] n (Med) Medikament nt, Arznei f; (addictive) Droge f; (narcotic) Rauschgift nt; **to be on ~s** drogensüchtig sein ▷ vt (mit Medikamenten) betäuben; **drug addict** n Rauschgiftsüchtige(r) mf; **drug dealer** n Drogenhändler(in) m(f); **druggist** n (US) Drogist(in) m(f); **drugstore** n (US) Drogerie f

drum [drʌm] n Trommel f; **~s** pl Schlagzeug nt; **drummer** n Schlagzeuger(in) m(f)

drunk [drʌŋk] pp of **drink** ▷ adj betrunken; **to get ~** sich betrinken ▷ n Betrunkene(r) mf; (alcoholic) Trinker(in) m(f); **drunk-driving** n (US) Trunkenheit f am Steuer; **drunken** adj betrunken, besoffen

dry [draɪ] adj trocken ▷ vt trocknen; (dishes, oneself, one's hands etc) abtrocknen ▷ vi trocknen, trocken werden; **dry out**

vi trocknen; **dry up** vi austrocknen; **dry-clean** vt chemisch reinigen; **dry-cleaning** n chemische Reinigung; **dryer** n Trockner m; (for hair) Föhn m; (over head) Trockenhaube f

DTP abbr = **desktop publishing** DTP nt

dual ['djuəl] adj doppelt; **~ carriageway** (Brit) zweispurige Schnellstraße f; **~ nationality** doppelte Staatsangehörigkeit

dubbed [dʌbd] adj (film) synchronisiert

dubious ['djuːbɪəs] adj zweifelhaft

duchess ['dʌtʃəs] n Herzogin f

duck [dʌk] n Ente f

dude [duːd] n (US fam) Typ m; **a cool ~** ein cooler Typ

due [djuː] adj (time) fällig; (fitting) angemessen; **in ~ course** zu gegebener Zeit; **~ to** infolge +gen, wegen +gen ▷ adv: **~ south/north** etc direkt nach Norden/Süden etc

dug [dʌg] pt, pp of **dig**

duke [djuːk] n Herzog m

dull [dʌl] adj (colour, light, weather) trübe; (boring) langweilig

duly ['djuːlɪ] adv ordnungsgemäß; (as expected) wie erwartet

dumb [dʌm] adj (pej) stumm; (pej: stupid) doof, blöde

dumb-bell ['dʌmbel] n Hantel f

dummy ['dʌmɪ] n (sham) Attrappe f; (in shop) Schaufensterpuppe f; (Brit: teat) Schnuller m; (fam: person) Dummkopf m ▷ adj unecht, Schein-; **~ run** Testlauf m

dump [dʌmp] n Abfallhaufen m; (fam: place) Kaff nt ▷ vt (lit, fig) abladen; (fam) **he ~ed her** er hat mir ihr Schluss gemacht

dumpling ['dʌmplɪŋ] n Kloß m, Knödel m

dune [djuːn] n Düne f

dung [dʌŋ] n (manure) Mist m
dungarees [dʌŋɡə'ri:z] npl
Latzhose f
dungeon ['dʌndʒən] n Kerker m
duplex ['dju:pleks] n
zweistöckige Wohnung; (US)
Doppelhaushälfte f
duplicate ['dju:plɪkɪt] n Dup-
likat nt ▷ ['dju:plɪkeɪt] vt (make
copies of) kopieren; (repeat)
wiederholen
durable ['djuərəbl] adj haltbar;
duration [djuə'reɪʃən] n Dauer f
during ['djuərɪŋ] prep (time)
während +gen
dusk [dʌsk] n Abenddämmerung f
dust [dʌst] n Staub m ▷ vt
abstauben; **dustbin** n (Brit)
Mülleimer m; **dustcart** n (Brit)
Müllwagen m; **duster** n
Staubtuch nt; **dust jacket** n
Schutzumschlag m; **dustman** n
(Brit) Müllmann m; **dustpan** n
Kehrschaufel f; **dusty** adj staubig
Dutch [dʌtʃ] adj holländisch ▷ n
(language) Holländisch nt; **to
speak/talk double ~** (fam)
Quatsch reden; **the ~** pl die
Holländer; **Dutchman** (pl **-men**)
n Holländer m; **Dutchwoman** (pl
-women) n Holländerin f
duty ['dju:tɪ] n Pflicht f; (task)
Aufgabe f; (tax) Zoll m; **on/off ~** im
Dienst/nicht im Dienst; **to be on
~** Dienst haben; **duty-free** adj
zollfrei; **~ shop** Dutyfreeshop m
duvet ['du:veɪ] n Federbett nt
DVD n abbr = **digital versatile
disk** DVD f; **DVD player** n
DVD-Player m; **DVD recorder** n
DVD-Rekorder m
dwelling ['dwelɪŋ] n Wohnung f
dwindle ['dwɪndl] vi schwinden
dye [daɪ] n Farbstoff m ▷ vt
färben
dynamic [daɪ'næmɪk] adj
dynamisch

dynamo ['daɪnəməʊ] n Dynamo m
dyslexia [dɪs'leksɪə] n Legasthenie
f; **dyslexic** adj legasthenisch; **to
be ~** Legastheniker(in) sein

e

E [iː] abbr = **east** (geo) O; abbr = **ecstasy** (drug) Ecstasy nt

E111 form n ~ Auslandskrankenschein m

each [iːtʃ] adj jeder/jede/jedes ▷ pron jeder/jede/jedes; **I'll have one of ~** ich nehme von jedem eins; **they ~ have a car** jeder von ihnen hat ein Auto; **~ other** einander, sich; **for/against ~ other** füreinander/gegeneinander ▷ adv je; **they cost 10 euros** ~ sie kosten je 10 Euro, sie kosten 10 Euro das Stück

eager [ˈiːɡəʳ] adj eifrig; **to be ~ to do sth** darauf brennen, etw zu tun

eagle [ˈiːɡl] n Adler m

ear [ɪəʳ] n Ohr nt; **earache** n Ohrenschmerzen pl; **eardrum** n Trommelfell nt

earl [ɜːl] n Graf m

early [ˈɜːlɪ] adj, adv früh; **to be 10 minutes** ~ 10 Minuten zu früh kommen; **at the earliest** frühestens; **in ~ June/2008** Anfang Juni/2008; **~ retirement** vorzeitiger Ruhestand; **~ warning system** Frühwarnsystem nt

earn [ɜːn] vt verdienen

earnest [ˈɜːnɪst] adj ernst; **in ~** im Ernst

earnings [ˈɜːnɪŋz] npl Verdienst m, Einkommen nt

earplug n Ohrenstöpsel m, Ohropax® nt; **earring** n Ohrring m

earth [ɜːθ] n Erde f; **what on ~ ...?** was in aller Welt ...? ▷ vt erden; **earthenware** n Tonwaren pl; **earthquake** n Erdbeben nt

earwig [ˈɪəwɪɡ] n Ohrwurm m

ease [iːz] vt (pain) lindern; (burden) erleichtern ▷ n (easiness) Leichtigkeit f; **to feel at ~** sich wohlfühlen; **to feel ill at ~** sich nicht wohlfühlen; **easily** [ˈiːzɪlɪ] adv leicht; **he is ~ the best** er ist mit Abstand die Beste

east [iːst] n Osten m; **to the ~ of** östlich von ▷ adv (go, face) nach Osten ▷ adj Ost-; **~ wind** Ostwind m; **eastbound** adj (in) Richtung Osten

Easter [ˈiːstəʳ] n Ostern nt; **at ~** zu Ostern; **Easter egg** n Osterei nt; **Easter Sunday** n Ostersonntag m

eastern [ˈiːstən] adj Ost-, östlich; **Eastern Europe** Osteuropa nt; **East Germany** n Ostdeutschland nt; **former ~ die** ehemalige DDR, die neuen Bundesländer; **eastwards** [ˈiːstwədz] adv nach Osten

easy [ˈiːzɪ] adj leicht; (task, solution) einfach; (life) bequem; (manner) ungezwungen; **easy-going** adj gelassen

eat [iːt] (ate, eaten) vt essen; (animal) fressen; **eat out** vi zum Essen ausgehen; **eat up** vt

aufessen; (animal) auffressen
eaten ['iːtn] pp of **eat**
eavesdrop ['iːvzdrɒp] vi (heimlich) lauschen; **to ~ on sb** jdn belauschen
e-book ['iːbʊk] n E-book nt
eccentric [ɪk'sentrɪk] adj exzentrisch
echo ['ekəʊ] (pl **-es**) n Echo nt
▷ vi widerhallen
e-cigarette ['iːsɪgəret] n E-Zigarette f
ecological [iːkə'lɒdʒɪkl] adj ökologisch; **~ disaster** Umweltkatastrophe f; **ecology** [i'kɒlədʒɪ] n Ökologie f
economic [iːkə'nɒmɪk] adj wirtschaftlich, Wirtschafts-; **~ aid** Wirtschaftshilfe f; **economical** adj wirtschaftlich; (person) sparsam; **economics** nsing o pl Wirtschaftswissenschaft f; **economist** [ɪ'kɒnəmɪst] n Wirtschaftswissenschaftler(in) m(f); **economize** [ɪ'kɒnəmaɪz] vi sparen (on an +dat); **economy** [ɪ'kɒnəmɪ] n (of state) Wirtschaft f; (thrift) Sparsamkeit f; **economy class** n (Aviat) Economyclass f
ecstasy ['ekstəsɪ] n Ekstase f; (drug) Ecstasy f
eczema ['eksɪmə] n Ekzem nt
edge [edʒ] n Rand m; (of knife) Schneide f; **on ~** nervös; **edgy** ['edʒɪ] adj nervös
edible ['edɪbl] adj essbar
Edinburgh ['edɪnbərə] n Edinburg nt
edit ['edɪt] vt (series, newspaper etc) herausgeben; (text) redigieren; (film) schneiden; (Inform) editieren; **edition** [ɪ'dɪʃən] n Ausgabe f; **editor** n Redakteur(in) m(f); (of series etc) Herausgeber(in) m(f); **editorial** [edɪ'tɔːrɪəl] adj Redaktions- ▷ n Leitartikel m
educate ['edjʊkeɪt] vt (child)

erziehen; (at school, university) ausbilden; (public) aufklären; **educated** adj gebildet; **education** [edjʊ'keɪʃən] n Erziehung f; (studies, training) Ausbildung f; (subject of study) Pädagogik f; (system) Schulwesen nt; (knowledge) Bildung f; **educational** adj pädagogisch; (instructive) lehrreich
eel [iːl] n Aal m
eerie ['ɪərɪ] adj unheimlich
effect [ɪ'fekt] n Wirkung f (on auf +akk); **to come into ~** in Kraft treten; **effective** adj wirksam, effektiv
effeminate [ɪ'femɪnət] adj (of man) tuntig (pej)
efficiency [ɪ'fɪʃənsɪ] n Leistungsfähigkeit f; (of method) Wirksamkeit f; **efficient** adj (Tech) leistungsfähig; (method) wirksam, effizient
effort ['efət] n Anstrengung f; (attempt) Versuch m; **to make an ~** sich anstrengen; **effortless** adj mühelos
e.g. abbr = **exempli gratia (for example)** z. B.
egg [eg] n Ei nt; **eggcup** n Eierbecher m; **eggplant** n (US) Aubergine f; **eggshell** n Eierschale f
ego ['iːgəʊ] (pl **-s**) n Ich nt; (self-esteem) Selbstbewusstsein nt; **ego(t)ist** ['egəʊ(t)ɪst] n Egozentriker(in) m(f)
Egypt ['iːdʒɪpt] n Ägypten nt; **Egyptian** [ɪ'dʒɪpʃən] adj ägyptisch ▷ n Ägypter(in) m(f)
eiderdown ['aɪdədaʊn] n Daunendecke f
eight [eɪt] num acht; **at the age of ~** im Alter von acht Jahren; **it's ~ (o'clock)** es ist acht Uhr ▷ n (a. bus etc) Acht f; (boat) Achter m; **eighteen** [eɪ'tiːn] num also achtzehn ▷ n Achtzehn f; see also **eight**

eighteenth adj achtzehnte(r, s); see also **eighth**; **eighth** [eɪtθ] adj achte(r, s); **the ~ of June** der achte Juni ▷ n (fraction) Achtel nt; **an ~ of a litre** ein Achtelliter; **eightieth** [ˈeɪtɪəθ] adj achtzigste(r, s); see also **eighth**; **eighty** [ˈeɪtɪ] num achtzig ▷ n Achtzig f; see also **eight**

Eire [ˈeərə] die Republik Irland

either [ˈaɪðə°] conj: **~ ... or** entweder ... oder ▷ pron: **~ of the two** eine(r, s) von beiden ▷ adj: **on ~ side** auf beiden Seiten ▷ adv: **I won't go ~** ich gehe auch nicht

eject [ɪˈdʒekt] vt ausstoßen; (person) vertreiben

elaborate [ɪˈlæbərət] adj (complex) kompliziert; (plan) ausgeklügelt; (decoration) kunstvoll ▷ vi [ɪˈlæbəreɪt] **could you ~ on that?** könntest du/könnten Sie mehr darüber sagen?

elastic [ɪˈlæstɪk] adj elastisch; **~ band** Gummiband nt

elbow [ˈelbəʊ] n Ellbogen m; **to give sb the ~** (fam) jdm den Laufpass geben

elder [ˈeldə°] adj (of two) älter ▷ n Ältere(r) mf; (Bot) Holunder m; **elderly** adj ältere(r, s); **~ people** ältere Leute; **eldest** [ˈeldɪst] adj älteste(r, s)

elect [ɪˈlekt] vt wählen; **he was ~ed chairman** er wurde zum Vorsitzenden gewählt; **election** [ɪˈlekʃən] n Wahl f; **election campaign** n Wahlkampf m; **electioneering** [ɪlekʃəˈnɪərɪŋ] n Wahlpropaganda f; **electorate** [ɪˈlektərɪt] n Wähler pl

electric [ɪˈlektrɪk] adj elektrisch; (car, motor, razor etc) Elektro-; **~ blanket** Heizdecke f; **~ cooker** Elektroherd m; **~ current** elektrischer Strom; **~ shock**

Stromschlag m; **electrical** adj elektrisch; **~ goods/appliances** Elektrogeräte; **electrician** [ɪlekˈtrɪʃən] n Elektriker(in) m(f); **electricity** [ɪlekˈtrɪsɪtɪ] n Elektrizität f; **electrocute** [ɪˈlektrəʊkjuːt] vt durch einen Stromschlag töten; **electronic** [ɪlekˈtrɒnɪk] adj elektronisch

elegance [ˈelɪgəns] n Eleganz f; **elegant** adj elegant

element [ˈelɪmənt] n Element nt; **an ~ of truth** ein Körnchen Wahrheit; **elementary** [elɪˈmentərɪ] adj einfach; (basic) grundlegend; **~ stage** Anfangsstadium nt; **~ school** (US) Grundschule f; **~ maths/French** Grundkenntnisse in Mathematik/Französisch

elephant [ˈelɪfənt] n Elefant m

elevator [ˈelɪveɪtə°] n (US) Fahrstuhl m

eleven [ɪˈlevn] num elf ▷ n (team, bus etc) Elf f see **eight**; **eleventh** [ɪˈlevnθ] adj elfte(r, s) ▷ n (fraction) Elftel nt see **eighth**

eligible [ˈelɪdʒəbl] adj infrage kommend; (for grant etc) berechtigt; **~ for a pension/competition** pensions-/teilnahmeberechtigt; **~ bachelor** begehrter Junggeselle

eliminate [ɪˈlɪmɪneɪt] vt ausschließen (from aus), ausschalten; (problem etc) beseitigen; **elimination** [ɪlɪmɪˈneɪʃən] n Ausschluss m (from aus); (of problem etc) Beseitigung f

elm [elm] n Ulme f

elope [ɪˈləʊp] vi durchbrennen (with sb mit jdm)

eloquent [ˈeləkwənt] adj redegewandt

else [els] adv: **anybody/anything ~** (in addition) sonst (noch) jemand/etwas; (other) ein anderer/etwas anderes; **somebody ~** jemand anders; **everyone ~** alle anderen; **or ~** sonst; **elsewhere** adv anderswo, woanders; (direction) woandershin

ELT abbr = **English Language Teaching**

email ['i:meɪl] vi, vt mailen (sth to sb jdm etw) ▷ n E-Mail f; **email address** n E-Mail-Adresse f

emancipated [ɪ'mænsɪpeɪtɪd] adj emanzipiert

embankment [ɪm'bæŋkmənt] n Böschung f; (for railway) Bahndamm m

embargo [ɪm'bɑːgəʊ] (pl **-es**) n Embargo nt

embark [ɪm'bɑːk] vi an Bord gehen

embarrass [ɪm'bærəs] vt in Verlegenheit bringen; **embarrassed** adj verlegen; **embarrassing** adj peinlich

embassy ['embəsɪ] n Botschaft f

embrace [ɪm'breɪs] vt umarmen ▷ n Umarmung f

embroider [ɪm'brɔɪdə°] vt besticken; **embroidery** n Stickerei f

embryo ['embrɪəʊ] (pl **-s**) n Embryo m

emerald ['emərəld] n Smaragd m

emerge [ɪ'mɜːdʒ] vi auftauchen; **it ~d that ...** es stellte sich heraus, dass ...

emergency [ɪ'mɜːdʒənsɪ] n Notfall m ▷ adj Not-; **~ exit** Notausgang m; **~ landing** Notlandung f; **~ room** (US) Unfallstation f; **~ service** Notdienst m; **~ stop** Vollbremsung f

emigrate ['emɪgreɪt] vi auswandern

emit [ɪ'mɪt] vt ausstoßen; (heat) abgeben

emoticon [ɪ'məʊtɪkən] n (Inform) Emoticon nt

emotion [ɪ'məʊʃən] n Emotion f, Gefühl nt; **emotional** adj (person) emotional; (experience, moment, scene) ergreifend

emperor ['empərə°] n Kaiser m

emphasis ['emfəsɪs] n Betonung f; **emphasize** ['emfəsaɪz] vt betonen; **emphatic**, **emphatically** [ɪm'fætɪk, -lɪ] adj, adv nachdrücklich

empire ['empaɪə°] n Reich nt

employ [ɪm'plɔɪ] vt beschäftigen; (hire) anstellen; (use) anwenden; **employee** [emplɔɪ'iː] n Angestellte(r) mf; **employer** n Arbeitgeber(in) m(f); **employment** n Beschäftigung f; (position) Stellung f; **employment agency** n Stellenvermittlung f

empress ['emprɪs] n Kaiserin f

empty ['emptɪ] adj leer ▷ vt (contents) leeren; (container) ausleeren

enable [ɪ'neɪbl] vt: **to ~ sb to do sth** es jdm ermöglichen, etw zu tun

enamel [ɪ'næməl] n Email nt; (of teeth) Zahnschmelz m

enchanting [ɪn'tʃɑːntɪŋ] adj bezaubernd

enclose [ɪn'kləʊz] vt einschließen; (in letter) beilegen (in, with dat); **enclosure** [ɪn'kləʊʒə°] n (for animals) Gehege nt; (in letter) Anlage f

encore ['ɒŋkɔː°] n Zugabe f

encounter [ɪn'kaʊntə°] n Begegnung f ▷ vt (person) begegnen +dat; (difficulties) stoßen auf +akk

encourage [ɪn'kʌrɪdʒ] vt ermutigen; **encouragement** n Ermutigung f

encyclopaedia
[ensaɪkləʊ'piːdɪə] n Lexikon nt, Enzyklopädie f

end [end] n Ende nt; (of film, play etc) Schluss m; (purpose) Zweck m; **at the ~ of May** Ende Mai; **in the ~** schließlich; **to come to an ~** zu Ende gehen ▷ vt beenden ▷ vi enden; **end up** vi enden

endanger [ɪn'deɪndʒə°] vt gefährden; **~ed species** vom Aussterben bedrohte Art

endeavour [ɪn'devə°] n Bemühung f ▷ vt sich bemühen (to do sth etw zu tun)

ending [endɪŋ] n (of book) Ausgang m; (last part) Schluss m; (of word) Endung f; **endless** ['endlɪs] adj endlos; (possibilities) unendlich

endurance [ɪn'djʊərəns] n Ausdauer f; **endure** [ɪn'djʊə°] vt ertragen

enemy ['enɪmɪ] n Feind(in) m(f) ▷ adj feindlich

energetic [enə'dʒetɪk] adj energiegeladen; (active) aktiv; **energy** ['enədʒɪ] n Energie f

enforce [ɪn'fɔːs] vt durchsetzen; (obedience) erzwingen

engage [ɪn'geɪdʒ] vt (employ) einstellen; (singer, performer) engagieren; **engaged** adj verlobt; (toilet, telephone line) besetzt; **to get ~** sich verloben (to mit); **engaged tone** n (Brit Tel) Belegtzeichen nt; **engagement** n (to marry) Verlobung f; **~ ring** Verlobungsring m; **engaging** adj gewinnend

engine [endʒɪn] n (Auto) Motor m; (Rail) Lokomotive f; **~ failure** (Auto) Motorschaden m; **~ trouble** (Auto) Defekt m am Motor; **engineer** [endʒɪ'nɪə°] n Ingenieur(in) m(f); (US Rail) Lokomotivführer(in) m(f);

engineering [endʒɪ'nɪərɪŋ] n Technik f; (mechanical ~) Maschinenbau m; (subject) Ingenieurwesen nt; **engine immobilizer** n (Auto) Wegfahrsperre f

England ['ɪŋglənd] n England nt; **English** adj englisch; **he's ~** er ist Engländer; **the ~ Channel** der Ärmelkanal ▷ n (language) Englisch nt; **in ~** auf Englisch; **to translate into ~** ins Englische übersetzen; (people) **the ~** pl die Engländer; **Englishman** (pl -**men**) n Engländer m; **Englishwoman** (pl -**women**) n Engländerin f

engrave [ɪn'greɪv] vt eingravieren; **engraving** n Stich m

engrossed [ɪn'grəʊst] adj vertieft (in sth in etw akk)

enigma [ɪ'nɪgmə] n Rätsel nt

enjoy [ɪn'dʒɔɪ] vt genießen; **~ reading** ich lese gern; **he ~s teasing her** es macht ihm Spaß, sie aufzuziehen; **did you ~ the film?** hat dir der Film gefallen?; **enjoyable** adj angenehm; (entertaining) unterhaltsam; **enjoyment** n Vergnügen nt; (stronger) Freude f (of an +dat)

enlarge [ɪn'lɑːdʒ] vt vergrößern; (expand) erweitern; **enlargement** n Vergrößerung f

enormous, enormously [ɪ'nɔːməs, -lɪ] adj, adv riesig, ungeheuer

enough [ɪ'nʌf] adj genug; **that's ~ das reicht!**; (stop it) Schluss damit!; **I've had ~** das hat mir gereicht; (to eat) ich bin satt ▷ adv genug, genügend

enquire [ɪn'kwaɪə°] vi sich erkundigen (about nach); **enquiry** [ɪn'kwaɪərɪ] n (question) Anfrage f; (for information) Erkundigung f (about über +akk); (investigation)

Untersuchung f; **"Enquiries"** „Auskunft"

enrol [ɪnˈrəʊl] vi sich einschreiben; (for course, school) sich anmelden; **enrolment** n Einschreibung f, Anmeldung f

en suite [ɒnˈswiːt] adj, n: **room with ~ (bathroom)** Zimmer nt mit eigenem Bad

ensure [ɪnˈʃʊə] vt sicherstellen

enter [ˈentə°] vt eintreten in +akk, betreten; (drive into) einfahren in +akk; (country) einreisen in +akk; (in list) eintragen; (Inform) eingeben; (race, contest) teilnehmen an +dat ▷ vi (towards speaker) hereinkommen; (away from speaker) hineingehen

enterprise [ˈentəpraɪz] n (Comm) Unternehmen nt

entertain [entəˈteɪn] vt (guest) bewirten; (amuse) unterhalten; **entertaining** adj unterhaltsam; **entertainment** n (amusement) Unterhaltung f

enthusiasm [ɪnˈθjuːzɪæzəm] n Begeisterung f; **enthusiastic** [ɪnθjuːzɪˈæstɪk] adj begeistert (about von)

entice [ɪnˈtaɪs] vt locken; (lead astray) verleiten

entire, entirely [ɪnˈtaɪə°, -lɪ] adj, adv ganz

entitle [ɪnˈtaɪtl] vt (qualify) berechtigen (to zu); (name) betiteln

entrance [ˈentrəns] n Eingang m; (for vehicles) Einfahrt f; (entering) Eintritt m; (Theat) Auftritt m; **entrance exam** n Aufnahmeprüfung f; **entrance fee** n Eintrittsgeld nt

entrust [ɪnˈtrʌst] vt: **to ~ sb with sth** jdm etw anvertrauen

entry [ˈentrɪ] n (way in) Eingang m; (entering) Eintritt m; (in vehicle) Einfahrt f; (into country) Einreise f;

(admission) Zutritt m; (in diary, accounts) Eintrag m; **"no ~"** „Eintritt verboten"; (for vehicles) „Einfahrt verboten"; **entry phone** n Türsprechanlage f

E-number n (food additive) E-Nummer f

envelope [ˈenvələʊp] n (Brief)umschlag m

enviable [ˈenvɪəbl] adj beneidenswert; **envious** [ˈenvɪəs] adj neidisch

environment [ɪnˈvaɪərənmənt] n Umgebung f; (ecology) Umwelt f; **environmental** [ɪnvaɪərənˈmentəl] adj Umwelt-; **~ pollution** Umweltverschmutzung f; **environmentalist** n Umweltschützer(in) m(f)

envy [ˈenvɪ] n Neid m (of auf +akk) ▷ vt beneiden (sb sth jdn um etw)

epic [ˈepɪk] n Epos nt; (film) Monumentalfilm m

epidemic [epɪˈdemɪk] n Epidemie f

epilepsy [ˈepɪlepsɪ] n Epilepsie f; **epileptic** [epɪˈleptɪk] adj epileptisch

episode [ˈepɪsəʊd] n Episode f; (TV) Folge f

epoch [ˈiːpɒk] n Zeitalter nt, Epoche f

equal [ˈiːkwl] adj gleich (to +dat) ▷ n Gleichgestellte(r) mf ▷ vt gleichen; (match) gleichkommen +dat; **two times two ~s four** zwei mal zwei ist gleich vier; **equality** [ɪˈkwɒlɪtɪ] n Gleichheit f; (equal rights) Gleichberechtigung f; **equalize** vi (Sport) ausgleichen; **equalizer** n (Sport) Ausgleichstreffer m; **equally** adv gleich; (on the other hand) andererseits; **equation** [ɪˈkweɪʒən] n (Math) Gleichung f

equator [ɪˈkweɪtə°] n Äquator m

equilibrium [iːkwɪˈlɪbriəm] *n* Gleichgewicht *nt*

equip [ɪˈkwɪp] *vt* ausrüsten; (*kitchen*) ausstatten; **equipment** *n* Ausrüstung *f*; (*for kitchen*) Ausstattung *f*; **electrical** ~ Elektrogeräte *pl*

equivalent [ɪˈkwɪvələnt] *adj* gleichwertig (*to dat*); (*corresponding*) entsprechend (*to dat*) ▷ *n* Äquivalent *nt*; (*amount*) gleiche Menge; (*in money*) Gegenwert *m*

era [ˈɪərə] *n* Ära *f*, Zeitalter *nt*

erase [ɪˈreɪz] *vt* ausradieren; (*tape, disk*) löschen; **eraser** *n* Radiergummi *m*

e-reader [ˈiːriːdər] *n* E-Book-Lesegerät *nt*

erect [ɪˈrekt] *adj* aufrecht ▷ *vt* (*building, monument*) errichten; (*tent*) aufstellen; **erection** *n* Errichtung *f*; (*Anat*) Erektion *f*

erode [ɪˈrəʊd] *vt* zerfressen; (*land*) auswaschen; (*rights, power*) aushöhlen; **erosion** [ɪˈrəʊʒən] *n* Erosion *f*

erotic [ɪˈrɒtɪk] *adj* erotisch

errand [ˈerənd] *n* Besorgung *f*

erratic [ɪˈrætɪk] *adj* (*behaviour*) unberechenbar; (*bus link etc*) unregelmäßig; (*performance*) unbeständig

error [ˈerə] *n* Fehler *m*; **in** ~ irrtümlicherweise; **error message** *n* (*Inform*) Fehlermeldung *f*

erupt [ɪˈrʌpt] *vi* ausbrechen

escalator [ˈeskəleɪtə] *n* Rolltreppe *f*

escalope [ˈeskələp] *n* Schnitzel *nt*

escape [ɪˈskeɪp] *n* Flucht *f*; (*from prison etc*) Ausbruch *m*; **to have a narrow** ~ gerade noch davonkommen; **there's no** ~ (*fig*) es gibt keinen Ausweg ▷ *vt*

(*pursuers*) entkommen +*dat*; (*punishment etc*) entgehen +*dat* ▷ *vi* (*from pursuers*) entkommen (*from dat*); (*from prison etc*) ausbrechen (*from dat*); (*leak: gas*) ausströmen; (*water*) auslaufen

escort [ˈeskɔːt] *n* (*companion*) Begleiter(in) *m(f)*; (*guard*) Eskorte *f* ▷ *vt* [ɪˈskɔːt] (*lady*) begleiten

especially [ɪˈspeʃəlɪ] *adv* besonders

espionage [ˈespɪənɑːʒ] *n* Spionage *f*

Esquire [ɪˈskwaɪə] *n* (*Brit: in address*): **J. Brown, Esq** Herrn J. Brown

essay [ˈeseɪ] *n* Aufsatz *m*; (*literary*) Essay *m*

essential [ɪˈsenʃəl] *adj* (*necessary*) unentbehrlich, unverzichtbar; (*basic*) wesentlich ▷ *n* **the** ~**s** *pl* das Wesentliche; **essentially** *adv* im Wesentlichen

establish [ɪˈstæblɪʃ] *vt* (*set up*) gründen; (*introduce*) einführen; (*relations*) aufnehmen; (*prove*) nachweisen; **to** ~ **that ...** feststellen, dass ...; **establishment** *n* Institution *f*; (*business*) Unternehmen *nt*

estate [ɪˈsteɪt] *n* Gut *nt*; (*of deceased*) Nachlass *m*; (*housing* ~) Siedlung *f*; (*country house*) Landsitz *m*; **estate agent** *n* (*Brit*) Grundstücksmakler(in) *m(f)*, Immobilienmakler(in) *m(f)*; **estate car** *n* (*Brit*) Kombiwagen *m*

estimate [ˈestɪmət] *n* Schätzung *f*; (*Comm: of price*) Kostenvoranschlag *m* ▷ [ˈestɪmeɪt] *vt* schätzen

Estonia [eˈstəʊnɪə] *n* Estland *nt*; **Estonian** [eˈstəʊnɪən] *adj* estnisch; ▷ *n* (*person*) Este *m*; Estin *f*; (*language*) Estnisch *nt*

estuary [ˈestjʊərɪ] *n* Mündung *f*

eternal, eternally [ɪˈtɜːnl, -nəlɪ]

adj, adv ewig; **eternity** n
Ewigkeit f
ethical ['eθɪkəl] adj ethisch;
ethics ['eθɪks] npl Ethik f
Ethiopia [iːθɪ'əʊpɪə] n Äthiopien
nt
ethnic ['eθnɪk] adj ethnisch;
(clothes etc) landesüblich;
~ **minority** ethnische Minderheit
e-ticket ['iːtɪkɪt] n E-Ticket nt
EU abbr = **European Union** EU f
euphemism ['juːfɪmɪzəm] n
Euphemismus m
euro ['jʊərəʊ] (pl -s) n (Fin) Euro
m; **Eurocheque** ['jʊərəʊtʃek] n
Euroscheck m; **Europe** ['jʊərəp] n
Europa nt; **European** [jʊərə'piːən]
adj europäisch; ~ **Parliament**
Europäisches Parlament; ~ **Union**
Europäische Union ▷ n
Europäer(in) m(f); **Eurosceptic**
['jʊərəʊskeptɪk] n
Euroskeptiker(in) m(f);
Eurotunnel n Eurotunnel m
evacuate [ɪ'vækjʊeɪt] vt (place)
räumen; (people) evakuieren
evade [ɪ'veɪd] vt ausweichen
+dat; (pursuers) sich entziehen +dat
evaluate [ɪ'væljʊeɪt] vt
auswerten
evaporate [ɪ'væpəreɪt] vi ver-
dampfen; (fig) verschwinden; **~d
milk** Kondensmilch f
even ['iːvən] adj (flat) eben;
(regular) gleichmäßig; (equal)
gleich; (number) gerade; **the score
is** ~ es steht unentschieden ▷ adv
sogar; ~ **you** selbst du sogar
du/Sie; ~ **if** selbst wenn, wenn
auch; ~ **though** obwohl; **not**
~ nicht einmal; ~ **better** noch
besser; **even out** vi (prices) sich
einpendeln
evening ['iːvnɪŋ] n Abend m; **in
the** ~ abends, am Abend; **this**
~ heute Abend; **evening class** n
Abendkurs m; **evening dress** n

(generally) Abendkleidung f;
(woman's) Abendkleid nt
evenly ['iːvənlɪ] adv gleichmäßig
event [ɪ'vent] n Ereignis nt;
(organized) Veranstaltung f; (Sport:
discipline) Disziplin f; **in the ~ of**
im Falle +gen; **eventful** adj
ereignisreich
eventual [ɪ'ventʃʊəl] adj (final)
letztendlich; **eventually**
[ɪ'ventʃʊəlɪ] adv (at last) am Ende;
(given time) schließlich
ever ['evə*] adv (at any time)
je(mals); **don't ~ do that again** tu
das ja nie wieder; **he's the best**
~ er ist der Beste, den es je
gegeben hat; **have you ~ been to
the States?** bist du schon einmal
in den Staaten gewesen?; **for**
~ (für) immer; **for ~ and ~** auf
immer und ewig; ~ **so ...** (fam)
äußerst ...; ~ **so drunk** ganz schön
betrunken
every ['evrɪ] adj jeder/jede/
jedes; ~ **day** jeden Tag; ~ **other
day** jeden zweiten Tag; ~ **five
days** alle fünf Tage; **I have
~ reason to believe that ...** ich
habe allen Grund anzunehmen,
dass ...; **everybody** pron jeder,
alle pl; **everyday** adj
(commonplace) alltäglich; (clothes,
language etc) Alltags-; **everyone**
pron jeder, alle pl; **everything**
pron alles; **everywhere** adv
überall; (with direction) überallhin
evidence ['evɪdəns] n Beweise
pl; (single piece) Beweis m;
(testimony) Aussage f; (signs)
Spuren pl; **evident, evidently** adj,
adv offensichtlich
evil ['iːvl] adj böse ▷ n Böse(s) nt;
an ~ ein Übel
evolution [iːvə'luːʃən] n Entwicklung f; (of life) Evolution f;
evolve [ɪ'vɒlv] vi sich entwickeln
ex- [eks] pref Ex-, ehemalig;

~boyfriend Exfreund m; **~wife** frühere Frau, Exfrau f; **ex** n (fam) Verflossene(r) mf, Ex mf

exact [ɪgˈzækt] adj genau; **exactly** adv genau; **not ~ fast** nicht gerade schnell

exaggerate [ɪgˈzædʒəreɪt] vt, vi übertreiben; **exaggerated** adj übertrieben; **exaggeration** n Übertreibung f

exam [ɪgˈzæm] n Prüfung f; **examination** [ɪgzæmɪˈneɪʃən] n (Med etc) Untersuchung f, Prüfung f; (at university) Examen nt; (at customs etc) Kontrolle f; **examine** [ɪgˈzæmɪn] vt untersuchen (for auf +akk); (check) kontrollieren, prüfen; **examiner** n Prüfer(in) m(f)

example [ɪgˈzɑːmpl] n Beispiel nt (of für +akk); **for ~** zum Beispiel

excavation [ekskəˈveɪʃən] n Ausgrabung f

exceed [ɪkˈsiːd] vt überschreiten, übertreffen; **exceedingly** adv äußerst

excel [ɪkˈsel] vt übertreffen; **he ~led himself** er hat sich selbst übertroffen ▷ vi sich auszeichnen (in in +dat, at bei); **excellent, excellently** [ˈeksələnt, -lɪ] adj, adv ausgezeichnet

except [ɪkˈsept] prep: **~ after +dat; ~ for** abgesehen von ▷ vt ausnehmen; **exception** [ɪkˈsepʃən] n Ausnahme f; **exceptional, exceptionally** [ɪkˈsepʃənl, -nəlɪ] adj, adv außergewöhnlich

excess [ekˈses] n Übermaß nt (of an +dat); **excess baggage** n Übergepäck nt; **excesses** npl Exzesse pl; (drink, sex) Ausschweifungen pl; **excessive, excessively** adj, adv übermäßig; **excess weight** n Übergewicht nt

exchange [ɪksˈtʃeɪndʒ] n Austausch m (for gegen); (of bought items) Umtausch m (for gegen); (Fin) Wechsel m; (Tel) Vermittlung f, Zentrale f ▷ vt austauschen; (goods) tauschen (for gegen); (bought items) umtauschen (for gegen); (money, blows) wechseln; **exchange rate** n Wechselkurs m

excite [ɪkˈsaɪt] vt erregen; **excited** adj aufgeregt; **to get ~** sich aufregen; **exciting** adj aufregend; (book, film) spannend

exclamation [ekskləˈmeɪʃən] n Ausruf m; **exclamation mark**, **exclamation point** (US) n Ausrufezeichen nt

exclude [ɪksˈkluːd] vt ausschließen; **exclusion** [ɪksˈkluːʒən] n Ausschluss m; **exclusive** [ɪksˈkluːsɪv] adj (select) exklusiv; (sole) ausschließlich; **exclusively** adv ausschließlich

excrement [ˈekskrɪmənt] n Kot m, Exkremente pl

excruciating [ɪksˈkruːʃɪeɪtɪŋ] adj fürchterlich, entsetzlich

excursion [ɪksˈkɜːʃən] n Ausflug m

excusable [ɪksˈkjuːzəbl] adj entschuldbar; **excuse** [ɪksˈkjuːz] vt entschuldigen; **~ me** Entschuldigung!; **to ~ sb for sth** jdm etw verzeihen; **to ~ sb from sth** jdn von etw befreien ▷ [ɪksˈkjuːs] n Entschuldigung f, Ausrede f

ex-directory [eksdaɪˈrektərɪ] adj: **to be ~** (Brit Tel) nicht im Telefonbuch stehen

execute [ˈeksɪkjuːt] vt (carry out) ausführen; (kill) hinrichten; **execution** n (killing) Hinrichtung f; (carrying out) Ausführung f; **executive** [ɪgˈzekjʊtɪv] n (Comm) leitender Angestellter, leitende Angestellte

exemplary [ɪgˈzemplərɪ] *adj* beispielhaft

exempt [ɪgˈzempt] *adj* befreit (from von) ▷ *vt* befreien

exercise [ˈeksəsaɪz] *n* (in school, sports) Übung *f*; (movement) Bewegung *f*; **to get more ~** mehr Sport treiben; **exercise bike** *n* Heimtrainer *m*; **exercise book** *n* Heft *nt*

exert [ɪgˈzɜːt] *vt* (influence) ausüben

exhaust [ɪgˈzɔːst] *n* (fumes) Abgase *pl*; (Auto) **~ (pipe)** Auspuff *m*; **exhausted** *adj* erschöpft; **exhausting** *adj* anstrengend

exhibit [ɪgˈzɪbɪt] *n* (in exhibition) Ausstellungsstück *nt*; **exhibition** [eksɪˈbɪʃən] *n* Ausstellung *f*; **exhibitionist** [eksɪˈbɪʃənɪst] *n* Selbstdarsteller(in) *m(f)*; **exhibitor** *n* Aussteller(in) *m(f)*

exhilarating [ɪgˈzɪləreɪtɪŋ] *adj* belebend, erregend

exile [ˈeksaɪl] *n* Exil *nt*; (person) Verbannte(r) *mf* ▷ *vt* verbannen

exist [ɪgˈzɪst] *vi* existieren; (live) leben (on von); **existence** *n* Existenz *f*; **to come into ~** entstehen; **existing** *adj* bestehend

exit [ˈeksɪt] *n* Ausgang *m*; (for vehicles) Ausfahrt *f*; **exit poll** *n* Umfrage direkt nach dem Wahlgang

exorbitant [ɪgˈzɔːbɪtənt] *adj* astronomisch

exotic [ɪgˈzɒtɪk] *adj* exotisch

expand [ɪksˈpænd] *vt* ausdehnen, erweitern ▷ *vi* sich ausdehnen; **expansion** [ɪksˈpænʃən] *n* Expansion *f*, Erweiterung *f*

expect [ɪksˈpekt] *vt* erwarten; (suppose) annehmen; **he ~s me to do it** er erwartet, dass ich es mache; **I ~ it'll rain** es wird wohl regnen; **I ~ so** ich denke schon

▷ *vi*: **she's ~ing** sie bekommt ein Kind

expedition [ekspɪˈdɪʃən] *n* Expedition *f*

expenditure [ɪkˈspendɪtʃəʳ] *n* Ausgaben *pl*

expense [ɪkˈspens] *n* Kosten *pl*; (single cost) Ausgabe *f*; **(business) ~s** *pl* Spesen *pl*; **at sb's ~** auf jds Kosten; **expensive** [ɪkˈspensɪv] *adj* teuer

experience [ɪkˈspɪərɪəns] *n* Erfahrung *f*; (particular incident) Erlebnis *nt*; **by/from ~** aus Erfahrung ▷ *vt* erfahren, erleben; (hardship) durchmachen; **experienced** *adj* erfahren

experiment [ɪkˈsperɪmənt] *n* Versuch *m*, Experiment *nt* ▷ *vi* experimentieren

expert [ˈekspɜːt] *n* Experte *m*, Expertin *f*; (professional) Fachmann *m*, Fachfrau *f*; (Jur) Sachverständige(r) *mf* ▷ *adj* fachmännisch, Fach-; **expertise** [ekspɜːˈtiːz] *n* Sachkenntnis *f*

expire [ɪkˈspaɪəʳ] *vi* (end) ablaufen; **expiry date** [ɪkˈspaɪəraɪdeɪt] *n* Verfallsdatum *nt*

explain [ɪksˈpleɪn] *vt* erklären (sth to sb jdm etw); **explanation** [ekspləˈneɪʃən] *n* Erklärung *f*

explicit [ɪksˈplɪsɪt] *adj* ausdrücklich, eindeutig

explode [ɪkˈspləʊd] *vi* explodieren

exploit [ɪkˈsplɔɪt] *vt* ausbeuten

explore [ɪkˈsplɔːʳ] *vt* erforschen

explosion [ɪkˈspləʊʒən] *n* Explosion *f*; **explosive** [ɪkˈspləʊsɪv] *adj* explosiv ▷ *n* Sprengstoff *m*

export [ekˈspɔːt] *vt, vi* exportieren ▷ [ˈekspɔːt] *n* Export *m* ▷ *adj* (trade) Export-

expose [ɪkˈspəʊz] *vt* (to danger)

etc) aussetzen (*to dat*); (*uncover*)
freilegen; (*impostor*) entlarven;
exposed *adj* (*position*)
ungeschützt; **exposure**
[ɪk'spəʊʒə*] *n* (*Med*)
Unterkühlung *f*; (*Foto: time*)
Belichtung(szeit) *f*; **24 ~5** 24
Aufnahmen
express [ɪk'spres] *adj* (*speedy*)
Express-, Schnell-; **~ delivery**
Eilzustellung *f* ▷ *n* (*Rail*)
Schnellzug *m* ▷ *vt* ausdrücken
▷ *vr:* **to ~ oneself** sich
ausdrücken; **expression**
[ɪk'spreʃən] *n* (*phrase*) Ausdruck
m; (*look*) Gesichtsausdruck *m*;
expressive *adj* ausdrucksvoll;
expressway *n* (*US*) Schnellstraße
f
extend [ɪk'stend] *vt* (*arms*)
ausstrecken; (*lengthen*) verlängern;
(*building*) vergrößern, ausbauen;
(*business, limits*) erweitern;
extension [ɪk'stenʃən] *n*
(*lengthening*) Verlängerung *f*; (*of
building*) Anbau *m*; (*Tel*) Anschluss
m; (*of business, limits*) Erweiterung
f; **extensive** [ɪk'stensɪv] *adj*
(*knowledge*) umfangreich; (*use*)
häufig; **extent** [ɪk'stent] *n*
(*length*) Länge *f*; (*size*) Ausdehnung
f; (*scope*) Umfang *m*, Ausmaß *nt*; **to
a certain/large ~** in
gewissem/hohem Maße
exterior [ek'stɪərɪə*] *n* Äußere(s)
nt
external [ek'stɜːnl] *adj* äußere-
re(r, s), Außen-; **externally** *adv*
äußerlich
extinct [ɪk'stɪŋkt] *adj* (*species*)
ausgestorben
extinguish [ɪk'stɪŋgwɪʃ] *vt*
löschen; **extinguisher** *n*
Löschgerät *nt*
extra ['ekstrə] *adj* zusätzlich;
~ charge Zuschlag *m*; **~ time**
(*Sport*) Verlängerung *f* ▷ *adv*

besonders; **~ large** (*clothing*)
übergroß ▷ *npl:* **~s** zusätzliche
Kosten *pl*; (*food*) Beilagen *pl*;
(*accessories*) Zubehör *nt*; (*for car etc*)
Extras *pl*
extract [ɪk'strækt] *vt* herausziehen (*from aus*); (*tooth*)
ziehen ▷ ['ekstrækt] *n* (*from book
etc*) Auszug *m*
extraordinary [ɪk'strɔːdnrɪ] *adj*
außerordentlich; (*unusual*)
ungewöhnlich; (*amazing*)
erstaunlich
extreme [ɪk'striːm] *adj* äußer-
ste(r, s); (*drastic*) extrem ▷ *n*
Extrem *nt*; **extremely** *adv*
äußerst, höchst; **extreme sports**
npl Extremsportarten *pl*;
extremist [ɪk'striːmɪst] *adj*
extremistisch ▷ *n* Extremist *m*
extricate ['ekstrɪkeɪt] *vt* befreien
(*from aus*)
extrovert ['ekstrəʊvɜːt] *adj*
extrovertiert
exuberance [ɪg'zuːbərəns] *n*
Überschwang *m*; **exuberant** *adj*
überschwänglich
exultation [egzəl'teɪʃən] *n* Jubel
m
eye [aɪ] *n* Auge *nt*; **to keep an
~ on sb/sth** auf jdn/etw
aufpassen ▷ *vt* mustern;
eyebrow *n* Augenbraue *f*;
eyelash *n* Wimper *f*; **eyelid** *n*
Augenlid *nt*; **eyeliner** *n* Eyeliner
m; **eyeopener** *n:* **that was an
~** das hat mir die Augen geöffnet;
eyeshadow *n* Lidschatten *m*;
eyesight *n* Sehkraft *f*; **eyesore** *n*
Schandfleck *m*; **eye witness** *n*
Augenzeuge *m*, Augenzeugin *f*

f

fabric ['fæbrɪk] n Stoff m
fabulous ['fæbjʊləs] adj
sagenhaft
façade [fə'sɑːd] n (a. fig) Fassade
f
face [feɪs] n Gesicht nt; (of clock)
Zifferblatt nt; (of mountain) Wand f;
in the ~ of trotz +gen; **to be ~ to
~** (people) einander
gegenüberstehen ▷ vt, vi (person)
gegenüberstehen +dat; (at table)
gegenübersitzen +dat; **to ~ north**
(room) nach Norden gehen; **to
~ (up to) the facts** den Tatsachen
ins Auge sehen; **to be ~d with sth**
mit etw konfrontiert sein; **face lift**
n Gesichtsstraffung f; (fig)
Verschönerung f; **face powder** n
Gesichtspuder m
facet ['fæsɪt] n (fig) Aspekt m
face value n Nennwert m
facial ['feɪʃəl] adj Gesichts- ▷ n
(fam) (kosmetische)
Gesichtsbehandlung

facilitate [fə'sɪlɪteɪt] vt
erleichtern
facility [fə'sɪlɪtɪ] n (building etc to
be used) Einrichtung f, Möglichkeit
f; (installation) Anlage f; (skill)
Gewandtheit f
fact [fækt] n Tatsache f; **as a
matter of ~, in ~** eigentlich,
tatsächlich
factor ['fæktə°] n Faktor m
factory ['fæktərɪ] n Fabrik f;
factory outlet n Fabrikverkauf m
factual ['fæktjʊəl] adj sachlich
faculty ['fækəltɪ] n Fähigkeit f;
(at university) Fakultät f; (US:
teaching staff) Lehrkörper m
fade [feɪd] vi (a. fig) verblassen;
faded adj verblasst, verblichen
faff about ['fæfəbaʊt] vi (Brit
fam) herumwursteln
fag [fæg] n (Brit fam: cigarette)
Kippe f; (US offensive) Schwule(r) m
Fahrenheit ['færənhaɪt] n
Fahrenheit
fail [feɪl] vt nicht bestehen
▷ vi versagen; (plan, marriage)
scheitern; (student) durchfallen;
(eyesight) nachlassen; **words ~ me**
ich bin sprachlos; **failing** n
Schwäche f; **failure** ['feɪljə°] n
(person) Versager(in) m(f); (act, a.
Tech) Versagen nt; (of engine etc)
Ausfall m; (of plan, marriage)
Scheitern nt
faint [feɪnt] adj schwach; (sound)
leise; (fam) **I haven't the ~est**
(idea) ich habe keinen blassen
Schimmer ▷ vi ohnmächtig
werden (with vor +dat); **faintness**
n (Med) Schwächegefühl nt
fair [feə°] adj (hair) (dunkel)blond;
(skin) hell; (just) gerecht, fair;
(reasonable) ganz ordentlich; (in
school) befriedigend; (weather)
schön; (wind) günstig; **a
~ number/amount of** ziemlich
viele/viel ▷ adv: **to play ~** fair

spielen; *(fig)* fair sein; **~ enough** in Ordnung! ▷ *n (fun~)* Jahrmarkt *m;* *(Comm)* Messe *f;* **fair-haired** *adj* (dunkel)blond; **fairly** *adv* *(honestly)* fair; *(rather)* ziemlich

fairy ['fɛərɪ] *n* Fee *f;* **fairy tale** *n* Märchen *nt*

faith [feɪθ] *n (trust)* Vertrauen *nt (in sb zu jdm);* *(Rel)* Glaube *m;* **faithful, faithfully** *adj, adv* treu; **Yours ~ly** Hochachtungsvoll

fake [feɪk] *n (thing)* Fälschung *f* ▷ *adj* vorgetäuscht ▷ *vt* fälschen

falcon ['fɔ:lkən] *n* Falke *m*

fall [fɔ:l] *(fell, fallen)* *vi* fallen; *(from a height, badly)* stürzen; **to ~ ill** krank werden; **to ~ asleep** einschlafen; **to ~ in love** sich verlieben ▷ *n* Fall *m;* *(accident, fig: of regime)* Sturz *m;* *(decrease)* Sinken *nt (in +gen);* *(US: autumn)* Herbst *m;* **fall apart** *vi* auseinanderfallen; **fall behind** *vi* zurückbleiben; *(with work, rent)* in Rückstand geraten; **fall down** *vi (person)* hinfallen; **fall off** *vi (decrease)* zurückgehen; **fall out** *vi (quarrel)* sich streiten; **fall over** *vi* hinfallen; **fall through** *vi (plan etc)* ins Wasser fallen

fallen ['fɔ:lən] *pp of* **fall**

fallout ['fɔ:laut] *n* radioaktiver Niederschlag, Fall-out *m*

false [fɔ:ls] *adj* falsch; *(artificial)* künstlich; **false alarm** *n* blinder Alarm; **false start** *n (Sport)* Fehlstart *m;* **false teeth** *npl* (künstliches) Gebiss

fame [feɪm] *n* Ruhm *m*

familiar [fə'mɪlɪə°] *adj* vertraut, bekannt; **to be ~ with** vertraut sein mit, gut kennen; **familiarity** [fəmɪlɪ'ærɪtɪ] *n* Vertrautheit *f*

family ['fæmɪlɪ] *n* Familie *f;* *(including relations)* Verwandtschaft

f; **family man** *n* Familienvater *m;* **family name** *n* Familienname *m,* Nachname *m;* **family practitioner** *n (US)* Allgemeinarzt *m,* Allgemeinärztin *f*

famine ['fæmɪn] *n* Hungersnot *f;* **famished** ['fæmɪʃt] *adj* ausgehungert

famous ['feɪməs] *adj* berühmt

fan [fæn] *n (hand-held)* Fächer *m;* *(Elec)* Ventilator *m;* *(admirer)* Fan *m*

fanatic [fə'nætɪk] *n* Fanatiker(in) *m(f)*

fancy ['fænsɪ] *adj (elaborate)* kunstvoll; *(unusual)* ausgefallen ▷ *vt (like)* gernhaben; **he fancies her** er steht auf sie; **~ that** stell dir vor!, so was!; **fancy dress** *n* Kostüm *nt,* Verkleidung *f*

fan heater ['fænhi:tə°] *n* Heizlüfter *m;* **fanlight** *n* Oberlicht *nt*

fan mail *n* Fanpost *f*

fantasise ['fæntəsaɪz] *vi* träumen *(about von);* **fantastic** [fæn'tæstɪk] *adj (a. fam)* fantastisch; **that's ~** *(fam)* das ist ja toll!; **fantasy** ['fæntəzɪ] *n* Fantasie *f*

far [fɑ:°] *(further o* farther, *furthest o* farthest*)* *adj* weit; **the ~ end of the room** das andere Ende des Zimmers; **the Far East** der Ferne Osten ▷ *adv* weit; **~ better** viel besser; **by ~ the best** bei weitem der/die/das Beste; **as ~ as ...** bis zum o zur ...; *(with place name)* bis nach ...; **as ~ as I'm concerned** was mich betrifft, von mir aus; **so ~** soweit, bisher; **faraway** *adj* weit entfernt; *(look)* verträumt

fare [fɛə°] *n* Fahrpreis *m;* *(money)* Fahrgeld *f*

farm [fɑ:m] *n* Bauernhof *m,* Farm *f;* **farmer** *n* Bauer *m,* Bäuerin *f,* Landwirt(in) *m(f);* **farmhouse**

Bauernhaus nt; **farming** n Landwirtschaft f; **farmland** n Ackerland nt; **farmyard** n Hof m

far-reaching ['fɑːriːtʃɪŋ] adj weit reichend; **far-sighted** adj weitsichtig; (fig) weitblickend

fart [fɑːt] n (fam) Furz m; **old ~** (fam: person) alter Sack ▷ vi (fam) furzen

farther ['fɑːðə*] adj, adv comparative of **far**; see **further**

farthest ['fɑːðɪst] adj, adv superlative of **far**; see **furthest**

fascinating ['fæsɪneɪtɪŋ] adj faszinierend; **fascination** n Faszination f

fascism ['fæʃɪzəm] n Faschismus m; **fascist** ['fæʃɪst] adj faschistisch ▷ Faschist(in) m(f)

fashion ['fæʃən] n (clothes) Mode f; (manner) Art (und Weise) f; **to be in ~** (in) Mode sein; **out of ~** unmodisch; **fashionable**, **fashionably** adj, adv (clothes, person) modisch; (author, pub etc) in Mode

fast [fɑːst] adj schnell; **to be ~** (clock) vorgehen ▷ adv schnell; (firmly) fest; **to be ~ asleep** fest schlafen ▷ n Fasten nt ▷ vi fasten; **fastback** n (Auto) Fließheck nt

fasten ['fɑːsn] vt (attach) befestigen (to an +dat); (do up) zumachen; **~ your seatbelts** bitte anschnallen; **fastener**, **fastening** n Verschluss m

fast food n Fast Food nt; **fast forward** n (for tape) Schnellvorlauf m; **fast lane** n Überholspur f

fat [fæt] adj dick; (meat) fett ▷ n Fett nt

fatal ['feɪtl] adj tödlich

fate [feɪt] n Schicksal nt

fat-free adj (food) fettfrei

father ['fɑːðə*] n Vater m; (priest)

Pfarrer m ▷ vt (child) zeugen; **Father Christmas** n der Weihnachtsmann; **father-in-law** (pl **fathers-in-law**) n Schwiegervater m

fatigue [fə'tiːg] n Ermüdung f

fattening ['fætnɪŋ] adj: **to be ~** dick machen; **fatty** ['fætɪ] adj (food) fettig

faucet ['fɔːsɪt] n (US) Wasserhahn m

fault [fɔːlt] n Fehler m; (Tech) Defekt m; (Elec) Störung f; (blame) Schuld f; **it's your ~** du bist daran schuld; **faulty** adj fehlerhaft; (Tech) defekt

favor (US), **favour** ['feɪvə*] n (approval) Gunst f; (kindness) Gefallen m; **in ~ of** für; **I'm in ~ of** (of going) ich bin dafür(, dass wir gehen); **to do sb a ~** jdm einen Gefallen tun ▷ vt (prefer) vorziehen; **favourable** adj günstig (to, for für); **favourite** ['feɪvərɪt] n Liebling m, Favorit(in) m(f) ▷ adj Lieblings-

fax [fæks] vt faxen ▷ n Fax nt; **fax number** n Faxnummer f

faze [feɪz] vt (fam) aus der Fassung bringen

FBI abbr = **Federal Bureau of Investigation** FBI nt

fear [fɪə*] n Angst f (of vor +dat) ▷ vt befürchten; **fearful** adj (timid) ängstlich, furchtsam; (terrible) fürchterlich; **fearless** adj furchtlos

feasible ['fiːzəbl] adj machbar

feast [fiːst] n Festessen nt

feather ['feðə*] n Feder f

feature ['fiːtʃə*] n (facial) (Gesichts)zug m; (characteristic) Merkmal nt; (of car etc) Ausstattungsmerkmal nt; (in the press) (Cine) Feature nt ▷ vt bringen, (als Besonderheit) zeigen; **feature film** n Spielfilm m

February ['februari] n Februar m; *see also* **September**

fed [fed] *pt, pp of* **feed**

federal ['fedərəl] *adj* Bundes-; **the Federal Republic of Germany** die Bundesrepublik Deutschland

fed-up [fed'ʌp] *adj*: **to be ~ with sth** etw satthaben; **I'm ~** ich habe die Nase voll

fee [fiː] n Gebühr f; (of doctor, lawyer) Honorar nt

feeble ['fiːbl] *adj* schwach

feed [fiːd] (**fed, fed**) vt (baby, animal) füttern; (support) ernähren ▷ n (for baby) Mahlzeit f; (for animals) Futter nt; (Inform: paper ~) Zufuhr f; **feed in** vt (information) eingeben; **feedback** n (information) Feed-back nt

feel [fiːl] (**felt, felt**) vt (sense) fühlen; (pain) empfinden; (touch) anfassen; (think) meinen ▷ vi (person) sich fühlen; **I ~ cold** mir ist kalt; **do you ~ like a walk?** hast du Lust, spazieren zu gehen?; **feeling** n Gefühl nt

feet [fiːt] pl of **foot**

fell [fel] pt of **fall** ▷ vt (tree) fällen

fellow ['feləʊ] n Kerl m, Typ m; **~ citizen** Mitbürger(in) m(f); **~ countryman** Landsmann m; **~ worker** Mitarbeiter(in) m(f)

felt [felt] pt, pp of **feel** ▷ n Filz m; **felt tip, felt-tip pen** n Filzstift m

female ['fiːmeɪl] n (of animals) Weibchen nt ▷ adj weiblich; **~ doctor** Ärztin f; **feminine** ['feminɪn] adj weiblich; **feminist** ['feminɪst] n Feminist(in) m(f) ▷ adj feministisch

fence [fens] n Zaun m

fencing n (Sport) Fechten nt

fender ['fendə°] n (US Auto) Kotflügel m

fennel ['fenl] n Fenchel m

fern [fɜːn] n Farn m

ferocious [fə'rəʊʃəs] adj wild

ferry ['feri] n Fähre f ▷ vt übersetzen

fertile ['fɜːtaɪl] adj fruchtbar; **fertility** [fə'tɪlɪti] n Fruchtbarkeit f; **fertilize** ['fɜːtɪlaɪz] vt (Bio) befruchten; (Agr: land) düngen; **fertilizer** n Dünger m

festival ['festɪvl] n (Rel) Fest nt; (Art, Mus) Festspiele pl; (pop music) Festival nt; **festive** ['festɪv] adj festlich; **festivities** [fe'stɪvɪtiz] n Feierlichkeiten pl

fetch [fetʃ] vt holen; (collect) abholen; (in sale, money) einbringen; **fetching** adj reizend

fetish ['fetɪʃ] n Fetisch m

fetus ['fiːtəs] n (US) Fötus m

fever ['fiːvə°] n Fieber nt; **feverish** adj (Med) fiebrig; (fig) fieberhaft

few [fjuː] adj, pron pl wenige pl; **a ~** pl ein paar; **fewer** adj weniger; **fewest** adj wenigste(r, s)

fiancé [fɪ'ãnseɪ] n Verlobte(r) m; **fiancée** n Verlobte f

fiasco [fɪ'æskəʊ] (pl **-s** o US **-es**) n Fiasko nt

fiber (US), **fibre** ['faɪbə°] n Faser f; (material) Faserstoff m

fickle ['fɪkl] adj unbeständig

fiction ['fɪkʃən] n (novels) Prosaliteratur f; **fictional** adj; **fictitious** [fɪk'tɪʃəs] adj erfunden

fiddle ['fɪdl] n Geige f; (trick) Betrug m ▷ vt (accounts, results) frisieren; **fiddle with** vt herumfummeln an +dat; **fiddly** adj knifflig

fidelity [fɪ'delɪti] n Treue f

fidget ['fɪdʒɪt] vi zappeln; **fidgety** adj zappelig

field [fiːld] n Feld nt; (grass-covered) Wiese f; (fig: of work) (Arbeits)gebiet nt

fierce [fɪəs] adj heftig; (animal, appearance) wild; (criticism, competition) scharf

fifteen [fɪfˈtiːn] num fünfzehn ▷ n Fünfzehn f; see also **eight**; **fifteenth** adj fünfzehnte(r, s); see also **eighth; fifth** [fɪfθ] adj fünfte(r, s) ▷ n (fraction) Fünftel nt; see also **eighth; fifty** [ˈfɪftɪ] num fünfzig ▷ n Fünfzig f; see also **eight; fiftieth** adj fünfzigste(r, s); see also **eighth**

fig [fɪg] n Feige f

fight [faɪt] (**fought, fought**) vi kämpfen (with, against gegen, for, over um) ▷ vt (person) kämpfen mit; (fig: disease, fire etc) bekämpfen ▷ n Kampf m; (brawl) Schlägerei f; (argument) Streit m; **fight back** vi zurückschlagen; **fight off** vt abwehren; **fighter** n Kämpfer(in) m(f)

figurative [ˈfɪgərətɪv] adj übertragen

figure [ˈfɪgə°] n (person) Gestalt f; (of person) Figur f; (number) Zahl f, Ziffer f; (amount) Betrag m; **a four-figure sum** eine vierstellige Summe ▷ vt (US: think) glauben ▷ vi (appear) erscheinen; **figure out** vt (work out) herausbekommen; **I can't figure him out** ich werde aus ihm nicht schlau; **figure skating** n Eiskunstlauf m

file [faɪl] n (tool) Feile f; (dossier) Akte f; (Inform) Datei f; (folder) Aktenordner m; **on ~** in den Akten ▷ vt (metal, nails) feilen; (papers) ablegen (under unter) ▷ vi: **to ~ in/out** hintereinander hereinkommen/hinausgehen; **filing cabinet** n Aktenschrank m

fill [fɪl] vt füllen; (post) plombieren; (post) besetzen; **fill in** vt (hole) auffüllen; (form) ausfüllen; (tell) informieren (on über); **fill out** vt (form) ausfüllen; **fill up** vi (Auto) volltanken

fillet [ˈfɪlɪt] n Filet nt

filling [ˈfɪlɪŋ] n (Gastr) Füllung f; (for tooth) Plombe f; **filling station** n Tankstelle f

film [fɪlm] n Film m ▷ vt (scene) filmen; **film star** n Filmstar m; **film studio** n Filmstudio nt

filter [ˈfɪltə°] n Filter m; (traffic lane) Abbiegespur f ▷ vt filtern

filth [fɪlθ] n Dreck m; **filthy** adj dreckig

fin [fɪn] n Flosse f

final [ˈfaɪnl] adj letzte(r, s); (stage, round) End-; (decision, version) endgültig; **~ score** Schlussstand m ▷ n (Sport) Endspiel nt; (competition) Finale nt; **~s** pl Abschlussexamen nt; **finalize** vt die endgültige Form geben +dat; **finally** adv (lastly) zuletzt; (eventually) schließlich, endlich

finance [faɪˈnæns] n Finanzwesen nt; **~s** pl Finanzen pl ▷ vt finanzieren; **financial** [faɪˈnænʃəl] adj finanziell; (adviser, crisis, policy etc) Finanz-

find [faɪnd] (**found, found**) vt finden; **he was found dead** er wurde tot aufgefunden; **I ~ myself in difficulties** ich befinde mich in Schwierigkeiten; **she ~s it difficult/easy** es fällt ihr schwer/leicht; **find out** vt herausfinden; **findings** npl (Jur) Ermittlungsergebnis nt; (of report, Med) Befund m

fine [faɪn] adj (thin) dünn, fein; (good) gut; (splendid) herrlich; (clothes) elegant; (weather) schön; **I'm ~** es geht mir gut; **that's ~** das ist OK ▷ adv (well) gut ▷ n (Jur) Geldstrafe f ▷ vt (Jur) mit einer Geldstrafe belegen; **fine arts** npl: **the ~** die schönen Künste pl;

finely adv (cut) dünn; (ground) fein

finger ['fɪŋgə°] n Finger m ▷ vt herumfingern an +dat; **fingernail** n Fingernagel m; **fingerprint** n Fingerabdruck m; **fingertip** n Fingerspitze f

finicky ['fɪnɪkɪ] adj (person) pingelig; (work) knifflig

finish ['fɪnɪʃ] n Ende nt; (Sport) Finish m; (line) Ziel nt; (of product) Verarbeitung f ▷ vt beenden; (book etc) zu Ende lesen; (food) aufessen; (drink) austrinken ▷ vi zu Ende gehen; (song, story) enden; (person) fertig sein; (stop) aufhören; **have you ~ed?** bist du fertig?; **to ~ first/second** (Sport) als erster/zweiter durchs Ziel gehen; **finishing line** n Ziellinie f

Finland ['fɪnlənd] n Finnland nt; **Finn** n Finne m, Finnin f; **Finnish** adj finnisch ▷ n (language) Finnisch nt

fir [fɜː°] n Tanne f

fire [faɪə°] n Feuer nt; (house etc) Brand m; **to set ~ to sth** etw in Brand stecken; **to be on ~** brennen ▷ vt (bullets, rockets) abfeuern; (fam: dismiss) feuern ▷ vi (Auto: engine) zünden; **to ~ at sb** auf jdn schießen; **fire alarm** n Feuermelder m; **fire brigade** n Feuerwehr f; **fire engine** n Feuerwehrauto nt; **fire escape** n Feuerleiter f; **fire extinguisher** n Feuerlöscher m; **firefighter** n Feuerwehrmann m, Feuerwehrfrau f; **fireman** n Feuerwehrmann m; **fireplace** n (offener) Kamin m; **fireproof** adj feuerfest; **fire station** n Feuerwache f; **firewood** n Brennholz nt; **fireworks** npl Feuerwerk nt

firm [fɜːm] adj fest; (person) **to be ~** entschlossen auftreten ▷ n Firma f

first [fɜːst] adj erste(r, s) ▷ adv (at first) zuerst; (firstly) erstens; (arrive, finish) als erste(r); (happen) zum ersten Mal; **~ of all** zuallererst ▷ n (person) Erste(r) m/f; (Auto: also) erster Gang; **at ~** zuerst, anfangs; **first aid** n erste Hilfe; **first-class** adj erstklassig; (compartment, ticket) erster Klasse; **~ mail** (Brit) bevorzugt beförderte Post ▷ adv (travel) erster Klasse; **first floor** n (Brit) erster Stock; (US) Erdgeschoss nt; **first lady** n (US) Frau f des Präsidenten; **firstly** adv erstens; **first name** n Vorname m; **first night** n (Theat) Premiere f; **first-rate** adj erstklassig

fir tree n Tannenbaum m

fish [fɪʃ] n Fisch m; **~ and chips** (Brit) frittierter Fisch mit Pommes frites ▷ vi fischen; (with rod) angeln; **to go ~ing** fischen/angeln gehen; **fishbone** n Gräte f; **fishcake** n Fischfrikadelle f; **fish farm** n Fischzucht f; **fish finger** n (Brit) Fischstäbchen nt; **fishing** ['fɪʃɪŋ] n Fischen nt; (with rod) Angeln nt; (as industry) Fischerei f; **fishing boat** n Fischerboot nt; **fishing line** n Angelschnur f; **fishing rod** n Angelrute f; **fishing village** n Fischerdorf nt; **fishmonger** ['fɪʃmʌŋgə°] n Fischhändler(in) m(f); **fish stick** n (US) Fischstäbchen nt; **fish tank** n Aquarium nt

fishy ['fɪʃɪ] adj (fam: suspicious) faul

fist [fɪst] n Faust f

fit [fɪt] adj (Med) gesund; (Sport) in Form, fit; (suitable) geeignet; **to keep ~** sich in Form halten ▷ vt passen +dat; (attach) anbringen (to an +dat); (install) einbauen (in +akk) ▷ vi passen; (in space, gap) hineinpassen ▷ n (of clothes) Sitz m; (Med) Anfall m; **it's a good ~** es

passt gut; **fit in** vt (accommodate)
unterbringen; (find time for)
einschieben ▷ vi (in space)
hineinpassen; (plans, ideas) passen;
he doesn't ~ (here) er passt nicht
hierher; **to ~ with sb's plans** sich
mit jds Plänen vereinbaren lassen
fitness n (Med) Gesundheit f;
(Sport) Fitness f; **fitness trainer** n
(Sport) Fitnesstrainer(in) m(f);
fitted carpet n Teppichboden m;
fitted kitchen n Einbauküche f;
fitting adj passend ▷ n (of dress)
Anprobe f; **~s** pl Ausstattung f

five [faɪv] num fünf ▷ n Fünf f;
see also **eight**; **fiver** n (Brit fam)
Fünfpfundschein m

fix [fɪks] vt befestigen (to an
+dat); (settle) festsetzen; (place,
time) ausmachen; (repair)
reparieren; **fixer** n (drug addict)
Fixer(in) m(f); **fixture** ['fɪkstʃə°]
n (Sport) Veranstaltung f; (match)
Spiel nt; (in building)
Installationsteil nt; **~s (and
fittings)** pl Ausstattung f

fizzy ['fɪzɪ] adj sprudelnd;
~ drink Limo f

flabbergasted ['flæbəgɑːstɪd]
adj (fam) platt

flabby ['flæbɪ] adj (fat) wabbelig

flag [flæg] n Fahne f; **flagstone** n
Steinplatte f

flake [fleɪk] n Flocke f ▷ vi: **to
~ (off)** abblättern

flamboyant [flæm'bɔɪənt] adj
extravagant

flame [fleɪm] n Flamme f; (person)
an old ~ eine alte Liebe

flan [flæn] n (fruit ~) Obstkuchen
m

flannel ['flænl] n Flanell m; (Brit:
face~) Waschlappen m; (fam: waffle)
Geschwafel nt ▷ vi herumlabern

flap [flæp] n Klappe f; (fam) **to be
in a ~** rotieren ▷ vt (wings)
schlagen mit ▷ vi flattern

flared [fleəd] adj (trousers) mit
Schlag; **flares** npl Schlaghose f

flash [flæʃ] n Blitz m; (news ~)
Kurzmeldung f; (Foto) Blitzlicht nt;
in a ~ im Nu ▷ vt: **to ~ one's
(head)lights** die Lichthupe
betätigen ▷ vi aufblinken;
(brightly) aufblitzen; **flashback** n
Rückblende f, Flashback m;
flashlight ['flæʃlaɪt] n (Photo)
Blitzlicht nt; (US: torch)
Taschenlampe f; **flashy** adj grell,
schrill; (pej) protzig

flat [flæt] adj flach; (surface) eben;
(drink) abgestanden; (tyre) platt;
(battery) leer; (refusal) glatt ▷ n
(Brit: rooms) Wohnung f ▷ (Auto)
Reifenpanne f; **flat screen** n
(Inform) Flachbildschirm m; **flatten**
vt platt machen, einebnen

flatter ['flætə°] vt schmeicheln
+dat; **flattering** adj
schmeichelhaft

flatware ['flætwɛə°] n (US)
Besteck nt

flavor (US), **flavour** ['fleɪvə°] n
Geschmack m ▷ vt Geschmack
geben +dat; (with spices) würzen;
flavouring n Aroma nt

flaw [flɔː] n Fehler m; **flawless**
adj fehlerlos; (complexion) makellos

flea [fliː] n Floh m

fled [fled] pt, pp of **flee**

flee [fliː] (**fled, fled**) vi fliehen

fleece [fliːs] n (of sheep) Vlies m;
(soft material) Fleece m; (jacket)
Fleecejacke f

fleet [fliːt] n Flotte f

Flemish ['flemɪʃ] adj flämisch
▷ n (language) Flämisch nt

flesh [fleʃ] n Fleisch nt

flew [fluː] pt of **fly**

flex [fleks] n (Brit Elec) Schnur
f

flexibility [fleksɪ'bɪlɪtɪ] n Bieg-
samkeit f; (fig) Flexibilität f;

flexible ['fleksɪbl] adj biegsam;

(plans, person) flexibel; **flexitime** *n* gleitende Arbeitszeit, Gleitzeit f

flicker ['flɪkə'] *vi* flackern; *(TV)* flimmern

flies [flaɪz] *pl of* **fly** ▷ *n*

flight [flaɪt] *n* Flug *m*; *(escape)* Flucht f; **~ of stairs** Treppe f; **flight attendant** *n* Flugbegleiter(in) *m(f)*; **flight recorder** *n* Flugschreiber *m*

flimsy ['flɪmzɪ] *adj* leicht gebaut, nicht stabil; *(thin)* hauchdünn; *(excuse)* fadenscheinig

fling [flɪŋ] *(flung, flung)* *vt* schleudern ▷ *n:* **to have a ~** eine (kurze) Affäre haben

flip [flɪp] *vt* schnippen; **to ~ a coin** eine Münze werfen; **flip through** *vt (book)* durchblättern; **flipchart** *n* Flipchart f

flipper ['flɪpə'] *n* Flosse f

flirt [flɜːt] *vi* flirten

float [fləʊt] *n (for fishing)* Schwimmer *m*; *(in procession)* Festwagen *m*; *(money)* Wechselgeld *nt* ▷ *vi* schwimmen; *(in air)* schweben

flock [flɒk] *n (of sheep) (Rel)* Herde f; *(of birds)* Schwarm *m*; *(of people)* Schar f

flog [flɒg] *vt* auspeitschen; *(Brit fam)* verscheuern

flood [flʌd] *n* Hochwasser *nt*, Überschwemmung f; *(fig)* Flut f ▷ *vt* überschwemmen; **floodlight** *n* Flutlicht *nt*; **floodlit** *adj (building)* angestrahlt

floor [flɔː'] *n* Fußboden *m*; *(storey)* Stock *m*; **ground ~** *(Brit)*, **first ~** *(US)* Erdgeschoss *nt*; **first ~** *(Brit)*, **second ~** *(US)* erster Stock; **floorboard** *n* Diele f

flop [flɒp] *n (fam: failure)* Reinfall *m*, Flop *m* ▷ *vi* misslingen, floppen

floppy disk ['flɒpɪ'dɪsk] *n* Diskette f

Florence ['flɒrəns] *n* Florenz *nt*

florist ['flɒrɪst] *n* Blumenhändler(in) *m(f)*; **florist's (shop)** ['flɒrɪsts] *n* Blumengeschäft *nt(f)*

flounder ['flaʊndə'] *n (fish)* Flunder f

flour [flaʊə'] *n* Mehl *nt*

flourish ['flʌrɪʃ] *vi* gedeihen; *(business)* gut laufen; *(boom)* florieren ▷ *vt (wave about)* schwenken; **flourishing** *adj* blühend

flow [fləʊ] *n* Fluss *m*; **to go with the ~** mit dem Strom schwimmen ▷ *vi* fließen

flower ['flaʊə'] *n* Blume f ▷ *vi* blühen; **flower bed** *n* Blumenbeet *nt*; **flowerpot** *n* Blumentopf *m*

flown [fləʊn] *pp of* **fly**

flu [fluː] *n (fam)* Grippe f

fluent *adj (Italian etc)* fließend; **to be ~ in German** fließend Deutsch sprechen

fluid ['fluːɪd] *n* Flüssigkeit f ▷ *adj* flüssig

flung [flʌŋ] *pt, pp of* **fling**

fluorescent [flʊə'resnt] *adj* fluoreszierend, Leucht-

flush [flʌʃ] *n (lavatory)* Wasserspülung f; *(blush)* Röte f ▷ *vi (lavatory)* spülen

flute [fluːt] *n* Flöte f

fly [flaɪ] *(flew, flown)* *vi, vt* fliegen; **how time flies** wie die Zeit vergeht! ▷ *n (insect)* Fliege f; **~/flies** *(pl) (on trousers)* Hosenschlitz *m*; **fly-drive** *n* Urlaub *m* mit Flug und Mietwagen; **flyover** *n (Brit)* Straßenüberführung f, Eisenbahnüberführung f; **flysheet** *n* Überzelt *nt*

FM *abbr* = **frequency modulation** ~ UKW

FO *abbr* = **Foreign Office** ≈ AA *nt*

foal [fəʊl] *n* Fohlen *nt*

foam [fəʊm] n Schaum m ▷ vi schäumen

fob off [fɒb ɒf] vt: **to fob sb off with sth** jdm etw andrehen

focus ['fəʊkəs] n Brennpunkt m; **in/out of ~** (photo) scharf/unscharf (camera) scharf/unscharf eingestellt ▷ vt (camera) scharf stellen ▷ vi sich konzentrieren (on auf +akk)

foetus ['fi:təs] n Fötus m

fog [fɒg] n Nebel m; **foggy** adj neblig; **fog light** n (Auto: at rear) Nebelschlussleuchte f

foil [fɔɪl] vt vereiteln ▷ n Folie f

fold [fəʊld] vt falten ▷ vi (fam: business) eingehen ▷ n Falte f; **fold up** vt (map etc) zusammenfalten; (chair etc) zusammenklappen ▷ vi (fam: business) eingehen; **folder** n (portfolio) Aktenmappe f; (pamphlet) Broschüre f; (Inform) Ordner m; **folding** adj zusammenklappbar; (bicycle, chair) Klapp-

folk [fəʊk] n Leute pl; (Mus) Folk m; **my ~s** pl (fam) meine Leute ▷ adj Volks-

follow ['fɒləʊ] vt folgen +dat; (pursue) verfolgen; (understand) folgen können +dat; (career, news etc) verfolgen; **as ~s** wie folgt ▷ vi (also on Twitter) folgen; (result) sich ergeben (from aus); **follow up** vt (request, rumour) nachgehen +dat, weiter verfolgen; **follower** n Anhänger(in) m(f); **following** adj folgend; **the ~ day** am (darauf)folgenden Tag ▷ prep nach; **follow up** n (event, book etc) Fortsetzung f

fond [fɒnd] adj: **to be ~ of** gernhaben; **fondly** adv (with love) liebevoll; **fondness** n (for things) Vorliebe f; (for people) Zuneigung f

fondue ['fɒndu:] n Fondue nt

font [fɒnt] n Taufbecken nt; (Typo) Schriftart f

food [fu:d] n Essen nt, Lebensmittel pl; (for animals) Futter nt; (groceries) Lebensmittel pl; **food poisoning** n Lebensmittelvergiftung f; **food processor** n Küchenmaschine f; **foodstuff** n Lebensmittel nt

fool [fu:l] n Idiot m, Narr m; **to make a ~ of oneself** sich blamieren ▷ vt (deceive) hereinlegen ▷ vi: **to ~ around** herumalbern; (waste time) herumtrödeln; **foolish** adj dumm; **foolproof** adj idiotensicher

foot [fʊt] (pl **feet** [fi:t]) n Fuß m; (measure) Fuß m (30,48 cm); **on ~** zu Fuß ▷ vt (bill) bezahlen; **foot-and-mouth disease** n Maul- und Klauenseuche f; **football** n Fußball m; (US: American ~) Football m; **footballer** n Fußballspieler(in) m(f); **footbridge** n Fußgängerbrücke f; **footing** n (hold) Halt m; **footlights** npl Rampenlicht nt; **footnote** n Fußnote f; **footpath** n Fußweg m; **footprint** n Fußabdruck m; **footwear** n Schuhwerk nt

○ **KEYWORD**

for [fɔː] prep 1 für; **is this for me?** ist das für mich?; **the train for London** der Zug nach London; **he went for the paper** er ging die Zeitung holen; **give it to me — what for?** gib es mir — warum?
2 (because of) wegen; **for this reason** aus diesem Grunde
3 (referring to distance) **there are roadworks for 5 km** die Baustelle ist 5 km lang; **we walked for miles** wir sind meilenweit gegangen

4 (referring to time) seit; (with future sense) für; **he was away for 2 years** er war zwei Jahre lang weg **5** (+infin clauses) **it is not for me to decide** das kann ich nicht entscheiden; **for this to be possible ...** damit dies möglich wird/wurde ...
6 (in spite of) trotz +gen o (inf) dat; **for all his complaints** obwohl er sich ständig beschwert
▷ conj denn

forbade [fəˈbæd] pt of **forbid**
forbid [fəˈbɪd] (**forbade**, **forbidden**) vt verbieten
force [fɔːs] n Kraft f; (compulsion) Zwang m, Gewalt; **to come into ~** in Kraft treten; **the Forces** pl die Streitkräfte ▷ vt zwingen; **forced** adj (smile) gezwungen; **~ landing** Notlandung f; **forceful** adj kraftvoll
forceps [ˈfɔːseps] npl Zange f
forearm [ˈfɔːrɑːm] n Unterarm m
forecast [ˈfɔːkɑːst] n voraussagen; (weather) vorhersagen ▷ n Vorhersage f
forefinger [ˈfɔːfɪŋɡə] n Zeigefinger m
foreground [ˈfɔːɡraʊnd] n Vordergrund m
forehand [ˈfɔːhænd] n (Sport) Vorhand f
forehead [ˈfɒrɪd, ˈfɔːhed] n Stirn f
foreign [ˈfɒrən] adj ausländisch; **foreigner** n Ausländer(in) m(f); **foreign exchange** n Devisen pl; **foreign language** n Fremdsprache f; **foreign minister** n Außenminister(in) m(f); **Foreign Office** n (Brit) Außenministerium nt; **Foreign Secretary** n (Brit) Außenminister(in) m(f); **foreign policy** n Außenpolitik f

foremost [ˈfɔːməʊst] adj erste(r, s); (leading) führend
forerunner [ˈfɔːrʌnə] n Vorläufer(in) m(f)
foresee [fɔːˈsiː] irr vt vorhersehen; **foreseeable** adj absehbar
forest [ˈfɒrɪst] n Wald m; **forestry** [ˈfɒrɪstrɪ] n Forstwirtschaft f
forever [fəˈrevə] adv für immer
forgave [fəˈɡeɪv] pt of **forgive**
forge [fɔːdʒ] n Schmiede f ▷ vt schmieden; (fake) fälschen; **forger** n Fälscher(in) m(f); **forgery** n Fälschung f
forget [fəˈɡet] (**forgot**, **forgotten**) vt, vi vergessen; **to ~ about sth** etw vergessen; **forgetful** adj vergesslich; **forgetfulness** n Vergesslichkeit f; **forget-me-not** n Vergissmeinnicht nt
forgive [fəˈɡɪv] (**forgave**, **forgiven**) irr vt verzeihen; **to ~ sb for sth** jdm etw verzeihen
forgot [fəˈɡɒt] pt of **forget**
forgotten [fəˈɡɒtn] pp of **forget**
fork [fɔːk] n Gabel f; (in road) Gabelung f ▷ vi (road) sich gabeln
form [fɔːm] n (shape) Form f, Klasse f; (document) Formular nt; (person) **to be in (good) ~** in Form sein ▷ vt bilden
formal [ˈfɔːməl] adj förmlich, formell; **formality** [fɔːˈmælɪtɪ] n Formalität f
format [ˈfɔːmæt] n Format nt ▷ vt (Inform) formatieren
former [ˈfɔːmə] adj frühere(r, s); (opposite of latter) erstere(r, s); **formerly** adv früher
formidable [ˈfɔːmɪdəbl] adj gewaltig; (opponent) stark
formula [ˈfɔːmjʊlə] n Formel f; **formulate** [ˈfɔːmjʊleɪt] vt formulieren

forth [fɔ:θ] adv: **and so ~** und so weiter; **forthcoming** [fɔ:θ'kʌmɪŋ] adj kommend, bevorstehend

fortieth ['fɔ:tɪəθ] adj vierzigste(r, s); see also **eighth**

fortnight ['fɔ:tnaɪt] n vierzehn Tage pl

fortress ['fɔ:trɪs] n Festung f

fortunate ['fɔ:tʃənɪt] adj glücklich; **I was ~** ich hatte Glück; **fortunately** adv zum Glück; **fortune** ['fɔ:tʃən] n (money) Vermögen nt; **good ~** Glück nt; **fortune-teller** n Wahrsager(in) m(f)

forty ['fɔ:tɪ] num vierzig ▷ n Vierzig f; see also **eight**

forward ['fɔ:wəd] adv vorwärts ▷ n (Sport) Stürmer(in) m(f) ▷ vt (send on) nachsenden; (Inform) weiterleiten; **forwards** adv vorwärts

fossick ['fɒsɪk] vi (Aust, NZ fam) suchen (for nach); **to ~ around** herumstöbern (fam); **to ~ for gold** nach Gold graben

foster child ['fɒstətʃaɪld] n Pflegekind nt; **foster parents** npl Pflegeeltern pl

fought [fɔ:t] pt, pp of **fight**

foul [faʊl] adj (weather) schlecht; (smell) übel ▷ n (Sport) Foul nt

found [faʊnd] pt, pp of **find** ▷ vt (establish) gründen; **foundations** [faʊn'deɪʃənz] npl Fundament nt

fountain ['faʊntɪn] n Springbrunnen m; **fountain pen** n Füller m

four [fɔ:°] num vier ▷ n Vier f; see also **eight**; **fourteen** ['fɔ:'ti:n] num vierzehn ▷ n Vierzehn f; see also **eight**; **fourteenth** adj vierzehnte(r, s); see also **eighth**; **fourth** [fɔ:θ] adj vierte(r, s); see also **eighth**

four-wheel drive n

Allradantrieb m; (car) Geländewagen m

fowl [faʊl] n Geflügel nt

fox [fɒks] n (a. fig) Fuchs m

fracking ['frækɪŋ] n Fracking nt

fraction ['frækʃən] n (Math) Bruch m; (part) Bruchteil m; **fracture** ['fræktʃə°] n (Med) Bruch m ▷ vt brechen

fragile ['frædʒaɪl] adj zerbrechlich

fragment ['frægmənt] n Bruchstück nt

fragrance ['freɪgrəns] n Duft m

frail [freɪl] adj gebrechlich

frame [freɪm] n Rahmen m; (of spectacles) Gestell nt; **~ of mind** Verfassung f ▷ vt einrahmen; **to ~ sb** (fam: incriminate) jdm etwas anhängen; **framework** n Rahmen m, Struktur f

France [frɑ:ns] n Frankreich nt

frank [fræŋk] adj offen

frankfurter ['fræŋkfɜ:tə°] n (Frankfurter) Würstchen nt

frankly ['fræŋklɪ] adv offen gesagt; **quite ~** ganz offen

frantic ['fræntɪk] adj (activity) hektisch; (effort) verzweifelt; **~ with worry** außer sich vor Sorge

fraud [frɔ:d] n (trickery) Betrug m; (person) Schwindler(in) m(f)

freak [fri:k] n Anomalie f; (animal, person) Missgeburt f; (fan: fan) Fan m, Freak m ▷ adj (conditions) außergewöhnlich, seltsam; **freak out** vi (fam) ausflippen

freckle ['frekl] n Sommersprosse f

free [fri:] adj, adv frei; (without payment) gratis, kostenlos; **for ~** umsonst ▷ vt befreien; **freebie** ['fri:bɪ] n (fam) Werbegeschenk nt; **it was a ~** es war gratis; **freedom** ['fri:dəm] n Freiheit f; **freefone** ['fri:fəʊn] adj: **a ~ number** eine gebührenfreie

Nummer; **free kick** n (Sport)
Freistoß m

freelance ['fri:lɑ:ns] adj
freiberuflich tätig; (artist)
freischaffend ▷ n Freiberufler(in)
m(f)

free-range ['fri:reɪndʒ] adj (hen)
frei laufend; **~ eggs** pl Freilandeier
pl

freeway ['fri:weɪ] n (US)
(gebührenfreie) Autobahn

freeze [fri:z] (**froze**, **frozen**) vi
(feel cold) frieren; (of lake etc)
zufrieren; (water etc) gefrieren ▷ vt
einfrieren; **freezer** n
Tiefkühltruhe f; (in fridge)
Gefrierfach nt; **freezing** adj
eiskalt; **I'm ~** mir ist eiskalt;
freezing point n Gefrierpunkt m

freight [freɪt] n (goods) Fracht f;
(money charged) Frachtgebühr f;
freight car n (US) Güterwagen m;
freight train n (US) Güterzug m

French [frentʃ] adj französisch
▷ n (language) Französisch nt; **the
~** pl die Franzosen; **French bean** n
grüne Bohne; **French bread** n
Baguette f; **French dressing** n
Vinaigrette f; **French fries** (US)
npl Pommes frites pl; **French kiss**
n Zungenkuss m; **Frenchman** (pl
-men) n Franzose m; **French
toast** n (US) in Ei und Milch
getunktes gebratenes Brot; **French
window(s)** n(pl) Balkontür f,
Terrassentür f; **Frenchwoman** (pl
-women) n Französin f

frequency ['fri:kwənsɪ] n
Häufigkeit f; (Phys) Frequenz f;
frequent ['fri:kwənt] adj häufig;
frequently adv häufig

fresco ['freskəʊ] n (pl **-es**) n Fresko
nt

fresh [freʃ] adj frisch; (new) neu;
freshen vi: **to ~ up** (person) sich
frisch machen; **fresher, freshman**
(pl **-men**) n Erstsemester nt;

freshwater fish n
Süßwasserfisch m

Fri abbr = **Friday** Fr

friction ['frɪkʃən] n (a. fig)
Reibung f

Friday ['fraɪdeɪ] n Freitag m; see
also **Tuesday**

fridge [frɪdʒ] n Kühlschrank m

fried [fraɪd] adj gebraten;
~ potatoes Bratkartoffeln pl;
~ egg Spiegelei nt; **~ rice**
gebratener Reis

friend [frend] n Freund(in) m(f);
(less close) Bekannte(r) mf; **to make
~s with sb** sich mit jdm
anfreunden; **we're good ~s** wir
sind gut befreundet; **friendly** adj
freundlich; **to be ~ with sb** mit
jdm befreundet sein ▷ n (Sport)
Freundschaftsspiel nt; **friendship**
['frendʃɪp] n Freundschaft f

fright [fraɪt] n Schrecken m;
frighten vt erschrecken; **to be
~ed** Angst haben; **frightening** adj
beängstigend

frill [frɪl] n Rüsche f; **~s** (fam)
Schnickschnack

fringe [frɪndʒ] n (edge) Rand m;
(on shawl etc) Fransen pl; (hair)
Pony m

frivolous ['frɪvələs] adj leichtsinnig; (remark) frivol

frizzy ['frɪzɪ] adj kraus

frog [frɒg] n Frosch m

 KEYWORD

from [frɒm] prep **1** (indicating
starting place) (indicating origin
etc) aus +dat; **a letter/telephone
call from my sister** ein
Brief/Anruf von meiner
Schwester; **where do you come
from?** woher kommen Sie?; **to
drink from the bottle** aus der
Flasche trinken

2 (*indicating time*) von ... an; (*past*) seit; **from one o'clock to o until o till two** von ein Uhr bis zwei; **from January (on)** ab Januar
3 (*indicating distance*) von ... (entfernt)
4 (*indicating price, number etc*) ab +*dat*; **from £10 to £10**; **there were from 20 to 30 people there** es waren zwischen 20 und 30 Leute da
5 (*indicating difference*) **he can't tell red from green** er kann nicht zwischen Rot und Grün unterscheiden; **to be different from sb/sth** anders sein als jd/etw
6 (*because of, based on*) **from what he says** aus dem, was er sagt; **weak from hunger** schwach vor Hunger

front [frʌnt] *n* Vorderseite *f*; (*of house*) Fassade *f*; (*in war, of weather*) Front *f*; (*at seaside*) Promenade *f*; **in ~, at the ~** vorne; **in ~ of** vor; **up ~** (*in advance*) vorher, im Voraus ▷ *adj* vordere(r, s), Vorder-; (*first*) vorderste(r, s); **~ door** Haustür *f*; **~ page** Titelseite *f*; **~ seat** Vordersitz *m*; **~ wheel** Vorderrad *m*
frontier ['frʌntɪə] *n* Grenze *f*
front-wheel drive *n* (*Auto*) Frontantrieb *m*
frost [frɒst] *n* Frost *m*; (*white ~*) Reif *m*; **frosting** *n* (*US*) Zuckerguss *m*; **frosty** *adj* frostig
froth [frɒθ] *n* Schaum *m*; **frothy** *adj* schaumig
frown [fraʊn] *vi* die Stirn runzeln
froze [frəʊz] *pt of* **freeze**
frozen ['frəʊzn] *pp of* **freeze** ▷ *adj* (*food*) tiefgekühlt, Tiefkühl-
fruit [fruːt] *n* (*as collective, a. type*) Obst *nt*; (*single~, a. fig*) Frucht *f*;

fruit machine *n* Spielautomat *m*;
fruit salad *n* Obstsalat *m*
frustrated [frʌˈstreɪtɪd] *adj* frustriert; **frustratration** *n* Frustration *f*, Frust *m*
fry [fraɪ] *vt* braten; **frying pan** *n* Bratpfanne *f*
fuchsia ['fjuːʃə] *n* Fuchsie *f*
fuck [fʌk] *vt* (*vulg*) ficken; **~ off** verpiss dich!; **fucking** *adj* (*vulg*) Scheiß-
fudge [fʌdʒ] *n* weiche Karamellsüßigkeit
fuel [fjʊəl] *n* Kraftstoff *m*; (*for heating*) Brennstoff *m*; **fuel consumption** *n* Kraftstoffverbrauch *m*; **fuel gauge** *n* Benzinuhr *f*; **fuel oil** *n* Gasöl *nt*; **fuel rod** *n* Brennstab *m*; **fuel tank** *n* Tank *m*; (*for oil*) Öltank *m*
fugitive ['fjuːdʒɪtɪv] *n* Flüchtling *m*
fulfil [fʊlˈfɪl] *vt* erfüllen
full [fʊl] *adj* voll; (*person: satisfied*) satt; (*member, employment*) vollständig; (*complete*) vollständig; **~ of ...** voller ... *gen*; **full beam** *n* (*Auto*) Fernlicht *nt*; **full moon** *n* Vollmond *m*; **full stop** *n* Punkt *m*; **full-time** *adj*; **~ job** Ganztagsarbeit *f*; **fully** *adv* völlig; (*recover*) voll und ganz; (*discuss*) ausführlich
fumble ['fʌmbl] *vi* herumfummeln (*with, at* an +*dat*)
fumes [fjuːmz] *npl* Dämpfe *pl*; (*of car*) Abgase *pl*
fun [fʌn] *n* Spaß *m*; **for ~** zum Spaß; **it's ~** es macht Spaß; **to make ~ of** sich lustig machen über +*akk*
function ['fʌŋkʃən] *n* Funktion *f*; (*event*) Feier *f*; (*reception*) Empfang *m* ▷ *vi* funktionieren; **function key** *n* (*Inform*) Funktionstaste *f*
fund [fʌnd] *n* Fonds *m*; **~s** *pl* Geldmittel *pl*

fundamental [fʌndə'mentl]
adj grundlegend; **fundamentally**
adv im Grunde

funding ['fʌndɪŋ] n finanzielle
Unterstützung

funeral ['fjuːnərəl] n Beerdigung f

funfair ['fʌnfeə°] n Jahrmarkt m

fungus ['fʌŋgəs] n (pl **fungi** o
funguses) n Pilz m

funicular [fjuː'nɪkjʊlə°] n Seilbahn f

funnel ['fʌnl] n Trichter m; (of
steamer) Schornstein m

funny ['fʌnɪ] adj (amusing)
komisch, lustig; (strange) seltsam

fur [fɜː°] n Pelz m; (of animal) Fell
nt

furious ['fjʊərɪəs] adj wütend
(with sb auf jdn)

furnished ['fɜːnɪʃd] adj möb-
liert; **furniture** ['fɜːnɪtʃə°] n
Möbel pl; **piece of ~** Möbelstück nt

further ['fɜːðə°] comparative of **far**
▷ adj weitere(r, s); **~ education**
Weiterbildung f; **until ~ notice** bis
auf weiteres ▷ adv weiter;
furthest ['fɜːðɪst] superlative of
far ▷ adj am weitesten entfernt
▷ adv am weitesten

fury ['fjʊərɪ] n Wut f

fuse [fjuːz] n (Elec) Sicherung f
▷ vi (Elec) durchbrennen; **fuse box**
n Sicherungskasten m

fuss [fʌs] n Theater nt; **to make a
~** (ein) Theater machen; **fussy** adj
(difficult) schwierig, kompliziert;
(attentive to detail) pingelig

future ['fjuːtʃə°] adj künftig ▷ n
Zukunft f

fuze (US) see **fuse**

fuzzy ['fʌzɪ] adj (indistinct)
verschwommen; (hair) kraus

g

gable ['geɪbl] n Giebel m

gadget ['gædʒɪt] n Vorrichtung f,
Gerät nt

Gaelic ['geɪlɪk] adj gälisch ▷ n
(language) Gälisch nt

gain [geɪn] vt (obtain, win)
gewinnen; (advantage, respect) sich
verschaffen; (wealth) erwerben;
(weight) zunehmen ▷ vi (improve)
gewinnen (in an +dat); (clock)
vorgehen ▷ n Gewinn m (in an
+dat)

gale [geɪl] n Sturm m

gall bladder ['gɔːlblædə°] n
Gallenblase f

gallery ['gælərɪ] n Galerie f,
Museum nt

gallon ['gælən] n Gallone f; ((Brit)
4.546 l, ((US) 3.79 l)

gallop ['gæləp] n Galopp m ▷ vi
galoppieren

gallstone ['gɔːlstəʊn] n Gallenstein m

Gambia ['gæmbɪə] *n* Gambia *nt*

gamble ['gæmbl] *vi* um Geld spielen, wetten ▷ *n*: **it's a ~** es ist riskant; **gambling** *n* Glücksspiel *nt*

game [geɪm] *n* Spiel *nt*; (*animals*) Wild *nt*; **a ~ of chess** eine Partie Schach; **~s** (*in school*) Sport *m*; **games console** *n* Spielkonsole *f*; **game show** *n* (*TV*) Gameshow *f*

gammon ['gæmən] *n* geräucherter Schinken

gang [gæŋ] *n* (*of criminals, youths*) Bande *f*, Gang *f*, Clique *f* ▷ *vt*: **to ~ up on** sich verschwören gegen

gangster ['gæŋstə°] *n* Gangster *m*

gangway ['gæŋweɪ] *n* (*for ship*) Gangway *f*, (*Brit: aisle*) Gang *m*, Gangway *f*

gap [gæp] *n* (*hole*) Lücke *f*; (*in time*) Pause *f*; (*in age*) Unterschied *m*

gap year *n* Jahr zwischen Schulabschluss und Studium, das oft zu Auslandsaufenthalten genutzt wird

garage ['gærɑːʒ] *n* Garage *f*; (*for repair*) (*Auto*)werkstatt *f*; (*for fuel*) Tankstelle *f*

garbage ['gɑːbɪdʒ] *n* (*US*) Müll *m*; (*fam: nonsense*) Quatsch *m*; **garbage can** *n* (*US*) Mülleimer *m*, (*outside*) Mülltonne *f*; **garbage truck** *n* (*US*) Müllwagen *m*

garden ['gɑːdn] *n* Garten *m*; (*public*) **~s** Park *m*; **garden centre** *n* Gartencenter *nt*; **gardener** *n* Gärtner(in) *m(f)*; **gardening** *n* Gartenarbeit *f*

gargle ['gɑːgl] *vi* gurgeln

gargoyle ['gɑːgɔɪl] *n* Wasserspeier *m*

garlic ['gɑːlɪk] *n* Knoblauch *m*; **garlic bread** *n* Knoblauchbrot *nt*; **garlic butter** *n* Knoblauchbutter *f*

gas [gæs] *n* Gas *nt*; (*US: petrol*)

Benzin *nt*; **to step on the ~** Gas geben; **gas cooker** *n* Gasherd *m*; **gas cylinder** *n* Gasflasche *f*; **gas fire** *n* Gasofen *m*

gasket ['gæskɪt] *n* Dichtung *f*

gas lighter *n* (*for cigarettes*) Gasfeuerzeug *nt*; **gas mask** *n* Gasmaske *f*; **gas meter** *n* Gaszähler *m*

gasoline ['gæsəliːn] *n* (*US*) Benzin *nt*

gasp [gɑːsp] *vi* keuchen; (*in surprise*) nach Luft schnappen

gas pedal *n* (*US*) Gaspedal *nt*; **gas pump** *n* (*US*) Zapfsäule *f*; **gas station** *n* (*US*) Tankstelle *f*; **gas tank** *n* (*US*) Benzintank *m*

gastric ['gæstrɪk] *adj* Magen-; **~ flu** Magen-Darm-Grippe *f*; **~ ulcer** *n* Magengeschwür *nt*

gasworks ['gæswɜːks] *n* Gaswerk *nt*

gate [geɪt] *n* Tor *nt*; (*barrier*) Schranke *f*; (*Aviat*) Gate *nt*, Flugsteig *m*

gateau ['gætəʊ] *n* (*pl* **gateaux**) *n* Torte *f*

gateway *n* Tor *nt*

gather ['gæðə°] *vt* (*collect*) sammeln; **to ~ speed** beschleunigen ▷ *vi* (*assemble*) sich versammeln; (*understand*) schließen (*from aus*); **gathering** *n* Versammlung *f*

gauge [geɪdʒ] *n* Meßgerät *nt*

gauze [gɔːz] *n* Gaze *f*; (*for bandages*) Mull *m*

gave [geɪv] *pt* of **give**

gay [geɪ] *adj* schwul; **~ marriage** (*fam*) Homoehe *f*

gaze [geɪz] *n* Blick *m* ▷ *vi* starren

GCSE *abbr* = **general certificate of secondary education** (*school*) Abschlussprüfung *f* der Sekundarstufe, ≈ mittlere Reife

gear [gɪə°] *n* (*Auto*) Gang *m*; (*equipment*) Ausrüstung *f*; (*clothes*)

Klamotten *pl*; **to change
~ schalten**; **gearbox** *n* Getriebe
nt; **gear change, gear shift** (US)
n Gangschaltung *f*; **gear lever,
gear stick** (US) *n* Schalthebel *m*
geese [gi:s] *pl of* **goose**
gel [dʒel] *n* Gel *nt* ▷ *vi* gelieren;
they really ~led sie verstanden
sich auf Anhieb
gem [dʒem] *n* Edelstein *m*; (*fig*)
Juwel *nt*
Gemini ['dʒemɪnɪ] *nsing* (*Astr*)
Zwillinge *pl*
gender ['dʒendə°] *n* Geschlecht
nt
gene [dʒi:n] *n* Gen *nt*
general ['dʒenərəl] *adj* allgemein; **~ knowledge**
Allgemeinbildung *f*; **~ election**
Parlamentswahlen *pl*; **generalize**
['dʒenrəlaɪz] *vi* verallgemeinern;
generally ['dʒenrəlɪ] *adv* im
Allgemeinen
generation [dʒenə'reɪʃən] *n*
Generation *f*; **generation gap** *n*
Generationsunterschied *m*
generator ['dʒenəreɪtə°] *n*
Generator *m*
generosity [dʒenə'rɒsɪtɪ] *n*
Großzügigkeit *f*; **generous**
['dʒenərəs] *adj* großzügig;
(*portion*) reichlich
genetic [dʒɪ'netɪk] *adj* genetisch;
~ research Genforschung *f*;
~ technology Gentechnik *f*;
genetically modified *adj*
gentechnisch verändert,
genmanipuliert; *see also* **GM**
Geneva [dʒɪ'ni:və] *n* Genf *nt*;
Lake ~ der Genfer See
genitals ['dʒenɪtlz] *npl* Ge-
schlechtsteile *pl*
genitive ['dʒenɪtɪv] *n* Genitiv *m*
genius ['dʒi:nɪəs] *n* Genie *nt*
genome [ʒi:nəʊm] *n* Genom *nt*
gentle ['dʒentl] *adj* sanft; (*touch*)
zart; **gentleman** (*pl* **-men**) *n*

Herr *m*; (*polite man*) Gentleman *m*
gents [dʒents] *n*: "**~**" (*lavatory*)
"Herren", **the ~** *pl* die
Herrentoilette
genuine ['dʒenjʊɪn] *adj* echt
geographical [dʒɪə'græfɪkəl]
adj geografisch; **geography**
[dʒɪ'ɒgrəfɪ] *n* Geografie *f*; (*at
school*) Erdkunde *f*
geological [dʒɪəʊ'lɒdʒɪkəl] *adj*
geologisch; **geology** [dʒɪ'ɒlədʒɪ]
n Geologie *f*
geometry [dʒɪ'ɒmɪtrɪ] *n*
Geometrie *f*
geranium [dʒɪ'reɪnɪəm] *n*
Geranie *f*
gerbil ['dʒɜ:bəl] *n* (*Zool*)
Wüstenrennmaus *f*
germ [dʒɜ:m] *n* Keim *m*; (*Med*)
Bazillus *m*
German ['dʒɜ:mən] *adj* deutsch;
she's ~ sie ist Deutsche;
~ shepherd Deutscher
Schäferhund ▷ *n* (*person*)
Deutsche(r) *mf*; (*language*) Deutsch
nt; **in ~** auf Deutsch; **German
measles** *n sing* Röteln *pl*;
Germany ['dʒɜ:mənɪ] *n*
Deutschland *nt*
gesture ['dʒestʃə°] *n* Geste *f*

🔘 **KEYWORD**

get [get] (*pt, pp* **got**, *pp* **gotten**
(US)) *vi* 1 (*become, be*) werden; **to
get old/tired** alt/müde werden;
to get married heiraten
2 (*go*) (an)kommen, gehen
3 (*begin*) **to get to know sb** jdn
kennenlernen; **let's get going** *o*
started! fangen wir an!
4 (*modal vb aux*) **you've got to do it**
du musst/Sie müssen es tun
▷ *vt* 1 **to get sth done** (*do*) etw
machen; (*have done*) etw machen
lassen; **to get sth going** *o* **to go**
etw in Gang bringen *o* bekommen;

to get sb to do sth jdn dazu
bringen, etw zu tun
2 (obtain: money, permission, results)
erhalten; (find: job, flat) finden;
(fetch: person, object) holen; **to get
sth for sb** jdm etw besorgen; **get
me Mr Jones, please!** (Tel)
verbinde/verbinden Sie mich bitte
mit Mr Jones; **get a life!** (annoyed)
mach dich mal locker!, reg dich
bloß ab!
3 (receive: present, letter)
bekommen, kriegen; (acquire:
reputation etc) erwerben
4 (catch) bekommen, kriegen; (hit:
target etc) treffen, erwischen; **get
him!** (to dog) fass!
5 (take, move) bringen; **to get sth
to sb** jdm etw bringen
6 (understand) verstehen; (hear)
mitbekommen; **I've got it!** ich
hab's!
7 (have, possess) **to have got sth**
etw haben
get about vi herumkommen,
(news) sich verbreiten
get across vi: **to sth** über etw akk
kommen; vt: **to get sth across**
(communicate) etw klarmachen
get along vi (people) (gut)
zurecht-/auskommen (with with);
(depart) sich akk auf den Weg
machen
get at vt (reach) herankommen
an +akk; (facts) herausbekommen;
what are you getting at? worauf
wollen Sie hinaus?, was meinst du
damit?; **to get at sb** (nag) an jdm
herumnörgeln
get away vi (leave) sich akk
davonmachen, wegkommen
(escape) **to get away from sth**
von etw dat entkommen; **to get
away with sth** mit etw davonkommen
get back vi (return)
zurückkommen; (Tel) **to get back**

to s.o. jdn zurückrufen
▷ vt zurückbekommen
get by vi (pass) vorbeikommen;
(manage) zurecht-/auskommen
(on) mit
get down vi (her)untergehen; **to
get down to** in Angriff nehmen,
(find time to do) kommen zu;
▷ vt (depress) fertigmachen; **it
gets me down** (fam) es macht
mich fertig; **to get sth down**
(write) etw aufschreiben
get in vi (train) ankommen; (arrive
home) heimkommen
get into vt (enter) hinein-/
hereinkommen in +akk; (car, train
etc) einsteigen in +akk; (clothes)
anziehen; (rage, panic etc) geraten
in +akk; **to get into trouble** in
Schwierigkeiten kommen
get off vi (from train etc)
aussteigen; (from horse etc)
absteigen; (fam: be enthusiastic) **to
get off on sth** auf etw abfahren;
▷ vt (stain, sticker)
los-/abbekommen; (clothes)
ausziehen
get on vi (progress)
vorankommen; (be friends)
auskommen; (age) alt werden;
(onto train etc) einsteigen; (onto
horse etc) aufsteigen
▷ vt etw +akk vorantreiben, mit
etw akk loslegen
get out vi (of house)
herauskommen; (of vehicle)
aussteigen; **get out!** raus!
▷ vt (take out) herausholen; (stain,
nail) herausbekommen
get out of vt (duty etc)
herumkommen um
get over vt (illness) sich akk
erholen von; (surprise) verkraften;
(news) fassen; (loss) sich abfinden
mit
get round vi herumkommen um;
vt (fig) (person) herumkriegen

get through vi (Tel) durchkommen (to) zu
get together vi zusammenkommen
get up vi aufstehen ▷ vt hinaufbringen; (go up) hinaufgehen; (organize) auf die Beine stellen
get up to vi (reach) erreichen; (prank etc) anstellen

getaway n Flucht f;
get-together n Treffen nt
Ghana ['gɑːnə] n Ghana nt
gherkin ['gɜːkɪn] n Gewürzgurke f
ghetto ['getəʊ] (pl -es) n Ghetto nt
ghost [gəʊst] n Gespenst nt; (of sb) Geist m
giant ['dʒaɪənt] n Riese m ▷ adj riesig
Gibraltar [dʒɪ'brɔːltə°] n Gibraltar nt
giddy ['gɪdɪ] adj schwindlig
gift [gɪft] n Geschenk nt; (talent) Begabung f; **gifted** adj begabt; **giftwrap** vt als Geschenk verpacken
gig [gɪg] n (performance) Gig m; (gigabyte) Gigabyte f
gigantic [dʒaɪ'gæntɪk] adj riesig
giggle ['gɪgl] vi kichern ▷ n Gekicher nt
gill [gɪl] n (of fish) Kieme f
gimmick ['gɪmɪk] n (for sales, publicity) Gag m
gin [dʒɪn] n Gin m
ginger ['dʒɪndʒə°] n Ingwer m ▷ adj (colour) kupferrot; (cat) rötlichgelb; **ginger ale** n Gingerale nt; **ginger beer** n Ingwerlimonade f; **gingerbread** n Lebkuchen m (mit Ingwergeschmack); **ginger(-haired)** adj rotbläulich
gingerly adv (move) vorsichtig

gipsy ['dʒɪpsɪ] n Zigeuner(in) m(f)
giraffe [dʒɪ'rɑːf] n Giraffe f
girl [gɜːl] n Mädchen nt; **girlfriend** n (feste) Freundin f; **girl guide** n (Brit), **girl scout** (US) Pfadfinderin f
gist [dʒɪst] n: **to get the ~ (of it)** das Wesentliche verstehen
give [gɪv] (gave, given) vt geben; (as present) schenken (to sb jdm); (state: name etc) angeben; (speech) halten; (blood) spenden; **to ~ sb sth** jdm etw geben/schenken ▷ vi (yield) nachgeben; **give away** vt (give free) verschenken; (secret) verraten; **give back** vt zurückgeben; **give in** vi aufgeben; **give up** vt, vi aufgeben; **give way** vi (collapse, yield) nachgeben; (traffic) die Vorfahrt beachten
given ['gɪvn] pp of **give** ▷ adj (fixed) festgesetzt; (certain) bestimmt; **~ name** (US) Vorname m ▷ conj: **~ that ...** angesichts der Tatsache, dass ...
glacier ['glæsɪə°] n Gletscher m
glad [glæd] adj froh (about über); **I was ~ to (hear) that ...** es hat mich gefreut, dass ...; **gladly** ['glædlɪ] adv gerne
glance [glɑːns] n Blick m ▷ vi einen Blick werfen (at auf +akk)
gland [glænd] n Drüse f; **glandular fever** n Drüsenfieber nt
glare [gleə°] n grelles Licht; (stare) stechender Blick ▷ vi (angrily) **to ~ at sb** jdn böse anstarren; **glaring** adj (mistake) krass
glass [glɑːs] n Glas nt; **~es** pl Brille f
glen [glen] n (Scot) enges Bergtal nt
glide [glaɪd] vi gleiten; (hover)

schweben; **glider** n Segelflugzeug nt; **gliding** n Segelfliegen nt

glimmer ['glɪmə°] n (of hope) Schimmer m

glimpse [glɪmps] n flüchtiger Blick

glitter ['glɪtə°] vi glitzern; (eyes) funkeln

glitzy ['glɪtsɪ] adj (fam) glanzvoll, Schickimicki-

global ['gləʊbəl] adj global, Welt-; **~ warming** die Erwärmung der Erdatmosphäre; **globe** [gləʊb] n (sphere) Kugel f; (world) Erdball m; (map) Globus m

gloomily ['gluːmɪlɪ], **gloomy** adv, adj düster

glorious ['glɔːrɪəs] adj (victory, past) ruhmreich; (weather, day) herrlich; **glory** ['glɔːrɪ] n Herrlichkeit f

gloss [glɒs] n (shine) Glanz m

glossary ['glɒsərɪ] n Glossar m

glossy ['glɒsɪ] adj (surface) glänzend ▷ n (magazine) Hochglanzmagazin nt

glove [glʌv] n Handschuh m; **glove compartment** n Handschuhfach nt

glow [gləʊ] vi glühen

glucose ['gluːkəʊs] n Traubenzucker m

glue [gluː] n Klebstoff m ▷ vt kleben

glutton ['glʌtn] n Vielfraß m; **a ~ for punishment** (fam) Masochist m

GM abbr = **genetically modified** Gen-; **GM crop** GV-Pflanzen pl; **~ foods** gentechnisch veränderte Lebensmittel

GMT abbr = **Greenwich Mean Time** WEZ f

go [gəʊ] (**went**, **gone**) vi gehen; (in vehicle, travel) fahren; (plane) fliegen; (road) führen (to nach); (depart: train, bus) (ab)fahren;

(person) (fort)gehen; (disappear) verschwinden; (time) vergehen; (function) gehen, funktionieren; (machine, engine) laufen; (fit, suit) passen (with zu); (fail) nachlassen; **I have to ~ to the doctor/to London** ich muss zum Arzt/nach London; **to ~ shopping** einkaufen gehen; **to ~ for a walk/swim** spazieren-/schwimmen gehen; **has he gone yet?** ist er schon weg?; **the wine ~es in the cupboard** der Wein kommt in den Schrank; **to get sth ~ing** etw in Gang setzen; **to keep ~ing** weitermachen; (machine etc) weiterlaufen; **how's the job ~ing?** was macht der Job?; **his memory/eyesight is going** sein Gedächtnis lässt nach/seine Augen werden schwach; **to ~ deaf/mad/grey** taub/verrückt/grau werden ▷ vb aux: **to be ~ing to do sth** etw tun werden; **I was ~ing to do it** ich wollte es tun ▷ n (pl -es) (attempt) Versuch m; **can I have another ~?** darf ich noch mal (probieren)?; **it's my ~** ich bin dran; **in one ~** auf einen Schlag; (drink) in einem Zug; **to ~ well/badly** gut/schlecht ankommen; **go in** vi hineingehen; **go into** vt (enter)

nach; **go down** vi (sun, ship) untergehen; (flood, temperature) zurückgehen; (price) sinken; **to ~ well/badly** gut/schlecht ankommen; **go in** vi hineingehen; **go into** vt (enter)

go after vt nachlaufen +dat; (in vehicle) nachfahren +dat; **go ahead** vi (in front) vorausgehen; (start) anfangen; **go away** vi weggehen; (on holiday, business) verreisen; **go back** vi (return) zurückgehen; **we ~ a long way** (fam) wir kennen uns schon ewig; **go by** vi vorbeigehen; (vehicle) vorbeifahren; (years, time) vergehen ▷ vt (judge by) gehen

hineingehen in +akk; (crash) fahren gegen, hineinfahren in +akk; **to ~ teaching/politics/the army** Lehrer werden/in die Politik gehen/zum Militär gehen; **go off** vi (depart) weggehen; (in vehicle) wegfahren; (lights) ausgehen; (milk etc) sauer werden; (gun, bomb, alarm) losgehen ▷ vt (dislike) nicht mehr mögen; **go on** vi (continue) weitergehen; (lights) angehen; **to ~ with** o doing **sth** etw weitermachen; **go out** vi (leave house) hinausgehen; (fire, light, person socially) ausgehen; **to ~ for a meal** essen gehen; **go up** vi (temperature, price) steigen; (lift) hochfahren; **go without** vt verzichten auf +akk; (food, sleep) auskommen ohne

go-ahead [ˈɡəʊəhed] adj (progressive) fortschrittlich ▷ n grünes Licht

goal [ɡəʊl] n (aim) Ziel nt; (Sport) Tor nt; **goalie, goalkeeper** n Torwart m, Torfrau f; **goalpost** n Torpfosten m

goat [ɡəʊt] n Ziege f

gob [ɡɒb] n (Brit fam) Maul nt; **shut your ~** halt's Maul! ▷ vi spucken; **gobsmacked** (fam: surprised) platt

god [ɡɒd] n Gott m; **thank God** Gott sei Dank; **godchild** (pl -children) n Patenkind nt; **goddaughter** n Patentochter f; **goddess** [ˈɡɒdes] n Göttin f; **godfather** n Pate m; **godmother** n Patin f; **godson** n Patensohn m

goggles npl Schutzbrille f; (for skiing) Skibrille f; (for diving) Taucherbrille f

going [ˈɡəʊɪŋ] adj (rate) üblich; **goings-on** npl Vorgänge pl

go-kart [ˈɡəʊkɑːt] n Gokart m

gold [ɡəʊld] n Gold nt; **golden** adj golden; **goldfish** n Goldfisch

m; **gold-plated** adj vergoldet

golf [ɡɒlf] n Golf nt; **golf ball** n Golfball m; **golf club** n Golfschläger m; (association) Golfklub m; **golf course** n Golfplatz m; **golfer** n Golfspieler(in) m(f)

gone [ɡɒn] pp of go; **he's ~** er ist weg ▷ prep: **just ~ three** kurz nach drei

good [ɡʊd] n (benefit) Wohl nt; (morally good things) Gute(s) nt; **for the ~ of** zum Wohle +gen; **it's for your own ~** es ist zu deinem/Ihrem Besten o Vorteil; **it's no ~** (doing sth) es hat keinen Sinn o Zweck; (thing) es taugt nichts; **for ~** für immer ▷ adj (better, best) gut; (suitable) passend; (thorough) gründlich; (well-behaved) brav; (kind) nett, lieb; **to be ~ at sport/maths** gut in Sport/Mathe sein; **to be no ~ at sport/maths** schlecht in Sport/Mathe sein; **it's ~ for you** es tut dir gut; **this is ~ for colds** das ist gut gegen Erkältungen; **too ~ to be true** zu schön, um wahr zu sein; **this is just not ~ enough** so geht das nicht; **a ~ three hours** gute drei Stunden; **~ morning/evening** guten Morgen/Abend; **~ night** gute Nacht; **to have a ~ time** sich gut amüsieren

goodbye [ɡʊdˈbaɪ] interj auf Wiedersehen

Good Friday n Karfreitag m

good-looking adj gut aussehend

goods [ɡʊdz] npl Waren pl, Güter pl; **goods train** n (Brit) Güterzug m

goodwill [ɡʊdˈwɪl] n Wohlwollen nt

google [ˈɡuːɡl] vt googeln

goose [ɡuːs] n (pl **geese**) n Gans f

▷ vt (fam) **to ~ s.o.** jdn in den Arsch kneifen; **gooseberry** ['guzbərɪ] n Stachelbeere f; **goose bumps** n, **goose pimples** npl Gänsehaut f

gorge [gɔ:dʒ] n Schlucht f

gorgeous ['gɔːdʒəs] adj wunderschön; **he's ~** er sieht toll aus

gorilla [gə'rɪlə] n Gorilla m

gossip ['gɒsɪp] n (talk) Klatsch m; (person) Klatschtante f ▷ vi klatschen, tratschen

got [gɒt] pt, pp of **get**

gotten ['gɒtn] (US) pp of **get**

govern ['gʌvən] vt regieren; (province etc) verwalten; **government** n Regierung f; **governor** n Gouverneur(in) m(f); **govt** abbr = **government** Regierung f

gown [gaʊn] n Abendkleid nt; (academic) Robe f

GP abbr = **General Practitioner** Allgemeinarzt, Allgemeinärztin

GPS n abbr = **global positioning system** GPS nt

grab [græb] vt packen; (person) schnappen

grace [greɪs] n Anmut f; (prayer) Tischgebet nt; **5 days' ~** 5 Tage Aufschub; **graceful** adj anmutig

grade [greɪd] n Niveau nt; (of goods) Güteklasse f; (mark) Note f; (US: year) Klasse f; **to make the ~** es schaffen; **grade crossing** n (US) Bahnübergang m; **grade school** n (US) Grundschule f

gradient ['greɪdɪənt] n (upward) Steigung f; (downward) Gefälle nt

gradual, gradually ['grædjʊəl, -lɪ] adj, adv allmählich

graduate n ['grædjʊɪt] n Uniabsolvent(in) m(f), Hochschulabsolvent(in) m(f) ▷ ['grædjʊeɪt] vi einen akademischen Grad erwerben

grain [greɪn] n (cereals) Getreide nt; (of corn, sand) Korn nt; (in wood) Maserung f

gram [græm] n Gramm nt

grammar ['græmə°] n Grammatik f; **grammar school** n (Brit) ≈ Gymnasium nt

gran [græn] n (fam) Oma f

grand [grænd] adj (pej) hochnäsig; (posh) vornehm ▷ n (fam) 1000 Pfund bzw. 1000 Dollar

grand(d)ad n (fam) Opa m; **granddaughter** n Enkelin f; **grandfather** n Großvater m; **grandma** n (fam) Oma f; **grandmother** n Großmutter f; **grandpa** n (fam) Opa m; **grandparents** npl Großeltern pl; **grandson** n Enkel m

grandstand n (Sport) Tribüne f

granny ['grænɪ] n (fam) Oma f

grant [grɑːnt] vt gewähren (sb sth jdm etw); **to take sth/sb for ~ed** jdn/etw als selbstverständlich hinnehmen ▷ n Subvention f, finanzielle Unterstützung f; (for university) Stipendium nt

grape [greɪp] n Weintraube f; **grapefruit** n Grapefruit f; **grape juice** n Traubensaft m

graph [grɑːf] n Diagramm nt; **graphic** ['græfɪk] adj grafisch; (description) anschaulich

grasp [grɑːsp] vt ergreifen; (understand) begreifen

grass [grɑːs] n Gras nt; (lawn) Rasen m; **grasshopper** n Heuschrecke f

grate [greɪt] n Feuerrost m ▷ vi kratzen ▷ vt (cheese) reiben

grateful, gratefully ['greɪtfʊl, -fəlɪ] adj, adv dankbar

grater ['greɪtə°] n Reibe f

gratifying ['grætɪfaɪɪŋ] adj erfreulich

gratitude ['grætɪtjuːd] n Dankbarkeit f

grave [greɪv] n Grab nt ▷ adj
ernst; (mistake) schwer

gravel [ˈgrævəl] n Kies m

graveyard [ˈgreɪvjɑːd] n Friedhof m

gravity [ˈgrævɪtɪ] n Schwerkraft
f; (seriousness) Ernst m

gravy [ˈgreɪvɪ] n Bratensoße f

gray [greɪ] adj (US) grau

graze [greɪz] vi (of animals)
grasen ▷ vt (touch) streifen; (Med)
abschürfen ▷ n (Med)
Abschürfung f

grease [griːs] n (fat) Fett nt;
(lubricant) Schmiere f ▷ vt
einfetten; (Tech) schmieren;

greasy [ˈgriːsɪ] adj fettig; (hands,
tools) schmierig; (fam: person)
schleimig

great [greɪt] adj groß; (fam: good)
großartig, super; **a ~ deal of** viel;
Great Britain n Großbritannien nt;
great-grandfather n Urgroßvater m; **great-grandmother** n
Urgroßmutter f; **greatly** adv sehr;
~ disappointed zutiefst
enttäuscht

Greece [griːs] n Griechenland nt

greed [griːd] n Gier f (for nach);
(for food) Gefräßigkeit f; **greedy**
adj gierig; (for food) gefräßig

Greek [griːk] adj griechisch ▷ n
(person) Grieche m, Griechin f;
(language) Griechisch nt; **it's all
~ to me** ich verstehe nur
Bahnhof

green [griːn] adj grün; **~ with
envy** grün/gelb vor Neid ▷ n
(colour; for golf) Grün nt; (village ~)
Dorfwiese f; **~s** (vegetables) grünes
Gemüse; **the Greens, the Green
Party** (Pol) die Grünen; **green card**
n (US: work permit)
Arbeitserlaubnis f; (Brit: for car)
grüne Versicherungskarte;
greengage n Reneklode f;

greengrocer n Obst- und
Gemüsehändler(in) m(f);

greenhouse n Gewächshaus nt;
~ effect Treibhauseffekt m;

Greenland n Grönland nt; **green
pepper** n grüner Paprika; **green
salad** n grüner Salat; **green tax**
n Ökosteuer f

Greenwich Mean Time
[ˈgrenɪdʒˈmiːntaɪm] n west-
europäische Zeit

greet [griːt] vt grüßen; **greeting**
n Gruß m

grew [gruː] pt of **grow**

grey [greɪ] adj grau; **grey-haired**
adj grauhaarig; **greyhound** n
Windhund m

grid [grɪd] n Gitter nt; **gridlock** n
Verkehrsinfarkt m; **gridlocked** adj
(roads) völlig verstopft; (talks)
festgefahren

grief [griːf] n Kummer m; (over
loss) Trauer f

grievance [ˈgriːvəns] n
Beschwerde f

grieve [griːv] vi trauern (for um)

grill [grɪl] n (on cooker) Grill m ▷ vt
grillen

grim [grɪm] adj (face, humour)
grimmig; (situation, prospects)
trostlos

grin [grɪn] n Grinsen nt ▷ vi
grinsen

grind [graɪnd] (**ground, ground**)
vt mahlen; (sharpen) schleifen; (US:
meat) durchdrehen, hacken

grip [grɪp] n Griff m; **get a
~** nimm dich zusammen!; **to get
to ~s with sth** etw in den Griff
bekommen ▷ vt packen; **gripping**
adj (exciting) spannend

groan [grəʊn] vi stöhnen (with
vor +dat)

grocer [ˈgrəʊsə°] n Lebensmit-
telhändler(in) m(f); **groceries** npl
Lebensmittel pl

groin [grɔɪn] n (Anat) Leiste f;

groin strain n (Med) Leistenbruch m

groom [gru:m] n Bräutigam m ▷ vt: **well ~ed** gepflegt

grope [grəʊp] vi tasten ▷ vt (sexually harrass) befummeln

gross [grəʊs] adj (coarse) derb; (extreme: negligence, error) grob; (disgusting) ekelhaft; (Comm) brutto; **~ national product** Bruttosozialprodukt nt; **~ salary** Bruttogehalt nt

grotty ['grɒtɪ] adj (fam) mies, vergammelt

ground [graʊnd] pt, pp of **grind** ▷ n Boden m, Erde f; (Sport) Platz m; **~s** pl (around house) (Garten)anlagen pl; (reasons) Gründe pl; (of coffee) Satz m; **on (the) ~s of** aufgrund von; **ground floor** n (Brit) Erdgeschoss nt; **ground meat** n (US) Hackfleisch nt

group [gru:p] n Gruppe f ▷ vt gruppieren

grouse [graʊs] (pl ~) n (bird) Schottisches Moorhuhn; (complaint) Nörgelei f

grow [grəʊ] (**grew, grown**) vi wachsen; (increase) zunehmen (in an); (become) werden; **to ~ old** alt werden; **to ~ into ...** sich entwickeln zu ... ▷ vt (crop, plant) ziehen; (commercially) anbauen; **I'm ~ing a beard** ich lasse mir einen Bart wachsen; **grow up** vi aufwachsen; (mature) erwachsen werden; **growing** adj wachsend; **a ~ number of people** immer mehr Leute

growl [graʊl] vi knurren

grown [grəʊn] pp of **grow**

grown-up [grəʊn'ʌp] adj erwachsen ▷ n Erwachsene(r) mf

growth [grəʊθ] n Wachstum nt; (increase) Zunahme f; (Med) Wucherung f

grubby ['grʌbɪ] adj schmuddelig

grudge [grʌdʒ] n Abneigung f (against gegen) ▷ vt: **to ~ sb sth** jdm etw nicht gönnen

gruelling ['grʊəlɪŋ] adj aufreibend; (pace) mörderisch

gruesome ['gru:səm] adj grausig

grumble ['grʌmbl] vi murren (about über +akk)

grumpy ['grʌmpɪ] adj (fam) mürrisch, grantig

grunt [grʌnt] vi grunzen

G-string ['dʒi:strɪŋ] n String m, Stringtanga m

guarantee [gærən'ti:] n Garantie f (of für); **it's still under ~** es ist noch Garantie darauf ▷ vt garantieren

guard [gɑ:d] n (sentry) Wache f; (in prison) Wärter(in) m(f); (Brit Rail) Schaffner(in) m(f) ▷ vt bewachen; **a closely ~ed secret** ein streng gehütetes Geheimnis

guardian ['gɑ:dɪən] n Vormund m; **~ angel** Schutzengel m

guess [ges] n Vermutung f; (estimate) Schätzung f; **have a ~** rate mal ▷ vt, vi raten; (estimate) schätzen; **I ~ you're right** du hast wohl recht; **I ~ so** ich glaube schon

guest [gest] n Gast m; **be my ~** nur zu!; **guest-house** n Pension f; **guest room** n Gästezimmer nt

guidance ['gaɪdəns] n (direction) Leitung f; (advice) Rat m; (counselling) Beratung f; **for your ~** zu Ihrer Orientierung; **guide** [gaɪd] n (person) Führer(in) m(f); (tour) Reiseleiter(in) m(f); (Brit: girl ~) Pfadfinderin f ▷ vt führen; **guidebook** n Reiseführer m; **guide dog** n Blindenhund m; **guided tour** n

Führung f (of durch); **guidelines**
npl Richtlinien pl

guilt [gɪlt] n Schuld f; **guilty** adj
schuldig (of gen); (look)
schuldbewusst; **to have a
~ conscience** ein schlechtes
Gewissen haben

guinea pig ['gɪnɪ pɪg] n
Meerschweinchen nt; (person)
Versuchskaninchen nt

guitar [gɪ'tɑː°] n Gitarre f

gulf [gʌlf] n Golf m; (gap) Kluft f;
Gulf States npl Golfstaaten pl

gull [gʌl] n Möwe f

gullible ['gʌlɪbl] adj
leichtgläubig

gulp [gʌlp] n (kräftiger) Schluck
▷ vi schlucken

gum [gʌm] n (around teeth, usu pl)
Zahnfleisch nt; (chewing ~)
Kaugummi m

gun [gʌn] n Schusswaffe f; (rifle)
Gewehr nt; (pistol) Pistole f;
gunfire n Schüsse pl,
Geschützfeuer nt; **gunpowder** n
Schießpulver nt; **gunshot** n
Schuss m

gush [gʌʃ] vi (heraus)strömen
(from aus)

gut [gʌt] n Darm m; **~s** pl
(intestines) Eingeweide; (courage)
Mumm m

gutter ['gʌtə°] n (for roof)
Dachrinne f; (in street) Rinnstein m,
Gosse f; **gutter press** n
Skandalpresse f

guy [gaɪ] n (man) Typ m, Kerl m; **~s**
pl (US) Leute pl

gym [dʒɪm] n Turnhalle f; (for
working out) Fitnesscenter nt;
gymnasium [dʒɪm'neɪzɪəm] n
Turnhalle f; **gymnastics**
[dʒɪm'næstɪks] nsing Turnen nt;
gym-toned adj durchtrainiert

gynaecologist [gaɪnɪ'kɒlədʒɪst]
n Frauenarzt m, Frauenärztin f,
Gynäkologe m, Gynäkologin f;

gynaecology n Gynäkologie f,
Frauenheilkunde f

gypsy ['dʒɪpsɪ] n Zigeuner(in)
m(f)

h

habit ['hæbɪt] n Gewohnheit f
hack [hæk] vt hacken; **hacker** n (Inform) Hacker(in) m(f)
had [hæd] pt, pp of **have**
haddock ['hædək] n Schellfisch m

hadn't ['hædnt] contr of **had not**
haemophiliac, **hemophiliac** (US) [hiːməʊ'fɪliæk] n Bluter(in) m(f);
haemorrhage, **hemorrhage** (US) ['hemərɪdʒ] n Blutung f ⊳ vi bluten; **haemorrhoids**, **hemorrhoids** (US) ['hemərɔɪdz] npl Hämorrhoiden pl
haggis ['hægɪs] n (Scot) mit gehackten Schafsinnereien und Haferschrot gefüllter Schafsmagen
Hague [heɪg] n: **the ~** Den Haag
hail [heɪl] n Hagel m ⊳ vi hageln ⊳ vt: **to ~ sb as sth** jdn als etw feiern; **hailstone** n Hagelkorn nt
hair [heə°] n Haar nt, Haare pl; **to do one's ~** sich frisieren; **to get**

one's ~ cut sich dat die Haare schneiden lassen; **hairbrush** n Haarbürste f; **hair conditioner** n Haarspülung f; **haircut** n Haarschnitt m; **to have a ~** sich dat die Haare schneiden lassen; **hairdo** (pl **-s**) n Frisur f; **hairdresser** n Friseur m, Friseuse f; **hairdryer** n Haartrockner m; (hand-held) Fön® m; (over head) Trockenhaube f; **hairgel** n Haargel nt; **hairpin** n Haarnadel f; **hair remover** n Enthaarungsmittel nt; **hair spray** n Haarspray nt; **hair straighteners** npl Haarglätter m; **hair style** n Frisur f; **hairy** adj haarig, behaart; (fam: dangerous) brenzlig
haka ['hɑːkɑ] n (NZ) Haka m (Ritualtanz der Maori); **dem Haka ähnliche Tanz, der vor allem von neuseeländischen Rugby-Teams vor Spielbeginn aufgeführt wird**
hake [heɪk] n Seehecht m
half [hɑːf] (pl **halves**) n Hälfte f; (Sport: of game) Halbzeit f; **to cut in ~** halbieren ⊳ adj halb; **three and a ~ pounds** dreieinhalb Pfund; **~ an hour, a ~ hour** eine halbe Stunde; **one and a ~** eineinhalb, anderthalb ⊳ adv halb, zur Hälfte; **~ past three, ~ three** halb vier; **at ~ past** um halb; **~ asleep** fast eingeschlafen; **she's ~ German** sie ist zur Hälfte Deutsche; **~ as big (as)** halb so groß (wie); **half board** n Halbpension f; **half fare** n halber Fahrpreis; **half-hearted** adj halbherzig; **half-hour** n halbe Stunde; **half pint** n ≈ Viertelliter m nt; **half price** n: **(at)** ~; **zum halben Preis**; **half-term** n (at school) Ferien pl in der Mitte des Trimesters; **half-time** n Halbzeit f; **halfway** adv auf halbem Wege
halibut ['hælɪbət] n Heilbutt m
hall [hɔːl] n (building) Halle f; (for

audience) Saal m; (entrance ~)
Flur m; (large) Diele f; **~ of
residence** (Brit) Studentenwohnheim nt

hallmark ['hɔːlmɑːk] n Stempel
m; (fig) Kennzeichen nt

hallo [hʌ'ləʊ] interj hallo

Hallowe'en [hæləʊ'iːn] n Halloween nt (Tag vor Allerheiligen, an
dem sich Kinder verkleiden und von Tür
zu Tür gehen)

○
○ **HALLOWE'EN**
○
○ **Hallowe'en** ist der 31. Oktober,
○ der Vorabend von Allerheiligen,
○ und nach altem Glauben der
○ Abend, an dem man Geister und
○ Hexen sehen kann. In
○ Großbritannien und vor allem in
○ den USA feiern die Kinder
○ Hallowe'en, indem sie sich
○ verkleiden und mit selbst
○ gemachten Laternen aus
○ Kürbissen von Tür zu Tür
○ ziehen.

halo ['heɪləʊ] (pl **-es**) n (of saint)
Heiligenschein m

halt [hɔːlt] n Pause f, Halt m; **to
come to a ~** zum Stillstand
kommen ▷ vt, vi anhalten

halve [hɑːv] vt halbieren

ham [hæm] n Schinken m; **~ and
eggs** Schinken mit Spiegelei

hamburger ['hæmbɜːgə°] n (Gastr)
Hamburger m

hammer ['hæmə°] n Hammer m
▷ vt, vi hämmern

hammock ['hæmək] n Hängematte f

hamper ['hæmpə°] vt behindern
▷ n (as gift) Geschenkkorb m; (for
picnic) Picknickkorb m

hamster ['hæmstə°] n
Hamster m

hand [hænd] n Hand f; (of clock,
instrument) Zeiger m; (in card game)

Blatt nt; **to be made by ~**
Handarbeit sein; **~s up!** Hände
hoch!; (at school) meldet euch!; **~s
off!** Finger weg!; **on the one ~ ...,
on the other ~ ...** einerseits ...,
andererseits ...; **to give sb a ~** jdm
helfen (with bei); **it's in his ~s** er
hat es in der Hand; **to be in good
~s** gut aufgehoben sein; **to get
out of ~** außer Kontrolle geraten
▷ vt (pass) reichen (to sb jdm);
hand down vt (tradition)
überliefern; (heirloom) vererben;
hand in vt einreichen; (at school,
university etc) abgeben; **hand out**
vt verteilen; **hand over** vt
übergeben

handbag n Handtasche f;
handbook n Handbuch nt;
handbrake n (Brit) Handbremse
f; **handcuffs** npl Handschellen pl;
handful n Handvoll f; **handheld
PC** n Handheld m

handicap ['hændɪkæp] n
Behinderung f, Handikap nt ▷ vt
benachteiligen

handicraft ['hændɪkrɑːft] n
Kunsthandwerk nt

handkerchief ['hæŋkətʃɪf] n
Taschentuch nt

handle ['hændl] n Griff m; (of
door) Klinke f; (of cup etc) Henkel m;
(for winding) Kurbel f ▷ vt (touch)
anfassen; (deal with: matter) sich
befassen mit; (people, machine etc)
umgehen mit; (situation, problem)
fertig werden mit; **handlebars** npl
Lenkstange f

hand luggage ['hændlʌgɪdʒ] n
Handgepäck nt; **handmade** adj
handgefertigt; **to be ~** Handarbeit
sein; **handout** n (sheet) Handout
nt, Thesenpapier nt; **handset** n
Hörer m; **please replace the
~** bitte legen Sie auf; **hands-free
phone** n Freisprechanlage f;
handshake n Händedruck m

handsome ['hænsəm] adj (man) gut aussehend

hands-on [hændz'ɒn] adj praxisorientiert; **~ experience** praktische Erfahrung

handwriting ['hændraɪtɪŋ] n Handschrift f

handy ['hændɪ] adj (useful) praktisch

hang [hæŋ] (hung, hung) vt (auf)hängen; (execute: hanged, hanged) hängen; **to ~ sth on sth** etw an etw akk hängen ▷ vi hängen ▷ n: **he's got the ~ of it** er hat den Dreh raus; **hang about** vi sich herumtreiben, rumhängen; **hang on** vi sich festhalten (to an +dat); (fam: wait) warten; **to ~ to sth** etw behalten; **hang up** vi (Tel) auflegen ▷ vt aufhängen

hangar ['hæŋə⁰] n Flugzeughalle f

hanger ['hæŋə⁰] n Kleiderbügel m

hang glider ['hæŋglaɪdə⁰] n (Flug)drachen m; (person) Drachenflieger(in) m(f); **hang-gliding** n Drachenfliegen nt

hangover ['hæŋəʊvə⁰] n (bad head) Kater m; (relic) Überbleibsel nt

hankie ['hæŋkɪ] n (fam) Taschentuch nt

happen ['hæpən] vi geschehen; (sth strange, unpleasant) passieren; **if anything should ~ to me** wenn mir etwas passieren sollte; **it won't ~ again** es wird nicht wieder vorkommen; **I ~ed to be passing** ich kam zufällig vorbei; **happening** n Ereignis nt, Happening nt

happily ['hæpɪlɪ] adv fröhlich, glücklich; (luckily) glücklicherweise; **happiness** ['hæpɪnəs] n Glück nt; **happy** ['hæpɪ] adj glücklich; (satisfied) **~ with sth** mit etw zufrieden;

(willing) **to be ~ to do sth** etw gerne tun; **Happy Christmas** fröhliche Weihnachten!; **Happy New Year** ein glückliches Neues Jahr!; **Happy Birthday** herzlichen Glückwunsch zum Geburtstag!; **happy hour** n Happy Hour f (Zeit, in der man in Bars Getränke zu günstigeren Preisen bekommt)

harass ['hærəs] vt (ständig) belästigen; **harassment** n Belästigung f; (at work) Mobbing nt; **sexual ~** sexuelle Belästigung

harbor (US), **harbour** ['hɑːbə⁰] n Hafen m

hard [hɑːd] adj hart; (difficult) schwer, schwierig; (harsh) hart(herzig); **don't be ~ on him** sei nicht zu streng zu ihm; **it's ~ to believe** es ist kaum zu glauben ▷ adv (work) schwer; (run) schnell; (rain, snow) stark; **to try ~/-er** sich dat große/mehr Mühe geben; **hardback** n gebundene Ausgabe; **hard-boiled** adj (egg) hart gekocht; **hard copy** n (Inform) Ausdruck m; **hard disk** n (Inform) Festplatte f; **harden** vt härten ▷ vi hart werden; **hardened** adj (person) abgehärtet (to gegen); **hard-hearted** adj hartherzig; **hardliner** n Hardliner(in) m(f); **hardly** ['hɑːdlɪ] adv kaum; **~ ever** fast nie; **hardship** ['hɑːdʃɪp] n Not f; **hard shoulder** n (Brit) Standspur f; **hardware** n (Inform) Hardware f, Haushalts- und Eisenwaren pl; **hard-working** adj fleißig, tüchtig

hare [heə⁰] n Hase m

harm [hɑːm] n Schaden m; (bodily) Verletzung f; **it wouldn't do any ~** es würde nicht schaden ▷ vt schaden +dat; (person) verletzen; **harmful** adj schädlich; **harmless** adj harmlos

harp [hɑːp] n Harfe f

harsh [hɑːʃ] *adj* (climate, voice) rau; (light, sound) grell; (severe) hart, streng

harvest ['hɑːvɪst] *n* Ernte *f*; (time) Erntezeit *f* ▷ *vt* ernten

has [hæz] *pres of* **have**

hash [hæʃ] *n* (Gastr) Haschee *nt*; (fam: hashish) Haschisch *nt*; **to make a ~ of sth** etw vermasseln; **hash browns** *npl* (US) = Kartoffelpuffer/Rösti mit Zwiebeln *pl*

hashtag ['hæʃtæg] *n* (on Twitter) Hashtag *m*

hassle ['hæsl] *n* Ärger *m*; (fuss) Theater *nt*; **no ~** kein Problem ▷ *vt* bedrängen

hasn't ['hæznt] *contr of* **has not**

haste [heɪst] *n* Eile *f*; **hastily**, **hasty** *adv, adj* hastig; (rash) vorschnell

hat [hæt] *n* Hut *m*

hatch [hætʃ] *n* (Naut) Luke *f*; (in house) Durchreiche *f*; **hatchback** ['hætʃbæk] *n* (car) Wagen *m* mit Hecktür

hate [heɪt] *vt* hassen; **I ~ doing this** ich mache das sehr ungern ▷ *n* Hass *m* (of *auf* +akk)

haul [hɔːl] *vt* ziehen, schleppen ▷ *n* (booty) Beute *f*; **haulage** ['hɔːlɪdʒ] *n* Transport *m*; (trade) Spedition *f*

O KEYWORD

have [hæv] (*pt, pp* **had**) *vb aux* **1** haben; (*esp with vbs of motion*) sein; **to have arrived/slept** angekommen sein/geschlafen haben; **to have been** gewesen sein; **having eaten** o **when he had eaten, he left** nachdem er gegessen hatte, ging er

2 (*in tag questions*) **you've done it, haven't you?** du hast/Sie haben es doch gemacht, oder nicht?

3 (*in short answers and questions*) **you've made a mistake — so I have/no I haven't** du hast/Sie haben einen Fehler gemacht — ja, stimmt/nein; **we haven't paid — yes we have!** wir haben nicht bezahlt — doch!; **I've been there before, have you?** ich war schon einmal da, du/Sie auch?

▷ *modal vb aux* (*be obliged*): **to have (got) to do sth** etw tun müssen; **you haven't to tell her** du darfst es ihr nicht erzählen

▷ *vt* **1** (*possess*) haben; **he has (got) blue eyes** er hat blaue Augen; **I have (got) an idea** ich habe eine Idee

2 (*referring to meals etc*) **to have breakfast/a cigarette** frühstücken/eine Zigarette rauchen

3 (*receive, obtain etc*) haben; **may I have your address?** kann ich deine/Ihre Adresse haben?; **to have a baby** ein Kind bekommen

4 (*maintain, allow*) **he will have it that he is right** er besteht darauf, dass er recht hat; **I won't have it** das lasse ich mir nicht bieten

5 to have sth done etw machen lassen; **to have sb do sth** jdn etw machen lassen; **he soon had them all laughing** er brachte sie alle zum Lachen

6 (*experience, suffer*) **she had her bag stolen** man hat ihr die Tasche gestohlen; **he had his arm broken** er hat sich den Arm gebrochen

7 (+*noun: take, hold etc*) **to have a walk/rest** spazieren gehen/sich ausruhen; **to have a meeting/party** eine Besprechung/Party haben; **have on** *vt* (*be wearing*) anhaben; (*have arranged*) vorhaben; (Brit) **you're having me on** du verarschst mich doch;

have out vt: **to have it out with sb** (settle problem) etw mit jdm bereden

Hawaii [hə'waɪiː] n Hawaii nt

hawk [hɔːk] n Habicht m

hay [heɪ] n Heu nt; **hay fever** n Heuschnupfen m

hazard ['hæzəd] n Gefahr f; (risk) Risiko nt; **hazardous** adj gefährlich; **~ waste** Sondermüll m; **hazard warning lights** npl Warnblinkanlage f

haze [heɪz] n Dunst m

hazelnut ['heɪzlnʌt] n Haselnuss f

hazy ['heɪzɪ] adj (misty) dunstig; (vague) verschwommen

he [hiː] pron er

head [hed] n Kopf m; (leader) Leiter(in) m(f); (at school) Schulleiter(in) m(f); **~ of state** Staatsoberhaupt nt; **at the ~ of** an der Spitze von; (tossing coin) **~s or tails?** Kopf oder Zahl? ▷ adj (leading) Ober-; **~ boy** Schulsprecher m; **~ girl** Schulsprecherin f ▷ vt anführen; (organization) leiten; **head for** vt zusteuern auf +akk; **he's heading for trouble** er wird Ärger bekommen

headache ['hedeɪk] n Kopfschmerzen pl, Kopfweh nt; **header** n (football) Kopfball m; (dive) Kopfsprung m; **headfirst** adj kopfüber; **headhunt** vt (Comm) abwerben; **heading** n Überschrift f; **headlamp**, **headlight** n Scheinwerfer m; **headline** n Schlagzeile f; **headmaster** n Schulleiter m; **headmistress** n Schulleiterin f; **head-on collision** adj Frontalzusammenstoß m; **headphones** npl Kopfhörer m; **headquarters** npl (of firm) Zentrale f; **headrest** n head

restraint n Kopfstütze f; **headscarf** (pl **-scarves**) n Kopftuch nt; **head teacher** n Schulleiter(in) m(f)

heal [hiːl] vt, vi heilen

health [helθ] n Gesundheit f; **good/bad for one's ~** gesund/ungesund; **your ~!** zum Wohl!; **~ and beauty** Wellness; **health centre** n Ärztezentrum nt; **health club** n Fitnesscenter nt; **health food** n Reformkost f; **~ shop**, **~ store** Bioladen m; **health insurance** n Krankenversicherung f; **health service** n Gesundheitswesen nt; **healthy** adj gesund

heap [hiːp] n Haufen m; **~s of** (fam) jede Menge ▷ vt, vi häufen

hear [hɪə°] (**heard**, **heard**) vt, vi hören; **to ~ about sth** von etw erfahren; **I've ~d of it/him** ich habe schon davon/von ihm gehört; **hearing** n Gehör nt; (Jur) Verhandlung f; **hearing aid** n Hörgerät nt; **hearsay** n: **from ~** vom Hörensagen

heart [hɑːt] n Herz nt; **to lose/take ~** den Mut verlieren/Mut fassen; **to learn by ~** auswendig lernen; (cards) **~s** Herz nt; **queen of ~s** Herzdame f; **heart attack** n Herzanfall m; **heartbeat** n Herzschlag m; **heartbreaking** adj herzzerreißend; **heartbroken** adj todunglücklich, untröstlich; **heartburn** n Sodbrennen nt; **heart failure** n Herzversagen nt; **heartfelt** adj tief empfunden; **heartless** adj herzlos; **heart-throb** n (fam) Schwarm m; **heart-to-heart** n offene Aussprache; **hearty** [hɑːtɪ] adj (meal, appetite) herzhaft; (welcome) herzlich

heat [hiːt] n Hitze f; (pleasant) Wärme f; (temperature) Temperatur f; *(Sport)* Vorlauf m ▷ vt *(house, room)* heizen; **heat up** vi warm werden ▷ vt aufwärmen; **heated** *adj* beheizt; *(fig)* hitzig; **heater** n Heizofen m; *(Auto)* Heizung f

heath [hi:θ] n *(Brit)* Heide f;

heather ['heðə⁰] n Heidekraut nt

heating ['hi:tɪŋ] n Heizung f; **heat resistant** *adj* hitzebeständig; **heatwave** n Hitzewelle f

heaven ['hevn] n Himmel m; **heavenly** *adj* himmlisch

heavily ['hevɪlɪ] *adv (rain, drink etc)* stark; **heavy** ['hevɪ] *adj* schwer; *(rain, traffic, smoker etc)* stark; **heavy goods vehicle** n Lastkraftwagen m

Hebrew ['hi:bru:] *adj* hebräisch ▷ n *(language)* Hebräisch nt

hectic ['hektɪk] *adj* hektisch

he'd [hi:d] *contr of* **he had; he would**

hedge [hedʒ] n Hecke f

hedgehog ['hedʒhɒg] n Igel m

heel [hi:l] n *(Anat)* Ferse f; *(of shoe)* Absatz m

hefty ['heftɪ] *adj* schwer; *(person)* stämmig; *(fine, amount)* saftig

height [haɪt] n Höhe f; *(of person)* Größe f

heir [eə⁰] n Erbe m; **heiress** ['eərɪs] n Erbin f

held [held] *pt, pp of* **hold**

helicopter ['helɪkɒptə⁰] n Hubschrauber m; **heliport** ['helɪpɔːt] n Hubschrauber-landeplatz m

hell [hel] n Hölle f; **go to ~** scher dich zum Teufel ▷ *interj* verdammt; **that's a ~ of a lot of money** das ist verdammt viel Geld

he'll [hi:l] *contr of* **he will; he shall**

hello [hʌ'ləʊ] *interj* hallo

helmet ['helmɪt] n Helm m

help [help] n Hilfe f ▷ vt, vi helfen +dat *(with bei)*; **to ~ sb (to) do sth** jdm helfen, etw zu tun; **can I ~?** kann ich (Ihnen) behilflich sein?; **I couldn't ~ laughing** ich musste einfach lachen; **I can't ~ it** ich kann nichts dafür; **~ yourself** bedienen Sie sich; **helpful** *adj (person)* hilfsbereit; *(useful)* nützlich; **helping** n Portion f; **helpless** *adj* hilflos

hem [hem] n Saum m

hemophiliac [hi:məʊ'fɪlɪæk] n *(US)* Bluter m; **hemorrhage** ['hemərɪdʒ] n *(US)* Blutung f; **hemorrhoids** ['hemərɔɪdz] npl *(US)* Hämorrhoiden pl

hen [hen] n Henne f

hen night n *(Brit)* Junggesellinnenabschied m

hence [hens] *adv (reason)* daher

henpecked ['henpekt] *adj:* **to be ~** unter dem Pantoffel stehen

hepatitis [hepə'taɪtɪs] n Hepatitis f

her [hɜː⁰] *adj* ihr; **she's hurt ~ leg** sie hat sich *dat* das Bein verletzt ▷ *pron (direct object)* sie; *(indirect object)* ihr; **do you know ~?** kennst du sie?; **can you help ~?** kannst du ihr helfen?; **it's ~** sie ist's

herb [hɜːb] n Kraut nt

herbal medicine ['hɜːbəl-] n Pflanzenheilkunde f; **herbal tea** n Kräutertee m

herd [hɜːd] n Herde f; **herd instinct** n Herdentrieb m

here [hɪə⁰] *adv* hier; *(to this place)* hierher; **come ~** komm her; **I won't be ~ for lunch** ich bin zum Mittagessen nicht da; **~ and there** hier und da, da und dort

hereditary [hɪ'redɪtərɪ] *adj* erblich; **hereditary disease** n Erbkrankheit f; **heritage** ['herɪtɪdʒ] n Erbe nt

hernia ['hɜ:nɪə] n Leistenbruch m, Eingeweidebruch m

hero ['hɪərəʊ] (pl -es) n Held m

heroin ['herəʊɪn] n Heroin nt

heroine ['herəʊɪn] n Heldin f; **heroism** ['herəʊɪzəm] n Heldentum nt

herring ['herɪŋ] n Hering m

hers [hɜ:z] pron ihre(r, s); **this is ~** das gehört ihr; **a friend of ~** ein Freund von ihr

herself [hɜ:'self] pron (reflexive) sich; **she's bought ~ a flat** sie hat sich eine Wohnung gekauft; **she needs it for ~** sie braucht es für sich (selbst); (emphatic) **she did it ~** sie hat es selbst gemacht; **(all) by ~** allein

he's [hi:z] contr of **he is**; **he has**

hesitant ['hezɪtənt] adj zögernd; **hesitate** ['hezɪteɪt] vi zögern; **don't ~ to ask** fragen Sie ruhig; **hesitation** n Zögern nt; **without ~** ohne zu zögern

heterosexual [hetərəʊ'sekʃʊəl] adj heterosexuell ▷ n Heterosexuelle(r) mf

HGV abbr = **heavy goods vehicle** LKW m

hi [haɪ] interj hi, hallo

hiccup ['hɪkʌp] n Schluckauf m; (minor problem) Problemchen nt; **to have (the) ~s** Schluckauf haben

hid [hɪd] pt of **hide**

hidden ['hɪdn] pp of **hide**

hide [haɪd] (hid, hidden) vt verstecken (from +dat); (feelings, truth) verbergen; (cover) verdecken ▷ vi sich verstecken (from vor +dat)

hideous ['hɪdɪəs] adj scheußlich

hiding ['haɪdɪŋ] n (beating) Tracht f Prügel; (concealment) **to be in ~** sich versteckt halten; **hiding place** n Versteck nt

hi-fi ['haɪfaɪ] n Hi-Fi nt; (system) Hi-Fi-Anlage f

high [haɪ] adj hoch; (wind) stark; (living) im großen Stil; (on drugs) high ▷ adv hoch ▷ n (Meteo) Hoch nt; **highchair** n Hochstuhl m; **higher** adj höher; **higher education** n Hochschulbildung f; **high flier** n Hochbegabte(r) mf; **high heels** npl Stöckelschuhe pl; **high jump** n Hochsprung m; **Highlands** npl (schottisches) Hochland nt; **highlight** n (in hair) Strähnchen nt; (fig) Höhepunkt m ▷ vt (with pen) hervorheben; **highlighter** n Textmarker m; **highly** adj hoch, sehr; **~ paid** hoch bezahlt; **I think ~ of him** ich habe eine hohe Meinung von ihm; **high-performance** adj Hochleistungs-; **high school** n (US) Highschool f, ≈ Gymnasium nt; **high-speed** adj Schnell-; **~ train** Hochgeschwindigkeitszug m; **high street** n Hauptstraße f; **high tech** adj Hightech- ▷ n Hightech nt; **high tide** n Flut f; **highway** n (US) ≈ Autobahn f; (Brit) Landstraße f

hijack ['haɪdʒæk] vt entführen, hijacken; **hijacker** n Entführer(in) m(f), Hijacker m

hike [haɪk] vi wandern ▷ n Wanderung f; **hiker** n Wanderer m, Wanderin f; **hiking** n Wandern nt

hilarious [hɪ'leərɪəs] adj zum Schreien komisch

hill [hɪl] n Hügel m; (higher) Berg m; **hilly** adj hügelig

him [hɪm] pron (direct object) ihn; (indirect object) ihm; **do you know ~?** kennst du ihn?; **can you help ~?** kannst du ihm helfen?; **it's ~** er ist's; **~ too** er auch

himself [hɪm'self] pron (reflexive) sich; **he's bought ~ a flat** er hat sich eine Wohnung gekauft; **he needs it for ~** er braucht es für sich (selbst); (emphatic) **he did it**

~ er hat es selbst gemacht; **(all) by ~** allein

hinder ['hɪndə°] vt behindern; **hindrance** n ['hɪndrəns] n Behinderung f

Hindu ['hɪnduː] adj hinduistisch ▷ n Hindu m; **Hinduism** ['hɪnduːɪzəm] n Hinduismus m

hinge [hɪndʒ] n Scharnier nt; (on door) Angel f

hint [hɪnt] n Wink m, Andeutung f; (trace) Spur f ▷ vi andeuten (at akk)

hip [hɪp] n Hüfte f

hippopotamus [hɪpə'pɒtəməs] n Nilpferd nt

hire ['haɪə°] vt (worker) anstellen; (car, bike etc) mieten ▷ n Miete f; **for ~** (taxi) frei; **hire car** n Mietwagen m; **hire charge** n Benutzungsgebühr f; **hire purchase** n Ratenkauf m

his [hɪz] adj sein; **he's hurt ~ leg** er hat sich dat das Bein verletzt ▷ pron seine(r, s); **it's ~** es gehört ihm; **a friend of ~** ein Freund von ihm

historic [hɪ'stɒrɪk] adj (significant) historisch; **historical** adj (monument etc) historisch; (studies etc) geschichtlich; **history** ['hɪstərɪ] n Geschichte f

hit [hɪt] n (blow) Schlag m; (on target) Treffer m; (successful film, CD etc) Hit m ▷ vt (hit, hit) schlagen; (bullet, stone etc) treffen; **the car ~ a tree** das Auto fuhr gegen einen Baum; **to ~ one's head on sth** sich dat den Kopf an etw dat stoßen; **hit (up)on** vt stoßen auf +akk; **hit-and-run** adj; **~ accident** Unfall m mit Fahrerflucht

hitch [hɪtʃ] vt (pull up) hochziehen ▷ n Schwierigkeit f; **without a ~** reibungslos

hitch-hike ['hɪtʃhaɪk] vi trampen; **hitch-hiker** n Tramper(in)

m(f); **hitchhiking** n Trampen nt

HIV abbr = **human immunodeficiency virus** HIV nt; **~ positive/negative** HIV-positiv/negativ

hive [haɪv] n Bienenstock m

HM abbr = **His/Her Majesty**

HMS abbr = **His/Her Majesty's Ship**

hoarse [hɔːs] adj heiser

hoax [həʊks] n Streich m, Jux m; (false alarm) blinder Alarm

hob [hɒb] n (of cooker) Kochfeld nt

hobble ['hɒbl] vi humpeln

hobby ['hɒbɪ] n Hobby nt

hobo ['həʊbəʊ] (pl **-es**) n (US) Penner(in) m(f)

hockey ['hɒkɪ] n Hockey nt

hold [həʊld] (**held, held**) vt halten; (contain) enthalten; (be able to contain) fassen; (post, office) innehaben; (value) behalten; (meeting) abhalten; (person as prisoner) gefangen halten; **to ~ one's breath** den Atem anhalten; **to ~ hands** Händchen halten; **~ the line** (Tel) bleiben Sie am Apparat ▷ vi (weather) sich halten; (in grasp) Halt m; (of ship, aircraft) Laderaum m; **hold back** vt zurückhalten; (keep secret) verheimlichen; **hold on** vi sich festhalten; (wait) warten; (Tel) dranbleiben; **to ~ to sth** etw festhalten; **hold out** vt ausstrecken; (offer) hinhalten; (offer) bieten ▷ vi durchhalten; **hold up** vt hochhalten; (support) stützen; (delay) aufhalten; **holdall** n Reisetasche f; **holder** n (person) Inhaber(in) m(f); **holdup** n (in traffic) Stau m; (robbery) Überfall m

hole [həʊl] n Loch nt; (of fox, rabbit) Bau m; **~ in the wall** (cash dispenser) Geldautomat m

holiday ['hɒlɪdeɪ] n (day off)
freier Tag; (public ~) Feiertag m;
(vacation) Urlaub m; (at school)
Ferien pl; **on ~** im Urlaub; **to go on
~** Urlaub machen; **holiday camp**
n Ferienlager nt; **holiday home** n
Ferienhaus nt; (flat)
Ferienwohnung f; **holidaymaker**
n Urlauber(in) m(f); **holiday
resort** n Ferienort m

Holland ['hɒlənd] n Holland nt

hollow ['hɒləʊ] adj hohl; (words)
leer ▷ n Vertiefung f

holly ['hɒlɪ] n Stechpalme f

holy ['həʊlɪ] adj heilig; **Holy
Week** n Karwoche f

home [həʊm] n Zuhause nt;
(area, country) Heimat f; (institution)
Heim nt; **at ~** zu Hause; **to make
oneself at ~** es sich dat bequem
machen; **away from ~** verreist
▷ adv: **to go ~** nach Hause
gehen/fahren; **home address** n
Heimatadresse f; **home country**
n Heimatland nt; **home game** n
(Sport) Heimspiel nt; **homeless** adj
obdachlos; **homely** adj häuslich;
(US: ugly) unscheinbar;
home-made adj selbst gemacht;
home movie n Amateurfilm m;
Home Office n (Brit)
Innenministerium nt

homeopathic adj (US) see
homoeopathic

home page ['həʊmpeɪdʒ] n
(Inform) Homepage f; **Home
Secretary** n (Brit)
Innenminister(in) m(f); **homesick**
adj: **to be ~** Heimweh haben;
home town n Heimatstadt f;
homework n Hausaufgaben pl

homicide ['hɒmɪsaɪd] n (US)
Totschlag m

homoeopathic
[həʊmɪəʊ'pæθɪk] adj
homöopathisch

homosexual [həʊməʊ'seksjʊəl]

adj homosexuell ▷ n Homosex-
uelle(r) mf

Honduras [hɒn'djʊərəs] n
Honduras nt

honest ['ɒnɪst] adj ehrlich;
honesty n Ehrlichkeit f

honey ['hʌnɪ] n Honig m;
honeycomb n Honigwabe f;
honeydew melon n
Honigmelone f; **honeymoon** n
Flitterwochen pl

Hong Kong [hɒŋ'kɒŋ] n
Hongkong nt

honor (US) see **honour**; **honorary**
['ɒnərərɪ] adj (member, title etc)
Ehren-, ehrenamtlich; **honour**
['ɒnə°] vt ehren; (cheque) einlösen;
(contract) einhalten ▷ n Ehre f; **in
~ of** zu Ehren von; **honourable** adj
ehrenhaft; **honours degree** n
akademischer Grad mit Prüfung im
Spezialfach

hood [hʊd] n Kapuze f; (Auto)
Verdeck nt; (US Auto) Kühlerhaube
f

hoof [huːf] n (pl hooves) n Huf
m

hook [hʊk] n Haken m; **hooked**
adj (keen) besessen (on von);
(drugs) abhängig sein (on von)

hooligan ['huːlɪgən] n Hooligan
m

hoot [huːt] vi (Auto) hupen

Hoover® ['huːvə] n Staubsauger
m; **hoover** vi, vt staubsaugen

hop [hɒp] vi hüpfen ▷ n (Bot)
Hopfen m

hope [həʊp] vt, vi hoffen (for auf
+akk); **I ~ so/~ not**
hoffentlich/hoffentlich nicht; **I
~ (that) we'll meet** ich hoffe, dass
wir uns sehen werden ▷ n
Hoffnung f; **there's no ~** es ist
aussichtslos; **hopeful** adj
hoffnungsvoll; **hopefully** adv (full
of hope) hoffnungsvoll; (I hope so)
hoffentlich; **hopeless** adj

hoffnungslos; (*incompetent*) miserabel

horizon [həˈraɪzn] n Horizont m; **horizontal** [hɒrɪˈzɒntl] adj horizontal

hormone [ˈhɔːməʊn] n Hormon nt

horn [hɔːn] n Horn nt; (*Auto*) Hupe f

hornet [ˈhɔːnɪt] n Hornisse f

horny [ˈhɔːnɪ] adj (*fam*) geil

horoscope [ˈhɒrəskəʊp] n Horoskop nt

horrible, horribly [ˈhɒrɪbl, -blɪ] adj, adv schrecklich; **horrid, horribly** [ˈhɒrɪd, -lɪ] adj, adv abscheulich; **horrify** [ˈhɒrɪfaɪ] vt entsetzen; **horror** [ˈhɒrəᵊ] n Entsetzen nt; **~s** (*things*) Schrecken pl

hors d'oeuvre [ɔːˈdɜːvr] n Vorspeise f

horse [hɔːs] n Pferd nt; **horse chestnut** n Rosskastanie f; **horsepower** n Pferdestärke f, PS nt; **horse racing** n Pferderennen nt; **horseradish** n Meerrettich m; **horse riding** n Reiten nt; **horseshoe** n Hufeisen nt

horticulture [ˈhɔːtɪkʌltʃəᵊ] n Gartenbau m

hose, hosepipe [həʊz, ˈhəʊzpaɪp] n Schlauch m

hospitable [hɒˈspɪtəbl] adj gastfreundlich

hospital [ˈhɒspɪtl] n Krankenhaus nt

hospitality [hɒspɪˈtælɪtɪ] n Gastfreundschaft f

host [həʊst] n Gastgeber m; (*TV: of show*) Moderator(in) m(f), Talkmaster(in) m(f) ▷ vt (*party*) geben; (*TV: TV show*) moderieren

hostage [ˈhɒstɪdʒ] n Geisel f

hostel [ˈhɒstəl] n Wohnheim nt; (*youth ~*) Jugendherberge f

hostess [ˈhəʊstɪs] n (*of a party*) Gastgeberin f

hostile [ˈhɒstaɪl] adj feindlich; **hostility** [hɒsˈtɪlɪtɪ] n Feindseligkeit f

hot [hɒt] adj heiß; (*drink, food, water*) warm; (*spiced*) scharf; **I'm (feeling)** ~ mir ist heiß; **hot cross bun** n Rosinenbrötchen mit einem Kreuz darauf, hauptsächlich zu Ostern gegessen; **hot dog** n Hotdog m

hotel [həʊˈtel] n Hotel nt; **hotel room** n Hotelzimmer nt

hothouse n Treibhaus nt; **hotline** n Hotline f; **hotplate** n Kochplatte f; **hotspot** n (*Inform*) Hotspot m; **hot-water bottle** n Wärmflasche f

hour [ˈaʊəᵊ] n Stunde f; **to wait for ~s** stundenlang warten; **~s** (*of shops etc*) Geschäftszeiten pl; **hourly** adj stündlich

house [haʊs] (*pl* **houses**) n Haus nt; **at my ~** bei mir (zu Hause); **to my ~** zu mir (nach Hause); **on the ~** auf Kosten des Hauses; **the House of Commons/Lords** das britische Unterhaus/Oberhaus; **the Houses of Parliament** das britische Parlamentsgebäude ▷ [haʊz] vt unterbringen; **houseboat** n Hausboot nt; **household** n Haushalt m; **~ appliance** Haushaltsgerät nt; **house-husband** n Hausmann m; **housekeeping** n Haushaltung f; (*money*) Haushaltsgeld nt; **house-trained** adj stubenrein; **house-warming (party)** n Einzugsparty f; **housewife** (*pl* **-wives**) n Hausfrau f; **house wine** n Hauswein m; **housework** n Hausarbeit f

housing [ˈhaʊzɪŋ] n (*houses*) Wohnungen pl; (*house building*) Wohnungsbau m; **housing**

benefit n Wohngeld nt; **housing development, housing estate** (Brit) n Wohnsiedlung f

hover ['hɒvə°] vi schweben; **hovercraft** n Luftkissenboot nt

how [haʊ] adv wie; **~ many** wie viele; **~ much** wie viel; **~ are you?** wie geht es Ihnen?; **~ are things?** wie geht's?; **~'s work?** was macht die Arbeit?; **~ about ...?** wie wäre es mit ...?; **however** [haʊ'evə°] conj (but) jedoch, aber ▷ adv (no matter how) wie ... auch; **~ much it costs** wie viel es auch kostet; **~ you do it** wie man es auch macht

howl [haʊl] vi heulen; **howler** ['haʊlə°] n (fam) grober Schnitzer

HP, hp (Brit) abbr = **hire purchase** Ratenkauf m ▷ abbr = **horsepower** PS

HQ abbr = **headquarters**

hubcap ['hʌbkæp] n Radkappe f

hug [hʌg] vt umarmen ▷ n Umarmung f

huge [hju:dʒ] adj riesig

hum [hʌm] vi, vt summen

human ['hju:mən] adj menschlich; **~ rights** Menschenrechte pl ▷ n: **~ (being)** Mensch m; **humanitarian** [hju:mænɪ'tɛərɪən] adj humanitär; **humanity** [hju:'mænɪtɪ] n Menschheit f; (kindliness) Menschlichkeit f; **humanities** Geisteswissenschaften pl

humble ['hʌmbl] adj demütig; (modest) bescheiden

humid ['hju:mɪd] adj feucht; **humidity** [hju:'mɪdɪtɪ] n (Luft)feuchtigkeit f

humiliate [hju:'mɪlɪeɪt] vt demütigen; **humiliation** [hju:mɪlɪ'eɪʃn] n Erniedrigung f, Demütigung f

humor (US) see **humour**;

humorous ['hju:mərəs] adj humorvoll; (story) lustig, witzig; **humour** ['hju:mə°] n Humor m; **sense of ~** Sinn m für Humor

hump [hʌmp] n Buckel m

hunch [hʌntʃ] n Gefühl nt, Ahnung f ▷ vt (back) krümmen; **hunchback** n Bucklige(r) mf

hundred ['hʌndrəd] num: **one ~, a ~** (ein)hundert; **a ~ and one** hundert(und)eins; **two ~** zweihundert; **hundredth** adj hundertste(r, s) ▷ n (fraction) Hundertstel nt; **hundredweight** n Zentner m (50,8 kg)

hung [hʌŋ] pt, pp of **hang**

Hungarian [hʌŋ'gɛərɪən] adj ungarisch ▷ n (person) Ungar(in) m(f); (language) Ungarisch nt; **Hungary** ['hʌŋgərɪ] n Ungarn nt

hunger ['hʌŋgə°] n Hunger m; **hungry** ['hʌŋgrɪ] adj hungrig; **to be ~** Hunger haben

hunk [hʌŋk] n (fam) gut gebauter Mann; **hunky** ['hʌŋkɪ] adj (fam) gut gebaut

hunt [hʌnt] n Jagd f; (search) Suche f (for nach) ▷ vt, vi jagen; (search) suchen (for nach); **hunting** n Jagen nt, Jagd f

hurdle ['hɜ:dl] n (a. fig) Hürde f; **the 400m ~s** der 400m-Hürdenlauf

hurl [hɜ:l] vt schleudern

hurricane ['hʌrɪkən] n Orkan m

hurried ['hʌrɪd] adj eilig; **hurry** ['hʌrɪ] n Eile f; **to be in a ~** es eilig haben; **there's no ~** es eilt nicht ▷ vi sich beeilen; **~ (up)** mach schnell! ▷ vt antreiben

hurt [hɜ:t] (**hurt, hurt**) vt wehtun +dat; (wound: person, feelings) verletzen; **I've ~ my arm** ich habe mir am Arm wehgetan ▷ vi wehtun; **my arm ~s** mir tut der Arm weh

h

husband ['hʌzbənd] n Ehemann m

husky ['hʌskɪ] adj rau ▷ n Schlittenhund m

hut [hʌt] n Hütte f

hyacinth ['haɪəsɪnθ] n Hyazinthe f

hybrid ['haɪbrɪd] n Kreuzung f; ~ car Hybridauto nt

hydroelectric ['haɪdrəʊɪ'lektrɪk] adj: ~ power station Wasserkraftwerk nt

hydrofoil ['haɪdrəʊfɔɪl] n Tragflächenboot nt

hydrogen ['haɪdrədʒən] n Wasserstoff m

hygiene ['haɪdʒiːn] n Hygiene f; **hygienic** [haɪ'dʒiːnɪk] adj hygienisch

hymn [hɪm] n Kirchenlied nt

hyperlink ['haɪpəlɪŋk] n Hyperlink m; **hypermarket** n Großmarkt m; **hypersensitive** adj überempfindlich

hyphen ['haɪfən] n Bindestrich m

hypnosis [hɪp'nəʊsɪs] n Hypnose f; **hypnotize** ['hɪpnətaɪz] vt hypnotisieren

hypochondriac [haɪpəʊ'kɒndriæk] n eingebildete(r) Kranke(r), eingebildete Kranke

hypocrisy [hɪ'pɒkrəsɪ] n Heuchelei f; **hypocrite** ['hɪpəkrɪt] n Heuchler(in) m(f)

hypodermic [haɪpə'dɜːmɪk] adj, n: ~ (needle) Spritze f

hypothetical [haɪpəʊ'θetɪkəl] adj hypothetisch

hysteria [hɪ'stɪərɪə] n Hysterie f; **hysterical** [hɪ'sterɪkəl] adj hysterisch; (amusing) zum Totlachen

---

◆

I

I [aɪ] pron ich

ice [aɪs] n Eis nt ▷ vt (cake) glasieren; **iceberg** n Eisberg m; **iceberg lettuce** n Eisbergsalat m; **icebox** n (US) Kühlschrank m; **icecold** adj eiskalt; **ice cream** n Eis nt; **ice cube** n Eiswürfel m; **iced** adj eisgekühlt; (coffee, tea) Eis-; (cake) glasiert; **ice hockey** n Eishockey nt

Iceland ['aɪslənd] n Island nt; **Icelander** n Isländer(in) m(f); **Icelandic** [aɪs'lændɪk] adj isländisch ▷ n (language) Isländisch nt

ice lolly ['aɪslɒlɪ] n (Brit) Eis nt am Stiel; **ice rink** n Kunsteisbahn f; **ice skating** n Schlittschuhlaufen nt

icing ['aɪsɪŋ] n (on cake) Zuckerguss m

icon ['aɪkɒn] n Ikone f; (Inform) Icon nt, Programmsymbol nt

icy ['aɪsɪ] adj (slippery) vereist; (cold) eisig

I'd [aɪd] contr of **I would; I had**

ID abbr = **identification** Ausweis m

idea [aɪ'dɪə] n Idee f; (**I've**) no ~ (ich habe) keine Ahnung; **that's my ~ of ...** so stelle ich mir ... vor

ideal [aɪ'dɪəl] n Ideal nt ▷ adj ideal; **ideally** adv ideal; (before statement) idealerweise

identical [aɪ'dentɪkəl] adj identisch; ~ **twins** eineiige Zwillinge

identify [aɪ'dentɪfaɪ] vt identifizieren; **identity** [aɪ'dentɪtɪ] n Identität f; **identity card** n Personalausweis m

idiom ['ɪdɪəm] n Redewendung f; **idiomatic** adj idiomatisch

idiot ['ɪdɪət] n Idiot(in) m(f)

idle ['aɪdl] adj (doing nothing) untätig; (worker) unbeschäftigt; (machines) außer Betrieb; (lazy) faul; (promise, threat) leer

idol ['aɪdl] n Idol nt; **idolize** ['aɪdəlaɪz] vt vergöttern

idyllic [ɪ'dɪlɪk] adj idyllisch

i.e. abbr = **id est** d.h.

⭕ **KEYWORD**

if [ɪf] conj **1** wenn; (in case also) falls; **if I were you** wenn ich Sie wäre
2 (although) (**even**) **if** (selbst o auch) wenn
3 (whether) ob
4 **if so/not** wenn ja/nicht; **if only ...** wenn ... doch nur ...; **if only I could** wenn ich doch nur könnte; see also **as**

ignition [ɪg'nɪʃən] n Zündung f; **ignition key** n (Auto) Zündschlüssel m

ignorance ['ɪgnərəns] n Unwissenheit f; **ignorant** adj

unwissend; **ignore** [ɪg'nɔːʳ] vt ignorieren, nicht beachten

I'll [aɪl] contr of **I will; I shall**

ill [ɪl] adj krank; **~ at ease** unbehaglich

illegal [ɪ'liːgəl] adj illegal

illegitimate [ɪlɪ'dʒɪtɪmət] adj unzulässig; (child) unehelich

illiterate [ɪ'lɪtərət] adj: **to be ~** Analphabet(in) sein

illness ['ɪlnəs] n Krankheit f

illuminate [ɪ'luːmɪneɪt] vt beleuchten; **illuminating** (remark) aufschlussreich

illusion [ɪ'luːʒən] n Illusion f; **to be under the ~ that ...** sich einbilden, dass ...

illustrate ['ɪləstreɪt] vt illustrieren; **illustration** n Abbildung f, Bild nt

I'm [aɪm] contr of **I am**

image ['ɪmɪdʒ] n Bild nt; (public ~) Image nt; **imaginable** [ɪ'mædʒɪnəbl] adj denkbar; **imaginary** [ɪ'mædʒɪnərɪ] adj eingebildet; **~ world** Fantasiewelt f; **imagination** [ɪmædʒɪ'neɪʃən] n Fantasie f; (mistaken) Einbildung f; **imaginative** [ɪ'mædʒɪnətɪv] adj fantasievoll; **imagine** [ɪ'mædʒɪn] vt sich vorstellen; (wrongly) sich einbilden; **~!** stell dir vor!

imam [ɪ'mɑːm] n Imam m

imitate ['ɪmɪteɪt] vt nachahmen, nachmachen; **imitation** n Nachahmung f ▷ adj imitiert, Kunst-

immaculate [ɪ'mækjʊlɪt] adj tadellos; (spotless) makellos

immature [ɪmə'tjʊəʳ] adj unreif

immediate [ɪ'miːdɪət] adj unmittelbar; (instant) sofortig; (reply) umgehend; **immediately** adv sofort

immense, immensely [ɪ'mens, -lɪ] adj, adv riesig, enorm

immersion heater [ɪˈmɜːʃn
hiːtə] n Boiler m
immigrant [ˈɪmɪɡrənt] n Einwanderer m, Einwanderin f;
immigration [ɪmɪˈɡreɪʃən] n
Einwanderung f; (facility)
Einwanderungskontrolle f
immobilize [ɪˈməʊbɪlaɪz] vt
lähmen; **immobilizer** n (Auto)
Wegfahrsperre f
immoral [ɪˈmɒrəl] adj
unmoralisch
immortal [ɪˈmɔːtl] adj
unsterblich
immune [ɪˈmjuːn] adj (Med)
immun (from, to gegen); **immune
system** n Immunsystem nt
impact [ˈɪmpækt] n Aufprall m;
(effect) Auswirkung f (on auf +akk)
impatience [ɪmˈpeɪʃəns] n
Ungeduld f; **impatient,
impatiently** adj, adv ungeduldig
impeccable [ɪmˈpekəbl] adj
tadellos
impede [ɪmˈpiːd] vt behindern
imperative [ɪmˈperətɪv] adj
unbedingt erforderlich ▷ n (Ling)
Imperativ m
imperfect [ɪmˈpɜːfɪkt] adj
unvollkommen; (goods) fehlerhaft
▷ n (Ling) Imperfekt nt;
imperfection [ɪmpəˈfekʃən] n
Unvollkommenheit f; (fault) Fehler
m
imperial [ɪmˈpɪəriəl] adj kaiserlich, Reichs-; **imperialism** n
Imperialismus m
impertinence [ɪmˈpɜːtɪnəns] n
Unverschämtheit f, Zumutung f;
impertinent adj unverschämt
implant [ɪmˈplɑːnt] n (Med)
Implantat nt
implausible [ɪmˈplɔːzəbl] adj
unglaubwürdig
implement [ˈɪmplɪmənt] n
Werkzeug nt, Gerät nt
▷ [ˈɪmplɪˈment] vt durchführen

implication [ɪmplɪˈkeɪʃən] n
Folge f, Auswirkung f; (logical)
Schlussfolgerung f; **implicit**
[ɪmˈplɪsɪt] adj implizit,
unausgesprochen; **imply**
[ɪmˈplaɪ] vt (indicate) andeuten;
(mean) bedeuten; **are you ~ing
that ...** wollen Sie damit sagen,
dass ...
impolite [ɪmpəˈlaɪt] adj
unhöflich
import [ɪmˈpɔːt] vt einführen,
importieren ▷ n [ˈɪmpɔːt] Einfuhr f, Import m
importance [ɪmˈpɔːtəns] n
Bedeutung f; **of no ~** unwichtig;
important adj wichtig (to sb für
jdn); (significant) bedeutend;
(influential) einflussreich
import duty [ˈɪmpɔːt djuːtɪ] n
Einfuhrzoll m; **import licence** n
Einfuhrgenehmigung f
impose [ɪmˈpəʊz] vt (conditions)
auferlegen (on dat); (penalty,
sanctions) verhängen (on gegen);
imposing [ɪmˈpəʊzɪŋ] adj eindrucksvoll, imposant
impossible [ɪmˈpɒsəbl] adj
unmöglich
impotence [ˈɪmpətəns] n
Machtlosigkeit f; (sexual)
Impotenz f; **impotent** adj
machtlos; (sexually) impotent
impractical [ɪmˈpræktɪkəl] adj
unpraktisch; (plan)
undurchführbar
impress [ɪmˈpres] vt beeindrucken; **impression** [ɪmˈpreʃən]
n Eindruck m; **impressive** adj
eindrucksvoll
imprison [ɪmˈprɪzn] vt inhaftieren; **imprisonment** n
Inhaftierung f
improbability [ɪmprɒbəˈbɪlɪtɪ]
n Unwahrscheinlichkeit f;
improbable [ɪmˈprɒbəbl] adj
unwahrscheinlich

improper [ɪmˈprɔpə*] *adj*
(*indecent*) unanständig; (*use*)
unsachgemäß

improve [ɪmˈpruːv] *vt*
verbessern ▷ *vi* sich verbessern,
besser werden; (*patient*)
Fortschritte machen;
improvement *n* Verbesserung *f*
(*in +gen; on gegenüber*); (*in
appearance*) Verschönerung *f*

improvise [ˈɪmprəvaɪz] *vt, vi*
improvisieren

impulse [ˈɪmpʌls] *n* Impuls *m*;
impulsive [ɪmˈpʌlsɪv] *adj*
impulsiv

O **KEYWORD**

in [ɪn] *prep* **1** (*indicating place,
position*) in +*dat*; (*with motion*) in
+*akk*; **in here/there** hier/dort; **in
London** in London; **in the United
States** in den Vereinigten Staaten
2 (*indicating time: during*) in +*dat*; **in
summer** im Sommer; **in 1988** (im
Jahre) 1988; **in the afternoon**
nachmittags, am Nachmittag
3 (*indicating time: in the space of*)
innerhalb von; **I'll see you in 2
weeks** o **in 2 weeks' time** ich sehe
dich/Sie in zwei Wochen
4 (*indicating manner, circumstances,
state etc*) in +*dat*; **in the sun/rain**
in der Sonne/im Regen; **in
English/French** auf
Englisch/Französisch; **in a
loud/soft voice** mit lauter/leiser
Stimme
5 (*with ratios, numbers*) **1 in 10** jeder
Zehnte; **20 pence in the pound** 20
Pence pro Pfund; **they lined up in
twos** sie stellten sich in
Zweierreihe auf
6 (*referring to people, works*) **the
disease is common in children**
die Krankheit ist bei Kindern
häufig; **in Dickens** bei Dickens;

we have a loyal friend in him er
ist uns ein treuer Freund
7 (*indicating profession etc*) **to be in
teaching/the army** Lehrer,
Lehrerin/beim Militär sein; **to be
in publishing** im Verlagswesen
arbeiten
8 (*with present participle*) **in saying
this, I ...** wenn ich das sage, ... ich;
in accepting this view, he ... weil
er diese Meinung akzeptierte, ...
er
▷ *adv*: **to be in** (*person: at home,
work*) da sein; (*train, ship, plane*)
angekommen sein; (*in fashion*) in
sein; **to ask sb in** jdn hereinbitten;
to run/limp *etc* **in**
hereingerannt/gehumpelt *etc*
kommen
▷ *n*: **the ins and outs** (*of proposal,
situation etc*) die Feinheiten

inability [ɪnəˈbɪlɪtɪ] *n* Unfähig-
keit *f*

inaccessible [ɪnækˈsesəbl] *adj*
(*a. fig*) unzugänglich

inaccurate [ɪnˈækjʊrɪt] *adj*
ungenau

inadequate [ɪnˈædɪkwət] *adj*
unzulänglich

inapplicable [ɪnəˈplɪkəbl] *adj*
unzutreffend

inappropriate [ɪnəˈprəʊprɪət]
adj unpassend; (*clothing*)
ungeeignet; (*remark*)
unangebracht

inborn [ˈɪnˈbɔːn] *adj* angeboren

incapable [ɪnˈkeɪpəbl] *adj*
unfähig (*of zu*); **to be ~ of doing
sth** nicht imstande sein, etw zu
tun

incense [ˈɪnsens] *n* Weihrauch
m

incentive [ɪnˈsentɪv] *n* Anreiz *m*

incessant, incessantly [ɪnˈsesnt,
-lɪ] *adj, adv* unaufhörlich

incest [ˈɪnsest] *n* Inzest *m*

inch [ɪntʃ] n Zoll m (2,54 cm)
incident ['ɪnsɪdənt] n Vorfall m; (disturbance) Zwischenfall m; **incidentally** [ɪnsɪ'dɛntlɪ] adv nebenbei bemerkt, übrigens
inclination [ɪnklɪ'neɪʃən] n Neigung f; **inclined** ['ɪnklaɪnd] adj: **to be ~ to do sth** dazu neigen, etw zu tun
include [ɪn'kluːd] vt einschließen; (on list, in group) aufnehmen; **including** prep einschließlich (+gen); **not ~ service** Bedienung nicht inbegriffen; **inclusive** [ɪn'kluːsɪv] adj einschließlich (+gen); (price) Pauschal-
incoherent [ɪnkəʊ'hɪərənt] adj zusammenhanglos
income ['ɪnkʌm] n Einkommen nt; (from business) Einkünfte pl; **income tax** n Einkommensteuer f; (on wages, salary) Lohnsteuer f; **incoming** ['ɪnkʌmɪŋ] adj ankommend; (mail) eingehend
incompatible [ɪnkəm'pætəbl] adj unvereinbar; (people) unverträglich; (Inform) nicht kompatibel
incompetent [ɪn'kɒmpɪtənt] adj unfähig
incomplete [ɪnkəm'pliːt] adj unvollständig
incomprehensible [ɪnkɒmprɪ'hensəbl] adj unverständlich
inconceivable [ɪnkən'siːvəbl] adj unvorstellbar
inconsiderate [ɪnkən'sɪdərət] adj rücksichtslos
inconsistency [ɪnkən'sɪstənsɪ] n Inkonsequenz f; (contradictory) Widersprüchlichkeit f; **inconsistent** adj inkonsequent; (contradictory) widersprüchlich; (work) unbeständig

inconvenience [ɪnkən'viːnɪəns] n Unannehmlichkeit f; (trouble) Umstände pl; **inconvenient** adj ungünstig, unbequem; (time) **it's ~ for me** es kommt mir ungelegen; **if it's not too ~ for you** wenn es dir/Ihnen passt
incorporate [ɪn'kɔːpəreɪt] vt aufnehmen (into in +akk); (include) enthalten
incorrect ['ɪnkərekt] adj falsch; (improper) unkorrekt
increase ['ɪnkriːs] n Zunahme f (in an +dat); (in amount, speed) Erhöhung f (in +gen) ▷ [ɪn'kriːs] vt (price, taxes, salary, speed etc) erhöhen; (wealth) vermehren; (number) vergrößern; (business) erweitern ▷ vi zunehmen (in an +dat); (prices) steigen; (in size) größer werden; (in number) sich vermehren; **increasingly** [ɪn'kriːsɪŋlɪ] adv zunehmend
incredible, incredibly [ɪn'kredəbl, -blɪ] adj, adv unglaublich; (very good) fantastisch
incredulous [ɪn'kredjʊləs] adj ungläubig, skeptisch
incriminate [ɪn'krɪmɪneɪt] vt belasten
incubator ['ɪnkjʊbeɪtə°] n Brutkasten m
incurable [ɪn'kjʊərəbl] adj unheilbar
indecent [ɪn'diːsnt] adj unanständig
indecisive [ɪndɪ'saɪsɪv] adj (person) unentschlossen; (result) nicht entscheidend
indeed [ɪn'diːd] adv tatsächlich; (as answer) allerdings; **very hot ~** wirklich sehr heiß
indefinite [ɪn'defɪnɪt] adj unbestimmt; **indefinitely** adv endlos; (postpone) auf unbestimmte Zeit

independence [ɪndɪˈpɛndəns] n Unabhängigkeit f

independent [ɪndɪˈpɛndənt] adj unabhängig (of von); (person) selbstständig

indescribable [ɪndɪˈskraɪbəbl] adj unbeschreiblich

index [ˈɪndɛks] n Index m, Verzeichnis nt; **index finger** n Zeigefinger m

India [ˈɪndɪə] n Indien nt; **Indian** [ˈɪndɪən] adj indisch; (Native American) indianisch ▷ n Inder(in) m(f); (Native American) Indianer(in) m(f); **Indian Ocean** n Indischer Ozean; **Indian summer** n Spätsommer m, Altweibersommer m

indicate [ˈɪndɪkeɪt] vt (show) zeigen; (instrument) anzeigen; (suggest) hinweisen auf +akk ▷ vi (Auto) blinken; **indication** [ɪndɪˈkeɪʃn] n (sign) Anzeichen nt (of für); **indicator** [ˈɪndɪkeɪtə°] n (Auto) Blinker m

indifferent [ɪnˈdɪfrənt] adj (not caring) gleichgültig (to, towards gegenüber); (mediocre) mittelmäßig

indigestible [ɪndɪˈdʒɛstəbl] adj unverdaulich; **indigestion** [ɪndɪˈdʒɛstʃən] n Verdauungsstörung f

indignity [ɪnˈdɪgnɪtɪ] n Demütigung f

indirect, indirectly [ɪndɪˈrɛkt, -lɪ] adj, adv indirekt

indiscreet [ɪndɪˈskriːt] adj indiskret

indispensable [ɪndɪˈspɛnsəbl] adj unentbehrlich

indisposed [ɪndɪˈspəʊzd] adj unwohl

indisputable [ɪndɪˈspjuːtəbl] adj unbestreitbar; (evidence) unanfechtbar

individual [ɪndɪˈvɪdjʊəl] n Einzelne(r) mf ▷ adj einzeln; (distinctive) eigen, individuell; **~ case** Einzelfall m; **individually** adv (separately) einzeln

Indonesia [ɪndəʊˈniːzjə] n Indonesien nt

indoor [ˈɪndɔː°] adj (shoes) Haus-; (plant, games) Zimmer-; (Sport: football, championship, record etc) Hallen-; **indoors** adv drinnen, im Haus

indulge [ɪnˈdʌldʒ] vi: **to ~ in sth** sich dat etw gönnen; **indulgence** n Nachsicht f; (enjoyment) (übermäßiger) Genuss; (luxury) Luxus m; **indulgent** adj nachsichtig (with gegenüber)

industrial [ɪnˈdʌstrɪəl] adj Industrie-, industriell; **~ estate** Industriegebiet nt; **industry** [ˈɪndəstrɪ] n Industrie f

inedible [ɪnˈɛdɪbl] adj nicht essbar, ungenießbar

ineffective [ɪnɪˈfɛktɪv] adj unwirksam, wirkungslos; **inefficient** [ɪnɪˈfɪʃənt] adj unwirksam; (use, machine) unwirtschaftlich; (method etc) unrationell

ineligible [ɪnˈɛlɪdʒəbl] adj nicht berechtigt (for zu)

inequality [ɪnɪˈkwɒlɪtɪ] n Ungleichheit f

inevitable [ɪnˈɛvɪtəbl] adj unvermeidlich; **inevitably** adv zwangsläufig

inexcusable [ɪnɪksˈkjuːzəbl]
adj unverzeihlich; **that's ~** das
kann man nicht verzeihen

inexpensive [ɪnɪksˈpɛnsɪv] *adj*
preisgünstig

inexperience [ɪnɪksˈpɪərɪəns]
n Unerfahrenheit *f*;
inexperienced *adj* unerfahren

inexplicable [ɪnɪksˈplɪkəbl] *adj*
unerklärlich

infallible [ɪnˈfæləbl] *adj*
unfehlbar

infamous [ˈɪnfəməs] *adj* (person)
berüchtigt (for wegen); (deed)
niederträchtig

infancy [ˈɪnfənsɪ] *n* frühe
Kindheit; **infant** [ˈɪnfənt] *n*
Säugling *m*; (small child)
Kleinkind *nt*; **infant school** *n*
Vorschule *f*

infatuated [ɪnˈfætjʊeɪtɪd] *adj*
vernarrt (with in +akk), verknallt
(with in +akk)

infect [ɪnˈfɛkt] *vt* (person)
anstecken; (wound) infizieren;
infection [ɪnˈfɛkʃən] *n* Infektion
f; **infectious** [ɪnˈfɛkʃəs] *adj*
ansteckend

inferior [ɪnˈfɪərɪə°] *adj* (in quality)
minderwertig; (in rank)
untergeordnet; **inferiority**
[ɪnfɪərɪˈɒrɪtɪ] *n* Minderwertigkeit
f; **~ complex** Minderwertigkeitskomplex *m*

infertile [ɪnˈfɜːtaɪl] *adj*
unfruchtbar

infidelity [ɪnfɪˈdɛlɪtɪ] *n* Untreue
f

infinite [ˈɪnfɪnɪt] *adj* unendlich

infinitive [ɪnˈfɪnɪtɪv] *n* (Ling)
Infinitiv *m*

infinity [ɪnˈfɪnɪtɪ] *n* Unend-
lichkeit *f*

infirmary [ɪnˈfɜːmərɪ] *n*
Krankenhaus *nt*

inflame [ɪnˈfleɪm] *vt* (Med)
entzünden; **inflammation**

[ɪnfləˈmeɪʃən] *n* (Med)
Entzündung *f*

inflatable [ɪnˈfleɪtəbl] *adj* auf-
blasbar; **~ dinghy** Schlauchboot
nt; **inflate** [ɪnˈfleɪt] *vt*
aufpumpen; (by blowing)
aufblasen; (prices) hochtreiben

inflation [ɪnˈfleɪʃən] *n* Inflation
f

inflexible [ɪnˈflɛksəbl] *adj*
unflexibel

inflict [ɪnˈflɪkt] *vt*: **to ~ sth on sb**
jdm etw zufügen; (punishment)
jdm etw auferlegen; (wound) jdm
etw beibringen

in-flight [ɪnˈflaɪt] *adj* (catering,
magazine) Bord-; **~ entertainment**
Bordprogramm *nt*

influence [ˈɪnflʊəns] *n* Einfluss
m (on auf +akk) ▷ *vt* beeinflussen;
influential [ɪnflʊˈɛnʃəl] *adj*
einflussreich

influenza [ɪnflʊˈɛnzə] *n* Grippe
f

inform [ɪnˈfɔːm] *vt* informieren
(of, about über +akk); **to keep sb
~ed** jdn auf dem Laufenden halten

informal [ɪnˈfɔːməl] *adj* zwanglos, ungezwungen

information [ɪnfəˈmeɪʃən] *n*
Auskunft *f*, Informationen *pl*; **for
your ~** zu deiner/Ihrer
Information; **further ~** weitere
Informationen, Weiteres;
information desk *n*
Auskunftsschalter *m*; **information
technology** *n* Informations-
technik *f*; **informative**
[ɪnˈfɔːmətɪv] *adj* aufschlussreich

infra-red [ɪnfrəˈrɛd] *adj* infrarot

infrastructure *n* Infrastruktur
f

infuriate [ɪnˈfjʊərɪeɪt] *vt* wütend
machen; **infuriating** *adj* äußerst
ärgerlich

infusion [ɪnˈfjuːʒən] *n* (herbal
tea) Aufguss *m*; (Med) Infusion *f*

ingenious [ɪn'dʒiːnɪəs] adj (person) erfinderisch; (device) raffiniert; (idea) genial

ingredient [ɪn'griːdɪənt] n (Gastr) Zutat f

inhabit [ɪn'hæbɪt] vt bewohnen; **inhabitant** n Einwohner(in) m(f)

inhale [ɪn'heɪl] vt einatmen; (cigarettes, Med) inhalieren; **inhaler** n Inhalationsgerät nt

inherit [ɪn'herɪt] vt erben; **inheritance** n Erbe nt

inhibited [ɪn'hɪbɪtɪd] adj gehemmt; **inhibition** [ɪnhɪ'bɪʃən] n Hemmung f

in-house [ɪn'haʊs] adj intern

inhuman [ɪn'hjuːmən] adj unmenschlich

initial [ɪ'nɪʃəl] adj anfänglich; ~ **stage** Anfangsstadium nt ▷ vt mit Initialen unterschreiben; **initially** adv anfangs; **initials** npl Initialen pl

initiative [ɪ'nɪʃətɪv] n Initiative f

inject [ɪn'dʒekt] vt (drug etc) einspritzen; **to ~ sb with sth** jdm etw (ein)spritzen; **injection** n Spritze f, Injektion f

in-joke [ɪn'dʒəʊk] n Insiderwitz m

injure [ɪn'dʒə*] vt verletzen; **to ~ one's leg** sich dat das Bein verletzen; **injury** [ɪn'dʒərɪ] n Verletzung f

injustice [ɪn'dʒʌstɪs] n Ungerechtigkeit f

ink [ɪŋk] n Tinte f; **ink-jet printer** n Tintenstrahldrucker m

inland [ɪn'lænd] adj Binnen- ▷ adv landeinwärts; **inland revenue** n (Brit) Finanzamt nt

in-laws [ɪn'lɔːz] npl (fam) Schwiegereltern pl

inline skates [ɪn'laɪnskeɪts] npl Inlineskates pl, Inliner pl

inmate [ɪn'meɪt] n Insasse m

inn [ɪn] n Gasthaus nt

innate [ɪ'neɪt] adj angeboren

inner [ɪn'ə*] adj innere(r, s); ~ **city** Innenstadt f

innocence ['ɪnəsns] n Unschuld f; **innocent** adj unschuldig

innovation [ɪnəʊ'veɪʃən] n Neuerung f

innumerable [ɪ'njuːmərəbl] adj unzählig

inoculate [ɪ'nɒkjʊleɪt] vt impfen (against gegen); **inoculation** [ɪnɒkjʊ'leɪʃən] n Impfung f

in-patient ['ɪnpeɪʃənt] n stationärer Patient, stationäre Patientin

input ['ɪnpʊt] n (contribution) Beitrag m; (Inform) Eingabe f

inquest ['ɪnkwest] n gerichtliche Untersuchung (einer Todesursache)

inquire [ɪn'kwaɪə*] see **enquire**; **inquiry** [ɪn'kwaɪərɪ] see **enquiry**

insane [ɪn'seɪn] adj wahnsinnig; (Med) geisteskrank; **insanity** [ɪn'sænɪtɪ] n Wahnsinn m

insatiable [ɪn'seɪʃəbl] adj unersättlich

inscription [ɪn'skrɪpʃən] n (on stone etc) Inschrift f

insect ['ɪnsekt] n Insekt nt; **insecticide** [ɪn'sektɪsaɪd] n Insektenbekämpfungsmittel nt; **insect repellent** n Insektenschutzmittel nt

insecure [ɪnsɪ'kjʊə*] adj (person) unsicher; (shelves) instabil

insensitive [ɪn'sensɪtɪv] adj unempfindlich (to gegen); (unfeeling) gefühllos; **insensitivity** [ɪnsensɪ'tɪvɪtɪ] n Unempfindlichkeit f (to gegen); (unfeeling nature) Gefühllosigkeit f

inseparable [ɪn'sepərəbl] adj unzertrennlich

insert [ɪn'sɜːt] vt einfügen; (coin) einwerfen; (key etc) hineinstecken

▷ n (in magazine) Beilage f;
insertion n (in text) Einfügen nt

inside [ɪnˈsaɪd] n: **the ~** das
Innere; (surface) die Innenseite;
from the ~ von innen innen; auf
innere(r, s), Innen-; **~ lane** (Auto)
Innenspur f; (Sport) Innenbahn f
▷ adv (place) innen; (direction)
hinein; **to go ~** hineingehen
▷ prep (place) in +dat; (into) in +akk
... hinein; (time, within) innerhalb
+gen; **inside out** adv verkehrt
herum; (know) in- und auswendig;
insider n Eingeweihte(r) mf,
Insider(in) m(f)

insight [ɪnˈsaɪt] n Einblick m
(into in +akk)

insignificant [ɪnsɪgˈnɪfɪkənt]
adj unbedeutend

insincere [ɪnsɪnˈsɪə°] adj un-
aufrichtig, falsch

insinuate [ɪnˈsɪnjʊeɪt] vt
andeuten; **insinuation**
[ɪnsɪnjʊˈeɪʃən] n Andeutung f

insist [ɪnˈsɪst] vi darauf bestehen;
to ~ on sth auf etw dat bestehen;
insistent adj hartnäckig

insoluble [ɪnˈsɒljʊbl] adj
unlösbar

insomnia [ɪnˈsɒmnɪə] n Schlaflosigkeit f

inspect [ɪnˈspekt] vt prüfen,
kontrollieren; **inspection**
Prüfung f; (check) Kontrolle f;
inspector n (police ~)
Inspektor(in) m(f); (senior)
Kommissar(in) m(f); (on bus etc)
Kontrolleur(in) m(f)

inspiration [ɪnspɪˈreɪʃən] n
Inspiration f; **inspire** [ɪnˈspaɪə°]
vt (respect) einflößen (in dat);
(person) inspirieren

install [ɪnˈstɔːl] vt (software)
installieren; (furnishings) einbauen

installment, **instalment**
[ɪnˈstɔːlmənt] n Rate f; (of story)
Folge f; **to pay in ~s** auf Raten

zahlen; **installment plan** n (US)
Ratenkauf m

instance [ˈɪnstəns] n (of
discrimination) Fall m; (example)
Beispiel nt (of für +akk); **for ~** zum
Beispiel

instant [ˈɪnstənt] n Augenblick
m ▷ adj sofortig; **instant coffee**
n löslicher Kaffee m; **instantly** adv
sofort

instead [ɪnˈsted] adv stattdes-
sen; **instead of** prep (an)statt
+gen; **~ of me** an meiner Stelle;
~ of going (an)statt zu gehen

instinct [ˈɪnstɪŋkt] n Instinkt m;
instinctive, instinctively
[ɪnˈstɪŋktɪv, -lɪ] adj, adv
instinktiv

institute [ˈɪnstɪtjuːt] n Institut
nt; **institution** [ɪnstɪˈtjuːʃən] n
(organisation) Institution f,
Einrichtung f; (home) Anstalt f

instruct [ɪnˈstrʌkt] vt anweisen;
instruction [ɪnˈstrʌkʃən] n
(teaching) Unterricht m; (command)
Anweisung f; **~s for use**
Gebrauchsanweisung f;
instructor n Lehrer(in) m(f); (US)
Dozent(in) m(f)

instrument [ˈɪnstrəmənt] n
Instrument nt; **instrument panel**
n Armaturenbrett nt

insufficient [ɪnsəˈfɪʃənt] adj
ungenügend

insulate [ˈɪnsjʊleɪt] vt (Elec)
isolieren; **insulating tape** n
Isolierband nt; **insulation**
[ɪnsjʊˈleɪʃən] n Isolierung f

insulin [ˈɪnsjʊlɪn] n Insulin nt

insult [ˈɪnsʌlt] n Beleidigung f
▷ [ɪnˈsʌlt] vt beleidigen;
insulting [ɪnˈsʌltɪŋ] adj
beleidigend

insurance [ɪnˈʃʊərəns] n Versicherung f; **~ company**
Versicherungsgesellschaft f;
~ policy Versicherungspolice f;

insure [ɪnˈʃʊəˀ] vt versichern (against gegen)

intact [ɪnˈtækt] adj intakt

intake [ˈɪnteɪk] n Aufnahme f

integrate [ˈɪntɪˈɡreɪt] vt integrieren (into in +akk); **integration** n Integration f

integrity [ɪnˈteɡrɪtɪ] n Integrität f, Ehrlichkeit f

intellect [ˈɪntɪlekt] n Intellekt m; **intellectual** [ɪntɪˈlektjʊəl] adj intellektuell; (interests etc) geistig

intelligence [ɪnˈtelɪdʒəns] n (understanding) Intelligenz f; **intelligent** adj intelligent

intend [ɪnˈtend] vt beabsichtigen; **to ~ to do sth** vorhaben, etw zu tun

intense [ɪnˈtens] adj intensiv; (pressure) enorm; (competition) heftig; **intensity** n Intensität f; **intensive** adj intensiv; **intensive care unit** n Intensivstation f; **intensive course** n Intensivkurs m

intent [ɪnˈtent] adj: **to be ~ on doing sth** fest entschlossen sein, etw zu tun; **intention** [ɪnˈtenʃən] n Absicht f; **intentional**, **intentionally** adj, adv absichtlich

interact [ɪntərˈækt] vi aufeinander einwirken; **interaction** n Interaktion f, Wechselwirkung f; **interactive** adj interaktiv

interchange [ˈɪntəˈtʃeɪndʒ] n (of motorways) Autobahnkreuz nt; **interchangeable** [ɪntəˈtʃeɪndʒəbl] adj austauschbar

intercity [ɪntəˈsɪtɪ] n Intercityzug m, IC m

intercom [ˈɪntəkɒm] n (Gegen)sprechanlage f

intercourse [ˈɪntəkɔːs] n (sexual) Geschlechtsverkehr m

interest [ˈɪntrest] n Interesse nt; (Fin: on money) Zinsen pl; (Comm: share) Anteil m; **to be of ~** von Interesse sein (to für) ▷ vt interessieren; **interested** adj interessiert (in an +dat); **to be ~ed in** sich interessieren für; **are you ~ in coming?** hast du Lust, mitzukommen?; **interest-free** adj zinsfrei; **interesting** adj interessant; **interest rate** n Zinssatz m

interface [ˈɪntəfeɪs] n (Inform) Schnittstelle f

interfere [ɪntəˈfɪəˀ] vi (meddle) sich einmischen (with, in in +akk); **interference** n Einmischung f; (TV, Radio) Störung f

interior [ɪnˈtɪərɪəˀ] adj Innen- ▷ n Innere(s) nt; (of car) Innenraum m; (of house) Innenausstattung f

intermediate [ɪntəˈmiːdɪət] adj Zwischen-; **~ stage** n Zwischenstadium nt

intermission [ɪntəˈmɪʃən] n Pause f

intern [ɪnˈtɜːn] n Assistent(in) m(f)

internal [ɪnˈtɜːnl] adj innere(r, s); (flight) Inlands-; **~ revenue** (US) Finanzamt nt; **internally** adv innen; (in body) innerlich

international [ɪntəˈnæʃnəl] adj international; **~ match** n Länderspiel nt; **~ flight** Auslandsflug m ▷ n (Sport: player) Nationalspieler(in) m(f)

Internet [ˈɪntənet] n (Inform) Internet nt; **Internet access** n Internetzugang m; **Internet auction** n Internetauktion f; **Internet banking** n Onlinebanking nt; **Internet café** n Internetcafé nt; **Internet connection** n Internetanschluss m; **Internet provider** n Internetprovider m

interpret [ɪnˈtɜːprɪt] vi, vt

(*translate*) dolmetschen; (*explain*) interpretieren; **interpretation** [ɪntɜːprɪˈteɪʃən] n Interpretation f; **interpreter** [ɪnˈtɜːprɪtə°] n Dolmetscher(in) m(f)

interrogate [ɪnˈterəgeɪt] vt verhören; **interrogation** n Verhör nt

interrupt [ɪntəˈrʌpt] vt unterbrechen; **interruption** [ɪntəˈrʌpʃən] n Unterbrechung f

intersection [ɪntəˈsekʃən] n (of roads) Kreuzung f

interstate [ˈɪntəˈsteɪt] n (US) zwischenstaatlich; ~ **highway** = Bundesautobahn f

interval [ˈɪntəvəl] n (space, time) Abstand m; (theatre etc) Pause f

intervene [ɪntəˈviːn] vi eingreifen (in in); **intervention** [ɪntəˈvenʃən] n Eingreifen nt; (Pol) Intervention f

interview [ˈɪntəvjuː] n Interview nt; (for job) Vorstellungsgespräch nt ▷ vt interviewen; (job applicant) ein Vorstellungsgespräch führen mit; **interviewer** n Interviewer(in) m(f)

intestine [ɪnˈtestɪn] n Darm m; ~s pl Eingeweide pl

intimate [ˈɪntɪmət] adj (friends) vertraut, eng; (atmosphere) gemütlich; (sexually) intim

intimidate [ɪnˈtɪmɪdeɪt] vt einschüchtern; **intimidation** n Einschüchterung f

into [ˈɪntə] prep in +akk; (crash) gegen; **to change ~ sth** (turn ~) zu etw werden; (put on) sich dat etw anziehen; **to translate ~ French** ins Französische übersetzen; **to be ~ sth** (fam) auf etw akk stehen

intolerable [ɪnˈtɒlərəbl] adj unerträglich

intolerant [ɪnˈtɒlərənt] adj intolerant

intoxicated [ɪnˈtɒksɪkeɪtid] adj betrunken; (fig) berauscht

intricate [ˈɪntrɪkət] adj kompliziert

intrigue [ɪnˈtriːɡ] vt faszinieren; **intriguing** adj faszinierend, fesselnd

introduce [ɪntrəˈdjuːs] vt (person) vorstellen (to sb jdm); (sth new) einführen (to in +akk); **introduction** [ɪntrəˈdʌkʃən] n Einführung f (to in +akk); (to book) Einleitung f (to zu); (to person) Vorstellung f

introvert [ˈɪntrəʊvɜːt] n Introvertierte(r) mf

intuition [ɪntjuːˈɪʃn] n Intuition f

invade [ɪnˈveɪd] vt einfallen in +akk

invalid [ˈɪnvəlɪd] n Kranke(r) mf; (disabled) Invalide m ▷ adj [ɪnˈvælɪd] (not valid) ungültig

invaluable [ɪnˈvæljʊəbl] adj äußerst wertvoll, unschätzbar

invariably [ɪnˈveərɪəblɪ] adv ständig; (every time) jedes Mal, ohne Ausnahme

invasion [ɪnˈveɪʒən] n Invasion f (of in +akk), Einfall m (of in +akk)

invent [ɪnˈvent] vt erfinden; **invention** [ɪnˈvenʃən] n Erfindung f; **inventor** n Erfinder(in) m(f)

inverted commas [ɪnˈvɜːtɪd ˈkɒməz] npl Anführungszeichen pl

invest [ɪnˈvest] vt, vi investieren (in in +akk)

investigate [ɪnˈvestɪgeɪt] vt untersuchen; **investigation** [ɪnvestɪˈgeɪʃən] n Untersuchung f (into +gen)

investment [ɪnˈvestmənt] n Investition f; **it's a good** ~ es ist eine gute Anlage; (it'll be useful) es macht sich bezahlt

invigorating [ɪnˈvɪɡəreɪtɪŋ] *adj* erfrischend, belebend; *(tonic)* stärkend

invisible [ɪnˈvɪzəbl] *adj* unsichtbar

invitation [ɪnvɪˈteɪʃən] *n* Einladung *f*; **invite** [ɪnˈvaɪt] *vt* einladen

invoice [ˈɪnvɔɪs] *n* *(bill)* Rechnung *f*

involuntary [ɪnˈvɒləntərɪ] *adj* unbeabsichtigt

involve [ɪnˈvɒlv] *vt* verwickeln *(in sth* in etw *akk); (entail)* zur Folge haben; **to be ~d in sth** *(participate in)* an etw *dat* beteiligt sein; **I'm not ~d** *(affected)* ich bin nicht betroffen

inward [ˈɪnwəd] *adj* innere(r, s); **inwardly** *adv* innerlich; **inwards** *adv* nach innen

iodine [ˈaɪədiːn] *n*· Jod *nt*

IOU [aɪəʊˈjuː] *abbr* = **I owe you** Schuldschein *m*

iPod® [ˈaɪpɒd] *n* iPod® *m*

IQ *abbr* = **intelligence quotient** IQ *m*

Iran [ɪˈrɑːn] *n* der Iran

Iraq [ɪˈrɑːk] *n* der Irak

Ireland [ˈaɪələnd] *n* Irland *nt*

iris [ˈaɪrɪs] *n* *(flower)* Schwertlilie *f*; *(of eye)* Iris *f*

Irish [ˈaɪrɪʃ] *adj* irisch; **~ coffee** Irish Coffee *m*; **~ Sea** die Irische See ▷ *n* *(language)* Irisch *nt*; **the ~ pl** die Iren *pl*; **Irishman** *(pl* **-men**) *n* Ire *m*; **Irishwoman** *(pl* **-women**) *n* Irin *f*

iron [ˈaɪən] *n* Eisen *nt*; *(for ironing)* Bügeleisen *nt* ▷ *adj* eisern ▷ *vt* bügeln

ironic(al) [aɪˈrɒnɪk(əl)] *adj* ironisch

ironing board *n* Bügelbrett *nt*

irony [ˈaɪrənɪ] *n* Ironie *f*

irrational [ɪˈræʃənl] *adj* irrational

irregular [ɪˈreɡjʊləʳ] *adj* unregelmäßig; *(shape)* ungleichmäßig

irrelevant [ɪˈreləvənt] *adj* belanglos, irrelevant

irreplaceable [ɪrɪˈpleɪsəbl] *adj* unersetzlich

irresistible [ɪrɪˈzɪstəbl] *adj* unwiderstehlich

irrespective [ɪrɪˈspektɪv ɒv] *prep* ungeachtet +*gen*

irresponsible [ɪrɪˈspɒnsəbl] *adj* verantwortungslos

irretrievable [ɪrɪˈtriːvəbl] *adv* unwiederbringlich; *(loss)* unersetzlich

irritable [ˈɪrɪtəbl] *adj* reizbar; **irritate** [ˈɪrɪteɪt] *vt* *(annoy)* ärgern; *(deliberately)* reizen; **irritation** [ɪrɪˈteɪʃən] *n* *(anger)* Ärger *m*; *(Med)* Reizung *f*

IRS *abbr* = **Internal Revenue Service** *(US)* Finanzamt *nt*

is [ɪz] *present of* **be** ist

Islam [ˈɪzlɑːm] *n* Islam *m*; **Islamic** [ɪzˈlæmɪk] *adj* islamisch

island [ˈaɪlənd] *n* Insel *f*; **Isle** [aɪl] *n* *(in names)* **the ~ of Man** die Insel Man; **the ~ of Wight** die Insel Wight; **the British ~s** die Britischen Inseln

isn't [ˈɪznt] *contr of* **is not**

isolate [ˈaɪsəleɪt] *vt* isolieren; **isolated** *adj* *(remote)* abgelegen; *(cut off)* abgeschnitten *(from* von); **an ~ case** ein Einzelfall; **isolation** [aɪsəˈleɪʃən] *n* Isolierung *f*

Israel [ˈɪzreɪl] *n* Israel *nt*; **Israeli** [ɪzˈreɪlɪ] *adj* israelisch ▷ *n* Israeli *m* of

issue [ˈɪʃuː] *n* *(matter)* Frage *f*; *(problem)* Problem *nt*; *(subject)* Thema *nt*; *(of newspaper etc)* Ausgabe *f*; **that's not the ~** darum geht es nicht ▷ *vt* ausgeben; *(document)* ausstellen; *(orders)* erteilen; *(book)* herausgeben

it [ɪt] *pron* **1** (*specific: subject*)
er/sie/es; (*direct object*) ihn/sie/es;
(*indirect object*) ihm/ihr/ihm;
about/from/in/of it
darüber/davon/darin/davon
2 (*impers*) es; **it's raining** es regnet;
it's Friday tomorrow morgen ist
Freitag; **who is it? — it's me** wer ist
da? — ich (bin's)

IT *abbr* = **information technology**
IT f

Italian [ɪ'tæljən] *adj* italienisch
▷ *n* Italiener(in) *m(f)*; (*language*)
Italienisch *nt*

italic [ɪ'tælɪk] *adj* kursiv ▷ *npl*: **in
~s** kursiv

Italy ['ɪtəlɪ] *n* Italien *nt*

itch [ɪtʃ] *n* Juckreiz *m*; **I have an
~** mich juckt es ▷ *vi* jucken; **he is
~ing to ...** es juckt ihn, zu ...; **itchy**
adj juckend

it'd ['ɪtd] *contr of* **it would; it had**

item ['aɪtəm] *n* (*article*)
Gegenstand *m*; (*in catalogue*)
Artikel *m*; (*on list, in accounts*)
Posten *m*; (*on agenda*) Punkt *m*; (*in
show programme*) Nummer *f*; (*in
news*) Bericht *m*; (*TV, radio*)
Meldung *f*

itinerary [aɪ'tɪnərərɪ] *n* Reiseroute *f*

it'll ['ɪtl] *contr of* **it will; it shall**

its [ɪts] *pron* sein; (*feminine form*)
ihr

it's [ɪts] *contr of* **it is; it has**

itself [ɪt'self] *pron* (*reflexive*) sich;
(*emphatic*) **the house** – das Haus
selbst o an sich; **by ~** allein; **the
door closes (by) –** die Tür schließt
sich von selbst

I've [aɪv] *contr of* **I have**

ivory ['aɪvərɪ] *n* Elfenbein *nt*

ivy ['aɪvɪ] *n* Efeu *m*

jab [dʒæb] *vt* (*needle, knife*)
stechen (*into in +akk*) ▷ *n* (*fam*)
Spritze *f*

jack [dʒæk] *n* (*Auto*) Wagenheber
m; (*Cards*) Bube *m*; **jack in** *vt* (*fam*)
aufgeben, hinschmeißen; **jack up**
vt (*car etc*) aufbocken

jacket ['dʒækɪt] *n* Jacke *f*; (*of
man's suit*) Jackett *nt*; (*of book*)
Schutzumschlag *m*; **jacket potato**
(*pl* **-es**) *n* (*in der Schale*)
gebackene Kartoffel

jack-knife ['dʒæknaɪf] (*pl*
jack-knives) *n* Klappmesser *nt*
▷ *vi* (*truck*) sich quer stellen

jackpot ['dʒækpɒt] *n* Jackpot *m*

Jacuzzi® [dʒə'ku:zɪ] *n* (*bath*)
Whirlpool® *m*

jail [dʒeɪl] *n* Gefängnis *nt* ▷ *vt*
einsperren

jam [dʒæm] *n* Konfitüre *f*,
Marmelade *f*; (*traffic ~*) Stau *m* ▷ *vt*
(*street*) verstopfen; (*machine*)

blockieren; **to be ~ed** (stuck) klemmen; **to ~ on the brakes** eine Vollbremsung machen

Jamaica [dʒə'meɪkə] n Jamaika nt

jam-packed adj proppenvoll

janitor ['dʒænɪtə*] n (US) Hausmeister(in) m(f)

Jan abbr = **January** Jan

January ['dʒænjʊərɪ] n Januar m

Japan [dʒə'pæn] n Japan nt; **Japanese** [dʒæpə'niːz] adj japanisch ▷ n (person) Japaner(in) m(f); (language) Japanisch nt

jar [dʒɑː*] n Glas nt

jaundice ['dʒɔːndɪs] n Gelbsucht f

javelin ['dʒævlɪn] n Speer m; (Sport) Speerwerfen nt

jaw [dʒɔː] n Kiefer m

jazz [dʒæz] n Jazz m

jealous ['dʒeləs] adj eifersüchtig (of auf +akk); **don't make me ~** mach mich nicht neidisch; **jealousy** n Eifersucht f

jeans [dʒiːnz] npl Jeans pl

Jeep® [dʒiːp] n Jeep® m

jelly ['dʒelɪ] n Gelee nt; (on meat) Gallert m; (dessert) Götterspeise f; (US: jam) Marmelade f; **jelly baby** n (sweet) Gummibärchen nt; **jellyfish** n Qualle f

jeopardize ['dʒepədaɪz] vt gefährden

jerk [dʒɜːk] n Ruck m; (fam: idiot) Trottel m ▷ vt ruckartig bewegen ▷ vi (rope) rucken; (muscles) zucken

Jerusalem [dʒə'ruːsələm] n Jerusalem nt

jet [dʒet] n (of water etc) Strahl m; (nozzle) Düse f; (aircraft) Düsenflugzeug nt; **jet foil** n Tragflächenboot nt; **jetlag** n Jetlag m (Müdigkeit nach langem Flug)

Jew [dʒuː] n Jude m, Jüdin f

jewel ['dʒuːəl] n Edelstein m; (esp fig) Juwel nt; **jeweller, jeweler** (US) n Juwelier(in) m(f); **jewellery, jewelry** (US) n Schmuck m

Jewish ['dʒuːɪʃ] adj jüdisch; **she's ~** sie ist Jüdin

jigsaw (puzzle) ['dʒɪgsɔː(pʌzl)] n Puzzle nt

jilt [dʒɪlt] vt den Laufpass geben +dat

jingle ['dʒɪŋgl] n (advert) Jingle m; (verse) Reim m

jitters ['dʒɪtəz] npl (fam) **to have the ~** Bammel haben; **jittery** adj (fam) ganz nervös

job [dʒɒb] n (piece of work) Arbeit f; (task) Aufgabe f; (occupation) Stellung f, Job m; **what's your ~?** was machen Sie beruflich?; **it's a good ~ you did that** gut, dass du das gemacht hast; **jobcentre** n Arbeitsvermittlungsstelle f, Arbeitsamt nt; **job-hunting** n: **to go ~** auf Arbeitssuche gehen; **jobless** adj arbeitslos; **job seeker** n Arbeitssuchende(r) mf; **jobseeker's allowance** n Arbeitslosengeld nt; **job-sharing** n Arbeitsplatzteilung f

jockey ['dʒɒkɪ] n Jockey m

jog [dʒɒg] vt (person) anstoßen ▷ vi (run) joggen; **jogging** n Jogging nt; **to go ~** joggen gehen

john [dʒɒn] n (US fam) Klo nt

join [dʒɔɪn] vt (put together) verbinden (to mit); (club etc) beitreten +dat; **to ~ sb** sich jdm anschließen; (sit with) sich zu jdm setzen ▷ vi (unite) sich vereinigen; (rivers) zusammenfließen ▷ n Verbindungsstelle f; (seam) Naht f; **join in** vi, vt mitmachen (sth bei etw)

joint [dʒɔɪnt] n (of bones) Gelenk nt; (in pipe etc) Verbindungsstelle f; (of meat) Braten m; (of marijuana)

Joint *m* ▷ *adj* gemeinsam; **joint account** *n* Gemeinschaftskonto *nt*; **jointly** *adv* gemeinsam

joke [dʒəʊk] *n* Witz *m*; (*prank*) Streich *m*; **for a ~** zum Spaß; **it's no ~** das ist nicht zum Lachen ▷ *vi* Witze machen; **you must be joking** das ist ja wohl nicht dein Ernst!

jolly ['dʒɒlɪ] *adj* lustig, vergnügt

Jordan ['dʒɔːdən] *n* (*country*) Jordanien *nt*; (*river*) Jordan *m*

jot down [dʒɒt daʊn] *vt* sich notieren; **jotter** *n* Notizbuch *nt*

journal ['dʒɜːnl] *n* (*diary*) Tagebuch *nt*; (*magazine*) Zeitschrift *f*; **journalism** *n* Journalismus *m*; **journalist** *n* Journalist(in) *m(f)*

journey ['dʒɜːnɪ] *n* Reise *f*; (*esp on stage, by car, train*) Fahrt *f*

joy [dʒɔɪ] *n* Freude *f* (*at über +akk*); **joystick** *n* (*Inform*) Joystick *m*; (*Aviat*) Steuerknüppel *m*

judge [dʒʌdʒ] *n* Richter(in) *m(f)*; (*Sport*) Punktrichter(in) *m(f)* ▷ *vt* beurteilen (*by* nach); **as far as I can ~** meinem Urteil nach ▷ *vi* urteilen (*by* nach); **judg(e)ment** *n* (*Jur*) Urteil *nt*; (*opinion*) Ansicht *f*; **an error of ~** Fehleinschätzung *f*

judo ['dʒuːdəʊ] *n* Judo *nt*

jug [dʒʌg] *n* Krug *m*

juggle ['dʒʌgl] *vi* (*lit, fig*) jonglieren (*with* mit)

juice [dʒuːs] *n* Saft *m*; **juicy** *adj* saftig; (*story, scandal*) pikant

July [dʒuːˈlaɪ] *n* Juli *m*; *see also* September

jumble ['dʒʌmbl] *n* Durcheinander *nt* ▷ *vt*: **to ~ (up)** durcheinanderwerfen; (*facts*) durcheinanderbringen; **jumble sale** *n* (*for charity*) Flohmarkt *m*, Wohltätigkeitsbasar *m*

jumbo ['dʒʌmbəʊ] *adj* (*sausage etc*) Riesen-; **jumbo jet** *n* Jumbojet *m*

jump [dʒʌmp] *vi* springen; (*nervously*) zusammenzucken; **to ~ to conclusions** voreilige Schlüsse ziehen; **to ~ from one thing to another** dauernd das Thema wechseln ▷ *vt* (*a. fig: omit*) überspringen; **to ~ the lights** bei Rot über die Kreuzung fahren; **to ~ the queue** sich vordrängen ▷ *n* Sprung *m*; (*for horses*) Hindernis *nt*; **jumper** *n* Pullover *m*; (*US: dress*) Trägerkleid *nt*; (*person, horse*) Springer(in) *m(f)*; **jumper cable** *n* (*US*), **jump lead** *n* (*Brit Auto*) Starthilfekabel *nt*

junction ['dʒʌŋkʃən] *n* (*of roads*) Kreuzung *f*; (*Rail*) Knotenpunkt *m*

June [dʒuːn] *n* Juni *m*; *see also* September

jungle ['dʒʌŋgl] *n* Dschungel *m*

junior ['dʒuːnɪə*] *adj* (*younger*) jünger; (*lower position*) untergeordnet (*to sb* jdm); **she's two years my ~** sie ist zwei Jahre jünger als ich; **junior high (school)** *n* (*US*) ≈ Mittelschule *f*; **junior school** *n* (*Brit*) Grundschule *f*

junk [dʒʌŋk] *n* (*trash*) Plunder *m*; **junk food** *n* Nahrungsmittel *pl* mit geringem Nährwert, Junkfood *nt*; **junkie** *n* (*fam*) Junkie *m*, Fixer(in) *m(f)*; (*fig: fan*) Freak *m*; **junk mail** *n* Reklame *f*; (*Inform*) Junkmail *f*; **junk shop** *n* Trödelladen *m*

jury ['dʒʊərɪ] *n* Geschworene *pl*; (*in competition*) Jury *f*

just [dʒʌst] *adj* gerecht ▷ *adv* (*recently*) gerade; (*exactly*) genau; **~ as expected** genau wie erwartet; **~ as nice** genauso nett; **~ in time** gerade noch rechtzeitig; (*immediately*) **~ before/after …** gleich vor/ nach …; (*small distance*) **~ round the corner** gleich um die Ecke; (*a little*

~ over an hour etwas mehr als eine Stunde; *(only)* **~ the two of us** nur wir beide; **~ a moment** Moment mal; *(absolutely, simply)* **it was ~ fantastic** es war einfach klasse; **~ about** so etwa; *(more or less)* mehr oder weniger; **~ about ready** fast fertig

justice ['dʒʌstɪs] *n* Gerechtigkeit *f;* **justifiable** [dʒʌstɪ'faɪəbl] *adj* berechtigt; **justifiably** *adv* zu Recht; **justify** ['dʒʌstɪfaɪ] *vt* rechtfertigen

jut [dʒʌt] *vi:* **to ~ (out)** herausragen

juvenile ['dʒuːvənaɪl] *n adj* Jugend-, jugendlich ▷ *n* Jugendliche(r) *mf*

k *abbr* = **thousand; 15k** 15 000
K *abbr* = **kilobyte** KB
kangaroo [kæŋgə'ruː] *n* Känguru *nt*
karaoke [kærɪ'əʊkɪ] *n* Karaoke *nt*
karate [kə'rɑːtɪ] *n* Karate *nt*
kart [kɑːt] *n* Gokart *m*
kayak ['kaɪæk] *n* Kajak *m* o *nt;* **kayaking** ['kaɪækɪŋ] *n* Kajak-fahren *nt*
Kazakhstan [kæzæk'stɑːn] *n* Kasachstan *nt*
kebab [kə'bæb] *n (shish ~)* Schaschlik *nt* o *m; (doner ~)* Kebab *m*
keel [kiːl] *n (Naut)* Kiel *m;* **keel over** *vi (boat)* kentern; *(person)* umkippen
keen [kiːn] *adj* begeistert *(on* von); *(hardworking)* eifrig; *(mind, wind)* scharf; *(interest, feeling)* stark; **to be ~ on sb** von jdm angetan sein; **she's ~ on riding** sie reitet

gern; **to be ~ to do** sth darauf
erpicht sein, etw zu tun
keep [kiːp] (**kept, kept**) vt
(*retain*) behalten; (*secret*) für sich
behalten; (*observe*) einhalten; (*promise*) halten; (*run: shop, diary,
accounts*) führen; (*animals*) halten;
(*support, family etc*) unterhalten,
versorgen; (*store*) aufbewahren; **to
~ sb waiting** jdn warten lassen; **to
~ sb from doing sth** jdn davon
abhalten, etw zu tun; **to ~ sth
clean/secret** etw sauber/geheim
halten; **"~ clear"** "(bitte) frei
halten"; **~ this to yourself**
behalten Sie das für sich ▷ vi
(*food*) sich halten; (*remain, with adj*)
bleiben; **~ quiet** sei ruhig!; **~ left**
links fahren; **~ doing sth**
(*repeatedly*) etw immer wieder tun;
~ at it mach weiter so!; **it ~s
happening** es passiert immer
wieder ▷ n (*livelihood*) Unterhalt
m; **keep back** vi zurückbleiben
▷ vt zurückhalten; (*information*)
verschweigen (*from sb* jdm); **keep
off** vt (*person, animal*) fernhalten;
"~ off the grass" "Betreten des
Rasens verboten"; **keep on** vi
weitermachen; (*walking*)
weitergehen; (*in car*) weiterfahren;
to ~ doing sth (*persistently*) etw
immer wieder tun ▷ vt (*coat etc*)
anbehalten; **keep out** vt nicht
hereinlassen ▷ vi draußen
bleiben; **~** (*on sign*) Eintritt
verboten; **keep to** vt (*road, path*)
bleiben auf +dat; (*plan etc*) sich
halten an +akk; **to ~ the point** bei
der Sache bleiben; **keep up** vi
Schritt halten (*with* mit) ▷ vt
(*maintain*) aufrechterhalten;
(*speed*) halten; **to ~ appearances**
den Schein wahren; **keep it up!**
(*fam*) weiter so!
keeper n (*museum etc*)
Aufseher(in) m(f); (*goal~*) Torwart

m; (*zoo ~*) Tierpfleger(in) m(f);
keep-fit n Fitnesstraining nt;
~ exercises Gymnastik f
kennel ['kenl] n Hundehütte f;
kennels n Hundepension f
Kenya ['kenjə] n Kenia nt
kept [kept] pt, pp of **keep**
kerb [kɜːb] n Randstein m
kerosene ['kerəsiːn] n (US)
Petroleum nt
ketchup ['ketʃəp] n Ketchup nt o
m
kettle ['ketl] n Kessel m
key [kiː] n Schlüssel m; (*of piano,
computer*) Taste f; (*Mus*) Tonart f;
(*for map etc*) Zeichenerklärung f
▷ vt: **to ~ (in)** (*Inform*) eingeben
▷ adj entscheidend; **keyboard** n
(*piano, computer*) Tastatur f;
keyhole n Schlüsselloch nt;
keypad n (*Inform*)
Nummernblock m; **keyring** n
Schlüsselring m
kick [kik] n Tritt m; (*Sport*) Stoß
m; **I get a ~ out of it** (*fam*) es turnt
mich an ▷ vt, vi treten; **kick out**
vt (*fam*) rausschmeißen (*of* aus);
kick-off n (*Sport*) Anstoß m
kid [kid] n (*child*) Kind nt ▷ vt
(*tease*) auf den Arm nehmen ▷ vi
Witze machen; **you're ~ding!**
das ist doch nicht dein Ernst!; **no
~ding** aber echt!
kidnap ['kidnæp] vt entführen;
kidnapper n Entführer(in) m(f);
kidnapping n Entführung f
kidney ['kidni] n Niere f; **kidney
machine** n künstliche Niere
kill [kil] vt töten; (*esp
intentionally*) umbringen; (*weeds*)
vernichten; **killer** n Mörder(in)
m(f)
kilo ['kiːləʊ] (*pl* **-s**) n Kilo nt;
kilobyte n Kilobyte nt;
kilogramme n Kilogramm nt;
kilometer (US), **kilometre** n
Kilometer m; **~s per hour**

Stundenkilometer pl; **kilowatt** n
Kilowatt nt

kilt [kɪlt] n Schottenrock m

kind [kaɪnd] adj nett, freundlich
(to zu) ▷ n Art f; (of coffee, cheese
etc) Sorte f; **what ~ of …?** was für
ein(e) …?; **this ~ of …** so ein(e) …;
~ of (+ adj) irgendwie

kindergarten ['kɪndəgɑːtn] n
Kindergarten m

kindly ['kaɪndlɪ] adj nett,
freundlich ▷ adv liebenswürdi-
gerweise; **kindness** ['kaɪndnəs]
n Freundlichkeit f

king [kɪŋ] n König m; **kingdom** n
Königreich nt; **kingfisher** n
Eisvogel m; **king-size** adj im
Großformat; (bed) extra groß

kipper ['kɪpə*] n Räucherhering
m

kiss [kɪs] n Kuss m; **~ of life**
Mund-zu-Mund-Beatmung f ▷ vt
küssen

kit [kɪt] n (equipment) Ausrüstung
f; (fam) Sachen pl; (sports ~)
Sportsachen pl; (belongings, clothes)
Sachen pl; (for building sth) Bausatz
m

kitchen ['kɪtʃɪn] n Küche f;
kitchen foil n Alufolie f; **kitchen
scales** n Küchenwaage f; **kitchen
unit** n Küchenschrank m;
kitchenware n Küchengeschirr
nt

kite [kaɪt] n Drachen m

kitten ['kɪtn] n Kätzchen nt

kiwi ['kiːwiː] n (fruit) Kiwi f

km abbr = **kilometres** km

knack [næk] n Dreh m, Trick m; to
get/have got the ~ den Dreh
herauskriegen/heraushaben;
knackered ['nækəd] adj (Brit fam)
fix und fertig, kaputt

knee [niː] n Knie nt; **kneecap** n
Kniescheibe f; **knee-jerk** adj
(reaction) reflexartig; **kneel** [niːl]
(knelt o kneeled, knelt o kneeled)

vi knien; (action, ~ down) sich
hinknien

knelt [nelt] pt, pp of **kneel**

knew [njuː] pt of **know**

knickers ['nɪkəz] npl (Brit fam)
Schlüpfer m

knife [naɪf] (pl **knives**) n Messer
nt

knight [naɪt] n Ritter m; (in
chess) Pferd nt, Springer m

knit [nɪt] vt, vi stricken; **knitting**
n (piece of work) Strickarbeit f;
(activity) Stricken nt; **knitting
needle** n Stricknadel f; **knitwear**
n Strickwaren pl

knob [nɒb] n (on door) Knauf m;
(on radio etc) Knopf m

knock [nɒk] vt (with hammer etc)
schlagen; (accidentally) stoßen; **to
~ one's head** sich an den Kopf
anschlagen ▷ vi klopfen (on, at an
+akk) ▷ n (blow) Schlag m; (on door)
Klopfen nt; **there was a ~ (at the
door)** es hat geklopft; **knock
down** vt (object) umstoßen; (with car)
(person) niederschlagen; (with car)
anfahren; (building) abreißen;
knock out vt (stun) bewusstlos
schlagen; (boxer) k.o. schlagen;
knock over vt umstoßen; (with
car) anfahren; **knocker** n
Türklopfer m; **knockout** n
Knockout m, K.o. m

knot [nɒt] n Knoten m

know [nəʊ] (**knew**, **known**) vt, vi
wissen; (be acquainted with: people,
places) kennen; (recognize)
erkennen; (language) können; **I'll
let you ~** ich sage dir Bescheid; **I
~ some French** ich kann etwas
Französisch; **to get to ~ sb** jdn
kennenlernen; **to be ~n** als
bekannt sein als; **know about** vi
Bescheid wissen über +akk;
(subject) sich auskennen in +dat;
(cars, horses etc) sich auskennen
mit; **know of** vt kennen; **not that**

I ~ nicht dass ich wüsste;
know-all n (fam) Klugscheißer m;
know-how nt Kenntnis f,
Know-how nt; **knowing** adj
wissend; (look, smile) vielsagend;
knowledge ['nɒlɪdʒ] n Wissen
nt; (of a subject) Kenntnisse pl; **to
(the best of) my ~** meines
Wissens
known [nəʊn] pp of **know**
knuckle ['nʌkl] n (Finger)knöchel m; (Gastr) Hachse f;
knuckle down vi sich an die
Arbeit machen
Koran [kɔ'rɑːn] n Koran m
Korea [kə'rɪə] n Korea nt
Kosovo ['kɒsɒvəʊ] n der Kosovo
kph abbr = **kilometres per hour**
km/h
Kremlin ['kremlɪn] n: **the ~** der
Kreml
Kurd [kɛːd] n Kurde m, Kurdin f;
Kurdish adj kurdisch
Kuwait [kʊ'weɪt] n Kuwait nt

L abbr (Brit Auto) = **learner**
LA abbr = **Los Angeles**
lab [læb] n (fam) Labor nt
label ['leɪbl] n Etikett nt; (tied)
Anhänger m; (adhesive) Aufkleber
m; (record ~) Label nt ▷ vt
etikettieren; (pej) abstempeln
laboratory [lə'bɒrətərɪ] n Labor
nt

- **LABOR DAY**

- Der **Labor Day** ist in den USA
- und Kanada der Name für den
- Tag der Arbeit. Er wird dort als
- gesetzlicher Feiertag am ersten
- Montag im September
- begangen.

laborious [lə'bɔːrɪəs] adj
mühsam; **labor** (US), **labour**
['leɪbə°] n Arbeit f; (Med) Wehen
pl; **to be in ~** Wehen haben ▷ adj

(Pol) Labour-; **~ Party** Labour Party f; **labor union** n (US) Gewerkschaft f; **labourer** n Arbeiter(in) m(f)

lace [leɪs] n (fabric) Spitze f; (of shoe) Schnürsenkel m ▷ vt: **to ~ (up)** zuschnüren

lack [læk] vt, vi: **to be ~ing** fehlen; **sb ~s o is ~ing sth** es fehlt jdm an etw dat; **we ~ the time** uns fehlt die Zeit ▷ n Mangel m (of +dat)

lacquer ['lækə] n Lack m; (Brit: hair ~) Haarspray nt

lad [læd] n Junge m

ladder ['lædə] n Leiter f; (in tight) Laufmasche f

laddish ['lædɪʃ] adj (Brit) machohaft

laden ['leɪdn] adj beladen (with mit)

ladies ['leɪdɪz], **ladies' room** n Damentoilette f

lad mag n Männerzeitschrift f

lady ['leɪdɪ] n Dame f; (as title) Lady f; **ladybird, ladybug** (US) n Marienkäfer m; **Ladyshave®** n Epiliergerät nt

lag [læg] vi: **to ~ (behind)** zurückliegen ▷ vt (pipes) isolieren

lager ['lɑːgə] n helles Bier; **~ lout** betrunkener Rowdy

lagging ['lægɪŋ] n Isolierung f

laid [leɪd] pt, pp of **lay**; **laid-back** adj (fam) cool, gelassen

lain [leɪn] pp of **lie**

lake [leɪk] n See m; **the Lake District** Seengebiet im Nordwesten Englands

lamb [læm] n Lamm nt; (meat) Lammfleisch nt; **lamb chop** n Lammkotelett nt

lame [leɪm] adj lahm; (excuse) faul; (argument) schwach

lament [lə'mɛnt] n Klage f ▷ vt beklagen

laminated ['læmɪneɪtɪd] adj beschichtet

lamp [læmp] n Lampe f; (in street) Laterne f; (in car) Licht nt; Scheinwerfer m; **lamppost** n Laternenpfahl m; **lampshade** n Lampenschirm m

land [lænd] n Land nt ▷ vi (from ship) an Land gehen; (Aviat) landen ▷ vt (passengers) absetzen; (goods) abladen; (plane) landen; **landing** n Landung f; (on stairs) Treppenabsatz m; **landing stage** n Landesteg m; **landing strip** n Landebahn f

landlady n Hauswirtin f, Vermieterin f; **landline** n Festnetz nt; **landlord** n (of house) Hauswirt m, Vermieter m; (of pub) Gastwirt m; **landmark** n Wahrzeichen nt; (event) Meilenstein m; **landowner** n Grundbesitzer(in) m(f); **landscape** n Landschaft f; (format) Querformat nt; **landslide** n (Geo) Erdrutsch m

lane [leɪn] n (in country) enge Landstraße, Weg m; (in town) Gasse f; (of motorway) Spur f; (Sport) Bahn f; **to get in ~** (in car) sich einordnen

language ['læŋgwɪdʒ] n Sprache f; (style) Ausdrucksweise f

lantern ['læntən] n Laterne f

lap [læp] n Schoß m; (in race) Runde f ▷ vt (in race) überholen

lapse [læps] n (mistake) Irrtum m; (moral) Fehltritt m ▷ vi ablaufen

laptop ['læptɒp] n Laptop m

large [lɑːdʒ] adj groß; **by and ~** im Großen und Ganzen; **largely** adv zum größten Teil; **large-scale** adj groß angelegt, Groß-

lark [lɑːk] n (bird) Lerche f

laryngitis [lærɪn'dʒaɪtɪs] n Kehlkopfentzündung f; **larynx** ['lærɪŋks] n Kehlkopf m

laser ['leɪzə*] n Laser m; **laser printer** n Laserdrucker m

lash [læʃ] vt peitschen; **lash out** vi (with fists) um sich schlagen; (spend money) sich in Unkosten stürzen (on mit)

lass [læs] n Mädchen nt

last [lɑːst] adj letzte(r, s); **the ~ but one** der/die/das vorletzte; **~ night** gestern Abend; **~ but not least** nicht zuletzt ▷ adv zuletzt; (last time) das letzte Mal; **at ~** endlich ▷ n (person) Letzte(r) m/f; (thing) Letzte(s) nt; **he was the ~ to leave** er ging als Letzter ▷ vi (continue) dauern; (remain in good condition) durchhalten; (remain good) sich halten; (money) ausreichen; **lasting** adj dauerhaft; (impression) nachhaltig; **lastly** adv schließlich; **last-minute** adj in letzter Minute; **last name** n Nachname m

late [leɪt] adj spät; (after proper time) zu spät; (train etc) verspätet; (dead) verstorben; **to be ~** zu spät kommen; (train etc) Verspätung haben ▷ adv spät; (after proper time) zu spät; **late availibility flight** n Last-Minute-Flug m; **lately** adv in letzter Zeit; **late opening** n verlängerte Öffnungszeiten pl; **later** ['leɪtə°] adj, adv später; **see you ~** bis später; **latest** ['leɪtɪst] adj späteste(r, s) (most recent) neueste(r, s) ▷ n: **the ~** (news) das Neueste; **at the ~** spätestens

Latin ['lætɪn] n Latein nt ▷ adj lateinisch; **Latin America** n Lateinamerika nt; **Latin-American** adj lateinamerikanisch ▷ n Lateinamerikaner(in) m(f)

latter ['lætə°] adj (second of two) letztere(r, s); (last: part, years) letzte(r, s), später

Latvia ['lætvɪə] n Lettland nt;

Latvian ['lætvɪən] ▷ adj lettisch; ▷ n (person) Lette m; Lettin f; (language) Lettisch nt

laugh [lɑːf] n Lachen nt; **for a ~** aus Spaß ▷ vi lachen (at, about über +akk); **to ~ at sb** sich über jdn lustig machen; **it's no ~ing matter** es ist nicht zum Lachen; **laughter** ['lɑːftə°] n Gelächter nt

launch [lɔːntʃ] n (launching, of ship) Stapellauf m; (of rocket) Abschuss m; (of product) Markteinführung f; (with hype) Lancierung f; (opening) Eröffnungsfeier f ▷ vt (ship) vom Stapel lassen; (rocket) abschießen; (product) einführen; (with hype) lancieren; (project) in Gang setzen

launder ['lɔːndə°] vt waschen und bügeln; (fig: money) waschen; **laundrette** [lɔːn'dret] n (Brit), **laundromat** ['lɔːndrəmæt] n (US) Waschsalon m; **laundry** ['lɔːndrɪ] n (place) Wäscherei f; (clothes) Wäsche f

lavatory ['lævətrɪ] n Toilette f

lavender ['lævɪndə°] n Lavendel m

lavish ['lævɪʃ] adj verschwenderisch; (furnishings etc) üppig; (gift) großzügig

law [lɔː] n Gesetz nt; (system) Recht nt; (for study) Jura; (of sport) Regel f; **against the ~** gesetzwidrig; **law-abiding** adj gesetzestreu; **law court** n Gerichtshof m; **lawful** adj rechtmäßig

lawn [lɔːn] n Rasen m; **lawnmower** n Rasenmäher m

lawsuit ['lɔːsuːt] n Prozess m; **lawyer** ['lɔːjə°] n Rechtsanwalt m, Rechtsanwältin f

laxative ['læksətɪv] n Abführmittel nt

lay [leɪ] pt of **lie** ▷ vt (laid, laid) legen; (table) decken; (vulg)

poppen, bumsen; (egg) legen ▷ adj
Laien-; **lay down** vt hinlegen; **lay
off** vt (workers) (vorübergehend)
entlassen; (stop attacking) in Ruhe
lassen; **lay on** vt (provide)
anbieten; (organize) veranstalten,
bereitstellen; **layabout** n
Faulenzer(in) m(f); **lay-by** n
Parkbucht f; (bigger) Parkplatz m

layer ['leɪə°] n Schicht f

layman ['leɪmən] n Laie m

layout ['leɪaʊt] n Gestaltung f,
(of book etc) Lay-out nt

laze [leɪz] vi faulenzen; **laziness**
['leɪzɪnɪs] n Faulheit f; **lazy**
['leɪzɪ] adj faul; (day, time)
gemütlich

lb abbr = **pound** Pfd.

lead [led] n Blei nt ▷ vt, vi [liːd]
(**led, led**) führen; (group etc) leiten;
to ~ the way vorangehen; **this is
~ing us nowhere** das bringt uns
nicht weiter ▷ [liːd] n (race)
Führung f; (distance, time ahead)
Vorsprung m (over vor +dat); (of
police) Spur f; (Theat) Hauptrolle f;
(dog's) Leine f; (Elec: flex) Leitung f;
lead astray vt irreführen; **lead
away** vt wegführen; **lead back** vi
zurückführen; **lead on** vt
anführen; **lead to** vt (street)
hinführen nach; (result in) führen
zu; **lead up to** vt (drive) führen zu

leaded ['ledɪd] adj (petrol)
verbleit

leader ['liːdə°] n Führer(in) m(f);
(of party) Vorsitzende(r) mf; (of
project, expedition) Leiter(in) m(f);
(Sport: in race) der/die Erste; (in
league) Tabellenführer m;
leadership ['liːdəʃɪp] n Führung
f

lead-free ['led'friː] adj (petrol)
bleifrei

leading ['liːdɪŋ] adj führend,
wichtig

leaf [liːf] (pl **leaves**) n Blatt nt;

leaflet ['liːflɪt] n Prospekt m;
(pamphlet) Flugblatt nt; (with
instructions) Merkblatt nt

league [liːg] n Bund m; (Sport)
Liga f

leak [liːk] n (gap) undichte Stelle;
(escape) Leck nt; **to take a ~** (fam)
pinkeln gehen ▷ vi (pipe etc)
undicht sein; (liquid etc) auslaufen;
leaky adj undicht

lean [liːn] adj (meat) mager; (face)
schmal; (person) drahtig ▷ vi
(**leant** o **leaned, leant** o **leaned**)
(not vertical) sich neigen; (rest) **to
~ against sth** sich an etw akk
lehnen; (support oneself) **to ~ on
sth** sich auf etw akk stützen ▷ vt
lehnen (on, against an +akk); **lean
back** vi sich zurücklehnen; **lean
forward** vi sich vorbeugen; **lean
over** vi sich hinüberbeugen; **lean
towards** vt tendieren zu

leant [lent] pt, pp of **lean**

leap [liːp] n Sprung m ▷ vi (**leapt**
o **leaped, leapt** o **leaped**)
springen; **leapt** [lept] pt, pp of
leap; **leap year** n Schaltjahr nt

learn [lɜːn] (**learnt** o **learned,
learnt** o **learned**) vt, vi lernen;
(find out) erfahren; **to ~ (how) to
swim** schwimmen lernen;
learned ['lɜːnɪd] adj gelehrt;
learner n Anfänger(in) m(f); (Brit:
driver) Fahrschüler(in) m(f)

learnt [lɜːnt] pt, pp of **learn**

lease [liːs] n (of land, premises etc)
Pacht f; (contract) Pachtvertrag m;
(of house, car etc) Miete f; (contract)
Mietvertrag m ▷ vt pachten;
(house, car etc) mieten; **lease out**
vt vermieten; **leasing** ['liːsɪŋ] n
Leasing nt

least [liːst] adj wenigste(r, s);
(slightest) geringste(r, s) ▷ adv am
wenigsten; **~ expensive**
billigste(r, s) ▷ n: **the ~** das
Mindeste; **not in the ~** nicht im

geringsten; **at ~** wenigstens; (with number) mindestens

leather ['lɛðə°] n Leder nt ▷ adj ledern, Leder-

leave [li:v] n (time off) Urlaub m; **on ~** auf Urlaub; **to take one's ~** Abschied nehmen (of von) ▷ vt (left, left) (place, person) verlassen; (not remove, not change) lassen; (~ behind: message, scar etc) hinterlassen; (forget) hinter sich lassen; (after death) hinterlassen (to sb jdm); (entrust) überlassen (to sb jdm); **to be left** (remain) übrig bleiben; **~ me alone** lass mich in Ruhe!; **don't ~ it to the last minute** warte nicht bis zur letzten Minute ▷ vi (weg)gehen, (weg)fahren; (on journey) abreisen; (bus, train) abfahren (for nach); **leave behind** vt zurücklassen; (scar etc) hinterlassen; (forget) hinter sich lassen; **leave out** vt auslassen; (person) ausschließen (of von)

leaves [li:vz] pl of **leaf**

leaving do ['li:vɪŋ du:] n Abschiedsfeier f

Lebanon ['lɛbənən] n: **the ~** der Libanon

lecture ['lɛktʃə°] n Vortrag m; (at university) Vorlesung f; **to give a ~** einen Vortrag/eine Vorlesung halten; **lecturer** n Dozent(in) m(f); **lecture theatre** n Hörsaal m

led [lɛd] pt, pp of **lead**

LED abbr = **light-emitting diode** Leuchtdiode f

ledge [lɛdʒ] n Leiste f; (window ~) Sims m or nt

leek [li:k] n Lauch m

left [lɛft] pt, pp of **leave** ▷ adj linke(r, s) ▷ adv (position) links; (movement) nach links ▷ n (side) linke Seite; **the Left** (Pol) die Linke; **on/to the ~** links (of von); **move/fall to the ~** nach links

rücken/fallen; **left-hand** adj linke(r, s); **~ bend** Linkskurve f; **~ drive** Linkssteuerung f; **left-handed** adj linkshändig; **left-hand side** n linke Seite

left-luggage locker n Gepäckschließfach nt; **left-luggage office** n Gepäckaufbewahrung f

leftovers npl Reste pl

left wing n linker Flügel; **left-wing** adj (Pol) linksgerichtet

leg [lɛg] n Bein nt; (of meat) Keule f

legacy ['lɛgəsɪ] n Erbe nt, Erbschaft f

legal ['li:gəl] adj Rechts-, rechtlich; (allowed) legal; (limit, age) gesetzlich; **~ aid** Rechtshilfe f; **legalize** vt legalisieren; **legally** adv legal

legend ['lɛdʒənd] n Legende f

legible, legibly ['lɛdʒəbl, -blɪ] adj, adv leserlich

legislation [lɛdʒɪs'leɪʃn] n Gesetze pl

legitimate [lɪ'dʒɪtɪmət] adj rechtmäßig, legitim

legroom ['lɛgrum] n Beinfreiheit f

leisure ['lɛʒə°] n (time) Freizeit f ▷ adj Freizeit-; **~ centre** Freizeitzentrum nt; **leisurely** ['lɛʒəlɪ] adj gemächlich

lemon ['lɛmən] n Zitrone f; **lemonade** [lɛmə'neɪd] n Limonade f; **lemon curd** n Brotaufstrich aus Zitronen, Butter, Eiern und Zucker; **lemon juice** n Zitronensaft m; **lemon sole** n Seezunge f

lend [lɛnd] (lent, lent) vt leihen; **to ~ sb sth** jdm etw leihen; **to (sb) ~ a hand** (jdm) behilflich sein; **lending library** n Leihbücherei f

length [lɛŋθ] n Länge f; **4 metres in ~** 4 Meter lang; **what**

~ **is it?** wie lange ist es?; **for any ~ of time** für längere Zeit; **at ~** (lengthily) ausführlich; **lengthen** ['leŋθən] vt verlängern; **lengthy** adj sehr lange; (dragging) langwierig

lenient ['liːnɪənt] adj nachsichtig

lens [lenz] n Linse f; (Foto) Objektiv nt

lent [lent] pt, pp of **lend**

Lent [lent] n Fastenzeit f

lentil ['lentl] n (Bot) Linse f

Leo ['liːəʊ] (pl **-s**) n (Astr) Löwe m

leopard ['lepəd] n Leopard m

lesbian ['lezbɪən] adj lesbisch ▷ n Lesbe f

less [les] adj, adv, n weniger; **~ and ~** immer weniger; (~ often) immer seltener; **lessen** ['lesn] vi abnehmen, nachlassen ▷ vt verringern; (pain) lindern; **lesser** ['lesə*] adj geringer; (amount) kleiner

lesson ['lesn] n (at school) Stunde f; (unit of study) Lektion f; (fig) Lehre f; (Rel) Lesung f; **~s start at 9** der Unterricht beginnt um 9

let [let] (let, let) vt lassen; (lease) vermieten; **to ~ sb have sth** jdm etw geben; **~'s go** gehen wir; **to ~ go (of sth)** (etw) loslassen; **let down** vt herunterlassen; (fail to help) im Stich lassen; (disappoint) enttäuschen; **let in** vt hereinlassen; **let off** vt (bomb) hochgehen lassen; (person) laufen lassen; **let out** vt hinauslassen; (secret) verraten; (scream etc) ausstoßen; **let up** vi nachlassen; (stop) aufhören

lethal ['liːθəl] adj tödlich

let's contr = **let us**

letter ['letə*] n (of alphabet) Buchstabe m; (message) Brief m; (official ~) Schreiben nt; **letter**

bomb n Briefbombe f; **letterbox** n Briefkasten m

lettuce ['letɪs] n Kopfsalat m

leukaemia, leukemia (US) [luːˈkiːmɪə] n Leukämie f

level ['levl] adj (horizontal) waagerecht; (ground) eben; (two things, two runners) auf selber Höhe; **to be ~ with sb/sth** mit jdm/etw auf gleicher Höhe sein; **~ on points** punktgleich ▷ adv (run etc) auf gleicher Höhe, gleich auf; **to draw ~** (in race) gleichziehen (with mit); (in game) ausgleichen ▷ n (altitude) Höhe f; (standard) Niveau nt; (amount, degree) Grad m; **to be on a ~ with** auf gleicher Höhe sein mit ▷ vt (ground) einebnen; **level crossing** n (Brit) (schienengleicher) Bahnübergang m; **level-headed** adj vernünftig

lever ['liːvə*, (US) 'levə*] n Hebel m; (fig) Druckmittel nt; **lever up** vt hochstemmen

liability [laɪəˈbɪlɪtɪ] n Haftung f; (burden) Belastung f; (obligation) Verpflichtung f; **liable** ['laɪəbl] adj: **to be ~ for sth** (responsible) für etw haften; **~ for tax** steuerpflichtig

liar ['laɪə*] n Lügner(in) m(f)

Lib Dem [lɪb'dem] abbr = **Liberal Democrat**

liberal ['lɪbərəl] adj (generous) großzügig; (broad-minded) liberal; **Liberal Democrat** n (Brit Pol) Liberaldemokrat(in) m(f) ▷ adj liberaldemokratisch

liberate ['lɪbəreɪt] vt befreien; **liberation** [lɪbəˈreɪʃn] n Befreiung f

Liberia [laɪˈbɪərɪə] n Liberia f

liberty ['lɪbətɪ] n Freiheit f

Libra ['liːbrə] n (Astr) Waage f

library ['laɪbrərɪ] n Bibliothek f; (lending ~) Bücherei f

Libya ['lɪbɪə] n Libyen nt

lice [laɪs] pl of **louse**

licence ['laɪsəns] n (permit)
Genehmigung f; (Comm) Lizenz f;
(driving ~) Führerschein m; **license**
['laɪsəns] n (US) see **licence** ▷ vt
genehmigen; **licensed** adj
(restaurant etc) mit
Schankerlaubnis; **license plate** n
(US Auto) Nummernschild nt;
licensing hours npl
Ausschankzeiten pl

lick [lɪk] vt lecken ▷ n Lecken
nt

licorice ['lɪkərɪs] n Lakritze f

lid [lɪd] n Deckel m; (eye~) Lid nt

lie [laɪ] n Lüge f; **~ detector**
Lügendetektor m ▷ vi lügen; **to
~ to sb** jdn belügen ▷ vi (lay, lain)
(rest, be situated) liegen; (~ down)
sich legen; (snow) liegen bleiben;
to be lying third an dritter Stelle
liegen; **lie about** vi herumliegen;
lie down vi sich hinlegen

Liechtenstein ['lɪktənstaɪn] n
Liechtenstein nt

lie in [laɪ'ɪn] n: **to have a
~** ausschlafen

life [laɪf] (pl **lives**) n Leben nt; **to
get ~** lebenslänglich bekommen;
there isn't much ~ here hier ist
nicht viel los; **how many lives
were lost?** wie viele sind ums
Leben gekommen?; **life assurance**
n Lebensversicherung f; **lifebelt** n
Rettungsring m; **lifeboat** n
Rettungsboot nt; **lifeguard** n
Bademeister(in) m(f),
Rettungsschwimmer(in) m(f); **life
insurance** n Lebensversicherung
f; **life jacket** n Schwimmweste f;
lifeless adj (dead) leblos; **lifelong**
adj lebenslang; **life preserver** n
(US) Rettungsring m; **life-saving**
adj lebensrettend; **life-size(d)** adj
in Lebensgröße; **life span** n
Lebensspanne f; **life style** n

Lebensstil m; **lifetime** n
Lebenszeit f

lift [lɪft] vt (hoch)heben; (ban)
aufheben ▷ n (Brit: elevator)
Aufzug m, Lift m; **to give sb a ~** jdn
im Auto mitnehmen; **lift up** vt
hochheben; **lift-off** n Start m

ligament ['lɪgəmənt] n Band nt

light [laɪt] (**lit** o **lighted, lit** o
lighted) vt beleuchten; (fire,
cigarette) anzünden ▷ n Licht nt;
(lamp) Lampe f; **~s** pl (Auto)
Beleuchtung f; (traffic ~s) Ampel f;
in the ~ of angesichts +gen ▷ adj
(bright) hell; (not heavy, easy) leicht;
(punishment) milde; (taxes) niedrig;
~ blue/green hellblau/hellgrün;
light up vt (illuminate) beleuchten
▷ vi (a. eyes) aufleuchten

light bulb n Glühbirne f

lighten ['laɪtn] vi hell werden
▷ vt (give light to) erhellen; (make
less heavy) leichter machen; (fig)
erleichtern

lighter ['laɪtə°] n (cigarette ~)
Feuerzeug nt

light-hearted adj unbeschwert;
lighthouse n Leuchtturm m;
lighting n Beleuchtung f; **lightly**
adv leicht; **light meter** n (Foto)
Belichtungsmesser m

lightning ['laɪtnɪŋ] n Blitz m

lightweight adj leicht

like [laɪk] vt mögen, gernhaben;
he ~s swimming er schwimmt
gern; **would you ~ ...?** hättest
du/hätten Sie gern ...?; **I'd ~ to go
home** ich möchte nach Hause
(gehen); **I don't ~ the film** der
Film gefällt mir nicht ▷ prep wie;
what's it/he ~? wie ist es/er?; **he
looks ~ you** er sieht dir/Ihnen
ähnlich; **~ that/this** so; **likeable**
['laɪkəbl] adj sympathisch

likelihood ['laɪklɪhʊd] n Wahrscheinlichkeit f; **likely** ['laɪklɪ]
adj wahrscheinlich; **the bus is**

~ **to be late** der Bus wird wahrscheinlich Verspätung haben; **he's not (at all) ~ to come** (höchst)wahrscheinlich kommt er nicht

like-minded ['laik'maindid] adj gleich gesinnt

likewise ['laikwaiz] adv ebenfalls; **to do ~** das Gleiche tun

liking ['laikiŋ] n (for person) Zuneigung f; (for type, things) Vorliebe f (for für)

lilac ['lailək] n Flieder m ▷ adj fliederfarben

lily ['lili] n Lilie f; **~ of the valley** Maiglöckchen nt

limb [lim] n Glied nt

limbo ['limbəʊ] n: **in ~** (plans) auf Eis gelegt

lime [laim] n (tree) Linde f; (fruit) Limone f; (substance) Kalk m; **lime juice** n Limonensaft m; **limelight** n (fig) Rampenlicht nt

limerick ['limərik] n Limerick m (fünfzeiliges komisches Gedicht)

limestone ['laimstəʊn] n Kalkstein m

limit ['limit] n Grenze f; (for pollution etc) Grenzwert m; **there's a ~ to that** dem sind Grenzen gesetzt; **to be over the ~** (speed) das Tempolimit überschreiten; (alcohol consumption) fahruntüchtig sein; **that's the ~** jetzt reicht's!, das ist die Höhe! ▷ vt beschränken (to auf +akk); (freedom, spending) einschränken; **limitation** [limi'teiʃən] n Beschränkung f; (of freedom, spending) Einschränkung f; **limited** adj begrenzt; **~ liability company** Gesellschaft f mit beschränkter Haftung, GmbH f; **public ~ company** Aktiengesellschaft f

limousine ['liməzi:n] n Limousine f

limp [limp] vi hinken ▷ adj schlaff

line [lain] n Linie f; (written) Zeile f; (rope) Leine f; (on face) Falte f; (row) Reihe f; (US: queue) Schlange f; (Rail) Bahnlinie f; (between A and B) Strecke f; (Tel) Leitung f; (range of items) Kollektion f; **hold the ~** bleiben Sie am Apparat; **to stand in ~** Schlange stehen; **in ~ with** in Übereinstimmung mit; **something along those ~s** etwas in dieser Art; **drop me a ~** schreib mir ein paar Zeilen; **~s** (Theat) Text m ▷ vt (clothes) füttern; (streets) säumen; **lined** adj (paper) liniert; (face) faltig; **line up** vi sich aufstellen; (US: form queue) sich anstellen

linen ['linin] n Leinen nt; (sheets etc) Wäsche f

liner ['lainə°] n Überseedampfer m, Passagierschiff nt

linger ['liŋgə°] vi verweilen; (smell) nicht weggehen

lingerie ['lænʒəri:] n Damenunterwäsche f

lining ['lainiŋ] n (of clothes) Futter nt; (brake ~) Bremsbelag m

link [liŋk] n (connection) Verbindung f; (of chain) Glied nt; (relationship) Beziehung f (with zu); (between events) Zusammenhang m; (Internet) Link m ▷ vt verbinden

lion ['laiən] n Löwe m; **lioness** n Löwin f

lip [lip] n Lippe f; **lipstick** n Lippenstift m

liqueur [li'kjʊə°] n Likör m

liquid ['likwid] n Flüssigkeit f ▷ adj flüssig

liquidate ['likwideit] vt liquidieren

liquidizer ['likwidaizə°] n Mixer m

liquor ['likə°] n Spirituosen pl

orice ['lɪkərɪs] n Lakritze f
bon ['lɪzbən] n Lissabon nt
p [lɪsp] vt, vi lispeln
st [lɪst] n Liste f ▷ vi (ship)
Schlagseite haben ▷ vt auflisten,
aufzählen; **~ed building** unter
Denkmalschutz stehendes
Gebäude
listen ['lɪsn] vi zuhören, horchen
(for sth auf etw akk); **listen to** vt
(person) zuhören +dat; (radio)
hören; (advice) hören auf; **listener**
n Zuhörer(in) m(f); (to radio)
Hörer(in) m(f)
lit [lɪt] pt, pp of **light**
liter ['liːtə*] n (US) Liter m
literacy ['lɪtərəsɪ] n Fähigkeit f
zu lesen und zu schreiben; **literal**
['lɪtərəl] adj (translation, meaning)
wörtlich; (actual) buchstäblich;
literally adv (translate, take sth)
wörtlich; (really) buchstäblich,
wirklich; **literary** ['lɪtərərɪ] adj
literarisch; (critic, journal etc)
Literatur-; (language) gehoben;
literature ['lɪtrɪtʃə*] n Literatur
f; (brochures etc)
Informationsmaterial nt
Lithuania [lɪθju'eɪnɪə] n Litauen
nt; **Lithuanian** [lɪθju'eɪnɪən]
▷ adj litauisch; ▷ n (person)
Litauer(in) m(f); (language)
Litauisch nt
litre ['liːtə*] n Liter m
litter ['lɪtə*] n Abfälle pl; (of
animals) Wurf m ▷ vt: **to be ~ed
with** übersät sein mit; **litter bin** n
Abfalleimer m
little ['lɪtl] adj (smaller,
smallest) klein; (in quantity)
wenig; **a ~ while ago** vor kurzer
Zeit ▷ adv, n (fewer, fewest)
wenig; **a ~** ein bisschen, ein
wenig; **as ~ as possible** so wenig
wie möglich; **for as ~ as £5** ab nur
5 Pfund; **I see very ~ of them** ich
sehe sie sehr selten; **~ by ~** nach

und nach; **little finger** n kleiner
Finger
live [laɪv] adj lebendig; (Elec)
geladen, unter Strom; (TV, Radio:
event) live; **~ broadcast**
Direktübertragung f ▷ [lɪv] vi
leben; (not die) überleben; (dwell)
wohnen; **you ~ and learn** man
lernt nie aus ▷ vt (life) führen; **to
~ a life of luxury** im Luxus leben;
live on vi weiterleben ▷ vt: **to
~ sth** von etw leben; (feed) sich von
etw ernähren; **to earn enough to
~** genug verdienen, um davon zu
leben; **live together** vi
zusammenleben; **live up to** vt
(reputation) gerecht werden +dat;
(expectations) entsprechen +dat;
live with vt (parents etc) wohnen
bei; (partner) zusammenleben mit;
(difficulty) **you'll just have to ~ it**
du musst dich/Sie müssen sich
eben damit abfinden
liveliness ['laɪvlɪnɪs] n Lebhaf-
tigkeit f; **lively** ['laɪvlɪ] adj
lebhaft
liver ['lɪvə*] n Leber f
lives [laɪvz] pl of **life**
livestock ['laɪvstɒk] n Vieh nt
living ['lɪvɪŋ] n Lebensunterhalt
m; **what do you do for a ~?** was
machen Sie beruflich? ▷ adj
lebend; **living room** n
Wohnzimmer nt
lizard ['lɪzəd] n Eidechse f
llama ['lɑːmə] n (Zool) Lama nt
load [ləud] n Last f; (Tech, fig)
Ladung f; (Tech, fig) Belastung f; **~s
of** (fam) massenhaft; **it was a ~ of
rubbish** (fam) es war
grottenschlecht ▷ vt (vehicle)
beladen; (Inform) laden; (film)
einlegen
loaf [ləuf] n (pl **loaves**) n: **a ~ of
bread** ein (Laib) Brot (m)nt
loan [ləun] n (item leant)
Leihgabe f; (Fin) Darlehen nt; **on**

~ geliehen ▷ vt leihen (to sb jdm)

loathe [ləʊð] vt verabscheuen

loaves [ləʊvz] pl of **loaf**

lobby ['lɒbɪ] n Vorhalle f; (Pol) Lobby f

lobster ['lɒbstə°] n Hummer m

local ['ləʊkəl] adj (traffic, time etc) Orts-; (radio, news, paper) Lokal-; (government, authority) Kommunal-; (anaesthetic) örtlich; ~ **call** (Tel) Ortsgespräch nt; ~ **elections** Kommunalwahlen pl; ~ **time** Ortszeit f; ~ **train** Nahverkehrszug m; **the ~ shops** die Geschäfte am Ort ▷ n (pub) Stammlokal nt; **the ~s** pl die Ortsansässigen pl; **locally** adv örtlich, am Ort

locate [ləʊˈkeɪt] vt (find) ausfindig machen; (position) legen; (establish) errichten; **to be ~d** sich befinden (in, at in +dat); **location** [ləʊˈkeɪʃən] n (position) Lage f; (Cine) Drehort m

loch [lɒx] n (Scot) See m

lock [lɒk] n Schloss nt; (Naut) Schleuse f; (of hair) Locke f ▷ vt (door etc) abschließen ▷ vi (door etc) sich abschließen lassen; (wheels) blockieren; **lock in** vt einschließen, einsperren; **lock out** vt aussperren; **lock up** vt (house) abschließen; (person) einsperren

locker ['lɒkə°] n Schließfach nt; **locker room** n (US) Umkleideraum m

locksmith ['lɒksmɪθ] n Schlosser(in) m(f)

locust ['ləʊkəst] n Heuschrecke f

lodge [lɒdʒ] n (small house) Pförtnerhaus nt; (porter's ~) Pförtnerloge f ▷ vi in Untermiete wohnen (with bei); (get stuck) stecken bleiben; **lodger** n Untermieter(in) m(f); **lodging** n Unterkunft f

loft [lɒft] n Dachboden m

log [lɒg] n Klotz m; (Naut) Log nt; **to keep a ~ of sth** über etw Buch führen; **log in, log on** vi (Inform) sich einloggen; **log off, log out** vi (Inform) sich ausloggen

logic ['lɒdʒɪk] n Logik f; **logical** adj logisch

login ['lɒgɪn] n (Inform) Log-in nt, Anmeldung f

logo ['ləʊgəʊ] (pl **-s**) n Logo nt

loin [lɔɪn] n Lende f

loiter ['lɔɪtə°] vi sich herumtreiben

lollipop ['lɒlɪpɒp] n Lutscher m; ~ **man/lady** (Brit) Schülerlotse m, Schülerlotsin f

lolly ['lɒlɪ] n Lutscher m

London ['lʌndən] n London nt; **Londoner** n Londoner(in) m(f)

loneliness ['ləʊnlɪnɪs] n Einsamkeit f; **lonely** ['ləʊnlɪ] adj; (esp US) **lonesome** ['ləʊnsəm] adj einsam

long [lɒŋ] adj lang; (distance) weit; **it's a ~ way** es ist weit (to nach); **for a ~ time** lange; **how ~ is the film?** wie lange dauert der Film?; **in the ~ run** auf die Dauer ▷ adv lange; **not for ~** nicht lange; ~ **ago** vor langer Zeit; **before ~** bald; **all day ~** den ganzen Tag; **no ~er** nicht mehr; **as ~ as** solange ▷ vi sich sehnen (for nach); (be waiting) sehnsüchtig warten (for auf); **long-distance call** n Ferngespräch nt; **long drink** n Longdrink m; **long-haul flight** n Langstreckenflug m; **longing** n Sehnsucht f (for nach); **longingly** adv sehnsüchtig; **longitude** ['lɒŋgɪtjuːd] n Länge f; **long jump** n Weitsprung m; **long-life milk** n H-Milch f; **long-range** adj Langstrecken-, Fern-; ~ **missile** Langstreckenrakete f; **long-sighted** adj weitsichtig; **long-standing** adj alt, langjährig; **long-term** adj

langfristig; *(car park, effect etc)* Langzeit-; ~ **unemployment** Langzeitarbeitslosigkeit *f*; **long wave** *n* Langwelle *f*

loo [luː] *n (Brit fam)* Klo *nt*

look [lʊk] *n* Blick *m*; *(appearance)* ~**s** *pl* Aussehen *nt*; **I'll have a** ~ ich schau mal nach; **to have a** ~ **at sth** sich *dat* etw ansehen; **can I have a** ~? darf ich mal sehen? ▷ *vi* schauen, gucken; *(with prep)* sehen; *(search)* nachsehen; *(appear)* aussehen; **(I'm just) ~ing** ich schaue nur; **it ~s like rain** es sieht nach Regen aus ▷ *vt*: ~ **what you've done** sieh dir mal an, was du da angestellt hast; *(appear)* **he ~s his age** man sieht ihm sein Alter an; **to ~ one's best** vorteilhaft aussehen; **look after** *vt (care for)* sorgen für; *(keep an eye on)* aufpassen auf +*akk*; **look at** *vt* ansehen, anschauen; **look back** *vi* sich umsehen; *(fig)* zurückblicken; **look down on** *vt (fig)* herabsehen auf +*akk*; **look for** *vt* suchen; **look forward to** *vt* sich freuen auf +*akk*; **look into** *vt (investigate)* untersuchen; **look out** *vi* hinaussehen *(of the window zum Fenster)*; *(watch out)* Ausschau halten *(for nach)*; *(be careful)* aufpassen, Acht geben *(for auf +akk)*; **~!** Vorsicht!; **look up** *vi* aufsehen ▷ *vt (word etc)* nachschlagen; **look up to** *vt* aufsehen zu

loony ['luːnɪ] *adj (fam)* bekloppt

loop [luːp] *n* Schleife *f*

loose [luːs] *adj* locker; *(knot, button)* lose; **loosen** *vt* lockern; *(knot)* lösen

loot [luːt] *n* Beute *f*

lop-sided ['lɒp'saɪdɪd] *adj* schief

lord [lɔːd] *n (ruler)* Herr *m*; *(Brit: title)* Lord *m*; **the Lord (God)** Gott der Herr; **the (House of) Lords** *(Brit)* das Oberhaus

lorry ['lɒrɪ] *n (Brit)* Lastwagen *m*

lose [luːz] *(lost, lost)* *vt* verlieren; *(chance)* verpassen; **to** ~ **weight** abnehmen ▷ *vi* verlieren; *(clock, watch)* nachgehen; **loser** *n* Verlierer(in) *m(f)*; **loss** [lɒs] *n* Verlust *m*; **lost** [lɒst] *pt, pp of* **lose**; **we're** ~ wir haben uns verlaufen ▷ *adj* verloren; **lost-and-found** *(US)*, **lost property (office)** *n* Fundbüro *nt*

lot [lɒt] *n (fam: batch)* Menge *f*, Haufen *m*, Stoß *m*; **this is the first** ~ das ist die erste Ladung; **a** ~ **viel(e)**; **a** ~ **of money** viel Geld; **~s of people** viele Leute; **the (whole)** ~ alles; *(people)* alle

lotion ['ləʊʃən] *n* Lotion *f*

lottery ['lɒtərɪ] *n* Lotterie *f*

loud [laʊd] *adj* laut; *(colour)* schreiend; **loudspeaker** *n* Lautsprecher *m*; *(of stereo)* Box *f*

lounge [laʊndʒ] *n* Wohnzimmer *nt*; *(in hotel)* Aufenthaltsraum *m*; *(at airport)* Warteraum *m* ▷ *vi* sich herumlümmeln

louse [laʊs] *(pl lice)* *n* Laus *f*; **lousy** ['laʊzɪ] *adj (fam)* lausig

lout [laʊt] *n* Rüpel *m*

lovable ['lʌvəbl] *adj* liebenswert

love [lʌv] *n* Liebe *f (of zu)*; *(person, address)* Liebling *m*, Schatz *m*; *(Sport)* null; **to be in** ~ verliebt sein *(with sb in jdn)*; **to fall in** ~ sich verlieben *(with sb in jdn)*; **to make** ~ *(sexually)* miteinander schlafen; **to make** ~ *(o with)* **sb** mit jdm schlafen; *(in letter)* **he sends his** ~ er lässt grüßen; **give her my** ~ grüße sie von mir; **~, Tom** liebe Grüße, Tom ▷ *vt (person)* lieben; *(activity)* sehr gerne mögen; **to** ~ **to do sth** etw für sein Leben gerne tun; **I'd** ~ **a cup of tea** ich hätte liebend gern eine Tasse Tee; **love affair** *n* (Liebes)verhältnis *nt*; **love letter**

Liebesbrief m; **love life** n Liebesleben nt; **lovely** ['lʌvlɪ] adj schön, wunderschön; (charming) reizend; **we had a ~ time** es war sehr schön; **lover** ['lʌvə] n Liebhaber(in) m(f); **loving** adj liebevoll

low [ləʊ] adj niedrig; (rank) niedere(r, s); (level, note, neckline) tief; (intelligence, density) gering; (quality, standard) schlecht; (not loud) leise; (depressed) niedergeschlagen; **we're ~ on petrol** wir haben kaum noch Benzin ▷ n (Meteo) Tief nt; **low-calorie** adj kalorienarm; **lowcut** adj (dress) tief ausgeschnitten; **low-emission** adj schadstoffarm; **lower** ['ləʊə⁰] adj niedriger; (storey, class etc) untere(r, s) ▷ vt herunterlassen; (eyes, price) senken; (pressure) verringern; **low-fat** adj fettarm; **low tide** [ləʊ'taɪd] n Ebbe f

loyal ['lɔɪəl] adj treu; **loyalty** n Treue f

lozenge ['lɒzɪndʒ] n Pastille f

Ltd abbr = **limited** ≈ GmbH f
lubricant ['lu:brɪkənt] n Schmiermittel nt, Gleitmittel nt
luck [lʌk] n Glück nt; **bad ~** Pech

nt; **luckily** adv glücklicherweise, zum Glück; **lucky** (number, day etc) Glücks-; **to be ~** Glück haben
ludicrous ['lu:dɪkrəs] adj grotesk
luggage ['lʌgɪdʒ] n Gepäck nt; **luggage compartment** n Gepäckraum m; **luggage rack** n Gepäcknetz nt
lukewarm ['lu:kwɔ:m] adj lauwarm
lullaby ['lʌləbaɪ] n Schlaflied nt
lumbago [lʌm'beɪgəʊ] n Hexenschuss m
luminous ['lu:mɪnəs] adj leuchtend
lump [lʌmp] n Klumpen m; (Med) Schwellung f; (in breast) Knoten m; (of sugar) Stück nt; **lump sum** n Pauschalsumme f; **lumpy** adj klumpig
lunacy ['lu:nəsɪ] n Wahnsinn m; **lunatic** ['lu:nətɪk] adj wahnsinnig ▷ n Wahnsinnige(r) mf
lunch, luncheon [lʌntʃ, -ən] n Mittagessen n; **to have ~** zu Mittag essen; **lunch break, lunch hour** n Mittagspause f; **lunchtime** n Mittagszeit f
lung [lʌŋ] n Lunge f
lurch [lɜːtʃ] n: **to leave sb in the ~** jdn im Stich lassen
lurid ['lʊərɪd] adj (colour) grell; (details) widerlich
lurk [lɜːk] vi lauern
lust [lʌst] n (sinnliche) Begierde f (for nach)
Luxembourg ['lʌksəmbɜːg] n Luxemburg nt; **Luxembourger** [lʌksəm'bɜːgə⁰] n Luxemburger(in) m(f)
luxurious [lʌg'ʒʊərɪəs] adj luxuriös, Luxus-; **luxury** ['lʌkʃərɪ] n (a. luxuries pl) Luxus m; **~ goods** Luxusgüter pl
lynx [lɪŋks] n Luchs m
lyrics ['lɪrɪks] npl Liedtext m

m

wütend, sauer (at auf +akk); (fam)
~ about (fond of) verrückt nach; **to
work like ~** wie verrückt arbeiten;
are you ~? spinnst du/spinnen
Sie?

madam ['mædəm] n gnädige
Frau

mad cow disease
[mæd'kaʊd'zi:z] n Rinder-
wahnsinn m; **maddening** adj
zum Verrücktwerden

made [meɪd] pt, pp of **make**

made-to-measure
['meɪdtə'meʒəᵊ] adj nach Maß;
~ suit Maßanzug m

madly ['mædlɪ] adv wie verrückt;
(with adj) wahnsinnig; **madman**
['mædmən] (pl **-men**) n
Verrückte(r) m; **madwoman**
['mædwʊmən] (pl **-women**) n
Verrückte f; **madness** ['mædnɪs]
n Wahnsinn m

magazine [mægə'zi:n] n
Zeitschrift f

maggot ['mægət] n Made f

magic ['mædʒɪk] n Magie f;
(activity) Zauberei f; (fig: effect)
Zauber m; **as if by ~** wie durch
Zauberei ▷ adj Zauber-; (powers)
magisch; **magician** [mə'dʒɪʃən]
n Zauberer m, Zaub(r)erin f

magnet ['mægnɪt] n Magnet m;
magnetic [mæg'netɪk] adj
magnetisch; **magnetism**
['mægnɪtɪzəm] n (fig)
Anziehungskraft f

magnificent, magnificently
[mæg'nɪfɪsənt, -lɪ] adj, adv
herrlich, großartig

magnify ['mægnɪfaɪ] vt vergrößern; **magnifying glass** n
Vergrößerungsglas nt, Lupe f

magpie ['mægpaɪ] n Elster f

maid [meɪd] n Dienstmädchen
nt; **maiden name** n
Mädchenname m; **maiden
voyage** n Jungfernfahrt f

m abbr = **metre** m

M abbr (street) = **Motorway** A; (size)
= **medium** M

MA abbr = **Master of Arts**
Magister Artium m

ma [mɑ:] n (fam) Mutti f

mac [mæk] n (Brit fam)
Regenmantel m

macaroon [mækə'ru:n] n
Makrone f

Macedonia [mæsɪdəʊnɪə] n
Mazedonien nt

machine [mə'ʃi:n] n Maschine f;
machine gun n
Maschinengewehr nt; **machinery**
[mə'ʃi:nərɪ] n Maschinen pl; (fig)
Apparat m; **machine washable**
adj waschmaschinenfest

mackerel ['mækrəl] n Makrele f

macro ['mækrəʊ] (pl **-s**) n
(Inform) Makro nt

mad [mæd] adj wahnsinnig,
verrückt; (dog) tollwütig; (angry)

mail [meɪl] n Post f; (e-mail) Mail f ▷ vt (post) aufgeben; (send) mit der Post schicken (to an +akk); **mailbox** n (US) Briefkasten m; (Inform) Mailbox f; **mailing list** n Adressenliste f; **mailman** n (pl -**men**) (US) Briefträger m; **mail order** n Bestellung f per Post; **mail order firm** n Versandhaus nt; **mailshot** n Mailing nt

main [meɪn] adj Haupt-; ~ **course** Hauptgericht nt; **the ~ thing** die Hauptsache ▷ n (pipe) Hauptleitung f; **mainframe** n Großrechner m; **mainland** n Festland nt; **mainly** adv hauptsächlich; **main road** n Hauptverkehrsstraße f; **main street** n (US) Hauptstraße f

maintain [meɪnˈteɪn] vt (keep up) aufrechterhalten; (machine, roads) instand halten; (service) warten; (claim) behaupten; **maintenance** [ˈmeɪntənəns] n Instandhaltung f; (Tech) Wartung f

maize [meɪz] n Mais m

majestic [məˈdʒestɪk] adj majestätisch; **majesty** [ˈmædʒɪstɪ] n Majestät f; **Your/His/Her Majesty** Eure/Seine/Ihre Majestät

major [ˈmeɪdʒə*] adj (bigger) größer; (important) bedeutend; ~ **part** Großteil m; (role) wichtige Rolle; ~ **road** Hauptverkehrsstraße f; (Mus) **A** ~ A-Dur nt ▷ vi (US) **to ~ in sth** etw im Hauptfach studieren

Majorca [məˈjɔːkə] n Mallorca nt

majority [məˈdʒɒrɪtɪ] n Mehrheit f; **to be in the ~** in der Mehrzahl sein

make [meɪk] n Marke f ▷ vt (**made**, made) machen; (manufacture) herstellen; (clothes) anfertigen; (dress) nähen; (soup)

zubereiten; (bread, cake) backen; (tea, coffee) kochen; (speech) halten; (earn) verdienen; (decision) treffen; **it's made of gold** es ist aus Gold; **to ~ sb do sth** jdn dazu bringen, etw zu tun; (force) jdn zwingen, etw zu tun; **she made us wait** sie ließ uns warten; **what ~s you think that?** wie kommen Sie darauf?; **it ~s the room look smaller** es lässt den Raum kleiner wirken; **to ~ (it to) the airport** (reach) den Flughafen erreichen; (in time) es zum Flughafen schaffen; **he never really made it** er hat es nie zu etwas gebracht; **she didn't ~ it through the night** sie hat die Nacht nicht überlebt; (calculate) **I ~ it 5/a quarter to six** nach meiner Rechnung kommt es auf 5 Pfund/nach meiner Uhr ist es dreiviertel sechs; **he's just made for this job** er ist für diese Arbeit wie geschaffen; **make for** vt zusteuern auf +akk; **make of** vt (think of) halten von; **I couldn't ~ anything of it** ich wurde daraus nicht schlau; **make off** vi sich davonmachen (with mit); **make out** ▷ vt (cheque) ausstellen; (list) aufstellen; (understand) verstehen; (discern) ausmachen; **to ~ (that) ...** es so hinstellen, als ob ...; **make up** vt (team etc) bilden; (face) schminken; (invent: story etc) erfinden; **to ~ one's mind** sich entscheiden; **to make (it) up with sb** sich mit jdm aussöhnen ▷ vi sich versöhnen; **make up for** vt ausgleichen; (time) aufholen

make-believe adj Fantasie-; **makeover** n gründliche Veränderung, Verschönerung f; **maker** n (Comm) Hersteller(in) m(f); **makeshift** adj behelfsmäßig; **make-up** n

Make-up nt, Schminke f; **making** ['meikiŋ] n Herstellung f

maladjusted [mælə'dʒʌstid] adj verhaltensgestört

malaria [mə'leəriə] n Malaria f

Malaysia [mə'leiziə] n Malaysia nt

male [meil] n Mann m; (animal) Männchen nt ▷ adj männlich; **~ chauvinist** Chauvi m, Macho m; **~ nurse** Krankenpfleger m

malfunction [mæl'fʌŋkʃən] vi nicht richtig funktionieren ▷ n Defekt m

malice ['mælis] n Bosheit f; **malicious** [mə'liʃəs] adj boshaft; (behaviour, action) böswillig; (damage) mutwillig

malignant [mə'lignənt] adj bösartig

mall [mɔ:l] n (US) Einkaufszentrum nt

malnutrition [mælnju:'trʃən] n Unterernährung f

malt [mɔ:lt] n Malz nt

Malta ['mɔ:ltə] n Malta nt; **Maltese** [mɔ:l'ti:z] adj maltesisch ▷ n (person) Malteser(in) m(f); (language) Maltesisch nt

maltreat [mæl'tri:t] vt schlecht behandeln; (violently) misshandeln

mammal ['mæməl] n Säugetier nt

mammoth ['mæməθ] n Mammut-, Riesen-

man [mæn] (pl **men**) n (male) Mann m; (human race) der Mensch, die Menschen pl; (in chess) Figur f ▷ vt besetzen

manage ['mænidʒ] vi zurechtkommen; **can you ~?** schaffst du es?; **to ~ without sth** ohne etw auskommen, auf etw verzichten können ▷ vt (control) leiten; (musician, sportsman) managen; (cope with) fertig werden mit; (task,

portion, climb etc) schaffen; **to ~ to do sth** es schaffen, etw zu tun; **manageable** adj (object) handlich; (task) zu bewältigen; **management** n Leitung f; (directors) Direktion f; (subject) Management nt, Betriebswirtschaft f; **management consultant** n Unternehmensberater(in) m(f); **manager** n Geschäftsführer(in) m(f); (departmental ~) Abteilungsleiter(in) m(f); (of branch, bank) Filialleiter(in) m(f); (of musician, sportsman) Manager(in) m(f); **managing director** n Geschäftsführer(in) m(f)

mane [mein] n Mähne f

maneuver (US) see **manoeuvre**

mango ['mæŋgəu] (pl **-es**) n Mango f

man-hour n Arbeitsstunde f

manhunt n Fahndung f

mania ['meiniə] n Manie f; **maniac** ['meiniæk] n Wahnsinnige(r) mf; (fan) Fanatiker(in) m(f)

manicure ['mænikjuə'] n Maniküre f

manipulate [mə'nipjuleit] vt manipulieren

mankind [mæn'kaind] n Menschheit f

manly ['mænli] adj männlich

man-made ['mænmeid] adj (product) künstlich

manner ['mænə'] n Art f; **in this ~** auf diese Art und Weise; **~s** pl Manieren pl

manoeuvre [mə'nu:və'] n Manöver nt ▷ vt, vi manövrieren

manor ['mænə'] n: **~ (house)** Herrenhaus nt

manpower ['mænpauə'] n Arbeitskräfte pl

mansion ['mænʃən] n Villa f; (of old family) Herrenhaus nt

manslaughter ['mænslɔ:təʳ] n
Totschlag m

mantelpiece ['mæntlpi:s] n
Kaminsims m

manual ['mænjʊəl] adj manuell,
Hand- ▷ n Handbuch nt

manufacture [mænju'fæktʃəʳ]
vt herstellen ▷ n Herstellung f;
manufacturer n Hersteller m

manure [mə'njʊəʳ] n Dung m;
(esp artificial) Dünger m

many ['meni] (**more, most**) adj,
pron viele; ~ **times** oft; **not**
~ **people** nicht viele Leute; **too**
~ **problems** zu viele Probleme

map [mæp] n Landkarte f; (of
town) Stadtplan m

maple ['meipl] n Ahorn m

marathon ['mærəθən] n Marathon m

marble ['mɑ:bl] n Marmor m; (for
playing) Murmel f

march [mɑ:tʃ] vi marschieren
▷ n Marsch m; (protest)
Demonstration f

March [mɑ:tʃ] n März m; see also
September

mare [meəʳ] n Stute f

margarine [mɑ:dʒə'ri:n] n
Margarine f

margin ['mɑ:dʒin] n Rand m;
(extra amount) Spielraum m;
(Comm) Gewinnspanne f;
marginal adj (difference etc)
geringfügig

marijuana [mærju'ɑ:nə] n
Marihuana nt

marine [mə'ri:n] adj Meeres-
marital ['mærɪtl] adj ehelich;
~ **status** Familienstand m

maritime ['mærɪtaim] adj See-

marjoram ['mɑ:dʒərəm] n
Majoran m

mark [mɑ:k] n (spot) Fleck m; (at
school) Note f; (sign) Zeichen nt
▷ vt (make ~) Flecken machen auf
+akk; (indicate) markieren;

(schoolwork) benoten, korrigieren,
Flecken machen auf +akk;
markedly ['mɑ:kidli] adv merk-
lich; (with comp adj) wesentlich;
marker n (in book) Lesezeichen nt;
(pen) Marker m

market ['mɑ:kit] n Markt m;
(stock ~) Börse f ▷ vt (Comm: new
product) auf den Markt bringen;
(goods) vertreiben; **marketing** n
Marketing nt; **market leader** n
Marktführer m; **market place** n
Marktplatz m; **market research** n
Marktforschung f

marmalade ['mɑ:məleid] n
Orangenmarmelade f

maroon [mə'ru:n] adj rötlich
braun

marquee [mɑ:'ki:] n großes Zelt

marriage ['mæridʒ] n Ehe f;
(wedding) Heirat f (to mit);
married ['mærid] adj (person)
verheiratet

marrow ['mærəʊ] n (bone ~)
Knochenmark nt; (vegetable) Kürbis
m

marry ['mæri] vt heiraten; (join)
trauen; (take as husband, wife)
heiraten ▷ vi: **to ~ / to get**
married heiraten

marsh [mɑ:ʃ] n Marsch f, Sumpf
m

marshal ['mɑ:ʃəl] n (at rally etc)
Ordner m; (US: police)
Bezirkspolizeichef m

martial arts ['mɑ:ʃəl'ɑ:ts] npl
Kampfsportarten pl

martyr ['mɑ:təʳ] n Märtyrer(in)
m(f)

marvel ['mɑ:vəl] n Wunder nt
▷ vi staunen (at über +akk);
marvellous, marvelous (US) adj
wunderbar

marzipan [mɑ:zi'pæn] n Marzipan nt o m

mascara [mæ'skɑ:rə] n Wimperntusche f

m

mascot ['mæskɒt] n Maskottchen nt
masculine ['mæskjʊlɪn] adj
männlich
mashed [mæʃt] adj ~ **potatoes**
pl Kartoffelbrei m, Kartoffelpüree
nt
mask [mɑːsk] n (a. inform) Maske
f ▷ vt (feelings) verbergen
masochist ['mæsəʊkɪst] n
Masochist(in) m(f)
mason ['meɪsn] n (stone~)
Steinmetz(in) m(f); ~ry
Mauerwerk nt
mass [mæs] n Masse f; (of people)
Menge f; (Rel) Messe f; **~es of**
massenhaft
massacre ['mæsəkə°] n Blutbad
nt
massage ['mæsɑːʒ] n Massage f
▷ vt massieren
massive ['mæsɪv] adj (powerful)
gewaltig; (very large) riesig
mass media ['mæsˈmiːdɪə] npl
Massenmedien pl; **mass-produce**
vt in Massenproduktion
herstellen; **mass production** n
Massenproduktion f
master ['mɑːstə°] n Herr m; (of
dog) Besitzer m, Herrchen nt;
(teacher) Lehrer m; (artist) Meister
m ▷ vt meistern; (language etc)
beherrschen; **masterly** adj
meisterhaft; **masterpiece** n
Meisterwerk nt
masturbate ['mæstəbeɪt] vi
masturbieren
mat [mæt] n Matte f; (for table)
Untersetzer m
match [mætʃ] n Streichholz
nt; (Sport) Wettkampf m; (ball
games) Spiel nt; (tennis) Match
nt ▷ vt (be like, suit) passen zu;
(equal) gleichkommen +dat
▷ vi zusammenpassen; **matchbox**
n Streichholzschachtel f;
matching adj (one item)

passend; (two items)
zusammenpassend
mate [meɪt] n (companion)
Kumpel m; (of animal) Weibchen
nt/Männchen nt ▷ vi sich paaren
material [mə'tɪərɪəl] n Material
nt; (for book etc, cloth) Stoff m;
materialistic [mətɪərɪə'lɪstɪk]
adj materialistisch; **materialize**
[mə'tɪərɪəlaɪz] vi zustande
kommen; (hope) wahr werden
maternal [mə'tɜːnl] adj
mütterlich; **maternity**
[mə'tɜːnɪtɪ] adj: ~ **dress**
Umstandskleid nt; ~ **leave**
Elternzeit f (der Mutter); ~ **ward**
Entbindungsstation f
math [mæθ] n (US fam) Mathe f;
mathematical [mæθə'mætɪkəl]
adj mathematisch; **mathematics**
[mæθə'mætɪks] nsing Mathematik
f; **maths** [mæθs] nsing (Brit fam)
Mathe f
matinée ['mætɪneɪ] n Nachmit-
tagsvorstellung f
matter ['mætə°] n (substance)
Materie f; (affair) Sache f; **a
personal** ~ eine persönliche
Angelegenheit; **a ~ of taste** eine
Frage des Geschmacks; **no
~ how/what** egal wie/was;
what's the ~? was ist los?; **as a
~ of fact** eigentlich; **a ~ of time**
eine Frage der Zeit ▷ vi darauf
ankommen, wichtig sein; **it
doesn't** ~ es macht nichts;
matter-of-fact adj sachlich,
nüchtern
mattress ['mætrəs] n Matratze f
mature [mə'tjʊə°] adj reif ▷ vi
reif werden; **maturity**
[mə'tjʊərɪtɪ] n Reife f
maximum ['mæksɪməm] adj
Höchst-, höchste (r, s); ~ **speed**
Höchstgeschwindigkeit f ▷ n
Maximum nt
may [meɪ] (**might**) vb aux (be

possible) können; (have permission)
dürfen; **it ~ rain** es könnte regnen;
~ I smoke? darf ich rauchen?; **it
~ not happen** es passiert
vielleicht gar nicht; **we ~ as well
go** wir können ruhig gehen
May [meɪ] n Mai m; see also
September
maybe ['meɪbiː] adv vielleicht
May Day ['meɪdeɪ] n der erste
Mai
mayo ['meɪəʊ] (US fam),
mayonnaise [meɪə'neɪz] n
Mayo f, Mayonnaise f, Majonäse
f
mayor [mɛəʳ] n Bürgermeister
m
maze [meɪz] n Irrgarten m; (fig)
Wirrwarr nt
MB abbr = **megabyte** MB nt

🔘 **KEYWORD**

me [miː] pron 1 (direct) mich; **it's
me** ich bin's
2 (indirect) mir; **give them to me**
gib sie mir
3 (after prep) (+akk) mich; (+dat)
mir; **with/without me** mit
mir/ohne mich

meadow ['medəʊ] n Wiese f
meal [miːl] n Essen nt, Mahlzeit
f; **to go out for a ~** essen gehen;
meal pack n (US) tiefgekühltes
Fertiggericht; **meal time** n
Essenszeit f
mean [miːn] (meant, meant) vt
(signify) bedeuten; (have in mind)
meinen; (intend) vorhaben; **I ~ it**
ich meine das ernst; **what do you
~ (by that)?** was willst du damit
sagen?; **to ~ to do sth** etw tun
wollen; **it was ~t for you** es war
für dich bestimmt; (o gedacht); **it
was ~t to be a joke** es sollte ein
Witz sein ▷ vi: **he ~s well** er

meint es gut ▷ adj (stingy) geizig;
(spiteful) gemein (to zu); **meaning**
['miːnɪŋ] n Bedeutung f; (of life,
poem) Sinn m; **meaningful** adj
sinnvoll; **meaningless** adj (text)
ohne Sinn
means [miːnz] (pl means) n
Mittel nt; (pl: funds) Mittel pl; **by
~ of** durch, mittels; **by all
~** selbstverständlich; **by no
~** keineswegs; **~ of transport**
Beförderungsmittel
meant [ment] pt, pp of **mean**
meantime ['miːntaɪm] adv: **in
the ~** inzwischen; **meanwhile**
[miːn'waɪl] adv inzwischen
measles ['miːzlz] nsing Masern
pl; **German ~** Röteln pl
measure ['meʒəʳ] vt, vi messen
▷ n (unit, device for measuring) Maß
nt; (step) Maßnahme f; **to take ~s**
Maßnahmen ergreifen;
measurement n (amount
measured) Maß nt
meat [miːt] n Fleisch nt;
meatball n Fleischbällchen nt
mechanic [mɪ'kænɪk] n
Mechaniker(in) m(f); **mechanical**
adj mechanisch; **mechanics** nsing
Mechanik f ▷ **mechanism**
['mekənɪzəm] n Mechanismus m
medal ['medl] n Medaille f;
(decoration) Orden m; **medalist**
(US), **medallist** ['medəlɪst] n
Medaillengewinner(in) m(f)
media ['miːdɪə] npl Medien pl
median strip ['miːdɪən strɪp] n
(US) Mittelstreifen m
mediate ['miːdɪeɪt] vi
vermitteln
medical ['medɪkl] adj
medizinisch; (treatment etc)
ärztlich; **~ student**
Medizinstudent(in) m(f) ▷ n
Untersuchung f; **Medicare**
['medɪkɛəʳ] n (US) Krankenkasse f
für ältere Leute; **medication**

[medɪˈkeɪʃən] n Medikamente pl;
to be on ~ Medikamente nehmen;
medicinal [meˈdɪsɪnl] adj Heil-;
medicine [ˈmedsɪn] n Arznei f;
(science) Medizin f

medieval [medɪˈiːvəl] adj
mittelalterlich

mediocre [miːdɪˈəʊkə°] adj
mittelmäßig

meditate [ˈmedɪteɪt] vi meditieren; (fig) nachdenken (on über
+akk)

Mediterranean
[medɪtəˈreɪnɪən] n (sea)
Mittelmeer nt; (region)
Mittelmeerraum m

medium [ˈmiːdɪəm] adj (quality,
size) mittlere(r, s); (steak)
halbdurch; **~ (dry)** (wine)
halbtrocken; **~ sized** mittelgroß;
~ wave Mittelwelle f ▷ n (pl
media) Medium nt; (means) Mittel
nt

meet [miːt] (**met, met**) vt
treffen; (by arrangement) sich
treffen mit; (difficulties) stoßen auf
+akk; (get to know) kennenlernen;
(requirement, demand) gerecht
werden +dat; (deadline) einhalten;
pleased to ~ you sehr angenehm!;
to ~ sb at the station jdn vom
Bahnhof abholen ▷ vi sich
treffen; (become acquainted) sich
kennenlernen; **we've met
(before)** wir kennen uns schon;
meet up vi sich treffen (with
mit); **meet with** vt (group)
zusammenkommen mit;
(difficulties, resistance etc) stoßen
auf +akk; **meeting** n Treffen nt;
(business ~) Besprechung f; (of
committee) Sitzung f; (assembly)
Versammlung f; **meeting
place, meeting point** n
Treffpunkt m

megabyte [ˈmegəbaɪt] n
Megabyte nt

melody [ˈmelədɪ] n Melodie f
melon [ˈmelən] n Melone f
melt [melt] vt, vi schmelzen
member [ˈmembə°] n Mitglied
nt; (of tribe, species) Angehörige(r)
mf; **Member of Parliament**
Parlamentsabgeordnete(r) mf;
membership n Mitgliedschaft f;
membership card n
Mitgliedskarte f
memento [məˈmentəʊ] (pl **-es**)
n Andenken nt (of an +akk)
memo [ˈmeməʊ] (pl **-s**) n
Mitteilung f, Memo nt; **memo pad**
n Notizblock m
memorable [ˈmemərəbl] adj
unvergesslich; **memorial**
[mɪˈmɔːrɪəl] n Denkmal nt (to
für); **memorize** [ˈmeməraɪz] vt
sich einprägen, auswendig lernen;
memory [ˈmemərɪ] n Gedächtnis nt; (Inform: of computer)
Speicher m; (sth recalled)
Erinnerung f; **in ~ of** zur
Erinnerung an +akk; **memory card**
n Speicherkarte f; **memory stick**
n (Inform) Memorystick® m
men [men] pl of **man**
menace [ˈmenɪs] n Bedrohung f;
(danger) Gefahr f
mend [mend] vt reparieren;
(clothes) flicken ▷ n: **on the ~** auf
dem Wege der Besserung
meningitis [menɪnˈdʒaɪtɪs] n
Hirnhautentzündung f
menopause [ˈmenəʊpɔːz] n
Wechseljahre pl
mental [ˈmentl] adj geistig;
mentality [menˈtælɪtɪ] n Mentalität f; **mentally** [ˈmentəlɪ] adv
geistig; **~ ill** geisteskrank
mention [ˈmenʃən] n Erwäh-
nung f ▷ vt erwähnen (to sb jdm
gegenüber); **don't ~ it** bitte sehr,
gern geschehen
menu [ˈmenjuː] n Speisekarte f;
(Inform) Menü nt

merchandise ['mɜːtʃəndaɪz] n Handelsware f; **merchant** ['mɜːtʃənt] adj Handels-

merciful ['mɜːsɪfʊl] adj gnädig; **mercifully** adv glücklicherweise

mercury ['mɜːkjʊrɪ] n Quecksilber nt

mercy ['mɜːsɪ] n Gnade f

mere [mɪəʳ] adj bloß; **merely** ['mɪəlɪ] adv bloß, lediglich

merge [mɜːdʒ] vi verschmelzen; (Auto) sich einfädeln; (Comm) fusionieren; **merger** n (Comm) Fusion f

meringue [məˈræŋ] n Baiser nt

merit ['merɪt] n Verdienst nt; (advantage) Vorzug m

merry ['merɪ] adj fröhlich; (fam: tipsy) angeheitert; **Merry Christmas** Fröhliche Weihnachten!; **merry-go-round** n Karussell nt

mess [mes] n Unordnung f; (muddle) Durcheinander nt; (dirty) Schweinerei f; (trouble) Schwierigkeiten pl; **in a ~** (muddled) Durcheinander nt; (untidy) unordentlich; (fig: person) in der Klemme; **to make a ~ of sth** etw verpfuschen; **to look a ~** unmöglich aussehen; **mess about** vi (tinker with) herummurksen (with an +dat); (play the fool) herumalbern; (do nothing in particular) herumgammeln; **mess up** vt verpfuschen; (make untidy) in Unordnung bringen; (dirty) schmutzig machen

message ['mesɪdʒ] n Mitteilung f, Nachricht f; (meaning) Botschaft f; **can I give him a ~?** kann ich ihm etwas ausrichten?; **please leave a ~** (on answerphones) bitte hinterlassen Sie eine Nachricht; **I get the ~** ich hab's verstanden

messenger ['mesɪndʒəʳ] n Bote m

messy ['mesɪ] adj (untidy) unordentlich; (situation etc) verfahren

met [met] pt, pp of **meet**

metal ['metl] n Metall nt; **metallic** [mɪˈtælɪk] adj metallisch

meteorology [miːtɪəˈrɒlədʒɪ] n Meteorologie f

meter ['miːtəʳ] n Zähler m; (parking meter) Parkuhr f; (US) see **metre**

method ['meθəd] n Methode f; **methodical** [mɪˈθɒdɪkəl] adj methodisch

meticulous [mɪˈtɪkjʊləs] adj (peinlich) genau

metre ['miːtəʳ] n Meter m or nt; **metric** ['metrɪk] adj metrisch; **~ system** Dezimalsystem nt

Mexico ['meksɪkəʊ] n Mexiko nt

mice [maɪs] pl of **mouse**

mickey ['mɪkɪ] n: **to take the ~ (out of sb)** (fam) (jdn) auf den Arm nehmen

microchip ['maɪkrəʊtʃɪp] n (Inform) Mikrochip m; **microphone** n Mikrofon nt; **microscope** n Mikroskop nt; **microwave (oven)** n Mikrowelle(nherd) f(m)

mid [mɪd] adj: **in ~ January** Mitte Januar; **he's in his ~ forties** er ist Mitte vierzig

midday ['mɪddeɪ] n Mittag m; **at ~** mittags

middle ['mɪdl] n Mitte f; (waist) Taille f; **in the ~ of** mitten in +dat; **to be in the ~ of doing sth** gerade dabei sein, etw zu tun ▷ adj mittlere(r, s), Mittel-; **the ~ one** der/die/das Mittlere; **middle-aged** adj mittleren Alters; **Middle Ages** npl: **the ~** das Mittelalter; **middle-class** adj mittelständisch; (bourgeois) bürgerlich; **middle classes** npl: **the ~** der Mittelstand; **Middle East** n: **the ~** der Nahe Osten; **middle name** n zweiter Vorname

Midlands ['mɪdləndz] npl: **the ~** Mittelengland nt

midnight ['mɪdnaɪt] n Mitternacht f

midst [mɪdst] n: **in the ~ of** mitten in +dat

midsummer ['mɪdsʌmə°] n Hochsommer m; **Midsummer's Day** Sommersonnenwende f

midway ['mɪdweɪ] adv auf halbem Wege; **~ through the film** nach der Hälfte des Films; **midweek** [mɪd'wiːk] adj, adv in der Mitte der Woche

midwife ['mɪdwaɪf] (pl **-wives**) n Hebamme f

midwinter [mɪd'wɪntə°] n tiefster Winter

might [maɪt] pt of **may**; (possibility) könnte; (permission) dürfte; (would) würde; **they ~ still come** sie könnten noch kommen; **he ~ have let me know** er hätte mir doch Bescheid sagen können; **I thought she ~ change her mind** ich dachte schon, sie würde sich anders entscheiden ▷ n Macht f, Kraft f

mighty ['maɪtɪ] adj gewaltig; (powerful) mächtig

migraine ['miːɡreɪn] n Migräne f

migrant ['maɪɡrənt] n (bird) Zugvogel m; **~ worker** Gastarbeiter(in) m(f); Migrant(in) m(f); **migrate** [maɪ'ɡreɪt] vi abwandern; (birds) nach Süden ziehen

mike [maɪk] n (fam) Mikro nt

Milan [mɪ'læn] n Mailand nt

mild [maɪld] adj mild; (person) sanft; **mildly** adv: **to put it**

~ gelinde gesagt; mildness n Milde f

mile [maɪl] n Meile f (= 1,609 km); **for ~s (and ~s)** = kilometerweit; **~s per hour** Meilen pro Stunde; **~s better than** hundertmal besser als; **mileage** n Meilen pl, Meilenzahl f; **mileometer** [maɪ'lɒmɪtə°] n = Kilometerzähler m; **milestone** n (a. fig) Meilenstein m

militant ['mɪlɪtənt] adj militant; **military** ['mɪlɪtərɪ] adj Militär-, militärisch

milk [mɪlk] n Milch f ▷ vt melken; **milk chocolate** n Vollmilchschokolade f; **milkman** (pl **-men**) n Milchmann m; **milk shake** n Milkshake m, Milchmixgetränk nt

mill [mɪl] n Mühle f; (factory) Fabrik f

millennium [mɪ'lenɪəm] n Jahrtausend nt

milligramme ['mɪlɪɡræm] n Milligramm nt; **milliliter** (US), **millilitre** n Milliliter m; **millimeter** (US), **millimetre** n Millimeter m

million [mɪljən] n Million f; **five ~** fünf Millionen; **~s of people** Millionen von Menschen; **millionaire** [mɪljə'nɛə°] n Millionär(in) m(f)

mime [maɪm] n Pantomime f ▷ vt, vi mimen; **mimic** ['mɪmɪk] n Imitator(in) m(f) ▷ vt, vi nachahmen; **mimicry** ['mɪmɪkrɪ] n Nachahmung f

mince [mɪns] vt (zer)hacken ▷ n (meat) Hackfleisch nt; **mincemeat** n süße Gebäckfüllung aus Rosinen, Äpfeln, Zucker, Gewürzen und Talg; **mince pie** n mit 'mincemeat' gefülltes süßes Weihnachtsgebäck

mind [maɪnd] n (intellect)

Verstand m; (also person) Geist m; **out of sight, out of ~** aus den Augen, aus dem Sinn; **he is out of his ~** er ist nicht bei Verstand; **to keep sth in ~** etw im Auge behalten; **do you have sth in ~?** denken Sie an etwas Besonderes?; **I've a lot on my ~** mich beschäftigt so vieles im Moment; **to change one's ~** es sich dat anders überlegen ⊳ vt (look after) aufpassen auf +akk; (object to) etwas haben gegen; **~ you, ...** allerdings ...; **I wouldn't ~ ...** ich hätte nichts gegen ...; **"~ the step"** „Vorsicht Stufe"; ⊳ vi etwas dagegen haben; **do you ~ if I ...** macht es Ihnen etwas aus, wenn ich ...; **I don't ~** es ist mir egal, meinetwegen; **never ~** macht nichts

mine [maɪn] pron meine(r, s); **this is ~** das gehört mir; **a friend of ~** ein Freund von mir ⊳ n (coalmine) Bergwerk nt; (Mil) Mine f; **miner** n Bergarbeiter(in) m(f)

mineral ['mɪnərəl] n Mineral nt; **mineral water** n Mineralwasser nt

mingle ['mɪŋɡl] vi sich mischen (with unter +akk)

miniature ['mɪnɪtʃə*] adj Miniatur-

minibar ['mɪnɪbɑː] n Minibar f; **minibus** n Kleinbus m; **minicab** n Kleintaxi nt

minimal ['mɪnɪml] adj minimal; **minimize** ['mɪnɪmaɪz] vt auf ein Minimum reduzieren; **minimum** ['mɪnɪməm] n Minimum nt ⊳ adj Mindest-

mining ['maɪnɪŋ] n Bergbau m

miniskirt n Minirock m

minister ['mɪnɪstə*] n (Pol) Minister(in) m(f); (Rel) Pastor(in) m(f), Pfarrer(in) m(f); **ministry** ['mɪnɪstrɪ] n (Pol) Ministerium nt

minor ['maɪnə*] adj kleiner; (insignificant) unbedeutend; (operation, offence) harmlos; **~ road** Nebenstraße f; (Mus) **A ~** a-Moll nt ⊳ n (Brit: under 18) Minderjährige(r) mf; **minority** [maɪˈnɒrɪtɪ] n Minderheit f

mint [mɪnt] n Minze f; (sweet) Pfefferminz(bonbon) nt; **mint sauce** n Minzsoße f

minus ['maɪnəs] prep minus; (without) ohne

minute [maɪˈnjuːt] adj winzig; **in ~ detail** genauestens ⊳ ['mɪnɪt] n Minute f; **just a ~** Moment mal; **any ~** jeden Augenblick; **~s** pl (of meeting) Protokoll nt

miracle ['mɪrəkl] n Wunder nt; **miraculous** [mɪˈrækjʊləs] adj unglaublich

mirage ['mɪrɑːʒ] n Fata Morgana f, Luftspiegelung f

mirror ['mɪrə*] n Spiegel m

misbehave [mɪsbɪˈheɪv] vi sich schlecht benehmen

miscalculation ['mɪskælkjʊˈleɪʃən] n Fehlkalkulation f; (misjudgement) Fehleinschätzung f

miscarriage ['mɪskærɪdʒ] n (Med) Fehlgeburt f

miscellaneous [mɪsɪˈleɪnɪəs] adj verschieden

mischief ['mɪstʃɪf] n Unfug m; **mischievous** ['mɪstʃɪvəs] adj (person) durchtrieben; (glance) verschmitzt

misconception [mɪskənˈsepʃən] n falsche Vorstellung

misconduct [mɪsˈkɒndʌkt] n Vergehen nt

miser ['maɪzə*] n Geizhals m

miserable ['mɪzərəbl] adj (person) todunglücklich; (conditions, life) elend; (pay, weather) miserabel

miserly ['maɪzəlɪ] adj geizig

misery ['mɪzərɪ] n Elend nt; (suffering) Qualen pl

misfit ['mɪsfɪt] n Außenseiter(in) m(f)

misfortune [mɪs'fɔːtʃən] n Pech nt

misguided [mɪs'gaɪdɪd] adj irrig; (optimism) unangebracht

misinform [mɪsɪn'fɔːm] vt falsch informieren

misinterpret [mɪsɪn'tɜːprɪt] vt falsch auslegen

misjudge [mɪs'dʒʌdʒ] vt falsch beurteilen

mislay [mɪs'leɪ] irr vt verlegen

mislead [mɪs'liːd] irr vt irreführen; **misleading** adj irreführend

misprint ['mɪsprɪnt] n Druckfehler m

mispronounce [mɪsprə'naʊns] vt falsch aussprechen

miss [mɪs] vt (fail to hit, catch) verfehlen; (not notice, hear) nicht mitbekommen; (be too late for) verpassen; (chance) versäumen; (regret the absence of) vermissen; **I ~ you** du fehlst mir ▷ vi nicht treffen; (shooting) danebentreffen; (ball, shot etc) danebenschießen; **miss out** vt auslassen ▷ vi: **to ~ on sth** etw verpassen

Miss [mɪs] n (unmarried woman) Fräulein nt

missile ['mɪsaɪl] n Geschoss nt; (rocket) Rakete f

missing ['mɪsɪŋ] adj (person) vermisst; (thing) fehlend; **to be/go ~** vermisst werden, fehlen

mission ['mɪʃən] n (Pol, Mil, Rel) Auftrag m, Mission f; **missionary** ['mɪʃənrɪ] n Missionar(in) m(f)

mist [mɪst] n (feiner) Nebel m; (haze) Dunst m; **mist over**, **mist up** vi sich beschlagen

mistake [mɪs'teɪk] n Fehler m; **by ~** aus Versehen ▷ irr vt

(mistook, mistaken)
(misunderstand) falsch verstehen; (mix up) verwechseln (for mit); **there's no mistaking ... ...** ist unverkennbar; (meaning) ... ist unmissverständlich; **mistaken** adj (idea, identity) falsch; **to be ~** sich irren, falschliegen

mistletoe ['mɪsltəʊ] n Mistel f

mistreat [mɪs'triːt] vt schlecht behandeln

mistress ['mɪstrɪs] n (lover) Geliebte f

mistrust [mɪs'trʌst] n Misstrauen nt (of gegen) ▷ vt misstrauen +dat

misty ['mɪstɪ] adj neblig; (hazy) dunstig

misunderstand [mɪsʌndə'stænd] irr vt, vi falsch verstehen; **misunderstanding** n Missverständnis nt; (disagreement) Differenz f

mitten ['mɪtn] n Fausthandschuh m

mix [mɪks] n (mixture) Mischung f ▷ vt mischen; (blend) vermischen (with mit); (drinks, music) mixen; **to ~ business with pleasure** das Angenehme mit dem Nützlichen verbinden ▷ vi (liquids) sich vermischen lassen; **mix up** vt (mix) zusammenmischen; (confuse) verwechseln (with mit); **mixed** adj gemischt; **a ~ bunch** eine bunt gemischte Truppe; **~ grill** Grill m; **~ vegetables** Mischgemüse nt; **mixer** n (for food) Mixer m; **mixture** ['mɪkstʃə] n Mischung f; (Med) Saft m; **mix-up** n Durcheinander nt, Missverständnis nt

ml abbr = **millilitre** ml

mm abbr = **millimetre** mm

moan [məʊn] n Stöhnen nt; (complaint) Gejammer nt ▷ vi

stöhnen; *(complain)* jammern, meckern *(about* über +*akk)*

mobile ['məʊbaɪl] *adj* beweglich; *(on wheels)* fahrbar ▷ *n (phone)* Handy *nt;* **mobile phone** *n* Mobiltelefon *nt,* Handy *nt;* **mobile-phone mast** Handymast *m*

mobility [məʊ'bɪlɪtɪ] *n* Beweglichkeit *f*

mock [mɒk] *vt* verspotten ▷ *adj* Schein-; **mockery** *n* Spott *m*

mod cons ['mɒd'kɒnz] *abbr* = **modern conveniences** (moderner) Komfort

mode [məʊd] *n* Art *f;* *(Inform)* Modus *m*

model ['mɒdl] *n* Modell *nt;* *(example)* Vorbild *nt; (fashion ~)* Model *nt* ▷ *adj (miniature)* Modell-; *(perfect)* Muster- ▷ *vt (make)* formen ▷ *vi:* **she ~s for Versace** sie arbeitet als Model bei Versace

modem ['məʊdem] *n* Modem *nt*

moderate ['mɒdərət] *adj* mäßig; *(views, politics)* gemäßigt; *(income, success)* mittelmäßig ▷ *n (Pol)* Gemäßigte(r) *mf* ▷ ['mɒdəreɪt] *vt* mäßigen; **moderation** [mɒdə'reɪʃən] *n* Mäßigung *f;* **in ~** mit Maßen

modern ['mɒdən] *adj* modern; **~ history** neuere Geschichte; **~ Greek** Neugriechisch *nt;* **modernize** ['mɒdənaɪz] *vt* modernisieren

modest ['mɒdɪst] *adj* bescheiden; **modesty** *n* Bescheidenheit *f*

modification [mɒdɪfɪ'keɪʃən] *n* Abänderung *f;* **modify** ['mɒdɪfaɪ] *vt* abändern

moist [mɒɪst] *adj* feucht; **moisten** ['mɒɪsn] *vt* befeuchten; **moisture** ['mɒɪstʃə*] *n* Feuchtigkeit *f;* **moisturizer** *n* Feuchtigkeitscreme *f*

molar ['məʊlə*] *n* Backenzahn *m*

mold (US) *see* **mould**

mole [məʊl] *n (spot)* Leberfleck *m; (animal)* Maulwurf *m*

molecule ['mɒlɪkjuːl] *n* Molekül *nt*

molest [məʊ'lest] *vt* belästigen

molt (US) *see* **moult**

molten ['məʊltən] *adj* geschmolzen

mom [mɒm] *n* (US) Mutti *f*

moment ['məʊmənt] *n* Moment *m,* Augenblick *m;* **just a ~** Moment mal; **at (a) the ~** im Augenblick; **in a ~** gleich

momentous [məʊ'mentəs] *adj* bedeutsam

Monaco ['mɒnəkəʊ] *n* Monaco *nt*

monarchy ['mɒnəkɪ] *n* Monarchie *f*

monastery ['mɒnəstrɪ] *n (for monks)* Kloster *nt*

Monday ['mʌndeɪ] *n* Montag *m; see also* **Tuesday**

monetary ['mʌnɪtərɪ] *adj (reform, policy, union)* Währungs-; **~ unit** Geldeinheit *f*

money ['mʌnɪ] *n* Geld *nt;* **to get one's ~'s worth** auf seine Kosten kommen; **money order** *n* Postanweisung *f*

mongrel ['mʌŋgrəl] *n* Promenadenmischung *f*

monitor ['mɒnɪtə*] *n (screen)* Monitor *m* ▷ *vt (progress etc)* überwachen; *(broadcasts)* abhören

monk [mʌŋk] *n* Mönch *m*

monkey ['mʌŋkɪ] *n* Affe *m;* **~ business** Unfug *m*

monopolize [mə'nɒpəlaɪz] *vt* monopolisieren; *(fig: person, thing)* in Beschlag nehmen; **monopoly** [mə'nɒpəlɪ] *n* Monopol *nt*

monotonous [mə'nɒtənəs] *adj* eintönig, monoton

monsoon [mɒn'suːn] *n* Monsun *m*

monster ['mɒnstə*] *n (animal,*

thing) Monstrum nt ▷ adj Riesen-;
monstrosity [mɒn'strɒsɪtɪ] n
Monstrosität f; (thing) Ungetüm
nt

Montenegro [mɒntɪ'niːgrəʊ] n
Montenegro nt

month [mʌnθ] n Monat m;
monthly adj monatlich; (ticket,
salary) Monats- ▷ adv monatlich
▷ n (magazine) Monatsschrift f

monty ['mɒntɪ] n: **to go the full**
~ (fam: strip) alle Hüllen fallen
lassen; (go the whole hog) aufs
Ganze gehen

monument ['mɒnjʊmənt] n
Denkmal nt (to für); **monumental**
[mɒnjʊ'mentl] adj (huge)
gewaltig

mood [muːd] n (of person)
Laune f; (a. general) Stimmung f;
to be in a good/bad
~ gute/schlechte Laune haben;
to be in the ~ for sth zu etw
aufgelegt sein; **I'm not in the**
~ ich fühle mich nicht danach;
moody adj launisch

moon [muːn] n Mond m; **to be**
over the ~ (fam) überglücklich
sein; **moonlight** n Mondlicht nt
▷ vi schwarzarbeiten; **moonlit**
adj (night, landscape) mondhell

moor [mɔː°] n Moor nt ▷ vt, vi
festmachen; **moorings** npl
Liegeplatz m; **moorland** n
Moorland nt, Heideland nt

moose [muːs] (pl -) n Elch m

mop [mɒp] n Mopp m; **mop up**
vt aufwischen

mope [məʊp] vi Trübsal blasen

moped ['məʊped] n (Brit) Moped
nt

moral ['mɒrəl] adj moralisch;
(values) sittlich ▷ n Moral f; **~s**
pl Moral f; **morale** [mɒ'rɑːl] n
Stimmung f, Moral f; **morality**
[mə'rælɪtɪ] n Moral f, Ethik f

morbid ['mɔːbɪd] adj krankhaft

○ **KEYWORD**

more [mɔː°] adj (greater in number
etc) mehr; (additional) noch mehr;
do you want (some) more tea?
möchtest du/möchten Sie noch
etwas Tee?; **I have no ~** oder **I don't**
have any more money ich habe
kein Geld mehr

▷ pron (greater amount) mehr;
(further or additional amount) noch
mehr; **is there any more?** gibt es
noch mehr?; (left over) ist noch
etwas da?; **there's no more** es ist
nichts mehr da

▷ adv mehr; **more**
dangerous/easily etc (than)
gefährlicher/einfacher etc (als);
more and more immer mehr;
more and more excited immer
aufgeregter; **more or less** mehr
oder weniger; **more than ever**
mehr denn je; **more beautiful**
than ever schöner denn je

moreish adj (food) **these crisps**
are really ~ ich kann mit diesen
Chips einfach nicht aufhören;
moreover adv außerdem

morgue [mɔːg] n Leichenschauhaus nt

morning ['mɔːnɪŋ] n Morgen m;
in the ~ am Morgen, morgens;
(tomorrow) morgen früh; **this**
~ heute morgen ▷ adj Morgen-;
(early) Früh-; (walk etc)
morgendlich; **morning after pill**
n die Pille danach; **morning**
sickness n Schwangerschaftsübelkeit f

Morocco [mə'rɒkəʊ] n Marokko
nt

moron ['mɔːrɒn] n (pej) Idiot(in)
m(f)

morphine ['mɔːfiːn] n Morphium nt

morsel ['mɔːsl] n Bissen m

mortal ['mɔːtl] adj sterblich; (wound) tödlich ▷ n Sterbliche(r) mf; **mortality** [mɔː'tælɪtɪ] n (death rate) Sterblichkeitsziffer f; **mortally** adv tödlich

mortgage ['mɔːgɪdʒ] n Hypothek f ▷ vt mit einer Hypothek belasten

mortified ['mɔːtɪfaɪd] adj: **I was ~** es war mir schrecklich peinlich

mortuary ['mɔːtjʊərɪ] n Leichenhalle f

mosaic [məʊ'zeɪɪk] n Mosaik nt

Moscow ['mɒskəʊ] n Moskau nt

Moslem ['mɒzləm] adj, n see **Muslim**

mosque [mɒsk] n Moschee f

mosquito [mɒs'kiːtəʊ] (pl **-es**) n (Stech)mücke f; (tropical) Moskito m; **~ net** Moskitonetz nt

moss [mɒs] n Moos nt

most [məʊst] adj meiste pl, die meisten; **in ~ cases** in den meisten Fällen ▷ adv (with verbs) am meisten; (with adj) …ste; (with adv) am …sten; (very) äußerst; **he ate (the) ~** er hat am meisten gegessen; **the ~ beautiful/interesting** der/die/das schönste/interessanteste; **~ interesting** hochinteressant! ▷ n das meiste, der größte Teil; (people) die meisten; **~ of the money/players** das meiste Geld/die meisten Spieler; **for the ~ part** zum größten Teil; **five at the ~** höchstens fünf; **to make the ~ of sth** etw voll ausnützen; **mostly** adv (most of the time) meistens; (mainly) hauptsächlich; (for the most part) größtenteils

MOT abbr = **Ministry of Transport**; **~ (test)** n TÜV m

motel [məʊ'tel] n Motel nt

moth [mɒθ] n Nachtfalter m; (wool-eating) Motte f; **mothball** n Mottenkugel f

mother ['mʌðə°] n Mutter f ▷ vt bemuttern; **mother-in-law** (pl **mothers-in-law**) n Schwiegermutter f; **mother-to-be** (pl **mothers-to-be**) n werdende Mutter

motif [məʊ'tiːf] n Motiv nt

motion ['məʊʃən] n Bewegung f; (in meeting) Antrag m; **motionless** adj bewegungslos

motivate ['məʊtɪveɪt] vt motivieren; **motive** ['məʊtɪv] n Motiv nt

motor ['məʊtə°] n Motor m; (fam: car) Auto nt ▷ adj Motor-; **Motorail train®** n (Brit) Autoreisezug m; **motorbike** n Motorrad nt; **motorboat** n Motorboot nt; **motorcycle** n Motorrad nt; **motor industry** n Automobilindustrie f; **motoring** ['məʊtərɪŋ] n Autofahren nt; **~ organization** Automobilklub m; **motorist** ['məʊtərɪst] n Autofahrer(in) m(f); **motor oil** n Motorenöl nt; **motor racing** n Autorennsport m; **motor scooter** n Motorroller m; **motor show** n Automobilausstellung f; **motor vehicle** n Kraftfahrzeug nt; **motorway** n (Brit) Autobahn f

motto ['mɒtəʊ] (pl **-es**) n Motto nt

mould [məʊld] n Form f; (mildew) Schimmel m ▷ vt (a. fig) formen; **mouldy** ['məʊldɪ] adj schimmelig

moult [məʊlt] vi sich mausern, haaren

mount [maʊnt] vt (horse) steigen auf +akk; (exhibition etc) organisieren; (painting) mit einem Passepartout versehen ▷ vi: **to ~ (up)** (an)steigen ▷ n Passepartout nt

mountain ['maʊntɪn] n Berg m;
mountain bike n Mountainbike
nt; **mountaineer** [maʊntɪ'nɪə°]
n Bergsteiger(in) m(f);
mountaineering [maʊntɪ'nɪərɪŋ]
n Bergsteigen nt; **mountainous**
adj bergig; **mountainside** n
Berghang m

mourn [mɔːn] vt betrauern ▷ vi
trauern (for um); **mourner** n
Trauernde(r) mf; **mournful** adj
trauervoll; **mourning** n Trauer f;
to be in ~ trauern (for um)

mouse [maʊs] (pl **mice**) n (a.
Inform) Maus f; **mouse mat**,
mouse pad (US) n Mauspad nt;
mouse trap n Mausefalle f

mousse [muːs] n (Gastr) Creme f;
(styling ~) Schaumfestiger m

moustache [mə'stɑːʃ] n
Schnurrbart m

mouth [maʊθ] n Mund m; (of
animal) Maul nt; (of cave) Eingang
m; (of bottle etc) Öffnung f; (of river)
Mündung f; **to keep one's ~ shut**
(fam) den Mund halten; **mouthful**
n (of drink) Schluck m; (of food)
Bissen m; **mouth organ** n
Mundharmonika f; **mouthwash** n
Mundwasser nt; **mouthwatering**
adj appetitlich, lecker

move [muːv] n (movement)
Bewegung f; (in game) Zug m; (step)
Schritt m; (moving house) Umzug m;
to make a ~ (in game) ziehen;
(leave) sich auf den Weg machen;
to get a ~ on (with sth) sich (mit
etw) beeilen ▷ vt bewegen;
(object) rücken; (car) wegfahren;
(transport: goods) befördern;
(people) transportieren; (in job)
versetzen; (emotionally) bewegen,
rühren; **I can't ~ it** (stuck, too heavy)
ich bringe es nicht von der Stelle;
to ~ (house) umziehen ▷ vi sich
bewegen; (change place) gehen;
(vehicle, ship) fahren; (move house,

town etc) umziehen; (in game)
ziehen; **move about** vi sich
bewegen; (travel) unterwegs sein;
move away vi weggehen; (move
town) wegziehen; **move in** vi (to
house) einziehen; **move off** vi
losfahren; **move on** vi
weitergehen; (vehicle)
weiterfahren; **move out** vi
ausziehen; **move up** vi (in queue
etc) aufrücken; **movement** n
Bewegung f

movie ['muːvɪ] n Film m; **the ~s**
(the cinema) das Kino; **movie
theatre** n (US) Kino nt

moving ['muːvɪŋ] adj (emotionally) ergreifend, berührend

mow [məʊ] (**mowed**, **mowed** or
mowed) vt mähen; **mower** n
(lawn~) Rasenmäher m

mown [məʊn] pp of **mow**

Mozambique [məʊzæm'biːk] n
Mosambik nt

MP abbr = **Member of Parliament**
Parlamentsabgeordnete(r) mf

mph abbr = **miles per hour** Meilen
pro Stunde

MPV abbr = **multi-purpose
vehicle** Mehrzweckfahrzeug nt

MP3 player [empiː'θriː 'pleɪə°]
n MP3-Player m

Mr [mɪstə°] n (written form of
address) Herr

Mrs ['mɪsɪz] n (written form of
address) Frau

Ms [məz] n (written form of address
for any woman, married or unmarried)
Frau

MS n abbr = **multiple sclerosis** MS
f

Mt abbr = **Mount** Berg m

much [mʌtʃ] (**more**, **most**) adj
viel; **we haven't got ~ time** wir
haben nicht viel Zeit; **how
~ money?** wie viel Geld? ▷ adv
viel; (with verb) sehr; **~ better** viel
besser; **I like it very ~** es gefällt

mir sehr gut; **I don't like it ~** ich mag es nicht besonders; **thank you very ~** danke sehr; **I thought as ~** das habe ich mir gedacht; **~ as I like him** so sehr ich ihn mag; **we don't see them ~** wir sehen sie nicht sehr oft; **~ the same** fast gleich ▷ n viel; **as ~ as you want** so viel du willst; **he's not ~ of a cook** er ist kein großer Koch

muck [mʌk] n (fam) Dreck m; **muck about** vi (fam) herumalbern; **muck up** vt (fam) dreckig machen; (spoil) vermasseln; **mucky** adj dreckig

mucus ['mjuːkəs] n Schleim m

mud [mʌd] n Schlamm m

muddle ['mʌdl] n Durcheinander nt; **to be in a ~** ganz durcheinander sein ▷ vt: **to ~ (up)** durcheinanderbringen; **muddled** adj konfus

muddy ['mʌdɪ] adj schlammig; (shoes) schmutzig; **mudguard** ['mʌdgɑːd] n Schutzblech nt

muesli ['muːzlɪ] n Müsli nt

muffin ['mʌfɪn] n Muffin m; (Brit) weiches, flaches Milchbrötchen aus Hefeteig, das meist getoastet und mit Butter gegessen wird

muffle ['mʌfl] vt (sound) dämpfen; **muffler** n (US) Schalldämpfer m

mug [mʌg] n (cup) Becher m; (fam: fool) Trottel m ▷ vt (attack and rob) überfallen; **mugging** n Raubüberfall m

muggy ['mʌgɪ] adj (weather) schwül

mule [mjuːl] n Maulesel m

mull over [mʌl 'əʊvə°] vt nachdenken über +akk

mulled [mʌld] adj: **~ wine** Glühwein m

multicolored (US), **multicoloured** ['mʌltɪˈkʌləd] adj bunt; **multicultural** adj

multikulturell; **multi-grade** adj: **~ oil** Mehrbereichsöl nt; **multilingual** adj mehrsprachig; **multinational** n (company) Multi m

multiple ['mʌltɪpl] n Vielfache(s) nt ▷ adj mehrfach; (several) mehrere; **multiple-choice (method)** n Multiple-Choice-Verfahren nt; **multiple sclerosis** ['mʌltɪplsklɪ'rəʊsɪs] n Multiple Sklerose f

multiplex ['mʌltɪpleks] adj, n: **~ (cinema)** Multiplexkino nt

multiplication [mʌltɪplɪ'keɪʃən] n Multiplikation f; **multiply** ['mʌltɪplaɪ] vt multiplizieren (by mit) ▷ vi sich vermehren

multi-purpose ['mʌltɪ'pɜːpəs] adj Mehrzweck-; **multistorey (car park)** n Parkhaus nt; **multitasking** n (Inform) Multitasking nt

mum [mʌm] n (fam: mother) Mutti f, Mami f

mumble ['mʌmbl] vt, vi murmeln

mummy ['mʌmɪ] n (dead body) Mumie f; (fam: mother) Mutti f, Mami f

mumps [mʌmps] nsing Mumps m

munch [mʌntʃ] vt, vi mampfen

Munich ['mjuːnɪk] n München nt

municipal [mjuː'nɪsɪpəl] adj städtisch

mural ['mjʊərəl] n Wandgemälde nt

murder ['mɜːdə°] n Mord m; **the traffic was ~** der Verkehr war die Hölle ▷ vt ermorden; **murderer** n Mörder(in) m(f)

murky ['mɜːkɪ] adj düster; (water) trüb

murmur ['mɜːmə°] vt, vi murmeln

muscle ['mʌsl] n Muskel m;
muscular ['mʌskjʊlə°] adj (strong)
muskulös; (cramp, pain etc) Muskel-
museum [mjuːˈzɪəm] n Museum
nt

mushroom ['mʌʃruːm] n (ess-
barer) Pilz; (button ~) Champignon
m ▷ vi (fig) emporschießen

mushy ['mʌʃi] adj breiig; **~ peas**
Erbsenmus nt

music ['mjuːzɪk] n Musik f;
(printed) Noten pl; **musical** adj
(sound) melodisch; (person)
musikalisch; **~ instrument**
Musikinstrument nt ▷ n (show)
Musical nt; **musically** adv
musikalisch; **musician**
[mjuːˈzɪʃən] n Musiker(in) m(f)

Muslim ['mʊzlɪm] adj
moslemisch ▷ n Moslem m,
Muslime f

mussel ['mʌsl] n Miesmuschel f

must [mʌst] (**had to, had to**) vb
aux (need to) müssen; (in negation)
dürfen; **I ~n't forget that** ich darf
das nicht vergessen; (certainty) **he
~ be there by now** er ist
inzwischen bestimmt schon da;
(assumption) **I ~ have lost it** ich
habe es wohl verloren; **~ you?**
muss das sein? ▷ n Muss nt

mustache ['mʌstæʃ] n (US)
Schnurrbart m

mustard ['mʌstəd] n Senf m; **to
cut the ~** es bringen

mustn't ['mʌsnt] contr of **must
not**

mutter ['mʌtə°] vt, vi
murmeln

mutton ['mʌtn] n Ham-
melfleisch nt

mutual ['mjuːtjʊəl] adj gegenseitig; **by ~ consent** in
gegenseitigem Einvernehmen

my [maɪ] adj mein; **I've hurt
~ leg** ich habe mir das Bein
verletzt

Myanmar ['maɪænmɑː] n
Myanmar nt

myself [maɪˈself] pron (reflexive)
mich akk, mir dat; **I've hurt ~** ich
habe mich verletzt; **I've bought
~ a flat** ich habe mir eine
Wohnung gekauft; **I need it for
~** ich brauche es für mich (selbst);
(emphatic) **I did it ~** ich habe es
selbst gemacht; **(all) by ~** allein

mysterious [mɪˈstɪərɪəs] adj
geheimnisvoll, mysteriös;
(inexplicable) rätselhaft; **mystery**
['mɪstərɪ] n Geheimnis nt; (puzzle)
Rätsel nt; **it's a ~ to me** es ist mir
schleierhaft; **mystify** [ˈmɪstɪfaɪ]
vt verblüffen

myth [mɪθ] n Mythos m; (fig:
untrue story) Märchen nt; **mythical**
adj mythisch; (fig: untrue)
erfunden; **mythology**
[mɪˈθɒlədʒɪ] n Mythologie f

n

N abbr = **north** N

nag [næg] vt, vi herumnörgeln (sb an jdm); **nagging** n Nörgelei f

nail [neɪl] n Nagel m ▷ vt nageln (to an); **nail down** vt festnageln; **nailbrush** n Nagelbürste f; **nail clippers** npl Nagelknipser m; **nailfile** n Nagelfeile f; **nail polish** n Nagellack m; **nail polish remover** n Nagellackentferner m; **nail scissors** npl Nagelschere f; **nail varnish** n Nagellack m

naïve [naɪˈiːv] adj naiv

naked [ˈneɪkɪd] adj nackt

name [neɪm] n Name m; **his ~ is ...** er heißt ...; **what's your ~?** wie heißen Sie?; (reputation) **to have a good/bad ~** einen guten/schlechten Ruf haben ▷ vt nennen (after nach); (sth new) benennen; (nominate) ernennen (as als/zu); **a boy ~d ...** ein Junge

namens ...; **namely** adv nämlich; **name plate** n Namensschild nt

nan bread [ˈnɑːnˈbred] n (warm serviertes) indisches Fladenbrot

nanny [ˈnænɪ] n Kindermädchen nt

nap [næp] n: **to have/take a ~** ein Nickerchen machen

napkin [ˈnæpkɪn] n (at table) Serviette f

Naples [ˈneɪplz] n Neapel nt

nappy [ˈnæpɪ] n (Brit) Windel f

narcotic [nɑːˈkɒtɪk] n Rauschgift nt

narrate [nəˈreɪt] vt erzählen; **narration** [nəˈreɪʃən] n Erzählung f; **narrative** [ˈnærətɪv] n Erzählung f; **narrator** [nəˈreɪtə*] n Erzähler(in) m(f)

narrow [ˈnærəʊ] adj eng, schmal; (victory, majority) knapp; **to have a ~ escape** mit knapper Not davonkommen ▷ vi sich verengen; **narrow down** vt einschränken (to sth auf etw akk); **narrow-minded** adj engstirnig

nasty [ˈnɑːstɪ] adj ekelhaft; (person) fies; (remark) gehässig; (accident, wound etc) schlimm

nation [ˈneɪʃən] n Nation f; **national** [ˈnæʃənl] adj national; **~ anthem** Nationalhymne f; **National Health Service** (Brit) staatlicher Gesundheitsdienst; **~ insurance** (Brit) Sozialversicherung f; **~ park** Nationalpark m; **~ service** Wehrdienst m; **~ socialism** (Hist) Nationalsozialismus m ▷ n Staatsbürger(in) m(f)

● **NATIONAL TRUST**
●
● Der **National Trust** ist ein 1895
● gegründeter Natur- und
● Denkmalschutzverband in
● Großbritannien, der Gebäude
● und Gelände von besonderem

n

◊ historischen oder ästhetischen
◊ Interesse erhält und der
◊ Öffentlichkeit zugänglich
◊ macht.

nationality [næʃ'nælɪtɪ] n
Staatsangehörigkeit f,
Nationalität f; **nationalize**
['næʃnəlaɪz] vt verstaatlichen;
nationwide adj, adv landesweit

native ['neɪtɪv] adj einheimisch;
(inborn) angeboren, natürlich;
Native American Indianer(in)
m(f); **~ country** Heimatland nt; **a**
~ German ein gebürtiger
Deutscher, eine gebürtige
Deutsche; **~ language**
Muttersprache f; **~ speaker**
Muttersprachler(in) m(f) ▷ n
Einheimische(r) mf; (in colonial
context) Eingeborene(r) mf

nativity play [nə'tɪvətɪpleɪ] n
Krippenspiel nt

NATO ['neɪtəʊ] acr = **North
Atlantic Treaty Organization**
Nato f

natural ['nætʃrəl] adj natürlich;
(law, science, forces etc) Natur-;
(inborn) angeboren; **~ gas** Erdgas
nt; **~ resources** Bodenschätze pl;
naturally adv natürlich; (by
nature) von Natur aus; **it comes
~ to her** es fällt ihr leicht

nature ['neɪtʃə°] n Natur f;
(type) Art f; **it is not in my ~** es
entspricht nicht meiner Art;
by ~ von Natur aus; **nature
reserve** n Naturschutzgebiet nt

naughty ['nɔːtɪ] adj (child)
ungezogen; (cheeky) frech

nausea ['nɔːsɪə] n Übelkeit f

nautical ['nɔːtɪkəl] adj nautisch;
~ mile Seemeile f

nave [neɪv] n Hauptschiff nt

navel ['neɪvəl] n Nabel m

navigate ['nævɪgeɪt] vi navi-
gieren; (in car) lotsen, dirigieren;

navigation [nævɪ'geɪʃən] n
Navigation f; (in car) Lotsen nt

navy ['neɪvɪ] n Marine f; **~ blue**
Marineblau nt

Nazi ['nɑːtsɪ] n Nazi m

NB abbr = **nota bene** NB

NE abbr = **northeast** NO

near [nɪə°] adj nahe; **in the
~ future** in nächster Zukunft; **that
was a ~ miss** (of thing) das war
knapp; (with price) **... or ~est offer**
Verhandlungsbasis ... ▷ adv in der
Nähe; **so ~** so nahe; **come ~er**
näher kommen; (event) näher
rücken ▷ prep: **~ (to)** (space) nahe
an +dat; (vicinity) in der Nähe +gen;
~ the sea nahe am Meer; **~ the
station** in der Nähe des Bahnhofs,
in Bahnhofsnähe; **nearby** adj
nahe gelegen ▷ adv in der Nähe;
nearly adv fast; **nearside** n
(Auto) Beifahrerseite f;
near-sighted adj kurzsichtig

neat [niːt] adj ordentlich; (work,
writing) sauber; (undiluted) pur

necessarily [nesə'serəlɪ] adv
notwendigerweise; **not ~** nicht
unbedingt; **necessary** ['nesəsərɪ]
adj notwendig, nötig; **it's ~ to ...**
man muss ...; **it's not ~ for him to
come** er braucht nicht
mitzukommen; **necessity**
[nɪ'sesɪtɪ] n Notwendigkeit f; **the
bare necessities** das absolut
Notwendigste; **there is no ~ to ...**
man braucht nicht (zu) ..., man
muss nicht ...

neck [nek] n Hals m; (size)
Halsweite f; **back of the ~** Nacken
m; **necklace** ['neklɪs] n
Halskette f; **necktie** n (US)
Krawatte f

nectarine ['nektərɪn] n Nektarine f

née [neɪ] adj geborene

need [niːd] n (requirement)
Bedürfnis nt (for für); (necessity)

Notwendigkeit f; (poverty) Not f; **to be in ~ of sth** etw brauchen; **if ~(s) be** wenn nötig; **there is no ~ to ...** man braucht nicht (zu) ..., man muss nicht ... ▷ vt brauchen; **I ~ to speak to you** ich muss mit dir reden; **you ~n't go** du brauchst nicht (zu) gehen, du musst nicht gehen

needle ['niːdl] n Nadel f

needless, needlessly ['niːdlɪs, -lɪ] adj, adv unnötig; **~ to say** selbstverständlich

needy ['niːdɪ] adj bedürftig

negative ['negǝtɪv] n (Ling) Verneinung f; (Foto) Negativ nt ▷ adj negativ; (answer) verneinend

neglect [nɪ'glekt] n Vernachlässigung f ▷ vt vernachlässigen; **to ~ to do sth** es versäumen, etw zu tun; **negligence** ['neglɪdʒǝns] n Nachlässigkeit f; **negligent** adj nachlässig

negligible ['neglɪdʒǝbl] adj unbedeutend; (amount) geringfügig

negotiate [nɪ'gǝuʃɪeɪt] vi verhandeln; **negotiation** [nɪgǝuʃɪ'eɪʃǝn] n Verhandlung f

neigh [neɪ] vi (horse) wiehern

neighbor (US), **neighbour** ['neɪbǝ*] n Nachbar(in) m(f); **neighbo(u)rhood** n Nachbarschaft f; **neighbo(u)ring** adj benachbart

neither ['naɪðǝ*] adj, pron keine(r, s) von beiden; **~ of you/us** keiner von euch/uns beiden ▷ adv: **~ ... nor ...** weder ... noch ... ▷ conj: **I'm not going - ~ am I** ich gehe nicht - ich auch nicht

neon ['niːɒn] n Neon nt; **~ sign** (advertisement) Leuchtreklame f

nephew ['nefjuː] n Neffe m

nerd [nɜːv] n (fam) Schwachkopf m; **he's a real computer ~** er ist ein totaler Computerfreak

nerve [nɜːv] n Nerv m; **he gets on my ~s** er geht mir auf die Nerven; (courage) **to keep/lose one's ~** die Nerven behalten/verlieren; (cheek) **to have the ~ to do sth** die Frechheit besitzen, etw zu tun; **nerve-racking** adj nervenaufreibend; **nervous** ['nɜːvǝs] adj (apprehensive) ängstlich; (on edge) nervös; **nervous breakdown** n Nervenzusammenbruch m

nest [nest] n Nest nt ▷ vi nisten

net [net] n Netz nt; **the Net** (Internet) das Internet; **on the ~** im Netz ▷ adj (price, weight) Netto-; **~ profit** Reingewinn m; **netball** n Netzball m

Netherlands ['neðǝlǝndz] npl: **the ~** die Niederlande pl

nettle ['netl] n Nessel f

network ['netwɜːk] n Netz nt; (TV, Radio) Sendenetz nt; (Inform) Netzwerk nt; **networking** n Networking nt (das Knüpfen und Pflegen von Kontakten, die dem beruflichen Fortkommen dienen)

neurosis [njuǝ'rǝusɪs] n Neurose f; **neurotic** [njuǝ'rɒtɪk] adj neurotisch

neuter ['njuːtǝ*] adj (Bio) geschlechtslos; (Ling) sächlich

neutral ['njuːtrǝl] adj neutral ▷ n (gear in car) Leerlauf m

never ['nevǝ*] adv nie(mals); **~ before** noch nie; **~ mind** macht nichts!; **never-ending** adj endlos; **nevertheless** [nevǝðǝ'les] adv trotzdem

new [njuː] adj neu; **this is all ~ to me** das ist für mich noch ungewohnt; **newcomer** n Neuankömmling m; (in job, subject) Neuling m

New England [njuː'ɪŋglǝnd] n Neuengland nt

Newfoundland ['nju:fəndlənd]
n Neufundland *nt*

newly ['nju:li] *adv* neu; ~ **made**
(*cake*) frisch gebacken;
newly-weds *npl* Frischvermählte
pl; **new moon** *n* Neumond *m*

news [nju:z] *nsing* (*item of* ~)
Nachricht *f*; (*Radio, TV*)
Nachrichten *pl*; **good** ~ ein
erfreuliche Nachricht; **what's the
~?** was gibt's Neues?; **have you
heard the ~?** hast du das Neueste
gehört?; **that's ~ to me** das ist mir
neu; **newsagent**, **news dealer**
(*US*) *n* Zeitungshändler(in) *m(f)*;
news bulletin *n*
Nachrichtensendung *f*; **news flash**
n Kurzmeldung *f*; **newsgroup** *n*
(*Inform*) Diskussionsforum *nt*,
Newsgroup *f*; **newsletter** *n*
Mitteilungsblatt *nt*; **newspaper**
['nju:speipə*] *n* Zeitung *f*

New Year ['nju:'jiə*] *n* das
neue Jahr; **Happy** ~ (ein) frohes
Neues Jahr!; (*toast*) Prosit
Neujahr!; **~'s Day** Neujahr *nt*,
Neujahrstag *m*; **~'s Eve**
Silvesterabend *m*; **~'s resolution**
guter Vorsatz fürs neue Jahr

New York [nju:'jɔːk] *n* New
York *nt*

New Zealand [nju:'zi:lənd] *n*
Neuseeland *nt* ⊳ *adj*
neuseeländisch; **New Zealander**
n Neuseeländer(in) *m(f)*

next [nekst] *adj* nächste(r, s);
the week after ~ übernächste
Woche; ~ **time I see him** wenn ich
ihn das nächste Mal sehe; **you're**
~ du bist jetzt dran ⊳ *adv* als
Nächstes; (*then*) dann, darauf; ~ **to**
neben *+dat*; ~ **to last** vorletzte(r,
s); ~ **to impossible** nahezu
unmöglich; **the** ~ **best thing** das
Nächstbeste; ~ **door** nebenan

NHS *abbr* = **National Health
Service**

Niagara Falls [naɪˈægrəˈfɔːlz]
npl Niagarafälle *pl*

nibble ['nɪbl] *vt* knabbern an
+dat; **nibbles** *npl* Knabberzeug *nt*

Nicaragua [nɪkəˈrægjuə] *n*
Nicaragua *nt*

nice [naɪs] *adj* nett, sympathisch;
(*taste, food, drink*) gut; (*weather*)
schön; ~ **and** ... schön ...; **be** ~ **to
him** sei nett zu ihm; **have a** ~ **day**
(*US*) schönen Tag noch!; **nicely** *adv*
nett; (*well*) gut; **that'll do** ~ das
genügt vollauf

nick [nɪk] *vt* (*fam: steal*) klauen;
(*capture*) schnappen

nickel ['nɪkl] *n* (*Chem*) Nickel *nt*;
(*US: coin*) Nickel *m*

nickname ['nɪkneɪm] *n*
Spitzname *m*

nicotine ['nɪkətiːn] *n* Nikotin *nt*;
nicotine patch *n* Nikotinpflaster
nt

niece [niːs] *n* Nichte *f*

Nigeria [naɪˈdʒɪərɪə] *n* Nigeria
nt

night [naɪt] *n* Nacht *f*; (*before bed*)
Abend *m*; **good** ~ gute Nacht!; **at**
(*o by*) ~ nachts; **to have an early**
~ früh schlafen gehen; **nightcap** *n*
Schlummertrunk *m*; **nightclub** *n*
Nachtklub *m*; **nightdress** *n*
Nachthemd *nt*; **nightie** ['naɪtɪ] *n*
(*fam*) Nachthemd *nt*

nightingale ['naɪtɪŋgeɪl] *n*
Nachtigall *f*

night life ['naɪtlaɪf] *n*
Nachtleben *nt*; **nightly** *adv* (*every
evening*) jeden Abend; (*every night*)
jede Nacht; **nightmare**
['naɪtmeə*] *n* Albtraum *m*;
nighttime *n* Nacht *f*; **at** ~ nachts

nil [nɪl] *n* (*Sport*) null

Nile [naɪl] *n* Nil *m*

nine [naɪn] *num* neun; ~ **times
out of ten** so gut wie immer ⊳ *n*
(*a. bus etc*) Neun *f*; *see also* **eight**;
nineteen [naɪn'tiːn] *num*

neunzehn ▷ n (a. bus etc) Neunzehn f; see also **eight**

nineteenth adj neunzehnte(r, s); see also **eighth**; **ninetieth** ['naıntıəθ] adj neunzigste(r, s); see also **eighth**; **ninety** ['naıntı] num neunzig ▷ n Neunzig f; see also **eight**; **ninth** [naınθ] adj neunte(r, s) ▷ n (fraction) Neuntel nt; see also **eighth**

nipple ['nıpl] n Brustwarze f

nitrogen ['naıtrədʒən] n Stickstoff m

◯ **KEYWORD**

no [nəʊ] (pl **noes**) adv (opposite of yes) nein; **to answer no** (to question) mit Nein antworten; (to request) Nein o nein sagen; **no thank you** nein, danke ▷ adj (not any) kein(e); **I have no money/time** ich habe kein Geld/keine Zeit; **"no smoking"** „Rauchen verboten" ▷ n Nein nt; (no vote) Neinstimme f

nobility [nəʊ'bılıtı] n Adel m;

noble ['nəʊbl] adj (rank) adlig; (quality) edel ▷ n Adlige(r) mf

nobody ['nəʊbədı] pron niemand; (emphatic) keiner; **~ knows** keiner weiß es; **~ else** sonst niemand, kein anderer ▷ n Niemand m

no-claims bonus [nəʊ'kleımzbəʊnəs] n Schadenfreiheitsrabatt m

nod [nɒd] vi, vt nicken; **nod off** vi einnicken

noise [nɔız] n (loud) Lärm m; (sound) Geräusch nt; **noisy** adj laut; (crowd) lärmend

nominate ['nɒmıneıt] vt (in election) aufstellen; (appoint) ernennen

nominative ['nɒmınətıv] n (Ling) Nominativ m

nominee [nɒmı'ni:] n Kandidat(in) m(f)

non- [nɒn] pref Nicht-; (with adj) nicht-, un-; **non-alcoholic** adj alkoholfrei

none [nʌn] pron keine(r, s); **~ of them** keiner von ihnen; **~ of it is any use** nichts davon ist brauchbar; **there are ~ left** es sind keine mehr da; (with comparative) **to be ~ the wiser** auch nicht schlauer sein; **I was ~ the worse for it** es hat mir nichts geschadet

nonentity [nɒ'nentıtı] n Null f

nonetheless [nʌnðə'les] adv nichtsdestoweniger, dennoch

non-event n Reinfall m; **non-existent** adj nicht vorhanden; **non-fiction** n Sachbücher pl; **non-iron** adj bügelfrei; **non-polluting** adj schadstofffrei; **non-resident** n: **"open to ~s"** „auch für Nichthotelgäste" adj: **~ bottle** Einwegflasche f **non-returnable** adj:

nonsense ['nɒnsəns] n Unsinn m; **don't talk ~** red keinen Unsinn

non-smoker [nɒn'sməʊkə*] n Nichtraucher(in) m(f);
non-smoking adj Nichtraucher-; **~ area** Nichtraucherbereich m; **nonstop** adj (train) durchgehend; (flight) Nonstop- ▷ adv (talk) ununterbrochen; (travel) ohne Unterbrechung; (fly) ohne Zwischenlandung; **non-violent** adj gewaltfrei

noodles ['nu:dlz] npl Nudeln pl

noon [nu:n] n Mittag m; **at ~** um 12 Uhr mittags

no one ['nəʊwʌn] pron niemand; (emphatic) keiner; **~ else** sonst niemand, kein anderer

nor [nɔ:] conj: **neither ... ~ ...**

weder ... noch ...; **I don't smoke,
~ does he** ich rauche nicht, er
auch nicht

norm [nɔːm] n Norm f

normal ['nɔːməl] adj normal; **to
get back to ~** sich wieder
normalisieren; **normally** adv
(usually) normalerweise

north [nɔːθ] n Norden m; **to the
~ of** nördlich von ▷ adv (go, face)
nach Norden ▷ adj Nord-; **~ wind**
Nordwind m; **North America** n
Nordamerika nt; **northbound** adj
(in) Richtung Norden; **northeast**
n Nordosten m; **to the ~ of**
nordöstlich von ▷ adv (go, face)
nach Nordosten ▷ adj Nordost-;
northern ['nɔːðən] adj nördlich;
~ France Nordfrankreich nt;
Northern Ireland n Nordirland
nt; **North Pole** n Nordpol m;
North Sea n Nordsee f;
northwards adv nach Norden;
northwest n Nordwesten m; **to
the ~ of** nordwestlich von ▷ adv
(go, face) nach Nordwesten ▷ adj
Nordwest-

Norway ['nɔːweɪ] n Norwegen
nt; **Norwegian** [nɔːˈwiːdʒən] adj
norwegisch ▷ n (person)
Norweger(in) m(f); (language)
Norwegisch nt

nos. abbr = **numbers** Nr.

nose [nəʊz] n Nase f; **nose
around** vi herumschnüffeln;
nosebleed n Nasenbluten nt;
nose-dive n Sturzflug m; **to take
a ~** abstürzen

nosey ['nəʊzɪ] see **nosy**

nostalgia [nɒsˈtældʒɪə] n Nos-
talgie f (for nach); **nostalgic** adj
nostalgisch

nostril ['nɒstrɪl] n Nasenloch nt

nosy ['nəʊzɪ] adj neugierig

not [nɒt] adv nicht; **~ a** kein;
~ one of them kein einziger von
ihnen; **he is ~ an expert** er ist kein

Experte; **I told him ~ to (do it)** ich
sagte ihm, er solle es nicht tun;
~ at all überhaupt nicht,
keineswegs; (don't mention it) gern
geschehen; **~ yet** noch nicht

notable ['nəʊtəbl] adj bemerkenswert; **note** [nəʊt] n (written)
Notiz f; (short letter) paar Zeilen pl;
(on scrap of paper) Zettel m;
(comment in book etc) Anmerkung f;
(bank~) Schein m; (Mus: sign) Note
f; (sound) Ton m; **to make a ~ of
sth** sich dat etw notieren; **~s** (of
lecture etc) Aufzeichnungen pl; **to
take ~s** sich dat Notizen machen
(of über +akk); **to ~** (notice)
bemerken (that dass); (write down)
notieren; **notebook** n Notizbuch
nt; (Inform) Notebook nt; **notepad**
n Notizblock m; **notepaper** n
Briefpapier nt

nothing ['nʌθɪŋ] n nichts; **~
but ...** lauter ...; **~ for umsonst; he
thinks ~ of it** er macht sich nichts
daraus

notice ['nəʊtɪs] n (announcement)
Bekanntmachung f; (on ~ board)
Anschlag m; (attention) Beachtung
f; (advance warning) Ankündigung f;
(to leave job, flat etc) Kündigung f;
at short ~ kurzfristig; **until
further ~** bis auf weiteres; **to give
sb ~** jdm kündigen; **to hand in
one's ~** kündigen; **to take (no)
~ of (sth)** etw (nicht) beachten;
take no ~ kümmere dich nicht
darum! ▷ vt bemerken;
noticeable adj erkennbar;
(visible) sichtbar; **to be ~** auffallen;
notice board n Anschlagtafel f

notification [nəʊtɪfɪˈkeɪʃən] n
Benachrichtigung f (of von); **notify**
['nəʊtɪfaɪ] vt benachrichtigen (of
von)

notion ['nəʊʃən] n Idee f

notorious [nəʊˈtɔːrɪəs] adj
berüchtigt

nought [nɔːt] n Null f
noun [naʊn] n Substantiv nt
nourish ['nʌrɪʃ] vt nähren;
  nourishing adj nahrhaft;
  nourishment n Nahrung f
novel ['nɒvəl] n Roman m ▷ adj
  neuartig; **novelist** n
  Schriftsteller(in) m(f); **novelty** n
  Neuheit f
November [nəʊ'vembə°] n
  November m; see also **September**
novice ['nɒvɪs] n Neuling m
now [naʊ] adv (at the moment)
  jetzt; (introductory phrase) also;
  right ~ jetzt gleich; **just ~** gerade;
  by ~ inzwischen; **from ~ on** ab
  jetzt; **~ and again** (o **then**) ab und
  zu; **nowadays** adv heutzutage
nowhere ['nəʊweə°] adv nirgends; **we're getting ~** wir
  kommen nicht weiter; **~ near**
  noch lange nicht
nozzle ['nɒzl] n Düse f
nuclear ['njuːklɪə°] adj (energy
  etc) Kern-; **~ power station**
  Kernkraftwerk nt; **nuclear waste**
  n Atommüll m
nude [njuːd] adj nackt ▷ n (person) Nackte(r) mf; (painting etc) Akt
  m
nudge [nʌdʒ] vt stupsen; **nudist**
  ['njuːdɪst] n Nudist(in) m(f),
  FKK-Anhänger(in) m(f); **nudist
  beach** n FKK-Strand m
nuisance ['njuːsns] n Ärgernis
  nt; (person) Plage f; **what a ~** wie
  ärgerlich!
nuke [njuːk] (US fam) n (bomb)
  Atombombe f ▷ vt eine
  Atombombe werfen auf +akk
numb [nʌm] adj taub, gefühllos
  ▷ vt betäuben
number ['nʌmbə°] n Nummer f;
  (Math) Zahl f; (quantity) (An)zahl f;
  in small/large ~s in
  kleinen/großen Mengen; **a ~ of
  times** mehrmals ▷ vt (give a

number to) nummerieren; (count)
  zählen (among zu); **his days are
  ~ed** seine Tage sind gezählt;
  number plate n (Brit Auto)
  Nummernschild nt
numeral ['njuːmərəl] n Ziffer f;
  numerical [njuː'merɪkəl] adj
  numerisch; (superiority)
  zahlenmäßig; **numerous**
  ['njuːmərəs] adj zahlreich
nun [nʌn] n Nonne f
Nuremberg ['njʊərəmbɜːg] n
  Nürnberg nt
nurse [nɜːs] n Krankenschwester
  f; (male~) Krankenpfleger m ▷ vt
  (patient) pflegen; (baby) stillen;
  nursery n Kinderzimmer nt; (for
  plants) Gärtnerei f; (tree)
  Baumschule f; **nursery rhyme** n
  Kinderreim m; **nursery school** n
  Kindergarten m; **~ teacher**
  Kindergärtner(in) m(f),
  Erzieher(in) m(f); **nursing** n
  (profession) Krankenpflege f;
  ~ home n Privatklinik f
nut [nʌt] n Nuss f; (Tech: for bolt)
  Mutter f; **nutcase** n (fam)
  Spinner(in) m(f); **nutcracker** n,
  nutcrackers npl Nussknacker m
nutmeg ['nʌtmeg] n Muskat m,
  Muskatnuss f
nutrient ['njuːtrɪənt] n Nährstoff
  m
nutrition [njuː'trɪʃən] n Ernährung f; **nutritious** [njuː'trɪʃəs]
  adj nahrhaft
nuts [nʌts] (fam) adj verrückt; **to
  be ~ about sth** nach etw verrückt
  sein ▷ npl (testicles) Eier pl
nutshell ['nʌtʃel] n Nussschale f;
  in a ~ kurz gesagt
nutter ['nʌtə°] n (fam)
  Spinner(in) m(f); **nutty** ['nʌtɪ]
  adj (fam) verrückt
NW abbr = **northwest** NW
nylon® ['naɪlɒn] n Nylon® nt
  ▷ adj Nylon-

n

O

O [əʊ] n (Tel) Null f

oak [əʊk] n Eiche f ▷ adj Eichen-

OAP abbr = **old-age pensioner** Rentner(in) m(f)

oar [ɔː] n Ruder nt

oasis [əʊˈeɪsɪs] n (pl **oases**) n Oase f

oatcake [ˈəʊtkeɪk] n Haferkeks m

oath [əʊθ] n (statement) Eid m

oats [əʊts] npl Hafer m; (Gastr) Haferflocken pl

obedience [əˈbiːdɪəns] n Gehorsam m; **obedient** adj gehorsam; **obey** [əˈbeɪ] vt, vi gehorchen +dat

object [ˈɒbdʒɪkt] n Gegenstand m; (abstract) Objekt nt; (purpose) Ziel nt ▷ [əbˈdʒekt] vi dagegen sein; (raise objection) Einwände erheben (to gegen); (morally) Anstoß nehmen (to an +dat); **do you ~ to my smoking?** haben Sie etwas dagegen, wenn ich rauche?; **objection** [əbˈdʒekʃən] n Einwand m

objective [əbˈdʒektɪv] n Ziel nt ▷ adj objektiv; **objectivity** [ɒbdʒekˈtɪvɪtɪ] n Objektivität f

obligation [ɒblɪˈɡeɪʃən] n (duty) Pflicht f; (commitment) Verpflichtung f; **no ~** unverbindlich; **obligatory** [əˈblɪɡətərɪ] adj obligatorisch; **oblige** [əˈblaɪdʒ] vt: **to ~ sb to do sth** jdn (dazu) zwingen, etw zu tun; **he felt ~d to accept the offer** er fühlte sich verpflichtet, das Angebot anzunehmen

oblique [əˈbliːk] adj schräg; (angle) schief

oboe [ˈəʊbəʊ] n Oboe f

obscene [əbˈsiːn] adj obszön

obscure [əbˈskjʊə] adj unklar; (unknown) unbekannt

observant [əbˈzɜːvənt] adj aufmerksam; **observation** [ɒbzəˈveɪʃən] n (watching) Beobachtung f; (remark) Bemerkung f; **observe** [əbˈzɜːv] vt (notice) bemerken; (watch) beobachten; (customs) einhalten

obsessed [əbˈsest] adj besessen (with an idea etc von einem Gedanken etc); **obsession** [əbˈseʃən] n Manie f

obsolete [ˈɒbsəliːt] adj veraltet

obstacle [ˈɒbstəkl] n Hindernis nt (to für); **to be an ~ to sth** einer Sache im Weg stehen

obstinate [ˈɒbstɪnət] adj hartnäckig

obstruct [əbˈstrʌkt] vt versperren; (pipe) verstopfen; (hinder) behindern, aufhalten; **obstruction** [əbˈstrʌkʃən] n Blockierung f; (of pipe) Verstopfung f; (obstacle) Hindernis nt

obtain [əbˈteɪn] vt erhalten; **obtainable** adj erhältlich

obvious ['ɒbvɪəs] *adj* offensichtlich; **it was ~ to me that ...** es war mir klar, dass ...; **obviously** *adj* offensichtlich

occasion [ə'keɪʒən] *n* Gelegenheit *f*; (*special event*) (großes) Ereignis *nt*; **on the ~** anlässlich +*gen*; **special ~** besonderer Anlass; **occasional, occasionally** *adj*, *adv* gelegentlich

occupant ['ɒkjʊpənt] *n* (*of house*) Bewohner(in) *m(f)*; (*of vehicle*) Insasse *m*, Insassin *f*; **occupation** [ɒkjʊ'peɪʃən] *n* Beruf *m*; (*pastime*) Beschäftigung *f*; (*of country etc*) Besetzung *f*; **occupied** *adj* (*country, seat, toilet*) besetzt; (*person*) beschäftigt; **to keep sb/oneself ~** jdn/sich beschäftigen; **occupy** ['ɒkjʊpaɪ] *vt* (*country*) besetzen; (*time*) beanspruchen; (*mind, person*) beschäftigen

occur [ə'kɜ:ˀ] *vi* vorkommen; **~ to sb** jdm einfallen; **occurrence** [ə'kʌrəns] *n* (*event*) Ereignis *nt*; (*presence*) Vorkommen *nt*

ocean ['əʊʃən] *n* Ozean *m*; (*US: sea*) das Meer *nt*

o'clock [ə'klɒk] *adv*: **5 ~** 5 Uhr; **at 10 ~** um 10 Uhr

octagon ['ɒktəgən] *n* Achteck *nt*

October [ɒk'təʊbəˀ] *n* Oktober *m*; *see also* **September**

octopus ['ɒktəpəs] *n* Tintenfisch *m*

odd [ɒd] *adj* (*strange*) sonderbar; (*not even*) ungerade; (*one missing*) einzeln; **to be the ~ one out** nicht dazugehören; **~ jobs** Gelegenheitsarbeiten *pl*; **odds** *npl* Chancen *pl*; **against all ~** entgegen allen Erwartungen; **~ and ends** (*fam*) Kleinkram *pl*

odometer [əʊ'dɒmətəˀ] *n* (*US Auto*) Meilenzähler *m*

odor (*US*), **odour** ['əʊdəˀ] *n* Geruch *m*

KEYWORD

of [ɒv, əv] *prep* **1** von +*dat* = use of *gen*; **the history of Germany** die Geschichte Deutschlands; **a friend of ours** ein Freund von uns; **a boy of 10** ein 10-jähriger Junge; **that was kind of you** das war sehr freundlich von Ihnen
2 (*expressing quantity, amount, dates etc*) **a kilo of flour** ein Kilo Mehl; **how much of this do you need?** wie viel brauchen Sie (davon)?; **there were 3 of them** (*people*) sie waren zu dritt; (*objects*) es gab 3 (davon); **a cup of tea/vase of flowers** eine Tasse Tee/Vase mit Blumen; **the 5th of July** der 5. Juli
3 (*from, out of*) aus; **a bridge made of wood** eine Holzbrücke, eine Brücke aus Holz

off [ɒf] *adv* (*away*) weg, fort; (*free*) frei; (*switch*) ausgeschaltet; (*milk*) sauer; **a mile ~** eine Meile entfernt; **I'm ~ now** ich gehe jetzt; **to have the day/Monday ~** heute/Montag freihaben; **the lights are ~** die Lichter sind aus; **the concert is ~** das Konzert fällt aus; **I got 10 % ~** ich habe 10 % Nachlass bekommen ▷ *prep* (*away from*) von; **to jump/fall ~ the roof** vom Dach springen/fallen; **to get ~ the bus** aus dem Bus aussteigen; **he's ~ work/school** er hat frei/schulfrei; **to take £20 ~ the price** den Preis um 20 Pfund herabsetzen

offence [ə'fɛns] *n* (*crime*) Straftat *f*; (*minor*) Vergehen *nt*; (*to feelings*) Kränkung *f*; **to cause/take ~** Anstoß

erregen/nehmen; **offend** [ə'fend]
vt kränken; (eye, ear) beleidigen;
offender n Straffällige(r) mf;
offense (US) see offence;
offensive [ə'fensɪv] adj anstößig;
(insulting) beleidigend; (smell) übel,
abstoßend ▷ n (Mil) Offensive f

offer ['ɒfə°] n Angebot nt; **on
~** (Comm) im Angebot ▷ vt
anbieten (to sb jdm); (money, a
chance etc) bieten

offhand [ɒf'hænd] adj lässig
▷ adv (say) auf Anhieb

office ['ɒfɪs] n Büro nt; (position)
Amt nt; **doctor's ~** (US) Arztpraxis
f; **office block** n Bürogebäude nt;
office hours npl Dienstzeit f;
(notice) Geschäftszeiten pl; **officer**
['ɒfɪsə°] n (Mil) Offizier(in) m(f);
(official) Polizeibeamte(r) m,
Polizeibeamtin f; **office worker**
['ɒfɪswɜːkə°] n Büroangestellte(r)
mf; **official** [ə'fɪʃəl] adj offiziell;
(report etc) amtlich; **~ language**
Amtssprache f ▷ n Beamte(r) m,
Beamtin f, Repräsentant(in)
m(f)

off-licence ['ɒflaɪsəns] n (Brit)
Wein- und Spirituosenhandlung f;
off-line adj (Inform) offline;
off-peak adj außerhalb der
Stoßzeiten; (rate, ticket) verbilligt;
off-putting adj abstoßend,
entmutigend, irritierend;
off-season adj außerhalb der
Saison

offshore ['ɒfʃɔː°] adj küstennah,
Küsten-; (oil rig) im Meer; **offside**
['ɒf'saɪd] n (Auto) Fahrerseite f;
(Sport) Abseits nt

often ['ɒfn] adv oft; **every so
~** von Zeit zu Zeit

oil [ɔɪl] n Öl nt ▷ vt ölen; **oil level**
n Ölstand m; **oil painting** n
Ölgemälde nt; **oil-rig** n
(Öl)bohrinsel f; **oil slick** n
Ölteppich m; **oil tanker** n

Öltanker m; (truck) Tankwagen m;
oily adj ölig; (skin, hair) fettig

ointment ['ɔɪntmənt] n Salbe f

OK, okay [əʊ'keɪ] adj (fam) okay,
in Ordnung; **that's ~ by** (o **with**)
me das ist mir recht

old [əʊld] adj alt; **old age** n Alter
nt; **~ pension** Rente f; **~ pensioner**
Rentner(in) m(f); **old-fashioned**
adj altmodisch; **old people's
home** n Altersheim nt

olive ['ɒlɪv] n Olive f; **olive oil** n
Olivenöl nt

Olympic [əʊ'lɪmpɪk] adj olym-
pisch; **the ~ Games, the ~s** pl die
Olympischen Spiele pl, die
Olympiade f

omelette ['ɒmlət] n Omelett nt

omission [əʊ'mɪʃən] n Auslas-
sung f; **omit** [əʊ'mɪt] vt
auslassen

KEYWORD

on [ɒn] prep 1 (indicating position)
auf +dat; (with vb of motion) auf
+akk; (on vertical surface, part of
body) an +dat/akk; **it's on the table**
es ist auf dem Tisch; **she put the
book on the table** sie legte das
Buch auf den Tisch; **on the left**
links

2 (indicating means, method,
condition etc) **on foot** (go, be) zu
Fuß; **on the train/plane** (go) mit
dem Zug/Flugzeug; (be) im
Zug/Flugzeug; **on the
telephone/television** am
Telefon/im Fernsehen; **to be on
drugs** Drogen nehmen; **to be on
holiday/business** im Urlaub/auf
Geschäftsreise sein

3 (referring to time) **on Friday** (am)
Freitag; **on Fridays** freitags; **on
June 20th** am 20. Juni; **a week on
Friday** Freitag in einer Woche; **on
arrival he ...** als er ankam, ... er ...

4 (*about, concerning*) über +*akk*
▷ *adv* **1** (*referring to dress*) an; **she put her boots/hat on** sie zog ihre Stiefel an/setzte ihren Hut auf
2 (*further, continuously*) weiter; **to walk on** weitergehen
▷ *adv* **1** (*functioning, of machine, TV, light*) an; (*tap*) aufgedreht; (*brakes*) angezogen; **is the meeting still on?** findet die Versammlung noch statt?; **there's a good film on** es läuft ein guter Film
2 **that's not on!** (*inf*) (*of behaviour*) das ist nicht drin!

once [wʌns] *adv* (*one time, in the past*) einmal; **at ~** sofort; (*at the same time*) gleichzeitig; **~ more** noch einmal; **for ~** ausnahmsweise (einmal); **~ in a while** ab und zu mal ▷ *conj* wenn ... einmal; **~ you've got used to it** sobald Sie sich daran gewöhnt haben

oncoming [ˈɒnkʌmɪŋ] *adj* entgegenkommend; **~ traffic** Gegenverkehr *m*

Ⓞ **KEYWORD**

one [wʌn] *num* eins; (*with noun, referring back to noun*) ein/eine/ein; **it is one (o'clock)** es ist eins, es ist ein Uhr; **one hundred and fifty** einhundertfünfzig
▷ *adj* **1** (*sole*) einzige(r, s); **the one book which** das einzige Buch, welches
2 (*same*) derselbe/dieselbe/ dasselbe; **they came in the one car** sie kamen alle in dem einen Auto
3 (*indef*) **one day I discovered ...** eines Tages bemerkte ich ...
▷ *pron* **1** eine(r, s); **do you have a red one?** haben Sie einen

roten/eine rote/ein rotes?; **this one** diese(r, s); **that one** der/die/das; **which one?** welche(r, s)?; **one by one** einzeln
2 **one another** einander; **do you two ever see one another?** seht ihr beide euch manchmal?
3 (*impers*) **one never knows** man kann nie wissen; **to cut one's finger** sich in den Finger schneiden

one-off *adj* einmalig ▷ *n*: **a ~** etwas Einmaliges; **one-parent family** *n* Einelternfamilie *f*; **one-piece** *adj* einteilig; **oneself** *pron* (*reflexive*) sich; **one-way** *adj*: **~ street** Einbahnstraße *f*; **~ ticket** (*US*) einfache Fahrkarte

onion [ˈʌnjən] *n* Zwiebel *f*

on-line [ˈɒnlaɪn] *adj* (*Inform*) online; **~ banking** Homebanking *nt*

only [ˈəʊnlɪ] *adv* nur; (*with time*) erst; **~ yesterday** erst gestern; **he's ~ four** er ist erst vier; **~ just arrived** erst angekommen
▷ *adj* einzige(r, s); **~ child** Einzelkind *nt*

o.n.o. *abbr* = **or nearest offer** VB

onside [ɒnˈsaɪd] *adv* (*Sport*) nicht im Abseits

onto [ˈɒntʊ] *prep* auf +*akk*; (*vertical surface*) an +*akk*; **to be ~ sb** jdm auf die Schliche gekommen sein

onwards [ˈɒnwədz] *adv* voran, vorwärts; **from today ~** von heute an, ab heute

open [ˈəʊpən] *adj* offen; **in the ~ air** im Freien; **~ to the public** für die Öffentlichkeit zugänglich; **the shop is ~ all day** das Geschäft hat den ganzen Tag offen ▷ *vt* öffnen, aufmachen; (*meeting, account, new building*)

eröffnen; (road) dem Verkehr
übergeben ▷ vi (door, window etc)
aufgehen, sich öffnen; (shop, bank)
öffnen, aufmachen; (begin)
anfangen (with mit); **open-air** adj
Freiluft-; **open day** n Tag m der
offenen Tür; **opening** n Öffnung
f; (beginning) Anfang m; (official, of
exhibition etc) Eröffnung f;
(opportunity) Möglichkeit f;
~ hours (o times) Öffnungszeiten
pl; **openly** adv offen;
open-minded adj aufgeschlossen; **open-plan** adj; **~ office**
Großraumbüro nt

opera ['ɔpərə] n Oper f; **opera
glasses** npl Operngläs nt; **opera
house** n Oper f, Opernhaus nt;
opera singer n Opernsänger(in)
m(f)

operate ['ɔpəreɪt] vt (machine)
bedienen; (brakes, lights) betätigen
▷ vi (machine) laufen; (bus etc)
verkehren (between zwischen); **to
~ (on sb)** (Med) (jdn) operieren;
operating theatre n
Operationssaal m; **operation**
[ɔpə'reɪʃən] n (of machine)
Bedienung f; (functioning)
Funktionieren nt; (Med) Operation
f (on an +dat); (undertaking)
Unternehmen nt; **in ~** (machine) in
Betrieb; **to have an ~** operiert
werden (for wegen); **operator**
['ɔpəreɪtə] n: **to phone the ~** die
Vermittlung anrufen

opinion [ə'pɪnjən] n Meinung f
(on zu); **in my ~** meiner Meinung
nach

opponent [ə'pəʊnənt] n Geg-
ner(in) m(f)

opportunity [ɔpə'tjuːnɪtɪ] n
Gelegenheit f

oppose [ə'pəʊz] vt sich
widersetzen +dat; (idea) ablehnen;
opposed adj: **to be ~ to sth**
gegen etw sein; **as ~ to** im

Gegensatz zu; **opposing** adj
(team) gegnerisch; (points of view)
entgegengesetzt

opposite ['ɔpəzɪt] adj (house)
gegenüberliegend; (direction)
entgegengesetzt; **the ~ sex** das
andere Geschlecht ▷ adv
gegenüber ▷ prep gegenüber
+dat; **~ me** mir gegenüber ▷ n
Gegenteil nt

opposition [ɔpə'zɪʃən] n
Widerstand m (to gegen); (Pol)
Opposition f

oppress [ə'pres] vt unterdrücken; **oppressive** adj (heat)
drückend

opt [ɔpt] vi: **to ~ for sth** sich für
etw entscheiden; **to ~ to do sth**
sich entscheiden, etw zu tun

optician [ɔp'tɪʃən] n Optiker(in)
m(f)

optimist ['ɔptɪmɪst] n Opti-
mist(in) m(f); **optimistic**
[ɔptɪ'mɪstɪk] adj optimistisch

option ['ɔpʃən] n Möglichkeit f;
(Comm) Option f; **to have no
~** keine Wahl haben; **optional** adj
freiwillig; **~ extras** (Auto) Extras
pl

or [ɔː°] conj oder; (otherwise)
sonst; (after neg) noch; **hurry up,
~ (else) we'll be late** beeil dich,
sonst kommen wir zu spät

oral ['ɔːrəl] adj mündlich; **~ sex**
Oralverkehr m ▷ n (exam)
Mündliche(s) nt; **oral surgeon** n
Kieferchirurg(in) m(f)

orange ['ɒrɪndʒ] n Orange f
▷ adj orangefarben; **orange juice**
n Orangensaft m

orbit ['ɔːbɪt] n Umlaufbahn f; **to
be out of ~** (fam) nicht zu
erreichen sein ▷ vt um umkreisen

orchard ['ɔːtʃəd] n Obstgarten m

orchestra ['ɔːkɪstrə] n Orchester nt; (US Theat) Parkett nt

orchid ['ɔːkɪd] n Orchidee f

ordeal [ɔː'diːl] n Tortur f; (emotional) Qual f

order ['ɔːdə'] n (sequence) Reihenfolge f; (good arrangement) Ordnung f; (command) Befehl m; (Jur) Anordnung f; (condition) Zustand m; (Comm, Bestellung f; **out of ~** (not functioning) außer Betrieb; (unsuitable) nicht angebracht; **in ~** (items) richtig geordnet; (all right) in Ordnung; **in ~ to do sth** um etw zu tun ▷ vt (arrange) ordnen; (command) befehlen; **to ~ sb to do sth** jdm befehlen, etw zu tun; (food, product) bestellen; **order form** n Bestellschein m

ordinary ['ɔːdnrɪ] adj gewöhnlich, normal; (average) durchschnittlich

ore [ɔː'] n Erz nt

organ ['ɔːgən] n (Mus) Orgel f; (Anat) Organ nt

organic [ɔː'gænɪk] adj organisch; (farming, vegetables) Bio-, Öko-; **~ farmer** Biobauer m, Biobäuerin f; **~ food** Biokost f

organization [ˌɔːgənaɪ'zeɪʃən] n Organisation f; (arrangement) Ordnung f; **organize** ['ɔːgənaɪz] vt organisieren; **organizer** n (elektronisches) Notizbuch

orgasm ['ɔːgæzəm] n Orgasmus m

orgy ['ɔːdʒɪ] n Orgie f

oriental [ˌɔːrɪ'entəl] adj orientalisch

orientation [ˌɔːrɪenteɪʃən] n Orientierung f

origin ['brɪdʒɪn] n Ursprung m; (of person) Herkunft f; **original** [ə'rɪdʒɪnl] adj (first) ursprünglich; (painting) original; (idea) originell ▷ n Original nt; **originality** [ərɪdʒɪ'nælɪtɪ] n Originalität f; **originally** adv ursprünglich

Orkneys ['ɔːknɪz] npl, **Orkney Islands** npl Orkneyinseln pl

ornament ['ɔːnəmənt] n Schmuckgegenstand m; **ornamental** [ɔːnə'mentl] adj dekorativ

orphan ['ɔːfən] n Waise f, Waisenkind nt; **orphanage** ['ɔːfənɪdʒ] n Waisenhaus nt

orthodox ['ɔːθədɒks] adj orthodox

orthopaedic, orthopedic (US) [ɔːθəʊ'piːdɪk] adj orthopädisch

ostentatious [ˌɒsten'teɪʃəs] adj protzig

ostrich ['ɒstrɪtʃ] n (Zool) Strauß m

other ['ʌðə'] adj, pron andere(r, s); **any ~ questions?** sonst noch Fragen?; **the ~ day** neulich; **every ~ day** jeden zweiten Tag; **any person ~ than him** alle außer ihm; **someone/something or ~** irgendjemand/irgendetwas; **otherwise** adv sonst; (differently) anders

OTT adj abbr = **over the top** übertrieben

otter ['ɒtə'] n Otter m

ought [ɔːt] vb aux (obligation) sollte; (probability) dürfte; (stronger) müsste; **you ~ to do that** du solltest/Sie sollten das tun; **he ~ to win** er müsste gewinnen; **that ~ to do** das müsste reichen

ounce [aʊns] n Unze f (28,35 g)

our [aʊə'] adj unser; **ours** pron unsere(r, s); **this is ~** das gehört uns; **a friend of ~** ein Freund von uns; **ourselves** pron (reflexive) uns; **we enjoyed ~** wir haben uns amüsiert; **we've got the house to ~** wir haben das Haus für uns; (emphatic) **we did it ~** wir haben es selbst gemacht; **(all) by ~ alone** allein

out [aʊt] adv hinaus/heraus; (not

indoors) draußen; (*not at home*) nicht zu Hause; (*not alight*) aus; (*unconscious*) bewusstlos; (*published*) herausgekommen; (*results*) bekannt gegeben; **have you been ~ yet?** warst du/waren Sie schon draußen?; **I was ~ when they called** ich war nicht da, als sie vorbeikamen; **to be ~ and about** unterwegs sein; **the sun is ~** die Sonne scheint; **the fire is ~** das Feuer ist ausgegangen; (*wrong*) **the calculation is (way) ~** die Kalkulation stimmt (ganz und gar) nicht; **they're ~ to get him** sie sind hinter ihm her ▷ *vt* (*fam*) outen

outback ['aʊtbæk] *n* (*in Australia*) **the ~** das Hinterland

outboard ['aʊtbɔːd] *adj*: **~ motor** Außenbordmotor *m*

outbreak ['aʊtbreɪk] *n* Ausbruch *m*

outburst ['aʊtbɜːst] *n* Ausbruch *m*

outcome ['aʊtkʌm] *n* Ergebnis *nt*

outcry ['aʊtkraɪ] *n* (*public protest*) Protestwelle *f* (*against* gegen)

outdo [aʊt'duː] *irr vt* übertreffen

outdoor [aʊt'dɔː] *adj* Außen-; (*Sport*) im Freien; **~ swimming pool** Freibad *nt*; **outdoors** [aʊt'dɔːz] *adv* draußen, im Freien

outer ['aʊtə] *adj* äußere(r, s); **outer space** *n* Weltraum *m*

outfit ['aʊtfɪt] *n* Ausrüstung *f*; (*clothes*) Kleidung *f*

outgoing ['aʊtgəʊɪŋ] *adj* kontaktfreudig

outgrow [aʊt'grəʊ] *irr vt* (*clothes*) herauswachsen aus

outing ['aʊtɪŋ] *n* Ausflug *m*

outlet ['aʊtlet] *n* Auslass *m*, Abfluss *m*; (*US*) Steckdose *f*; (*shop*) Verkaufsstelle *f*

outline ['aʊtlaɪn] *n* Umriss *m*; (*summary*) Abriss *m*

outlive [aʊt'lɪv] *vt* überleben

outlook ['aʊtlʊk] *n* Aussicht(en) *f*(*pl*); (*prospects*) Aussichten *pl*; (*attitude*) Einstellung *f* (*on* zu)

outnumber [aʊt'nʌmbə] *vt* zahlenmäßig überlegen sein +*dat*; **~ed** zahlenmäßig unterlegen

out of ['aʊtɒv] *prep* (*motion, motive, origin*) aus; (*position, away from*) außerhalb +*gen*; **~ danger/sight/breath** außer Gefahr/Sicht/Atem; **made ~ wood** aus Holz gemacht; **we are ~ bread** wir haben kein Brot mehr; **out-of-date** *adj* veraltet; **out-of-the-way** *adj* abgelegen

outpatient ['aʊtpeɪʃənt] *n* ambulanter Patient, ambulante Patientin

output ['aʊtpʊt] *n* Produktion *f*; (*of engine*) Leistung *f*; (*Inform*) Ausgabe *f*

outrage ['aʊtreɪdʒ] *n* (*great anger*) Empörung *f* (*at* über); (*wicked deed*) Schandtat *f*; (*crime*) Verbrechen *nt*; (*indecency*) Skandal *m*; **outrageous** [aʊt'reɪdʒəs] *adj* unerhört; (*clothes, behaviour etc*) unmöglich, schrill

outright ['aʊtraɪt] *adv* (*killed*) sofort ▷ *adj* total; (*denial*) völlig; (*winner*) unbestritten

outside [aʊt'saɪd] *n* Außenseite *f*; **on the ~** außen ▷ *adj* äußere(r, s), Außen-; (*chance*) sehr gering ▷ *adv* außen; **to go ~** nach draußen gehen ▷ *prep* außerhalb +*gen*; **outsider** *n* Außenseiter(in) *m(f)*

outskirts ['aʊtskɜːts] *npl* (*of town*) Stadtrand *m*

outstanding [aʊt'stændɪŋ] *adj* hervorragend; (*debts etc*) ausstehend

outward ['aʊtwəd] *adj* äußere(r, s); **~ journey** Hinfahrt *f*;

outwardly adv nach außen hin;
outwards adv nach außen
oval ['əʊvəl] adj oval
ovary ['əʊvərɪ] n Eierstock m
ovation [əʊ'veɪʃən] n Ovation f,
Applaus m
oven ['ʌvn] n Backofen m; **oven glove** n Topfhandschuh m;
ovenproof adj feuerfest;
oven-ready adj bratfertig
over ['əʊvə°] prep (position) über +dat; (motion) über +akk; **they spent a long time ~ it** sie haben lange dazu gebraucht; **from all ~ England** aus ganz England;
~ £20 mehr als 20 Pfund; **~ the phone/radio** am Telefon/im Radio; **to talk ~ a glass of wine** sich bei einem Glas Wein unterhalten; **~ and above this** darüber hinaus; **~ the summer** während des Sommers ▷ adv (across) hinüber/herüber; (match, play etc) zu Ende; (left) übrig; (more) mehr; **~ there/in America** da drüben/drüben in Amerika; **~ to you** du bist/Sie sind dran; **it's (all) ~ between us** es ist aus zwischen uns; **~ and ~ again** immer wieder; **to start (all) ~ again** noch einmal von vorn anfangen; **children of 8 and ~** Kinder ab 8 Jahren
over- ['əʊvə°] pref über-
overall ['əʊvərɔːl] n (Brit) Kittel m ▷ adj (situation) allgemein; (length) Gesamt-; **~ majority** absolute Mehrheit ▷ adv insgesamt; **overalls** npl Overall m
overboard ['əʊvəbɔːd] adv über Bord
overbooked [əʊvə'bʊkt] adj überbucht; **overbooking** n Überbuchung f
overcharge [əʊvə'tʃɑːdʒ] vt zu viel verlangen von

overcoat ['əʊvəkəʊt] n Wintermantel m
overcome [əʊvə'kʌm] irr vt überwinden; **~ by sleep/emotion** von Schlaf/Rührung übermannt; **we shall ~** wir werden siegen
overcooked [əʊvə'kʊkt] adj verkocht; (meat) zu lange gebraten
overcrowded [əʊvə'kraʊdɪd] adj überfüllt
overdo [əʊvə'duː] irr vt übertreiben; **overdone** [əʊvə'dʌn] adj übertrieben; (food) zu lange gekocht; (meat) zu lange gebraten
overdose ['əʊvədəʊs] n Überdosis f
overdraft ['əʊvədrɑːft] n Kontoüberziehung f; **overdrawn** [əʊvə'drɔːn] adj überzogen
overdue [əʊvə'djuː] adj überfällig
overestimate [əʊvər'estɪmeɪt] vt überschätzen
overexpose [əʊvərɪks'pəʊz] vt (Foto) überbelichten
overflow [əʊvə'fləʊ] vi überlaufen
overhead ['əʊvəhed] adj (Aviat) ~ **locker** Gepäckfach nt; ~ **projector** n Overheadprojektor m; ~ **railway** Hochbahn f ▷ [əʊvə'hed] adv oben; **overhead**, (Brit) **overheads** n (Comm) allgemeine Geschäftskosten pl
overhear [əʊvə'hɪə°] irr vt zufällig mit anhören
overheat [əʊvə'hiːt] vi (engine) heiß laufen
overjoyed [əʊvə'dʒɔɪd] adj überglücklich (at über)
overland ['əʊvəlænd] adj Überland- ▷ [əʊvə'lænd] adv (travel) über Land
overlap [əʊvə'læp] vi (dates etc) sich überschneiden; (objects) sich teilweise decken

overload [əʊvə'ləʊd] vt
überladen

overlook [əʊvə'lʊk] vt (view from
above) überblicken; (not notice)
übersehen; (pardon) hinwegsehen
über +akk

overnight [əʊvə'naɪt] adj (jour-
ney, train) Nacht-; **~ bag**
Reisetasche f; **~ stay**
Übernachtung f ▷ adv über Nacht

overpass ['əʊvəpɑːs] n
Überführung f

overpay [əʊvə'peɪ] vt
überbezahlen

overrule [əʊvə'ruːl] vt verwerfen; (decision) aufheben

overseas [əʊvə'siːz] adj Über-
see-; ausländisch; (fam) Auslands-
▷ adv (go) nach Übersee; (live,
work) in Übersee

oversee [əʊvə'siː] irr vt
beaufsichtigen

overshadow [əʊvə'ʃædəʊ] vt
überschatten

overshoot [əʊvə'ʃuːt] irr vt
(runway) hinausschießen über
+akk; (turning) vorbeifahren
+dat

oversight ['əʊvəsaɪt] n Versehen nt

oversimplify [əʊvə'sɪmplɪfaɪ]
vt zu sehr vereinfachen

oversleep [əʊvə'sliːp] irr vi
verschlafen

overtake [əʊvə'teɪk] irr vt, vi
überholen

overtime ['əʊvətaɪm] n Überstunden pl

overturn [əʊvə'tɜːn] vt, vi
umkippen

overweight [əʊvə'weɪt] adj: **to
be ~** Übergewicht haben

overwhelm [əʊvə'welm] vt
überwältigen; **overwhelming** adj
überwältigend

overwork [əʊvə'wɜːk] n
Überarbeitung f ▷ vi sich

überarbeiten; **overworked** adj
überarbeitet

owe [əʊ] vt schulden; **to ~ sth to
sb** (money) jdm etw schulden;
(favour etc) jdm etw verdanken;
how much do I ~ you? was bin ich
dir/Ihnen schuldig?; **owing to**
prep wegen +gen

owl [aʊl] n Eule f

own [əʊn] vt besitzen ▷ adj eigen;
on one's ~ allein; **he has a flat of
his ~** er hat eine eigene Wohung;
own up vi: **to ~ to sth** etw
zugeben; **owner** n Besitzer(in)
m(f); (of business) Inhaber(in) m(f);
ownership n Besitz m; **under
new ~** unter neuer Leitung

ox [ɒks] (pl **oxen**) n Ochse m;
oxtail ['ɒksteɪl] n Ochsen-
schwanz m; **~ soup**
Ochsenschwanzsuppe f

oxygen ['ɒksɪdʒən] n Sauerstoff
m

oyster ['ɔɪstə°] n Auster f

oz abbr = **ounces** Unzen pl

Oz ['ɒz] n (fam) Australien nt

ozone ['əʊzəʊn] n Ozon nt;
~ layer Ozonschicht f

p

p *abbr* = **page** S.; *abbr* = **penny, pence**

p.a. *abbr* = **per annum**

pace [peɪs] *n* (*speed*) Tempo *nt*; (*step*) Schritt *m*; **pacemaker** *n* (*Med*) Schrittmacher *m*

Pacific [pəˈsɪfɪk] *n*: **the ~ (Ocean)** der Pazifik; **Pacific Standard Time** *n* pazifische Zeit

pacifier [ˈpæsɪfaɪə] *n* (*US: for baby*) Schnuller *m*

pack [pæk] *n* (*of cards*) Spiel *nt*; (*esp US: of cigarettes*) Schachtel *f*; (*gang*) Bande *f*; (*US: backpack*) Rucksack *m* ▷ *vt* (*case*) packen; (*clothes*) einpacken ▷ *vi* (*for holiday*) packen; **pack in** *vt* (*Brit fam: job*) hinschmeißen; **package** [ˈpækɪdʒ] *n* (*a. Inform, fig*) Paket *nt*; **package deal** *n* Pauschalangebot *nt*; **package holiday, package tour** *n* Pauschalreise *f*; **packaging** *n* (*material*) Verpackung *f*; **packed lunch** *n* (*Brit*) Lunchpaket *nt*; **packet** *n* Päckchen *nt*; (*of cigarettes*) Schachtel *f*

pad [pæd] *n* (*of paper*) Schreibblock *m*; (*padding*) Polster *nt*; **padded envelope** *n* wattierter Umschlag; **padding** *n* (*material*) Polsterung *f*

paddle [ˈpædl] *n* (*for boat*) Paddel *nt* ▷ *vi* (*in boat*) paddeln; **paddling pool** *n* (*Brit*) Planschbecken *nt*

padlock [ˈpædlɒk] *n* Vorhängeschloss *nt*

page [peɪdʒ] *n* (*of book etc*) Seite *f*

pager [ˈpeɪdʒə] *n* Piepser *m*

paid [peɪd] *pt, pp of* **pay** ▷ *adj* bezahlt

pain [peɪn] *n* Schmerz *m*; **to be in ~** Schmerzen haben; **she's a (real) ~** sie nervt; **painful** *adj* (*physically*) schmerzhaft; (*embarrassing*) peinlich; **painkiller** *n* schmerzstillendes Mittel

painstaking *adj* sorgfältig

paint [peɪnt] *n* Farbe *f* ▷ *vt* anstreichen; (*picture*) malen; **paintbrush** *n* Pinsel *m*; **painter** *n* Maler(in) *m(f)*; **painting** *n* (*picture*) Bild *nt*, Gemälde *nt*

pair [peə°] *n* Paar *nt*; **a ~ of shoes** ein Paar Schuhe; **a ~ of scissors** eine Schere; **a ~ of trousers** eine Hose

pajamas [pəˈdʒɑːməz] *npl* (*US*) Schlafanzug *m*

Pakistan [ˌpɑːkɪˈstɑːn] *n* Pakistan *nt*

pal [pæl] *n* (*fam*) Kumpel *m*

palace [ˈpæləs] *n* Palast *m*

pale [peɪl] *adj* (*face*) blass, bleich; (*colour*) hell

palm [pɑːm] (*of hand*) Handfläche *f*; **~ (tree)** Palme *f*; **palmtop** (*computer*) *n* Palmtop(computer) *m*

pamper ['pæmpə'] vt
verhätscheln

pan [pæn] n (saucepan) Topf m;
(frying pan) Pfanne f; **pancake**
['pænkeɪk] n Pfannkuchen m;
Pancake Day n (Brit)
Fastnachtsdienstag m

pandemic [pæn'demɪk] n Pandemie f

panel ['pænl] n (of wood) Tafel f;
(in discussion) Diskussionsteil-
nehmer pl; (in jury) Jurymitglieder
pl

panic ['pænɪk] n Panik f ⊳ vi in
Panik geraten; **panicky** ['pænɪkɪ]
adj panisch

pansy ['pænzɪ] n (flower)
Stiefmütterchen nt

panties ['pæntɪz] npl (Damen)-
slip m

pantomime ['pæntəmaɪm] n
(Brit) um die Weihnachtszeit
aufgeführte Märchenkomödie

pants [pænts] npl Unterhose f;
(esp US: trousers) Hose f

pantyhose ['pæntɪhəʊz] npl
(US) Strumpfhose f; **panty-liner** n
Slipeinlage f

paper ['peɪpə'] n Papier nt;
(newspaper) Zeitung f; (exam)
Klausur f; (for reading at conference)
Referat nt; **~s** pl (identity papers)
Papiere pl; **~ bag** Papiertüte f;
~ cup Pappbecher m ⊳ vt (wall)
tapezieren; **paperback** n
Taschenbuch nt; **paper clip** n
Büroklammer f; **paper feed** n (of
printer) Papiereinzug m; **paper
round : to do a ~** Zeitungen
austragen; **paperwork** n
Schreibarbeit f

parachute ['pærəʃuːt] n Fallschirm m ⊳ vi abspringen

paracetamol [pærə'siːtəmɒl] n
(tablet) Paracetamoltablette
f

parade [pə'reɪd] n (procession)

Umzug m; (Mil) Parade f ⊳ vi
vorbeimarschieren

paradise ['pærədaɪs] n Paradies
nt

paragliding ['pærəglaɪdɪŋ] n
Gleitschirmfliegen nt

paragraph ['pærəgrɑːf] n Absatz
m

parallel ['pærəlel] adj parallel
⊳ n (Math, fig) Parallele f

paralyze ['pærəlaɪz] vt lähmen;
(fig) lahmlegen

paranoid ['pærənɔɪd] adj
paranoid

paraphrase ['pærəfreɪz] vt
umschreiben; (sth spoken) anders
ausdrücken

parasailing ['pærəseɪlɪŋ] n
Parasailing n

parasol ['pærəsɒl] n Sonnenschirm m

parcel ['pɑːsl] n Paket nt

pardon ['pɑːdn] n (Jur)
Begnadigung f; **~ me/I beg your
~** verzeih/verzeihen Sie bitte;
(objection) aber ich bitte dich/Sie; **I
beg your ~?/~ me?** wie bitte?

parent ['pɛərənt] n Elternteil m;
~s pl Eltern pl; **~-in-law** pl
Schwiegereltern pl; **parental**
[pə'rɛntl] adj elterlich, Eltern-

parish ['pærɪʃ] n Gemeinde f

park [pɑːk] n Park m ⊳ vt, vi
parken; **parking** n Parken nt; **"no
~"**, **"Parken verboten"**; **parking
brake** n (US) Handbremse f;
parking disc n Parkscheibe f;
parking fine n Geldbuße f für
falsches Parken; **parking lights**
npl (US) Standlicht nt; **parking lot**
n (US) Parkplatz m; **parking meter**
n Parkuhr f; **parking place**,
parking space n Parkplatz m;
parking ticket n Strafzettel m

parliament ['pɑːləmənt] n Parlament nt

parrot ['pærət] n Papagei m

parsley ['pɑːslɪ] n Petersilie f

parsnip ['pɑːsnɪp] n Pastinake f (längliches, weißes Wurzelgemüse)

part [pɑːt] n Teil m; (of machine) Teil nt; (Theat) Rolle f; (US: in hair) Scheitel m; **to take ~** teilnehmen (in an +dat); **for the most ~** zum größten Teil ▷ adj Teil- ▷ vt (separate) trennen; (hair) scheiteln ▷ vi (people) sich trennen

partial ['pɑːʃəl] adj (incomplete) teilweise, Teil-

participant [pɑːˈtɪsɪpənt] n Teilnehmer(in) m(f); **participate** [pɑːˈtɪsɪpeɪt] vi teilnehmen (in an +dat)

particular [pəˈtɪkjʊləˈ] adj (specific) bestimmt; (exact) genau; (fussy) eigen; **in ~** insbesondere ▷ n **~s** pl (details) Einzelheiten pl; (about person) Personalien pl; **particularly** adv besonders

parting ['pɑːtɪŋ] n (farewell) Abschied m; (Brit: in hair) Scheitel m

partly ['pɑːtlɪ] adv teilweise

partner ['pɑːtnəˈ] n Partner(in) m(f); **partnership** n Partnerschaft f

partridge ['pɑːtrɪdʒ] n Rebhuhn nt

part-time ['pɑːˈtaɪm] adj Teilzeit- ▷ **to work ~** Teilzeit arbeiten

party ['pɑːtɪ] n (celebration) Party f; (Pol, Jur) Partei f; (group) Gruppe f ▷ vi feiern

pass [pɑːs] vt (on foot) vorbeigehen an +dat; (in car etc) vorbeifahren an +dat; (time) verbringen; (exam) bestehen; (law) verabschieden; **to ~ sth to sb**, **to ~ sb sth** jdm etw reichen; **to ~ the ball to sb** jdm den Ball zuspielen ▷ vi (on foot) vorbeigehen; (in car etc) vorbeifahren; (years) vergehen; (in exam) bestehen ▷ n (document) Ausweis m; (Sport) Pass m; **pass**

away vi (die) verscheiden; **pass by** vi (on foot) vorbeigehen; (in car etc) vorbeifahren ▷ vt (on foot) vorbeigehen an +dat; (in car etc) vorbeifahren an +dat; **pass on** vt weitergeben (to an +akk); (disease) übertragen (to auf +akk); **pass out** vi (faint) ohnmächtig werden; **pass round** vt herumreichen

passage ['pæsɪdʒ] n (corridor) Gang m; (in book, music) Passage f; **passageway** n Durchgang m

passenger ['pæsɪndʒəˈ] n Passagier(in) m(f); (on bus) Fahrgast m; (on train) Reisende(r) mf; (in car) Mitfahrer(in) m(f)

passer-by ['pɑːsəˈbaɪ] (pl **passers-by**) n Passant(in) m(f)

passion ['pæʃən] n Leidenschaft f; **passionate** ['pæʃənɪt] adj leidenschaftlich; **passion fruit** n Passionsfrucht f

passive ['pæsɪv] adj passiv; **~ smoking** Passivrauchen nt ▷ n: **~ (voice)** (Ling) Passiv nt

passport ['pɑːspɔːt] n (Reise)pass m; **passport control** n Passkontrolle f

password ['pɑːswɜːd] n (Inform) Passwort nt

past [pɑːst] n Vergangenheit f ▷ adv (by) vorbei; **it's five ~** es ist fünf nach ▷ adj (years) vergangen; (president etc) ehemalig; **in the ~ two months** in den letzten zwei Monaten ▷ prep (telling time) nach; **half ~ 10** halb 11; **to go ~ sth** an etw dat vorbeigehen/-fahren

pasta ['pæstə] n Nudeln pl

paste [peɪst] vt (stick) kleben; (Inform) einfügen ▷ n (glue) Kleister m

pastime ['pɑːstaɪm] n Zeitvertreib m

pastry ['peɪstrɪ] n Teig m; (cake) Stückchen

pasty ['pæstɪ] n (Brit) Pastete f

patch [pætʃ] n (area) Fleck m; (for mending) Flicken ▷ vt flicken; **patchy** adj (uneven) ungleichmäßig

pâté ['pæteɪ] n Pastete f

paternal [pə'tɜːnl] adj väterlich; **~ grandmother** Großmutter f väterlicherseits; **paternity leave** [pə'tɜːnɪtɪːv] n Elternzeit f (des Vaters)

path [pɑːθ] n (a. Inform) Pfad m; (a. fig) Weg m

pathetic [pə'θetɪk] adj (bad) kläglich, erbärmlich; **it's ~** es ist zum Heulen

patience ['peɪʃəns] n Geduld f; (Brit Cards) Patience f; **patient** adj geduldig ▷ n Patient(in) m(f)

patio ['pætɪəʊ] n Terrasse f

patriotic [pætrɪ'ɒtɪk] adj patriotisch

patrol car [pə'trəʊlkɑː°] n Streifenwagen m; **patrolman** (pl **-men**) n (US) Streifenpolizist m

patron ['peɪtrən] n (sponsor) Förderer m, Förderin f; (in shop) Kunde m, Kundin f

patronize ['pætrənaɪz] vt (treat condescendingly) von oben herab behandeln; **patronizing** adj (attitude) herablassend

pattern ['pætən] n Muster nt

pause [pɔːz] n Pause f ▷ vi (speaker) innehalten

pavement n (Brit) Bürgersteig m; (US) Pflaster nt

pay [peɪ] (**paid, paid**) vt bezahlen; **he paid (me) £20 for it** er hat (mir) 20 Pfund dafür gezahlt; **to ~ attention** Acht geben (to auf +akk); **to ~ sb a visit** jdn besuchen ▷ vi zahlen; (be profitable) sich bezahlt machen; **to ~ for sth** etw bezahlen ▷ n Bezahlung f, Lohn m; **pay back** vt (money) zurückzahlen; **pay in** vt (into account) einzahlen; **payable**

adj zahlbar; (due) fällig; **payday** n Zahltag m; **payee** [peɪ'iː] n Zahlungsempfänger(in) m(f); **payment** n Bezahlung f; (money) Zahlung f; **pay-per-view** adj Pay-per-View-; **pay phone** n Münzfernsprecher m; **pay TV** n Pay-TV nt

PC abbr = **personal computer** PC m; abbr = **politically correct** politisch korrekt

PDA abbr = **personal digital assistant** PDA m

PE abbr = **physical education** (school) Sport m

pea [piː] n Erbse f

peace [piːs] n Frieden m; **peaceful** adj friedlich

peach [piːtʃ] n Pfirsich m

peacock ['piːkɒk] n Pfau m

peak [piːk] n (of mountain) Gipfel m; (fig) Höhepunkt m; **peak period** n Stoßzeit f; (season) Hochsaison

peanut ['piːnʌt] n Erdnuss f; **peanut butter** n Erdnussbutter f

pear [peə°] n Birne f

pearl [pɜːl] n Perle f

pebble ['pebl] n Kiesel m

pecan ['piːkæn] n Pekannuss f

peck [pek] vt, vi picken; **peckish** adj (Brit fam) ein bisschen hungrig

peculiar [pɪ'kjuːlɪə°] adj (odd) seltsam; **~ to** charakteristisch für; **peculiarity** [pɪkjʊlɪ'ærɪtɪ] n (singular quality) Besonderheit f; (strangeness) Eigenartigkeit f

pedal ['pedl] n Pedal nt

pedestrian [pɪ'destrɪən] n Fußgänger(in) m(f); **pedestrian crossing** n Fußgängerüberweg m

pee [piː] vi (fam) pinkeln

peel [piːl] n Schale f ▷ vt schälen ▷ vi (paint etc) abblättern; (skin etc) sich schälen

peer [pɪə°] n Gleichaltrige(r) mf ▷ vi starren

peg [peg] n (for coat etc) Haken m; (for tent) Hering m; **(clothes)** ~ (Wäsche)klammer f

pelvis ['pelvɪs] n Becken nt

pen [pen] n (ball-point) Kuli m, Kugelschreiber; (fountain ~) Füller m

penalize ['pi:nəlaɪz] vt (punish) bestrafen; **penalty** ['penltɪ] n (punishment) Strafe f; (in football) Elfmeter m

pence [pens] pl of **penny**

pencil ['pensl] n Bleistift m; **pencil sharpener** n (Bleistift)spitzer m

penetrate ['penɪtreɪt] vt durchdringen; (enter into) eindringen in +akk

penfriend ['penfrend] n Brieffreund(in) m(f)

penguin ['peŋgwɪn] n Pinguin m

penicillin [penɪ'sɪlɪn] n Penizillin nt

peninsula [pɪ'nɪnsjʊlə] n Halbinsel f

penis ['pi:nɪs] n Penis m

penknife ['pennaɪf] n (pl **penknives**) Taschenmesser nt

penny ['penɪ] n (pl **pence** o **pennies**) n (Brit) Penny m; (US) Centstück nt

pension ['penʃən] n Rente f; (for civil servants, executives etc) Pension f; **pensioner** n Rentner(in) m(f); **pension plan, pension scheme** n Rentenversicherung f

penultimate [pɪ'nʌltɪmət] adj vorletzte(r, s)

people ['pi:pl] npl (persons) Leute pl; (von Staat) Volk nt; (inhabitants) Bevölkerung f; **people carrier** n Minivan m

pepper ['pepə°] n Pfeffer m; (vegetable) Paprika m; **peppermint** n (sweet) Pfefferminz nt

per [pɜ:°] prep pro; ~ **annum** pro Jahr; ~ **cent** Prozent nt

percentage [pə'sentɪdʒ] n Prozentsatz m

perceptible [pə'septəbl] adj wahrnehmbar

percolator ['pɜ:kəleɪtə°] n Kaffeemaschine f

percussion [pə'kʌʃən] n (Mus) Schlagzeug nt

perfect ['pɜ:fɪkt] adj perfekt; (utter) völlig ▷ [pə'fekt] vt vervollkommnen; **perfectly** adv perfekt; (utterly) völlig

perform [pə'fɔ:m] vt (task) ausführen; (play) aufführen; (Med: operation) durchführen ▷ vi (Theat) auftreten; **performance** n (show) Vorstellung f; (efficiency) Leistung f

perfume ['pɜ:fju:m] n Duft m; (substance) Parfüm nt

perhaps [pə'hæps] adv vielleicht

period ['pɪərɪəd] n (length of time) Zeit f; (in history) Zeitalter nt; (school) Stunde f; (Med) Periode f; (US: full stop) Punkt m; **for a ~ of three years** für einen Zeitraum von drei Jahren; **periodical** [pɪərɪ'ɒdɪkəl] n Zeitschrift f

peripheral [pə'rɪfərəl] n (Inform) Peripheriegerät nt

perjury ['pɜ:dʒərɪ] n Meineid m

perm [pɜ:m] n Dauerwelle f

permanent, permanently ['pɜ:mənənt, -lɪ] adj, adv ständig

permission [pə'mɪʃən] n Erlaubnis f; **permit** ['pɜ:mɪt] n Genehmigung f ▷ [pə'mɪt] vt erlauben, zulassen; **to ~ sb to do sth** jdm erlauben, etw zu tun

persecute ['pɜ:sɪkju:t] vt verfolgen

perseverance [pɜ:sɪ'vɪərəns] n Ausdauer f

persist [pə'sɪst] vi (in belief etc) bleiben (in bei); (rain, smell) andauern; **persistent** adj beharrlich

P

person ['pɜːsn] n Mensch m; (in official context) Person f; **in ~** persönlich; **personal** adj persönlich; (private) privat; **personality** [pɜːsə'nælɪtɪ] n Persönlichkeit f; **personal organizer** n Organizer m; **personal stereo** (pl -s) n Walkman® m; **personnel** [pɜːsə'nel] n Personal nt

perspective [pə'spektɪv] n Perspektive f

persuade [pə'sweɪd] vt überreden; (convince) überzeugen; **persuasive** [pə'sweɪsɪv] adj überzeugend

perverse [pə'vɜːs] adj eigensinnig; abwegig; **pervert** ['pɜːvɜːt] n Perverse(r) mf ▷ [pə'vɜːt] vt (morally) verderben; **perverted** [pə'vɜːtɪd] adj pervers

pessimist ['pesɪmɪst] n Pessimist(in) m(f); **pessimistic** [pesɪ'mɪstɪk] adj pessimistisch

pest [pest] n (insect) Schädling m; (fig: person) Nervensäge f; (thing) Plage f; **pester** ['pestə°] vt plagen; **pesticide** ['pestɪsaɪd] n Schädlingsbekämpfungsmittel nt

pet [pet] n (animal) Haustier nt; (person) Liebling m

petal ['petl] n Blütenblatt nt

petition [pə'tɪʃən] n Petition f

petrol ['petrəl] n (Brit) Benzin nt; **petrol pump** n (at garage) Zapfsäule f; **petrol station** n Tankstelle f; **petrol tank** n Benzintank m

pharmacy ['fɑːməsɪ] n (shop) Apotheke f; (science) Pharmazie f

phase [feɪz] n Phase f

PhD abbr = **Doctor of Philosophy** Dr. phil; (dissertation) Doktorarbeit f; **to do one's ~** promovieren

pheasant ['feznt] n Fasan m

phenomenon [fɪ'nɒmɪnən] (pl **phenomena**) n Phänomen nt

Philippines ['fɪlɪpiːnz] npl Philippinen pl

philosophical [fɪlə'sɒfɪkəl] adj philosophisch; (fig) gelassen; **philosophy** [fɪ'lɒsəfɪ] n Philosophie f

phone [fəun] n Telefon nt ▷ vt, vi anrufen; **phone book** n Telefonbuch nt; **phone bill** n Telefonrechnung f; **phone booth**, **phone box** (Brit) n Telefonzelle f; **phonecall** n Telefonanruf m; **phonecard** n Telefonkarte f; **phone-in** n Rundfunkprogramm, bei dem Hörer anrufen können; **phone number** n Telefonnummer f

photo ['fəutəu] (pl -s) n Foto nt; **photo booth** n Fotoautomat m; **photocopier** ['fəutəu'kɒpɪə°] n Kopiergerät nt; **photocopy** ['fəutəukɒpɪ] n Fotokopie f ▷ vt fotokopieren; **photograph** ['fəutəgrɑːf] n Fotografie f, Aufnahme f ▷ vt fotografieren; **photographer** [fə'tɒgrəfə°] n Fotograf(in) m(f); **photography** [fə'tɒgrəfɪ] n Fotografie f

phrase [freɪz] n (expression) Redewendung f, Ausdruck m; . **phrase book** n Sprachführer m

physical ['fɪzɪkəl] adj (bodily) körperlich, physisch ▷ n ärztliche Untersuchung; **physically** adv (bodily) körperlich, physisch; **~ handicapped** körperbehindert

physics ['fɪzɪks] nsing Physik f

physiotherapy [fɪzɪə'θerəpɪ] n Physiotherapie f

physique [fɪ'ziːk] n Körperbau m

piano ['pjɑːnəu] (pl -s) n Klavier nt

pick [pɪk] vt (flowers, fruit) pflücken; (choose) auswählen; (team) aufstellen; **pick out** vt auswählen; **pick up** vt (lift up) aufheben; (collect) abholen; (learn) lernen

pickle ['pɪkl] n (food) (Mixed) Pickles pl ▷ vt einlegen

pickpocket ['pɪkpɒkɪt] n Taschendieb(in) m(f)

picnic ['pɪknɪk] n Picknick nt

picture ['pɪktʃə°] n Bild nt; **to go to the ~s** (Brit) ins Kino gehen ▷ vt (visualize) sich vorstellen; **picture book** n Bilderbuch nt; **picturesque** [pɪktʃə'rɛsk] adj malerisch

pie [paɪ] n (meat) Pastete f; (fruit) Kuchen m

piece [piːs] n Stück nt; (part) Teil nt; (in chess) Figur f; (in draughts) Stein m; **a ~ of cake** ein Stück Kuchen; **to fall to ~s** auseinanderfallen

pier [pɪə°] n Pier m

pierce [pɪəs] vt durchstechen, durchbohren; (cold, sound) durchdringen; **pierced** adj (part of body) gepierct; **piercing** adj durchdringend

pig [pɪg] n Schwein nt

pigeon ['pɪdʒən] n Taube f; **pigeonhole** n (compartment) Ablegefach nt

piggy ['pɪgɪ] adj (fam) verfressen; **pigheaded** ['pɪg'hɛdɪd] adj dickköpfig; **piglet** ['pɪglət] n Ferkel nt; **pigsty** ['pɪgstaɪ] n Schweinestall m; **pigtail** ['pɪgteɪl] n Zopf m

pile [paɪl] n (heap) Haufen m; (one on top of another) Stapel m; **pile up** vi (accumulate) sich anhäufen

piles [paɪlz] npl Hämorr(ho)iden pl

pile-up ['paɪlʌp] n (Auto) Massenkarambolage f

pilgrim ['pɪlgrɪm] n Pilger(in) m(f)

pill [pɪl] n Tablette f; **the ~** die (Antibaby)pille; **to be on the ~** die Pille nehmen

pillar ['pɪlə°] n Pfeiler m

pillow ['pɪləʊ] n (Kopf)kissen nt; **pillowcase** n (Kopf)kissenbezug m

pilot ['paɪlət] n (Aviat) Pilot(in) m(f)

pimple ['pɪmpl] n Pickel m

pin [pɪn] n (for fixing) Nadel f; (in sewing) Stecknadel f; (Tech) Stift m; **I've got ~s and needles in my leg** mein Bein ist mir eingeschlafen ▷ vt (fix with ~) heften (to an +akk)

PIN [pɪn] acr = **personal identification number** **~ (number)** PIN f, Geheimzahl f

pinch [pɪntʃ] n (of salt) Prise f ▷ vt zwicken; (fam: steal) klauen ▷ vi (shoe) drücken

pine [paɪn] n Kiefer f

pineapple ['paɪnæpl] n Ananas f

pink [pɪŋk] adj rosa

pinstripe(d) ['pɪnstraɪp(t)] adj Nadelstreifen-

pint [paɪnt] n Pint nt (Brit: 0,57 l, US: 0,473l); (Brit: glass of beer) Bier nt

pious ['paɪəs] adj fromm

pip [pɪp] n (of fruit) Kern m

pipe [paɪp] n (for smoking) Pfeife f; (for water, gas) Rohrleitung f

pirate ['paɪərɪt] n Pirat(in) m(f); **pirated copy** n Raubkopie f

Pisces ['paɪsiːz] nsing (Astr) Fische pl; **she's a ~** sie ist Fisch

piss [pɪs] vi (vulg) pissen ▷ n (vulg) Pisse f; **to take the ~ out of sb** jdn verarschen; **piss off** vi (vulg) sich verpissen; **~!** verpiss dich!; **pissed** adj (Brit fam: drunk) sturzbesoffen; (US fam: annoyed) stocksauer

pistachio [pɪ'stɑːʃɪəʊ] n (pl **-s**) Pistazie f

piste [piːst] n (Ski) Piste f

pistol ['pɪstl] n Pistole f

pit [pɪt] n (hole) Grube f; (coalmine) Zeche f; **the ~s** (motor racing) die Box; **to be the ~s** (fam) grottenschlecht sein

pitch [pɪtʃ] n (Sport) Spielfeld nt; (Mus: of instrument) Tonlage f; (of voice) Stimmlage f ▷ vt (tent)

aufschlagen; (throw) werfen;
pitch-black adj pechschwarz
pitcher ['pɪtʃə*] n (US: jug) Krug m
pitiful ['pɪtɪful] adj (contemptible)
jämmerlich
pitta bread ['pɪtə] n Pittabrot nt
pity ['pɪtɪ] n Mitleid nt; **what a**
~ wie schade; **it's a** ~ es ist schade
▷ vt Mitleid haben mit
pizza ['piːtsə] n Pizza f
place [pleɪs] n m (spot, in text)
Stelle f; (town etc) Ort; (house) Haus
nt; (position, seat, on course) Platz m;
~ **of birth** Geburtsort m; **at my**
~ bei mir; **in third** ~ auf dem dritten
Platz; **to three decimal** ~s bis auf
drei Stellen nach dem Komma; **out
of** ~ nicht an der richtigen Stelle;
(fig: remark) unangebracht; **in** ~ **of**
anstelle von; **in the first** ~ (firstly)
erstens; (immediately) gleich; (in any
case) überhaupt ▷ vt (put) stellen,
setzen; (lay flat) legen; (advertisement) setzen (in in +akk); (Comm:
order) aufgeben; **place mat** n Set nt
plague [pleɪg] n Pest f
plaice [pleɪs] n Scholle f
plain [pleɪn] adj (clear) klar,
deutlich; (simple) einfach; (not
beautiful) unattraktiv; (yoghurt)
Natur-; (Brit: chocolate)
(Zart)bitter- ▷ n Ebene f; **plainly**
adv (frankly) offen; (simply) einfach;
(obviously) eindeutig
plait [plæt] n Zopf m ▷ vt
flechten
plan [plæn] n Plan m; (for essay
etc) Konzept nt ▷ vt planen; **to**
~ **to do sth, to** ~ **on doing sth**
vorhaben, etw zu tun ▷ vi planen
plane [pleɪn] n (aircraft)
Flugzeug nt; (tool) Hobel m
planet ['plænɪt] n Planet m
plank [plæŋk] n Brett nt
plant [plɑːnt] n Pflanze f;
(equipment) Maschinen pl; (factory)
Werk nt ▷ vt (tree etc) pflanzen;

plantation [plæn'teɪʃən] n Plan-
tage f
plaque [plæk] n Gedenktafel f;
(on teeth) Zahnbelag m
plaster ['plɑːstə*] n (Brit Med:
sticking ~) Pflaster nt; (on wall)
Verputz m; **to have one's arm in**
~ den Arm in Gips haben
plastered ['plɑːstəd] adj (fam)
besoffen; **to get** (absolutely)
~ sich besaufen
plastic ['plæstɪk] n Kunststoff m,
Plastik nt ▷ adj Plastik-; **to pay with**
~ mit Kreditkarte
bezahlen ▷ adj Plastik-; **plastic
bag** n Plastiktüte f; **plastic
surgery** n plastische Chirurgie f
plate [pleɪt] n (for food) Teller m;
(flat sheet) Platte f; (plaque) Schild
nt
platform ['plætfɔːm] n (Rail)
Bahnsteig m; (at meeting) Podium
nt
platinum ['plætɪnəm] n Platin nt
play [pleɪ] n Spiel n; (Theat)
(Theater)stück nt ▷ vt spielen
gegen; **to** ~ **the piano** Klavier
spielen; **to** ~ **a part in** (fig) eine
Rolle spielen bei ▷ vi spielen;
play at vt: **what are you ~ing at?**
was soll das?; **play back** vt
abspielen; **play down** vt
herunterspielen
playacting n Schauspielerei f;
playback n Wiedergabe f; **player**
n Spieler(in) m(f); **playful** adj
(person) verspielt; (remark)
scherzhaft; **playground** n
Spielplatz m; (in school) Schulhof m;
playgroup n Spielgruppe f;
playing card n Spielkarte f;
playing field n Sportplatz m;
playmate n Spielkamerad(in)
m(f); **playwright** n
Dramatiker(in) m(f)
plc abbr = **public limited company**
AG f

plea [pliː] n Bitte f (for um)

plead [pliːd] vi dringend bitten (with sb jdn); (Jur) to ~ guilty sich schuldig bekennen

pleasant, pleasantly ['pleznt, -lı] adj, adv angenehm

please [pliːz] adv bitte; more tea? - yes, ~ noch Tee? - ja, bitte ▷ vt (be agreeable to) gefallen +dat; ~ yourself wie du willst/Sie wollen; **pleased** adj zufrieden; (glad) erfreut; ~ to meet you freut mich, angenehm; **pleasing** adj erfreulich; **pleasure** ['pleʒəʳ] n Vergnügen nt, Freude f; **it's a ~** gern geschehen

pledge [pledʒ] n Versprechen nt ▷ vt versprechen

plenty ['plentı] n: ~ of eine Menge, viel(e); to be ~ genug sein, reichen; **I've got ~** habe mehr als genug ▷ adv (US fam) ganz schön

pliable ['plaıəbl] adj biegsam

pliers ['plaıəz] npl (Kombi)zange f

plimsoll ['plımsəl] n (Brit) Turnschuh m

plonk [plɒŋk] n (Brit fam: wine) billiger Wein ▷ vt: to ~ sth (down) etw hinknallen

plot [plɒt] n (of story) Handlung f; (conspiracy) Komplott nt; (of land) Stück n Land, Grundstück nt ▷ vi ein Komplott schmieden

plough, plow (US) [plaυ] n Pflug m ▷ vt, vi (Agr) pflügen; **ploughman's lunch** n (Brit) in einer Kneipe serviertes Gericht aus Käse, Brot, Mixed Pickles etc

pluck [plʌk] vt (eyebrows, guitar) zupfen; (chicken) rupfen; **pluck up** vt: to ~ (one's) courage Mut aufbringen

plug [plʌg] n (for sink, bath) Stöpsel m; (Elec) Stecker m; (Auto) (Zünd)kerze f; (fam: publicity)

Schleichwerbung f ▷ vt (fam: advertise) Reklame machen für; **plug in** vt anschließen

plum [plʌm] n Pflaume f ▷ adj (fam: job etc) Super-

plumber ['plʌməʳ] n Klempner(in) m(f); **plumbing** ['plʌmıŋ] n (fittings) Leitungen pl; (craft) Installieren nt

plump [plʌmp] adj rundlich

plunge [plʌndʒ] vt (knife) stoßen; (into water) tauchen ▷ vi stürzen; (into water) tauchen

plural ['plυərəl] n Plural m

plus [plʌs] prep plus; (as well as) und ▷ adj Plus-; **20 ~** mehr als 20 ▷ n (fig) Plus nt

plywood ['plaıwυd] n Sperrholz nt

pm abbr = **post meridiem; at 3 ~** um 3 Uhr nachmittags; **at 8 ~** um 8 Uhr abends

pneumonia [njuːˈməυnıə] n Lungenentzündung f

poached ['pəυtʃt] adj (egg) pochiert, verloren

PO Box n abbr = **post office box** Postfach m

pocket ['pɒkıt] n Tasche f ▷ vt (put in ~) einstecken; **pocketbook** n (US: wallet) Brieftasche f; **pocket calculator** n Taschenrechner m; **pocket money** n Taschengeld nt

podcast ['pɒdkɑːst] n Podcast m

poem ['pəυəm] n Gedicht nt; **poet** ['pəυıt] n Dichter(in) m(f); **poetic** [pəυˈetık] adj poetisch; **poetry** ['pəυıtrı] n (art) Dichtung f; (poems) Gedichte pl

point [pɔınt] n Punkt m; (spot) Stelle f; (sharp tip) Spitze f; (moment) Zeitpunkt m; (purpose) Zweck m; (idea) Argument nt; (decimal) Dezimalstelle f; **~s pl** (Rail) Weiche f; **~ of view** Standpunkt m; **three ~ two** drei Komma zwei; **at some ~** irgendwann (mal); **to get**

to the ~ zur Sache kommen;
there's no ~ es hat keinen Sinn; **I
was on the ~ of leaving** ich wollte
gerade gehen ▷ vt *(gun etc)*
richten *(at auf +akk)*; **to ~ one's
finger at** mit dem Finger zeigen
auf +akk ▷ vi *(with finger etc)*
zeigen *(at, to auf +akk)*; **point out**
vt *(indicate)* aufzeigen; *(mention)*
hinweisen auf +akk; **pointed** adj
spitz; *(question)* gezielt; **pointer** n
(on dial) Zeiger m; *(tip)* Hinweis m;
pointless adj sinnlos

poison ['pɔɪzn] n Gift nt ▷ vt
vergiften; **poisonous** adj giftig

poke [pəʊk] vt *(with stick, finger)*
stoßen, stupsen; *(put)* stecken

Poland ['pəʊlənd] n Polen nt

polar ['pəʊlə°] adj Polar-, polar;
~ bear Eisbär m

pole [pəʊl] n Stange f; *(Geo, Elec)*
Pol m

Pole [pəʊl] n Pole m, Polin f

pole vault n Stabhochsprung m

police [pə'liːs] n Polizei f; **police
car** n Polizeiwagen m; **policeman**
(pl -men) n Polizist m; **police
station** n *(Polizei)*wache f;
policewoman *(pl -women)* n
Polizistin f

policy ['pɒlɪsɪ] n *(plan)* Politik f;
(principle) Grundsatz m; *(insurance
~)* *(Versicherungs)*police f

polio ['pəʊlɪəʊ] n Kinderlähmung f

polish ['pɒlɪʃ] n *(for furniture)*
Politur f; *(for floor)* Wachs nt; *(for
shoes)* Creme f; *(shine)* Glanz m;
(fig) Schliff m ▷ vt polieren;
(shoes) putzen; *(fig)* den letzten
Schliff geben +dat

Polish ['pəʊlɪʃ] adj polnisch ▷ n
Polnisch nt

polite [pə'laɪt] adj höflich;
politeness n Höflichkeit f

political, politically [pə'lɪtɪkəl, -lɪ]
adj, adv politisch; **~ly correct**
politisch korrekt; **politician**

politician n Politiker(in) m(f);
politics ['pɒlɪtɪks] nsing o pl
Politik f

poll [pəʊl] n *(election)* Wahl f;
(opinion ~) Umfrage f

pollen ['pɒlən] n Pollen m,
Blütenstaub m; **pollen count** n
Pollenflug m

polling station ['pəʊlɪŋsteɪʃən]
n Wahllokal nt

pollute [pə'luːt] vt verschmutzen; **pollution** [pə'luːʃən] n
Verschmutzung f

pompous ['pɒmpəs] adj aufge-
blasen; *(language)* geschwollen

pond [pɒnd] n Teich m

pony ['pəʊnɪ] n Pony nt;
ponytail n Pferdeschwanz m

poodle ['puːdl] n Pudel m

pool [puːl] n *(swimming ~)*
Schwimmbad nt; *(private)*
Swimmingpool m; *(of spilt liquid,
blood)* Lache f; *(game)* Poolbillard
nt ▷ vt *(money etc)*
zusammenlegen

poor [pɔː°] adj arm; *(not good)*
schlecht ▷ npl; **the ~** die Armen
pl; **poorly** adv *(badly)* schlecht
▷ adj *(Brit)* krank

pop [pɒp] n *(music)* Pop m; *(noise)*
Knall m ▷ vt *(put)* stecken;
(balloon) platzen lassen ▷ vi
(balloon) platzen; *(cork)* knallen; **to
~ in** *(person)* vorbeischauen; **pop
concert** n Popkonzert nt;
popcorn n Popcorn nt

Pope [pəʊp] n Papst m

pop group ['pɒpgruːp] n
Popgruppe f; **pop music** n
Popmusik f

poppy ['pɒpɪ] n Mohn m

Popsicle® ['pɒpsɪkl] n *(US)* Eis
nt am Stiel

pop star ['pɒpstɑː°] n Popstar m

popular ['pɒpjʊlə°] adj *(well-
liked)* beliebt *(with bei)*;
(widespread) weit verbreitet

population [pɒpjʊ'leɪʃən] n Bevölkerung f; (of town) Einwohner pl

porcelain ['pɔːslɪn] n Porzellan nt

porch [pɔːtʃ] n Vorbau m; (US: verandah) Veranda f

porcupine [pɔːkjʊpaɪn] n Stachelschwein nt

pork [pɔːk] n Schweinefleisch nt; **pork chop** n Schweinekotelett; **pork pie** n Schweinefleischpastete f

porn [pɔːn] n Porno m; **pornographic** [pɔːnə'græfɪk] adj pornografisch; **pornography** [pɔː'nɒgrəfɪ] n Pornografie f

porridge ['pɒrɪdʒ] n Haferbrei m

port [pɔːt] n (harbour) Hafen m; (town) Hafenstadt f; (Naut: left side) Backbord nt; (wine) Portwein m; (Inform) Anschluss m

portable ['pɔːtəbl] adj tragbar; (radio) Koffer-

portal ['pɔːtl] n (Inform) Portal nt

porter ['pɔːtə°] n Pförtner(in) m(f); (for luggage) Gepäckträger m

porthole ['pɔːthəʊl] n Bullauge nt

portion ['pɔːʃən] n Teil m; (of food) Portion f

portrait ['pɔːtrɪt] n Porträt nt

portray [pɔː'treɪ] vt darstellen

Portugal ['pɔːtʃʊgl] n Portugal nt; **Portuguese** [pɔːtʃʊ'giːz] adj portugiesisch ⊳ n Portugiese m, Portugiesin f; (language) Portugiesisch nt

pose [pəʊz] n Haltung f ⊳ vi posieren ⊳ vt (threat, problem) darstellen

posh [pɒʃ] adj (fam) piekfein

position [pə'zɪʃən] n Stellung f; (place) Position f, Lage f; (job) Stelle f; (opinion) Standpunkt m; **to be in a ~ to do sth** in der Lage sein, etw zu tun; **in third ~** auf dem dritten Platz ⊳ vt aufstellen; (Inform:

cursor) positionieren

positive ['pɒzɪtɪv] adj positiv; (convinced) sicher

possess [pə'zes] vt besitzen; **possession** [pə'zeʃən] n ~(s pl) Besitz m; **possessive** adj (person) besitzergreifend

possibility [pɒsə'bɪlɪtɪ] n Möglichkeit f; **possible** ['pɒsəbl] adj möglich; **if ~** wenn möglich; **as big/soon as ~** so groß/bald wie möglich; **possibly** adv (perhaps) vielleicht; **I've done all I ~ can** ich habe mein Möglichstes getan

post [pəʊst] n (mail) Post f; (pole) Pfosten m; (job) Stelle f ⊳ vt (letters) aufgeben; (on website) posten; **to keep sb ~ed** jdn auf dem Laufenden halten; **postage** ['pəʊstɪdʒ] n Porto nt; **~ and packing** Porto und Verpackung; **postal** adj Post-; (Brit) **~ order** Postanweisung f; **postbox** n Briefkasten m; **postcard** n Postkarte f; **postcode** n (Brit) Postleitzahl f

poster ['pəʊstə°] n Plakat nt, Poster nt

postgraduate [pəʊst'grædjuɪt] n jmd, der seine Studien auch nach dem ersten akademischen Grad weiterführt

postman ['pəʊstmən] (pl **-men**) n Briefträger m; **postmark** n Poststempel m

postmortem [pəʊst'mɔːtəm] n Autopsie f

post office ['pəʊstɒfɪs] n Post® f

postpone [pə'spəʊn] vt verschieben (till auf +akk)

posture ['pɒstʃə°] n Haltung f

pot [pɒt] n Topf m; (tea-, coffee ~) Kanne f; (fam: marijuana) Pot m ⊳ vt (plant) eintopfen

potato [pə'teɪtəʊ] (pl **-es**) n Kartoffel f; **potato chips** (US) npl Kartoffelchips pl; **potato peeler** n Kartoffelschäler m

potent ['pəʊtənt] *adj* stark

potential [pəʊ'tenʃəl] *adj*
potenziell ▷ *n* Potenzial *nt*;
potentially *adv* potenziell

pothole ['pɒthəʊl] *n* Höhle *f*; (in road) Schlagloch *nt*

potter about ['pɒtərəbaʊt] *vi*
herumhantieren

pottery ['pɒtərɪ] *n* (objects)
Töpferwaren *pl*

potty ['pɒtɪ] *adj* (Brit fam)
verrückt ▷ *n* Töpfchen *nt*

poultry ['pəʊltrɪ] *n* Geflügel
nt

pounce [paʊns] *vi*: **to ~ on** sich
stürzen auf +akk

pound [paʊnd] *n* (money) Pfund
nt; (weight) Pfund *nt* (0,454 kg); **a
~ of cherries** ein Pfund Kirschen;
ten-~ note Zehnpfundschein
m

pour [pɔ:ʳ] *vt* (liquid) gießen; (rice,
sugar etc) schütten; **to ~ sb sth**
(drink) jdm etw eingießen;
pouring *adj* (rain) strömend

poverty ['pɒvətɪ] *n* Armut *f*

powder ['paʊdəʳ] *n* Pulver *nt*;
(cosmetic) Puder *m*; **powdered
milk** *n* Milchpulver *nt*; **powder
room** *n* Damentoilette *f*

power ['paʊəʳ] *n* Macht *f*;
(ability) Fähigkeit *f*; (strength)
Stärke *f*; (Elec) Strom *m*; **to be in
~** an der Macht sein ▷ *vt*
betreiben, antreiben;
power-assisted steering *n*
Servolenkung *f*; **power cut** *n*
Stromausfall *m*; **powerful** *adj*
(politician etc) mächtig; (engine,
government) stark; (argument)
durchschlagend; **powerless** *adj*
machtlos; **power station** *n*
Kraftwerk *nt*

p&p *abbr* = **postage and packing**

PR *abbr* = **public relations** ▷ *abbr* =
proportional representation

practical, practically ['præktɪkəl,

-lɪ] *adj, adv* praktisch; **practice**
['præktɪs] *n* (training) Übung *f*;
(custom) Gewohnheit *f*; (doctor's,
lawyer's) Praxis *f*; **in ~** (in reality) in
der Praxis; **out of ~** außer Übung;
to put sth into ~ etw in die Praxis
umsetzen ▷ *vt, vi* (US) see
practise; practise ['præktɪs] *vt*
(instrument, movement) üben;
(profession) ausüben ▷ *vi* üben;
(doctor, lawyer) praktizieren

Prague [prɑːg] *n* Prag *nt*

praise [preɪz] *n* Lob *nt* ▷ *vt*
loben

pram [præm] *n* (Brit)
Kinderwagen *m*

prawn [prɔːn] *n* Garnele *f*,
Krabbe *f*; **prawn crackers** *pl*
Krabbenchips *pl*

pray [preɪ] *vi* beten; **to ~ for sth**
(fig) stark auf etw akk hoffen;
prayer ['preəʳ] *n* Gebet *nt*

pre- [priː] *pref* vor-, prä-

preach [priːtʃ] *vi* predigen

prearrange [priːə'reɪndʒ] *vt* im
Voraus vereinbaren

precaution [prɪ'kɔːʃən] *n* Vor-
sichtsmaßnahme *f*

precede [prɪ'siːd] *vt* vorausgehen +dat; **preceding** *adj*
vorhergehend

precinct ['priːsɪŋkt] *n* (Brit:
pedestrian ~) Fußgängerzone *f*;
(Brit: shopping ~) Einkaufsviertel *nt*;
(US: district) Bezirk *m*

precious ['preʃəs] *adj* kostbar;
~ stone Edelstein *m*

précis ['preɪsiː] *n* Zusammenfassung *f*

precise, precisely [prɪ'saɪs, -lɪ]
adj, adv genau

precondition [priːkən'dɪʃən] *n*
Vorbedingung *f*

predecessor ['priːdɪsesəʳ] *n*
Vorgänger(in) *m(f)*

predicament [prɪ'dɪkəmənt] *n*
missliche Lage

predict [prɪ'dɪkt] vt voraussagen; **predictable** adj vorhersehbar; (person) berechenbar

predominant [prɪ'dɒmɪnənt] adj vorherrschend; **predominantly** adv überwiegend

preface ['prefɪs] n Vorwort nt

prefer [prɪ'fɜː'] vt vorziehen (to dat), lieber mögen (to als); **to ~ to do sth** etw lieber tun; **preferably** ['prefrəblɪ] adv vorzugsweise, am liebsten; **preference** ['prefərəns] n (liking) Vorliebe f; **preferential** [prefə'renʃəl] adj: **to get ~ treatment** bevorzugt behandelt werden

prefix ['priːfɪks] n (US Tel) Vorwahl f

pregnancy ['pregnənsɪ] n Schwangerschaft f; **pregnant** ['pregnənt] adj schwanger; **two months ~** im zweiten Monat schwanger

prejudice ['predʒʊdɪs] n Vorurteil nt; **prejudiced** adj (person) voreingenommen

preliminary [prɪ'lɪmɪnərɪ] adj (measures) vorbereitend; (results) vorläufig; (remarks) einleitend

premature ['premətʃʊə] adj vorzeitig; (hasty) voreilig

premiere ['premɪɛə'] n Premiere f

premises ['premɪsɪz] npl (offices) Räumlichkeiten pl; (of factory, school) Gelände nt

premium-rate ['priːmɪəmreɪt] adj (Tel) zum Höchsttarif

preoccupied [priː'ɒkjʊpaɪd] adj: **to be ~ with sth** mit etw sehr beschäftigt sein

prepaid [priː'peɪd] adj vorausbezahlt; (envelope) frankiert

preparation [prepə'reɪʃən] n Vorbereitung f; **prepare** [prɪ'peə'] vt vorbereiten (for auf +akk); (food)

zubereiten; **to be ~d to do sth** bereit sein, etw zu tun ▷ vi sich vorbereiten (for auf +akk)

prerequisite [priː'rekwɪzɪt] n Voraussetzung f

prescribe [prɪ'skraɪb] vt vorschreiben; (Med) verschreiben; **prescription** [prɪ'skrɪpʃən] n Rezept nt

presence ['prezns] n Gegenwart f, **present** ['preznt] adj (in attendance) anwesend (at bei); (current) gegenwärtig; **~ tense** Gegenwart f, Präsens nt ▷ n Gegenwart f; (gift) Geschenk nt; **at ~** zurzeit ▷ [prɪ'zent] vt (TV, Radio) präsentieren; (problem) darstellen; (report etc) vorlegen; **to ~ sb with sth** jdm etw überreichen; **present-day** adj heutig; **presently** adv bald; (at present) zurzeit

preservative [prɪ'zɜːvətɪv] n Konservierungsmittel nt; **preserve** [prɪ'zɜːv] vt erhalten; (food) einmachen, konservieren

president ['prezɪdənt] n Präsident(in) m(f); **presidential** [prezɪ'denʃəl] adj Präsidenten-; (election) Präsidentschafts-

press [pres] n (newspapers, machine) Presse f ▷ vt (push) drücken; **to ~ a button** auf einen Knopf drücken ▷ vi (push) drücken; **pressing** adj dringend; **press-stud** n Druckknopf m; **press-up** n (Brit) Liegestütz m; **pressure** ['preʃə'] n Druck m; **to be under ~** unter Druck stehen; **to put ~ on sb** jdn unter Druck setzen; **pressure cooker** n Schnellkochtopf m; **pressurize** ['preʃəraɪz] vt (person) unter Druck setzen

presumably [prɪ'zjuːməblɪ] adv vermutlich; **presume** [prɪ'zjuːm] vt, vi annehmen

presumptuous [prɪˈzʌmptʃʊəs] adj anmaßend

presuppose [priːsəˈpəʊz] vt voraussetzen

pretend [prɪˈtend] vt: **to ~ that** so tun als ob; **to ~ to do sth** vorgeben, etw zu tun ▷ vi: **she's ~ing** sie tut nur so

pretentious [prɪˈtenʃəs] adj anmaßend; (person) wichtigtuerisch

pretty [ˈprɪtɪ] adj hübsch ▷ adv ziemlich

prevent [prɪˈvent] vt verhindern; **to ~ sb from doing sth** jdn daran hindern, etw zu tun

preview [ˈpriːvjuː] n (Cine) Voraufführung f; (trailer) Vorschau f

previous [ˈpriːvɪəs], **-ly** adj, adv früher

prey [preɪ] n Beute f

price [praɪs] n Preis m ▷ vt: **it's ~d at £10** es ist mit 10 Pfund ausgezeichnet; **priceless** adj unbezahlbar; **price list** n Preisliste f; **price tag** n Preisschild nt

prick [prɪk] n Stich m; (vulg: penis) Schwanz m; (vulg: person) Arsch m ▷ vt stechen in +akk; **to ~ one's finger** sich dat in den Finger stechen; **prickly** [ˈprɪklɪ] adj stachelig

pride [praɪd] n Stolz m; (arrogance) Hochmut m ▷ vt: **to ~ one-self on sth** auf etw akk stolz sein

priest [priːst] n Priester m

primarily [ˈpraɪmərɪlɪ] adv vorwiegend; **primary** [ˈpraɪmərɪ] adj Haupt-; **~ education** Grundschulausbildung f; **~ school** Grundschule f

prime [praɪm] adj Haupt-; (excellent) erstklassig ▷ n: **in one's ~** in den besten Jahren; **prime minister** n Premierminister(in) m(f); **prime time** n (TV) Hauptsendezeit f

primitive [ˈprɪmɪtɪv] adj primitiv

primrose [ˈprɪmrəʊz] n Schlüsselblume f

prince [prɪns] n Prinz m; (ruler) Fürst m; **princess** [prɪnˈses] n Prinzessin f; Fürstin f

principal [ˈprɪnsɪpəl] adj Haupt-, wichtigste(r, s) ▷ n (school) Rektor(in) m(f)

principle [ˈprɪnsəpl] n Prinzip nt; **in ~** im Prinzip; **on ~** aus Prinzip

print [prɪnt] n (picture) Druck m; (Foto) Abzug m; (made by feet, fingers) Abdruck m; **out of ~** vergriffen ▷ vt drucken; (photo) abziehen; (write in block letters) in Druckschrift schreiben; **print out** vt (Inform) ausdrucken; **printed matter** n Drucksache f; **printer** n Drucker m; **printout** n (Inform) Ausdruck m

prior [ˈpraɪə³] adj früher; **a ~ engagement** eine vorher getroffene Verabredung; **~ to sth** vor etw dat; **~ to going abroad, she had ...** bevor sie ins Ausland ging, hatte sie ...

priority [praɪˈɒrɪtɪ] n (thing having precedence) Priorität f

prison [ˈprɪzn] n Gefängnis nt; **prisoner** n Gefangene(r) m/f; **~ of war** Kriegsgefangene(r) m/f

privacy [ˈprɪvəsɪ] n Privatleben nt; **private** [ˈpraɪvɪt] adj privat; (confidential) vertraulich ▷ n einfacher Soldat; **in ~** privat; **privately** adv privat; (confidentially) vertraulich; **privatize** [ˈpraɪvətaɪz] vt privatisieren

privilege [ˈprɪvɪlɪdʒ] n Privileg nt; **privileged** adj privilegiert

prize [praɪz] n Preis m; **prize money** n Preisgeld nt; **prizewinner** n Gewinner(in) m(f); **prizewinning** adj preisgekrönt

pro [prəʊ] (pl **-s**) n (professional) Profi m; **the ~s and cons** pl das Für und Wider

pro- [prəʊ] pref pro-

probability [prɒbəˈbɪlətɪ] n Wahrscheinlichkeit f; **probable, probably** [ˈprɒbəbl, -blɪ] adj, adv wahrscheinlich

probation [prəˈbeɪʃən] n Probezeit f; (Jur) Bewährung f

probe [prəʊb] n (investigation) Untersuchung f ▷ vt untersuchen

problem [ˈprɒbləm] n Problem nt; **no ~** kein Problem!

procedure [prəˈsiːdʒə°] n Verfahren nt

proceed [prəˈsiːd] vi (continue) fortfahren; (set about sth) vorgehen ▷ vt: **to ~ to do sth**, etw zu tun anfangen; **proceedings** npl (Jur) Verfahren nt; **proceeds** [ˈprəʊsiːdz] npl Erlös m

process [ˈprəʊses] n Prozess m, Vorgang m; (method) Verfahren nt ▷ vt (application etc) bearbeiten; (food, data) verarbeiten; (film) entwickeln

procession [prəˈseʃən] n Umzug m

processor [ˈprəʊsesə°] n (Inform) Prozessor m; (Gastr) Küchenmaschine f

produce [ˈprɒdjuːs] n (Agr) Produkte pl, Erzeugnisse pl ▷ [prəˈdjuːs] vt (manufacture) herstellen, produzieren; (on farm) erzeugen; (film, play, record) produzieren; (cause) hervorrufen; (evidence, results) liefern; **producer** n (manufacturer) Hersteller(in) m(f); (of film, play, record) Produzent(in) m(f); **product** [ˈprɒdʌkt] n Produkt nt, Erzeugnis nt; **production** [prəˈdʌkʃən] n Produktion f; (Theat) Inszenierung f; **productive** [prəˈdʌktɪv] adj produktiv; (land) ertragreich

prof [prɒf] n (fam) Prof m

profession [prəˈfeʃən] n Beruf m; **professional** [prəˈfeʃənl] n Profi m ▷ adj beruflich; (expert) fachlich; (sportsman, actor etc) Berufs-

professor [prəˈfesə°] n Professor(in) m(f); (US: lecturer) Dozent(in) m(f)

proficient [prəˈfɪʃənt] adj kompetent (in in +dat)

profile [ˈprəʊfaɪl] n Profil nt; **to keep a low ~** sich rarmachen

profit [ˈprɒfɪt] n Gewinn m ▷ vi profitieren (by, from von); **profitable** adj rentabel

profound [prəˈfaʊnd] adj tief; (idea, thinker) tiefgründig; (knowledge) profund

program [ˈprəʊgræm] n (Inform) Programm nt; (US) see **programme** ▷ vt (Inform) programmieren; (US) see **programme**

programme [ˈprəʊgræm] n Programm nt; (TV, Radio) Sendung f ▷ vt programmieren; **programmer** n Programmierer(in) m(f); **programming** n (Inform) Programmieren nt; **~ language** Programmiersprache f

progress [ˈprəʊgres] n Fortschritt m; **to make ~** Fortschritte machen ▷ [prəˈgres] vi (work, illness etc) fortschreiten; (improve) Fortschritte machen; **progressive** [prəˈgresɪv] adj (person, policy) fortschrittlich; **progressively** [prəˈgresɪvlɪ] adv zunehmend

prohibit [prəˈhɪbɪt] vt verbieten

project [ˈprɒdʒekt] n Projekt nt

projector [prəˈdʒektə°] n Projektor m

prolong [prəˈlɒŋ] vt verlängern

prom [prɒm] n (at seaside) Promenade f; (Brit: concert) Konzert nt (bei dem ein Großteil des Publikums im Parkett Stehplätze hat); (US:

P

dance) Ball für die Schüler und
Studenten von Highschools oder
Colleges

prominent ['prɒmɪnənt] adj
(politician, actor etc) prominent;
(easily seen) auffallend

promiscuous [prə'mɪskjʊəs]
adj promisk

promise ['prɒmɪs] n Versprechen nt ▷ vt versprechen; to
~ sb sth jdm etw versprechen; to
~ to do sth versprechen, etw zu
tun ▷ vi versprechen; **promising**
adj vielversprechend

promote [prə'məʊt] vt (in rank)
befördern; (help on) fördern;
(Comm) werben für; **promotion**
[prə'məʊʃən] n (in rank)
Beförderung f; (Comm) Werbung f
(of für)

prompt [prɒmpt] adj prompt;
(punctual) pünktlich ▷ adv: **at two
o'clock ~** Punkt zwei Uhr ▷ vt
(Theat: actor) soufflieren +dat

prone [prəʊn] adj: to be ~ to sth
zu etw neigen

pronounce [prə'naʊns] vt
(word) aussprechen; **pronounced**
adj ausgeprägt; **pronunciation**
[prənʌnsɪ'eɪʃən] n Aussprache f

proof [pruːf] n Beweis m; (of
alcohol) Alkoholgehalt m

prop [prɒp] n Stütze f; (Theat)
Requisit nt ▷ vt: **to ~ sth
against sth** etw gegen etw
lehnen; **prop up** vt stützen; (fig)
unterstützen

proper ['prɒpə'] adj richtig;
(morally correct) anständig

property ['prɒpətɪ] n (possession)
Eigentum nt; (house) Haus nt; (land)
Grundbesitz m; (characteristic)
Eigenschaft f

proportion [prə'pɔːʃən] n
Verhältnis nt; (share) Teil m; **~s** pl
(size) Proportionen pl; **in ~ to** im
Verhältnis zu; **proportional** adj

proportional; **~ representation**
Verhältniswahlrecht nt

proposal [prə'pəʊzl] n Vorschlag
m; ~ **(of marriage)** (Heirats)antrag
m; **propose** [prə'pəʊz] vt
vorschlagen ▷ vi (offer marriage)
einen Heiratsantrag machen (to sb
jdm)

proprietor [prə'praɪətə'] n
Besitzer(in) m(f); (of pub, hotel)
Inhaber(in) m(f)

prose [prəʊz] n Prosa f

prosecute ['prɒsɪkjuːt] vt verfolgen (for wegen)

prospect ['prɒspekt] n Aussicht
f

prosperity [prɒ'sperɪtɪ] n
Wohlstand m; **prosperous** adj
wohlhabend; (business) gut
gehend

prostitute ['prɒstɪtjuːt] n Prostituierte(r) mf

protect [prə'tekt] vt schützen
(from, against vor +dat, gegen);
protection [prə'tekʃən] n Schutz
m (from, against vor +dat, gegen);
protective adj beschützend;
(clothing etc) Schutz-

protein ['prəʊtiːn] n Protein nt

protest ['prəʊtest] n Protest m;
(demonstration)
Protestkundgebung f ▷ [prə'test]
vi protestieren (against gegen);
(demonstrate) demonstrieren

Protestant ['prɒtəstənt] adj
protestantisch ▷ n Protestant(in)
m(f)

proud, proudly [praʊd, -lɪ] adj,
adv stolz (of auf +akk)

prove [pruːv] vt beweisen; (turn
out to be) sich erweisen als

proverb ['prɒvɜːb] n Sprichwort
nt

provide [prə'vaɪd] vt zur
Verfügung stellen; (drinks, music
etc) sorgen für; (person) versorgen
(with mit); **provide for** vt (family

etc) sorgen für; **provided** conj:
~ **(that)** vorausgesetzt, dass;
provider n (Inform) Provider m
provision [prə'vɪʒən] n (condition) Bestimmung f; ~**s** pl (food)
Proviant m
provisional, provisionally
[prə'vɪʒənl, -l] adj, adv
provisorisch
provoke [prə'vəʊk] vt
provozieren; (cause) hervorrufen
proximity [prɒk'sɪmɪtɪ] n Nähe f
prudent ['pru:dənt] adj klug;
(person) umsichtig
prudish ['pru:dɪʃ] adj prüde
prune [pru:n] n Backpflaume f
▷ vt (tree etc) zurechtstutzen
PS abbr = postscript PS nt
psalm [sɑ:m] n Psalm m
pseudo- ['sju:dəʊ] adj pseudo-,
Pseudo-; **pseudonym** ['sju:də-
nɪm] n Pseudonym nt
PST abbr = Pacific Standard Time
psychiatric [saɪkɪ'ætrɪk] adj
psychiatrisch; (illness) psychisch;
psychiatrist [saɪ'kaɪətrɪst] n
Psychiater(in) m(f); **psychiatry**
[saɪ'kaɪətrɪ] n Psychiatrie f;
psychic ['saɪkɪk] adj über-
sinnlich; **I'm not ~** ich kann keine
Gedanken lesen; **psychoanalysis**
[saɪkəʊə'næləsɪs] n Psychoanalyse f; **psychoanalyst**
[saɪkəʊ'ænəlɪst] n Psychoanaly-
tiker(in) m(f); **psychological** [saɪ-
kə'lɒdʒɪkəl] adj psychologisch;
psychology [saɪ'kɒlədʒɪ] n Psychologie f; **psychopath** ['saɪkəʊ-
pæθ] n Psychopath(in) m(f)
pt abbr = pint
pto abbr = please turn over b.w.
pub [pʌb] n (Brit) Kneipe f

● PUB
●
● Ein **pub** ist ein Gasthaus mit
● einer Lizenz zum Ausschank von

● alkoholischen Getränken. Ein
● „Pub" besteht meist aus
● verschiedenen gemütlichen
● (**lounge, snug**) oder
● einfacheren (**public bar**)
● Räumen, in denen oft auch
● Spiele wie Darts, Domino und
● Poolbillard zur Verfügung
● stehen. In „Pubs" werden vor
● allem mittags auch Mahlzeiten
● angeboten (**pub lunch**). Die
● Sperrstunde wurde 2005
● aufgehoben. Dennoch sind
● „Pubs" oft nur von 11 bis 23 Uhr
● geöffnet. Nachmittags bleiben
● sie häufig geschlossen.

puberty ['pju:bətɪ] n Pubertät
f
public ['pʌblɪk] n: **the (general)**
~ die (breite) Öffentlichkeit; **in**
~ in der Öffentlichkeit ▷ adj
öffentlich; (relating to the State)
Staats-; ~ **convenience** (Brit)
öffentliche Toilette; ~ **holiday**
gesetzlicher Feiertag; ~ **opinion**
die öffentliche Meinung;
~ **relations** pl
Öffentlichkeitsarbeit f, Public
Relations pl; ~ **school** (Brit)
Privatschule f; **publication**
[pʌblɪ'keɪʃən] n Veröffentlichung
f; **publicity** [pʌb'lɪsɪtɪ] n
Publicity f; (advertisements)
Werbung f; **publish** ['pʌblɪʃ] vt
veröffentlichen; **publisher** n
Verleger(in) m(f); (company) Verlag
m; **publishing** n Verlagswesen nt
pub lunch ['pʌblʌntʃ] n (oft
einfacheres) Mittagessen in einer
Kneipe
pudding ['pʊdɪŋ] n (course)
Nachtisch m
puddle ['pʌdl] n Pfütze f
puff [pʌf] vi (pant) schnaufen
puffin ['pʌfɪn] n Papageien-
taucher m

puff paste (US), **puff pastry**
['pʌf'peɪstrɪ] n Blätterteig m

pull [pʊl] n Ziehen nt; **to give sth
a ~** an etw dat ziehen ▷ vt (cart,
tooth) ziehen; (rope, handle) ziehen
an +dat; (fam: date) abschleppen;
to ~ a muscle sich dat einen
Muskel zerren; **to ~ sb's leg** jdn
auf den Arm nehmen ▷ vi ziehen;
pull apart vt (separate)
auseinanderziehen; **pull down** vt
(blind) herunterziehen; (house)
abreißen; **pull in** vi hineinfahren;
(stop) anhalten; **pull off** vt (deal
etc) zuwege bringen; (clothes)
ausziehen; **pull on** vt (clothes)
anziehen; **pull out** vi (car from
lane) ausscheren; (train) abfahren;
(withdraw) aussteigen (of aus) ▷ vt
herausziehen; (tooth) ziehen;
(troops) abziehen; **pull round**, **pull
through** vi durchkommen; **pull
up** vt (raise) hochziehen; (chair)
heranziehen ▷ vi anhalten

pullover ['pʊləʊvə°] n Pullover m

pulp [pʌlp] n Brei m; (of fruit)
Fruchtfleisch nt

pulpit ['pʊlpɪt] n Kanzel f

pulse [pʌls] n Puls m

pump [pʌmp] n Pumpe f; (in
petrol station) Zapfsäule f; **pump up**
vt (tyre etc) aufpumpen

pumpkin ['pʌmpkɪn] n Kürbis m

pun [pʌn] n Wortspiel nt

punch [pʌntʃ] n (blow)
(Faust)schlag m; (tool) Locher m;
(hot drink) Punsch m; (cold drink)
Bowle f ▷ vt (strike) schlagen;
(ticket, paper) lochen

punctual, **punctually**
['pʌŋktjʊəl, -ɪ] adj, adv
pünktlich

punctuation [pʌŋktjʊ'eɪʃən] n
Interpunktion f; **punctuation
mark** n Satzzeichen nt

puncture ['pʌŋktʃə°] n (flat tyre)
Reifenpanne f

punish ['pʌnɪʃ] vt bestrafen;
punishment n Strafe f; (action)
Bestrafung f

pupil ['pju:pl] n (school)
Schüler(in) m(f)

puppet ['pʌpɪt] n Marionette f

puppy ['pʌpɪ] n junger Hund

purchase ['pɜːtʃɪs] n Kauf m ▷ vt
kaufen

pure [pjʊə°] adj rein; (clean)
sauber; (utter) pur; **purely**
['pjʊəlɪ] adv rein; **purify**
['pjʊərɪfaɪ] vt reinigen; **purity**
['pjʊərɪtɪ] n Reinheit f

purple ['pɜːpl] adj violett

purpose ['pɜːpəs] n Zweck m; (of
person) Absicht f; **on ~** absichtlich

purr [pɜː°] vi (cat) schnurren

purse [pɜːs] n Geldbeutel m; (US:
handbag) Handtasche f

pursue [pə'sju:] vt (person, car)
verfolgen; (hobby, studies)
nachgehen +dat; **pursuit**
[pə'sju:t] n (chase) Verfolgung f;
(occupation) Beschäftigung f;
(hobby) Hobby nt

pus [pʌs] n Eiter m

push [pʊʃ] n Stoß m ▷ vt (person)
stoßen; (car, chair etc) schieben;
(button) drücken; (drugs) dealen
▷ vi (in crowd) drängeln; **push in** vi
(in queue) sich vordrängeln; **push
off** vi (fam: leave) abhauen; **push
on** vi (with job) weitermachen;
push up vt (prices) hochtreiben;
pushchair n (Brit)
Sport(kinder)wagen m; **pusher** n
(of drugs) Dealer(in) m(f); **push-up**
n (US) Liegestütz m; **pushy** adj
(fam) aufdringlich, penetrant

put [pʊt] (**put**, **put**) vt turn;
(upright) stellen; (flat) legen;
(express) ausdrücken; (write)
schreiben; **he ~ his hand in his
pocket** er steckte die Hand in die
Tasche; **he ~ his hand on her
shoulder** er legte ihr die Hand auf

die Schulter; **to ~ money into one's account** Geld auf sein Konto einzahlen; **put aside** vt (money) zurücklegen; **put away** vt (tidy away) wegräumen; **put back** vt zurücklegen; (clock) zurückstellen; **put down** vt (in writing) aufschreiben; (Brit: animal) einschläfern; (rebellion) niederschlagen; **to put the phone down** (den Hörer) auflegen; **to put one's name down for sth** sich für etw eintragen; **put forward** vt (idea) vorbringen; (name) vorschlagen; (clock) vorstellen; **put in** vt (install) einbauen; (submit) einreichen; **put off** vt (switch off) ausschalten; (postpone) verschieben; **to put sb off doing sth** jdn davon abbringen, etw zu tun; **put on** vt (switch on) anmachen; (clothes) anziehen; (hat, glasses) aufsetzen; (make-up, CD) auflegen; (play) aufführen; **to put the kettle on** Wasser aufsetzen; **to put weight on** zunehmen; **put out** vt (hand, foot) ausstrecken; (light, cigarette) ausmachen; (building) errichten; (price) erhöhen; (person) unterbringen; **to ~ with** sich abfinden mit; **I won't ~ with it** das lasse ich mir nicht gefallen
putt [pʌt] vt, vi (Sport) putten
puzzle [ˈpʌzl] n Rätsel nt; (toy) Geduldsspiel nt; (jigsaw) ~ Puzzle nt ⊳ vt vor ein Rätsel stellen; **it ~s me** es ist mir ein Rätsel; **puzzling** adj rätselhaft
pyjamas [prˈdʒɑːməz] npl Schlafanzug m
pylon [ˈpaɪlən] n Mast m
pyramid [ˈpɪrəmɪd] n Pyramide f

q

quack [kwæk] vi quaken
quaint [kweɪnt] adj (idea, tradition) kurios; (picturesque) malerisch
qualification [ˌkwɒlɪfɪˈkeɪʃən] n (for job) Qualifikation f; (from school, university) Abschluss m; **qualified** [ˈkwɒlɪfaɪd] adj (for job) qualifiziert; **qualify** vt (limit) einschränken; **to be qualified to do sth** berechtigt sein, etw zu tun ⊳ vi (finish training) seine Ausbildung abschließen; (contest etc) sich qualifizieren
quality [ˈkwɒlɪtɪ] n Qualität f; (characteristic) Eigenschaft f
quantity [ˈkwɒntɪtɪ] n Menge f, Quantität f
quarantine [ˈkwɒrəntiːn] n Quarantäne f
quarrel [ˈkwɒrəl] n Streit m ⊳ vi sich streiten
quarter [ˈkwɔːtə°] n Viertel nt;

(of year) Vierteljahr nt; (US: coin) Vierteldollar m; **a ~ of an hour** eine Viertelstunde; **~ to/past** (Brit) (o **~ of/after** (US)) **three** Viertel vor/nach drei ▷ vt vierteln; **quarter final** n Viertelfinale nt; **quarters** npl (Mil) Quartier nt

quartet [kwɔː'tet] n Quartett nt

quay [kiː] n Kai m

queasy ['kwiːzɪ] adj: **I feel ~** mir ist übel

queen [kwiːn] n Königin f; (in cards, chess) Dame f

queer [kwɪə°] adj (strange) seltsam, sonderbar; (pej: homosexual) schwul ▷ n (pej) Schwule(r) m

quench [kwentʃ] vt (thirst) löschen

query ['kwɪərɪ] n Frage f ▷ vt infrage stellen; (bill) reklamieren

question ['kwestʃən] n Frage f; **that's out of the ~** das kommt nicht infrage ▷ vt (person) befragen; (suspect) verhören; (express doubt about) bezweifeln; **questionable** adj zweifelhaft; (improper) fragwürdig; **question mark** n Fragezeichen nt; **questionnaire** [kwestʃə'nɛə°] n Fragebogen m

queue [kjuː] n (Brit) Schlange f; **to jump the ~** sich vordrängeln ▷ vi: **to ~ (up)** Schlange stehen

quibble ['kwɪbl] vi kleinlich sein; (argue) streiten

quiche [kiːʃ] n Quiche f

quick [kwɪk] adj schnell; (short) kurz; **be ~** mach schnell!; **quickly** adv schnell

quid [kwɪd] (pl **quid**) n (Brit fam) Pfund nt; **20 ~** 20 Pfund

quiet ['kwaɪət] adj (not noisy) leise; (peaceful, calm) still, ruhig; **be ~** sei still!; **to keep ~ about sth** über etw akk nichts sagen ▷ n

Stille f, Ruhe f; **quiet down** (US), **quieten down** ['kwaɪətən'daʊn] vi sich beruhigen ▷ vt beruhigen; **quietly** adv leise; (calmly) ruhig

quilt [kwɪlt] n (Stepp)decke f

quit [kwɪt] (quit o **quitted, quit** o **quitted**) vt (leave) verlassen; (job) aufgeben; **to ~ doing sth** aufhören, etw zu tun ▷ vi (resign) kündigen

quite [kwaɪt] adv (fairly) ziemlich; (completely) ganz, völlig; **I don't ~ understand** ich verstehe das nicht ganz; **a few** ziemlich viele; **~ so** richtig!

quits [kwɪts] adj: **to be ~ with sb** mit jdm quitt sein

quiver ['kwɪvə°] vi zittern

quiz [kwɪz] n (competition) Quiz nt

quota ['kwəʊtə] n Anteil m; (Comm, Pol) Quote f

quotation [kwəʊ'teɪʃən] n Zitat nt; (price) Kostenvoranschlag m; **quotation marks** npl Anführungszeichen pl; **quote** [kwəʊt] vt (text, author) zitieren; (price) nennen ▷ n Zitat nt; (price) Kostenvoranschlag m; **in ~s** in Anführungszeichen

r

rabbi ['ræbaɪ] n Rabbiner m
rabbit ['ræbɪt] n Kaninchen nt
rabies ['reɪbiːz] nsing Tollwut f
raccoon [rə'kuːn] n Waschbär m
race [reɪs] n (competition) Rennen nt; (people) Rasse f ▷ vt um die Wette laufen/fahren ▷ vi (rush) rennen; **racecourse** n Rennbahn f; **racehorse** n Rennpferd nt; **racetrack** n Rennbahn f
racial ['reɪʃəl] adj Rassen-; **~ discrimination** Rassendiskriminierung f
racing ['reɪsɪŋ] n (horse) **~** Pferderennen nt; (motor) **~** Autorennen nt; **racing car** n Rennwagen m
racism ['reɪsɪzəm] n Rassismus m; **racist** n Rassist(in) m(f) ▷ adj rassistisch
rack [ræk] n Ständer m, Gestell nt ▷ vt: **to ~ one's brains** sich dat den Kopf zerbrechen

racket ['rækɪt] n (Sport) Schläger m; (noise) Krach m
radar ['reɪdɑ:°] n Radar nt o m; **radar trap** n Radarfalle f
radiation [reɪdɪ'eɪʃən] n (radioactive) Strahlung f
radiator ['reɪdɪeɪtə°] n Heizkörper m; (Auto) Kühler m
radical ['rædɪkəl] adj radikal
radio ['reɪdɪəʊ] (pl **-s**) n Rundfunk m, Radio nt
radioactivity [reɪdɪəʊæk'tɪvɪtɪ] n Radioaktivität f
radio alarm ['reɪdɪəʊə'lɑ:m] n Radiowecker m; **radio station** n Rundfunksstation f
radiotherapy [reɪdɪəʊ'θerəpɪ] n Strahlenbehandlung f
radish ['rædɪʃ] n Radieschen nt
radius ['reɪdɪəs] n Radius m; **within a five-mile ~** im Umkreis von fünf Meilen (of um)
raffle ['ræfl] n Tombola f; **raffle ticket** n Los nt
raft [rɑ:ft] n Floß nt
rag [ræg] n Lumpen m; (for cleaning) Lappen m
rage [reɪdʒ] n Wut f; **to be all the ~** der letzte Schrei sein ▷ vi toben; (disease) wüten
raid [reɪd] n Überfall m (on auf +akk); (by police) Razzia f (on gegen) ▷ vt (bank etc) überfallen; (by police) eine Razzia machen in +dat
rail [reɪl] n (on stairs, balcony etc) Geländer nt; (of ship) Reling f (Rail) Schiene f; **railcard** n (Brit) Bahncard® f; **railing** n Geländer nt; **~s** pl (fence) Zaun m; **railroad** n (US) Eisenbahn f; **railroad station** n (US) Bahnhof m; **railway** n (Brit) Eisenbahn f; **railway line** n Bahnlinie f; (track) Gleis m; **railway station** n Bahnhof m
rain [reɪn] n Regen m ▷ vi regnen; **it's ~ing** es regnet; **rainbow** n Regenbogen m;

raincoat n Regenmantel m;
rainfall n Niederschlag m;
rainforest n Regenwald m; **rainy**
adj regnerisch
raise [reɪz] n (US: of wages/salary)
Gehalts-/Lohnerhöhung f ▷ vt
(lift) hochheben; (increase)
erhöhen; (family) großziehen;
(livestock) züchten; (money)
aufbringen; (objection) erheben; **to
~ one's voice** laut werden
raisin [ˈreɪzən] n Rosine f
rally [ˈrælɪ] n (Pol) Kundgebung f;
(Auto) Rallye f; (Tennis) Ballwechsel
m
RAM [ræm] acr = **random access
memory** RAM m
ramble [ˈræmbl] n Wanderung f
▷ vi (walk) wandern; (talk)
schwafeln
ramp [ræmp] n Rampe f
ran [ræn] pt of **run**
ranch [rɑːntʃ] n Ranch f
rancid [ˈrænsɪd] adj ranzig
random [ˈrændəm] adj
willkürlich ▷ n: **at ~** (choose)
willkürlich; (fire) ziellos
rang [ræŋ] pt of **ring**
range [reɪndʒ] n (selection)
Auswahl f (of an +dat); (Comm)
Sortiment nt (of an +dat); (of
missile, telescope) Reichweite f; (of
mountains) Kette f; **in this price
~** in dieser Preisklasse ▷ vi: **to
~ from ... to ...** gehen von ... bis ...;
(temperature, sizes, prices) liegen
zwischen ... und ...
rank [ræŋk] n (Mil) Rang m; (social
position) Stand m ▷ vt einstufen
ransom [ˈrænsəm] n Lösegeld nt
rap [ræp] n (Mus) Rap m
rape [reɪp] n Vergewaltigung f
▷ vt vergewaltigen
rapid, rapidly [ˈræpɪd, -lɪ] adj, adv
schnell
rapist [ˈreɪpɪst] n Vergewaltiger
m

rare [reə°] adj selten, rar;
(especially good) vortrefflich; (steak)
blutig; **rarely** adv selten; **rarity**
[ˈreərɪtɪ] n Seltenheit f
rash [ræʃ] adj unbesonnen ▷ n
(Med) (Haut)ausschlag m
rasher [ˈræʃə°] n: **~ of bacon**
(Speck)scheibe f
raspberry [ˈrɑːzbərɪ] n Himbeere f
rat [ræt] n Ratte f; (pej: person)
Schwein nt
rate [reɪt] n (proportion, frequency)
Rate f; (speed) Tempo nt; **~ of
exchange** (Wechsel)kurs m; **~ of
inflation** Inflationsrate f; **~ of
interest** Zinssatz m; **at any ~** auf
jeden Fall ▷ vt (evaluate)
einschätzen (as als)
rather [ˈrɑːðə°] adv (in preference)
lieber; (fairly) ziemlich; **I'd ~ stay
here** ich würde lieber hierbleiben;
I'd ~ not lieber nicht; **or ~** (more
accurately) vielmehr
ratio [ˈreɪʃɪəʊ] (pl **-s**) n Verhältnis
nt
rational [ˈræʃənl] adj rational;
rationalize [ˈræʃnəlaɪz] vt
rationalisieren
rattle [ˈrætl] n (toy) Rassel f ▷ vt
(keys, coins) klimpern mit; (person)
durcheinanderbringen ▷ vi (window) klappern; (bottles) klirren;
rattle off vt herunterrasseln;
rattlesnake n Klapperschlange
f
rave [reɪv] vi (talk wildly)
fantasieren; (rage) toben; (enthuse)
schwärmen (about von) ▷ n (Brit:
event) Raveparty f
raven [ˈreɪvn] n Rabe m
raving [ˈreɪvɪŋ] adv: **~ mad** total
verrückt
ravishing [ˈrævɪʃɪŋ] adj
hinreißend
raw [rɔː] adj (food) roh; (skin)
wund; (climate) rau

ray [reɪ] n (of light) Strahl m; **~ of hope** Hoffnungsschimmer m

razor ['reɪzə°] n Rasierapparat m; **razor blade** n Rasierklinge f

Rd n abbr = **road** Str.

re [riː] prep (Comm) betreffend +gen

RE abbr = **religious education**

reach [riːtʃ] n: **within/out of (sb's) ~** in/außer (jds) Reichweite; **within easy ~ of the shops** nicht weit von den Geschäften ▷ vt (arrive at, contact) erreichen; (come down/up as far as) reichen bis zu; (contact) **can you ~ it?** kommst du/kommen Sie dran?; **reach for** vt greifen nach; **reach out** vi die Hand ausstrecken; **to ~ for** greifen nach

react [riːˈækt] vi reagieren (to auf +akk); **reaction** [riːˈækʃən] n Reaktion f (to auf +akk); **reactor** [riːˈæktə°] n Reaktor m

read [riːd] (read, read) vt lesen; (meter) ablesen; **to ~ sth to sb** jdm etw vorlesen ▷ vi lesen; **to ~ to sb** jdm vorlesen; **it ~s well** es liest sich gut; **it ~s as follows** es lautet folgendermaßen; **read out** vt vorlesen; **read through** vt durchlesen; **read up on** vt nachlesen über +akk; **readable** adj (book) lesenswert; (handwriting) lesbar; **reader** n Leser(in) m(f); **readership** n Leserschaft f

readily ['rɛdɪlɪ] adv (willingly) bereitwillig; **~ available** leicht erhältlich

reading ['riːdɪŋ] n (action) Lesen nt; (from meter) Zählerstand m; **reading glasses** npl Lesebrille f; **reading lamp** n Leselampe f; **reading list** n Leseliste f; **reading matter** n Lektüre f

readjust [riːəˈdʒʌst] vt (mechanism etc) neu einstellen ▷ vi sich wieder anpassen (to an +akk)

ready ['rɛdɪ] adj fertig, bereit; **to**

be ~ to do sth (willing) bereit sein, etw zu tun; **are you ~ to go?** bist du so weit?; **to get sth ~** etw fertig machen; **to get (oneself) ~** sich fertig machen; **ready cash** n Bargeld nt; **ready-made** adj (product) Fertig-; (clothes) Konfektions-; **~ meal** n Fertiggericht nt

real [rɪəl] adj wirklich; (actual) eigentlich; (genuine) echt; (idiot etc) richtig ▷ adv (fam, esp US) echt; **for ~** echt; **this time it's for ~** diesmal ist es ernst; **get ~** sei realistisch!; **real ale** n Ale nt; **real estate** n Immobilien pl

realistic, realistically [rɪəˈlɪstɪk, -əlɪ] adj, adv realistisch; **reality** [riːˈælɪtɪ] n Wirklichkeit f; **in ~** in Wirklichkeit; **reality TV** n Reality-TV nt; **realization** [rɪələˈreɪʃən] n (awareness) Erkenntnis f; **realize** ['rɪəlaɪz] vt (understand) begreifen; (plan, idea) realisieren; **I ~d (that) ...** mir wurde klar, dass ...

really ['rɪəlɪ] adv wirklich

real time [rɪəl'taɪm] n (Inform) **in ~** in Echtzeit

realtor ['rɪəltɔː°] n (US) Grundstücksmakler(in) m(f)

rearm [riːˈɑːm] vi wieder aufrüsten

rearrange [riːəˈreɪndʒ] vt (furniture, system) umstellen; (meeting) verlegen (for auf +akk)

rear-view mirror ['rɪəˈvjuːˈmɪrə°] n Rückspiegel m; **rear window** n (Auto) Heckscheibe f

reappear [riːəˈpɪə°] vi wieder erscheinen

rear [rɪə°] adj hintere(r, s), Hinter- ▷ n (of building, vehicle) hinterer Teil; **at the ~ of** hinten +dat; (inside) hinten in +dat; **rear light** n (Auto) Rücklicht nt

reason ['ri:zn] n (cause) Grund m
(for für); (ability to think) Verstand
m; (common sense) Vernunft f; **for
some ~** aus irgendeinem Grund
▷ vi: **to ~ with sb** mit jdm
vernünftig reden; **reasonable** adj
(person, price) vernünftig; (offer)
akzeptabel; (chance) reell; (food,
weather) ganz gut; **reasonably** adv
vernünftig; (fairly) ziemlich

reassure [ri:ə'ʃʊə⁰] vt beruhigen; **she ~d me that ...** sie
versicherte mir, dass ...

rebel ['rebl] n Rebell(in) m(f)
▷ [ri'bel] vi rebellieren; **rebellion**
[ri'beliən] n Aufstand m

reboot [ri:'bu:t] vt, vi (Inform)
rebooten

rebound [ri'baʊnd] vi (ball etc)
zurückprallen

rebuild [ri'bild] irr vt wieder
aufbauen

recall [ri'kɔ:l] vt (remember) sich
erinnern an +akk; (call back)
zurückrufen

recap ['ri:kæp] vt, vi
rekapitulieren

receipt [ri'si:t] n (document)
Quittung f; (receiving) Empfang m;
~s pl (money) Einnahmen pl

receive [ri'si:v] vt (news etc)
erhalten, bekommen; (visitor)
empfangen; **receiver** n (Tel)
Hörer m; (Radio) Empfänger m

recent [ri:snt] adj (event) vor
Kurzem stattgefunden; (photo)
neueste(r,s); (invention) neu; **in
~ years** in den letzten Jahren;
recently adv vor Kurzem; (in the
last few days or weeks) in letzter Zeit

reception [ri'sepʃən] n Empfang
m; **receptionist** n (in hotel)
Empfangschef m, Empfangsdame f;
(woman in firm) Empfangsdame f;
(Med) Sprechstundenhilfe f

recess [ri'ses] n (in wall) Nische
f; (US: in school) Pause f

recession [ri'seʃən] n Rezession
f

recharge [ri:'tʃɑ:dʒ] vt (battery)
aufladen; **rechargeable**
[ri:'tʃɑ:dʒəbl] adj wiederaufladbar

recipe ['resipi] n Rezept nt (for
für)

recipient [ri'sipiənt] n
Empfänger(in) m(f)

reciprocal [ri'siprəkəl] adj
gegenseitig

recite [ri'sait] vt vortragen;
(details) aufzählen

reckless ['rekləs] adj leichtsinnig; (driving) gefährlich

reckon ['rekən] vt (calculate)
schätzen; (think) glauben ▷ vi: **to
~ with/on** rechnen mit

reclaim [ri'kleim] vt (baggage)
abholen; (expenses, tax)
zurückverlangen

recline [ri'klain] vi (person) sich
zurücklehnen; **reclining seat** n
Liegesitz m

recognition [rekəg'niʃən] n
(acknowledgement) Anerkennung f;
in ~ of in Anerkennung +gen;
recognize ['rekəgnaiz] vt
erkennen; (approve officially)
anerkennen

recommend [rekə'mend] vt
empfehlen; **recommendation**
[rekəmen'deiʃən] n Empfehlung f

reconfirm [ri:kən'fɜ:m] vt (flight
etc) rückbestätigen

reconsider [ri:kən'sidə⁰] vt noch
einmal überdenken ▷ vi es sich
dat noch einmal überlegen

reconstruct [ri:kən'strʌkt] vt
wieder aufbauen; (crime)
rekonstruieren

record ['rekɔ:d] n (Mus)
(Schall)platte f; (best performance)
Rekord m; **~s** pl (files) Akten pl; **to
keep a ~ of** Buch führen über +akk
▷ adj (time etc) Rekord- ▷ [ri'kɔ:d]
vt (write down) aufzeichnen; (on

tape etc) aufnehmen; **~ed message**
Ansage f; **recorded delivery** n
(Brit) **by ~** per Einschreiben

recorder [rɪˈkɔːdə*] n (Mus)
Blockflöte f; **(cassette)**
~ (Kassetten)rekorder m;

recording [rɪˈkɔːdɪŋ] n (on tape
etc) Aufnahme f; **record player**
[ˈrekɔːdpleɪə*] n Plattenspieler m

recover [rɪˈkʌvə*] vt (money, item)
zurückbekommen; (appetite,
strength) wiedergewinnen ▷ vi
sich erholen

recreation [rekrɪˈeɪʃən] n
Erholung f; **recreational** adj
Freizeit-; **~ vehicle** (US)
Wohnmobil n

recruit [rɪˈkruːt] n (Mil)
Rekrut(in) m(f); (in firm,
organization) neues Mitglied ▷ vt
(Mil) rekrutieren; (members)
anwerben; (staff) einstellen;
recruitment agency n
Personalagentur f

rectangle [ˈrektæŋgl] n
Rechteck nt; **rectangular**
[rekˈtæŋgulə*] adj rechteckig

rectify [ˈrektɪfaɪ] vt berichtigen

recuperate [rɪˈkuːpəreɪt] vi sich
erholen

recyclable [riːˈsaɪkləbl] adj
recycelbar, wiederverwertbar

recycle [riːˈsaɪkl] vt recyceln,
wiederverwerten; **~d paper**
Recyclingpapier nt; **recycling** n
Recycling nt, Wiederverwertung f

red [red] adj col ▷ n: **in the ~**
in den roten Zahlen; **Red Cross** n
Rotes Kreuz; **red cabbage** n
Rotkohl m; **redcurrant** n (rote)
Johannisbeere

redeem [rɪˈdiːm] vt (Comm)
einlösen

red-handed [redˈhændɪd] adj:
to catch sb ~ jdn auf frischer Tat
ertappen; **redhead** n
Rothaarige(r) mf

redial [riːˈdaɪəl] vt, vi nochmals
wählen

redirect [riːdaɪˈrekt] vt (traffic)
umleiten; (forward) nachsenden

red light [redˈlaɪt] n (traffic
signal) rotes Licht; **to go through
the ~** bei Rot über die Ampel
fahren; **red meat** n
Rind-, Lamm-, Rehfleisch

redo [riːˈduː] irr vt nochmals
machen

reduce [rɪˈdjuːs] vt reduzieren
(to auf +akk, by um); **reduction**
[rɪˈdʌkʃən] n Reduzierung f; (in
price) Ermäßigung f

redundant [rɪˈdʌndənt] adj
überflüssig; **to be made
~** entlassen werden

red wine [redˈwaɪn] n Rotwein
m

reef [riːf] n Riff nt

reel [riːl] n Spule f; (on fishing rod)
Rolle f; **reel off** vt herunterrasseln

ref [ref] n (fam: referee) Schiri m

refectory [rɪˈfektərɪ] n (at
college) Mensa f

refer [rɪˈfɜː*] vt: **to ~ sb to sb/sth**
jdn an jdn/etw verweisen; **to
~ sth to sb** (query, problem) etw an
jdn weiterleiten ▷ vi: **to ~ to**
(mention, allude to) sich beziehen
auf +akk; (book) nachschlagen in
+dat

referee [refəˈriː] n Schiedsrich-
ter(in) m(f); (in boxing) Ringrichter
m; (Brit: for job) Referenz f

reference [ˈrefrəns] n (allusion)
Anspielung f (to auf +akk); (for job)
Referenz f; (in book) Verweis m;
~ (number) (in document)
Aktenzeichen nt; **with ~ to** mit
Bezug auf +akk; **reference book** n
Nachschlagewerk nt

referendum [refəˈrendəm] (pl
referenda) n Referendum n

refill [ˈriːfɪl] vt [riːˈfɪl] nachfüllen
▷ n (for ballpoint pen) Ersatzmine f

refine [rɪ'faɪn] vt (purify)
raffinieren; (improve) verfeinern;
refined adj (genteel) fein

reflect [rɪ'flekt] vt reflektieren;
(fig) widerspiegeln ▷ vi
nachdenken (on über +akk);
reflection [rɪ'flekʃən] n (image)
Spiegelbild nt; (thought)
Überlegung f; **on ~** nach reiflicher
Überlegung

reflex ['riːfleks] n Reflex m

reform [rɪ'fɔːm] n Reform f ▷ vt
reformieren; (person) bessern

refrain [rɪ'freɪn] vi: **to ~ from
doing sth** es unterlassen, etw zu
tun

refresh [rɪ'freʃ] vt erfrischen;
refresher course n
Auffrischungskurs m; **refreshing**
adj erfrischend; **refreshments** npl
Erfrischungen pl

refrigerator [rɪ'frɪdʒəreɪtə°] n
Kühlschrank m

refuel [riː'fjʊəl] vt, vi auftanken

refugee [refjʊ'dʒiː] n Flüchtling
m

refund ['riːfʌnd] n (of money)
Rückerstattung f; **to get a ~ (on
sth)** sein Geld (für etw)
zurückbekommen ▷ [rɪ'fʌnd] vt
zurückerstatten

refusal [rɪ'fjuːzəl] n (to do sth)
Weigerung f; **refuse** ['refjuːs] n
Müll m, Abfall m ▷ [rɪ'fjuːz] vt
ablehnen; **to ~ sb sth** jdm etw
verweigern; **to ~ to do sth** sich
weigern, etw zu tun ▷ vi sich
weigern

regain [rɪ'geɪn] vt wiedergewinnen, wiedererlangen; **to
~ consciousness** wieder zu
Bewusstsein kommen

regard [rɪ'gɑːd] n: **with ~ to** in
Bezug auf +akk; **in this ~** in dieser
Hinsicht; **~s** (at end of letter) mit
freundlichen Grüßen; **give my ~s
to ...** viele Grüße an ... +akk ▷ vt:

to ~ sb/sth as sth jdn/etw als etw
betrachten; **as ~s ...** was ...
betrifft; **regarding** prep bezüglich
+gen; **regardless** adj: **~ of** ohne
Rücksicht auf +akk ▷ adv
trotzdem; **to carry on ~** einfach
weitermachen

regime [reɪ'ʒiːm] n (Pol) Regime
nt

region ['riːdʒən] n (of country)
Region f, Gebiet nt; **in the ~ of**
(about) ungefähr; **regional** adj
regional

register ['redʒɪstə°] n Register
nt; (school) Namensliste f ▷ vt
(with an authority) registrieren
lassen; (birth, death, vehicle)
anmelden ▷ vi (at hotel, for course)
sich anmelden; (at university) sich
einschreiben; **registered** adj
eingetragen; (letter)
eingeschrieben; **by ~ post** per
Einschreiben; **registration**
[redʒɪ'streɪʃən] n (for course)
Anmeldung f; (at university)
Einschreibung f; (Auto: number)
(polizeiliches) Kennzeichen;
registration form n
Anmeldeformular nt; **registration
number** n (Auto) (polizeiliches)
Kennzeichen; **registry office**
['redʒɪstrɪɒfɪs] n Standesamt nt

regret [rɪ'gret] n Bedauern nt
▷ vt bedauern; **regrettable** adj
bedauerlich

regular ['regjʊlə°] adj regelmäßig; (size) normal ▷ n (client)
Stammkunde m, Stammkundin f;
(in bar) Stammgast m; (petrol)
Normalbenzin nt; **regularly** adv
regelmäßig

regulate ['regjʊleɪt] vt
regulieren; (using rules) regeln;
regulation [regjʊ'leɪʃən] n (rule)
Vorschrift f

rehabilitation [riːəbɪlɪ'teɪʃən]
n Rehabilitation f

rehearsal [rɪ'hɜːsəl] n Probe f;
rehearse vt, vi proben

reign [reɪn] n Herrschaft f ▷ vi
herrschen (over über +akk)

reimburse [riːɪm'bɜːs] vt (person) entschädigen; (expenses)
zurückerstatten

reindeer ['reɪndɪə*] n Rentier nt

reinforce [riːɪn'fɔːs] vt
verstärken

reinstate [riːɪn'steɪt] vt
(employee) wieder einstellen;
(passage in text) wieder aufnehmen

reject ['riːdʒekt] n (Comm
Ausschussartikel m ▷ [rɪ'dʒekt]
vt ablehnen; **rejection**
[rɪ'dʒekʃən] n Ablehnung f

relapse [rɪ'læps] n Rückfall m

relate [rɪ'leɪt] vt (story) erzählen;
(connect) in Verbindung bringen (to
mit) ▷ vi: **to ~ to** (refer) sich
beziehen auf +akk; **related** adj
verwandt (to mit); **relation**
[rɪ'leɪʃən] n (relative) Verwandte(r)
mf; (connection) Beziehung f; **~s** pl
(dealings) Beziehungen pl;
relationship n (connection)
Beziehung f; (between people)
Verhältnis nt

relative ['relətɪv] n Verwandte(r)
mf ▷ adj relativ; **relatively** adv
relativ, verhältnismäßig

relax [rɪ'læks] vi sich
entspannen; **~!** reg dich nicht auf!
▷ vt (grip, conditions) lockern;
relaxation [riːlæk'seɪʃən] n (rest)
Entspannung f; **relaxed** adj
entspannt; **relaxing** adj
entspannend

release [rɪ'liːs] n (from prison)
Entlassung f; **new/recent ~** (film,
CD) Neuerscheinung f ▷ vt
(animal, hostage) freilassen;
(prisoner) entlassen; (handbrake)
lösen; (news) veröffentlichen;
(film, CD) herausbringen

relent [rɪ'lent] vi nachgeben;

relentless, relentlessly adj, adv
(merciless) erbarmungslos;
(neverending) unaufhörlich

relevance ['reləvəns] n
Relevanz f (to für); **relevant** adj
relevant (to für)

reliable, reliably [rɪ'laɪəbl, -blɪ]
adj, adv zuverlässig; **reliant**
[rɪ'laɪənt] adj: **~ on** abhängig von

relic ['relɪk] n (from past) Relikt n

relief [rɪ'liːf] n (from anxiety, pain)
Erleichterung f; (assistance) Hilfe f;
relieve [rɪ'liːv] vt (pain) lindern;
(boredom) überwinden; (take over
from) ablösen; **I'm ~d** ich bin
erleichtert

religion [rɪ'lɪdʒən] n Religion f;
religious [rɪ'lɪdʒəs] adj religiös

relish ['relɪʃ] n (for food) würzige
Soße ▷ vt (enjoy) genießen; **I
don't ~ the thought of it** der
Gedanke behagt mir gar nicht

reluctant [rɪ'lʌktənt] adj
widerwillig; **to be ~ to do sth** etw
nur ungern tun; **reluctantly** adv
widerwillig

rely on [rɪ'laɪ ɒn] vt sich
verlassen auf +akk; (depend on)
abhängig sein von

remain [rɪ'meɪn] vi bleiben; (be
left over) übrig bleiben; **remainder**
n (a. Math) Rest m; **remaining** adj
übrig; **remains** npl Überreste pl

remark [rɪ'mɑːk] n Bemerkung f
▷ vt: **to ~ that** bemerken, dass
▷ vi: **to ~ on sth** über etw akk eine
Bemerkung machen; **remarkable,
remarkably** adj, adv
bemerkenswert

remarry [riː'mærɪ] vi wieder
heiraten

remedy ['remədɪ] n Mittel nt (for
gegen) ▷ vt abhelfen +dat

remember [rɪ'membə*] vt sich
erinnern an +akk; **to ~ to do sth**
daran denken, etw zu tun; **I
~ seeing her** ich erinnere mich

daran, sie gesehen zu haben; **I must ~ that** das muss ich mir merken ▷ *vi* sich erinnern

Remembrance Day
[rɪˈmembrənsˈdeɪ] *n* (Brit) = Volkstrauertag *m*

○ **REMEMBRANCE DAY**
○
○ **Remembrance Sunday/Day** ist
○ der britische Gedenktag für die
○ Gefallenen der beiden
○ Weltkriege und anderer Kriege.
○ Er fällt auf einen Sonntag vor
○ oder nach dem 11. November
○ (am 11.11.1918 endete der Erste
○ Weltkrieg) und wird mit einer
○ Schweigeminute,
○ Kranzniederlegungen an
○ Kriegerdenkmälern und dem
○ Tragen von Anstecknadeln in
○ Form einer Mohnblume
○ begangen.

remind [rɪˈmaɪnd] *vt*: **to ~ sb of/about sb/sth** jdn an jdn/etw erinnern; **to ~ sb to do sth** jdn daran erinnern, etw zu tun; **that ~s me** dabei fällt mir ein ...; **reminder** (*to pay*) Mahnung *f*

reminisce [remɪˈnɪs] *vi* in Erinnerungen schwelgen (*about an* +akk); **reminiscent** [remɪˈnɪsənt] *adj*: **to be ~ of** erinnern an +akk

remittance [rɪˈmɪtəns] *n* Überweisung *f* (*to* an +akk)

remnant [ˈremnənt] *adj* (place) Rest *m*

remote [rɪˈməʊt] *adj* (place) abgelegen; (slight) gering ▷ *n* (TV) Fernbedienung *f*; **remote control** *n* Fernsteuerung *f*; (device) Fernbedienung *f*

removal [rɪˈmuːvəl] *n* Entfernung *f*; (Brit: move from house) Umzug *m*; **removal firm** *n* (Brit) Spedition *f*; **remove** [rɪˈmuːv] *vt* entfernen; (lid) abnehmen;

(clothes) ausziehen; (doubt, suspicion) zerstreuen

rename [riːˈneɪm] *vt* umbenennen

renew [rɪˈnjuː] *vt* erneuern; (licence, passport, library book) verlängern lassen; **renewable** *adj* (energy) erneuerbar

renounce [rɪˈnaʊns] *vt* verzichten auf +akk; (faith, opinion) abschwören +dat

renovate [ˈrenəveɪt] *vt* renovieren

renowned [rɪˈnaʊnd] *adj* berühmt (for für)

rent [rent] *n* Miete *f*; **for ~** (US) zu vermieten ▷ *vt* (as hirer, tenant) mieten; (as owner) vermieten; **~ed car** Mietwagen *m*; **rent out** *vt* vermieten; **rental** *n* Miete *f*; (for car, TV etc) Leihgebühr *f* ▷ *adj* Miet-

reorganize [riːˈɔːgənaɪz] *vt* umorganisieren

rep [rep] *n* Vertreter(in) *m(f)*

repair [rɪˈpeəʳ] *n* Reparatur *f* ▷ *vt* reparieren; (damage) wiedergutmachen; **repair kit** *n* Flickzeug *nt*

repay [riːˈpeɪ] irr *vt* (money) zurückzahlen; **to ~ sb for sth** (fig) sich bei jdm für etw revanchieren

repeat [rɪˈpiːt] *n* (Radio, TV) Wiederholung *f* ▷ *vt* wiederholen; **repetition** [repəˈtɪʃən] *n* Wiederholung *f*; **repetitive** [rɪˈpetɪtɪv] *adj* sich wiederholend

rephrase [riːˈfreɪz] *vt* anders formulieren

replace [rɪˈpleɪs] *vt* ersetzen (with durch); (put back) zurückstellen, zurücklegen; **replacement** *n* (thing, person) Ersatz *m*; (temporarily in job) Vertretung *f*; **replacement part** *n* Ersatzteil *nt*

replay [ˈriːpleɪ] *n*: (action)

~ Wiederholung f ▷ [ri:'pleɪ] vt (game) wiederholen

replica ['replɪkə] n Kopie f

reply [rɪ'plaɪ] n Antwort f ▷ vi antworten; **to ~ to sb/sth** jdm/auf etw akk antworten ▷ vt: **to ~ that** antworten, dass

report [rɪ'pɔːt] n Bericht m; (school) Zeugnis nt ▷ vt (tell) berichten; (give information against) melden; (to police) anzeigen ▷ vi (present oneself) sich melden; **to ~ sick** sich krankmelden; **report card** n (US: school) Zeugnis nt; **reporter** n Reporter(in) m(f)

represent [reprɪ'zent] vt darstellen; (speak for) vertreten; **representation** [reprɪzen'teɪʃən] n (picture etc) Darstellung f; **representative** [reprɪ'zentətɪv] n Vertreter(in) m(f); (US Pol) Abgeordnete(r) mf ▷ adj repräsentativ (of für)

reprimand ['reprɪmɑːnd] n Tadel m ▷ vt tadeln

reprint ['riːprɪnt] n Nachdruck m

reproduce [riːprə'djuːs] vt (copy) reproduzieren ▷ vi (Bio) sich fortpflanzen; **reproduction** [riːprə'dʌkʃən] n (copy) Reproduktion f; (Bio) Fortpflanzung f

reptile ['reptaɪl] n Reptil nt

republic [rɪ'pʌblɪk] n Republik f; **republican** adj republikanisch ▷ n Republikaner(in) m(f)

repulsive [rɪ'pʌlsɪv] adj abstoßend

reputable ['repjʊtəbl] adj seriös

reputation [repjʊ'teɪʃən] n Ruf m; **he has a ~ for being difficult** er hat den Ruf, schwierig zu sein

request [rɪ'kwest] n Bitte f (for um); **on ~** auf Wunsch ▷ vt bitten um; **to ~ sb to do sth** jdn bitten, etw zu tun

require [rɪ'kwaɪə°] vt (need)

brauchen; (desire) verlangen; **what qualifications are ~d?** welche Qualifikationen sind erforderlich?; **required** adj erforderlich; **requirement** n (condition) Anforderung f; (need) Bedingung f

rerun ['riːrʌn] n Wiederholung f

rescue ['reskjuː] n Rettung f; **to come to sb's ~** jdm zu Hilfe kommen ▷ vt retten; **rescue party** n Rettungsmannschaft f

research [rɪ'sɜːtʃ] n Forschung f ▷ vi forschen (into über +akk) ▷ vt erforschen; **researcher** n Forscher(in) m(f)

resemblance [rɪ'zembləns] n Ähnlichkeit f (to mit); **resemble** [rɪ'zembl] vt ähneln +dat

resent [rɪ'zent] vt übel nehmen

reservation [rezə'veɪʃən] n (booking) Reservierung f; (doubt) Vorbehalt m; **I have a ~** (in hotel, restaurant) ich habe reserviert; **reserve** [rɪ'zɜːv] n (store) Vorrat m (of an +dat); (manner) Zurückhaltung f; (Sport) Reservespieler(in) m(f); (game ~) Naturschutzgebiet nt ▷ vt (book in advance) reservieren; **reserved** adj reserviert

reservoir ['rezəvwɑː°] n (for water) Reservoir nt

reside [rɪ'zaɪd] vi wohnen; **residence** ['rezɪdəns] n Wohnsitz m; (living) Aufenthalt m; **~ permit** n Aufenthaltsgenehmigung f; **~ hall** n Studentenwohnheim nt; **resident** ['rezɪdənt] n (in house) Bewohner(in) m(f); (in town, area) Einwohner(in) m(f)

resign [rɪ'zaɪn] vt (post) zurücktreten von; (job) kündigen ▷ vi (from post) zurücktreten; (from job) kündigen; **resignation** [rezɪg'neɪʃən] n (from post)

Rücktritt m; (from job) Kündigung f; **resigned** adj resigniert; **he is ~ to it** er hat sich damit abgefunden

resist [rɪˈzɪst] vt widerstehen +dat; **resistance** n Widerstand m (to gegen)

resit [riːˈsɪt] (Brit) irr vt wiederholen ▷ [ˈriːsɪt] n Wiederholungsprüfung f

resolution [rezəˈluːʃən] n (intention) Vorsatz m; (decision) Beschluss m

resolve [rɪˈzɒlv] vt (problem) lösen

resort [rɪˈzɔːt] n (holiday ~) Urlaubsort m; (health ~) Kurort m; **as a last ~** als letzter Ausweg ▷ vi: **to ~ to** greifen zu +dat; (violence) anwenden

resources [rɪˈsɔːsɪz] npl (money) (Geld)mittel pl; (mineral ~) Bodenschätze pl

respect [rɪˈspekt] n Respekt m (for vor +dat); (consideration) Rücksicht f (for auf +akk); **with ~ to** in Bezug auf +akk; **in this ~** in dieser Hinsicht; **with all due ~** bei allem Respekt ▷ vt respektieren; **respectable** [rɪˈspektəbl] adj (person, family) angesehen; (district) anständig; (achievement, result) beachtlich; **respected** [rɪˈspektɪd] adj angesehen

respective [rɪˈspektɪv] adj jeweilig; **respectively** adv: **5 % and 10 % ~** 5 % beziehungsweise 10 %

respiratory [rɪˈspɪrətərɪ] adj: **~ problems** (o **trouble**) Atembeschwerden pl

respond [rɪˈspɒnd] vi antworten (to auf +akk); (react) reagieren (to auf +akk); (to treatment) ansprechen (to auf +akk); **response** [rɪˈspɒns] n Antwort f; (reaction) Reaktion f; **in ~ to** als Antwort auf +akk

responsibility [rɪspɒnsəˈbɪlɪtɪ] n Verantwortung f; **that's her ~** dafür ist sie verantwortlich; **responsible** [rɪˈspɒnsəbl] adj verantwortlich (for für); (trustworthy) verantwortungsbewusst; (job) verantwortungsvoll

rest [rest] n (relaxation) Ruhe f; (break) Pause f; (remainder) Rest m; **to have** (o **take**) **a ~** sich ausruhen; (break) Pause machen; **the ~ of the wine/the people** der Rest des Weins/der Leute ▷ vi (relax) sich ausruhen; (lean) lehnen (on, against an +dat, gegen)

restaurant [ˈrestərɒnt] n Restaurant m; **restaurant car** n (Brit) Speisewagen m

restful [ˈrestfʊl] adj (holiday etc) erholsam, ruhig; **restless** [ˈrestləs] adj unruhig

restore [rɪˈstɔːʳ] vt (painting, building) restaurieren; (order) wiederherstellen; (give back) zurückgeben

restrain [rɪˈstreɪn] vt (person, feelings) zurückhalten; **to ~ oneself** sich beherrschen

restrict [rɪˈstrɪkt] vt beschränken (to auf +akk); **restricted** adj beschränkt; **restriction** [rɪˈstrɪkʃən] n Einschränkung f (on +gen)

rest room [ˈrestruːm] n (US) Toilette f

result [rɪˈzʌlt] n Ergebnis nt; (consequence) Folge f; **as a ~ of** infolge +gen ▷ vi: **to ~ in** führen zu; **to ~ from** sich ergeben aus

resume [rɪˈzjuːm] vt (work, negotiations) wieder aufnehmen; (journey) fortsetzen

résumé [ˈrezjʊmeɪ] n Zusammenfassung f; (US: curriculum vitae) Lebenslauf m

resuscitate [rɪˈsʌsɪteɪt] vt
wiederbeleben

retail [ˈriːteɪl] adv im
Einzelhandel; **retailer** n
Einzelhändler(in) m(f)

retain [rɪˈteɪn] vt behalten; (heat)
halten

rethink [riːˈθɪŋk] irr vt noch
einmal überdenken

retire [rɪˈtaɪəʳ] vi (from work) in
den Ruhestand treten; (withdraw)
sich zurückziehen; **retired** adj
(person) pensioniert; **retirement** n
(time of life) Ruhestand m;
retirement age n Rentenalter nt

retrace [riːˈtreɪs] vt
zurückverfolgen

retrain [riːˈtreɪn] vi sich
umschulen lassen

retreat [rɪˈtriːt] n (Mil) Rückzug
m (from aus); (refuge) Zufluchtsort
m ▷ vi (Mil) sich zurückziehen;
(step back) zurückweichen

retrieve [rɪˈtriːv] vt (recover)
wiederbekommen; (rescue) retten;
(data) abrufen

retrospect [ˈretrəʊspekt] n: **in
~** rückblickend; **retrospective**
[retrəʊˈspektɪv] adj rückblickend;
(pay rise) rückwirkend

return [rɪˈtɜːn] n (going back)
Rückkehr f; (giving back)
Rückgabe f; (profit) Gewinn m;
(Brit: ~ ticket) Rückfahrkarte f;
(plane ticket) Rückflugticket nt;
(Tennis) Return m; **in ~** als
Gegenleistung (for für); **many
happy ~s (of the day)** herzlichen
Glückwunsch zum Geburtstag!
▷ vi (person) zurückkehren;
(doubts, symptoms) wieder
auftreten; **to ~ to school/work**
wieder in die Schule/die Arbeit
gehen ▷ vt (give back)
zurückgeben; **I ~ed his call** ich
habe ihn zurückgerufen;
returnable adj (bottle) Pfand-;

return flight n (Brit) Rückflug m;
(both ways) Hin- und Rückflug m;
return key n (Inform)
Eingabetaste f; **return ticket** n
(Brit) Rückflugkarte f; (for plane)
Rückflugticket nt

retweet [riːˈtwiːt] vt (on Twitter)
retweeten

reunification [riːjuːnɪfɪˈkeɪʃən]
n Wiedervereinigung f

reunion [riːˈjuːnjən] n (party)
Treffen nt; (family) Revanche f;
wieder vereinigen

reunite [riːjuːˈnaɪt] vt
wieder vereinigen

reusable [riːˈjuːzəbl] adj
wiederverwendbar

reveal [rɪˈviːl] vt (make known)
enthüllen; (secret) verraten; (show)
zeigen; **revealing** adj
aufschlussreich; (dress) freizügig

revenge [rɪˈvendʒ] n Rache f; (in
game) Revanche f; **to take ~ on sb
(for sth)** sich an jdm (für etw)
rächen

revenue [ˈrevənjuː] n Einnahmen pl

reverse [rɪˈvɜːs] n (back)
Rückseite f; (opposite) Gegenteil nt;
(Auto) ~ (gear) Rückwärtsgang m
▷ adj: **in ~ order** in umgekehrter
Reihenfolge ▷ vt (order)
umkehren; (decision) umstoßen;
(car) zurücksetzen ▷ vi (Auto)
rückwärtsfahren

review [rɪˈvjuː] n (of book, film
etc) Rezension f; Kritik f; **to be
under ~** überprüft werden ▷ vt
(book, film etc) rezensieren;
(re-examine) überprüfen

revise [rɪˈvaɪz] vt revidieren;
(text) überarbeiten; (Brit: in school)
wiederholen ▷ vi (Brit: in school)
(für eine Prüfung) lernen; **revision**
[rɪˈvɪʒən] n (of text)
Überarbeitung f; (Brit: in school)
Wiederholung f

revitalize [riːˈvaɪtəlaɪz] vt neu
beleben

revive [rɪ'vaɪv] vt (person) wiederbeleben; (tradition, interest) wieder aufleben lassen ▷ vi (regain consciousness) wieder zu sich kommen

revolt [rɪ'vəʊlt] n Aufstand m; **revolting** adj widerlich

revolution [revə'lu:ʃən] n (Pol, fig) Revolution f; (turn) Umdrehung f; **revolutionary** adj revolutionär ▷ n Revolutionär(in) m(f)

revolve [rɪ'vɒlv] vi sich drehen (around um); **revolver** n Revolver m; **revolving door** n Drehtür f

reward [rɪ'wɔ:d] n Belohnung f ▷ vt belohnen; **rewarding** adj lohnend

rewind [ri:'waɪnd] irr vt (tape) zurückspulen

rewritable [ri:'raɪtəbl] adj (CD, DVD) wiederbeschreibbar; **rewrite** irr vt (write again; recast) umschreiben

rheumatism ['ru:mətɪzəm] n Rheuma nt

Rhine [raɪn] n Rhein m

rhinoceros [raɪ'nɒsərəs] n Nashorn nt

Rhodes [rəʊdz] n Rhodos nt

rhubarb ['ru:bɑ:b] n Rhabarber m

rhyme [raɪm] n Reim m ▷ vi sich reimen (with auf +akk)

rhythm ['rɪðəm] n Rhythmus m

rib [rɪb] n Rippe f

ribbon ['rɪbən] n Band nt

rice [raɪs] n Reis m; **rice pudding** n Milchreis m

rich [rɪtʃ] adj reich; (food) schwer ▷ npl: **the ~** die Reichen pl

rickety ['rɪkɪtɪ] adj wackelig

rid [rɪd] (**rid, rid**) vt: **to get ~ of sb/sth** jdn/etw loswerden

ridden ['rɪdn] pp of ride

riddle ['rɪdl] n Rätsel nt

ride [raɪd] (**rode, ridden**) vt (horse) reiten; (bicycle) fahren ▷ vi

(on horse) reiten; (on bike) fahren ▷ n (in vehicle, on bike) Fahrt f; (on horse) (Aus)ritt m; **to go for a ~** (in car, on bike) spazieren fahren; (on horse) reiten gehen; **to take sb for a ~** (fam) jdn verarschen; **rider** n (on horse) Reiter(in) m(f); (on bike) Fahrer(in) m(f)

ridiculous [rɪ'dɪkjʊləs] adj lächerlich; **don't be ~** red keinen Unsinn!

riding ['raɪdɪŋ] n Reiten nt; **to go ~** reiten gehen ▷ adj Reit-

rifle ['raɪfl] n Gewehr nt

rig [rɪg] n: **oil ~** Bohrinsel f ▷ vt (election etc) manipulieren

right [raɪt] adj (correct, just) richtig; (opposite of left) rechte(r, s); (clothes, job etc) passend; **to be ~** (person) recht haben; (clock) richtig gehen; **that's ~** das stimmt! ▷ n Recht nt (to auf +akk); (side) rechte Seite; **the Right** (Pol) die Rechte; **to take a ~** (Auto) rechts abbiegen; **on the ~** rechts (of von); **to the ~** nach rechts; (on the ~) rechts (of von) ▷ adv (towards the ~) nach rechts; (directly) direkt; (exactly) genau; **to turn ~** (Auto) rechts abbiegen; **~ away** sofort; **~ now** im Moment; (immediately) sofort; **right angle** n rechter Winkel; **right-hand drive** n Rechtssteuerung f ▷ adj rechtsgesteuert; **right-handed** adj: **he is ~** er ist Rechtshänder; **right-hand side** n rechte Seite; **on the ~** auf der rechten Seite; **rightly** adv zu Recht; **right of way** n: **to have ~** (Auto) Vorfahrt haben; **right wing** n (Pol, Sport) rechter Flügel; **right-wing** adj Rechts-; **~ extremist** Rechtsradikale(r) mf

rigid ['rɪdʒɪd] adj (stiff) starr; (strict) streng

rigorous, rigorously ['rɪgərəs, -lɪ] adj, adv streng

rim [rɪm] n (of cup etc) Rand m; (of wheel) Felge f

rind [raɪnd] n (of cheese) Rinde f; (of bacon) Schwarte f; (of fruit) Schale f

ring [rɪŋ] (rang, rung) vt, vi (bell) läuten; (Tel) anrufen ⊳ n (on finger, in boxing) Ring m; (circle) Kreis m; (at circus) Manege f; **to give sb a ~** (Tel) jdn anrufen; **ring back** vt, vi zurückrufen; **ring up** vt, vi anrufen

ring binder n Ringbuch nt
ringleader n Anführer(in) m(f)
ring road n (Brit) Umgehungsstraße f
ringtone n Klingelton m
rink [rɪŋk] n (ice ~) Eisbahn f; (for roller-skating) Rollschuhbahn f
rinse [rɪns] vt spülen
riot ['raɪət] n Aufruhr m

rip [rɪp] n Riss m ⊳ vt zerreißen; **to ~ sth open** etw aufreißen ⊳ vi reißen; **rip off** vt (fam: person) übers Ohr hauen; **rip up** vt zerreißen

ripe [raɪp] adj (fruit) reif; **ripen** vi reifen

rip-off ['rɪpɒf] n: **that's a ~** (fam: too expensive) das ist Wucher

rise [raɪz] (rose, risen) vi (from sitting, lying) aufstehen; (sun) aufgehen; (prices, temperature) steigen; (ground) ansteigen; (in revolt) sich erheben ⊳ n (increase) Anstieg m (in +gen); (pay ~) Gehaltserhöhung f (to power, fame) Aufstieg m (to zu); (slope) Steigung f; **risen** ['rɪzn] pp of **rise**

risk [rɪsk] n Risiko nt ⊳ vt riskieren; **to ~ doing sth** es riskieren, etw zu tun; **risky** adj riskant

risotto [rɪ'zɒtəʊ] (pl **-s**) n Risotto nt

ritual ['rɪtjʊəl] n Ritual nt ⊳ adj rituell

rival ['raɪvəl] n Rivale m, Rivalin f (for um); (Comm) Konkurrent(in) m(f); **rivalry** n Rivalität f; (Comm, Sport) Konkurrenz f

river ['rɪvə°] n Fluss m; **the River Thames** (Brit), **the Thames River** (US) die Themse; **riverside** n Flussufer nt ⊳ adj am Flussufer

road [rəʊd] n Straße f; (fig) Weg m; **on the ~** (travelling) unterwegs, dem Auto/Bus etc fahren; **roadblock** n Straßensperre f; **roadmap** n Straßenkarte f; **road rage** n aggressives Verhalten im Straßenverkehr; **roadside** n: **at (o by) the ~** am Straßenrand; **roadsign** n Verkehrsschild nt; **road tax** n Kraftfahrzeugsteuer f; **roadworks** npl Bauarbeiten pl; **roadworthy** adj fahrtüchtig

roar [rɔː°] n (of person, lion) Brüllen nt; (von Verkehr) Donnern nt ⊳ vi (person, lion) brüllen (with vor +dat)

roast [rəʊst] n Braten m ⊳ adj: **~ beef** Rinderbraten m; **~ chicken** Brathähnchen nt; **~ pork** Schweinebraten m; **~ potatoes** pl im Backofen gebratene Kartoffeln ⊳ vt (meat) braten

rob [rɒb] vt bestehlen; (bank, shop) ausrauben; **robber** n Räuber(in) m(f); **robbery** n Raub m

robe [rəʊb] n (US: dressing gown) Morgenrock m; (of judge, priest etc) Robe f, Talar m

robin ['rɒbɪn] n Rotkehlchen nt
robot ['rəʊbɒt] n Roboter m
robust [rəʊ'bʌst] adj robust; (defence) stark

rock [rɒk] n (substance) Stein m; (boulder) Felsbrocken m; (Mus) Rock m; **stick of ~** (Brit) Zuckerstange f; **on the ~s** (drink)

mit Eis; (marriage) gescheitert
▷ vt, vi (swing) schaukeln; (dance)
rocken; **rock climbing** n Klettern
nt; **to go ~** klettern gehen
rocket ['rɔkɪt] n Rakete f; (in
salad) Rucola m
rocking chair ['rɔkɪŋtʃeə°] n
Schaukelstuhl m
rocky ['rɔkɪ] adj (landscape) felsig;
(path) steinig
rod [rɔd] n (bar) Stange f; (fishing
~) Rute f
rode [rəʊd] pt of **ride**
rogue [rəʊg] n Schurke m,
Gauner m
role [rəʊl] n Rolle f; **role model** n
Vorbild n
roll [rəʊl] n (of film, paper etc)
Rolle f; (bread ~) Brötchen nt ▷ vt
(move by ~ing) rollen; (cigarette)
drehen ▷ vi (move by ~ing) rollen;
(ship) schlingern; (camera) laufen;
roll out vt (pastry) ausrollen; **roll
over** vi (person) sich umdrehen;
roll up vi (fam: arrive) antanzen
▷ vt (carpet) aufrollen; **to roll
one's sleeves up** die Ärmel
hochkrempeln
roller n (hair ~) (Locken)wickler m;
Rollerblades® n(f) m(f); **Roman
blading** n Inlineskaten
nt; **roller coaster** n Achterbahn f;
roller skates npl Rollschuhe pl;
roller-skating n Rollschuhlaufen
nt; **rolling pin** n Nudelholz nt;
roll-on (deodorant) n Deoroller
m

ROM [rɔm] acr = **read only
memory** ROM m
Roman ['rəʊmən] adj römisch
▷ n Römer(in) m(f); **Roman
Catholic** adj römisch-katholisch
▷ n Katholik(in) m(f)
romance [rəʊˈmæns] n Romantik f; (love affair) Romanze f
Romania [rəʊˈmeɪnɪə] n
Rumänien nt; **Romanian** adj

rumänisch ▷ n Rumäne m,
Rumänin f; (language) Rumänisch
nt
romantic [rəʊˈmæntɪk] adj
romantisch
roof [ruːf] n Dach nt; **roof rack** n
Dachgepäckträger m
rook [rʊk] n (in chess) Turm m
room [ruːm] n Zimmer nt, Raum
m; (large, for gatherings etc) Saal m;
(space) Platz m; (fig) Spielraum m;
to make ~ for Platz machen für;
roommate n Zimmergenosse m,
Zimmergenossin f;
Mitbewohner(in) m(f); **room
service** n Zimmerservice m;
roomy adj geräumig; (garment)
weit
root [ruːt] n Wurzel f; **root out** vt
(eradicate) ausrotten; **root
vegetable** n Wurzelgemüse nt
rope [rəʊp] n Seil nt; **to know
the ~s** (fam) sich auskennen
rort [rɔːt] (Aust, NZ fam) n
Betrugsschema nt, Abzocke f (fam)
▷ vt austricksen (fam); (money)
abschöpfen
rose [rəʊz] pt of **rise** ▷ n Rose f
rosé ['rəʊzeɪ] n Rosé(wein) m
rot [rɔt] vi verfaulen
rota ['rəʊtə] n (Brit) Dienstplan m
rotate [rəʊˈteɪt] vt (turn) rotieren
lassen ▷ vi rotieren
rotten ['rɔtn] adj (decayed) faul;
(mean) gemein; (unpleasant)
scheußlich; (ill) elend
rough [rʌf] adj (not smooth) rau;
(path) uneben; (coarse, violent)
grob; (crossing) stürmisch; (without
comforts) hart; (unfinished,
makeshift) grob; (approximate)
ungefähr; **~ draft** Rohentwurf m; **I
have a ~ idea** ich habe eine
ungefähre Vorstellung ▷ adv: **to
sleep ~** im Freien schlafen ▷ vt:
to ~ it primitiv leben; **roughly** adv
grob; (approximately) ungefähr

round [raʊnd] *adj* rund ▷ *adv*: **all ~** (on all sides) rundherum; **the long way ~** der längere Weg; **I'll be ~ at 8** ich werde um acht Uhr da sein; **the other way ~** umgekehrt ▷ *prep* (surrounding) um (... herum); **~ (about)** (approximately) ungefähr; **~ the corner** um die Ecke; **to go ~ the world** um die Welt reisen; **she lives ~ here** sie wohnt hier in der Gegend ▷ *n* Runde *f*; (of bread, toast) Scheibe *f*; **it's my ~** (of drinks) die Runde geht auf mich ▷ *vt* (corner) biegen um; **round off** *vt* abrunden; **round up** *vt* (number, price) aufrunden

roundabout *n* (Brit Auto) Kreisverkehr *m*; (Brit: merry-go-round) Karussell *nt* ▷ *adj* umständlich; **round-the-clock** *adj* rund um die Uhr; **round trip** *n* Rundreise *f*; **round-trip ticket** *n* (US) Rückfahrkarte *f*; (for plane) Rückflugticket *nt*

rouse [raʊz] *vt* (from sleep) wecken

route [ruːt] *n* Route *f*; (bus, train etc service) Linie *f*; (fig) Weg *m*

router [ˈruːtəʳ] *n* (Inform) Router *m*

routine [ruːˈtiːn] *n* Routine *f* ▷ *adj* Routine-

row[1] [rəʊ] *n* (line) Reihe *f*; **three times in a ~** dreimal hintereinander ▷ *vt, vi* (boat) rudern ▷ [raʊ] *n* (noise) Krach *m*; (dispute) Streit *m*

rowboat [ˈrəʊbəʊt] *n* (US) Ruderboot *nt*

row house [ˈrəʊhaʊs] *n* (US) Reihenhaus *nt*

rowing [ˈrəʊɪŋ] *n* Rudern *nt*; **rowing boat** *n* (Brit) Ruderboot *nt*; **rowing machine** *n* Rudergerät *nt*

royal [ˈrɔɪəl] *adj* königlich; **royalty** *n* (family) Mitglieder *pl* der königlichen Familie; **royalties**

pl (from book, music) Tantiemen *pl*

RSPCA *abbr* = **Royal Society for the Prevention of Cruelty to Animals** *britischer* Tierschutzverein

RSPCC *abbr* = **Royal Society for the Prevention of Cruelty to Children** *britischer* Kinderschutzverein

RSVP *abbr* = **répondez s'il vous plaît** u. A. w. g.

rub [rʌb] *vt* reiben; **rub in** *vt* einmassieren; **rub out** *vt* (with eraser) ausradieren

rubber [ˈrʌbəʳ] *n* Gummi *m*; (Brit: eraser) Radiergummi *m*; (US fam: contraceptive) Gummi *m*; **rubber band** *n* Gummiband *nt*; **rubber stamp** *n* Stempel *m*

rubbish [ˈrʌbɪʃ] *n* Abfall *m*; (nonsense) Quatsch *m*; (poor-quality thing) Mist *m*; **don't talk ~** red keinen Unsinn!; **rubbish bin** *n* Mülleimer *m*; **rubbish dump** *n* Müllabladeplatz *m*

rubble [ˈrʌbl] *n* Schutt *m*

ruby [ˈruːbɪ] *n* (stone) Rubin *m*

rucksack [ˈrʌksæk] *n* Rucksack *m*

rude [ruːd] *adj* (impolite) unhöflich; (indecent) unanständig

rug [rʌɡ] *n* Teppich *m*; (next to bed) Bettvorleger *m*; (for knees) Wolldecke *f*

rugby [ˈrʌɡbɪ] *n* Rugby *nt*

rugged [ˈrʌɡɪd] *adj* (coastline) zerklüftet; (features) markant

ruin [ˈruːɪn] *n* Ruine *f*; (financial, social) Ruin *m* ▷ *vt* ruinieren

rule [ruːl] *n* Regel *f*; (governing) Herrschaft *f*; **as a ~** in der Regel ▷ *vt, vi* (govern) regieren; (decide) entscheiden; **ruler** *n* Lineal *nt*; (person) Herrscher(in) *m(f)*

rum [rʌm] *n* Rum *m*

rumble [ˈrʌmbl] *vi* (stomach) knurren; (train, truck) rumpeln

rummage [ˈrʌmɪdʒ] *vi*: **~ (around)** herumstöbern

rumor (US), **rumour** ['ru:mə°] n
Gerücht nt

run [rʌn] (**ran, run**) vt (race,
distance) laufen; (machine, engine,
computer program, water) laufen
lassen; (manage) leiten, führen;
(car) unterhalten; **I ran her home**
ich habe sie nach Hause gefahren
▷ vi laufen; (move quickly) rennen;
(bus, train) laufen; (path etc)
verlaufen; (machine, engine,
computer program) laufen; (flow)
fließen; (colours, make-up)
verlaufen; **to ~ for President** für
die Präsidentschaft kandidieren;
to be ~ing low knapp werden;
my nose is ~ing mir läuft die
Nase; **it ~s in the family** es liegt in
der Familie ▷ n (on foot) Lauf m;
(in car) Spazierfahrt f; (series) Reihe
f; (sudden demand) Ansturm m (on
auf +akk); (in tights) Laufmasche f;
(in cricket, baseball) Lauf m; **to go
for a ~** laufen gehen; (in car) eine
Spazierfahrt machen; **in the long
~** auf die Dauer; **on the ~** auf der
Flucht (from vor +dat); **run about**
vi herumlaufen; **run away** vi
weglaufen; **run down** vt (with car)
umfahren; (criticize)
heruntermachen; **to be ~** (tired)
abgespannt sein; **run into** vt
(meet) zufällig treffen; (problem)
stoßen auf +akk; **run off** vi
weglaufen; **run out** vi (person)
hinausrennen; (liquid) auslaufen;
(lease, time) ablaufen; (money,
supplies) ausgehen; **he ran ~ of
money** ihm ging das Geld aus; **run
over** vt (with car) überfahren; **run
up** vt (debt, bill) machen

rung [rʌŋ] pp of **ring**

runner ['rʌnə°] n (athlete)
Läufer(in) m(f); **to do a ~** (fam)
wegrennen; **runner bean** n (Brit)
Stangenbohne f

running ['rʌnɪŋ] n (Sport) Laufen

nt; (management) Leitung f,
Führung f ▷ adj (water) fließend;
~ costs Betriebskosten pl; (for car)
Unterhaltskosten pl; **3 days** ~ 3
Tage hintereinander

runny ['rʌnɪ] adj (food) flüssig;
(nose) laufend

runway ['rʌnweɪ] n Start- und
Landebahn f

rural ['rʊərəl] adj ländlich

rush [rʌʃ] n Eile f; (for tickets etc)
Ansturm m (for auf +akk); **to be in a
~** es eilig haben; **there's no ~** es
eilt nicht ▷ vt (do too quickly)
hastig machen; (meal) hastig
essen; **to ~ sb to hospital** jdn auf
dem schnellsten Weg ins
Krankenhaus bringen; **don't ~ me**
dräng mich nicht ▷ vi (hurry)
eilen; **don't ~** lass dir Zeit; **rush
hour** n Hauptverkehrszeit f

rusk [rʌsk] n Zwieback m

Russia ['rʌʃə] n Russland nt;
Russian adj russisch ▷ n Russe
m, Russin f; (language) Russisch nt

rust [rʌst] n Rost m ▷ vi rosten;
rustproof ['rʌstpru:f] adj rostfrei; **rusty** ['rʌstɪ] adj rostig

ruthless ['ru:θləs] adj rücksichtslos; (treatment, criticism)
schonungslos

rye [raɪ] n Roggen m; **rye bread**
n Roggenbrot nt

S

S *abbr* = **south** S

sabotage ['sæbətɑːʒ] *vt* sabotieren

sachet ['sæʃeɪ] *n* Päckchen *nt*

sack [sæk] *n* (*bag*) Sack *m*; **to get the ~** (*fam*) rausgeschmissen werden ▷ *vt* (*fam*) rausschmeißen

sacred ['seɪkrɪd] *adj* heilig

sacrifice ['sækrɪfaɪs] *n* Opfer *nt* ▷ *vt* opfern

sad [sæd] *adj* traurig

saddle ['sædl] *n* Sattel *m*

sadistic [sə'dɪstɪk] *adj* sadistisch

sadly ['sædlɪ] *adv* (*unfortunately*) leider

safari [sə'fɑːrɪ] *n* Safari *m*

safe [seɪf] *adj* (*free from danger*) sicher; (*out of danger*) in Sicherheit; (*careful*) vorsichtig; **have a ~ journey** gute Fahrt! ▷ *n* Safe *m*; **safeguard** *n* Schutz *m* ▷ *vt* schützen (*against* vor +*dat*); **safely** *adv* sicher; (*arrive*) wohlbehalten;

(*drive*) vorsichtig; **safety** *n* Sicherheit *f*; **safety belt** *n* Sicherheitsgurt *m*; **safety pin** *n* Sicherheitsnadel *f*

Sagittarius [sædʒɪ'teərɪəs] *n* (*Astr*) Schütze *m*

Sahara [sə'hɑːrə] *n*: **the ~ (Desert)** die (Wüste) Sahara

said [sed] *pt, pp of* **say**

sail [seɪl] *n* Segel *nt*; **to set ~** losfahren (*for* nach) ▷ *vi* (*in yacht*) segeln; (*on ship*) mit dem Schiff fahren; (*ship*) auslaufen (*for* nach) ▷ *vt* (*yacht*) segeln mit; (*ship*) steuern; **sailboat** *n* (*US*) Segelboot *nt*; **sailing** *n*: **to go ~** segeln gehen; **sailing boat** *n* (*Brit*) Segelboot *nt*; **sailor** *n* Seemann *m*; (*in navy*) Matrose *m*

saint [seɪnt] *n* Heilige(r) *mf*

sake [seɪk] *n*: **for the ~ of** um +*gen* ... willen; **for your ~** deinetwegen, dir zuliebe

salad ['sæləd] *n* Salat *m*; **salad cream** *n* (*Brit*) majonäseartige Salatsoße; **salad dressing** *n* Salatsoße *f*

salary ['sælərɪ] *n* Gehalt *nt*

sale [seɪl] *n* Verkauf *m*; (*at reduced prices*) Ausverkauf *m*; **the ~s** *pl* (*in summer, winter*) der Schlussverkauf; **for ~** zu verkaufen; **sales clerk** *n* (*US*) Verkäufer(in) *m(f)*; **salesman** (*pl* **-men**) *n* Verkäufer *m*; (*rep*) Vertreter *m*; **sales rep** *n* Vertreter(in) *m(f)*; **sales tax** *n* (*US*) Verkaufssteuer *f*; **saleswoman** (*pl* **-women**) *n* Verkäuferin *f*; (*rep*) Vertreterin *f*

salmon ['sæmən] *n* Lachs *m*

saloon [sə'luːn] *n* (*ship's lounge*) Salon *m*; (*US*: *bar*) Kneipe *f*

salt [sɔːlt] *n* Salz *nt* ▷ *vt* (*flavour*) salzen; (*roads*) mit Salz streuen; **salt cellar**, **salt shaker** (*US*) *n* Salzstreuer *m*; **salty** *adj* salzig

salvage ['sælvɪdʒ] vt bergen (from aus); (fig) retten

same [seɪm] adj: **the ~** (similar) der/die/das gleiche, die gleichen pl; (identical) der-/die-/dasselbe, dieselben pl; **they live in the ~ house** sie wohnen im selben Haus ▷ pron: **the ~** (similar) der/die/das Gleiche, die Gleichen pl; (identical) der-/die-/dasselbe, dieselben pl; **all the ~** trotzdem; **the ~ to you** gleichfalls; **it's all the ~ to me** es ist mir egal ▷ adv: **the ~** gleich; **they look the ~** sie sehen gleich aus

sample ['sɑːmpl] n Probe f; (of fabric) Muster nt ▷ vt probieren

sanctions ['sæŋkʃənz] npl (Pol) Sanktionen pl

sanctuary ['sæŋktjʊərɪ] n (refuge) Zuflucht f; (for animals) Schutzgebiet nt

sand [sænd] n Sand m

sandal ['sændl] n Sandale f

sandpaper n Sandpapier nt ▷ vt schmirgeln

sandwich ['sænwɪdʒ] n Sandwich nt

sandy ['sændɪ] adj (full of sand) sandig; **~ beach** Sandstrand m

sane [seɪn] adj geistig gesund, normal; (sensible) vernünftig

sang [sæŋ] pt of **sing**

sanitary ['sænɪtərɪ] adj hygienisch; **sanitary napkin** (US), **sanitary towel** n Damenbinde f

sank [sæŋk] pt of **sink**

Santa (Claus) ['sæntə('klɔːz)] n der Weihnachtsmann

sarcastic [sɑːˈkæstɪk] adj sarkastisch

sardine [sɑːˈdiːn] n Sardine f

Sardinia [sɑːˈdɪnɪə] n Sardinien nt

sari [ˈsɑːrɪ] n Sari m (von indischen Frauen getragenes Gewand)

sat [sæt] pt, pp of **sit**

Sat abbr = **Saturday** Sa.

satellite ['sætəlaɪt] n Satellit m; **satellite dish** n Satellitenschüssel f; **satellite TV** n Satellitenfernsehen nt

satin ['sætɪn] n Satin m

satisfaction [sætɪsˈfækʃən] n (contentment) Zufriedenheit f; **is that to your ~?** bist du/sind Sie damit zufrieden?; **satisfactory** [sætɪsˈfæktərɪ] adj zufriedenstellend; **satisfied** ['sætɪsfaɪd] adj zufrieden (with mit); **satisfy** ['sætɪsfaɪ] vt zufriedenstellen; (convince) überzeugen; (conditions) erfüllen; (need, demand) befriedigen; **satisfying** adj befriedigend

Saturday ['sætədeɪ] n Samstag m, Sonnabend m; see also **Tuesday**

sauce [sɔːs] n Soße f; **saucepan** n Kochtopf m; **saucer** n Untertasse f

saucy ['sɔːsɪ] adj frech

Saudi Arabia ['saʊdɪə'reɪbɪə] n Saudi-Arabien nt

sauna ['sɔːnə] n Sauna f

sausage ['sɒsɪdʒ] n Wurst f; **sausage roll** n mit Wurst gefülltes Blätterteigröllchen

savage ['sævɪdʒ] adj (person, attack) brutal; (animal) wild

save [seɪv] vt (rescue) retten (from vor +dat); (money, time, electricity etc) sparen; (strength) schonen; (Inform) speichern; **to ~ sb's life** jdm das Leben retten ▷ vi sparen ▷ n (in football) Parade f; **save up** vi sparen (for auf +akk); **saving** n (of money) Sparen nt; **~s** pl Ersparnisse pl; **~s account** n Sparkonto nt

savory (US), **savoury** ['seɪvərɪ] adj (not sweet) pikant

saw [sɔː] (**sawed, sawn**) vt, vi sägen ▷ n (tool) Säge f ▷ pt of **see**; **sawdust** n Sägemehl nt

saxophone ['sæksəfəʊn] n
Saxophon nt

say [seɪ] (**said, said**) vt sagen (to
sb jdm); (prayer) sprechen; **what
does the letter ~?** in den
Brief?; **the rules ~ that ...** in den
Regeln heißt es, dass ...; **he's said
to be rich** er soll reich sein ▷ n: **to
have a ~ in sth** bei etw ein
Mitspracherecht haben ▷ adv
zum Beispiel; **saying** n
Sprichwort nt

scab [skæb] n (on cut) Schorf m

scaffolding ['skæfəʊldɪŋ] n
(Bau)gerüst nt

scale [skeɪl] n (of map etc)
Maßstab m; (on thermometer etc)
Skala f; (of pay) Tarifsystem nt;
(Mus) Tonleiter f; (of fish, snake)
Schuppe f; **to ~** maßstabsgerecht;
on a large/small ~ in
großem/kleinem Umfang; **scales**
npl (for weighing) Waage f

scalp [skælp] n Kopfhaut f

scan [skæn] vt (examine) genau
prüfen; (read quickly) überfliegen;
(Inform) scannen ▷ n (Med)
Ultraschall m; **scan in** vt (Inform)
einscannen

scandal ['skændl] n Skandal m;
scandalous adj skandalös

Scandinavia [skændɪ'neɪvɪə] n
Skandinavien nt; **Scandinavian**
adj skandinavisch ▷ n Skandi-
navier(in) m(f)

scanner ['skænə°] n Scanner m

scapegoat ['skeɪpgəʊt] n
Sündenbock m

scar [skɑː°] n Narbe f

scarce ['skeəs] adj selten; (in
short supply) knapp; **scarcely** adv
kaum

scare ['skeə°] n (general alarm)
Panik f ▷ vt erschrecken; **to be ~d**
Angst haben (of +dat)

scarf [skɑːf] (pl **-scarves**) n Schal
m; (on head) Kopftuch nt

scarlet ['skɑːlət] adj schar-
lachrot; **scarlet fever** n Scharlach
m

scary ['skeərɪ] adj (film, story)
gruselig

scatter ['skætə°] vt verstreuen;
(seed, gravel) streuen; (disperse)
auseinandertreiben

scene [siːn] n (location) Ort m;
(division of play) (Theat) Szene f;
(view) Anblick m; **to make a ~** eine
Szene machen; **scenery** ['siːnərɪ]
n (landscape) Landschaft f; (Theat)
Kulissen pl; **scenic** ['siːnɪk] adj
(landscape) malerisch; **~ route**
landschaftlich schöne Strecke

scent [sent] n (perfume) Parfüm
nt; (smell) Duft m

sceptical ['skeptɪkəl] adj
skeptisch

schedule ['ʃedjuːl, 'skedʒʊəl] n
(plan) Programm nt; (of work)
Zeitplan m; (list) Liste f; (US: of
trains, buses, air traffic)
Fahr-, Flugplan m; **on
~** planmäßig; **to be behind ~ with
sth** mit etw in Verzug sein ▷ vt:
**the meeting is ~d for next
Monday** die Besprechung ist für
nächsten Montag angesetzt;
scheduled adj (departure, arrival)
planmäßig; **~ flight** Linienflug m

scheme [skiːm] n (plan) Plan m;
(project) Projekt nt; (dishonest)
Intrige f ▷ vi intrigieren

schizophrenic [skɪtsə'frenɪk]
adj schizophren

scholar ['skɒlə°] n Gelehrte(r)
mf; **scholarship** n (grant)
Stipendium nt

school [skuːl] n Schule f;
(university department) Fachbereich
m; (US: university) Universität f;
school bag n Schultasche f;
schoolbook n Schulbuch nt;
schoolboy n Schüler m; **school
bus** n Schulbus m; **schoolgirl** n

s

Schülerin f; **schoolteacher** n
Lehrer(in) m(f); **schoolwork** n
Schularbeiten pl

sciatica [saɪˈætɪkə] n Ischias m

science [ˈsaɪəns] n Wissenschaft
f; (natural ~) Naturwissenschaft f;
science fiction n Sciencefiction
f; **scientific** [saɪənˈtɪfɪk] adj
wissenschaftlich; **scientist**
[ˈsaɪəntɪst] n Wissenschaftler(in)
m(f); (in natural sciences)
Naturwissenschaftler(in) m(f)

scissors [ˈsɪzəz] npl Schere f

scone [skɒn] n kleines süßes
Hefebrötchen mit oder ohne Rosinen,
das mit Butter oder Dickrahm und
Marmelade gegessen wird

scoop [skuːp] n (exclusive story)
Exklusivbericht m; **a ~ of
ice-cream** eine Kugel Eis ▷ vt: to
~ **(up)** schaufeln

scooter [ˈskuːtə°] n (Motor)-
roller m; (toy) (Tret)roller m

scope [skəʊp] n Umfang m;
(opportunity) Möglichkeit f

score [skɔː°] n (Sport) Spielstand
m; (final result) Spielergebnis nt; (in
quiz etc) Punktestand m; (Mus)
Partitur f; **to keep (the)
~** mitzählen ▷ vt (goal) schießen;
(points) punkten ▷ vi (keep ~)
mitzählen; **scoreboard** n
Anzeigetafel f

scorn [skɔːn] n Verachtung f;
scornful adj verächtlich

Scorpio [ˈskɔːpɪəʊ] (pl **-s**) n (Astr)
Skorpion m

scorpion [ˈskɔːpɪən] n Skorpion
m

Scot [skɒt] n Schotte m, Schottin
f; **Scotch** [skɒtʃ] n (whisky)
schottischer Whisky, Scotch m

Scotch tape® n (US) Tesafilm® m

Scotland [ˈskɒtlənd] n Schottland nt; **Scotsman** (pl **-men**) n
Schotte m; **Scotswoman** (pl
-women) n Schottin f; **Scottish**

adj schottisch

scout [skaʊt] n (boy ~) Pfadfinder
m

scowl [skaʊl] vi finster blicken

scrambled eggs npl Rührei nt

scrap [skræp] n (bit) Stückchen
nt, Fetzen m; (metal) Schrott m ▷ vt
(car) verschrotten; (plan)
verwerfen; **scrapbook** n
Sammelalbum nt

scrape [skreɪp] n (scratch)
Kratzer m ▷ vt (car) schrammen;
(wall) streifen; **to ~ one's knee**
sich das Knie schürfen; **scrape
through** vi (exam) mit knapper
Not bestehen

scrap heap [ˈskræphiːp] n
Schrotthaufen m; **scrap metal** n
Schrott m; **scrap paper** n
Schmierpapier nt

scratch [skrætʃ] n (mark) Kratzer
m; **to start from ~** von vorne
anfangen ▷ vt kratzen; (car)
zerkratzen; **to ~ one's arm** sich
am Arm kratzen ▷ vi kratzen;
(~ oneself) sich kratzen

scream [skriːm] n Schrei m ▷ vi
schreien (with vor +dat); **to ~ at sb**
jdn anschreien

screen [skriːn] n (TV, Inform)
Bildschirm m; (Cine) Leinwand f
▷ vt (protect) abschirmen; (hide)
verdecken; (film) zeigen;
(applicants, luggage) überprüfen;
screenplay n Drehbuch nt;
screensaver n (Inform)
Bildschirmschoner m; **screenshot**
n (Inform) Screenshot n

screw [skruː] n Schraube f ▷ vt
(vulg: have sex with) ficken; **to ~ sth
to sth** etw an etw akk schrauben;
to ~ off/on (lid)
ab-/aufschrauben; **screw up** vt
(paper) zusammenknüllen; (make a
mess of) vermasseln; **screwdriver**
n Schraubenzieher m; **screw top**
n Schraubverschluss m

scribble ['skrɪbl] vt, vi kritzeln
script [skrɪpt] n (of play) Text m; (of film) Drehbuch nt; (style of writing) Schrift f
scroll down ['skrəʊl'daʊn] vi (Inform) runterscrollen; **scroll up** vi (Inform) raufscrollen; **scroll bar** n (Inform) Scrollbar f
scrub [skrʌb] vt schrubben; **scrubbing brush**, **scrub brush** (US) n Scheuerbürste f
scruffy ['skrʌfɪ] adj vergammelt
scrupulous ['skruːpjʊləs, -lɪ] adj, adv gewissenhaft; (painstaking) peinlich genau
scuba-diving ['skuːbədaɪvɪŋ] n Sporttauchen nt
sculptor ['skʌlptə°] n Bildhauer(in) m(f); **sculpture** ['skʌlptʃə°] n (Art) Bildhauerei f; (statue) Skulptur f
sea [siː] n Meer nt, See f; **seafood** n Meeresfrüchte pl; **sea front** n Strandpromenade f; **seagull** n Möwe f
seal [siːl] n (animal) Robbe f; (stamp, impression) Siegel nt; (Tech) Verschluss m; (ring etc) Dichtung f ▷ vt versiegeln; (envelope) zukleben
seam [siːm] n Naht f
search [sɜːtʃ] n Suche f (for nach); **to do a ~ for** (Inform) suchen nach; **in ~ of** auf der Suche nach ▷ vi suchen (for nach) ▷ vt durchsuchen; **search engine** n (Inform) Suchmaschine f
seashell ['siːʃel] n Muschel f; **seashore** n Strand m; **seasick** adj seekrank; **seaside** n: **at the ~** am Meer; **to go to the ~** ans Meer fahren; **seaside resort** n Seebad nt
season ['siːzn] n Jahreszeit f; (Comm) Saison f; **high/low**

~ Hoch-/Nebensaison f ▷ vt (flavour) würzen
seasoning n Gewürz nt
season ticket n (Rail) Zeitkarte f; (Theat) Abonnement nt; (Sport) Dauerkarte f
seat [siːt] n (place) Platz m; (chair) Sitz m; **take a ~** setzen Sie sich ▷ vt: **the hall ~s 300** der Saal hat 300 Sitzplätze; **please be ~ed** bitte setzen Sie sich; **to remain ~ed** sitzen bleiben; **seat belt** n Sicherheitsgurt m
sea view ['siːvjuː] n Seeblick m; **seaweed** n Seetang m
secluded [sɪ'kluːdɪd] adj abgelegen
second ['sekənd] adj zweite(r, s); **the ~ of June** der zweite Juni ▷ adv (in ~ position) an zweiter Stelle; (secondly) zweitens; **he came ~** er ist Zweiter geworden ▷ n (of time) Sekunde f; (moment) Augenblick m; ~ (gear) der zweite Gang; (~ helping) zweite Portion; **just a ~** (einen) Augenblick!; **secondary** adj (less important) zweitrangig; **~ education** höhere Schulbildung f; **~ school** n weiterführende Schule; **second-class** adj (ticket) zweiter Klasse; **~ stamp** Briefmarke für nicht bevorzugt beförderte Sendungen ▷ adv (travel) zweiter Klasse; **second-hand** adj, adv gebraucht; (information) aus zweiter Hand; **secondly** adv zweitens; **second-rate** adj (pej) zweitklassig
secret ['siːkrət] n Geheimnis nt ▷ adj geheim; (admirer) heimlich
secretary ['sekrətrɪ] n Sekretär(in) m(f); (minister) Minister(in) m(f); **Secretary of State** n (US) Außenminister(in) m(f); **secretary's office** n Sekretariat nt

secretive ['siːkrətɪv] adj (person) geheimnistuerisch; **secretly** ['siːkrətlɪ] adv heimlich

sect [sekt] n Sekte f

section ['sekʃən] n (part) Teil m; (of document) Abschnitt m; (department) Abteilung f

secure [sɪ'kjʊə] adj (safe) sicher (from vor +dat); (firmly fixed) fest ▷ vt (make firm) befestigen; (window, door) fest verschließen; **securely** adv fest; (safely) sicher; **security** [sɪ'kjʊərɪtɪ] n Sicherheit f

sedative ['sedətɪv] n Beruhigungsmittel nt

seduce [sɪ'djuːs] vt verführen; **seductive** [sɪ'dʌktɪv] adj verführerisch; (offer) verlockend

see [siː] (saw, seen) vt sehen; (understand) verstehen; (check) nachsehen; (accompany) bringen; (visit) besuchen; (talk to) sprechen; **to ~ the doctor** zum Arzt gehen; **to ~ sb home** jdn nach Hause begleiten; **I saw him swimming** ich habe ihn schwimmen sehen; **~ you** tschüs!; **~ you on Friday** bis Freitag! ▷ vi sehen; (understand) verstehen; (check) nachsehen; (you) ~ siehst du!; **we'll ~** mal sehen; **see about** vt (attend to) sich kümmern um; **see off** vt (say goodbye to) verabschieden; **see out** vt (show out) zur Tür bringen; **see through** vt: **to see sth through** etw zu Ende bringen; **to ~ sb/sth** jdn/etw durchschauen; **see to** vt sich kümmern um; **~ it that ...** sieh zu, dass ...

seed [siːd] n (of plant) Samen m; (in fruit) Kern m; **seedless** adj kernlos

seedy ['siːdɪ] adj zwielichtig

seek [siːk] (sought, sought) vt suchen; (fame) streben nach; **to ~ sb's advice** jdn um Rat fragen

seem [siːm] vi scheinen; **he ~s (to be) honest** er scheint ehrlich zu sein; **it ~s to me that ...** es scheint mir, dass ...

seen [siːn] pp of **see**

seesaw ['siːsɔː] n Wippe f

see-through adj durchsichtig

segment ['segmənt] n Teil m

seize [siːz] vt packen; (confiscate) beschlagnahmen; (opportunity, power) ergreifen

seldom ['seldəm] adv selten

select [sɪ'lekt] adj (exclusive) exklusiv ▷ vt auswählen; **selection** [sɪ'lekʃən] n Auswahl f (of an +dat); **selective** adj (choosy) wählerisch

self [self] (pl **selves**) n Selbst nt, Ich nt; **he's his old ~ again** er ist wieder ganz der Alte;

self-adhesive adj selbstklebend; **self-assured** adj selbstsicher; **self-catering** adj für Selbstversorger; **self-centred** adj egozentrisch; **self-confidence** n Selbstbewusstsein nt;

self-confident adj selbstbewusst; **self-conscious** adj befangen, verklemmt; **self-control** n Selbstbeherrschung f; **self-defence** n Selbstverteidigung f; **self-employed** adj selbstständig; **self-evident** adj offensichtlich

selfie ['selfi] n Selfie nt

selfish [selfɪʃ], **selfishly** ['selfɪʃ, -lɪ] adj, adv egoistisch, selbstsüchtig; **selfless, selflessly** adj, adv selbstlos

self-pity [self'pɪtɪ] n Selbstmitleid nt; **self-portrait** n Selbstporträt nt; **self-respect** n Selbstachtung f; **self-service** n Selbstbedienung f ▷ adj Selbstbedienungs-

sell [sel] (sold, sold) vt verkaufen; **to ~ sb sth, to ~ sth to**

sb jdm etw verkaufen; **do you ~ postcards?** haben Sie Postkarten? ▷ vi (product) sich verkaufen; **sell out** vt: **to be sold ~** ausverkauft sein; **sell-by date** n Haltbarkeitsdatum nt

Sellotape® ['seləteɪp] n (Brit) Tesafilm® m

semester [sɪ'mestə°] n Semester nt

semi ['semɪ] n (Brit: house) Doppelhaushälfte f; **semicircle** n Halbkreis m; **semicolon** n Semikolon nt; **semidetached (house)** n (Brit) Doppelhaushälfte f; **semifinal** n Halbfinale nt

seminar ['semɪnɑː°] n Seminar nt

semiskimmed milk ['semɪskɪmd'mɪlk] n Halbfettmilch f

senate ['senət] n Senat m; **senator** n Senator(in) m(f)

send [send] (**sent, sent**) vt schicken; **to ~ sb sth, to ~ sth to sb** jdm etw schicken; **~ her my best wishes** grüße sie von mir; **send away** vt wegschicken ▷ vi: **to ~ for** anfordern; **send back** vt zurückschicken; **send for** vt (person) holen lassen; (by post) anfordern; **send off** vt (by post) abschicken; **send out** vt (invitations etc) verschicken ▷ vi: **to ~ for sth** etw holen lassen

sender ['sendə°] n Absender(in) m(f)

senior ['siːnɪə°] adj (older) älter; (high-ranking) höher; (pupils) älter; **he is ~ to me** er ist mir übergeordnet ▷ n: **he's eight years my ~** er ist acht Jahre älter als ich; **senior citizen** n Senior(in) m(f)

sensation [sen'seɪʃən] n Gefühl nt; (excitement, person, thing)

Sensation f; **sensational** adj sensationell

sense [sens] n (faculty, meaning) Sinn m; (feeling) Gefühl nt; (understanding) Verstand m; **~ of smell/taste** Geruchs-/Geschmackssinn m; **to have a ~ of humour** Humor haben; **to make ~** (sentence etc) einen Sinn ergeben; (be sensible) Sinn machen; **in a ~** gewissermaßen ▷ vt spüren; **senseless** adj (stupid) sinnlos

sensible, sensibly ['sensəbl, -blɪ] adj, adv vernünftig

sensitive ['sensɪtɪv] adj empfindlich (to gegen); (easily hurt) sensibel; (subject) heikel

sensual ['sensjʊəl] adj sinnlich

sensuous ['sensjʊəs] adj sinnlich

sent [sent] pt, pp of **send**

sentence ['sentəns] n (Ling) Satz m; (Jur) Strafe f ▷ vt verurteilen (to zu)

sentiment ['sentɪmənt] n (sentimentality) Sentimentalität f; (opinion) Ansicht f; **sentimental** [sentɪ'mentl] adj sentimental

separate ['seprət] adj getrennt, separat; (individual) einzeln ▷ vt ['sepəreɪt] vt trennen (from von); **they are ~d** (couple) sie leben getrennt ▷ vi sich trennen; **separately** adv getrennt; (singly) einzeln

September [sep'tembə°] n September m; **in ~** im September; **on the 2nd of ~** am 2. September; **at the beginning/in the middle/at the end of ~** Anfang/Mitte/Ende September; **last/next ~** letzten/nächsten September

septic ['septɪk] adj vereitert

sequel ['siːkwəl] n (to film, book) Fortsetzung f (to von)

sequence ['siːkwəns] n (order)
Reihenfolge f

Serbia ['sɜːbjə] n Serbien nt

sergeant ['saːdʒənt] n Polizei-
meister(in) m(f); (Mil)
Feldwebel(in) m(f)

serial ['sɪərɪəl] n (TV) Serie f; (in
newspaper etc) Fortsetzungsroman
m ▷ adj (Inform) seriell; ~ **number**
Seriennummer f

series ['sɪəriːz] nsing Reihe f; (TV,
Radio) Serie f

serious ['sɪərɪəs] adj ernst;
(injury, illness, mistake) schwer;
(discussion) ernsthaft; **are you ~?**
ist das dein Ernst?; **seriously** adv
ernsthaft; (hurt) schwer; **~? im**
Ernst?; **to take sb ~** jdn ernst
nehmen

sermon ['sɜːmən] n (Rel) Predigt f

servant ['sɜːvənt] n Diener(in)
m(f); **serve** [sɜːv] vt (customer)
bedienen; (food) servieren; (in a
country etc) dienen +dat; (sentence)
verbüßen; **I'm being ~d** ich werde
schon bedient; **it ~s him right** es
geschieht ihm recht ▷ vi dienen
(as als), aufschlagen ▷ n
Aufschlag m

server n (Inform) Server m

service ['sɜːvɪs] n (in shop, hotel)
Bedienung f; (activity, amenity)
Dienstleistung f; (set of dishes)
Service nt; (Auto) Inspektion f;
(Tech) Wartung f; (Rel)
Gottesdienst m, Aufschlag m;
train/bus ~ Zug-/Busverbindung
f; **"~ not included"** „Bedienung
nicht inbegriffen" ▷ vt (Auto, Tech)
warten; **service area** n (on
motorway) Raststätte f (mit
Tankstelle); **service charge** n
Bedienung f; **service provider** n
(Inform) Provider m; **service
station** n Tankstelle f

session ['seʃən] n (of court,
assembly) Sitzung f

set [set] (**set, set**) vt (place)
stellen; (lay flat) legen; (arrange)
anordnen; (table) decken; (trap,
record) aufstellen; (time, price)
festsetzen; (watch, alarm) stellen
(for auf +akk); **to ~ sb a task** jdm
eine Aufgabe stellen; **to ~ free**
freilassen; **to ~ a good example**
ein gutes Beispiel geben; **the
novel is ~ in London** der Roman
spielt in London ▷ vi (sun)
untergehen; (become hard) fest
werden; (bone)
zusammenwachsen ▷ n (collection
of things) Satz m; (of cutlery,
furniture) Garnitur f; (group of
people) Kreis m; (Radio, TV) Apparat
m, Satz m; (Theat) Bühnenbild nt;
(Cine) (Film)kulisse f ▷ adj (agreed,
prescribed) festgelegt; (ready)
bereit; ~ **meal** Menü nt; **set aside**
vt (money) beiseitelegen; (time)
einplanen; **set off** vi aufbrechen
(for nach); (alarm) auslösen;
(enhance) hervorheben; **set out** vi
aufbrechen (for nach) ▷ vt (chairs,
chesspieces etc) aufstellen; (state)
darlegen; ~ **to do sth** (intend)
beabsichtigen, etw zu tun; **set up**
vt (firm, organization) gründen;
(stall, tent, camera) aufbauen;
(meeting) vereinbaren ▷ vt **to ~ as
a doctor** sich als Arzt niederlassen

setback n Rückschlag m

settee [se'tiː] n Sofa nt, Couch f

setting ['setɪŋ] n (of novel, film)
Schauplatz m; (surroundings)
Umgebung f

settle ['setl] vt (bill, debt)
begleichen; (dispute) beilegen;
(question) klären; (stomach)
beruhigen ▷ vi: **to ~ (down)** (feel
at home) sich einleben; (calm down)
sich beruhigen; **settle in** vi (in
place) sich einleben; (in job) sich
eingewöhnen; **settle up** vi
(be)zahlen; **to ~ with sb** mit jdm

abrechnen; **settlement** n (of bill, debt) Begleichung f; (colony) Siedlung f; **to reach a ~** sich einigen

setup ['setʌp] n (organization) Organisation f; (situation) Situation f

seven ['sevn] num sieben ▷ n Sieben f; see also **eight**; **seventeen** ['sevn'tiːn] num siebzehn ▷ n Siebzehn f; see also **eight**; **seventeenth** adj siebzehnte(r, s); see also **eighth**; **seventh** ['sevnθ] adj siebte(r, s) ▷ n (fraction) Siebtel nt; see also **eighth**; **seventieth** ['sevntɪɪθ] adj siebzigste(r, s); see also **eighth**; **seventy** ['sevntɪ] num siebzig; **~-one** einundsiebzig ▷ n Siebzig f; **to be in one's seventies** in den Siebzigern sein; see also **eight**

several ['sevrəl] adj, pron mehrere

severe [sɪ'vɪə*] adj (strict) streng; (serious) schwer; (pain) stark; (winter) hart; **severely** adv (harshly) hart; (seriously) schwer

sew [səʊ] (**sewed, sewn**) vt, vi nähen

sewage ['suːɪdʒ] n Abwasser nt; **sewer** ['sʊə*] n Abwasserkanal m; **sewing** ['səʊɪŋ] n Nähen nt; **sewing machine** n Nähmaschine f

sewn [səʊn] pp of **sew**

sex [seks] n Sex m; (gender) Geschlecht nt; **to have ~** Sex haben (with mit); **sexism** ['seksɪzəm] n Sexismus m; **sexist** ['seksɪst] adj sexistisch ▷ n Sexist(in) m(f); **sex life** n Sex(ual)leben nt

sexual ['seksjʊəl] adj sexuell; **~ discrimination/harassment** sexuelle Diskriminierung/ Belästigung; **~ intercourse** Geschlechtsverkehr m; **sexuality**

[seksjʊ'ælɪtɪ] n Sexualität f; **sexually** adv sexuell

sexy ['seksɪ] adj sexy, geil

Seychelles [seɪ'ʃelz] npl Seychellen pl

shabby ['ʃæbɪ] adj schäbig

shack [ʃæk] n Hütte f

shade [ʃeɪd] n (shadow) Schatten m; (for lamp) (Lampen)schirm m; (colour) Farbton m; **~s** (US: sunglasses) Sonnenbrille f ▷ vt (from sun) abschirmen; (in drawing) schattieren

shadow ['ʃædəʊ] n Schatten m

shady ['ʃeɪdɪ] adj schattig; (fig) zwielichtig

shake [ʃeɪk] (**shook, shaken**) vt schütteln; (shock) erschüttern; **to ~ hands with sb** jdm die Hand geben; **to ~ one's head** den Kopf schütteln ▷ vi (tremble) zittern; (building, ground) schwanken; **shake off** vt abschütteln; **shaken** ['ʃeɪkn] pp of **shake**; **shaky** ['ʃeɪkɪ] adj (trembling) zittrig; (table, chair, position) wackelig; (fig) unsicher

shall [ʃæl] (**should**) vb aux werden; (in questions) sollen; **I ~ do my best** ich werde mein Bestes tun; **~ I come too?** soll ich mitkommen?; **where ~ we go?** wo gehen wir hin?

shallow ['ʃæləʊ] adj (a. fig) seicht; (person) oberflächlich

shame [ʃeɪm] n (feeling of ~) Scham f; (disgrace) Schande f; **what a ~!** wie schade!; **~ on you!** schäm dich/schämen Sie sich!; **it's a ~ that ...** schade, dass ...

shampoo [ʃæm'puː] n Shampoo nt; **to have a ~ and set** sich die Haare waschen und legen lassen ▷ vt (hair) waschen; (carpet) schamponieren

shandy ['ʃændɪ] n Radler m, Alsterwasser nt

shan't [ʃɑːnt] contr of **shall not**

shape [ʃeɪp] n Form f; (unidentified figure) Gestalt f; **in the ~ of** in Form +gen; **to be in good ~** (healthwise) in guter Verfassung sein; **to take ~** (plan, idea) Gestalt annehmen ▷ vt (clay, person) formen; **-shaped** [ʃeɪpt] suf -förmig; **shapeless** adj formlos

share [ʃɛəʳ] n Anteil +dat (in, of an m); (Fin) Aktie f ▷ vt, vi teilen; **shareholder** n Aktionär(in) m(f)

shark [ʃɑːk] n (Zool) Haifisch m

sharp [ʃɑːp] adj scharf; (pin) spitz; (person) scharfsinnig; (pain) heftig; (increase, fall) abrupt; **C/F ~** (Mus) Cis/Dis nt ▷ adv: **at 2 o'clock ~** Punkt 2 Uhr; **sharpen** vt (knife) schärfen; (pencil) spitzen; **sharpener** n (pencil ~) Spitzer m

shatter [ʃætəʳ] vt zerschmettern; (fig) zerstören ▷ vi zerspringen; **shattered** adj (exhausted) kaputt

shave [ʃeɪv] vt (**shaved** o **shaven**) vt rasieren ▷ vi sich rasieren ▷ n Rasur f; **that was a close ~** (fig) das war knapp; **shave off** vt: **to shave one's beard off** sich den Bart abrasieren; **shaven** [ʃeɪvn] pp of **shave** ▷ adj (head) kahl geschoren; **shaver** n (Elec) Rasierapparat m; **shaving brush** n Rasierpinsel m; **shaving foam** n Rasierschaum m; **shaving tackle** n Rasierzeug nt

shawl [ʃɔːl] n Tuch nt

she [ʃiː] pron sie

shed [ʃed] (**shed, shed**) n Schuppen m ▷ vt (tears, blood) vergießen; (hair, leaves) verlieren

she'd [ʃiːd] contr of **she had; she would**

sheep [ʃiːp] (pl -) n Schaf nt; **sheepdog** n Schäferhund m; **sheepskin** n Schaffell nt

sheer [ʃɪəʳ] adj (madness) rein;

(steep) steil; **by ~ chance** rein zufällig

sheet [ʃiːt] n (on bed) Betttuch nt; (of paper) Blatt nt; (of metal) Platte f; (of glass) Scheibe f; **a ~ of paper** ein Blatt Papier

shelf [ʃelf] (pl **shelves**) n Bücherbord nt, Regal nt; **shelves** pl (item of furniture) Regal nt

she'll [ʃiːl] contr of **she will; she shall**

shell [ʃel] n (of egg, nut) Schale f; (sea~) Muschel f ▷ vt (peas, nuts) schälen; **shellfish** n (as food) Meeresfrüchte pl

shelter [ʃeltəʳ] n (protection) Schutz m; (accommodation) Unterkunft f; (bus ~) Wartehäuschen nt ▷ vt schützen (from vor +dat) ▷ vi sich unterstellen; **sheltered** adj (spot) geschützt; (life) behütet

shelve [ʃelv] vt (fig) aufschieben; **shelves** pl of **shelf**

shepherd [ʃepəd] n Schäfer m; **shepherd's pie** n Hackfleischauflauf mit Decke aus Kartoffelpüree

sherry [ʃerɪ] n Sherry m

she's [ʃiːz] contr of **she is; she has**

shield [ʃiːld] n Schild m; (fig) Schutz m ▷ vt schützen (from vor +dat)

shift [ʃɪft] n (change) Veränderung f; (period at work, workers) Schicht f; (on keyboard) Umschalttaste f ▷ vt (furniture etc) verrücken; (stain) entfernen; **to ~ gear(s)** (US Aut) schalten ▷ vi (move) sich bewegen; (move up) rutschen; **shift key** n Umschalttaste f

shin [ʃɪn] n Schienbein nt

shine [ʃaɪn] (**shone, shone**) vi (be shiny) glänzen; (sun) scheinen; (lamp) leuchten ▷ vt (polish) polieren ▷ n Glanz m

shingles ['ʃɪŋglz] *nsing* (Med) Gürtelrose *f*

shiny ['ʃaɪnɪ] *adj* glänzend

ship [ʃɪp] *n* Schiff *nt* ▷ *vt* (send) versenden; (by ship) verschiffen; **shipment** *n* (goods) Sendung *f*; (sent by ship) Ladung *f*; **shipwreck** *n* Schiffbruch *m*; **shipyard** *n* Werft *f*

shirt [ʃɜːt] *n* Hemd *nt*

shit [ʃɪt] *n* (vulg) Scheiße *f*; (person) Arschloch *nt*; **~!** Scheiße!

shitty ['ʃɪtɪ] *adj* (fam) beschissen

shiver ['ʃɪvə°] *vi* zittern (with vor +dat)

shock [ʃɒk] *n* (mental, emotional) Schock *m*; **to be in ~** unter Schock stehen; **to get a ~** (Elec) einen Schlag bekommen ▷ *vt* schockieren; **shock absorber** *n* Stoßdämpfer *m*; **shocked** *adj* schockiert (by über +akk); **shocking** *adj* schockierend; (awful) furchtbar

shoe [ʃuː] *n* Schuh *m*; **shoelace** *n* Schnürsenkel *m*; **shoe polish** *n* Schuhcreme *f*

shone [ʃɒn] *pt, pp of* **shine**

shonky ['ʃɒŋkɪ] *adj* (Aust, NZ fam) schäbig; (work) stümperhaft

shook [ʃʊk] *pt of* **shake**

shoot [ʃuːt] (shot, shot) *vt* (wound) anschießen; (kill) erschießen; (Cine) drehen; (fam: heroin) drücken ▷ *vi* (with gun, move quickly) schießen; **to ~ at sb** auf jdn schießen ▷ *n* (of plant) Trieb *m*; **shooting** *n* (exchange of gunfire) Schießerei *f*; (killing) Erschießung *f*

shop [ʃɒp] *n* Geschäft *nt*, Laden *m* ▷ *vi* einkaufen; **shop assistant** *n* Verkäufer(in) *m(f)*; **shopkeeper** *n* Geschäftsinhaber(in) *m(f)*; **shoplifting** *n* Ladendiebstahl *m*; **shopper** *n* Käufer(in) *m(f)*; **shopping** *n* (activity) Einkaufen

nt; (goods) Einkäufe *pl*; **to do the ~** einkaufen; **to go ~** einkaufen gehen; **shopping bag** *n* Einkaufstasche *f*; **shopping cart** (US) Einkaufswagen *m*; **shopping center** (US), **shopping centre** *n* Einkaufszentrum *nt*; **shopping list** *n* Einkaufszettel *m*; **shopping trolley** *n* (Brit) Einkaufswagen *m*; **shop window** *n* Schaufenster *nt*

shore [ʃɔː°] *n* Ufer *nt*; **on ~** an Land

short [ʃɔːt] *adj* kurz; (person) klein; **to be ~ of money** knapp bei Kasse sein; **to be ~ of time** wenig Zeit haben; **~ of breath** kurzatmig; **to ~** (holiday) abbrechen; **we are two ~** wir haben zwei zu wenig; **it's ~ for …** das ist die Kurzform von … ▷ *n* (drink, Elec) Kurze(r) *m*; **shortage** *n* Knappheit *f* (of an +dat); **shortbread** *n* Buttergebäck *nt*; **short circuit** *n* Kurzschluss *m*; **shortcut** *n* (quicker route) Abkürzung *f*; (Inform) Shortcut *m*; **shorten** *vt* kürzen; (in time) verkürzen; **shorthand** *n* Stenografie *f*; **shortlist** *n*: **to be on the ~** in der engeren Wahl sein; **short-lived** *adj* kurzlebig; **shortly** *adv* bald; **shorts** *npl* Shorts *pl*; **short-sighted** *adj* (a. fig) kurzsichtig; **short-sleeved** *adj* kurzärmelig; **short-stay car park** *n* Kurzzeitparkplatz *m*; **short story** *n* Kurzgeschichte *f*; **short-term** *adj* kurzfristig; **short wave** *n* Kurzwelle *f*

shot [ʃɒt] *pt, pp of* **shoot** ▷ *n* (from gun, in football) Schuss *m*; (Foto, Cine) Aufnahme *f*; (injection) Spritze *f*; (of alcohol) Schuss *m*

should [ʃʊd] *pt of* **shall** ▷ *vb aux*: **I ~ go now** ich sollte jetzt gehen; **what ~ I do?** was soll ich tun?; **you ~n't have said that** das hättest du/hätten Sie nicht sagen sollen; **that ~ be enough** das müsste reichen

shoulder ['ʃəʊldə] n Schulter f

shouldn't ['ʃʊdnt] contr of **should not**

should've ['ʃʊdəv] contr of **should have**

shout [ʃaʊt] n Schrei m; (call) Ruf m ▷ vt rufen; (order) brüllen ▷ vi schreien; **to ~ at** anschreien; **to ~ for help** um Hilfe rufen

shove [ʃʌv] vt (person) schubsen; (car, table etc) schieben ▷ vi (in crowd) drängeln

shovel ['ʃʌvl] n Schaufel f ▷ vt schaufeln

show [ʃəʊ] (**showed, shown**) vt zeigen; **to ~ sb sth, to ~ sth to sb** jdm etw zeigen; **to ~ sb in** jdn hereinführen; **to ~ sb out** jdn zur Tür bringen ▷ n (Cine, Theat) Vorstellung f; (TV) Show f; (exhibition) Ausstellung f; **show off** vi (pej) angeben; **show round** vt herumführen; **to show sb round the house/the town** jdm das Haus/die Stadt zeigen; **show up** vi (arrive) auftauchen

shower ['ʃaʊə*] n Dusche f; (rain) Schauer m; **to have** (o **take**) **a ~** duschen ▷ vi (wash) duschen; **shower gel** n Duschgel nt

showing ['ʃəʊɪŋ] n (Cine) Vorstellung f

shown [ʃəʊn] pp of **show**

showroom ['ʃəʊruːm] n Ausstellungsraum m

shrank [ʃræŋk] pt of **shrink**

shred [ʃred] n (of paper, fabric) Fetzen m ▷ vt (in shredder) (im Reißwolf) zerkleinern; **shredder** n (for paper) Reißwolf m

shrimp [ʃrɪmp] n Garnele f

shrink [ʃrɪŋk] (**shrank, shrunk**) vi schrumpfen; (clothes) eingehen

shrivel ['ʃrɪvl] vi **to ~ (up)** schrumpfen; (skin) runzlig werden; (plant) welken

Shrove Tuesday ['ʃrəʊv'tjuːzdeɪ] n Fastnachtsdienstag m

shrub [ʃrʌb] n Busch m, Strauch m

shrug [ʃrʌg] vt, vi **to ~ (one's shoulders)** die Achseln zucken

shrunk [ʃrʌŋk] pp of **shrink**

shudder ['ʃʌdə*] vi schaudern; (ground, building) beben

shuffle ['ʃʌfl] vt, vi mischen

shut [ʃʌt] (**shut, shut**) vt zumachen, schließen; **~ your face!** (fam) halt den Mund! ▷ vi schließen ▷ adj geschlossen; **we're ~** wir haben geschlossen; **shut down** vt schließen; (computer) ausschalten ▷ vi schließen; (computer) sich ausschalten; **shut in** vt einschließen; **shut off** vt (lock out) aussperren; **to shut oneself out** sich aussperren; **shut up** vt (lock up) abschließen; (silence) zum Schweigen bringen ▷ vi (keep quiet) den Mund halten; **~! halt den Mund!**; **shutter** n (on window) (Fenster)laden m; **shutter release** n Auslöser m; **shutter speed** n Belichtungszeit f

shuttle bus ['ʃʌtlbʌs] n Shuttlebus m

shuttlecock ['ʃʌtlkɒk] n Federball m

shuttle service ['ʃʌtlsɜːvɪs] n Pendelverkehr m

shy [ʃaɪ] adj schüchtern; (animal) scheu

Siberia [saɪ'bɪərɪə] n Sibirien nt

Sicily ['sɪsɪlɪ] n Sizilien nt

sick [sɪk] adj krank; (joke) makaber; **to be ~** (Brit: vomit) sich übergeben; **to be off ~** wegen Krankheit fehlen; **I feel ~** mir ist schlecht; **to be ~ of sb/sth** jdn/etw satthaben; **it makes me**

~ (fig) es ekelt mich an; **sickbag** n Spucktüte f; **sick leave** n: **to be on** ~ krankgeschrieben sein; **sickness** n Krankheit f; (Brit: nausea) Übelkeit f; **sickness benefit** n (Brit) Krankengeld nt

side [saɪd] n Seite f; (of road) Rand m; (of mountain) Hang m; (Sport) Mannschaft f; **by my** ~ neben mir; ~ **by** ~ nebeneinander ▷ adj (door) Seiten-; **sideboard** n Anrichte f; **sideburns** npl Koteletten pl; **side dish** n Beilage f; **side effect** n Nebenwirkung f; **sidelight** n (Brit Auto) Parklicht nt; **side order** n Beilage f; **side road** n Nebenstraße f; **side street** n Seitenstraße f; **sidewalk** n (US) Bürgersteig m; **sideways** adv seitwärts

sieve [sɪv] n Sieb nt

sift [sɪft] vt (flour etc) sieben

sigh [saɪ] vi seufzen

sight [saɪt] n (power of seeing) Sehvermögen nt; (view, thing seen) Anblick m; ~**s** pl (of city etc) Sehenswürdigkeiten pl; **to have bad** ~ schlecht sehen; **to lose** ~ **of** aus den Augen verlieren; **out of** ~ außer Sicht; **sightseeing** n: **to go** ~ Sehenswürdigkeiten besichtigen; ~ **tour** Rundfahrt f

sign [saɪn] n Zeichen nt; (notice, road ~) Schild nt ▷ vt unterschreiben ▷ vi unterschreiben; **to** ~ **for sth** den Empfang einer Sache gen bestätigen; **to** ~ **in/out** sich ein-/austragen; **sign on** vi (Brit: register as unemployed) sich arbeitslos melden; **sign up** vi (for course) sich einschreiben; (Mil) sich verpflichten

signal ['sɪgnl] n Signal nt ▷ vi (car driver) blinken

signature ['sɪgnətʃə*] n Unterschrift f

significant [sɪg'nɪfɪkənt] adj (important) bedeutend, wichtig; (meaning sth) bedeutsam; **significantly** adv (considerably) bedeutend

sign language ['saɪnlæŋgwɪdʒ] n Zeichensprache f; **signpost** n Wegweiser m

silence ['saɪləns] n Stille f; (of person) Schweigen nt; ~**!** Ruhe! ▷ vt zum Schweigen bringen; **silent** adj still; (taciturn) schweigsam; **she remained** ~ sie schwieg

silk [sɪlk] n Seide f ▷ adj Seiden-

silly ['sɪlɪ] adj dumm, albern; **don't do anything** ~ mach keine Dummheiten; **the** ~ **season** das Sommerloch

silver ['sɪlvə*] n Silber nt; (coins) Silbermünzen pl ▷ adj Silber-, silbern; **silver-plated** adj versilbert; **silver wedding** n silberne Hochzeit

SIM card ['sɪm-] n (Tel) SIM-Karte f

similar ['sɪmɪlə*] adj ähnlich (to dat); **similarity** [sɪmɪ'lærɪtɪ] n Ähnlichkeit f (to mit); **similarly** adv (equally) ebenso

simple ['sɪmpl] adj einfach; (unsophisticated) schlicht; **simplify** ['sɪmplɪfaɪ] vt vereinfachen; **simply** adv einfach; (merely) bloß; (dress) schlicht

simulate ['sɪmjʊleɪt] vt simulieren

simultaneous, simultaneously [sɪməl'teɪnɪəs, -lɪ] adj, adv gleichzeitig

sin [sɪn] n Sünde f ▷ vi sündigen

since [sɪns] adv seitdem; (in the meantime) inzwischen ▷ prep seit +dat; **ever** ~ **1995** schon seit 1995 ▷ conj (time) seit, seitdem; (because) da, weil; **ever** ~ **I've known her** seit ich sie kenne; **it's ages** ~ **I've seen him** ich habe ihn seit Langem nicht mehr gesehen

s

sincere [sɪn'sɪə°] adj aufrichtig; **sincerely** adv aufrichtig; **Yours ~** mit freundlichen Grüßen

sing [sɪŋ] (**sang, sung**) vt, vi singen

Singapore [sɪŋgə'pɔː°] n Singapur nt

singer ['sɪŋə°] n Sänger(in) m(f)

single ['sɪŋgl] adj (one only) einzig; (not double) einfach; (bed, room) Einzel-; (unmarried) ledig; (Brit: ticket) einfach ▷ n (Brit: ticket) einfache Fahrkarte; (Mus) Single f; **a ~ to London, please** (Brit Rail) einfach nach London, bitte; **single out** vt (choose) auswählen; **single-handed, single-handedly** adv im Alleingang; **single parent** n Alleinerziehende(r) mf; **single supplement** n (for hotel room) Einzelzimmerzuschlag m

singular ['sɪŋgjʊlə°] n Singular m

sinister ['sɪnɪstə°] adj unheimlich

sink [sɪŋk] (**sank, sunk**) vt versenken; (ship) vi sinken ▷ n Spülbecken nt; (in bathroom) Waschbecken nt

sip [sɪp] vt nippen an +dat

sir [sɜː°] n **yes, ~** ja(, mein Herr); **can I help you, ~?** kann ich Ihnen helfen?; **Sir James** (title) Sir James

sister ['sɪstə°] n Schwester f; (Brit: nurse) Oberschwester f; **sister-in-law** (pl **sisters-in-law**) n Schwägerin f

sit [sɪt] (**sat, sat**) vi (be sitting) sitzen; (~ down) sich setzen; (committee, court) tagen ▷ vt (Brit: exam) machen; **sit down** vi sich hinsetzen; **sit up** vi (from lying position) sich aufsetzen

sitcom ['sɪtkɒm] n Situationskomödie f

site [saɪt] n Platz m; (building ~) Baustelle f; (web~) Site f

sitting ['sɪtɪŋ] n (meeting, for portrait) Sitzung f; **sitting room** n Wohnzimmer nt

situated ['sɪtjʊeɪtɪd] adj: **to be ~** liegen

situation [sɪtjʊ'eɪʃən] n (circumstances) Situation f, Lage f; (job) Stelle f; **"~s vacant/wanted"** (Brit) „Stellenangebote/Stellengesuche"

six [sɪks] num sechs ▷ n Sechs f; see also **eight**; **sixpack** n (of beer etc) Sechserpack nt; **sixteen** ['sɪks'tiːn] num sechzehn ▷ n Sechzehn f; see also **eight**; **sixteenth** adj sechzehnte(r, s); see also **eighth**; **sixth** [sɪksθ] adj sechste(r, s); **~ form** (Brit) ▷ n Oberstufe f ▷ n (fraction) Sechstel nt; see also **eighth**; **sixtieth** ['sɪkstɪɪθ] adj sechzigste(r, s); see also **eighth**; **sixty** ['sɪkstɪ] num sechzig; **~-one** einundsechzig ▷ n Sechzig f; **to be in one's sixties** in den Sechzigern sein; see also **eight**

size [saɪz] n Größe f; **what ~ are you?** welche Größe hast du/haben Sie?; **a ~ too big** eine Nummer zu groß

sizzle ['sɪzl] vi (Gastr) brutzeln

skate [skeɪt] n Schlittschuh m; (roller ~) Rollschuh m ▷ vi Schlittschuh laufen; (roller~) Rollschuh laufen; **skateboard** n Skateboard nt; **skating** n Eislauf m; (roller~) Rollschuhlauf m; **skating rink** n Eisbahn f; (for roller-skating) Rollschuhbahn f

skeleton ['skelɪtn] n (a. fig) Skelett nt

skeptical n (US) see **sceptical**

sketch [sketʃ] n Skizze f; (Theat) Sketch m ▷ vt skizzieren; **sketchbook** n Skizzenbuch nt

ski [skiː] n Ski m ▷ vi Ski laufen; **ski boot** n Skistiefel m

skid [skɪd] vi (Auto) schleudern

skier ['skiːəᵃ] n Skiläufer(in) m(f);
skiing n Skilaufen nt; **to go ~** Ski
laufen gehen; **~ holiday** Skiurlaub
m; **skiing instructor** n
Skilehrer(in) m(f)

skilful, skilfully ['skɪlful, -fəlɪ]
adj, adv geschickt

ski-lift ['skiːlɪft] n Skilift m

skill [skɪl] n Geschick nt; (acquired
technique) Fertigkeit f; **skilled** adj
geschickt (at, in in +dat); (worker)
Fach-; (work) fachmännisch

skim [skɪm] vt: **to ~ (off)** (fat etc)
abschöpfen; **to ~ (through)** (read)
überfliegen; **skimmed milk** n
Magermilch f

skin [skɪn] n Haut f; (fur) Fell nt;
(peel) Schale f; **skin diving** n
Sporttauchen nt; **skinny** adj dünn

skip [skɪp] vi hüpfen; (with rope)
seilspringen ▷ vt (miss out)
überspringen; (meal) ausfallen
lassen; (school, lesson) schwänzen

ski pants ['skiːpænts] npl
Skihose f; **ski pass** n Skipass m;
ski pole n Skistock m; **ski resort**
n Skiort m

skirt [skɜːt] n Rock m

ski run ['skiːrʌn] n (Ski)abfahrt
f; **ski stick** n Skistock m; **ski tow**
n Schlepplift m

skittle ['skɪtl] n Kegel m; **~s**
(game) Kegeln nt

skive [skaɪv] vi: **to ~ (off)** (Brit)
(from school) schwänzen; (from
work) blaumachen

skull [skʌl] n Schädel m

sky [skaɪ] n Himmel m;
skydiving n Fallschirmspringen
nt; **skylight** n Dachfenster nt;
skyscraper n Wolkenkratzer m

slam [slæm] vt (door) zuschlagen;
slam on vt: **to slam the brakes
on** voll auf die Bremse treten

slander ['slɑːndəᵃ] n Verleumdung f ▷ vt verleumden

slang [slæŋ] n Slang m

slap [slæp] n Klaps m; (across face)
Ohrfeige f ▷ vt schlagen; **to ~ sb's
face** jdn ohrfeigen

slash [slæʃ] n (punctuation mark)
Schrägstrich m ▷ vt (face, tyre)
aufschlitzen; (prices) stark
herabsetzen

slate [sleɪt] n (rock) Schiefer m;
(roof ~) Schieferplatte f

slaughter ['slɔːtəᵃ] vt (animals)
schlachten; (people) abschlachten

Slav [slɑːv] adj slawisch ▷ n
Slawe m, Slawin f

slave [sleɪv] n Sklave m, Sklavin f;
slave away vi schuften;
slave-driver n (fam)
Sklaventreiber(in) m(f); **slavery**
['sleɪvərɪ] n Sklaverei f

sleaze [sliːz] n (corruption)
Korruption f; **sleazy** adj (bar,
district) zwielichtig

sledge [sledʒ] n Schlitten m

sleep [sliːp] (slept, slept) vi
schlafen; **to ~ with sb** mit jdm
schlafen ▷ n Schlaf m; **to put to
~** (animal) einschläfern; **sleep in** vi
(lie in) ausschlafen; **sleeper** n
(Rail: train) Schlafwagenzug m;
(carriage) Schlafwagen m; **sleeping
bag** n Schlafsack m; **sleeping car**
n Schlafwagen m; **sleeping pill** n
Schlaftablette f; **sleepless** adj
schlaflos; **sleepover** n Übernachtung f (bei Freunden etc); **sleepy** adj
schläfrig; (place) verschlafen

sleet [sliːt] n Schneeregen m

sleeve [sliːv] n Ärmel m;
sleeveless adj ärmellos

sleigh [sleɪ] n (Pferde)schlitten m

slender ['slendəᵃ] adj schlank; (fig)
gering

slept [slept] pt, pp of **sleep**

slice [slaɪs] n Scheibe f; (of cake,
tart, pizza) Stück nt ▷ vt: **to ~ (up)**
in Scheiben schneiden; **sliced
bread** n geschnittenes Brot

slid [slɪd] *pt, pp of* **slide**

slide [slaɪd] (**slid, slid**) *vt* gleiten lassen; (*push*) schieben ▷ *vi* gleiten; (*slip*) rutschen ▷ *n* (*Foto*) Dia *nt*; (*in playground*) Rutschbahn *f*; (*Brit: for hair*) Spange *f*

slight [slaɪt] *adj* leicht; (*problem, difference*) klein; **not in the ~est** nicht im Geringsten; **slightly** *adv* etwas; (*injured*) leicht

slim [slɪm] *adj* (*person*) schlank; (*book*) dünn; (*chance, hope*) gering ▷ *vi* abnehmen

slime [slaɪm] *n* Schleim *m*; **slimy** *adj* schleimig

sling [slɪŋ] (**slung, slung**) *vt* werfen ▷ *n* (*for arm*) Schlinge *f*

slip [slɪp] *n* (*mistake*) Flüchtigkeitsfehler *m*; **~ of paper** Zettel *m* ▷ *vt* (*put*) stecken; **to ~ on/off** (*garment*) an-/ausziehen; **it ~ped my mind** ich habe es vergessen ▷ *vi* (*lose balance*) (aus)rutschen; **slip away** *vi* (*leave*) sich wegstehlen; **slipper** *n* Hausschuh *m*; **slippery** *adj* (*path, road*) glatt; (*soap, fish*) glitschig; **slip-road** *n* (*Brit: onto motorway*) Auffahrt *f*; (*off motorway*) Ausfahrt *f*

slit [slɪt] (**slit, slit**) *vt* aufschlitzen ▷ *n* Schlitz *m*

slope [sləʊp] *n* Neigung *f*; (*side of hill*) Hang *m* ▷ *vi* (*be sloping*) schräg sein; **sloping** *adj* (*floor, roof*) schräg

sloppy [ˈslɒpɪ] *adj* (*careless*) schlampig; (*sentimental*) rührselig

slot [slɒt] *n* (*opening*) Schlitz *m*; (*Inform*) Steckplatz *m*; **we have a ~ free at 2** (*free time*) um 2 ist noch ein Termin frei; **slot machine** *n* Automat *m*; (*for gambling*) Spielautomat *m*

Slovak [ˈsləʊvæk] *adj* slowakisch ▷ *n* (*person*) Slowake *m*, Slowakin *f*; (*language*) Slowakisch *nt*; **Slovakia** [sləʊˈvækɪə] *n* Slowakei *f*

Slovene [ˈsləʊviːn], **Slovenian** [sləʊˈviːnɪən] *adj* slowenisch ▷ *n* (*person*) Slowene *m*, Slowenin *f*; (*language*) Slowenisch *nt*; **Slovenia** [sləʊˈviːnɪə] *n* Slowenien *nt*

slow [sləʊ] *adj* langsam; (*business*) flau; **to be ~** (*clock*) nachgehen; (*stupid*) begriffsstutzig sein; **slow down** *vi* langsamer werden; (*when driving/walking*) langsamer fahren/gehen; **slowly** *adv* langsam; **slow motion** *n*: **in ~** in Zeitlupe

slug [slʌg] *n* (*Zool*) Nacktschnecke *f*

slum [slʌm] *n* Slum *m*

slump [slʌmp] *n* Rückgang *m* (*in* an +*dat*) ▷ *vi* (*onto chair etc*) sich fallen lassen; (*prices*) stürzen

slung [slʌŋ] *pt, pp of* **sling**

slur [slɜː°] *n* (*insult*) Verleumdung *f*; **slurred** [slɜːd] *adj* undeutlich

slush [slʌʃ] *n* (*snow*) Schneematsch *m*

slut [slʌt] *n* (*pej*) Schlampe *f*

smack [smæk] *n* Klaps *m* ▷ *vt*: **to ~ sb** jdm einen Klaps geben ▷ *vi*: **to ~ of** riechen nach

small [smɔːl] *adj* klein; **small ads** *npl* (*Brit*) Kleinanzeigen *pl*; **small change** *n* Kleingeld *nt*; **small letters** *npl*: **in ~** in Kleinbuchstaben; **smallpox** *n* Pocken *pl*; **small print** *n*: **the ~** das Kleingedruckte; **small-scale** *adj* (*map*) in kleinem Maßstab; **small talk** *n* Konversation *f*, Smalltalk *m*

smart [smɑːt] *adj* (*elegant*) schick; (*clever*) clever; **smartarse**, **smartass** (US) *n* (*fam*) Klugscheißer (in) *m(f)*; **smart card** *n* Chipkarte *f*; **smartly** *adv* (*dressed*) schick; **smartphone** *n* (*Tel*) Smartphone *nt*

smash [smæʃ] *n* (*car crash*) Zusammenstoß *m*, Schmetterball m ▷ vt (break) zerschlagen; (fig: record) brechen, deutlich übertreffen ▷ vi (break) zerbrechen; **to ~ into** (car) krachen gegen

smear [smɪə°] n (mark) Fleck m; (Med) Abstrich m; (fig) Verleumdung f ▷ vt (spread) schmieren; (make dirty) beschmieren; (fig) verleumden

smell [smel] (**smelt** o **smelled**, **smelt** o **smelled**) vt riechen ▷ vi riechen (of nach); (unpleasantly) stinken ▷ n Geruch m; (unpleasant) Gestank m; **smelly** adj übel riechend; **smelt** [smelt] pt, pp of **smell**

smile [smaɪl] n Lächeln nt ▷ vi lächeln; **to ~ at sb** jdn anlächeln

smock [smɒk] n Kittel m

smog [smɒg] n Smog m

smoke [sməʊk] n Rauch m ▷ vt rauchen; (food) räuchern ▷ vi rauchen; **smoke alarm** n Rauchmelder m; **smoked** adj (food) geräuchert; **smoke-free** adj (zone, building) rauchfrei; **smoker** n Raucher(in) m(f); **smoking** n Rauchen nt; **"no ~"** „Rauchen verboten"

smooth [smu:ð] adj glatt; (flight, crossing) ruhig; (movement) geschmeidig; (without problems) reibungslos; (pej: person) aalglatt ▷ vt (hair, dress) glatt streichen; (surface) glätten; **smoothly** adv reibungslos; **to run ~** (engine) ruhig laufen

smudge [smʌdʒ] vt (writing, lipstick) verschmieren

smug [smʌg] adj selbstgefällig

smuggle ['smʌgl] vt schmuggeln; **to ~ in/out** herein-/herausschmuggeln

smutty ['smʌtɪ] adj (obscene) schmutzig

snack [snæk] n Imbiss m; **to have**

a ~ eine Kleinigkeit essen; **snack bar** n Imbissstube f

snail [sneɪl] n Schnecke f; **snail mail** n (fam) Schneckenpost f

snake [sneɪk] n Schlange f

snap [snæp] n (photo) Schnappschuss m ▷ adj (decision) spontan ▷ vt (break) zerbrechen; (rope) zerreißen ▷ vi (break) brechen; (rope) reißen; (bite) schnappen (at nach); **snap off** vt (break) abbrechen; **snap fastener** n (US) Druckknopf m; **snapshot** n Schnappschuss m

snatch [snætʃ] vt (grab) schnappen

sneak [sni:k] vi (move) schleichen; **sneakers** npl (US) Turnschuhe pl

sneeze [sni:z] vi niesen

sniff [snɪf] vi schniefen; (smell) schnüffeln (at an +dat) ▷ vt schnuppern an +dat; (glue) schnüffeln

snob [snɒb] n Snob m; **snobbish** adj versnobt

snog [snɒg] vi, vt knutschen

snooker ['snu:kə°] n Snooker nt

snoop [snu:p] vi: **to ~ (around)** (herum)schnüffeln

snooze [snu:z] n, vi: **to (have a) ~** ein Nickerchen machen

snore [snɔ:°] vi schnarchen

snorkel ['snɔ:kl] n Schnorchel m; **snorkelling** n Schnorcheln nt; **to go ~** schnorcheln gehen

snout [snaʊt] n Schnauze f

snow [snəʊ] n Schnee m ▷ vi schneien; **snowball** n Schneeball m; **snowboard** n Snowboard nt; **snowboarding** n Snowboarding nt; **snowdrift** n Schneewehe f; **snowdrop** n Schneeglöckchen nt; **snowflake** n Schneeflocke f; **snowman** (pl **-men**) n Schneemann m; **snowplough**,

snowplow (US) n Schneepflug m;
snowstorm n Schneesturm m;
snowy adj (region) schneereich;
(landscape) verschneit
snug [snʌg] adj (person, place)
gemütlich
snuggle up ['snʌglʌp] vi: to
~ **to sb** sich an jdn ankuscheln

O **KEYWORD**

so [səʊ] adv **1** (thus) so; (likewise)
auch; **so saying he walked away**
indem er das sagte, ging er; **if so**
wenn ja; **I didn't do it — you did
so!** ich hab dies nicht gemacht —
hast du wohl!; **so do I, so am I** etc
ich auch; **so it is!** tatsächlich!; **I
hope/think so** hoffentlich/ich
glaube schon; **so far** bis jetzt
2 (in comparisons etc: to such a
degree) so; **so quickly/big (that)**
so schnell/groß, dass; **I'm so glad
to see you** ich freue mich so,
dich/Sie zu sehen
3 so many so viele; **so much work**
so viel Arbeit; **I love you so much**
ich liebe dich so sehr
4 (phrases) so or etwa 10; **so
long!** (inf) (goodbye) tschüss!
▷ conj **1** (expressing purpose) **so as to**
um ... zu; **so (that)** damit
2 (expressing result) also; **so I was
right after all** ich hatte also doch
recht; **so you see ...** wie du
siehst/Sie sehen ...

soak [səʊk] vt durchnässen;
(leave in liquid) einweichen; **I'm ~ed**
ich bin klatschnass; **soaking** adj:
~ **(wet)** klatschnass
soap [səʊp] n Seife f; **soap
(opera)** n Seifenoper f; **soap
powder** n Waschpulver nt
sob [sɒb] vi schluchzen
sober ['səʊbə°] adj nüchtern;
sober up vi nüchtern werden

so-called ['səʊ'kɔːld] adj
sogenannt
soccer ['sɒkə°] n Fußball m
sociable ['səʊʃəbl] adj gesellig
social ['səʊʃəl] adj sozial;
(sociable) gesellig; **socialist** adj
sozialistisch ▷ n Sozialist(in)
m(f); **socialize** vi unter die Leute
gehen; **social media** n Social
Media pl; **social networking** n
Netzwerken nt; **social security** n
(Brit) Sozialhilfe f; (US)
Sozialversicherung f
society [sə'saɪətɪ] n Gesellschaft
f; (club) Verein m
sock [sɒk] n Socke f
socket ['sɒkɪt] n (Elec) Steckdose
f
soda ['səʊdə] n (~ water) Soda f;
(US: pop) Limo f; **soda water** n
Sodawasser nt
sofa ['səʊfə] n Sofa nt; **sofa bed**
n Schlafcouch f
soft [sɒft] adj weich; (quiet) leise;
(lighting) gedämpft; (kind)
gutmütig; (weak) nachgiebig;
~ **drink** alkoholfreies Getränk;
softly adv sanft; (quietly) leise;
software n (Inform) Software f
soil [sɔɪl] n Erde f; (ground) Boden m
solar ['səʊlə°] adj Sonnen-, Solar-
solarium [sə'lɛərɪəm] n
Solarium f
sold [səʊld] pt, pp of **sell**
soldier ['səʊldʒə°] n Soldat(in)
m(f)
sole [səʊl] n Sohle f; (fish)
Seezunge f ▷ vt besohlen ▷ adj
einzig; (owner, responsibility)
alleinig; **solely** adv nur
solemn ['sɒləm] adj feierlich;
(person) ernst
solicitor [sə'lɪsɪtə°] n (Brit)
Rechtsanwalt m, Rechtsanwältin f
solid ['sɒlɪd] adj (hard) fest; (gold,
oak etc) massiv; (~ly built) solide;
(meal) kräftig

solitary ['sɒlɪtərɪ] adj einsam; (single) einzeln; **solitude** ['sɒlɪtjuːd] n Einsamkeit f

solo ['səʊləʊ] n (Mus) Solo nt

soluble ['sɒljʊbl] adj löslich; **solution** [sə'luːʃən] n Lösung f (to +gen); **solve** [sɒlv] vt lösen

somber (US), **sombre** ['sɒmbə°] adj düster

KEYWORD

some [sʌm] adj 1 (a certain amount o number of) einige; (a few) ein paar; (with singular nouns) etwas; **some tea/biscuits** etwas Tee/ein paar Kekse; **I've got some money, but not much** ich habe ein bisschen Geld, aber nicht viel

2 (certain: in contrasts) manche(r, s); **some people say that ...** manche Leute sagen, dass ...

3 (unspecified) irgendein(e); **some woman was asking for you** da hat eine Frau nach dir/Ihnen gefragt; **some day** eines Tages; **some day next week** irgendwann nächste Woche

▷ pron 1 (a certain number) einige; **have you got some?** hast du/haben Sie welche?

2 (a certain amount) etwas; **I've read some of the book** ich habe das Buch teilweise gelesen

▷ adv: **some 10 people** etwa 10 Leute

somebody pron jemand; ~ **(or other)** irgendjemand; ~ **else** jemand anders; **someday** adv irgendwann; **somehow** adv irgendwie; **someone** pron see **somebody**; **someplace** adv (US) see **somewhere**; **something** ['sʌmθɪŋ] pron etwas; ~ **(or other)** irgendetwas; ~ **else** etwas anderes; ~ **nice** etwas Nettes;

would you like ~ **to drink?** möchtest du/möchten Sie etwas trinken? ▷ adv: ~ **like 20** ungefähr 20; **sometime** adv irgendwann; **sometimes** adv manchmal; **somewhat** adv ein wenig; **somewhere** adv irgendwo; (to a place) irgendwohin; ~ **else** irgendwo anders; (to another place) irgendwo anders hin

son [sʌn] n Sohn m

song [sɒŋ] n Lied nt; Song m

son-in-law ['sʌnɪnlɔː] (pl **sons-in-law**) n Schwiegersohn m

soon [suːn] adv bald; (early) früh; **too** ~ zu früh; **as** ~ **as I ...** sobald ich ...; **as** ~ **as possible** so bald wie möglich; **sooner** adv (time) früher; (for preference) lieber

soot [sʊt] n Ruß m

soothe [suːð] vt beruhigen; (pain) lindern

sophisticated [sə'fɪstɪkeɪtɪd] adj (person) kultiviert; (machine) hoch entwickelt; (plan) ausgeklügelt

sophomore ['sɒfəmɔː°] n (US) College-Student(in) m(f) im zweiten Jahr

soppy ['sɒpɪ] adj (fam) rührselig

soprano [sə'prɑːnəʊ] n Sopran m

sore [sɔː°] adj: **to be** ~ wehtun; **to have a** ~ **throat** Halsschmerzen haben ▷ n wunde Stelle

sorrow ['sɒrəʊ] n Kummer m

sorry ['sɒrɪ] adj (sight, figure) traurig; **(I'm)** ~ (excusing) Entschuldigung!; **I'm** ~ (regretful) es tut mir leid; ~? wie bitte?; **I feel** ~ **for him** er tut mir leid

sort [sɔːt] n Art f; **what** ~ **of film is it?** was für ein Film ist das?; **a** ~ **of** eine Art +gen; **all** ~**s of things** alles Mögliche ▷ adv: ~ **of** (fam) irgendwie ▷ vt sortieren; **everything's** ~**ed** (dealt with) alles ist geregelt; **sort out** vt (classify etc) sortieren; (problems) lösen

sought [sɔːt] pt, pp of **seek**

soul [səʊl] n Seele f; (music) Soul m

sound [saʊnd] adj (healthy) gesund; (safe) sicher; (sensible) vernünftig; (theory) stichhaltig; (thrashing) tüchtig ▷ n (noise) Geräusch nt; (Mus) Klang m; (TV) Ton m ▷ vt: **to ~ the alarm** Alarm schlagen; **to ~ one's horn** hupen ▷ vi (seem) klingen (like wie); **soundcard** n (Inform) Soundkarte f; **sound effects** npl Klangeffekte pl; **soundproof** adj schalldicht; **soundtrack** n (of film) Filmmusik f, Soundtrack m

soup [suːp] n Suppe f

sour ['saʊə°] adj sauer; (fig) mürrisch

source [sɔːs] n Quelle f; (fig) Ursprung m

sour cream [saʊə'kriːm] n saure Sahne

south [saʊθ] n Süden m; **to the ~ of** südlich von ▷ adv (go, face) nach Süden ▷ adj Süd-; **South Africa** n Südafrika nt; **South African** adj südafrikanisch ▷ n Südafrikaner(in) m(f); **South America** n Südamerika nt; **South American** adj südamerikanisch ▷ n Südamerikaner(in) m(f); **southbound** adj (in) Richtung Süden; **southern** ['sʌðən] adj Süd-, südlich; **~ Europe** Südeuropa nt; **southwards** ['saʊθwədz] adv nach Süden

souvenir [suːvə'nɪə°] n Andenken nt (of an +akk)

sow [saʊ] (**sowed, sown** o **sowed**) vt (a. fig) säen; (field) besäen ▷ n [saʊ] (pig) Sau f

soya bean ['sɔɪə'biːn] n Sojabohne f

soy sauce ['sɔɪ'sɔːs] n Sojasoße f

spa [spɑː] n (place) Kurort m

space [speɪs] n (room) Platz m, Raum m; (outer ~) Weltraum m; (gap) Zwischenraum m; (for parking) Lücke f; **space bar** n Leertaste f; **spacecraft** (pl -) n Raumschiff nt; **space ship** n Raumschiff nt; **space shuttle** n Raumfähre f

spacing ['speɪsɪŋ] n (in text) Zeilenabstand m; **double ~** zweizeiliger Abstand

spacious ['speɪʃəs] adj geräumig

spade [speɪd] n Spaten m; **~s** Pik nt

spaghetti [spə'getɪ] nsing Spaghetti pl

Spain [speɪn] n Spanien nt

spam [spæm] n (Inform) Spam m

Spaniard ['spænɪəd] n Spanier(in) m(f); **Spanish** ['spænɪʃ] adj spanisch ▷ n (language) Spanisch nt

spanner ['spænə°] n (Brit) Schraubenschlüssel m

spare [speə°] adj (as replacement) Ersatz-; **~ part** Ersatzteil nt; **~ room** Gästezimmer nt; **~ time** Freizeit f; **~ tyre** Ersatzreifen m ▷ n (~ part) Ersatzteil m ▷ vt (lives, feelings) verschonen; **can you ~ (me) a moment?** hättest du/hätten Sie einen Moment Zeit?

spark [spɑːk] n Funke m; **sparkle** ['spɑːkl] vi funkeln; **sparkling wine** n Schaumwein m, Sekt m; **spark plug** n [spɑːkplʌg] n Zündkerze f

sparrow ['spærəʊ] n Spatz m

sparse [spɑːs] adj spärlich; **sparsely** adv: **~ populated** dünn besiedelt

spasm ['spæzəm] n Krampf m

spat [spæt] pt, pp of **spit**

speak [spiːk] (**spoke, spoken**) vt sprechen; **can you ~ French?** sprechen Sie Französisch?; **to**

~ one's mind seine Meinung sagen ▷ vi sprechen (to mit, zu); (make speech) reden; **~ing** (Tel) am Apparat; **so to ~** sozusagen; **~ for yourself** das meinst auch nur du!; **speak up** vi (louder) lauter sprechen; **speaker** n Sprecher(in) m(f); (public ~) Redner(in) m(f); (loud~) Lautsprecher m, Box f

special ['spɛʃəl] adj besondere(r, s), speziell ▷ n (on menu) Tagesgericht nt; (TV, Radio) Sondersendung f; **special delivery** n Eilzustellung f; **special effects** npl Spezialeffekte pl; **specialist** n Spezialist(in) m(f); (Tech) Fachmann m, Fachfrau f; (Med) Facharzt m, Fachärztin f; **speciality** [spɛʃi'ælɪtɪ] n Spezialität f; **specialize** vi sich spezialisieren (in auf +akk); **specially** adv besonders; (specifically) extra; **special offer** n Sonderangebot nt; **specialty** n (US) see **speciality**

species ['spiːʃiːz] nsing Art f

specific [spə'sɪfɪk] adj besonders; (precise) genau; **specify** ['spɛsɪfaɪ] vt genau angeben

specimen ['spɛsɪmən] n (sample) Probe f; (example) Exemplar nt

specs [spɛks] npl (fam) Brille f

spectacle [spɛktəkl] n Schauspiel nt

spectacles npl Brille f

spectacular [spɛk'tækjʊlə°] adj spektakulär

spectator [spɛk'teɪtə°] n Zuschauer(in) m(f)

sped [spɛd] pt, pp of **speed**

speech [spiːtʃ] n (address) Rede f; (faculty) Sprache f; **to make a ~** eine Rede halten; **speechless** adj sprachlos (with vor +dat)

speed [spiːd] n (speed o speeded, sped o speeded) vi rasen; (exceed

~ limit) zu schnell fahren ▷ n Geschwindigkeit f; (of film) Lichtempfindlichkeit f; **speed up** vt beschleunigen ▷ vi schneller werden/fahren; (drive faster) schneller fahren; **speedboat** n Rennboot nt; **speed bump** n Bodenschwelle f; **speed camera** n Blitzgerät nt; **speed limit** n Geschwindigkeitsbegrenzung f; **speedometer** [spɪ'dɒmɪtə°] n Tachometer m; **speed trap** n Radarfalle f; **speedy** adj schnell

spell [spɛl] (**spelt** o **spelled**, **spelt** o **spelled**) vt buchstabieren; **how do you ~ ...?** wie schreibt man ...? ▷ n (period) Weile f; (enchantment) Zauber m; **a cold/hot ~** (weather) ein Kälteeinbruch/eine Hitzewelle; **spellchecker** n (Inform) Rechtschreibprüfung f; **spelling** n Rechtschreibung f; (of a word) Schreibweise f; **~ mistake** Schreibfehler m

spelt [spɛlt] pt, pp of **spell**

spend [spɛnd] (**spent, spent**) vt (money) ausgeben (on für); (time) verbringen; **spending money** n Taschengeld nt

spent [spɛnt] pt, pp of **spend**

sperm [spɜːm] n Sperma nt

sphere [sfɪə°] n (globe) Kugel f; (fig) Sphäre f

spice [spaɪs] n Gewürz nt; (fig) Würze f ▷ vt würzen; **spicy** ['spaɪsɪ] adj würzig; (fig) pikant

spider ['spaɪdə°] n Spinne f

spike [spaɪk] n (on railing etc) Spitze f; (on shoe, tyre) Spike m

spill [spɪl] (**spilt** o **spilled**, **spilt** o **spilled**) vt verschütten

spin [spɪn] (**spun, spun**) vt (turn) sich drehen; (washing) schleudern; **my head is ~ning** mir dreht sich alles ▷ vt (turn) drehen; (coin) hochwerfen ▷ n (turn) Drehung f

spinach ['spɪnɪtʃ] n Spinat m

spin doctor n Spindoktor m
(Verantwortlicher für die
schönrednerische Öffentlichkeitsarbeit
besonders von Politikern)

spin-drier ['spɪndraɪə°] n
Wäscheschleuder f; **spin-dry** vt
schleudern

spine [spaɪn] n Rückgrat nt; (of
animal, plant) Stachel m; (of book)
Rücken m

spiral ['spaɪrəl] n Spirale f ▷ adj
spiralförmig; **spiral staircase** n
Wendeltreppe f

spire ['spaɪə°] n Turmspitze f

spirit ['spɪrɪt] n (essence, soul)
Geist m; (humour, mood) Stimmung
f; (courage) Mut m; (verve) Elan m;
~s pl (drinks) Spirituosen pl

spiritual ['spɪrɪtjʊəl] adj geistig;
(Rel) geistlich

spit [spɪt] (spat, spat) vi
spucken ▷ n (for roasting)
(Brat)spieß m; (saliva) Spucke f;
spit out vt ausspucken

spite [spaɪt] n Boshaftigkeit f; **in
~ of** trotz +gen; **spiteful** adj
boshaft

spitting image ['spɪtɪŋ'ɪmɪdʒ]
n: **he's the ~ of you** er ist
dir/Ihnen wie aus dem Gesicht
geschnitten

splash [splæʃ] vt (person, object)
bespritzen ▷ vi (liquid) spritzen
(play in water) planschen

splendid ['splendɪd] adj herrlich

splinter ['splɪntə°] n Splitter
m

split [splɪt] (split, split) vt (stone,
wood) spalten; (share) teilen ▷ vi
(stone, wood) sich spalten; (seam)
platzen ▷ n (in stone, wood) Spalt
m; (in clothing) Riss m; (fig)
Spaltung f; **split up** vi (couple) sich
trennen ▷ vt (divide up) aufteilen;
split ends npl (Haar)spliss m;
splitting adj (headache) rasend

spoil [spɔɪl] (spoiled o spoilt,

spoiled o **spoilt**) vt verderben;
(child) verwöhnen ▷ vi (food)
verderben

spoilt [spɔɪlt] pt, pp of **spoil**

spoke [spəʊk] pt of **speak** ▷ n
Speiche f

spoken ['spəʊkən] pp of **speak**

spokesperson ['spəʊkspɜːsən]
(pl -**people**) n Sprecher(in) m(f)

sponge [spʌndʒ] n (for washing)
Schwamm m; **sponge bag** n
Kulturbeutel m; **sponge cake** n
Biskuitkuchen m

sponsor ['spɒnsə°] n (of event,
programme) Sponsor(in) m(f) ▷ vt
unterstützen; (event, programme)
sponsern

spontaneous, spontaneously
[spɒn'teɪnɪəs, -lɪ] adj, adv
spontan

spool [spuːl] n Spule f

spoon [spuːn] n Löffel m

sport [spɔːt] n Sport m; **sports
car** n Sportwagen m; **sports
centre** n Sportzentrum nt;
sports club n Sportverein m;
sportsman (pl -**men**) n Sportler
m; **sportswear** n Sportkleidung f;
sportswoman (pl -**women**) n
Sportlerin f; **sporty** adj sportlich

spot [spɒt] n (dot) Punkt m; (of
paint, blood etc) Fleck m; (place)
Stelle f; (pimple) Pickel m; **on the
~ vor Ort; (at once) auf der Stelle
▷ vt (notice) entdecken; (difference)
erkennen; **spotless** adj (clean)
blitzsauber; **spotlight** n (lamp)
Scheinwerfer m; **spotty** adj
(pimply) pickelig

spouse [spaʊs] n Gatte m,
Gattin f

spout [spaʊt] n Schnabel m

sprain [spreɪn] n Verstauchung
f ▷ vt: **to ~ one's ankle** sich den
Knöchel verstauchen

sprang [spræŋ] pt of **spring**

spray [spreɪ] n (liquid in can)

Spray nt o m; (~ (can)) Spraydose f
▷ vt (plant, insects) besprühen;
(car) spritzen

spread [sprɛd] **(spread, spread)**
vt (open out) ausbreiten; (news,
disease) verbreiten; (butter, jam)
streichen; (bread, surface)
bestreichen ▷ vi (news, disease,
fire) sich verbreiten ▷ n (of disease,
religion etc) Verbreitung f; (for bread)
Aufstrich m; **spreadsheet** n
(Inform) Tabellenkalkulation f

spring [sprɪŋ] **(sprang, sprung)**
vi (leap) springen ▷ n (season)
Frühling m; (coil) Feder f; (water)
Quelle f; **springboard** n
Sprungbrett nt; **spring onion** n
(Brit) Frühlingszwiebel f; **spring
roll** n (Brit) Frühlingsrolle f;
springy adj (mattress) federnd

sprinkle ['sprɪŋkl] vt streuen;
(liquid) (be)träufeln; **to ~ sth with
sth** etw mit etw bestreuen; (with
liquid) etw mit etw besprengen;
sprinkler n (for lawn)
Rasensprenger m; (for fire)
Sprinkler m

sprint [sprɪnt] vi rennen; (Sport)
sprinten

sprout [spraʊt] n (of plant) Trieb
m; (from seed) Keim m; (Brussels)
~s pl Rosenkohl m ▷ vi sprießen

sprung [sprʌŋ] pp of **spring**

spun [spʌn] pt, pp of **spin**

spy [spaɪ] n Spion(in) m(f) ▷ vi
spionieren; **to ~ on sb** jdm
nachspionieren ▷ vt erspähen

squad [skwɒd] n (Sport) Kader m;
(police ~) Kommando nt

square [skwɛə*] n (shape)
Quadrat nt; (open space) Platz m;
(on chessboard etc) Feld nt ▷ adj (in
shape) quadratisch; **2 ~ metres** 2
Quadratmeter; **2 metres ~** 2 Meter
im Quadrat ▷ vt: **3 ~d** 3 hoch 2;
square root n Quadratwurzel f

squash [skwɒʃ] n (drink)

Fruchtsaftgetränk nt; (Sport)
Squash nt; (US: vegetable) Kürbis m
▷ vt zerquetschen

squat [skwɒt] vi (be crouching)
hocken; **to ~ (down)** sich
(hin)hocken

squeak [skwiːk] vi (door, shoes
etc) quietschen; (animal) quieken

squeal [skwiːl] vi (person)
kreischen (with vor +dat)

squeeze [skwiːz] vt drücken;
(orange) auspressen ▷ vi: **to ~ into
the car** sich in den Wagen
hineinzwängen; **squeeze up** vi
(on bench etc) zusammenrücken

squid [skwɪd] n Tintenfisch m

squint [skwɪnt] vi schielen; (in
bright light) blinzeln

squirrel ['skwɪrəl] n Eichhörnchen nt

squirt [skwɜːt] vt, vi (liquid)
spritzen

Sri Lanka [sriːˈlæŋkə] n Sri
Lanka nt

st abbr = **stone** Gewichtseinheit (6,35
kg)

St abbr = **saint** St.; = **street** Str.

stab [stæb] vt (person) einstechen
auf +akk; (to death) erstechen;
stabbing adj (pain) stechend

stabilize ['steɪbɪlaɪz] vt
stabilisieren ▷ vi sich
stabilisieren

stable ['steɪbl] n Stall m ▷ adj
stabil

stack [stæk] n (pile) Stapel m
▷ vt: **to ~ (up)** (auf)stapeln

stadium ['steɪdɪəm] n Stadion
nt

staff [stɑːf] n (personnel) Personal
nt, Lehrkräfte pl

stag [stæg] n Hirsch m

stag night n (Brit)
Junggesellenabschied m

stage [steɪdʒ] n (Theat) Bühne f;
(of project, life etc) Stadium nt; (of
journey) Etappe f; **at this ~** zu

diesem Zeitpunkt ▷ vt (Theat) aufführen, inszenieren; (demonstration) veranstalten

stagger ['stægə°] vi wanken ▷ vt (amaze) verblüffen; **staggering** adj amazing) umwerfend; (amount, price) schwindelerregend

stagnate [stæg'neɪt] vi (fig) stagnieren

stain [steɪn] n Fleck m; **stained-glass window** n Buntglasfenster nt; **stainless steel** n rostfreier Stahl; **stain remover** n Fleck(en)entferner m

stair [steə°] n (Treppen)stufe f; **~s** pl Treppe f; **staircase** n Treppe f

stake [steɪk] n (post) Pfahl m; (in betting) Einsatz m; (Fin) Anteil m (in an +dat); **to be at ~** auf dem Spiel stehen

stale [steɪl] adj (bread) alt; (beer) schal

stalk [stɔːk] n Stiel m ▷ vt (wild animal) sich anpirschen an +akk; (person) nachstellen +dat

stall [stɔːl] n (in market) (Verkaufs)stand m; (in stable) Box f; **~s** pl (Theat) Parkett nt ▷ vt (engine) abwürgen ▷ vi (driver) den Motor abwürgen; (car) stehen bleiben; (delay) Zeit schinden

stamina ['stæmɪnə] n Durchhaltevermögen nt

stammer ['stæmə°] vi, vt stottern

stamp [stæmp] n (postage ~) Briefmarke f; (for document) Stempel m ▷ vt (passport etc) stempeln; (mail) frankieren; **stamped addressed envelope** n frankierter Rückumschlag

stand [stænd] (stood, stood) vi stehen; (as candidate) kandidieren ▷ vt (place) stellen; (endure) aushalten; **I can't ~ her** ich kann sie nicht ausstehen ▷ n (stall)

Stand m; (seats in stadium) Tribüne f; (for coats, bicycles) Ständer m; (for small objects) Gestell nt; **stand around** vi herumstehen; **stand by** vi (be ready) sich bereithalten; (be inactive) danebenstehen ▷ vt (fig: person) halten zu; (decision, promise) stehen zu; **stand for** vt (represent) stehen für; (tolerate) hinnehmen; **stand in for** vt einspringen für; **stand out** vi (be noticeable) auffallen; **stand up** vi (get up) aufstehen ▷ vt (girlfriend, boyfriend) versetzen; **stand up for** vt sich einsetzen für; **stand up to** vt: **to ~ to sb** jdm die Stirn bieten

standard ['stændəd] n (norm) Norm f; **~ of living** Lebensstandard m ▷ adj Standard-

standardize ['stændədaɪz] vt vereinheitlichen

stand-by ['stændbaɪ] n (thing in reserve) Reserve f; **on ~** in Bereitschaft ▷ adj (flight, ticket) Stand-by-; **standing order** n (at bank) Dauerauftrag m; **standpoint** ['stændpɔɪnt] n Standpunkt m; **standstill** ['stændstɪl] n Stillstand m; **to come to a ~** stehen bleiben; (fig) zum Erliegen kommen

stank [stæŋk] pt of stink

staple ['steɪpl] n (for paper) Heftklammer f ▷ vt heften (to an +akk); **stapler** n Hefter m

star [stɑː°] n Stern m; (person) Star m ▷ vt: **the film ~s Hugh Grant** der Film zeigt Hugh Grant in der Hauptrolle ▷ vi die Hauptrolle spielen

starch [stɑːtʃ] n Stärke f

stare [steə°] vi starren; **to ~ at** anstarren

starfish ['stɑːfɪʃ] n Seestern m

star sign ['stɑːsaɪn] n Sternzeichen nt

start [stɑːt] n (beginning) Anfang m, Beginn m; (Sport) Start m; (lead) Vorsprung m; **from the ~** von Anfang an ⊳ vt anfangen; (car, engine) starten; (business, family) gründen; **to ~ to do sth, to ~ doing sth** anfangen, etw zu tun ⊳ vi (begin) anfangen; (car) anspringen; (on journey) aufbrechen; (Sport) starten; (jump) zusammenfahren; **~ing from Monday** ab Montag; **start off** vt (discussion, process etc) anfangen, beginnen ⊳ vi (begin) anfangen, beginnen; (on journey) aufbrechen; **start over** vi (US) wieder anfangen; **start up** vi (in business) anfangen ⊳ vt (car, engine) starten; (business) gründen; **starter** n (Brit: first course) Vorspeise f; (Auto) Anlasser m; **starting point** n (a. fig) Ausgangspunkt m

startle ['stɑːtl] vt erschrecken; **startling** adj überraschend

starve [stɑːv] vi hungern; (to death) verhungern; **I'm starving** ich habe einen Riesenhunger

state [steɪt] n (condition) Zustand m; (Pol) Staat m; **the (United) States** die (Vereinigten) Staaten ⊳ adj Staats-; (control, education) staatlich ⊳ vt erklären; (facts, name etc) angeben; **stated** adj (fixed) festgesetzt

statement ['steɪtmənt] n (official declaration) Erklärung f; (to police) Aussage f; (from bank) Kontoauszug m

state-of-the-art [steɪtəvðiːˈɑːt] adj hochmodern, auf dem neuesten Stand der Technik

static ['stætɪk] adj (unchanging) konstant

station ['steɪʃən] n (for trains, buses) Bahnhof m; (underground ~) Station f; (police ~, fire ~) Wache f;

(TV, Radio) Sender m ⊳ vt (Mil) stationieren

stationer's ['steɪʃənəz] n: **~ (shop)** Schreibwarengeschäft nt; **stationery** n Schreibwaren pl

station wagon ['steɪʃənwægən] n (US) Kombiwagen m

statistics [stəˈtɪstɪks] nsing (science) Statistik f; (figures) Statistiken pl

statue ['stætjuː] n Statue f

status ['steɪtəs] n Status m; (prestige) Ansehen nt; **status bar** n (Inform) Statuszeile f

stay [steɪ] n Aufenthalt m ⊳ vi bleiben; (with friends, in hotel) wohnen (with bei); **to ~ the night** übernachten; **stay away** vi wegbleiben; **to ~ from sb** sich von jdm fernhalten; **stay behind** vi zurückbleiben; (at work) länger bleiben; **stay in** vi (at home) zu Hause bleiben; **stay out** vi (not come home) wegbleiben; **stay up** vi (at night) aufbleiben

steady ['stedɪ] adj (speed) gleichmäßig; (progress, increase) stetig; (job, income, girlfriend) fest; (worker) zuverlässig; (hand) ruhig; **they've been going ~ for two years** sie sind seit zwei Jahren fest zusammen ⊳ vt (nerves) beruhigen; **to ~ oneself** Halt finden

steak [steɪk] n Steak nt; (of fish) Filet nt

steal [stiːl] (**stole, stolen**) vt stehlen; **to ~ sth from sb** jdm etw stehlen

steam [stiːm] n Dampf m ⊳ vt (Gastr) dämpfen; **steam up** vi (window) beschlagen; **steamer** n (Gastr) Dampfkochtopf m; (ship) Dampfer m; **steam iron** n Dampfbügeleisen nt

steel [stiːl] n Stahl m ⊳ adj Stahl-

steep [sti:p] adj steil

steeple ['sti:pl] n Kirchturm m

steer [stɪə°] vt, vi steuern; (car, bike etc) lenken; **steering** n (Auto) Lenkung f; **steering wheel** n Steuer nt, Lenkrad nt

stem [stem] n (of plant, glass) Stiel m

step [step] n Schritt m; (stair) Stufe f; (measure) Maßnahme f; **~ by ~** Schritt für Schritt ▷ vi treten; **~ this way, please** hier entlang, bitte; **step down** vi (resign) zurücktreten

stepbrother n Stiefbruder m; **stepchild** (pl **-children**) n Stiefkind nt; **stepfather** n Stiefvater m

stepladder n Trittleiter f

stepmother n Stiefmutter f; **stepsister** n Stiefschwester f

stereo ['stɛrɪəʊ] (pl **-s**) n: **~ (system)** Stereoanlage f

sterile ['stɛraɪl] adj steril; **sterilize** ['stɛrɪlaɪz] vt sterilisieren

sterling ['stɜːlɪŋ] n (Fin) das Pfund Sterling

stew [stju:] n Eintopf m

steward ['stjuːəd] n (on plane, ship) Steward m; **stewardess** n Stewardess f

stick [stɪk] (stuck, stuck) vt (with glue etc) kleben; (pin etc) stecken; (fam: put) tun ▷ vi (get jammed) klemmen; (hold fast) haften ▷ n Stock m; (hockey ~) Schläger m; (of chalk) Stück nt; (of celery, rhubarb) Stange f; **stick out** vt: **to stick one's tongue out (at sb)** (jdm) die Zunge herausstrecken ▷ vi (protrude) vorstehen; (ears) abstehen; (be noticeable) auffallen; **stick to** vt (rules, plan etc) sich halten an +akk; **sticker** ['stɪkə°] n Aufkleber m; **sticky** ['stɪkɪ] adj klebrig;

(weather) schwül; **~ label** Aufkleber m; **~ tape** Klebeband nt

stiff [stɪf] adj steif

stifle ['staɪfl] vt (yawn etc, opposition) unterdrücken; **stifling** adj drückend

still [stɪl] adj still; (drink) ohne Kohlensäure ▷ adv (yet, even now) (immer) noch; (all the same) immerhin; (sit, stand) still; **he ~ doesn't believe me** er glaubt mir immer noch nicht; **keep ~** halt still; **bigger/better ~** noch größer/besser

still life (pl **still lives**) n Stillleben nt

stimulate ['stɪmjʊleɪt] vt anregen, stimulieren; **stimulating** adj anregend

sting [stɪŋ] (stung, stung) vt (wound with ~) stechen ▷ vi (eyes, ointment etc) brennen ▷ n (insect wound) Stich m

stingy ['stɪndʒɪ] adj (fam) geizig

stink [stɪŋk] (stank, stunk) vi stinken (of nach) ▷ n Gestank m

stir [stɜ:°] vt (mix) (um)rühren; **stir up** vt (mob) aufhetzen; (memories) wachrufen; **to ~ trouble** Unruhe stiften; **stir-fry** vt (unter Rühren) kurz anbraten

stitch [stɪtʃ] n (in sewing) Stich m; (in knitting) Masche f; **to have a ~ (pain)** Seitenstechen haben; **he had to have ~es** er musste genäht werden; **she had her ~es out** ihr wurden die Fäden gezogen; **to be in ~es** (fam) sich kaputtlachen ▷ vt nähen; **stitch up** vt (hole, wound) nähen

stock [stɒk] n (supply) Vorrat m (of an +dat); (of shop) Bestand m; (for soup etc) Brühe f; **~s and shares** pl Aktien und Wertpapiere pl; **to be in/out of ~** vorrätig/nicht vorrätig sein; **to**

take ~ Inventur machen; (fig) Bilanz ziehen ▷ vt (keep in shop) führen; **stock up** vi sich eindecken (on, with mit)

stockbroker n Börsenmakler(in) m(f)

stock cube n Brühwurfel m

stock exchange n Börse f

stocking ['stɒkɪŋ] n Strumpf m

stock market ['stɒkmɑːkɪt] n Börse f

stole [stəʊl] pt of **steal**; **stolen** ['stəʊlən] pp of **steal**

stomach ['stʌmək] n Magen m; (belly) Bauch m; **on an empty ~** auf leeren Magen; **stomach-ache** n Magenschmerzen pl; **stomach upset** n Magenverstimmung f

stone [stəʊn] n Stein m; (seed) Kern m, Stein m; (weight) britische Gewichtseinheit (6,35 kg) ▷ adj Stein-, aus Stein; **stony** adj (ground) steinig

stood [stʊd] pt, pp of **stand**

stool [stuːl] n Hocker m

stop [stɒp] n Halt m; (for bus, tram, train) Haltestelle f; **to come to a ~** anhalten ▷ vt (vehicle, passer-by) anhalten; (put an end to) ein Ende machen +dat; (cease) aufhören mit; (prevent from happening) verhindern; (bleeding) stillen; (engine, machine) abstellen; (payments) einstellen; (cheque) sperren; **to ~ doing sth** aufhören, etw zu tun; **to ~ sb (from) doing sth** jdn daran hindern, etw zu tun; **~ it** hör auf (damit)! ▷ vi (vehicle) anhalten; (during journey) Halt machen; (pedestrian, clock, heart) stehen bleiben; (rain, noise) aufhören; (stay) bleiben; **stop by** vi vorbeischauen; **stop over** vi Halt machen; (overnight) übernachten; **stopgap** n Provisorium nt, Zwischenlösung f; **stopover** n (on journey)

Zwischenstation f; **stopper** n Stöpsel m; **stop sign** n Stoppschild nt; **stopwatch** n Stoppuhr f

storage ['stɔːrɪdʒ] n Lagerung f; **store** [stɔː°] n (supply) Vorrat m (of an +dat); (place for storage) Lager nt; (large shop) Kaufhaus nt; (US: shop) Geschäft nt ▷ vt lagern; (Inform) speichern; **storecard** n Kundenkreditkarte f; **storeroom** n Lagerraum m

storey ['stɔːrɪ] n (Brit) Stock m, Stockwerk nt

storm [stɔːm] n Sturm m; (thunder~) Gewitter nt ▷ vi (with movement) stürmen; **stormy** adj stürmisch

story ['stɔːrɪ] n Geschichte f; (plot) Handlung f; (US: of building) Stock m, Stockwerk nt

stout [staʊt] adj (fat) korpulent

stove [stəʊv] n Herd m; (for heating) Ofen m

stow [stəʊ] vt verstauen; **stowaway** n blinder Passagier

straight [streɪt] adj (not curved) gerade; (hair) glatt; (honest) ehrlich (with zu); (fam: heterosexual) hetero ▷ adv (directly) direkt; (immediately) sofort; (drink) pur; (think) klar; **~ ahead** geradeaus; **to go ~ on** geradeaus weitergehen/weiterfahren; **straightaway** adv sofort; **straightforward** adj einfach; (person) aufrichtig, unkompliziert

strain [streɪn] n Belastung f ▷ vt (eyes) überanstrengen; (rope, relationship) belasten; (vegetables) abgießen; **to ~ a muscle** sich einen Muskel zerren; **strained** adj (laugh, smile) gezwungen; (relations) gespannt; **~ muscle** Muskelzerrung f; **strainer** n Sieb nt

strand [strænd] n (of wool) Faden

m; (of hair) Strähne f ▷ vt: **to be
(left) ~ed** (person) festsitzen

strange [streɪndʒ] adj seltsam;
(unfamiliar) fremd; **strangely** adv
seltsam; ~ **enough**
seltsamerweise; **stranger** n
Fremde(r) mf; **I'm a ~ here** ich bin
hier fremd

strangle ['stræŋgl] vt (kill)
erdrosseln

strap [stræp] n Riemen m; (on
dress etc) Träger m; (on watch) Band
nt ▷ vt (fasten) festschnallen (to an
+dat); **strapless** adj trägerlos

strategy ['strætɪdʒɪ] n Strategie
f

straw [strɔː] n Stroh nt; (drinking
~) Strohhalm m

strawberry n Erdbeere f

stray [streɪ] n streunendes Tier
▷ adj (cat, dog) streunend ▷ vi
streunen

streak [striːk] n (of colour, dirt)
Streifen m; (in hair) Strähne f; (in
character) Zug m

stream [striːm] n (flow of liquid)
Strom m; (brook) Bach m ▷ vi
strömen; **streamer** n (of paper)
Luftschlange f

street [striːt] n Straße f;
streetcar n (US) Straßenbahn f;
street lamp, **street light** n
Straßenlaterne f; **street map** n
Stadtplan m

strength [streŋθ] n Kraft f,
Stärke f; **strengthen** vt
verstärken; (fig) stärken

strenuous ['strenjʊəs] adj
anstrengend

stress [stres] n Stress m; (on
word) Betonung f; **to be under
~** im Stress sein ▷ vt betonen;
(put under ~) stressen; **stressed**
adj: ~ **(out)** gestresst

stretch [stretʃ] n (of land) Stück
nt; (of road) Strecke f ▷ vt (material,
shoes) dehnen; (rope, canvas)

spannen; (person in job etc) fordern;
to ~ one's legs (walk) sich die
Beine vertreten ▷ vi (person) sich
strecken; (area) sich erstrecken (to
bis zu); **stretch out** vi: **to stretch
one's hand/legs out** die
Hand/die Beine ausstrecken,
ausstrecken ▷ vi (reach) sich
strecken; (lie down) sich
ausstrecken; **stretcher** n
Tragbahre f

strict, **strictly** [strɪkt, -lɪ] adj, adv
(severe(ly)) streng; (exact(ly)) genau;
~ **speaking** genauer gesagt

strike [straɪk] (**struck, struck**) vt
(match) anzünden; (hit) schlagen;
(find) finden; **it struck me as
strange** es kam mir seltsam vor
▷ vi (stop work) streiken; (attack)
zuschlagen; (clock) schlagen ▷ n
(by workers) Streik m; **to be on
~** streiken; **strike up** vt
(conversation) anfangen;
(friendship) schließen; **striking** adj
auffallend

string [strɪŋ] n (for tying) Schnur
f; (Mus, Tennis) Saite f; **the ~s** pl
(section of orchestra) die Streicher pl

strip [strɪp] n Streifen m; (Brit: of
footballer etc) Trikot nt ▷ vi
(undress) sich ausziehen, strippen

stripe [straɪp] n Streifen m;
striped adj gestreift

stripper ['strɪpə°] n Stripper(in)
m(f); (paint ~) Farbentferner m

strip-search ['strɪpsɜːtʃ] n
Leibesvisitation f (bei der man sich
ausziehen muss)

striptease ['strɪptiːz] n Striptease m

stroke [strəʊk] n (Med, Tennis etc)
Schlag m; (of pen, brush) Strich m
▷ vt streicheln

stroll [strəʊl] n Spaziergang m
▷ vi schlendern; **stroller** n (US: for
baby) Buggy m

strong [strɒŋ] adj stark; (healthy)

robust; (wall, table) stabil; (shoes) fest; (influence, chance) groß; **strongly** adv stark; (believe) fest; (constructed) stabil

struck [strʌk] pt, pp of **strike**

structural, structurally ['strʌktʃərəl, -lɪ] adj strukturell; **structure** ['strʌktʃə'] n Struktur f; (building, bridge) Konstruktion f, Bau m

struggle ['strʌgl] n Kampf m (for um) ▷ vi (fight) kämpfen (for um); (do sth with difficulty) groß; abmühen; **to ~ to do sth** sich abmühen, etw zu tun

stub [stʌb] n (of cigarette) Kippe f; (of ticket, cheque) Abschnitt m ▷ vt: **to ~ one's toe** sich dat den Zeh stoßen (on an +dat)

stubble ['stʌbl] n Stoppelbart m; (field) Stoppeln pl

stubborn ['stʌbən] adj (person) stur

stuck [stʌk] pt, pp of **stick** ▷ adj: **to be ~** (jammed) klemmen; (at a loss) nicht mehr weiterwissen; **to get ~** (car in snow etc) stecken bleiben

student ['stjuːdənt] n Student(in) m(f), Schüler(in) m(f)

studio ['stjuːdɪəʊ] (pl -s) n Studio nt

studious ['stjuːdɪəs] adj fleißig

study ['stʌdɪ] n (investigation) Untersuchung f; (room) Arbeitszimmer nt ▷ vt, vi studieren

stuff [stʌf] n Zeug nt, Sachen pl ▷ vt (push) stopfen; (Gastr) füllen; **to ~ oneself** (fam) sich vollstopfen; **stuffing** n (Gastr) Füllung f

stuffy ['stʌfɪ] adj (room) stickig; (person) spießig

stumble ['stʌmbl] vi stolpern; (when speaking) stocken

stun [stʌn] vt (shock) fassungslos

machen; **I was ~ned** ich war fassungslos (o völlig überrascht)

stung [stʌŋ] pt, pp of **sting**

stunk [stʌŋk] pp of **stink**

stunning ['stʌnɪŋ] adj (marvellous) fantastisch; (beautiful) atemberaubend; (very surprising, shocking) überwältigend; unfassbar

stunt [stʌnt] n (Cine) Stunt m

stupid ['stjuːpɪd] adj dumm; **stupidity** [stjuː'pɪdɪtɪ] n Dummheit f

sturdy ['stɜːdɪ] adj robust; (building, car) stabil

stutter ['stʌtə'] vi, vt stottern

stye [staɪ] n (Med) Gerstenkorn nt

style [staɪl] n Stil m ▷ vt (hair) stylen; **styling mousse** n Schaumfestiger m; **stylish** ['staɪlɪʃ] adj elegant, schick

subconscious [sʌb'kɒnʃəs] adj unterbewusst ▷ n: **the ~** das Unterbewusstsein

subdivide [sʌbdɪ'vaɪd] vt unterteilen

subject ['sʌbdʒɪkt] n (topic) Thema nt; (in school) Fach nt; (citizen) Staatsangehörige(r) mf; (of kingdom) Untertan(in) m(f); (Ling) Subjekt nt; **to change the ~** das Thema wechseln ▷ adj [səb'dʒekt]: **to be ~ to** (dependent on) abhängen von; (under control of) unterworfen sein +dat

subjective [səb'dʒektɪv] adj subjektiv

sublet [sʌb'let] irr vt untervermieten (to an +akk)

submarine [sʌbmə'riːn] n U-Boot nt

submerge [səb'mɜːdʒ] vt (put in water) eintauchen ▷ vi tauchen

submit [səb'mɪt] vt (application, claim) einreichen ▷ vi (surrender) sich ergeben

subordinate [sə'bɔːdɪnət] adj

untergeordnet (to +dat) ▷ n Untergebene(r) mf

subscribe [səbˈskraɪb] vi: **to ~ to** (magazine etc) abonnieren; **subscription** [səbˈskrɪpʃən] n (to magazine etc) Abonnement nt; (to club etc) (Mitglieds)beitrag m

subsequent [ˈsʌbsɪkwənt] adj nach(folgend); **subsequently** adv später, anschließend

subside [səbˈsaɪd] vi (floods) zurückgehen; (storm) sich legen; (building) sich senken

substance [ˈsʌbstəns] n Substanz f

substantial [səbˈstænʃəl] adj beträchtlich; (improvement) wesentlich; (meal) reichhaltig; (furniture) solide

substitute [ˈsʌbstɪtjuːt] n Ersatz m; (Sport) Ersatzspieler(in) m(f) ▷ vt: **to ~ A for B** B durch A ersetzen

subtitle [ˈsʌbtaɪtl] n Untertitel m

subtle [ˈsʌtl] adj (difference, taste) fein; (plan) raffiniert

subtotal [ˈsʌbtəʊtl] n Zwischensumme f

subtract [səbˈtrækt] vt abziehen (from von)

suburb [ˈsʌbɜːb] n Vorort m; **in the ~s** am Stadtrand; **suburban** [səˈbɜːbən] adj vorstädtisch, Vorstadt-

subway [ˈsʌbweɪ] n (Brit) Unterführung f; (US Rail) U-Bahn f

succeed [səkˈsiːd] vi erfolgreich sein; **he ~ed (in doing it)** es gelang ihm(, es zu tun) ▷ vt nachfolgen +dat; **succeeding** adj nachfolgend; **success** [səkˈses] n Erfolg m; **successful, successfully** adj, adv erfolgreich

successive [səkˈsesɪv] adj aufeinanderfolgend; **successor** n Nachfolger(in) m(f)

succulent [ˈsʌkjʊlənt] adj saftig

succumb [səˈkʌm] vi erliegen (to +dat)

such [sʌtʃ] adj solche(r, s); **~ a book** so ein Buch, ein solches Buch; **it was ~ a success that ...** es war solch ein Erfolg, dass ...; **~ as** wie ▷ adv so; **~ a hot day** so ein heißer Tag ▷ pron: **as ~** als solche(r, s)

suck [sʌk] vt (toffee etc) lutschen; (liquid) saugen; **it ~s** (fam) das ist beschissen

Sudan [suːˈdɑːn] n: **(the)** ~ der Sudan

sudden [ˈsʌdn] adj plötzlich; **all of a** ~ ganz plötzlich; **suddenly** adv plötzlich

sudoku [suˈdəʊkuː] n Sudoku nt

sue [suː] vt verklagen

suede [sweɪd] n Wildleder nt

suffer [ˈsʌfəʳ] vt erleiden ▷ vi leiden; **to ~ from** (Med) leiden an +dat

sufficient, sufficiently [səˈfɪʃənt, -lɪ] adj, adv ausreichend

suffocate [ˈsʌfəkeɪt] vt, vi ersticken

sugar [ˈʃʊgəʳ] n Zucker m ▷ vt zuckern; **sugar bowl** n Zuckerdose f; **sugary** adj (sweet) süß

suggest [səˈdʒest] vt vorschlagen; (imply) andeuten; **I ~ saying nothing** ich schlage vor, nichts zu sagen; **suggestion** n (proposal) Vorschlag m; **suggestive** adj vielsagend; (sexually) anzüglich

suicide [ˈsuːɪsaɪd] n (act) Selbstmord m; **suicide bomber** n Selbstmordattentäter(in) m(f); **suicide bombing** n Selbstmordattentat nt

suit [suːt] n (man's clothes) Anzug m; (lady's clothes) Kostüm nt; (Cards) Farbe f ▷ vt (be convenient for) passen +dat; (clothes, colour) stehen +dat; (climate, food) bekommen +dat; **suitable** adj geeignet (for für); **suitcase** n Koffer m

suite [swiːt] n (of rooms) Suite f; (sofa and chairs) Sitzgarnitur f

sulk [sʌlk] vi schmollen; **sulky** adj eingeschnappt

sultana [sʌlˈtɑːnə] n (raisin) Sultanine f

sum [sʌm] n Summe f; (money a.) Betrag m; (calculation) Rechenaufgabe f; **sum up** vt, vi (summarize) zusammenfassen

summarize [ˈsʌməraɪz] vt, vi zusammenfassen; **summary** n Zusammenfassung f

summer [ˈsʌmə*] n Sommer m; **summer camp** n (US) Ferienlager nt; **summer holidays** n Sommerferien pl; **summertime** n: **in (the) ~** im Sommer

summit [ˈsʌmɪt] n (a. Pol) Gipfel m

summon [ˈsʌmən] vt (doctor, fire brigade etc) rufen; (to one's office) zitieren; **summon up** vt (courage, strength) zusammennehmen

summons [ˈsʌmənz] nsing (Jur) Vorladung f

sumptuous [ˈsʌmptjʊəs] adj luxuriös; (meal) üppig

sun [sʌn] n Sonne f ▷ vt: **to ~ oneself** sich sonnen

Sun abbr = **Sunday** So.

sunbathe vi sich sonnen; **sunbathing** nt Sonnenbaden nt; **sunbed** n Sonnenbank f; **sunblock** n Sunblocker m; **sunburn** n Sonnenbrand m; **sunburnt** adj: **to be/get ~** einen Sonnenbrand haben/bekommen

sundae [ˈsʌndeɪ] n Eisbecher m

Sunday [ˈsʌndɪ] n Sonntag m; see also **Tuesday**

sung [sʌŋ] pp of **sing**

sunglasses [ˈsʌnɡlɑːsɪz] npl

Sonnenbrille f; **sunhat** n Sonnenhut m

sunk [sʌŋk] pp of **sink**

sunlamp [ˈsʌnlæmp] n Höhensonne f; **sunlight** n Sonnenlicht nt; **sunny** [ˈsʌnɪ] adj sonnig; **sun protection factor** n Lichtschutzfaktor m; **sunrise** n Sonnenaufgang m; **sunroof** n (Auto) Schiebedach nt; **sunscreen** n Sonnenschutzmittel nt; **sunset** n Sonnenuntergang m; **sunshade** n Sonnenschirm m; **sunshine** n Sonnenschein m; **sunstroke** n (Sonnen)stich m; **suntan** n (Sonnen)bräune f; **to get/have a ~** braun werden/sein; **~ lotion** (o oil) Sonnenöl nt

super [ˈsuːpə*] adj (fam) toll

superb, superbly [suːˈpɜːb, -lɪ] adj, adv ausgezeichnet

superficial, superficially [suːpəˈfɪʃəl, -ɪ] adj, adv oberflächlich

superfluous [sʊˈpɜːfluəs] adj überflüssig

superglue [ˈsuːpəɡluː] n Sekundenkleber m

superior [sʊˈpɪərɪə*] adj (better) besser (to als); (higher in rank) höhergestellt (to als), höher ▷ n (in rank) Vorgesetzte(r) mf

supermarket [ˈsuːpəmɑːkɪt] n Supermarkt m

supersede [suːpəˈsiːd] vt ablösen

supersonic [suːpəˈsɒnɪk] adj Überschall-

superstition [suːpəˈstɪʃən] n Aberglaube m; **superstitious** [suːpəˈstɪʃəs] adj abergläubisch

superstore [ˈsuːpəstɔː*] n Verbrauchermarkt m

supervise [ˈsuːpəvaɪz] vt beaufsichtigen; **supervisor** [ˈsuːpəvaɪzə] n Aufsicht f; (at university) Doktorvater m

supper ['sʌpə°] n Abendessen nt; (late-night snack) Imbiss

supplement ['sʌplɪmənt] n (extra payment) Zuschlag m; (of newspaper) Beilage f ▷ vt ergänzen; **supplementary** [sʌplɪ'mentərɪ] adj zusätzlich

supplier [sə'plaɪə°] n Lieferant(in) m(f); **supply** [sə'plaɪ] vt (deliver) liefern; (drinks, music etc) sorgen für; **to ~ sb with sth** (provide) jdn mit etw versorgen ▷ n (stock) Vorrat m (of an +dat)

support [sə'pɔ:t] n Unterstützung f; (Tech) Stütze f ▷ vt (hold up) tragen, stützen; (provide for) ernähren, unterhalten; (speak in favour of) unterstützen; **he ~s Manchester United** er ist Manchester-United-Fan

suppose [sə'pəʊz] vt (assume) annehmen; **I ~ so** ich denke schon; **I ~ not** wahrscheinlich nicht; **you're not ~d to smoke here** du darfst/Sie dürfen hier nicht rauchen; **supposedly** [sə'pəʊzɪdlɪ] adv angeblich; **supposing** conj angenommen

suppress [sə'pres] vt unterdrücken

surcharge ['sɜ:tʃɑːdʒ] n Zuschlag m

sure [ʃʊə°] adj sicher; **I'm (not) ~** ich bin mir (nicht) sicher; **make ~ you lock up** vergiss/vergessen Sie nicht abzuschließen ▷ adv: **~!** klar!; **~ enough** tatsächlich; **surely** adv: **~ you don't mean it?** das ist nicht dein/Ihr Ernst, oder?

surf [sɜ:f] n Brandung f ▷ vt: **to ~ the net** im Internet surfen

surface ['sɜ:fɪs] n Oberfläche f ▷ vi auftauchen; **surface mail** n: **by ~** auf dem Land-/Seeweg

surfboard ['sɜ:fbɔ:d] n Surfbrett nt; **surfer** n Surfer(in) m(f);

surfing n Surfen nt; **to go ~** surfen gehen

surgeon ['sɜ:dʒən] n Chirurg(in) m(f); **surgery** ['sɜ:dʒərɪ] n (operation) Operation f; (room) Praxis f, Sprechzimmer nt; (consulting time) Sprechstunde f; **to have ~** operiert werden

surname ['sɜ:neɪm] n Nachname m

surpass [sɜ:'pɑ:s] vt übertreffen

surplus ['sɜ:pləs] n Überschuss m (of an +dat)

surprise [sə'praɪz] n Überraschung f ▷ vt überraschen; **surprising** adj überraschend; **surprisingly** adv überraschenderweise, erstaunlicherweise

surrender [sə'rendə°] vi sich ergeben (to +dat) ▷ vt (weapon, passport) abgeben

surround [sə'raʊnd] vt umgeben; (stand all round) umringen; **surrounding** adj (countryside) umliegend ▷ n **~s** pl Umgebung f

survey ['sɜ:veɪ] n (opinion poll) Umfrage f; (of literature etc) Überblick m (of über +akk); (of land) Vermessung f ▷ [sɜ:'veɪ] vt (look out over) überblicken; (land) vermessen

survive [sə'vaɪv] vt, vi überleben

susceptible [sə'septəbl] adj empfänglich (to für); (Med) anfällig (to für)

sushi ['su:ʃɪ] n Sushi nt

suspect ['sʌspekt] n Verdächtige(r) m(f) adj verdächtig ▷ [sə'spekt] vt verdächtigen (of +gen); (think likely) vermuten

suspend [sə'spend] vt (from work) suspendieren; (payment) vorübergehend einstellen; (player) sperren; (hang up) aufhängen; **suspender** n (Brit) Strumpfhalter

m; **~s** *pl* (US: for trousers)
Hosenträger *pl*
suspense [sə'spɛns] *n* Spannung *f*
suspicious [sə'spɪʃəs] *adj*
misstrauisch (of sb/sth jdm/etw
gegenüber); (causing suspicion)
verdächtig
SUV *abbr* = **sport utility vehicle**
SUV *m*, Geländewagen *m*
swallow ['swɒləʊ] *n* (bird)
Schwalbe *f* ▷ *vt*, *vi* schlucken
swam [swæm] *pt of* **swim**
swamp [swɒmp] *n* Sumpf *m*
swan [swɒn] *n* Schwan *m*
swap [swɒp] *vt*, *vi* tauschen; **to
~ sth for sth** etw gegen etw
eintauschen
sway [sweɪ] *vi* schwanken
swear [sweə°] *(swore,
sworn)* *vi* (promise) schwören;
(curse) fluchen; **to ~ at sb** jdn
beschimpfen; **swear by** *vt* (have
faith in) schwören auf +akk;
swearword *n* Fluch *m*
sweat [swɛt] *n* Schweiß *m* ▷ *vi*
schwitzen; **sweatband** *n*
Schweißband *nt*; **sweater** *n*
Pullover *m*; **sweatshirt** *n*
Sweatshirt *nt*; **sweaty** *adj*
verschwitzt
swede [swiːd] *n* Steckrübe *f*
Swede [swiːd] *n* Schwede *m*,
Schwedin *f*; **Sweden** *n* Schweden
nt; **Swedish** *adj* schwedisch ▷ *n*
(language) Schwedisch *nt*
sweep [swiːp] *(swept, swept)*
vt, *vi* (with brush) kehren, fegen;
sweep up *vt* (dirt etc) zusammenkehren, zusammenfegen
sweet [swiːt] *n* (Brit: candy)
Bonbon *nt*; (dessert) Nachtisch *m*
▷ *adj* süß; (kind) lieb;
sweet-and-sour *adj* süßsauer;
sweetcorn *n* Mais *m*; **sweeten** *vt*
(tea etc) süßen; **sweetener** *n*
(substance) Süßstoff *m*; **sweet**

potato *n* Süßkartoffel *f*
swell [swɛl] *(swelled, swollen* o
swelled) *vi*: **to ~ (up)**
(an)schwellen ▷ *adj* (US fam) toll;
swelling *n* (Med) Schwellung *f*
sweltering ['swɛltərɪŋ] *adj* (heat)
drückend
swept [swɛpt] *pt, pp of* **sweep**
swift [swɪft] *adj* schnell
swig [swɪg] *n* (fam) Schluck *m*
swim [swɪm] *(swam, swum)* *vi*
schwimmen ▷ *n*: **to go for a
~** schwimmen gehen; **swimmer** *n*
Schwimmer(in) *m(f)*; **swimming** *n*
Schwimmen *nt*; **to go
~** schwimmen gehen; **swimming
cap** *n* (Brit) Badekappe *f*;
swimming costume *n* (Brit)
Badeanzug *m*; **swimming pool** *n*
Schwimmbad *nt*; (private, in hotel)
Swimmingpool *m*; **swimming
trunks** *npl* (Brit) Badehose *f*;
swimsuit *n* Badeanzug *m*
swindle ['swɪndl] *vt* betrügen
(out of um)
swine [swaɪn] *n* (person)
Schwein *nt*; **swine flu** *n*
Schweinegrippe *f*
swing [swɪŋ] *(swung, swung)*
vt, *vi* (object) schwingen ▷ *n* (for
child) Schaukel *f*
swipe [swaɪp] *vt* (credit card etc)
durchziehen; (fam: steal) klauen;
swipe card *n* Magnetkarte *f*
Swiss [swɪs] *adj* schweizerisch
▷ *n* Schweizer(in) *m(f)*
switch [swɪtʃ] *n* (Elec) Schalter *m*
▷ *vi* (change) wechseln (to zu);
switch off *vt* abschalten,
ausschalten; **switch on** *vt*
anschalten, einschalten;
switchboard *n* (Tel) Vermittlung *f*
Switzerland ['swɪtsələnd] *n* die
Schweiz
swivel ['swɪvl] *vi* sich drehen
▷ *vt* drehen
swollen ['swəʊlən] *pp of* **swell**

▷ adj (Med) geschwollen; (stomach) aufgebläht

swop [swɒp] see **swap**

sword [sɔːd] n Schwert nt

swore [swɔː°] pt of **swear**

sworn [swɔːn] pp of **swear**

swot [swɒt] vi (Brit fam) büffeln (for für)

swum [swʌm] pp of **swim**

swung [swʌŋ] pt, pp of **swing**

syllable ['sɪləbl] n Silbe f

syllabus ['sɪləbəs] n Lehrplan m

symbol ['sɪmbəl] n Symbol nt; **symbolic** [sɪm'bɒlɪk] adj symbolisch; **symbolize** vt symbolisieren

symmetrical [sɪ'metrɪkəl] adj symmetrisch

sympathetic [sɪmpə'θetɪk] adj mitfühlend; (understanding) verständnisvoll; **sympathize** ['sɪmpəθaɪz] vi mitfühlen (with sb mit jdm); **sympathy** ['sɪmpəθɪ] n Mitleid nt; (after death) Beileid nt; (understanding) Verständnis nt

symphony ['sɪmfənɪ] n Sinfonie f

symptom ['sɪmptəm] n (a. fig) Symptom nt

synagogue ['sɪnəgɒg] n Synagoge f

synonym ['sɪnənɪm] n Synonym nt; **synonymous** [sɪ'nɒnɪməs] adj synonym (with mit)

synthetic [sɪn'θetɪk] adj (material) synthetisch

syphilis ['sɪfɪlɪs] n Syphilis f

Syria ['sɪrɪə] n Syrien nt

syringe [sɪ'rɪndʒ] n Spritze f

system ['sɪstəm] n System nt; **systematic** [sɪstə'mætɪk] adj systematisch; **system disk** n (Inform) Systemdiskette f; **system(s) software** n (Inform) Systemsoftware f

t

tab [tæb] n (for hanging up coat etc) Aufhänger m; (Inform) Tabulator m; **to pick up the ~** (fam) die Rechnung übernehmen

table ['teɪbl] n Tisch m; (list) Tabelle f; **~ of contents** Inhaltsverzeichnis nt; **tablecloth** n Tischdecke f; **tablelamp** n Tischlampe f; **tablemat** n Set nt; **tablespoon** n Servierlöffel m; (in recipes) Esslöffel m

tablet ['tæblət] n (Med) Tablette f; (Inform) Tablet nt

table tennis ['teɪbltenɪs] n Tischtennis nt

tabloid ['tæblɔɪd] n Boulevardzeitung f

taboo [tə'buː] n Tabu nt ▷ adj tabu

tacit, tacitly ['tæsɪt, -lɪ] adj, adv stillschweigend

tack [tæk] n (small nail) Stift m; (US: thumb-) Reißzwecke f

tackle ['tækl] n (Sport) Angriff m; (equipment) Ausrüstung f ▷ vt (deal with) in Angriff nehmen; (Sport) angreifen; (verbally) zur Rede stellen (about wegen)

tacky ['tækɪ] adj trashig, heruntergekommen

tact [tækt] n Takt m; **tactful, tactfully** adj, adv taktvoll; **tactic(s)** ['tæktɪk(s)] n(pl) Taktik f; **tactless, tactlessly** ['tæktləs, -lɪ] adj, adv taktlos

tag [tæg] n (label) Schild nt; (with maker's name) Etikett nt

Tahiti [tɑːˈhiːtɪ] n Tahiti nt

tail [teɪl] n Schwanz m; **heads or ~s?** Kopf oder Zahl?; **tailback** n (Brit) Rückstau m; **taillight** n (Auto) Rücklicht nt

tailor ['teɪlə'] n Schneider(in) m(f)

tailpipe ['teɪlpaɪp] n (US Auto) Auspuffrohr nt

tainted ['teɪntɪd] adj (US: food) verdorben

Taiwan [taɪˈwæn] n Taiwan nt

take [teɪk] (**took, taken**) vt nehmen; (~ along with one) mitnehmen; (~ to a place) bringen; (subtract) abziehen (from von); (capture: person) fassen; (gain, obtain) bekommen; (Fin, Comm) einnehmen; (train, taxi) nehmen, fahren mit; (trip, walk, holiday, exam, course, photo) machen; (bath) nehmen; (phone call) entgegennehmen; (decision, precautions) treffen; (risk) eingehen; (advice, job) annehmen; (consume) zu sich nehmen; (tablets) nehmen; (heat, pain) ertragen; (react to) aufnehmen; (have room for) Platz haben für; **I'll ~ it** (item in shop) ich nehme es; **how long does it ~?** wie lange dauert es?; **it ~s 4 hours** man braucht 4 Stunden; **do you ~ sugar?** nimmst

du/nehmen Sie Zucker?; **I ~ it that ...** ich nehme an, dass ...; **to ~ part in** teilnehmen an +dat; **to ~ place** stattfinden; **take after** vt nachschlagen +dat; **take along** vt mitnehmen; **take apart** vt auseinandernehmen; **take away** vt (remove) wegnehmen (from sb jdm); (subtract) abziehen (from von); **take back** vt (return) zurückbringen; (retract) zurücknehmen; (remind) zurückversetzen (to in +akk); **take down** vt (picture, curtains) abnehmen; (write down) aufschreiben; **take in** vt (understand) begreifen; (give accommodation to) aufnehmen; (deceive) hereinlegen; (include) einschließen; (show, film etc) mitnehmen; **take off** vi (plane) starten ▷ vt (clothing) ausziehen; (hat, lid) abnehmen; (deduct) abziehen; (Brit: imitate) nachmachen; **to take a day off** sich einen Tag freinehmen; **take on** vt (undertake) übernehmen; (employ) einstellen; (Sport) antreten gegen; **take out** vt (wallet etc) herausnehmen; (person, dog) ausführen; (insurance) abschließen; (money from bank) abheben; (book from library) ausleihen; **take over** vt übernehmen ▷ vi: **he took over (from me)** er hat mich abgelöst; **take to** vt: **I've taken to her/it** ich mag sie/es; **to ~ doing sth** (begin) anfangen, etw zu tun; **take up** vt (carpet) hochnehmen; (space) einnehmen; (time) in Anspruch nehmen; (hobby) anfangen mit; (new job) antreten; (offer) annehmen

takeaway n (Brit: meal) Essen nt zum Mitnehmen

taken ['teɪkn] pp of **take** ▷ adj

(seat) besetzt; **to be ~ with** angetan sein von

takeoff ['teɪkɒf] n (Aviat) Start m; (imitation) Nachahmung f; **takeout** (US) see **takeaway**; **takeover** n (Comm) Übernahme f

takings ['teɪkɪŋz] npl Einnahmen pl

tale [teɪl] n Geschichte f

talent ['tælənt] n Talent nt; **talented** adj begabt

talk [tɔːk] n (conversation) Gespräch nt; (rumour) Gerede nt; (to audience) Vortrag m ▷ vi (have conversation) sich unterhalten; **to ~ to** (o **with**) sb (about sth) mit jdm (über etw akk) sprechen ▷ vt (language) sprechen; (nonsense) reden; (politics, business) reden über +akk; **to ~ sb into doing/out of doing sth** jdn überreden/jdm ausreden, etw zu tun; **talk over** vt besprechen

talkative adj gesprächig; **talk show** n Talkshow f

tall [tɔːl] adj groß; (building, tree) hoch; **he is 6ft ~** er ist 1,80m groß

tame [teɪm] adj zahm; (joke, story) fade ▷ vt (animal) zähmen

tampon ['tæmpɒn] n Tampon m

tan [tæn] n (on skin) (Sonnen)bräune f; **to get/have a ~** braun werden/sein ▷ vi braun werden

tangerine [tændʒəˈriːn] n Mandarine f

tango ['tæŋɡəʊ] n Tango m

tank [tæŋk] n Tank m; (for fish) Aquarium nt; (Mil) Panzer m

tanker ['tæŋkə°] n (ship) Tanker m; (vehicle) Tankwagen m

tanned [tænd] adj (by sun) braun

tantalizing ['tæntəlaɪzɪŋ] adj verlockend

Tanzania [tænzəˈnɪə] n Tansania nt

tap [tæp] n (for water) Hahn m ▷ vt, vi (strike) klopfen; **to ~ sb on the shoulder** jdm auf die Schulter klopfen; **tap-dance** vi steppen

tape [teɪp] n (adhesive ~) Klebeband nt; (for tape recorder) Tonband nt; (cassette) Kassette f; (video) Video nt ▷ vt (record) aufnehmen; **tape up** vt (parcel) zukleben; **tape measure** n Maßband nt; **tape recorder** n Tonbandgerät nt

tapestry ['tæpɪstrɪ] n Wandteppich m

tap water ['tæpwɔːtə°] n Leitungswasser nt

target ['tɑːgɪt] n Ziel nt; (board) Zielscheibe f; **target group** n Zielgruppe f

tariff ['tærɪf] n (price list) Preisliste f; (tax) Zoll m

tarmac ['tɑːmæk] n (Aviat) Rollfeld nt

tart [tɑːt] n (fruit ~) (Obst)kuchen m; (small) (Obst)törtchen nt; (fam, pej: prostitute) Nutte f; (fam: promiscuous person) Schlampe f

tartan ['tɑːtən] n Schottenkaro nt; (material) Schottenstoff m

tartar(e) sauce ['tɑːtəˈsɔːs] n Remouladensoße f

task [tɑːsk] n Aufgabe f; (duty) Pflicht f; **taskbar** n (Inform) Taskbar f

Tasmania [tæzˈmeɪnɪə] n Tasmanien nt

taste [teɪst] n Geschmack m; (sense of ~) Geschmackssinn m; (small quantity) Kostprobe f; **it has a strange ~** es schmeckt komisch ▷ vt schmecken; (try) probieren ▷ vi (food) schmecken (of nach); **to ~ good/strange** gut/komisch schmecken; **tasteful, tastefully** adj, adv geschmackvoll; **tasteless, tastelessly** adj, adv geschmacklos; **tasty** adj lecker

tattered ['tætəd] adj (clothes) zerlumpt; (fam: person) angespannt; **I'm absolutely ~** ich bin mit den Nerven am Ende

tattoo [tə'tu:] n (on skin) Tätowierung f

taught [tɔ:t] pt, pp of **teach**

Taurus ['tɔ:rəs] n (Astr) Stier m

tax [tæks] n Steuer f (on auf +akk) ▷ vt besteuern; **taxable** adj steuerpflichtig; **taxation** [tæk'seɪʃən] n Besteuerung f; **tax bracket** n Steuerklasse f; **tax disc** n (Brit Auto) Steuermarke f; **tax-free** adj steuerfrei

taxi ['tæksɪ] n Taxi nt ▷ vi (plane) rollen; **taxi driver** n Taxifahrer(in) m(f); **taxi rank** (Brit), **taxi stand** n Taxistand m

tax return n Steuererklärung f

tea [ti:] n Tee m; (afternoon ~) ≈ Kaffee und Kuchen; (meal) frühes Abendessen; **teabag** n Teebeutel m; **tea break** n (Tee)pause f

teach [ti:tʃ] (**taught**, **taught**) vt (person, subject) unterrichten; **to ~ sb (how) to dance** jdm das Tanzen beibringen ▷ vi unterrichten; **teacher** n Lehrer(in) m(f); **teaching** n (activity) Unterrichten nt; (profession) Lehrberuf m

teacup ['ti:kʌp] n Teetasse f

team [ti:m] n (Sport) Mannschaft f, Team nt; **teamwork** n Teamarbeit f

teapot ['ti:pɒt] n Teekanne f

tear [tɪə*] n (in eye) Träne f

tear [tɛə*] (**tore**, **torn**) vt zerreißen; **to ~ a muscle** sich einen Muskel zerren n (in material etc) Riss m; **tear down** vt (building) abreißen; **tear up** vt (paper) zerreißen

tearoom ['ti:rʊm] n Teestube f,

Café, in dem in erster Linie Tee serviert wird

tease [ti:z] vt (person) necken (about wegen)

tea set n Teeservice nt; **teashop** n Teestube f; **teaspoon** n Teelöffel m; **tea towel** n Geschirrtuch nt

technical ['tɛknɪkəl] adj technisch; (knowledge, term, dictionary) Fach-; **technically** adv technisch; **technique** [tɛk'ni:k] n Technik f

techno ['tɛknəʊ] n Techno f

technological [tɛknə'lɒdʒɪkəl] adj technologisch; **technology** [tɛk'nɒlədʒɪ] n Technologie f, Technik f

tedious ['ti:dɪəs] adj langweilig

teen(age) ['ti:n(eɪdʒ)] adj (fashions etc) Teenager-; **teenager** n Teenager m; **teens** [ti:nz] npl: **in one's ~** im Teenageralter

teeth [ti:θ] pl of **tooth**

teetotal ['ti:'təʊtl] adj abstinent

telegraph pole ['tɛlɪgrɑ:fpəʊl] n (Brit) Telegrafenmast m

telephone ['tɛlɪfəʊn] n Telefon nt ▷ vi telefonieren ▷ vt anrufen; **telephone banking** n Telefonbanking nt; **telephone book** n Telefonbuch nt; **telephone booth**, **telephone box** (Brit) n Telefonzelle f; **telephone call** n Telefonanruf m; **telephone directory** n Telefonbuch nt; **telephone number** n Telefonnummer f

telephoto lens ['tɛlɪfəʊtəʊ'lɛnz] n Teleobjektiv nt

telescope ['tɛlɪskəʊp] n Teleskop nt

televise ['tɛlɪvaɪz] vt im Fernsehen übertragen; **television** ['tɛlɪvɪʒən] n Fernsehen nt; **television programme** n Fernsehsendung f; **television (set)** n Fernseher m

teleworking ['teliwɜːkɪŋ] n
Telearbeit f

tell [tel] (**told, told**) vt (*say,
inform*) sagen (*sb sth* jdm etw);
(*story*) erzählen; (*truth*) sagen;
(*difference*) erkennen; (*reveal secret*)
verraten; **to ~ sb about sth** jdm
von etw erzählen; **to ~ sth from
sth** etw von etw unterscheiden
▷ vi (*be sure*) wissen; **tell apart** vt
unterscheiden; **tell off** vt
schimpfen

telling adj aufschlussreich

telly ['teli] n (*Brit fam*) Glotze f; **on
(the) ~** in der Glotze

temp [temp] n Aushilfskraft f
▷ vi als Aushilfskraft arbeiten

temper ['tempə°] n (*anger*) Wut f;
(*mood*) Laune f; **to lose one's ~** die
Beherrschung verlieren; **to have a
bad ~** jähzornig sein;
temperamental
[temprə'mentl] adj (*moody*)
launisch

temperature ['temprɪtʃə°] n
Temperatur f; (*Med: high* ~) Fieber
nt; **to have a ~** Fieber haben

temple ['templ] n Tempel m;
(*Anat*) Schläfe f

temporarily ['tempərərɪlɪ] adv
vorübergehend; **temporary**
['tempərərɪ] adj vorübergehend;
(*road, building*) provisorisch

tempt [tempt] vt in Versuchung
führen; **I'm ~ed to accept** ich bin
versucht anzunehmen;
temptation [temp'teɪʃən] n
Versuchung f; **tempting** adj
verlockend

ten [ten] num zehn ▷ n Zehn f;
see also **eight**

tenant ['tenənt] n Mieter(in)
m(f); (*of land*) Pächter(in) m(f)

tend [tend] vi: **to ~ to do sth**
(*person*) dazu neigen, etw zu tun;
to ~ towards neigen zu;
tendency ['tendənsi] n Tendenz

f; **to have a ~ to do sth** (*person*)
dazu neigen, etw zu tun

tender ['tendə°] adj (*loving*)
zärtlich; (*sore*) empfindlich; (*meat*)
zart

tendon ['tendən] n Sehne f

Tenerife [tenə'riːf] n Teneriffa nt

tenner ['tenə°] n (*Brit fam: note*)
Zehnpfundschein m; (*amount*) zehn
Pfund

tennis ['tenɪs] n Tennis nt;
tennis ball n Tennisball m; **tennis
court** n Tennisplatz m; **tennis
racket** n Tennisschläger m

tenor ['tenə°] n Tenor m

tenpin bowling, tenpins (US)
['tenpɪn'bəʊlɪŋ, 'tenpɪnz] n
Bowling nt

tense [tens] adj angespannt;
(*stretched tight*) gespannt; **tension**
['tenʃən] n Spannung f; (*strain*)
Anspannung f

tent [tent] n Zelt nt

tenth [tenθ] adj zehnte(r, s) ▷ n
(*fraction*) Zehntel nt; see also **eighth**

tent peg n Hering m; **tent pole**
n Zeltstange f

term [tɜːm] n (*in school, at
university*) Trimester nt; (*expression*)
Ausdruck m; **~s** pl (*conditions*)
Bedingungen pl; **to be on good ~s
with sb** mit jdm gut auskommen;
to come to ~s with sth sich mit
etw abfinden; **in the long/short
~** langfristig/kurzfristig; **in ~s
of ...** was ... betrifft

terminal ['tɜːmɪnl] n (*bus ~ etc*)
Endstation f; (*Aviat*) Terminal m;
(*Inform*) Terminal nt; (*Elec*) Pol m
▷ adj (*Med*) unheilbar; **terminally**
adv (*ill*) unheilbar

terminate ['tɜːmɪneɪt] vt (*contract*) lösen; (*pregnancy*) abbrechen
▷ vi (*train, bus*) enden

terminology [tɜːmɪ'nɒlədʒɪ] n
Terminologie f

terrace ['terəs] n (*of houses*)

Häuserreihe f; (in garden etc)
Terrasse f; **terraced** adj (garden)
terrassenförmig angelegt;
terraced house n (Brit)
Reihenhaus nt

terrible ['terǝbl] adj schrecklich
terrific [tǝ'rɪfɪk] adj (very good)
fantastisch
terrify ['terɪfaɪ] vt erschrecken;
to be terrified schreckliche Angst
haben (of vor +dat)
territory ['terɪtǝrɪ] n Gebiet nt
terror ['terǝ*] n Schrecken m;
(Pol) Terror m; **terrorism** n
Terrorismus m; **terrorist** n
Terrorist(in) m(f)
test [test] n Test m, Klassenarbeit
f; (driving) Prüfung f; **to put to
the ~** auf die Probe stellen ▷ vt
testen, prüfen; (patience, courage
etc) auf die Probe stellen
Testament ['testǝmǝnt] n: **the
Old/New ~** das Alte/Neue
Testament
test-drive ['testdraɪv] vt Probe
fahren
testicle ['testɪkl] n Hoden m
testify ['testɪfaɪ] vi (Jur)
aussagen
test tube ['testtju:b] n
Reagenzglas nt
tetanus ['tetǝnǝs] n Tetanus m
text [tekst] n Text m; (of
document) Wortlaut m; (sent by
mobile phone) SMS f ▷ vt (message)
simsen, SMSen; SMSen; jdm
simsen, jdm eine SMS schicken;
I'll ~ it to you ich schicke es dir per
SMS
textbook n Lehrbuch nt
texting ['tekstɪŋ] n SMS-
Messaging nt; **text message** n
SMS f; **text messaging** n
SMS-Messaging nt
texture ['tekstʃǝ*] n
Beschaffenheit f
Thailand ['taɪlænd] n Thailand nt

Thames [temz] n Themse f
than [ðæn] prep, conj als;
bigger/faster ~ me
größer/schneller als ich; **I'd rather
walk ~ drive** ich gehe lieber zu
Fuß als mit dem Auto
thank [θæŋk] vt danken +dat;
~ you danke; **~ you very much**
vielen Dank; **thankful** adj
dankbar; **thankfully** adv (luckily)
zum Glück; **thankless** adj
undankbar; **thanks** npl Dank m;
~ dankel; **~ to** dank +gen

⁕ **THANKSGIVING DAY**
⁕
⁕ **Thanksgiving (Day)** ist ein
⁕ Feiertag in den USA, der auf den
⁕ vierten Donnerstag im
⁕ November fällt. Er soll daran
⁕ erinnern, wie die Pilgerväter die
⁕ gute Ernte im Jahre 1621
⁕ feierten. In Kanada gibt es einen
⁕ ähnlichen Erntedanktag (der
⁕ aber nichts mit den Pilgervätern
⁕ zu tun hat) am zweiten Montag
⁕ im Oktober.

⭕ **KEYWORD**

that [ðæt, ðǝt] (pl those) adj (demonstrative)
(pl those) der/die/das, jene(r, s);
that one das da
▷ pron 1 (demonstrative) (pl those)
das; **who's/what's that?** wer ist
da/was ist das?; **is that you?** bist
du/sind Sie das?; **that's what he
said** genau das hat er gesagt;
what happened after that? was
passierte danach?; **that is** das
heißt
2 (relative) (subj) der/die/das, die;
(direct obj) den/die/das, die;
(indirect obj) dem/der/dem, denen;
all (that) I have alles, was ich
habe
3 (relative) (of time); **the day (that)**

an dem Tag, als; **the winter (that) he came** in dem Winter, in dem er kam

▷ *conj* dass; **he thought that I was ill** er dachte, dass ich krank sei, er dachte, ich sei krank

▷ *adv* (*demonstrative*) so; **I can't work that much** ich kann nicht so viel arbeiten

that's [ðæts] *contr of* **that is; that has**

thaw [θɔː] *vi* tauen; (*frozen food*) auftauen ▷ *vt* auftauen lassen

◯ **KEYWORD**

the [ðə, ðiː] *def art* **1** der/die/das; **to play the piano/violin** Klavier/Geige spielen; **I'm going to the butcher's/the cinema** ich gehe zum Fleischer/ins Kino; **Elizabeth the First** Elisabeth die Erste

2 (+*adj to form noun*) das, die; **the rich and the poor** die Reichen und die Armen

3 (*in comparisons*) **the more he works the more he earns** je mehr er arbeitet, desto mehr verdient er

theater (*US*), **theatre** ['θɪətə°] *n* Theater *nt*; (*for lectures etc*) Saal *m*

theft [θɛft] *n* Diebstahl *m*

their [ðɛə°] *adj* ihr; (*unidentified person*) sein; **they cleaned ~ teeth** sie putzten sich die Zähne; **someone has left ~ umbrella here** jemand hat seinen Schirm hier vergessen; **theirs** *pron* ihre(r, s); (*unidentified person*) seine(r, s); **a friend of ~** ein Freund von ihnen; **someone has left ~ here** jemand hat seins hier liegen lassen

them [ðem, ðəm] *pron* (*direct object*) sie; (*indirect object*) ihnen;

(*unidentified person*) ihn/ihm, sie/ihr; **do you know ~?** kennst du/kennen Sie sie?; **can you help ~?** kannst du/können Sie ihnen helfen?; **it's ~** sie sind's; **if anyone has a problem you should help ~** wenn jemand ein Problem hat, solltest du/sollten Sie ihm helfen

theme [θiːm] *n* Thema *nt*; (*Mus*) Motiv *nt*; **~ park** Themenpark *m*; **~ song** Titelmusik *f*

themselves [ðəm'sɛlvz] *pron* sich; **they hurt ~** sie haben sich verletzt; **they were not there** sie selbst waren nicht da; **they did it ~** sie haben es selbst gemacht; **they are not dangerous in ~** an sich sind sie nicht gefährlich; (**all**) **by ~** allein

then [ðɛn] *adv* (*at that time*) damals; (*next*) dann; (*therefore*) also; (*furthermore*) ferner; **from ~ on** von da an; **by ~** bis dahin ▷ *adj* damalig

theoretical, **theoretically** [θɪə'rɛtɪkəl, -lɪ] *adj*, *adv* theoretisch

theory ['θɪərɪ] *n* Theorie *f*; **in ~** theoretisch

therapy ['θɛrəpɪ] *n* Therapie *f*

◯ **KEYWORD**

there [ðɛə°] *adv* **1 there is/there are** es *o* da ist/sind; (*there exists/exist also*) es gibt; **there are 3 of them** (*people, things*) es gibt 3 davon; **there has been an accident** da war ein Unfall

2 (*place*) da, dort; (*direction*) dahin, dorthin; **put it in/on there** leg es dahinein/dorthinauf

3 there, there (*esp to child*) na, na

thereabouts *adv* (*approximately*) so ungefähr; **therefore** *adv* daher, deshalb

thermometer [θəˈmɒmɪtə°] n Thermometer nt

Thermos® [ˈθɜːməs] n: ~ **(flask)** Thermosflasche® f

these [ðiːz] pron, adj diese; **I don't like ~ apples** ich mag diese Äpfel nicht; ~ **are not my books** das sind nicht meine Bücher

thesis [ˈθiːsɪs] (pl **theses**) n (for PhD) Doktorarbeit f

they [ðeɪ] pron pl sie; (people in general) man; (unidentified person) er/sie; ~ **are rich** sie sind reich; ~ **say that ...** man sagt, dass ...; **if anyone looks at this, ~ will see that ...** wenn sich jemand dies ansieht, wird er erkennen, dass ...

they'd [ðeɪd] contr of **they had; they would**

they'll [ðeɪl] contr of **they will; they shall**

they've [ðeɪv] contr of **they have**

thick [θɪk] adj dick; (fog) dicht; (liquid) dickflüssig; (stupid) dumm; **thicken** vi (fog) dichter werden; (sauce) dick werden ▷ vt (sauce) eindicken

thief [θiːf] (pl **thieves**) n Dieb(in) m(f)

thigh [θaɪ] n Oberschenkel m

thimble [ˈθɪmbl] n Fingerhut m

thin [θɪn] adj dünn

thing [θɪŋ] n Ding nt; (affair) Sache f; **my ~s** pl meine Sachen pl; **how are ~s?** wie geht's?; **I can't see a ~** ich kann nichts sehen; **he knows a ~ or two about cars** er kennt sich mit Autos aus

think [θɪŋk] (thought, thought) vt, vi denken; (believe) meinen; **I ~ so** ich denke schon; **I don't ~ so** ich glaube nicht; **think about** vt denken an +akk; (reflect on) nachdenken über +akk; (have opinion of) halten von; **think of** vt denken an +akk; (devise) sich ausdenken; (have opinion of) halten

von; (remember) sich erinnern an +akk; **think over** vt überdenken; **think up** vt sich ausdenken

third [θɜːd] adj dritte(r, s); **the Third World** ▷ n (fraction) Drittel nt; **in ~ (gear)** im dritten Gang; see also **eight; thirdly** adv drittens; **third-party insurance** n Haftpflichtversicherung f

thirst [θɜːst] n Durst m (for nach); **thirsty** adj: **to be ~** Durst haben

thirteen [θɜːˈtiːn] num dreizehn ▷ n Dreizehn f; see also **eight; thirteenth** adj dreizehnte(r, s); see also **eight; thirtieth** [ˈθɜːtɪɪθ] adj dreißigste(r, s); see also **eight; thirty** [ˈθɜːtɪ] num dreißig; **~-one** einunddreißig ▷ n Dreißig f; **to be in one's thirties** in den Dreißigern sein; see also **eight**

KEYWORD

this [ðɪs] adj (demonstrative) (pl **these**) diese(r, s); **this evening** heute Abend; **this one** diese(r, s) (da)
▷ pron (demonstrative) (pl **these**) dies, das; **who/what is this?** wer/was ist das?; **this is where I live** hier wohne ich; **this is what he said** das hat er gesagt; **this is Mr Brown** dies ist Mr Brown; (on telephone) hier ist Mr Brown
▷ adv (demonstrative) **this high/long** etc so groß/lang etc

thistle [ˈθɪsl] n Distel f

thong [θɒŋ] n String m

thorn [θɔːn] n Dorn m, Stachel m

thorough [ˈθʌrə] adj gründlich; **thoroughly** adv gründlich; (agree etc) völlig

those [ðəʊz] pron die da, jene; ~ **who** diejenigen, die ▷ adj die, jene

though [ðəʊ] *conj* obwohl; **as ~** als ob ▷ *adv* aber

thought [θɔːt] *pt, pp of* **think** ▷ *n* Gedanke *m*; *(thinking)* Überlegung *f*; **thoughtful** *adj (kind)* rücksichtsvoll; *(attentive)* aufmerksam; *(in Gedanken versunken)* nachdenklich; **thoughtless** *adj (unkind)* rücksichtslos, gedankenlos

thousand ['θaʊzənd] *num:* **(one) ~, a ~** tausend; **five ~** fünftausend; **~s of** Tausende von

thrash [θræʃ] *vt (hit)* verprügeln; *(defeat)* vernichtend schlagen

thread [θrɛd] *n* Faden *m* ▷ *vt (needle)* einfädeln; *(beads)* auffädeln

threat [θrɛt] *n* Drohung *f*; *(danger)* Bedrohung *f* (**to** für); **threaten** *vi* bedrohen; **threatening** *adj* bedrohlich

three [θriː] *num* drei ▷ *n* Drei *f*; *see also* **eight; three-dimensional** *adj* dreidimensional; **three-piece suit** *n* Anzug *m* mit Weste; **three-quarters** *npl* drei Viertel *pl*

threshold ['θrɛʃhəʊld] *n* Schwelle *f*

threw [θruː] *pt of* **throw**

thrifty ['θrɪftɪ] *adj* sparsam

thrilled [θrɪld] *adj:* **to be ~ (with sth)** sich *(über etw akk)* riesig freuen; **thriller** *n* Thriller *m*; **thrilling** *adj* aufregend

thrive [θraɪv] *vi* gedeihen *(on* bei); *(fig, business)* florieren

throat [θrəʊt] *n* Hals *m*, Kehle *f*

throbbing ['θrɒbɪŋ] *adj (pain, headache)* pochend

thrombosis [θrɒm'bəʊsɪs] *n* Thrombose *f*; **deep vein ~** tiefe Venenthrombose *f*

throne [θrəʊn] *n* Thron *m*

through [θruː] *prep* durch; *(time)* während +*gen*; *(because of)* aus, durch; *(US: up to and including)* bis;

arranged **~ him** durch ihn arrangiert ▷ *adv* durch; **to put sb ~** *(Tel)* jdn verbinden (**to** mit) ▷ *adj (ticket, train)* durchgehend; **~ flight** Direktflug *m*; **to be ~ with sb/sth** mit jdm/etw fertig sein;

throughout [θruː'aʊt] *prep (place)* überall in +*dat*; *(time)* während +*gen*; **~ the night** die ganze Nacht hindurch ▷ *adv* überall; *(time)* die ganze Zeit

throw [θrəʊ] **(threw, thrown)** *vt* werfen; *(rider)* abwerfen; *(party)* geben; **to ~ sth to sb, to ~ sb sth** jdm etw zuwerfen; **I was ~n by his question** seine Frage hat mich aus dem Konzept gebracht ▷ *n* Wurf *m*; **throw away** *vt* wegwerfen; **throw in** *vt (include)* dazugeben; **throw out** *vt (unwanted object)* wegwerfen; *(person)* hinauswerfen *(of* aus); **throw up** *vt, vi (fam: vomit)* sich übergeben; **throw-in** *n* Einwurf *m*

thrown [θrəʊn] *pp of* **throw**

thru (US) *see* **through**

thrush [θrʌʃ] *n* Drossel *f*

thrust [θrʌst] **(thrust, thrust)** *vt, vi (push)* stoßen

thruway ['θruːweɪ] *n* (US) Schnellstraße *f*

thumb [θʌm] *n* Daumen *m* ▷ *vt:* **to ~ a lift** per Anhalter fahren; **thumbtack** *n* (US) Reißzwecke *f*

thunder ['θʌndə] *n* Donner *m* ▷ *vi* donnern; **thunderstorm** *n* Gewitter *nt*

Thur(s) *abbr* = **Thursday** Do.

Thursday ['θɜːzdɪ] *n* Donnerstag *m*; *see also* **Tuesday**

thus [ðʌs] *adv (in this way)* so; *(therefore)* somit, also

thyme [taɪm] *n* Thymian *m*

Tibet [tɪ'bɛt] *n* Tibet *nt*

tick [tɪk] *n* (Brit: mark) Häkchen *nt* ▷ *vt (name)* abhaken; *(box, answer)* ankreuzen ▷ *vi (clock)* ticken

ticket ['tɪkɪt] n (for train, bus) (Fahr)karte f; (plane ~) Flugschein m, Ticket nt; (for theatre, match, museum etc) (Eintritts)karte f; (for ~) (Preis)schild nt; (raffle ~) Los nt; (for car park) Parkschein m; (for traffic offence) Strafzettel m; **ticket collector**, **ticket inspector** (Brit) n Fahrkartenkontrolleur m(f); **ticket machine** (for public transport) Fahrkartenautomat m; (in car park) Parkscheinautomat m; **ticket office** n (Rail) Fahrkartenschalter m; (Theat) Kasse f

tickle ['tɪkl] vt kitzeln; **ticklish** ['tɪklɪʃ] adj kitzlig

tide [taɪd] n Gezeiten pl; **the ~ is in/out** es ist Flut/Ebbe

tidy ['taɪdɪ] adj ordentlich ▷ vt aufräumen; **tidy up** vt, vi aufräumen

tie [taɪ] n (neck~) Krawatte f; (Sport) Unentschieden nt; (bond) Bindung f ▷ vt (attach, do up) binden (to an +akk); (~ together) zusammenbinden; (knot) machen ▷ vi (Sport) unentschieden spielen; **tie down** vt festbinden (to an +dat); (fig) binden; **tie up** vt (dog) anbinden; (parcel) verschnüren; (shoelace) binden; (boat) festmachen; **I'm tied up** (fig) ich bin beschäftigt

tiger ['taɪgə²] n Tiger m

tight [taɪt] adj (clothes) eng; (knot) fest; (screw, lid) fest sitzend; (control, security measures) streng; (timewise) knapp; (schedule) eng ▷ adv (shut) fest; (pull) stramm; **hold ~** festhalten!; **sleep ~** schlaf gut!; **tighten** vt (knot, rope, screw) fest ziehen; (control) verschärfen ▷ vi (knot, rope, screw) sich festziehen; (control) sich verschärfen; **tightly** adv (hold) fest; (cling) dicht; (control) streng; **tightrope** n Hochseil nt; **tights** npl (Brit) Strumpfhose f

tile [taɪl] n (on roof) Dachziegel m;

(on wall, floor) Fliese f; **tiled** adj (roof) Ziegel-; (floor, wall) gefliest

till [tɪl] n Kasse f ▷ prep, conj see **until**

tilt [tɪlt] vt kippen; (head) neigen ▷ vi sich neigen

time [taɪm] n Zeit f; (occasion) Mal nt; (Mus) Takt m; **local ~** Ortszeit; **what ~ is it?**, **what's the ~?** wie spät ist es?, wie viel Uhr ist es?; **to take one's ~** (over sth) sich (bei etw) Zeit lassen; **to have a good ~** Spaß haben; **in two weeks' ~** in zwei Wochen; **at ~s** manchmal; **at the same ~** gleichzeitig; **all the ~** die ganze Zeit; **by the ~ he ...** bis er ...; (in past) als er ...; **for the ~ being** vorläufig; **in ~** (not late) rechtzeitig; **on ~** pünktlich; **the first ~** das erste Mal; **this ~** diesmal; **five ~s** fünfmal; **five x six** fünf mal sechs; **four ~s a year** viermal im Jahr; **three at a ~** drei auf einmal ▷ vt (with stopwatch) stoppen; **you ~d that well** das hast du/haben Sie gut getimt; **time difference** n Zeitunterschied m; **time limit** n Frist f; **timer** n Timer m; (switch) Schaltuhr f; **time-saving** adj zeitsparend; **time switch** n Schaltuhr f; **timetable** n (for public transport) Fahrplan m; (school) Stundenplan m; **time zone** n Zeitzone f

timid ['tɪmɪd] adj ängstlich

timing ['taɪmɪŋ] n (coordination) Timing nt, zeitliche Abstimmung

tin [tɪn] n (metal) Blech nt; (Brit: can) Dose f; **tinfoil** n Alufolie f; **tinned** [tɪnd] adj (Brit) aus der Dose; **tin opener** n (Brit) Dosenöffner m

tinsel ['tɪnsəl] n ~ Lametta nt

tint [tɪnt] n (Farb)ton m; (in hair) Tönung f; **tinted** adj getönt

tiny ['taɪnɪ] adj winzig

tip [tɪp] n (money) Trinkgeld nt; (hint) Tipp m; (end) Spitze f; (of cigarette) Filter m; (Brit: rubbish ~) Müllkippe f ▷ vt (waiter) Trinkgeld geben +dat; **tip over** vt, vi (overturn) umkippen

tipsy ['tɪpsɪ] adj beschwipst

tiptoe ['tɪptəʊ] n: **on ~** auf Zehenspitzen

tire ['taɪə²] n (US) see **tyre** ▷ vt müde machen ▷ vi müde werden; **tired** adj müde; **to be ~ of sb/sth** jdn/etw satthaben; **to be ~ of doing sth** es satthaben, etw zu tun; **tireless, tirelessly** adv unermüdlich; **tiresome** adj lästig; **tiring** adj ermüdend

Tirol [tɪ'rəʊl] see **Tyrol**

tissue ['tɪʃu:] n (Anat) Gewebe nt; (paper handkerchief) Tempotaschentuch® nt; **tissue paper** n Seidenpapier nt

tit [tɪt] n (bird) Meise f; (fam: breast) Titte f

title ['taɪtl] n Titel m

titter ['tɪtə] vi kichern

○ **KEYWORD**

to [tu:, tə] prep 1 (direction) zu, nach; **I go to France/school** ich gehe nach Frankreich/zur Schule; **to the left** nach links

2 (as far as) bis

3 (with expressions of time) vor; **a quarter to 5** Viertel vor 5

4 (for, of) für; **secretary to the director** Sekretärin des Direktors

5 (expressing indirect object) **to give sth to sb** jdm etw geben; **to talk to sb** mit jdm sprechen; **I sold it to a friend** ich habe es einem Freund verkauft

6 (in relation to) zu; **30 miles to the gallon** 30 Meilen pro Gallone

7 (purpose, result) zu; **to my surprise** zu meiner Überraschung ▷ with vb 1 (infin) to go/eat gehen/essen; **to want to do sth** etw tun wollen; **to try/start to do sth** versuchen/anfangen, etw zu tun; **he has a lot to lose** er hat viel zu verlieren

2 (with vb omitted) **I don't want to** ich will (es) nicht

3 (purpose, result) um; **I did it to help you** ich tat es, um dir/Ihnen zu helfen

4 (after adj etc) ready to use gebrauchsfertig; **too old/young to ...** zu alt/jung, um ... zu ... ▷ adv: **push/pull the door to** die Tür zuschieben/zuziehen

toad [təʊd] n Kröte f; **toadstool** n Giftpilz m

toast [təʊst] n (bread, drink) Toast m; **a piece** (o **slice**) **of ~** eine Scheibe Toast; **to propose a ~ to sb** einen Toast auf jdn ausbringen ▷ vt (bread) toasten; (person) trinken auf +akk; **toaster** n Toaster m

tobacco [tə'bækəʊ] (pl **-es**) n Tabak m; **tobacconist's** [tə'bækənɪsts] n: ~ **(shop)** Tabakladen m

toboggan [tə'bɒgən] n Schlitten m

today [tə'deɪ] adv heute; **a week ~** heute in einer Woche; **~'s newspaper** die Zeitung von heute

toddler ['tɒdlə²] n Kleinkind nt

toe [təʊ] n Zehe f, Zeh m; **toenail** n Zehennagel m

toffee ['tɒfɪ] n (sweet) Karamellbonbon nt; **toffee apple** n kandierter Apfel; **toffee-nosed** adj hochnäsig

tofu ['təʊfu:] n Tofu m

together [tə'geðə²] adv

zusammen; **I tied them ~** ich habe sie zusammengebunden

toilet ['tɔɪlət] n Toilette f; **to go to the ~** auf die Toilette gehen; **toilet bag** n Kulturbeutel m; **toilet paper** n Toilettenpapier nt; **toiletries** ['tɔɪlətrɪz] npl Toilettenartikel pl; **toilet roll** n Rolle f Toilettenpapier

token ['təʊkən] n Marke f; (in casino) Spielmarke f; (voucher, gift ~) Gutschein m; (sign) Zeichen nt

Tokyo ['təʊkiəʊ] n Tokio nt

told [təʊld] pt, pp of **tell**

tolerant ['tɒlərənt] adj tolerant (of gegenüber); **tolerate** ['tɒləreɪt] vt tolerieren; (noise, pain, heat) ertragen

toll [təʊl] n (charge) Gebühr f; **the death ~** die Zahl der Toten; **toll-free** adj, adv (US Tel) gebührenfrei; **toll road** n gebührenpflichtige Straße

tomato [tə'mɑːtəʊ] (pl **-es**) n Tomate f; **tomato juice** n Tomatensaft m; **tomato ketchup** n Tomatenketchup m o nt; **tomato sauce** n Tomatensoße f; (Brit: ketchup) Tomatenketchup m o nt

tomb [tuːm] n Grabmal nt; **tombstone** n Grabstein m

tomorrow [tə'mɒrəʊ] adv morgen; **~ morning** morgen früh; **~ evening** morgen Abend; **the day after ~** übermorgen; **a week (from) ~/~ week** morgen in einer Woche

ton [tʌn] n (Brit) Tonne f (1016 kg); (US) Tonne f (907 kg); **~s of books** (fam) eine Menge Bücher

tone [təʊn] n Ton m; **tone down** vt mäßigen; **toner** ['təʊnə*] n (for printer) Toner m; **toner cartridge** n Tonerpatrone f

tongs [tɒŋz] npl Zange f; (curling ~) Lockenstab m

tongue [tʌŋ] n Zunge f

tonic ['tɒnɪk] n (Med) Stärkungsmittel nt; **~ (water)** Tonic nt; **gin and ~** Gin m Tonic

tonight [tə'naɪt] adv heute Abend; (during night) heute Nacht

tonsils ['tɒnslz] n Mandeln pl; **tonsillitis** [tɒnsɪ'laɪtɪs] n Mandelentzündung f

too [tuː] adv zu; (also) auch; **~ fast** zu schnell; **~ much/many** zu viel/viele; **me ~** ich auch; **she liked it ~** ihr gefiel es auch

took [tʊk] pt of **take**

tool [tuːl] n Werkzeug nt; **toolbar** n (Inform) Symbolleiste f; **toolbox** n Werkzeugkasten m

tooth [tuːθ] (pl **teeth**) n Zahn m; **toothache** n Zahnschmerzen pl; **toothbrush** n Zahnbürste f; **toothpaste** n Zahnpasta f; **toothpick** n Zahnstocher m

top [tɒp] n (of tower, class, company etc) Spitze f; (of mountain) Gipfel m; (of tree) Krone f; (of street) oberes Ende; (of tube, pen) Kappe f; (of box) Deckel m; (of bikini) Oberteil nt; (sleeveless) Top nt; **at the ~ of the page** oben auf der Seite; **at the ~ of the league** an der Spitze der Liga; **on ~** oben; **~ of** auf +dat; (in addition to) zusätzlich zu; **in ~ (gear)** im höchsten Gang; **over the ~** übertrieben ▷ adj (floor, shelf) oberste(r, s); (price, note) höchste(r, s); (best) Spitzen-; (pupil, school) beste(r, s) ▷ vt (exceed) übersteigen; (be better than) übertreffen; (league) an erster Stelle liegen in +dat; **~ped with cream** mit Sahne obendrauf; **top up** vt auffüllen; **can I top you up?** darf ich dir nachschenken?

topic ['tɒpɪk] n Thema nt; **topical** adj aktuell

topless ['tɒpləs] adj, adv oben ohne

topping ['tɒpɪŋ] n (on top of pizza, ice-cream etc) Belag m, Garnierung f

top-secret ['tɒp'si:krət] adj streng geheim

torch [tɔːtʃ] n (Brit) Taschenlampe f

tore [tɔː'] pt of **tear**

torment ['tɔːment] vt quälen

torn [tɔːn] pp of **tear**

tornado [tɔː'neɪdəʊ] (pl **-es**) n Tornado m

torrential [tə'renʃəl] adj (rain) sintflutartig

tortoise ['tɔːtəs] n Schildkröte f

torture ['tɔːtʃə'] n Folter f; (fig) Qual f ▷ vt foltern

Tory ['tɔːrɪ] (Brit) n Tory m, Konservative(r) mf ▷ adj Tory-

toss [tɒs] vt (throw) werfen; (salad) anmachen; **to ~ a coin** eine Münze werfen ▷ n: **I don't give a ~** (fam) es ist mir scheißegal

total ['təʊtl] n (of figures, money) Gesamtsumme f; **a ~ of 30** insgesamt 30; **in ~** insgesamt ▷ adj total; (sum etc) Gesamt- ▷ vt (amount to) sich belaufen auf +akk; **totally** adv total

touch [tʌtʃ] n (act of ~ing) Berührung f; (sense of ~) Tastsinn m; (trace) Spur f; **to be/keep in ~ with sb** mit jdm in Verbindung stehen/bleiben; **to get in ~ with sb** sich mit jdm in Verbindung setzen; **to lose ~ with sb** den Kontakt zu jdm verlieren ▷ vt (feel) berühren; (emotionally) bewegen; **touch on** vt (topic) berühren; **touchdown** n (Aviat) Landung f; (Sport) Touchdown m; **touching** adj (moving) rührend; **touch screen** n Touchscreen m, Berührungsbildschirm m; **touchy** adj empfindlich, zickig

tough [tʌf] adj hart; (meat) zäh; (material) robust; (meat) zäh

tour [tʊə'] n Tour f (of durch); (of town, building) Rundgang m (of durch); (of pop group etc) Tournee f ▷ vt eine Tour/einen Rundgang/eine Tournee machen durch ▷ vi (on holiday) umherreisen; **tour guide** n Reiseleiter(in) m(f)

tourism ['tʊərɪzəm] n Tourismus m, Fremdenverkehr m; **tourist** n Tourist(in) m(f); **tourist class** n Touristenklasse f; **tourist guide** n (book) Reiseführer m; (person) Fremdenführer(in) m(f); **tourist office** n Fremdenverkehrsamt nt

tournament ['tʊənəmənt] n Turnier nt

tour operator ['tʊərɒpəreɪtə'] n Reiseveranstalter m

tow [təʊ] vt abschleppen; (caravan, trailer) ziehen; **tow away** vt abschleppen

towards [tə'wɔːdz] prep: **~ me** mir entgegen, auf mich zu; **we walked ~ the station** wir gingen in Richtung Bahnhof; **my feelings ~ him** meine Gefühle ihm gegenüber; **she was kind ~ me** sie war nett zu mir

towel ['taʊəl] n Handtuch nt

tower ['taʊə'] n Turm m; **tower block** n (Brit) Hochhaus nt

town [taʊn] n Stadt f; **town center** (US), **town centre** n Stadtmitte f, Stadtzentrum nt; **town hall** n Rathaus nt

towrope ['təʊrəʊp] n Abschleppseil nt; **tow truck** n (US) Abschleppwagen m

toxic ['tɒksɪk] adj giftig, Gift-

toy [tɔɪ] n Spielzeug nt; **toy with** vt spielen mit; **toyshop** n Spielwarengeschäft nt

trace [treɪs] n Spur f; **without**

~ spurlos ▷ vt (find) ausfindig machen; **tracing paper** n Pauspapier nt

track [træk] n (mark) Spur f; (path) Weg m; (Rail) Gleis nt; (on CD, record) Stück nt; **to keep/lose ~ of sb/sth** jdn/etw behalten/aus den Augen verlieren; **track down** vt ausfindig machen; **trackball** n (Inform) Trackball m; **tracksuit** n Trainingsanzug m

tractor ['træktə°] n Traktor m

trade [treɪd] n (commerce) Handel m; (business) Geschäft nt; (skilled job) Handwerk nt ▷ vi handeln (in mit) ▷ vt (exchange) tauschen (for gegen); **trademark** n Warenzeichen nt; **tradesman** (pl -men) n (shopkeeper) Geschäftsmann m; (workman) Handwerker m; **trade(s) union** n (Brit) Gewerkschaft f

tradition [trə'dɪʃən] n Tradition f; **traditional, traditionally** adj, adv traditionell

traffic ['træfɪk] n Verkehr m; (pej: trading) Handel m (in mit); **traffic circle** n (US) Kreisverkehr m; **traffic island** n Verkehrsinsel f; **traffic jam** n Stau m; **traffic lights** npl Verkehrsampel f; **traffic warden** n (Brit) ≈ Politesse f

tragedy ['trædʒədɪ] n Tragödie f; **tragic** ['trædʒɪk] adj tragisch

trail [treɪl] n Spur f; (path) Weg m ▷ vt (follow) verfolgen; (drag) schleppen; (drag behind) hinter sich herziehen; (Sport) zurückliegen hinter +dat ▷ vi (hang loosely) schleifen; (Sport) weit zurückliegen; **trailer** n Anhänger m; (US: caravan) Wohnwagen m; (Cine) Trailer m

train [treɪn] n (Rail) Zug m ▷ vt (teach) ausbilden; (Sport) trainieren ▷ vi (Sport) trainieren; **to ~ as** (o **to be**) **a teacher** eine Ausbildung als Lehrer machen; **trained** adj (person, voice) ausgebildet; **trainee** n Auszubildende(r) mf; (academic, practical) Praktikant(in) m(f); **traineeship** n Praktikum nt; **trainer** n (Sport) Trainer(in) m(f); **~s** (Brit: shoes) Turnschuhe pl; **training** n Ausbildung f; (Sport) Training nt; **train station** n Bahnhof m

tram ['træm] n (Brit) Straßenbahn f

tramp [træmp] n Landstreicher(in) m(f) ▷ vi trotten

tranquillizer ['træŋkwɪlaɪzə°] n Beruhigungsmittel nt

transaction (piece of business) Geschäft nt

transatlantic ['trænzæt'læntɪk] adj transatlantisch; **~ flight** Transatlantikflug m

transfer ['trænsfə°] n (of money) Überweisung f; (US: ticket) Umsteigekarte f ▷ [træns'fɜ:°] vt (money) überweisen (to sb an jdn); (patient) verlegen; (employee) versetzen; (Sport) transferieren ▷ vi (on journey) umsteigen; **transferable** [træns'fɜ:rəbl] adj übertragbar

transform [træns'fɔːm] vt umwandeln; **transformation** [trænsfə'meɪʃən] n Umwandlung f

transfusion [træns'fjuːʒən] n Transfusion f

transistor [træn'zɪstə°] n Transistor m; **~ (radio)** Transistorradio nt

transition [træn'zɪʃən] n Übergang m (from ... to von ... zu)

transit lounge ['trænzɪtlaʊndʒ] n Transitraum m; **transit passenger** n Transitreisende(r) mf

translate [trænz'leɪt] vt, vi
übersetzen; **translation**
[trænz'leɪʃən] n Übersetzung f;
translator [trænz'leɪtə*] n
Übersetzer(in) m(f)
transmission [trænz'mɪʃən] n
(Auto) Getriebe nt
transparent [træns'pærənt] adj
durchsichtig; (fig) offenkundig
transplant [træns'plɑːnt] (Med)
vt transplantieren ▷ ['trænsplɑːnt]
n (operation) Transplantation f
transport ['trænspɔːt] n (of
goods, people) Beförderung f; **public
~** öffentliche Verkehrsmittel pl
▷ [træns'pɔːt] vt befördern,
transportieren; **transportation**
[trænspɔː'teɪʃən] n see **transport**
trap [træp] n Falle f ▷ vt: **to be
~ped** (in snow, job etc) festsitzen
trash [træʃ] n (book, film etc)
Schund m; (US: refuse) Abfall m;
trash can n (US) Abfalleimer m;
trashy adj niveaulos; (novel)
Schund-
traumatic [trɔː'mætɪk] adj
traumatisch
travel ['trævl] n Reisen nt ▷ vi
(journey) reisen ▷ vt (distance)
zurücklegen; (country) bereisen;
travel agency, **travel agent** n
(company) Reisebüro nt; **traveler**
(US) see **traveller**; **traveler's
check** (US) see **traveller's cheque**;
travel insurance n
Reiseversicherung f; **traveller** n
Reisende(r) mf; **traveller's cheque**
n (Brit) Reisescheck m; **travelsick**
n reisekrank
tray [treɪ] n Tablett nt; (for mail
etc) Ablage f; (of printer, photocopier)
Fach nt
tread [tred] n (on tyre) Profil nt;
tread on [tred] (**trod, trodden**)
vt treten auf +akk
treasure ['treʒə*] n Schatz m
▷ vt schätzen

treat [triːt] n besondere Freude;
it's my ~ das geht auf meine
Kosten ▷ vt behandeln; **to ~ sb
(to sth)** jdn (zu etw) einladen; **to
~ oneself to sth** sich etw leisten;
treatment ['triːtmənt] n
Behandlung f
treaty ['triːtɪ] n Vertrag m
tree [triː] n Baum m
tremble ['trembl] vi zittern
tremendous [trə'mendəs] adj
gewaltig; (fam: very good) toll
trench [trentʃ] n Graben m
trend [trend] n Tendenz f;
(fashion) Mode f, Trend m; **trendy**
adj trendy
trespass ['trespəs] vi: **"no ~ing"**
„Betreten verboten"
trial ['traɪəl] n (Jur) Prozess m;
(test) Versuch m; **by ~ and error**
durch Ausprobieren; **trial period**
n (for employee) Probezeit f
triangle ['traɪæŋgl] n Dreieck nt;
(Mus) Triangel m; **triangular**
[traɪ'æŋgjʊlə*] adj dreieckig
tribe [traɪb] n Stamm m
trick [trɪk] n Trick m; (mischief)
Streich m ▷ vt hereinlegen
tricky ['trɪkɪ] adj (difficult)
schwierig, heikel; (situation)
verzwickt
trifle ['traɪfl] n Kleinigkeit f; (Brit
Gastr) Trifle nt (Nachspeise aus
Biskuit, Wackelpudding, Obst,
Vanillesoße und Sahne)
trigger ['trɪgə*] n (of gun) Abzug
m ▷ vt: **to ~ (off)** auslösen
trim [trɪm] vt (hair, beard)
nachschneiden; (nails) schneiden;
(hedge) stutzen ▷ n: **just a ~,
please** nur etwas nachschneiden,
bitte; **trimmings** npl (decorations)
Verzierungen pl; (extras) Zubehör
nt; (Gastr) Beilagen pl
trip [trɪp] n Reise f; (outing)
Ausflug m ▷ vi stolpern (over über
+akk)

triple ['trɪpl] *adj* dreifach ▷ *adv*:
~ the price dreimal so teuer ▷ *vi*
sich verdreifachen; **triplet**
['trɪplɪt] *n* Drilling *m*

tripod ['traɪpɒd] *n* (*Foto*) Stativ *nt*

trite [traɪt] *adj* banal

triumph ['traɪʌmf] *n* Triumph *m*

trivial ['trɪvɪəl] *adj* trivial

trod [trɒd] *pt of* **tread**

trodden *pp of* **tread**

trolley ['trɒlɪ] *n* (*Brit: in shop*)
Einkaufswagen *m*; (*for luggage*)
Kofferkuli *m*; (*serving*) Teewagen *m*

trombone [trɒm'bəʊn] *n*
Posaune *f*

troops [tru:ps] *npl* (*Mil*) Truppen *pl*

trophy ['trəʊfɪ] *n* Trophäe *f*

tropical ['trɒpɪkl] *adj* tropisch

trouble ['trʌbl] *n* (*problems*)
Schwierigkeiten *pl*; (*worry*) Sorgen
pl; (*effort*) Mühe *f*; (*unrest*) Unruhen
pl; (*Med*) Beschwerden *pl*; **to be in
~** in Schwierigkeiten sein; **to get
into ~** (*with authority*) Ärger
bekommen; **to make
~** Schwierigkeiten machen ▷ *vt*
(*worry*) beunruhigen; (*disturb*)
stören; **my back's troubling me**
mein Rücken macht mir zu
schaffen; **sorry to ~ you** ich muss
dich/Sie leider kurz stören;
troubled *adj* (*worried*)
beunruhigt; **trouble-free** *adj*
problemlos; **troublemaker** *n*
Unruhestifter(in) *m(f)*;
troublesome *adj* lästig

trousers ['traʊzəz] *npl* Hose *f*

trout [traʊt] *n* Forelle *f*

truck [trʌk] *n* Lastwagen *m*; (*Brit
Rail*) Güterwagen *m*; **trucker** *n*
(*US: driver*) Lastwagenfahrer(in)
m(f)

true [tru:] *adj* (*factually correct*)
wahr; (*genuine*) echt; **to come**

~ wahr werden

truly ['tru:lɪ] *adv* wirklich; **Yours
~** (*in letter*) mit freundlichen
Grüßen

trumpet ['trʌmpɪt] *n* Trompete *f*

trunk [trʌŋk] *n* (*of tree*) Stamm
m; (*Anat*) Rumpf *m*; (*of elephant*)
Rüssel *m*; (*piece of luggage*)
Überseekoffer *m*; (*US Auto*)
Kofferraum *m*; **trunks** *npl*:
(swimming) ~ Badehose *f*

trust [trʌst] *n* (*confidence*)
Vertrauen *nt* (*in zu*) ▷ *vt* vertrauen
+*dat*; **trusting** *adj* vertrauensvoll;
trustworthy *adj*
vertrauenswürdig

truth [tru:θ] *n* Wahrheit *f*;
truthful *adj* ehrlich; (*statement*)
wahrheitsgemäß

try [traɪ] *n* Versuch *m* ▷ *vt*
(*attempt*) versuchen; (*~ out*)
ausprobieren; (*sample*) probieren;
(*Jur: person*) vor Gericht stellen;
(*courage, patience*) auf die Probe
stellen ▷ *vi* versuchen; (*make
effort*) sich bemühen; **~ and come**
versuch zu kommen; **try on** *vt*
(*clothes*) anprobieren; **try out** *vt*
ausprobieren

T-shirt ['ti:ʃɜːt] *n* T-Shirt *nt*

tub [tʌb] *n* (*for ice-cream,
margarine*) Becher *m*

tube [tju:b] *n* (*pipe*) Rohr *nt*; (*of
rubber, plastic*) Schlauch *m*; (*for
toothpaste, glue etc*) Tube *f*; **the
~** (*in London*) die U-Bahn

tube station ['tju:bsteɪʃən] *n*
U-Bahn-Station *f*

tuck [tʌk] *vt* (*put*) stecken; **tuck
in** *vt* (*shirt*) in die Hose stecken;
(*blanket*) feststecken; (*person*)
zudecken ▷ *vi* (*eat*) zulangen

tucker ['tʌkə] *n* (*Aust, NZ fam*)
Essen *nt*, Fressalien *pl* (*fam*)

Tue(s) *abbr* = **Tuesday** Di.

Tuesday ['tju:zdɪ] *n* Dienstag *m*;

on ~ (am) Dienstag; **on ~s**
dienstags; **this/last/next
~** diesen/letzten/nächsten
Dienstag; **(on) ~ morning/
afternoon/evening (am)**
Dienstagmorgen/-nachmittag/
-abend; **every ~** jeden
Dienstag; **a week on ~/~ week**
Dienstag in einer Woche

tug [tʌg] vt ziehen; **she ~ged his
sleeve** sie zog an seinem Ärmel
▷ vi ziehen (at an +dat)

tuition [tjuːˈɪʃən] n Unterricht m;
(US: fees) Studiengebühren pl;
~ fees pl Studiengebühren pl

tulip ['tjuːlɪp] n Tulpe f

tumble ['tʌmbl] vi (person, prices)
fallen; **tumble dryer** n
Wäschetrockner m; **tumbler** n
(glass) (Becher)glas nt

tummy ['tʌmɪ] n (fam) Bauch m;
tummyache n (fam) Bauchweh nt

tumor (US), **tumour** ['tjuːməʳ]
n Tumor m

tuna ['tjuːnə] n Thunfisch m

tune [tjuːn] n Melodie f; **to be
in/out of ~** (instrument)
gestimmt/verstimmt sein; (singer)
richtig/falsch singen ▷ vt
(instrument) stimmen; (radio)
einstellen (to auf +akk); **tuner** n
(in stereo system) Tuner m

Tunisia [tjuːˈnɪzɪə] n Tunesien
nt

tunnel ['tʌnl] n Tunnel m;
(under road, railway) Unterführung
f

turban ['tɜːbən] n Turban m

turbulence ['tɜːbjʊləns] n
(Aviat) Turbulenzen pl; **turbulent**
adj stürmisch

Turk [tɜːk] n Türke m, Türkin f

turkey ['tɜːkɪ] n Truthahn m

Turkey ['tɜːkɪ] n die Türkei;
Turkish adj türkisch ▷ n (language) Türkisch nt

turmoil ['tɜːmɔɪl] n Aufruhr m

turn [tɜːn] n (rotation) Drehung f;
(performance) Nummer f; **to make
a left ~** nach links abbiegen; **at
the ~ of the century** um die
Jahrhundertwende; **it's your ~** du
bist/Sie sind dran; **in ~, by ~s**
abwechselnd; **to take ~s** sich
abwechseln ▷ vt (wheel, key, screw)
drehen; (to face other way)
umdrehen; (corner) biegen um;
(page) umblättern; (transform)
verwandeln (into in +akk) ▷ vi
(rotate) sich drehen; (to face other
way) sich umdrehen; (change
direction: driver, car) abbiegen;
(become) werden; (weather)
umschlagen; **to ~ into sth**
(become) sich in etw akk
verwandeln; **to ~ cold/green**
kalt/grün werden; **to ~ left/right**
links/rechts abbiegen; **turn away**
vt (person) abweisen; **turn back** vt
(person) zurückweisen ▷ vi (go
back) umkehren; **turn down** vt
(refuse) ablehnen; (radio, TV) leiser
stellen; (heating) kleiner stellen;
turn off vi abbiegen ▷ vt (switch
off) ausschalten; (tap) zudrehen;
(engine, electricity) abstellen; **turn
on** vt (switch on) einschalten; (tap)
aufdrehen; (engine, electricity)
anstellen; (fam: person) anmachen,
antörnen; **turn out** vt (light)
ausmachen; (pockets) leeren ▷ vi
(develop) sich entwickeln; **as it
turned out** wie sich herausstellte;
turn over vi umdrehen; (page)
umblättern ▷ vi (person) sich
umdrehen; (car) sich
überschlagen; (TV) umschalten (to
auf +akk); **turn round** vt (to face
other way) umdrehen ▷ vi (person)
sich umdrehen; (go back)
umkehren; **turn to** vt sich
zuwenden (+dat); **turn up** vi
(person, lost object) auftauchen ▷ vt
(radio, TV) lauter stellen; (heating)

höher stellen; **turning** n (in road)
Abzweigung f; **turning point** n
Wendepunkt m

turnip ['tɜːnɪp] n Rübe f

turnover ['tɜːnəʊvə] n (Fin)
Umsatz m

turnpike ['tɜːnpaɪk] n (US)
gebührenpflichtige Autobahn

turntable ['tɜːntͤibl] n (on
record player) Plattenteller m

turn-up ['tɜːnʌp] n (Brit: on
trousers) Aufschlag m

turquoise ['tɜːkwɔɪz] adj türkis

turtle ['tɜːtl] n (Brit)
Wasserschildkröte f; (US)
Schildkröte f

tutor ['tjuːtə] n (private)
Privatlehrer(in) m(f); (Brit: at
university) Tutor(in) m(f)

tux [tʌks] , **tuxedo** [tʌk'siːdəʊ]
(pl -s) n (US) Smoking m

TV ['tiːviː] n Fernsehen nt; (~ set)
Fernseher m; **to watch
~** fernsehen; **on ~** im Fernsehen
▷ adj Fernseh-; (~) **programme**
Fernsehsendung f

tweed [twiːd] n Tweed m

tweet [twiːt] vi (on Twitter)
twittern

tweezers ['twiːzəz] npl Pinzette
f

twelfth [twelfθ] adj zwölfte(r, s);
see also **eighth** ▷ num zwölf ▷ n
Zwölf f; see also
eight

twentieth ['twentiːθ] adj
zwanzigste(r, s); see also **eighth**; **twenty** ['twenti] num zwanzig;
~-one einundzwanzig ▷ n
Zwanzig f; **to be in one's twenties**
in den Zwanzigern sein; see also
eight

twice [twaɪs] adv zweimal; **~ as
much/many** doppelt so viel/viele

twig [twɪg] n Zweig m

twilight ['twaɪlaɪt] n (in evening)
Dämmerung f

twin [twɪn] n Zwilling m ▷ adj
(brother etc) Zwillings-; **~ beds** zwei
Einzelbetten ▷ vt: **York is ~ned
with Münster** York ist eine
Partnerstadt von Münster

twinge [twɪndʒ] n (pain)
stechender Schmerz

twinkle ['twɪŋkl] vi funkeln

twin room ['twɪnˈruːm] n
Zweibettzimmer nt; **twin town** n
Partnerstadt f

twist [twɪst] vt (turn) drehen,
winden; (distort) verdrehen; **I've
~ed my ankle** ich bin mit dem Fuß
umgeknickt

two [tuː] num zwei; **to break sth
in ~** etw in zwei Teile brechen ▷ n
Zwei f; **the ~ of them** die beiden;
see also **eight**; **two-dimensional**
adj zweidimensional, (fig)
oberflächlich; **two-faced** adj
falsch, heuchlerisch; **two-piece**
adj zweiteilig; **two-way** adj:
~ traffic Gegenverkehr

type [taɪp] n (sort) Art f; (typeface)
Schrift(art) f; **what ~ of car is it?**
was für ein Auto ist das?; **he's not
my ~** er ist nicht mein Typ;
typeface n Schrift(art) f;
typewriter n Schreibmaschine f

typhoid ['taɪfɔɪd] n Typhus m

typhoon [taɪ'fuːn] n Taifun m

typical ['tɪpɪkəl] adj typisch (of
für)

typing error ['taɪpɪŋerə] n
Tippfehler m

tyre [taɪə] n (Brit) Reifen m; **tyre
pressure** n Reifendruck m

Tyrol [tɪ'rəʊl] n: **the ~** Tirol nt

U

UFO ['juːfəʊ] *acr* = **unidentified flying object** Ufo *nt*

Uganda [juːˈgændə] *n* Uganda *nt*

ugly ['ʌglɪ] *adj* hässlich

UHT *adj abbr* = **ultra-heat treated** ~ **milk** H-Milch *f*

UK *abbr* = **United Kingdom**

Ukraine [juːˈkreɪn] *n*: **the** ~ die Ukraine

ulcer ['ʌlsə⁰] *n* Geschwür *nt*

ulterior [ʌlˈtɪərɪə⁰] *adj*: ~ **motive** Hintergedanke *m*

ultimate ['ʌltɪmət] *adj* (final) letzte(r, s); (authority) höchste(r, s); **ultimately** *adv* letzten Endes; (eventually) schließlich; **ultimatum** [ʌltɪˈmeɪtəm] *n* Ultimatum *nt*

ultra- ['ʌltrə] *pref* ultra-

ultrasound ['ʌltrəsaʊnd] *n* (Med) Ultraschall *m*

umbrella [ʌmˈbrelə] *n* Schirm *m*

umpire ['ʌmpaɪə⁰] *n* Schiedsrichter(in) *m(f)*

umpteen ['ʌmptiːn] *num* (fam) zig; ~ **times** zigmal

un- [ʌn] *pref* un-

UN *n sing abbr* = **United Nations** VN, Vereinte Nationen *pl*

unable [ʌnˈeɪbl] *adj*: **to be** ~ **to do sth** etw nicht tun können

unacceptable [ʌnəˈkseptəbl] *adj* unannehmbar

unaccountably [ʌnəˈkaʊntəblɪ] *adv* unerklärlicherweise

unaccustomed [ʌnəˈkʌstəmd] *adj*: **to be** ~ **to sth** etw nicht gewohnt sein

unanimous, unanimously [juːˈnænɪməs, -lɪ] *adj, adv* einmütig

unattached [ʌnəˈtætʃt] *adj* (without partner) ungebunden

unattended [ʌnəˈtendɪd] *adj* (luggage, car) unbeaufsichtigt

unauthorized [ʌnˈɔːθəraɪzd] *adj* unbefugt

unavailable [ʌnəˈveɪləbl] *adj* nicht erhältlich; (person) nicht erreichbar

unavoidable [ʌnəˈvɔɪdəbl] *adj* unvermeidlich

unaware [ʌnəˈweə⁰] *adj*: **to be** ~ **of sth** sich einer Sache *dat* nicht bewusst sein; **I was** ~ **that ...** ich wusste nicht, dass ...

unbalanced [ʌnˈbælənst] *adj* unausgewogen; (mentally) gestört

unbearable [ʌnˈbeərəbl] *adj* unerträglich

unbeatable [ʌnˈbiːtəbl] *adj* unschlagbar

unbelievable [ʌnbɪˈliːvəbl] *adj* unglaublich

unblock [ʌnˈblɒk] *vt* (pipe) frei machen

unbutton [ʌnˈbʌtn] *vt* aufknöpfen

uncertain [ʌn'sɜːtən] adj
unsicher

uncle ['ʌŋkl] n Onkel m

uncomfortable [ʌn'kʌmfətəbl]
adj unbequem

unconditional [ʌnkən'dɪʃənl]
adj bedingungslos

unconscious [ʌn'kɒnʃəs]
(Med) bewusstlos; **to be ~ of sth**
sich einer Sache dat nicht bewusst
sein; **unconsciously** adv
unbewusst

uncork [ʌn'kɔːk] vt entkorken

uncover [ʌn'kʌvə°] vt
aufdecken

undecided [ʌndɪ'saɪdɪd] adj
unschlüssig

undeniable [ʌndɪ'naɪəbl] adj
unbestreitbar

under ['ʌndə°] prep (beneath)
unter +dat; (with motion) unter
+akk; **children ~ eight** Kinder
unter acht; **~ an hour** weniger als
eine Stunde ▷ adv (beneath)
unten; (with motion) darunter;
children aged eight and ~ Kinder
bis zu acht Jahren; **under-age** adj
minderjährig

undercarriage ['ʌndəkærɪdʒ] n
Fahrgestell nt

underdog ['ʌndədɒg] n (outsider)
Außenseiter(in) m(f)

underdone [ʌndə'dʌn] adj
(Gastr) nicht gar, durch;
(deliberately) nicht durchgebraten

underestimate [ʌndər-
'estɪmeɪt] vt unterschätzen

underexposed [ʌndəriks'pəʊzd]
adj (Foto) unterbelichtet

undergo [ʌndə'gəʊ] irr vt
(experience) durchmachen;
(operation, test) sich unterziehen
+dat

undergraduate [ʌndə'grædjʊət]
n Student(in) m(f)

underground ['ʌndəgraʊnd] adj
unterirdisch ▷ n (Brit Rail) U-Bahn

f; **underground station** n
U-Bahn-Station f

underlie [ʌndə'laɪ] irr vt
zugrunde liegen +dat

underline [ʌndə'laɪn] vt
unterstreichen

underlying [ʌndə'laɪɪŋ] adj
zugrunde liegend

underneath [ʌndə'niːθ] prep
unter; (with motion) unter +akk
▷ adv darunter

underpants ['ʌndəpænts] npl
Unterhose f; **undershirt**
['ʌndəʃɜːt] n (US) Unterhemd nt;
undershorts ['ʌndəʃɔːts] npl (US)
Unterhose f

understand [ʌndə'stænd] irr vt,
vi verstehen; **I ~ that ...** (been told)
ich habe gehört, dass ...;
(sympathize) ich habe Verständnis
dafür, dass ...; **to make oneself
understood** sich verständlich
machen; **understandable** adj
verständlich; **understanding** adj
verständnisvoll

undertake [ʌndə'teɪk] irr vt
(task) übernehmen; **to ~ to do sth**
sich verpflichten, etw zu tun;
undertaker n Leichenbestat-
ter(in) m(f); **~'s (firm)**
Bestattungsinstitut nt

underwater [ʌndə'wɔːtə°] adv
unter Wasser ▷ adj Unterwasser-

underwear ['ʌndəweə°] n
Unterwäsche f

undesirable [ʌndɪ'zaɪərəbl] adj
unerwünscht

undo [ʌn'duː] irr vt (unfasten)
aufmachen; (work)
zunichtemachen; (Inform)
rückgängig machen

undoubtedly [ʌn'daʊtɪdlɪ] adv
zweifellos

undress [ʌn'dres] vt ausziehen;
to get ~ed sich ausziehen ▷ vi
sich ausziehen

undue [ʌn'djuː] adj übermäßig

u

unduly [ʌn'dju:lɪ] adv übermäßig

unearth [ʌn'ɜ:θ] vt (dig up) ausgraben; (find) aufstöbern

unease [ʌn'i:z] n Unbehagen nt; **uneasy** adj (person) unbehaglich; **I'm ~ about it** mir ist nicht wohl dabei

unemployed [ʌnɪm'plɔɪd] adj arbeitslos ▷ ▷ npl: **the ~** die Arbeitslosen pl; **unemployment** [ʌnɪm'plɔɪmənt] n Arbeitslosigkeit f; **unemployment benefit** n Arbeitslosengeld nt

unequal [ʌn'i:kwəl] adj ungleich

uneven [ʌn'i:vən] adj (surface, road) uneben; (contest) ungleich

unexpected [ʌnɪk'spektɪd] adj unerwartet

unfair [ʌn'fɛəʳ] adj unfair

unfamiliar [ʌnfə'mɪljəʳ] adj: **to be ~ with sb/sth** jdn/etw nicht kennen

unfasten [ʌn'fɑ:sn] vt aufmachen

unfit [ʌn'fɪt] adj ungeeignet (for für); (in bad health) nicht fit

unforeseen [ʌnfɔ:'si:n] adj unvorhergesehen

unforgettable [ʌnfə'getəbl] adj unvergesslich

unforgivable [ʌnfə'gɪvəbl] adj unverzeihlich

unfortunate [ʌn'fɔ:tʃnət] adj (unlucky) unglücklich; **it is ~ that ...** es ist bedauerlich, dass ...; **unfortunately** adv leider

unfounded [ʌn'faʊndɪd] adj unbegründet

unhappy [ʌn'hæpɪ] adj (sad) unglücklich, unzufrieden; **to be ~ with sth** mit etw unzufrieden sein

unhealthy [ʌn'helθɪ] adj ungesund

unheard-of [ʌn'hɜ:dɒv] adj

(unknown) gänzlich unbekannt; (outrageous) unerhört

unhelpful [ʌn'helpful] adj nicht hilfreich

unhitch [ʌn'hɪtʃ] vt (caravan, trailer) abkoppeln

unhurt [ʌn'hɜ:t] adj unverletzt

uniform ['ju:nɪfɔ:m] n Uniform f ▷ adj einheitlich

unify ['ju:nɪfaɪ] vt vereinigen

unimportant [ʌnɪm'pɔ:tənt]-adj unwichtig

uninhabited [ʌnɪn'hæbɪtɪd] adj unbewohnt

uninstall [ʌnɪn'stɔ:l] vt (Inform) deinstallieren

unintentional [ʌnɪn'tenʃənl] adj unabsichtlich

union ['ju:njən] n (uniting) Vereinigung f; (alliance) Union f; **Union Jack** n Union Jack m (britische Nationalflagge)

unique [ju:'ni:k] adj einzigartig

unit ['ju:nɪt] n Einheit f; (of system, machine) Teil nt; (in school) Lektion f

unite [ju:'naɪt] vt vereinigen; **the United Kingdom** das Vereinigte Königreich; **the United Nations** pl die Vereinten Nationen pl; **the United States (of America)** pl die Vereinigten Staaten (von Amerika) pl ▷ vi sich vereinigen

universe ['ju:nɪvɜ:s] n Universum nt

university [ju:nɪ'vɜ:sɪtɪ] n Universität f

unkind [ʌn'kaɪnd] adj unfreundlich (to zu)

unknown [ʌn'nəʊn] adj unbekannt (to +dat)

unleaded [ʌn'ledɪd] adj bleifrei

unless [ən'les] conj es sei denn, wenn ... nicht; **don't do it ~ I tell you to** mach das nicht, es sei denn, ich sage es dir; **~ I'm**

mistaken ... wenn ich mich nicht irre ...

unlicensed [ʌnˈlaɪsənst] *adj* (to sell alcohol) ohne Lizenz

unlike [ʌnˈlaɪk] *prep* (in contrast to) im Gegensatz zu; **it's ~ her to be late** es sieht ihr gar nicht ähnlich, zu spät zu kommen; **unlikely** [ʌnˈlaɪkli] *adj* unwahrscheinlich

unload [ʌnˈləʊd] *vt* ausladen

unlock [ʌnˈlɒk] *vt* aufschließen

unlucky [ʌnˈlʌki] *adj* unglücklich; **to be ~** Pech haben

unmistakable [ʌnmɪˈsteɪkəbl] *adj* unverkennbar

unnecessary [ʌnˈnesəsəri] *adj* unnötig

unobtainable [ʌnəbˈteɪnəbl] *adj* nicht erhältlich

unoccupied [ʌnˈɒkjʊpaɪd] *adj* (seat) frei; (building, room) leer stehend

unpack [ʌnˈpæk] *vt, vi* auspacken

unpleasant [ʌnˈpleznt] *adj* unangenehm

unplug [ʌnˈplʌg] *vt*: **to ~ sth** den Stecker von etw herausziehen

unprecedented [ʌnˈpresɪdəntɪd] *adj* beispiellos

unpredictable [ʌnprɪˈdɪktəbl] *adj* (person, weather) unberechenbar

unreasonable [ʌnˈriːznəbl] *adj* unvernünftig; (demand) übertrieben

unreliable [ʌnrɪˈlaɪəbl] *adj* unzuverlässig

unsafe [ʌnˈseɪf] *adj* nicht sicher; (dangerous) gefährlich

unscrew [ʌnˈskruː] *vt* abschrauben

unsightly [ʌnˈsaɪtli] *adj* unansehnlich

unskilled [ʌnˈskɪld] *adj* (worker) ungelernt

unsuccessful [ʌnsəkˈsesfʊl] *adj* erfolglos

unsuitable [ʌnˈsuːtəbl] *adj* ungeeignet (for für)

until [ənˈtɪl] *prep* bis; **not ~ erst: from Monday ~ Friday** von Montag bis Freitag; **he didn't come home ~ midnight** er kam erst um Mitternacht nach Hause; **~ then** bis dahin ▷ *conj* bis; **she won't come ~ you invite her** sie kommt erst, wenn du sie einlädst/wenn Sie sie einladen

unusual, unusually [ʌnˈjuːʒʊəl, -i] *adj, adv* ungewöhnlich

unwanted [ʌnˈwɒntɪd] *adj* unerwünscht, ungewollt

unwell [ʌnˈwel] *adj* krank; **to feel ~** sich nicht wohlfühlen

unwilling [ʌnˈwɪlɪŋ] *adj*: **to be ~ to do sth** nicht bereit sein, etw zu tun

unwind [ʌnˈwaɪnd] *irr vt* abwickeln ▷ *vi* (relax) sich entspannen

unwrap [ʌnˈræp] *vt* auspacken

unzip [ʌnˈzɪp] *vt* den Reißverschluss aufmachen an +*dat*; (Inform) entzippen

○ KEYWORD

up [ʌp] *prep*: **to be up sth** oben auf etw *dat* sein; **to go up sth** (auf) etw *akk* hinaufgehen; **go up that road** gehen Sie die Straße hinauf

▷ *adv* **1** (upwards, higher) oben; **put it up a bit higher** stell es etwas weiter nach oben; **up there** da oben, dort oben; **up above** hoch oben

2 to be up (out of bed) auf sein; (prices, level) gestiegen sein; (building, tent) stehen

3 up to (as far as) bis; **up to now** bis jetzt

4 to be up to (depending on): **it's up to you** das hängt von dir ab; (equal to): **he's not up to it** (job, task etc) er ist dem nicht gewachsen; (inf: be doing) (showing disapproval, suspicion) **what is he up to?** was führt er im Schilde?; **his work is not up to the required standard** seine Arbeit entspricht nicht dem geforderten Niveau
▷ n: **ups and downs** (in life, career) Höhen und Tiefen pl

upbringing ['ʌpbrɪŋɪŋ] n Erziehung f

update [ʌp'deɪt] n (list etc) Aktualisierung f; (software) Update nt ▷ vt (list etc, person) auf den neuesten Stand bringen, aktualisieren

upgrade [ʌp'greɪd] vt (computer) aufrüsten; **we were ~d** das Hotel hat uns ein besseres Zimmer gegeben

upheaval [ʌp'hiːvəl] n Aufruhr m; (Pol) Umbruch m

uphill [ʌp'hɪl] adv bergauf

upload [ʌp'ləʊd] vt hochladen

upon [ə'pɒn] prep see **on**

upper ['ʌpə'] adj obere(r, s); (arm, deck) Ober-

upright ['ʌpraɪt] adj, adv aufrecht

uprising ['ʌpraɪzɪŋ] n Aufstand m

upset [ʌp'sɛt] irr vt (overturn) umkippen; (disturb) aufregen; (sadden) bestürzen; (offend) kränken; (plans) durcheinanderbringen ▷ adj (disturbed) aufgeregt; (sad) bestürzt; (offended) gekränkt; **~ stomach** ['ʌpsɛt] Magenverstimmung f

upside down [ʌpsaɪd'daʊn] adv verkehrt herum; (fig) drunter und drüber; **to turn sth ~** (box etc) etw umdrehen/durchwühlen

[ʌp'stɛəz] adv oben; (go, take) nach oben

up-to-date ['ʌptə'deɪt] adj modern; (fashion, information) aktuell; **to keep sb ~** jdn auf dem Laufenden halten

upwards ['ʌpwədz] adv nach oben

urban ['ɜːbən] adj städtisch, Stadt-

urge [ɜːdʒ] n Drang m ▷ vt: **to ~ sb to do sth** jdn drängen, etw zu tun; **urgent, urgently** ['ɜːdʒənt, -lɪ] adj, adv dringend

urine ['jʊərɪn] n Urin m

URL abbr = **uniform resource locator** (Inform) URL-Adresse f

us [ʌs] pron uns; **do they know ~?** kennen sie uns?; **can he help ~?** kann er uns helfen?; **it's ~** wir sind's; **both of ~** wir beide

US, USA nsing abbr = **United States (of America)** USA pl

USB stick [juː'esbiː'stɪk] n USB-Stick m

use [juːs] n (using) Gebrauch m; (for specific purpose) Benutzung f; **to make ~ of** Gebrauch machen von; **in/out of ~** in/außer Gebrauch; **it's no ~ (doing that)** es hat keinen Zweck(, das zu tun); **it's (of) no ~ to me** das kann ich nicht brauchen ▷ [juːz] vt benutzen, gebrauchen; (for specific purpose) verwenden; (method) anwenden; **use up** vt aufbrauchen

used [juːzd] adj (secondhand) gebraucht ▷ vb aux: **to be ~d to sb/sth** an jdn/etw gewöhnt sein; **to get ~d to sb/sth** sich an jdn/etw gewöhnen; **she ~d to live here** sie hat früher mal hier gewohnt; **useful** adj nützlich; **useless** adj nutzlos; (unusable) unbrauchbar; (pointless) zwecklos; **user** ['juːzə'] n Benutzer(in) m(f);

user-friendly adj
benutzerfreundlich; **username** n
Benutzername
usual ['juːʒʊəl] adj üblich,
gewöhnlich; **as ~** wie üblich;
usually adv normalerweise
ute ['juːt] n (Aust, NZ fam)
Kleintransporter m
utensil [juːˈtensl] n Gerät nt
uterus ['juːtərəs] n Gebärmutter
f
utilize ['juːtɪlaɪz] vt verwenden
utmost ['ʌtməʊst] adj äußerst;
to do one's ~ sein Möglichstes
tun
utter ['ʌtə°] adj völlig ▷ vt von
sich geben; **utterly** adv völlig
U-turn ['juːtɜːn] n (Auto) Wende
f; **to do a ~** wenden; (fig) eine
Kehrtwendung machen

V

vacancy ['veɪkənsɪ] n (job)
offene Stelle; (room) freies Zimmer;
vacant ['veɪkənt] adj (room,
toilet) frei; (post) offen; (building)
leer stehend; **vacate** [vəˈkeɪt] vt
(room, building) räumen; (seat) frei
machen
vacation [vəˈkeɪʃən] n (US)
Ferien pl, Urlaub m; (at university)
(Semester)ferien pl; **to go on ~** in
Urlaub fahren; **~ course**
Ferienkurs m
vaccinate ['væksɪneɪt] vt
impfen; **vaccination**
[væksɪˈneɪʃən] n Impfung f; **~ card**
Impfpass m
vacuum ['vækjʊm] n Vakuum nt
▷ vt, vi (staub)saugen; **vacuum
(cleaner)** n Staubsauger m
vagina [vəˈdʒaɪnə] n Scheide f
vague [veɪɡ] adj (imprecise) vage;
(resemblance) entfernt; **vaguely**
adv in etwa, irgendwie

vain [veɪn] adj (attempt) vergeblich; (conceited) eitel; **in ~** vergeblich, umsonst; **vainly** adv (in vain) vergeblich

valentine (card) ['væləntaɪn(kɑːd)] n Valentinskarte f; **Valentine's Day** n Valentinstag m

valid ['vælɪd] adj (ticket, passport etc) gültig; (argument) stichhaltig; (claim) berechtigt

valley ['vælɪ] n Tal nt

valuable ['væljʊəbl] adj wertvoll; (time) kostbar; **valuables** npl Wertsachen pl

value ['væljuː] n Wert m ▷ vt (appreciate) schätzen; **value added tax** n Mehrwertsteuer f

valve [vælv] n Ventil nt

van [væn] n (Auto) Lieferwagen m

vanilla [və'nɪlə] n Vanille f

vanish ['vænɪʃ] vi verschwinden

vanity ['vænɪtɪ] n Eitelkeit f; **vanity case** n Schminkkoffer m

vapor (US), **vapour** ['veɪpə°] n (mist) Dunst m; (steam) Dampf m

variable ['vɛərɪəbl] adj (weather, mood) unbeständig; (quality) unterschiedlich; (speed, height) regulierbar; **varied** ['vɛərɪd] adj (interests, selection) vielseitig; (career) bewegt; (work, diet) abwechslungsreich; **variety** [və'raɪətɪ] n (diversity) Abwechslung f; (assortment) Vielfalt f (of an +dat); (type) Art f; **various** ['vɛərɪəs] adj verschieden

varnish ['vɑːnɪʃ] n Lack m ▷ vt lackieren

vary ['vɛərɪ] vt (alter) verändern ▷ vi (be different) unterschiedlich sein; (fluctuate) sich verändern; (prices) schwanken

vase [vɑːz, ?? veɪz] (US) n Vase f

vast [vɑːst] adj riesig; (area) weit

VAT [væt] abbr = **value added tax** Mehrwertsteuer f, MwSt.

Vatican ['vætɪkən] n: **the ~** der Vatikan

VCR [viːsiːˈɑː°] abbr = **video cassette recorder** Videorekorder m

VD [viːˈdiː] abbr = **venereal disease** Geschlechtskrankheit f

VDU [viːdiːˈjuː] abbr = **visual display unit**

veal [viːl] n Kalbfleisch nt

vegan ['viːgən] n Veganer(in) m(f)

vegetable ['vedʒtəbl] n Gemüse nt

vegetarian [vedʒɪ'tɛərɪən] n Vegetarier(in) m(f) ▷ adj vegetarisch

veggie ['vedʒɪ] n (fam) Vegetarier(in) m(f); Gemüse nt ▷ adj vegetarisch; **veggieburger** n Veggieburger m, Gemüseburger m

vehicle ['viːɪkl] n Fahrzeug nt

veil [veɪl] n Schleier m

vein [veɪn] n Ader f

Velcro® ['velkrəʊ] n Klettband nt

velvet ['velvɪt] n Samt m

vending machine ['vendɪŋməʃiːn] n Automat m

venetian blind [vɪ'niːʃən'blaɪnd] n Jalousie f

Venezuela [vene'zweɪlə] n Venezuela nt

Venice ['venɪs] n Venedig nt

venison ['venɪsn] n Rehfleisch nt

vent [vent] n Öffnung f

ventilate ['ventɪleɪt] vt lüften; **ventilation** [ventɪ'leɪʃən] n Belüftung f; **ventilator** ['ventɪleɪtə°] n (in room) Ventilator m; **to be on a ~** (Med) künstlich beatmet werden

venture ['ventʃə°] n (project)

Unternehmung f; (Comm)
Unternehmen nt ▷ vi (go) (sich)
wagen
venue ['venju:] n (for concert etc)
Veranstaltungsort m; (Sport)
Austragungsort m
verb [vɜːb] n Verb nt; **verbal** adj
(agreement) mündlich; (skills)
sprachlich; **verbally** adv
mündlich
verdict ['vɜːdɪkt] n Urteil nt
verge [vɜːdʒ] n (of road)
(Straßen)rand m; **to be on the ~ of
doing sth** im Begriff sein, etw zu
tun ▷ vi: **to ~ on** grenzen an +akk
verification [verɪfɪ'keɪʃən] n
(confirmation) Bestätigung f;
(check) Überprüfung f; **verify**
['verɪfaɪ] vt (confirm) bestätigen;
(check) überprüfen
vermin ['vɜːmɪn] npl Schädlinge
pl; (insects) Ungeziefer nt
verruca [ve'ruːkə] n Warze f
versatile ['vɜːsətaɪl] adj
vielseitig
verse [vɜːs] n (poetry) Poesie f;
(stanza) Strophe f
version ['vɜːʃən] n Version f
versus ['vɜːsəs] prep gegen
vertical ['vɜːtɪkəl] adj senkrecht,
vertikal
very ['verɪ] adv sehr; **~ much** sehr
▷ adj: **the ~ book I need** genau
das Buch, das ich brauche; **at that
~ moment** gerade in dem
Augenblick; **at the ~ top** ganz
oben; **the ~ best** der/die/das
Allerbeste
vest [vest] n (Brit) Unterhemd nt;
(US: waistcoat) Weste f
vet [vet] n Tierarzt m, Tierärztin f
veto ['viːtəʊ] n (pl **-es**) n Veto nt
▷ vt sein Veto einlegen gegen
VHF abbr = **very high frequency**
UKW
via ['vaɪə] prep über +akk
viable ['vaɪəbl] adj (plan)

realisierbar; (company) rentabel
vibrate [vaɪ'breɪt] vi vibrieren;
vibration [vaɪ'breɪʃən] n
Vibration f
vicar ['vɪkə*] n Pfarrer(in) m(f)
vice [vaɪs] n (evil) Laster nt; (Tech)
Schraubstock m ▷ pref Vize-;
~-chairman stellvertretender
Vorsitzender; **~-president**
Vizepräsident(in) m(f)
vice versa ['vaɪs'vɜːsə] adv
umgekehrt
vicinity [vɪ'sɪnɪtɪ] n: **in the ~** in
der Nähe (of +gen)
vicious ['vɪʃəs] adj (violent)
brutal; (malicious) gemein; **vicious
circle** n Teufelskreis m
victim ['vɪktɪm] n Opfer nt
Victorian [vɪk'tɔːrɪən] adj
viktorianisch
victory ['vɪktərɪ] n Sieg m
video ['vɪdɪəʊ] adj (pl **-s**) Video-
▷ n Video nt; (recorder)
Videorekorder m ▷ vt (auf Video)
aufnehmen; **video camera** n
Videokamera f; **video cassette** n
Videokassette f; **video clip** n
Videoclip m; **video game** n
Videospiel nt; **videophone** n
Bildtelefon nt; **video recorder** n
Videorekorder m; **video shop** n
Videothek f; **videotape** n
Videoband nt ▷ vt (auf Video)
aufnehmen
Vienna [vɪ'enə] n Wien nt
Vietnam [vjet'næm] n Vietnam
nt
view [vjuː] n (sight) Blick m (of auf
+akk); (vista) Aussicht f; (opinion)
Ansicht f, Meinung f; **in ~ of**
angesichts +gen ▷ vt (situation,
event) betrachten; (house)
besichtigen; **viewer** n (for slides)
Diabetrachter m; (TV)
Zuschauer(in) m(f); **viewpoint** n
(fig) Standpunkt m
vigilant ['vɪdʒɪlənt] adj wachsam

vile [vaɪl] *adj* abscheulich; *(weather, food)* scheußlich

village [ˈvɪlɪdʒ] *n* Dorf *nt*; **villager** *n* Dorfbewohner(in) *m(f)*

villain [ˈvɪlən] *n* Schurke *m*; *(in film, story)* Bösewicht *m*

vine [vaɪn] *n* (Wein)rebe *f*

vinegar [ˈvɪnɪgəʳ] *n* Essig *m*

vineyard [ˈvɪnjəd] *n* Weinberg *m*

vintage [ˈvɪntɪdʒ] *n* *(of wine)* Jahrgang *m*; **vintage wine** *n* edler Wein

vinyl [ˈvaɪnɪl] *n* Vinyl *nt*

viola [vɪˈəʊlə] *n* Bratsche *f*

violate [ˈvaɪəleɪt] *vt* *(treaty)* brechen; *(rights, rule)* verletzen

violence [ˈvaɪələns] *n* *(brutality)* Gewalt *f*; *(of person)* Gewalttätigkeit *f*; **violent** *adj* *(brutal)* brutal; *(death)* gewaltsam

violet [ˈvaɪələt] *n* Veilchen *nt*

violin [vaɪəˈlɪn] *n* Geige *f*, Violine *f*

VIP *abbr* = **very important person** VIP *mf*

viral [ˈvaɪərəl] *adj* *(Inform)* viral

virgin [ˈvɜːdʒɪn] *n* Jungfrau *f*

Virgo [ˈvɜːgəʊ] *n* *(Astr)* Jungfrau *f*

virile [ˈvɪraɪl] *adj* *(man)* männlich

virtual [ˈvɜːtjʊəl] *adj* *(Inform)* virtuell; **virtually** *adv* praktisch; **virtual reality** *n* virtuelle Realität

virtue [ˈvɜːtjuː] *n* Tugend *f*; **by ~ of** aufgrund +*gen*; **virtuous** [ˈvɜːtjʊəs] *adj* tugendhaft

virus [ˈvaɪrəs] *n* *(Med, Inform)* Virus *m*

visa [ˈviːzə] *n* Visum *nt*

visibility [vɪzɪˈbɪlɪtɪ] *n* *(Meteo)* Sichtweite *f*; **good/poor ~** gute/schlechte Sicht; **visible** [ˈvɪzəbl] *adj* sichtbar; *(evident)* sichtlich; **visibly** *adv* sichtlich

vision [ˈvɪʒən] *n* Sehvermögen *nt*; *(foresight)* Weitblick *m*; *(dream, image)* Vision *f*

visit [ˈvɪzɪt] *n* Besuch *m*; *(stay)* Aufenthalt *m* ▷ *vt* besuchen; **visiting hours** *npl* Besuchszeiten *pl*; **visitor** *n* Besucher(in) *m(f)*; **~s' book** Gästebuch *nt*; **visitor centre** *n* Informationszentrum *nt*

visor [ˈvaɪzəʳ] *n* *(on helmet)* Visier *nt*; *(Auto)* Blende *f*

visual [ˈvɪzjʊəl] *adj* Seh-; *(image, joke)* visuell; **~ aid** Anschauungsmaterial *nt*; **~ display unit** Monitor *m*; **visualize** *vt* sich vorstellen; **visually** *adv* visuell; **~ impaired** sehbehindert

vital [ˈvaɪtl] *adj* *(essential)* unerlässlich, wesentlich; *(argument, moment)* entscheidend; **vitality** [vaɪˈtælɪtɪ] *n* Vitalität *f*; **vitally** *adv* äußerst

vitamin [ˈvɪtəmɪn] *n* Vitamin *nt*

vivacious [vɪˈveɪʃəs] *adj* lebhaft

vivid [ˈvɪvɪd] *adj* *(description)* anschaulich; *(memory)* lebhaft; *(colour)* leuchtend

V-neck [ˈviːnek] *n* V-Ausschnitt *m*

vocabulary [vəʊˈkæbjʊlərɪ] *n* Wortschatz *m*, Vokabular *nt*

vocal [ˈvəʊkəl] *adj* *(of the voice)* Stimm-; *(group)* Gesangs-; *(protest, person)* lautstark

vocation [vəʊˈkeɪʃən] *n* Berufung *f*; **vocational** *adj* Berufs-

vodka [ˈvɒdkə] *n* Wodka *m*

voice [vɔɪs] *n* Stimme *f* ▷ *vt* äußern; **voice mail** *n* Voicemail *f*

void [vɔɪd] *n* Leere *f* ▷ *adj* *(Jur)* ungültig; **~ of** *(ganz)* ohne

volcano [vɒlˈkeɪnəʊ] *(pl* **-es**) *n* Vulkan *m*

volley [ˈvɒlɪ] *n* *(Tennis)* Volley *m*; **volleyball** *n* Volleyball *m*

volt [vəʊlt] *n* Volt *nt*; **voltage** *n* Spannung *f*

volume [ˈvɒljuːm] *n* *(of sound)* Lautstärke *f*; *(space occupied by sth)*

Volumen nt; (size, amount) Umfang m; (book) Band m; **volume control** n Lautstärkeregler m

voluntary, voluntarily ['vɒləntərɪ, -lɪ] adj, adv freiwillig; (unpaid) ehrenamtlich; **volunteer** [vɒlən'tɪə°] n Freiwillige(r) mf ▷ vi sich freiwillig melden ▷ vt: **to ~ to do sth** sich anbieten, etw zu tun

voluptuous [və'lʌptjʊəs] adj sinnlich

vomit ['vɒmɪt] vi sich übergeben

vote [vəʊt] n Stimme f; (ballot) Wahl f; (result) Abstimmungsergebnis nt; (right to vote) Wahlrecht nt ▷ vt (elect) wählen; **they ~d him chairman** sie wählten ihn zum Vorsitzenden ▷ vi wählen; **to ~ for/against sth** für/gegen etw stimmen; **voter** n Wähler(in) m(f)

voucher ['vaʊtʃə°] n Gutschein m

vow [vaʊ] n Gelöbnis nt ▷ vt: **to ~ to do sth** geloben, etw zu tun

vowel ['vaʊəl] n Vokal m

voyage ['vɔɪɪdʒ] n Reise f

vulgar ['vʌlgə°] adj vulgär, ordinär

vulnerable ['vʌlnərəbl] adj verwundbar; (sensitive) verletzlich

vulture ['vʌltʃə°] n Geier m

W abbr = west W

wade [weɪd] vi (in water) waten

wafer ['weɪfə°] n Waffel f; (Rel) Hostie f; **wafer-thin** adj hauchdünn

waffle ['wɒfl] n Waffel f; (Brit fam: empty talk) Geschwafel nt ▷ vi (Brit fam) schwafeln

wag [wæg] vt (tail) wedeln mit

wage [weɪdʒ] n Lohn m

waggon (Brit), **wagon** ['wægən] n (horse-drawn) Fuhrwerk nt; (Brit Rail) Waggon m; (US Auto) Wagen m

waist [weɪst] n Taille f; **waistcoat** n (Brit) Weste f; **waistline** n Taille f

wait [weɪt] n Wartezeit f ▷ vi warten (for auf +akk); **to ~ and see** abwarten; **~ a minute** Moment mall; **wait up** vi aufbleiben

waiter n Kellner m; **~!** Herr Ober!

waiting n: **"no ~"** „Halteverbot";

waiting list n Warteliste f;
waiting room n (Med)
Wartezimmer nt; (Rail) Wartesaal
m

waitress n Kellnerin f

wake [weɪk] (**woke** o **waked**,
woken o **waked**) vt wecken ▷ vi
aufwachen; **wake up** vt
aufwecken ▷ vi aufwachen;
wake-up call n (Tel) Weckruf m

Wales ['weɪlz] n Wales nt

walk [wɔːk] n Spaziergang m;
(ramble) Wanderung f; (route) Weg
m; **to go for a ~** spazieren gehen;
it's only a five-minute ~ es sind
nur fünf Minuten zu Fuß ▷ vi
gehen; (stroll) spazieren gehen;
(ramble) wandern ▷ vt (dog)
ausführen; **walking** n: **to go
~ wandern**; **walking shoes** npl
Wanderschuhe pl; **walking stick** n
Spazierstock m

Walkman® (pl -s) n Walkman®
m

wall [wɔːl] n (inside) Wand f;
(outside) Mauer f

wallet ['wɒlɪt] n Brieftasche
f

wallpaper ['wɔːlpeɪpə'] n
Tapete f; (Inform)
Bildschirmhintergrund m ▷ vt
tapezieren

walnut ['wɔːlnʌt] n (nut)
Walnuss f

waltz [wɔːlts] n Walzer m

wander ['wɒndə'] vi (person)
herumwandern

want [wɒnt] n (lack) Mangel m
(of an +dat); (need) Bedürfnis nt; **for
~ of** aus Mangel an +dat ▷ vt
(desire) wollen; (need) brauchen; **I
~ to stay here** ich will hier
bleiben; **he doesn't ~ to** er will
nicht

WAP phone ['wæpfəʊn] n
WAP-Handy nt

war [wɔː'] n Krieg m

ward [wɔːd] n (in hospital)
Station f; (child) Mündel nt

warden ['wɔːdən] n Aufseher(in)
m(f); (in youth hostel) Herbergsvater
m, Herbergsmutter f

wardrobe ['wɔːdrəʊb] n
Kleiderschrank m

warehouse ['wɛəhaʊs] n
Lagerhaus nt

warfare ['wɔːfɛə'] n Krieg m;
(techniques) Kriegsführung f

warm [wɔːm] adj warm;
(welcome) herzlich; **I'm ~** mir ist
warm ▷ vt wärmen; (food)
aufwärmen; **warm over** vt (US:
food) aufwärmen; **warm up** vt
(food) aufwärmen; (room)
erwärmen ▷ vi (food, room) warm
werden; (Sport) sich aufwärmen;
warmly adv warm; (welcome)
herzlich; **warmth** n Wärme f; (of
welcome) Herzlichkeit f

warn [wɔːn] vt warnen (of,
against vor +dat); **to ~ sb not to do
sth** jdn davor warnen, etw zu tun;
warning n Warnung f; **warning
light** n Warnlicht nt; **warning
triangle** n (Auto) Warndreieck nt

warranty ['wɒrəntɪ] n Garantie
f

wart [wɔːt] n Warze f

wary ['wɛərɪ] adj vorsichtig;
(suspicious) misstrauisch

was [wɒz, wəz] pt of **be**

wash [wɒʃ] n: **to have a ~** sich
waschen; **it's in the ~** es ist in der
Wäsche ▷ vt waschen; (plates,
glasses etc) abwaschen; **to ~ one's
hands** sich dat die Hände
waschen; **to ~ the dishes** (das
Geschirr) abwaschen ▷ vi (clean
oneself) sich waschen; **wash off** vt
abwaschen; **wash up** vi (Brit:
wash dishes) abwaschen; (US: clean
oneself) sich waschen; **washable**
adj waschbar; **washbag** n (US)
Kulturbeutel m; **washbasin** n

Waschbecken nt; **washcloth** n (US) Waschlappen m; **washer** n (Tech) Dichtungsring m; (washing machine) Waschmaschine f; **washing** n (laundry) Wäsche f; **washing machine** n Waschmaschine f; **washing powder** n Waschpulver nt; **washing-up** n (Brit) Abwasch m; **to do the ~** abwaschen; **washing-up liquid** n (Brit) Spülmittel nt; **washroom** n (US) Toilette f

wasn't ['wɒznt] contr of **was not**

wasp [wɒsp] n Wespe f

waste [weist] n (materials) Abfall m; (wasting) Verschwendung f; **it's a ~ of time** das ist Zeitverschwendung ▷ adj (superfluous) überschüssig ▷ vt verschwenden (on an +akk); (opportunity) vertun; **waste bin** n Abfalleimer m; **wastepaper basket** n Papierkorb m

watch [wɒtʃ] n (timepiece) (Armband)uhr f ▷ vt (observe) beobachten, (guard) aufpassen auf +akk; (film, play, programme) sich dat ansehen; **to ~ TV** fernsehen ▷ vi zusehen; (guard) Wache halten; **to ~ for sb/sth** nach jdm/etw Ausschau halten; **~ out** pass auf!; **watchdog** n Wachhund m; (fig) Aufsichtsbehörde f; **watchful** adj wachsam

water ['wɔːtə°] n Wasser nt ▷ vt (plant) gießen ▷ vi (eye) tränen; **my mouth is ~ing** mir läuft das Wasser im Mund zusammen; **water down** vt verdünnen; **watercolor** (US), **watercolour** n (painting) Aquarell nt; (paint) Wasserfarbe f; **watercress** n (Brunnen)kresse f; **waterfall** n Wasserfall m; **watering can** n Gießkanne f; **water level** n

Wasserstand m; **watermelon** n Wassermelone f; **waterproof** adj wasserdicht; **water-skiing** n Wasserskilaufen nt; **water sports** npl Wassersport m; **watertight** adj wasserdicht; **water wings** npl Schwimmflügel pl; **watery** adj wässerig

wave [weiv] n Welle f ▷ vt (move to and fro) schwenken; (hand, flag) winken mit ▷ vi (person) winken; (flag) wehen; **wavelength** n Wellenlänge f; **to be on the same ~** (fig) die gleiche Wellenlänge haben; **wavy** ['weivɪ] adj wellig

wax [wæks] n Wachs nt; (in ear) Ohrenschmalz m

way [wei] n Weg m; (direction) Richtung f; (manner) Art f; **can you tell me the ~ to ... ?** wie komme ich (am besten) zu ... ?; **we went the wrong ~** wir sind in die falsche Richtung gefahren/gegangen; **to lose one's ~** sich verirren; **to make ~ for sb/sth** jdm/etw Platz machen; **to get one's own ~** seinen Willen durchsetzen; **"give ~"** (Auto) "Vorfahrt achten"; **the other ~ round** andersherum; **one ~ or another** irgendwie; **in a ~** in gewisser Weise; **in the ~** im Weg; **by the ~** übrigens; **"~ in"** "Eingang"; **"~ out"** "Ausgang"; **no ~** (fam) kommt nicht infrage!

we [wiː] pron wir

weak [wiːk] adj schwach; **weaken** vt schwächen ▷ vi schwächer werden

wealth [welθ] n Reichtum m; **wealthy** adj reich

weapon ['wepən] n Waffe f

wear [weə°] (pt wore, worn) vt (have on) tragen; **what shall I ~?** was soll ich anziehen? ▷ vi (become worn) sich abnutzen ▷ n: **~ (and tear)** Abnutzung f; **wear**

w

off vi (diminish) nachlassen; **wear out** vt abnutzen; (person) erschöpfen ▷ vi sich abnutzen

weather ['weðə'] n Wetter nt; **I'm feeling under the ~** ich fühle mich nicht ganz wohl; **weather forecast** n Wettervorhersage f

weave [wi:v] (**wove** o **weaved**, **woven** o **weaved**) vt (cloth) weben; (basket etc) flechten

web [web] n (a. fig) Netz nt; **the Web** das Web, das Internet; **webcam** ['webkæm] n Webcam f; **web page** n Webseite f; **website** n Website f

we'd [wi:d] contr of **we had; we would**

Wed abbr = **Wednesday** Mi.

wedding ['wedɪŋ] n Hochzeit f; **wedding anniversary** n Hochzeitstag m; **wedding dress** n Hochzeitskleid nt; **wedding ring** n Ehering m

wedding shower n (US) Party für die zukünftige Braut

wedge [wedʒ] n (under door etc) Keil m; (of cheese etc) Stück nt, Ecke f

Wednesday ['wenzdeɪ] n Mittwoch m; see also **Tuesday**

wee [wi:] adj klein ▷ vi (fam) Pipi machen

weed [wi:d] n Unkraut nt ▷ vt jäten

week [wi:k] n Woche f; **twice a ~** zweimal in der Woche; **a ~ on Friday/Friday ~** Freitag in einer Woche; **a ~ last Friday** letzten Freitag vor einer Woche; **in two ~s' time, in two ~s** in zwei Wochen; **for ~s** wochenlang; **weekday** n Wochentag m; **weekend** n Wochenende nt; **weekend break** n Wochenendurlaub m; **weekly** adv,

adv wöchentlich; (magazine) Wochen-

weep [wi:p] (**wept, wept**) vi weinen

weigh [weɪ] vt, vi wiegen; **it ~s 20 kilos** es wiegt 20 Kilo; **weigh up** vt abwägen; (person) einschätzen; **weight** [weɪt] n Gewicht nt; **to lose/put on ~** abnehmen/zunehmen; **weightlifting** n Gewichtheben nt; **weight training** n Krafttraining nt; **weighty** adj (important) schwerwiegend

weird [wɪəd] adj seltsam; **weirdo** ['wɪədəʊ] n Spinner(in) m(f)

welcome ['welkəm] n Empfang m ▷ adj willkommen; (news) angenehm; **~ to London** willkommen in London! ▷ vt begrüßen; **welcoming** adj freundlich

welfare ['welfeə'] n Wohl nt; (US: social security) Sozialhilfe f; **welfare state** n Wohlfahrtsstaat m

well [wel] n Brunnen m ▷ adj (in good health) gesund; **are you ~?** geht es dir/Ihnen gut?; **to feel ~** sich wohlfühlen; **get ~ soon** gute Besserung! ▷ interj nun; **~, I don't know** nun, ich weiß nicht ▷ adv gut; **~ done** gut gemacht!; **it may ~ be** das kann wohl sein; **as ~** (in addition) auch; **~ over 60** weit über 60

we'll [wi:l] contr of **we will; we shall**

well-behaved [welbɪ'heɪvd] adj brav; **well-being** n Wohl nt; **well-built** adj (person) gut gebaut; **well-done** adj (steak) durchgebraten; **well-earned** adj wohlverdient

wellingtons ['welɪŋtənz] npl Gummistiefel pl

well-known [wel'nəʊn] adj bekannt; **well-off** adj (wealthy)

wohlhabend; **well-paid** adj gut
bezahlt
Welsh [welʃ] adj walisisch ▷ n
(language) Walisisch nt; **the ~** pl die
Waliser pl; **Welshman** (pl **-men**) n
Waliser m; **Welshwoman** (pl
-women) n Waliserin f
went [went] pt of **go**
wept [wept] pt, pp of **weep**
were [wɜː] pt of **be**
we're [wɪə°] contr of **we are**
weren't [wɜːnt] contr of **were not**
west [west] n Westen m; **the
West** (Pol) der Westen ▷ adv (go,
face) nach Westen ▷ adj West-;
westbound adj (in) Richtung
Westen; **western** adj
West-, westlich; **Western Europe**
Westeuropa nt ▷ n (Cine) Western
m; **West Germany** n: **(the
former)** ~ (das ehemalige)
Westdeutschland,
Westdeutschland n; **westwards**
['westwədz] adv nach Westen
wet [wet] **(wet, wet)** vt: **to
~ oneself** in die Hose machen
▷ adj nass, feucht; **"~ paint"**
„frisch gestrichen"; **wet suit** n
Taucheranzug m
we've [wiːv] contr of **we have**
whale [weɪl] n Wal m
wharf [wɔːf] (pl **-s** o **wharves**) n
Kai m

what [wɒt] adj **1** (in questions)
welche(r, s) was für ein(e);
what size is it? welche Größe ist
das?; **2** (in exclamations) was für ein(e);
what a mess! was für ein
Durcheinander!
▷ pron (interrogative/relative) was;
what are you doing? was machst
du/machen Sie gerade?; **what are
you talking about?** wovon redest

du/reden Sie?; **what's your
name?** wie heißt du/heißen Sie?;
what is it called? wie heißt das?;
what about ...? wie wär's mit ...?;
I saw what you did ich habe
gesehen, was du gemacht
hast/Sie gemacht haben
▷ excl (disbelieving) wie, was;
what, no coffee! wie, kein
Kaffee?; **I've crashed the car —
what!** ich hatte einen
Autounfall — was!

whatever pron: **I'll do ~ you
want** ich tue alles, was du
willst/Sie wollen; **~ he says** egal,
was er sagt
what's [wɒts] contr of **what is;
what has**
wheat [wiːt] n Weizen m
wheel [wiːl] n Rad nt; (steering
wheel) Lenkrad nt ▷ vt (bicycle,
trolley) schieben; **wheelbarrow** n
Schubkarren m; **wheelchair** n
Rollstuhl m; **wheel clamp** n
Parkkralle f

when [wen] adv wann
▷ conj **1** (at, during, after the time
that) wenn; (in past) als; **she was
reading when I came in** sie las,
als ich hereinkam; **be careful
when you cross the road** sei
vorsichtig, wenn du über die
Straße gehst/seien Sie vorsichtig,
wenn Sie über die Straße gehen
2 (on, at which) als; **on the day
when I met him** an dem Tag, an
dem ich ihn traf
3 (whereas) wo ... doch

whenever adv (every time) immer
wenn; **come ~ you like** komm,
wann immer du willst/kommen
Sie, wann immer sie wollen

w

where [wɛə°] adv wo; **~ are you going?** wohin gehst du/gehen Sie?; **~ are you from?** woher kommst du/kommen Sie? ▷ conj wo; **that's ~ I used to live** da habe ich früher gewohnt; **whereabouts** [wɛərə'bauts] adv wo ▷ n pl ['wɛərəbauts] Aufenthaltsort m; **whereas** [wɛər'æz] conj während, wohingegen; **whereby** adv wodurch; **wherever** [wɛər'evə°] conj wo immer; **~ that may be** wo immer das sein mag; **~ I go** überall, wohin ich gehe

whether ['wɛðə°] conj ob

⊙ **KEYWORD**

which [wɪtʃ] adj 1 (interrogative) (direct, indirect) welche(r, s); **which one?** welche(r, s)?
2 **in which case** in diesem Fall; **by which time** zu dieser Zeit
▷ pron 1 (interrogative) welche(r, s); (of people also) wer
2 (relative) der/die/das; (referring to people) was; **the apple which you ate/which is on the table** der Apfel, den du gegessen hast/der auf dem Tisch liegt; **he said he saw her, which is true** er sagte, er habe sie gesehen, was auch stimmt

whichever adj, pron welche(r, s) auch immer

while [waɪl] n: **a ~** eine Weile; **for a ~** eine Zeit lang; **a short ~ ago** vor Kurzem ▷ conj während; (although) obwohl

whine [waɪn] vi (person) jammern

whip [wɪp] n Peitsche f ▷ vt (beat) peitschen; **~ped cream** Schlagsahne f

whirl [wɜːl] vt, vi herumwirbeln;

whirlpool n (in river, sea) Strudel m; (pool) Whirlpool m

whisk [wɪsk] n Schneebesen m ▷ vt (cream etc) schlagen

whisker [wɪskə°] n (of animal) Schnurrhaar nt; **~s** pl (of man) Backenbart m

whisk(e)y ['wɪski] n Whisky m

whisper ['wɪspə°] vi, vt flüstern; **to ~ sth to sb** jdm etw zuflüstern

whistle ['wɪsl] n Pfiff m; (instrument) Pfeife f ▷ vt, vi pfeifen

white [waɪt] n (of egg) Eiweiß nt; (of eye) Weiße nt ▷ adj weiß; (with fear) blass; (coffee) mit Milch/Sahne; **White House** n: **the ~** das Weiße Haus; **white lie** n Notlüge f; **white meat** n helles Fleisch; **white sauce** n weiße Soße; **white water rafting** n Rafting nt; **white wine** n Weißwein m

Whitsun ['wɪtsn] n Pfingsten nt

⊙ **KEYWORD**

who [huː] pron 1 (interrogative) wer; (akk) wen; (dat) wem; **who is it?, who's there?** wer ist da?
2 (relative) der/die/das; **the woman/man who spoke to me** die Frau/der Mann, die/der mit mir sprach

whoever [huː'evə°] pron wer auch immer; **~ you choose** wen auch immer du wählst/Sie wählen

whole [həʊl] adj ganz ▷ n Ganze(s) nt; **the ~ of my family** meine ganze Familie; **on the ~** im Großen und Ganzen; **wholefood** n (Brit) Vollwertkost f; **~ store** Bioladen m; **wholeheartedly** adv voll und ganz; **wholemeal** adj (Brit) Vollkorn-; **wholesale** adv (buy, sell) im Großhandel; **wholesome**

adj gesund; **whole wheat** *adj* Vollkorn-; **wholly** ['həʊlɪ] *adv* völlig

---

KEYWORD

whom [huːm] *pron* **1** (*interrogative*) (*akk*) wen; (*dat*) wem; **whom did you see?** wen hast du/haben Sie gesehen?; **to whom did you give it?** wem hast du/haben Sie es gegeben? **2** (*relative*) (*akk*) den/die/das; (*dat*) dem/der/dem; **the man whom I saw/to whom I spoke** der Mann, den ich sah/mit dem ich sprach

whooping cough ['huːpɪŋkɒf] *n* Keuchhusten *m*

whose [huːz] *adj* (*in questions*) wessen; (*in relative clauses*) dessen/deren/dessen, deren *pl*; **~ bike is that?** wessen Fahrrad ist das? ▷ *pron* (*in questions*) wessen; **~ is this?** wem gehört das?

KEYWORD

why [waɪ] *adv* warum, weshalb ▷ *conj* warum, weshalb; **that's not why I'm here** ich bin nicht deswegen hier; **that's the reason why** deshalb ▷ *excl* (*expressing surprise, shock*) na so was; (*explaining*) also dann; **why, it's you!** na so was, du bist/Sie sind es!

wicked ['wɪkɪd] *adj* böse; (*fam: great*) geil

wide [waɪd] *adj* breit; (*skirt, trousers*) weit; (*selection*) groß ▷ *adv* weit; **wide-angle lens** *n* Weitwinkelobjektiv *nt*; **wide-awake** *adj* hellwach; **widely** *adv* weit; **~ known**

allgemein bekannt; **widen** *vt* verbreitern; (*fig*) erweitern; **wide-open** *adj* weit offen; **widescreen TV** *n* Breitbildfernseher *m*; **widespread** *adj* weit verbreitet

widow ['wɪdəʊ] *n* Witwe *f*; **widowed** *adj* verwitwet; **widower** *n* Witwer *m*

width [wɪdθ] *n* Breite *f*

wife [waɪf] (*pl* **wives**) *n* (Ehe)frau *f*

Wi-Fi ['waɪfaɪ] *n* Wi-Fi *nt*

wig [wɪɡ] *n* Perücke *f*

wiggle ['wɪɡl] *vt* wackeln mit

wild [waɪld] *adj* wild; (*violent*) heftig; (*plan, idea*) verrückt ▷ *n*: **in the ~** in freier Wildbahn; **wildlife** *n* Tier- und Pflanzenwelt *f*; **wildly** *adv* wild; (*exaggerated*) maßlos

---

KEYWORD

will [wɪl] *vb aux* **1** (*forms future tense*) werden; **I will finish it tomorrow** ich mache es morgen zu Ende **2** (*in conjectures, predictions*) he will o **he'll be there by now** er dürfte jetzt da sein; **that will be the postman** das wird der Postbote sein **3** (*in commands, requests, offers*) **will you be quiet!** sei/seien Sie endlich still!; **will you help me?** hilfst du/helfen Sie mir?; **will you have a cup of tea?** trinkst du/trinken Sie eine Tasse Tee?; **I won't put up with it!** das lasse ich mir nicht gefallen! ▷ *vt* wollen ▷ *n* Wille *m*; (*jur*) Testament *nt*

willing *adj* bereitwillig; **to be ~ to do sth** bereit sein, etw zu tun; **willingly** *adv* gern(e)

willow ['wɪləʊ] *n* Weide *f*

w

willpower ['wɪlpaʊə°] n Willenskraft f

wimp [wɪmp] n Weichei nt

win [wɪn] (**won, won**) vt, vi gewinnen ▷ n Sieg m; **win over**, **win round** vt für sich gewinnen

wind [waɪnd] (**wound, wound**) vt (rope, bandage) wickeln; **wind down** vt (car window) herunterkurbeln; **wind up** vt (clock) aufziehen; (car window) hochkurbeln; (meeting, speech) abschließen; (person) aufziehen, ärgern

wind [wɪnd] n Wind m; (Med) Blähungen pl; **wind farm** n Windpark m; **wind instrument** n Blasinstrument nt; **windmill** n Windmühle f

window ['wɪndəʊ] n Fenster nt; (counter) Schalter m; **~ of opportunity** Chance f, Gelegenheit f; **window box** n Blumenkasten m; **windowpane** n Fensterscheibe f; **window-shopping** n: **to go ~** einen Schaufensterbummel machen; **windowsill** n Fensterbrett nt

windpipe ['wɪndpaɪp] n Luftröhre f; **windscreen** n (Brit) Windschutzscheibe f; **windscreen wiper** n (Brit) Scheibenwischer m; **windshield** n (US) Windschutzscheibe f; **windshield wiper** n (US) Scheibenwischer m; **windsurfer** n Windsurfer(in) m(f); (board) Surfbrett nt; **windsurfing** n Windsurfen nt; **wind turbine** n Windturbine f

windy ['wɪndɪ] adj windig

wine [waɪn] n Wein m; **wine bar** n Weinlokal nt; **wineglass** n Weinglas nt; **wine list** n Weinkarte f; **wine tasting** n (event) Weinprobe f

wing [wɪŋ] n Flügel m; (Brit Auto) Kotflügel m; **~s** pl (Theat) Kulissen pl

wink [wɪŋk] vi zwinkern; **to ~ at sb** jdm zuzwinkern

winner ['wɪnə°] n Gewinner(in) m(f); (Sport) Sieger(in) m(f); **winning** adj (team, horse etc) siegreich; **~ number** Gewinnzahl f ▷ n **~s** pl Gewinn m

winter ['wɪntə°] n Winter m; **winter sports** npl Wintersport m; **wint(e)ry** ['wɪntrɪ] adj winterlich

wipe [waɪp] vt abwischen; **to ~ one's nose** sich dat die Nase putzen; **to ~ one's feet** (on mat) sich dat die Schuhe abtreten; **wipe off** vt abwischen; **wipe out** vt (destroy) vernichten; (data, debt) löschen; (epidemic etc) ausrotten

wire ['waɪə°] n Draht m; (Elec) Leitung f; (US: telegram) Telegramm nt ▷ vt (plug in) anschließen; (US Tel) telegrafieren (sb sth jdm etw); **wireless** ['waɪələs] adj drahtlos

wisdom ['wɪzdəm] n Weisheit f; **wisdom tooth** n Weisheitszahn m

wise, wisely [waɪz, -lɪ] adj, adv weise

wish [wɪʃ] n Wunsch m (for nach); **with best ~es** (in letter) herzliche Grüße ▷ vt wünschen, wollen; **to ~ sb good luck/Merry Christmas** jdm viel Glück/frohe Weihnachten wünschen; **I ~ I'd never seen him** ich wünschte, ich hätte ihn nie gesehen

witch [wɪtʃ] n Hexe f

○ **KEYWORD**

with [wɪð] prep **1** (accompanying, in the company of) mit; **we stayed with friends** wir übernachteten bei Freunden; **I'll be with you in a minute** einen Augenblick, ich bin sofort da; **I'm not with you** (*I don't understand*) das verstehe ich nicht; **to be with it** (*inf*) (*up-to-date*) auf dem Laufenden sein; (*alert*) (voll) da sein *inf*

2 (*descriptive, indicating manner etc*) mit; **the man with the grey hat** der Mann mit dem grauen Hut; **red with anger** rot vor Wut

withdraw [wɪðˈdrɔ:] *irr vt* zurückziehen; (*money*) abheben; (*comment*) zurücknehmen ▷ *vi* sich zurückziehen

wither [ˈwɪðə°] *vi* (*plant*) verwelken

withhold [wɪðˈhəʊld] *irr vt* vorenthalten (*from sb* jdm)

within [wɪðˈɪn] *prep* innerhalb +*gen*; **~ walking distance** zu Fuß erreichbar

without [wɪðˈaʊt] *prep* ohne; **~ asking** ohne zu fragen

withstand [wɪðˈstænd] *irr vt* standhalten +*dat*

witness [ˈwɪtnəs] *n* Zeuge *m*, Zeugin *f* ▷ *vt* Zeuge sein; **witness box, witness stand** (US) *n* Zeugenstand *m*

witty [ˈwɪtɪ] *adj* geistreich

wives [waɪvz] *pl of* **wife**

WMD *abbr* = **weapon of mass destruction** Massenvernichtungswaffe

wobble [ˈwɒbl] *vi* wackeln; **wobbly** *adj* wackelig

wok [wɒk] *n* Wok *m*

woke [wəʊk] *pt of* **wake**

woken [ˈwəʊkn] *pp of* **wake**

wolf [wʊlf] (*pl* **wolves**) *n* Wolf *m*

woman [ˈwʊmən] (*pl* **women**) *n* Frau *f*

womb [wu:m] *n* Gebärmutter *f*

women [ˈwɪmɪn] *pl of* **woman**

won [wʌn] *pt, pp of* **win**

wonder [ˈwʌndə°] *n* (*marvel*) Wunder *nt*; (*surprise*) Staunen *nt* ▷ *vt*, *vi* (*speculate*) sich fragen; **I ~ what/if ...** ich frage mich, was/ob ...; **wonderful**, **wonderfully** *adj*, *adv* wunderbar

won't [wəʊnt] *contr of* **will not**

wood [wʊd] *n* Holz *nt*; **~s** Wald *m*; **wooden** *adj* Holz-; (*fig*) hölzern; **woodpecker** *n* Specht *m*; **woodwork** *n* (*wooden parts*) Holzteile *pl*; (*in school*) Werken *nt*

wool [wʊl] *n* Wolle *f*, **woollen**, **woolen** (US) *adj* Woll-

word [wɜ:d] *n* Wort *nt*; (*promise*) Ehrenwort *nt*; **~s** *pl* (*of song*) Text *m*; **to have a ~ with sb** mit jdm sprechen; **in other ~s** mit anderen Worten ▷ *vt* formulieren; **wording** *n* Wortlaut *m*, Formulierung *f*; **word processing** *n* Textverarbeitung *f*; **word processor** *n* (*program*) Textverarbeitungsprogramm *nt*

wore [wɔ:°] *pt of* **wear**

work [wɜ:k] *n* Arbeit *f*; (*of art, literature*) Werk *nt*; **~ of art** Kunstwerk *nt*; **he's at ~** er ist in/auf der Arbeit; **out of ~** arbeitslos ▷ *vi* arbeiten (*at, on* an +*dat*); (*machine, plan*) funktionieren; (*medicine*) wirken; (*succeed*) klappen ▷ *vt* (*machine*) bedienen; **work out** *vi* (*plan*) klappen; (*sum*) aufgehen; (*person*) trainieren ▷ *vt* (*price, speed etc*) ausrechnen; (*plan*) ausarbeiten; **work up** *vt*: **to get worked up** sich aufregen; **workaholic** [wɜ:kəˈhɒlɪk] *n* Arbeitstier *nt*; **worker** *n* Arbeiter(in) *m(f)*; **working class** *n* Arbeiterklasse *f*; **workman** (*pl* -**men**) *n* Handwerker *m*; **workout** *n* (*Sport*) Fitnesstraining *nt*, Konditionstraining *nt*; **work permit** *n* Arbeitserlaubnis *f*;

w

workplace n Arbeitsplatz m;
workshop n Werkstatt f;
(meeting) Workshop m; **work
station** n (Inform) Workstation
f

world [wɜːld] n Welt f; **world
championship** n Weltmeisterschaft f; **World War** n: ~ **I/II, the
First/Second** ~ der Erste/Zweite
Weltkrieg; **world-wide** adj, adv
weltweit; **World Wide Web** n
World Wide Web nt

worm [wɜːm] n Wurm m

worn [wɔːn] pp of **wear** ▷ adj
(clothes) abgetragen; (tyre)
abgefahren; **worn-out** adj
abgenutzt; (person) erschöpft

worried [ˈwʌrɪd] adj besorgt; **be
~ about** sich dat Sorgen machen
um; **worry** [ˈwʌrɪ] n Sorge f ▷ vt
Sorgen machen +dat ▷ vi sich
Sorgen machen (about um); **don't
~!** keine Sorge!; **worrying** adj
beunruhigend

worse [wɜːs] adj comparative of
bad; schlechter; (pain, mistake etc)
schlimmer ▷ adv comparative of
badly; schlechter; **worsen** vt
verschlechtern ▷ vi sich
verschlechtern

worship [ˈwɜːʃɪp] vt anbeten,
anhimmeln

worst [wɜːst] adj superlative of
bad; schlechteste(r, s); (pain,
mistake etc) schlimmste(r, s) ▷ adv
superlative of **badly**; am
schlechtesten ▷ n: **the ~ is over**
das Schlimmste ist vorbei; **at (the)
~** schlimmstenfalls

worth [wɜːθ] n Wert m; **£10 ~ of
food** Essen für 10 Pfund ▷ adj: **it is
~ £50** es ist 50 Pfund wert;
~ seeing sehenswert; **it's ~ it**
(rewarding) es lohnt sich;
worthless adj wertlos;
worthwhile adj lohnend,
lohnenswert; **worthy** [ˈwɜːðɪ]

adj (deserving respect) würdig; **to
be ~ of sth** etw verdienen

O **KEYWORD**

would [wʊd] vb aux 1 (conditional
tense) **if you asked him he would
do it** wenn du ihn fragtest/Sie ihn
fragten, würde er es tun; **if you
had asked him he would have
done it** wenn du ihn gefragt
hättest/Sie ihn gefragt hätten,
hätte er es getan
2 (in offers, invitations, requests)
would you like a biscuit?
möchtest du/möchten Sie einen
Keks?; **would you ask him to
come in?** würdest du/würden Sie
ihn bitte hereinbitten?
3 (in indirect speech) **I said I would
do it** ich sagte, ich würde es tun
4 (emphatic) **it WOULD have to
snow today!** es musste ja
ausgerechnet heute schneien!
5 (insistence) **she wouldn't behave**
sie wollte sich partout nicht
anständig benehmen
6 (conjecture) **it would have been
midnight** es mag ungefähr
Mitternacht gewesen sein; **it
would seem so** es sieht wohl so
aus
7 (indicating habit) **he would go
there on Mondays** er ging jeden
Montag dorthin

wouldn't [ˈwʊdnt] contr of
would not

would've [ˈwʊdəv] contr of
would have

wound [wuːnd] n Wunde f ▷ vt
verwunden; (fig) verletzen
▷ [waʊnd] pt, pp of **wind**

wove [wəʊv] pt of **weave**

woven [ˈwəʊvn] pp of **weave**

wrap [ræp] vt (parcel, present)
einwickeln; **to ~ sth round sth**

etw um etw wickeln; **wrap up** *vt*
(*parcel, present*) einwickeln ▷ *vi*
(*dress warmly*) sich warm anziehen;
wrapper *n* (*of sweet*) Papier *nt*;
wrapping paper *n* Packpapier *nt*;
(*giftwrap*) Geschenkpapier *nt*
wreath [riːθ] *n* Kranz *m*
wreck [rek] *n* (*ship, plane, car*)
Wrack *nt*; **a nervous ~** ein
Nervenbündel *m* ▷ *vt* (*car*) zu
Schrott fahren; (*fig*) zerstören;
wreckage ['rekɪdʒ] *n* Trümmer *pl*
wrench [rentʃ] *n* (*tool*)
Schraubenschlüssel *m*
wrestling ['reslɪŋ] *n* Ringen *nt*
wring out ['rɪŋ'aʊt] (**wrung,
wrung**) *vt* auswringen
wrinkle ['rɪŋkl] *n* Falte *f*
wrist [rɪst] *n* Handgelenk *nt*;
wristwatch *n* Armbanduhr *f*
write [raɪt] (**wrote, written**) *vt*
schreiben; (*cheque*) ausstellen ▷ *vi*
schreiben; **to ~ to sb** jdm
schreiben; **write down** *vt*
aufschreiben; **write off** *vt* (*debt,
person*) abschreiben; (*car*) zu
Schrott fahren ▷ *vi*: **to ~ off for
sth** etw anfordern; **write out** *vt*
(*name etc*) ausschreiben; (*cheque*)
ausstellen; **write-protected** *adj*
(*Inform*) schreibgeschützt; **writer**
n Verfasser(in) *m(f)*; (*author*)
Schriftsteller(in) *m(f)*; **writing** *n*
Schrift *f*; (*profession*) Schreiben *nt*;
in ~ schriftlich; **writing paper** *n*
Schreibpapier *nt*
written ['rɪtən] *pp of* **write**
wrong [rɒŋ] *adj* (*incorrect*) falsch;
(*morally*) unrecht; **you're ~** du
hast/Sie haben unrecht; **what's
~ with your leg?** was ist mit
deinem/Ihrem Bein los?; **you've
got the ~ number** du bist/Sie sind
falsch verbunden; **I dialled the
~ number** ich habe mich
verwählt; **don't get me ~**
versteh/verstehen Sie mich

nicht falsch; **to go ~** (*plan*)
schiefgehen; **wrongly** *adv* falsch;
(*unjustly*) zu Unrecht
wrote [rəʊt] *pt of* **write**
WWW *abbr* = **World Wide Web**
WWW

X

y

xenophobia [zenəˈfəʊbɪə] *n*
Ausländerfeindlichkeit *f*

XL *abbr* = **extra large** XL, übergroß

Xmas [ˈkrɪsməs] *n* Weihnachten
nt

X-ray [ˈeksreɪ] *n (picture)*
Röntgenaufnahme *f* ▷ *vt* röntgen

xylophone [ˈzaɪləfəʊn] *n* Xylo

yacht [jɒt] *n* Jacht *f*; **yachting** *n*
Segeln *nt*; **to go** ~ segeln gehen

yam [jæm] *n (US)* Süßkartoffel
f

yard [jɑːd] *n* Hof *m*; *(US: garden)*
Garten *m*; *(measure)* Yard *nt* (0,91 m)

yd *abbr* = **yard(s)**

year [ˈjɪə*] *n* Jahr *nt*; **this/last/
next** ~ dieses/letztes/nächstes
Jahr; **he is 28 ~s old** er ist 28 Jahre
alt; **~s ago** vor Jahren; **a
five-year-old** ein(e)
Fünfjährige(r); **yearly** *adj, adv*
jährlich

yearn [jɜːn] *vi* sich sehnen *(for
nach +dat)*; **to ~ to do sth** sich
danach sehnen, etw zu tun

yeast [jiːst] *n* Hefe *f*

yell [jel] *vi, vt* schreien; **to ~ at sb**
jdn anschreien

yellow [ˈjeləʊ] *adj* gelb; ~ **card**

(*Sport*) gelbe Karte; **~ fever**
Gelbfieber nt; **~ line** (*Brit*)
Halteverbot nt; **double ~ line** (*Brit*)
~ absolutes Halteverbot; **the**
Yellow Pages® pl die Gelben
Seiten pl

yes [jes] adv ja; (*answering*
negative question) doch; **to say ~ to**
sth ja zu etw sagen ▷ n ja nt

yesterday ['jestədeɪ] adv
gestern; **~ morning/evening**
gestern Morgen/Abend; **the day**
before ~ vorgestern; **~'s**
newspaper die Zeitung von
gestern

yet [jet] adv (*still*) noch; (*up to*
now) bis jetzt; (*in a question:*
already) schon; **he hasn't arrived**
~ er ist noch nicht gekommen;
have you finished ~? bist du/sind
Sie schon fertig?; **~ again** schon
wieder; **as ~** bis jetzt ▷ conj doch

yield [jiːld] n Ertrag m ▷ vt
(*result, crop*) hervorbringen; (*profit,*
interest) bringen ▷ vi nachgeben
(*to +dat*); (*Mil*) sich ergeben (*to*
+dat); **"~"** (US Aut) "Vorfahrt
beachten"

yoga ['jəʊgə] n Yoga nt

yog(h)urt ['jɒgət] n Jog(h)urt m

yolk [jəʊk] n Eigelb nt

Yorkshire pudding
['jɔːkʃə'pʊdɪŋ] n gebackener
Eierteig, der meist zum Roastbeef
gegessen wird

🅞 **KEYWORD**

you [juː] pron **1** (*subj, in*
comparisons) (*familiar form*) (*sg*) du;
(*pl*) ihr; (*in letters*) Du, Ihr; (*polite*
form) Sie; **you Germans** ihr
Deutschen; **she's younger than**
you sie ist jünger als du/ihr/Sie
2 (*direct object, after prep +akk*)
(*familiar form*) (*sg*) dich; (*pl*) euch;
(*in letters*) Dich, Euch; (*polite form*)

Sie; **I know you** ich kenne
dich/euch/Sie
3 (*indirect object, after prep +dat*)
(*familiar form*) (*sg*) dir; (*pl*) euch; (*in*
letters) Dir, Euch; (*polite form*)
Ihnen; **I gave it to you** ich gab es
dir/euch/Ihnen
4 (*impers*) (*one*) (*subj*) man; (*direct*
object) einen; (*indirect object*)
einem; **fresh air does you good**
frische Luft tut (einem) gut

you'd [juːd] contr of **you had; you**
would; ~ better leave du
solltest/Sie sollten gehen

you'll [juːl] contr of **you will; you**
shall

young [jʌŋ] adj jung ▷ n die
~ pl (**~ people**) die jungen Leute pl;
(*animals*) die Jungen pl; **youngster**
['jʌŋstə°] n Jugendliche(r)
mf

your ['jɔː°] adj sing dein; polite
form Ihr; pl euer; polite form Ihr;
have you hurt ~ leg? hast du
dir/haben Sie sich das Bein
verletzt?

you're ['jʊə°] contr of **you are**

yours ['jɔːz] pron sing deine(r, s);
polite form Ihre(r, s); pl eure(r, s);
polite form Ihre(r, s); **is this ~?**
gehört das dir/Ihnen?; **a friend of**
~ ein Freund von dir/Ihnen

yourself [jɔː'self] pron sing dich;
polite form sich; **have you hurt ~?**
hast du dir/haben Sie sich
verletzt?; **did you do it ~?** hast
du/haben Sie es selbst gemacht?;
(**all) by ~** allein; **yourselves** pron
pl euch; polite form sich; **have you**
hurt ~? habt ihr euch/haben Sie
sich verletzt?; **did you do it ~?**
habt ihr/haben Sie es selbst
gemacht?; (**all) by ~** allein

youth [juːθ] n (*period*) Jugend f;
(*young man*) junger Mann; (*young*
people) Jugend f; **youth group** n

Jugendgruppe f; **youth hostel** n
Jugendherberge f
you've [ju:v] *contr of* **you have**
yucky ['jʌkɪ] *adj (fam)* eklig
yummy ['jʌmɪ] *adj (fam)* lecker
yuppie, yuppy ['jʌpɪ] n Yuppie
m

Z

zap [zæp] *vt (Inform)* löschen; *(in
computer game)* abknallen ▷ *vi (TV)*
zappen; **zapper** n *(TV)*
Fernbedienung f; **zapping** n *(TV)*
ständiges Umschalten, Zapping nt
zebra ['zebrə, ?? 'zi:brə] *(US)* n
Zebra nt; **zebra crossing** n *(Brit)*
Zebrastreifen m
zero [zɪərəʊ] *(pl* **-es)** n Null f; **10
degrees below -** 10 Grad unter
null
zest [zest] n *(enthusiasm)*
Begeisterung f
zigzag ['zɪgzæg] n Zickzack m
▷ *vi (person, vehicle)* im Zickzack
gehen/fahren; *(path)* im Zickzack
verlaufen
zinc [zɪŋk] n Zink nt
zip [zɪp] n *(Brit)* Reißverschluss m
▷ *vt:* **to - (up)** den Reißverschluss
zumachen; *(Inform)* zippen; **zip
code** n *(US)* Postleitzahl f; **zip
disk®** n *(Inform)* ZIP-Diskette® f;

Zip drive® n (Inform)
ZIP-Laufwerk® nt; **Zip file®** n
(Inform) ZIP-Datei® f; **zipper** n
(US) Reißverschluss m
zit [zɪt] n (fam) Pickel m
zodiac ['zəʊdɪæk] n Tierkreis m;
sign of the ~ Tierkreiszeichen
nt
zone [zəʊn] n Zone f; (area)
Gebiet nt; (in town) Bezirk m
zoo [zuː] n Zoo m
zoom [zuːm] vi (move fast)
brausen, sausen ▷ n: **~ (lens)**
Zoomobjektiv nt; **zoom in** vi
(Foto) heranzoomen (on an +akk)
zucchini [zuːˈkiːnɪ] (pl **-(s)**) n
(US) Zucchini f

z

Collins

easy learning French

Easy Learning French Dictionary
978-0-00-753096-0   £9.99

Easy Learning French Grammar
978-0-00-814199-8   £7.99

Easy Learning French Verbs
978-0-00-815841-5   £7.99

**Easy Learning Complete French Grammar,
Verbs and Vocabulary**
(3 books in 1) 978-0-00-814172-1   £12.99

Easy Learning French Grammar & Practice
978-0-00-814163-9   £9.99

Easy Learning French Verbs & Practice
978-0-00-814208-7   £10.99

Available to buy from all good booksellers and online.
Many titles are also available as ebooks.
www.collins.co.uk/languagesupport

       facebook.com/collinsdictionary

       @collinsdict

MORE THAN TWO MILLION EASY LEARNING BOOKS SOLD

BESTSELLING BILINGUAL DICTIONARIES

Collins

easy learning Spanish

Easy Learning Spanish Dictionary 978-0-00-753094-6	£9.99
Easy Learning Spanish Grammar 978-0-00-814201-8	£7.99
Easy Learning Spanish Verbs 978-0-00-815843-9	£7.99
Easy Learning Complete Spanish Grammar, **Verbs and Vocabulary** (3 books in 1) 978-0-00-814173-8	£12.99
Easy Learning Spanish Grammar & Practice 978-0-00-814164-6	£9.99
Easy Learning Spanish Verbs & Practice 978-0-00-814209-4	£10.99

Available to buy from all good booksellers and online.
Many titles are also available as ebooks.
www.collins.co.uk/languagesupport

 facebook.com/collinsdictionary

 @collinsdict

Collins

easy learning German

Easy Learning German Dictionary
978-0-00-753095-3 £9.99

Easy Learning German Grammar
978-0-00-814200-1 £7.99

Easy Learning German Verbs
978-0-00-815842-2 £7.99

**Easy Learning Complete German Grammar,
Verbs and Vocabulary**
(3 books in 1) 978-0-00-814178-3 £12.99

Easy Learning German Grammar & Practice
978-0-00-814165-3 £10.99

Available to buy from all good booksellers and online.
Many titles are also available as ebooks.
www.collins.co.uk/languagesupport

facebook.com/collinsdictionary

@collinsdict

Collins

easy learning Italian

Easy Learning Italian Dictionary 978-0-00-753093-9	£10.99
Easy Learning Italian Grammar 978-0-00-814202-5	£7.99
Easy Learning Italian Verbs 978-0-00-815844-6	£7.99
Easy Learning Complete Italian Grammar, Verbs and Vocabulary (3 books in 1) 978-0-00-814175-2	£12.99
Easy Learning Italian Grammar & Practice 978-0-00-814166-0	£10.99

Available to buy from all good booksellers and online.
Many titles are also available as ebooks.
www.collins.co.uk/languagesupport

facebook.com/collinsdictionary

@collinsdict